UNIVERSITY CASEBOOK SERIES

FEDERAL INCOME TAXATION OF CORPORATIONS

SECOND EDITION

by

PAUL R. MCDANIEL
Professor of Law
Director of Graduate Tax Program
New York University School of Law

MARTIN J. MCMAHON, JR.
Clarence J. TeSelle Professor of Law
University of Florida

DANIEL L. SIMMONS
Professor of Law
University of California at Davis

NEW YORK, NEW YORK

FOUNDATION PRESS

1999

395 Hudson Street
New York, NY 10014
Phone Toll Free 1–877–888–1330
Fax (212) 367–6799
fdpress.com

Printed in the United States of America

ISBN 1–56662–774–5

TEXT IS PRINTED ON 10% POST CONSUMER RECYCLED PAPER

1st Reprint — 2001

PREFACE

This book covers the federal income taxation of corporations. It is excerpted from our larger work, *Federal Income Taxation of Business Organizations, 3d Ed.* (Foundation Press, 1999), for use in courses that cover only corporate taxation, separately from the study of taxation of partnerships. In a course, or coordinated sequence of courses, covering partnerships, S corporations, and C corporations, *Federal Income Taxation of Business Organizations, 3d Ed.* should be used for comprehensive coverage. Chapters 1-17 of this volume are substantially identical to chapters 10-26 in *Federal Income Taxation of Business Organizations*, with the exception of the elimination of some cross references and the inclusion in Chapter 2, Section 1 of this book of a substantial portion of the material from Chapter 1, Section 2 of *Federal Income Taxation of Business Organizations*.

Like *Federal Income Taxation of Business Organizations*, this work is selective rather than encyclopedic. The detailed nature of the statutory and regulatory provisions and number of fact specific cases and rulings preclude encyclopedic analysis, particularly where largely historical issues are concerned. Accordingly, both students and instructors must bear in mind that the cases and rulings discussed in connection with any particular issue in many instances are only examples of a much larger body of law. Nevertheless, it is impossible to cover the entire volume in detail in any single course.

Depending on the level of detail covered, this volume can be used in a variety of courses covering corporate taxation at either the J.D. or LL.M. level. The arrangement in outline format of both the subdivisions within the chapters and the detailed Illustrative Material following the principal cases is intended to facilitate the assignment by the instructor of only selected portions of the material on any particular topic when the book is employed in survey course on corporate taxation. At the same time, the text presents detailed discussion of complex issues in the proper statutory structural context for coverage in more advanced courses.

We recognize that teachers of courses dealing with federal income taxation of corporations approach their courses with different objectives in mind and use different techniques for handling the materials. In selecting and organizing the materials, we have attempted to maximize the usefulness of these materials for whatever approach the teacher wishes to adopt—an intensive technical analysis, a problem oriented method, a consideration of the policies that underlie the technical tax structure, or a survey of the principal elements of the federal income taxation of corporations. While the selection of principal cases and the numerous examples discussed in the Illustrative Material can, in effect, serve as problems for students and class discussion, many instructors choose to cover corporate taxation by using a series of detailed problems for class discussion. We have not provided any sets of questions or problems within the materials themselves because the nature of the questions which will be appropriate will vary greatly with the type of course for which the materials are being utilized.

Like its companion volumes, *Federal Income Taxation of Partnerships and S Corporations, 3d Ed.* and *Federal Income Taxation, 4th Ed.*, this book charts a course between those books that employ primarily textual explanation and those that rely for the most part on cases. Most chapters and sections of chapters are introduced by a textual discussion or outline of the basic issues and structure of the statute governing treatment of the particular item or transaction covered in the chapter or section. Principal cases have been included to illustrate key concepts not governed by a detailed statutory provision, as well as to illustrate how the courts have utilized the technical tools at their disposal. We have recognized, however, that the dramatic changes in the statutory structure in the past decade and a half, particularly those in the Tax Reform Act of 1986—the changing magnitude of the capital gain preference, repeal of the *General Utilities* rule providing nonrecognition of gain upon the distribution of property by a corporation, and the flattening of the personal income tax rates, resulting in a maximum individual rate barely above the maximum corporate rate—have changed dramatically the important issues. As a result, many cases long used in teaching materials are no longer helpful to students, even though they remain valid precedents. Thus the statutory changes have made it impossible to include a judicial decision as a principal case to illustrate the application of a significant number of Code provisions. Accordingly, in many chapters the "principal case" is an excerpt from a congressional committee report or a Revenue Ruling, which helps the student understand the reasons underlying changes in the statute, as well as providing a road map to assist in mastering the detailed statutory provisions.

In the Illustrative Material, which follows the principal cases, we have attempted to provide sufficient discussion of rulings and cases to give an insight into the endless variety of factual situations to which the highly technical provisions of the Internal Revenue Code governing corporate taxation must be applied. The Illustrative Material also provides important historical background and discussion of sequential amendments to particular sections of the Code and regulations necessary to understand the significance of the current Code provisions. The breadth and detail of the Illustrative Material is such that many instructors may wish to assign only portions of it depending on the scope of the particular course. To assist in selective use of Illustrative Material, we have endeavored generally to arrange the Illustrative Material from the general to the more specific as the outline format progresses.

Of course, the Internal Revenue Code and Treasury Regulations are the centerpiece of any course in federal taxation. This text is intended to be used in conjunction with either a complete set of the Code and regulations or one of the several available edited versions of the Code and regulations. The statutory and regulatory references at the head of each topic are not intended to be exhaustive. Rather, they represent only the essential sections of the Code and regulations which the student must understand to obtain the framework for the cases and materials under the particular topic. We have not undertaken completely to explain the operation of the Code and regulations in the textual notes and Illustrative Material. The student must work with the statute and regulatory material before undertaking the examination of its application in the materials in this volume.

This book is divided into seven Parts, which are further subdivided into chapters. Each Part, in general, represents a block of material in which we think most instructors in a particular course will chose to cover all of the chapters, although the depth of the coverage within each chapter may differ with the overall scope of the course. Many instructors will cover more than one Part in a particular course. Alternatively, the entire volume could be used as a source book, without particular assignments, in an advanced problem oriented course in business planning.

Part I (Chapters 1-8) covers basic corporate taxation: the corporate income tax, classification, formation, capital structure, dividends, redemptions, and liquidations (except in connection with acquisitions). These materials generally will be combined with other Parts as one element in a broader course, although they may be used for a separate two hour course in basic corporate taxation. Part II (Chapter 9) covers Subchapter S. This Part typically will be combined with Part I in course in basic corporate taxation, but in an LL.M. program, it might be combined with material from subsequent parts in an advanced corporate tax course.

Part III (Chapter 10) covers affiliated corporations and consolidated returns. Most books, if they cover this material at all, include it near the end of the book. We have placed the material on consolidated returns immediately following Subchapter S because we believe both Parts reflect a common theme – application of aggregate theory as opposed to separate entity theory in the taxation of corporate income, albeit in differing manners and to limited extents. Thus, it might be logical to close a course in basic corporate taxation with some discussion of both Subchapter S and consolidated returns. Alternatively, a basic course might close with Subchapter S and an advanced course, dealing primarily with acquisitions, might begin with consolidated returns, the rules respecting which play an important part in structuring acquisition transactions. (The authors generally have begun their courses on corporate acquisitions and reorganizations with consolidated returns). Finally, some instructors may choose to skip this Chapter.

Part IV (Chapters 11 through 13) covers taxable and tax free mergers and acquisitions. This Part (particularly Chapter 12 dealing with bootstrap acquisitions) relates back to, and builds upon, concepts explored in Part I. Part V (Chapters 14 and 15) covers single corporation reorganizations and corporate divisions (§ 355). Part VI (Chapter 16) covers carryover of corporate attributes in acquisitions and reorganizations. These three Parts (as well as Part III) may be combined into a two or three credit hour course in advanced corporate taxation. Alternatively portions of Parts III, IV, and V may be combined with Part I (and possibly Part II) in a four hour course covering corporate taxation generally. Experience has proven, however, that it is difficult to cover all of the topics discussed in these Parts in a four credit hour course. To facilitate selective use of the materials on tax-free acquisitive reorganizations, the first two sections of Chapter 13 provide an overview of corporate reorganizations and the important judicial and administrative limitations superimposed on the statute, while the remaining sections individually examine in detail each different form of acquisition technique. Some instructors may chose to cover only the first two sections in a basic corporate taxation course.

Part VII (Chapter 17) covers penalty taxes and collapsible corporations. We expect that only a few courses, primarily advanced corporate taxation courses in LL.M. programs, will cover this Part in conjunction with more discrete division of the earlier parts into a greater number of courses having a more narrowly focused scope. Some limited reference to these materials may be in order in J.D. level courses in corporate taxation.

As to editorial matters, the statutory references throughout are to the 1986 Code, except where the text expressly indicates otherwise. References in the cases and other primary sources to the 1954 and 1939 Codes and prior statutes have been edited to conform them to the 1986 Code. Generally the practice is to omit the earlier citation and instead refer to the matter as "the former version," or "the predecessor," or to give the current relevant 1986 Code section if there has been significant change in the statutory language. But if a significant change has occurred, that fact is noted and the prior language is given. Footnotes in cases and materials frequently have been omitted. Where retained the original numbering of the footnotes has been kept so that, in many instances, the footnote numbers are not consecutive. Editorial footnotes for cases and materials are so designated and are indicated by an asterisk. References to Tax Court Memorandum decisions are to the number assigned by the Tax Court and not to any particular commercial publication. In general, references to the Code, regulations, cases and rulings are current as of December 31, 1998.

We are indebted to Jennifer Bailey, Pietro Canestrelli, and Krista Schumpert for research and editorial assistance.

PAUL R. MCDANIEL
MARTIN J. MCMAHON, JR.
DANIEL L. SIMMONS

April, 1999

HUGH J. AULT: AN APPRECIATION

This edition marks the end of Hugh Ault's participation in *Federal Income Taxation of Corporations*. We, his co-authors and colleagues, have benefited enormously from his challenging intellect, his humor and his personal kindness. We missed him greatly in the preparation of this edition and we shall miss him in future ones. But Hugh Ault has made an indelible mark on this volume and much of his remarkable input is present here and will be for every edition to come. We are proud to dedicate this edition to Hugh Ault, a penetrating scholar ans wonderful friend.

PAUL R. MCDANIEL
MARTIN J. MCMAHON, JR.
DANIEL L. SIMMONS

April, 1999

*

ACKNOWLEDGEMENTS

We gratefully acknowledge the permission extended by the following publishers to reprint excerpts from the materials listed below which appear in this edition.

Excerpt From:	Page
Joseph Pechman, Federal Tax Policy, Fifth Ed. Copyright © 1987, The Brookings Institution. Reprinted with permission of the Brookings Institution.	10, 25
Untangling the Income Tax, by David F. Bradford, Cambridge Mass.: Harvard University Press, Copyright © 1980 by the President and Fellows of Harvard College. Reprinted by permisssion of the publisher.	14
Richard Musgrave and Peggy Musgrave, Public Finance in Theory and Practice, Fifth Edition. Copyright © 1989, McGraw-Hill Publishing Company. Reprinted with permission of the McGraw-Hill Companies.	17
McClure, Must Corporate Income be Taxed Twice, Copyright © 1979, The Brookings Institution. Reprinted with permission of the Brookings Institution.	21
The American Law Institute, Federal Income Tax Project: Subchapter C Proposals on Corporate Acquisitions and Dispositions (W. Andrews Reporter). Copyright © 1982 by the American Law Institute. Reprinted with permission.	32

*

SUMMARY OF CONTENTS

*

TABLE OF CONTENTS

TABLE OF INTERNAL REVENUE CODE SECTIONS

UNITED STATES

UNITED STATES CODE ANNOTATED

26 U.S.C.A.—Internal Revenue Code

UNITED STATES CODE ANNOTATED

26 U.S.C.A.—Internal Revenue Code

UNITED STATES CODE ANNOTATED

26 U.S.C.A.—Internal Revenue Code

UNITED STATES CODE ANNOTATED

26 U.S.C.A.—Internal Revenue Code

UNITED STATES CODE ANNOTATED

26 U.S.C.A.—Internal Revenue Code

UNITED STATES CODE ANNOTATED

26 U.S.C.A.—Internal Revenue Code

UNITED STATES CODE ANNOTATED

26 U.S.C.A.—Internal Revenue Code

UNITED STATES CODE ANNOTATED

26 U.S.C.A.—Internal Revenue Code

UNITED STATES CODE ANNOTATED

26 U.S.C.A.—Internal Revenue Code

UNITED STATES CODE ANNOTATED
26 U.S.C.A.—Internal Revenue Code

UNITED STATES CODE ANNOTATED

26 U.S.C.A.—Internal Revenue Code

UNITED STATES CODE ANNOTATED

26 U.S.C.A.—Internal Revenue Code

UNITED STATES CODE ANNOTATED

26 U.S.C.A.—Internal Revenue Code

UNITED STATES CODE ANNOTATED

26 U.S.C.A.—Internal Revenue Code

UNITED STATES CODE ANNOTATED

26 U.S.C.A.—Internal Revenue Code

UNITED STATES CODE ANNOTATED

26 U.S.C.A.—Internal Revenue Code

UNITED STATES CODE ANNOTATED

26 U.S.C.A.—Internal Revenue Code

UNITED STATES CODE ANNOTATED

26 U.S.C.A.—Internal Revenue Code

UNITED STATES CODE ANNOTATED

26 U.S.C.A.—Internal Revenue Code

UNITED STATES CODE ANNOTATED
26 U.S.C.A.—Internal Revenue Code

UNITED STATES CODE ANNOTATED

26 U.S.C.A.—Internal Revenue Code

Sec.	This Work Page
453	77
453	84
453	85
453	179
453	198
453	234
453	284
453	342
453	410
453	425
453	473
453	474
453	490
453	530
453	578
453	804
453(b)(1)	344
453(b)(2)	473
453(c)	80
453(c)	84
453(d)	85
453(f)(4)	473
453(f)(4)	490
453(f)(4)	578
453(f)(6)	80
453(f)(6)	84
453(g)	80
453(g)	85
453(h)	342
453(h)	411
453(h)	467
453(h)	473
453(h)	474
453(h)	480
453(h)(1)	578
453(h)(1)(A)—(h)(1)(C)	338
453(h)(2)	338
453(i)	85
453(i)(2)	473
453(j)(2)	343
453(j)(2)	344
453(k)(2)	473
453A	458
453B	342
453B	410
453B	473
453B(a)	77
453B(d)	345
453B(h)	409
453B(h)	411
465	396
465	794
465(a)(1)(B)	4
465(c)(3)(B)	396
469	4
469	219
469	384
469	396
469(h)(4)	4
469(j)(1)	4
469(j)(2)	4
481	426
481	735
482	66
482	67
482	68
482	69
482	70
482	71
482	72
482	123
482	128
482	227
482	396
482	432
482	433
482	437
482	438
482	439
483	168
483	175
483	177
483	602
483	603
483(a)	177
483(b)	177
501	435
501	436
501(c)(3)	714
511—514	49
531	131
531	187
531	780
531—537	187
531—537	779
531—537	780
532	780
532(b)(1)	794
532(c)	782
533	790
533(a)	783
534	790
534(c)	790
535	788
535(c)	783
535(c)	784
537(a)(2)	787
537(b)(1)	787
537(b)(4)	786
541	791
541	793
541—547	187
541—547	779
541—547	791
542(a)	791
542(a)(2)	791
542(a)(2)	795
543(a)(1)(C)	792
543(a)(3)	792
543(a)(4)	792

UNITED STATES CODE ANNOTATED

26 U.S.C.A.—Internal Revenue Code

Sec.	This Work Page
543(a)(6)	793
543(a)(7)	792
544(a)(2)	791
545	793
545(b)(6)	793
547	794
561—563	790
611	7
641(d)	369
663(c)	368
664	368
683	79
704(b)	388
704(b)	408
704(c)	429
704(e)(1)	395
704(e)(2)	395
704(e)(3)	395
705	449
706(d)	393
721	121
721	122
721(b)	79
722	408
734	428
736(a)	429
743	468
751	410
751	429
751(b)	428
752(a)	408
851—855	49
856—860	49
860A—860G	49
902	66
936	444
951	63
1001	74
1001	518
1001	600
1001	773
1014	37
1014	77
1014	289
1014	290
1014	325
1014	773
1015	773
1017	197
1017	655
1031	75
1031	198
1031	338
1031	450
1031	804
1031(b)	84
1031(b)	645
1031(b)	650
1032	4
1032	74
1032	76
1032	78
1032	123
1032	183
1032	197
1032	460
1032	581
1032	607
1032	616
1032	624
1032	625
1032	635
1032	654
1032	656
1032	648
1033	735
1036	648
1036	649
1041	444
1041	502
1059	227
1059	231
1059	232
1059	236
1059	513
1059	514
1059(a)	271
1059(a)	286
1059(a)(2)	231
1059(c)	231
1059(d)(1)	231
1059(d)(6)	232
1059(e)(1)	232
1059(e)(1)	271
1059(e)(1)(A)(iii)(I)	243
1059(e)(1)(A)(iii)(II)	286
1059(e)(2)	232
1059(e)(2)	514
1059(e)(2)	725
1059(e)(3)	232
1059(f)	232
1060	342
1060	343
1060	467
1060	468
1060	469
1060	470
1060	471
1060	486
1060(a)	471
1060(c)	343
1201	4
1211	160
1211	204
1211(a)	158
1211(a)	333
1211(b)	158
1212	197
1212	734
1212(a)	3

UNITED STATES CODE ANNOTATED

26 U.S.C.A.—Internal Revenue Code

UNITED STATES CODE ANNOTATED
26 U.S.C.A.—Internal Revenue Code

UNITED STATES CODE ANNOTATED
26 U.S.C.A.—Internal Revenue Code

UNITED STATES CODE ANNOTATED

26 U.S.C.A.—Internal Revenue Code

UNITED STATES CODE ANNOTATED

26 U.S.C.A.—Internal Revenue Code

*

TABLE OF TREASURY REGULATIONS

TEMPORARY TREASURY REGULATIONS

PROPOSED TREASURY REGULATIONS

PROPOSED TREASURY REGULATIONS

TREASURY REGULATIONS

TREASURY REGULATIONS

TREASURY REGULATIONS

TREASURY REGULATIONS

TREASURY REGULATIONS

TREASURY REGULATIONS

TREASURY REGULATIONS

TREASURY REGULATIONS

TREASURY REGULATIONS

TREASURY REGULATIONS

TREASURY REGULATIONS

*

TABLE OF CASES AND RULINGS

Principal cases are in bold type. Non-principal cases are in roman type. References are to Pages.

FEDERAL INCOME TAXATION OF CORPORATIONS

*

PART I

TAXATION OF CORPORATIONS AND SHAREHOLDERS

CHAPTER 1

TAXATION OF CORPORATE INCOME

SECTION 1. THE REGULAR CORPORATE INCOME TAX

Unlike partnerships, which are not taxpaying entities but generally are treated as an aggregate of the partners who pay tax on their shares of partnership income, corporations are taxpaying entities, separate and distinct from their shareholders. Except in certain limited situations, a corporation must pay an income tax on its profits even if the corporation currently or subsequently distributes those profits to its shareholders as dividends taxable to them individually as a part of their taxable income.[1]

1. For 1994, over 4.3 million corporate income tax returns were filed. Approximately 2.4 million returns reported net income in an aggregate amount of nearly $739.5 billion. The remaining returns reported operating losses of approximately $162.2 billion. Before allowing credits, corporations owing tax paid income taxes of more than $172.8 billion; the allowance of nearly $37 billion of credits, however, reduced net income tax receipts to $135.5 billion. 17 SOI Bulletin No. 1, pp. 51, 67–68 (Summer 1997). In spite of the Code's preference for pass-through entities, the number of corporate returns filed annually has steadily increased since 1986 (with the exception of 1988). Id. at 51.

The corporate income tax predates the current individual income tax. The modern corporate income tax originated in 1909, four years before the adoption of the Sixteenth Amendment and the broad based individual income tax which it made possible. In Flint v. Stone Tracy Company, 220 U.S. 107 (1911), the Supreme Court upheld the 1909 corporate income tax against a constitutional challenge alleging that it was a direct tax that was not apportioned among the states according to population as required by Article I, Section 9, Clause 4 of the Constitution. Rather, the Court held that the corporate income tax was an excise tax on the privilege of doing business in the corporate form.

Ever since the enactment of the individual income tax in 1913, corporate income generally has been taxed twice, first when earned by the corporation and again when distributed to the shareholders as dividends or in liquidation. There have been some exceptions: prior to 1936 there was a partial exclusion of dividends under the individual income tax, and during 1936 and 1937 corporations were allowed a deduction for the amount of dividends paid out to shareholders. From 1954 through 1986 individuals were permitted by former § 116 to exclude from income a relatively small portion of dividends received (the original exclusion was $50; this amount had increased to $100 per taxpayer immediately prior to repeal of the exclusion). In addition, from 1954 until 1963 shareholders were allowed a credit equal to 4 percent of dividends received (in excess of the exclusion).[2]

Under current law the most significant exception to taxation of the corporation as a separate entity is the election under Subchapter S (§§ 1361–1379) to treat the corporation as a pass-through entity with gains and losses being reported on the shareholders' individual returns.[3] A number of restrictive conditions limit the availability of this election. Corporations that do not make an election under subchapter S, which are the majority of corporations, are called "C corporations;" corporations which make the election are called "S corporations."

The policy decision to treat a corporation as a tax-paying entity separate and distinct from its shareholders entails certain structural requirements. A separate rate structure, currently specified in § 11, is applicable to corporations. The rate of tax on corporate income has varied over the years.[4] Currently, the rates are: 15 percent on the first $50,000 of

2. See Shoup, The Dividend Exclusion and Credit in the Revenue Code of 1954, 8 Nat'l Tax J. 136 (1955).

3. Subchapter S applies only to "small business corporations" having a limited number of shareholders. While Subchapter S is loosely referred to as permitting a corporation to elect to be taxed as a partnership, the operational effects under the Subchapter differ somewhat from partnership treatment. Subchapter S is discussed in Chapter 9.

4. In 1909, when the corporate income tax was introduced, the rate was 1%. During World War I, it reached 12%; a 40% top rate was applicable during World War II; and a 52% rate was imposed during the Korean War. In 1964, the rate was reduced to 50% for that year and to 48% beginning in 1965. The rates and brackets were modified several times during the 1970's and 1980's. See J. Pechman, Federal Tax Policy, 135–137, 302–305, 321–322 (5th ed. 1987).

For many years the corporate income tax provided a relatively large portion of federal tax receipts, being as much as 42.2 percent in 1929, 36.8 percent in 1944, and 32.4 percent

taxable income, 25 percent on next $25,000, 34 percent on taxable income between $75,000 and $10 million, and 35 percent of taxable income in excess of $10 million. If taxable income exceeds $100,000, a five percent surtax is imposed on the excess over $100,000 up to a maximum additional tax of $11,750, which occurs when taxable income reaches $335,000. If a corporation has taxable income over $15 million, a three percent surtax is imposed on the excess over $15 million, up to a maximum additional tax of $100,000, which occurs when taxable income reaches $18.33 million. The purposes of these surtaxes are to phase-out the benefit of the graduated rates for corporations having taxable incomes in excess of $100,000, so that corporations with taxable income exceeding $18.33 million pay a 35 percent flat rate. As with any phase-out technique, corporations in the phase-out ranges are subject to a marginal rate in excess of the statutory rate that would otherwise apply. The marginal rate structure of the regular corporate tax, as a result of the phase-outs, is as follows:

15% on first $50,000

25% on next $25,000 ($75,000)

34% on next $25,000 ($100,000)

39% on next $235,000 ($335,000)

34% on next $9,765,000 ($10 million)

35% on next $5,000,000 ($15 million)

38% on next $3,333,333 ($18.333 million)

35% above $18,333,333 million

Taxable income of a corporation basically is determined by applying the same rules that govern taxation of individuals, so that the gross income rules, the deduction rules, the accounting provisions, and the capital gain and loss provisions are all pertinent.[5] But there are a number of important variations from these basic income tax provisions that are applicable only to corporations. Thus, for example, application of the deduction sections, such as § 162(a) and § 165(a), to corporations generally is guided by the premise that all corporations are engaged in trade or business. In addition, there are a number of special provisions that apply only to corporations, such as the dividends received deduction in § 243 for intercorporate dividends, which effectively excludes all or part of such dividends from a corporation's taxable income. The treatment of capital gains and losses recognized by corporations also differs. Under § 1212(a), capital losses are allowed only to the extent of capital gains, with a five-year carryover and a

in 1954. In more recent years, however, the percentage of federal tax receipts attributable to the corporate income tax has fallen. By 1960 corporate taxes were only 24.8 percent of total receipts; by 1980 only 13.9 percent; and from 1982 through 1995 ranged from 8 to 10 percent.

5. As with individuals, corporations are subject to the alternative minimum tax provided by § 55 through § 59 in any year in which the alternative minimum tax exceeds the regular tax. The alternative minimum tax rate for corporations is 20 percent, and the tax is imposed on "alternative minimum taxable income," a tax base that differs substantially from "taxable income".

three-year carryback of any excess losses. Section 1201 provides that for any year in which the maximum tax rate under § 11 exceeds 35 percent (excluding the 5 percent and 3 percent surtaxes), the maximum rate of tax on long term capital gains is limited to 35 percent. At present, corporate rates do not exceed 35 percent so this provision has no impact.[6]

The non-applicability to most corporations of the passive activity loss rules of § 469 is a very significant difference between individual and corporate taxation. Section 469 applies to a closely held C corporation, defined in §§ 469(j)(1) and 465(a)(1)(B) as a C corporation more than 50 percent of the stock of which is held at some time during the last half of the taxable year by five or fewer persons, taking into account certain attribution rules. It also applies to "personal service corporations" defined in § 469(j)(2). Section 469 does not apply to S corporations, but it does apply to the shareholders in taking into account their shares of S corporation income or loss. Special rules govern the determination of whether a closely held C corporation or personal service corporation "materially participates" in an activity. See I.R.C. § 469(h)(4).

The rules governing choice of accounting methods and taxable years also differ for corporations. Most C corporations are required to use the accrual method of accounting. Exceptions are provided for corporations with average annual gross receipts of less than $5 million and for personal service corporations. See I.R.C. § 448. Although most C corporations are free to choose any taxable year, personal service corporations and S corporations generally are required to adopt a calendar year. See I.R.C. §§ 441(i), 1378(b). These corporations may adopt a fiscal year, however, if the corporation can establish a business purpose for the fiscal year or if it makes an election under § 444, which requires that the corporation make an advance deposit of taxes.

Special problems also result from transactions unique to the corporate form, such as the tax consequences to a corporation of the issuance of its stock or of dealings by it in its stock. Section 1032 solves this problem by providing that a corporation does not realize income upon the sale or issuance of its own shares for money, property, or services. Further, there is the necessity of classifying as either stock or debt the securities issued by a corporation, since payment of interest generates a deduction to the corporation under § 163 while the distribution of a dividend does not. This classification issue, which is considered in Chapter 4, is a matter of considerable controversy.

Because the corporation is a separate tax entity, rules must be provided to specify the tax treatment for various events in the life of the corporation, e.g., upon the formation of the corporation. In general, if an individual, group of individuals or partnership desires to incorporate a

6. Of course, there is nothing to prevent Congress from amending § 1201 to provide a higher maximum rate of tax on capital gains at the same time it amends § 11 to increase the general rate. Conversely, § 1201 might be amended to provide, as it did prior to the 1986 Act, for a maximum tax rate on capital gains lower than the then current maximum rate under § 11.

business and accordingly transfers the assets to a corporation formed for that purpose, no gain or loss will result from the change in the form of the ownership of the assets. The transferor now owns stock of a corporation holding the assets instead of holding the assets themselves; but the Code expressly provides that any gain or loss inherent in those assets is not to be recognized when they are so exchanged for stock. The transferor's basis for the assets now becomes the basis for the stock, and this asset basis likewise carries over to the corporation and becomes its basis for the assets. The rules governing formation of a corporation are discussed in Chapters 3 and 4.

Problems also arise as to the proper tax relationship between the ongoing corporation and its shareholders. The corporation may distribute cash, property, or its own stock. It is necessary to establish a standard for ascertaining the extent to which distributions represent corporate earnings, and thus are appropriately taxed to the shareholders as dividends, or a return of capital which should be applied against the basis of the shareholder's stock and taxable as gain if the distribution exceeds that basis. It also is necessary to decide whether the distribution of property by the corporation is an event which should result in the recognition of gain or loss to the corporation when the property is either appreciated or depreciated. The rules governing the tax treatment of dividends are considered in Chapter 5. Special problems presented by dividends paid in the distributing corporation's own stock are discussed in Chapter 7.

Some of the shares of a shareholder, or all of the shares of some shareholders, may be redeemed by the corporation for cash or other property. In this case it is necessary to determine whether the transaction more nearly resembles a sale of the stock, thereby giving rise to recovery of basis and capital gain treatment, or a dividend with the attendant ordinary income consequences. It also is necessary to determine whether it is appropriate for the corporation to recognize gain or loss if property, rather than cash, is distributed to the shareholder in such a transaction. The rules required to determine the proper tax treatment of these transactions at the corporate and the shareholder level are considered in Chapter 6.

The shareholders later may decide to sell or liquidate the corporation. Again, it is necessary to provide rules for determining the gain or loss realized in such cases, and whether that gain or loss will be recognized at the corporate level, the shareholder level, or both. Special rules may be appropriate if the liquidated corporation is a subsidiary corporation, most of the stock of which is owned by another corporation. In this case nonrecognition of gain and loss to both corporations may be appropriate. Furthermore, consideration must be given to treatment of sales and purchases of corporate assets in connection with a liquidation. The purchase of all of the stock of a corporation and the purchase of all of its assets as a going business may be alternatives from a non-tax perspective. To what extent should the tax system treat these transactions identically and to what extent should the form chosen by the parties govern the transaction? Chapters 8 and 11 consider these matters.

It would be possible to "integrate" the tax treatment of the corporation with the tax treatment of its shareholders. Thus, it is not essential to an income tax system that corporations be subject to a separate tax structure, in the sense that both the corporation and its shareholders bear tax on the same income. The tax systems of some countries have varying degrees of integration of the corporate and individual income taxes. The policy arguments for a separate corporate income tax versus integration of the taxation of corporations and their shareholders are discussed later in this Chapter. The limited integration offered by Subchapter S is considered in Chapter 9.

New rules would be required if the corporate and individual income taxes were integrated, but one method of understanding the United States corporate tax structure is to consider which of the present rules are required because of the policy decision to treat the corporation as a taxpaying entity independent of its shareholders. Also, note the situations in which there has been a decision to depart from the separate tax treatment of corporations and shareholders, as in Subchapter S. A different set of rules has been shaped for this purpose. Are these situations an appropriate part of an otherwise separate structure, or are they aberrations inconsistent with that separate structure? In addition, which rules in the corporate tax area result from the decision not to tax the appreciation in the value of property, including stock in a corporation, on an accrual basis? Which rules result from the decision to accord special treatment to capital gains and losses? Which rules stem from a decision to aid "small business"? What other policy decisions may have influenced the rules?

Still another way of viewing the materials is from the standpoint of business planning requirements. What are the various routes to implement a given business decision when tax consequences are taken into consideration? Which are more or less expensive from a tax standpoint? In which situations do business needs appear to have shaped the tax rules, and conversely, in which situations has the development of the tax law determined the manner in which business transactions are carried out? The materials on the sale and purchase of the corporate business in Chapters 11 and 12, acquisitive tax free reorganizations in Chapter 13, single corporation reorganizations in Chapter 14, and corporate divisions in Chapter 15 raise planning as well as structural questions.

SECTION 2. THE ALTERNATIVE MINIMUM TAX

INTERNAL REVENUE CODE: Sections 53(a)-(c); 55(a)-(c), (d)(2); 56(a), (c)(1), (g); 57(a).

The alternative minimum tax (AMT) applies both to individuals and to corporations (other than S Corporations and small business corporations), but certain structural features of the AMT make it a much more important consideration for corporate taxpayers than for individual taxpayers. Most individuals do not have to make AMT computations each year. On the other hand, the possibility that a corporation may be liable for the AMT is so significant that most corporations must make AMT computations on an annual basis even though no AMT liability may arise for the year. The purpose of the AMT is to assure that a taxpayer with substantial economic income cannot escape significant tax liability through exclusions, deductions, and credits that are provided under the regular tax as incentives for economic behavior which Congress intends to encourage rather than which serve to measure economic income accurately. See S.Rep. No. 99–313, 99th Cong. 2d Sess. 518–20 (1986).

Mechanically, under § 55(a) the AMT is an "add on" tax, but structurally the AMT is a "shadow" tax system that applies a lower uniform rate to a more broadly defined tax base than is used in computing the regular income tax. The corporation generally is required to pay the greater of the regular income tax or the AMT.

1. *AMT Rate and Exclusion*

Generally speaking, the tax base for the AMT is the corporation's regular taxable income increased by the "tax preferences" specified in § 57 and adjusted as required under § 56 by recomputing certain deductions, such as ACRS depreciation under § 168, to negate to some extent the acceleration of these deductions which is provided under the regular income tax. The resulting tax base is termed "alternative minimum taxable income" (AMTI) and, after an allowance of an exemption, AMTI is taxed at a flat 20 percent rate. I.R.C. § 55(b)(1)(B). The exemption allowed to a corporation is $40,000, but it is reduced by 25 percent of the amount by which the corporation's AMTI exceeds $150,000. I.R.C. § 55(d)(2), (3). Thus, for a corporation with AMTI of $310,000 or more, no exemption is available. As a result of the phase-out of the $40,000 AMT exemption, the corporate AMT marginal rate structure is as follows:

0% on first $40,000

20% on next $110,000 ($150,000)

25% on next $160,000 ($310,000)

20% above $310,000

The amount of tax resulting from this computation is termed "tentative minimum tax" by § 55(b). Technically, the AMT liability is the amount by which this tentative minimum tax exceeds regular tax liability for the year. Thus in a year in which the corporation is liable for AMT it also is liable for regular tax.

2. *Alternative Minimum Taxable Income*

AMTI is computed by adding back to taxable income the preference items listed in § 57 including the following: (1) solid mineral (but not oil and gas) depletion allowances under § 611 to the extent that the deductions exceed the taxpayer's basis for the property at the end of the year (this applies only to percentage depletion, but not to all percentage depletion over cost depletion); (2) a portion of the amount by which intangible drilling and development costs deducted under § 263(c) for drilling oil, gas or geothermal steam wells exceeds net income from such wells for the year; (3) interest on private activity bonds exempt from tax under § 103; and (4) certain accelerated depreciation taken on property placed in service before 1987.

Regular taxable income is also adjusted by the items described in § 56. The complex adjustments of § 56 may either increase or decrease AMTI relative to taxable income, and may produce different results in different years. For example, § 56(a)(1) prescribes that in computing AMTI, taxable income is "adjusted" by recomputing depreciation of tangible personal property applying the 150 percent declining balance method, switching to straight line.[7] (Most tangible personal property is depreciated for regular tax purposes under the 200 percent declining balance method, switching to straight line; real estate is depreciated using the straight line method for both regular tax and AMT purposes. Section 168(b)(3) and (5) provide an irrevocable election for regular tax purposes to depreciate property otherwise eligible for 200 percent declining balance using 150 percent declining balance in order to conform regular tax and AMT depreciation deductions.) As a result of the different capital recovery method, AMTI is increased relative to regular taxable income in the early years of an asset's cost recovery period, but is decreased relative to regular taxable income in later years. Section 56(a)(2) and (3) prescribe other timing adjustments relating to mine exploration and development expenses and long term construction contracts. In addition, for AMT purposes, a special net operating loss carryover rule, prescribed in § 56(d), must be used instead of the normal net operative loss carryover rule of § 172. Under § 56(d), a net operating loss carryover is not permitted to reduce AMTI to zero; the maximum AMT net operating loss carryover deduction equals 90 percent of AMTI without regard to the deduction. Under § 56(a)(5) pollution control facilities are depreciated for AMTI purposes using the straight line method over the appropriate capital recovery period of § 168.[8]

The complexities caused by the AMT extend beyond the face of its own provisions. For example, § 56(a)(6) recognizes that property may have a different basis for AMT purposes than for regular tax purposes because of the slower cost recovery permitted under the AMT. Thus, the gain or loss on the sale of property often is different for AMT purposes than for regular tax purposes. This result always will be true if depreciable property is sold prior to full cost recovery under the AMT.

The most complex, and most significant, adjustment, however, is the "adjusted current earnings" (ACE) adjustment in § 56(g). This provision adds to AMTI an amount equal to 75 percent of the excess of the

7. For property placed in service before January 1, 1999, depreciation is recomputed using the longer recovery periods of the alternative depreciation schedule of § 168(g).

8. For regular tax purposes, the cost of certified pollution control facilities may be amortized over a 60 month period. I.R.C. § 169. With respect to property placed in service before January 1, 1998, the § 56 adjustment for AMTI was determined using the alternative depreciation system of § 168(g). I.R.C. § 56(a)(5).

corporation's "adjusted current earnings" over its AMTI (computed without reference to the ACE adjustment or the AMT net operating loss deduction). If AMTI exceeds adjusted current earnings, then the ACE adjustment is negative. "Adjusted current earnings" is defined in § 56(g)(4) as AMTI with several enumerated adjustments. These adjustments are intended to cause AMTI more accurately to reflect the corporation's economic income. In enacting the AMT Congress was particularly concerned with taxing corporations that report earnings to shareholders and pay dividends but have no taxable income under the regular tax. See S.Rep. No. 99–313, 99th Cong. 2d Sess. 519 (1986).

3. *Credit Against Regular Tax*

Many of the adjustments in § 56 and tax preferences in § 57 that are taken into account in computing AMTI reflect timing differences with respect to regular taxable income rather than permanent exclusions from taxable income. As a consequence, prior years' AMT is treated to some extent as a prepayment of the current year's regular taxes. To the extent that regular taxable income in any year exceeds tentative AMT as defined in § 55(b), § 53 allows a portion of AMT liability for prior years as a credit against regular tax liability. For corporations, the creditable portion of the prior minimum tax paid is limited to a portion of prior AMT liability attributable to adjustments and preferences includable in AMTI. I.R.C. § 53(d)(1)(A) and (B)(iv). Here it is important that mechanically AMT is not the entire amount resulting from multiplying AMTI by the AMT tax rate but only the amount by which tentative AMT exceeds regular tax liability for the year. AMT from any number of prior years may be credited against regular tax in a particular year, but the carryover credit available for future years is, of course, reduced by the amount of the credit claimed. I.R.C. § 53(a). The carryover credit is available in the first year the corporation incurs regular income tax liability regardless of whether or not the items that gave rise to prior AMT liability are brought back into the regular income tax base in that year. The operation of the credit can be illustrated by the following example. Suppose that in year one an accelerated deduction of $100 reduces regular taxable income and is treated as a tax preference item subject to the AMT. In a later year, regular taxable income will be $100 higher than it would have been if the deduction had not been accelerated. The additional $35 of regular tax on the $100 can be partially offset by a credit of $20 of minimum tax paid in year one.

4. *Exemption for Small Corporations*

Under § 55(e), for tax years beginning after December 31, 1997 certain "small corporations" are not subject to the AMT. A corporation qualifies as a small corporation if its average annual gross receipts for the preceding three taxable years do not exceed $5 million. Once a corporation qualifies as a small corporation under the $5 million test, it will remain a small corporation not subject to AMT as long as its average gross receipts for the preceding three taxable years do not exceed $7.5 million. I.R.C. § 55(e)(1)(A). In addition, under § 55(e)(1)(C) any newly formed corporation will be treated as a small corporation in its first taxable year, regardless of the amount of its gross receipts. In applying these provisions, a corporation will be aggregated with a group of corporations under common control that is treated as a single employer for purposes of § 414(c) or treated as a continuation of a predecessor entity. I.R.C. §§ 55(e)(1)(D), 448(c)(2) and (3). If a corporation ceases to qualify as a "small corporation", in general, the AMT is calculated by requiring adjustments to capital recovery items such as depreciation and amortization of pollution control facilities only with respect to property placed in service after the date on which the corporation lost its status as a small corporation. See I.R.C. § 55(e)(2).

SECTION 3. SELECTED TAX POLICY ISSUES

A. THE INCIDENCE OF THE CORPORATION INCOME TAX

Joseph Pechman, Federal Tax Policy

The Brookings Institution (Fifth ed. 1987).

There is no more controversial issue in taxation than the question, "Who bears the corporation income tax?" On this question, both economists and businessmen differ among themselves. The following quotations are representative of these divergent views:

Corporate taxes are simply costs, and the method of their assessment does not change this fact. Costs must be paid by the public in prices, and corporate taxes are thus, in effect, concealed sales taxes. (Enders M. Voorhees, chairman of the Finance Committee, U.S. Steel Corporation, address before the Controllers' Institute of America, New York, September 21, 1943.)

The initial or short-run incidence of the corporate income tax seems to be largely on corporations and their stockholders. * * * There seems to be little foundation for the belief that a large part of the corporate tax comes out of wages or is passed on to consumers in the same way that a selective excise [tax] tends to be shifted to buyers. (Richard Goode, The Corporation Income Tax, Wiley, 1951, pp. 71–72.)

* * * The corporation profits tax is almost entirely shifted: the government simply uses the corporation as a tax collector. (Kenneth E. Boulding, The Organizational Revolution, Harper, 1953, p. 277.)

It is hard to avoid the conclusion that plausible alternative sets of assumptions about the relevant elasticities all yield results in which capital bears very close to 100 percent of the [corporate] tax burden. (Arnold C. Harberger, "The Incidence of the Corporation Income Tax," Journal of Political Economy, vol. 70, June 1962, p. 234.)

* * * An increase in the [corporate] tax is shifted fully through short-run adjustments to prevent a decline in the net rate of return [on corporate

investment], and * * * these adjustments are maintained subsequently. (Marian Krzyzaniak and Richard A. Musgrave, The Shifting of the Corporation Income Tax, Johns Hopkins Press, 1963, p. 65.)

* * * There is no inter-sector inefficiency resulting from the imposition of the corporate profits tax with the interest deductibility provision. Nor is there any misallocation between safe and risky industries. From an efficiency point of view, the whole corporate profits tax structure is just like a lump sum tax on corporations. (Joseph E. Stiglitz, "Taxation, Corporate Financial Policy, and the Cost of Capital," Journal of Public Economics, vol. 2, February 1973, p. 33.)

* * * If the net rate of return is given in the international market place, the burden of a tax on the income from capital in one country will not (in the middle or long run) end up being borne by capital (which can flee) but by other factors of production (land, labor, and to a degree, perhaps, old fixed capital). (Arnold C. Harberger, "The State of the Corporate Tax: Who Pays It? Should It Be Replaced?" in Charls E. Walker and Mark A. Bloomfield, eds., New Directions in Federal Tax Policy for the 1980s, Ballinger, 1983.)

Unfortunately, economics has not yet provided a scientific basis for accepting or rejecting one side or the other. This section presents the logic of each view and summarizes the evidence.

The Shifting Mechanism

One reason for the sharply divergent views is that the opponents frequently do not refer to the same type of shifting. It is important to distinguish between short-and long-run shifting and the mechanisms through which they operate. The "short run" is defined by economists as a period too short for firms to adjust their capital to changing demand and supply conditions. The "long run" is a period in which capital can be adjusted.

THE SHORT RUN. The classical view in economics is that the corporation income tax cannot be shifted in the short run. The argument is as follows: all business firms, whether they are competitive or monopolistic, seek to maximize net profits. This maximum occurs when output and prices are set at the point where the cost of producing an additional unit is exactly equal to the additional revenue obtained from the sale of that unit. In the short run, a tax on economic profit should make no difference in this decision. The output and price that maximized the firm's profits before the tax will continue to maximize profits after the tax is imposed. (This follows from simple arithmetic. If a series of figures is reduced by the same percentage, the figure that was highest before will be the highest after.)

The opposite view is that today's markets are characterized neither by perfect competition nor by monopoly; instead, they show considerable imperfection and mutual interdependence or oligopoly. In such markets, business firms may set their prices at the level that covers their full costs plus a margin for profits. Alternatively, the firms are described as aiming at an after-tax target rate of return on their invested capital. Under the cost-plus behavior, the firm treats the tax as an element of cost and raises its price to recover the tax. (Public utilities are usually able to shift the tax in this way, because state rate-making agencies treat the corporation tax as a cost.) Similarly, if the firm's objective is the after-tax target rate of return, imposition of a tax or an increase in the tax rate—by reducing the rate of return on invested capital—will have to be accounted for in making output and price decisions. To preserve the target rate of return, the tax must be shifted forward to consumers or backward to the workers or partly forward and partly backward.

It is also argued that the competitive models are irrelevant in most markets where one or a few large firms exercise a substantial degree of leadership. In such markets, efficient producers raise their prices to recover the tax, and the tax merely forms an "umbrella" that permits less efficient or marginal producers to survive.

When business managers are asked about their pricing policies, they often say that they shift the corporation income tax. However, even if business firms intend to shift the tax, there is some doubt about their ability to shift it fully in the short run. In the first place, the tax depends on the outcome of business operations during an entire year. Businessmen can only guess the ratio of the tax to their gross receipts, and it is hard to conceive of their setting a price that would recover the precise amount of tax they will eventually pay. (If shifting were possible, there would be some instances of firms shifting more than 100 percent of the tax, but few economists believe that overshifting actually occurs.)

Second, businessmen know that should they attempt to recover the corporation income tax through higher prices (or lower wages), other firms would not necessarily do the same. Some firms make no profit or have large loss carry-overs and thus pay no tax; among other firms, the ratio of tax to gross receipts differs. In multiproduct firms, the producer has even less basis for judging the ratio of tax to gross receipts for each product. All these possibilities increase the uncertainty of response by other firms and make the attempt to shift part or all of the corporation income tax hazardous.

THE LONG RUN. In the long run, the corporation income tax influences investment by reducing the rate of return on corporate equity. If the corporation income tax is not shifted in the short run, net after-tax rates of return are depressed, and the incentive to undertake corporate investment is thereby reduced. After-tax rates of return tend to be equalized with those in the noncorporate sector, but in the process corporate capital and output will have been permanently reduced. Thus, if there is no short-run shifting and if the supply of capital is fixed, the burden of the tax falls on the owners of capital in general. If the depressed rate of return on capital reduces investment, productivity of labor decreases and at least part of the tax may be borne by workers.

Where investment is financed by borrowing, the corporation tax cannot affect investment decisions because interest on debt is a deductible expense. If the marginal investment of a firm is fully financed by debt, the corporation tax becomes a lump-sum tax on profits generated by previous investments and is borne entirely by the owners of the corporation, the stockholders. In view of the recent large increase in debt financing (see the section on equity and debt finance below), a substantial proportion of the corporation income tax may now rest on stockholders and not be diffused to owners of capital in general through the shifting process just described.

THE CORPORATION TAX IN AN OPEN ECONOMY. The foregoing analysis assumed that the corporation tax was imposed in a closed economy. In an open economy, the rate of return on capital is set in the international marketplace. If the tax in one country is higher than it is elsewhere, capital will move to other countries until the rate of return is raised to the international level. Thus the burden of the tax would not be borne by capital but by other factors of production (land, labor, and old fixed capital) that cannot move. Since labor is the largest input into corporate products, wage earners would bear most of the burden of the corporation tax through lower real wages.

In the years immediately after World War II, most countries imposed tight capital controls and currencies were not convertible. As capital controls were dismantled and many foreign currencies other than the U.S. dollar became acceptable in international transactions, the open economy model became more realistic. During this later period, the effective corporation tax rates have been declining in the United States. It follows that recent U.S. tax policy has probably reduced any adverse effect of the corporation income tax on real wages, not increased it as some allege.

The Evidence

The evidence on the incidence of the corporation income tax is inconclusive. The data do not permit a clear determination of the factors affecting price and wage decisions. Different authors examining the same set of facts have come to diametrically opposite conclusions.

Over the long run, unincorporated business has not grown at the expense of incorporated business in the United States. Corporations accounted for 58.7 percent of the national income originating in the business sector in 1929; their share reached 75.6 percent in 1986 * * *. Much of the increase came from the relative decline in industries, particularly farming, in which corporations are not important; but even in the rest of the economy, there is no indication of a shift away from the corporate form of organization. The advantages of doing business in the corporate form far outweigh whatever deterrent effects the corporation tax might have on corporate investment.

Beyond this, the data are conflicting. On the one hand, before-and after-tax rates of return reported by corporations have been higher since the end of World War II than in the late 1920s, when the corporation income tax was much lower * * *. On the other hand, except for recession years, the share of pre-tax property income (profits, interest, and capital consumption allowances) in the corporate gross product changed little

* * *. Corporations have been able to increase their before-tax profits enough to avoid a reduction in the after-tax return without increasing their share of income in the corporate sector. This suggests that corporations have increased pre-tax rates of return not by marking up prices or lowering wages, but by making more efficient use of their capital. But what might have occurred without the tax is unknown, and its long-run effect remains unclear.

The burden of corporate taxation borne by individuals is strikingly different under the different incidence assumptions. The tax is regressive in the lower income classes and mildly progressive in the higher ones if as much as one-half is shifted forward to consumers in the form of higher prices and the remainder is borne by owners of capital in general. If the entire tax is borne by capital, progressivity increases in the higher income classes * * *. (141–146)

David Bradford, Untangling the Income Tax*

Harvard University Press (1987).

Confusion between nominal and real incidence is particularly common in the case of the corporation income tax. There is no doubt that this tax is borne by persons, not by the institutions that file the tax returns and send in the checks. But there is doubt and controversy about how the corporation income tax affects the burdens on individuals in their roles as workers, consumers, savers, and so on. The problem of determining the true incidence of the corporation income tax is a classic in public finance. In a famous treatment of the problem, Arnold Harberger (1962)** conceived of the tax as an extra levy on the use of capital (machines, buildings, inventories, and so on) in the corporate sector. His analysis of the tax has been so widely accepted that it can now be considered the traditional view.

As with an excise tax on telephone calls, a levy on an input to a single sector—in this case, capital services in the corporate sector—discourages the use of that input and leads to shifts in prices for inputs and outputs throughout the economy. (The price of capital services can be thought of as the interest rate a borrower must pay a lender for the use of the funds required to purchase and maintain a building, a machine, a bit of inventory, and the like.) Just as the process of adjustment of wages, prices, output, and employment generates the ultimate distribution of the burden of a tax on telephone calls, a similar process spreads the burden of a tax on corporate capital. The distribution after full adjustment of the economy has taken place will depend on the details of how demand for the outputs of the corporate sector varies with the prices of goods produced there and how the

** [Ed.: Harberger, The Incidence of the Corporate Income Tax, 70 J.Pol.Econ. 215 (1962).]

corporate and noncorporate sectors make use of the services of capital and labor.

Two things are clear in Harberger's characterization of the situation. First, no special burden can result for owners of capital employed in the corporate sector (corporate shareholders). Because resources are free to move between sectors, they must receive the same return in both. Economists use the term "shifting" to describe the difference between the nominal and the real incidence of a tax. In this instance, the tax on uses of capital in the corporate sector will certainly be shifted. The question is: onto whom? Second, the tax must be shifted to individuals in some combination of their roles as capitalists (owners of wealth) and workers. (Consumers as such can bear no special burden in the Harberger model, because he does not distinguish purchasers of corporate goods from purchasers of noncorporate goods.) That is, the tax will change both the after-tax return to savers and the wages received by workers. It is even possible that a tax on the use of capital in the corporate sector could raise the wages of workers (if lots of capital and not many workers are released by the tax-induced contraction of the corporate sector), in which case we would say capitalists (who might, of course, also be workers) bear more than 100 percent of the tax. Similarly, it is theoretically possible that capitalists could gain from the tax.

Harberger's famous conclusion, based on educated guesses about critical features of the production technology and demand behavior, was that the tax probably did not affect the wages of workers. The tax was thus probably borne entirely by individuals as owners of wealth and not as workers. The technique employed by Harberger involved describing mathematically the interrelationships of demand and supply throughout the economy, along with the ways in which inputs are combined by firms to produce goods and services.[2] Since the time of Harberger's first contributions, advances in computer technology have allowed other researchers to produce greatly refined versions of his analysis (see Ballard et al., 1985).*

More recent treatments have been able to distinguish many different industries, to allow for interindustry transactions, to recognize the existence of many other taxes, and to include individual workers/consumers of varying types. The primary inputs, however, have in most cases been held to two: capital and labor. These detailed models, increasingly comprehensive in coverage, have typically supported Harberger's original conclusion about the incidence of a tax on the use of capital by corporations.

I have been careful in this discussion to refer to a tax "on the use of capital by corporations," rather than to the corporation income tax. In recent years the view of the corporation income tax has been changing (see

2. The technique is referred to as "general equilibrium analysis," because of its attempt to encompass all the balancing relationships in the economy and thereby account for the full range of ripple effects of a policy change.

* [Ed.: Ballard, Shoven & Whalley, General Equilibrium Computations of the Marginal Welfare Cost of Taxes in the United States, 75 Am.Econ.Rev. 128 (March 1985).]

Bradford, 1980b).** Although researchers are not challenging the correctness of the earlier work as to the effect of a tax on corporate capital, they have begun to question the adequacy of conceiving of the corporation income tax as a tax on corporate capital. They emphasize the importance of looking at the details of the tax as it affects various transactions, such as payment of dividends or undertaking an investment project. These details can be analyzed correctly only if the corporation income tax is seen as an element in the income tax system as a whole, that is, jointly with the personal income tax. Together, the two sets of rules determine how the corporation tax influences investment and financial decisions, employment practices, and so on.

This rethinking can be related to the view I have often encountered among business people, that the corporation income tax amounts to a sales tax applied to corporations. To some extent this view is simply an expression of the point already emphasized here: taxes paid by corporations are borne not by institutions as such, nor by their stockholders as such, but by a wide class of individuals. The proceeds from a company's sales must cover taxes paid by the company, the cost of hired inputs (including labor and capital), and a residual profit or loss accruing to the owners of the company. In a competitive economy, owners will insist on receiving a competitive return, including compensation for bearing risk. (If they do not get it, they will change the firm's decisions.) Conversely, owners who regularly earn supernormal profits find them eroded by the entry of competitor firms. The tendency of the system is toward a situation in which owners who contribute capital to firms obtain a return equivalent to that of owners who hire out their capital-not more, not less. (Equivalent return is not necessarily the identical return. There are typically differences in risk.)

Thus taxes paid by corporations must ultimately be reflected in changes in prices paid by customers and received by suppliers (including suppliers of finance and of labor services). This is true whether the tax is a sales tax, a corporation income tax, or a payroll tax. Whether the tax that is labeled a corporation income tax is equivalent to a sales tax on corporations depends on the details. A cash-flow tax of the sort proposed by Henry Aaron and Harvey Galper* would be based effectively on the difference between the sales and purchases of the corporate sector to and from the noncorporate economy. It would thus, indeed, have the character of a corporate sales tax. Yet a tax levied on the income of corporations, calculated according to accrual-income principles except with no deduction for interest paid (or taxation of interest received), would clearly be a double tax on corporate income and not equivalent to a sales tax. The effect of the existing system * * * with its deduction for corporate interest paid, its accelerated depreciation of investment, investment tax credit, inadequate

** [Ed.: Bradford, "The Economics of Tax Policy Towards Saving," in The Government and Capital Formation (G. von Furstenberg ed. 1980).]

* [Ed.: Aaron & Galper, Reforming the Federal Tax System, 24 Tax Notes 285 (1984).]

inflation indexing, and so on, is unfortunately, difficult to determine. (136–139)

B. INTEGRATION OF THE CORPORATION AND PERSONAL INCOME TAXES

Every industrialized country has been required to deal with the policy questions of whether a corporation should pay an income tax separate from, and in addition to, that on its shareholders; whether the corporate and individual income taxes should be fully "integrated," so that only a single tax at the shareholder level ultimately is borne by income earned in corporate form; or whether some in-between position should be adopted. The United States has chosen a system of completely separate taxation of corporations and shareholders, except in those limited circumstances in which a corporation can, and does, make a Subchapter S election. Furthermore, certain provisions of the 1986 Act, particularly those dealing with distributions of property by the corporation to its shareholders, whether as dividends or in liquidation (see pages 202 and 303) were designed to strengthen the system of double taxation of corporate profits. Other industrialized countries have reached policy decisions falling somewhere between the poles of completely separate taxation and full integration. The following materials present background on this subject, review the recent history of treatment of this issue in the United States, and give a brief survey of some positions which have been taken in other countries.

(1) ROLE OF THE CORPORATE INCOME TAX

Richard Musgrave and Peggy Musgrave, Public Finance in Theory and Practice

McGraw–Hill, Inc. 5th Ed. 1988.

The role of the corporation tax in a good tax system is by no means obvious. If the appropriate tax base is viewed in terms of consumption, there is clearly no case for a corporation tax. Corporate source income should then become taxable only if and when it is distributed and spent by the recipient. But the case for a corporation tax may be questioned even in the context of an income-based approach. Here taxation at the corporate level may be viewed as a mere device for integrating corporate source income into the individual income tax, or it may be viewed as an additional "absolute" tax on corporate source income, to be imposed before net income is allocated to the shareholder. Under U.S. law, the latter view continues to apply. The federal corporation tax of [35] percent is taken out first and cannot be credited against the shareholder's personal income tax on dividend income. Proposals to integrate corporate income into the individual income tax were rejected in the tax reform of 1986.

The Integrationist View

Those who take the integrationist position view the problem of taxation at the corporate level merely as a way of including all corporate-source income in the individual income tax base. Their basic proposition is that in the end, all taxes must be borne by people and that the concept of equitable taxation can be applied to people only. Moreover, they hold that income should be taxed as a whole under a global income concept, independently of its source. Proceeding on the assumption that the corporation income tax falls on profits, they criticize such a tax because profits when distributed are taxed twice—first at the corporation level under the corporation tax and then at the personal level as dividends under the individual income tax.

Consider taxpayer A who pays personal income tax at the 28 percent rate. Her share in the profits of corporation X is $100 on which the corporation pays a tax of $34. The remainder, or $66, is distributed in dividends to A, who then pays an income tax of $18.48. The combined tax equals $52.48. In the absence of a corporation tax, the income tax paid on $100 of dividends would have been $28, thus leaving an "excess tax" of $24.48. Next consider shareholder B, who pays personal income tax at a rate of 15 percent. For him, the combined tax equals $34 plus $9.90, or $43.90. The income tax under an integrated system would have been $15, thus leaving an excess tax of $28.90, somewhat above that of A. Failure to integrate imposes an additional burden and that burden per dollar of corporate source income is larger for the smaller shareholder whose individual income tax is lower. At the same time, note that dividends are likely to comprise a larger share of A's than of B's income. This being the case, the extra tax as a percent of total income may be larger for A than for B. However this may be, the extra tax is unjustified from the integrationist's point of view, because all income (including that derived from corporate source) should be taxed at the same rate. In place of the corporation tax, there should be source withholding of individual income tax on corporate source income.

The preceding illustration has assumed that profits after tax are in fact distributed as dividends. In reality such is not the case, because at least half of profits after corporation tax tend to be retained. In the absence of imputing retained earnings to the shareholder (as would be the case under the integrated system) the corporation tax thus serves the purpose of reaching retained earnings. * * *

The Absolutist View

Those who take an opposing position believe that the integrationist approach rests on an unrealistic view of the corporation. The large widely held corporation—which accounts for the great bulk of corporation tax revenue—is not a mere conduit for personal income. It is a legal entity with an existence of its own, a powerful factor in economic and social decision making, operated by a professional management subject to little control by the individual shareholder. From this it is concluded that being a separate entity, the corporation also has a separate taxable capacity which is properly subject to a separate and absolute tax. Whether profits after tax are distributed or retained is irrelevant in this context.

This "absolute" or "classical" view of the tax is hardly tenable. Corporations do indeed act as distinct decision-making units, only more or less vaguely related to the wishes of the shareholders, thus calling for a regulatory policy at the corporate rather than the shareholder level. Moreover, tax devices may be useful under certain circumstances for such regulatory purposes. However, this is quite a different matter from proposing that a corporation has an ability to pay of its own and should be subject to a distinct tax.[2] Obviously, all taxes must in the end fall on somebody, i.e., on natural persons. Corporate profits are part of the income of the shareholders and, in the spirit of the accretion approach to the income tax, should be taxed as part of their income. There is no reason why they should either bear an extra tax or be given preferred treatment.

Once more, note that this view of the corporation tax rests on the assumption that the tax falls on profits and is not passed on to consumers or wage earners. To the extent that such shifting occurs, the intent of the absolutists to impose an extra tax on corporate source income is thwarted. The tax, in this case, becomes an inferior and arbitrary sales or wages tax, without a rational place in an equitable tax structure.[3]

Other Reasons for Corporation Tax

Even though there is no valid argument for an absolute corporation tax on individual ability-to-pay grounds, a number of other considerations might justify such a tax. However, it would hardly be of the same order of magnitude or structure as the federal profits tax.

Benefit Considerations. Corporations may be called upon to pay a benefit tax. Government renders many services which benefit business operations by reducing costs, broadening markets, facilitating financial transactions, and so forth. Most of these services, however, do not accrue solely to corporations but to other forms of business organization as well. The rationale would therefore be for a general tax on business operations rather than for a tax on corporations only. Although there are certain governmental costs incurred in connection with corporations in particular, these costs are a minor factor and hardly justify a tax. The privilege of operation under limited liability is, of course, of tremendous value to corporations, but the institution of limited liability as such is practically costless to society and hence does not justify imposition of a benefit tax.

2. One may, of course, speak of the ability of a corporation to pay a certain tax without going bankrupt or without curtailing its operations. The concept of capacity to pay as used in this sense, however, relates to the economic effects of the tax rather than to ability to pay as used in the context of equity considerations.

3. It is inferior because the implicit rates of sales or payroll taxation will vary arbitrarily with the profit-sales ratio (margin) or the profits-wage bill ratio of particular corporations.

The purpose of benefit taxes is to allocate the cost of public services rendered, not to charge for costless benefits.

To the extent that a benefit tax is appropriate, two further questions arise. One relates to the level at which such a tax should be imposed. Since most public services which accrue as benefits to business are rendered at the state and local levels, it is evident that such a tax would not be primarily a federal matter. The other relates to the appropriate tax base. This will differ with the service rendered, but in most cases it will not be profits. Thus, real property would best reflect the value of fire protection; employment would reflect the input of school expenditures; transportation would reflect road services; and so forth. If a general proxy is to be used, total costs incurred in the state or locality might be the best overall measure, with value added (which includes profits as well as other factor costs) being a second possibility.

Regulatory Objectives. A different case for an absolute corporation tax may be made if the tax is viewed as an instrument of control over corporate behavior. The appropriate form of corporation tax then depends on the particular policy objective that is to be accomplished.

1. The control of monopoly has been traditionally undertaken through regulatory devices, but a tax approach might be used. This, however, would not call for a general tax on profits, which would not be effective in correcting monopolistic behavior. Rather, it would call for a more complex tax, related to the degree of monopolistic restriction.

2. If it were desired to restrict the absolute size of firms or bigness (which is not the same as restricting monopoly or market shares), a tax might again be used for this purpose. Here, a progressive business tax would be called for. The reason for progression, however, would not be ability to pay, as in the individual income tax. Large firms might be owned by small investors and small firms might be owned by wealthy investors. Rather, progression would be used to discriminate against the large firm and curtail what are considered to be undesirable social effects of bigness. The question then arises about whether such a tax should not be on asset size or sales rather than on profits. Even if bigness is held undesirable, it is not a reason for penalizing the profitable big firm in particular.

Although we have no full-fledged experience with such an approach (a progressive corporation tax was recommended by the Roosevelt administration in 1936 but rejected), a limited application is found in the three-rate schedule which applies various lower rates to small firms. * * *

3. An excess profits tax may be imposed in periods of emergency (such as wars) when direct controls over wages and prices are needed. Wage constraints under such conditions cannot be applied effectively without corresponding profit constraints, and a tax on excess profits is a helpful tool in this connection. The United States imposed such a tax in both world wars as well as during the Korean war. Although sound in principle, the excess profits tax is difficult to administer since excess profits are not readily defined. Such profits may be measured by comparison with a base

period, but inequities may result from differences in initial position; or, a standard rate of return may be used, in which case risk differentials can hardly be overlooked, thus posing the difficult problem of what rates are appropriate for what industries.

A different type of situation in which a selective excess profits tax may be called for was created by the recent oil crisis and the removal of price controls on oil, leading to the imposition of a windfall profits tax.

4. As a stimulus to capital formation and growth, it may be desirable to encourage corporate saving and to discourage dividend distribution. This objective may be accomplished by imposing a tax on dividends paid out while exempting earnings retained. Alternatively, it may be held desirable to encourage corporate distributions and to discourage retentions in order to improve the functioning of the capital market or to increase consumption expenditures. This goal may be achieved by imposing a tax on undistributed profits while exempting profits which are paid out as dividends. Such a tax was imposed in the late thirties with the intention of stimulating consumer spending.

5. Finally, the corporation tax may be used to provide incentives or disincentives to investment, as distinct from corporate savings. Devices like accelerated depreciation and, prior to 1986, the investment tax credit may be used for this purpose, and they may be applied on a cyclical or a secular basis. * * * [I]t should be noted here that such incentives may also be given directly—i.e., in the form of investment subsidies or grants—rather than as relief under the profits tax.

In all, these considerations suggest that tax instruments may be helpful devices in controlling corporate behavior but in most cases, a form of taxation would be required which differs from the profits tax. (371–375)

(2) ISSUES IN CORPORATE TAX INTEGRATION

The following reading, excerpts from books by Charles McLure and Joseph Pechman, respectively, explores first the policy issues involved in the integration of the corporate and individual income taxes, and second, devices to accomplish that integration.

Charles McLure, Must Corporate Income Be Taxed Twice?

The Brookings Institution (1979).

Integration of the corporate and individual income taxes [is] a policy long favored by some public finance economists, but * * * to most Americans, and perhaps even to most economists, lawyers, accountants, politicians, and public officials, integration is so novel that they would have considerable difficulty in answering such questions as: What is integration? What are its advantages? Why the * * * interest in integration? Not to mention: How is integration achieved? What are the issues of tax policy it involves? Are there any unusual practical problems? This book is primarily devoted to the second group of questions. But for background it will be useful to answer the first three questions briefly and give some indication of the importance of the others, as well as to consider some terminology.

* * *

Pros and Cons of Integration

Those who object to the pattern of taxation resulting from the separate, unintegrated income taxes on income originating in investments in corporate shares argue that the separate taxation of corporate-source income is logically indefensible, that it creates both horizontal and vertical inequities, that it distorts the allocation of investment between the corporate sector and the noncorporate sector, that it encourages corporations to rely too heavily on debt financing and retain too great a share of net corporate income, and that it depresses the nation's rates of capital accumulation and economic growth. Against this rather impressive list of indictments, it is countered that the separate taxation of corporate income can be defended on basic tax principles, especially because it adds significantly to the progressivity of the income tax; that the distortions of resource allocation and corporate financial policy have not been firmly documented and would not be very important, in any event; and that integration of the income taxes, because it would encourage distribution of corporate profits, is likely to increase the rates of private capital accumulation and economic growth only if the substantial loss of revenue it would entail were made up in a distinctly regressive way—or not made up at all. Furthermore, say the skeptics, full integration, having never been tried in any country and having been rejected explicitly in at least two, involves considerable practical problems, and even dividend relief, which they view as inequitable, raises many problems, as European experience shows.

Interest in Integration

Interest in integration, which had largely been dormant in the United States since the penalty tax on undistributed profits was repealed in 1939, can be traced to the confluence of several forces. Perhaps the most visible of these has been the much-discussed capital shortage.[12] Businessmen (and some economists) have argued that the tax system in general, and the double taxation of corporate dividends in particular, is responsible for what they take to be an undesirable shortfall in capital formation. Relief from double taxation of dividends, they argue, would go far in relieving the capital shortage.

A second important reason for the * * * interest in integration is the increased tendency for other developed countries to provide at least partial dividend relief. In 1965 France began to allow shareholders credit for half the corporate tax attributable to dividends, and in 1973 the United Kingdom returned to a system of partial relief from double taxation of dividends

12. This is not the place to attempt to judge whether the "capital shortage" is real or imaginary (or indeed what the term is intended to mean). * * *

after using a classical system from 1965 to 1973. Finally, on January 1, 1977, West Germany, which since 1953 had applied a lower rate of tax to dividends than to retentions, became the first member of the European Community to provide complete relief from the double taxation of dividends.*

* * *

Policy Issues in Integration

The three most obvious issues in the debate over integration are whether or not to have some kind of integration; if so, whether it should involve all corporate income or only distributed income; and whether integration or dividend relief should be complete or only partial. But positions on these basic issues depend crucially on how less obvious questions are resolved.

First, corporations, like other business taxpayers, benefit from an array of tax preferences that reduces the effective rate of taxation of corporate economic income * * *. The proper treatment of tax preferences, usually overlooked in elementary discussions of integration and dividend relief, permeates any detailed discussion of dividend relief, and it can do so for integration, too, if a decision is not made at an early stage to eliminate all preferences from the tax code. Among the policy questions that must be settled are whether tax preferences should be eliminated so far as corporate-source income is concerned, passed through to shareholders on all corporate-source income, or passed through only on income that is not distributed; and, beyond that, whether exclusion preferences (such as interest on municipal bonds) and deductible preferences (such as the excess of accelerated depreciation over economic depreciation) should be treated differently from creditable preferences (such as the investment tax credit). Additional questions that must be addressed, especially in the case of dividend relief, include whether preference income is to be assumed to be paid out, or "stacked," first (so that dividends are attributed initially to tax-preferred income) or last (so that dividends are attributed initially to

* [Ed.: The two-rate or "split-rate" system is not currently employed as the sole method of integration in any major industrialized country. As discussed below, however, Germany has employed a split-rate system in conjunction with its imputation system.

The imputation system is utilized, for example, in France, The United Kingdom, Belgium, Ireland and Canada, with each system producing variations on the method. Thus, France gives the shareholder a credit for 50% of the dividend, which credit is grossed-up. The United Kingdom similarly gives a credit of approximately 50%. Canada provides a dividend credit, but the credit is unrelated to the tax paid, if any, at the corporate level. Germany is the only industrialized country which completely integrates the corporate and individual taxes with respect to distributed dividends. Germany also employs a split-rate system in connection with its imputation system. Thus, a higher rate of tax is imposed on undistributed corporate profits than on profits distributed as dividend distributions. The corporate tax on distributed profits is then credited by the shareholder, with the amount of the credit being included in income (grossed-up). See Ault and Radler, The German Corporation Tax Reform Law 1977 (1976).

The classical one-rate system is in effect, for example, in the Netherlands, Switzerland and the United States.]

fully taxed income) or to be split proportionately between dividends and retentions. Whereas economic reasoning may point to certain answers to some of these questions, administrative realities may point elsewhere.

* * * [D]ecisions on the treatment of preferences (especially rules for stacking and washout) involve serious questions of economic policy and not mere technical details. Commercial banks and regulated public utilities, for example, would be hit hard by a system that washed out tax preferences (especially if the foreign tax credit were treated as a preference), even if preference income were stacked last. Considerations such as this may help to explain the adoption of liberal stacking and transition rules in Europe.

Second, some 20 to 25 percent of all corporate stock is held by tax-exempt organizations, including pension funds, foundations, and educational and religious organizations.[18] Should the burden of the corporate income tax be removed from these otherwise tax-exempt organizations if the income taxes are integrated? (The revenue consequences of doing so is enormous * * * under total integration).[19]

Third, any scheme involving integration of the corporation and personal income taxes will have important implications for other components of the income tax system. In some cases the relation will be direct * * *. In other instances the tie will be less direct, but still very strong; full integration, for example, may be unacceptable without a withholding tax levied at the corporate level at a rate that is coordinated with the top marginal rate under the personal income tax. Furthermore, whether any form of integration is politically acceptable will depend on the tax reforms that accompany it. Dividend relief, for example, would substantially reduce the distributional progressivity of the tax system and would be acceptable among liberals only if packaged with a large reduction of the tax preferences currently enjoyed by high-income households; total integration, by comparison, because it would reach retained earnings on a current basis, might be acceptable to this group even if accompanied by less extensive tax reform.

Fourth, any form of integration involves incredibly complicated questions about the proper taxation of international flows of corporate earnings. How, for example, should dividends flowing between two countries that provide dividend relief be taxed? Should the relief be granted by the source country or the residence country? Does it matter whether direct or portfolio investment is involved? What if the two countries employ different means of providing dividend relief? What if only one country allows dividend relief and the other has a classical system? A fully integrated system? These basic

18. This estimate is based on figures for the receipt of dividends contained in Marshall E. Blume, Jean Crockett, and Irwin Friend, "Stockownership in the United States: Characteristics and Trends," Survey of Current Business, vol. 54 (November 1974), pp. 16–40.

19. See Simon, Tax Reform, pp. 3856–57, and Break and Pechman, Federal Tax Reform: The Impossible Dream? p. 103.

questions must be settled—and the answers agreed upon by the countries—before it is possible to proceed to technical problems of implementation.*

* * *

International Considerations

One of the few subjects commonly encountered by tax economists that is more complicated than integration is the tax treatment of income flowing across international boundaries; unfortunately the proper tax treatment of such income poses major problems for either integration or dividend relief. Clearly, international tax relations are simplest if all countries employ classical systems. But the United States' most important trading partners use tax systems that provide at least partial relief from the double taxation of dividends; therefore, it may become increasingly difficult to negotiate tax treaties if the United States retains an unintegrated classical system. Yet international considerations, as well as administrative difficulties, tend to militate against the adoption of full integration. Given the present interpretation of "reciprocity" in double taxation conventions, the difficulty of not allowing the benefits of integration to foreign shareholders in U.S. firms might dictate against the use of the dividend-paid deduction method of dividend relief, which many observers find to be the most natural and most easily administered approach if appraised only in terms of its domestic attributes. Thus the very choice between the shareholder credit approach and the dividend-paid deduction might be in large part predetermined by U.S. treaty obligations and foreign practices. Unless the United States could persuade other major countries to change from the shareholder credit approach to the dividend-paid deduction (or the equivalent split-rate system), use of the second approach might be effectively foreclosed.

J. Pechman, Federal Tax Policy

The Brookings Institution (Fifth ed. 1987).

Taxation of corporate earnings continues to be controversial. Some people regard taxation of total profits under the corporation tax and of distributed profits under the individual income tax as inequitable. Others believe that taxation of the corporation as a separate entity is justified. Whether something needs to be done depends on an evaluation of the economic issues discussed earlier and on the effect of the proposed changes on the distribution of tax burdens. The problem is tricky and there is no easy solution.

The Additional Burden on Dividends

On the assumption that all, or a significant portion, of the corporation tax rests on the stockholder, the effect of the tax is to impose the heaviest

* ([Ed.: See Ault, Corporate Integration, Tax Treaties, and the Division of the International Tax Base, 47 Tax L. Rev. 565 (1995).]

burden on dividends received by persons in the lowest income classes. This can be seen by examining the illustrative calculations in table 5–9, which show the total and additional tax burden on stockholders who receive $66 of dividends under present tax rates. Given the present rate of 34 percent, the corporation income before tax from which the $66 of dividends were paid must have amounted to $100. If this $100 had been subject to individual income tax rates only, the tax on these dividends would go from zero at the bottom of the income scale to 33 percent in the zone where the benefit of the first bracket rate and the exemption are phased out * * * and 28 percent at the top. With the corporation tax, the combined individual and corporation income tax increases from $34 for those subject to a zero rate to $55.78 for those subject to the 33 percent rate and $52.48 for those subject to the 28 percent rate (table 5–9, column 6).

Table 5–9. Additional Burden of the Corporation Income Tax on $100 of Corporation Income [a]

Dollars

Marginal individual income tax rate (percent) (1)	*Corporate income before tax* (2)	*Corporation tax at 34 percent* (3)	*Dividends received by stockholders* (4)	*Stockholder's individual income tax* (5)	*Total tax burden* (6)	*Additional burden of the corporation tax* (7)
0	100	34	66	0	34.00	34.00
10	100	34	66	6.60	40.60	30.60
20	100	34	66	13.20	47.20	27.20
28	100	34	66	18.48	52.48	24.48
33	100	34	66	21.78	55.78	22.78
40	100	34	66	26.40	60.40	20.40
50	100	34	66	33.00	67.00	17.00

Column 3 = 0.34 × column 2.
Column 4 = column 2 − column 3.
Column 5 = column 4 × column 1.
Column 6 = column 3 + column 5.
Column 7 = column 6 − column 1 × column 2.
a. Assumes that corporation income after tax is devoted entirely to the payment of dividend.

However, the *additional* burden resulting from the corporation tax falls as income rises. For example, the taxpayer subject to a zero individual rate would have paid no tax on the $66 of dividends; the additional corporation income tax burden in this case is the full $34 tax. By contrast, a taxpayer subject to the 28 percent rate pays an individual income tax of $18.48 on the dividend, and the total tax burden on the original $100 of corporate earnings is $52.48. But since the taxpayer would have to pay $28.00 under the individual income tax in any case, the additional burden is only $24.48. For the taxpayer subject to the 33 percent rate, the additional burden is $22.78 (table 5–9, column 7).

One test of an equitable method of moderating or eliminating the additional tax burden on dividends is to ask whether the method removes a uniform percentage of the additional burden shown in table 5–9. If the percentage removed is the same for dividend recipients in every individual income tax bracket, the method deals evenly at all levels. Deviations from a constant percentage indicate the dividend recipients who are favored or penalized by the method.

A second test is whether the method increases or reduces the progressivity of the tax system as a whole. Since corporate ownership is heavily concentrated in the high income classes * * *, moderation or reduction of the additional tax burden on dividends alone would reduce progressivity, unless the change were accompanied by rate increases or revisions in the individual income tax base to prevent large tax cuts for the minority of taxpayers who have large stockholdings.

Methods of Integration

Five methods of integrating the corporation and individual income taxes have been used at various times in different countries: (1) a dividend-received credit for individuals; (2) a deduction for dividends paid by the corporation in computing the corporation income tax; (3) a "split-rate" corporation income tax, which applies a higher tax rate to undistributed than to distributed corporate earnings; (4) a method that considers all or a portion of the corporation income tax to be withholding on dividends at the source; and (5) an exclusion of all or a portion of the dividends received from the individual income tax base. These methods would only partially integrate the corporation and individual income taxes because the relief would be given only to distributed earnings. A sixth method would be to treat all corporations like partnerships and tax their income to the stockholders whether distributed or not. This is the only method that would fully integrate the corporation and individual income taxes on both distributed and undistributed corporate earnings and would rely entirely on the individual income tax for the taxation of corporate profits. Of the various methods, the second, third, fourth, and sixth would remove the same proportion of the additional burden of the corporation tax at all individual income levels. All the methods would make the federal tax system less progressive without offsetting changes. It is assumed that there is no shifting of the corporation income tax.

THE DIVIDEND-RECEIVED CREDIT. Under this method, dividend recipients are allowed to deduct a percentage of their dividends as a credit against their individual income tax. Between 1954 and 1963, U.S. taxpayers were allowed a credit of 4 percent for dividends after a $50 exclusion ($100 for joint returns).

Although the credit grants the same relief on a dollar of dividends at all income levels, it removes an increasing proportion of the additional burden of the corporation tax as incomes rise. For those subject to a zero rate, the credit is worthless. For a taxpayer subject to a 10 percent rate, the 4 percent credit would remove 8.6 percent of the additional burden, and for a taxpayer subject to the maximum 33 percent rate, the credit would remove 11.6 percent (table 5–10). This regressive pattern of relief led to its repeal.

Table 5–10. Portion of the Additional Burden of the Corporation Income Tax Removed by the 4 Percent Dividend–Received Credit

Marginal individual income tax rate (percent) (1)	*Additional burden resulting from corporation tax (dollars)* (2)	*Dividend-received credit (dollars)* (3)	*Percentage of additional burden removed by the dividend credit* (4)
0	34.00	a	a
10	30.60	2.64	8.6
20	27.20	2.64	9.7
28	24.48	2.64	10.8
33	22.78	2.64	11.6
40	20.40	2.64	12.9
50	17.00	2.64	15.5

Column 2 = column 7 of table 5–9.
Column 3 = 4 percent of $66.
Column 4 = column 3 − column 2.
a. The credit has no value for those subject to a zero tax rate.

THE DIVIDEND-PAID DEDUCTION. This is the simplest method of dealing with the problem; it was used in the United States in 1936 and 1937 as a basis for a surtax on corporate earnings. Corporations deduct from their taxable income all or a portion of the dividends they pay out, and the corporation tax applies to the remainder. Table 5–11 shows the relief that would be granted under this method if the corporation were allowed a deduction of 25 percent of dividends paid. As shown in column 6, the relief would be 17.9 percent of the additional tax imposed by the corporation income tax at all income levels.

Table 5–11. Portion of the Additional Burden of the Corporation Income Tax Removed by the Dividend–Paid Deduction

Assuming the corporation deducts 25 percent of dividends paid					
		Tax benefit of dividend-paid deduction (dollars)			
Marginal individual income tax rate (percent) (1)	*Additional burden resulting from corporation tax (dollars)* (2)	*Reduced corporation tax (paid to stock-holders as additional dividends)* (3)	*Tax on additional dividends* (4)	*Net benefit* (5)	*Percentage of additional burden removed by the dividend–paid deduction* (6)
0	34.00	6.09	0	6.09	17.9
10	30.60	6.09	0.61	5.48	17.9
20	27.20	6.09	1.22	4.87	17.9
28	24.48	6.09	1.71	4.38	17.9
33	22.78	6.09	2.01	4.08	17.9
40	20.40	6.09	2.44	3.65	17.9
50	17.00	6.09	3.05	3.04	17.9

Column 2 = column 7 of table 5–9.
Column 3 = amount of additional dividends corporations could pay out with a 25 percent dividend-paid deduction.
Column 4 = column 1 × column 3.
Column 5 = column 3 − column 4.
Column 6 = column 5 − column 2.

Aside from granting the same proportionate relief at all income levels, the dividend-paid [deduction] has the merit of treating dividends like interest. (If a full deduction were allowed, the treatment would be identical.) This would increase the attractiveness of equity financing by corporations.

The surtax on undistributed profits raised a storm of protest when it was used briefly in the United States during the 1930s. Corporations complained that by encouraging payouts of earnings it reduced their ability to save and invest at a time when the market for corporate equities was almost dried up. The method is also criticized on the ground that it discourages internal financing by corporations and might reduce total saving and investment. On the other hand, some believe it unwise to permit corporations to avoid the capital markets for financing their investment programs. Forcing them "to stand the test of the marketplace" might exercise a desirable restraint on bigness and also give investors more control over the disposition of their funds.

An alternative method of equalizing the treatment of dividends and interest would be to eliminate the deduction for interest in computing the taxable income of corporations. Since the base of the tax would be raised, the tax rate could be reduced substantially. * * * Such a plan has merit if a separate tax on corporate capital—whether financed by debt or equity capital—is justified. Such a tax has not been seriously considered in the United States because it would drastically alter the distribution of the corporation tax burden among firms and industries. In general, manufacturing corporations, which rely mainly on equity capital, would benefit; utilities and transportation and financial companies, which rely heavily on borrowed capital, would pay much higher taxes.

THE SPLIT-RATE CORPORATION INCOME TAX. A number of countries tax undistributed earnings at a higher rate than distributed earnings. This split-rate plan is similar in effect to a deduction for dividends paid. For example, a 50–25 percent split rate would be equivalent to a 50 percent tax on total corporate earnings with a deduction of 50 percent for dividends paid. The percentages actually used by various countries differ greatly, reflecting the absence of accepted criteria for establishing the split rates. The split-rate system is used in Austria, Japan, Norway, and other countries.

THE IMPUTATION METHOD. Under this method, all or a portion of the individual income tax is regarded as having been paid at the source (through the corporation tax). For example, if 10 percent of the dividend were regarded as having been withheld, a shareholder receiving a $66 dividend would "gross up" the dividend by adding $6.60 (0.10 x 66) to taxable income and then take the $6.60 as a credit against tax. In this illustration, the portion of the additional burden of the corporation income tax removed is 19.4 percent at all income levels (table 5–12). Thus, with a corporate rate of 34 percent, a dividend gross-up of 10 percent at the individual level is somewhat more generous than a 25 percent dividend deduction at the corporate level (compare column 6 of tables 5–11 and 5–12).

Table 5–12. Portion of the Additional Burden of the Corporation Income Tax Removed by the Imputation Method

Assuming 10 percent of dividends received regarded as withheld

		Withholding credit (dollars)			
Marginal individual income tax rate (percent) (1)	*Additional burden resulting from corporation tax (dollars)* (2)	*Amount withheld at source* (3)	*Tax on amount withheld* (4)	*Net credit* (5)	*Percentage of additional burden removed by the dividend credit* (6)
0	34.00	6.60	0	6.60	19.4
10	30.60	6.60	0.66	5.94	19.4
20	27.20	6.60	1.32	5.28	19.4
28	24.48	6.60	1.85	4.75	19.4
33	22.78	6.60	2.18	4.42	19.4
40	20.40	6.60	2.64	3.96	19.4
50	17.00	6.60	3.30	3.30	19.4

Column 2 = column 7 of table 5–9.
Column 3 = 10 percent of $66.
Column 4 = column 1 × column 3.
Column 5 = column 3 − column 4.
Column 6 = column 5 ÷ column 2.

The imputation method achieves the same result as the dividend-paid deduction for corporations but is likely to discourage corporate saving somewhat less. This advantage frequently makes the imputation method more attractive, even though it is more difficult to understand and would also complicate the individual income tax return. Variants of the imputation method are used in a number of countries, including the United Kingdom, France, Italy, and West Germany.

THE DIVIDEND EXCLUSION. This method permits individual income taxpayers to exclude all or a portion of their dividends from taxable income. In the United States, between 1964 and 1986 there was an individual exclusion of $100 ($200 on joint returns), which was a vestige of the compromise adopted when the 4 percent dividend credit was repealed. The [exclusion] was eliminated beginning in 1987, when the tax base was broadened to provide revenue for rate reductions. Like the dividend-received credit, the exclusion grants an increasing amount of relief on a dollar of dividends as incomes rise. Accordingly, it cannot remove the same proportion of the additional tax burden at all levels of income.

THE PARTNERSHIP METHOD, OR FULL INTEGRATION. The most far-reaching solution is to regard the income of corporations as belonging to their stockholders in the year in which it is earned, regardless of whether the earnings are distributed. The corporation income tax as such would be abolished, but a tax would be retained at the corporate level as a withholding device for the individual income tax. Stockholders would pay individual income tax on their prorated share of the earnings of corporations in which they held stock and would receive credit for the amount of tax withheld at the source, just as in the case of wages and salaries.

This method would automatically apply the correct individual income tax rates to all corporate earnings and thus equalize the tax rates on corporate and noncorporate earnings. It would also be less regressive and less costly than partial integration for dividends alone, because retained as well as distributed corporate earnings would be subject to the individual income tax.

A major drawback of the plan is that, unless the withholding rate was set at a high level, some stockholders would not have funds to pay tax on earnings they did not receive. This would force them to liquidate security holdings or apply pressure on corporations to distribute a much larger portion of their retained earnings. In the former case, stock ownership among people with modest means would be discouraged; in the latter, corporate saving would be reduced.

Treatment approximating this method is available under present law for closely held corporations with no more than thirty-five shareholders. These corporations operate much like partnerships and can arrange to distribute enough earnings to the partners to avoid forced liquidations. The decision to be treated like a partnership for tax purposes is made only if it is advantageous to the shareholders. Experts agree that it would not be practical to extend the partnership method to large, publicly held corporations with complex capital structures, frequent changes in ownership, and thousands or millions of stockholders.

A procedure that would approximate the effect of the partnership method and avoid its liquidity problems would be to permit corporations to allocate all or a portion of their undistributed earnings to their shareholders. The corporation income tax would be converted to a withholding tax for the individual income tax, and the corporate rate would be set at the top-bracket individual income tax rate. Shareholders would include the allocated dividends as well as cash dividends in their taxable income and would deduct the amount of tax withheld as a credit against their income tax. The only difference between this procedure and the original partnership method is that the allocation of earnings by corporations to shareholders would not be mandatory. But since shareholders would be denied immediate credit for the withheld tax, the pressure on corporate management to allocate all undistributed earnings would probably be irresistible. The procedure, which was originally proposed by a Canadian Royal Commission in 1966, has merit (if a separate corporation tax is considered inappropriate), but it has not been seriously considered anywhere.

ILLUSTRATIVE MATERIAL

A. GENERAL

Although there was some political interest in integration of the corporate and personal income taxes and/or dividend relief in the mid 1970s, over the past two decades interest in integration has been tepid at best, as tax policy attention at various times has focused on matters of rate reductions, dealing with the effect of inflation in constructing capital cost recovery provisions, and finally, in the mid–1980's, to broadening the tax base. In the Tax Reform Act of 1986 Congress adopted several provisions that strengthened the double taxation system, e.g., repealing the so-called *General Utilities* rule, which previously had permitted corporations to distribute appreciated property to their shareholders without recognition of corporate level gain. When the double taxation system was threatened by a rapid proliferation of publicly traded limited partnerships, portending a move by business to "self-help" integration, Congress intervened in 1987 by enacting § 7704, discussed at page 46, which taxes unincorporated publicly traded business entities as corporations.

This declining interest in integration also coincided with a growing appreciation of the extraordinarily complex and difficult technical issues which would be entailed in implementing any form of integration system. See McLure, A Status Report on Tax Integration in the United States, 31 Nat'l Tax J. 313 (1978). Moreover, it became apparent that various components of the political process had strongly differing interests in the extent and characteristics of any form of integration that might be adopted. See McClure and Surrey, Integration of Income Taxes: Issues For Debate, 55 Harv.Bus.Rev. 169 (Sept.-Oct. 1977). Academic interest in the issue, however, has continued. Furthermore, as a practical matter, integration is rapidly becoming relevant only with respect to publicly traded businesses. With the enactment of limited liability company statutes in virtually every state, owners of a closely held business can enjoy the important attributes of a corporation for state law purposes while achieving pass-through single level tax status. See page 40. Nevertheless, the issue continues to be important because the relatively small number of publicly traded corporations earn a dominant share of overall business profits.

How does the issue of who economically bears the burden of the corporate tax relate to the desirability of integration? Would integration be less appropriate if the burden is shifted primarily to workers or consumers than it would be if the burden is borne primarily by shareholders?

B. AMERICAN LAW INSTITUTE STUDY REPORTER'S PROPOSALS

Among the arguments made in favor of integration is that the current double taxation system distorts the corporation's choice as to whether to fund new investment by issuing shares to raise equity capital or by borrowing. This problem was addressed by Professor William Andrews, the Reporter for the American Law Institute, Federal Income Tax Project, Subchapter C: Proposals on Corporate Acquisitions and Dispositions (1980), in his Study on Distributions (1980), published with the adopted ALI proposals. Professor Andrews adopted a different approach to the proper relationship between the corporate and individual tax systems as reflected in the following excerpt:

"Most of the troubles with existing law arise from two main uncompensated biases: 1) the bias against new equity investment, and 2) the bias in favor of nondividend distributions. The main proposals in this Study are to alleviate those biases by providing relief for the former and imposing a compensatory excise on the latter. If these proposals were adopted, all distributions would be subjected to more nearly comparable tax burdens, and contributions to corporate equity (negative distributions) would attract a comparable benefit (negative burden). In such a system, the difficult definitional problems with which present law struggles would be eliminated or reduced substantially in significance.

"While the proposals complement one another in important ways, an effort has been made to analyze and present them separately, as follows:

"1) *Relief for new equity*. Reporter's Proposal R1 is to relieve the bias against new equity by provision of a deduction based on newly contributed equity capital. The main proposal is for a corporate dividends-paid deduction, limited to a specified rate on the amount of net newly contributed equity capital, akin to the interest deduction that would have resulted from a debt investment. Adoption of this proposal would move a long way toward eliminating problems of differentiation between debt and equity, since it would attach comparable tax consequences to any investment of outside funds.

"The main problem in implementing this proposal is defining net newly contributed investment in a manner that will exclude mere refinancing of accumulated earnings or previously contributed capital. This problem would be minimized if an appropriate tax burden were imposed generally on nondividend distributions.

"2) *Nondividend distributions*. Reporter's Proposal R2 would deal with the present bias in favor of nondividend distributions by imposing some increased tax on them. One possibility would be to impute redemption distributions pro rata to continuing shareholders, as if they had received a dividend and used it to buy out redeeming shareholders. The proposal offered is simply to impose a flat-rate, compensatory excise on nondividend distributions, to be withheld and paid over to the government by the distributing corporation.

"Adoption of this proposal would take much of the pressure off questions of dividend equivalence, with which present law struggles, and make it possible to be much more lenient about stock dividends and spin-offs, and the bailout opportunities they generate under existing law.

"3) *Intercorporate investments and distributions*. A corporation can now purchase dividend-paying stock of another corporation and enjoy 85 or 100 percent exemption from corporate income tax on the dividends received from this investment. A purchase of shares from noncorporate shareholders represents an indirect way of distributing funds out of corporate solution, and the intercorporate dividend deduction operates to contract the corporate income tax base accordingly, but all without any distribution, as such, by either corporation. Reporter's Proposal R3 would distinguish between direct and mere portfolio investment. In the case of portfolio investment, the dividend-received deduction and cognate provisions would be made inapplicable; with respect to direct investment those provisions would continue in effect, but purchases of shares would be treated as nondividend distributions subject to the compensatory excise in Reporter's Proposal R2." (353–355)

Note how the ALI Subchapter C Study Reporter's proposals deal with the transition problem that would arise if an integration proposal were adopted. Assuming that the shareholders bear some substantial portion of the corporate tax and that such tax burden is capitalized into, i.e., depresses, the value of corporate stock and hence the price at which the current owners purchased the stock, adoption of full integration or dividend relief would give rise to a windfall economic gain for those shareholders. By limiting relief to the portion of the yield on new equity which approximates interest, the Reporter's approach eliminates this problem. How does the proposal for a corporate level excise tax on nondividend distributions increase the fairness or the efficiency of taxation of corporate income? It appears that the perceived problem is that a greater price can be obtained for shares sold back to the corporation than for shares sold to another investor because the other investor could be expected to discount the value of the shares to an amount below the value of a proportionate amount of the corporation's assets to reflect the double taxation of a flow of dividends from those assets. Are the ALI Reporter's proposals intended to solve the same problems as are perceived by those who favor integration?

C. TREASURY DEPARTMENT STUDY

In January of 1992 the Treasury Department released a comprehensive study on integration of the corporate and individual income tax systems. United States Department of the Treasury, Report on Integration of The Individual and Corporate Tax Systems: Taxing Business Income Once (1992). The Report concluded that integration of the corporate and individual taxes would reduce three economic distortions inherent in the classical corporate tax system. First, the current incentive to invest in non-corporate rather than corporate businesses would be reduced. A correlative effect would be the elimination of "self-help integration" through disincorporation. Second, elimination of the double taxation of earnings from corporate equity investment would reduce the tax incentive to finance new corporate investment with debt rather than equity. Finally, integration would reduce the incentive to retain earnings in some cases, and in other cases to repurchase shares with borrowed funds in order to avoid the double tax on distribution of corporate profits.

The Report focused on the basic operation of three prototype systems: (1) a dividend exclusion system; (2) a shareholder allocation system; and (3) a Comprehensive Business Income Tax (CBIT) system. An imputation credit system was discussed but was not proposed. The Treasury Department recommended further study of the relatively simple dividend exclusion model and the CBIT prototype.

Under the dividend exclusion prototype, the corporate income tax would continue in effect much in its current form. Distributions to shareholders, however, would be tax-free. The primary technical complexity of the dividend exclusion model is the need to maintain an Excludable Distributions Account (EDA) at the corporate level. The EDA would be credited with an amount equal to the income on which the corporation paid taxes and only distributions charged against the EDA would be eligible for exemption at the shareholder level. Such a rule is necessitated, in part, by the existence of tax preferences, such as accelerated depreciation and expensing of certain capital outlays, in the corporate income tax. These preferences sometimes are viewed as effectively reducing the rate of corporate taxation, or, alternatively, as effectively exempting some of the corporation's income from taxation. Since income sheltered from corporate taxation by preferences would not augment the EDA, distributions of such income would be taxable to shareholders. In addition, because gains from the sale of stock in some part generally represent retained earnings, some mechanism is necessary to ameliorate double taxation caused by taxing gains from the sale of stock. To deal with this issue, the Treasury Report proposed a Dividend Reinvestment Plan (DRIP) election under which the corporation and shareholders could deem earnings to have been distributed by the corporation and recontributed by the shareholders, thereby effecting an increase in the shareholders' bases in their stock. By recommending a dividend exclusion model, the report avoids the need to reexamine some basic policy decisions regarding the treatment of distributions to tax-exempt organizations. In order to insure that all corporate income is taxed at least once, tax-exempt organizations, such as charities and pension funds owning stock in a taxable corporation, might have to be taxed if relief from double taxation were effected at the corporate level rather than at the shareholder level.[9]

Presumably because the dividend exclusion prototype, while eliminating the double tax on corporate income, does not eliminate all differences between debt and equity financing,[10] the Treasury Report sets forth the more radical CBIT prototype. The distinctive feature of the CBIT is the denial of the interest deduction for both corporate and unincorporated businesses, coupled with an exemption for interest income. Under the

9. The Report recommends that the exclusion of interest and dividend income be extended to nonresident alien shareholders only through tax treaties. See Ault, Corporate Integration and Tax Treaties: Where Do We Go From Here?, 4 Tax Note Int'l 545 (March 16, 1992); Doernberg, International Aspects of Individual and Corporate Tax Integration, 4 Tax Notes Int'l 535 (March 26, 1992).

10. Under the dividend exclusion prototype system, dividends are not deductible by the corporation but are excludable by the shareholder. Interest, however, is deductible by the corporation but includable by the creditor. While facially there appears to be a single level of tax on both interest and dividends, when a tax exempt organization is the lender the interest income escapes taxation at both the corporate and investor levels.

CBIT, corporations, partnerships, and proprietorships all would pay an entity level tax on their profits, but both dividends and interest would be tax exempt to the recipient.[11] It appears that the Treasury Department's CBIT prototype does not provide for a deduction for reasonable compensation to owner/employees, such as partners and proprietors, instead relying on an exemption from the CBIT for small businesses "[b]ecause it is difficult to separate returns to capital from returns to labor in the case of very small businesses." Failure to provide such a deduction is a problem whenever the owner-employee is in a marginal tax bracket less than the CBIT rate, which was proposed to be 31 percent (equal to the then maximum individual rate). In such cases the CBIT could overtax the owner/employee unless the small business exception applied.

The Treasury Department Report examines, but recommends against adoption of a full imputation model, in other words, treating all corporations the same as partnerships and taxing the shareholders currently on their respective shares of corporate income, without regard to distributions. Such a system, the report concludes, would be too complex to administer. The Treasury Department likewise rejected an imputation credit system, which in effect treats the corporate income tax largely as a refundable withholding tax on corporate distributions, as too complex. Since the latter is the mechanism employed by most industrialized countries that have adopted integration systems, the Treasury's conclusion is somewhat puzzling.

In opting to recommend two systems that levy a flat rate entity level tax on business profits and exempt from tax distributions representing the yield on capital investment, the Treasury Department appears to have decided implicitly that income from capital largely should be taxed at a flat rate, rather than at progressive rates. This conclusion is re-enforced by the Treasury's rejection of the shareholder allocation and imputation credit systems, both of which can be structured to preserve principles of progressive taxation. Indeed, the arguments in favor of either of the systems include the preservation of taxation of dividends at the shareholder's personal tax rate. The traditional equity criterion of tax policy has been subordinated in the Treasury Report. Instead, the Treasury Department appears to have given primacy to administrability and economic efficiency criteria.

The concept of taxing some types of income at flat rates, whether higher or lower than the maximum marginal rate applying to other types of income, previously has not received an imprimatur of approval from any branch of the government. Some analogy might lie, however, in the provisions that between 1969 and 1981 imposed a maximum rate of 50 percent on income from services, and the provisions in effect from 1954 until 1978 imposing a maximum rate of 25 percent on capital gains (limited to $50,000 of gains after 1969).

11. The Report recommends that the exemption for interest and dividend income be extended to nonresident alien shareholders and bondholders only through tax treaties.

Notwithstanding the rejection by the Treasury Department of the imputation credit system for integration of the corporate and individual income taxes, the American Law Institute developed a report concerning an imputation credit prototype for integration. Under the ALI's model, the corporate income tax would be converted into a withholding tax on shareholder income taxes on corporate distributions. For purposes of computing shareholders' incomes, distributions would be grossed-up by the amount of taxes "withheld" by the corporation. Because the withholding tax would be creditable against income from other sources and refundable to the extent it exceeded taxes on income from other sources, progressivity at the shareholder level could be preserved. Unlike the Treasury Department proposals, the ALI draft proposals provide for a limited pass-through to shareholders of certain tax preferences. Like the Treasury Department Report, the ALI proposal recognizes that some relief for capital gains realized on the sale of corporate stock may be appropriate to relieve the double tax on retained earnings. Thus the ALI also recommends a constructive dividend-reinvestment rule. In addition, the ALI report proposed other rules to coordinate the imputation credit system with the capital loss limitation rules, which should be relaxed, and the § 1014 step-up in basis at death, which should be denied in an amount (roughly speaking) equal to any dividends (grossed-up by withholding taxes) that could be distributed to the heirs on which taxes had been withheld.

Finally, because the ALI proposals, unlike the Treasury Department Report, tax corporate earnings at the shareholder's rate, the elimination of even a single level of tax on corporate earnings distributed to tax-exempt shareholders must be considered. Although the ALI proposals take no position on the treatment of tax-exempt organizations generally, the proposals include the imposition of tax on both the interest and dividend income of tax-exempt entities, while allowing them the credit for corporate taxes paid with respect to the dividend income and another credit for taxes withheld on the interest income. The ALI proposals include a separate corporate interest withholding tax with respect to interest paid by corporations; although interest would remain deductible in computing taxable income, corporations would pay a flat rate tax on interest payments made and recipients of interest would receive a credit for this tax although their interest income would not be grossed-up by the withholding tax paid by the corporation. The purpose of this rather complex rule is to equalize the treatment of debt and equity investments by tax-exempt entities. Because of this limited goal, the ALI proposals make no recommendation regarding the tax rate that should be imposed on tax-exempt entities, and note that if the rate were set at zero and, as recommended, both credits are refundable, no tax would be imposed on corporate earnings distributed as either dividends or interest to tax-exempt shareholders. Rules dealing with foreign shareholders and bondholders in domestic corporations would be similarly structured, with a Foreign Investor's Tax imposed at the corporate level on interest and dividends paid to foreign investors (and gains realized by foreign investors on sales of securities in domestic corporations) and a refundable credit against that tax at the shareholder level. Again, the ALI proposes no recommendation regarding the tax rate.

Notwithstanding these more recent expressions of interest in integrating the corporate and individual income tax systems, there is little likelihood that any comprehensive integration system will be adopted in the near future unless, as proposed by a number of Republican congressional leaders in the early 1990s, the entire tax system is revised to abandon income taxation in favor of a consumption tax. Simply to repeal either the corporate level of tax or the shareholder level of tax would involve very substantial revenue losses. If integration were to be revenue neutral, a substantial increase in individual income tax rates or repeal of tax preferences would be required.

CHAPTER 2

IDENTIFYING TAXABLE CORPORATE ENTITIES

Under current law, corporate income in the highest income bracket is taxed at a marginal rate of 35 percent (although surtax rates applicable to certain lower income brackets result in effective marginal rates as high as 39 percent), and the maximum individual marginal tax rate is 39.6 percent. At differing income levels, however, a significant rate differential may exist between the corporate and individual rates, but the relationship cannot be described as systematic. A maximum corporate tax rate that approaches the maximum individual tax rate of 39.6 percent, coupled with the double taxation of corporate earnings, serves as a disincentive to organizing businesses in the corporate form unless nontax factors strongly indicate that the corporate form is necessary or desirable.

Prior to the 1986 Act, the maximum individual rate exceeded the maximum corporate rate by a substantial amount. In addition, although corporate earnings were taxed twice, if the distribution of earnings was delayed until liquidation of the corporation or of the shareholder's entire interest in the corporation, the shareholder level tax was incurred at preferential rates for long-term capital gains that were even more generous than the current preference. These factors, coupled with the pre–1987 statutory provisions that permitted corporations to distribute appreciated property to shareholders without recognizing a corporate level taxable gain on the appreciation, served as a strong tax inducement to incorporate a profitable business venture that was going to accumulate and reinvest earnings, even if no nontax factors indicated that incorporation was preferable to the partnership or sole proprietorship form. Conversely, if the venture was expected to produce a tax loss, for example a business experiencing tax losses in its early years in part because of tax preferences, it was advantageous to be taxed as a partnership or sole proprietorship, even though the use of the corporate form would have been desirable to accomplish some nontax objective.

The pre–1987 incentive for individuals to shift income to a corporation (or obtain other tax benefits available only in corporate form) gave rise to controversies regarding whether income should be taxed to the corporation or directly to its owners. The materials in this chapter examine the resolution of this issue in several contexts. Under the current rate structure, however, in many instances the positions of the government and the taxpayer may be reversed, i.e., the government may seek to tax income at the corporate rather than the individual rate; individual taxpayers may have the opposite objective.

SECTION 1. WHAT IS A "CORPORATION" UNDER THE INCOME TAX?

INTERNAL REVENUE CODE: Sections 7701(a)(3); 7704.

REGULATIONS: Sections 301.7701–1(a) and (b),–2(a), (b)(1)-(7), –3(a), (b)(1), (c)(1)(i)-(iv),–4(a)-(c).

A business may be conducted by an entity that under the law of the state or foreign nation in which the entity is organized is a corporation, a partnership, or neither a corporation nor a partnership, for example, a limited liability company (LLC) or a business trust. For federal income tax purposes, however, Treas. Reg. § 301.7701–2 provides that a business entity with two or more members is classified as either a partnership or a corporation. For this purpose the term "business entity" is very broad. See Treas. Reg. § 301.7701–1(a)(2). It includes not only corporations, partnerships (both limited and general), and limited liability companies formally organized as such under state law, but also less formally organized associations as well as business trusts. Under Treas. Reg. § 301.7701–2(b), any business organized as a "corporation" under relevant state or federal law automatically is classified as a corporation for federal income tax purposes, as are insurance companies and most banks. Treas. Reg. § 301.7701–2(b)(8) lists specified foreign entities that are *per se* corporations for federal income tax purposes.

A "business entity" that is not listed in Treas. Reg. § 301.7701–2(b) is classified as a partnership. Treas. Reg. § 301.7701–3(a) and (b). An entity that is classified as a partnership may elect to be taxed as a corporation, Treas. Reg. § 301.7701–3(a), but if no election is made, the entity is by default classified as a partnership. Treas. Reg. § 301.7701–3(b). Treas. Reg. § 301.7701–4 distinguishes businesses, financial operations, and ventures taxed as partnerships from trusts established for the protection and conservation of property (which may include a trade or business operated by the trust as a sole proprietor).

Rules and Regulations, Department of the Treasury, Internal Revenue Service, Simplification of Entity Classification Rules

T.D. 8697, 1997–1 I.C.B. 215.

Explanation of Provisions

Section 7701(a)(2) of the Code defines a partnership to include a syndicate, group, pool, joint venture, or other unincorporated organization, through or by means of which any business, financial operation, or venture is carried on, and that is not a trust or estate or a corporation. Section

7701(a)(3) defines a corporation to include associations, joint-stock companies, and insurance companies.

The existing regulations for classifying business organizations as associations (which are taxable as corporations under section 7701(a)(3)) or as partnerships under section 7701(a)(2) are based on the historical differences under local law between partnerships and corporations. Treasury and the IRS believe that those rules have become increasingly formalistic. This document replaces those rules with a much simpler approach that generally is elective.

As stated in the preamble to the proposed regulations, in light of the increased flexibility under an elective regime for the creation of organizations classified as partnerships, Treasury and the IRS will continue to monitor carefully the uses of partnerships in the international context and will take appropriate action when partnerships are used to achieve results that are inconsistent with the policies and rules of particular Code provisions or of U.S. tax treaties.

A. *Summary of the Regulations*

Section 301.7701–1 provides an overview of the rules applicable in determining an organization's classification for federal tax purposes. The first step in the classification process is to determine whether there is a separate entity for federal tax purposes. The regulations explain that certain joint undertakings that are not entities under local law may nonetheless constitute separate entities for federal tax purposes; however, not all entities formed under local law are recognized as separate entities for federal tax purposes. Whether an organization is treated as an entity for federal tax purposes is a matter of federal tax law, and does not affect the rights and obligations of its owners under local law. For example, if a domestic limited liability company with a single individual owner is disregarded as an entity separate from its owner under § 301.7701–3, its individual owner is subject to federal income tax as if the company's business was operated as a sole proprietorship.

An organization that is recognized as a separate entity for federal tax purposes is either a trust or a business entity (unless a provision of the Code expressly provides for special treatment, such as the Qualified Settlement Fund rules (§ 1.468B) or the Real Estate Mortgage Investment Conduit (REMIC) rules, see section 860A(a)). The regulations provide that trusts generally do not have associates or an objective to carry on business for profit. The distinctions between trusts and business entities, although restated, are not changed by these regulations.

Section 301.7701–2 clarifies that business entities that are classified as corporations for federal tax purposes include corporations denominated as such under applicable law, as well as associations, joint-stock companies, insurance companies, organizations that conduct certain banking activities, organizations wholly owned by a State, organizations that are taxable as corporations under a provision of the Code other than section 7701(a)(3), and certain organizations formed under the laws of a foreign jurisdiction (including a U.S. possession, territory, or commonwealth).

* * *

Any business entity that is not required to be treated as a corporation for federal tax purposes (referred to in the regulation as an eligible entity) may choose its classification under the rules of § 301.7701–3. Those rules provide that an eligible entity with at least two members can be classified as either a partnership or an association, and that an eligible entity with a single member can be classified as an association or can be disregarded as an entity separate from its owner. * * *

In order to provide most eligible entities with the classification they would choose without requiring them to file an election, the regulations provide default classification rules that aim to match taxpayers' expectations (and thus reduce the number of elections that will be needed). The regulations adopt a passthrough default for domestic entities, under which a newly formed eligible entity will be classified as a partnership if it has at least two members, or will be disregarded as an entity separate from its owner if it has a single owner. The default for foreign entities is based on whether the members have limited liability. Thus a foreign eligible entity will be classified as an association if all members have limited liability. A foreign eligible entity will be classified as a partnership if it has two or more members and at least one member does not have limited liability; the entity will be disregarded as an entity separate from its owner if it has a single owner and that owner does not have limited liability. Finally, the default classification for an existing entity is the classification that the entity claimed immediately prior to the effective date of these regulations. An entity's default classification continues until the entity elects to change its classification by means of an affirmative election.

An eligible entity may affirmatively elect its classification on Form 8832, Entity Classification Election. The regulations require that the election be signed by each member of the entity or any officer, manager, or member of the entity who is authorized to make the election and who represents to having such authorization under penalties of perjury. An election will not be accepted unless it includes all of the required information * * * .

Taxpayers are reminded that a change in classification, no matter how achieved, will have certain tax consequences that must be reported. For example, if an organization classified as an association elects to be classified as a partnership, the organization and its owners must recognize gain, if any, under the rules applicable to liquidations of corporations.

B. Discussion of Comments on the General Approach and Scope of the Regulations

Several comments requested clarification with regard to the rules for determining when an owner of an interest in an organization will be respected as a bona fide owner for federal tax purposes. Some commentators * * * relying on Rev. Rul. 93–4, 1993–1 C.B. 225, suggested that if two wholly-owned subsidiaries of a common parent were the owners of an organization, those owners would not be respected as bona fide owners and the organization would be treated as having only one owner (the common parent). Although the determination of whether an organization has more than one owner is based on all the facts and circumstances, the fact that some or all of the owners of an organization are under common control does not require the common parent to be treated as the sole owner. Consistent with this approach, Rev. Rul. 93–4 treated two wholly owned subsidiaries as associates and then classified the foreign entity based on the four corporate characteristics under section 7701. While these four factors will no longer apply with the adoption of the regulations, determining whether the subsidiaries are associates continues to be an issue.

* * *

C. *Discussion of Comments Relating to the Elective Regime*

Most of the commentators agreed that the default rules included in the proposed regulations generally would match taxpayers' expectations. **

Some commentators requested that taxpayers be allowed to make classification elections with their first tax returns. The regulations retain the requirement that elections be made at the beginning of the taxable year. Treasury and the IRS continue to believe that it is appropriate to determine an entity's classification at the time that it begins its operations. Taxpayers can specify the date on which an election will be effective, provided that date is not more than 75 days prior to the date on which the election is filed (irrespective of when the interest was acquired) and not more than 12 months after the date the election was filed. * * *

The regulations limit the ability of an entity to make multiple classification elections by prohibiting more than one election to change an entity's classification during any sixty month period. * * * [T]he regulations permit the Commissioner to waive the application of the sixty month limitation by letter ruling. However, waivers will not be granted unless there has been more than a fifty percent ownership change. The sixty month limitation only applies to a change in classification by election; the limitation does not apply if the organization's business is actually transferred to another entity.

* * *

ILLUSTRATIVE MATERIAL

A. HISTORICAL BACKGROUND

For many years prior to 1997, under a prior version of Treas. Reg. § 301.7701–2 (the "*Kintner*" regulations) six characteristics were taken into account as the criteria for distinguishing corporations from other organizations: (1) the presence of associates; (2) an objective to carry on business and divide the gains therefrom; (3) continuity of life, i.e., the death, resignation, etc. of a member does not cause the dissolution of the organization; (4) centralization of management, i.e., fewer than all the members have exclusive authority to make management decisions; (5) limited liability; and (6) free transferability of interests. To be classified as an association taxable as a corporation, the organization must have had more corporate than noncorporate characteristics. The corporate characteristics common to the types of organization being compared were ignored, and since the presence of associates and an objective to carry on a business for profit are common to both corporations and partnerships, the determination whether an organization is an association taxable as a corporation or is a partnership was be made with reference only to the other four characteristics.

The *Kintner* regulations evolved from a series of judicial decisions and amendments to the regulations over a period of nearly thirty years. In Morrissey v. Commissioner, 296 U.S. 344 (1935), a number of investors formed a real estate trust to construct and operate a golf course. After examining the organization and operation of the trust, the Supreme Court determined that it more nearly resembled a corporation than an ordinary trust and that under the statutory predecessor of § 7701(a)(3) such resemblance was sufficient to tax the trust as a corporation. The characteristics that the Supreme Court identified as those relevant in determining whether the trust resembled a corporation were those later incorporated into the *Kintner* regulations. Subsequently, some taxpayers used *Morrissey* and the early classification Regulations based on the case as a sword to seek corporate treatment for their unincorporated organizations. Doctors and other professionals, who were prevented by state law from incorporating and thus could not obtain the benefits of qualified pension and profit-sharing plans, formed associations intended to qualify as "corporations" under the tests in the *Morrissey* case. These entities were sustained as corporations for tax purposes. See, e.g., United States v. Kintner, 216 F.2d 418 (9th Cir.1954). In *Kintner,* the taxpayer, along with other doctors with whom he was associated in a medical partnership, formed an unincorporated association for the practice of medicine and established a pension plan. The articles of association attempted to give the organization the "attributes of a corporation" as defined in *Morrissey.* Applying the *Morrissey* tests, the District Court found the association taxable as a corporation. The Court of Appeals affirmed, rejecting the Government's contention that because of a state law prohibition against the practice of medicine by a corporation, the organization could not be classified as an association taxable as a corporation for federal tax purposes. The Internal Revenue Service refused to follow *Kintner* and in November, 1960 promulgated the former version of Treas. Reg. § 301.7701–2, which came to be known as the *Kintner* regulations, providing a series of more refined tests of "corporateness" based on the *Morrissey* decision.

Starting in the 1970s the test of the *Kintner* regulations was applied to limited partnerships. The inquiry virtually always resulted in classification as a partnership. See, e.g., Larson v. Commissioner, 66 T.C. 159 (1976). When starting in the late 1980s it was applied to limited liability companies, the test could result in classification as either a corporation of a partnership, depending on the exact provisions of the articles of the limited liability company, see, e.g., Rev. Rul. 93–98, 1993–1 C.B. 233. The conventional wisdom was that the classification rules had, in substance, effectively become elective. For this reason, the current expressly elective classification rules for unincorporated entities were adopted in 1997.

B. BUSINESS TRUSTS

1. *General*

Treas. Reg. § 301.7701–4(a) and (b) through (c) distinguish between "ordinary" trusts, whose purposes are the protection or conservation of trust property, and trusts which are in effect a joint enterprise of the beneficiaries to conduct a business for profit and which will be classified as either a partnership or a corporation under Treas. Reg. § 301.7701–2 and –3. No cases have been decided or rulings issued under the current version of Treas. Reg. § 301.7701–4, but a number of cases were decided under the prior version of the classification rulings. In most of those cases the question of whether the trust was an "ordinary trust" or a business association taxable as a corporation usually turned on whether the trust beneficiaries were in fact business associates. For example, in Outlaw v. United States, 494 F.2d 1376 (Ct.Cl.1974), a trust was formed to own and manage some 10,000 acres of farm land and employed 18 to 20 full time plus 60 to 70 temporary workers to engage in a full scale agricultural operation. The trust had 27 original investors, which increased over time to 41 investors; its objective was to carry on a business of owning, developing and exploiting agricultural lands for income; its existence continued notwithstanding the withdrawal, death, bankruptcy, etc. of an investor); all decisions were made by an operating committee akin to a corporate board of directors; the investor-beneficiaries were liable only to the extent of their proportionate interests in the trust assets; and the investors could freely transfer their interests after giving notice to the trustee. Based on these facts, the trust was a business entity taxable as a corporation.

See also Rev.Rul. 80–75, 1980–1 C.B. 314 (trust established by promoter to conduct business activity and to which beneficiaries contributed cash in exchange for income interests and remainder to person designated by holder of income interest was classified as a business association); Estate of Bedell v. Commissioner, 86 T.C. 1207 (1986)(testamentary trust which conducted a manufacturing business lacked "associates" because the beneficiaries had "not planned a common effort or entered into a combination for the conduct of a business enterprise,“ only a few of the beneficiaries participated in trust affairs, and their interests were not transferrable); Elm Street Realty Trust v. Commissioner, 76 T.C. 803 (1981)(A)(inter vivos estate planning trust which received rent from net lease of real estate had business objective because trustee had the power to sell real estate and purchase and improve other real estate; the trust, however, lacked associates because donee beneficiaries had no role in creation of trust, only limited powers to participate in the trust's activities, and beneficial interests were transferable only under restrictive conditions). Hynes v. Commissioner, 74 T.C. 1266 (1980), held that a trust created to develop and sell real estate was to be taxed as an association even though the grantor held 100 percent of the beneficial interest; the term "associates" in the regulations encompasses "one-person corporations."

Under current Treas. Reg. § 301.7701–4, a trust such as those involved in *Outlaw* and *Estate of Bedell* would be classified as a business entity rather than as an ordinary trust, and under Treas. Reg. § 301.7701–2 and–3 then would be classified as a partnership unless it elected to be taxed as a corporation.

2. *Liquidating Trusts*

Treas. Reg. § 301.7701–4(d) provides a special rule for "liquidating" trusts which will not be held to be associations taxable as corporations as long as the primary purpose of the trust is the liquidation and distribution of the assets transferred to it. See Abraham v. United States, 406 F.2d 1259 (6th Cir.1969), where the court found the trust to be an association taxable as a corporation and not a liquidating trust; the trustees were given broad powers to conduct the prior business, although the powers were not actually exercised. In Walker v. United States, 194 F.Supp. 522 (D.Mass. 1961), an irrevocable trust was set up to hold property, an office building, as part of a family settlement of a dispute over the property. The court found the arrangement was a trust; it had centralized management but no transferability of interests or continuity of life because of the power of the beneficiaries to revoke the arrangement. The purpose of the trust was the liquidation of the property and not the carrying on of business for profit. See also Rev.Rul. 75–379, 1975–2 C.B. 505, and Rev.Rul. 63–228, 1963–2 C.B. 229, finding certain trusts which engaged in business activities to fall within the "liquidation" exception; Rev.Proc. 82–58, 1982–2 C.B. 847, amplified by Rev.Proc. 91–15, 1991–1 C.B. 484 (guidelines for advance rulings on classification of liquidation trusts).

C. PUBLICLY TRADED PARTNERSHIPS AND LIMITED LIABILITY COMPANIES

1. *General*

As noted in the preamble to the "check-a-box" entity classification regulations, the regulations apply only to those entities the classification of which is not specified by a Code section. Section 7704 generally treats as a corporation any partnership the interests in which are traded on an established securities market or are readily tradable on a secondary market or a substantial equivalent of a secondary market. Because under state law general partnership interests cannot be traded, the provision in fact only applies to limited partnerships and limited liability companies. The legislative history explains that a secondary market exists if prices are regularly quoted by brokers or dealers who are making a market for such interest. Occasional accommodation trades of partnership interests, a buy-sell agreement between the partners (without more), or the occasional repurchase or redemption by the partnership or acquisition by a general partner of partnership interests will not be treated as a secondary market or the equivalent thereof. However, if the partners have regular and ongoing opportunities to dispose of their interests, the interests are tradable on the equivalent of a secondary market. Meaningful restrictions imposed on the right to transfer partnership interests may preclude classification as a corporation, even if some interests are actually traded. See H.Rep. 100–495, 100th Cong., 1st Sess. 943–950 (1987).

As a corollary to § 7704, Congress amended § 469, dealing with limitations on deductions from passive activities, to provide that net income from any publicly traded limited partnership is treated as portfolio income (like dividends and interest) rather than passive activity income solely for purposes of applying § 469. Net losses from any publicly traded limited partnership may not offset either portfolio income (including net income from another publicly traded limited partnership) or net income from other passive activities, but instead must be separately carried-over and may be deducted only against net income from the same publicly traded limited partnership in future years. I.R.C. § 469(g). See H.Rep. 100–3545, 100th Cong., 1st Sess. 951–52 (1987). This provision extends to publicly traded limited partnerships even if they are specially excepted from the rules of § 7704. Generally under § 469, all items with respect to limited partnership interests are considered to be passive activity income or loss.

2. *Meaning of "Publicly Traded"*

Treas. Reg. 301.7704–1(b) provides definitions of the statutory terms "established securities market" and "readily tradable on a secondary market or the substantial equivalent of a secondary market." Established securities markets include not only exchanges, but also interdealer quotation systems. A secondary market or a substantial equivalent of a secondary market exists if the partners are readily able to buy, sell, or exchange their interests in a manner that is economically comparable to trading on an established securities market. Interests are readily tradable on a secondary market or its equivalent if (1) firm quote trading exists, even if only one person makes available bid or offer quotes; (2) the holder of an interest has a readily available, regular and ongoing opportunity to sell or exchange such interest through a public means of obtaining or providing information of offers to buy, sell, or exchange interests; or (3) buyers and sellers have the opportunity to buy, sell, or exchange interests in a time frame and with the regularity and continuity that the existence of a market maker would provide. Interests are not readily tradable, however, unless the partnership participates in establishing the market or recognizes transfers by admission of purchasers to the partnership or recognizing their rights as transferees. Treas. Reg. § 301.7704–1(d). A redemption or repurchase plan can result in partnership interests being publicly traded.

The Regulations provide several "safe harbors." Treas. Reg. § 301.7704–1(e) disregards transfers in which the transferee has a transferred basis, transfers at death, transfers between family members, transfers pursuant to certain redemption agreements, and certain other transfers in determining whether there is public trading of the partnership interests. The most broadly applicable safe harbor excludes from the definition of publicly traded partnership so-called "private placements"—that is, any partnership whose interests were not registered under the Securities Act of 1933, but only if the partnership does not have more than 100 members. Treas. Reg. § 301.7704–1(h).

In addition, a partnership will not be considered to be traded on the substantial equivalent of a secondary market for any year in which no more than two percent of the total interests in partnership capital or profits is sold or disposed of in transactions other than private transfers, qualifying redemptions, certain other safe harbors. Treas. Reg. § 301.7704–1(j). It is clear from § 7704(f), dealing with the effect of a partnership becoming a corporation, that § 7704 contemplates the possibility that a partnership which is initially recognized as such might in a subsequent year become a corporation under § 7704. The "lack of actual trading" safe harbor, which applies on a year-by-year basis, suggests further that a partnership might be considered to be a corporation in one year and a partnership in the next, when it meets the safe harbor. This result could give rise to a constructive liquidation of the "corporation" with tax consequences to the entity and the investors or, conversely, the constructive formation of a new corporation.

3. *Exceptions*

A broad exception to § 7704 allows publicly traded limited partnerships more than ninety percent of whose gross income is from certain "passive sources" to continue to be treated as partnerships. Qualified income for this purpose, with some narrow exceptions, includes interest, dividends, real property rents, gain from the sale of real property, and income and gains from the exploration, development, extraction, processing, refining, etc. of oil and gas or any other natural resource. While the legislative history is silent as to the reason for this exception, it presumably is based on the historic use of limited partnerships in organizing such ventures and the availability of conduit taxation for other entity forms (e.g., real estate investment trusts) making investments of this type.

An additional exception permits publicly traded partnerships that were in existence on December 31, 1987 to continue to be treated as partnerships as long as they do not add a "substantial new line of business." See I.R.C. § 7704(g).

D. FOREIGN BUSINESS ENTITIES

Treas. Reg. § 301.7701–2(b)(8) lists certain foreign business entities (including entities organized in U.S. possessions, territories, and commonwealths) that are classified as *per se* corporations. The listed organizations are limited liability entities, such as the British Public Limited Company, the French Societe Anonyme, and the German Aktiengesellschaft. Other foreign entities can elect under Treas. Reg. § 301.7701–3(a) whether to be treated as a partnership or as a corporation. In contrast to the partnership default classification rules for domestic organizations, under Treas. Reg. § 301.7701–3(b)(2) the default rule for foreign entities is based on whether the members have limited liability. A foreign entity is classified as an association if all members have limited liability, but it is classified as a partnership if it has two or more members and at least one member does not have limited liability. If a foreign entity has only one owner, who does not have limited liability, the entity is disregarded.

E. SPECIAL CLASSES OF CORPORATIONS

1. *Conduit Corporations Relieved of Federal Tax*

Regulated investment companies investing in securities—mutual funds—are in effect relieved of corporate tax liability as respects the dividends and capital gains from their stock investments if they currently distribute this income to their shareholders. A mutual fund to this extent is thus treated as a conduit rather than a taxable entity. See I.R.C. §§ 851–855.

In 1960 Congress extended conduit treatment to real estate investment trusts (REITs) otherwise taxable as corporations (see §§ 856–860); and in 1986 conduit treatment was extended to real estate mortgage investment conduits (REMICs)(§§ 860A–860G).

2. *Other Special Corporate Treatment*

Certain classes of corporations are given special treatment as respects the computation or treatment of taxable income, e.g., banks, insurance companies, and foreign corporations; or exemption from tax, e.g., the various tax-exempt organizations (as to which, however, the corporate income tax is applicable to the extent of "unrelated business taxable income," I.R.C. §§ 511–514).

SECTION 2. REGARD AND DISREGARD OF THE CORPORATE ENTITY

Prior to the late 1980s, a combination of tax and nontax factors led many individuals to choose to operate businesses, whether closely held or publicly held, as C corporations subject to the double tax regime. More recently, the development of the limited liability company business form, coupled with the adoption of the check-a-box classification regulations, and the current rate structure have strongly influenced individuals to conduct closely held businesses in a from subject to the partnership taxation rules of subchapter K, particularly if capital is a material income producing factor. Even if a corporate structure is desired, the shareholders often elect to be taxed under Subchapter S, which eliminates the corporate level tax and results in the corporation's income being taxed directly to the shareholders. In both of these instances, the question of whether business income or deductions properly are attributable to the entity or directly to the owners does not arise. In the classic C corporation, however, the question of whether particular items of income or deduction are properly attributable to the corporation or directly to the shareholders is very important. Under the current rate structures (taking into account the preferential treatment of capital gains) and statutory scheme, the C corporation is the form of choice only for publicly traded businesses, which are forced into the C corporation regime, and businesses whose income is derived primarily from personal services (largely because the C corporation form has certain advantages over the other forms with regard to the provision of tax-free fringe benefits to the shareholder-employees). Most of the case law regarding this issue, however, developed in the context of closely held businesses in which capital was a material income producing factor.

Strong v. Commissioner*

Tax Court of the United States, 1976.
66 T.C. 12.

■ TANNENWALD, JUDGE: * * *

Petitioners formed a partnership for the purpose of constructing and operating an apartment complex on real estate contributed by several partners. In order to obtain financing for the project, it was necessary to transfer the property to a corporation wholly owned by the partnership so that mortgage loans could be made at an interest rate in excess of the limit imposed by State usury laws on loans to individuals. Construction and operation of the apartments generated net operating losses during the years in issue which were reported on the partnership's returns and as distributive shares on the individual returns of the petitioners. The respondent determined that the corporation, as owner of the property, was the proper party to report those losses. Petitioners allege that the corporation was a nominee whose ownership should be disregarded for tax purposes. The crux of petitioners' case is that the corporation was merely a sham or device used for the purpose of avoiding the New York usury statute, that it performed no acts other than those essential to that function, and that to treat it as the actual owner of the property would be to exalt form over substance.

The use of sham or dummy corporations to avoid application of the usury laws is a recognized practice in New York. Hoffman v. Lee Nashem Motors, Inc., 20 N.Y.2d 513, 231 N.E.2d 765, 285 N.Y.S.2d 68 (1967) * * *. There is no doubt that petitioners sought to do business in partnership form and that the corporation was, at least in their eyes, a mere tool or conduit. Their argument is not without some appeal, but we conclude that it should not be accepted.

The principal guidepost on the road to recognition of the corporate entity is Moline Properties v. Commissioner, 319 U.S. 436 (1943). In that case, a corporation was organized as part of a transaction which included

* [Ed.: The decision was affirmed by memorandum, 553 F.2d 94 (2d Cir.1977).]

the transfer of mortgaged property to it by the shareholder, the assumption by it of the outstanding mortgages, and the transfer of its stock to a voting trustee named by the mortgagee as security for additional advances. Later the indebtedness was repaid and the shareholder reacquired control of the corporation. Thereafter it mortgaged and sold some of the property it held, and leased another portion. The Court held that the corporation was a separate entity from its inception, and stated its rule of decision as follows:

> The doctrine of corporate entity fills a useful purpose in business life. Whether the purpose be to gain an advantage under the law of the state of incorporation or to avoid or to comply with the demands of creditors or to serve the creator's personal or undisclosed convenience, *so long as that purpose is the equivalent of business activity or is followed by the carrying on of business by the corporation,* the corporation remains a separate taxable entity. * * * In Burnet v. Commonwealth Improvement Co., 287 U.S. 415, this Court appraised the relation between a corporation and its sole stockholder and held taxable to the corporation a profit on a sale to its stockholder. This was because the taxpayer had adopted the corporate form for purposes of his own. The choice of the advantages of incorporation to do business, it was held, required the acceptance of the tax disadvantages. [319 U.S. at 438–439. Fn. refs. omitted; emphasis supplied.]

Cases following *Moline Properties* have generally held that the income from property must be taxed to the corporate owner and will not be attributed to the shareholders, unless the corporation is a *purely passive dummy* or is used for a tax-avoidance purpose. Harrison Property Management Co. v. United States, 475 F.2d 623 (Ct.Cl.1973); Taylor v. Commissioner, 445 F.2d 455 (1st Cir.1971); National Investors Corp. v. Hoey, 144 F.2d 466 (2d Cir.1944) * * *. This is particularly true where the demand that the corporate entity be ignored emanates from the shareholders of a closely held corporation. See Harrison Property Management Co. v. United States, supra at 626; David F. Bolger, 59 T.C. 760, 767 n. 4 (1973).[8] It has been suggested that the prevailing approach misses the point by focusing (as do the parties herein) on the viability of the corporate entity rather than the situs of real beneficial or economic ownership. Kurtz & Kopp, "Taxability of Straw Corporations in Real Estate Transactions," 22 Tax Lawyer 647 (1969). However, the thrust of the case law, as we read it, is to leave the door open to the argument that a corporation played a purely nominal or "straw" role in a transaction, while closing it firmly against any contention that a corporation may be disregarded simply because it is the creature of its shareholders. * * *

8. See also Higgins v. Smith, 308 U.S. 473 (1940). Cf. Colin v. Altman, 39 App. Div.2d 200, 333 N.Y.S.2d 432, 433–434 (1st Dept.1972): "the corporate veil is never pierced for the benefit of the corporation or its stockholders. * * * [The sole stockholder] is not the corporation either in law or fact and, having elected to take the advantages [of incorporation], it is not inequitable to subject him to the disabilities consequent upon his election."

The Supreme Court has held that shareholder domination, even to the extent that a corporation could be said to lack beneficial ownership of its assets and income, is insufficient to permit taxpayers to ignore the corporation's existence. National Carbide Corp. v. Commissioner, 336 U.S. 422, 433–434 (1949); Moline Properties v. Commissioner, supra. The Court of Appeals for the Second Circuit, to which appeal will lie herein, has similarly refused to disregard the interposition of a corporate entity between shareholders and their property, except where the corporation has not purported to deal with the property in its own right. The focus is on business purpose or activity with respect to the particular property whose ownership is in question.

In Paymer v. Commissioner, 150 F.2d 334 (2d Cir.1945), two brothers formed a pair of corporations (Raymep and Westrich) to which they transferred legal title to certain real estate. Their purpose was to deter execution against the property by their individual creditors. Neither corporation engaged in any business activity except that Raymep obtained a loan and as part security "assigned to the lender all the lessor's rights, profits and interest in two leases on the property and covenanted that they were in full force and effect and that it was the sole lessor." 150 F.2d at 336. Westrich was disregarded on the ground that it "was at all times but a passive dummy which did nothing but take and hold title to the real estate conveyed to it. It served no business purpose *in connection with the property.*" 150 F.2d at 337. (Emphasis added.) Raymep, however, was not disregarded, because it did perform a business function as the owner of the property.

In Jackson v. Commissioner, 233 F.2d 289 (2d Cir.1956), affg. 24 T.C. 1 (1955), the Court of Appeals disregarded holding companies which lacked separate business purpose or activity, stating that the situation was encompassed within the foregoing language in its opinion in *Paymer* and further observing:

> A natural person may be used to receive income which in fact is another's. So, too, a corporation, although for other purposes a jural entity distinct from its stockholders, may be used as a mere dummy to receive income which in fact is the income of the stockholders or of someone else; in such circumstances, the company will be disregarded. [233 F.2d at 290 n. 2.]

Finally, in Commissioner v. State–Adams Corp., 283 F.2d 395 (2d Cir.1960), revg. 32 T.C. 365 (1959)(which involved a different factual situation), the court characterized its holding in *Paymer* as "nothing more than a restatement of the fundamental rule that income from real estate held in the name of a nominee will be taxed to the beneficial owner, not to the nominee." 283 F.2d at 398 (fn. ref. omitted). The mere fact that some of the documents herein speak in terms of a corporate nominee is not sufficient to bring petitioners within the exception to the general rule. Harrison Property Management Co. v. United States, supra; Collins v. United States, supra * * *.

In short, a corporate "straw" may be used to separate apparent from actual ownership of property, without incurring the tax consequences of an actual transfer; but to prevent evasion or abuse of the two-tiered tax structure, a taxpayer's claim that his controlled corporation should be disregarded will be closely scrutinized. If the corporation was intended to, or did in fact, act in its own name with respect to property, its ownership thereof will not be disregarded.

The degree of corporate purpose and activity requiring recognition of the corporation as a separate entity is extremely low. Thus, it has been stated that "a determination whether a corporation is to be considered as doing business is not necessarily dependent upon the quantum of business" and that the business activity may be "minimal." See Britt v. United States, 431 F.2d 227, 235, 237 (5th Cir.1970).

In this case, the corporation's purpose and activities were sufficient to require recognition of its separate ownership of the property in question and, a fortiori, of its existence as a taxable entity. The purpose to avoid State usury laws is a "business purpose" within the meaning of *Moline Properties*. Collins v. United States, supra; David F. Bolger, supra.[9] The corporation had broad, unrestricted powers under its charter. Compare Collins v. United States, supra. Its activities were more extensive than those which required recognition of Raymep in Paymer v. Commissioner, supra. Like Raymep, it borrowed money on the security of rents; in addition, it mortgaged the property itself and it received and applied the loan proceeds. It engaged in the foregoing activities on more than one occasion and is more vulnerable than was the corporation in Collins v. United States, supra, which was also formed to avoid usury law restrictions and placed only a single mortgage. These activities, carried out in its own name, go beyond "transactions essential to the holding and transferring of title." See Taylor v. Commissioner, 445 F.2d at 457. The fact that the corporation in this case, unlike those in other cases, did not enter into any leases does not, in our opinion, constitute a sufficient basis for distinguishing their thrust.[10]

Furthermore, the corporation was otherwise treated by the partnership in a manner inconsistent with petitioners' contention that the two were the same entity. The partnership agreement required that deeds, loan agreements, and mortgages "executed by or on behalf of the partnership" be signed by both Jones and Strong; property standing in the corporate name was so dealt with on Jones' signature alone. Separation of title to the various parcels permitted the creation of mutual easements, an act which would have been prevented by the doctrine of merger had the properties been under common ownership. See Parsons v. Johnson, 68 N.Y. 62 (1877);

9. See also Daniel E. Rogers, T.C. Memo. 1975–289.

10. In Raymep Realty Corp., 7 T.C.M. 262 (1948), relied upon by petitioners we held the execution of a lease in the name of a corporate nominee titleholder did not require the corporation to be recognized as a taxable entity. We characterized that single act as "a purely nominal adjunct to the holding of title." Here, by contrast, the business activity was the raison d'être of the corporation.

Snyder v. Monroe County, 2 Misc.2d 946, 153 N.Y.S.2d 479, 486 (1956), affd. mem. 6 A.D.2d 854, 175 N.Y.S.2d 1008 (4th Dept.1958). The corporation applied for and received insurance on the property in its own name.

Finally, although not determinative, an element to be considered is the fact that the corporate vehicle in this case, whatever the parties' intentions, carried with it the usual baggage attending incorporation, including limitation of the shareholders' personal liability during construction. Jones alone was potentially responsible (as guarantor) for repayment of the construction loans.

In the final analysis, the corporation herein fits the mold articulated in Collins v. United States, supra:

> The fact remains, however, that the corporation did exist and did perform the function intended of it until the permanent loan was consummated. It was more than a business convenience, it was a business necessity to plaintiffs' enterprise. As such, it came into being. As such, it served the purpose of its creation. [386 F.Supp. at 21.]
>
> The fact that the purpose and use of the corporation was limited in scope is beside the point. See Sam Siegel, 45 T.C. 566, 577 (1966).

The tide of judicial history is too strong to enable petitioners to prevail, albeit that the activities of the corporation were substantially less than those involved in most of the decided cases with the exception of Collins v. United States, supra.

Having set up a separate entity through which to conduct their affairs, petitioners must live with the tax consequences of that choice. Indeed, the very exigency which led to the use of the corporation serves to emphasize its separate existence. See Moline Properties v. Commissioner, 319 U.S. at 440; David F. Bolger, 59 T.C. at 766. Our conclusion is not based upon any failure of the petitioners to turn square corners with respondent; they consistently made clear their intention to prevent separate taxation of the corporation if legally possible. They took most precautions consistent with business exigency to achieve that end. We simply hold that their goal was not attainable in this case.

Reviewed by the Court.

Decisions will be entered for the respondent.

Commissioner v. Bollinger

Supreme Court of the United States, 1988.
485 U.S. 340.

■ JUSTICE SCALIA delivered the opinion of the Court.

Petitioner the Commissioner of Internal Revenue challenges a decision by the United States Court of Appeals for the Sixth Circuit holding that a corporation which held record title to real property as agent for the corporation's shareholders was not the owner of the property for purposes of federal income taxation. 807 F.2d 65 (1986). We granted certiorari, 482 U.S. 913, 107 S.Ct. 3183, 96 L.Ed.2d 672 (1987), to resolve a conflict in the courts of appeals over the tax treatment of corporations purporting to be agents for their shareholders. Compare George v. Commissioner, 803 F.2d 144, 148–149 (C.A.5 1986), cert. pending, No. 86–1152; Frink v. Commissioner, 798 F.2d 106, 109–110 (C.A.4 1986), cert. pending, No. 86–1151.

I

Respondent Jesse C. Bollinger, Jr., developed, either individually or in partnership with some or all of the other respondents, eight apartment complexes in Lexington, Kentucky. (For convenience we will refer to all the ventures as "partnerships.") Bollinger initiated development of the first apartment complex, Creek side North Apartments, in 1968. The Massachusetts Mutual Life Insurance Company agreed to provide permanent financing by lending $1,075,000 to "the corporate nominee of Jesse C. Bollinger, Jr." at an annual interest rate of eight percent, secured by a mortgage on the property and a personal guaranty from Bollinger. The loan commitment was structured in this fashion because Kentucky's usury law at the time limited the annual interest rate for noncorporate borrowers to seven percent. Ky.Rev.Stat. §§ 360.010, 360.025 (1972). Lenders willing to provide money only at higher rates required the nominal debtor and record title holder of mortgaged property to be a corporate nominee of the true owner and borrower. On October 14, 1968, Bollinger incorporated Creekside, Inc., under the laws of Kentucky; he was the only stockholder. The next day, Bollinger and Creekside, Inc., entered into a written agreement which provided that the corporation would hold title to the apartment complex as Bollinger's agent for the sole purpose of securing financing, and would convey, assign, or encumber the property and disburse the proceeds thereof only as directed by Bollinger; that Creekside, Inc., had no obligation to maintain the property or assume any liability by reason of the execution of promissory notes or otherwise; and that Bollinger would indemnify and hold the corporation harmless from any liability it might sustain as his agent and nominee.

Having secured the commitment for permanent financing, Bollinger, acting through Creekside, Inc., borrowed the construction funds for the apartment complex from Citizens Fidelity Bank and Trust Company. Creekside, Inc., executed all necessary loan documents including the promissory note and mortgage, and transferred all loan proceeds to Bollinger's individual construction account. Bollinger acted as general contractor for the construction, hired the necessary employees, and paid the expenses out of the construction account. When construction was completed, Bollinger obtained, again through Creekside, Inc., permanent financing from Massachusetts Mutual Life in accordance with the earlier loan commitment. These loan proceeds were used to pay off the Citizens Fidelity construction loan. Bollinger hired a resident manager to rent the apartments, execute leases with tenants, collect and deposit the rents, and maintain operating records. The manager deposited all rental receipts into, and paid all operating expenses from, an operating account, which was first opened in the name of Creekside, Inc., but was later changed to "Creekside Apartments, a partnership." The operation of Creekside North Apartments generated losses for the taxable years 1969, 1971, 1972, 1973, and 1974, and ordinary income for the years 1970, 1975, 1976, and 1977. Throughout, the income and losses were reported by Bollinger on his individual income tax returns.

Following a substantially identical pattern, seven other apartment complexes were developed by respondents through seven separate partnerships. For each venture, a partnership executed a nominee agreement with Creekside, Inc., to obtain financing. (For one of the ventures, a different Kentucky corporation, Cloisters, Inc., in which Bollinger had a 50 percent interest, acted as the borrower and titleholder. For convenience, we will refer to both Creekside and Cloisters as "the corporation.") The corporation transferred the construction loan proceeds to the partnership's construction account, and the partnership hired a construction supervisor who oversaw construction. Upon completion of construction, each partnership actively managed its apartment complex, depositing all rental receipts into, and paying all expenses from, a separate partnership account for each apartment complex. The corporation had no assets, liabilities, employees, or bank accounts. In every case, the lenders regarded the partnership as the owner of the apartments and were aware that the corporation was acting as agent of the partnership in holding record title. The partnerships reported the income and losses generated by the apartment complexes on their partnership tax returns, and respondents reported their distributive share of the partnership income and losses on their individual tax returns.

The Commissioner of Internal Revenue disallowed the losses reported by respondents, on the ground that the standards set out in National Carbide Corp. v. Commissioner, 336 U.S. 422, 69 S.Ct. 726, 93 L.Ed. 779 (1949), were not met. The Commissioner contended that *National Carbide* required a corporation to have an arm's length relationship with its shareholders before it could be recognized as their agent. Although not all respondents were shareholders of the corporation, the Commissioner took the position that the funds the partnerships disbursed to pay expenses should be deemed contributions to the corporation's capital, thereby making all respondents constructive stockholders. Since, in the Commissioner's view, the corporation rather than its shareholders owned the real estate, any losses sustained by the ventures were attributable to the corporation and not respondents. Respondents sought a redetermination in the United States Tax Court. The Tax Court held that the corporations were the agents of the partnerships and should be disregarded for tax purposes. Bollinger v. Commissioner, 48 TCM 1443 (1984), ¶ 84, 560 P-H Memo TC. On appeal, the United States Court of Appeals for the Sixth Circuit affirmed. 807 F.2d 65 (1986). We granted the Commissioner's petition for certiorari.

II

For federal income tax purposes, gain or loss from the sale or use of property is attributable to the owner of the property. See Helvering v.

Horst, 311 U.S. 112, 116–117, 61 S.Ct. 144, 147, 85 L.Ed. 75 (1940); Blair v. Commissioner, 300 U.S. 5, 12, 57 S.Ct. 330, 333, 81 L.Ed. 465 (1937) * * *. The problem we face here is that two different taxpayers can plausibly be regarded as the owner. Neither the Internal Revenue Code nor the regulations promulgated by the Secretary of the Treasury provide significant guidance as to which should be selected. It is common ground between the parties, however, that if a corporation holds title to property as agent for a partnership, then for tax purposes the partnership and not the corporation is the owner. Given agreement on that premise, one would suppose that there would be agreement upon the conclusion as well. For each of respondents' apartment complexes, an agency agreement expressly provided that the corporation would "hold such property as nominee and agent for" the partnership, App. to Pet. for Cert. 21a, n. 4, and that the partnership would have sole control of and responsibility for the apartment complex. The partnership in each instance was identified as the principal and owner of the property during financing, construction, and operation. The lenders, contractors, managers, employees, and tenants—all who had contact with the development—knew that the corporation was merely the agent of the partnership, if they knew of the existence of the corporation at all. In each instance the relationship between the corporation and the partnership was, in both form and substance, an agency with the partnership as principal.

The Commissioner contends, however, that the normal indicia of agency cannot suffice for tax purposes when, as here, the alleged principals are the controlling shareholders of the alleged agent corporation. That, it asserts, would undermine the principle of Moline Properties v. Commissioner, 319 U.S. 436, 63 S.Ct. 1132, 87 L.Ed. 1499 (1943), which held that a corporation is a separate taxable entity even if it has only one shareholder who exercises total control over its affairs. Obviously, *Moline*'s separate-entity principle would be significantly compromised if shareholders of closely held corporations could, by clothing the corporation with some attributes of agency with respect to particular assets, leave themselves free at the end of the tax year to make a claim—perhaps even a good-faith claim—of either agent or owner status, depending upon which choice turns out to minimize their tax liability. The Commissioner does not have the resources to audit and litigate the many cases in which agency status could be thought debatable. Hence, the Commissioner argues, in this shareholder context he can reasonably demand that the taxpayer meet a prophylactically clear test of agency.

We agree with that principle, but the question remains whether the test the Commissioner proposes is appropriate. The parties have debated at length the significance of our opinion in *National Carbide Corp. v. Commissioner,* supra. In that case, three corporations that were wholly owned subsidiaries of another corporation agreed to operate their production plants as "agents" for the parent, transferring to it all profits except for a nominal sum. The subsidiaries reported as gross income only this sum, but the Commissioner concluded that they should be taxed on the entirety of the profits because they were not really agents. We agreed, reasoning first, that the mere fact of the parent's control over the subsidiaries did not establish the existence of an agency, since such control is typical of all shareholder-corporation relationships, id., 336 U.S. at 429–434, 69 S.Ct., at 730–732; and second, that the agreements to pay the parent all profits above a nominal amount were not determinative since income must be taxed to those who actually earn it without regard to anticipatory assignment, id., at 435–436, 69 S.Ct., at 733–734. We acknowledged, however, that there was such a thing as "a true corporate agent * * * of [an] owner-principal," id. at 437, 69 S.Ct., at 734, and proceeded to set forth four indicia and two requirements of such status, the sum of which has become known in the lore of federal income tax law as the "six *National Carbide* factors":

> "[1] Whether the corporation operates in the name and for the account of the principal, [2] binds the principal by its actions, [3] transmits money received to the principal, and [4] whether receipt of income is attributable to the services of employees of the principal and to assets belonging to the principal are some of the relevant considerations in determining whether a true agency exists. [5] If the corporation is a true agent, its relations with its principal must not be dependent upon the fact that it is owned by the principal, if such is the case. [6] Its business purpose must be the carrying on of the normal duties of an agent." Id., at 437, 69 S.Ct., at 734 (footnotes omitted).

We readily discerned that these factors led to a conclusion of nonagency in *National Carbide* itself. There each subsidiary had represented to its customers that it (not the parent) was the company manufacturing and selling its products; each had sought to shield the parent from service of legal process; and the operations had used thousands of the subsidiaries' employees and nearly $20 million worth of property and equipment listed as assets on the subsidiaries' books. * * *

The Commissioner contends that the last two *National Carbide* factors are not satisfied in the present case. To take the last first: The Commissioner argues that here the corporation's business purpose with respect to the property at issue was not "the carrying on of the normal duties of an agent," since it was acting not as the agent but rather as the owner of the property for purposes of Kentucky's usury laws. We do not agree. It assuredly was not acting as the owner in fact, since respondents represented themselves as the principals to all parties concerned with the loans. Indeed, it was the lenders themselves who required the use of a corporate nominee. Nor does it make any sense to adopt a contrary-to-fact legal presumption that the corporation was the principal, imposing a federal tax sanction for the apparent evasion of Kentucky's usury law. To begin with, the Commissioner has not established that these transactions were an evasion. Respondents assert without contradiction that use of agency arrangements in order to permit higher interest was common practice, and it is by no means clear that the practice violated the spirit of the Kentucky law, much less its letter. It might well be thought that the borrower does not generally require usury protection in a transaction sophisticated enough to employ a corporate agent—assuredly not the normal *modus operandi* of the loan shark. That the statute positively envisioned corporate nominees is suggested by a provision which forbids charging the higher corporate interest rates "to a corporation, the principal asset of which shall be the ownership of a one (1) or two (2) family dwelling," Ky.Rev.Stat. § 360.025(2)(1987)—which would seem to prevent use of the nominee device for ordinary home-mortgage loans. In any event, even if the transaction did run afoul of the usury law, Kentucky, like most States, regards only the lender as the usurer, and the borrower as the victim. See Ky.Rev.Stat. § 360.020 (1987)(lender liable to borrower for civil penalty), § 360.990 (lender guilty of misdemeanor). Since the Kentucky statute imposed no penalties upon the borrower for allowing himself to be victimized, nor treated him as *in pari delictu,* but to the contrary enabled him to pay back the principal without any interest, and to sue for double the amount of interest already paid (plus attorney's fees), see Ky.Rev.Stat. § 360.020 (1972), the United States would hardly be vindicating Kentucky law by depriving the usury victim of tax advantages he would otherwise enjoy. In sum, we see no basis in either fact or policy for holding that the corporation was the principal because of the nature of its participation in the loans.

Of more general importance is the Commissioner's contention that the arrangements here violate the fifth *National Carbide* factor—that the corporate agent's "relations with its principal must not be dependent upon the fact that it is owned by the principal." The Commissioner asserts that this cannot be satisfied unless the corporate agent and its shareholder principal have an "arm's-length relationship" that includes the payment of a fee for agency services. The meaning of *National Carbide's* fifth factor is, at the risk of understatement, not entirely clear. Ultimately, the relations between a corporate agent and its owner-principal are *always* dependent upon the fact of ownership, in that the owner can cause the relations to be altered or terminated at any time. Plainly that is not what was meant, since on that interpretation all subsidiary-parent agencies would be invalid for tax purposes, a position which the *National Carbide* opinion specifically disavowed. We think the fifth *National Carbide* factor—so much more abstract than the others—was no more and no less than a generalized statement of the concern, expressed earlier in our own discussion, that the separate-entity doctrine of *Moline* not be subverted.

In any case, we decline to parse the text of *National Carbide* as though that were itself the governing statute. As noted earlier, it is uncontested that the law attributes tax consequences of property held by a genuine agent to the principal; and we agree that it is reasonable for the Commissioner to demand unequivocal evidence of genuineness in the corporation-shareholder context, in order to prevent evasion of *Moline.* We see no basis, however, for holding that unequivocal evidence can only consist of the rigid requirements (arm's-length dealing plus agency fee) that the Commissioner suggests. Neither of those is demanded by the law of agency, which permits agents to be unpaid family members, friends, or associates. See Restatement (Second) of Agency §§ 16, 21, 22 (1958). It seems to us that the genuineness of the agency relationship is adequately assured, and tax-avoiding manipulation adequately avoided, when the fact that the corporation is acting as agent for its shareholders with respect to a particular asset is set forth in a written agreement at the time the asset is acquired, the corporation functions as agent and not principal with respect to the asset for all purposes, and the corporation is held out as the agent and not principal in all dealings with third parties relating to the asset. Since these requirements were met here, the judgment of the Court of Appeals is

Affirmed.

ILLUSTRATIVE MATERIAL

A. APPLICATION OF THE BUSINESS ACTIVITY TEST

1. *General*

In cases involving the issue whether a corporation should be taxed as a separate entity, the taxpayer and the Commissioner may be on different sides, depending on the tax stakes involved. Thus, for example, a taxpayer whose personal tax bracket exceeds the corporate rate will urge that the corporation be recognized for tax purposes so as to postpone imposition of his higher individual rate on the income; the Commissioner may seek to disregard the corporate entity. Conversely, as in *Strong* and *Bollinger,* the taxpayer who seeks to deduct directly losses that result from activities of the "corporation" or who utilizes the corporate form only for nominal purposes, will urge that the formal existence of the corporation be ignored; the Commissioner will assert that the activities of the corporation warrant its recognition as a separate taxable entity. Historically, taxpayers generally had little success in attempts to assert that the corporation which they created should be disregarded for tax purposes; the courts generally upheld the Commissioner's position that the activities of the corporation were sufficient to warrant its being regarded as a separate entity for tax purposes. (Note that even in *Bollinger,* in which the taxpayer prevailed, the corporation was not ignored for tax purposes; it was treated as the shareholders' agent.) On the other hand, the corporate entity should be disregarded to prevent tax avoidance. The following cases illustrate the results reached by the courts in this area.

2. *Insufficient Business Activity—Corporate Entity Disregarded*

In Greenberg v. Commissioner, 62 T.C. 331 (1974), aff'd per curiam, 526 F.2d 588 (4th Cir.1975), two individuals formed five corporations to develop large residential subdivisions. All the corporations performed identical functions. Following a disagreement between the two shareholders, four corporations were liquidated, and one of the shareholders was redeemed out of the remaining corporation. The taxpayer was left as the sole shareholder of the remaining corporation. The taxpayer reported capital gains on the amounts received in liquidation of the four corporations. The court held that the four liquidated corporations were merely shams; all the income earned by those corporations was the income of the continuing corporation; and the amounts distributed to the taxpayer were simply a dividend: "These [liquidated] corporations served no purpose except to obtain a tax benefit which is not 'business' sufficient to grant them recognition as separate 'taxworthy' entities for Federal tax purposes." (345) See also Kimbrell v. Commissioner, 371 F.2d 897 (5th Cir.1967)(Commissioner's contention upheld that corporations involved were "mere depositories" for the individual shareholder's income where the corporation engaged in no business activities but merely received the income for the services performed by the individual taxpayer); Patterson v. Commissioner, T.C. Memo. 1966–239, aff'd per curiam, 68–2 USTC ¶ 9471 (2d Cir. 1968)(the corporation performed no useful function and the taxpayer, a professional boxer, "simply did not put flesh on the bones of the corporate skeleton").

In Noonan v. Commissioner, 52 T.C. 907 (1969), aff'd per curiam, 451 F.2d 992 (9th Cir.1971), a corporation received income as a limited partner from a business enterprise in which the sole shareholder was a general partner. The Tax Court acknowledged that the corporation had been properly organized, but it refused to recognize the separate corporate entity where the record was devoid of evidence showing any active business purpose.

3. *Sufficient Business Activity—Corporate Entity Respected*

(a) *General*

In situations similar to that in Strong v. Commissioner, the courts have rejected taxpayers' attempts to have a corporation holding title to real estate disregarded and treated as a "mere dummy" for tax purposes. In Bolger v. Commissioner, 59 T.C. 760 (1973), the taxpayer was engaged in real estate investment and finance. The taxpayer would locate a building which a business desired to lease. The following transactions would take place, often all on the same day: Taxpayer would organize a nominally capitalized corporation with the shareholders being himself and other individuals; the corporation would purchase the building and enter into a lease with the user; the corporation would then issue its notes, secured by a mortgage on the property and an assignment of the lease, to an institutional lender to obtain funds for the purchase. The term of the mortgage notes and the primary term of the lease were usually coextensive. The mortgage provided that the property could be transferred, with the transferees being obligated to fulfill the terms of the mortgage and the lease except that the transferees would assume no personal financial obligation for the payment of principal and interest on the note. Such transferees were also obligated to keep the corporation in existence. Immediately after these transactions, the corporation would then convey the property to its shareholders subject to the lease and mortgage and without any cash payment to the corporation. The transferee shareholders would assume the corporation's obligation under the lease and mortgage, but they had no personal liability thereon except to the extent of the property they received. The taxpayers claimed that they were entitled to the depreciation deductions generated by the properties. The Commissioner asserted that only the corporation had a depreciable interest in the property. The court first held that both at the time the corporation was created and after the transfer of the property to the shareholders, the corporation was a viable business entity. Although at the latter point the corporation was stripped of its assets and, by virtue of its various agreements could not engage in any business activity, the court held it was sufficient that the corporation continued to be liable on its obligations to the lender and remained in existence with full powers to own property and transact business. The court went on to hold, however, that because of the transfer of the property to the shareholders the individual taxpayers were entitled to the depreciation deductions. The case presaged the Tax Court's position in *Strong* that there is very little room for a taxpayer successfully to assert disregard of the corporate form which the taxpayer has adopted.

See also Tomlinson v. Miles, 316 F.2d 710 (5th Cir.1963)(corporation formed to hold title to real estate to facilitate its ultimate sale held taxable on the gain from such sales although the corporation held title "for the use and benefit" of the shareholders); Taylor v. Commissioner, 445 F.2d 455 (1st Cir.1971)(opening of a checking account and the execution of deeds and a mortgage constituted "business activity"): "If [the corporation] were to serve only as a straw, it should have only performed those transactions essential to the holding and transferring of title." (457); Commissioner v. State–Adams Corp., 283 F.2d 395 (2d Cir.1960)(court rejected the taxpayer's argument that the holding of title did not warrant recognition of the corporate entity since the corporate functions of collecting money with respect to the land constituted "business activity"); Britt v. United States, 431 F.2d 227 (5th Cir.1970)(where the court held, for the taxpayer, that the corporation was a separate entity since the corporate activity in signing notes and collecting dividends constituted "business activity").

Recognition of the corporate entity because the corporation conducts sufficient business activity does not preclude a *Bollinger* type argument that the corporation nevertheless was acting merely as the agent of its shareholders.

(b) *Investment Activity*

Taxpayers have sometimes been successful in having their corporations recognized as separate entities under the *Moline Properties* concept of "business activity" even though the corporate function consisted only of a single investment asset rather than active business operations. In Siegel v. Commissioner, 45 T.C. 566 (1966) (A), the taxpayer, wishing to limit his potential liability, established a Panamanian corporation to invest in a farm joint venture in Cuba. The taxpayer had no immediate need for the profits and his plan at the time of the incorporation was ultimately "to obtain the fruits of the venture through liquidation of the corporation". Although the other members of the joint venture actively participated in the farming operation, the corporation's only activity was to receive money from the venture, deposit it in its account, and periodically invest and reinvest the funds in the Cuban farming venture. The Tax Court concluded that there was a sufficient amount of business activity: "Nor may it be said that [the corporation's] minimal activity did not constitute the conduct of business. The point is that [the corporation] was formed for only a limited purpose, namely, to invest in the joint venture * * *."[1] See also Bateman v. United States, 490 F.2d 549 (9th Cir.1973)(corporation which owned a limited partnership interest in a partnership in which its sole shareholder was active and conducted no business other than this passive investment was treated as a separate taxable entity based on the trial court's finding that the business purpose for the corporation was to build a cash reserve fund to buy out retiring or deceased partners' interests).

B. IRRELEVANCE OF ACTUAL DIRECTION OF CORPORATE ACTIVITIES

In attempting to have the corporation disregarded for tax purposes, the Commissioner has argued unsuccessfully that the corporation is not engaged in "business activity" in cases in which the shareholder-owner has completely dominated the corporate activities. For example, in Bass v. Commissioner, 50 T.C. 595 (1968), the taxpayer organized a Swiss corporation to which he transferred working interests in oil and gas leases. The Commissioner attempted to discount the business actions of the corporation on the theory that the taxpayer "actually made the business decisions for the corporation." The Tax Court concluded that the corporation was a viable business entity since it had "acted" like a genuine corporation in paying the expenses of the business and filing returns. The *Bass* opinion emphasized the Supreme Court's language in National Carbide Corp. v. Commissioner, 336 U.S. 422 (1949), that "the fact that the owner retains direction of its affairs down to the minutest detail * * * [makes] no difference tax-wise." A like result was reached in Ross Glove Co. v. Commissioner, 60 T.C. 569 (1973) (A).

After failing in an attempt to prevent the classification of professional service corporations as corporations for tax purposes, see e.g., Kurzner v. United States, 413 F.2d 97 (5th Cir.1969), the Commissioner began to attack professional service corporations generally on the basis that such corporations were shams that did not actually earn their incomes. However, as long as corporate formalities were followed and the shareholder-employees respected the corporate form in conducting business, the Commissioner met with little success. Compare Achiro v. Commissioner, 77 T.C. 881 (1981)(corporate form of management services company respected at taxpayer's behest even though shareholders were sole employees and primary purpose of forming corporation was to reduce income taxes) with Jones v. Commissioner, 64 T.C. 1066 (1975)(court reporter who formed personal service corporation taxed individually because court rules required reporter to be an individual rather than a corporation).

1. Section 951, added in 1962, would now deal with the situation in *Siegel* to the extent that the utilization of a foreign rather than a domestic corporation was involved.

C. APPLICATION OF THE AGENCY RATIONALE

The *Moline Properties* doctrine makes it difficult to disregard the corporate entity if the corporation conducts any business, particularly because the requisite activity threshold is low. Taxpayers often have sought to achieve the same result as is produced by the disregard of corporate entity theory on the ground that a principal-agent relationship exists between the shareholder and the corporation. Therefore the income involved is the shareholder's rather than the corporation's. As explained in the *Bollinger* opinion, this argument was based on language in National Carbide Corp. v. Commissioner, 336 U.S. 422, 437–39 (1949).

Prior to the *Bollinger* decision, most cases turned on application of the fifth *National Carbide* factor, whether the relations between the principal and the agent depended on the principal's ownership of the agent. For example, in Harrison Property Management Co., Inc. v. United States, 475 F.2d 623 (Ct.Cl.1973), three partners transferred title to oil-bearing property to the corporation, retaining all beneficial rights and interests in the property in themselves. The primary reason for the formation of the corporation was the orderly management of the property in the event of the death of one of the individuals. The corporation received the income from oil leases, paid expenses incident thereto, and filed a fiduciary income tax return showing all net income distributed to the three individuals. The individuals reported the amounts in their individual returns. The Commissioner contended that the corporation should be treated as a separate entity and was taxable on the income. The court first held that the corporation was a taxable entity under the *Moline Properties* test and then rejected the taxpayer's alternative contention that an agency relationship existed between the corporation and the three individuals:

"*National Carbide* makes it clear that the formal designation of 'agency agreement' is not conclusive; the significant criteria, as we understand them, are whether the so-called 'agent' would have made the agreement if the so-called 'principals' were not its owners, and conversely whether the 'principals' would have undertaken the arrangement if the 'agent' were not their corporate creature. * * *

"[W]e do not doubt that the present plaintiffs fail the test. It is inconceivable that Harrison Property Management Co., Inc. would have made its alleged 'agency' contract with property owners other than its own shareholders, the Harrisons, or that the latter would have agreed to such an arrangement with the corporation if they did not own and control it. Obviously the agreement was deliberately drawn, in conjunction with the special provisions of the corporate charter, so that the company would service its owners alone, and was made solely because they were its owners. The entire operating arrangement was custom-made for that very purpose. * * * In other words, all of the corporation's relations with the beneficial owners of the managed property were wholly dependent on the fact that they were the sole shareholders. * * * " (625–628)

The Courts of Appeals decisions preceding *Bollinger* viewed the six *National Carbide* factors as being of greater importance than did the

Supreme Court in *Bollinger*, and also emphasized the fifth factor. Roccaforte v. Commissioner, 708 F.2d 986 (5th Cir.1983), rev'g, 77 T.C. 263 (1981), held that while the first four factors were relevant, in order to establish an agency relationship it was mandatory that the final two factors—relations between the principal and agent must be arms' length and the business purpose of the corporation must be to carry on the normal duties of an agent—be met. Because the Tax Court had found that the relations between the shareholders and the corporation were dependent on the fact that the "agent" was owned by the principals, the court held that a true agency had not been established. The facts upon which the nonarms' length relationship conclusion was based were that the corporation was owned by its shareholders in the same percentages which the shareholders held their interests in the partnership which they claimed owned the property for tax purposes, the sole function of the "agent" was to borrow money in avoidance of state usury laws, and it was not compensated for its services. Similar results were reached in Ourisman v. Commissioner, 760 F.2d 541 (4th Cir.1985); Vaughn v. United States, 740 F.2d 941 (Fed.Cir. 1984); Jones v. Commissioner, 640 F.2d 745 (5th Cir.1981); Frink v. Commissioner, 798 F.2d 106 (4th Cir.1986), vacated 485 U.S. 973 (1988); George v. Commissioner, 803 F.2d 144 (5th Cir.1986), vacated 485 U.S. 973 (1988). In all of these cases the court concluded that a corporation which is not compensated and which is owned by one or more of its principals could not be a true agent under the fifth *National Carbide* factor.

Several Courts of Appeals decisions, however, applied an agency rationale to avoid corporate taxation. In general, these decisions focused on the fact that the corporation was not owned proportionately by the principals. The Sixth Circuit in its opinion in *Bollinger* distinguished *Roccaforte* because in *Bollinger* the corporation's stock was not owned by the same individuals who claimed to be the principals. 807 F.2d 65 (6th Cir.1986). See also Moncrief v. United States, 730 F.2d 276 (5th Cir.1984)(corporation wholly owned by 25 percent partner was true agent of partnership; *Roccaforte* distinguished); Raphan v. United States, 759 F.2d 879 (Fed.Cir.1985) (principals owned no stock of agent corporation).

Are the above Courts of Appeals decisions of any relevance after *Bollinger* or does the *Bollinger* opinion signal that form will control? The opinion stresses that a written agency agreement, the terms of which are respected, should be sufficient to establish the agency. Apparently these facts should suffice even in the case of an individual claiming that her wholly owned corporation is her agent. If so, the analysis in *Harrison Property Management Co.*, at page 64, is no longer valid. From the perspective of preventing tax avoidance through self-serving labeling of transactions, which is the preferable rule, that in *Bollinger* or that in *Harrison Property Management Co.?* Is one test more administrable than the other? If no written agreement exists should the agency argument be rejected on the grounds that form has not been followed, or should the courts engage in a facts and circumstances search for a "real" agency relationship? Heaton v. Commissioner, T.C. Memo. 1989–459, held that under *Bollinger* the absence of a written agency agreement was fatal to the taxpayer's agency claim, but the court also examined other factors to find that the taxpayer failed to satisfy every one of the *Bollinger* standards. The importance of form under the *Bollinger* standards also was emphasized in Greenberg v. Commissioner, T.C. Memo. 1989–12.

In re LeBlanc, 79 A.F.T.R.2d 97–754 (Bkrtcy.E.D.La.1997), held that *Bollinger* did not merely establish a safe harbor but established a definite standard, although less stringent than the *National Carbide* test, that must be met for a genuine agency relationship to exist. According to the *LeBlanc* court, the tripartite *Bollinger* test requires: "(1) 'the fact that the corporation is acting as agent for its shareholders with respect to a particular asset is set forth in a written agreement at the time the asset is acquired'; (2) 'the corporation functions as agent ... with respect to the asset for all purposes'; and (3) 'the corporation is held out as the agent ... in all dealings with third parties relating to the asset.' "

In First Chicago Corp. v. Commissioner, 96 T.C. 421 (1991), the Tax Court returned to the *National Carbide* factors to reject the taxpayer's argument that stock of a foreign corporation owned by various subsidiary members of an affiliated group of corporations was owned by the subsidiaries as agents for the parent corporation (which claimed a foreign tax credit under § 902 of the Code which is only available to a 10% stockholder of a foreign corporation). The Tax Court focused specifically on the last two *National Carbide* factors. In Bramblett v. Commissioner, 960 F.2d 526 (5th Cir.1992), a partnership sold land to a corporation owned by the partners. The corporation then developed and sold the land. The Commissioner denied the partnership capital gains treatment on the sale of the land, claiming that the corporation was acting as the partnership's agent in developing the land. In holding that the corporation was not the agent of the partnership, the Court of Appeals treated the *National Carbide* factors as the primary test for an agency relationship, and described *Bollinger* as a case involving additional factors that may indicate an agency relationship exists.

Apart from the broader issue of what factors generally establish a true agency relationship or, conversely, preclude a true agency relationship, is the *Bollinger* opinion flawed on its particular facts in finding an agency relationship? The sole purpose and activity of the corporation was to obtain a loan at a rate that would have been usurious under state law if the loan had been made to an individual. According to the opinion in *Bollinger,* the individual rather than the corporation was taxed because the corporation was a genuine agent. If that is true, then the principal—an individual—was the true borrower, and the loan was usurious under state law. Thus the lender would have violated state law. In Commissioner v. First Security Bank of Utah, N.A., 405 U.S. 394 (1972), the Supreme Court refused to apply § 482, discussed below, to tax a bank on income received by a commonly controlled insurance company. A key element in the Court's reasoning was that it would have been illegal for the bank to have received the income. Is *Bollinger* inconsistent with *First Security Bank of Utah?*

SECTION 3. REALLOCATION OF INCOME

INTERNAL REVENUE CODE: Section 482.

Section 482 authorizes the Commissioner to reallocate items of income, deduction, or credit among two or more organizations, trades or businesses under common control when necessary to prevent evasion of taxes or clearly to reflect income. This provision may apply in a variety of contexts, but the common theme is that when related entities deal with one another at less than arm's length the Commissioner can adjust their taxable incomes to reflect the income that each would have earned had they dealt at arm's length. Thus an increase in the income of one of the related parties, reflecting a payment which would have been made in an arm's length relationship but which was not made, must be accompanied by a correlative deduction or capitalized item for the other related party. Treas. Reg. § 1.482–1(g)(2).[2]

The extensive Regulations under § 482 are intended to ensure that taxpayers clearly reflect income attributable to controlled transactions by placing commonly controlled taxpayers on "a tax parity with an uncontrolled taxpayer by determining the true taxable income of the controlled taxpayer." Treas. Reg. § 1.482–1(a)(1). True taxable income results from a transaction under an "arm's length" standard, which attempts to equate the results of a controlled transaction with the result that would have occurred if uncontrolled taxpayers had engaged in the same transaction under similar circumstances. Treas. Reg. § 1.482–2(b)(1). The Regulations provide various methods which, if followed, are deemed to result in an arm's length price. See Treas. Regs. §§ 1.482–2 (loans, services, and rents), 1.482–3 (sales of tangible property), and 1.482–4 (sales of intangible property). Although § 482 does not authorize taxpayers to invoke its terms to reallocate income or deductions, Treas. Reg. § 1.482–1(a)(3) permits a taxpayer to report income on a return using prices that vary from the prices actually charged in a controlled transaction in order to reflect an arm's length result. A section 482 reallocation makes sense only if the parties involved are subject to significantly different tax rates or regimes. Thus, § 482 is employed primarily in the international context. In some instances, however, the provision is invoked by the Commissioner in the purely domestic context.

ILLUSTRATIVE MATERIAL

A. APPLICATION TO TRANSACTIONS INVOLVING INDIVIDUAL SHAREHOLDERS AND THEIR CONTROLLED CORPORATIONS

In the context of transactions involving individual shareholders and their controlled corporations, § 482 has been applied to dealings such as

2. Treas. Reg. § 1.482–1(g) permits taxpayers whose incomes have been adjusted under § 482 to make payments or setoffs reflecting the adjustments without further tax consequences. See Rev.Proc. 65–17, 1965–1 C.B. 833; Rev. Proc. 82–80, 1982–1 C.B. 89.

leases at inadequate or excessive rent and to dealings between commonly controlled corporations at an inadequate or at an excessive price, such as the sale of goods or services from X Corporation to Y Corporation, both of which are owned by the same shareholders. See, e.g., Fegan v. Commissioner, 71 T.C. 791 (1979)(79 percent shareholder of a corporation leased a motel to the corporation for less than its fair rental value); Peck v. Commissioner, 752 F.2d 469 (9th Cir.1985)(reallocation due to less than arm's length rental).

Virtually all of the case law involving the application of § 482 arose prior to the dramatic changes in the rate structure in 1986. Accordingly, most of the cases involved an allocation of income from a corporation to individual shareholders. Under the rate structure of the late 1980s and early 1990s, in which corporate rates exceeded the maximum individual rate the situations that were likely to raise § 482 issues were different. Between 1986 and 1993, the Commissioner had the incentive only to allocate income from the individual shareholders to the corporation. More recent changes to the rate structure, introducing maximum marginal rates higher than the maximum corporate rate and a significant capital gains preference, however, may lead to a renewal of the historic pattern. The following cases (involving both income allocations to and from corporations) illustrate how the Commissioner and the courts have applied § 482 in the individual shareholder-corporation context.

In Cooper v. Commissioner, 64 T.C. 576 (1975), the taxpayer transferred a construction business to a corporation and retained the depreciable assets. The taxpayer did not charge the corporation with any rent. The court upheld the Commissioner's allocation of the fair rental value of the depreciable assets to the individual taxpayer under § 482; the taxpayer was still engaged in a trade or business by virtue of retention of assets essential to the conduct of the construction business. See also Powers v. Commissioner, 724 F.2d 64 (7th Cir.1983)(shareholder leased property from one corporation at greater than arm's length rental and subleased to another corporation at less than arm's length rental; reallocations from both corporations to shareholder upheld).

Section 482 can be applied to allocate gross income. Treas. Regs. § 1.482–1(f)(1)(ii). In Procacci v. Commissioner, 94 T.C. 397 (1990), a partnership leased a golf course to a corporation controlled by the partners. Because the corporation's operating expenses to third parties exceeded its available funds, the corporation paid no rent to the partnership. The Commissioner invoked § 482 to allocate rental income to the partnership. The court rejected the taxpayer's argument that § 482 could not be applied to reallocate income from a taxpayer with net operating losses, but nevertheless held that the Commissioner's § 482 allocation was improper. At the time the partnership acquired the golf course, it had physically deteriorated. The partnership's goals were to improve the course to "championship status," to enhance the value of adjacent land that the partnership planned to develop, and to enable the partnership profitably to develop golf condominiums on the golf course property. Since, under the circumstances, operating expenses of the golf course were too high to permit its profitable operation, an unrelated lessee would have demanded a subsidy from the partnership. Accordingly, on the facts, the court found that a zero rental was an arm's length amount.

In some situations in which § 482 might be invoked, other principles are applied. These other rules do not necessarily require correlative adjustments such as those required under § 482. Thus, when an employee-shareholder is paid an excessive salary, the Internal Revenue Service often simply disallows a deduction to the corporation under § 162(a)(1) rather than invoking § 482. When a shareholder purchases or leases property from a corporation at a bargain price, the Service asserts that the bargain element is a dividend to the shareholder. See page 223. Finally, below market rate of interest loans are subject to the rules of § 7872, although § 482 also may be relevant. See Treas. Reg. § 1.482–2(a).

B. THE EXISTENCE OF "CONTROL"

In a case in which two unrelated taxpayers each owned 50 percent of the stock in a subsidiary corporation, the Tax Court originally held that the predecessor of § 482 was not applicable since the subsidiary was not "controlled" by the same interests despite the fact that the taxpayers were acting in furtherance of their common purposes. Lake Erie & Pittsburg Railway Co. v. Commissioner, 5 T.C. 558 (1945). The Service initially acquiesced in this decision (1945 C.B. 5), but in 1965 reexamined its position and indicated that it would no longer follow the *Lake Erie* holding. Rev.Rul. 65–142, 1965–1 C.B. 223. *Lake Erie* was likewise rejected by B. Forman Co. v. Commissioner, 453 F.2d 1144 (2d Cir.1972). In that case, two unrelated corporations formed a subsidiary, in which they each owned 50 percent of the stock, to build and operate a shopping center next to their department stores. The court held § 482 was applicable to allow the Commissioner to allocate to the shareholders interest income on non-interest bearing loans made to the subsidiary: "Whether [the two shareholders] are regarded as a partnership or joint venture, *de facto,* in forming [the subsidiary], the conclusion is inescapable that they acted in concert in making loans without interest to a corporation, all of whose stock they owned and all of whose directors and officers were their alter egos. They were not competitors in their dealings with one another or with [the subsidiary]. Their interests in [the subsidiary] were identical. When the Commissioner withdrew his acquiescence in *Lake Erie,* he gave reality of control as one of the reasons for doing so * * *. We agree." (1155)

The existence of control is a practical rather than formalistic question. In Hall v. Commissioner, 32 T.C. 390 (1959), the taxpayer as a sole proprietorship sold goods manufactured by him to a foreign corporation at a price considerably below his usual list price, the stock of the corporation according to the taxpayer being owned by his son and another. The court said that § 482 was applicable regardless of the legal ownership of the stock, since the taxpayer in fact exercised control over the corporation and dominated it. The court therefore allocated a part of the corporation's income to the taxpayer by treating the sales as if made in accordance with the taxpayer's list prices. In Ach v. Commissioner, 358 F.2d 342 (6th Cir.1966), the proprietor of a profitable clothing business sold the assets of a dress business to a corporation with loss carryovers controlled by her son. The Government argued that the sale should be ignored completely and the income from the dress business taxed directly to the proprietor. The Tax Court refused to take this approach, ("The corporation was actually in existence, and there was a genuine transfer of assets to it that were actually used in the conduct of the dress business," 42 T.C. 114, 123 (1964)), but went on to allocate 70 percent of the profits of the dress business to the proprietor because of her continuing management activities. The Court of Appeals sustained the allocation.

C. INADEQUATE SALARY PAID TO SHAREHOLDER–EMPLOYEES

1. *Background*

When individual rates substantially exceed corporate tax rates, as was the case prior to 1987, a sole shareholder, who is also the principal officer of his corporation, might not take any salary from the corporation, planning instead to build up the value of the corporation and then sell the stock, paying tax at capital gain rates. This raises the question of whether § 482 permits the Commissioner to allocate a fair salary to the shareholder (which the employee is then treated as having been recontributed to the corporation) on which the shareholder-employee must pay tax. Can the Commissioner also apply the principles of § 61 and Lucas v. Earl, 281 U.S. 111 (1930), to tax the corporation's income to the shareholder-employee? Similar issues have arisen in situations in which the corporation is a personal services corporation through which the shareholder-employee renders services that he previously performed as a sole proprietor. Since 1986, however, an individual has had a much reduced incentive to avoid taking a salary from his wholly-owned corporation except to the extent of the benefit provided by the 15 and 25 percent corporate rate brackets.

2. *Application of Section 482*

In some cases the Commissioner has successfully applied § 482 to a shareholder serving as an employee of a controlled corporation for an inadequate salary, thereby artificially inflating the corporation's income. See, e.g., Rubin v. Commissioner, 429 F.2d 650 (2d Cir.1970), on remand, 56 T.C. 1155 (1971), aff'd per curiam, 460 F.2d 1216 (2d Cir.1972); Borge v. Commissioner, 405 F.2d 673 (2d Cir.1968). However, the Commissioner has not always been successful.

In Foglesong v. Commissioner, T.C. Memo. 1976–294, the taxpayer was a sales representative for a pipe company. He formed a corporation which issued 98 percent of its common stock to him. The taxpayer's children were issued preferred stock with a stated value of $400. Thereafter the corporation entered into an employment contract with the taxpayer and into contracts with the pipe manufacturers for whom the taxpayer sold pipe products; commissions earned on sales were paid by the manufacturers directly to the corporation, from which the taxpayer received a salary. The taxpayer's compensation over the next several years was less than two-thirds of the commissions paid to the corporation, which had no other employees or sources of income. During that period dividends of $32,000 were paid on the preferred stock; no dividends were paid on the common stock. The Tax Court weighed the legitimate business purposes for the arrangement against its tax avoidance potential and held that the taxpayer so controlled and directed the earning of the income of the corporation that he was personally taxable on 98 percent of such income under the principles of Lucas v. Earl.

On appeal, the Seventh Circuit Court of Appeals vacated and remanded the case. 621 F.2d 865 (7th Cir.1980). The Court of Appeals concluded that applying § 61 was imprecise and directed the Tax Court to reconsider the case based on the Commissioner's power to reallocate income under § 482. On remand, the Tax Court held that § 482 was properly applied to allocate 98 percent of the corporation's income to the taxpayer because his salary was unreasonably low. 77 T.C. 1102 (1981). The Tax Court applied its earlier decision in Keller v. Commissioner, 77 T.C. 1014 (1981), to hold that the requisite "two organizations" existed: Foglesong was in the trade or business of selling pipe as an employee of the corporation, and the corporation was in the trade or business of selling pipe (through the efforts of Foglesong). The taxpayer appealed again, and the Court of Appeals vacated and remanded the decision a second time. A different panel held that § 482 could not be invoked to allocate income from a personal service corporation to its shareholder-employee who performs services solely for the corporation. The Court of Appeals did not consider the "two organizations" requirement to have been met.

The Internal Revenue Service does not follow the second Court of Appeals decision in *Foglesong*. Rev.Rul. 88–38, 1988–1 C.B. 246. Similarly, notwithstanding the reversal by the Seventh Circuit in *Foglesong*, the Tax Court continues to hold that § 482 can be applied to allocate income between a corporation and a shareholder-employee who performs services solely for a controlled corporation, at least where appeal does not lie to the Seventh Circuit. See Haag v. Commissioner, 88 T.C. 604 (1987)(income of professional service corporation reallocated to physician-sole shareholder who drew nominal salary).

In determining whether a reallocation of income is appropriate under § 482, the inquiry is whether the shareholder-employee's total compensation (including salary, bonuses, deferred compensation, and other fringe benefits) approximates the amount he would have received absent incorporation of the business. See Keller v. Commissioner, 77 T.C. 1014 (1981), aff'd, 723 F.2d 58 (10th Cir.1983)(§ 482 applicable, but on facts no reallocation was warranted because total compensation approximated preincorporation earnings).

3. *Applicability of Assignment of Income Principles*

Because it relies on § 482 in cases of nominal compensation to controlling-shareholder employees, the Tax Court applies § 61 and Lucas v. Earl only in the cases in which the corporation does not control the income. In Johnson v. Commissioner, 78 T.C. 882 (1982), aff'd by order, 734 F.2d 20 (9th Cir.1984), the Tax Court promulgated a two part test for determining when the corporation controls the income: "First, the service-performer employee must be just that—an employee of the corporation whom the corporation has the right to direct or control in some meaningful sense. Second, there must exist between the corporation and the person or entity using the services a contract or other similar indicium recognizing the corporation's controlling position." (891) In that case the individual taxpayer, a professional basketball player, was held to control the income because even though the team for which he played paid the salary directly to the corporation, the only contract was between the player and the team. In contrast, in *Haag,* supra, the corporation was treated as controlling the income, because the individual and corporation entered into an employment contract and the recipients of services treated the services as being rendered by the corporation.

Sargent v. Commissioner, 929 F.2d 1252 (8th Cir.1991), rev'g 93 T.C. 572 (1989), distinguished *Johnson* and reached a result similar to *Haag* in treating a professional hockey player as an employee of his professional service corporation. The Tax Court held that the taxpayer was an employee of the hockey team because the requirements of team play meant that the taxpayer was under the direction and control of the team. The Court of Appeals reversed the Tax Court because the corporation was formed for a bona fide business purpose, the taxpayer was a contractually-bound employee of the corporation, and the corporation had a recognized contract of employment with the hockey team.

For other cases in which the assignment of income principles rather than § 482 have been invoked compare Ronan State Bank v. Commissioner, 62 T.C. 27 (1974)(bank marketed credit life insurance through its employees but, believing that it was prohibited from engaging in the insurance business under state law, it assigned that business to its two principal shareholders who reported the commission income; the Tax Court upheld the Commissioner's allocation of the commission income to the bank solely under § 61 principles, thus avoiding the Supreme Court decision in Commissioner v. First Security Bank of Utah N.A., 405 U.S. 394 (1972), that § 482 could not be employed to allocate income to a corporation where it would have been illegal for the corporation to have received that income directly) with Salyersville National Bank v. United States, 613 F.2d 650 (6th Cir.1980)(no reallocation under § 482 on facts substantially similar to *Ronan State Bank,* citing *First Security Bank of Utah*).

What difference in result does it make whether the theory of the reallocation is the disregard of the intervening corporate entity, § 61 principles, or the application of § 482?

4. *Section 269A—Reallocation of Personal Service Corporation Income*

In Keller v. Commissioner, page 71, the physician shareholder of the professional service corporation involved in the case had been a partner in a medical partnership prior to formation of the corporation. Thereafter, Dr. Keller's professional service corporation was substituted for him as a partner. The purpose of this arrangement was to permit Dr. Keller to custom tailor a deferred compensation and fringe benefit plan for himself, which could permit evasion of the nondiscrimination rules with respect to pension plans and statutory fringe benefits. Congress responded to the *Keller* decision with the enactment of § 269A. See H.R.Rep. No. 97–760, 97th Cong., 2d Sess. 633–34 (1982). This provision authorizes reallocation of income from a personal service corporation to the employee-owner if (1) the principal purpose of forming or using the corporation is the avoidance of federal income tax by reducing the income of any employee-owner; (2) the corporation performs substantially all of its services on behalf of *one* other corporation, person, or partnership; and (3) substantially all of the services provided by the corporation are performed by employees who own more than 10 percent of the stock. Thus, § 269A does not apply to personal services corporations with more than one customer, which is normally the case or, for example, if ten physicians form a corporation to provide emergency room services exclusively to one hospital and each physician owns 10 percent of the stock. For the mechanics of the reallocation under § 269A, see Prop. Reg. § 1.269A–1 (1983). As noted previously, the 1982 Act made several changes in the treatment of qualified deferred compensation plans that greatly reduced the tax benefits from personal service corporations. These changes have reduced the number of incorporations to which § 269A might be applied.

CHAPTER 3

FORMATION OF THE CORPORATION

SECTION 1. RECEIPT OF STOCK FOR PROPERTY

A. BASIC PRINCIPLES

INTERNAL REVENUE CODE: Sections 351; 357; 358(a), (b)(1); 362(a); 1032; 1223(1), (2).

REGULATIONS: Sections 1.351–1(a),(c); 1.358–2(b)(2); 1.1032–1(a), (d).

When its requirements are met, § 351 permits the incorporation of a proprietorship, a partnership, or a new business without the recognition of gain, and prevents the recognition of loss. Under § 351, gain or loss is not recognized on the transfer of property to a corporation solely in exchange for stock[1] of the corporation if the transferor or transferors own at least 80 percent of the stock of the transferee corporation immediately after the transaction. Section 358 provides that the basis of stock received in exchange for property contributed to the corporation in a nonrecognition transaction under § 351 will be the same as the basis of property transferred to the corporation. Section 362(a) generally provides the corporation with a basis in the property equal to the transferor's basis.

In the absence of § 351, incorporation would constitute a taxable exchange under § 1001 since the transferor's change of status from the owner of an asset to the owner of shares of a corporation that owns the asset is a realization event. Burnet v. Commonwealth Improvement Co., 287 U.S. 415 (1932). Section 351 is intended to defer recognition of gain or loss in "transactions where gain or loss may have accrued in a constitutional sense, but where in popular and economic sense there has been a mere change in the form of ownership and the taxpayer has not really 'cashed in' on the theoretical gain, or closed out a losing venture." Portland Oil Co. v. Commissioner, 109 F.2d 479, 488 (1st Cir.1940). This "tax-free" incorporation is important where the assets to be transferred to the corporation have increased in value so that a gain would be present on a taxable exchange. The section also permits the tax-free creation of a subsidiary corporation by another corporation. In addition, it permits the transfer of property to an existing corporation without the recognition of gain, either where the existing corporation is controlled by an individual or by a corporation.

1. Prior to an amendment in 1989, § 351 nonrecognition treatment also applied if the corporation issued "securities," generally long-term debt, along with stock. As a result of the amendment, the transfer of appreciated property for anything other than stock is a recognition event.

In the situations covered by § 351, if the taxpayer is seeking the advantage of nonrecognition of gain on the transfer, the conditions of the section represent requirements to be satisfied. But the taxpayer may have a different goal. If the assets to be transferred have depreciated in value, so that a loss would be realized on their transfer, the transferor may be seeking recognition. If § 351 applies, however, the loss will not be recognized. Here, the conditions of § 351 represent factors to be avoided if the loss is to be obtained. Similarly, since the corporation takes over the transferor's basis if § 351 applies, the taxpayer may in some limited cases be willing to recognize gain in order to obtain for the corporation a depreciable basis equal to the fair market value of the transferred assets instead of the lower basis that it would obtain if the gain were not recognized. Here also, the conditions of the section must be avoided if such a stepped-up basis is to be obtained. Section 351 is applicable regardless of the intent of the taxpayer if the conditions of the section are in fact satisfied. Gus Russell, Inc. v. Commissioner, 36 T.C. 965 (1961).

Although by its terms § 351(a) applies only if the transferor receives stock as the sole consideration for the transfer of property to a controlled corporation, § 351(b) allows for the receipt of cash or other property—"boot" in tax jargon. The transferor's realized gain is recognized to the extent of money and the fair market value of property received as boot. (In both respects, § 351 operates in much the same manner as § 1031). Loss, however, is never recognized even though boot may be present. I.R.C. § 351(b)(2). However, under § 358(a) the transferor's basis in stock received is adjusted to reflect the receipt and taxation of the boot. The corporation's basis in property received is increased by gain recognized to the transferor. I.R.C. § 362(a).

Generally, § 351 provides nonrecognition regardless of whether the transferor receives common stock, preferred stock, or a hybrid, such as participating preferred stock. Under § 351(g), added in 1997, certain types of preferred stock that have characteristics that cause the stock more nearly to resemble debt are treated as boot. If a particular transferor receives only disqualified preferred stock, § 351 does not apply to that transferor at all.

The main requirement of § 351, apart from the question of boot, is acquisition of control by the transferors. As defined in § 368(c), control requires that the transferors own at least 80 percent of the stock of the transferee corporation immediately after the exchange. This requirement normally will be satisfied on an incorporation, with problems arising only if there is an immediate transfer of stock to a person not transferring property to the corporation. As a result, the control requirement is most significant with respect to transfers to an existing corporation.

Where incorporation of a proprietorship or partnership is contemplated, it is very likely that the properties involved will be subject to liabilities. Since ordinarily the assumption of a liability or the taking of property subject to a liability is regarded as consideration moving from the transferee to the transferor in the amount of the liability, the application of this rule to § 351 transactions in many cases would produce boot in the amount of the liabilities. The presence of boot in the form of assumed liabilities, giving rise to the possibility of taxable gain, would impede the free transition from the unincorporated to the corporate form, thereby frustrating the underlying policy of § 351. Consequently, § 357 provides that the assumption of a liability or the acquisition of property subject to a liability does not constitute boot for the purpose of § 351, unless a tax avoidance scheme is involved or unless the liabilities assumed exceed the basis of the property transferred. While the liability is not considered boot, its assumption by the corporation has the effect of the receipt of money by the stockholder. Accordingly, § 358(d) provides that for basis purposes liabilities are treated as money, which has the effect of decreasing the transferor's basis for the stock received in the exchange.

Nonrecognition principles also apply to the corporate transferee. Section 1032 provides nonrecognition treatment to a corporate transferee on the issuance of its stock in exchange for property or services. Under § 362(a)(1) the basis of transferred property in the hands of the transferee corporation is the same as the basis of the transferred property in the hands of the transferor, plus any gain recognized to the transferor on the exchange.

Suppose A transfers an apartment building worth $100,000 but with an adjusted basis of $10,000, to a newly created corporation in return for its stock. A's basis for the stock is $10,000 under § 358(a). The corporation's basis for the apartment building under § 362(a)(1) is likewise $10,000. If the corporation had been in existence and had issued both stock and $30,000 cash for the apartment, A would have had a recognized gain of $30,000 (the extent of the boot, assuming that the value of the stock was $70,000 and assuming that no dividend was involved), a basis of $10,000 for the stock, and a basis of $30,000 for the cash; the corporation would have had a basis of $40,000 ($10,000 basis in transferor A's hands plus gain of $30,000 recognized to A). If for some reason, such as lack of control because of a prearranged transfer of some of the stock, the incorporation was not under § 351 at all, the entire gain would be recognized, and the basis of the apartment in the corporation's hands under general cost principles would be the fair market value of the stock issued for the assets. Treas. Reg. § 1.1032–1(d). The fair market value of the assets would be relevant in determining that value, though it would not be controlling. Rev.Rul. 56–100, 1956–1 C.B. 624.

The corporation's basis under § 362(a) is thus dependent on the basis of the transferring stockholders and the amount of gain, if any, that is recognized to them. It does not depend upon nor is it affected by any actual cost that the corporation may have. Hence, in the immediately preceding example, where the corporation paid out $30,000 cash as well as stock, if the basis of the stockholder for the apartment house had been higher than the value of the stock and the cash received so that the stockholder realized but did not recognize a loss, the corporation's basis for the apartment house would still be the same as that of the stockholder. The corporation's basis for the apartment house would not be increased by the $30,000 cash that it paid. The loss, not being recognized, would not reduce that basis.

Sections 1223(1) and (2), following the basis provisions, give both the stockholder and the corporation the holding period of the assets transferred to the corporation. The stock obtains such holding period and may on a sale be treated as held for the period of the transferred property only if the property was itself a capital asset or an asset that could obtain capital gain treatment under § 1231.

If § 351 is applicable, the combined effect of the two basis provisions, §§ 358(a) and 362(a)(1), is to produce the possibility of two gains or two losses where only one existed before. However, a subsequent recognition of the stockholder's gain may be postponed if the stock is later transferred in a tax-free transaction, e.g., a reorganization. Furthermore, if the stock is held by the transferor until death, one of the two gains or losses is eliminated by the rule of § 1014, which provides for a basis equal to the value of the stock at the date of death.

ILLUSTRATIVE MATERIAL

A. THE CORPORATION'S ASSET BASIS: MULTIPLE ASSET TRANSFERS

When a shareholder exchanges more than one item of property solely for stock in a § 351 transfer, the corporation's basis in each item of property is the same as it was in the hands of the shareholder. See P.A. Birren & Son v. Commissioner, 116 F.2d 718 (7th Cir.1940); Gunn v. Commissioner, 25 T.C. 424, 438 (1955), aff'd per curiam, 244 F.2d 408 (10th Cir.1957). Thus, for example, if the shareholder transfers Blackacre, with a basis of $100 and a fair market value of $300 and Whiteacre with a basis of $200 and a fair market value of $300, the basis of each property remains the same. The aggregate basis of $300 is not reallocated among the properties. The problems encountered in allocating basis increases attributable to the transferor's recognized gain when multiple assets are involved are discussed at page 83.

B. "PROPERTY": CASH AND PROMISSORY NOTES

For purposes of § 351, "property" includes not only cash, Rev.Rul. 69–357, 1969–1 C.B. 101, but also accounts receivable, regardless of whether the transferor used the cash or accrual method of accounting, Rev. Rul. 80–198, 1980–2 C.B. 113, as well as § 453 installment notes. Under Treas. Reg. § 1.453–9(c)(2), in general no gain or loss results from the transfer of installment obligations to a corporation in an exchange to which § 351 applies despite the fact that part of the tax on the installment gain may in effect be shifted to the other shareholders. However, if the obligor on the installment obligation is the corporation *itself,* then the § 351 transaction constitutes a "satisfaction" of the installment obligation under § 453B(a) and results in a tax to the transferor. Rev.Rul. 73–423, 1973–2 C.B. 161, following dicta in Jack Ammann Photogrammetric Engineers, Inc. v. Commissioner, 341 F.2d 466 (5th Cir.1965).

Because § 351 may apply to transfers to a preexisting corporation as well as to transfers to a newly organized corporation, provided the control requirement is met, the question of whether the transfer of indebtedness of the corporation in exchange for stock qualifies can arise. Sections 351(d)(2) and (3) provide that stock issued to satisfy an indebtedness of the issuing corporation not evidenced by a security, or to pay interest on indebtedness of the issuing corporation, is not considered as issued in return for property. Similarly, § 351(e)(2) provides that § 351 is not applicable if a corporation in a bankruptcy or insolvency proceeding transfers assets to another corporation and then distributes the stock received to its creditors. The transaction is treated as if the assets had first been distributed to the creditors and the creditors had then transferred the property to the new corporation.

C. ALLOCATION OF BASIS TO STOCK

The stockholders' basis in the stock must be allocated among stock of different classes in proportion to the fair market values of the stock in each class. I.R.C. § 358(b)(1); Treas. Reg. § 1.358–2(b)(2). Thus, for example, if A transfers real property with a basis of $20 and fair market value of $100 to X, a controlled corporation, in a nonrecognition transaction under § 351, and A receives in exchange common stock with a value of $80 and preferred stock with a value of $20, A's substituted basis in the common stock is $16 ($20 × $80/$100) and A's substituted basis in the preferred stock is $4 ($20 × $20/100). The stockholder cannot allocate the basis of some transferred assets to one block of stock, for example, preferred stock, and the lower basis of other assets to another block of stock. See Rev.Rul. 85–164, 1985–2 C.B. 117.

D. TAX CONSEQUENCES TO THE CORPORATION ISSUING STOCK

Section 1032, which applies both to newly-issued stock and treasury stock, provides that the issuance of its own stock is not a taxable event for the corporation. Treas. Reg. § 1.1032–1(d) provides that the basis of the property acquired by the corporation in exchange for its stock is its "cost" to the corporation—the fair market value of the property acquired—unless the transaction falls under § 351 or the reorganization nonrecognition sections, which generally provide for a carryover of basis from the transferor. The cost basis equals fair market value rule applies even when the corporation acquires property in a transaction in which it reissues treasury stock that it previously purchased for less than its fair market value at the time it is reissued. Thus, § 1032 provides nonrecognition of the "profit" realized by a corporation purchasing and reissuing its own shares. See Rev.Rul. 74–503, 1974–2 C.B. 117.

E. SECURITIES "SWAP FUNDS"

Should the § 351 tax-free treatment cover all transfers to controlled corporations? Suppose that an individual owns a large amount of a particular stock that has greatly appreciated in value. The taxpayer would like to diversify that investment but feels that the tax on capital gains is too high a price to pay for diversification. There are many other individuals in a similar situation, but with different stocks. An investment house forms a regulated investment company (mutual fund)—which is a corporation for federal tax purposes—and invites an exchange of the stocks of the individuals in return for stock of the fund. This exchange would provide the individuals with the desired diversification, since they would now have, through their participation in the mutual fund, an interest in many different stocks, including their former shares. In 1960, the Internal Revenue Service issued letter rulings to the effect that such a transaction would qualify under § 351. The investment funds organized to achieve such purposes were known as "swap funds." In Rev.Proc. 62–32, 1962–2 C.B. 527, the Internal Revenue Service announced that it would no longer issue rulings on such transactions. However, swap funds continued to flourish, relying upon the opinions of counsel that § 351 made the transaction tax-free to the transferors. In 1966, the Treasury issued proposed regulations to the effect that future swap fund transactions would constitute taxable exchanges. In 1966, Congress ratified the tax-free treatment of transfers to swap funds that were made prior to June 30, 1967, but excluded "investment companies" from the definition of "corporation" under § 351 for transfers after that date. In 1976, the statutory structure, but not the result, was changed. Section 351(e) now provides that § 351 does not apply to transfers to investment companies. As a result, gain or loss is recognized by the transferors in such transactions.[2]

Treas. Reg. § 1.351–1(c) provides that a transferee will be considered to be to an "investment company" if the transaction results, directly or indirectly, in a diversification of the transferor's interest and the transferee is a regulated investment company, a real estate investment trust, or a corporation more than 80 percent of the value of the assets of which is held in readily marketable stocks or securities or similar transferable interests. Under Treas. Reg. § 1.351–1(c)(5), a transaction ordinarily results in diversification "if two or more persons transfer nonidentical assets to a corporation in the exchange." The Internal Revenue Service has taken the position that the requirement that two or more persons transfer nonidentical assets to the corporation is satisfied if one group of transferors transfer the stock of a single corporation and another group transfers cash. Rev.Rul. 87–27, 1987–1 C.B. 134. The statutory changes and the regulations thus extend to situations beyond the mutual fund problem that caused those changes.

In Rev.Rul. 88–32, 1988–1 C.B. 113, the Internal Revenue Service ruled that a transfer of stock does not result in diversification unless diversification is the result of a nonrecognition transaction. Thus, there is no proscribed diversification if the transferor transfers stock of a single corporation to a controlled investment company that sells the stock in a

2. Section 683 provides similar rules for transfers to trusts used as swap funds and § 721(b) deals with diversification through partnership formation.

taxable transaction and reinvests the sales proceeds in a diverse portfolio of stock.

B. "SOLELY FOR STOCK"—THE RECEIPT OF OTHER PROPERTY

INTERNAL REVENUE CODE: Sections 351(b), (g); 267(a)(1), (b)(2), (c), (d); 453(c), (f)(6), (g); 1239.

REGULATIONS: Sections 1.301–1(1); 1.351–2.

PROPOSED REGULATIONS: Section 1.453–1(f)(1)(iii), (f)(3)(ii).

The nonrecognition rule of § 351(a) is limited to an exchange of property "solely for stock" of the controlled corporation. Section 351(b) permits the receipt of other property, but requires that the transferor recognize gain to the extent of the fair market value of other property plus the amount of money received. The basis rules of § 358 adjust the transferor's basis in the stock of the controlled corporation to account for boot by decreasing basis in an amount equal to the fair market value of property and the amount of money received, and increasing basis by the amount of any gain recognized. The transferee corporation's basis in transferred assets is also increased under § 362(a) by the amount of gain recognized by the transferor on the § 351 exchange.

In some circumstances, a taxpayer may desire to treat the transfer of property to a controlled corporation as a "sale" rather than as an exchange governed by § 351. If the taxpayer has property that has declined in value, a "sale" may be desirable to enable the transferor to recognize a loss on the depreciated assets. Sale treatment may be achieved only if the property is transferred in exchange for property other than stock or only for nonqualified preferred stock (as defined in § 351(g)). If the transaction qualifies as a § 351 transaction, even where boot is received, no loss can be recognized in the transaction.

Under certain circumstances, if there is a significant differential between the individual capital gains rate and the corporate tax rate, a transferor might be willing to pay a capital gain tax on the sale of appreciated assets to permit the corporation to obtain a step-up in basis for the assets, thereby reducing in some circumstances potential ordinary income upon subsequent sales of the property by the corporation, or providing higher depreciation or capital recovery deductions against ordinary income (but see § 1239). The receipt of "property" other than stock in a § 351 transaction would provide the same increase in basis to the extent of gain recognized under § 351(b).

Where property is transferred to a controlled corporation for stock and debt obligations, whether or not the debt is a security, no part of the transaction constitutes a sale with a resulting recognition of loss. The debt instrument constitutes "other property" (boot) and the tax consequences thus are governed by § 351(a) and (b). Under § 351(g), added in 1997, certain types of preferred stock that have characteristics that cause the stock more nearly to resemble debt also are treated as boot. Gain is recognized on the transaction to the extent of the fair market value of other property, but no loss is recognized. The taxpayer cannot alter these tax consequences by attempting to denominate part of the transaction as a "sale" of some assets and the balance as a transfer under § 351. See, e.g., Nye v. Commissioner, 50 T.C. 203 (1968).

Where the transferor receives only cash or property (and no stock), the transaction is a sale or exchange and gain or loss will be recognized accordingly. Thus the taxpayer can achieve sale treatment by transferring property for debt instruments ("securities") rather than stock. However, if the transferor is in control of the corporation sale treatment will not be accorded the transaction if the purported debt instrument is in fact "equity" (see page 130), thus bringing § 351 into play. In addition, a shareholder who transfers depreciated property to the corporation and who receives only nonqualified preferred stock (as defined in § 351(g)) may recognize the loss, notwithstanding that for some other purposes, the preferred stock might be "equity."

Revenue Ruling 68–55

1968–1 C.B. 140.

Advice has been requested as to the correct method of determining the amount and character of the gain to be recognized by Corporation *X* under section 351(b) of the Internal Revenue Code of 1954 under the circumstances described below.

Corporation *Y* was organized by *X* and *A*, an individual who owned no stock in *X*. *A* transferred 20*x* dollars to *Y* in exchange for stock of *Y* having a fair market value of 20*x* dollars and *X* transferred to *Y* three separate assets and received in exchange stock of *Y* having a fair market value of 100*x* dollars plus cash of 10*x* dollars.

In accordance with the facts set forth in the table below if *X* had sold at fair market value each of the three assets it transferred to *Y*, the result would have been as follows:

	Asset I	*Asset II*	*Asset III*
Character of asset	Capital asset held more than 6 months.	Capital asset held not more than 6 months.	Section 1245 property.
Fair market value	$22*x*	$33*x*	$55*x*
Adjusted basis	40*x*	20*x*	25*x*
Gain (loss)	($18*x*)	$13*x*	$30*x*
Character of gain or loss	Long-term capital loss.	Short-term capital gain.	Ordinary income.

The facts in the instant case disclose that with respect to the section 1245 property the depreciation subject to recapture exceeds the amount of gain that would be recognized on a sale at fair market value. Therefore, all of such gain would be treated as ordinary income under section 1245(a)(1) of the Code.

Under section 351(a) of the Code, no gain or loss is recognized if property is transferred to a corporation solely in exchange for its stock and immediately after the exchange the transferor is in control of the corporation. If section 351(a) of the Code would apply to an exchange but for the fact that there is received, in addition to the property permitted to be received without recognition of gain, other property or money, then under section 351(b) of the Code gain (if any) to the recipient will be recognized, but in an amount not in excess of the sum of such money and the fair market value of such other property received, and no loss to the recipient will be recognized.

The first question presented is how to determine the amount of gain to be recognized under section 351(b) of the Code. The general rule is that each asset transferred must be considered to have been separately exchanged. See the authorities cited in Revenue Ruling 67–192, C.B. 1967–2, 140, and in Revenue Ruling 68–23, [1968–1 C.B. 144] * * *. Thus, for purposes of making computations under section 351(b) of the Code, it is not proper to total the bases of the various assets transferred and to subtract this total from the fair market value of the total consideration received in the exchange. Moreover, any treatment other than an asset-by-asset approach would have the effect of allowing losses that are specifically disallowed by section 351(b)(2) of the Code.

The second question presented is how, for purposes of making computations under section 351(b) of the Code, to allocate the cash and stock received to the amount realized as to each asset transferred in the exchange. The asset-by-asset approach for computing the amount of gain realized in the exchange requires that for this purpose the fair market value of each category of consideration received must be separately allocated to the transferred assets in proportion to the relative fair market values of the transferred assets. See section 1.1245–4(c)(1) of the Income Tax Regulations which, for the same reasons, requires that for purposes of computing the amount of gain to which section 1245 of the Code applies each category of consideration received must be allocated to the properties transferred in proportion to their relative fair market values.

Accordingly, the amount and character of the gain recognized in the exchange should be computed as follows:

	Total	*Asset I*	*Asset II*	*Asset III*
Fair market value of asset transferred	\$110x	\$22x	\$33x	\$55x
Percent of total fair market value	—	20%	30%	50%
Fair market value of Y stock received in exchange	\$100x	\$20x	\$30x	\$50x
Cash received in exchange	10x	2x	3x	5x
Amount realized	\$110x	\$22x	\$33x	\$55x
Adjusted basis	—	40x	20x	25x
Gain (loss) realized	—	(\$18x)	\$13x	\$30x

Under section 351(b)(2) of the Code the loss of 18x dollars realized on the exchange of Asset Number I is not recognized. Such loss may not be used to offset the gains realized on the exchanges of the other assets. Under section 351(b)(1) of the Code, the gain of 13*x* dollars realized on the exchange of Asset Number II will be recognized as short-term capital gain in the amount of 3*x* dollars, the amount of cash received. Under sections 351(b)(1) and 1245(b)(3) of the Code, the gain of 30*x* dollars realized on the exchange of Asset Number III will be recognized as ordinary income in the amount of 5*x* dollars, the amount of cash received.

ILLUSTRATIVE MATERIAL

A. THE CORPORATION'S BASIS

If no gain is recognized, the corporation takes a transferred basis from the shareholder in each separate asset under § 362(a)(1). This transferred basis is increased by the transferor's recognized gain, which requires an allocation of the gain to different assets. Rev.Rul. 68–55 applies the principle of Williams v. McGowan, 152 F.2d 570 (2d Cir.1945), requiring the seller of multiple assets to compute gain or loss on an asset-by-asset basis to § 351 transactions involving boot. See also Rev.Rul. 67–192, 1967–2 C.B. 140; Treas. Reg. § 1.1245–4(c). Although the regulations under § 362 are silent on the issue, and no Revenue Ruling directly addresses the point, this comminution rule also should apply to determine adjustments to the corporation's basis in the transferred assets. The amount of gain allocated to each asset for purposes of the basis adjustment required by § 362(a) should be the amount of gain recognized by the seller with respect to that asset under Rev. Rul. 68–55. Thus the corporation's basis in each of the assets involved in Rev. Rul. 68–55 should be as follows:

	Asset I	Asset II	Asset III
Transferor's Basis	$40x	$20x	$25x
Transferor's Gain	____	$ 3x	$ 5x
Corporation's Basis	$40x	$23x	$30x

Note that there is no basis adjustment to Asset I, because with respect to that asset the transferor realized an unrecognized loss.

B. EXCHANGE OF PROPERTY FOR CORPORATE DEBT

1. *Sale Versus Exchange Treatment*

In Burr Oaks Corp. v. Commissioner, 365 F.2d 24 (7th Cir.1966), three individuals transferred land to a controlled corporation and received in exchange therefore three two-year 6 percent notes each in the amount of $110,000 (although the land was found to be worth only one-half of the face value of the notes). The taxpayers asserted that the transaction was a sale, but the Tax Court found the transaction was an equity contribution to the corporation and the notes were treated as preferred stock rather than debt. The paid-in capital of the corporation was only $4,500 at a time that the corporation incurred "liabilities" of eighty times that amount. The Court of Appeals upheld the Tax Court: "When the payment to the transferors is dependent on the success of an untried undercapitalized business with uncertain prospects, a strong inference arises that the transfer is an equity contribution." The requirements of § 351 being otherwise met, the corporation received only a transferred basis in the land transferred to the corporation. The opposite result was reached in Gyro Engineering Corp. v. United States, 417 F.2d 437 (9th Cir.1969). The principal stockholders transferred three apartment buildings to a corporation for $30,000 cash and $2,343,000 in notes. The transaction was treated as a sale and not as a contribution to capital since the property was generating revenue sufficient to pay the notes. See also J.I. Morgan, Inc. v. Commissioner, 30 T.C. 881 (1958) (A), rev'd and remanded on other issues, 272 F.2d 936 (9th Cir.1959)(sustaining a "sale" of assets by a majority stockholder to his corporation in return for an installment contract payable in seven years); Piedmont Corp. v. Commissioner, 388 F.2d 886 (4th Cir.1968)(corporation with paid-in capital of $60 acquired from its two stockholders options to purchase land, giving unsecured notes therefor with terms ranging from three to seven years; corporation exercised the options and sold the land; Tax Court upheld the Commissioner's contention that the notes were equity, but the Court of Appeals reversed and upheld sale treatment, concluding that the notes represented valid debt).

In Adams v. Commissioner, 58 T.C. 41 (1972), the taxpayer was a minority stockholder in a corporation (Western). He individually owned some uranium property that he desired to sell to Western, but Western could not buy because of credit restrictions. The taxpayer formed a new wholly-owned corporation (Wyoming) and within 3 days sold his uranium property to Wyoming for a $1 million, 2–year note. Wyoming then leased the property to Western and received a $945,000 advance royalty that was used to pay off the taxpayer's note. The taxpayer reported the payment as long-term capital gain and the corporation included the amount of the note in its basis for cost depletion purposes. While the court upheld the Commissioner's treatment of the transaction under § 351, since both the creation of Wyoming and the "sale" of the uranium property to it were "interdependent steps" in the formation of Wyoming, the note was treated as boot under § 351(b) and not as equity as urged by the Commissioner. See also D'Angelo Associates, Inc. v. Commissioner, page 111.

2. *Installment Sale Treatment*

The receipt of corporate debt obligations as boot by the shareholder may not require the immediate recognition of gain. A disposition of property for payments that are received after the close of the taxable year in which disposition occurs is an installment sale subject to deferred recognition of gain under the rules of § 453. Under § 453(c) the gain recognized with respect to any payment in an installment sale is an amount that bears the same ratio to the payment as the gross profit on the installment sale bears to the total contract price. Section 453(f)(6) provides, with respect to a like-kind exchange under § 1031(b), that payments and total contract price do not include property that may be received without recognition of gain. Prop. Reg. § 1.453–1(f)(3)(ii) (1984) applies the rules of § 453(f)(6) to a § 351 exchange. Prop. Reg. § 1.453–1(f)(1)(iii)(1984) allocates the transferor's basis in transferred property first to the stock received without recognition under § 351, to the extent of the fair market value of the stock. Any remaining basis is used to offset gain recognized on the installment sale. In effect, neither payments nor total contract price include stock permitted to be received under § 351 without recognition of gain.

Assume, for example, that A transfers property with an adjusted basis of $40 and a fair market value of $100 to a corporation controlled by A in exchange for stock worth $70 and a note for $30, payable in three annual installments, with adequate interest, beginning in the year following the transfer. Because under Treas. Reg. § 1.1001–1(g) the amount realized upon receipt of the note is $30, § 351(b) requires that A recognize $30 of A's $60 realized gain. Under § 453, however, since "payments" do not include the stock received in the year of the exchange, no gain is recognized immediately. Under the proposed regulations, A's $40 basis is allocated to the stock, leaving no basis to reduce gain on the installment sale. Recognition is deferred until the receipt of each $10 payment whereupon A recognizes the full $10 ($10 × $30/$30). Alternatively, if A's basis in the property transferred were $85 dollars, $70 of basis would be allocated to the stock, leaving $15 of basis to offset A's installment gain. A would recognize $15 of gain under § 351(b) but the recognition would be deferred under § 453. A would recognize $5 of gain on each $10 payment ($10 × $15/$30).

Prop. Reg. § 1.453–1(f)(3)(ii)(1984) provides that the transferor's basis in stock as determined under § 358 includes the deferred gain to be recognized under the installment method. Thus in the first example above, A's basis in the stock is $40 consisting of A's basis in the property transferred increased by the gain recognized and decreased by the fair market value of the note. A's basis in the second example is $70. With respect to the transferee corporation's basis under § 362(a), however, Prop. Reg. § 1.453–1(f)(3)(ii)(1984) provides that the transferor's recognized gain under the installment method will not be included in the transferee's basis until the deferred gain is actually recognized by the transferor. Section 453(d) allows the transferor to elect out of installment sale treatment in which case the full fair market value of the note is recognized as gain in the year of the exchange. The election would permit the corporation immediately to step-up its basis in the transferred property under § 362(a).

Section 453(g) restricts use of the installment method in the case of a transfer of depreciable property to a corporation if the transferor owns more than 50 percent of the stock of the corporation, a transaction to which § 1239 applies. See Guenther v. Commissioner, T.C. Memo. 1995–280 (the fact that in the absence of § 453(g) a related purchaser would be entitled to claim depreciation on a stepped up basis is a factor in determining whether transfer was motivated by tax avoidance). In addition, § 453(i) requires immediate recognition of any gain subject to depreciation recapture under § 1245 or § 1250. Thus installment treatment frequently is not available for transfers of depreciable property. In addition, § 453 does not apply to transfers of inventory or property held for sale to customers. Installment sale treatment also is not available if the securities received by the transferor are publicly traded.

C. PREFERRED STOCK AS BOOT

Section 351(g), enacted in 1997, treats certain "nonqualified preferred stock" as other property, requiring recognition of gain under § 351(b) to the extent of the fair market value of the nonqualified preferred stock. A transferor who receives only nonqualified preferred stock recognizes either gain or loss because § 351 does not apply to the transferor. But a transferor who also receives some other stock, either common or preferred, in addition to nonqualified preferred stock is subject to the loss disallowance rule of § 351(b). Nonqualified preferred stock is preferred stock that has significant characteristics that cause it to resemble debt. Determining whether stock is "nonqualified preferred stock" is a two step process. First, the stock must be "preferred stock." For this purpose, preferred stock is stock that is limited and preferred as to dividends, and which does not participate in corporate growth. I.R.C. § 351(g)(3)(A). Thus, participating preferred stock, because its rights are not limited and it participates in corporate growth, cannot be nonqualified preferred stock. Second, the preferred stock is "nonqualified" only if the issuer or a related person, within a 20 year period of issue, (1) may be required by the holder to redeem the stock, (2) is required to redeem the stock, or (3) has a right to redeem the stock, and, in any of those three instances it is more likely than not that the right to redeem will be exercised. I.R.C. § 351(g)(2). Preferred stock also is nonqualified preferred stock if the dividend rate is determined in whole or in part by reference to interest rates, commodity prices, or similar indices.

D. THE RECEIPT OF STOCK OPTIONS AND OTHER CONTINGENT INTERESTS

Treas. Reg. § 1.351–1(a)(1)(ii) provides that stock rights or stock warrants are not "stock" for § 351 purposes. In Hamrick v. Commissioner, 43 T.C. 21 (1964)(Acq. in result only, 1966–2 C.B. 5), the taxpayer transferred property to a controlled corporation in exchange for stock plus a contingent right to additional stock dependent upon the performance of the corporation. The Tax Court held that the taxpayer's subsequent receipt of the contingent stock qualified for nonrecognition treatment under § 351. The Tax Court followed the decision in Carlberg v. United States, 281 F.2d 507 (8th Cir.1960), holding that transferable contingent rights to receive stock were stock for purposes of § 354 (nonrecognition treatment for an exchange of stock for stock in corporate reorganizations). In both cases the opinions conclude that the contingent rights received by the taxpayers could represent either stock or nothing at all. The Internal Revenue Service has indicated that it will follow the result of *Hamrick,* but only because the rights received by the taxpayer were nonassignable and nonmarketable, and could only give rise to the receipt of additional stock by one who was a party to the transfer. Rev.Rul. 66–112, 1966–1 C.B. 68, 70.

E. TRANSFERS OF DEPRECIABLE PROPERTY: DEPRECIATION RECAPTURE AND SECTION 1239

Sections 1245(b)(3) and 1250(d)(3) provide that there is no recapture of depreciation in § 351 transactions except to the extent of the gain required to be recognized by § 351(b).

If there is a significant differential between the individual capital gains rate and the corporate tax rate, a taxpayer owning an asset with a low basis but a high value, but with little or no recapture ordinary income potential, might attempt to step-up the basis for depreciation by selling the asset to another taxpayer under the taxpayer's control, the larger depreciation deductions offsetting the capital gain. When the sale is between a corporation and a more than 50 percent stockholder, § 1239 meets this problem by providing ordinary income treatment on the sale. Section 1239 applies to the gain recognized under § 351(b)(boot) and thus also to the gain required to be recognized under § 357(c) (liabilities in excess of basis). Rev.Rul. 60–302, 1960–2 C.B. 223; Alderman v. Commissioner, 55 T.C. 662 (1971). Section 1239 does not apply, however, to sales or boot taxed under § 351(b) if the shareholder involved in the transaction owns 50 percent or less of the corporation's stock.

F. RECEIPT OF STOCK DISPROPORTIONATE TO PROPERTY TRANSFERRED

The 1939 Code predecessor of § 351 required that for the section to be applicable the nonrecognition property received by each transferor had to be substantially in proportion to the transferor's interest in the transferred property prior to the exchange. The 1954 Code dropped the proportionate interest requirement as a factor in the nonrecognition of gain, but retained it as a factor indicating the possible existence of compensation or a gift. See the cross-references in § 351(h)(3) and (4). Treas. Reg. § 1.351–1(b)(1) states that "in appropriate cases" the stock will be treated as if first received in proportion to assets transferred, and then transferred to the ultimate recipients by way of gift or compensation if the facts so warrant. However, Rev.Rul. 76–454, 1976–2 C.B. 102, applied Treas. Reg. § 1.351–1(b)(1) to find a dividend in a situation in which a stockholder and his controlled corporation formed a new corporation with the stockholder receiving a disproportionately large amount of the stock of the newly formed corporation.

G. TRANSFERS TO CONTROLLED CORPORATIONS

1. *Dividend Distributions*

Since § 351 applies to transfers to an existing corporation, as well as to transfers to form a new corporation, a taxpayer might be tempted to combine a transfer of property with a distribution of cash. For example, a sole stockholder transfers a capital asset worth $10,000 to a corporation for $10,000 fair market value of stock plus $1,000 cash. The $1,000 cash could be classified as a dividend under § 301 rather than being considered as boot resulting in capital gain. While § 351(h) does not include a cross-reference to the dividend sections, it would seem that dividend treatment is appropriate in such a case. See Treas. Reg. §§ 1.351–2(d) and 1.301–1(1).

If property worth $10,000 is sold by a sole stockholder to an existing corporation for $10,000 cash, the transaction presumably is a sale. However, if the stockholder cannot establish a business purpose for the transfer, the stockholder might be regarded as making a contribution to capital of $10,000 and receiving a dividend of $10,000. But see Curry v. Commissioner, 43 T.C. 667 (1965) (NA), where the court summarily disposed of the Commissioner's contention that there was no "business purpose" for a sale of real estate to a controlled corporation: "It would seem that the mere desire to sell, even if the sole purpose was to realize capital gains, should be a sufficient business purpose (assuming always that the substance complies with the form). * * * Indeed, it is difficult to imagine what added business purpose respondent would require for a sale of property." (695)

2. *Contributions to Capital*

If a stockholder, without receiving shares of stock in return, contributes additional capital to the corporation in the form of assets that have appreciated or depreciated in value, presumably no gain or loss will be regarded as realized since nothing is received in return. Moreover, even if a constructive "exchange" were regarded as present because of the increase in value resulting to the existing shares, cf. Scanlon v. Commissioner, 42 B.T.A. 997, § 351 would usually be applicable to provide nonrecognition treatment. The transferor adds the basis of the contributed property to the basis for his stock; the corporation under § 362(a)(2) uses the transferor's basis. If property is transferred as a contribution to capital by persons other than stockholders, as in situations in which a community organization transfers property to a corporation to induce it to locate in the area, the corporation may exclude the contribution under § 118 and under § 362(c) the corporation's basis in the property is zero.

3. *Treatment of Corporation Transferring Appreciated Property as Boot*

Section 351(f) provides that in the case of a § 351 transaction gain is to be recognized under § 311(b) on a transfer by the corporation of appreciated property as a part of the exchange. Section 311(b) requires recognition of gain as if the property transferred by the corporation had been sold for its fair market value. Thus corporate level gain will be recognized on a transfer of appreciated property to a stockholder as boot in a § 351 exchange.

This provision is most likely to come into play when transfers are made to a preexisting corporation, but it could apply in a formation as well. Suppose A and B want to form a corporation that they will own equally to operate Blackacre, which is owned by A and has a fair market value of $1,000 and Whiteacre, which is owned by B and has a fair market value of $800. To incorporate with equal contributions, in addition to contributing Whiteacre, B also contributes marketable securities with a basis of $20 and a fair market value of $100, which the corporation distributes to A. (As a result of the contribution of the marketable securities by B and their distribution to A, each of A and B has contributed a net amount of $1,000.) In addition to A being required to account for $100 of boot under § 351(b), the corporation will recognize a gain of $80 under § 351(f).

SECTION 2. "SOLELY" FOR STOCK: ASSUMPTION OF LIABILITIES

INTERNAL REVENUE CODE: Sections 357; 358(d).

REGULATIONS: Sections 1.357–1,–2; 1.358–3.

Under § 357(a), the assumption of a liability, or receipt of property subject to a liability, is not treated as the receipt of money or other property. Section 357(a) is subject to two exceptions. Section 357(b), enacted in 1939 as part of the original provision, treats liabilities as boot if either (1) a tax avoidance purpose is present or (2) there is no bona fide business purpose for transferring the liabilities. Second, under § 357(c), enacted in 1954, if the amount of liabilities assumed exceeds the basis of the property transferred, gain results to the extent of such excess, regardless of the purpose of the debt or the assumption. For purposes of determining the transferor's basis in nonrecognition property received in the exchange, § 358(d) treats the assumption of a liability of the transferor or a transfer of property subject to a liability as the receipt of cash by the transferor, without regard to how the debt is treated under § 357. The result is a reduction in the transferor's basis to the extent of the liability.

Suppose that A owned an asset worth $100,000, which cost $10,000 and was subject to a mortgage of $50,000 to secure a bank loan of $50,000 obtained by A in a separate transaction. If A is permitted to transfer the asset to a controlled corporation subject to the liability without recognition of gain, A avoids tax on $40,000, the difference between A's original investment of $10,000 and the $50,000 cash received by A from the borrowing. The problem is resolved by § 357(c)(1). The gain is capital or ordinary according to the ratio of capital assets to ordinary assets transferred. Treas. Reg. § 1.357–2(b). In turn, the basis of the corporation is increased by the gain recognized.

Even if § 357(c) is not applicable, under § 357(b) the total amount of liabilities assumed or to which transferred property is subject is treated as money received unless the taxpayer can show that the principal purpose of the assumption or transfer subject to liabilities was not tax avoidance and that the purpose was a bona fide business purpose. Section 357(b)(2) adds that the taxpayer must meet the burden of proof by "the clear preponderance of the evidence." Under the express terms of the statute, if any liability is found to be transferred to the corporation for the forbidden tax avoidance purpose, or without a bona fide business purpose, all liabilities are treated as money. Treas. Reg. § 1.357–1(c). Treas. Reg. § 1.351–3(a)(6) and (b)(7) require both the transferor and the transferee corporation to describe on their income tax returns for the year of the transfer the business reason of each with respect to the corporation's assumption of liabilities.

Peracchi v. Commissioner

United States Court of Appeals, Ninth Circuit, 1998.
143 F.3d 487.

■ KOZINSKI, CIRCUIT JUDGE:

We must unscramble a Rubik's Cube of corporate tax law to determine the basis of a note contributed by a taxpayer to his wholly-owned corporation.

The Transaction

The taxpayer, Donald Peracchi, needed to contribute additional capital to his closely-held corporation (NAC) to comply with Nevada's minimum premium-to-asset ratio for insurance companies. Peracchi contributed two parcels of real estate. The parcels were encumbered with liabilities which together exceeded Peracchi's total basis in the properties by more than half a million dollars. As we discuss in detail below, under section 357(c), contributing property with liabilities in excess of basis can trigger immediate recognition of gain in the amount of the excess. In an effort to avoid this, Peracchi also executed a promissory note, promising to pay NAC $1,060,000 over a term of ten years at 11% interest. Peracchi maintains that the note has a basis equal to its face amount, thereby making his total basis in the property contributed greater than the total liabilities. If this is so, he will have extracted himself from the quicksand of section 357(c) and owe no immediate tax on the transfer of property to NAC. The IRS, though, maintains that (1) the note is not genuine indebtedness and should be treated as an unenforceable gift; and (2) even if the note is genuine, it does not increase Peracchi's basis in the property contributed.

The parties are not splitting hairs: Peracchi claims the basis of the note is $1,060,000, its face value, while the IRS argues that the note has a basis of zero. If Peracchi is right, he pays no immediate tax on the half a million dollars by which the debts on the land he contributed exceed his basis in the land; if the IRS is right, the note becomes irrelevant for tax purposes and Peracchi must recognize an immediate gain on the half million. The fact that the IRS and Peracchi are so far apart suggests they are looking at the transaction through different colored lenses. To figure out whether Peracchi's lens is rose-tinted or clear, it is useful to take a guided tour of sections 351 and 357 and the tax law principles undergirding them.

Into the Lobster Pot: Section 351[2]

The Code tries to make organizing a corporation pain-free from a tax point of view. A capital contribution is, in tax lingo, a "nonrecognition"

2. "Decisions to embrace the corporate form of organization should be carefully considered, since a corporation is like a lobster pot: easy to enter, difficult to live in, and

event: A shareholder can generally contribute capital without recognizing gain on the exchange. * * * See I.R.C. § 351. So long as the shareholders contributing the property remain in control of the corporation after the exchange, section 351 applies: It doesn't matter if the capital contribution occurs at the creation of the corporation or if—as here—the company is already up and running. * * *

Gain Deferral: Section 358(a)

* * * [W]hen a shareholder like Peracchi contributes property to a corporation in a nonrecognition transaction, * * * the shareholder must substitute the basis of that property for what would otherwise be the cost basis of the stock.[6] This preserves the gain for recognition at a later day: The gain is built into the shareholder's new basis in the stock, and he will recognize income when he disposes of the stock.

The fact that gain is deferred rather than extinguished doesn't diminish the importance of questions relating to basis and the timing of recognition. In tax, as in comedy, timing matters. Most taxpayers would much prefer to pay tax on contributed property years later-when they sell their stock-rather than when they contribute the property.[7] Thus what Peracchi is seeking here is gain deferral: He wants the gain to be recognized only when he disposes of some or all of his stock.

Continuity of Investment: Boot and section 351(b)

* * * [T]he central exception to nonrecognition for section 351 transactions comes into play when the taxpayer receives "boot"—money or property other than stock in the corporation—in exchange for the property contributed. See I.R.C. § 351(b). Boot is recognized as taxable income because it represents a partial cashing out. * * *

Peracchi did not receive boot in return for the property he contributed. But that doesn't end the inquiry: We must consider whether Peracchi has cashed out in some other way which would warrant treating part of the transaction as taxable boot.

Assumption of Liabilities: Section 357(a)

The property Peracchi contributed to NAC was encumbered by liabilities. Contribution of leveraged property makes things trickier from a tax perspective. When a shareholder contributes property encumbered by debt, the corporation usually assumes the debt. And the Code normally treats discharging a liability the same as receiving money: The taxpayer improves his economic position by the same amount either way. See I.R.C.

painful to get out of." Boris I. Bittker & James S. Eustice, Federal Income Taxation of Corporations and Shareholders ¶ 2.01[3] (6th ed.1997) (footnotes omitted) (hereinafter Bittker & Eustice).

6. See I.R.C. § 358(a) * * * .

7. Of course, should the taxpayers be lucky enough to die before disposing of the stock, their heirs would take a stepped-up basis in the stock equal to its fair market value as of the date of death. See I.R.C. § 1014.

§ 61(a)(12). NAC's assumption of the liabilities attached to Peracchi's property therefore could theoretically be viewed as the receipt of money, which would be taxable boot. See United States v. Hendler, 303 U.S. 564, 58 S.Ct. 655, 82 L.Ed. 1018 (1938).

The Code takes a different tack. Requiring shareholders like Peracchi to recognize gain any time a corporation assumes a liability in connection with a capital contribution would greatly diminish the nonrecognition benefit section 351 is meant to confer. Section 357(a) thus takes a lenient view of the assumption of liability: A shareholder engaging in a section 351 transaction does not have to treat the assumption of liability as boot, even if the corporation assumes his obligation to pay. * * *

This nonrecognition does not mean that the potential gain disappears. Once again, the basis provisions kick in to reflect the transfer of gain from the shareholder to the corporation: The shareholder's substitute basis in the stock received is decreased by the amount of the liability assumed by the corporation. See I.R.C. § 358(d), (a). The adjustment preserves the gain for recognition when the shareholder sells his stock in the company, since his taxable gain will be the difference between the (new lower) basis and the sale price of the stock.

Sasquatch and The Negative Basis Problem: Section 357(c)

Highly leveraged property presents a peculiar problem in the section 351 context. Suppose a shareholder organizes a corporation and contributes as its only asset a building with a basis of $50, a fair market value of $100, and mortgage debt of $90. Section 351 says that the shareholder does not recognize any gain on the transaction. Under section 358, the shareholder takes a substitute basis of $50 in the stock, then adjusts it downward under section 357 by $90 to reflect the assumption of liability. This leaves him with a basis of minus $40. A negative basis properly preserves the gain built into the property: If the shareholder turns around and sells the stock the next day for $10 (the difference between the fair market value and the debt), he would face $50 in gain, the same amount as if he sold the property without first encasing it in a corporate shell.[8]

But skeptics say that negative basis, like Bigfoot, doesn't exist. Compare Easson v. Commissioner, 33 T.C. 963, 970 (1960) (there's no such thing as a negative basis) with Easson v. Commissioner, 294 F.2d 653, 657–58 (9th Cir.1961) (yes, Virginia, there is a negative basis). Basis normally operates as a cost recovery system: Depreciation deductions reduce basis, and when basis hits zero, the property cannot be depreciated farther. At a more basic level, it seems incongruous to attribute a negative value to a figure that normally represents one's investment in an asset. Some commentators nevertheless argue that when basis operates merely to measure potential gain (as it does here), allowing negative basis may be perfectly appropriate and consistent with the tax policy underlying nonrecognition

8. If the taxpayer sells the property outright, his amount realized includes the full amount of the mortgage debt* * * and the result is as follows: Amount realized ($10 cash + $90 debt) − $50 Basis = $50 gain.

transactions. See, e.g., J. Clifton Fleming, Jr., The Highly Avoidable Section 357(c): A Case Study in Traps for the Unwary and Some Positive Thoughts About Negative Basis, 16 J. Corp. L. 1, 27–30 (1990). Whatever the merits of this debate, it seems that section 357(c) was enacted to eliminate the possibility of negative basis. * * *

Section 357(c) prevents negative basis by forcing a shareholder to recognize gain to the extent liabilities exceed basis. Thus, if a shareholder contributes a building with a basis of $50 and liabilities of $90, he does not receive stock with a basis of minus $40. Instead, he takes a basis of zero and must recognize a $40 gain.

Peracchi sought to contribute two parcels of real property to NAC in a section 351 transaction. Standing alone the contribution would have run afoul of section 357(c): The property he wanted to contribute had liabilities in excess of basis, and Peracchi would have had to recognize gain to the extent of the excess, or $566,807:[10]

	Liabilities	Basis
Property #1	1,386,655	349,774
Property #2	161,558	631,632
	1,548,213	981,406
Liabilities	1,548,213	
Basis	981,406	
Excess (357(c))	566,907	

The Grift: Boosting Basis with a Promissory Note

Peracchi tried to dig himself out of this tax hole by contributing a personal note with a face amount of $1,060,000 along with the real property. Peracchi maintains that the note has a basis in his hands equal to its face value. If he's right, we must add the basis of the note to the basis of the real property. Taken together, the aggregate basis in the property contributed would exceed the aggregate liabilities:

	Liabilities	Basis
Property #1	1,386,655	349,774
Property #2	161,558	631,632
Note	0	1,060,000
	1,548,213	2.041,406

Under Peracchi's theory, then, the aggregate liabilities no longer exceed the aggregate basis, and section 357(c) no longer triggers any gain. The government argues, however, that the note has a zero basis. If so, the note would not affect the tax consequences of the transaction, and Peracchi's $566,807 in gain would be taxable immediately.[11]

10. Peracchi remained personally liable on the debts encumbering the property transferred to NAC. NAC took the property subject to the debts, however, which is enough to trigger gain under the plain language of section 357(c). See Owen v. Commissioner, 881 F.2d 832, 835–36 (9th Cir.1989).

11. The government does not dispute that the note and the two parcels of real estate were contributed as part of the same transaction for purposes of section 351. Their

Are Promises Truly Free?

Which brings us (phew!) to the issue before us: Does Peracchi's note have a basis in Peracchi's hands for purposes of section 357(c)?[12] The language of the Code gives us little to work with. The logical place to start is with the definition of basis. Section 1012 provides that "[t]he basis of property shall be the cost of such property. . . ." But "cost" is nowhere defined. What does it cost Peracchi to write the note and contribute it to his corporation? The IRS argues tersely that the "taxpayers in the instant case incurred no cost in issuing their own note to NAC, so their basis in the note was zero." Brief for Appellee at 41. See Alderman v. Commissioner, 55 T.C. 662, 665 (1971); Rev. Rul. 68–629, 1968–2 C.B. 154, 155.[13] Building on this premise, the IRS makes Peracchi out to be a grifter: He holds an unenforceable promise to pay himself money, since the corporation will not collect on it unless he says so.

It's true that all Peracchi did was make out a promise to pay on a piece of paper, mark it in the corporate minutes and enter it on the corporate books. It is also true that nothing will cause the corporation to enforce the note against Peracchi so long as Peracchi remains in control. But the IRS ignores the possibility that NAC may go bankrupt, an event that would suddenly make the note highly significant. Peracchi and NAC are separated by the corporate form, and this gossamer curtain makes a difference in the shell game of C Corp organization and reorganization. Contributing the note puts a million dollar nut within the corporate shell, exposing Peracchi to the cruel nutcracker of corporate creditors in the event NAC goes bankrupt. And it does so to the tune of $1,060,000, the full face amount of the note. Without the note, no matter how deeply the corporation went into debt, creditors could not reach Peracchi's personal assets. With the note on the books, however, creditors can reach into Peracchi's pocket by enforcing the note as an unliquidated asset of the corporation.

The key to solving this puzzle, then, is to ask whether bankruptcy is significant enough a contingency to confer substantial economic effect on this transaction. If the risk of bankruptcy is important enough to be recognized, Peracchi should get basis in the note: He will have increased his exposure to the risks of the business—and thus his economic invest-

bases must therefore be aggregated for purposes of section 357(c).

12. Peracchi owned all the voting stock of NAC both before and after the exchange, so the control requirement of section 351 is satisfied. * * * Peracchi did not receive any stock in return for the property contributed, so it could be argued that the exchange was not "solely in exchange for stock" as required by section 351. Courts have consistently recognized, however, that issuing stock in this situation would be a meaningless gesture: Because Peracchi is the sole shareholder of NAC, issuing additional stock would not affect his economic position relative to other shareholders. See, e.g., Jackson v. Commissioner, 708 F.2d 1402, 1405 (9th Cir.1983).

13. We would face a different case had the Treasury promulgated a regulation interpreting section 357(c). A revenue ruling is entitled to some deference as the stated litigating position of the agency which enforces the tax code, but not nearly as much as a regulation. Ruling 68–629 offers no rationale, let alone a reasonable one, for its holding that it costs a taxpayer nothing to write a promissory note, and thus deserves little weight.

ment in NAC—by $1,060,000. If bankruptcy is so remote that there is no realistic possibility it will ever occur, we can ignore the potential economic effect of the note as speculative and treat it as merely an unenforceable promise to contribute capital in the future.

When the question is posed this way, the answer is clear. Peracchi's obligation on the note was not conditioned on NAC's remaining solvent. It represents a new and substantial increase in Peracchi's investment in the corporation.[14] The Code seems to recognize that economic exposure of the shareholder is the ultimate measuring rod of a shareholder's investment. * * * Peracchi therefore is entitled to a step-up in basis to the extent he will be subjected to economic loss if the underlying investment turns unprofitable. * * *

The economics of the transaction also support Peracchi's view of the matter. The transaction here does not differ substantively from others that would certainly give Peracchi a boost in basis. For example, Peracchi could have borrowed $1 million from a bank and contributed the cash to NAC along with the properties. Because cash has a basis equal to face value, Peracchi would not have faced any section 357(c) gain. NAC could then have purchased the note from the bank for $1 million which, assuming the bank's original assessment of Peracchi's creditworthiness was accurate, would be the fair market value of the note. In the end the corporation would hold a million dollar note from Peracchi—just like it does now—and Peracchi would face no section 357(c) gain.[15] The only economic difference between the transaction just described and the transaction Peracchi actually engaged in is the additional costs that would accompany getting a loan from the bank. Peracchi incurs a "cost" of $1 million when he promises to pay the note to the bank; the cost is not diminished here by the fact that the transferor controls the initial transferee. The experts seem to agree: "Section 357(c) can be avoided by a transfer of enough cash to eliminate any excess of liabilities over basis; and since a note given by a solvent obligor in purchasing property is routinely treated as the equivalent of cash in determining the basis of the property, it seems reasonable to give it the same treatment in determining the basis of the property transferred in a § 351 exchange." Bittker & Eustice ¶ 3.06[4][b].

We are aware of the mischief that can result when taxpayers are permitted to calculate basis in excess of their true economic investment. * * * [W]e do not believe our holding will have such pernicious effects. First, and most significantly, by increasing the taxpayer's personal expo-

14. We confine our holding to a case such as this where the note is contributed to an operating business which is subject to a non-trivial risk of bankruptcy or receivership. NAC is not, for example, a shell corporation or a passive investment company; Peracchi got into this mess in the first place because NAC was in financial trouble and needed more assets to meet Nevada's minimum premium-to-asset ratio for insurance companies.

15. * * * We readily acknowledge that our assumptions fall apart if the shareholder isn't creditworthy. Here, the government has stipulated that Peracchi's net worth far exceeds the value of the note, so creditworthiness is not at issue. But we limit our holding to cases where the note is in fact worth approximately its face value.

sure, the contribution of a valid, unconditional promissory note has substantial economic effects which reflect his true economic investment in the enterprise. * * * Peracchi will have to pay the full amount of the note with after-tax dollars if NAC's economic situation heads south. Second, [i]t is the pass-through of losses that makes artificial increases in equity interests of particular concern. * * * We don't have to tread quite so lightly in the C Corp context, since a C Corp doesn't funnel losses to the shareholder.[16] * * *

We find further support for Peracchi's view by looking at the alternative: What would happen if the note had a zero basis? The IRS points out that the basis of the note in the hands of the corporation is the same as it was in the hands of the taxpayer. Accordingly, if the note has a zero basis for Peracchi, so too for NAC. See I.R.C. § 362(a).[17] But what happens if NAC—perhaps facing the threat of an involuntary petition for bankruptcy—turns around and sells Peracchi's note to a third party for its fair market value? According to the IRS's theory, NAC would take a carryover basis of zero in the note and would have to recognize $1,060,000 in phantom gain on the subsequent exchange, even though the note did not appreciate in value one bit. That can't be the right result.

Accordingly, we hold that Peracchi has a basis of $1,060,000 in the note he wrote to NAC. The aggregate basis exceeds the liabilities of the properties transferred to NAC under section 351, and Peracchi need not recognize any section 357(c) gain.

Genuine Indebtedness or Sham?

The Tax Court never reached the issue of Peracchi's basis in the note. Instead, it ruled for the Commissioner on the ground that the note is not genuine indebtedness. The court emphasized two facts which it believed supported the view that the note is a sham: (1) NAC's decision whether to collect on the note is wholly controlled by Peracchi and (2) Peracchi missed the first two years of payments, yet NAC did not accelerate the debt. These facts certainly do suggest that Peracchi paid imperfect attention to his obligations under the note, as frequently happens when debtor and creditor are under common control. But we believe the proper way to approach the

16. Our holding therefore does not extend to the partnership or S Corp context.

17. But see Lessinger v. Commissioner, 872 F.2d 519 (2d Cir.1989). In *Lessinger*, the Second Circuit analyzed a similar transaction. It agreed with the IRS's (faulty) premise that the note had a zero basis in the taxpayer's hands. But then, brushing aside the language of section 362(a), the court concluded that the note had a basis in the corporation's hands equal to its face value. The court held that this was enough to dispel any section 357(c) gain to the taxpayer, proving that two wrongs sometimes do add up to a right.

We agree with the IRS that *Lessinger's* approach is untenable. Section 357(c) contemplates measuring basis of the property contributed in the hands of the taxpayer, not the corporation. Section 357 appears in the midst of the Code sections dealing with the effect of capital contributions on the shareholder; sections 361 et seq., on the other hand, deal with the effect on a corporation, and section 362 defines the basis of property contributed in the hands of the corporation. Because we hold that the note has a face value basis to the shareholder for purposes of section 357(c), however, we reach the same result as *Lessinger*.

genuine indebtedness question is to look at the face of the note and consider whether Peracchi's legal obligation is illusory. And it is not. First, the note's bona fides are adequate: The IRS has stipulated that Peracchi is creditworthy and likely to have the funds to pay the note; the note bears a market rate of interest commensurate with his creditworthiness; the note has a fixed term. Second, the IRS does not argue that the value of the note is anything other than its face value; nothing in the record suggests NAC couldn't borrow against the note to raise cash. Lastly, the note is fully transferable and enforceable by third parties, such as hostile creditors. On the basis of these facts we hold that the note is an ordinary, negotiable, recourse obligation which must be treated as genuine debt for tax purposes. * * *

The IRS argues that the note is nevertheless a sham because it was executed simply to avoid tax. Tax avoidance is a valid concern in this context; section 357(a) does provide the opportunity for a bailout transaction of sorts. For example, a taxpayer with an unencumbered building he wants to sell could take out a nonrecourse mortgage, pocket the proceeds, and contribute the property to a newly organized corporation. Although the gain would be preserved for later recognition, the taxpayer would have partially cashed out his economic investment in the property: By taking out a nonrecourse mortgage, the economic risk of loss would be transferred to the lender. Section 357(b) addresses this sort of bailout by requiring the recognition of gain if the transaction lacks a business purpose.

Peracchi's capital contribution is not a bailout. Peracchi contributed the buildings to NAC because the company needed additional capital, and the contribution of the note was part of that transaction. The IRS, in fact, stipulated that the contribution had a business purpose. Bailout potential exists regardless of whether the taxpayer contributes a note along with the property; section 357(b), not 357(c), is the sword the Service must use to attack bailout transactions.

* * *

The Aftermath

We take a final look at the result to make sure we have not placed our stamp of approval on some sort of exotic tax shelter. We hold that Peracchi is entitled to a step up in basis for the face value of the note, just as if he contributed cash to the corporation. See I.R.C. § 358. If Peracchi does in fact keep his promise and pay off the note with after tax dollars, the tax result is perfectly appropriate: NAC receives cash, and the increase in basis Peracchi took for the original contribution is justified. Peracchi has less potential gain, but he paid for it in real dollars.

But what if, as the IRS fears, NAC never does enforce the note? If NAC goes bankrupt, the note will be an asset of the estate enforceable for the benefit of creditors, and Peracchi will eventually be forced to pay in after tax dollars. Peracchi will undoubtedly have worked the deferral mechanism of section 351 to his advantage, but this is not inappropriate where the taxpayer is on the hook in both form and substance for enough cash to offset the excess of liabilities over basis. By increasing his personal exposure to the creditors of NAC, Peracchi has increased his economic investment in the corporation, and a corresponding increase in basis is wholly justified.[20]

Conclusion

We hold that Peracchi has a basis of $1,060,000 in the note, its face value. As such, the aggregate liabilities of the property contributed to NAC do not exceed its basis, and Peracchi does not recognize any § 357(c) gain. The decision of the Tax Court is REVERSED. The case is remanded for entry of judgment in favor of Peracchi.

■ FERNANDEZ, CIRCUIT JUDGE, Dissenting:

Is there something that a taxpayer, who has borrowed hundreds of thousands of dollars more than his basis in his property, can do to avoid taxation when he transfers the property? Yes, says Peracchi, because by using a very clever argument he can avoid the strictures of 26 U.S.C. § 357(c). He need only make a promise to pay by giving a "good," though unsecured, promissory note to his corporation when he transfers the property to it. That is true even though the property remains subject to the encumbrances. How can that be? Well, by preparing a promissory note the taxpayer simply creates basis without cost to himself. But see 26 U.S.C. § 1012; Rev. Rul. 68–629, 1968–2 C.B. 154; Alderman v. Commissioner, 55 T.C. 662, 665 (1971). Thus he can extract a large part of the value of the property, pocket the funds, use them, divest himself of the property, and pay the tax another day, if ever at all.

But as with all magical solutions, the taxpayer must know the proper incantations and make the correct movements. He cannot just transfer the property to the corporation and promise, or be obligated, to pay off the encumbrances. That would not change the fact that the property was still subject to those encumbrances. According to Peracchi, the thaumaturgy that will save him from taxes proceeds in two simple steps. He must first prepare a ritualistic writing—an unsecured promissory note in an amount equal to or more than the excess of the encumbrances over the basis. He must then give that writing to his corporation. That is all.[1] But is not that just a "promise to pay," which "does not represent the paying out or reduction of assets?" Don E. Williams Co. v. Commissioner, 429 U.S. 569,

20. What happens if NAC does not go bankrupt, but merely writes off the note instead? Peracchi would then face discharge of indebtedness income to the tune of $1,060,000. This would put Peracchi in a worse position than when he started, since discharge of indebtedness is normally treated as ordinary income. Peracchi, having increased his basis in the stock of the corporation by $1,060,000 would receive a capital loss (or less capital gain) to that extent. But the shift in character of the income will normally work to the disadvantage of a taxpayer in Peracchi's situation.

1. What is even better, he need not even make payments on the note until after the IRS catches up with him. I, by the way, am dubious about the proposition that the Tax Court clearly erred when it held that the note was not even a genuine indebtedness.

583 * * * (1977). Never mind, he says. He has nonetheless increased the total basis of the property transferred and avoided the tax. I understand the temptation to embrace that argument, but I see no real support for it in the law.

Peracchi says a lot about economic realities. I see nothing real about that maneuver. I see, rather, a bit of sortilege that would have made Merlin envious. The taxpayer has created something—basis—out of nothing.

Thus, I respectfully dissent.

Revenue Ruling 95–74

1995–2 C.B. 36.

ISSUES

(1) Are the liabilities assumed by S in the § 351 exchange described below liabilities for purposes of §§ 357(c)(1) and 358(d)?

(2) Once assumed by S. how will the liabilities in the § 351 exchange described below be treated?

FACTS

Corporation P is an accrual basis, calendar-year corporation engaged in various ongoing businesses, one of which includes the operation of a manufacturing plant (the Manufacturing Business). The plant is located on land purchased by P many years before. The land was not contaminated by any hazardous waste when P purchased it. However, as a result of plant operations, certain environmental liabilities, such as potential soil and groundwater remediation, are now associated with the land.

In Year 1, for bona fide business purposes, P engages in an exchange to which § 351 of the Internal Revenue Code applies by transferring substantially all of the assets associated with the Manufacturing Business, including the manufacturing plant and the land on which the plant is located, to a newly formed corporation S, in exchange for all of the stock of S and for S's assumption of the liabilities associated with the Manufacturing Business, including the environmental liabilities associated with the land. P has no plan or intention to dispose of (or have S issue) any S stock. S is an accrual basis, calendar-year taxpayer.

P did not undertake any environmental remediation efforts in connection with the land transferred to S before the transfer and did not deduct or capitalize any amount with respect to the contingent environmental liabilities associated with the transferred land.

In Year 3, S undertakes soil and groundwater remediation efforts relating to the land transferred in the § 351 exchange and incurs costs (within the meaning of the economic performance rules of § 461(h)) as a result of those remediation efforts. Of the total amount of costs incurred, a portion would have constituted ordinary and necessary business expenses that are deductible under § 162 and the remaining portion would have constituted capital expenditures under § 263 if there had not been a § 351 exchange and the costs for remediation efforts had been incurred by P. See Rev. Rul. 94–38, 1994–1 C.B. 35 (discussing the treatment of certain environmental remediation costs).

LAW AND ANALYSIS

Issue 1: Section 351(a) provides that no gain or loss shall be recognized if property is transferred to a corporation solely in exchange for stock and immediately after the exchange the transferor is in control of the corporation.

Section 357(a) provides a general rule that a transferee corporation's assumption of a transferor's liability in a § 351 exchange will not be treated as money or other property received by the transferor. Section 357(b) provides an exception to the general rule of § 357(a) when it appears that the principal purpose of the transferor in having the liability assumed was avoidance of Federal income tax on the exchange or, if not such purpose, was not a bona fide business purpose.

Section 357(c)(1) provides a second exception to the general rule of § 357(a). Section 357(c)(1) provides that if the sum of the liabilities the transferee corporation assumes and takes property subject to exceeds the total of the adjusted basis of the property the transferor transfers to the corporation pursuant to the exchange, then the excess shall be considered as gain from the sale or exchange of the property.

For purposes of applying the exception in § 357(c)(1), § 357(c)(3)(A) provides that a liability the payment of which would give rise to a deduction (or would be described in § 736(a)) is excluded. This special rule does not apply, however, to any liability to the extent that the incurrence of the liability resulted in the creation of, or an increase in, the basis of any property. Section 357(c)(3)(B).

Section 358(a)(1) provides that in a § 351 exchange the basis of the property permitted to be received under § 351 without the recognition of gain or loss shall be the same as that of the property exchanged, decreased by (i) the fair market value of any other property (except money) received by the transferor, (ii) the amount of any money received by the transferor, and (iii) the amount of loss to the transferor which was recognized on such exchange, and increased by (i) the amount which was treated as a dividend and (ii) the amount of gain to the transferor which was recognized on such exchange (not including any portion of such gain which was treated as a dividend).

Section 358(d)(1) provides that where, as part of the consideration to the transferor, another party to the exchange assumed a liability of the transferor, such assumption (in the amount of the liability) shall, for purposes of § 358, be treated as money received by the transferor on the exchange. Section 358(d)(2) provides that § 358(d)(1) does not apply to any liability excluded under § 357(c)(3).

* * *

A number of cases concerning cash basis taxpayers were litigated in the 1970s with respect to the definition of "liabilities" for purposes of § 357(c)(1), with sometimes conflicting analyses and results. * * * In response to this litigation, Congress enacted § 357(c)(3) to address the concern that the inclusion in the § 357(c)(1) determination of certain deductible liabilities resulted in "unforeseen and unintended tax difficulties for certain cash basis taxpayers who incorporate a going business." S.Rep. No. 1263, 95th Cong., 2d Sess. 184–85 (1978), 1978–3 C.B. 482–83.

Congress concluded that including in the § 357(c)(1) determination liabilities that have not yet been taken into account by the transferor results in an overstatement of liabilities of, and potential inappropriate gain recognition to, the transferor because the transferor has not received the corresponding deduction or other corresponding tax benefit. Id. To prevent this result, Congress enacted § 357(c)(3)(A) to exclude certain deductible liabilities from the scope of § 357(c), as long as the liabilities had not resulted in the creation of, or an increase in, the basis of any property (as provided in § 357(c)(3)(B)). * * *

While § 357(c)(3) explicitly addresses liabilities that give rise to deductible items, the same principle applies to liabilities that give rise to capital expenditures as well. Including in the § 357(c)(1) determination those liabilities that have not yet given rise to capital expenditures (and thus have not yet created or increased basis) with respect to the property of the transferor prior to the transfer also would result in an overstatement of liabilities. Thus, such liabilities also appropriately are excluded in determining liabilities for purposes of § 357(c)(1). Cf. * * * Rev. Rul. 88–77, 1988–2 C.B. 129 (accrued but unpaid expenses and accounts payable are not liabilities of a cash basis partnership for purposes of computing the adjusted basis of a partner's interest for purposes of § 752).

In this case, the contingent environmental liabilities assumed by S had not yet been taken into account by P prior to the transfer (and therefore had neither given rise to deductions for P nor resulted in the creation of, or increase in, basis in any property of P). As a result, the contingent environmental liabilities are not included in determining whether the amount of the liabilities assumed by S exceeds the adjusted basis of the property transferred by P pursuant to § 357(c)(1).

Due to the parallel constructions and interrelated function and mechanics of §§ 357 and 358, liabilities that are not included in the determination under § 357(c)(1) also are not included in the § 358 determination of the transferor's basis in the stock received in the § 351 exchange. * * * Therefore, the contingent environmental liabilities assumed by S are not treated as money received by P under § 358 for purposes of determining P's basis in the stock of S received in the exchange.

Issue 2: In Holdcroft Transp. Co. v. Commissioner, 153 F.2d 323 (8th Cir.1946), the Court of Appeals for the Eighth Circuit held that, after a transfer pursuant to the predecessor to § 351, the payments by a transferee corporation were not deductible even though the transferor partnership would have been entitled to deductions for the payments had the partnership actually made the payments. The court stated generally that the expense of settling claims or liabilities of a predecessor entity did not arise as an operating expense or loss of the business of the transferee but was a part of the cost of acquiring the predecessor's property, and the fact that the claims were contingent and unliquidated at the time of the acquisition was not of controlling consequence.

In Rev. Rul. 80–198, 1980–2 C.B. 113, an individual transferred all of the assets and liabilities of a sole proprietorship, which included accounts payable and accounts receivable, to a new corporation in exchange for all of its stock. The revenue ruling holds, subject to certain limitations, that the transfer qualifies as an exchange within the meaning of § 351(a) and that the transferee corporation will report in its income the accounts receivable as collected and will be allowed deductions under § 162 for the payments it makes to satisfy the accounts payable. In reaching these holdings, the revenue ruling makes reference to the specific congressional intent of § 351(a) to facilitate the incorporation of an ongoing business by making the incorporation tax free. The ruling states that this intent would be equally frustrated if either the transferor were taxed on the transfer of the accounts receivable or the transferee were not allowed a deduction for payment of the accounts payable. * * *

The present case is analogous to the situation in Rev. Rul. 80–198. For business reasons, P transferred in a § 351 exchange substantially all of the assets and liabilities associated with the Manufacturing Business to S, in exchange for all of its stock, and P intends to remain in control of S. The costs S incurs to remediate the land would have been deductible in part and capitalized in part had P continued the Manufacturing Business and incurred those costs to remediate the land. The congressional intent to facilitate necessary business readjustments would be frustrated by not according to S the ability to deduct or capitalize the expenses of the ongoing business.

Therefore, on these facts, the Internal Revenue Service will not follow the decision in Holdcroft Transp. Co. v. Commissioner, 153 F.2d 323 (8th Cir.1946). Accordingly, the contingent environmental liabilities assumed from P are deductible as business expenses under § 162 or are capitalized under § 263, as appropriate, by S under S's method of accounting (determined as if S has owned the land for the period and in the same manner as it was owned by P).

HOLDINGS

(1) The liabilities assumed by S in the § 351 exchange described above are not liabilities for purposes of § 357(c)(1) and § 358(d) because the liabilities had not yet been taken into account by P prior to the transfer (and therefore had neither given rise to deductions for P nor resulted in the creation of, or increase in, basis in any property of P).

(2) The liabilities assumed by S in the § 351 exchange described above are deductible by S as business expenses under § 162 or are capital expenditures under § 263, as appropriate, under S's method of accounting

(determined as if S has owned the land for the period and in the same manner as it was owned by P).

ILLUSTRATIVE MATERIAL

A. EFFECT OF TRANSFEROR'S CONTINUED LIABILITY

Rosen v. Commissioner, 62 T.C. 11 (1974), aff'd by order, 515 F.2d 507 (3d Cir.1975), held that § 357(c) applies even in situations in which the transferor remains personally liable on the obligation assumed by the transferee corporation. The Tax Court held that there is no requirement in § 357(c) that the transferor be relieved of liability. In Owen v. Commissioner, 881 F.2d 832 (9th Cir.1989), cited in footnote 10 of the *Peracchi* opinion, the Ninth Circuit followed the Tax Court's approach in *Rosen*. In *Owen*, the taxpayers incorporated a partnership by transferring partnership assets subject to liabilities in excess of basis. The liabilities had been personally guaranteed by the transferors who remained liable for the full amount of the debt. The court held that the transferors' continuing personal liability for the loans secured by the transferred property is irrelevant. Section 357(c) applies as long as the property received by the corporation is subject to the debt.

B. CONTRIBUTION OF SHAREHOLDER'S PROMISSORY NOTE: DETERMINATION OF TRANSFEROR'S BASIS

The effect on the determination of gain under § 357(c) of the transferor of encumbered property giving the corporation his own promissory note was not an issue of first impression in *Peracchi*. Several courts have confronted the issue, and each has analyzed it differently. The Tax Court first faced the issue in Alderman v. Commissioner, 55 T.C. 662 (1971), where, as in *Peracchi*, the taxpayers transferred assets to their corporation, which assumed liabilities in excess of the transferors' basis for the assets. In order to increase the assets of the corporation and avoid gain under § 357(c), the taxpayers executed a note payable to the corporation in an amount slightly in excess of the amount by which the assumed liabilities exceeded the basis of the transferred assets. The Tax Court held that the basis of the note was zero, since the taxpayers incurred no cost in making it. Gain therefore resulted under § 357(c). Presumably, payment of the note in *Alderman* would provide additional basis for the stock in the stockholders' hands as additional capital is actually contributed to the corporation. The corporation would not be required to recognize gain on this capital contribution. In Rev.Rul. 68–629, 1968–2 C.B. 154, the IRS followed the result in *Alderman*.

In Lessinger v. Commissioner, 872 F.2d 519 (2d Cir.1989), however, the Court of Appeals for the Second Circuit refused to follow *Alderman*. Lessinger transferred the assets of a sole proprietorship to his wholly owned corporation in a transaction to which § 351 applied. The proprietorship was insolvent in that its liabilities exceeded the value of transferred assets. Liabilities also exceeded Lessinger's basis in the transferred assets.

The transferee corporation created a "loan receivable" due from Lessinger on the corporate books in the amount that the liabilities of the proprietorship exceeded the value of the transferred assets. Reversing the Tax Court (85 T.C. 824 (1985)), the Court of Appeals held that Lessinger was not required by § 357(c) to recognize gain, but followed a different path of reasoning than the Ninth Circuit Court of Appeals did in *Peracchi*. The Second Circuit agreed with the *Alderman* holding that a taxpayer has no basis in the taxpayer's own promise to pay, but also concluded that the basis of Lessinger's obligation in the hands of the corporate transferee was equal to the face amount of the obligation. The court reasoned that the transferee corporation "incurred a cost in the transaction involving the transfer of the obligation by taking on the liabilities of the proprietorship that exceeded its assets." The court also pointed out that unless the corporation had a basis in Lessinger's obligation, it would have to recognize gain on payment of the debt. The court then held that "where the transferor undertakes genuine personal liability to the transferee, 'adjusted basis' in § 357(c) refers to the transferee's basis in the obligation which is its face amount." (526) Finally, the court also noted that Lessinger did not avoid recognition of real gain on the transaction because of his liability to the corporation.

The Second Circuit's reasoning in *Lessinger* is questionable. First, in total disregard of § 362(a), the court concluded that the corporation took a basis in the transferor's promissory note equal to its face amount. Second, since the payments on the note should be treated as capital contributions, the corporation will not recognize any gain as it receives payments. Third, the court's reasoning that gain under § 357(c) is computed with reference to the transferee's basis in the transferred property rather than the transferor's basis is contrary to the otherwise universally accepted rule that gain is computed with reference to the transferor's basis.

Neither the Tax Court's decision in *Alderman* nor the Ninth Circuit's decision in *Peracchi* is clearly correct or clearly erroneous. *Alderman* follows the statutory pattern of Subchapter C quite literally, without resort to general principles of taxation. *Peracchi*, on the other hand, superimposes on Subchapter C the general principle that payment with a promissory note is treated the same as payment in cash. From this perspective it should not matter whether a taxpayer, on the one hand, transfers property and cash to a corporation in exchange for stock or, on the other hand, transfers property and a promissory note in exchange for stock. If the exchange were a taxable transaction, the tax consequences to both the shareholder and corporation would be identical in each case. Why the results should differ between the cases in a § 351 transaction is not readily apparent.

C. THE CORPORATION'S BASIS

When a single asset is transferred in a situation to which § 357(c) applies, determination of the corporation's basis is not difficult. But where multiple assets are transferred—a common situation because the contribution of improved real estate involves two separate assets, the building and the land under it—determining the basis of each asset to the corporation under § 362(a) is very difficult. If § 357(b) applies to treat liabilities as boot, the recognition of gain is no different than in the case of cash or other property. Thus the basis increase for the corporation with respect to each asset equals the gain recognized to the transferor with respect to that asset. Allocation of gain recognized by the transferor under § 357(c), however, presents different issues.

The principle of Rev.Rul. 68–55, page 81, upon which the allocation of § 351(b) gain among assets for purposes of the basis adjustment in § 362(a)(1) is based, does not help because, unlike § 351(b) gain, § 357(c) gain is not computed asset-by-asset. Gain under § 357(c) results only when aggregate liabilities assumed by the corporation exceed the aggregate basis of all transferred assets. If a liability is secured by a particular asset, however, gain recognized by the transferor under § 357(c) with respect to the liability reasonably might be allocated solely to the encumbered asset. But in many cases this simplified allocation method will be unavailing. For example, assume that A transfers two assets to X, a controlled corporation. One asset is real property with a fair market value of $75 and a basis of $15, and the second asset is equipment with a value of $25 and a basis of $30. X assumes unsecured liabilities of $50, which requires that A recognize $5 of gain under § 357(c). Here the recognized gain occurs because in the aggregate the basis of transferred assets is less than liabilities. Unlike the case in which boot is received, the recognized gain is not attributable to specific assets. Nonetheless, an allocation of A's $5 gain to the real property rather than an apportionment between the two assets has some appeal because the allocation will not cause an increase in the difference between the fair market value and adjusted basis of any asset. This same logic would indicate that if a single transferor transfers two or more appreciated assets and recognizes gain under § 357(c), the basis adjustment should be made by apportioning the gain among the assets relative to amount by which the fair market value of each asset exceed its basis. The regulations are silent regarding these question, but see Treas. Reg. § 1.357–2(b) (suggesting that the basis increase be allocated in proportion to the fair market values of the assets), however, and the Internal Revenue Service has never issued a revenue ruling on point.

D. ACCOUNTS PAYABLE

As described in Rev. Rul. 95–74, prior to the Revenue Act of 1978 special problems were present when accounts receivable and accounts payable were transferred by a cash method taxpayer in a § 351 transaction. Since the accounts receivable would not have been included in income at the time of the transfer, their tax basis in the hands of the transferor is zero. On the other hand, the accounts payable, by definition not yet paid or deducted by a cash method taxpayer, would, under the literal language of § 357(c), constitute "liabilities" assumed by the corporation in the incorporation transaction. As a result, a cash method taxpayer could realize income in a § 351 transaction if the accounts payable were transferred to a corporation in connection with accounts receivable or other assets with a low tax basis. Raich v. Commissioner, 46 T.C. 604 (1966). The courts struggled with different approaches to avoid this result, see, e.g., Focht v. Commissioner, 68 T.C. 223 (1977)(the Tax Court abandoned its position in *Raich* and held that cash method payables are not liabilities under § 357(c) to the extent the payables would be deductible when paid), until the Revenue Act of 1978 added § 357(c)(3), providing that liabilities which would give rise to a deduction on payment are not considered for purposes of § 357(c)(1), and § 358(d)(2), which provides that such liabilities are not treated as cash received for purposes of determining the transferor's basis in stock or securities received.

Accounts payable that are treated as not being liabilities by § 357(c)(3) typically include cash method trade accounts payable and other cash method liabilities, such as interest and taxes, which relate to the transferred trade or business. Whether a transferor is a cash method taxpayer is determined separately for each item. For example, a taxpayer using a hybrid method of accounting, which utilizes inventories and the accrual method in computing income from purchases and sales and which utilizes the cash method in computing all other items of income and expenses, is considered a cash method taxpayer for purposes of applying § 357(c) to accounts payable for items computed on the cash method of accounting, but not with respect to liabilities relating to inventory. See Staff of the Joint Committee on Taxation, General Explanation of the Revenue Act of 1978, 218–20 (Comm.Print 1978).

Not all of the potential problems with payables are resolved by § 357(c)(3). In Orr v. Commissioner, 78 T.C. 1059 (1982), which arose before the effective date of § 357(c)(3), the taxpayer transferred to a newly formed corporation customers' cash deposits for travel received in the course of taxpayer's business as a travel agent. The deposits were refundable and had not been taken into income by the taxpayer. The taxpayer's liability to refund deposits exceeded the amount of cash, and hence the basis of property, transferred to the new corporation. The Tax Court held that the taxpayer recognized gain under § 357(c)(1) to the extent the liabilities exceeded the taxpayer's basis in transferred property. The Tax Court refused to allow nonrecognition under its decision in *Focht* because refunds of the deposits would not have been deductible by the taxpayer. Presumably the same result would be reached under § 357(c)(3).

E. ASSUMPTION OF TRANSFEROR'S DEBT TO TRANSFEREE CORPORATION

In Kniffen v. Commissioner, 39 T.C. 553 (1962)(Acq.), the taxpayer transferred assets and liabilities of a sole proprietorship to a pre-existing corporation. Among the liabilities assumed by the corporation was a debt from the taxpayer to the corporation. The assumption eliminated the taxpayer's debt by operation of law. The Commissioner asserted that the taxpayer realized cancellation of indebtedness income as boot under § 351(b) and that there was no assumption of debt to bring § 357 into play. The court held for the taxpayer; the debt was assumed and then discharged so that § 357(c) applied. Under the current statutory pattern, however, it appears that § 108(e)(4) would require the recognition of discharge of indebtedness income (unless otherwise not recognized under § 108) if the transferor "controls" the transferee corporation (control for his purpose being defined in § 267(b), which provides a more than 50 percent of value test for control).

F. SECTION 357(b) SITUATIONS

1. *Liabilities Incurred Shortly Before Transfer*

The scope of § 357(b) is not entirely clear. An assumption of liabilities incurred initially to acquire business assets transferred to the transferee should satisfy the bona fide business purpose requirement. See Jewell v. United States, 330 F.2d 761 (9th Cir.1964)(not applying the predecessor of § 357(b) to the transfer of assets to a corporation that assumed notes due from the taxpayer to a trust). Suppose, however, that a liability, such as a loan from a bank, is incurred just before a transfer of property to a controlled corporation so that the stockholder obtains cash, the corporation assumes the debt, and then pays the bank. The whole transaction really is equivalent to a payment of cash for the property by the corporation to the stockholder, and the assumption of the liability in such a case would appear to fall under § 357(b). For example, in Drybrough v. Commissioner, 376 F.2d 350 (6th Cir.1967), the taxpayer in 1957 transferred real estate to four corporations, each assuming a portion of the mortgage debt on the property that had been incurred in 1953. Another property was transferred to a fifth corporation subject to a mortgage that had been placed on the property in 1957, just three months prior to the transfer. The proceeds of the 1957 mortgage had been invested in tax-exempt bonds. About one-half of the 1953 mortgage proceeds had been used to pay off an earlier indebtedness and most of the balance was also invested in tax-exempt bonds. The court held that the assumption of the 1953 indebtedness was not governed by § 357(b); the use to which the proceeds of the mortgage were put was not relevant in determining whether there was a tax avoidance purpose on the exchange. There was a valid business purpose for placing the real estate subject to the mortgage in the corporation. On the other hand, the assumption of the 1957 indebtedness was governed by § 357(b); the creation of the debt was directly in anticipation of having the corporation assume the indebtedness and constituted a plan to avoid recognition of gain. See also Bryan v. Commissioner, 281 F.2d 238 (4th Cir.1960)(finding a tax avoidance purpose and lack of business purpose on transfer of real estate to a controlled corporation subject to liabilities incurred just prior to the transfer; the court, however, treated as boot only the amount of the liabilities in excess of basis, although the case arose prior to the enactment of § 357(c)); Thompson v. Campbell, 64–2 U.S.T.C. ¶ 9659 (N.D.Tex.1964), aff'd per curiam, 353 F.2d 787 (5th Cir.1965)(transfer to a controlled corporation of assets subject to liabilities incurred the day before incorporation resulted in boot under § 357(b)).

In some cases a borrowing immediately before the transfer has been found not to run afoul of the business purpose requirement. In Easson v. Commissioner, 33 T.C. 963 (1960), rev'd on other grounds, 294 F.2d 653 (9th Cir.1961), the Tax Court construed the predecessor of § 357(b) not to apply on the facts of the case to a mortgage placed on the assets shortly before incorporation because the taxpayer had a valid business purpose for the corporate assumption of the mortgage (i.e., insulation of personal assets from potential liabilities and facilitation of management of the real estate and estate planning), and the corporation was an active business entity. In Rev.Rul. 79–258, 1979–2 C.B. 143, the Internal Revenue Service concluded that in a type (D) reorganization (discussed at page 664), a nonrecognition transaction that is also subject to § 357, there was no tax avoidance motive where the transferor refinanced a portion of an existing long-term debt on the eve of assumption of the debt by the transferee corporation. The refinanced indebtedness was attributable to business assets received by the transferee.

2. *Personal Nonbusiness–related Liabilities*

Section 357(b) also has been applied to treat assumed debt as money in cases involving the assumption of personal nonbusiness liabilities of the transferor. In Estate of Stoll v. Commissioner, 38 T.C. 223 (1962), the taxpayer transferred all the assets of a newspaper business to a corporation, which assumed a $1,015,000 liability of the taxpayer. To the extent of $600,000, the liability represented a refinancing that took place just prior to the incorporation and was secured by property transferred to the corporation. The $415,000 balance of the liability was secured by life insurance policies on the taxpayer's life that were not transferred to the corporation. The Tax Court held that the predecessor of § 357(b) applied to treat the $415,000 of indebtedness as boot because there was no business purpose for the assumption of the liability by the corporation and the liability was not related to the business transfer. However, the predecessor of § 357(b) did not apply to treat the $600,000 liability as boot. (Note that § 357(b)(1) now requires that the total liability be treated as boot if there is a tax avoidance purpose or if there is no bona fide business purpose for the assumption of any liability). In Campbell v. Wheeler, 342 F.2d 837 (5th Cir.1965), the taxpayer transferred a partnership interest to a corporation subject to liabilities that had been incurred just prior to the transfer in order to pay the personal income tax liability of the taxpayer. The court held that the transaction was governed by § 357(b) and the amount of the liabilities assumed constituted boot.

In Simpson v. Commissioner, 43 T.C. 900 (1965) (A), the taxpayer transferred the assets of two department stores, cash, and stock exchange traded securities to a corporation in a § 351 transaction. The corporation also assumed liabilities in an amount that was slightly less than the aggregate basis of the assets transferred. Most of the liabilities were liens against the publicly traded stock, and the purpose of transferring the stock to the corporation was to reduce the taxpayer's personal income taxes. The Commissioner asserted that § 357(b) applied, but the court held that the arrangement of the assumption of liabilities in an amount slightly less than basis in order to avoid § 357(c) was not a tax avoidance purpose.

SECTION 3. THE "CONTROL" REQUIREMENT

INTERNAL REVENUE CODE: Sections 351(a); 368(c).

REGULATIONS: Section 1.351–1(a).

American Bantam Car Co. v. Commissioner*

Tax Court of the United States, 1948.
11 T.C. 397.

[A group of individuals, called the "associates," purchased the assets of a bankrupt automobile company in 1935. The "associates" then organized the taxpayer corporation in 1936 to take over the assets. The associates were to transfer the assets (subject to certain liabilities) to the corporation in return for 300,000 shares of no par common stock. Ninety thousand shares of the preferred stock of the corporation (each share having three votes) were to be sold to the public through underwriters at $10 a share. The underwriters were to receive as compensation, in addition to discounts and commissions, certain amounts of the common stock issued to the associates based on a schedule determined by the progress of the sale of the preferred stock. The transfer of the assets to the corporation was made on June 3, 1936, in return for the common stock. On June 8, 1936, the associates and the underwriters agreed on the details of the compensation schedule. On August 16, 1936, the associates placed their 300,000 common stock shares in escrow until the public offering of the preferred stock was completed. In October 1937, the associates, pursuant to the agreement, transferred to the underwriters 87,900 common stock shares and the underwriters sold 1,008 of these shares to the public. As a consequence of the underwriters' stock sales, the associates held 212,100 shares of the common stock (less than 80%), the underwriters held 86,892 shares, and the public 1,008 shares. The public also held 83,618 shares of preferred stock. The issue before the court was the corporation's basis for depreciation of the acquired assets in the years 1942 and 1943. The taxpayer claimed depreciation should be based on cost to the taxpayer in 1936, i.e., the market value of the assets in 1936; the Commissioner claimed depreciation should be based on the basis of the assets in the hands of the associates prior to the transfer to the taxpayer, which basis was lower than the 1936 fair market value. The determination of the basis turned on the question whether the original transfer qualified under section 351. If all the elements of the transaction were taken together under a step transaction approach, then the associates were not in control and the corporation received a stepped-up basis for the assets; if the 1936 and 1937 transactions were treated as separate, then the associates were in control "immediately

* Ed.: The decision was affirmed per curiam, 177 F.2d 513 (3d Cir.1949).

after" the initial stock transaction and section 351 would apply to carry over the old basis of the assets to the corporation.]

During all of 1936 the associates retained ownership over the 300,000 shares of common stock and during that interval the underwriters sold only 14,757 shares of preferred stock which did not entitle them to any common stock under the agreement of June 8, 1936. The corporation's by-laws provided that each share of preferred stock should have three votes while each share of common stock should have one vote. Therefore, at the end of 1936, out of 344,271 possible stock votes, the total combined voting power of all outstanding stock, the associates owned 300,000 or over 80 per cent. It was not until October 1937 when the [underwriters] received 87,900 shares of the associates' common stock in fulfillment of the underwriting agreement that the associates lost "control" of petitioner within the statutory definition of the word. Retention of "control" for such a duration of time satisfies the governing provision of [section 351]. * * *

In determining whether a series of steps are to be treated as a single indivisible transaction or should retain their separate entity, the courts use a variety of tests. Paul, Selected Studies in Federal Taxation, 2d series, pages 200–254. Among the factors considered are the intent of the parties, the time element, and the pragmatic test of the ultimate result. An important test is that of mutual interdependence. Were the steps so interdependent that the legal relations created by one transaction would have been fruitless without a completion of the series?

Using these tests as a basis for their decisions the courts in Hazeltine Corp. v. Commissioner, 89 F.2d 513, and Bassick v. Commissioner, 85 F.2d 8, treated the series of steps involved in each case as parts of a unified transaction and therefore determined that the transferors of assets to the new corporation did not acquire the requisite control. An analysis of the fact situations involved shows salient distinguishing features from the present facts. In each of the above cases there was a written contract prior both to the organization of the new corporation and the exchange of assets for stock which bound the transferors unconditionally to assign part of the stock acquired to third parties after the exchange. Thus at the moment of the exchange the recipient of the stock did not own it, but held it subject to a binding contractual obligation to transfer a portion. The court in each case thought that the incorporation and exchange would never have been agreed upon without the supplemental agreement turning over stock to a third party. In such situations it is logical for the courts to say that the exchange and the subsequent transfer are part of one and the same transaction so that the transferor never actually owned the shares he later assigned.

A close examination of the facts surrounding the exchange in the present case makes it clear that the exchange of assets for stock and the subsequent transfer of a portion of that stock to [the underwriters] therein involved should not be considered part of the same transaction so as to deprive the associates of "control" immediately after the exchange. The facts are distinguishable from those existing in the *Hazeltine* and *Bassick* cases on three grounds. First, there was no written contract prior to the exchange binding the associates to transfer stock to the underwriters. At the most there was an informal oral understanding of a general plan contemplating the organization of a new corporation, the exchange of assets for stock, and marketing of preferred stock of the new corporation to the public. A written contract providing for the transfer of shares from the associates to the underwriters did not come until five days after the exchange. Secondly, when the transfer of shares to the underwriters was embodied specifically in a formal contract, the underwriters received no absolute right to ownership of the common stock, but only when, as and if, certain percentages of preferred stock were sold. How clearly contingent was the nature of their rights is illustrated by the fact only one underwriter, Grant, met the terms of the agreement and became entitled to any shares. Thirdly, the necessity of placing the 300,000 shares in escrow with a bank is indicative of complete ownership of such stock by the associates following the exchange.

The standard required by the courts to enable them to say that a series of steps are interdependent and thus should be viewed as a single transaction do not exist here. It is true all the steps may have been contemplated under the same general plan of May 1936; yet the contemplated arrangement for the sale of preferred stock to the public was entirely secondary and supplemental to the principal goal of the plan—to organize the new corporation and exchange its stock for the Austin assets. * * *

Thus we conclude that in the present case the exchange of assets for stock between the associates and petitioner on June 3, 1936, was a separate completed transaction distinct from the subsequent transfer of common stock to [the underwriters] so that the associates were in control of petitioner immediately after the exchange within the provisions of [section 351]. * * *

D'Angelo Associates, Inc. v. Commissioner

Tax Court of the United States, 1978.
70 T.C. 121.

■ WILBUR, J. * * *

This controversy has its origin in events occurring during June 1960. Petitioner was organized on June 21, 1960. Shortly thereafter, initial capital in the amount of $15,000 in cash was transferred to petitioner by Dr. D'Angelo, and petitioner issued 60 shares of common stock, 10 shares to Mrs. D'Angelo and 10 shares each in the names of the five D'Angelo children. On June 30, 1960, Dr. and Mrs. D'Angelo, in a transaction formally designated a sale, transferred various property to petitioner, including the building and equipment whose basis is now at issue. In exchange for this property, the D'Angelos received $15,000 in cash; the assumption by petitioner of a liability of the D'Angelos, secured by a mortgage on property transferred to petitioner; and a 6 percent interest bearing demand note payable to Dr. D'Angelo in the amount of $96,727.85.

Thereafter, in claiming depreciation, petitioner treated the transfer as a sale.

We must determine the proper basis for depreciation of the rental property (building and equipment) transferred to petitioner. This issue depends on whether or not section 351 applies to the transfer of this property to the petitioner. Section 351 applies when property is conveyed to a corporation solely in exchange for stock or securities,* and immediately after the exchange, the transferors control the corporation. If section 351 is applicable, petitioner must depreciate the transferred assets using the transferors' basis. See section 362(a)(1). If section 351 is inapplicable, and the transfer of assets to petitioner was, as petitioner contends, a sale, depreciation would be based on the purchase price of those assets, a figure concededly greater than the transferors' adjusted basis. Petitioner would accordingly realize larger depreciation deductions. * * *

Respondent contends that the transfer of the rental property to petitioner was pursuant to a nontaxable exchange under section 351(a). He argues that the transfer of cash for stock and the exchange of the rental property for cash and notes were contemporaneous events that were in substance integral parts of a single transaction. * * *

Petitioner, on the other hand, contends that section 351 is inapplicable to the transfer for several reasons. Petitioner asserts that the transfer of the rental property was a transaction separate from the contributions of cash and should be characterized as a taxable sale. Petitioner argues that Dr. and Mrs. D'Angelo never owned more than 10 of the 60 shares outstanding in petitioner (the 50 shares constituting "control" being issued to non-transferors prior to the sale) * * *

For the following reasons, we agree with respondent.

a. *Sale or Exchange:* It is well established that the economic substance of a transaction must govern for tax purposes rather than the time sequence or form in which the transaction is cast. Gregory v. Helvering, 293 U.S. 465 (1935). Where a series of closely related steps are taken pursuant to a plan to achieve an intended result, the transaction must be viewed as an integrated whole for tax purposes. See Redwing Carriers, Inc. v. Tomlinson, 399 F.2d 652, 658 (5th Cir.1968); Atlee v. Commissioner, 67 T.C. 395 (1976).

Petitioner has failed to convince us that a sale took place. The events significant to the creation of petitioner occurred almost simultaneously. The formation of petitioner, the transfer of $15,000 cash to petitioner for the issuance of 60 shares of stock, and the transfer of the rental property to petitioner for the return of the $15,000 in cash and the notes all occurred within an interval of less than 10 days. See section 1.351–1(a)(1), Income Tax Regs. The evidence demonstrates that these steps were integral parts

* [Ed.: Before October 2, 1989, debt securities could be received without recognition of gain in a § 351 transaction.]

of a plan designed by Dr. D'Angelo to transfer the assets used primarily in his dental practice from individual to corporate ownership.

Any reason for petitioner's existence would have vanished absent the transfer of the rental property in accordance with the overall plan. * * * We believe this record demonstrates a continuing interest by Dr. D'Angelo in the transferred rental property consistent with the policy underlying the nonrecognition provisions of section 351 and unlike that contemplated by a sale. See Portland Oil Co. v. Commissioner, 109 F.2d 479, 488 (1st Cir. 1940), cert. denied 310 U.S. 650 (1940) * * *.

Sequential protocol is of marginal relevance in determining whether contemporaneous events should be viewed as a single integrated transaction or as independent transactions. Rather, the boundaries are defined by including events contemplated for the success of the business plans from which they emanate. Commissioner v. Court Holding Co., 324 U.S. 331 (1945); United States v. Cumberland Public Service Co., 338 U.S. 451 (1950). In this light it is clear that the success of the corporate undertaking motivated both the transfer of cash for stock and the transfer of the rental property for the corporate obligation. As we noted in Nye v. Commissioner, 50 T.C. 203, 212 (1968):

> [T]hey gave no reason why the transaction was divided into two parts, the transfer of cash for stock and the purported sale of the business assets for the note. Such evidence might have confirmed that the form in which the transaction was cast was consistent with its true nature. * * * Lack of such evidence is worthy of note because it fails to negate the inference to be drawn from other facts indicating that the two parts of the transaction were inseparably related. * * * In the absence of evidence of a business reason for dividing the transaction, we conclude that a separate sale has not been shown. [Citations omitted]

b. *Control:* We view the events before us as equivalent to the formation and capitalization of the corporation, followed by a gift to the D'Angelo children of the controlling interest when Dr. and Mrs. D'Angelo caused petitioner to directly issue the 50 shares to the children. At the end of the series of transactions on June 30, 1960, all of the assets remaining in the corporation were contributed by Dr. and Mrs. D'Angelo, including the $15,000 in cash.[6] This cash was in the possession of Dr. and Mrs. D'Angelo

6. In all likelihood, the $15,000 in cash remained in the corporation, and was evidenced by the $15,000 demand note payable to Dr. D'Angelo issued by petitioner on June 30, 1960, the same day the $96,727.85 note was issued. Under this assumption the consideration received from petitioner corresponds with the stated "sales" price; if the cash was distributed as well as the $15,000 note, there is an unexplained $15,000 discrepancy. Accordingly, we find that no adjustment in the adjusted basis of the rental property is needed on account of the $15,000 cash. Additionally, since the $15,000 note is a security for the same reasons we find the $96,-727.85 note a security (see infra), no adjustment in basis would be required.

If in fact, the $15,000 was returned to the D'Angelos along with the $15,000 demand note, the same result would be required, since the consideration for the transfer of the rental property would be the $15,000 note (along with the stock and oth-

both before and after the transfers with the petitioner merely issuing stock directly to Mrs. D'Angelo and in the names of the children. The D'Angelo children did not purchase the stock issued in their names, but were simply the beneficiaries of a gift from their parents.[7]

The loss of control of petitioner resulting from the gift of stock does not preclude the application of section 351(a), which requires that the transferors be in control of the transferee corporation "immediately after the exchange." This requirement is satisfied where, as here, the transferors transfer by gift the stock they were entitled to receive in exchange for the property they transferred to the corporation, regardless of whether such disposition was planned before or after acquiring control. See Wilgard Realty Co. v. Commissioner, 127 F.2d 514, 516 (2d Cir.1942), affg. 43 B.T.A. 557 (1941), cert. denied 317 U.S. 655 (1942); Stanton v. United States, 512 F.2d 13, 17 (3d Cir.1975) * * *. The issuance of the stock by petitioner to the D'Angelo children is the direct consequence of "the absolute right" of Dr. and Mrs. D'Angelo to designate who would receive all of the stock. Stanton v. United States, supra, at 17; Wilgard Realty Co. v. Commissioner, supra, at 516. Since it is possession of this power which is essential under section 351 for control, it follows that the transferors herein, Dr. and Mrs. D'Angelo were in control of petitioner immediately after the exchange. See American Bantam Car Co. v. Commissioner, 11 T.C. 397 (1948), affd. per curiam 177 F.2d 513 (3d Cir.1949), cert. denied 339 U.S. 920 (1950).

Petitioner nevertheless argues that since the stock was issued directly to Mrs. D'Angelo and the children, Dr. D'Angelo never held any stock in the corporation. We recognize that the *Wilgard* decision was predicated on the transferor's freedom of action *after* he acquired the stock, and that Fahs v. Florida Machine & Foundry Co., 168 F.2d 957 (5th Cir.1948) may be read to support petitioner's viewpoint. * * * Additionally, in Mojonnier & Sons, Inc. v. Commissioner, 12 T.C. 837 (1949), in distinguishing *Wilgard,* this Court stated:

> In the instant proceeding, however, the stock, exclusive of the 1,490 shares issued to Mojonnier and his wife, was not issued to the transferors and then conveyed by them to members of their

er notes), rather than the contemporaneous return of the same $15,000 contributed a few days earlier.

We also note that petitioner does not contend that the assumption of liability for the mortgage by petitioner should be treated as money received by the transferors by reason of sec. 357(b).

7. As noted earlier, the stock was issued to Dr. D'Angelo as trustee for the children pursuant to the New York State Uniform Gift to Minors Act. Respondent does not argue that the transferors retained control because the trust was illusory or because of the powers Dr. D'Angelo exercised as trustee. In view of respondent's position, we assume for purposes of this case that the trustee acted independently and solely on behalf of the best interests of the beneficiaries, although there is considerable evidence to the contrary. We therefore do not base our decision to any extent on the circumstance that Dr. D'Angelo as trustee acted on behalf of the children; the result would be precisely the same if the children had reached majority when the stock was issued and received title to the stock in their own names.

> family, but was issued directly to the members of the family in accordance with the plan and offer of F.E. Mojonnier. Thus, the transferors were never the owners or holders of a sufficient amount of stock to place them in "control" of the corporation within the meaning of [the predecessor of section 351]. * * *

Nevertheless, the decisions in both *Wilgard* and *Stanton* were clearly predicated on the power of the transferor to designate who will receive the stock rather than the precise moment that the power was exercised. These cases do not turn on whether the tune Dr. D'Angelo called was written in two/four time, but on his power to call the tune. And it is on this score that both Florida Machine & Foundry Co. and Mojonnier & Sons, Inc., are distinguishable from *Wilgard, Stanton,* and the facts before us.[8] Cf. Culligan Water Conditioning of Tri–Cities, Inc., v. United States, 567 F.2d 867 (9th Cir.1978); Intermountain Lumber Co. v. Commissioner, 65 T.C. 1025 (1976).

* * *

We conclude * * * that section 351(a) therefore applies to the transfers of rental property as contended by the respondent.

ILLUSTRATIVE MATERIAL

A. CONTROL IMMEDIATELY AFTER THE TRANSFER

In Mojonnier & Sons, Inc. v. Commissioner, 12 T.C. 837 (1949) (NA), discussed in *D'Angelo,* a father had agreed that if his sons and a foreman worked in his business they would receive some stock when he incorporated his business a few years later. On that later incorporation, shares of stock were issued directly to the sons and foreman, so that the father received less than 80 percent of the stock. The court held, with the taxpayer, that § 351 did not apply in view of the absence of control. It rejected the Commissioner's argument that the father should be regarded as receiving all of the stock and then making gifts to the others, the court stating that the transfers of stock were not gifts but rewards for past services and,

8. If immediately prior to forming the corporation, five-sixths of the rental properties was given to the children and transferred to the corporation in return for the controlling interest (along with their parents' remaining one-sixth interest) petitioner's basis would be the basis of Dr. and Mrs. D'Angelo. Similarly, if the transfers were made directly to the corporation by Dr. and Mrs. D'Angelo in return for stock and the stock then given to the children, petitioner does not seriously contend section 351 would be inapplicable. That this transaction has been squeezed into the seemingly non-existent time interval between these two situations surely cannot produce a different result. Cf. sec. 1.351–1(b)(1), Income Tax Regs., and S.Rept. No. 1622, to accompany H.R. 8300 (Pub.L. No. 591), 83d Cong., 2d Sess. 264, 265 (1954), which, although not addressing the control problem directly, at least suggest the result we reach. Additionally, the prior precedents, by making the power to designate the distributee of the stock dispositive, avoid potential abuses inherent in options that would otherwise be available to taxpayers. Bittker & Eustice, Federal Income Taxation of Corporations and Shareholders, par. 3.01, p. 3–4 (3d ed. 1971). Culligan Water Conditioning of Tri–Cities, Inc. v. United States, 567 F.2d 867 (9th Cir. 1978).

moreover, had been made directly to the others in accordance with the prior agreement. In May Broadcasting Co. v. United States, 200 F.2d 852 (8th Cir.1953), a transfer of a radio station to a newly formed corporation for its stock and then a sale of one-fourth of the stock to a third party, who also contributed cash to the corporation, was held not to be a § 351 exchange since the sale was pursuant to a contract existing at the time of incorporation, although the requirement of Federal Communications Commission approval delayed the sale until nine months after the first transaction.

Commissioner v. National Bellas Hess, Inc., 220 F.2d 415 (8th Cir. 1955), is similar to the *American Bantam* case, in that an unexercised option held by the employees of the transferee corporation to purchase some stock from the transferors did not prevent control from residing in the transferors; nor did a sale of stock to the public within three months. In Federal Grain Corp. v. Commissioner, 18 B.T.A. 242 (1929), an agreement that the transferors would place the stock of the corporation in a voting trust for five years was said not to defeat the "control" of the transferors, since the definition of "control" relates to ownership of stock rather than actual control through the exercise of voting rights.

Intermountain Lumber Co. v. Commissioner, 65 T.C. 1025 (1976), held that the requisite control immediately after the exchange was not present where, as part of the incorporation transaction, the transferor was obligated under an agreement of sale to sell almost half of the shares of the corporation to a third party. The court formulated the control requirement of § 351 as follows: "A determination of 'ownership,' as that term is used in section 368(c) and for purposes of control under section 351, depends upon the obligations and freedom of action of the transferee with respect to the stock when he acquired it from the corporation. * * * If the [stockholder], as part of the transaction by which the shares were acquired, has irrevocably foregone or relinquished at that time the legal right to determine whether to keep the shares, ownership in such shares is lacking for purposes of section 351. By contrast, if there are no restrictions upon freedom of action at the time he acquires the shares, it is immaterial how soon thereafter the [stockholder] elects to dispose of his stock or whether such disposition is in accord with a preconceived plan not amounting to a binding obligation." (1031)

Since the stockholder was under an obligation to sell the shares, § 351 was not applicable and the corporate transferee obtained a stepped-up basis in the property involved in the transaction. The third party in *Intermountain* did not transfer property to the corporation in the transaction.

Under the standard of *Intermountain,* did the taxpayer in *D'Angelo* retain control immediately after the corporation's issuance of stock to his children?

B. WHO ARE THE TRANSFERORS?

1. *General*

Section 351 applies when one or more persons who transfer property to the corporation are in control immediately after the transfer. The control requirement thus requires identification of the group of transferors who are to be counted.

In some cases taxpayers have attempted to count existing stockholders as members of the control group in order to classify an exchange of appreciated property for stock by non-controlling persons as a nonrecognition transaction under § 351. For example, in Estate of Kamborian v. Commissioner, 469 F.2d 219 (1st Cir.1972), the taxpayers holding 76 percent of the stock of a corporation transferred appreciated property to the corporation in exchange for additional stock. A trust that held 13 percent of the stock of the transferee corporation purchased a small number of shares for cash in an attempt to qualify the transfer under § 351. The taxpayers claimed that the trust was a transferor so that together the combined holdings of transferors exceeded 80 percent. The court held that it is "permissible to consider transfers by other owners only if those transfers were, in economic terms, sufficiently related to * * * make all of the transfers parts of a single transaction." The court added that, "The trustees' desire to help the [other] stockholders avoid taxes, warrantably found by the Tax Court to have been the primary motive for the trust's purchase cannot be used to make a single transaction out of otherwise unrelated transfers."

In Rev.Rul. 79–70, 1979–1 C.B. 144, X Corporation transferred property to newly organized Y Corporation and, pursuant to a prearranged binding contract, sold 40 percent of the Y stock to Z Corporation. Simultaneously, Z purchased securities for cash from Y. The Ruling held that Z Corporation was not a transferor of property because it received only securities from Y. Z's ownership of the Y stock acquired by purchase from X Corporation could not be counted in determining whether the control requirement of § 351 was satisfied. Since Z therefore received only securities for cash and was not a stockholder prior to the exchange, it was not a member of the control group for § 351 purposes. X was the only transferor of property, it received only 60 percent of the stock, and the transaction therefore did not qualify under § 351.

On the other hand, Rev.Rul. 79–194, 1979–1 C.B. 145, held that a prearranged sale between two transferors of property for stock does not affect the control requirement. Z Corporation transferred property to Newco for 80 percent of Newco stock. A group of investors transferred property for 20 percent of Newco stock. Following the transfers to Newco, Z sold stock to the investors. At the end of the transaction, Z owned 49 percent of the Newco stock. The Ruling held that since Z and the investors were transferors, the persons transferring property to Newco in exchange for Newco stock owned 100 percent of Newco stock immediately after the exchange. However, where the investor group transferred property in exchange for only 1 percent of the Newco stock, with Z receiving 99 percent, the investors' stock ownership was not sufficient to qualify them as transferors of property and thus the control requirement was not satisfied because of the subsequent sale of stock by Z to the investors.

Rev.Rul. 84–44, 1984–1 C.B. 105, provides that § 351 is not applicable to the transferor of property to a corporate subsidiary in exchange for stock of the transferee subsidiary's parent corporation, which is in turn controlled by the transferor. However, the same result can be accomplished by restructuring the transaction as a transfer to the controlled parent corporation first, followed by a transfer by the parent corporation in exchange for stock of its controlled subsidiary. Rev.Rul. 83–34, 1983–1 C.B. 79, holds that although these transfers may be undertaken pursuant to an integrated plan, each transfer is treated as a separate transaction that satisfies § 351. See also Rev.Rul. 83–156, 1983–2 C.B. 66, holding that § 351 applies to a transfer of assets to a wholly owned subsidiary that then transfers the assets to a partnership. Compare Rev.Rul. 70–140, 1970–1 C.B. 73 (no § 351 treatment for the transfer of assets of a sole proprietorship to a controlled corporation followed immediately by an exchange of the stock of the controlled corporation for the stock of another corporation; because of the integrated nature of the two transactions, the original transferor was not in control.)

Although nonrecognition of gain or loss under § 351 is based in principle on the transferors' continued investment in the transferred property, and requires a continued proprietary interest in the transferee corporation through the receipt of stock representing control, there is no express requirement that the transferors maintain a continued interest in the transferred assets.

2. *Underwriting Situations*

In the *American Bantam Car. Co.* case the Commissioner might have accepted the taxpayer's unitary view of the transaction, but have replied that viewing the transaction unitarily, the public stockholders and the underwriter were "transferors of property" to be counted in the control group so that § 368(c) and § 351 nevertheless were satisfied, especially since the shares they held were being counted in determining the total against which the requisite 80 percent was to be computed. In Rev.Rul. 78–294, 1978–2 C.B. 141, the Service first held that purchasers of stock sold by a corporation through an underwriter could be considered part of the control group for purposes of § 351. In 1996, Rev.Rul. 78–294 was superseded by regulations. Treas. Reg. § 1.351–1(a)(3) provides that if a person acquires stock from an underwriter in exchange for cash in a "qualified underwriting transaction," for purposes of § 351 the person who purchases the stock from the underwriter is treated as transferring the cash directly to the corporation in exchange for the stock and the underwriter's role in the transaction is disregarded. A "qualified underwriting transaction" is an underwriting in which a corporation issues stock for cash in which either the underwriter is an agent of the corporation or the underwriter's ownership of stock is transitory.

C. CONTROL WHEN THERE ARE MULTIPLE CLASSES OF STOCK

The existence of multiple classes of voting stock requires a determination regarding the relative voting power of each class in order to determine whether the transferors of property are in control. There is little available guidance regarding the meaning of "total combined voting power of all classes of stock entitled to vote." In Rev.Rul. 63–234, 1963–2 C.B. 148, the Internal Revenue Service ruled under § 368(c)(in a type (D) reorganization) that preferred stock which entitled its holders to elect two of twelve directors was voting stock in that "it conferred upon the holders of such stock the right to significant participation in the management of the affairs of the corporation." The Service relied on its earlier ruling in I.T. 3896, 1948–1 C.B. 72 (declared obsolete in Rev.Rul. 68–100, 1968–1 C.B. 572), which considered voting control for purposes of membership in an affiliated group, holding that the voting power of preferred stock was in proportion to the number of directors elected by the preferred stockholders. Thus preferred stock with the right to elect two of twelve directors possessed 2/12, or 16.7 percent of voting control. See also Rev.Rul. 69–126, 1969–1 C.B. 218, applying the same analysis for purposes of defining voting control under § 1504. Under this standard, a stockholder who receives common stock for services might receive more than 20 percent of the common stock by value without defeating § 351 nonrecognition treatment for transferors of property if the common stock transferred to the service stockholder represents a separate class of stock with limited voting rights.

The Internal Revenue Service also has ruled in Rev.Rul. 59–259, 1959–2 C.B. 115, that "control" under § 368(c) requires that in addition to 80 percent of the combined voting power of all classes of voting stock, the transferor stockholders must also own 80 percent of the number of shares of *each* class of nonvoting stock. Ownership of 80 percent of the total number of shares outstanding is not sufficient.

Nonqualified preferred stock, as defined in § 351(g), is treated as property other than stock for purposes of determining whether the transferor of property received in exchange for such stock recognizes gain or loss in a § 351 transaction. See page 86. Nevertheless, except to the extent otherwise provided by regulations, nonqualified preferred stock is treated as stock for purposes of determining whether the control requirement has been met and the transaction as a whole qualifies under § 351(a). See S.Rep. No. 174, 105th Cong, 2d Sess. 206 (1998).

D. CONTINUITY OF INTEREST

There is no express requirement that the transferor in a § 351 exchange maintain a continued interest in the transferred property. See Rev.Rul. 83–34, 1983–1 C.B. 79 (§ 351 transfer to a controlled subsidiary followed by a transfer of the property to another subsidiary pursuant to an integrated plan); Rev.Rul. 83–156, 1983–2 C.B. 66 (§ 351 transfer to a controlled subsidiary followed by a transfer of the property to a partnership).

In Rev.Rul. 84–71, 1984–1 C.B. 106, P, a public corporation, wanted to acquire the stock of T Corporation. A, who held 14 percent of T's stock, was willing to participate only in a nonrecognition transaction. The remainder of T's stockholders would accept cash. P and A formed new S Corporation.

P transferred sufficient cash to purchase 86 percent of the T stock and A transferred his T stock in a transaction qualified under § 351. S transferred the cash to a new subsidiary, again under § 351. The new subsidiary used the cash to acquire T stock from the remaining T stockholders. The transaction could not have qualified for tax-free reorganization treatment to A because of a lack of continuity of interest, see page 526. The Ruling, however, states that application of § 351 to transfers that are part of the larger transaction will not be precluded by the fact that the larger acquisitive reorganization is taxable due to the absence of the continuity of interest in transferred assets that is required in corporate reorganizations.

SECTION 4. RECEIPT OF STOCK FOR SERVICES

INTERNAL REVENUE CODE: Section 83; 351(d)(1).

REGULATIONS: Sections 1.351–1(a)(1), (2), Exs. (2) and (3).

Section § 351 applies only to the transfer of "property" in exchange for stock. Section 351(d)(1) specifically provides that stock issued for services is not issued for property. Section 83 applies to stock issued for services. Thus, the shareholder who receives the stock for services realizes ordinary income equal to the fair market value of the stock. If the stock is subject to a substantial risk of forfeiture or other restrictions that prevent it from being fully vested, § 83 provides rules for determining the year in which the value of the stock interest must be included in income. Pursuant to § 83(h), the corporation will be able to deduct the fair market value of the stock if the services provided by the transferee were not capital in nature. See also Treas. Reg. § 1.83–6. Otherwise the corporation will capitalize the value of the stock. If a single transferor transfers both property and services for stock, the transaction must be bifurcated and treated as the receipt of stock for property of equivalent value and the receipt of stock for services. Thus the transferor may be accorded nonrecognition under § 351 with respect to the stock received for property even though the receipt of the remainder of the stock is taxable under § 61 and § 83.

ILLUSTRATIVE MATERIAL

A. EFFECT OF STOCK FOR SERVICES ON OTHER TRANSFERORS

The presence of a transfer of services to the corporation for stock will not defeat the § 351 transaction as to other parties unless the transferor of services receives more than 20 percent of the stock since transferors of "property" would still be in "control" of the corporation. See Mojonnier & Sons, Inc. v. Commissioner, 12 T.C. 837 (1949) (NA)(§ 351 did not apply to any transferor where upon incorporation of a sole proprietorship former employees received more than 20 percent of stock in consideration for past services). A transferor of services who receives more than 20 percent of the stock for his services and who also transfers some property to the corporation for stock will qualify as a "transferor of property," so that both the stock received for services and the stock received for property will be counted in determining whether the control test is met. However, Treas. Reg. § 1.351–1(a)(ii) warns that if the primary purpose of the property transfer is to qualify the stock received for services and the property transferred constitutes only a "relatively small value" in comparison to the value of the services stock, the services stock will not be counted in determining the control group. Rev.Proc. 76–22, 1976–1 C.B. 562, indicates that for advance ruling purposes the property transferred will not be considered to be of "relatively small value" if it has a value equal to at least 10 percent of the value of the stock received for services by the person providing services (i.e., the value of the property is at least 9.09 percent of the total value of the stock received).

B. "PROPERTY" DISTINGUISHED FROM SERVICES AND SERVICE FLAVORED ASSETS

"Property" for § 351 purposes does not include all interests that may be considered property interests for other purposes. The question whether assets that have been produced as the result of the taxpayer's personal efforts constitute "property" for purposes of § 351 is identical to that encountered in exchanges of property for a partnership interest accorded nonrecognition treatment under § 721, and is similar, but not identical, to that encountered in connection with whether an asset constitutes "property" for purposes of capital gain treatment under § 1221. Thus, the term "property" includes secret processes and formulae whether patentable or not. Rev.Rul. 64–56, 1964–1 (Part 1) C.B. 133. Under that Ruling, if the transferred information qualifies as property, then § 351 applies even though services are to be performed in connection with the transfer; the services, however, must be ancillary and subsidiary to the property transfer. Continuing technical assistance, employee training, and construction assistance will ordinarily be considered services for purposes of § 351 transfers. Rev.Rul. 71–564, 1971–2 C.B. 179, holds that trade secrets are property for purposes of § 351 transfers as long as the transferee corporation receives an exclusive right to the trade secret until it becomes public knowledge and is no longer protectable under applicable law. E.I. Du Pont de Nemours & Co. v. United States, 471 F.2d 1211 (Ct.Cl.1973), held, however, that the transfer of a royalty free, nonexclusive license qualified as a transfer of "property" in a § 351 exchange. The fact that a taxable transfer of the nonexclusive license would not have qualified for capital gain treatment did not prevent § 351 from applying.

Rev.Rul. 70–45, 1970–1 C.B. 17, provides that business goodwill is property. In Rev.Rul. 79–288, 1979–2 C.B. 139, the Internal Revenue Service ruled further that a corporate name registered in a foreign country and protected under the laws of the foreign country is property for § 351 purposes, but that an unregistered, unprotected name with no goodwill value is not property.

In United States v. Frazell, 335 F.2d 487 (5th Cir.1964), a geologist entered into an agreement under which he was to identify potentially productive oil and gas properties, using several oil maps that he owned. Frazell was paid for his services and was to receive a specified interest in the properties after the other venturers had recovered certain costs. Eventually, instead of an interest in the properties, he received stock in a corporation to which the properties had been transferred. One of the court's alternative holdings was that Frazell realized ordinary income under § 351 on the theory that, if the stock were a substitution for the partnership interest originally contemplated, it would be compensation for services (and not received in exchange for "property"), and hence taxable under § 351. To the extent that the geological maps constituted "property," the taxpayer was entitled to § 351 nonrecognition treatment as to these items.

In James v. Commissioner, 53 T.C. 63 (1969), the taxpayer and one Talbot entered into an agreement to develop a real estate project. Talbot was to contribute land and the taxpayer was to promote the project and obtain the necessary FHA commitment and financing for the project. The taxpayer obtained the commitments in the name of the corporation and the taxpayer and Talbot then transferred the land and financing commitments to a corporation. The stock of the corporation was issued 50–50 to taxpayer and Talbot. The taxpayer argued that he had transferred contract rights (analogous to patents or secret processes) to the corporation and therefore § 351 controlled. Following *Frazell,* the court held that the stock was received for services and was therefore ordinary income to the taxpayer. Furthermore, the only transferor of "property" was Talbot, who owned only 50 percent of the stock after the transaction. Thus § 351 did not apply to Talbot's transfer because the 80 percent control test was not met and taxable gain resulted.

James was distinguished in United States v. Stafford, 727 F.2d 1043 (11th Cir.1984), which held that an unenforceable letter of intent to provide financing was property under § 721, which provides for nonrecognition of gain or loss on the contribution of property to a partnership. The court indicated that it would reach the same result under § 351. The court pointed out that Stafford had developed the letter of intent for his own account and owned the letter of intent individually. The financing commitment in *James* was in the name of the corporation.

In Hospital Corp. of America v. Commissioner, 81 T.C. 520, 587–590 (1983), the Tax Court held that the transfer of an opportunity to negotiate a management contract in Saudi Arabia was not the transfer of "property". In Roberts Company, Inc. v. Commissioner, 5 T.C. 1 (1945), however, a contingent fee agreement in favor of attorneys conveying an interest in land in the event of a successful litigation was held to constitute a property interest in the land involved, so that the attorneys could qualify as transferors of property.

C. TREATMENT OF THE CORPORATION

Whether a corporation issues stock in exchange for services in a § 351 transaction upon its formation or after the corporation is formed, the treatment of the corporation is the same. The corporation recognizes no gain under § 1032 and is entitled to a deduction under § 162 or to capitalize the value of the stock as the cost of the asset to which the services for which the stock was issued are related. Justification for the corporation claiming a deduction or acquiring basis while not recognizing any income is not self-evident.

Suppose a corporation pays an employee a bonus in the form of its stock, which it had previously purchased in the market and whose value is in excess of the basis of the stock. While presumably the value of the stock would otherwise be a deductible expense (see § 83(h)), does the nonrecognition treatment of § 1032 relieving the gain from inclusion (Treas. Reg. § 1.1032–1(a)(last sentence)) bring into play § 265, which disallows expenses allocable to income "wholly exempt"? Clearly there has been an "exchange" of the stock for the value of services, which fixed the value of the stock. See International Freighting Corp. v. Commissioner, 135 F.2d 310 (2d Cir.1943). In Hercules Powder Co. v. United States, 180 F.Supp. 363 (Ct.Cl.1960), after holding that stock so distributed did not result in gain to the corporation under the pre–§ 1032 regulations, the court then allowed the deduction as against the Commissioner's assertion of the rule of § 265:

"We think that the words 'gives rise to neither taxable gain nor deductible loss' in the regulation concerning the original issue of shares did not create an exemption of income from taxation. That could not be accomplished by regulation. That language must mean that such an issue does not give rise to income, within the meaning of [§ 61]." (367)

Subsequently, the Internal Revenue Service ruled that a transfer of appreciated stock or newly issued stock to employees as compensation for services is fully deductible under § 162. Although not discussing § 265, the Rulings stated that the nonrecognition provisions of § 1032 have no effect on business expense deductions otherwise allowable under § 162. Rev.Rul. 62–217, 1962–2 C.B. 59; Rev.Rul. 69–75, 1969–1 C.B. 52.

SECTION 5. "PROPERTY" AND MIDSTREAM TRANSFERS OF INCOME ITEMS

INTERNAL REVENUE CODE: Sections 446(b); 482.

Foster v. Commissioner

United States Court of Appeals, Ninth Circuit, 1985.
756 F.2d 1430.

■ J. BLAINE ANDERSON, CIRCUIT JUDGE:

In 1955, Jack Foster and his three sons formed a partnership, T. Jack Foster and Sons (Partnership), for the general purpose of dealing in property, with Jack as the managing partner. In 1958, the Partnership began to investigate the reclamation potential of Brewer's Island, a 2,600 acre undeveloped and partially submerged tract of land located about 12 miles south of San Francisco. After commissioning engineering studies, the Partnership determined that the tract could be transformed into a self-contained city (Foster City) of 35,000.

In December, 1959, the Partnership acquired an option to purchase the property for $12.8 million; in May, 1960, it secured enabling legislation from the California legislature for a municipal improvement district known as Estero, which was coterminous with Brewer's Island; and, in August, 1960, it exercised its option to purchase the tract. Thereafter, the Partnership and Estero began developing the property by neighborhood.

* * *

C. *Application of § 482 to the Disposition of Property Acquired in a Nonrecognition Transaction*

The first of the nine neighborhoods to be developed was Neighborhood One. In October, 1962, before any sales to builders were consummated, the Partnership transferred an undivided one-quarter interest in 127 acres of Neighborhood One to each of four newly formed corporations as tenants in common. Each of the four corporations, referred to collectively by the Tax Court as the Alphabets, was solely owned by one of the Fosters.

In August, 1966, the Partnership transferred 311 lots in Neighborhood Four, which had been improved to a lesser extent than Neighborhood One, to Foster Enterprises, a corporation owned by the Fosters in equal shares. Foster Enterprises, which was incorporated in 1960 to take title to a hotel in Hawaii, had accumulated a net operating loss of $1.2 million.

The Neighborhood One transaction was an exchange of property for stock under § 351. The Neighborhood Four transaction was a contribution to capital under § 1032. Under both sections, neither the transferor nor the transferee recognize gain or loss on the transfer, and the basis of the property does not change. The transferee therefore inherits the potential gain or loss inherent in the property at the time of its transfer.

The Tax Court was correct in its determination that the Commissioner may employ § 482 to reallocate income derived from the disposition of property previously acquired in a nonrecognition transaction. Rooney v. United States, 305 F.2d 681, 686 (9th Cir.1962)(Section 482 will control when it conflicts with § 351 as long as the discretion of the Commissioner in reallocating is not abused.); Treas.Reg. § 1.482–1(d)(5)(1984). see also Stewart v. Commissioner, 714 F.2d 977, 989 (9th Cir.1983).

D. *Section 482 Reallocation*

The Tax Court, pursuant to § 482, reallocated all the income from the sale of the lots in Neighborhood One and Neighborhood Four from the

Alphabets and Foster Enterprises to the Partnership. The income reallocated was divided into two parts, income due to appreciation in value before the transfers and income due to appreciation after the transfers.

1. *Pre-transfer Appreciation*

The Tax Court reallocated the income attributable to appreciation before the transfers on the ground that the purpose of the transfers was to avoid taxes. It found that A.O. Champlin, the Fosters' long-time tax advisor, decided it was advantageous from a tax standpoint for the Fosters to undertake the development of Foster City in a partnership form. Losses incurred during the early years could then be used by the partners to reduce income on their personal tax returns. Later, as the land was developed, certain lots were transferred from the Partnership to its controlled entities in an effort to shift income. As noted by the Tax Court, "only highly appreciated inventory pregnant with income was conveyed." Foster, 80 T.C. at 179. Moreover, according to the testimony of Champlin, the value of money on hand to the Fosters far exceeded any interest that might eventually have to be paid on a tax deficiency, particularly when the rate of interest charged by the Government was less than that charged by commercial banks.

In the case of the Alphabets, which were formed within a month of the transfer, the Tax Court determined that the object was to shift from the Partnership the income from the sale of the lots and split it among taxpayers subject to a lower rate of tax. The Fosters argue that the transfer could not have been tax motivated because it would have increased taxes; the income reported by the Alphabets was not offset by any losses, whereas if the income had been reported by the Partnership, it would have been offset by the operating losses which the Partnership claimed on its returns. The Tax Court, however, found that "the tax savings to an individual realized by preserving a partnership loss may very well exceed the tax cost to his corporation incurred by reporting the income." Id., 80 T.C. at 173.

The Fosters contend that although the Neighborhood Four transfer may have resulted in a tax saving, it was made for a business purpose. There was evidence that Rex Johnson, a senior vice president of Republic National Bank who was in charge of monitoring the Fosters' account, insisted that the lots be conveyed to Foster Enterprises as a condition to Republic's renewing the Partnership's loans. The Tax Court discounted this as the motivation behind the transfer, and we find its reasoning persuasive.

Foster Enterprises was not indebted to Republic. It had borrowed money from Likins–Foster Honolulu Corporation and Roy Turner Associates, Ltd., a subsidiary of Likins–Foster. Both Likins–Foster and the Partnership were indebted to Republic.

According to Johnson, the transfer was necessary to improve the liquidity of Foster Enterprises and thereby (1) enhance the collectibility of the indebtedness of Likins–Foster to Republic, (2) improve the bank's security in the Likins–Foster stock, and (3) insulate the bank from the fortunes of the Foster partnership. The Tax Court, however, found that a special audit report prepared by the bank stated that the Likins–Foster loans were being paid according to schedule. Moreover, if Johnson were concerned about the ability of Likins–Foster to repay its loan, it would have made more sense to transfer the lots directly to that corporation because it was the Likins–Foster stock that had been pledged as security. The transfer of the lots obviously weakened the Partnership's ability to repay its loan to Republic, noted the Tax Court, and certainly exacerbated its cash flow problem.

The sales proceeds were not used by Foster Enterprises to liquidate its debts to Likins–Foster and Turner Associates. Rather, they were loaned to the Partnership to further develop Foster City. Although Foster Enterprises still had an asset, it was now, continued the Tax Court, an unsecured receivable from the Partnership. Collectibility was therefore dependent upon the Partnership's overall success with the Foster City undertaking, precisely the risk against which Johnson ostensibly wanted to protect.

The Tax Court found that the purpose of the Neighborhood Four transaction was to shift to Foster Enterprises the income earned from the sale of the lots so that it could be absorbed by that corporation's losses. The record contains ample evidence to support the Tax Court's conclusions concerning both the Neighborhood Four and the Neighborhood One transactions. We therefore find that the Commissioner did not abuse his discretion in reallocating to the Partnership that portion of the sales income due to appreciation before the date of transfer. See Rooney v. United States, 305 F.2d 681, 684–85 (9th Cir.1962).

2. *Post-transfer Appreciation*

Because Neighborhoods One and Four were both further developed after the transfers, a part of the income derived from the sale of lots was created after the transfer date. The Tax Court concluded that Estero was controlled by the Partnership, and was used by it as its instrument for the development of Foster City. Thus Estero's efforts were to be viewed as those of the Partnership, and the gain was to be attributed to it.

Estero, a Municipal Improvement District, was created in 1960 by a special act of the California legislature. It was authorized to tax and to issue tax-exempt bonds to finance its activities in reclaiming and improving Brewer's Island. It was also vested with a broad array of general governmental powers. As enumerated by the Tax Court:

> It was empowered to reclaim land, make provision for street lighting, sewage, storm drainage, garbage and water service, and parks and playgrounds. It was also empowered to construct small craft harbors, provide fire and police protection, condemn land, enter into contracts, and make and enforce such regulations as were necessary and proper to the exercise of its enumerated powers. A violation of such regulation constituted a misdemeanor.

Foster, 80 T.C. at 58.

We agree with the Tax Court that during the years in issue, the Fosters, as the principal landowners and developers, controlled Estero. Indeed, the California Supreme Court has recognized that the Estero Act was designed by the California legislature to place control of the district in the landowner/developer. Cooper v. Leslie Salt Co., 70 Cal.2d 627, 451 P.2d 406, 408–409, 75 Cal.Rptr. 766, 768–769, cert. denied, 396 U.S. 821, 90 S.Ct. 62, 24 L.Ed.2d 72 (1969). The Tax Court stated:

> There is no question that Estero added value to Brewer's Island. However, it never realized that value because it did not own the land or receive the proceeds from its sale. All we are deciding here is whether the value added by Estero is allocable to the Foster partnership because of the legislatively conferred control that the partnership exercised over the district. To answer that question in the affirmative does not require that we ignore Estero's legal identity as a public agency.

Foster, 80 T.C. at 169. Estero was the Partnership's creature, used by it to improve the land and thus increase its value. That is what it was designed to be and do. Because it is a public body, validly created, its own income, if any, belongs to it, and would not be allocable to some other entity.

* * *

The Tax Court stated that its finding that the Partnership controlled Estero did not conflict with the district's status as a "juristic entity," and therefore [Commissioner v. Birch Ranch & Oil Co., 192 F.2d 924 (9th Cir.1951)] was inapposite. 80 T.C. at 169. We agree. The primary question here is not whether Estero is an independent entity. The primary question is whether the Commissioner can allocate to the Partnership the income arising from value created by Estero that would have gone to the Partnership but for the transfers to the Alphabets and Foster Enterprises. The Alphabets' and Foster Enterprises' function was to divert what would normally be the income of the Partnership away from it and to the Alphabets and Foster Enterprises. If the transfers had not been made, the income in question would not have been Estero's; it would have been that of the Partnership. The relationship between the Partnership and its creatures, the Alphabets and Foster Enterprises, was precisely the same, whether the appreciation in value occurred before the transfers or after them. Under section 482, the Commissioner may allocate income earned subsequent to the income evading event or transfer. The fact that some of it is attributable to a time following the transfers makes no difference. Because Estero did not own the land, the gain in value would never accrue to Estero, but would have accrued to the Partnership, the landowner, but for the transfers. By the transfers, the Partnership shifted that income away from itself and to the Alphabets, which had nothing, and to Foster Enterprises, which had large losses from unrelated ventures. By that device, the Partnership sought to get out from under large tax liabilities and yet retain control of Foster City. Under § 482, the Commissioner could reallocate to the Partnership the income that the Partnership had shifted to the Alphabets and Foster Enterprises. The transfers had no business function; their purpose was tax avoidance. The Tax Court properly upheld the Commissioner's reallocation.

* * *

E. *Penalty*

The Tax Court affirmed the Commissioner's assessment of a penalty against Jack and Gladys Foster for negligent or intentional disregard of income tax rules and regulations. 26 U.S.C. § 6653(a)(1976). We vacate the assessment. This is a case of first impression with no clear authority to guide the decision makers as to the major and complex issues. The positions taken by the Fosters were reasonably debatable. Under all of the circumstances, we do not believe it can be fairly said that the Fosters acted negligently or intentionally in disregard of the law.

AFFIRMED in part, VACATED in part.

ILLUSTRATIVE MATERIAL

A. SECTION 482 ALLOCATIONS

Although the Ninth Circuit held in *Foster* that § 482 overrides § 351, allowing the Commissioner to allocate subsequent income back to the transferor or previously incurred expenses to the transferee corporation, other court decisions have held that § 482 could not be applied to override a nonrecognition provision. See Ruddick Corp. v. United States, 643 F.2d 747 (Ct.Cl.1981). Treas. Reg. § 1.482–1(f)(1)(iii) now expressly provides that § 482 may be applied to override § 351.

B. ASSIGNMENT OF INCOME

In the case of a transfer to the corporation of contract rights or other property with accrued but uncollected income, the Commissioner has invoked assignment of income principles to force the transferor to recognize earned income on the transfer of the right to collect that income. See Weinberg v. Commissioner, 44 T.C. 233 (1965), aff'd per curiam sub nom. Commissioner v. Sugar Daddy, Inc., 386 F.2d 836 (9th Cir.1967). Hempt Bros., Inc. v. United States, 490 F.2d 1172 (3d Cir.1974), held that application of the assignment of income doctrine to tax the transfer of receivables by a cash method taxpayer would frustrate the policy of § 351, which is to facilitate incorporation of a going business. Rev.Rul. 80–198, 1980–2 C.B. 113, adopts the holding of *Hempt Brothers,* but adds that assignment of income principles will apply to tax the transfer of receivables if that is the only asset transferred to the corporation. Pursuant to § 362(a), the corporation will have a zero basis in the receivables and will thus be required to recognize on collection the full amount as income.

C. TAX BENEFIT RULE

Suppose a deduction for expenses has been taken by the proprietor of a previously unincorporated business that subsequently is transferred to a corporation in a § 351 transaction. Can the Service assert that the tax benefit rule is applicable to require income inclusion of the previously deducted items of the unincorporated business. Hillsboro National Bank v. Commissioner, 460 U.S. 370 (1983), held that the tax benefit rule did not apply to the transferor of previously expensed property transferred to another party in a transaction in which the transferee took a transferred basis (a corporate liquidation governed by a now repealed provision). This result is appropriate in a § 351 transaction because the corporation takes a transferred basis under § 362(a). If, on the other hand, the transaction provides the transferee with a stepped-up basis, then application of the tax benefit rule to "recapture" the prior deduction is appropriate. See United States v. Bliss Dairy, Inc., a case consolidated with *Hillsboro National Bank.*

D. CHANGE OF ACCOUNTING METHOD

The Commissioner may invoke her powers under § 446(b) to require proper accounting for income as between the transferor and the transferee corporation. In Palmer v. Commissioner, 267 F.2d 434 (9th Cir.1959), the transferor was forced to switch from the completed contract method to the percentage of completion method of accounting for long term construction contracts when it attempted to transfer the contracts to a controlled corporation before payment for completed work came due. Mathis v. United States, 430 F.2d 158 (7th Cir.1970), however, rejected the Commissioner's assertion of § 446(b) to force the transferor off of the completed contract method since both the transferor and transferee were paying tax at the same corporate rates on the income in question.

CHAPTER 4

THE CAPITAL STRUCTURE OF THE CORPORATION

SECTION 1. DEBT VERSUS EQUITY

The tax treatment of the various forms that an investment in a corporation can take is a central issue in the pattern of corporate taxation. Unlike in the partnership situation, the return on capital invested in ownership interests in the corporation, i.e., corporate stock, is subject to two levels of tax, once in the hands of the corporation and again when dividends are distributed to individual shareholders. On the other hand, the return on an investment in a corporation as a creditor, i.e., the interest paid by the corporation for the funds advanced, is only subject to a single level of tax since the interest payment, unlike a dividend, is deductible by the corporation and thus avoids the corporate level tax. Moreover, if the investor is a tax-exempt entity, such as a pension fund, debt classification generally eliminates the yield from the corporate tax base entirely.

This tax "bias" in favor of investment as a creditor has been a source of great strain on the tax system. Taxpayers and their advisors have attempted to structure obligations that qualify as debt for tax purposes, with the attendant single level of tax on the return, while at the same time giving the investor an opportunity to participate in the growth of the business enterprise—a typical aspect of an ownership or equity investment.

As an investment matter, the investor generally is indifferent to the formal classification of the investment instrument. From the investment perspective, the question is the yield on the investment in relation to the level of risk involved and the formal classification of the return as "interest" or "dividend" is not a matter of concern (except, of course, from a tax point of view). As a general matter, the higher the level of legal and economic protection provided in the instrument, the lower the investment return. In addition, given the imagination of the marketers of financial products, the possible combinations of ownership and creditor interests in a particular financial instrument are almost infinite.

The development of tax principles in this area has lagged far behind the development of investment products. This lag may be traceable to two causes. In the first place, the legal rules for the classification of investment instruments as debt or equity have developed primarily in the context of small, closely held corporations in cases in which the investors were both shareholders and "lenders." The method of analysis developed by the courts in that context has been largely inadequate to deal with situations such as large venture capital firms investing in an emerging business or the issuance of highly complex and sophisticated financial instruments by publicly traded companies. Secondly, and closely related, is the fact that, in developing the debt-equity rules, the courts generally have applied an "all or nothing" approach. That is, a particular instrument is either a debt instrument in its entirety for tax purposes or an equity instrument in its entirety. This approach, of course, is totally at odds with the various combinations of debt and equity features which can be employed in a particular financial instrument. Nonetheless, except when Congress has been willing to provide a legislative alternative (which in a few situations it has been forced to do), the all-or-nothing approach continues to prevail. This approach has made it relatively easy for sophisticated investors and their equally sophisticated tax advisors to craft instruments which combine the desirable legal features of ownership and creditor status with the most advantageous tax treatment.

The material in this chapter first considers the "traditional" debt-equity classification issues primarily as they have developed in the context of closely-held corporations. It then deals with the classification issues which are raised by more complex financial instruments and the more specific Congressional responses to those issues.

As the materials are considered, keep in mind the issues raised by the proposals for the integration of corporation and personal taxes discussed in Chapter 1. Which of the problems encountered in this Chapter would disappear under integration? What new issues would be raised?

The present distinction between debt and equity capital presents the corporation and its investors with different tax issues and planning possibilities. As respects the corporation issuing the obligation,[1] if the obligation is debt, interest is deductible, retirement at a discount may result in cancellation of indebtedness income, or retirement at a premium may provide an additional interest deduction. If the obligation is stock, dividends are not deductible and generally the corporation does not recognize income or loss on retirement. Retention of earnings to retire debt generally will not run afoul of the § 531 penalty tax on improperly accumulated earnings, see page 780, but such retention might result in that tax in the case of stock. Also the availability of the deduction for original issue discount requires that the obligation be classified as debt; no such deduction is allowed for the issuance of stock.

Gain or loss recognized by a corporate or individual stockholder on the sale, exchange or retirement of stock will be capital gain or loss. Loss incurred on worthless stock also is a capital loss. However, § 1244 allows individuals an ordinary loss on stock in certain small business companies, and a corporation is allowed an ordinary loss on the worthless stock of a controlled subsidiary. Gain or loss recognized on the sale, exchange or retirement of a debt obligation is also capital to a corporate or individual

1. The term "obligation" is used in the following materials to include stock, debt, and instruments with attributes of both stock and debt whose proper classification is in doubt.

holder (unless there is an element of original issue or market discount involved). Loss on a worthless debt obligation that is classified as a "security" is treated as a capital loss to both the corporate and individual holder. For this purpose, a debt obligation is a "security" if it is in registered form or has coupons attached. No loss is allowed in the case of a worthless debt which is a "registration required debt" but which has not been registered. I.R.C. § 165(j). An individual's loss on a debt obligation that is not a security is a short-term capital loss, unless the debt arose in the individual's trade or business, in which case the loss is ordinary. Loss incurred by a corporate holder on a nonsecurity debt obligation is ordinary. See I.R.C. §§ 165(g), 166(a) and (d). Loss incurred by a corporate holder with respect to worthless securities of a controlled subsidiary generally is ordinary. I.R.C. § 165(g)(3).

Payments on an obligation will also produce different tax results for the holder depending on the character of the obligation. If the payment constitutes interest it will be includible in the recipient's income whether or not the corporation has earnings and profits, whereas inclusion as a dividend depends on the presence of earnings and profits. If a corporation holds the obligation, the intercorporate dividends received deduction under § 243 (see page 227) depends on the presence of a "dividend," which requires that the obligation be treated as stock. If the advances to the corporation are regarded as contributions to capital, i.e., additional stock investment, repayment usually will be a dividend to the stockholder, but if regarded as loans, the repayment will not be taxable. Where the obligation is retired, if it is stock, the retirement under some circumstances will be a dividend under § 301; if a debt, retirement will produce capital gain or loss (in the absence of original issue discount or premium).

The preceding discussion is not exhaustive, and there are other facets to the problem. For example, the classification of the obligation as stock or debt is important under the reorganization provisions to both the investor and the corporation. Also, if a foreign subsidiary is involved, the classification will be important, for example, with respect to the foreign tax credit. Classification of the obligation as stock or debt also is important in determining the applicability of the personal holding company tax. See page 790.

A. DEDUCTIBLE INTEREST OR NONDEDUCTIBLE DIVIDEND DISTRIBUTION: GENERAL PRINCIPLES GOVERNING CLASSIFICATION AS DEBT OR EQUITY

INTERNAL REVENUE CODE: Section 385.

Attempts in Congress to define debt and equity when the 1954 Code was enacted were rejected by the Senate. The Senate Finance Committee Report stated that "any attempt to write into the statute precise definitions which will classify for tax purposes the many types of corporate stocks and securities will be frustrated by the numerous characteristics of an interchangeable nature which can be given to these instruments." S.Rep.

No. 1622, 83d Cong., 2d Sess. 42 (1954). In the 1969 Act, however, Congress enacted § 385 in an attempt to transfer the problem of definition to the Treasury.

Excerpt from GENERAL EXPLANATION OF THE TAX REFORM ACT OF 1969, Joint Committee on Internal Revenue Taxation (1970):

"*Explanation of* [§ 385].—The Act deals with the [debt-equity] problems * * * by adding two different provisions to the tax laws, one which is of general application under the tax laws and a second which relates only to corporate acquisitions.

"The first of these [§ 385] provides the Secretary of the Treasury or his delegate with specific statutory authority to promulgate regulatory guidelines, to the extent necessary or appropriate, for determining whether a corporate obligation constitutes stock or indebtedness for all purposes of the Internal Revenue Code. These guidelines are to set forth factors to be taken into account in determining in a particular factual situation whether a debtor-creditor relationship exists or whether a corporation-shareholder relationship exists. The provision specifies certain factors which may be taken into account in these guidelines. However, it is not intended that only these factors be included in the guidelines or that, in a particular situation, any of these factors must be included in the guidelines, or that any of the factors which are included by statute must necessarily be given any more weight than other factors added by regulations. The factors specifically listed are as follows:

(1) Whether there is a written unconditional promise to pay on demand or on a specified date a sum certain in money in return for an adequate consideration in money or money's worth, and to pay a fixed rate of interest;

(2) Whether there is subordination to, or preference over, any indebtedness of the corporation;

(3) The ratio of debt to equity of the corporation;

(4) Whether there is convertibility into the stock of the corporation; and

(5) The relationship between holdings of stock in the corporation and holdings of the interest in question.

"In developing these guidelines, the Secretary of the Treasury is not bound or limited by the specific rules which the Act provides for distinguishing debt from equity in the corporate acquisition context [§ 279]. Thus, an obligation the interest on which is not disallowed under the corporate acquisition section nevertheless might be found to constitute equity (and hence the interest disallowed) under the general debt-equity regulatory guidelines. Moreover, unlike the rules provided [§ 279] in a corporate acquisition context, which deal only with the allowability of the interest deduction, the guidelines to be promulgated by the Secretary of the Treasury are applicable for all purposes of the Internal Revenue Code." (123–24.)

The final § 385 regulations were issued in December 1980, applicable to instruments issued after April 30, 1981. T.D. 7747, 1981–1 C.B. 141. The effective date was extended several times and the regulations were withdrawn on August 5, 1983. T.D. 7920, 1983–2 C.B. 69. The regulations focused primarily on proportionality and valuation as the keys to debt/equity distinctions. An instrument in the form of debt which was not held in proportion to stock was generally treated as debt. Proportionately held obligations were treated as debt if the debt was not excessive (thin capitalization), the interest rate was commercially reasonable, or if interest was not reasonable, the obligation was issued for money repayable at a fixed time. Although elegant in structure and theoretical underpinning, the regulations were difficult to apply in the myriad of situations which they were required to cover. The § 385 regulations expired under the weight of their complexity, particularly in the small business context, and because enterprising taxpayers developed financial instruments that would have successfully taken advantage of the regulations' bright line classification of hybrid instruments. See Rev.Rul. 83–98, 1983–2 C.B. 40. No new regulations have been issued under § 385, and the debt versus equity classification issue thus continues to turn on judicial authority.

Slappey Drive Industrial Park v. United States

United States Court of Appeals, Fifth Circuit, 1977.
561 F.2d 572.

■ GOLDBERG, CIRCUIT JUDGE.

This tax refund suit involves seven closely held real estate development corporations that Spencer C. Walden, Jr. organized and manages. The first issue * * * is whether certain purported debts that the corporations owed their shareholders should be treated for tax purposes as contributions to capital. * * * The district court, Cairo Developers, Inc. v. United States, D.C., 381 F.Supp. 431, resolved [the] issue in the government's favor. We affirm.

I. Facts

Spencer C. Walden, Jr. is a successful real estate developer in Albany, Georgia, a city of some 100,000 located less than 50 miles southeast of Plains. Acting primarily through the partnership of Walden & Kirkland, Walden has developed numerous residential subdivisions and various commercial properties. This case concerns a subset of his activities.

Among the properties Walden has developed are several tracts originally owned by his father-in-law, J.T. Haley, and Haley's descendants. With Walden directing organizational efforts, members of the Haley family formed six corporations over a fifteen year period. Those corporations were Pecan Haven, Inc. (Pecan Haven), Lake Park, Inc. (Lake Park), Sherwood Acres, Inc. (Sherwood), Lake Park Additions, Inc. (Additions), Forest Estates, Inc. (Forest Estates) and Slappey Drive Industrial Park, Inc. (Slappey). Each of these is a party to this case. The other corporate party is

Cairo Developers, Inc. (Cairo Developers), which Walden formed in conjunction with two individuals not members of the J.T. Haley family.

Walden was the moving force behind each of these corporations. He was president of each enterprise, and his partnership, Walden & Kirkland, handled their development work. All but Slappey were to develop residential subdivisions; Slappey's project was an industrial park.

On this appeal the government * * * contends that purported debts that each corporation owed its shareholders should receive equity treatment. The debts arose from eight transfers of land (ostensibly credit sales) and three transfers of money (ostensibly loans) that the shareholders made to the corporations. [Ed.: The gain on transfers of property for notes would be subject to current taxation under post–1989 law, see page 74. The court's discussion of the debt-equity issue remains relevant.] We develop the facts relevant to these contentions by discussing the corporations in the order of their incorporation, referring to the contested transfers by alphabetical labels.

Pecan Haven. Pecan Haven was formed in June 1947. The shareholders were Walden (1 share), his wife Cornelia Haley Walden (59 shares) and her twin sister Loretta Haley (60 shares). They paid $12,000 for their shares. Pecan Haven developed several tracts obtained from Loretta and Cornelia and later developed a tract purchased from their father J.T. Haley.

Transfer A occurred July 26, 1960. Spencer Walden transferred 69.435 acres to the corporation in exchange for its $65,000 five-year 3% installment notes. Appellants assert that the corporation's book net worth at that time was $83,000 and that its "true" net worth, taking into account the appreciated value of its real estate holdings, was $476,000. The corporation failed to make timely payments of principal or interest, and $20,000 remains outstanding.

Lake Park. J.T. Haley's three children—Joel T. Haley, Jr., Cornelia and Loretta—organized Lake Park in November 1950 intending to develop lands they held jointly. They took equal shares of the corporation's stock, for which they paid a total of $28,000. The corporate books reflected the contributions as $9,000 paid-in capital and $19,000 paid-in surplus. The corporation immediately acquired land from its shareholders that it developed.

Transfer B occurred September 7, 1954. The shareholders transferred 100 acres to the corporation in exchange for $10,000 cash and a $40,000 demand note bearing 4% interest. Appellants contend that at the time of the transfer the corporation's net worth was $50,000 and that its "true" net worth was $78,000. Lake Park made irregular principal payments and retired the note in 1959. The corporation did not pay interest as provided in the note, making only a single $2,500 interest payment in 1956.

Sherwood. The Lake Park shareholders—Joel, Cornelia and Loretta—formed Sherwood in September 1954. Each took one-third of the new corporation's stock, for which they paid a total of $21,000. The next day they made transfer C, conveying to the corporation 48 acres in which each owned a one-third undivided interest. In exchange the corporation paid $6,000 cash and an $18,000 demand note bearing 4% interest. The corporation made irregular principal payments and a single interest payment, retiring the debt in 1960.

By the time of the second contested Sherwood transaction, Joel had died, leaving to his wife Katherine and his two children equal portions of his stock and the remaining property owned in conjunction with the other shareholders. This new lineup of shareholders made transfer D in January 1960. In exchange for 126.48 acres, the corporation issued five-year 3% notes to each shareholder totaling $189,720.02. Appellants assert that at that time the corporation had a book net worth of $62,000 and a "true" net worth of $206,000. Sherwood made irregular principal and interest payments, and a $32,000 balance remains outstanding.

Transfer E occurred in December 1964 when Sherwood's shareholders conveyed an additional 84.252 acres to the corporation. In exchange they received five-year 5% notes totaling $126,000. Appellants contend that the corporation had a $117,000 book net worth and a $240,000 "true" net worth. In September 1965 the corporation retired the notes held by Katherine and her two children. The corporation has made no payments on the notes held by Loretta and Cornelia. The corporation made an interest payment to Katherine and her children in 1965 and made annual interest payments to Loretta and Cornelia from 1967 through 1971. * * *

Additions. In June 1959 Loretta, Cornelia and Katherine formed Additions, each taking one-third of its shares and contributing a total of $36,900 paid-in capital. Katherine's two children did not participate. The shareholders and Katherine's children immediately made transfer F, conveying 268.8 acres to the corporation in exchange for five-year 3% notes totaling $368,200.[8] The corporation made no principal or interest payments until 1964. From 1964 until 1969 it made annual interest payments. It has made a single principal payment, for $5,000 in 1965.

Transaction G occurred August 2, 1961. Loretta advanced the corporation $61,250, taking in return its one-year 5% note. The corporation made its first payment on the note in 1964 and retired the note in 1965.

After conducting a topographical survey of the land it had received from its shareholders in 1959, Additions discovered that nearly three acres could not be incorporated into the planned residential subdivision because of drainage problems. The corporation abandoned its initial plan regarding this tract and did not subdivide it into lots. The corporation did not break the parcel out separately on its books but carried it in the same account that included all undeveloped land. In 1963 Georgia Power Company approached Additions and bought two acres for a substation, and the City of Albany contacted Additions and purchased the remainder of the tract for a pumping station. Georgia Power paid $7,500 for its parcel and the city

8. The notes of Cornelia, Loretta and Katherine were subordinated to the children's notes.

$2,500. Additions claims that this land had been held for investment, making capital gains treatment appropriate.

Forest Estates. In September 1959 Loretta Haley and Marjorie Scherberger formed Forest Estates, each taking half its stock, for which they paid a total of $25,000. They immediately effected transfer H, conveying to the corporation 43.93 acres that they owned jointly in exchange for five-year 4% notes totaling $100,000. Forest Estates made no principal payments on the notes until 1971, and $70,000 remains outstanding. The corporation made small and irregular interest payments from 1961 through 1967. Forest Estates suffered losses in 1965 and 1966 and apparently abandoned development plans.

Cairo Developers. Spencer C. Walden, Jr., George M. Kirkland, Jr., and J. Norwood Clark formed Cairo Developers in April 1961. Kirkland was Walden's partner in Walden & Kirkland. Clark was a real estate broker from Cairo, Georgia, who owned the bulk of the land that Cairo Developers was to develop. Each organizer took one-third of the corporation's stock, paying in a total of $5,100. From May 1961 through January 1964, the corporation received ostensible loans from the three shareholders, the Walden & Kirkland partnership, a corporation that Walden and Kirkland owned, and two of Walden's children. These advances together constitute transfer J. Most of these notes were due in one year; a few were payable on demand. The corporation made no payments of principal or interest until 1971.

Slappey. On July 7, 1962, Cornelia Haley Walden organized Slappey, paying $9,000 for all its issued stock. On July 9 she transferred the stock in equal segments to her three children. The next day Cornelia made transfer K, conveying 80.78 acres to the corporation in exchange for $6,366.50 cash and an eight-year 4% note for $75,000. Slappey planned to develop the land for industrial and commercial establishments. The corporation made irregular principal and interest payments, failing to pay the debt on its due date.

Transfer L occurred May 27, 1963. Each of the three shareholders advanced the corporation $5,000 in exchange for one-year 6% notes. Slappey has made no payments of principal or interest on these notes.

Overview. We may assume, as appellants contend, that in each ostensible sale of property to a corporation the price reflected the fair market value.[11] Nonetheless, the recurring pattern in regard to all the loans has been the corporations' failure to adhere to the announced repayment schedules. Although the corporations did make some principal and interest payments, in not a single case did the payments conform to the terms included in the notes. In addition, Spencer Walden's deposition testimony makes clear that the creditor-shareholders viewed their situation not at all as normal creditors would. The shareholders entered no objections to the passing of payment dates and requested payments only when the corpora-

11. We note also that the ostensible lenders took no security interests in the transferred property or otherwise and that, with a single exception, see note 8 supra, the debts at issue were not subordinated to other corporate obligations.

tions had "plenty of cash." In explaining the willingness to tolerate delinquencies even when interest was not being paid, Walden candidly stated that the individuals were more concerned with their status as shareholders than in their status as creditors.

II. Debt–equity

The tax code provides widely disparate treatment of debt and equity. In regard to a typical transfer at issue here, involving an individual's transfer of property to his corporation in exchange for the instrument in question, the classification as debt or equity may affect the taxation of the original transaction,[12] the resulting bases and hence the taxation of subsequent transfers,[13] and the taxation of payments the corporation makes to the shareholder with respect to the instrument.[14] In the case at bar debt classification would greatly benefit the taxpayers.

Unfortunately, the great disparity in the tax treatment of debt and equity does not derive from a clear distinction between those concepts. The problem is particularly acute in the case of close corporations, because the participants often have broad latitude to cast their contributions in whatever form they choose. Taxpayers have often sought debt's advantageous tax treatment for transactions that in substance more closely resembled the kind of arrangement Congress envisioned when it enacted the equity provisions. See Nassau Lens Co. v. Commissioner, 308 F.2d 39, 44–46 (2d Cir.1962)(Marshall, J.). Thus, the labels that parties attach to their transactions provide no guarantee of the appropriate tax treatment. See, e.g., Tyler v. Tomlinson, 414 F.2d 844, 850 (5th Cir.1969); Berkowitz v. United States, 411 F.2d 818, 820 (5th Cir.1969).

Articulating the essential difference between the two types of arrangement that Congress treated so differently is no easy task. Generally, shareholders place their money "at the risk of the business" while lenders seek a more reliable return. See Midland Distributors, Inc. v. United States, 481 F.2d 730, 733 (5th Cir.1973); Dillin v. United States, 433 F.2d 1097, 1103 (5th Cir.1970). That statement of course glosses over a good many considerations with which even the most inexperienced investor is abundantly familiar. A purchaser of General Motors stock may bear much

12. See I.R.C. § 351. That section provides that no gain or loss is recognized when persons transfer property to their controlled corporation solely in exchange for "stock or securities." The term "stock" would include the instruments here if they were characterized as equity. The term "securities" might or might not extend to them if characterized as debt; the term encompasses some debt instruments but not others. * * *

13. See, e.g., I.R.C. § 362. In the instant case the transferring shareholders' bases in their land were significantly lower than the sales prices. Thus the difference between new basis and carryover basis is important.

14. The corporation may deduct interest on indebtedness, see I.R.C. § 163, but if the transaction is characterized as equity, ostensible interest payments become non-deductible dividends. In general, the recipient is not taxable on loan principal payments but is taxable if the transaction constitutes equity; in that instance the purported principal payments come in for dividend treatment. See I.R.C. § 316.

less risk than a bona fide lender to a small corporation. See Fin Hay Realty Co. v. United States, 398 F.2d 694, 697 (3d Cir.1968).

Nevertheless, the "risk of the business" formulation has provided a shorthand description that courts have repeatedly invoked. Contributors of capital undertake the risk because of the potential return, in the form of profits and enhanced value, on their underlying investment. Lenders, on the other hand, undertake a degree of risk because of the expectancy of timely repayment with interest. Because a lender unrelated to the corporation stands to earn only a fixed amount of interest, he usually is unwilling to bear a substantial risk of corporate failure or to commit his funds for a prolonged period. A person ordinarily would not advance funds likely to be repaid only if the venture is successful without demanding the potential enhanced return associated with an equity investment. See Curry v. United States, 396 F.2d 630, 634 (5th Cir.), cert. denied, 393 U.S. 967, 89 S.Ct. 401, 21 L.Ed.2d 375 (1968); DuGro Frozen Foods, Inc. v. United States, 481 F.2d 1271, 1272 (5th Cir.1973).

These considerations provide only imperfect guidance when the issue relates to a shareholder's purported loan to his own corporation, the usual situation encountered in debt-equity cases. It is well established that shareholders may loan money to their corporations and achieve corresponding tax treatment. See United States v. Snyder Bros. Co., 367 F.2d 980, 983 (5th Cir.1966), cert. denied, 386 U.S. 956, 87 S.Ct. 1021, 18 L.Ed.2d 104 (1967); Rowan v. United States, 219 F.2d 51 (5th Cir.1955). When making such loans they could hardly be expected to ignore their shareholder status; their motivations will not match those of potential lenders who have no underlying equity interest. The "risk of the business" standard, though, continues to provide a backdrop for our analysis. While we should not expect a creditor-shareholder to evidence motivations and behavior conforming perfectly to those of a mere creditor, neither should we abandon the effort to determine whether the challenged transaction is in substance a contribution to capital masquerading as debt.[15]

Rather than attempt to measure concrete cases against an abstract formulation of the overriding test, we have identified numerous observable criteria that help place a given transaction on one side of the line or the other. We have always recognized, however, that the various factors are not equally significant. "The object of the inquiry is not to count factors, but to evaluate them." Tyler v. Tomlinson, 414 F.2d 844, 848 (5th Cir.1969). Each case turns on its own facts; differing circumstances may bring different factors to the fore. See In re Indian Lake Estates, Inc., 448 F.2d 574, 579 (5th Cir.1971); Tomlinson v. The 1661 Corp., 377 F.2d 291, 295 (5th Cir.1967).

15. In emphasizing the usefulness of comparing the challenged transaction to the type arrangement that a disinterested lender would have entered, the Third Circuit has noted that disregarding the shareholder-lender's personal interest in his own corporation is fairer than presumptively construing all such transactions adversely to the shareholder. See Fin Hay Realty Co. v. United States, 398 F.2d 694, 697 (3d Cir.1968).

With that preliminary caveat, we note the factors that prior cases have identified:

(1) the names given to the certificates evidencing the indebtedness;

(2) the presence or absence of a fixed maturity date;

(3) the source of payments;

(4) the right to enforce payment of principal and interest;

(5) participation in management flowing as a result;

(6) the status of the contribution in relation to regular corporate creditors;

(7) the intent of the parties;

(8) "thin" or adequate capitalization;

(9) identity of interest between creditor and stockholder;

(10) source of interest payments;

(11) the ability of the corporation to obtain loans from outside lending institutions;

(12) the extent to which the advance was used to acquire capital assets; and

(13) the failure of the debtor to repay on the due date or to seek a postponement.

Estate of Mixon v. United States, 464 F.2d 394, 402 (5th Cir.1972).[16] As indicated above, these factors are but tools for discerning whether a transaction more closely resembles the type arrangement for which Congress provided debt or equity treatment.[17]

In the case at bar the most telling of the *Mixon* factors is the corporate debtors' consistent failure to repay the debts on the due dates or to seek postponements. More generally, that failure and the corresponding absence of timely interest payments combine with Walden's testimony regarding the parties' view of their relationship to make clear that these transactions were in substance not at all the type arrangements for which debt treatment is appropriate.

The individuals' failure to insist upon timely repayment or satisfactory renegotiation indicates that the compensation they sought went beyond the announced interest rate, for an investor would not ordinarily undertake such a risk for so limited a return. See Tyler v. Tomlinson, 414 F.2d 844, 850 (5th Cir.1969). The failure to insist that the corporations pay the interest that the agreements provided underscores the inference; "a true

16. The list is not exhaustive; our cases undoubtedly mention considerations that have yet to take a number. * * *

17. The issue is primarily one of law. We must uphold the district court's findings of basic facts unless clearly erroneous, but the ultimate characterization of the transactions as debt or equity receives no such protection. See Estate of Mixon v. United States, 464 F.2d 394, 402–03 (5th Cir.1972).

lender is concerned with interest." Curry v. United States, 396 F.2d 630, 634 (5th Cir.), cert. denied, 393 U.S. 967, 89 S.Ct. 401, 21 L.Ed.2d 375 (1968). See also National Carbide Corp. v. Commissioner, 336 U.S. 422, 435 n. 16, 69 S.Ct. 726, 93 L.Ed. 779 (1949). When a corporate contributor seeks no interest, it becomes abundantly clear that the compensation he seeks is that of an equity interest: a share of the profits or an increase in the value of his shareholdings. See Estate of Mixon v. United States, 464 F.2d 394, 409 (5th Cir.1972).

Walden's testimony confirms these conclusions. He acknowledged that the individuals sought payments of principal or interest only when the corporations had "plenty of cash" and that the investors did so because they were more concerned with their status as shareholders than as creditors. That statement of how the individuals viewed their situation corresponds almost perfectly to the classic equity situation. A corporation normally declares dividends only when it has "plenty of cash." Shareholders ordinarily acquiesce in such dividend policies because their primary concern is the health and long-term success of the enterprise. Walden's statement indicates that the individuals here possessed precisely those motivations and that they believed it appropriate for the corporations to decide when to make payments on the same basis that corporations customarily make dividend decisions. See Berkowitz v. United States, 411 F.2d 818, 821 (5th Cir.1969). The taxpayers' pattern of conduct belies any intention to structure their affairs as parties to a debt transaction ordinarily would. In the circumstances here, these factors indicate that all the transactions should be characterized for tax purposes as equity arrangements.

In reaching this conclusion we have not ignored the other factors our cases have identified. Appellants place particular reliance on the intent of the parties. Here, appellants contend, the form in which the parties cast the transactions conclusively demonstrates their intent to create a debt relationship. In relying so heavily on this factor, however, appellants misconceive its import. The question is not whether the parties intended to call their transaction "debt" and thus to achieve advantageous tax treatment; that a person wants to pay less tax rather than more provides little basis for discerning how much tax Congress decided he should pay. Instead, the relevant inquiry is the actual manner, not the form, in which the parties intended to structure their relationship. If the intended structuring accords with the type arrangement that qualifies for taxation as debt, that intent supports a finding of debt. Here, however, the parties intended to structure their relationship in a manner placing funds at the prolonged risk of the businesses; they intended decisions whether to make payments on the advances to be based on the criteria usually associated with dividend decisions. To the extent that intent is relevant, it favors equity classification.[18]

18. Walden testified that the corporations intended to repay the indebtedness. Even accepting that testimony as true, the parties' conduct makes clear that they intended to repay only after a prolonged period, at which time repayment would be likely only

Another *Mixon* factor to which appellants look for support is the extent to which the advance was used to acquire capital assets. They argue that here the corporations used none of the advances for that purpose. Instead, appellants note, the corporations used the contributions primarily for land, which constitutes the inventory of these real estate development firms. Whatever force this factor might have in other settings, appellants here can garner little support from it. Most of these advances, while perhaps not used for capital assets, nonetheless served "to finance initial operations." Plantation Patterns, Inc. v. Commissioner, 462 F.2d 712, 722 (5th Cir. 1972). See Aqualane Shores, Inc. v. Commissioner, 269 F.2d 116 (5th Cir.1959)(shareholder's credit "sale" of land to real estate development corporation held to constitute equity contribution). Providing the bulk of the necessary first assets without which a corporation could not begin functioning is as traditional a usage of capital contributions as is purchasing "capital assets."

Another factor from *Mixon* that sometimes proves most instructive is the identity of interest between creditor and stockholder. Courts and commentators have often discussed this criterion under the rubric "proportionality." When each shareholder owns the same proportion of the company's stock as he does of the ostensible shareholder debt, the parties' framing of the transaction contributes little to the analysis. See Fin Hay Realty Co. v. United States, 398 F.2d 694 (3d Cir.1968). In that situation the owners' decision regarding how much of their contribution to cast as equity and how much as debt does not affect the distribution of control over the company. Non-tax considerations may play little role in the choice, and reviewing courts accordingly must scrutinize carefully the resulting transaction. When, on the other hand, an individual holds different percentages of the corporation's stock and shareholder debt, the casting of debt in that form ordinarily will affect substantial non-tax interests. There is thus reason to believe that the parties' debt characterization has substance as well as form.[19]

Appellants argue in the case at bar that many of the challenged transfers exhibited imperfect proportionality and that some displayed none at all.[20] While that argument would carry weight in the usual case, it has

if the enterprises have proved successful. Thus they intended to repay in the same sense that corporations might intend their dividends eventually to total up to the original price of the stock. Walden's testimony in this regard provides only the barest support for debt classification.

19. Even when a corporation incurs bona fide debt, of course, the opportunity to advance the funds and earn the corresponding return provides both tax and other advantages to the shareholder. Individual shareholders may therefore insist upon receiving their share of such advantages. Thus "proportionality" justifies courts in applying careful examination of the transactions but is not necessarily inconsistent with a finding of bona fide debt.

20. Transfers B, C, H and L exhibited perfect proportionality; each shareholder took the same percentage of shareholder debt as he or she held of the corporation's stock. Transfers D and E originally showed complete proportionality but became somewhat disproportional when the corporations made principal payments in different amounts to the different shareholders. Transfer F was not completely proportional; Katherine's children made loans but held no shares. Treating Katherine and her children as a unit, howev-

little force here. The disproportional holdings all occurred among close relatives. Although we do not treat the various shareholding members of the J.T. Haley family as an indivisible unit, neither do we treat them as unrelated individuals. For all that appears in this record, relations among the various family members were completely harmonious. Because shareholding family members were thus less likely to attribute major significance to departures from strict equality in their positions, the instances of disproportionate debt and equity holdings provide a much weaker inference than they ordinarily would that the ostensible debt was in fact what it purported to be.[21]

Finally, appellants strenuously urge that the level of the corporations' capitalization does not undermine their position. We have not, however, based our decision on the inadequacy of the corporate capitalization. While some of the purported loans were made to corporations with woefully inadequate capital, others were not. In some cases, as the taxpayers note, capitalization was adequate.[22] These facts strengthen our conclusion as to

er, transfer F exhibited perfect proportionality. Similarly, transfer K evidenced no proportionality but was totally proportional treating Cornelia and her children as a unit. Transfer J was only roughly proportional. While different shareholders (or their businesses) made advances at different times, each of the three equal shareholders put up roughly one-third of the funds when considered in conjunction with their other loans to the corporation. Transfer G was not proportional; a one-third shareholder made the entire advance. Transfer A was completely disproportional; Spencer made the loan but held no stock.

21. In Estate of Mixon v. United States, 464 F.2d 394 (5th Cir.1972), we examined proportionality by looking to the family attribution provisions of I.R.C. § 318. See 464 F.2d at 398 n. 3, 409. Even using those provisions to increase the individual's shareholdings, he held only 15.3% of the corporation's stock while making 80% of the challenged advance. Thus taking the view of attribution most favorable to the government in that case, the low proportionality favored the taxpayer.

In the case at bar, unlike in *Mixon,* the approach taken to attribution affects the direction in which the proportionality factor cuts. We think the proper approach is the practical one outlined in the text. Rather than rigidly apply the § 318 attribution rules—an approach that *Mixon* does not require and that would contravene the limitation of that section to "those provisions * * * to which [it is] expressly made applicable," I.R.C. § 318(a)—we treat the familial relationships as factors affecting the impact to be accorded the results of the proportionality inquiry. We of course accord careful scrutiny to intra-family transactions. See Dillin v. United States, 433 F.2d 1097, 1103 (5th Cir. 1970).

22. Taxpayers urge that these businesses involved little risk and therefore needed little capital. The apparent failure of Forest Estates, however, belies their assertion. The ventures incurred development expenses running into six figures and required as much as two or three years to begin receiving any revenues by selling lots. These considerations demonstrate the inadequacy of, for example, the initial capitalizations of $5,100 for Cairo Developers, $9,000 for Slappey, and $21,000 for Sherwood. Thus the capitalization factor favors the government with respect to transfers made to those corporations upon their formation.

In regard to transfers made at later times, however, we agree with appellants that net worth, not initial capitalization, provides the relevant data. See Tomlinson v. The 1661 Corp., 377 F.2d 291, 299 n. 18 (5th Cir.1967). At the time of transfer E. Sherwood's net worth was $117,000. That figure would become much greater if we were to take into account the appreciated value of Sherwood's real estate holdings or if we added the amounts of the earlier purported debts (originating from transfers C and D) that we reclassify as equity. We need not decide the propriety of these steps, for we agree with appellants that in any event Sherwood's capi-

some transactions, weaken it for others. They do not, however, suffice to change the conclusion we have derived from the parties' pattern of conduct and from Walden's testimony.[23]

Because the parties to the transactions in question intended to conduct and did conduct their affairs in a manner that the tax code labels equity rather than debt, taxation of the transactions as equity is appropriate. Contrary to appellants' assertions, in reaching that result we do not disapprove their decisions concerning how to organize the corporations, and we do not substitute our business judgment for theirs. We merely announce the tax consequences that attach to their decisions. While appellants are correct that they were free to decide without our supervision how much of the corporate financing to derive from loans and how much from capital contributions, they were not free to decide for themselves what tax consequences would attach to their conduct. * * *

CONCLUSION

The district court properly characterized the eleven purported corporate debts as contributions to capital. * * * The district court's decision is Affirmed.

ILLUSTRATIVE MATERIAL

A. THE NATURE OF THE INQUIRY

1. *Generally*

Gilbert v. Commissioner, 248 F.2d 399 (2d Cir.1957), was one of the first cases to apply a multi-factor approach to the debt versus equity issue. The court in *Gilbert* identified debt as an unqualified obligation to pay a sum certain at a reasonably close fixed maturity date along with a fixed percentage in interest payable regardless of the debtor's income or lack thereof. The courts, following the *Gilbert* analysis, began to search for factors which would help to distinguish the unqualified obligation to repay from an equity investment. As a result, formidable lists of factors began to be developed against which obligations could be measured to determine if they more resembled debt or equity. At one point, this "factor check-off list" approach threatened to become as mechanical as the earlier obsession

talization at the time of transfer E was adequate.

23. The *Mixon* factors not discussed in text carry little weight in this case. The source of principal and interest payments and the questionable availability of similar loans from outside lenders provide slight support to the government. That most of the obligations possessed fixed maturity dates would favor appellants had they not consistently ignored those dates. Similarly, the individuals' legal right to enforce payment does not aid appellants in light of the apparent understanding, as manifested in observable behavior, that they would not enforce those rights. The lenders already controlled corporate management; that they derived no more control as a result of the ostensible loans does not cut against the equity classification. See Dillin v. United States, 433 F.2d 1097, 1101 (5th Cir. 1970). Finally, that appellants did not subordinate their loans to other corporate obligations, see note 11 supra, provides slight support for appellants but does not undermine the conclusion we have drawn from the more significant indicia discussed in text.

with debt-equity ratios. However, it is now settled that the trier of fact must weigh the various factors in the light of the entire evidence presented and not give undue weight to any one factor. The courts' refusal to sanction a relatively mechanical test such as the debt-equity ratio, however, has resulted in a great deal of uncertainty for tax advisors and the government, with the inevitable consequence that a substantial amount of litigation has been generated in the debt-equity area.

2. *The Relevance of Evidentiary "Factors"*

In analyzing debt-equity cases under the factors listed in *Slappey Drive Industrial Park,* it is tempting to categorize the cases which involve a given factor showing, for example, that in some cases the factor of subordination of shareholder loans resulted in a finding of equity, but in other cases it did not prevent a finding of debt. The temptation to create such legal shopping lists must be resisted. It is the factors *in relationship* which appear to determine the results in debt-equity cases, even in those cases in which the court may emphasize particular factors. For instance, if a court considers subordination significant, it is generally subordination in relation to the absence of other factors that would demonstrate debt which is determinative, not subordination as such. It is important to recognize that each of the factors considered by the courts contributes in varying degree to the resolution of the classification issue. For example, in Fin Hay Realty Co. v. United States, 398 F.2d 694 (3d Cir.1968), the court listed sixteen factors to be considered in distinguishing debt from equity, but described the factors as "only aids in answering the ultimate question whether the investment, analyzed in terms of its economic reality, constitutes risk capital entirely subject to the fortunes of the corporate venture or represents a strict debtor-creditor relationship. Since there is often an element of risk in a loan, just as there is an element of risk in an equity investment, the conflicting elements do not end at a clear line in all cases * * *."

In Lane v. United States, 742 F.2d 1311 (11th Cir.1984), the court stated: "In order for an advance of funds to be considered a debt rather than equity, the courts have stressed that a reasonable expectation of repayment must exist which does not depend solely on the success of the borrower's business." The taxpayer advanced funds to three failing corporations for demand notes, many of which contained no provision for the payment of interest. The taxpayer testified in the trial court that he expected repayment when the corporations were in a position to retransfer the funds without damage to their ongoing businesses. The court concluded from the taxpayer's testimony that repayment was dependent upon the success of the business. As a consequence the advances constituted equity rather than debt.

On the other hand, Tomlinson v. 1661 Corp., 377 F.2d 291 (5th Cir.1967), held that shareholder advances constituted debt. The shareholders advanced funds to their corporation on a pro-rata basis, with a resulting debt-equity ratio of approximately 4:1. The evidence indicated that the corporation could have borrowed from outside sources but would have had to have paid a higher rate of interest to do so. The shareholder notes were subordinated only to secured mortgage debt. The interest was accrued but unpaid; however, interest was cumulative and all interest had to be paid before dividends could be paid. The proportionality of debt and equity was not conclusive because the debt was freely transferable whereas the stock was not because of shareholder agreements, and thus the proportionality could be destroyed at any time. Even including third party mortgage debt, the debt-equity ratio was only 14.6:1. The court declined to speculate on the business reasons for the nonpayment of interest.

In American Underwriters, Inc. v. Commissioner, T.C. Memo. 1996–548, the taxpayer corporation lent another corporation under control of a common shareholder over $15,000,000 to support cross collateralization agreements and loan guarantees with respect to leveraged speculative securities investment activities in which both corporations were engaged. The advances were recorded on the corporation's books as demand loans, but bore no interest, and were not evidenced by any instruments. Notwithstanding these lack of formalities and an absence of evidence of the borrower's actual net worth or debt-to-equity ratio, the court found the advances to constitute true debt. Among the factors that favored debt classification were the absence of a direct stock ownership interest in the borrower by the lender and the absence of any formal exercise of management control (even though both corporations were controlled and operated by the same individual). The result in this case is somewhat surprising. On similar facts, other decisions have found not only that there was no valid indebtedness, but also have found such loans to constitute a disguised dividend by the "lender" to the common shareholder coupled with a constructive capital contribution from the common shareholder to the "borrower." See page 226.

In Hardman v. United States, 827 F.2d 1409 (9th Cir.1987), a shareholder "sold" property to a controlled corporation in exchange for an assumption of liabilities plus a note for one-third of the corporate profits on its disposition of the property. The distribution of a portion of the sales proceeds to the shareholder was treated as repayment of the note, resulting in long-term capital gain attributable to the shareholder's sale of the property to the corporation. The note was true debt, not equity, because payment of the note was not dependent on the fortunes of the business nor did the note lack a fixed maturity date since repayment was tied to "a fairly certain event—sale of the property."

3. *Standard of Review*

Since debt-equity cases turn on factual issues, the Courts of Appeals generally treat the trial court's conclusion as a finding of fact which under Fed.R.Civ.P. 52(a) can be set aside only if it is clearly erroneous. See, e.g., Charter Wire, Inc. v. United States, 309 F.2d 878 (7th Cir.1962); Adelson v. United States, 737 F.2d 1569 (Fed.Cir.1984); Roth Steel Tube Co. v. Commissioner, 800 F.2d 625 (6th Cir.1986); Hardman v. U.S. 827 F.2d 1409 (9th Cir.1987).

In the Fifth and Eleventh Circuits, however, the ultimate inference from the facts as to whether an obligation constitutes debt or equity is a matter of law, not of fact. See Alterman Foods, Inc. v. United States, 505 F.2d 873 (5th Cir.1974); Lane v. United States, 742 F.2d 1311 (11th Cir.1984); Slappey Drive Industrial Park, footnote 17, at page 140. In the Eighth Circuit, the issue is considered to be one of mixed law and fact. J.S. Biritz Construction Co. v. Commissioner, 387 F.2d 451 (8th Cir.1967).

Consistent with the view that the inquiry is inherently factual, the Internal Revenue Service will not "ordinarily" rule on whether advances to a corporation constitute debt or equity. See, e.g., Rev.Proc. 98–3, § 4.01(30), 1998–1 C.B. 100.

B. ANALYSIS OF PARTICULAR FACTORS

1. *Proportion of Debt to Stockholdings*

When debt and equity obligations are held in the same proportion individual stockholders are, apart from tax considerations, indifferent with respect to whether distributions from the corporation are made in the form of interest or dividends. In the event of cash flow problems which make the payment of the fixed obligations of debt instruments difficult for the corporation, controlling stockholders who hold debt obligations in the same proportion as equity may forego repayment rather than threaten the continued value of their equity investment. In all cases, therefore, it can be said that payment of proportionately held debt is subject to the fortunes of the business. But the pro rata holding of debt and equity is not an absolute barrier to recognition of debt status, even when a sole stockholder is present. Whether proportionately held debt obligations will be paid in a timely fashion depends on other factors such as the existence of adequate equity capital to insure debt repayment or an income stream sufficient to meet payments of interest and principal. Compare Wilshire & Western Sandwiches, Inc. v. Commissioner, 175 F.2d 718 (9th Cir.1949), with Reed v. Commissioner, 242 F.2d 334 (2d Cir.1957). In some cases, the absence of proportional holdings of stock and debt has been considered as a factor favoring debt status. Adelson v. United States, 737 F.2d 1569 (Fed.Cir.1984)(taxpayer advances to clients in which the taxpayer held only a minor equity interest treated as debt; taxpayer was dealing with client companies as an outsider whose dominant motive was not to further an equity interest in the companies).

2. *Thin Capitalization*

A high proportion of debt relative to shareholder equity is an indication that the corporation lacks reserves to pay interest and principal on debt when corporate income is insufficient to meet current payments. In such a case, the debt holders' potential recovery is subject to entrepreneurial risk as repayment is dependent on the success of the venture. Thus a high ratio of debt to equity is a factor favoring equity classification. See John Kelley Co. v. Commissioner, 326 U.S. 521 (1946)(subordinated convertible debentures were true debt because the corporation was not "thinly capitalized").

While generally the decisions mention the debt-equity ratio, they offer little discussion of the rules governing its determination. In *Slappey Drive Industrial Park,* the court looked at the relation of the debt both to the book value of the corporation's assets and to their actual fair market value. In Bauer v. Commissioner, 748 F.2d 1365 (9th Cir.1984), the court held that the debt to equity ratio compares total liabilities to the stockholders' equity which includes both initial paid-in capital plus accumulated earnings. The court reversed the Tax Court's holding that shareholder loans were contributions to capital. The Tax Court had based its holding, in part, on a stipulation by the parties that the corporate debt/equity ratio was 92 to 1, the ratio of liabilities to the shareholders' initial capital contributions. Comparing liabilities with total shareholder equity, determined by including both paid in capital and accumulated earnings, produced debt to equity ratios ranging from 2 to 1 to 8 to 1.

In determining the ratio of debt to equity, courts may consider all of the outstanding indebtedness of the corporation even though it is typically shareholder debt which is being tested for equity equivalence. Thus an outstanding bank loan can have an influence on the "thinness" of the corporation's capital structure. See, e.g., Berkowitz v. United States, 411 F.2d 818 (5th Cir.1969).

A high ratio of debt to equity is not automatically fatal to debt status. In Bradshaw v. United States, 683 F.2d 365 (Ct.Cl.1982), notwithstanding a very high ratio of debt to equity (the corporation's capital consisted of an automobile valued at $4,500), the court classified as debt five notes, each in the face amount of $50,000, given to a sole shareholder of the debtor corporation in exchange for real property transferred to the corporation by the shareholder. The court emphasized the fact that the corporation's cash flow was sufficient to meet its obligations under the notes to pay interest and principal on fixed dates and that the corporation paid principal and interest on the notes when due.

3. *Subordination to Other Creditors*

In P.M. Finance Corp. v. Commissioner, 302 F.2d 786 (3d Cir.1962), the court held that shareholder "loans" were equity by placing heavy reliance on the fact that the loans were subordinated to all "present and future bank loans." Complete subordination, the court noted, "tends to wipe out a most significant characteristic of the creditor-debtor relationship, the right to share with general creditors in the assets in the event of dissolution or liquidation, * * * but it also destroys another basic attribute of creditor status: i.e., the power to demand payment at a fixed maturity date." (790) Subordination, however, is not invariably fatal to debt classification. See Jones v. United States, 659 F.2d 618 (5th Cir.1981)(debt status upheld despite state regulations requiring subordination to insurance corporation's policy holders); Federal Express Corp. v. United States, 645 F.Supp. 1281 (W.D.Tenn.1986)(debt status sustained for obligations subordinate only to senior debt; the challenged obligations were negotiated at arm's length by sophisticated institutional investors and were on a parity with trade debt).

4. *Intent, Business Purpose and Tax Avoidance*

Although courts frequently list the taxpayer's "intent" as a factor in determining whether an obligation constitutes debt or equity, most cases recognize that "intent" is simply a way of stating the conclusion, and examine more objective factors to determine the debt-equity status of the particular obligation. In general, earlier cases in which taxpayer "intent" or "business purpose" appeared to take on an independent status have not been followed. See, e.g., Gooding Amusement Co. v. Commissioner, 236 F.2d 159 (6th Cir.1956); Tomlinson v. 1661 Corp., 377 F.2d 291 (5th Cir.1967). In Estate of Mixon v. United States, 464 F.2d 394 (5th Cir.1972), however, the court sustained the taxpayer's treatment of an interest-free shareholder advance to a bank, as required by bank examiners, as debt under a 13-factor analysis; the court indicated that where the objective signs point in all directions, the trial court was correct in looking to the subjective intent of the parties to decide which direction to follow. (407)

5. *Absence of New Investment*

If a corporation has been in existence for some time, and then issues a dividend in the form of a debt obligation, or, by recapitalization, issues a debt obligation in exchange for previously outstanding stock, the Commissioner has attempted to treat the new obligation as stock on the ground that there is no new investment to permit the obligation to be considered as debt. Compare Sayles Finishing Plants, Inc. v. United States, 399 F.2d 214 (Ct.Cl.1968)(notes issued for stock in a reorganization constituted equity because no new funds were added to the corporation by issuing the debt and the only benefit to the business was the obtaining of the interest deduction) with Monon Railroad v. Commissioner, 55 T.C. 345 (1970)(A)(debentures issued to acquire outstanding shares of stock were valid debt; it was not necessary that new funds be received by the corporation in exchange for the debt where other factors pointed to debt classification).

C. SHAREHOLDER–GUARANTEED LOANS

Suppose that instead of borrowing from a shareholder, the corporation borrows from a commercial lending institution, which agrees to make the loan only upon the condition that the shareholder personally guarantees the corporate obligation. Does such an arrangement escape the debt-equity imbroglio? In Murphy Logging Co. v. United States, 378 F.2d 222 (9th Cir.1967), two partners formed a corporation which purchased logging equipment from the partnership. The corporation borrowed money from a bank to make the acquisition and the shareholders guaranteed the bank note. The Commissioner treated the transaction as if the bank loan had gone directly from the bank to the shareholders, who had then made a contribution to the capital of the corporation in a § 351 transaction.

Payments by the corporation on the bank loan then were treated as constructive dividends to the shareholders (who presumably would also be treated as having made the bank payments, with possible corresponding interest deductions to the shareholders individually). The District Court upheld the Commissioner, 239 F.Supp. 794 (D.Or.1965). The Court of Appeals, however, reversed and held that the debt ran from the bank to the corporation and allowed the corporate interest deduction. Although the shareholders had placed only $1,500 in the corporation and had sold the equipment to the corporation for $238,150, the court included the integrity and reputation of the shareholders as intangible assets to be considered in valuing the equity capital of the corporation. With this factor added, the court concluded that there was no thin capitalization. In addition, the transaction by which the corporation acquired the logging equipment was treated as a sale rather than a § 351 transaction, which permitted the corporation to use a cost basis for the equipment. See also Smyers v. Commissioner, 57 T.C. 189 (1971) (in the absence of thin capitalization, the shareholder guarantee did not convert a loan to equity even though it was "reasonable to assume that these unsecured loans would not have been made without petitioners' guarantee").

A contrary result was reached in Plantation Patterns, Inc. v. Commissioner, 462 F.2d 712 (5th Cir.1972). Mrs. Jemison owned all the shares of stock of the taxpayer corporation, which had been capitalized at $5,000. Exercise of the elements of ownership of the shares, however, was dominated by Mr. Jemison, her husband. The taxpayer corporation acquired the business of another corporation and issued notes to the shareholders of the acquired corporation in a transaction that called for a purchase price of almost $650,000 in excess of the book net worth of the acquired corporation. All but $100,000 of the notes were subordinated to the corporate debt of the taxpayer, but the notes were personally guaranteed by Mr. Jemison. The debt-equity ratio of the taxpayer corporation was 100.5:1. The court held that the notes were in fact those of the guarantor, Mr. Jemison, which he contributed as capital to the corporation; therefore, the interest deduction was disallowed to the taxpayer corporation. Mrs Jemison, the shareholder, correspondingly, received dividends on the note payments. The court based its decision on the facts that the notes were used to purchase capital assets of the taxpayer corporation; the guarantee by Mr. Jemison was essential to the transaction; subordination was present; the complete identity of interest between the shareholder and the guarantor, Mr. Jemison being regarded as the "constructive owner" of his wife's shares; and no value was given to the intangible financial skills of Mr. Jemison in determining the debt-equity ratio. On the last point the court stated: "[W]e conclude that intangible assets such as those claimed for Mr. Jemison have no place in assessing debt-equity ratio unless it can be shown by convincing evidence that the intangible asset has a direct and primary relationship to the well-being of the corporation. Additionally, it is clear to us that the assets sought to be valued must be something more than management skills and normal business contacts. These are expected of management in the direction of any corporation."

The existence of a shareholder guarantee should not be fatal to treating a bank loan as true debt if it can be established that the bank probably would have made the loan in any event, and the guarantee was only additional security for the bank or part of the bank's general policy of requiring shareholder guarantees on loans to closely held corporations.

D. LOANS BETWEEN RELATED CORPORATIONS

Transactions between parent and subsidiary corporations also give rise to debt-equity problems. In Jack Daniel Distillery v. United States, 379 F.2d 569 (Ct.Cl.1967), the taxpayer, a subsidiary, issued its $3.5 million note to its parent corporation to reflect an advance of that amount by the parent corporation. The parent corporation also contributed another $2 million in cash to the capital of the subsidiary. The court held that the subsidiary's note was a valid debt obligation because it was an unconditional obligation to pay regardless of earnings; interest was accrued for both book and tax purposes; the note was subordinated only to specific debts and not to creditors generally; the subsidiary had the ability to, and did in fact, borrow from unrelated banks (the parent having borrowed the $3.5 million contributed to the subsidiary with knowledge on the part of the lenders that the funds were going to be utilized by the subsidiary); further advances to the subsidiary were not necessary and the loan was repaid in full; despite the fact that the note was unsecured, there was a reasonable expectation that the amounts would be repaid; and substantial equity contributions had been made by the parent.

But in National Farmers Union Service Corp. v. United States, 400 F.2d 483 (10th Cir.1968), a parent's advance to a subsidiary was treated as an equity contribution where there was no acceleration clause, the note was unsecured, the funds were used to supply capital, some notes were canceled prior to maturity, the likelihood of repayment was remote, no sinking fund had been established, and a third party would not have made the loan. Although the parent had borrowed the money which was transferred to the subsidiary, the lenders did not know that the funds were going to be placed in the subsidiary, thus distinguishing the case from *Jack Daniel,* supra. On similar grounds, the court in Roth Steel Tube Co. v. Commissioner, 800 F.2d 625 (6th Cir.1986), upheld the Tax Court's ruling that advances to a 62 percent subsidiary, acquired by the taxpayer following a bankruptcy reorganization, were contributions to capital. The appellate court stated that neither the fact that 38 percent of the subsidiary's stock was owned by shareholders who did not make proportionate advances, nor the fact that the advances were used for operating funds, was sufficient justification for rejecting the Tax Court's determination that the advances were equity.

Related problems arise with respect to advances between brother-sister corporations. In Stinnett's Pontiac Service, Inc. v. Commissioner, 730 F.2d 634 (11th Cir.1984), the court denied the taxpayer corporation's bad debt deduction for advances to another corporation owned in part by the taxpayer's 74 percent shareholder. The purported loans lacked a fixed maturity date, no interest payments were made, there was no written evidence of indebtedness for a majority of the loans, repayment was subordinate to other creditors, and the borrower was thinly capitalized. The court held that the advances represented a contribution to capital. The court also held that the advances were taxable dividends to the taxpayer's major shareholder because the shareholder benefited from the advances in the form of an economic improvement in the shareholder's equity interest in the borrower. The court reached the opposite conclusion on similar facts in Mills v. Internal Revenue Service, 840 F.2d 229 (4th Cir.1988). The court was impressed with the group's regular history of repaying intercorporate advances and the testimony of the controlling shareholders that the advances were intended as loans.

E. TRANSMUTATION OF DEBT TO EQUITY

Even if an obligation represents a valid debt obligation at the time of its issue, its character can change to equity as the result of the passage of time or a change in circumstances. For example, in Cuyuna Realty Co. v. United States, 382 F.2d 298 (Ct.Cl.1967), the taxpayer corporation between 1912 and 1914 incurred debt to its parent corporation of over $1.4 million. Interest was accrued but never paid. In 1956 the parent forgave the unpaid accrued interest and principal because the taxpayer had been insolvent since its organization and future repayment was impossible. The Commissioner disallowed the interest deduction to the taxpayer for the years beginning in 1952. The court upheld the Commissioner, concluding that, while the notes were intended to create a valid debt in the 1912–1914 period, they had changed their character to equity. No debtor-creditor relation existed long before 1956 since there was no maturity date, there was thin capitalization, no attempts were made to enforce the creditor's rights, and no outside lender would have made the loans: "A rule that the original intention of the parties should control the character of an instrument for all time would be completely inconsistent with the purpose of the statute. Interest, like an ordinary business expense, is allowed as a deduction from income because it is a cost of producing income. It ceases to be a real cost, if with the passage of time it becomes apparent that the parties had no intention of continuing the debtor-creditor relationship." (301)

In Edwards v. Commissioner, 415 F.2d 578 (10th Cir.1969), the taxpayer acquired a corporation for $75,000, with $5,000 of the purchase price being allocated to acquisition of the stock of the acquired corporation and $70,000 to the acquisition of the corporation's notes in the face amount of $241,904 that had been issued by the acquired corporation to its previous sole shareholder. The acquired corporation proved successful and the notes were repaid out of earnings. The taxpayer treated the amounts received as long-term capital gains under the predecessor to § 1271(a). The Commissioner asserted that the payments constituted dividends. The Commissioner did not contest that the notes were originally valid corporate debt, but argued that they changed to equity in the hands of the taxpayer. The court held that the notes represented debt in the hands of the taxpayer and that the predecessor to § 1271(a) applied. The court found that there was no sham, no thin capitalization, and the purchase by the taxpayer did not convert the notes to equity. Under current law, the notes would have been market discount obligations, and the gain recognized upon retirement would have been taxed as ordinary income under § 1276, discussed at page 180. Thus, the incentive of the Commissioner to challenge the transactions on debt versus equity grounds would be lessened, but not completely eliminated.

Similarly, in Imperial Car Distributors, Inc. v. Commissioner, 427 F.2d 1334 (3d Cir.1970), four investors acquired the stock of the taxpayer corporation from the former owner for $2,000. For an additional $2,000 the investors also acquired notes of the corporation with a face value of $120,000 previously issued to the former owner. New notes were then issued by the corporation pro rata to the investors to replace the former notes. Payments to retire the notes were treated as capital gains by the investors under the predecessor to § 1271(a) and the taxpayer corporation deducted the interest on the notes. The Commissioner conceded that the original notes were valid debt, but urged that the notes became part of the capital of the taxpayer upon their transfer to the investors. The court held that the notes constituted valid debt obligations, reversing a Tax Court determination to the contrary, concluding that where a debt was valid when originally issued, the later transfer did not change its character to equity. Under current law, the new notes would have been original discount obligations, requiring current accrual of interest income by the holders over the term of the notes. See page 168.

F. TAXPAYER EFFORTS TO RECLASSIFY OBLIGATIONS

The classification problem can be presented in reverse, with the taxpayer claiming that an instrument issued as stock is really debt or that an instrument that on its face is a debt instrument really is stock. Section 385(c)(1), enacted in 1992, provides that the characterization by the issuer of an instrument as stock or debt is binding on both the issuer and all of the holders of the instrument (but not on the Commissioner). However, § 385(c)(2) permits a holder of an instrument—but not the issuing corporation—to adopt an inconsistent treatment if the holder discloses the inconsistent treatment on the holder's tax return.

1. *Reclassification of Stock as Debt*

In Lee Telephone Co. v. Commissioner, 260 F.2d 114 (4th Cir.1958), the court rejected the taxpayer's attempt to classify as debt shares of preferred stock issued to finance an expanding telephone business after a public utility commission thought that the debt ratio had grown too large; the shares had a sinking fund but otherwise closely resembled stock. Similarly, in Miele v. Commissioner, 56 T.C. 556 (1971) (A), aff'd by order, 474 F.2d 1338 (3d Cir.1973), a corporation decided to purchase a new barge but needed a guarantee from the United States Maritime Commission on a first mortgage loan in order to make the acquisition. The Maritime Commission required $150,000 of additional capital from private sources before it would guarantee the loan and the corporation issued preferred stock to shareholders in proportion to their common stock holdings to secure the needed funds. Subsequently, the preferred stock was redeemed pro rata, and the taxpayer shareholder treated the preferred stock as debt in order to avoid dividend treatment under § 301. The court held the taxpayers to their classification.

In Bowersock Mills & Power Co. v. Commissioner, 172 F.2d 904 (10th Cir.1949), a closely held corporation issued preferred stock to its bondholders in a recapitalization. The rights of the preferred shareholders were secured by the common stock, which would be transferred to the preferred shareholders upon default. The corporation was permitted to treat the preferred stockholders as creditors of the corporation and deduct the dividends on the preferred stock as interest. Section 385(c) overrules *Bowersock Mills & Power*.

2. *Reclassification of Debt as Equity*

Taxpayers sometimes have obtained a classification of debt instruments different from the formal characterization the parties themselves initially gave to the instruments. For example, in Mercantile Bank & Trust Co. v. United States, 147 F.Supp. 956 (Ct.Cl.1957), a bank, prohibited by state law from issuing preferred stock, issued a "capital note" to the Reconstruction Finance Corporation ("RFC") which closely resembled the usual preferred stock instrument taken by the RFC. The court, with one dissent, permitted the bank to claim that the instrument was stock for excess profits tax purposes. But in Zilkha & Sons, Inc. v. Commissioner, 52 T.C. 607 (1969) (A), where shareholders were urging that hybrid securities constituted preferred stock (the corporation having no earnings and profits, so that all payments with respect to the securities would have constituted nontaxable distributions), the court upheld the Commissioner's determination that the securities constituted debt resulting in taxation of payments received by the security holders as interest. See also J.A. Maurer, Inc. v. Commissioner, 30 T.C. 1273 (1958) (A)(corporation successfully asserted that advances by a shareholder in the form of debt constituted equity capital, so that no cancellation of indebtedness income resulted on the settlement of the advances for less than their face amount); Joseph Lupowitz Sons, Inc. v. Commissioner, 497 F.2d 862 (3d Cir.1974)(taxpayer successfully argued that open account advances were contributions to capital and not loans thus avoiding imputation of interest income).

G. CONVERTIBLE OBLIGATIONS, HYBRID SECURITIES, AND OTHER FINANCIAL INSTRUMENTS

1. *Convertible Obligations*

With debt instruments that are convertible into corporate stock, an investor may achieve both the certainty of a fixed payment of principal and interest, and the potential to share in economic growth if the corporation is successful. From the point of view of the corporation, hybrid securities are a way to attract investors interested in long term appreciation while providing deductible interest payments to the issuer. Convertibility is listed in § 385 as one of the facts and circumstances to be considered in determining whether a financial instrument is debt or equity.

Rev.Rul. 83–98, 1983–2 C.B. 40, considered a hybrid instrument referred to as an "adjustable rate convertible note" (ARCN). Under the facts of the ruling, X Corporation, with a single class of common stock outstanding, issued $10 million of ARCNs. An ARCN could be purchased for $1,000 of cash or 50 shares of X stock, which at the time of the offering was worth $1,000. At the option of the holder, each ARCN was convertible into 50 shares of stock. Otherwise, the ARCN would pay $600 at the end of the 20 year term of the note. The ARCN was callable for $600 by X at any time after the first two years. X was required to pay annual interest on each ARCN equal to the dividends paid on 50 shares of X stock, plus 2 percent of the issue price ($20). The interest was not to be less than $60 nor more than $175 in any year. In order to qualify the instrument as debt under the then § 385 regulations, the ARCN was designed so that the present value of its debt features was worth more than one-half of its $1,000 issue price. The Internal Revenue Service held that the ARCNs were equity. The Service found that the ARCNs were structured so that under most likely eventualities they would be converted into common stock and therefore did not represent a promise to pay a sum certain. The Service also noted that the guaranteed annual interest of $60 per $1,000 of capital was unreasonably low in comparison to the return available on nonconvertible, noncontingent instruments; based on the level of dividends on X common stock, more than 65 percent of the potential annual yield on the instruments was discretionary; and the instruments were subordinate to the claims of general creditors.

In Rev.Rul. 85–119, 1985–2 C.B. 60, the Internal Revenue Service allowed interest deductions for payments with respect to publicly traded subordinated notes with a mandatory conversion feature adopted to comply with banking regulations. At maturity the notes were convertible into stock of the issuing corporation with a value at the time of conversion equal to the principal of the notes. However, if a note holder elected not to accept stock, the issuer was required to undertake a secondary stock offering on the open market and deliver cash to the note holder in an amount equal to the note principal. The notes required quarterly interest payments in an amount that varied with the market rate payable on comparable subordinated instruments. Debt treatment was supported by the facts that the notes were publicly held and not in proportion to equity ownership; interest was payable without regard to earnings; the notes had a fixed maturity at the end of a limited period of time; the issuer was not thinly capitalized; note holders had no vote or participation in management; and, as distinguished from Rev.Rul. 83–98 supra, the amount of stock to be issued in exchange for the notes at maturity was based on the face amount of the notes rather than the value of stock. These debt factors outweighed the fact that the notes were subordinated to other creditors, but not equity interests, and were in form payable only in the issuer's stock.

Totally apart from the traditional debt versus equity classification standards, pursuant to § 163(*l*), interest payments are not deductible if conversion into equity is required by the terms of the debt obligation, or if the issuer or a related person has the option to make payments of a substantial portion of interest or principal in the form of equity interests in the issuer or a related person. Interest or principal payable, at the option of the holder, in equity interests in the issuing corporation or a related party will be subject to § 163(*l*) if there is a "substantial certainty" that the option will be exercised.

2. *Bifurcation of Debt and Equity Features*

(a) *Court Decisions*

In two cases, the courts bifurcated the debt and equity components of a single financial instrument. In Helvering v. Richmond, F. & P. R.R. Co., 90 F.2d 971 (4th Cir.1937), the corporation was allowed an interest deduction for guaranteed 7 percent dividends paid on preferred stock, but payments in excess of the guarantee were treated as dividends, a return on equity. The preferred stock provided for participation in corporate earnings above the 7 percent guaranteed dividends and possessed full voting rights. The guaranteed dividends were a first lien on corporate assets and took precedence over all creditors, including general creditors.

In Farley Realty Corp. v. Commissioner, 279 F.2d 701 (2d Cir.1960), the corporation borrowed money from a nonshareholder to acquire a building. The obligation required fixed payments of interest and had a fixed maturity date. In addition, the obligation holder was entitled to 50 percent of the appreciation on sale of the building, whether this event occurred before or after the maturity date. The Commissioner allowed the corporation to deduct fixed interest payments on the loan but disallowed any deduction for payment in settlement of the creditor's interest in appreciation.

In contrast, in Rev.Rul. 83–51, 1983–1 C.B. 48, the Internal Revenue Service held that contingent interest in the form of shared appreciation paid by the borrower to the mortgagee on a home residence loan was deductible interest. The loans provided for a fixed interest rate plus 40 percent of the appreciation on sale of the residence or at the end of the 10 year term of the loan. The Ruling described the interest as ascertainable because it was dependent on fixed events. The Ruling expressly provides that it is not applicable in a commercial context.

(b) *Bifurcation by Statute*

(i) *Section 385*

Section 385(a) authorizes regulations classifying obligations as debt in part and equity in part. The legislative history indicates that "such treatment may be appropriate in circumstances where a debt instrument provides for payments that are dependent to a significant extent (whether in whole or in part) on corporate performance, whether through equity kickers, contingent interest, significant deferral of payment, subordination, or an interest rate sufficiently high to suggest a significant risk of default." H.Rep. No. 101–247, 101st Cong., 1st Sess. 1235–1236 (1989). No regulations under this provision have been proposed.

(ii) *Excess Interest Paid To Related Tax Exempt Persons*

Another example of a sort of bifurcation related to thin capitalization concepts is found in § 163(j). Under that section, "excess" interest paid to related parties who are tax-exempt may not be deducted currently by the paying corporation if the corporation has a debt-equity ratio in excess of 1.5 to 1. The provision is applicable to interest paid to more than 50 percent shareholders who are domestic tax-exempt organizations or foreign persons who are not subject to United States tax on interest payments. "Excess" interest is defined as interest in excess of 50 percent of the corporation's adjusted taxable income. Excess interest can be carried forward indefinitely and deducted in subsequent years to the extent the 50 percentage threshold is not met in those years. In addition, the 50 percent limitation itself can be carried forward for three years.

The Congressional concern here was that the corporation's earnings were being "stripped" out in the form of deductible interest payments but not being taxed in the hands of the tax exempt recipients. In effect, the portion of the interest which is disallowed is included in the corporate tax base in the same way as earnings used to pay dividends.

H. PLANNING CONSIDERATIONS

In view of the number of factors considered by the courts in resolving debt-equity cases and the unpredictable weight given to any particular factor, the tax advisor faces a difficult problem in advising clients as to the proper mix of debt and equity in determining the capital structure of a corporation. In some cases, the client simply may wish to avoid any problem and take his entire investment in the corporation in the form of equity interests. Where other corporate planning considerations—or the more adventurous nature of the client—indicate the use of debt, the tax planning problems are more difficult.

Some of the various factors in the debt-equity equation are clearly within the control of the taxpayer. Thus, proper attention to the form of the debt obligation should create no problem. But how, for example, can the tax advisor establish that outside lenders would have made a loan, a factor which many of the cases consider significant? Here it would be important at the outset to determine through an analysis of the corporation's projected cash flow and operating capital requirements that a bank would have considered a loan under these circumstances and perhaps some documentation from a bank that it would have made such a loan. Other factors may be more difficult to control. For example, where shareholder debt is to be combined with some outside financing, a bank may insist on subordination of the shareholder debt and this factor cannot be "planned around".

Once the formalities indicating a debtor-creditor relationship between the corporation and its shareholders are established, it is important that the formalities be followed. For example, interest and principal should in fact be paid according to the terms of the instrument. But here the planning considerations become more complicated. While payment of principal may be helpful in establishing the debt character of the obligation, it also exposes the shareholder to the risk of dividend taxation should the tax advisor have "guessed wrong" on the debt-equity question. Would it be better to provide in the original instrument that no principal payments will be made for a period of time, with larger payments to be made later in the term of the note? If such a course is taken, however, the taxpayer loses the argument that principal payments were in fact made, a factor sometimes stressed by the courts. On the other hand, even if principal payments are postponed, complete assurance is still not possible. Even though the corporation has been audited and the loans accepted as debt for purposes of the interest deduction, the Service could still challenge the status of the obligation in subsequent years when principal payments are made. In the end, there is no sure escape from the difficult decisions which the current status of the tax law on debt and equity require.

B. DEDUCTIONS FOR LOSS OF INVESTMENT IN A CORPORATION

INTERNAL REVENUE CODE: Sections 165(g); 166(a); (b), (d), (e); 1244; 1271(a)(1).

REGULATIONS: Sections 1.166–5, –9; 1.1244–1(a), (c), (d), –2(a)–(b).

The capital versus ordinary distinction is important to both individual and corporate taxpayers who suffer losses as well as to individuals who realize gains. Deduction of corporate capital losses is limited to the taxpayer's capital gains. I.R.C. § 1211(a). Capital loss deductions of noncorporate taxpayers are limited to the taxpayer's capital gains plus $3,000 annually. I.R.C. § 1211(b).

Section 165(g) in general treats a loss on worthless "*securities*" as a capital loss. In contrast, § 166(a) provides ordinary loss treatment on debts not represented by securities. Section 166(d), however, requires short-term capital loss treatment for *nonbusiness bad debt* held by a noncorporate taxpayer. For purposes of § 165(g), "securities" is defined to include stock, rights to acquire stock, and any bond, debenture, note, or other evidence of indebtedness issued by a corporation (or a governmental entity) which is in registered form or has interest coupons attached. I.R.C. § 165(g)(2). An obligation is in registered form if the rights to principal and stated interest are transferable through a book entry system maintained by the issuer. See, e.g., Treas. Reg. § 5f.103–1(c). Section 163(f) disallows an interest deduction with respect to obligations issued by a person other than an individual which are offered to the public unless the obligation is in registered form.[2] If a "registration required obligation" is not issued in

2. There is an exception for obligations which are not held by a United States person on which interest is payable only outside of the United States, so-called "Eurodollar" obligations. I.R.C. § 163(f)(2)(B).

registered form, § 165(j) further disallows a deduction for any loss sustained by the holder.

Section 1244 allows a stockholder to treat a loss on certain small business stock, called § 1244 stock, as an ordinary loss rather than a capital loss, whether the loss is attributable to worthlessness or realized upon a sale of the stock. This ordinary loss treatment is limited to $50,000 per year, or $100,000 on a joint return. The ordinary loss treatment is available only to the individual (or individuals who are members of a partnership) to whom the stock was issued.

Under § 165(g)(3), the corporate holder of a worthless security of an "affiliated corporation" is entitled to ordinary loss treatment. A corporation is an affiliated corporation for this purpose if the corporate security holder directly owns 80 percent of the voting power of all classes of stock entitled to vote and 80 percent of the stock of each class of nonvoting stock. In addition, the affiliated corporation must have derived 90 percent of its aggregate gross receipts for all taxable years from sources other than passive investments such as rents, royalties, dividends and interest. Treas. Reg. § 1.165–5(d)(2)(iii) provides that the term gross receipts includes all corporate receipts without reduction for the cost of goods sold, except that gross receipts from the sale or exchange of stock or securities are taken into account only to the extent of the gains from such sales.

Section 1271(a)(1) provides that amounts received on the retirement of any debt instrument issued by a corporation are considered to have been received in an exchange, thus providing the exchange element prerequisite for capital gain or loss treatment. The provision does not independently characterize gain or loss. Under § 1271(a), gain or loss on retirement of a debt instrument that is a capital asset in the hands of the debt-holder will be treated as gain or loss on the exchange of the capital asset resulting in capital gain or loss treatment; gain or loss on retirement of a debt obligation that is not a capital asset is ordinary. A debt is "retired" for this purpose even if the debt is settled for less than its full amount. McClain v. Commissioner, 311 U.S. 527 (1941). Section 1272, however, requires current inclusion as ordinary income of original discount attributable to the bond; and § 1276 requires ordinary income treatment of any market discount realized upon retirement of a corporate bond. See Section 2. of this Chapter.

As a result of these provisions, the following is the general pattern of loss treatment for *individuals* on the worthlessness of their investments in corporations:

1. Stocks, bonds, and other securities generally result in capital losses, allowable in full but only against capital gains plus $3,000 of ordinary income, with an unlimited carryover of excess losses.

2. Nonbusiness bad debts not represented by "securities", i.e., advances and notes not qualifying under § 165(g)(2)(C), result in short-term capital losses, also allowable in full but only against capital gains (and offset first against short-term gains) and $3,000 of ordinary income with an unlimited carryover of excess losses.

3. Business bad debts not represented by "securities" (as defined in § 165(g)(2)(C)), i.e., advances related to a trade or business of the investor, result in ordinary losses under § 166(a), allowable in full against ordinary income or capital gain and are included in the net operating loss deduction.

4. Section 1244 small business stock losses and § 1242 small business investment company stock losses result in ordinary losses, allowable in full against ordinary income or capital gain and are included in the net operating loss deduction.

The following is the general pattern of loss treatment for *corporations* when their investments in other corporations become worthless:

1. Stocks, bonds, and other securities (except those in certain subsidiaries) result in long-term capital losses, allowable in full but only against capital gains with a three year carryback and a five year carryforward.

2. Bad debts not represented by "securities," i.e., advances and notes not described in § 165(g)(2)(C), result in ordinary losses, allowable in full against ordinary income or capital gain and includable in the net operating loss deduction.

3. Stocks or securities in affiliated (80 percent owned) operating subsidiaries result in ordinary losses (under § 165(g)(3)), allowable in full against ordinary income or capital gain and includable in the net operating loss deduction. (If the stock is not worthless, then on liquidation of the subsidiary no loss is allowed on the stock under § 332 but the subsidiary's asset bases and its net operating losses are carried over to the parent.)

4. Certain corporations, such as small business investment companies and banks, have special rules providing ordinary losses in some situations.

Thus, classification of a loss as a bad debt for a corporation, or a business bad debt for an individual, remains important to obtain ordinary loss treatment. Deduction of a capital loss on an equity investment or a loss on a nonbusiness bad debt is limited by § 1211.

ILLUSTRATIVE MATERIAL

A. DEBT–EQUITY ASPECTS

The initial question to be answered in considering the loss character of shareholder advances to a corporation not represented by a security is whether the corporate obligation involved is classified as debt or equity. The rules of § 166 are applicable only if a true debt is created. If the advances are found to constitute a contribution to capital, the capital loss limitations of § 165(g) are generally applicable and the issue of business versus nonbusiness bad debt is not reached. The characterization of an advance as debt or equity for purposes of § 166 requires the same analysis used to determine whether payments with respect to an obligation are dividends or deductible interest, discussed in Section 1.A of this Chapter. Compare Thompson v. Commissioner, 73 T.C. 878 (1980)(A)(advances from shareholders evidenced by written demand notes treated as contributions to capital; small amount of initial capital compared to amounts claimed as debt indicated that the corporation was undercapitalized; no evidence that the holders had ever demanded payment; advances were proportionate to stockholdings; no evidence that the stockholders contemplated a demand for repayment); Recklitis v. Commissioner, 91 T.C. 874 (1988)(cash advances to controlled corporation held to be contributions to capital; the advances were interest free, contained no specific repayment terms, and were not evidenced by a written agreement) with Adelson v. United States, 737 F.2d 1569 (Fed.Cir.1984)(advances to client companies in which taxpayer held only minor equity interests held to be debt).

B. BUSINESS VERSUS NONBUSINESS BAD DEBT

If the advance qualifies as a debt, and hence is not a contribution to capital, and the debt is not evidenced by a security, the next questions are whether the noncorporate debtor-investor is engaged in a trade or business and whether the taxpayer has established the necessary degree of connection between the debt and the business to qualify the debt as a business bad debt. If these two tests are met, the loss falls under §§ 166(a) and (b) as a business bad debt and avoids the limitation of § 166(d).

1. *Protection of Employment Versus Protection of Investment.*

Most frequently, the question of whether a debt is a business bad debt or a nonbusiness bad debt arises when a shareholder-employee makes a loan to the corporation. Employment by the corporation clearly constitutes a trade or business, so the crucial inquiry is whether the loan was "proximate" to the taxpayer's activity as an employee or the taxpayer's activity as a shareholder. See Treas. Reg. § 1.166–5. The seminal case on this issue is United States v. Generes, 405 U.S. 93 (1972).

In *Generes*, the Supreme Court held that a debt qualifies as a business bad debt only if the taxpayer's "dominant" motivation was preservation of his business, i.e., employment rather than preservation of the value of his equity investment in the corporation. A "significant" business motivation, if not dominant, is not sufficient. The taxpayer in *Generes* lent several hundred thousand dollars to a corporation in which he owned 44 percent of the stock and from which he earned an annual salary of approximately $12,000 as a part-time employee. (He was a full time employee of a bank at a salary of $19,000.) He had invested approximately $39,000 in stock of the corporation. The Supreme Court held that it was unreasonable to think that the taxpayer's dominant motive was preservation of his salary, rather than his investment.

As one factor in the determination, the *Generes* opinion stressed the relation between the taxpayer's after-tax salary—$7,000 in that case—and the amount of his investment. In Adelson v. United States, 737 F.2d 1569 (Fed.Cir.1984), the court concluded that the dominant motive test of *Generes* required the trial court to compare the potential risk and reward of the taxpayer's equity interest in client companies to which the taxpayer advanced funds with the taxpayer's interest in his salary as a financial consultant. On remand, the Claims Court found that the taxpayer's dominant motive was business, but the Court of Appeals again remanded the case to the Claims Court for specific findings comparing the potential profits that might have inured to the taxpayer's business interest with the potential profits from the taxpayer's equity interests. The court stressed, however, that determination of dominant motive does not necessarily depend upon a mathematical analysis of relative benefits. Adelson v. United States, 782 F.2d 1010 (Fed.Cir.1986). On remand, after reevaluating the record, the Claims Court determined that the taxpayer established that advances to three corporations were business debts, but did not prove that loans to three other corporations had a dominant business motive. Adelson v. United States, 12 Cl.Ct. 231 (1987). The Claims Court based its determinations on a specific comparison of the taxpayer's potential fee income with the potential return on the taxpayer's equity investment in each corporation.

In Bowers v. Commissioner, 716 F.2d 1047 (4th Cir.1983), the taxpayer advanced funds to a major client of the taxpayer's real estate brokerage firm. The taxpayer's corporation derived commission income from transactions undertaken by the debtor corporation and a substantial part of the commission income was paid to the taxpayer as an employee. Reversing the Tax Court, the Court of Appeals allowed the taxpayer to claim a business bad debt deduction when the taxpayer's claim for repayment of the advances became worthless. The court concluded that the taxpayer's dominant motive in making the advances was to protect the income of his controlled corporation and thereby the taxpayer's own enhanced employment income. Thus, the debt was a business bad debt. On somewhat similar facts, however, business bad debt treatment was denied in Tennessee Securities, Inc. v. Commissioner, 674 F.2d 570 (6th Cir.1982). The taxpayers in *Tennessee Securities* were the principal shareholders of a stock brokerage corporation. The taxpayers individually guaranteed loans to an unrelated corporation which they hoped would undertake a public stock offering utilizing the taxpayer's brokerage corporation as the underwriter. When the debtor corporation declared bankruptcy, the taxpayers caused their brokerage corporation to make payments in satisfaction of the taxpayers' guarantees. The court upheld the Commissioner's determination that the taxpayers recognized ordinary income when their corporation satisfied the taxpayers' obligation under their guarantees. In addition, the court held that since the taxpayers' guarantees were given to enhance their investment in their brokerage corporation, their loss on payment of the guarantees was a nonbusiness bad debt.

The court in Litwin v. United States, 983 F.2d 997 (10th Cir.1993), allowed bad debt deductions for advances and payments on guarantees with respect to the taxpayer's closely held corporation. The court held that the taxpayer principally formed the corporation to earn a salary, be employed, and remain useful to society. The fact that salary payments to the taxpayer had been deferred for the full three year existence of the corporation did not affect the court's holding. The court was satisfied with evidence that the taxpayer had intended to draw his salary in the future.

In Estate of Mann, 731 F.2d 267 (5th Cir.1984), the taxpayer established his dominant business motive under the *Generes* standard and was allowed a business bad debt deduction for advances to his brother's corporation in which the taxpayer had only a negligible stock interest. The taxpayer had earned substantial commissions from his brother's corporation which had utilized the taxpayer as a broker in several corporate acquisitions. The court upheld the Tax Court's findings that the taxpayer's advances were motivated by the taxpayer's interest in protecting his brokerage commissions.

2. *Is the Taxpayer Engaged in a "Trade or Business"—The Promoter Cases*

In Whipple v. Commissioner, 373 U.S. 193 (1963), the Supreme Court considered whether an investor was engaged in a trade or business. The court denied a business bad debt deduction for advances made by the taxpayer to a company which he had formed and to which he had leased property he owned:

"Devoting one's time and energies to the affairs of a corporation is not of itself, and without more, a trade or business of the person so engaged. Though such activities may produce income, profit or gain in the form of dividends or enhancement in the value of an investment, this return is distinctive to the process of investing and is generated by the successful operation of the corporation's business as distinguished from the trade or business of the taxpayer himself. When the only return is that of an investor, the taxpayer has not satisfied his burden of demonstrating that he is engaged in a trade or business since investing is not a trade or business and the return to the taxpayer, though substantially the product of his services, legally arises not from his own trade or business but from that of the corporation. Even if the taxpayer demonstrates an independent trade or business of his own, care must be taken to distinguish bad debt losses arising from his own business and those actually arising from activities peculiar to an investor concerned with, and participating in, the conduct of the corporate business.

"If full-time service to one corporation does not alone amount to a trade or business, which it does not, it is difficult to understand how the same service to many corporations would suffice. To be sure, the presence of more than one corporation might lend support to a finding that the taxpayer was engaged in a regular course of promoting corporations for a fee or commission * * * or for a profit on their sale * * *, but in such cases there is compensation other than the normal investor's return, income received directly for his own services rather than indirectly through the corporate enterprise * * *. On the other hand, since the Tax Court found, and the petitioner does not dispute, that there was no intention here of developing the corporations as going businesses for sale to customers in the ordinary course, the case before us inexorably rests upon the claim that one who actively engages in serving his own corporations for the purpose of creating future income though those enterprises is in a trade or business. That argument is untenable * * *." (202–203)

Despite the suggestion in *Whipple* that promotional services provided to a number of corporations might constitute a trade or business, subsequent cases have in general refused to find a trade or business in such situations. See, e.g., Townshend v. United States, 384 F.2d 1008 (Ct.Cl. 1967) (over a 20–year period the taxpayer had investigated a number of business opportunities and had organized five corporations; although he was considered a "promoter" for securities law purposes, the court refused to allow a business bad debt deduction for advances made by the taxpayer; there was no showing that fees or commissions from promotional activities were received and the taxpayer realized no profits from a quick turnover of the investments). A few cases have allowed a business bad debt deduction, however. See Elliott v. United States, 268 F.Supp. 521 (D.Or.1967) (taxpayer's advances to a wholly-owned corporation qualified for business bad debt treatment on a finding that he was in the business of seeking out business opportunities which he could successfully promote or finance; in a 12–year period the taxpayer made five loans and four investments); In re Farrington, 111 B.R. 342 (Bkrtcy.N.D.Okl.1990), aff'd 91–1 U.S.T.C. ¶ 50,115 (N.D. Okla. 1991) (advances from 49 percent shareholder to corporation were treated as business bad debts because taxpayer was in the business of "promoting, organizing and financing businesses for resale;" over 12 year period, he organized, purchased, and sold eleven separate businesses).

3. *Shareholder Guarantee of Corporate Debts*

In Putnam v. Commissioner, 352 U.S. 82 (1956), the Supreme Court held that payments by a guarantor because of the default of the primary obligor are subject to the limitations of § 166 and are thus deductible only as capital losses unless the obligation can qualify as a business bad debt: "The familiar rule is that, *instanter* upon the payment by the guarantor of the debt, the debtor's obligation to the creditor becomes an obligation to the guarantor, not a new debt, but by subrogation, the result of the shift of the original debt from the creditor to the guarantor who steps into the creditor's shoes. Thus, the loss sustained by the guarantor unable to recover from the debtor is by its very nature a loss from the worthlessness of a debt." (85)

Some cases decided soon after *Putnam* did not apply the holding in that case if the payment in connection with the guarantee did not result in a right to subrogation under state law, see, e.g., Rietzke v. Commissioner, 40 T.C. 443 (1963), but the weight of authority held that § 166 applied to payments on guarantees regardless of whether a state law right of subrogation exists, see, e.g., Stratmore v. United States, 420 F.2d 461 (3d Cir. 1970). The legislative history of the 1976 amendments to § 166 explains that one of the purposes of those changes was to eliminate this distinction; § 166 applies whether or not the guarantor has a right of subrogation. Thus, Treas. Reg. § 1.166–9 draws no such distinction. The only effect of a right of subrogation is to affect the timing of the guarantor's deduction. See Staff of the Joint Committee on Taxation, General Explanation of the Tax Reform Act of 1976, pp. 156–157 (Comm. Print 1976). See also Black Gold Energy Corporation v. Commissioner, 99 T.C. 482 (1992), aff'd by order, 33 F.3d 62 (10th Cir. 1994), in which the Tax Court held that only an actual payment made pursuant to a guarantee can give rise to a deduction under § 166; the accrual basis taxpayer was not allowed a bad debt deduction in the year all events fixed the amount of the liability, nor was the taxpayer allowed to claim a bad debt deduction for the amount of a note given to the creditor as a result of the guarantee.

Because the guarantor's deduction is a bad debt deduction, it may be claimed only upon the worthlessness of the guarantor's right of subrogation against the primary obligor. Thus, in Intergraph Corp. v. Commissioner, 106 T.C. 312 (1996), aff'd by order, 121 F.3d 723 (11th Cir.1997), the taxpayer's deduction for paying a guarantee of its Japanese subsidiary's debt was denied because the subrogation right was not worthless. Even though the corporate primary obligor was insolvent at the time the guarantee was satisfied, the subsidiary continued to conduct business as a going concern.

The *Putnam* decision does not itself insure that payments made by a stockholder in satisfaction of a guarantee of corporate debt will be deductible as a nonbusiness bad debt under § 166. If a stockholder's guarantee of a loan from an outside lender is found to be a substitute for the infusion of additional equity capital, the stockholder's payment under the guarantee will be treated as a capital contribution. See Lane v. United States, 742 F.2d 1311 (11th Cir.1984)(applying the 13–factor test of *Slappey Drive Industrial Park* to distinguish debt from equity, the court concluded that the stockholder's intent at the time the guarantees were extended was to use the guarantees as short-term substitutes for more capital stock; the stockholder's payment was treated as a contribution to capital); Casco Bank & Trust Co. v. United States, 544 F.2d 528 (1st Cir.1976) (stockholder advances to corporation in order to avoid default on bonds guaranteed by the stockholder were held to be equity contributions; the stockholder's deduction of a nonbusiness bad debt was not allowed because at the time of the stockholder advances, there was little reasonable expectation that the stockholder would be repaid). In such a case the shareholder is allowed a bad debt deduction only when the shareholder's stock becomes worthless, not at the time the loan guarantee is satisfied. The amount of the § 165 loss deduction for worthless stock is augmented by the amount of the payment, which is added to the basis of the stock at the time the guarantee is satisfied.

Treas. Reg. § 1.166–9(a) and (b) expressly provides that § 166 and not § 163 applies to all payments made with respect to guarantees, including interest. See Brooks v. Commissioner, T.C. Memo. 1990–259, n.6.

C. ORDINARY LOSS ON STOCK

1. *Section 1244 Stock*

Section 1244 allows a stockholder to treat losses recognized from the sale or worthlessness of stock in certain small corporations, called § 1244 stock, as an ordinary loss rather than a capital loss. The loss is also available in computing the stockholder's net operating loss deduction. This ordinary loss treatment is limited to $50,000 per year, or $100,000 on a joint return. Ordinary loss treatment under § 1244 is available only to the individual (not including a trust) or partnership to whom the stock was issued, and in the case of a partnership the loss may be passed through to the individual partners with the dollar limitations applying at the partner level.

Section 1244 stock is defined essentially as stock of a "small business corporation." The stock must be issued for money or other property, other than stocks or securities and, under Treas. Reg. § 1.1244(c)–1(f), other than for services. It is important that stock actually be issued in exchange for each separate contribution to the corporation. See Pierce v. Commissioner, T.C. Memo. 1989–647(§ 1244 does not apply to the portion of basis of § 1244 stock attributable to additional capital contributions to corporation made after issuance of stock, even though § 1244 would have applied if additional shares had been issued in exchange for the additional contributions). In Adams v. Commissioner, 74 T.C. 4 (1980), § 1244 stock issued to a third party was reacquired by the corporation and then reissued to the taxpayer. Ordinary loss treatment was not allowed to the taxpayer when the stock became worthless. The taxpayer failed to demonstrate that the stock purchase price paid by the taxpayer was anything more than a substitution for capital paid out by the corporation on reacquisition of stock from the first holder. There was no net flow of funds into the corporation.

A corporation is a "small business corporation" if, at the time of the issuance of the stock for which an ordinary loss is claimed, the aggregate amount of equity capital received by the corporation does not exceed $1 million. If a qualified corporation issues common stock in excess of $1 million, Treas. Reg. § 1.1244(c)–2(b)(2) provides for designation of shares which were issued before the limit was exceeded as "§ 1244 stock."

If a corporation is a small business corporation when the stock was issued, it may lose that status thereafter without disqualifying the stock previously issued. The number of shareholders or the existence of several classes of stock is not material. In addition to being a small business corporation, however, the corporation also must have derived more than 50 percent of its gross receipts from operating income for a period up to five years prior to the loss on the stock, unless its deductions exceed its gross income. I.R.C. § 1244(c)(1)(C) and (2)(C). Treas. Reg. § 1.1244(c)–1(e)(2) provides that, even if deductions exceed gross income, ordinary loss treatment will be denied if the corporation is not "largely an operating company". The validity of the regulations was upheld and ordinary loss treatment denied in Davenport v. Commissioner, 70 T.C. 922 (1978), in which the corporation derived more than 50 percent of its aggregate gross receipts from interest during the five years preceding the loss, but during those years its deductions exceeded gross income; seven dissenters would have held for the taxpayer on the basis that the corporation was a small loan company and hence was an "operating company" even though its income was interest income. Special provisions regarding § 1244 stock cover stock dividends, recapitalizations, and reorganizations and disallow any loss attributable to property with a basis in excess of the value of property contributed to the corporation in exchange for § 1244 stock.

Since the benefits of § 1244 do not extend to debt, the provision creates an advantage for equity capital, which must be weighed against the present tax advantages accorded to debt obligations.

Taxpayer attempts to avoid the limitations of § 166 by having their insolvent corporate debtors issue § 1244 stock on which an ordinary loss was then claimed have been unsuccessful. See, e.g., Hollenbeck v. Commissioner, 50 T.C. 740 (1968), aff'd, 422 F.2d 2 (9th Cir.1970) (stock received in exchange for release of purported debt obligation did not qualify because the "debt" was found to be equity). In addition, notes issued in exchange for § 1244 stock do not receive ordinary loss treatment. Benak v. Commissioner, 77 T.C. 1213 (1981) (worthless note issued on redemption of § 1244 resulted in non-business bad debt treatment).

2. *Small Business Investment Company Stock*

The Small Business Investment Act of 1958 authorized the formation of small business investment companies organized to provide equity capital to small businesses through the purchase of their convertible debentures. These small business investment companies are private corporations with a paid-in capital and surplus of at least $300,000. The Small Business Administration is authorized to lend such a company up to $150,000 through the purchase of the latter's subordinated debentures. Under § 1242, if a stockholder investing in the stock of a small business investment company suffers a loss on the stock, the loss is treated as an ordinary loss and may be utilized in a net operating loss deduction. Also, under § 1243, if the small business investment company itself suffers a loss on stock acquired by it pursuant to the conversion privilege on convertible debentures, the loss is treated as ordinary.

D. LOSS ON SURRENDER OF STOCK VERSUS CONTRIBUTION TO CAPITAL

In Commissioner v. Fink, 483 U.S. 89 (1987), the Supreme Court held that controlling stockholders cannot recognize a loss on the surrender of a portion of their stock to the corporation. The taxpayers, husband and wife, owned 72.5 percent of the common stock of the corporation. They surrendered some of their shares, reducing their ownership interest to 68.5 percent in order to make the corporation's capital structure more attractive to outside investors. The taxpayers claimed an ordinary loss under § 165 to the extent of the basis in their surrendered shares. The Sixth Circuit allowed the taxpayers' loss deduction by treating each share of stock as a separate investment, adopting a "fragmented" view of stock ownership under which gain or loss is recognized separately on the sale or other disposition of each share of stock. Fink v. Commissioner, 789 F.2d 427, 431–432 (6th Cir.1986). The Supreme Court, however, treated the controlling stockholders' stock as a unitary investment:

"A shareholder who surrenders a portion of his shares to the corporation has parted with an asset, but that alone does not entitle him to an immediate deduction. Indeed, if the shareholder owns less than 100 percent of the corporation's shares, any non pro rata contribution to the corporation's capital will reduce the net worth of the contributing shareholder. A shareholder who surrenders stock thus is similar to one who forgives or surrenders a debt owed to him by the corporation; the latter gives up interest, principal, and also potential voting power in the event of insolvency or bankruptcy. But * * * such forgiveness of corporate debt is treated as a contribution to capital rather than a current deduction. * * * The Finks' voluntary surrender of shares, like a shareholder's voluntary forgiveness of debt owed by the corporation, closely resembles an investment or contribution to capital * * *." (96–97)

For cases prior to *Fink* that reached the same result, see Frantz v. Commissioner, 784 F.2d 119 (2d Cir.1986) (controlling stockholder's voluntary surrender of preferred stock for the purpose of enhancing the value of retained common stock treated as a contribution to capital; because the overall change in the taxpayer's retained interest in the company was minuscule compared to the interest surrendered, there was no justification for treating the change in value as a capital loss, much less as an ordinary one); Schleppy v. Commissioner, 601 F.2d 196 (5th Cir.1979) (non pro rata surrender of stock to improve financial condition of the corporation did not result in an immediate ordinary loss); Tilford v. Commissioner, 705 F.2d 828 (6th Cir.1983) (stockholder denied a capital loss deduction on the transfer of stock to corporate employees; the court upheld Treas. Reg. § 1.83–6(d), which provides that a stockholder transfer of stock to an employee for services rendered to the corporation shall be treated as a stockholder contribution to the corporation's capital followed by a transfer of property to the employee).

SECTION 2. BOND DISCOUNT AND PREMIUM

A. ORIGINAL ISSUE DISCOUNT

INTERNAL REVENUE CODE: Sections 163(e); 483; 1272(a); 1273; 1274(a)–(d); 1274A; 1275(a)(1), (a)(2), (b), (c).

Tax Reform Act of 1984 General Explanation of the Revenue Provisions

Staff of the Joint Committee on Taxation 108 (1984).

[Pre–1984] Law

Timing of inclusion and deduction of interest: The OID rules

If, in a lending transaction, the borrower receives less than the amount to be repaid at the loan's maturity, the difference represents "discount." Discount performs the same function as stated interest; that is, it compensates the lender for the use of its money. Sections 1232A and 163(e) of [pre–1984] law (the "OID rules") generally required the holder of a discount debt obligation to include in income annually a portion of the original issue discount on the obligation, and allowed the issuer to deduct a corresponding amount, irrespective of whether the cash method or the accrual method of accounting was used.[7]

Original issue discount was defined as the excess of an obligation's stated redemption price at maturity over its issue price. This amount was allocated over the life of the obligation through a series of adjustments to the issue price for each "bond period" (generally, each one-year period beginning on the issue date of the bond and each anniversary). The adjustment to the issue price for each bond period was determined by multiplying the "adjusted issue price" (the issue price increased by adjustments prior to the beginning of the bond period) by the obligation's yield to maturity, and then subtracting the interest payable during the bond period. The adjustment to the issue price for any bond period was the amount of OID allocated to that bond period.

The OID rules did not apply to obligations issued by individuals,[8] obligations with a maturity of one year or less, or obligations issued in exchange for property where neither the obligation nor the property received for it was traded on an established securities exchange.

Measurement of interest in deferred-payment transactions involving property: the imputed interest rules

A deferred-payment sale of property exempt from the OID rules was generally subject to the unstated interest rules of § 483. If the parties to the transaction failed to state a minimum "safe-harbor" rate of interest to be paid on the loan by the purchaser-borrower, § 483 recharacterized a portion of the principal amount as unstated interest. This "imputation" of interest was performed by assuming that interest accrued at a rate higher than the safe-harbor rate.

The safe-harbor rate was a simple interest rate; the imputation rate was a compound rate. The safe-harbor and imputation rates were 9 percent

7. The premise of the OID rules was that an OID obligation should be treated in the same manner as a nondiscount obligation requiring current payments of interest for tax purposes. To accomplish this result, the rules in essence treated the borrower as having paid the lender the annual unpaid interest accruing on the outstanding principal balance of the loan, which amount the borrower was allowed to deduct as interest expense and the lender was required to include in income. The lender was then deemed to have lent this amount back to the borrower, who in subsequent periods was deemed to pay interest on this amount as well as on the principal balance. This concept of accruing interest on unpaid interest is commonly referred to as the "economic accrual" of interest, or interest "compounding."

8. Prior to 1982, the OID provisions applied only to corporate and taxable government obligations. The Tax Equity and Fiscal Responsibility Act of 1982 (TEFRA) extended these provisions to noncorporate obligations other than those of individuals.

and 10 percent, respectively, when the Act became law. The safe-harbor interest rate applicable to certain transfers of land between members of the same family was 6 percent.

* * *

If interest was imputed under § 483, a portion of each deferred payment was treated as unstated interest. The allocation between unstated interest and principal was made on the basis of the size of the deferred payment in relation to the total deferred payments. Amounts characterized as unstated interest were included in the income of the lender in the year the deferred payment was received (in the case of a cash method taxpayer) or due (in the case of an accrual method taxpayer). The borrower correspondingly deducted the imputed interest in the year the payment was made or due.

Reasons for Change

Mismatching and noneconomic accrual of interest

Enacted in 1969, the OID rules were designed to eliminate the distortions caused by the mismatching of income and deductions by lenders and borrowers in discount lending transactions. Prior to that time, an accrual method borrower could deduct deferred interest payable to a cash method lender prior to the period in which the lender included the interest in income. Although the OID rules prevented mismatching in many situations, the potential for distortion continued to exist where the obligation was excepted from the OID rules. Some taxpayers attempted to exploit these exceptions, particularly the exception relating to nontraded obligations issued for nontraded property, to achieve deferral of tax on interest income and accelerated deductions of interest expense.

For example, in a typical transaction, real estate, machinery, or other depreciable property was purchased for a promissory note providing that interest accrued annually but was not payable until the note matured. The issuer, who used the accrual method of accounting, would claim annual interest deductions for accrued but unpaid interest. The holder, a cash method taxpayer, would defer interest income until it was actually received.

Such a mismatching of income and deductions had serious revenue consequences, since the present value of the income included by the lender in the later period was less than the present value of the deductions claimed by the borrower. The greater the length of time between the borrower's deduction and the lender's inclusion, the greater the loss of tax revenues.

This revenue loss was magnified if the accrual-method purchaser computed its interest deduction using a noneconomic formula such as straight-line amortization, simple interest, or the "Rule of 78's". In Rev. Rul. 83–84, 1983–1 C.B. 9, the Internal Revenue Service stated that interest may be deducted only to the extent it has accrued economically, using a constant yield-to-maturity formula. Some taxpayers, however, took the position that the ruling incorrectly interpreted existing law. Other taxpayers construed the ruling narrowly, as applying only to the precise facts set forth in the ruling.

In light of the significant distortions occurring under prior law, both in the form of mismatching of interest income and deductions and in the form of noneconomic accruals of interest, Congress believed it appropriate to extend the periodic inclusion and deduction rules of sections 1232A and 163(e) of prior law to nontraded debt instruments issued for nontraded property. The same policy objectives that led to the application of these rules to interest on traded debt instruments or instruments issued for cash—namely, better compliance by holders and clearer reflection of income—were believed to apply equally in the case of nontraded instruments issued for nontraded property.

The principal obstacle to applying the OID rules to a transaction in which neither side is traded is the difficulty of determining the issue price of the debt instrument directly. Both the issue price and the redemption price of an instrument must be known to compute the amount of OID. In a transaction involving the issuance of an note for cash, the issue price is simply the amount of cash received. Where the issuer receives nontraded property, however, the fair market value of the property determines the obligation's issue price.[14] Using a "facts and circumstances," case-by-case analysis to determine fair market value in these situations was considered impracticable. Congress believed that the valuation problem could best be resolved by incorporating into the OID rules a mechanism for testing the adequacy of interest in a sale of property already present in the Code—the unstated interest rules of section 483—with certain modifications. An approximation of the maximum fair market value of property (and hence the issue price of the obligation issued in exchange for it) could be arrived at by assuming a minimum rate of interest which parties dealing at arm's-length and without tax motivations could be expected to agree upon.

* * *

Finally, Congress believed there was no justification for continuing the exemption from the OID rules for holders of obligations not constituting capital assets in the holder's hands. Sales of ordinary income assets may involve deferred interest to the same degree as sales of capital assets, and the timing of income in such sales is as important as its character.

While acknowledging the complexity of the OID rules, Congress believed that the rules could be extended to a broader range of transactions without disrupting the routine, legitimate transactions of individuals or small businesses, which might have difficulty applying the rules. The Act exempts many such routine transactions.

Mismeasurement of interest in transactions involving nontraded property

14. The issue price of the obligation in such a transaction is the value of the property received by the issuer, less any cash down payment made to the holder.

Congress recognized that, under prior law, it was possible for taxpayers in a sale of nontraded property for nontraded debt to achieve unwarranted tax benefits not only by mismatching interest income and deductions, but by manipulating the principal amount of the debt. This could be accomplished by artificially fixing interest at a below-market rate. Although economically the parties were in the same position as if interest had been accurately stated, significant tax advantages often resulted from characterizing the transaction as involving a lower rate of interest and a larger loan principal amount. If recognized for tax purposes, this mischaracterization of interest as principal resulted in an overstatement of the sales price and tax basis of the property. In cases where the property was a capital asset in the hands of the seller, the seller was able to convert interest income, which should have been taxable as ordinary income in the year it accrued, into capital gain taxable at lower rates (and, under the installment method provided in sec. 453, generally only as installment payments were made). If the property was depreciable in the hands of the purchaser, the inflated basis enabled the purchaser to claim excessive cost recovery (ACRS) deductions * * *.

These same tax advantages accrued to taxpayers who engaged in low-interest transactions entirely for nontax reasons.

Explanation of Provisions

a. Extension of OID rules

Overview

The Act extends the rules for periodic inclusion and deduction of original issue discount by lenders and borrowers to debt instruments that are issued for property that is not publicly traded, and that are themselves not publicly traded. The Act also repeals * * * the exemption from the income accrual requirement for cash-method holders of obligations not constituting capital assets in the holder's hands. Exceptions from the rules are provided to ensure that they will not apply to * * * *de minimis* transactions * * *.

If either the debt instrument or the property for which it is exchanged is publicly traded, the amount of OID is determined as under [pre–1984] law. The market value of the traded side determines the issue price of the obligation, and the excess of the redemption price over the issue price is original issue discount. Where neither side is traded, the transaction is tested for the adequacy of stated interest in a manner similar to that prescribed in section 483 of [pre–1984] law.

If the stated rate of interest is not equal to or greater than a safe-harbor rate, the issue price is determined by imputing interest to the transaction at a higher rate. The safe-harbor rate and the imputation rate are equal to * * * [the "applicable Federal rate,"] a rate based on the yields of marketable securities of the United States government. [Ed.: The original 1984 legislation imputed interest of 120 percent of the applicable federal rate if the parties failed to specify interest of at least 110 percent of the applicable federal rate. The 1988 Act adopted the applicable federal rate as both the safe-harbor and imputed interest rate.]

* * *

Regulatory authority

The Act authorizes the Treasury Department to issue regulations dealing with the treatment of transactions involving varying interest rates, put or call options, indefinite maturities, contingent payments, assumptions of debt instruments, or other circumstances.

* * *

ILLUSTRATIVE MATERIAL

A. ECONOMIC ACCRUAL OF INTEREST

Since 1984, § 1272 has required that original issue discount be accounted for by both the issuer and holder of the bond as the interest reflected by the discount economically accrues, i.e., on a compounding, or constant interest, basis. Ratable deduction and inclusion of original issue discount, which was the rule prior to 1984, did not accurately reflect the economic accrual of interest over the life of the bond. For example, a three-year bond with a face amount of $1,265.32 issued for $1,000 reflects an interest rate of 8 percent, compounded semiannually (or an effective annual rate of 8.16 percent). Accounting for the $265.32 of original issue discount ratably over the three years would result in a deduction of $88.44 each year for three years. However, in economic terms, the original issue discount transaction is the same as if the borrower had borrowed additional money each year to pay interest. Interest in each period is computed on the original principal plus the borrowed interest. Using a constant interest rate, the amount of the interest should be lower in the early years and then grow as the outstanding "principal" of the loan increases due to the interest which has been "borrowed" back.[3] This calculation allows the interest expense to be "compounded", i.e., interest is charged on the interest which is borrowed back. The following table illustrates the difference between ratable treatment and economic accrual treatment.

	Ratable Interest	Economic Interest	"Principal" Outstanding
Year 1	$88.44	$81.60	$1,081.60
Year 2	$88.44	$88.26	$1,169.86
Year 3	$88.44	$95.46	$1,265.32

Under § 1272(a)(3) and (5), original issue discount is calculated by determining the "yield to maturity" based on semiannual compounding (8 percent in the above example). Under Treas. Reg. § 1.1272–1(b)(1)(i), the

3. This would be the result when a three-year note required annual interest payments but provided that in any year in which interest was not paid, the unpaid interest would be added to principal and would bear interest at the rate stated in the note.

original issue discount for any accrual period is calculated first by determining the yield to maturity of the debt instrument, that is, "the discount rate that, when used in computing the present value of all principal and interest payments to be made under the debt instrument produces an amount equal to the issue price of the debt instrument." Then, under Treas. Reg. § 1.1272–1(b)(1)(ii), an accrual period must be determined, which can be any interval not exceeding one year. The regulations point out that the computation of yield is simplified if the accrual periods correspond to the intervals between payment dates provided by the terms of the debt instrument. The original issue discount allocable to each accrual period is the adjusted issue price of the instrument multiplied by the yield to maturity of the debt instrument, reduced by the amount of qualified stated interest allocable to the accrual period. Treas. Reg. § 1.1272–1(b)(1)(iii). "Adjusted issue price" is the original issue price increased by accrued but unpaid original issue discount and decreased by payments. Treas. Reg. § 1.1275–1(b). "Qualified stated interest" is interest that is unconditionally payable at a fixed rate at least annually. Treas. Reg. § 1.1273–1(c). See Rev. Rul. 95–70, 1995–2 C.B. 124 (scheduled interest payments are not "unconditionally payable," as required to qualify as "qualified stated interest," merely because failure to pay the interest when due results in either (1) the corporate issuer being required to forgo dividend payments or (2) past due payments accruing interest at a rate two points higher than the stated yield).

The holder of an original issue discount bond is required to include the daily portions of original issue discount for each day the bond is held. I.R.C. § 1272(a)(1). The daily portion is determined by ratably allocating to each day in a semiannual accrual period the interest increment occurring during that period. I.R.C. § 1272(a)(3). The issuer deducts original issue discount in the same manner. I.R.C. § 163(e).

The bond holder's basis in the original issue discount obligation is increased to reflect the amount included in income by the holder. I.R.C. § 1272(d)(2). If the holder of the obligation disposes of it before maturity, the purchaser steps into the original bondholder's shoes with respect to the remaining original issue discount attributable to the bond. The original bondholder treats any amount received in excess of the adjusted basis as gain on disposition; the second owner is entitled to deduct any such excess over the remaining life of the bond from the amount of original issue discount otherwise required to be included in income. I.R.C. § 1272(a)(7).

Under these principles, assuming that the bond in the above example was issued on December 31st of year 0 and the issuer chose to apply semiannual compounding, at the beginning of year 3 the adjusted issue price is $1,169.86, reflecting the original issue price of $1,000 and the accrued interest for years 1 and 2. The amount of original issue discount deducted by the borrower and included by the lender for year 3 is $95.46.

B. ORIGINAL ISSUE DISCOUNT OBLIGATIONS ISSUED FOR PROPERTY

1. *Publicly Traded Bonds or Property*

When A sells property to B in a transaction in which some of the payments for the property are deferred, two separate economic transactions are involved. A is both selling the property to B and loaning B the amount of the unpaid purchase price, while B is correspondingly purchasing the property and simultaneously borrowing the unpaid purchase price from A. Original issue discount is present if the stated principal amount of B's obligation is greater than the fair market value of the transferred property.

Section 1273(b)(3) provides that original issue discount arises in the case of bonds issued for property when either the bonds or the property (in the form of stock or securities) are traded on an established securities market and the face amount of the bonds issued exceeds the fair market value of the property received. Treas. Reg. § 1.1273–2(f) provides that property is traded on an established market if it is traded on a recognized exchange, or if the property appears on a system of general circulation that provides a reasonable basis to determine fair market value through dissemination of either price quotations or reports of recent sales.

2. *Obligations Issued for Other Property*

Presumably the restriction of the original issue discount rules in the 1969 Act to situations involving bonds or property traded on an established securities market was for administrative convenience to avoid the difficult valuation problems faced by the courts in the pre–1969 cases. As described in the Joint Committee Staff's General Explanation of the Tax Reform Act of 1984, before 1984 the approach of the Code to this problem was to impute interest under § 483 to each payment made in the case of a deferred payment sale in which stated interest was inadequate. In § 1274 Congress dealt with the valuation issue by using the present value of obligations determined by a fixed rate of return as the reference point.

In effect, § 1274 requires that if the stated interest in sales of property on a deferred basis is less than a stipulated interest rate—the rate paid on Federal obligations with a similar maturity[4]—the original issue discount rules apply. For purposes of determining the issue price of the original issue discount obligation, the present value of all payments to be made under the instrument is calculated on the basis of the applicable federal rate. The resulting difference between the hypothetical issue price and the actual payments to be made under the instrument is original issue discount which must be currently included by the seller and deducted by the buyer using a constant interest rate as described at page 173.

The following example illustrates the application of § 1274. Suppose that A agrees to sell property to X Corp. for $1,000,000 on the following

4. The applicable Federal rate is determined on a monthly basis. The rate used is the lowest Federal rate for similar obligations in effect in the 3 months prior to the date of the contract of sale. I.R.C. § 1274(d)(2).

terms. Payment for the property will be due three years from the date of the sale and will bear simple interest at 8 percent with all interest to be paid at the end of the third year. Assume that the applicable federal rate is 9 percent. The first question is whether the obligation bears "adequate stated interest." It does not since (a) the stated rate is only 8 percent, (b) the interest is not compounded, and (c) the interest is only payable at the maturity of the obligation. By using a below-market interest rate, A and B have attempted to convert a portion of the financing transaction into a sales transaction. Thus, under § 1274(a)(2), the "imputed principal amount" is treated as the issue price for purposes of determining the original issue discount. The imputed principal amount is defined in § 1274(b) as the present value of all payments due on the debt instrument, using as a discount rate the applicable federal rate. On this basis, the present value of the $1,240,000 payment to be made in year 3 is $952,191. This amount is then treated as the issue price of the obligation for purposes of determining the original issue discount on the financing portion of the transaction and as the sales price for the sales portion of the transaction.

Section 1274 thus isolates the unstated interest element in the transaction, using the applicable federal rate as the applicable norm. The resulting computation indicates that economically A sold the property to B for $952,191 and loaned B that amount in return for a promise to pay $1,240,000 in three years reflecting a 9 percent interest rate, compounded semiannually. B has a basis of $952,191 in the property for purposes of depreciation and sale. On the financing side of the transaction, A is required to include currently the appropriate amount of original issue discount income and B is given a deduction for a corresponding amount, thus matching deduction and inclusion.

If the rate of interest charged and payable at least annually under the contract had been equal to the applicable federal rate (or 9 percent in the case of a qualified instrument to which § 1274A(a) applies) compounded semi-annually, the original issue discount rules would not have applied to recalculate the sales price.[5] The agreed price for the property would determine A's gain on the sales portion of the transaction and B's basis for the property. The interest deduction and interest income would likewise be matched because the interest payments must be made currently to prevent the application of the original issue discount rules, thus requiring current inclusion by the cash method seller.

By using the applicable federal rate to identify the interest element of the transaction, § 1274 avoids the necessity of directly valuing nontraded property for purposes of calculating the original issue discount. In effect, it requires the buyer and seller to use at least the appropriate federal rate on the financing portion of the transaction. The remainder of the payments are then considered to be the price paid for the underlying property. The

5. Under § 1274(d)(1)(D), regulations may be promulgated to permit the taxpayer to use a rate lower than the applicable Federal rate if it can be established that it would have been possible for the taxpayer to borrow in an arm's length transaction at such lower rate.

section thus works backward from a given interest rate to calculate the current value of the property.

3. *Exceptions to Section 1274 and the Application of Section 483*

Section 1274A(a) and (b) provides that the discount rate for purposes of § 1274 is not to exceed 9 percent, compounded semiannually, if the stated principal of the obligation is not in excess of $2.8 million, as adjusted for inflation since 1989,[6] and the obligation is not issued as consideration for the sale or exchange of certain tangible personal property used in a trade or business. Property for which this exception is not applicable is "§ 38 property" within the meaning of § 48(b), which, in general, includes depreciable machinery and equipment and certain limited classes of improvements to real property.

Some deferred payment sales are not subject to § 1274: sale of a farm by an individual or small business for less than $1 million; the sale of a principal residence; any sale or exchange of property if the total amount receivable under the obligation does not exceed $250,000; and certain sales of patents to the extent the sale price is contingent on income from the patent. Transactions not covered by § 1274 are subject to the imputed interest rules of § 483.

With some exceptions, the amount of imputed interest is calculated for purposes of § 483 in the same manner as under § 1274. Imputed interest under § 483 is the difference between issue price and the present value of the payments required by the obligation using the applicable federal rate, compounded semiannually, as the discount rate. I.R.C. § 483(b). Unlike original issue discount under § 1274, however, imputed interest under § 483 is taken into account by a cash method taxpayer only when payment is received or paid, and by an accrual method taxpayer when payment is due. Treas. Reg. § 1.483–2(a)(1)(ii). Unstated interest must be allocated to each payment using the constant interest method of § 1272(a). I.R.C. § 483(a).

Under § 1274A(c), interest on an obligation subject to § 1274 may be reported on the cash method if the stated principal does not exceed $2 million, as adjusted for inflation since 1989.[7] Cash method reporting must be elected by both the lender and borrower. The election is available only if the lender does not use the accrual accounting method and is not a dealer with respect to the property.

C. ORIGINAL ISSUE DISCOUNT AND CONVERTIBLE DEBENTURES

Debentures can be issued with warrants attached, or convertible bonds can be issued with the bondholder given the right to acquire common or preferred stock in the corporation. Economically, some portion of the original issue price of convertible securities should be attributable to the

6. For 1998 the inflation adjusted ceiling was $3,823,100, Rev. Rul. 97–56, 1997–52 I.R.B. 10.

7. For 1998, the inflation adjusted amount was $2,730,800. Rev. Rul. 97–56, 1997–52 I.R.B. 10.

value of the warrants or conversion features, and thus, even though the instrument is issued for a price equal to its redemption value, in theory it bears OID. Nevertheless, Treas. Regs. § 1.163–3(a) and § 1.1273–2(j) provide that, in the case of convertible obligations, no original issue discount is created with respect to the conversion feature if the option price approximates the value of the stock at the time the instrument is issued. All of the consideration is deemed to be paid for the debt portion of the transaction. Hunt Foods and Industries, Inc. v. Commissioner, 57 T.C. 633 (1972), aff'd per curiam, 496 F.2d 532 (9th Cir.1974), sustained the validity of the predecessor of Treas. Reg. § 1.1273–2(j), and held that no original issue discount was created with respect to the conversion feature in the case of convertible debt obligations; no interest deduction was allowed to the issuing corporation. AMF Inc. v. United States, 476 F.2d 1351 (Ct.Cl.1973), is to the same effect. In Honeywell Inc. v. Commissioner, 87 T.C. 624 (1986) (A), the Tax Court applied the same theory to the bonds of a foreign finance subsidiary convertible into common stock of its parent corporation. The court refused to reduce the issue price of the bonds by the value of the conversion feature.

Section 1273(c)(2) and Treas. Reg. § 1.1273–2(h) provide different treatment for obligations issued as part of an investment unit package that includes a separate option, security or other severable property such as stock warrants. The price paid for the package must be apportioned among its components, and the original issue price of the obligation includes only the consideration paid for the debt portion of the package.

D. CONTINGENT INTEREST AND VARIABLE RATE INTEREST

In the case of obligations issued for cash or marketable securities, original issue discount is the difference between the issue price of the obligation and the amount to be paid at maturity. In the case of obligations issued for property subject to § 1274, the computation of original issue discount depends upon the present value of all payments under the note. Both of these computations require knowledge of the time and amount of payments under the obligations. Determination of the amount of original issue discount is more complex when either the time or amount of payment under the obligation is contingent on some future event, such as the performance of property transferred in exchange for the obligation, or when the interest rate stated in the obligation is variable in accordance with some outside measure of interest, such as the prime rate of a specific financial institution.

1. *Contingent Payments*

Treas. Reg. § 1.1275–4 applies the OID rules to contingent obligations on the basis of simplifying assumptions. In the case of a publicly traded instrument, generally speaking, the yield on the contingent obligation is determined and a payment schedule to produce that yield is then fixed. Treas. Reg. § 1.1275–4(b). The yield on the instrument is the yield at which the issuer would issue a fixed rate debt instrument with terms and conditions similar to the contingent payment debt instrument. The issuer's determination of yield and projected payments generally will be respected, but the yield must be reasonable and may not be less than the applicable federal rate (AFR). For market-based payments, projected payments equal the forward price of the payments. For non-market-based payments, projected payments are the expected amount of the payments as of the issue date. Projected payments rather than actual payments are used to determine the adjusted issue price of the debt instrument, the holder's basis in the debt instrument, and the amount of any contingent payment treated as made on the scheduled retirement of the debt instrument. If actual payments are larger or smaller than projected, adjustments—greater accruals, offsets to accruals, or loss deductions—must be made.

Treas. Reg. § 1.1275–4(c) provides special rules applicable to a nonpublicly traded debt instruments issued in a purchase or exchange for nonpublicly traded property. Noncontingent payments are treated as a separate debt instrument that is subject to the rules applicable to noncontingent debt instruments. Contingent payments are taken into account separately when made. The portion of each contingent payment that is principal is determined by discounting the payment from the payment date to the issue date at the AFR (determined on the instrument's issue date); the remainder of the payment is treated as interest.

Under Treas. Reg. § 1.1274–2(g), the issue price of a contingent payment debt instrument that is issued in exchange for nonpublicly traded property, for example, real estate, does not include any contingent payments due under the instrument. Thus, in computing the basis of the property, the buyer initially takes into account only the noncontingent payments due under the instrument. As contingent payments treated as principal are made, the buyer increases the basis in the property. See T.D. 8674, 1996–2 C.B. 84, 88. Nevertheless, if such a sale is not reported under the § 453 installment method, the amount realized by the seller is not the issue price of the instrument determined under Treas. Reg. § 1.1274–2(g), which does not take into account the contingent payments. The amount realized is the sum of the issue price of the noncontingent payments plus the fair market value of the contingent payments. Treas. Reg. § 1.1001–1(g)(2)(ii).

2. *Variable Interest Rates*

Rather than stating a fixed rate of interest, debt obligations commonly will base the interest rate on some external publicly available standard such as the prime rate of a particular financial institution or the London Interbank Offered Rate (LIBOR). Treas. Reg. § 1.1275–5 provides rules for obligations that qualify as "variable rate debt instruments." In general, the interest paid on a variable rate debt instrument is treated as qualified stated interest. Thus, there will be no original issue discount if the instrument is issued for a price that equals the stated redemption price and the variable interest is paid periodically. If an instrument fails to qualify as a variable rate debt instrument, interest is treated as contingent interest subject to the rules discussed in subsection 1 above.

Variable rate debt instruments include only instruments that (1) provide for noncontingent principal payments at least equal to the issue price and (2) provide for a stated interest rate that is some combination of a current "qualified floating rate" or "objective rate." Treas. Reg. § 1.1275–5(a)(2)–(4). A "qualified floating rate" is an interest like rate based on an identifiable standard such as the applicable Federal rate or LIBOR. Treas. Reg. § 1.1275–5(b)(1). An "objective rate" is a rate that is determinable from a qualified floating rate, such as LIBOR plus 200 basis points, or from the yield or change in price of actively traded property (other than a foreign currency). Treas. Reg. § 1.1275–5(c)(1). Treas. Reg. § 1.1275–5(a)(3) allows the use of a single rate, one or more qualified floating rates, a fixed single rate followed by a qualified floating rate, a qualified floating rate followed by a second qualified floating rate, an objective rate, or a single fixed rate followed by a qualified inverse floating rate.

In computing original issue discount for any accrual period, a variable interest rate is treated as qualified stated interest. Thus, the variable rate is used to reduce (or eliminate) the amount of original issue discount in an accrual period just as a fixed rate does. See Treas. Reg. § 1.1275–5(e).

E. MARKET DISCOUNT

There is an interest element similar to original issue discount present on the purchase of a debt obligation in the market for a price below its stated redemption price. Section 1276, enacted in 1984, insures that this "market discount" is treated as ordinary income on disposition of the bond.

Market discount is defined in § 1278(a)(2) as the excess of the stated redemption price at maturity over the taxpayer's basis in the bond upon acquisition. Gain on any disposition of a market discount bond is treated as ordinary income to the extent of the accrued market discount. I.R.C. § 1276(a)(1). For purposes of determining the portion of the gain attributable to market discount upon disposition or retirement of the obligation, market discount accrues ratably for each day the holder owns the bond. I.R.C. § 1276(b)(1). Alternatively, the bondholder may elect under § 1276(b)(2) to accrue market discount using the economic accrual method of § 1272(a).

F. HIGH YIELD DISCOUNT OBLIGATIONS

Section 163(e)(5) requires bifurcation of the return on so-called "high yield discount obligations" into an interest portion and, for some purposes, a dividend portion. In response to the wave of leveraged buy-outs in the early 1980s, Congress expressed the view that heavily discounted bonds sufficiently resemble equity to be treated as preferred stock when the bonds provide a high rate of interest which is not actually paid for long periods of time. H.Rep. No. 101–247, 101st Cong., 1st Sess. 1220 (1989). The legislative history points out that the long-term deferral of interest on original issue discount bonds is riskier than other forms of debt investment and that the presence of a high rate of return suggests that payment of interest is dependent on the profitability of the issuer's business. As a result,

§ 163(e)(5) disallows entirely the interest deduction for a portion of the original issue discount on a "high yield original issue discount obligation," and defers the interest deduction on the remainder until the interest is actually paid. The holder of a high yield original issue discount obligation must continue to report the accrued original issue discount as income over the term of the obligation as required by § 1272, but a corporate holder is permitted to treat the disqualified portion of the accrued original issue discount as a dividend for purposes of the dividends received deduction of §§ 243–246A. Thus, to a limited extent, the disqualified portion of the return on a high yield original issue discount obligation is treated as a dividend while a portion of the return is given interest treatment, though with deduction deferred to actual payment.

A high yield original issue discount obligation is defined in § 163(i) as an obligation with a term in excess of five years, which has a yield to maturity in excess of the "applicable federal rate" plus five percent, and which has significant original issue discount. In highly simplified terms, an obligation has significant original issue discount if in any period ending more than five years after the obligation is issued, the obligation has accrued but unpaid interest in excess of the amount of the obligation's annual yield to maturity. I.R.C. § 163(i)(2). This disqualified portion of a high yield original issue discount obligation (the portion for which no current interest deduction is allowed and which is treated as a dividend to a corporate holder) is the lesser of the original issue discount of the obligation or the amount by which original issue discount exceeds the applicable federal rate plus six percent. I.R.C. § 163(e)(5)(C). Thus actual interest paid, plus original issue discount up to the applicable federal rate plus six percent, remains deductible as interest, but only when actually paid. The excess is given the equivalent of dividend treatment.

B. BOND PREMIUM

INTERNAL REVENUE CODE: Sections 171(a), (b); 249.

REGULATIONS: Section 1.61–12(c)(2).

ILLUSTRATIVE MATERIAL

A. PREMIUM AT ORIGINAL ISSUE

The issuer of a bond with a stated interest rate in excess of prevailing market rates may be in a position to demand a premium for the bond, i.e., consideration in excess of the stated principal amount of the bond. As to the creditor, the premium in effect reduces the interest income. Section 171 provides an election to the creditor to amortize premium over the term of the obligation using the constant interest method of § 1272(a). See Treas. Reg. § 1.1272–2. The election is irrevocable absent the consent of the Commissioner and applies to all bonds held by the taxpayer. See I.R.C. § 171(c). Section 171(b) requires the holder to amortize bond premium over the full term to maturity, even though the bond may be callable at an earlier date.

Bond premium received upon the initial issuance of a bond is income to the issuer under Treas. Reg. § 1.61–12(c)(2), which provides that the issuer takes bond premium into account as an offset to its interest deduction under the constant interest method.

Bond premium may also arise as the creditor pays an additional consideration for the privilege of converting the obligation into stock. Section 171(b)(1) excludes from bond premium "any amount attributable to the conversion features."

B. PREMIUM PAID BY THE ISSUER ON REDEMPTION

Bond premium paid by the issuer on redemption of an obligation is deductible by the issuer as additional interest on the obligation. In the case of convertible obligations, however, § 249 limits the deduction for redemption premium to an amount representing a "normal call premium" on obligations that are not convertible. The balance is a capital transaction. Thus, in the case of bond premium paid to redeem convertible bonds, the creditor is not allowed to amortize any portion of the premium attributable to the conversion feature, nor is the issuer allowed an interest deduction for that portion of a premium paid upon redemption of its bonds which is attributable to the conversion feature. This result presumably corresponds to the parallel treatment of original issue discount between issuer and holder, discussed at page 182 . However, the treatment of the convertibility feature is different as between original issue discount and bond premium in the case of convertible bonds. The regulations adopt the view that in the case of convertible bonds, the conversion feature is not separable from the debt for purposes of determining original issue discount, hence preventing a larger original issue discount from resulting; on the other hand, in the case of bond premium the conversion feature is deemed under the Code to be a feature separable from the debt portion of the obligation and hence the amount, if any, attributable to the conversion element is not deductible as interest.

In Tandy Corp. v. United States, 626 F.2d 1186 (5th Cir.1980), the court denied a deduction under § 163 for premium on conversion of debt into stock. The taxpayer claimed that the excess of the fair market value of the stock issued over the face of the bonds was deductible as interest. The court concluded that under the terms of the indenture conversion extinguished the obligation to pay accrued interest or bond premium. Thus no accrued interest or bond premium was involved. The court did not consider the application of § 249.

In National Can Corp. v. United States, 687 F.2d 1107 (7th Cir.1982), an overseas finance subsidiary issued debentures convertible into the stock of its parent corporation. The parent redeemed its subsidiary's debentures with its own stock, the fair market value of which exceeded the issue price of the debentures. The parent claimed a deduction for the difference as premium under §§ 171 and 162. The parent corporation argued that the limitation of § 171(b)(1) applied only to obligations convertible into the stock of the issuing corporation, and not to obligations convertible into the stock of another. The court broadly interpreted § 171(b)(1) to limit deduction of premium attributable to any conversion feature. The court concluded that the premium was due to the unexercised conversion feature of the bonds so that amortization of premium was barred by § 171(b)(1) and Treas. Reg. § 1.171–2(c). The court also disallowed the taxpayer's claimed deduction under § 162, holding that under § 1032 the corporation recognizes no gain or loss when it issues stock in satisfaction of a conversion obligation of the bonds of a subsidiary. In the District Court the taxpayer also asserted that the value of the conversion feature at the time the bonds were issued reduced the issue price of the bonds thereby creating amortizable original issue discount in an amount equal to the value of the conversion rights. The District Court refused to treat the conversion rights as a separate asset capable of valuation apart from the debt component of the bonds. National Can Corp. v. United States, 520 F.Supp. 567 (N.D.Ill.1981). The taxpayer abandoned this claim on appeal.

In Head Ski Co., Inc. v. United States, 323 F.Supp. 1383 (D.Md.1971), aff'd per curiam, 454 F.2d 732 (4th Cir.1972), the court held, contrary to the position of the Internal Revenue Service, that the premium paid to repurchase convertible debentures constituted an ordinary and necessary business expense under the law as it existed prior to the enactment of § 249 in the Tax Reform Act of 1969. The Service then revoked its prior position, and stated that it would follow the decisions in Roberts & Porter, Inc. v. Commissioner, 307 F.2d 745 (7th Cir.1962), and *Head Ski Co.* in situations not covered by § 249. On the other hand, the Service apparently will challenge deductibility where the premium paid is unreasonable in amount. Rev.Rul. 74–210, 1974–1 C.B. 48.

CHAPTER 5

DIVIDEND DISTRIBUTIONS

SECTION 1. INTRODUCTION

The income tax treatment of corporate distributions to the shareholder is a complex matter and the rules must be traced through many sections. The starting point is § 301(a), which generally covers all distributions of property by a corporation to its shareholders in their capacity as shareholders. There are, however, important exceptions: (1) the distribution of stock or rights to stock of the corporation is not considered a distribution of "property" for this purpose, and (2) distributions in redemption of stock under certain circumstances and complete liquidations are not considered § 301 distributions. Thus, § 301(a), as the general rule, is applicable to a broader range of distributions than just dividends in the corporate law sense. Section 301(a) refers to § 301(c), which classifies distributions within the ambit of § 301 between dividends in the tax sense, which are included directly in gross income (§ 301(c)(1)), and distributions that are not dividends in the tax sense, which are treated as a return of capital applied against the stock basis (§ 301(c)(2)), and if in excess of that basis usually are treated as gain from the sale or exchange of property (§ 301(c)(3)), thus bringing the capital gain provisions into play. Section 61(a)(7) also requires that dividends in the tax sense be included in gross income.

Section 243(a)(1) provides a corporation that is a shareholder in another corporation with a deduction equal to 70 percent of intercorporate dividends received; section 243(c) increases the deduction to 80 percent if the shareholder corporation owns at least twenty percent of the stock of the payor corporation; and section 243(a)(3) extends this deduction to 100 percent for affiliated corporations that so elect. There are numerous limitations on the intercorporate dividends received deduction, which is discussed in Section 4 of this Chapter.

Section 316(a) provides the tax definition of a dividend. This definition is in terms of the "earnings and profits" of the corporation. The statutory dividend test is two-fold: any distribution to a shareholder is a dividend if it is out of either (1) earnings and profits accumulated after February 28, 1913, or (2) earnings and profits of the current year regardless of a lack of, or deficit in, accumulated earnings and profits. Earnings and profits differ substantially from taxable income, being more akin to net income in a financial accounting sense. But, because some significant adjustments to earned surplus in the corporate sense are not taken into account in computing earnings and profits, it is not entirely accurate to say that the taxability of the shareholder depends essentially on the earned surplus account of the corporation.

If the distributing corporation has neither current earnings and profits nor earnings and profits accumulated after February 28, 1913, so that there is not a dividend in the tax sense, then the distribution is applied against the basis of the recipient shareholder's stock under § 301(c)(2), and any excess is taxed as a capital gain under § 301(c)(3).

Section 316(a) eliminates most tracing requirements by specifying in the second sentence that if any earnings and profits exist, the distribution is deemed to be out of such earnings and profits rather than from any other source, and first from the most recently accumulated earnings and profits. But while tracing difficulties are largely avoided, the problem of ascertaining the amount of a corporation's earnings and profits remains. If the earnings and profits of the current year exceed the distribution, the amount of the accumulated earnings and profits is irrelevant. If accumulated earnings and profits are present, the precise determination of the earnings and profits of the current year is likewise unnecessary. But in some situations the precise dollar amount of either current or accumulated earnings and profits may be crucial and it is here that the exact scope of the statutory phrase "earnings and profits" must be determined. As will be seen, the phrase is only partially defined in § 312, thus requiring extensive judicial and administrative interpretation.

Section 301(b) determines the amount of the distribution in situations in which property or liabilities are involved, and § 301(d) establishes the basis of the distributed property in the shareholder's hands.

The scope of § 301(a) is qualified by various other sections dealing with corporate distributions, as the cross-references in § 301(f) indicate. Section 302 provides sale or exchange treatment for specified distributions *in redemption of stock*. If § 302 applies, capital gain or loss normally is recognized. Section 331 provides sale or exchange treatment for distributions in complete liquidation of the corporation; and § 302(b)(4) does the same for distributions to noncorporate shareholders in partial liquidation of the corporation. The definitions of complete and partial liquidations are tax words of art that are somewhat confusing. Certain distributions in corporate reorganizations also are specially treated (§§ 354 et seq.), as are certain distributions in redemption of stock to pay death taxes (§ 303) and involving related corporations (§ 304).

Sections 305, 306, and 307 relate to the distribution of a "stock dividend." In general, these sections treat the distribution as a nontaxable event for the shareholder. However, there are many exceptions that can cause the receipt of the stock dividend to be taxable. In addition, some stock dividends, though they possess a nontaxable character on receipt, may on disposition generate ordinary income to the extent of the amount realized rather than capital gain.

This statutory pattern provides many opportunities for controversies to flourish. Dividend distributions produce ordinary income to the recipient. The shareholder's basis in his stock cannot be offset against dividend distributions. Liquidations, whether partial or complete, and certain stock redemptions achieve sale or exchange treatment in which the shareholder may apply the basis of the redeemed stock against the amount realized. Any gain is capital gain, against which capital losses may be deducted, and which may be taxed at a preferential rate if capital gains exceed capital losses for the year. But since a transaction cast in the form of a partial liquidation or other stock redemption may amount realistically to no more than the distribution of a dividend, the line is not crystal clear. The differing treatment of dividends, on the one hand, and liquidations, partial liquidations, and redemptions, on the other hand, is of great significance. Furthermore, the statutory exemption from taxation as current ordinary income of the receipt of many stock dividends may provide the shareholder with the opportunity to create capital gain situations through the later sale of the dividend stock unless effective safeguards to prevent this tactic were placed in the statute.

Another facet of the taxation of corporate distributions that has shaped the historical development of Subchapter C should be noted at this point. Where the corporate earnings have not been realized but are represented by appreciation in value of corporate assets, realization by the corporation of that appreciation will produce a corporate level tax on the profit. The corporation then will be faced with distributing its earnings to its shareholders subject to the statutory provisions governing the various methods whereby corporate earnings are transformed into cash in the shareholders' hands. But the corporation-shareholder group may desire to avoid the double tax inherent in this system by avoiding the initial corporation tax. If the appreciated asset is distributed in kind to the shareholders, has realization of profit to the corporation and hence the corporate tax been avoided? For many years prior to the enactment of the 1954 Code, this was a troublesome question. In 1954, the predecessors of § 311 and § 336 were enacted specifically to provide for nonrecognition treatment to the corporation with respect to gain or loss inherent in distributed assets, whether by dividend, redemption, or liquidation.

Over the years, numerous limitations were imposed on nonrecognition of gain with respect to distributed property. Finally, the Tax Reform Act of 1986 amended § 311 and § 336 to require that *gain* be recognized by the corporation on the distribution of property, other than in liquidation of the corporation, and that both *gain and loss* be recognized on liquidating distributions. Much of the logic behind the shape of the current provisions, and some of the historical cases to be encountered in the following chapters can be understood only if these former rules are kept in mind. As § 311 was tightened to limit nonrecognition on distributions of appreciated property, corporate taxpayers attempted to devise increasingly complex schemes to come within the remaining nonrecognition rules, and the courts and Congress were forced to respond. Since 1986, corporate taxpayers have continued to seek holes in the recognition rules of § 311 so as to avoid the tax on appreciation at the corporate level.

The background of controversial areas involves two other statutory provisions, relating to the corporation rather than the shareholder, which appear in the Code outside of Subchapter C. If corporations are taxed at rates lower than individuals, retention of corporate earnings and consequent postponement of the shareholder tax are the inevitable results of the treatment of the corporation as a taxpaying entity. As a force in the other direction, the Code contains in §§ 531–537 a special tax (at 39.6 percent) on a corporation that accumulates its earnings for the purpose of avoiding the imposition of the individual tax on its shareholders. Such a special tax presents its own problems of application. By its presence it also precipitates some of the controversial transactions mentioned above when the accumulation of earnings approaches the danger zone created by the § 531 accumulated earnings tax, since the shareholders will then usually act to draw some of the earnings out of the corporation. If the accumulation of earnings largely reflects passive investments of a closely-held corporation, such as the holding of stocks and other securities, even if the special § 531 tax can be avoided, another special 39.6 (percent tax the "personal holding company tax") may be imposed on the undistributed income if the passive income receipts meet the objective standards of §§ 541–547.

These penalty taxes were enacted at a time when the maximum rate of tax on individual income substantially exceeded the maximum rate of tax on corporate income, thereby giving rise to an incentive to earn income through a corporation which retained that income. Under the present rate structure, with the maximum individual rates only slightly higher than the maximum corporate rates, there generally is little incentive to cause earnings that might otherwise be realized directly by an individual to be realized and accumulated by a corporation. In these circumstances, the reason for these penalty taxes has largely disappeared, although they remain as traps for the unwary. The provisions could perhaps be justified as enforcing a policy decision to impose a "double" tax on corporate profits on a reasonably current basis, but historically their function was to prevent accumulations at lower corporate rates.

The material in this chapter deals with cash and property dividend distributions by the ongoing corporation with respect to its continuing shareholders. Subsequent chapters deal with stock dividends, corporate distributions in redemption of stock, distributions in liquidation of the corporation, and the accumulated earnings tax and the personal holding company tax.

SECTION 2. DIVIDEND DISTRIBUTIONS IN GENERAL

INTERNAL REVENUE CODE: Sections 61(a)(7); 301(a), (b), (c); 312(a), (c), (f)(1)(omitting subparagraph (A)), (k)(1)–(3), (*l*), (n)(2), (4), (5); 316(a); 317(a).

REGULATIONS: Sections 1.301–1(a), (c); 1.312–6(a), (b), (d); 1.312–7(b)(1); 1.316–1(a)(1), (e), Ex. (1); 1.316–2(a), (b), (c).

Mazzocchi Bus Co., Inc. v. Commissioner

United States Court of Appeals, Third Circuit, 1994.
14 F.3d 923.

■ BECKER, CIRCUIT JUDGE.

This appeal is from a decision of the United States Tax Court which upheld the Commissioner's determination of federal income tax deficiencies for the years 1974 through 1979 against Mazzocchi Bus Co., Inc. ("MBC"), a closely-held corporation; [and] Nicholas Mazzocchi ("Mazzocchi"), its controlling shareholder * * *. The Commissioner's determination stems from Mazzocchi's diversion of receipts totalling more than $700,000 from MBC for his personal use and benefit during the years in question, taken together with his failure to report that income on both his and MBC's tax returns.

The principal question presented by the appeal is whether MBC, a corporation using the cash method of accounting for computing its income taxes, should be entitled to use the accrual method for calculating its earnings and profits.[2] As applied to the facts, the question is whether the tax court correctly held that the earnings and profits of MBC during the taxable years in question should not be reduced by income taxes, penalties, and interest owed but not paid by the corporation during those years. Relying on a reasonable Treasury regulation directly on point, we conclude that the tax court properly held that MBC must use the same accounting method for calculating its earnings and profits as it uses in calculating its income taxes. * * * [W]e will affirm.

I. FACTS AND PROCEDURAL HISTORY

Mazzocchi was the president and controlling shareholder of MBC, which engaged in the school bus transportation business. During the years in question, MBC failed to record in its cash receipts books numerous checks constituting large payments for transportation services MBC provided several schools, and concomitantly failed to report those checks as receipts on its income tax returns. * * *

The omitted checks were mainly customer checks issued to Mazzocchi and/or MBC, 60 of which contained the single endorsement of Mazzocchi and 19 of which contained the initial endorsement of MBC followed by the second endorsement of Mazzocchi. As MBC's president, Mazzocchi was able surreptitiously (without the knowledge of corporate accountants or other officers) to negotiate these checks * * * thus affecting [sic] the diversion. * * *

The IRS ultimately commenced a criminal investigation of the business affairs of MBC and Mazzocchi, leading to Mazzocchi's indictment for income tax evasion [and subsequent guilty plea]. * * * Later, in 1986, the Commissioner determined that Mazzocchi had diverted money from MBC

2. Under the cash method of accounting, the taxpayer reports income when received and expenditures when paid. In contrast, under the accrual method of accounting, the taxpayer reports income when the right to receive payment has accrued and the obligation to make payment has been established. Under § 446 the taxpayer may select one of several accounting methods, including the cash or accrual method, to compute taxable income, so long as it reflects income accurately and the taxpayer uses the same method to keep its books. But the Internal Revenue Code is mute about the accounting method a taxpayer must use for computing its earnings and profits.

for his personal use and benefit and had failed to report it both on the joint returns he filed with his wife and on MBC's tax returns. Consequently, the Commissioner assessed the tax deficiencies and additions for fraud to the taxes against Mazzocchi and MBC which are at issue here.

The taxpayers challenged the Commissioner's deficiency determinations in the tax court, but the tax court rejected their efforts and held for the Commissioner. * * *

Mazzocchi additionally argued to the tax court that the earnings and profits of MBC, a cash basis taxpayer, should be reduced in the years at issue by the amount of accrued but unpaid taxes, penalties, and interest attributable to its income tax deficiencies for those years. This argument is premised on the Code's treatment of corporate distributions out of earnings and profits as ordinary income but its differing treatment of corporate distributions in excess of earnings and profits as either a return of capital or a capital gain, depending on the taxpayer's basis in the corporate securities. Had Mazzocchi prevailed on that point, then some unspecified portion of the income Mazzocchi diverted from MBC (depending on MBC's earnings and profits in the relevant tax years, an issue the tax court did not resolve) would represent some combination of a nontaxable return of capital and a capital gain with respect to Mazzocchi (in turn depending on his basis in the corporate securities), instead of a constructive dividend taxable at ordinary income tax rates. The tax court, however, rejected his argument, reasoning that there was no basis to adjust earnings and profits for unpaid expenses incurred by MBC, a cash basis taxpayer.

* * *

[W]e chiefly focus on Mazzocchi's contention that a cash basis corporation should be allowed to deduct accrued but unpaid tax liabilities from its earnings and profits. * * *

II. DISCUSSION

A.

* * *

The Code generally treats corporate distributions (or dividends) out of earnings and profits as ordinary income to the shareholder taxpayer. But if a corporation pays a dividend which exceeds its earnings and profits (as measured by § 316(a)), the Code treats that portion of the dividend as a nontaxable return of capital to the shareholder taxpayer to the extent of the taxpayer's basis in the securities, and as a capital gain to the taxpayer once the taxpayer's basis is exhausted. See I.R.C. §§ 301(c), 316(a). * * * From the perspective of Mazzocchi's tax liability, characterizing the income as return of capital and/or capital gain is favorable since a return of capital is nontaxable and, as [capital gains, may be taxed at a lower rate than ordinary income].

The framework described above is relevant to this case because diverted corporate funds are treated as a constructive dividend to the taxpayer and, to the same extent, augment the corporation's taxable income (and hence its earnings and profits). See I.R.C. § 316(a)(defining a dividend as a distribution of property out of earnings and profits) * * *. In other words, the Code would treat the funds Mazzocchi diverted as income to MBC (inflating its earnings and profits), which income MBC then straightaway constructively disbursed to Mazzocchi as dividends.

Thus, assuming MBC did not suffer lost earnings and profits in the relevant years, a determination of a deficiency would increase MBC's earnings and profits by the amount of the deficiency and render all the diverted funds ordinary income to Mazzocchi. See I.R.C. § 301(c)(1). If MBC were able to reduce its earnings and profits by deducting therefrom the accrued (but unpaid) tax liabilities assessed against it in this action, the result would likely be to convert much of the constructive distribution to Mazzocchi into either a nontaxable return of capital or a capital gain, depending on Mazzocchi's basis in MBC shares. Thereby Mazzocchi's federal income tax deficiency and, correspondingly, the penalties and interest assessed against him, would be substantially reduced.

Of course, if MBC is not allowed to deduct the accrued tax liability from its earnings and profits in the relevant years, as a cash basis taxpayer it will be able to deduct those sums from its earnings and profits in the year it pays its back taxes. Accordingly, what is at issue here is only the timing of MBC's deduction of the income tax deficiency, penalties, and interest from its earnings and profits; under the cash basis method MBC would deduct it in the year paid (probably 1994), whereas under the accrual method it would deduct in each of the respective years 1975 through 1979 the amount accrued in that year.

To sustain his contention that a cash basis corporation may not employ the accrual method for determining its earnings and profits, the Commissioner principally relies on Treasury Regulation § 1.312–6 ("Earnings and Profits"[5]). Specifically, § 1.312–6 provides in relevant part:

> In determining the amount of earnings and profits * * * due consideration must be given to the facts, and, while mere bookkeeping entries increasing or decreasing surplus will not be conclu-

5. The term "earnings and profits" is used in various sections of the Code (its predominant use is in the treatment of dividend distributions by corporations), but is not defined therein. The Commissioner, however, has issued various regulations and revenue rulings in an effort to define it. * * * Briefly, earnings and profits are calculated by first adding to taxable income: "all income exempted by statute, income not taxable by the Federal Government under the Constitution [and] items includable in gross income under [the Code]," Treas.Reg. § 1.312–6(b); certain items which a corporation may deduct in computing taxable income (such as percentage depletion and dividends received); and deductions based on artificial timing (such as accelerated depreciation and deferred income). Then, earnings and profits are reduced by items like expenses and losses which a corporation may not deduct from its taxable income (for instance, federal income taxes and, notably, capital losses in past years disallowed as deductions from taxable income under Subchapter P of the Code, see Treas.Reg. § 1.312–7(b)(1)). Finally, various unusual financial transactions (for example, corporate distributions or changes in capital structure) may affect earnings and profits. * * *

> sive, the amount of the earnings and profits in any case will be dependent upon the method of accounting properly employed in computing taxable income * * *. *For instance, a corporation keeping its books and filing its income tax returns * * * on the cash receipts and disbursement basis may not use the accrual basis in determining its earnings and profits.* * * *

Id. (emphasis added). As the Commissioner points out, we owe substantial deference to regulations issued by the agency Congress entrusted to administer the statute. See, e.g., Cottage Sav. Ass'n v. Commissioner, 499 U.S. 554 (1991)("[W]e must defer to [the Commissioner's] regulatory interpretations of the Code so long as they are reasonable.").

We note in this regard that the Supreme Court approved a precursor to § 1.312–6(a) in Commissioner v. South Tex. Lumber Co., 333 U.S. 496 (1948), reh'g denied, 334 U.S. 813 (1948). Although that case arose under the excess profits tax, that tax used the same "accumulated earnings and profits" language which is contained in the current § 316. * * * In upholding a Treasury Regulation in pertinent respects remarkably similar to the one at issue here,[6] the Court rejected an attempt by a corporation which kept the relevant portion of its books using the installment method to use the accrual method in computing its earnings and profits[.] * * *

We owe the regulation heightened deference on account of its protracted history. See Cottage Sav. Ass'n, 499 U.S. at 560–62 * * *. The Commissioner adhered to the IRS' longstanding practice when he first promulgated the regulation at issue here in 1955. See T.D. 6152, 1955–2 C.B. 61, 104–05 (promulgating the regulation);[7] T.D. 5059, 1941–2 C.B. 125, 125–26 (Treasury decision issued to tax collectors containing virtually the identical language later incorporated into § 1.312–6(a)); G.C.M. 2951, VII–1 C.B. 160, 160–61 (General Counsel Memorandum 1928); see also I.T. 3253, 1939–1 C.B. 178, 178–79 (corporation keeping its books on the accrual basis may deduct accrued taxes in the computation of its earnings and profits).

The tax court has also long adhered to the view that a cash basis taxpayer cannot deduct accrued but unpaid taxes from earnings and profits. * * *

Nonetheless, several old court of appeals opinions have come out otherwise, holding that a cash-basis corporation may deduct accrued but unpaid taxes from its earnings and profits. See Demmon v. United States, 321 F.2d 203, 204–06 (7th Cir.1963); Drybrough v. Commissioner, 238 F.2d 735, 738–40 (6th Cir.1956) * * *. The Commissioner's brief and the tax court, see, e.g., Webb v. Commissioner, 67 T.C. 1008, 1018 (1977), with

6. Compare § 29.115–3 of Regulations 111 ("In determining the amount of earnings or profits * * * due consideration must be given to the facts, and, while mere bookkeeping entries increasing or decreasing surplus will not be conclusive, the amount of the earnings or profits in any case will be dependent upon the method of accounting properly employed in computing net income."), reprinted in South Tex. Lumber, 333 U.S. at 500 n. 6, 68 S.Ct. at 698 n. 6 with Treas.Reg. § 1.312–6(a), quoted supra at 928.

7. Treasury Regulation § 1.312–6 (1955) is, in all pertinent respects, identical to the current version.

whom we side, both provide incisive criticisms of the reasoning those appellate decisions utilized and advance cogent arguments why the applicable Treasury regulation is a reasonable construction of the Code which should govern the resolution of this question.[10]

B.

Drybrough primarily relied on cases which had allowed accrual method corporations to reduce earnings and profits by the amount of disputed federal taxes despite the fact that an accrual corporation generally cannot deduct disputed taxes from its income. Building on the reasoning those cases employed, the court in *Drybrough* engrafted a more discernible distortion onto the Code when it concluded that cash method corporations should also be permitted to reduce earnings and profits by the amount of accrued taxes. * * * We decline to brandish those ancient cases to fashion a similar rule * * *. The Commissioner forcefully argues, and we agree, that one objectionable departure from normal tax accounting practices does not justify another.[11]

We also take issue with the rationale expressed in *Drybrough* that general corporate law and accounting concepts of dividends and impairment of capital control the computation of earnings and profits for purposes of federal taxation. * * * As the tax court observed in *Webb*, *Drybrough* evidently "assumes that there must be some correlation between general corporate law concepts of capital and earning surplus and the Federal income tax concepts of capital and earnings and profits, an assumption which is not correct." *Webb*, 67 T.C. at 1020–21. Similarly, the Eighth Circuit Court of Appeals held in *Alworth Trust* that it is improper to "read[ ]into the definition of 'dividend' [in the income tax context] the general law relating to the right of a corporation to declare dividends." 136 F.2d at 814. Given the disparate purposes behind the federal tax code and the corporate law impairment of capital doctrine, we agree.

* * *

The Seventh Circuit Court of Appeals in *Demmon*, supra, relied upon *Drybrough* * * * in resolving that "both reason and authority" support the argument that a cash basis corporation may deduct its accrued and unpaid

10. None of these appellate decisions considered the Treasury regulation which controls the outcome of this case, even though it was in effect when the later two decisions (*Demmon* and *Drybrough*) were handed down.

11. Moreover, like the tax court, we discern no basis for differentiating between accrued taxes and other accrued liabilities when it comes to computing earnings and profits. See *Webb*, 67 T.C. at 1019. Besides our aforementioned deference to § 1.312–6, which contains no exception for tax liabilities, we believe that granting tax (as opposed to other) liabilities special treatment would institute inconsistent accounting methods (the cash method for most items but the accrual method for tax liabilities) for items taken into account in computing earnings and profits. Such special treatment would unnecessarily add complexity to the Code, undesirably distort earnings and profits, and unjustifiably engraft an unprincipled exception onto the Code.

taxes in computing earnings and profits. * * * [I]nsofar as we believe *Drybrough* to be flawed, we think so is *Demmon*.

* * *

C.

Finally, we consider Mazzocchi's assertion that "[c]ourts which have reduced earnings and profits by accrued but unpaid income tax liability have done so with the understanding that earnings and profits are intended to provide a measure of the ability of the Corporation to make distributions which are not out of its capital." That much is certainly true, but even if a Treasury regulation did not tie our hands, it is far from clear that the cash method does not accomplish that goal equally well. Earnings and profits ideally represent what the corporation has earned, whether during that fiscal year or since its inception, in excess of capital invested in it. But we think that in many cases, contrary to the suggestion of Mazzocchi, the cash method accurately reflects that amount, for it treats as earnings and profits the difference between the amount of cash received or gained and the amount of cash spent, depleted, or lost that year.

The cash basis method is not always meticulously accurate, as is illustrated by the case sub judice: a corporation may be deemed to have earnings and profits in one year although in a later year it has to pay taxes (or judgments, liabilities, or other losses) attributable to income earned in the earlier year, which exaggerates in the earlier year (but, by the same token, understates in the later year) the corporation's ability to distribute dividends. But the accrual system also has its drawbacks from an economic perspective. To take but one example, since the corporation has not yet collected the receipts it has accrued, it cannot distribute them (unless it takes out a loan with the accrued income as security, but economically that would be equivalent to selling the accrued income for present cash, rendering the modified accrual method akin to the cash method), and thus the accrual system may also overstate in the current year (and conversely understate in a later year) the corporation's ability to distribute dividends. In short, neither the cash nor the accrual method of accounting may accurately represent in an economic sense the amount of net assets that a corporation has available to distribute as dividends to its shareholders during any given year. Some inaccuracies inhere in the administrative necessity artificially to divide time into discrete years for tax purposes.

We find several significant drawbacks to Mazzocchi's suggested approach allowing a corporate taxpayer the freedom to choose which accounting system to use for calculating earnings and profits irrespective of the accounting method it uses to calculate its taxable income. First, it would tend to skew substantially the payment of taxes in favor of the taxpayer's shareholders, as the taxpayer will choose whichever method minimizes its shareholders' tax liability. * * * Second, to allow the choice would impose upon the Commissioner the burden of maintaining—and auditing—two sets of books for each taxpayer electing inconsistent accounting methods for income and earnings and profits purposes.

* * *

D.

In conclusion, we hold that the tax court correctly rejected Mazzocchi's argument that the earnings and profits of MBC, a cash basis corporation, should be reduced by the amount of accrued but unpaid taxes, penalties, and interest attributable to its income tax deficiencies for the years in issue. To preclude the distortion of tax liability and to spare the Commissioner the concomitant onerous bookkeeping tasks which would follow from a corporation's using one accounting method to compute income while using a different accounting method to calculate earnings and profits, § 1.312–6(a) of the Treasury regulations has long provided that a corporation must use the same accounting method in calculating earnings and profits as it uses in determining its taxable income. * * *

ILLUSTRATIVE MATERIAL

A. DISTRIBUTIONS OUT OF EARNINGS AND PROFITS

1. *General*

Treas. Reg. § 1.316–2 provides rules for ascertaining the source of a distribution. Under the regulations, the accumulated earnings and profits are significant only if the earnings and profits of the current year do not cover the total distributions for the year. See Treas. Reg. § 1.316–1(a)(1). In the latter event, the current earnings and profits are prorated among all of the year's cash distributions and the remaining amount of the distributions is charged against accumulated earnings and profits as of the beginning of the year in the order in which the distributions were made. Although the regulations do not expressly apply this rule if one or more of the distributions is of property, no other rule is provided to govern such a case, and logically the same rule should be applied. See G.C.M. 36,138 (Jan. 15, 1975) (so interpreting Treas. Reg. § 1.316–2). But if there is no overall loss for the year, no proration is made. Suppose that as of January 1, Y Corporation had no accumulated earnings and profits. From January 1 through June 30 it had operating profits (for earnings and profits purposes) of $50,000, and on July 1 it distributed $40,000 in cash to its shareholders. As of December 31, Y Corporation had only $30,000 of current earnings and profits for the year. Only $30,000 of the July 1 distribution is taxable as a dividend because current earnings and profits always are determined at the end of the year without regard to distributions during the year, not at the time of the distribution.

If the operating result for the current year is a loss, so no current earnings and profits exist, then a distribution during the year will be charged against accumulated earnings and profits computed to the date of the distribution. If the actual current earnings and profits or loss to the date of the distribution cannot be ascertained, then the current loss of the year is prorated and applied to the accumulated earnings and profits as of the beginning of the year. See Rev.Rul. 74–164, 1974–1 C.B. 74, for examples applying the foregoing rules. Suppose that on January 1, X Corporation had accumulated earnings and profits of $40,000. For the period January 1 through June 30, it had an operating loss (for earnings and profits purposes) of $50,000, but as of December 31, it had current earnings and profits for the year of $10,000. On July 1, X Corporation distributed $50,000 of cash to its shareholders. Even though as of July 1, the operating loss incurred during the first half of the year would have eliminated the accumulated earnings and profits if the corporate books had been closed at that time, the entire distribution is a dividend. Since the corporation did not in fact incur a loss for the year, but rather earned $10,000, the loss accrued as of July 1 did not reduce accumulated earnings and profits, which as of July 1 remained $40,000.

Allocation of earnings and profits among distributions with respect to different classes of stock presents more difficult problems where one class of stock has dividend priorities established by the corporate charter. Rev. Rul. 69–440, 1969–2 C.B. 46, involved a corporation that had three classes of stock, the first two of which had priority with respect to dividend payments. The corporation distributed amounts to the first two classes of stock in excess of earnings and profits. The Ruling held that if the preferred stock, the first priority stock, had dividend priority under the corporate charter, then earnings and profits were first to be allocated to all of the dividends paid on the preferred stock. If this treatment exhausted earnings and profits and distributions were made with respect to other classes of stock, then those distributions simply reduced the basis of that stock.

2. *Timing of Dividend Inclusion*

A dividend is included in the shareholder's gross income when "received," regardless of whether the shareholder uses the cash receipts or accrual method. See Commissioner v. American Light & Traction Co., 156 F.2d 398 (7th Cir.1946), relying on the rule in Treas. Reg. § 1.301–1(b), and rejecting the other possible dates such as declaration or record; Rev.Rul. 64–290, 1964–2 C.B. 465. See also Caruth Corp. v. United States, 865 F.2d 644 (5th Cir.1989)(dividend on stock transferred by charitable gift after declaration date but before record date was taxable to charitable donee, not donor). Similarly, the date of payment (and not the date of declaration) is the date of distribution from the standpoint of the corporation and, accordingly, dividends are taken into account to reduce earnings and profits in the year of payment. Rev.Rul. 62–131, 1962–2 C.B. 94; Bush Bros. & Co. v. Commissioner, 73 T.C. 424 (1979), aff'd, 668 F.2d 252 (6th Cir.1982). Dividend checks payable and mailed on December 31 affect earnings and profits for the corporation in that year, even though the shareholder does not include the dividend in income until the following year. Rev.Rul. 65–23, 1965–1 C.B. 520.

B. DISTRIBUTIONS NOT OUT OF EARNINGS AND PROFITS

A distribution that is not "out of earnings and profits," because there are neither earnings and profits of the current year nor accumulations since February 28, 1913, or because total distributions exceed available earnings and profits is applied first to reduce the shareholder's basis for the stock to zero under § 301(c)(2), and any excess results in capital gain under § 301(c)(3). Johnson v. United States, 435 F.2d 1257 (4th Cir.1971), held that a taxpayer who had several blocks of stock with different bases was required to treat a distribution on the stock not out of earnings and profits as made pro rata among the blocks of stock in order to determine the gain realized by the taxpayer on the distribution; the taxpayer was not allowed to aggregate the total basis in the stock and offset that total against the amount of the distribution.

Distributions traceable to pre-March 1, 1913 profits are likewise treated as a return of capital. Since § 316(a) provides that for tax purposes all of the earnings and profits accumulated after February 28, 1913 must be distributed before a distribution may be regarded as out of the pre-March 1, 1913 profits, the latter type of distributions are unlikely to occur in the case of profitable corporations.

C. DETERMINATION OF EARNINGS AND PROFITS

1. *General*

The earnings and profits of a year are not synonymous with either taxable income or book net income. Accumulated earnings and profits is not earned surplus in the corporate sense, but the aggregate of annual earnings and profits, as adjusted for distributions and certain other transactions involving shareholders. Although the Code does not comprehensively define the term "earnings and profits," numerous statutory rules governing the determination of earnings and profits move the concept closer to economic income than to either taxable or book income. Nevertheless, the starting point for computing earnings and profits is taxable income, which must then be adjusted to take into account income items excluded from taxable income, expenses (not chargeable to a capital account) that are disallowed as deductions, and myriad differences regarding the timing of income and deductions. Taxable income is used as a starting point, in part, because it is an amount that must be computed in any event based on an ascertainable standard. However, taxable income must be adjusted to account for items of economic income and expenditure not reflected in the income tax base.

2. *Treatment of Special Income Items*

Most items of wholly or partially exempt income, such as tax-exempt interest, life insurance proceeds, and intercorporate domestic dividends, are included in earnings and profits. Treas. Reg. § 1.312–6(b). But some items excluded from gross income also are excluded in the computation of earnings and profits. For example, those subsidies or payments to a corporation regarded as nontaxable contributions to capital under § 118 do not enter into earnings and profits, Rev.Rul. 66–353, 1966–2 C.B. 111. If receipts are treated as contributions to capital rather than as taxable income for services, and thus have no effect on earnings and profits, no depreciation deduction is allowed with respect to the property under Rev.Rul. 66–353, and hence earnings and profits in subsequent years would be increased correspondingly. Although there is no express authority on point, § 312(f)(1) should exclude from earnings and profits amounts received on the issuance of the corporation's own stock or stock options, which are excluded from income by § 1032.

A bad debt previously deducted without an income tax benefit, but which nevertheless reduced earnings and profits, increases earnings and profits on its recovery. Rev.Rul. 58–546, 1958–2 C.B. 143.

Cancellation of an indebtedness of the corporation increases earnings and profits if the cancellation results in taxable income. Schweppe v. Commissioner, 168 F.2d 284 (9th Cir.1948), aff'g 8 T.C. 1224 (1947). The same is true if the cancellation is excluded from income because of the tax benefit rule. Rev.Rul. 58–546, supra. But if the cancellation is excluded from income under § 108 and there is a corresponding basis adjustment under § 1017, then no current increase in earnings and profits results from the cancellation. I.R.C. § 312(1); see also Rev.Rul. 58–546, supra. To the extent that there is no basis reduction, however, earnings and profits must be increased, even though other tax attributes are reduced under § 108(b).

3. *Treatment of Deduction Items*

Most deduction items disallowed in computing taxable income are nonetheless subtracted in determining earnings and profits. Such items include federal income taxes, unreasonable compensation (to the extent not recharacterized as a dividend), excess charitable contributions, disallowed capital losses, and deductions disallowed on grounds of public policy under § 162(c), (e), (f), and (g). See Rev.Rul. 77–442, 1977–2 C.B. 264; see also Rev.Rul. 71–165, 1971–1 C.B. 111 (amortizable bond premium on tax-exempt bonds that is nondeductible under § 171(a)(2) reduces earnings and profits in the year to which the amortizable bond premium is attributable).

A net operating loss carryover deduction does not reduce current earnings and profits because the adjustment to earnings and profits was made in the year the loss was incurred. The same is true with respect to capital loss carryovers under § 1212.

Some deductions permitted in computing taxable income are eliminated in computing earnings and profits. Treas. Reg. § 1.312–6(c) provides that a percentage depletion deduction allowed in computing taxable income must be adjusted to the cost depletion method for the computation of earnings and profits. Similarly, the intercorporate dividends received deduction under § 243 is disallowed. Although a charitable contribution deduction equal to the fair market value of property donated to charity may be allowable under § 170, Rev.Rul. 78–123, 1978–1 C.B. 87, held that a corporation's earnings and profits are reduced only by the adjusted basis of the property since the appreciation element had never entered into earnings and profits. Kaplan v. Commissioner, 43 T.C. 580 (1965)(NA), is to the contrary and in our view is incorrect.

4. *Treatment of Matters of Timing*

As discussed in *Mazzocchi Bus Co.*, except where the Code otherwise specifically so provides, the timing of earnings and profits adjustments is determined by the accounting method used by the corporation in computing taxable income. See Treas. Reg. § 1.312–6(a), first sentence; see also Bangor & Aroostook R. Co. v. Commissioner, 193 F.2d 827 (1st Cir.1951). Thus, for example, a reserve for estimated future expenses, while proper under accounting principles, would not reduce earnings and profits if not deductible for tax purposes. See also Rev.Rul. 66–35, 1966–1 C.B. 63 (amortizable bond premium and bond discount on taxable bonds are reflected in earnings and profits in the same year in which includible or deductible in computing taxable income); Rev.Rul. 60–123, 1960–1 C.B. 145 (corporation deducted interest and taxes for tax purposes, but capitalized such items on its books for regulatory purposes; held, such items are deductible in computing earnings and profits in the same manner and year as allowed for purposes of computing taxable income).

Section 312(f)(1) directs that realized gains and losses be taken into account in computing earnings and profits in the year that they are recognized. Thus, for example, gain deferred on a like-kind exchange under § 1031 does not increase earnings and profits. On the other hand, when gain realized on the sale of property is reported on the installment basis under § 453, § 312(n)(5) directs that the entire gain is added to earnings and profits in the year of the sale, rather than as each installment is received. If it later is determined that the taxpayer realized an overall loss on the transaction, earnings and profits are decreased in the subsequent year. Luckman v. Commissioner, 56 T.C. 1216 (1971).

In computing taxable income, accelerated depreciation deductions are allowed under § 168, and § 179 permits a limited amount of certain capital expenses to be deducted currently. In computing earnings and profits, however, § 312(k)(3) provides that: (1) amounts expensed under § 179 must be deducted ratably over a five-year period; and (2) depreciation deductions for tangible property to which § 168 applies must be computed under the less rapid alternative depreciation system of § 168(g)(2). Section 312(k) is designed to prevent the distribution of nontaxable dividends attributable to the excess of accelerated depreciation over the lesser amount of depreciation considered more accurately to reflect economic decline in value. See S.Rep. No. 91–552, 91st Cong., 1st Sess. 176 (1969). Under Treas. Reg. § 1.312–15(a), § 312(k) also applies to amortization under §§ 169, 184, 187, 188, or "any similar provision."

Because depreciation is allowed at a different rate for earnings and profits purposes, depreciable property has a different basis for this purpose. Accordingly, the gain or loss on the sale of depreciable property for earnings and profits purposes will differ from the taxable gain or loss. Also, because depreciation on manufacturing plant and equipment must be treated as an inventory cost under § 263A, inventories will differ for earnings and profits purposes from those used in computing taxable income.

Section 312(n) requires a number of other adjustments to earnings and profits to reflect more accurately a corporation's economic gain or loss. Among the most significant are that: (1) earnings and profits be increased annually by the "LIFO recapture amount," which generally speaking is tantamount to requiring that earnings and profits be computed using only the first in-first out (FIFO) inventory method; and (2) deductible intangible drilling and development costs and solid mineral exploration and development costs be capitalized and amortized in future years.

5. *Effect of Stock Option Transactions*

In Luckman v. Commissioner, 418 F.2d 381 (7th Cir.1969), a shareholder received from a corporation a cash distribution that he treated as a nontaxable return of capital. In prior years, the corporation had sold stock to its employees under "restricted stock options" at a purchase price that was about $3.4 million less than the fair market value of the stock at the time of sale. Under a now repealed provision, the employees were not taxed on the discount. The taxpayer nevertheless argued that the difference between the option price and the fair market value reduced the earnings and profits of the corporation, creating a deficit in the corporation's earnings and profits account, and thus rendered the distributions received by the taxpayer nontaxable. The Tax Court held that earnings and profits were not reduced as the result of the exercise of the stock options (50 T.C. 619 (1968)), but the Court of Appeals reversed:

"As used in federal taxation, [the earnings and profits] concept represents an attempt to separate those corporate distributions with respect to stock which represent returns of capital contributed by the stockholders from those distributions which represent gain derived from the initial investment by virtue of the conduct of business. The crucial issue is whether a given transaction has a real effect upon the portion of corporate net worth which is not representative of distributed capital and which results from its conduct of business. In order to make this determination it is necessary to scrutinize the economic effects of the particular transaction as well as its character and relation to the corporate business. * * *"

"Had the compensation been paid in cash and then used to purchase stock, there could be no question that the corporation had incurred a true economic expense which reduced earnings and profits. The amount of corporate assets available for distribution to those who owned the stock at the time of the transaction is reduced to the same extent in either case. The economic effect of the two transactions is identical." (383–84) Accord Divine v. Commissioner, 500 F.2d 1041 (2d Cir.1974), rev'g 59 T.C. 152 (1972).

Stock options that are governed by § 422 or by § 83 and Treas. Reg. § 1.421–6 should produce the same result as in *Luckman*.

6. *Federal Income Tax Costs*

Following Treas. Reg. § 1.312–6(a), first sentence, which provides for computation of earnings and profits using the taxpayer's method of accounting, an accrual method corporation takes federal income taxes into account in determining earnings and profits in the year to which the taxes relate, even in the case of a deficiency that is not discovered and paid until a later year. Deutsch v. Commissioner, 38 T.C. 118 (1962). An income tax refund arising from a net operating loss carryback is taken into account for purposes of earnings and profits in the year in which the net operating loss occurred, not in the year to which it is carried back. *Deutsch,* supra; Rev.Rul. 64–146, 1964–1 (Part 1) C.B. 129.

As discussed in *Mazzocchi Bus Co.*, however, the treatment of federal income taxes for cash method corporations has proved troublesome. *Mazzocchi Bus Co.* followed Helvering v. Alworth Trust, 136 F.2d 812 (8th Cir.1943), Webb v. Commissioner, 67 T.C. 1008 (1977), aff'd per curiam, 572 F.2d 135 (5th Cir.1978), and Rev.Rul. 70–609, 1970–2 C.B. 78, in holding that a cash method corporation could not subtract the federal income taxes until the year paid, and refused to follow Drybrough v. Commissioner, 238 F.2d 735 (6th Cir.1956), and Demmon v. United States, 321 F.2d 203 (7th Cir.1963), which permitted subtraction in the year to which the taxes related. Since Congress has narrowed the types of C Corporations that can use the cash method of accounting, the problem now is of diminished importance. But for those C corporations that can use the cash method of accounting, the *Mazzocchi Bus Co.* approach produces a result more consistent with the purposes of the earnings and profits concept.

7. *Effect of Distributions*

Accumulated earnings and profits represents a running account, which is based upon the algebraic sum of the yearly earnings and profits or loss figures from the commencement of the corporate life, reduced by distributions chargeable to earnings and profits. Thus, distributions of taxable dividends reduce the accumulated earnings and profits. I.R.C. § 312(a). Deficits in the accumulated earnings and profits resulting from operating losses must be made up by subsequent earnings and profits before the account will be on the plus side. But an impairment of capital resulting from capital distributions need not be restored. Hence a distribution treated as a dividend under corporation law but not constituting a dividend for tax purposes because the requisite earnings and profits do not exist, does not produce a deficit in the earnings and profits account and does not prevent subsequent earnings from producing a plus figure for accumulated earnings and profits. Meyer v. Commissioner, 7 T.C. 1381 (1946)(involving stock redemptions); Estate of Uris v. Commissioner, 605 F.2d 1258 (2d Cir.1979)(same result; deficit in earnings and profits can be created only by operating losses).

The cancellation by a corporation of a shareholder's debt to the corporation is a distribution of property to the shareholder that reduces earnings and profits, Shephard v. Commissioner, 340 F.2d 27 (6th Cir. 1965). In Maher v. Commissioner, 55 T.C. 441 (1970) (NA), the Tax Court held that the assumption of a shareholder's liability on a note constituted a distribution that was the equivalent of money and was therefore a taxable dividend in the year of the assumption to the extent of earnings and profits, which were reduced accordingly. The Court of Appeals reversed, holding that a dividend resulted, not in the year the liability was assumed, but in the year payments were actually made by the corporation on the principal obligation; the taxpayer had remained secondarily liable on the note assumed by the corporation and hence the dividend arose only at the time of payment. 469 F.2d 225 (8th Cir.1972). The Internal Revenue Service announced in Rev.Rul. 77–360, 1977–2 C.B. 86, that it would follow the Court of Appeals decision in cases involving similar facts. The Tax Court approach is the correct one; once the corporation incurred the debt, a claim on the corporations' earnings was created and its capacity to distribute dividends was reduced at that time.

Rev.Proc. 75–17, 1975–1 C.B. 677, provides guidelines for the treatment of distributions that are claimed to be nontaxable in whole or in part.

D. PARENT AND SUBSIDIARY EARNINGS AND PROFITS

The earnings and profits of parent and subsidiary corporations that do not file consolidated returns are generally not consolidated for purposes of determining whether distributions by the parent corporation to its shareholders are out of earnings and profits and hence taxable as dividends. (As discussed at page 462, members of an affiliated group of corporations filing consolidated returns do combine the earnings and profits of the group.) As a result, in the non-consolidated return context, it is possible for the parent corporation to make distributions to its shareholders that will not be treated as dividends despite the existence of earnings and profits in the subsidiary corporation.

Suppose that X Corporation, which has earnings and profits, wishes to make cash available to a shareholder but the shareholder does not want the distribution treated as a dividend. The shareholder transfers the stock of X Corporation to Y Corporation, a newly formed holding company, in a § 351 exchange. Y Corporation then obtains a loan from a bank, secured by the X Corporation stock, and distributes the loan proceeds to the shareholder. Dividends are then paid by X Corporation to Y Corporation, which it uses to pay off the bank loan. Assuming that the distribution by Y Corporation to the shareholders is made in a taxable year that ends before dividends are paid to it by X Corporation, and if the form of the transaction is respected, the taxpayer would have achieved return of basis treatment (§ 301(c)(2)) for what is in effect a distribution of the subsidiary's profits. However, Rev.Rul. 80–239, 1980–2 C.B. 103, held that the distribution from Y Corporation was in fact a disguised dividend paid by X Corporation. Section 304, discussed at page 272, was amended in 1982 specifically to govern such transactions, and reaches substantially the same result as the Ruling through different mechanics.

SECTION 3. DISTRIBUTION OF A DIVIDEND IN KIND

INTERNAL REVENUE CODE: Sections 301(a), (b), (c), (d); 311; 312(a)(3), (b), (c); 336(b).

In General Utilities & Operating Co. v. Helvering, 296 U.S. 200 (1935), the taxpayer corporation distributed to its three shareholders 19,090 shares of stock in another corporation, Islands Edison Co., which had a basis to the distributing corporation of $1,900 but which was worth approximately $1,071,426. The dividend was declared as payable in the stock of the Islands Edison Co., and the distribution was made after the corporation became aware that another corporation wished to purchase its Islands Edison stock. The distributing corporation's purpose was to avoid paying a corporate tax on the gain on the sale of the stock. The Commissioner sought to tax General Utilities & Operating Co. on the appreciation inherent in the stock at the time of the distribution on a number of different theories, including that the dividend was in effect a cash dividend that created a debt that was discharged by the transfer of appreciated property. The Supreme Court upheld the decisions of the lower courts that the taxpayer corporation did not realize any gain because there was no sale; the dividend was payable directly in stock, not in cash, and thus no debt ever arose.

Notwithstanding that the actual issue on appeal in *General Utilities* was narrower,[1] the case generally came to be regarded as standing for the proposition that no gain or loss ever was realized by a corporation that distributed property as a dividend. The Commissioner steadily attacked this rule, but his arguments were consistently rejected by the courts. See, e.g., Transport, Trading & Terminal Corp. v. Commissioner, 9 T.C. 247 (1947)(NA), rev'd on other issues, 176 F.2d 570 (2d Cir.1949).

In the 1954 revision of the Internal Revenue Code Congress codified the *General Utilities* approach in former versions of § 311, governing distributions not in liquidation, and § 336, governing distributions in liquidation of the corporation. These sections provided for nonrecognition of both gain and loss at the corporate level on the distribution of property by a corporation. Over the next thirty years, however, Congress slowly but steadily added exceptions to the nonrecognition of gain rule in § 311 (and to a lesser extent § 336), while leaving nonrecognition of losses wholly intact. By 1984, the exceptions had nearly swallowed the general rule as recognition of gain was extended to almost all dividend and redemption distributions of appreciated property. Nonrecognition generally was limited to partial liquidation distributions received by certain individuals and dividend or redemption distributions of capital (or § 1231) assets if specific

1. The Supreme Court declined to consider the Commissioner's argument that the taxpayer in effect sold the Island Edison Co. stock to the buyer, followed by a distribution of the proceeds to the shareholders, because the argument was not raised before the trial court.

restrictive conditions had been met. Nonrecognition to the corporation on liquidating distributions as provided under § 336, however, continued unchanged. The reason given for the 1984 amendments to § 311, in Staff of the Joint Committee on Taxation, General Explanation of the Tax Reform Act of 1984, 98th Cong., 2d Sess. (Comm.Print, Dec. 31, 1984), was straightforward:

"Under a double tax system, corporate income generally is taxed twice. Such income is taxed first to the corporation that earns it. It is taxed a second time to the ultimate shareholders of such corporation when it is distributed to them. Any failure to treat distributions of appreciated property as taxable events to the distributing corporation, however, provided opportunities for deferring, or even avoiding, corporate level tax. The Congress believed that such a result was inappropriate under a double-tax system." (148–149).

This explanation left something to be desired. If virtual repeal of the *General Utilities* doctrine was necessary to protect the double tax system, why were any exceptions to recognition retained in § 311, and why should § 336 continue to provide nearly complete nonrecognition of gain and loss at the corporate level on liquidating distributions? Congress responded to this inconsistency in the Tax Reform Act of 1986 by replacing the *General Utilities* rule with one of gain recognition on distributions of appreciated property by a corporation.

House Ways and Means Committee Report, Tax Reform Act of 1986

H.Rep. No. 99–426, 99th Cong., 1st Sess., 281–82 (1985).

The committee believes that the *General Utilities* rule, * * * produces many incongruities and inequities in the tax system. First, the rule may create significant distortions in business behavior. Economically, a liquidating distribution is indistinguishable from a nonliquidating distribution; yet the Code provides a substantial preference for the former. A corporation acquiring the assets of a liquidating corporation is able to obtain a basis in assets equal to their fair market value, although the transferor recognizes no gain (other than possibly recapture amounts) on the sale. The tax benefits may make the assets more valuable in the hands of the transferee than in the hands of the present owner. The effect may be to induce corporations with substantial appreciated assets to liquidate and transfer their assets to other corporations for tax reasons, when economic considerations might indicate a different course of action. Accordingly, the *General Utilities* rule may be responsible, at least in part, for the dramatic increase in corporate mergers and acquisitions in recent years. The committee believes that the Code should not artificially encourage corporate liquidations and acquisitions, and believes that repeal of the *General Utilities* rule is a major step towards that goal.

Second, the *General Utilities* rule tends to undermine the corporate income tax. Under normally applicable tax principles, nonrecognition of gain is available only if the transferee takes a carryover basis in the transferred property, thus assuring that a tax will eventually be collected on the appreciation. Where the *General Utilities* rule applies, assets generally are permitted to leave corporate solution and to take a stepped-up basis in the hands of the transferee without the imposition of a corporate-level tax. Thus, the effect of the rule is to grant a permanent exemption from the corporate income tax.

ILLUSTRATIVE MATERIAL

A. SCOPE OF RECOGNITION AT THE CORPORATE LEVEL

1. *General*

Section 311(a) continues to set forth a general rule of nonrecognition at the corporate level for distributions by a corporation "with respect to its stock" of its stock (or rights to acquire its stock) and "property." Section 311(b) then reverses this rule if the distribution is subject to § 301 or § 302 *and* the fair market value of the property exceeds its basis to the corporation. In such cases, the corporation is required to recognize gain as if it had sold the property to the distributee at fair market value. Section 311(a) continues to prevent the recognition of a loss.

In Pope & Talbot, Inc. v. Commissioner, 104 T.C. 574 (1995), the taxpayer transferred property to a newly formed limited partnership in which its shareholders were the limited partners. The taxpayer argued that the gain recognized under § 311 should be computed with reference to the fair market value of the property received by the shareholders, i.e., the aggregate fair market value of the partnership interests, rather than by the fair market value of the distributed property if sold as an entirety. The court rejected this argument, finding that it would undermine the purposes of § 311. On further proceedings in *Pope & Talbot*, the Tax Court held that the trading value of the distributed limited partnership interests was relevant, but not determinative, in valuing the land. Because the aggregate trading value of the limited partnership units was less than the value of the land, the court found that the land should be valued at the lower end of the possible range of values for the land itself. T.C. Memo. 1997–116. The Tax Court's decision was affirmed, 162 F.3d 1236 (9th Cir. 1999).

2. *Character of Gain*

Section 311(b) specifies that gain should be recognized as if the corporation had sold the distributed property. This rule should control characterization of the gain as ordinary or capital, as well as its amount. Thus, gain recognized by the corporation on the distribution of appreciated capital assets can be offset by recognized capital losses. See I.R.C. § 1211. Gain on the distribution of § 1231 assets may be capital or ordinary, subject to the § 1231 computation and the applicability of the various recapture rules (primarily § 1245). Section 1239 may recharacterize gain as ordinary when the property is distributed to a more than 50 percent shareholder (taking into account attribution) in whose hands the property is depreciable.

3. *Losses*

The 1986 Act did not eliminate all of the anomalies in the treatment of property distributions by corporations. Section 336 allows the recognition of loss at the corporate level, subject to certain exceptions, on liquidating distributions. But under § 311, no loss is allowed when depreciated property is distributed. Suppose that X Corporation purchased two parcels of land: Tract 1 for $5,000 in 1997, and Tract 2 for $7,000 in 1998. In 1999, when each parcel had a fair market value of $6,000, X Corporation distributed both parcels as a dividend. X Corporation cannot offset the loss on Tract 2 against the gain on Tract 1.

Since X Corp. cannot offset the loss against the gain, can the nonrecognition of the loss on Tract 2 be sidestepped by selling it to the shareholders? A sale might be accomplished in either of two ways. First, the shareholders could pay the corporation cash for the property. Alternatively, the corporation could declare a $6,000 cash dividend, thereby creating a debt to the shareholders, and then distribute the property in satisfaction of the debt. If the debt is bona fide and the subsequent transfer of property in satisfaction of the debt is an independent transaction, a loss should be allowed on the disposition of the property. But if the two distributions are related and the step transaction doctrine is applied to integrate the transactions, the loss would be disallowed by § 311(a).

If a sale is to a more than fifty percent shareholder, § 267(a)(1) disallows any loss at the corporate level. But if the shareholder later sells the property at a gain, pursuant to § 267(d) the gain will not be recognized to the extent of the previously disallowed loss. Section 311 does not permit the transferee in effect to use the disallowed loss in this fashion. If § 311 were amended to provide for recognition of loss to the distributing corporation, should § 267 apply to disallow the loss in proper circumstances?

Congress did not explain why the 1986 revisions retained the *General Utilities* rule as to current distributions of depreciated property. Is there any sound policy reason for denying the loss deduction? Since under § 301(d) the shareholder's basis for distributed property is its fair market value at the time of distribution, the loss is eliminated forever. The disallowance of the loss may be avoided by selling the property to a third party and distributing the proceeds to the shareholders or, assuming § 267 does not apply, by selling the property to the shareholders. In the first case, however, the shareholders may desire the actual property, not its equivalent value. In the second case, the transaction is economically different. Perhaps the unarticulated reason for disallowing the recognition of losses is Congressional concern with tax avoidance transactions in closely held corporations. If the tax avoidance potential of allowing corporations a loss on distributions of property to majority shareholders is the concern, it would appear that the problem could have been addressed by subjecting losses at the corporate level resulting from distributions to shareholders to the same rules that govern losses realized on sales to shareholders.

4. *Distributions of Encumbered Property*

The distribution of property subject to a lien, whether or not the shareholder expressly assumes the corporation's liability, results in realization of the same amount of gain as would have been realized if the property had been sold by the corporation. To deal with situations in which the amount of the lien exceeds the fair market value of the property, § 311(b)(2), through a cross reference to § 336(b), provides that for this purpose the fair market value of the property will be treated as not less than the amount of the liability. If the corporate debt secured by the property is nonrecourse, this rule is merely duplicative of § 7701(g). See also Commissioner v. Tufts, 461 U.S. 300 (1983). But if a recourse liability that is greater than the fair market value of the property is assumed by the shareholder, the rule in § 311(b) converts what might otherwise be ordinary income from discharge of indebtedness under Treas. Reg. § 1.1001-2(a)(2) into gain from the sale or exchange of property.

B. THE EFFECT OF DIVIDENDS IN KIND ON EARNINGS AND PROFITS

Accounting for the proper adjustments to earnings and profits as a result of dividends in kind entails several steps. Because a distribution in kind of appreciated property results in the recognition of gain to the corporation under § 311, earnings and profits automatically should be increased by the recognized gain under the normal rules basing earnings and profits on taxable income. See I.R.C. § 312(f)(1). Redundantly, § 312(b)(1) requires that earnings and profits be increased in the amount by which the fair market of the distributed property exceeds its basis. Read literally, § 312(b)(1) results in a double addition to earnings and profits; it is unlikely, however, that it will be so interpreted. The distribution itself requires a downward adjustment to earnings and profits in an amount equal to the fair market value of the distributed property. See I.R.C. §§ 312(a)(3) and 312(b)(2). Why are earnings and profits increased by only the gain but decreased by the fair market value of the distributed property?

Note that § 312(b)(1) excepts from the rule requiring an increase in earnings and profits the distribution of the corporation's own promissory note. Similarly, § 311(b) excepts such a distribution from its gain recognition rule. The distribution, however, does effect a reduction in earnings and profits. The upward adjustment occurs when the corporation earns the income used to pay the indebtedness; there is no downward adjustment when the note is paid.

If depreciated property is distributed, § 312(a)(3) allows earnings and profits to be reduced by the basis of the property, even though § 311(a) disallows recognition of the loss. Note that as far as the net effect on earnings and profits is concerned, this treatment achieves the same result as allowing the loss and reducing earnings and profits by the fair market value of the distributed property.

In determining the extent to which any distributions (including that of the property itself) made during the year are taxable as dividends, the increase in current earnings and profits for the year resulting from the recognized gain attributable to the distribution of property is taken into account in the same manner as any other income item for the year as provided in Treas. Reg. § 1.316–2. Thus the current earnings and profits resulting from a distribution of appreciated property may be used to support dividend treatment of a portion of an unrelated cash distribution. Suppose that X Corporation has neither accumulated nor current earnings and profits except as generated by property distributions during the current year. During the year it distributes property having a fair market value of $100 and a basis of $20 to Shareholder A and $100 cash to Shareholder B. Forty dollars ($40) of the distribution to each shareholder is a dividend. In G.C.M. 36,138 (Jan. 15, 1975), the Service so interpreted Treas. Reg. § 1.316–2.

If the distributed property is subject to liens or the distributee shareholder assumes a corporate liability in connection with the distribution, § 312(c) requires that a "proper adjustment" be made. Treas. Reg. § 1.312–3 interprets the statutory language to mean that the downward adjustment to earnings and profits under § 312(a) or § 312(b) to reflect the distribution should be reduced by the amount of the liability. Because of the manner in which Treas. Reg. § 1.316–2 apportions earnings and profits among distributions during the year to determine the extent to which each distribution is a dividend, the result is not always the same as simply increasing current earnings and profits by the amount of the liability and then making the § 312(a) and § 312(b) adjustments to reflect the distribution.

C. TREATMENT OF SHAREHOLDERS

Section 301(b)(1) provides that in the case of both corporate and individual shareholders the amount of any distribution that is a dividend is the fair market value of the distributed property. However, where the property is subject to a lien or the shareholder assumes a corporate indebtedness in connection with the distribution, § 301(b)(2) directs that the amount of the distribution be reduced by the amount of the debt. In all cases, nevertheless, the shareholder's basis in the distributed property is its fair market value. I.R.C. § 301(d). But see Tabbi v. Commissioner, T.C. Memo. 1995–463 (daughter of shareholder took a zero basis in property received from controlled corporation, as an indirect gift from father, because father did not report transfer as a constructive dividend to him). Suppose that a corporation with sufficient earnings and profits to support dividend treatment of the entire distribution distributes property having a fair market value of $100, subject to a mortgage of $60. The shareholder has a dividend of $40, but takes a basis in the distributed property of $100. If the shareholder then sells the property for $40 cash, with the purchaser assuming the $60 mortgage, the shareholder realizes no gain. Why is this the correct result?

D. DISTRIBUTION OF RIGHTS TO PURCHASE STOCK OF ANOTHER CORPORATION

Prior to the enactment of the 1954 Code, Palmer v. Commissioner, 302 U.S. 63 (1937), held that the issuance by a corporation of rights to purchase stock in another corporation was not a dividend at the time of issuance. In light of the broad definition of "property" provided in § 317(a), however, rights to purchase stock of another corporation are "property" and are currently taxable as a dividend under § 301. Rev.Rul. 70–521, 1970–2 C.B. 72; Weigl v. Commissioner, 84 T.C. 1192 (1985). Section 311(b) requires the distributing corporation to recognize gain in the amount by which the fair market value of the rights exceeds its basis in the rights; a correlative increase in earnings and profits is required. Under current § 312(a)(3) and 312(b)(2), the distributing corporation reduces earnings and profits by the fair market value of the rights.

E. DISTRIBUTION OF CORPORATION'S OWN SECURITIES

1. *Debt Instruments*

Suppose that a corporation distributes its own promissory note in the face amount of $10,000. As far as the shareholder is concerned, a distribution of the corporation's own debt instrument generally is treated in the same manner as any other distribution of property. Section 301(b), which appears to provide that the amount of the distribution is the fair market value of the instrument, and § 301(d), which appears to give the shareholder a fair market value basis in the distributed obligation, must be coordinated with the OID rules of §§ 1271–1275. (See Chapter 13, Section 2.) Pursuant to § 1275(a)(4) and Treas. Reg. § 1.1001–1(g), the "amount" of the distribution for purposes of § 301(b) is the "issue price" of the obligation determined under § 1273 or § 1274. If the instrument is publicly traded upon issue, its issue price equals its fair market value. I.R.C. § 1273(b); Treas. Reg. § 1.1273–2(b)(1). If the debt obligation is not publicly traded, the issue price is determined under § 1274 with reference to the sum of the present values (discounted at the appropriate AFR) of all payments due under the obligation. If the stated principal amount does not exceed the present value of the future payment at the appropriate AFR, then the stated principal amount is the issue price; otherwise, the issue price equals the discounted present value of the payments. The issue price, so determined, then becomes the shareholder's initial basis in the instrument. As long as the instrument bears interest, payable at least annually, at the appropriate AFR for its term, however, the issue price will be the stated principal amount of the obligation, which should be treated as its fair market value.

The distributing corporation receives substantially different treatment when it distributes its own debt instrument than it does when it distributes other property. Because its basis for its own promissory note presumably is zero, if the general rule applied, the distributing corporation might be required to recognize gain. However, the parenthetical in § 311(b)(1)(A) provides nonrecognition treatment to the distributing corporation. Earnings and profits adjustments are governed by § 312(a)(2), which reduces earnings and profits by the face amount of an obligation other than an obligation bearing original issue discount (OID). If the distributed instrument bears OID, then earnings and profits are reduced only by the "issue price." For purposes of applying § 312(a)(2), § 312(*o*) incorporates the OID rules. Section 1275(a)(4) treats an OID instrument distributed by a corporation with respect to its stock as an OID instrument issued in exchange for property. Therefor, as in the case of the shareholder, § 1274 applies. As a result, earnings and profits are reduced by the lesser of the "issue price" of the obligation or its face amount. See S.Rep. No. 98–169, 98th Cong., 2d Sess. 188–89 (1984).

Discount obligations distributed to shareholders in a § 301 distribution are thereafter subject to the OID rules, as if they had been issued for cash equal to their issue price at the time of distribution. When the corporation deducts interest on the obligation under § 163(e) as it economically accrues, earnings and profits eventually will be charged with the full face amount of the obligation.

2. *Stock or rights to acquire stock*

Distributions to shareholders of a corporation's own stock or rights to purchase such stock generally are not subject to the rules of § 301 and § 311. Special rules under § 305 apply to these situations. See Chapter 15.

SECTION 4. DISGUISED DIVIDENDS

INTERNAL REVENUE CODE: Sections 61(a)(7); 301(a), (b); 316(a); 317(a).

REGULATIONS: Sections 1.162–7; 1.301–1(c), (j), (m).

Ireland v. United States

United States Court of Appeals, Fifth Circuit, 1980.
621 F.2d 731.

■ AINSWORTH, CIRCUIT JUDGE:

Appellant Charles W. Ireland ("Ireland") used aircraft provided by his company to travel between his home and the firm's headquarters. The Internal Revenue Service ("IRS") assessed additional income to Ireland in the amount of the alleged value of the plane rides. After paying the resulting deficiency, Ireland brought suit in district court seeking a refund. The district court upheld the assessment and denied the refund. Ireland therefore appeals. We affirm the district court's holding that the value of the plane trips is taxable income to Ireland, but disagree, however, with the method used by the IRS and adopted by the district court in calculating the value. Accordingly, we remand for further proceedings in that regard.

Ireland was employed by Birmingham Slag Company in 1939. Virtually all of the stock in the company was owned by members of appellant's family. Working his way through the corporate ladder, appellant became the president of the firm in 1951. In 1956, Birmingham Slag merged with Vulcan Detinning Company to form Vulcan Material Company ("Vulcan"), with Ireland as its president. Since the merger, Vulcan has been a publicly held corporation with its principal office in Birmingham, Alabama.

* * *

[Eventually, Ireland became Chairman of the Board of Directors of Vulcan and Bernard Monaghan became President of Vulcan. Ireland and Monaghan differed in their views of corporate policy. Lower management personnel bypassed the corporate chain of command and brought problems directly to Ireland. The resulting conflict interfered with the efficient operation of the company. To resolve the deleterious effect of the conflict between Monaghan and Ireland, Monaghan was given sole control over the company's daily operations while Ireland concentrated on the development of long-range policies. To make Ireland less accessible to Vulcan's management personnel, thereby forcing them to deal directly with Monaghan, Ireland left the Vulcan's Birmingham office.]

Ireland moved from Birmingham to Lynn Haven, Florida, in 1965, to a home owned by his wife. After the move, Vulcan paid for his long-distance calls to the Birmingham office as well as the cost of office supplies used in conjunction with a business office maintained in appellant's Lynn Haven home.

While in Lynn Haven, Ireland had frequent occasion to travel to Birmingham in order to attend meetings of the executive committee or the Board of Directors. Ireland also traveled to various other locations in conjunction with certain business deals * * *. Whenever Ireland desired, the company would arrange for one of its airplanes to fly to Panama City, the nearest airport to Lynn Haven, to pick up Ireland. The cost of these flights was borne by Vulcan. On occasion, Ireland's family or friends would travel with him on the flights on a space-available basis.

* * *

Ireland raises two issues on appeal. First, he challenges the district court's finding that the value of the airplane flights provided by Vulcan constituted income to him. Ireland contends that the flights were not regular commuting expenses because he was forced to move to Lynn Haven in order to solve the management crisis resulting from his personal conflict with Monaghan. Assuming the district court was correct on the first issue, Ireland also argues that the method of determining the value of the flights was improper. We address these issues in order.

The Value of the Flights as Income

* * * Under section 61(a)(7), gross income includes the receipt of any dividend. A dividend under the Code is "any distribution of property made by a corporation to its shareholders." 26 U.S.C. § 316(a). There is no

requirement that the dividend be formally declared or even intended by the corporation. Loftin and Woodard, Inc. v. United States, 577 F.2d 1206, 1214 (5th Cir.1978) * * * . Accordingly, an expenditure made by a corporation for the personal benefit of a stockholder, or the use by the shareholder of corporate-owned facilities for his personal benefit, may result in the taxpayer being found to have received a constructive dividend. See, e. g., Commissioner v. Riss, 374 F.2d 161, 170 (8th Cir.1967)(taxpayer's use of company-owned automobile); Nicholls, North, Buse Co. v. Commissioner, 56 T.C. 1225 (1971)(use of boat purchased by company and used by taxpayer's son for predominantly personal purposes); International Artists, Ltd. v. Commissioner, 55 T.C. 94, 105–08 (1970)(use of residence provided by corporation). * * *

In determining whether a constructive dividend has been made, "(t)he crucial concept * * * is that the corporation conferred an economic benefit on the stockholder without expectation of repayment." United States v. Smith, 418 F.2d 589, 593 (5th Cir.1969). * * * Of course, economic benefit per se is not the only factor determining taxability. In order for a company-provided benefit to be treated as income, the item must primarily benefit taxpayer's personal interests as opposed to the business interests of the corporation. * * * The district court found that the airplane flights between Panama City and Birmingham were in the nature of commuting expenses and therefore the flights primarily served Ireland's personal interests.

* * *

Our consideration of the nature of the traveling expenses incurred in the present case is aided by the Supreme Court's landmark decision in Commissioner v. Flowers, 326 U.S. 465, 66 S.Ct. 250 * * *(1946). In *Flowers*, the taxpayer was an attorney practicing in Jackson, Mississippi. He received an offer of employment from a railroad company located in Mobile, Alabama. He accepted the position with an understanding that he would continue to reside in Jackson where he had an established home and community of friends. Thereafter, Flowers lived in Jackson, but traveled to Mobile frequently. He sought to deduct the costs of commuting between Jackson and Mobile. The Supreme Court denied the deduction. Focusing on the business purpose for his living arrangement, the Court noted that Flowers' decision to reside in Jackson served no interest of the railroad company, but reflected only his personal preferences. * * * Since the costs occasioned by Flowers' lengthy commute did not aid the corporation, the expense was personal and not deductible.

The threshold question presented in this case is somewhat different from that posed in *Flowers*. Here, we first must determine whether the value of flights provided by a company can be included in income under section 61, whereas in *Flowers*, the Court considered the deductibility of traveling expenses incurred by the taxpayer. Despite the different focus, both questions turn on the nature of the traveling expense. The Court in *Flowers* held that if traveling expenses were personal, no deduction was permitted. Similarly, if a company provides facilities that allow a taxpayer to avoid incurring an otherwise personal expense, then the value of the services rendered must be included in income in the absence of an overriding business purpose. *Flowers* necessarily determined that traveling expenses such as those encountered in that case are personal. As items of personal expense, *Flowers* implicitly holds that they cannot be provided directly by a company, in the absence of a business purpose, without the taxpayer including in income the value received.

Appellant does not disagree with the principle that a taxpayer's use of company-provided facilities for personal commuting should be included in income. Rather, Ireland seeks to distinguish *Flowers* by arguing that his decision to reside in Lynn Haven was based on business reasons. Specifically, Ireland contends that he moved * * * in order to serve Vulcan's interests in having him physically separated from Monaghan. The district court acknowledged the relevancy of Vulcan's interest in the separation, but rejected it as the basis of appellant's move. * * * [T]he district court found that Vulcan's corporate interest could have been equally well served by Ireland "establishing an office in his home in Birmingham and instructing subordinate officials to communicate with Monaghan and not with [Ireland.]" Under this view, Ireland's move to Lynn Haven was based on personal concerns so that the increase in traveling costs was also personal, as in *Flowers*.

* * * On the basis of the evidence presented, it cannot be said that Ireland was directed by Vulcan to leave Birmingham. Any conclusion of business purpose in this regard is pure surmise. Accordingly, the record adequately supports the district court's finding that the move, while indirectly benefitting Vulcan, was primarily personal in nature so that the transportation expenses between Lynn Haven and Birmingham were personal, as was the case in *Flowers*. Therefore, the value of the company-provided flights was properly included in Ireland's income for the 1970 tax year.

Valuing the Flights

Having resolved the threshold question, we now must consider whether the district court properly determined the value of the flights. As an initial matter, we note that the parties agree on the basic principle controlling the determination of value. As the Government states in its brief, "the amount of income attributable to taxpayer by reason of his personal use of the corporate aircraft is measured by the fair market value of obtaining similar services or facilities in an arms-length transaction in the open market." (Appellee's brief, p. 20) In light of the acknowledged standard, it is surprising that the IRS chose to base its measure not on the fair market value of some comparable service, but on an allocable portion of the total cost of operating Vulcan's air fleet. Specifically, the IRS first determined the total cost of operating Vulcan's entire fleet, including charges for depreciation, during 1970. That figure was divided by the total number of miles flown by Vulcan's planes to arrive at a cost per mile figure. The IRS calculated its assessment of value by multiplying the number of miles Ireland flew for personal trips by the cost per mile figure.

The Government's position is that the total cost method based on the corporation's costs of operating its airplanes is an adequate measure of value, and that Ireland did not introduce sufficient evidence of superior alternative methods of valuation to overcome the presumptive correctness of the IRS method. It is clear, however, that the total cost approach is not the preferred approach. Fair market value of the services received is the overriding concept in the measurement of a constructive dividend and "(t)he equation of value with costs, is therefore, not the norm but the exception." Loftin and Woodard, supra, 577 F.2d at 1223.

Despite the preference for a fair market value approach, the taxpayer has the burden of proving that the assessment was incorrect. * * * At trial, Ireland introduced competent evidence demonstrating the cost of charter air service. Specifically, appellant introduced an exhibit showing charter rates from six different companies including mileage rates, hourly charges, deadhead charges, overnight rates, as well as discounts available for volume customers. * * *

The Government contends that charter air service is not comparable to the company-provided flights. The Government presents a number of factors showing the differences between the two. First, the company planes were "on-call" and could be obtained by Ireland with little prior notice. Second, the charter service did not have the same "aura of distinction" that one could achieve by traveling on company planes. Third, the planes available for charter were not necessarily of the same quality as Vulcan's planes especially since the company occasionally provided Ireland with the use of its Lear jet. Finally, Vulcan's planes, in accordance with company policy, had two pilots to minimize the risk of accidents, whereas charter planes would have been piloted by a single person. The Government contends that these points when considered together create a sufficient distinction to require a finding that charter flights were not comparable to the company-provided trips.

We believe that the Government's argument too narrowly construes the concept of comparability. * * * The general nature of the service was air transportation in a private airplane at a time and place determined by Ireland. Certainly, the type of transportation afforded Ireland differs qualitatively from commercial passenger flights where service is limited to a few predetermined flights. Yet, charter service adequately falls within the guidelines mentioned above. * * *

Our analysis is underscored by a brief consideration of the inequities in the Government's model. By basing its calculation on Vulcan's total cost of operating the airplanes, the model ties the determination of value to an arbitrary figure. Much of the total cost figure is a charge for certain fixed costs such as depreciation. The fixed costs allocable to Ireland's personal trips would depend on the total use of Vulcan's planes in any given year. Thus, in a year with heavy business travel, Ireland's share of the fixed costs would be lower than in a year with less business travel. This variation has no basis in any commercial reality or actual value to Ireland. While such an inequity might be acceptable in circumstances with no readily acceptable comparable service, this is not the situation in this case. * * *

The IRS' mandate in this case is only to assess a reasonable amount of taxes based on the approximate value of the services rendered to Ireland by Vulcan. Determination of that value is not capable of mathematical exactitude, and reasonableness should play a prominent role. We hold that Ireland presented sufficient evidence demonstrating the inherent comparability of charter air flights to the services provided by Vulcan. Value of the flights should properly have been based on a comparison with existing charter rates in the year in question. We remand the determination of value so that the district court can assess the evidence and arrive at a proper figure for the value.

ILLUSTRATIVE MATERIAL

A. CONSTRUCTIVE DIVIDENDS IN GENERAL

1. *Generally*

As long as sufficient earnings and profits exist for a distribution to be characterized as a dividend under § 316(a), any distribution to a shareholder in the capacity of a shareholder that is not excluded from dividend treatment under § 301(f) will be taxed as a dividend, even if not distributed in proportion to stock ownership. See Treas. Reg. § 1.301–1(c). If there is a direct benefit to an individual shareholder as a result of the corporate payment, the benefit is a dividend for tax purposes—a so-called "constructive" or "disguised" dividend—although it may not be a formal dividend as far as state corporation law is concerned. In Paramount–Richards Theatres v. Commissioner, 153 F.2d 602 (5th Cir.1946), the court described this doctrine as follows:

"Corporate earnings may constitute a dividend notwithstanding that the formalities of a dividend declaration are not observed; that the distribution is not recorded on the corporate books as such; that it is not in proportion to stockholdings, or even that some of the stockholders do not participate in its benefits. Nothing in the statute or decisions warrants the view that a dividend distribution loses its character as such and becomes a deductible business expense merely because stockholders do not benefit equally from the distribution." (604)

In many cases, as in *Ireland*, a disguised dividend is in the form of a benefit obtained by the shareholder as a result of corporate action not involving an actual monetary distribution to the shareholder, such as permitting the shareholder to use an automobile or personal residence owned by the corporation. In many of these cases the corporation nevertheless claims a deduction as an ordinary and necessary business expense for its costs incurred in providing the benefit to the shareholder. At the same time, the shareholder often does not report any income.

In some situations there may be a payment to the shareholder that nominally is termed interest, rent, compensation, or something else, but which is recharacterized as a dividend based on the true substance of the transaction. In these cases, for the most part, the principal issue is deductibility to the corporation of the payment. Interest, compensation and rent are deductible by the corporation, but dividends are not deductible. The shareholder would be taxed on the payment as ordinary income regardless of the characterization.

In other situations the corporation may make a clearly nondeductible distribution to the shareholder that the shareholder claims is nevertheless a nontaxable receipt, such as loan proceeds or a return of capital. Hutchins Standard Service, Inc. v. Commissioner, T.C. Memo. 1981–33, held that repayment of a purported loan from the shareholder to the corporation, which was recharacterized as an equity contribution, was a dividend.

While in some cases nonreporting by the shareholder may be based on a good faith belief that the distribution was a loan or that nothing of value was received from the corporation, many cases involve deliberate tax avoidance. There is an increasing tendency for the courts to impose negligence and civil fraud penalties in cases in which the corporation distributes cash to the shareholder or corporate expenditures provide a clear economic benefit to the shareholder and the shareholder fails to include the value of the benefit in income. See, e.g., Hagaman v. Commissioner, 958 F.2d 684 (6th Cir.1992)(fraud penalty imposed because shareholder diverted cash receipts of corporation for payment of personal expenses and did not report distribution as income); McCabe v. Commissioner, T.C. Memo. 1985–34, aff'd by order, 780 F.2d 1027 (9th Cir. 1985) (penalties for negligence and for instituting primarily for delay Tax Court proceedings contesting deficiency imposed in case in which shareholder did not report as income payment by corporation of shareholder's personal travel expenses).

As discussed in *Ireland*, if an expenditure serves a corporate purpose, even though a shareholder is benefitted, the payment of an expense by the corporation may not be a constructive dividend. In Magnon v. Commissioner, 73 T.C. 980, 993–94 (1980) (A), the Tax Court explained the test as follows: "Where a corporation confers an economic benefit on a shareholder without the expectation of repayment, that benefit becomes a constructive dividend, taxable to the shareholder, even though neither the corporation nor the shareholder intended a dividend. However, 'not every corporate expenditure which incidentally confers economic benefit on a shareholder is a constructive dividend.' The crucial test of the existence of a constructive dividend is whether the 'distribution was primarily for the benefit of the shareholder.' "Applying this standard, the court found that corporate payments for construction work on the shareholder's residence were constructive dividends but that payments to another corporation owned by the shareholder, which were made to further the payor corporation's business, were not.[2]

Pittman v. Commissioner, 100 F.3d 1308 (7th Cir.1996), held that if funds have been diverted from the corporation to a shareholder, a deficiency based on a constructive dividend must be upheld unless the shareholder proves that he received no personal benefit. The absence of a corporate business purpose for an expenditure made at the direction of a sole shareholder alone may be sufficient to establish that the expenditure is a constructive dividend to the shareholder, without any separate demonstration of an actual benefit to the shareholder. See United States v. Mews, 923 F.2d 67 (7th Cir.1991) (upholding shareholder's conviction for criminal tax fraud for failure to report constructive dividends). In King's Court Mobile Home Park, Inc. v. Commissioner, 98 T.C. 511 (1992), a controlling shareholder-officer of the taxpayer diverted rental income from the corporation to himself. The corporation, on an amended return, included the amount of the diverted funds in income and claimed an offsetting deduction for wages. The court denied the deduction and treated the amount as a dividend because the taxpayers failed to establish the corporation's intent to compensate its shareholder-officer.

2. *Significance of earnings and profits*

As with the case of formally declared dividends, a constructive distribution is a dividend for tax purposes only to the extent that the corporation has either accumulated or current earnings and profits. In Truesdell v. Commissioner, 89 T.C. 1280 (1987) (A), the Tax Court rejected the Commissioner's argument that corporate income diverted to a sole shareholder's personal account was taxable in full without regard to the corporation's earnings and profits, and instead applied constructive dividend analysis. In so doing the Tax Court followed the approach adopted by the Ninth Circuit in Simon v. Commissioner, 248 F.2d 869 (8th Cir.1957). In *Simon,* black market profits not reported by the corporation and diverted to the shareholders were taxable to the latter only to the extent of corporate earnings and profits. But if a shareholder's diversion of corporate income is more in the nature of embezzlement or diversion of funds to defraud other shareholders or corporate creditors, some cases treat the diverted funds as fully taxable rather than as corporate distributions. See Leaf v. Commissioner, 33 T.C. 1093 (1960), aff'd per curiam, 295 F.2d 503 (6th Cir.1961); Weir v. Commissioner, 283 F.2d 675 (6th Cir.1960). If the Commissioner asserts that a constructive distribution is taxable in full as a dividend, the taxpayer bears the burden of establishing that the corporation had insufficient earnings and profits to support treatment of the entire distribution as a dividend. DiZenzo v. Commissioner, 348 F.2d 122 (2d Cir.1965).

2. Compare Stinnett's Pontiac Service, Inc. v. Commissioner, 730 F.2d 634 (11th Cir.1984), discussed at page 226.

B. COMPENSATION TO SHAREHOLDERS

1. *Salary and Bonuses*

Disguised dividends frequently take the form of excessive salary and bonus payments made to shareholder-employees. Recharacterization of excessive salaries and compensation to shareholder-employees is facilitated by § 162(a)(1), allowing a deduction of "a reasonable allowance for salaries or other compensation for personal services actually rendered." Treas. Reg. § 1.162–7(b)(1) re-enforces this message by specifically providing that "[a]n ostensible salary paid by a corporation may be a dividend on its stock." Recharacterization of purported compensation as dividends of necessity turn on the particular facts of each case. Although there are many formulations of the relevant factors, the following are among those most frequently enumerated: (1) the extent and importance of the shareholder-employee's role in corporate management and activities; (2) the comparability of the purported compensation with that paid to employees performing similar services for other employers; (3) the size, complexity, and economic condition (profitability) of the corporate business; (4) the relationship of the purported compensation to shareholdings (e.g., proportionality); and (5) the corporation's dividend policy. See Elliotts, Inc. v. Commissioner, 716 F.2d 1241 (9th Cir.1983), in which the court also considered whether the corporate profits remaining after paying the purported compensation would provide an acceptable rate of return to a hypothetical investment in the corporation's stock by an outside investor.

In Charles McCandless Tile Service v. United States, 422 F.2d 1336 (Ct.Cl.1970), the Claims Court recharacterized as dividends a portion of the compensation paid to shareholder-employees, even though the amount of the compensation was found to be reasonable, because the corporation had a history of paying little or no dividends. Other courts declined to follow this "automatic dividend" rule, see, e.g., Laure v. Commissioner, 70 T.C. 1087 (1978) (A), aff'd, 653 F.2d 253 (6th Cir.1981); Charles Schneider & Co. v. Commissioner, 500 F.2d 148 (8th Cir.1974); and Edwin's, Inc. v. United States, 501 F.2d 675 (7th Cir.1974). In Rev.Rul. 79–8, 1979–1 C.B. 92, the Internal Revenue Service announced that it too would eschew an "automatic dividend" rule, concluding that although "the failure of a closely held corporation to pay more than an insubstantial portion of its earnings as dividends on its stock is a very important consideration," deductions for compensation to shareholder-employees found to be otherwise reasonable in amount will not be denied solely on that ground.

Contingent compensation to shareholder-employees based on corporate profitability, particularly when combined with infrequent dividend payments or compensation in proportion to shareholdings, often results in recharacterization of the contingent compensation as dividends. See, e.g., Charles Schneider & Co., Inc., supra; Paul E. Kummer Realty Co. v. Commissioner, 511 F.2d 313 (8th Cir.1975). Contingent compensation arrangements are accorded some protection by Treas. Reg. § 1.162–7(b)(2), which provides that a deduction will be allowed for otherwise excessive compensation paid under an arm's length contingent compensation agreement the terms of which are reasonable at the time it is entered into. See Kennedy v. Commissioner, 671 F.2d 167 (6th Cir.1982)(contingent compensation reasonable where not in proportion to shareholdings); *Elliotts, Inc.*, supra. The underlying rationale for recognizing contingent compensation contracts in the case of shareholder-employees is not as strong as in cases involving nonshareholder employees. A principal shareholder needs no additional incentive to give his best efforts in managing his business. This fact was noted in University Chevrolet Co. v. Commissioner, 16 T.C. 1452, 1455 (1951), aff'd 199 F.2d 629 (5th Cir.1952), as follows: "For the sole owner to pay himself a bonus to do his best in managing his own business is nonsense." However, although contingent compensation contracts between a corporation and its sole shareholder may be suspect, under the *Moline Properties* doctrine, discussed at page 49, which treats a corporation and its shareholders as separate entities, such contracts cannot be subjected to an automatic dividend rule. See also Comtec Systems, Inc. v. Commissioner, T.C. Memo. 1995–4 (allowing a deduction for "catch-up" compensation paid to president-sole shareholder of corporation to compensate him for inadequate compensation in prior years).

2. *Fees for Services*

Tulia Feedlot, Inc. v. United States, 513 F.2d 800 (5th Cir.1975), held that payments by a corporation to shareholders in consideration of guaranteeing corporate debts were constructive dividends because the fees had no reasonable connection with the amount of loans guaranteed. For a subsequent year, however, the taxpayer prevailed in a different forum because it established that the guarantees were necessary to obtain the loans, the guarantees would not have been given without the payment of fees to the guarantor shareholders, and the fees were paid in proportion to the amount of debt guaranteed rather than in proportion to shareholdings. Tulia Feedlot, Inc. v. United States, 3 Cl.Ct. 364 (1983). See also Olton Feed Yard, Inc. v. United States, 592 F.2d 272 (5th Cir.1979) (loan guarantee fees paid to shareholders were constructive dividends because payments were proportionate to stock ownership in a profitable corporation that never paid any dividends).

C. LOANS TO SHAREHOLDERS

1. *Loan versus distribution*

The question whether shareholder withdrawals from a corporation constitute loans or dividends also frequently arises. In such cases the ultimate factual inquiries are whether there is a reasonable expectation of repayment and an intent to enforce the repayment of the disbursed funds. Compare Pierce v. Commissioner, 61 T.C. 424 (1974)(A) (advances to shareholders were loans because an intent to repay was found and substantial repayments were in fact made) with Electric & Neon, Inc. v. Commissioner, 56 T.C. 1324 (1971) (A), aff'd by order, 496 F.2d 876 (5th Cir. 1974) (advances were dividends rather than loans because there was no express obligation evidencing the indebtedness and it was unrealistic to expect that the corporation would demand payment from its 97 percent shareholder).

To ascertain these subjective facts, the courts examine numerous subsidiary "objective" facts and circumstances. Among the most important "objective" facts are the following: (1) the extent of shareholder control over the corporation; (2) limitations on the amount that could be disbursed to the shareholder, (3) the retained earnings and dividend history of the corporation; (4) the size of the withdrawals; (5) the presence or absence of conventional indicia of debt, such as promissory notes with a determinable maturity date, collateral, and provision for interest; (6) the treatment of the advances in the corporate records; (7) the history of payment of interest and principal; (8) the shareholder's ability to repay the funds: (9) whether the corporation sought to enforce the debt: and (10) the shareholder's use of the funds. See, e.g., Crowley v. Commissioner, 962 F.2d 1077 (1st Cir.1992); Busch v. Commissioner, 728 F.2d 945 (7th Cir.1984). These factors are similar to those used to distinguish debt from equity in the case of shareholder contributions, discussed in Chapter 13, Section 1 and, as is the case there, no one factor is determinative. For example, in Turner v. Commissioner, T.C. Memo. 1985–159, aff'd 812 F.2d 650 (11th Cir.1987), advances to the shareholder were loans because they were evidenced by interest bearing notes, secured by mortgages, treated as loans by independent auditors, and the corporation credited shareholder-employee's salary against the debt. However, other advances initially debited to an "advance" account but subsequently credited and reclassified as business expenses were constructive dividends because there was no evidence of intent to repay the amounts; other advances evidenced only by a book account entry as "due from officers" were dividends.

On the other hand, in Livernois Trust v. Commissioner, 433 F.2d 879 (6th Cir.1970), the existence of demand notes bearing 6 percent interest did not control the characterization of advances to a shareholder as loans rather than dividends. In Crowley v. Commissioner, 962 F.2d 1077 (1st Cir.1992), withdrawals by a minority shareholder were treated as constructive dividends rather than loans, even though the shareholder had made some repayments in a subsequent year; the shareholder's unrestricted withdrawal privilege was determinative.

2. *Below Market Rate of Interest Loans*

Section 7872 requires the imputation of a dividend if a corporation makes a below-market or interest-free loan to a shareholder. The shareholder may then be entitled to an offsetting interest deduction under § 163. The deductibility of such imputed interest by the shareholder, however, is subject to all of the limitations that generally apply to the deductibility of the interest depending on the use to which the loan proceeds are applied by the shareholder. See, e.g., § 163(d) (limiting deductions for investment interest); § 163(h) (disallowing deductions for personal interest); § 263A(f) (requiring capitalization of certain production period interest); § 265 (disallowing deduction of interest incurred with respect to tax-free bonds); § 469 (restrictions on deductions of passive losses). The corporation recognizes interest income but, of course, obtains no offsetting deductions for the imputed dividend. When the loan is payable on demand, both payments are deemed to have been made on December 31st of each year the loan is outstanding, and the amount of the dividend and the deemed interest payment equals the forgone interest for the year. I.R.C. § 7872(a). But if the loan is for a specified term, § 7872(b) provides that the dividend distribution is made on the date the loan is made, and its amount is determined by subtracting the net present value, using a specified discount rate, of the payment due to the corporation from the amount of the loan; the imputed interest payments are treated as occurring over the term of the loan by applying OID principles, discussed in Chapter 13, Section 2.

In KTA–Tator, Inc. v. Commissioner, 108 T.C. 100 (1997), a corporation made advances to its shareholders to finance the construction of real estate projects owned by the shareholders. No interest was charged during the construction period and the amounts were recorded on corporate books as "advances." Upon completion of the construction period, the advances were converted to interest bearing loans with a specific amortization schedule. Under § 7872, the advances were treated as interest free demand shareholder loans during the construction period, resulting in the realization of interest income by the corporation without any deduction for the deemed dividend distributions to the shareholders.

D. CORPORATE EXPENDITURES RESULTING IN ECONOMIC BENEFIT TO SHAREHOLDERS

1. *General*

Corporate expenses ostensibly incurred in furtherance of the business enterprise have been found to be nondeductible constructive dividends because of the personal benefits derived therefrom by the shareholders in a variety of circumstances. Constructive dividends often take the form of the rent free use of corporate property by shareholders for personal purposes. See, e.g., Dean v. Commissioner, 187 F.2d 1019 (3d Cir.1951) (rent free use of residence owned by corporation). In Melvin v. Commissioner, 88 T.C. 63 (1987), aff'd on other grounds, 894 F.2d 1072 (9th Cir.1990) shareholders obtained the use of corporate vehicles for personal purposes by reimbursing the corporation for its costs incurred with respect to the automobiles. The shareholders were found to have a dividend equal to the amount by which the fair rental values of the automobiles exceeded the reimbursements paid to the corporation.

Expenditures for goods and services delivered to shareholders, for which there is no expectation of payment in return, are another frequently encountered example of constructive dividends. See, e.g., Gibbs v. Tomlinson, 362 F.2d 394 (5th Cir.1966) (improvements to a shareholder's land); Greenspon v. Commissioner, 229 F.2d 947 (8th Cir.1956) (landscaping and maintenance of the sole stockholder's home). The same principle applies to payments of a shareholder's personal living expenses. See, e.g., Meridian Wood Products Co., Inc. v. United States, 725 F.2d 1183 (9th Cir.1984) (shareholder's personal travel and entertainment expenses); Larkin v. Commissioner, 394 F.2d 494 (1st Cir.1968) (payments for health plan covering shareholder-officers, since the benefits were not related to services as employees). But see Gill v. Commissioner, T.C. Memo. 1994–92 (treating a contribution by a corporation to a shareholder-employee's IRA account as additional compensation, not a constructive dividend), aff'd on other grounds, 76 F.3d 378 (6th Cir. 1996); Ghosn v. Commissioner, T.C. Memo. 1995–192 (corporate payments of sole shareholder/employee's personal expenses constituted additional compensation, not a dividend, because stated salary was extraordinarily low).

Not all corporate expenditures that benefit shareholders are found to be constructive dividends. In Ciaravella v. Commissioner, T.C. Memo 1998–31, the shareholder's wholly owned corporation made payments to the shareholder to sponsor the shareholder's race car activities. The shareholder's race car carried the corporation's logo as a sponsor. The court concluded that the payments represented advertising expenditures that benefited the corporate business. A portion of the corporation's deduction for the expenditure, however, was disallowed as unreasonable. In Weigel v. Commissioner, T.C. Memo. 1996–485, a corporation that leased real property from its sole shareholder made leasehold improvements to the property. The value of the improvements was not a constructive dividend because the lease was for an extended period at a commercially reasonable rent and the improvements were for the use and benefit of the corporation.

2. *Valuation of Constructive Distributions Attributable to Corporate Expenditures*

As demonstrated in *Ireland*, the fair rental value is the generally preferred measure of the amount of a dividend if the shareholder receives the rent free use of corporate property for personal purposes. In the absence of reliable evidence of this value, or as a starting point, however, the Internal Revenue Service and the courts frequently use the costs incurred by the corporation to provide such property as a surrogate for the fair rental value. In contrast to the *Ireland* decision, Cirelli v. Commissioner, 82 T.C. 335 (1984), held that the amount of a constructive dividend equaled the expenses of maintaining a yacht that were disallowed as corporate deductions. The court acknowledged that the proper measure of the dividend was fair rental value of the property, but it did not apply that measure because the taxpayer failed to prove that the fair rental value was less than the disallowed expenses.

3. *Payment of Shareholder's Debts*

Payment by a corporation of a shareholder's debt generally constitutes a constructive dividend. See Sachs v. Commissioner, 277 F.2d 879 (8th Cir.1960) (corporate payment of fine imposed on stockholder-president for filing a false corporate tax return, where he and his brothers owned almost all of stock). In Gaines v. Commissioner, T.C. Memo. 1982–731, a corporation paid expenses incurred by a predecessor partnership. Because the court found that the debts of the predecessor partnership had not been assumed by the corporation upon formation, the payment constituted a constructive dividend to the shareholders who were the partners. If there is a corporate purpose for the payment, however, it might not be a dividend even though the shareholder is also benefitted. In Dolese v. United States, 605 F.2d 1146 (10th Cir.1979), the payment by four corporations of legal fees incurred by their shareholder with respect to his divorce were held to be constructive dividends. But the portion of those legal fees that related to clarification of an injunction, issued in the course of the divorce proceedings, restraining the corporations from engaging in any transactions outside the ordinary course of business was not a constructive dividend because those costs were incurred to resist actions that were detrimental to the corporation.

Mere corporate liability on the obligation does not preclude treatment of payment as a constructive dividend. In Yelencsics v. Commissioner, 74 T.C. 1513 (1980) (A), a corporation cosigned a note with its shareholder without receiving any consideration and without any corporate business purpose. When the corporation paid the note, the shareholder received a constructive dividend. Constructive dividends likewise may result if corporate funds are used to discharge an obligation that the shareholder had personally guaranteed. See Wortham Machinery Co. v. United States, 521 F.2d 160 (10th Cir.1975). Miller v. Commissioner, T.C. Memo. 1984–448, found a constructive dividend in a case in which a medical professional corporation paid a debt of a bankrupt hospital that had been guaranteed by the corporation's sole shareholder even though the purpose of the loan was to enable the doctor to practice at the hospital through the corporation.

4. *Insurance on Shareholders' Lives*

If the shareholder, or the beneficiaries designated by the shareholder, have irrevocable rights in a life insurance policy payment of premiums by the corporation constitutes a dividend. See, e.g., Genshaft v. Commissioner, 64 T.C. 282 (1975) (A). On the other hand, if the corporation is the owner and beneficiary no dividend results from premium payments. In Casale v. Commissioner, 247 F.2d 440 (2d Cir.1957), a corporation obtained an insurance policy on its principal shareholder, who was also president of the corporation, to fund its liability under a deferred compensation contract with the shareholder. The corporation was the beneficiary of the policy and the shareholder-president had only a contractual right to future payments. Thus, there was no dividend to the shareholder.Rev.Rul. 59–184, 1959–1 C.B. 65, follows *Casale*.

The receipt of the insurance proceeds by the corporation on the death of the insured is not taxable income to it under § 101 (although the proceeds are includable in alternative minimum taxable income). If the insurance proceeds are then distributed by the corporation to the shareholders on the death of the insured, the tax consequences depend on the distribution transaction. If the corporation possesses all of the incidents of ownership of a life insurance policy, but it names a shareholder as a beneficiary, the results are unclear. Golden v. Commissioner, 113 F.2d 590 (3d Cir.1940), held that the receipt of the insurance policy proceeds by the shareholders from a trust for their benefit that was the named beneficiary of the policy constituted a dividend. On essentially similar facts, however, Ducros v. Commissioner, 272 F.2d 49 (6th Cir.1959), held that the proceeds were exempt to the recipients under § 101, and not a dividend, since the distribution was made directly to them by the insurance company. In Rev.Rul. 61–134, 1961–2 C.B. 250, the Internal Revenue Service announced that it would not follow *Ducros* but would apply the rule of *Golden* to cases like *Ducros*. Subsequently, Estate of Horne v. Commissioner, 64 T.C. 1020 (1975), reached the same result as *Ducros*, on the reasoning that for estate tax purposes, the deceased controlling shareholder was treated as owning the policy directly and it would be inconsistent to treat the policy proceeds as a corporate distribution. (In a footnote, the Tax Court suggested that the payment of the insurance to the named beneficiaries might have been a dividend to the deceased shareholder's estate, a question that was not before the court.) Subsequently, the IRS acquiesced in the result in *Estate of Horne*, 1980–2 C.B. 1, but did not modify or revoke Rev. Rul. 61–134, which takes a position directly opposite of *Estate of Horne*.

5. *Charitable Contributions*

A charitable contribution by a closely held corporation could be viewed as a constructive dividend to the controlling shareholders of the corporation if the contribution served only the personal charitable interests of the shareholders. But Knott v. Commissioner, 67 T.C. 681 (1977), and Rev.Rul. 79–9, 1979–1 C.B. 125, held that the shareholder's interest in seeing the corporation make a particular charitable contribution is not sufficient to warrant constructive dividend treatment.

Payments by subsidiaries to parent corporations that are tax-exempt institutions have been held to be dividends and not deductible charitable contributions. See, e.g., Crosby Valve & Gage Co. v. Commissioner, 380 F.2d 146 (1st Cir.1967).

E. BARGAIN TRANSACTIONS

A sale of property to a shareholder at a price below fair market value results in the "bargain" element being taxed as a dividend. In Honigman v. Commissioner, 466 F.2d 69 (6th Cir.1972), the shareholder purchased a hotel from the corporation for $661,000. The Internal Revenue Service on audit took the position that the hotel was worth $1,300,000 and asserted the tax on the excess of that amount over the actual purchase price as a dividend. Appraisal evidence submitted at the trial showed a range of values between $625,000 and $1,300,000. The Tax Court, affirmed by the Court of Appeals, found the fair market value of the property was $830,000 and accordingly taxed $169,000 as a dividend. The Court of Appeals rejected the taxpayer's argument that in a bargain purchase situation there must be an intent to distribute a dividend before dividend characterization of the bargain element is possible.

Leases of corporate property to shareholders at less than fair rental value similarly result in constructive dividends. A lease by a corporation to a stockholder of a theater at a rental obviously too low in view of the profits from the property was held to result in the profits being taxed to the corporation and then to the shareholder as a dividend. 58th Street Plaza Theatre, Inc. v. Commissioner, 195 F.2d 724 (2d Cir.1952).

A lease of the shareholder's property to the corporation for a rental in excess of fair rental value also gives rise to a constructive dividend. For example, in Lucas v. Commissioner, 71 T.C. 838 (1979), aff'd 657 F.2d 841 (6th Cir.1981), the shareholders leased a coal deposit from a third party for a royalty of 25 cents per ton and subleased the coal to another party who agreed to pay royalties of 50 cents per ton on coal sold to the lessors' wholly owned corporation and 25 cents per ton on coal sold to unrelated parties. The additional 25 cents per ton royalty on coal sold to the corporation was held to be a dividend from the corporation. See also Omholt v. Commissioner, 60 T.C. 541 (1973) (A) (excessive royalty payments)

F. INDIRECT BENEFITS TO SHAREHOLDERS: PAYMENTS TO SHAREHOLDER'S RELATIVES

1. *General*

A distribution of money or property to a relative of a shareholder that serves a personal purpose of the shareholder rather than a corporate business purpose can be a constructive dividend to the shareholder, even though the shareholder personally did not receive anything. See, e.g., Snyder v. Commissioner, T.C. Memo. 1983–692 (shareholder received constructive dividends as a result of use of corporation's automobiles by shareholder's daughters for nonbusiness purpose, payment by corporation to shareholder's son of salary in excess of the amount deductible under § 162(a)(1) as reasonable compensation, payment by corporation of credit card charges incurred by shareholder's son to pay living expenses while at college, and payment of alimony to shareholder's ex-wife). Constructive dividends of this nature arise most commonly when a corporation pays excessive compensation to a relative of a shareholder and the corporation's deduction is disallowed under § 162(a)(1). The distributee relative is then treated as having received a tax free gift, and the shareholder may be liable for a gift tax as well. See Caledonian Record Publishing Co., Inc. v. United States, 579 F.Supp. 449 (D.Vt.1983)(excessive compensation paid to the controlling shareholder's son was a gift to the son; I.R.S. did not assert deficiency against father based on constructive dividend theory). But see Smith v. Manning, 189 F.2d 345 (3d Cir.1951)(excessive salaries paid by father to daughters taxed to daughters as compensation, notwithstanding disallowance of father's deduction).

In Speer v. Commissioner, T.C. Memo. 1996–323, the Home Shopping Network entered into a contract for data processing services with a corporation wholly owned by the son of the HSN's majority shareholder. The contract provided for fees to the son's corporation equal to one percent of HSN's gross profits. Because the son actually designed data processing software, the contract was on arm's-length terms, important unrelated minority HSN shareholders did not object, believing it to be fair, and the contract served a valid business purpose, the court rejected the Commissioner's argument that a constructive dividend to the HSN majority shareholder resulted from the contract. In Lanier v. Commissioner, T.C. Memo 1998–7, the court held that there was no constructive dividend from a contribution to a political campaign committee supporting the shareholders' son. The campaign committee was a separate legal entity. As a result, the contribution did not satisfy any direct obligations of the shareholders' son, and the economic benefit of the contribution accrued to a legal entity distinct from the shareholders or their family.

A bargain sale of property to a relative of a shareholder will be a constructive dividend to the shareholder if the transaction occurred by virtue of the shareholder's position as a shareholder and was personally motivated, as opposed to being an arm's length bargain between the corporation and the shareholder's relative. In Baumer v. United States, 580 F.2d 863 (5th Cir.1978), a corporation granted an option to the sole shareholder's son to purchase an undivided one-half interest in a tract of land for an amount equal to approximately one-half of the corporation's cost. At that time the possibility of developing the tract was ripe. The consideration for the option was substantially below its fair market value. The transaction was motivated by the sole shareholder's desire to make recompense for having advised his son not to purchase the property at a time prior to its purchase by the corporation. The court held that the dividend occurred at the time the option was granted, but because the value of the option was unascertainable at that time, the open transaction doctrine should be applied. Thus the option was valued with reference to the amount received by the son on the sale of the property immediately after the exercise of the option in a later year; the amount of the distribution was the price paid by the ultimate buyer minus the amount paid by the son for the option, and the distribution was taxable in that year.

2. *Payments to Surviving Spouses*

Corporate distributions to shareholder-surviving spouses after the death of their spouse-executives raise a number of issues. If the payment is characterized as additional salary for the past services of the executive, the amount is taxable to the surviving spouse and deductible by the corporation. On the other hand, if the payment qualifies as a gift, it is tax-free to the recipient, and the corporation's deduction is limited by § 274(b). Finally, if the payment is viewed as a dividend distribution, it is taxable to the recipient and nondeductible by the corporation. Resolution of these issues is fact specific, and no one factor is determinative. For example, Rubber Associates, Inc. v. Commissioner, 335 F.2d 75 (6th Cir.1964), held that a payment was deductible deferred compensation rather than a dividend distribution because it was made as part of a plan to pay additional compensation for the past services of deceased officer-shareholders. In contrast, Barbourville Brick Co. v. Commissioner, 37 T.C. 7 (1961), held that payments to a widow who was the principal shareholder were dividends, not deductible expenses, despite the fact that they were related in amount to her husband's previous salary.

G. TRANSACTIONS BETWEEN RELATED CORPORATIONS

Transactions between commonly controlled corporations, for example, the lease or sale of property or the provision of services for inadequate consideration, the making of a loan, etc., may involve constructive dividend issues. Most cases involve loans between related corporations in which the Commissioner attempts to treat the entire loan as a constructive distribution by the "lender" to the controlling shareholder coupled with a capital contribution by the shareholder to the "borrower." Not all loans between related corporations are susceptible to such recharacterization. The "loan" first must be found not to constitute bona fide indebtedness. Even then, a constructive dividend to the shareholder will be found only if the shareholder receives a direct benefit, distinct from an indirect benefit as a shareholder, from the making of the loan.

Transfers that discharge an obligation of the shareholder generally are found to serve a shareholder purpose. See, e.g., Gilbert v. Commissioner, 74 T.C. 60 (1980) (purported loan the proceeds of which were used to redeem stock of other 50 percent shareholder was constructive dividend to continuing shareholder); Stinnett's Pontiac Service, Inc. v. Commissioner, 730 F.2d 634 (11th Cir.1984) (loan to related corporation satisfying common shareholder's obligation to make additional capital contributions to "borrower" corporation was a constructive dividend). Transfers to a related corporation that serve a corporate business purpose generally escape constructive dividend treatment. See, e.g., Magnon v. Commissioner, 73 T.C. 980 (1980) (A) (no constructive dividend because loan was bona fide and for purpose of improving relations with lender's largest customer, who desired that common shareholder of lender and borrower establish new, separate business); Mills v. Internal Revenue Service, 840 F.2d 229 (4th Cir.1988) (no constructive dividend because purpose of loan was to further financial stability of integrated business conducted through related corporations). In Davis v. Commissioner, T.C. Memo. 1995–283, the court articulated a four factor test to determine whether a purported loan from one corporation to another commonly controlled corporation is a constructive dividend to the common shareholder: (1) Was the common shareholder able to use the transferor as a source of risk capital for the transferee without using his or her personal resources; (2) could the common shareholder carry on a business with extremely thin capitalization without having his or her personal funds subordinated to the transferee's indebtedness; (3) was the value of the common shareholder's equity interest in the transferee enhanced by the transfer; and (4) was the common shareholder relieved of potential liability on personal guarantees or loans made to the transferee that were repaid with the transferred funds? See also Schwartz v. Commissioner, 69 T.C. 877 (1978) (no constructive dividend resulted from intercorporate transfers between six commonly controlled corporations in a case in which the transfers were pursuant to consolidated bankruptcy proceedings even though the transferred funds were used to discharge debts of the related corporations guaranteed by the shareholder).

A sale of property from one commonly controlled corporation to another at less than an arm's-length price may be treated as if the selling corporation had made a distribution in an amount equal to the bargain element to its shareholders who in turn contributed that amount to the capital of the buying corporation. Rev.Rul. 69–630, 1969–2 C.B. 112, held that this result automatically followed if as a result of a tax avoidance transaction, § 482 was applied to reallocate income between the related corporations to reflect an arm's-length price. The case law usually has applied this approach when there has been an intentional diversion of funds from one corporation to the other. See Sparks Nugget, Inc. v. Commissioner, 458 F.2d 631 (9th Cir.1972) (constructive dividend found in a case of excessive rentals were paid in a transaction between related corporations); Arnold v. Commissioner, T.C. Memo. 1994–97 (constructive dividend to the owner of commonly controlled corporations resulted from a sale and leaseback between corporations at a bargain price because the transaction was structured to benefit the shareholder). Contra, White Tool and Machine Co. v. Commissioner, T.C. Memo. 1980–443, aff'd 677 F.2d 528 (6th Cir.1982) (no constructive dividend to common shareholder although corporation paid excessive rent to related corporation; reallocation of income under § 482 was adequate remedy).

Rev.Rul. 78–83, 1978–1 C.B. 79, involving the diversion of funds from one sister corporation to another to avoid foreign exchange control restrictions, indicated that the "constructive distribution-contribution to capital" analysis applies even though there was no motive to allocate income or deductions improperly.

SECTION 5. INTERCORPORATE DIVIDENDS

INTERNAL REVENUE CODE: Sections 243(a), (b)(1) and (2), (c); 246(c); 246A; 301(e); 1059.

Corporate shareholders of domestic corporations may in effect exclude all or a portion of dividend income they receive. Prior to 1936 all intercorporate dividends were excluded in full. Taxation of a portion of intercorporate dividends was introduced in that year, reflecting a general policy in the early 1930's of discouraging complicated corporate structures. Under current law, however, the tax on intercorporate dividends affects primarily investments in public corporations by other corporations. These investments generally have little to do with corporate operating structures.

Without some exclusion, successive taxation of a dividend as it passed from corporation to corporation in a chain of corporations would result in multiple taxation of the dividend and leave very little for the ultimate individual shareholder. However, if the corporate shareholder has an insubstantial degree of ownership or control of the distributing corporation the argument in favor of relief from corporate taxation of dividend income is not as strong. For example, if a corporation has excess cash to invest on a short-term basis, it can be argued that the tax treatment of the corporation's investment return should not depend on whether the short-term investment is in portfolio stock or certificates of deposit. On the other hand, interest is deductible by the payor and dividends are not, so that if one believes that there should be only one tax imposed as long as earnings remain in corporate solution, the dividends received deduction is appropriate even in short-term investment situations.

If one corporation owns 80 percent or more of the voting stock and 80 percent or more in value of the stock of another corporation, these affiliated corporations may file a consolidated return, which eliminates dividends paid by the subsidiary to the parent in computing their consolidated taxable income. See I.R.C. §§ 1501–1505. See Chapter 19, Section 2. If affiliated corporations choose not to file consolidated returns, the parent nevertheless may deduct an amount equal to all dividends received from the subsidiary, subject to the conditions and limitations of § 243(b). See Treas. Reg. § 1.243–4.

For many years prior to the 1986 Act, § 243(a) granted a deduction equal to 85 percent of intercorporate dividends received by any corporation that did not elect to file a consolidated return or qualify for the 100 percent deduction under § 243(b). The 1986 Act reduced this intercorporate dividend received deduction to 80 percent to offset the revenue effect of lower corporate tax rates introduced by the 1986 Act. The 1987 Act further amended § 243(a) and added § 243(c), thereby reducing the intercorporate dividend deduction to 70 percent for corporations that do not own 20 percent or more (in value and voting power) of the distributing corporation's stock. Thus, a higher rate of tax is imposed on dividends received on what might be broadly viewed as "portfolio" investments.

The maximum rate of tax on intercorporate dividends is 10.5 percent (35 percent times the 30 percent of the dividend included in income). However, the dividend received deduction creates a difference between earnings and profits and taxable income, thus potentially bringing the alternative minimum tax (AMT) into play even for corporations qualifying for a 100 percent dividend received deduction. See I.R.C. §§ 55 and 56(g), discussed at page 6. If the AMT applies, the maximum tax rate on intercorporate dividends is somewhat higher than under the regular tax.

The availability of the intercorporate dividend deduction creates a variety of tax arbitrage opportunities for corporations. Statutory provisions designed to limit the tax arbitrage benefits of transactions structured to take advantage of the dividends received deduction are explored in the following material.

ILLUSTRATIVE MATERIAL

A. DEBT FINANCED PORTFOLIO STOCK

One tax arbitrage situation involves debt-financed acquisitions of dividend-paying stock. For example, X Corporation borrows $1,000,000, agreeing to pay 10 percent interest, and purchases, at par, $1,000,000 of preferred stock paying annual dividends of 10 percent. X Corporation will realize no pretax gain or loss because the interest expense equals the dividend income. However, if the interest paid to finance the acquisition and 70 percent of the dividends received from the debt-financed portfolio stock are both deductible, then the corporation will have an after-tax profit, even if the stock does not increase in value, because it will recognize income of $100,000, but claim $170,000 of deductions. For example, if X Corporation were in the 35 percent marginal tax bracket, the excess deductions would yield tax savings of $24,500 (35 percent × $70,000).

Section 246A reduces the intercorporate dividend received deduction by the percentage of the corporation's portfolio stock that was debt financed during the applicable measuring period.[3] Thus, for example, if the acquisition is three-quarters debt financed, the dividends received deduction is reduced by 75 percent. The dividends received deduction is never reduced, however, by an amount in excess of the interest deduction attributable to the debt that financed the portfolio stock. Section 246A(c)(2) defines "portfolio stock" in such a way that the provision generally does not apply to dividends received by a corporation that owns stock representing at least 50 percent of the total value and the total voting power of the outstanding stock of the distributing corporation. Section 246A also does not apply to dividends paid by certain closely-held corporations.

Is the problem addressed by § 246A created by the dividends received deduction or by the interest deduction? Compare the approach adopted in § 279, discussed at page 489, which disallows the interest deduction for certain acquisition indebtedness.

B. DIVIDEND–RELATED LOSSES: MINIMUM HOLDING PERIOD

A corporation's basis in stock generally is unaffected by the receipt of an intercorporate dividend. Section 301(c)(2) requires a reduction in basis for the portion of a distribution that is not a dividend and, therefore, is treated as a return of capital. However, § 301(c)(2) does not apply to the untaxed portion of intercorporate dividends. The intercorporate dividend exclusion is intended to prevent double taxation at the corporate level, and reducing basis by the amount of the exclusion would only postpone the exaction of such double tax.

Arguably, however, the intercorporate dividend deduction coupled with short-term holding of stock purchased in anticipation of receiving a dividend creates inappropriate tax arbitrage benefits. For example, suppose X Corporation realized a $500,000 capital gain and no offsetting capital loss during its current tax year. Shortly before the end of its taxable year, X Corporation purchases 10,000 shares of Z Corporation stock for $1,000,000.

3. H Enterprises International, Inc. v. Commissioner, T.C. Memo. 1998–97, held that § 246A may be applied in cases in which one member of an affiliated group of corporations incurs the borrowing and another member of the group purchases the portfolio stock. In that case a subsidiary corporation borrowed funds that it then distributed to its parent corporation, which in turn used the distributed loan proceeds to purchase the portfolio stock.

Before the close of its taxable year, X Corporation (1) receives a $200,000 dividend on its Z Corporation shares, and (2) sells its Z Corporation shares for $800,000 (the value of the shares having declined as a result of the dividend). X Corporation realizes a $200,000 loss on disposition of the Z Corporation shares because its basis in the stock was not reduced by the intercorporate dividend received. This transaction is uneconomic because the dividend income is offset by the resulting capital loss. However, X Corporation pays tax at an effective rate of 10.5 percent on the $200,000 intercorporate dividend received (resulting in a tax of $24,500), while using the loss to offset a $200,000 capital gain that otherwise would have been taxed at the rate of 35 percent (saving $70,000 of tax). Thus, the transaction produces an after-tax benefit of $45,500.

Section 246(c) is aimed at such transactions and provides that the dividends received deduction is not allowed with respect to any dividends on any share of stock that is held for less than 45 days during the 90 day period beginning on the date that is 45 days before the date on which the stock becomes ex-dividend. (Under stock exchange rules, stock generally becomes ex-dividend three business days before the "record date" for paying dividends.) For preferred stock, if the dividends received are attributable to a period in excess of 366 days, the holding period is extended to 90 days during the 180 day period beginning on the date that is 90 days before the date on which the stock becomes ex-dividend.

Section 246(c)(4) tolls the taxpayer's holding period of stock for any period in which its risk of loss is diminished through a put option, contract to sell, or short position. See Treas. Reg. § 1.246–5. In Progressive Corp. v. United States, 970 F.2d 188 (6th Cir.1992), the taxpayer acquired stock in anticipation of dividend distributions, and simultaneously held both put and call options on the stock at the same strike price. The taxpayer also acquired stock ex-dividend and simultaneously held in-the-money call options on the stock. Reversing the District Court, the Sixth Circuit held that the taxpayer's holding period was tolled under § 246(c)(3) during the period it held the options. The District Court had misapplied Treas. Reg. § 1.246–3(d)(2) by concluding that the holding period is tolled only when the taxpayer is in a true "short position," i.e., had borrowed and sold the stock and did not own any similar shares with which to satisfy its outstanding obligation to return a like number of shares.

Debt-equity classification issues can be important under § 246(c). Rev. Rul. 94–28, 1994–1 C.B. 86, involved an instrument that was classified as debt for state corporate law purposes but as stock for federal income tax purposes. The instrument provided for a payment of a fixed amount on a stated date. Accordingly, the corporate purchaser of this instrument had an "option to sell" or was under a "contractual obligation to sell" within the meaning of § 246(c)(4)(A). Thus, the 45–day holding period of § 246A(c)(1)(A) was stayed.

Would it be preferable to approach the basic problem addressed by § 243(c) by denying the loss deduction if the purchase and sale are closely related in time to a dividend payment?

C. BASIS REDUCTION FOR EXTRAORDINARY DIVIDENDS

1. *General*

Congress considered § 246(c) to be inadequate to deal with the tax avoidance possibilities created by the availability of the dividends received deduction for extraordinarily large dividends. If an extraordinary dividend was expected to be paid on stock of another corporation, the corporation owning the stock would be willing to hold the stock for the period required to avoid the limitation in § 246(c). In response, Congress enacted § 1059, which it justified as follows:

"When a stock pays an extraordinary dividend, the acquisition of the stock often may be viewed as the acquisition of two assets: the right to the distributions to be made with respect to the stock and the underlying stock itself. In instances in which the acquisition of stock is the acquisition of two assets, the committee concludes that it is appropriate to reduce the basis of the underlying stock to reflect the value of the distribution not taxed to the corporate distributee. In the committee's view, the failure of [prior] law to apply a two-asset analysis in cases of extraordinary distributions when the taxpayer's holding period in the stock is short, leads to tax arbitrage opportunities * * *." H.Rep. No. 98–342, 98th Cong., 2d Sess. 1186 (1984).

Section 1059 requires that a corporate shareholder that receives an "extraordinary dividend" on stock that it has not held for more than two years before the dividend announcement date must reduce the basis of the stock (but not below zero) by the amount of the untaxed portion of the dividend. This basis reduction is treated as occurring at the beginning of the ex-dividend date of the extraordinary dividend. I.R.C. § 1059(d)(1). To the extent that the untaxed portion of any extraordinary dividend exceeds the shareholder's basis for the stock, the excess is taxed as gain on the sale of the stock in the taxable year in which the extraordinary dividend is received (in addition to gain otherwise recognized). I.R.C. § 1059(a)(2). The amount by which the basis of the stock is reduced is intended to represent the portion of the cost of the "two assets" allocated to the extraordinary dividend. The "basis" of the extraordinary dividend is never recovered because the dividends received deduction is allowed in its place. Because there is no untaxed portion of the dividend if § 246(c) applies, § 1059 operates only if the holding period requirement of § 246(c) has been met.

Section 1059(c) defines an extraordinary dividend in terms of the size of the dividend in relation to the shareholder's adjusted basis in its stock (after taking into any account prior basis reductions under § 1059), subject to an alternative test using fair market value instead of basis at the taxpayer's election. (For the application of the alternative test, see Rev.Rul. 88–49, 1988–1 C.B. 297.) A dividend is extraordinary if aggregate dividends received in any 85 day period exceed 10 percent of the basis of common stock, or 5 percent of the basis of preferred stock, with respect to which the dividends were paid. Furthermore, if aggregate dividends paid with respect to stock in any one year period exceed 20 percent of the corporate shareholder's basis for the stock, then all such dividends are aggregated and considered to be an extraordinary dividend.

Section 1059(e)(1) treats certain distributions as *per se* extraordinary dividends. This rule applies to any distribution (without regard to the holding period for the stock or the relative magnitude of the distribution) to a corporate shareholder in partial liquidation of the distributing corporation (as defined in § 302(e), discussed at page 260). Any redemption of stock that is non-pro rata (irrespective of the holding period of the stock or the relative size of the distribution) is treated as an extraordinary distribution.[4] Finally, § 1059(f) treats as extraordinary all dividends on preferred stock if according to the terms of the stock the dividend rate declines over time or the issue price exceeds the liquidation or redemption value.

2. *Exceptions*

There are a few exceptions to § 1059. Section 1059(d)(6) generally exempts from the rules of § 1059 distributions to a corporate shareholder that has held the stock of the distributing corporation for the entire period the distributing corporation (and any predecessor corporation) has been in existence. Section 1059(e)(2) provides that the basis reduction rules do not apply to distributions between members of an affiliated group filing consolidated returns or to distributions that constitute qualifying dividends within the meaning of § 243(b)(1), except to the extent the dividends are attributable to pre-affiliation earnings or appreciation of the payor corporation. The § 1059(d)(6) and § 1059(e)(2) exceptions do not apply, however, to distributions in partial liquidations or non pro rata redemptions treated as extraordinary dividends under § 1059(e)(1). Treas. Reg. § 1.1059(e)–1.

3. *Special Rules for Preferred Stock*

Because under the general rule a preferred stock that pays a greater than 5–percent dividend within any period of 85 days or less is paying an extraordinary dividend, a 6–percent preferred stock dividend that is paid once annually would be extraordinary. On the other hand, a preferred stock that paid four quarterly 5–percent dividends, which on an annual basis is a substantially higher percentage, would not be subject to a basis adjustment under the general rule. To provide relief for preferred stock like the 6–percent preferred stock in the above example, § 1059(e)(3) applies a special rule to preferred stock that pays dividends at a fixed rate not less often than annually, provided it was not purchased when dividends were in arrears. If the taxpayer holds the stock for more than 5 years, no dividends received by the shareholder will be treated as extraordinary dividends, and therefore no basis reduction will be required, if during the period the shareholder held the stock the dividend rate did not exceed an annualized rate of 15 percent of the lower of (a) the taxpayer's adjusted basis or (b) the liquidation preference of the stock. However, if the actual rate of return

4. Stock redemptions that are treated as dividends as a result of option attribution under § 318(a)(4), see page 241, also are *per se* extraordinary dividends, as are distributions in corporate reorganizations that are treated as dividends due to option attribution. The purpose of these two rules is to prevent the use of options to cause a distribution to a corporate shareholder that would otherwise result in sale or exchange treatment to benefit from the dividends received deduction.

from dividends on qualifying preferred stock during this period exceeds 15 percent, no relief is available and all of the dividends are extraordinary dividends.

If the corporate taxpayer does not hold the stock for 5 years, dividends announced during the two year period after the purchase (but not thereafter) are extraordinary to the extent they exceed the dividends "earned" by the taxpayer. To determine whether the taxpayer's dividends received exceed the dividends it earned, the taxpayer's "actual dividend rate" is computed. The actual dividend rate is the average annual amount of dividends received (or deemed received under § 305 or any other provision) during the period the taxpayer owned the stock, computed as a return on the taxpayer's adjusted basis or, if less, the stock's liquidation preference. This is then compared to the stock's "stated dividend rate," which is the return represented by the annual fixed preferred dividends payable on the stock. If the actual dividend rate exceeds the stated dividend rate, a portion of each dividend received or deemed received will be an extraordinary dividend, and basis will be reduced by the untaxed portion of such dividend. The Conference Committee Report, Tax Reform Act of 1986, H.Rep. No. 99–841, 99th Cong., 2d Sess., Vol. II, 165 (1986) provides the following example of this determination:

"[A]ssume that on January 1, 1987, a corporation purchases for $1,000 ten shares of preferred stock having a liquidation preference of $100 per share and paying fixed preferred dividends of $6 per share to shareholders of record on March 31 and September 30 of each year. If the taxpayer does not elect to have the special rule apply, the basic rule would generally require the taxpayer to reduce the basis in the stock by the untaxed portion of each dividend received prior to the expiration of the two-year holding period. This is because a dividend exceeding 5 percent of adjusted basis (or fair market value, if shown to the satisfaction of the Secretary) paid semi-annually is an extraordinary dividend under the general rule. However, [the] special rule will apply to the preferred stock. Under this provision, the taxpayer's stated dividend rate is 12 percent ($12/$100). If the taxpayer sells the stock on October 1, 1988, (after holding the stock for 1.75 years) and no dividends in excess of the fixed preferred dividends have been paid, its actual dividend rate will be 13.7 percent ($240/$1,000 divided by 1.75). This 13.7 percent exceeds the 12 percent stated dividend rate by 1.7. This excess, as a fraction of the actual dividend rate, is 12.4 percent (1.7 divided by 13.7). Accordingly, each of the dividends will be treated as an extraordinary dividend described in § 1059(a) to the extent of 0.74 per share ($6 × 12.4 percent). However, if the corporation does not sell the stock until January 1, 1989, and no dividends in excess of the fixed preferred dividends have been paid, its 'actual dividend rate' will be 12 percent ($240/$1000 divided by 2.0). This does not exceed the stated dividend rate; accordingly, no portion of any dividend will be treated as an extraordinary dividend."

D. EARNINGS AND PROFITS RECALCULATION FOR DISTRIBUTIONS TO TWENTY PERCENT CORPORATE SHAREHOLDER

Section 301(e) provides a special rule for determining the portion of any distribution that is not a dividend to a corporate shareholder holding at least 20 percent, by either voting power or value, of the stock of the distributing corporation. When § 301(e) applies, earnings and profits of the distributing corporation are computed without regard to § 312(n), discussed at page 199, except the adjustments described in § 312(n)(7), relating to redemptions of corporate stock are taken into account. Section 312(n), in general, requires that certain income items that are deferred for purposes of computing taxable income, be taken into account in an earlier year in computing earnings and profits. Thus, the effect of § 301(e) is to convert a distribution that otherwise might have been wholly a dividend, subject to the intercorporate dividends received deduction, into a return of capital under § 301(c)(2), reducing the distributee's basis in its stock, or giving rise to a gain under § 301(c)(3). This narrow provision is aimed at certain manipulative devices involving the distribution of an extraordinary dividend followed by the sale of subsidiary stock after the subsidiary has realized an economic gain but before the subsidiary corresponding taxable gain has been recognized, such as in the case of an installment sale under § 453. See H.Rep. No. 98–861, 98th Cong., 1st Sess. 842 (1984).

E. DIVIDENDS DISTRIBUTED IN CONNECTION WITH THE SALE OF A CORPORATE BUSINESS

When a subsidiary corporation pays a dividend to its parent shortly before the sale of the stock of the subsidiary by the parent, the issue arises whether the distribution is a dividend eligible for the dividends received deduction under § 243 or is to be treated as a portion of the amount realized on the sale of the stock, and, therefore, ineligible for the deduction. The result can differ depending on the facts and circumstances surrounding the distribution. This matter is discussed in detail at page 507.

CHAPTER 6

STOCK REDEMPTIONS

SECTION 1. INTRODUCTION

INTERNAL REVENUE CODE: Sections 302(a), (b)(1)–(4), (c)(1), (d), (e); 311; 317; 318.

REGULATIONS: Sections 1.302–1(a), –2.

When a shareholder sells stock back to the issuing corporation, it is necessary to determine whether the transaction more nearly resembles a sale of stock or a dividend distribution. If the transaction is thought more nearly to resemble a sale, the shareholder should be entitled to a recovery of basis with respect to the surrendered shares and capital gain or loss treatment. Since liquidating distributions generally are entitled to capital gain treatment under § 331, similar treatment clearly is appropriate if all of a shareholder's shares are sold back to the issuing corporation. Such treatment likewise appears to be appropriate if the shareholder's voting power and right to earnings are substantially reduced. But if there is no significant change in the voting rights or the share of earnings of the corporation to which a shareholder is entitled, the distribution is more like a normal dividend distribution and ordinary income treatment for the entire amount received, with no return of capital aspect, is appropriate.

Section 302(a) distinguishes those sales of stock back to the issuing corporation that are entitled to capital gain treatment from those that more nearly resemble dividends. That section provides that a redemption is a capital gain or loss transaction as respects the shareholder if the transaction meets one of the tests of § 302(b). This treatment results from the language in § 302(a) that treats the redemption proceeds as "payment in exchange for the stock." If the transaction does not meet one of those tests, then the amounts distributed by the corporation in redemption of the stock are treated by § 302(d) as distributions of property under § 301, and, if earnings and profits are present, constitute dividend distributions.

The stakes turning on the classification of a redemption under these rules are high as far as individual shareholders are concerned. Dividend treatment sweeps the entire distribution under the rates applicable to ordinary income. Redemption treatment results in no income to the extent of the shareholder's basis in the redeemed shares and taxation of the excess as capital gain, which can be offset by capital losses and which may be subject to tax at a lower preferential rate to the extent of net long-term capital gains for the taxable year.

If a corporation is the redeemed shareholder, the consequences turning on characterization under § 302 can be important because dividend characterization qualifies the distribution for the intercorporate dividends received deduction under § 243 (see page 227). But a disproportionate redemption that does not qualify for sale or exchange treatment under § 302(b), and which therefore is eligible for the § 243 dividends received deduction, is an extraordinary dividend with respect to which the basis of any remaining stock must be reduced under § 1059.

Subsections (b)(2) and (3) furnish two reasonably specific rules for identifying a redemption eligible for sale or exchange treatment: the § 302(b)(2) test of a substantially disproportionate redemption applicable if the particular shareholder retains some stock after the redemption, with the degree of disproportion specified in mathematical terms; and the § 302(b)(3) termination test applicable if all of the stock of the particular shareholder is redeemed. If these tests are not met, resort must be made to the vague, and possibly subjective, test of § 302(b)(1)—a redemption is treated as a capital transaction if it is not essentially equivalent to a dividend. In applying all three of these tests, shareholders are treated as owning not only those shares of stock actually owned by them, but also any shares in the corporation owned by certain family members and related entities. See I.R.C. §§ 302(c)(1), 318; Treas. Reg. § 1.301-1(a).

In addition, § 302(b)(4) provides that a redemption of stock held by an individual shareholder in partial liquidation of the corporation will be entitled to exchange treatment. This provision differs from §§ 302(b)(1) through (b)(3) in that, while those provisions are applied by examining the effect of the distribution at the shareholder level, § 302(b)(4) examines the distribution from the perspective of the distributing corporation to determine whether exchange treatment is appropriate for the shareholders.

Finally, § 303, which is intended to relieve the perceived hardship of treating redemptions to pay estate taxes as a dividend, permits exchange treatment with respect to redemptions of certain stock held by a deceased shareholder's estate even though § 302(b) is inapplicable.

ILLUSTRATIVE MATERIAL

A. EFFECT ON EARNINGS AND PROFITS

The impact on earnings and profits of a redemption distribution subject to § 302 is important because any reduction in earnings and profits caused by the distribution will reduce the potential "pool" of earnings and profits available for subsequent distributions taxable as dividends under §§ 301 and 316. If a redemption fails to qualify under § 302(a) and is treated as a § 301 distribution, earnings and profits are reduced under § 312(a) by the amount of the distribution. But if the redemption qualifies for exchange treatment under § 302(a) or § 303, then § 312(n)(7) provides that the portion of the distribution chargeable to earnings and profits cannot exceed the ratable share of the earnings and profits attributable to the redeemed stock. For example, if a corporation with $100,000 of earnings and profits redeemed 10 percent of its stock for $15,000, the maximum charge to earnings and profits would be $10,000. If the stock had a par value or stated value of more than $5,000, the charge to earnings and profits would be reduced commensurately.

The legislative history of § 312(n)(7) provides some guidelines for dealing with situations if the statute is unclear. First, no amount of earnings and profits generally should be attributable to nonconvertible preferred stock, unless the distribution includes dividend arrearages. H.Rep. No. 98–861, 98th Cong., 2d Sess. 840 (1984). Presumably, however, the amount of any redemption premium might reduce earnings and profits. Second, earnings and profits are not to be reduced by more than the amount distributed. S.Rep. No. 98–169, 98th Cong., 2d Sess. 202 (1984). Thus, for example, if a corporation with $100,000 of accumulated earnings and profits redeemed 10 percent of its stock for $9,500, the *maximum* charge to earnings and profits would be $9,500. And if there is paid-in capital attributable to the redeemed stock, the actual charge will be less—if the stated value of the redeemed stock were $1,000, the charge to earnings and profits would be only $8,500. However, if the stock were redeemed in exchange for property having a basis of $12,000 and a fair market value of $9,500, § 312(a)(3) appears to permit earnings and profits to be reduced by $11,000 (assuming again that the stated value of the stock was $1,000), the additional $2,500 reduction in earnings and profits reflecting the economic loss on the property for which a deduction is barred by § 311(a). See Rev. Rul. 70–531, 1970–2 C.B. 76.

If current earnings and profits are not sufficient to cover both ordinary dividend distributions and redemptions made in the same year, the ordinary dividend distributions are treated as the first distributions out of earnings and profits. Rev.Rul. 74–339, 1974–2 C.B. 103; Baker v. United States, 460 F.2d 827 (8th Cir.1972) (a dissent would have treated the ordinary dividends and the redemption distributions on a pro rata basis as far as earnings and profits were concerned).

B. REDEMPTION WITH PROPERTY

A distribution of appreciated property by a corporation to a shareholder results in taxable gain at the corporate level, regardless of whether the distribution is treated as a redemption or as a distribution to which § 301 applies. I.R.C. § 311(b). If stock is redeemed in exchange for depreciated property, however, § 311(a) disallows recognition of any realized loss.

C. REDEMPTION OF SECURITIES OTHER THAN STOCK

Section 301(a) refers to a distribution to a shareholder with "respect to its stock." Treas. Reg. § 1.301–1(c) states that § 302 is not applicable unless the distribution is to the shareholder in his capacity as a shareholder. Hence the redemption of a debt instrument from a stockholder is not governed by either § 301 or § 302, but instead falls under the general rules governing the disposition of debt instruments. As a consequence, the rules relating to the classification of corporate obligations as stock or debt are important here.

D. SECTION 305 ASPECTS OF STOCK REDEMPTIONS

A stock redemption can bring § 305 into play since it involves an increase in the proportionate interest in the corporation for those shareholders whose stock is not redeemed. See page 312.

E. "GREENMAIL"

Due to Congressional concern that corporations might deduct expenses incurred to redeem stock in order to fight hostile takeover attempts, the 1986 Act added § 162(k), denying any deduction for all expenses incurred with respect to any redemption, not just those that are made in the course of fighting a hostile takeover. See S.Rep. No. 99–426, 99th Cong., 2d Sess. 248–49 (1987); H.Rep. No. 99–841, 99th Cong., 2d Sess. II–168–69 (1987). In 1996, § 162(k) was amended to apply to any repurchase from a 10 percent or more owner, whether the repurchase is treated as a sale or as a dividend and whether or not the repurchase is in connection with a reorganization. On the other hand, § 162(k) also was amended so that it does not apply to disallow interest deductions on debt incurred to finance the repurchase or deductions for amortizable fees, such as investment banking fees, incurred in connection with such a loan.

SECTION 2. SUBSTANTIALLY DISPROPORTIONATE REDEMPTIONS

INTERNAL REVENUE CODE: Sections 302(a), (b)(2), (c)(1); 318.

REGULATIONS: Section 1.302–3.

Section 302(b)(2) provides a mathematical test for disproportionate redemptions to qualify for sale or exchange treatment under § 302(a). The test involves two ingredients: one, the shareholder's percentage ownership of voting stock after the redemption must be less than 80 percent of his percentage ownership before the redemption (and also a like reduction in ownership of common stock if some of the common stock is non-voting); and two, after the redemption the shareholder must own less than 50 percent of the voting stock of the corporation. Even without this 50 percent requirement, the reduction in size of the shareholding in the corporation required under the 80 percent rule can be quite large. Because the 80 percent test is based on comparing the percentage of outstanding shares of the corporation owned by the shareholder after the redemption to the percentage of outstanding shares of the corporation owned by the shareholder before the redemption, a redemption of merely a fraction of a percent more than 20 percent of the shareholder's stock does not qualify. For example, a shareholder owning 60 shares of stock of a corporation having 100 shares outstanding must have at least 24 shares redeemed to meet the 80 percent test—a 40 percent reduction in the number of shares held by the redeemed shareholder. In order to qualify under § 302(b)(2), after the redemption the shareholder's percentage ownership must have been reduced to below 48 percent (80 percent of 60 percent), taking into account the reduced number of shares outstanding as a result of the redemption.

Revenue Ruling 87–88

1987–2 C.B. 81.

ISSUE

If shares of both voting and nonvoting common stock are redeemed from a shareholder in one transaction, are the two classes aggregated for purposes of applying the substantially disproportionate requirement in section 302(b)(2)(C) of the Internal Revenue Code?

FACTS

X corporation had outstanding 10 shares of voting common stock and 30 shares of nonvoting common stock. The fair market values of a share of voting common stock and a share of nonvoting common stock are approximately equal. A owned 6 shares of X voting common stock and all the nonvoting common stock. The remaining 4 shares of the X voting common stock were held by persons unrelated to A within the meaning of section 318(a) of the Code.

X redeemed 3 shares of voting common stock and 27 shares of nonvoting common stock from A in a single transaction. Thereafter, A owned 3 shares of X voting common stock and 3 shares of nonvoting common stock. The ownership of the remaining 4 shares of X voting common stock was unchanged.

LAW AND ANALYSIS

If a distribution in redemption of stock qualifies under section 302(b)(2) of the Code as substantially disproportionate, the distribution is treated under section 302(a) as a payment in exchange for the stock redeemed.

Under section 302(b)(2)(B) and (C) of the Code, a distribution is substantially disproportionate if (i) the shareholder owns less than 50 percent of the total combined voting power of the corporation immediately after the redemption, (ii) immediately after the redemption the ratio of voting stock owned by the shareholder to all the voting stock of the corporation is less than 80 percent of the same ratio immediately before the redemption, and (iii) immediately after the redemption the ratio of common stock owned by the shareholder to all of the common stock of the corporation (whether voting or nonvoting) is less than 80 percent of the same ratio immediately before the redemption.

Under section 302(b)(2)(C) of the Code, if more than one class of common stock is outstanding, the determination in (iii) above is made by reference to fair market value. Section 302(b)(2) applies to a redemption of both voting stock and other stock (although not to the redemption solely of nonvoting stock). Section 1.302–3(a) of the Income Tax Regulations.

With regard to requirements (i) and (ii) described above, after the redemption, A owned less than 50 percent of the voting power of X (43 percent), and A's voting power was reduced to less than 80 percent of the percentage of voting power in X that A owned before the redemption (from 60 percent to 43 percent for a reduction to 72 percent of the preredemption level).

With regard to requirement (iii) above, section 302(b)(2)(C) of the Code provides that, if there is more than one class of common stock outstanding, the fair market value of all of the common stock (voting and nonvoting) will govern the determination of whether there has been the requisite reduction in common stock ownership. The fact that this test is based on fair market value and is applied by reference to all of the common stock of the corporation suggests that the requirement concerning reduction in common stock ownership is to be applied on an aggregate basis rather than on a class-by-class basis. Thus, the fact that A has no reduction in interest with regard to the nonvoting common stock and continues to own 100 percent of this stock does not prevent the redemption of this class of stock from qualifying under section 302(b)(2) when the whole transaction meets section 302(b)(2) requirements. To conclude otherwise would require that, notwithstanding a redemption of one class of common stock in an amount sufficient to reduce the shareholder's aggregate common stock ownership by more than 20 percent in value, every other class of common stock owned by the shareholder must be subject to a redemption.

Prior to the redemption, A owned 90 percent of the total fair market value of all the outstanding X common stock (36 out of the 40 shares of voting and nonvoting common stock). After the redemption, A owned 60 percent of the total fair market value of all the X common stock (6 out of 10 shares). The reduction in ownership (from 90 percent to 60 percent) was a reduction to less than 80 percent of the fraction that A previously owned of the total fair market value of all the X common stock.

HOLDING

If more than one class of common stock is outstanding, the provisions of section 302(b)(2)(C) of the Code are applied in an aggregate and not a class-by-class manner. Accordingly, the redemption by X of 3 shares of voting common stock and 27 shares of nonvoting common stock qualifies as substantially disproportionate within the meaning of section 302(b)(2), even though A continues to own 100 percent of the outstanding nonvoting common stock.

ILLUSTRATIVE MATERIAL

A. REDEMPTION OF STOCK OTHER THAN VOTING COMMON STOCK

Under Treas. Reg. § 1.302–3, a redemption of either common or preferred non-voting stock may qualify under § 302(b)(2) only if there is a simultaneous redemption of voting stock. A redemption of non-voting stock (preferred or common) alone, however, may not qualify under § 302(b)(2); such a transaction is governed by § 302(b)(1) and § 302(b)(3).

The next to last sentence of § 302(b)(2)(C) does not require that common stock be redeemed in all cases. Rev.Rul. 81–41, 1981–1 C.B. 121, held that § 302(b)(2) could apply to a redemption solely of voting preferred stock if the shareholder did not own any common stock before or after the redemption. If the shareholder owns common stock, however, even if nonvoting, sufficient common stock to meet the 80 percent test must be redeemed along with sufficient voting stock, whether common or preferred, to meet the 50 percent test. There is no requirement that after the redemption the shareholder hold less than 50 percent of the *value* of the common stock.

B. CONSTRUCTIVE STOCK OWNERSHIP

Under § 302(c)(1), the attribution of stock ownership rules of § 318(a) respecting closely related family members and entities are applicable in determining whether the § 302(b)(2) tests have been met; the proportionate or disproportionate character of the distribution is tested by reference to the entire group of related parties. The network of attributed ownership can be quite wide under § 318(a). The attribution rules primarily deal with four situations:

(1) Under § 318(a)(1), stock is attributed between *family members* standing in the specified familial relationships;

(2) Section 318(a)(2) attributes the ownership of stock held by *entities*—partnerships, estates, trusts, and corporations respectively—to the partners, beneficiaries, and shareholders owning 50 percent or more of the stock of a corporation;

(3) Section 318(a)(3) attributes stock owned by a partner, beneficiary, or shareholder owning 50 percent or more of the stock of a corporation to the "entity" if the stipulated relationships are present;

(4) Section 318(a)(4) treats a taxpayer as owning any stock that the taxpayer has an option to purchase.

In applying these rules, § 318(a)(5)(A) treats stock that is *constructively* owned by virtue of the application of the attribution rules as if it were *actually owned* for the purpose of reattribution. Thus, for example, if A is the beneficiary of a trust, stock owned by the trust would be attributed to A under § 318(a)(2)(B). Under § 318(a)(5)(A) that stock would then be considered as actually owned by A for "reattributing" the stock to A's parents under § 318(a)(1).

There are, however, some limits to the reattribution of constructively owned stock. Section 318(a)(5)(B) provides that the stock constructively owned by virtue of the application of the family attribution rules will not be considered as actually owned for purposes of its reattribution under those rules. Thus, stock owned by A that is attributed to A's parents under § 318(a)(1) will not be reattributed through A's parents to A's brother or sister (there is no direct attribution between siblings). Similarly, if stock is attributed to a partnership, estate, etc., under § 318(a)(3), it will not then be reattributed to another partner, beneficiary, etc., under § 318(a)(2). These limitations on reattribution eliminate so-called "sideways" attribution.

Application of the attribution rules sometimes may help a taxpayer. Suppose that the husband owns voting common stock and the wife owns non-voting preferred stock. Some of the wife's preferred stock is redeemed in connection with a transaction in which part of the husband's common stock is redeemed and the husband's redemption meets the requirements of § 302(b)(2). Section 302(b)(2) applies to qualify the wife's redemption. Rev.Rul. 77–237, 1977–2 C.B. 88. On the other hand, if the attribution rules make another the constructive owner of stock actually held by the taxpayer, the attribution does not reduce the taxpayer's "real" ownership for purposes of testing the disproportionality of the distribution. Northwestern Steel and Supply Co. v. Commissioner, 60 T.C. 356 (1973). For example if A, who owns 50 shares of stock, and B, who owns 40 shares of stock, are parent and child, A is deemed to own B's 40 shares in addition to her own 50 shares; correspondingly B is deemed to own A's 50 shares. Thus, in testing a redemption of shares from either or both of A and B under § 302(b)(2), both A and B are deemed to own 90 shares before the transaction.

In applying the option attribution rules, Treas. Reg. § 1.302–3(a) provides that options to purchase unissued stock from the corporation are disregarded. However, Rev.Rul. 68–601, 1968–2 C.B. 124, held that the holder of warrants and convertible debentures was deemed to hold the option shares, but that such shares were not to be counted in determining the percentage of stock owned by other shareholders. Henry T. Patterson Trust v. United States, 729 F.2d 1089 (6th Cir.1984), is to the contrary. In that case, a shareholder other than the shareholder whose stock was redeemed was treated as owning stock that he had an option to purchase from the corporation for purposes of determining the percentage of stock owned by the redeemed shareholder. As a result, as urged by the shareholder, § 302(b)(2) applied. See also Sorem v. Commissioner, 334 F.2d 275 (10th Cir.1964) (employees holding stock options on unissued stock treated as owning stock). Rev.Rul. 89–64, 1989–1 C.B. 91, held that the holder of an option to purchase shares from the corporation was deemed to hold the option shares even though the option was by its terms not exercisable until a future date.

C. SERIES OF DISTRIBUTIONS

Section 302(b)(2)(D) requires the taxpayer to treat a series of redemptions made pursuant to a plan as a single redemption in testing the disproportionality of the redemption. See Blount v. Commissioner, 425 F.2d 921 (2d Cir.1969). Rev.Rul. 85–14, 1985–1 C.B. 92, held that the existence of a "plan" does not require an agreement between two or more shareholders, but may be satisfied by "a design by a single redeemed shareholder to arrange a redemption as part of a sequence of events that ultimately restores to such shareholder the control that was apparently reduced in the redemption." In the Ruling, A held 1,466 out of 2,031 shares of the corporation, or 72.18 percent. On January 1, B, who held 210 shares that were to be repurchased by the corporation upon his retirement pursuant to a stock repurchase agreement, announced that he would retire on March 22. A then caused the corporation to redeem 902 of his shares on March 15, reducing his interest to 49.96 percent. One week later, when B's shares were redeemed, A's interest was increased to 61.37 percent (564 out of 919 shares). The Ruling held that the reduction in A's interest was not to be measured immediately following the redemption of his shares, but only after the redemption of B's shares. But Glacier State Electric Supply Co. v. Commissioner, 80 T.C. 1047 (1983), held that a possible future redemption upon the death of a shareholder pursuant to a buy-sell agreement should not be considered as part of a "plan" in testing whether a current redemption met the test of § 302(b)(2).

Because of the availability of the § 243 intercorporate dividend received deduction, a corporate shareholder frequently prefers to characterize a distribution as a dividend rather than as a § 302 redemption. In Bleily & Collishaw, Inc. v. Commissioner, 72 T.C. 751 (1979), aff'd by order, 647 F.2d 169 (9th Cir.1981), all of the shares of stock of another corporation held by a corporate shareholder were redeemed in seven installments over a six month period. Each of the first six installments left the shareholder with slightly more than 80 percent of the percentage ownership of stock that it held before that redemption. The shareholder claimed that each of the six distributions was a distribution under § 301 rather than § 302(a). Finding that there was a firm and fixed plan to eliminate the shareholder from the corporation, the Tax Court treated all of the installments as part of a single distribution in redemption of all of the taxpayer's shares under § 302(b)(3).

D. BASIS CONSIDERATIONS

If a redemption fails to qualify for exchange treatment under § 302(a) and the distribution is a dividend, the basis of the redeemed stock is not relevant in computing the shareholder's income. Under Treas. Reg. § 1.302–2(c), the basis of the redeemed stock is added to the basis of the other stock held by the taxpayer.

Redemption distributions to a shareholder that is a corporation and which are treated as dividends because of option attribution under § 318(a)(4) are extraordinary dividends under § 1059(e)(1)(A)(iii)(I). The corporate recipient is required to reduce the basis of its remaining stock to the extent that the dividend was not taxed by virtue of the § 243 dividends received deduction. See page 231.

SECTION 3. TERMINATION OF A SHAREHOLDER'S INTEREST

INTERNAL REVENUE CODE: Sections 302(b)(3), (c); 318.

REGULATIONS: Section 1.302–4.

Since the termination of a shareholder's interest is an example of a substantially disproportionate distribution, § 302(b)(3), treating a redemption in complete termination of a shareholder's interest as an exchange, initially appears to add little to the operation of § 302(b). It does, however, serve two major functions. First, it permits the redemption of non-voting stock to qualify for capital gain treatment without resort to the vague "not essentially equivalent to a dividend" test of § 302(b)(1). Second, if all of the stock actually owned by a shareholder is redeemed, § 302(c) permits the family attribution rules of § 318(a)(1) to be disregarded in determining if the shareholder's interest has been completely terminated. This waiver of the family attribution rules is not available under § 302(b)(2).

ILLUSTRATIVE MATERIAL

A. SERIAL REDEMPTIONS

A frequent issue under § 302(b)(3) is the treatment of redemptions of less than all of a shareholder's stock in each of a series of redemptions where the ultimate result is the complete termination of the shareholder's interest. If there is a firm and fixed plan to eliminate the shareholder from the corporation, the component redemptions will be treated as a single redemption of the shareholder's entire interest. The plan does not need to be enforceable or in writing, but it must be more than a handshake. Bleily & Collishaw, Inc. v. Commissioner, 72 T.C. 751 (1979), aff'd by order, 647 F.2d 169 (9th Cir.1981). If the time frame for the redemption is vague and the redeemed shareholder retains control over corporate affairs in the interim, however, the individual transactions will not be aggregated; the preliminary redemptions will be treated as § 301 distributions. Benjamin v. Commissioner, 592 F.2d 1259 (5th Cir.1979); Johnston v. Commissioner, 77 T.C. 679 (1981)(individual redemptions were essentially equivalent to dividends if redemption plan not consistently followed).

If all of a shareholder's stock is redeemed for the corporation's promissory note, the question arises of whether the note is debt or equity. See Lisle v. Commissioner, T.C. Memo. 1976–140 (finding twenty year notes secured by escrow of stock to be true debt). If the note is found to be equity rather than a debt instrument, the "complete termination" required by § 302(b)(3) is not present, and each principal payment must be tested separately against the various § 302(b) tests to determine whether redemption treatment is available.

B. WAIVER OF FAMILY ATTRIBUTION

1. *General*

Whether a shareholder's interest has been completely terminated as required by § 302(c)(1) is tested after applying the attribution rules of § 318(a). However, § 302(c)(2)(A) provides that the *family* attribution rules do not apply if the distributee has no further interest other than as a creditor and if the distributee files an agreement to notify the Internal

Revenue Service of any subsequent acquisition of such an interest (which would retroactively disqualify the redemption if acquired within ten years from the distribution).

Under § 302(c)(2)(B), the waiver of family attribution rules may not be available if the redeemed stock was acquired by the distributee within the preceding 10–year period from a related person (a person whose stock would be attributable to the distributee). Thus, a complete termination under § 302(b)(3) is not available to a husband-distributee who received the redeemed stock from his wife within the 10–year period. Waiver of family attribution also is unavailable if within the 10–year period the distributee gave stock to a related person (e.g., the wife above is the distributee). The limitation of § 302(c)(2)(B), however, does not apply unless one of the principal purposes of the acquisition or disposition was tax avoidance. See § 302(c)(2)(B), flush language, and Treas. Reg. § 1.302–4(g), last sentence.

2. *Tax Avoidance Transactions*

The Internal Revenue Service has issued a number of rulings dealing with the question of whether transfers of stock between related parties within ten years of the redemption were tax avoidance transactions. Rev. Rul. 77–293, 1977–2 C.B. 91, held that tax avoidance was not present in a case in which a father made a gift of a part of his stock to his son concurrently with a redemption of the remainder of the stock from the father. The purpose of the gift was to give the son control of the corporation in connection with the transfer to him of management responsibility. In Rev.Rul. 85–19, 1985–1 C.B. 94, a minority shareholder first sold to his father, the controlling shareholder, a number of shares received from the father by gift two years earlier, and the corporation then immediately redeemed the son's remaining shares, which he had acquired by bequest. The Ruling held that there was no tax avoidance motive present and suggests that tax avoidance exists only if the transferor seeks to retain indirect control, such as by transferring stock to a spouse prior to a redemption of all of the shares actually owned, or if the transfer is in contemplation of a redemption of the shares from the transferee. See also Rev.Rul. 79–67, 1979–1 C.B. 128 (distribution of stock from estate to beneficiary to qualify redemption from beneficiary under § 302(b)(3) is not tax avoidance); Rev.Rul. 82–129, 1982–2 C.B. 76 (partition of stock held as community property is not a transfer).

3. *Waiver of Family Attribution By Entities*

Prior to 1982, when § 302(c)(2)(C) was enacted, there was significant controversy regarding the type of taxpayer entitled to take advantage of the waiver of the family attribution rules. For example, suppose A owns 50 percent of the stock of X Corporation and Trust T, created by a deceased aunt for the benefit of A's children, owns 50 percent. Under § 318, A's children are deemed to own A's stock and the trust is deemed to own the stock of the children. If all of the stock actually owned by the trust is redeemed, can the trust take advantage of the waiver of the family attribution rules provided in § 302(c)(2) and treat the redemption as a complete termination under § 302(b)(3)? Rev.Rul. 59–233, 1959–2 C.B. 106, held that the waiver of the family attribution rules applied only if the distributee in the redemption was deemed to own stock under the family attribution rules. Since the last step in the attribution involved in the Ruling was not a "*family*" attribution, the exception did not apply. See also Rev.Rul. 68–388, 1968–2 C.B. 122. (In contrast, a redemption from A would have qualified because in that case, the family attribution would have been the last link in the chain and the waiver of attribution in § 302(c)(2) would have been effective.)

The Tax Court rejected the Internal Revenue Service's narrow interpretation of the waiver of family attribution rules. See, e.g., Crawford v. Commissioner, 59 T.C. 830 (1973)(NA) (estate permitted to waive family attribution rules); Rodgers P. Johnson Trust v. Commissioner, 71 T.C. 941 (1979)(A) (trust permitted to waive family attribution). In Rickey v. United States, 592 F.2d 1251 (5th Cir.1979), the court went a step further and held that an estate could waive the *entity* attribution rules if all of the stock owned by the estate was redeemed but the beneficiary continued to be an actual shareholder. David Metzger Trust v. Commissioner, 76 T.C. 42 (1981), aff'd, 693 F.2d 459 (5th Cir.1982), held to the contrary.

Section 302(c)(2)(C) permits waiver of the family attribution rules in situations like *Crawford* and *Johnson Trust*. The attribution rules may be waived if after the redemption neither the entity (trust, estate, partnership or corporation) nor the beneficiaries, partners or shareholders hold an interest in the redeeming corporation and if both agree not to acquire such an interest in the stipulated ten-year period. Under § 302(c)(2)(C), only the *family* attribution rules may be waived; the attribution rules between entity and beneficiary may not be waived. The Conference Committee Report accompanying the 1982 Act stated that the amendment to § 302(c) was intended to overrule *Rickey*. H.Rep. No. 97–760, 97th Cong., 2d Sess. 546 (1982).

4. *Timely Filing of Waiver Agreement*

Treas. Reg. § 1.302–4(a)(1) provides that the agreement required by § 302(c)(2) must be filed with the tax return reporting the redemption distribution, but the courts have been much more lenient in their interpretation of the requirement. See, e.g., United States v. Van Keppel, 321 F.2d 717 (10th Cir.1963) (agreement filed over one year after the tax return was due, but not before issuance of a notice of deficiency, as timely); Fehrs v. United States, 556 F.2d 1019 (Ct.Cl.1977) (agreement filed seven years after redemption held timely). But Robin Haft Trust v. Commissioner, 62 T.C. 145 (1974), vacated on other grounds, 510 F.2d 43 (1st Cir.1975), held that agreements filed after an adverse Tax Court decision were not timely.

5. *Retention of Prohibited Interest*

Section 302(c)(2)(A) conditions the availability of the waiver of family attribution rules on the redeemed shareholder retaining no interest in the corporation, including an interest as an officer, director, or employee, other than an interest as a creditor. The Internal Revenue Service has been strict in its interpretation of what constitutes a prohibited "interest" in the corporation on the part of the redeemed shareholder, and the courts have generally upheld the Commissioner's position.

Whether post-redemption employment of a former shareholder by the corporation precludes availability of the waiver may depend on the nature of the employment. Service as a common law employee invariably has been found to be a prohibited interest even though the former shareholder's compensation was not contingent on corporate profits and he did not manage the corporation. See Cerone v. Commissioner, 87 T.C. 1 (1986) (employment at significantly reduced salary as bartender and cashier in restaurant/bar); Seda v. Commissioner, 82 T.C. 484 (1984) (employment at fixed salary even though no fact finding as torole in management); Rev. Rul. 56–556, 1956–2 C.B. 177 (compensation is irrelevant; employment is *per se* a prohibited interest). If the employment is in the capacity of an independent contractor, the answer is less certain. Rev.Rul. 70–104, 1970–1 C.B. 66, held that a five-year "consulting contract" was a prohibited interest without examining the particular services to be provided and the terms of compensation. The Tax Court, however, applies a facts and circumstances test based on "whether the former stockholder has either retained a financial stake in the corporation or continued to control the corporation and benefit by its operations." Lynch v. Commissioner, 83 T.C. 597, 605 (1984), rev'd, 801 F.2d 1176 (9th Cir.1986). Compare Chertkof v. Commissioner, 72 T.C. 1113 (1979), aff'd, 649 F.2d 264 (4th Cir.1981), in which the Tax Court found a prohibited interest because the former shareholder had provided management services as an independent contractor, with Estate of Lennard v. Commissioner, 61 T.C. 554 (1974) (NA), in which the court held that rendering accounting services as an independent contractor was not a prohibited interest.

In *Lynch,* supra, the Ninth Circuit rejected the Tax Court's facts and circumstances test in favor of a *per se* prohibition on post-redemption provision of services to the corporation. This *per se* rule was then applied to deny waiver of family attribution because the former shareholder provided nonmanagement services as an independent contractor for $500 per month. The Ninth Circuit expressly rejected the Tax Court's *Estate of Lennard* decision, and held that no qualitative judgments regarding the value of the retained interest are permissible. See also the concurring opinion in *Seda,* supra, in which eight Tax Court judges supported application of a *per se* rule.

Suppose that the redeemed shareholder retains or reacquires voting power in a fiduciary capacity. Rev.Rul. 81–233, 1981–2 C.B. 83, held that a redeemed shareholder who within ten years became a custodian under the Uniform Gift to Minors Act with respect to stock given to his children by the shareholder's parents had acquired a prohibited interest because he had the power to vote the stock. See also Rev.Rul. 71–426, 1971–2 C.B. 173 (stock of the corporation was owned by a mother and her four children, with the children's stock held by a voting trust; retention by the mother of the position as voting trustee was a prohibited interest). If the fiduciary position is as an executor or testamentary trustee, however, the Service has ruled that the exception for interests acquired by bequest or inheritance applies. Rev.Rul. 79–334, 1979–2 C.B. 127 (testamentary trustee); Rev.Rul. 72–380, 1972–2 C.B. 201 (executor of estate).

The statute allows the redeemed shareholder to remain as a "creditor" of the corporation, thus raising the issue whether obligations issued in the redemption constitute debt or equity. Treas. Reg. § 1.302–4(d) specifies conditions that must be met for the redeemed shareholder's interest as a creditor to be respected as such. See, e.g., Dunn v. Commissioner, 615 F.2d 578 (2d Cir.1980) (interest was as a "creditor" despite restrictions pursuant to automobile dealers franchise agreement on the payment of the obligations issued in the redemption if payment would leave inadequate working capital); *Estate of Lennard,* supra (subordination of the obligation to bank loans did not prevent "creditor" status notwithstanding Treas. Reg. § 1.302–4(d)). For the Internal Revenue Service guidelines on issuing advance rulings if stock is redeemed with notes, see Rev.Proc. 98–3, §§ 3.01(16)–(18), 4.01(21) 1998–1 I.R.B. 100. See also Treas. Reg. § 1.302–4(e) (acquisition of assets of corporation to enforce creditor's rights is not prohibited interest; reacquisition of stock in enforcing creditor's rights is prohibited interest). Rev.Rul. 59–119, 1959–1 C.B. 68, held that if the shareholder retained the right to have a member of the law firm representing him serve on the board of directors of the corporation to protect his interests as a creditor and to determine that the conditions of the stock redemption agreement were being observed, the "limited" directorship by an agent prevented the application of § 302(c)(2)(A). Compare Rev.Rul. 76–524, 1976–2 C.B. 94 (continuing as director and officer does not prevent redemption from qualifying under § 302(b)(3) if waiver of family attribution is not necessary for complete termination).

Rev.Rul. 77–467, 1977–2 C.B. 92, held that a redeemed shareholder could lease real estate to the corporation and the lease would not be a prohibited interest if the rent was not dependent on corporate earnings. Rev.Rul. 84–135, 1984–2 C.B. 80, held that the right to receive a lifetime pension under a pre-existing unfunded nonqualified pension plan was not a prohibited interest. Are these interests any less a continuing interest in the corporation than employment in a nonmanagerial capacity for a fixed salary?

C. BASIS OF STOCK REDEEMED IN NONQUALIFYING TRANSACTION

If a redemption is treated as a § 301 distribution under § 302(d), the basis of the redeemed shares is allocated to the shareholder's remaining shares. If the shareholder's actual interest is completely terminated but, due to the family attribution rules, the shareholder's entire interest has not been terminated, the basis of the redeemed shares should be added to the basis of the related person whose shares were attributed to the redeemed shareholder. Treas. Reg. § 1.302–2(c); see also, Levin v. Commissioner, 385 F.2d 521 (2d Cir.1967) (basis of parent's redeemed shares added to basis of son's shares).

SECTION 4. DISTRIBUTIONS NOT "ESSENTIALLY EQUIVALENT TO A DIVIDEND"

INTERNAL REVENUE CODE: Sections 302(b)(1), (c)(1); 318.

REGULATIONS: Section 1.302–2.

United States v. Davis

Supreme Court of the United States, 1970.
397 U.S. 301.

■ MR. JUSTICE MARSHALL delivered the opinion of the Court.

In 1945, taxpayer and E.B. Bradley organized a corporation. In exchange for property transferred to the new company, Bradley received 500 shares of common stock, and taxpayer and his wife similarly each received 250 such shares. Shortly thereafter, taxpayer made an additional contribution to the corporation, purchasing 1,000 shares of preferred stock at a par value of $25 per share.

The purpose of this latter transaction was to increase the company's working capital and thereby to qualify for a loan previously negotiated through the Reconstruction Finance Corporation. It was understood that the corporation would redeem the preferred stock when the RFC loan had been repaid. Although in the interim taxpayer bought Bradley's 500 shares and divided them between his son and daughter, the total capitalization of the company remained the same until 1963. That year, after the loan was fully repaid and in accordance with the original understanding, the company redeemed taxpayer's preferred stock.

In his 1963 personal income tax return taxpayer did not report the $25,000 received by him upon the redemption of his preferred stock as income. Rather, taxpayer considered the redemption as a sale of his preferred stock to the company—a capital gains transaction under § 302 of the Internal Revenue Code of 1954 resulting in no tax since taxpayer's basis in the stock equaled the amount he received for it. The Commissioner of Internal Revenue, however, did not approve this tax treatment. According to the Commissioner, the redemption of taxpayer's stock was essentially equivalent to a dividend and was thus taxable as ordinary income under §§ 301 and 316 of the Code. Taxpayer paid the resulting deficiency and brought this suit for a refund. The District Court ruled in his favor, 274 F.Supp. 466 (M.D.Tenn.1967), and on appeal the Court of Appeals affirmed. 408 F.2d 1139 (6th Cir.1969).

The Court of Appeals held that the $25,000 received by taxpayer was "not essentially equivalent to a dividend" within the meaning of that phrase in § 302(b)(1) of the Code because the redemption was the final step in a course of action that had a legitimate business (as opposed to a tax avoidance) purpose. That holding represents only one of a variety of treatments accorded similar transactions under § 302(b)(1) in the circuit courts of appeals.[2] We granted certiorari, 396 U.S. 815, 90 S.Ct. 88 (1969), in order to resolve this recurring tax question involving stock redemptions by closely held corporations. We reverse.

I

The Internal Revenue Code of 1954 provides generally in §§ 301 and 316 for the tax treatment of distributions by a corporation to its shareholders; under those provisions, a distribution is includable in a taxpayer's gross income as a dividend out of earnings and profits to the extent such earnings exist. There are exceptions to the application of these general provisions, however, and among them are those found in § 302 involving certain distributions for redeemed stock. The basic question in this case is whether the $25,000 distribution by the corporation to taxpayer falls under that section—more specifically, whether its legitimate business motivation qualifies the distribution under § 302(b)(1) of the Code. Preliminarily, however, we must consider the relationship between § 302(b)(1) and the rules regarding the attribution of stock ownership found in § 318(a) of the Code.

Under subsection (a) of § 302, a distribution is treated as "payment in exchange for the stock," thus qualifying for capital gains rather than ordinary income treatment, if the conditions contained in any one of the four paragraphs of subsection (b) are met. In addition to paragraph (1)'s "not essentially equivalent to a dividend" test, capital gains treatment is available where (2) the taxpayer's voting strength is substantially diminished, (3) his interest in the company is completely terminated, or (4) certain railroad stock is redeemed. Paragraph (4) is not involved here, and taxpayer admits that paragraphs (2) and (3) do not apply. Moreover, taxpayer agrees that for the purposes of §§ 302(b)(2) and (3) the attribution rules of § 318(a) apply and he is considered to own the 750 outstanding shares of common stock held by his wife and children in addition to the 250 shares in his own name.

Taxpayer, however, argues that the attribution rules do not apply in considering whether a distribution is essentially equivalent to a dividend under § 302(b)(1). According to taxpayer, he should thus be considered to own only 25 percent of the corporation's common stock, and the distribu-

2. Only the Second Circuit has unequivocally adopted the Commissioner's view and held irrelevant the motivation of the redemption. See Levin v. Commissioner, 385 F.2d 521 (1967). * * *

The other courts of appeals that have passed on the question are apparently willing to give at least some weight under § 302(b)(1) to the business motivation of a distribution and redemption. See, e.g., Commissioner v. Berenbaum, 369 F.2d 337 (C.A.10th Cir.1966); Kerr v. Commissioner, 326 F.2d 225 (9th Cir.1964) . * * * Even among those courts that consider business purpose, however, it is generally required that the business purpose be related, not to the issuance of the stock, but to the redemption of it. * * *

tion would then qualify under § 302(b)(1) since it was not pro rata or proportionate to his stock interest, the fundamental test of dividend equivalency. See Treas.Reg. 1.302–2(b). However, the plain language of the statute compels rejection of the argument. In subsection (c) of § 302, the attribution rules are made specifically applicable "in determining the ownership of stock for purposes of this section." Applying this language, both courts below held that § 318(a) applies to all of § 302, including § 302(b)(1)—a view in accord with the decisions of the other courts of appeals, a longstanding treasury regulation,[5] and the opinion of the leading commentators.[7]

Against this weight of authority, taxpayer argues that the result under paragraph (1) should be different because there is no explicit reference to stock ownership as there is in paragraphs (2) and (3). Neither that fact, however, nor the purpose and history of § 302(b)(1) support taxpayer's argument. The attribution rules—designed to provide a clear answer to what would otherwise be a difficult tax question—formed part of the tax bill that was subsequently enacted as the 1954 Code. As is discussed further, infra, the bill as passed by the House of Representatives contained no provision comparable to § 302(b)(1). When that provision was added in the Senate, no purpose was evidenced to restrict the applicability of § 318(a). Rather, the attribution rules continued to be made specifically applicable to the entire section, and we believe that Congress intended that they be taken into account wherever ownership of stock was relevant.

Indeed, it was necessary that the attribution rules apply to § 302(b)(1) unless they were to be effectively eliminated from consideration with regard to §§ 302(b)(2) and (3) also. For if a transaction failed to qualify under one of those sections solely because of the attribution rules, it would according to taxpayer's argument nonetheless qualify under § 302(b)(1). We cannot agree that Congress intended so to nullify its explicit directive. We conclude, therefore, that the attribution rules of § 318(a) do apply; and, for the purposes of deciding whether a distribution is "not essentially equivalent to a dividend" under § 302(b)(1), taxpayer must be deemed the owner of all 1,000 shares of the company's common stock.

II

After application of the stock ownership attribution rules, this case viewed most simply involves a sole stockholder who causes part of his shares to be redeemed by the corporation. We conclude that such a redemption is always "essentially equivalent to a dividend" within the meaning of that phrase in § 302(b)(1)[8] and therefore do not reach the

5. See Treas.Reg. 1.302–2(b).

7. See B. Bittker & J. Eustice, Federal Income Taxation of Corporations and Shareholders 292 n. 32 (2d ed. 1966).

8. Of course, this just means that a distribution in redemption to a sole shareholder will be treated under the general provisions of § 301, and it will only be taxed as a dividend under § 316 to the extent that there are earnings and profits.

Government's alternative argument that in any event the distribution should not on the facts of this case qualify for capital gains treatment.[9]

The predecessor of § 302(b)(1) came into the tax law as § 201(d) of the Revenue Act of 1921, 42 Stat. 228:

> "A stock dividend shall not be subject to tax but if after the distribution of any such dividend the corporation proceeds to cancel or redeem its stock at such time and in such manner as to make the distribution and cancellation or redemption essentially equivalent to the distribution of a taxable dividend, the amount received in redemption or cancellation of the stock shall be treated as a taxable dividend. * * * "

Enacted in response to this Court's decision that pro rata stock dividends do not constitute taxable income, Eisner v. Macomber, 252 U.S. 189, 40 S.Ct. 189 (1920), the provision had the obvious purpose of preventing a corporation from avoiding dividend tax treatment by distributing earnings to its shareholders in two transactions—a pro rata stock dividend followed by a pro rata redemption—that would have the same economic consequences as a simple dividend. Congress, however, soon recognized that even without a prior stock dividend essentially the same result could be effected whereby any corporation, "especially one which has only a few stockholders, might be able to make a distribution to its stockholders which would have the same effect as a taxable dividend." H.R.Rep. No. 1, 69th Cong., 1st Sess., 5. In order to cover this situation, the law was amended to apply "(whether or not such stock was issued as a stock dividend)" whenever a distribution in redemption of stock was made "at such time and in such manner" that it was essentially equivalent to a taxable dividend. Revenue Act of 1926, § 201(g), 44 Stat. 11.

This provision of the 1926 Act was carried forward in each subsequent revenue act and finally became § 115(g)(1) of the Internal Revenue Code of 1939. Unfortunately, however, the policies encompassed within the general language of § 115(g)(1) and its predecessors were not clear, and there resulted much confusion in the tax law. At first, courts assumed that the provision was aimed at tax avoidance schemes and sought only to determine whether such a scheme existed. See, e.g., Commissioner v. Quackenbos, 78 F.2d 156 (2d Cir.1935). Although later the emphasis changed and the focus was more on the effect of the distribution, many courts continued to find that distributions otherwise like a dividend were not "essentially equivalent" if, for example, they were motivated by a sufficiently strong nontax business purpose. See cases cited n. 2, supra. There was general disagreement, however, about what would qualify as such a purpose, and the result was a case-by-case determination with each case decided "on the

9. The Government argues that even if business purpose were relevant under § 302(b)(1), the business purpose present here related only to the original investment and not at all to the necessity for redemption. See cases cited, n. 2, supra. Under either view, taxpayer does not lose his basis in the preferred stock. Under Treas.Reg. 1.302–2(c) that basis is applied to taxpayer's common stock.

basis of the particular facts of the transaction in question." Bains v. United States, 153 Ct.Cl. 599, 603, 289 F.2d 644, 646 (1961).

By the time of the general revision resulting in the Internal Revenue Code of 1954, the draftsmen were faced with what has aptly been described as "the morass created by the decisions." Ballenger v. United States, 301 F.2d 192, 196 (4th Cir.1962). In an effort to eliminate "the considerable confusion which exists in this area" and thereby to facilitate tax planning, H.R.Rep. No. 1337, 83d Cong., 2d Sess., 35, the authors of the new Code sought to provide objective tests to govern the tax consequences of stock redemptions. Thus, the tax bill passed by the House of Representatives contained no "essentially equivalent" language. Rather, it provided for "safe harbors" where capital gains treatment would be accorded to corporate redemptions that met the conditions now found in §§ 302(b)(2) and (3) of the Code.

It was in the Senate Finance Committee's consideration of the tax bill that § 302(b)(1) was added, and Congress thereby provided that capital gains treatment should be available "if the redemption is not essentially equivalent to a dividend." Taxpayer argues that the purpose was to continue "existing law," and there is support in the legislative history that § 302(b)(1) reverted "in part" or "in general" to the "essentially equivalent" provision of § 115(g)(1) of the 1939 Code. According to the Government, even under the old law it would have been improper for the Court of Appeals to rely on "a business purpose for the redemption" and "an absence of the proscribed tax avoidance purpose to bail out dividends at favorable tax rates." See Northup v. United States, 240 F.2d 304, 307 (2d Cir.1957); Smith v. United States, 121 F.2d 692, 695 (3d Cir.1941); cf. Commissioner v. Estate of Bedford, 325 U.S. 283 (1945). However, we need not decide that question, for we find from the history of the 1954 revisions and the purpose of § 302(b)(1) that Congress intended more than merely to re-enact the prior law.

In explaining the reason for adding the "essentially equivalent" test, the Senate Committee stated that the House provisions "appeared unnecessarily restrictive, particularly, in the case of redemptions of preferred stock which might be called by the corporation without the shareholder having any control over when the redemption may take place." S.Rep. No. 1622, 83d Cong., 2d Sess., 44. This explanation gives no indication that the purpose behind the redemption should affect the result.[10] Rather, in its more detailed technical evaluation of § 302(b)(1), the Senate Committee reported as follows:

"The test intended to be incorporated in the interpretation of paragraph (1) is in general that currently employed under section 115(g)(1) of the 1939 Code. Your committee further intends that in applying this test for the future * * * the inquiry will be devoted solely to the question of

10. See Bittker & Eustice, supra, n. 7 at 291: "It is not easy to give § 302(b)(1) an expansive construction in view of this indication that its major function was the narrow one of immunizing redemptions of minority holdings of preferred stock."

whether or not the transaction by its nature may properly be characterized as a sale of stock by the redeeming shareholder to the corporation. For this purpose the presence or absence of earnings and profits of the corporation is not material. Example: X, the sole shareholder of a corporation having no earnings or profits causes the corporation to redeem half of its stock. Paragraph (1) does not apply to such redemption notwithstanding the absence of earnings and profits." S.Rep. No. 1622, supra, at 234.

The intended scope of § 302(b)(1) as revealed by this legislative history is certainly not free from doubt. However, we agree with the Government that by making the sole inquiry relevant for the future the narrow one whether the redemption could be characterized as a sale, Congress was apparently rejecting past court decisions that had also considered factors indicating the presence or absence of a tax-avoidance motive.[11] At least that is the implication of the example given. Congress clearly mandated that pro rata distributions be treated under the general rules laid down in §§ 301 and 316 rather than under § 302, and nothing suggests that there should be a different result if there were a "business purpose" for the redemption. Indeed, just the opposite inference must be drawn since there would not likely be a tax-avoidance purpose in a situation where there were no earnings or profits. We conclude that the Court of Appeals was therefore wrong in looking for a business purpose and considering it in deciding whether the redemption was equivalent to a dividend. Rather, we agree with the Court of Appeals for the Second Circuit that "the business purpose of a transaction is irrelevant in determining dividend equivalence" under § 302(b)(1). Hasbrook v. United States, 343 F.2d 811, 814 (1965).

Taxpayer strongly argues that to treat the redemption involved here as essentially equivalent to a dividend is to elevate form over substance. Thus, taxpayer argues, had he not bought Bradley's shares or had he made a subordinated loan to the company instead of buying preferred stock, he could have gotten back his $25,000 with favorable tax treatment. However, the difference between form and substance in the tax law is largely problematical, and taxpayer's complaints have little to do with whether a business purpose is relevant under § 302(b)(1). It was clearly proper for Congress to treat distributions generally as taxable dividends when made out of earnings and profits and then to prevent avoidance of that result

11. This rejection is confirmed by the Committee's acceptance of the House treatment of distributions involving corporate contractions—a factor present in many of the earlier "business purpose" redemptions. In describing its action, the Committee stated as follows:

> "Your committee, as did the House bill, separates into their significant elements the kind of transactions now incoherently aggregated in the definition of a partial liquidation. Those distributions which may have capital-gain characteristics *because they are not made pro rata* among the various shareholders, would be subjected, at the shareholder level, to the separate tests described in [§§ 301 to 318]. On the other hand, those distributions characterized by what happens solely at the corporate level by reason of the assets distributed would be included as within the concept of a partial liquidation." S.Rep. No. 1622, supra, at 49. (Emphasis added.)

without regard to motivation where the distribution is in exchange for redeemed stock.

We conclude that that is what Congress did when enacting § 302(b)(1). If a corporation distributes property as a simple dividend, the effect is to transfer the property from the company to its shareholders without a change in the relative economic interests or rights of the stockholders. Where a redemption has that same effect, it cannot be said to have satisfied the "not essentially equivalent to a dividend" requirement of § 302(b)(1). Rather, to qualify for preferred treatment under that section, a redemption must result in a meaningful reduction of the shareholder's proportionate interest in the corporation. Clearly, taxpayer here, who (after application of the attribution rules) was the sole shareholder of the corporation both before and after the redemption, did not qualify under this test. The decision of the Court of Appeals must therefore be reversed and the case remanded to the District Court for dismissal of the complaint.

It is so ordered.

■ MR. JUSTICE DOUGLAS, with whom THE CHIEF JUSTICE and MR. JUSTICE BRENNAN concur, dissenting.

I agree with the District Court, 274 F.Supp. 466, and with the Court of Appeals, 408 F.2d 1139, that respondent's contribution of working capital in the amount of $25,000 in exchange for 1,000 shares of preferred stock with a par value of $25 was made in order for the corporation to obtain a loan from the RFC and that the preferred stock was to be redeemed when the loan was repaid. For the reasons stated by the two lower courts, this redemption was not "essentially equivalent to a dividend," for the bona fide business purpose of the redemption belies the payment of a dividend. As stated by the Court of Appeals:

"Although closely-held corporations call for close scrutiny under the tax law, we will not, under the facts and circumstances of this case, allow mechanical attribution rules to transform a legitimate corporate transaction into a tax avoidance scheme." 408 F.2d, at 1143–1144.

When the Court holds it was a dividend, it effectively cancels § 302(b)(1) from the Code. This result is not a matter of conjecture, for the Court says that in the case of closely held or one-man corporations a redemption of stock is "always" equivalent to a dividend. I would leave such revision to the Congress.

ILLUSTRATIVE MATERIAL

A. GENERAL

If a shareholder is unable to meet the "safe haven" requirements of § 302(b)(2) or § 302(b)(3), the shareholder still may fall back on the general language of § 302(b)(1), allowing capital gain treatment to distributions found to be not essentially equivalent to a dividend. But the *Davis* case makes the task of the shareholder attempting to fit the transaction under § 302(b)(1) very difficult. First, the Court's holding that the attribution rules of § 318 apply to § 302(b)(1) situations means that the shareholder in a closely-held corporate context almost invariably will be deemed to own a higher percentage of stock than is actually owned, and hence the distribution to the shareholder will more likely have or approach the pro rata character of a dividend distribution. See, e.g., Title Insurance and Trust Co. v. United States, 484 F.2d 462 (9th Cir.1973); Johnson v. United States, 434 F.2d 340 (8th Cir.1970); and Rev.Rul. 71–261, 1971–1 C.B. 108, all situations in which, by virtue of the application of the attribution rules, the shareholder was deemed to own 100 percent of the stock of the corporation and hence the distribution was treated as a dividend. (Indeed, in some cases the interaction of the attribution rules and the redemption can actually *increase* the redeemed shareholder's interest after the redemption, see, e.g., Sawelson v. Commissioner, 61 T.C. 109 (1973).) Second, the Court's elimination of the "business purpose" factor in determining dividend equivalence under § 302(b)(1) removes from consideration any argument based on the reasons for the redemption (presumably including "shareholder" purposes, see Nicholson v. Commissioner, 17 T.C. 1399 (1952)), and focuses attention solely on the "effect" of the distribution. Here the factors discussed below, some of which were developed in the prior case law dealing with dividend equivalence, remain relevant after *Davis,* with the exception of those cases whose result turned on a finding of "business purpose" for the redemption.

Could the taxpayer in Davis have avoided the dividend result if, instead of receiving the preferred stock, he had made a subordinated loan to the corporation of $25,000?

B. "MEANINGFUL REDUCTION" IN THE SHAREHOLDER'S INTEREST

1. *Voting Stock*

(a) Effect on Control

In attempting to give some content to the "meaningful reduction" standard set forth by the Supreme Court in *Davis,* subsequent cases and Rulings have focused principally on the effect that the redemption has on the shareholder's voting control of the corporation. Thus in Rev.Rul. 75–502, 1975–2 C.B. 111, a redemption that reduced the shareholder's voting stock interest in the corporation from 57 percent to 50 percent, the other 50 percent being held by a single unrelated shareholder, qualified as a meaningful reduction. The Ruling indicated that if the redemption had not reduced the shareholder's interest in the voting stock to 50 percent or less, then § 302(b)(1) would not have been applicable. See Rev.Rul. 77–218, 1977–1 C.B. 81 (8 percent reduction in actual and constructive ownership that left the shareholder with more than 50 percent of the voting stock because of the attribution rules was not a meaningful reduction even though all of the shares actually owned by the taxpayer were redeemed). Benjamin v. Commissioner, 66 T.C. 1084 (1976), aff'd, 592 F.2d 1259 (5th Cir.1979), involving a redemption of voting preferred stock, found that the redemption did not qualify under § 302(b)(1) because of the shareholder's continuing voting control over the corporation after the redemption. The facts that the shareholder's interest in the net worth of the corporation and the right to participate in its earnings were reduced were not sufficient since "the retention of absolute voting control in the present case outweighs any other considerations". (66 T.C. at 1111).

Situations involving redemptions of voting stock held by minority shareholders are analyzed similarly. In Rev.Rul. 76–364, 1976–2 C.B. 91, the shareholder held 27 percent of the voting stock of the corporation and three other unrelated shareholders each had a 24.3 percent interest. A redemption that reduced the shareholder's 27 percent interest to 22.27 percent was held to be a meaningful reduction since through the redemption the shareholder lost the ability to control the corporation by acting in conjunction with only one of the other shareholders. See also Rev.Rul. 75–512, 1975–2 C.B. 112 (a reduction from 30 percent actual and constructive ownership to 24.3 percent constructive ownership qualified under § 302(b)(1) because all of the shares actually owned were redeemed). Compare Rev.Rul. 76–385, 1976–2 C.B. 92 (the shareholder had a .0001118 percent interest in a publicly held corporation, and thus effectively no control at all with respect to the operation of the corporation; a 3.3 percent reduction in share ownership was meaningful); Rev.Rul. 81–289, 1981–2 C.B. 82 (redemption of 2 percent of stock of shareholder holding less than 1 percent of publicly traded corporation's outstanding stock was essentially equivalent to a dividend because simultaneous redemptions from other shareholders resulted in total redemption of 2 percent of corporation's outstanding stock).

Roebling v. Commissioner, 77 T.C. 30 (1981), involved the redemption of voting preferred stock pursuant to a plan of the corporation to redeem all of its outstanding preferred stock over a number of years. Before the series of redemptions commenced, the shareholder held 91.94 percent of the preferred stock and 39.6 percent of the common stock, which gave her 57.12 percent of the total voting shares. If the plan had been carried out in full, the shareholder would have been left with less than forty percent of the voting stock of the corporation, which had approximately 500 shareholders. For the years in question, however, the shareholder's voting power was only reduced to 43.28 percent. Because the shareholder's voting power was reduced from majority control to less than 50 percent, the court concluded that the reduction was meaningful. This conclusion was reenforced by the reduction in the percentage of total dividend distributions that would be receivable by the taxpayer as a result of the redemption.

Rickey v. United States, 427 F.Supp. 484 (W.D.La.1976), aff'd on other grounds, 592 F.2d 1251 (5th Cir.1979), held that a reduction in voting stock from 72 percent to 58 percent was a qualifying redemption because the shareholder lost the ability to control the two-thirds vote necessary for certain corporate actions under the state corporation law. Henry T. Patterson Trust v. United States, 729 F.2d 1089 (6th Cir.1984), reached the same result in a case in which the shareholder's interest was reduced from 80 percent to 60 percent. This analysis was rejected in Rev.Rul. 78–401, 1978–

2 C.B. 127, which held that a reduction from 90 percent to 60 percent did not qualify under § 302(b)(1); the shareholder still had the right to control the day-to-day operations of the corporation and the fact that he gave up the right to control actions requiring a two-thirds vote under state corporation law was not sufficient.

(b) Effect of "Family Hostility" on Application of Constructive Stock Ownership Rules

If, after the redemption, the shareholder's directly owned stock is insufficient to provide control but the shareholder is deemed to own over 50 percent of the voting stock because of the attribution rules, she is still treated as the controlling shareholder for purposes of testing the meaningful reduction in the shareholder's interest. See, e.g., Fehrs Finance Co. v. Commissioner, 487 F.2d 184 (8th Cir.1973); Rev.Rul. 77–218, supra. While *Davis* indicates that the attribution rules apply in such a situation, *Davis* could be viewed as permitting this shareholder to argue that where the related parties in fact were in disagreement, the attribution rules should not be applied in testing control. Several pre-*Davis* cases had adopted this approach. See, e.g., Estate of Squier v. Commissioner, 35 T.C. 950 (1961) (NA). In the first case to raise the issue following *Davis,* however, the Tax Court held that the *Davis* view of the attribution rules precluded applying a "family fight" exception. Robin Haft Trust v. Commissioner, 61 T.C. 398 (1973). The Court of Appeals reversed (510 F.2d 43 (1st Cir.1975)) and remanded the case for consideration of whether "the existence of family discord [tended] to negate the presumption that taxpayers would exert continuing control over the corporation despite the redemption." In Rev. Rul. 80–26, 1980–1 C.B. 66, the Internal Revenue Service announced that it would not follow the Court of Appeals decision in *Robin Haft Trust* on the theory that a "family hostility" exception to the attribution rules is inconsistent with both *Davis* and the legislative history of § 302(b)(1). Likewise, the Fifth Circuit, in David Metzger Trust v. Commissioner, 693 F.2d 459 (5th Cir.1982), held that there is no family hostility exception to the attribution rules.

The Tax Court rejected any possibility of a family hostility or "bad blood" exception to the application of the § 318 attribution rules in Niedermeyer v. Commissioner, 62 T.C. 280 (1974), aff'd per curiam 535 F.2d 500 (9th Cir.1976). Subsequently, in Cerone v. Commissioner, 87 T.C. 1, 22 (1986), the Tax Court described the relevance of family hostility as follows:

"First, the attribution rules are plainly and straightforwardly applied. Second, a determination is made whether there has been a reduction in the stockholder's proportionate interest in the corporation. If not, the inquiry ends because, if there is no change in the stockholder's interest, dividend equivalency results. If there has been a reduction, then all of the facts and circumstances must be examined to see if the reduction was meaningful under *United States v. Davis,* supra. It is at this point, *and only then,* that family hostility becomes an appropriate factor for consideration." Since the shareholder's interest in *Cerone* was not reduced, this version of the family hostility doctrine was, on the facts, inapplicable.

The circumscribed family hostility doctrine of *Cerone* could lead to unusual results. Suppose the stock of X Corp. is held as follows: A, 41 shares; B, 34 shares; C, 17 shares; and D, 8 shares. A and B are parent and child, but the shareholders are otherwise unrelated. If there was "bad blood" between A and B, a redemption of as few as one of B's shares might qualify under § 301(b)(1). But if ten shares were redeemed from each of B and C, the redemption never could qualify because, taking into account the attribution rules, B's ownership increased from 75 percent to 81.25 percent, even though actual ownership was reduced from 34 percent to 24 percent and A alone now holds actual voting control of the corporation. See Henry T. Patterson Trust v. United States, 729 F.2d 1089 (6th Cir.1984), in which all of the stock actually owned by the taxpayer was redeemed; in an alternative holding the court concluded that due to family hostility there was a meaningful reduction even though after applying the attribution rules, the taxpayer's interest was reduced only from 97 percent to 93 percent.

2. *Non–Voting Stock*

If a redemption of non-voting stock is involved, the "meaningful reduction" is tested in terms of the change in the shareholder's rights with respect to the corporation's earnings and profits and assets on liquidation. See Himmel v. Commissioner, 338 F.2d 815 (2d Cir.1964), analyzing the "complex of shareholder rights" in a situation involving a multi-class capitalization. Rev.Rul. 77–426, 1977–2 C.B. 87, held that any redemption of non-voting preferred stock constituted a meaningful reduction for purposes of § 302(b)(1) because the stockholder did not hold directly or indirectly any voting common stock. The rights given up in the redemption were permanently lost and not retained through continuing common stock ownership.

On the other hand, if a preferred shareholder continues to own common stock, achieving a meaningful reduction with respect to a redemption of nonvoting preferred stock is much more difficult. For example in Hays v. Commissioner, T.C. Memo. 1971–95, the taxpayer owned 80 percent of the common stock of the corporation and all of the preferred stock. A redemption of 10 percent of the preferred stock was found to result in a dividend to the shareholder: "The redemption of 300 out of 3,000 shares of preferred stock held by Hays could not be termed 'meaningful.' Also, whatever significance the reduction might have standing alone, its importance is diminished upon consideration of the fact that Hays remained owner of 80 percent of the common stock in [the corporation]. Thus while his right to earnings and profits via the preferred stock was reduced * * *, he continued to have access to 80 percent of that amount via his common stock. Since Hays owned the overwhelming majority of the common, the only voting stock, his ability to declare dividends was assured." (382)

Rev.Rul. 85–106, 1985–2 C.B. 116, involved a redemption of two-thirds of a shareholder's non-voting preferred stock. Prior to the redemption, the shareholder, which was a trust, held directly approximately 18 percent of each of the nonvoting preferred stock and nonvoting common stock and, by attribution from its sole beneficiary, approximately 18 percent of the voting common stock. The ruling held that the redemption was essentially equivalent to a dividend because, after taking into account attribution, the redeemed shareholder's potential for participating in a control group by aligning itself with two other stockholders, who together held 38 percent of the voting common stock, was not reduced.

3. *Comparative Dividend Analysis*

Another approach to the problem of dividend equivalence is to compare the distribution on redemption with the distribution of a similar amount as a hypothetical dividend. See Himmel v. Commissioner, 338 F.2d 815 (2d Cir.1964) (receipt of substantially larger distribution than would have been received as dividend indicates that redemption is not essentially equivalent to a dividend). While the *Davis* opinion does not discuss this so-called "comparative dividend" method, it is not necessarily inconsistent with the Court's focus on the effect rather than the purpose of the distribution. However, the cases decided since *Davis* do not use comparative dividend analysis of redemptions. Brown v. United States, 477 F.2d 599 (6th Cir. 1973), held the approach inconsistent with *Davis,* and in Rev.Rul. 85–106, 1985–2 C.B. 116, the Internal Revenue Service rejected the use of comparative dividend analysis. But see Grabowski Trust v. Commissioner, 58 T.C. 650 (1972), finding comparative dividend analysis relevant after *Davis.*

Do the developments since *Davis* indicate that in the redemption area Congress should rely exclusively on mechanical tests such as that in § 302(b)(2)?

C. Insufficient Earnings and Profits

Suppose a distribution in redemption of stock is made under circumstances that would make it essentially equivalent to a dividend, but there are no current or accumulated earnings and profits. Treas. Reg. § 1.302–2(a) states that, despite the verbal difficulty of calling the distribution "essentially equivalent to a dividend," it should nevertheless be placed under §§ 302(d) and 301(c) rather than § 302(a). The distribution would thus be applied against the basis of *all* of the distributee's stock, rather than only the redeemed stock, and taxable gain results only if his entire basis is exceeded.

SECTION 5. PARTIAL LIQUIDATIONS

INTERNAL REVENUE CODE: Sections 302(b)(4), (e).

REGULATIONS: Section 1.346–1,–2,–3.

Section 302(b)(4) extends sale or exchange treatment to redemptions of stock from *individual* shareholders in "partial liquidation" of the distributing corporation. The term "partial liquidation" is defined in § 302(e), and that definition makes clear that unlike the redemptions described in §§ 302(b)(1) through (b)(3), which focus upon the effect of the distribution to the shareholder, whether a distribution qualifies as a partial liquidation is determined with reference to its effect on the corporation. Although the statutory language of § 302(e)(1) refers to a distribution "not essentially equivalent to a dividend (determined at the corporate level rather than at the shareholder level)," § 302(e) is in fact concerned primarily, perhaps exclusively, with the concept of a distribution in connection with a "corporate contraction." The lineage of § 302(e) can be traced through former § 346(a)(2) of the 1954 Code back to provisions of the 1939 Code. The provision was described in the Conference Committee Report accompanying its enactment as "continuing" the law under former § 346(a)(2). See S.Rep. No. 83–1622, 83rd Cong., 2d Sess. 49, 261–2 (1954). The case law under the 1939 Code had focused on corporate contraction as the test for a partial liquidation. See, e.g., Blaschka v. United States, 393 F.2d 983 (Ct.Cl.1968) (distribution was essentially equivalent to a dividend "in that there was no contraction of [the corporation's] business") ; see also Treas. Reg. § 1.346–1(a) ("genuine contraction of the corporate business"). While there is relatively little recent case law with respect to the "contraction" doctrine, the Internal Revenue Service has issued a number of rulings that provide guidelines in the area, and the case law under the 1939 Code continues to be relevant under § 302(e)(1). See H.Rep. No. 97–760, 97th Cong.2d Sess. 530 (1982).

Section 302(e)(2) provides a mechanical safe harbor rule that satisfies the not essentially equivalent to a dividend requirement under § 302(e)(1) if it is met. If the distribution consists of *all* of the assets, or the proceeds from the sale, of an *active* trade or business conducted for at least five years (which was not acquired by the corporation within the five year period in a taxable transaction), *and* after the distribution the corporation continues to conduct an *active* trade or business with a similar five year history, the distribution is not essentially equivalent to a dividend.

As in the other redemption situations, classification of a transaction as a partial liquidation is important to the shareholders to permit a recovery of basis, absorb otherwise realized capital losses, and take advantage of the preferential rates accorded long-term capital gains.

Estate of Chandler v. Commissioner*

Tax Court of the United States, 1954.
22 T.C. 1158.

[All of the petitioners were stockholders of Chandler–Singleton Company (hereinafter referred to as the Company), a Tennessee corporation

* [Ed.: The Tax Court's decision was affirmed, 228 F.2d 909 (6th Cir.1955), the court stating that the finding as to dividend equivalence was a finding of fact sustained by the

organized on May 9, 1923. The capital stock of the Company consisted of 500 shares of common stock of $100 par value, all of which was outstanding until November 7, 1946. The stock was essentially all held by the Chandler family group. From its organization until February 28, 1946, the Company was engaged in the operation of a general department store in Maryville, Tennessee. It had a ladies' ready-to-wear department, men's department, children's department, piece goods department, and a bargain basement.

Chandler was the president and manager of the Company. At the beginning of 1944 he was in very poor health. John W. Bush was the secretary of the Company, but until 1944 he had not been particularly active in its affairs. On January 1, 1944, he became assistant manager of the Company. By profession he was a civil engineer, but at that time he was unemployed due to a change in the administration of the City of Knoxville, Tennessee. During 1944 and 1945 Chandler was sick most of the time. In his absence John W. Bush managed the department store.

John W. Bush did not like being a merchant and decided to return to engineering. In November 1945 he informed Chandler that he was resigning as manager at the end of the year. Chandler, feeling unable to manage the department store himself, decided to sell.

At a stockholders' meeting held on February 20, 1946, it was unanimously agreed that the Company should accept an offer to purchase its merchandise, furniture and fixtures, and lease. The sale was consummated and the Company ceased operating the department store on February 28, 1946. The purchaser, Arthur's Incorporated, moved in that night and began operating the store the following day.

Chandler had worked hard in the department store and had no outside interest. He wanted something to do and did not want to get out of business entirely. It was planned that a ladies' ready-to-wear store would be opened by the Company to be managed by Clara T. McConnell (now Clara M. Register) who had managed the ladies' ready-to-wear department of the department store. Thirty shares of stock in the Company owned by Chandler's wife were cancelled on April 5, 1946. Ten of these shares were issued to Clara McConnell on April 13, 1946, in order that she might have an interest in the Company whose store she was going to manage. A men's store, to be eventually taken over by the eldest son of John and Margaret Bush, was also contemplated. It was thought that approximately half of the assets of the Company would be needed for each of the two stores.

About the first of June, 1946, the Company obtained space for the ladies' ready-to-wear store about one-half block from the old department store and the store was opened on September 23, 1946.

The ladies' ready-to-wear store was about the same size as that department in the former department store. The department store had occupied 8,000 to 9,000 square feet of floor space, had employed 10 to 20 persons, and had carried fire insurance in the amount of $65,000 on its

evidence. Some courts, however, would call this a conclusion of law.]

stock and fixtures. The new store had approximately 1,800 square feet of floor space, employed four to six persons, and carried fire insurance in the amount of $10,000.

A special meeting of the stockholders was held on September 28, 1946, the minutes of which read in part as follows:

"The Chairman explained that the purpose of the meeting was to authorize partial liquidation for the following reasons:

"The old business was sold and plans were developed to go back into business, operating two stores, a ladies' ready-to-wear business and a men's store. The ladies' ready-to-wear store has been opened and is now operating. Up to now, we have been unable to negotiate a lease for a suitable location, and, after considerable thought, it has been decided to abandon the idea of operating an exclusive men's shop and operate only the one store at the present time. It appears that requirements of the one store will be approximately one-half the capital now invested in Chandler's, Inc.

"Upon motion of Margaret Chandler Bush, seconded by J.W. Bush, and unanimously carried, the officials were authorized and instructed to redeem from each shareholder one-half of his stock, paying therefor the book value, which is approximately $269.00 per share."

On November 7, 1946, each stockholder turned in one-half of his stock in return for cash, the total distributed being $67,250.

The amount of cash and United States Bonds possessed by the Company at the beginning of 1946 exceeded the amount required for the current operation of the business by approximately $45,000. Between January 1 and February 28, 1946, the Company's earned surplus increased by $39,460.44 out of which the Company paid dividends in the amount of $12,500. To the extent of at least $58,027.91, the excess cash possessed by the Company prior to the November 7 distribution was not created by a reduction in the amount of capital needed to operate the Company's business.

Petitioners reported the excess of the payments received over the cost of the stock in their individual income tax returns as capital gain. Respondent treated the payments, to the extent of the earned surplus of $58,027.91, as dividends and taxed them to the petitioners as ordinary income.

The acquisition and cancellation of one-half the Company's stock in 1946 was done at such a time and in such a manner as to make the distribution and cancellation essentially equivalent to the distribution of a taxable dividend to the extent of $58,027.91.]

OPINION

■ BRUCE, JUDGE: Respondent contends that the Company's pro rata distribution in redemption of half its capital stock at book value was made at such a time and in such a manner as to make the distribution essentially equivalent to the distribution of a taxable dividend to the extent of earnings and profits. If respondent's contention is correct the distribution to the extent of earnings and profits loses [its capital gain status and is treated as a taxable dividend].

A cancellation or redemption by a corporation of all of the stock of a particular shareholder has been held not to be essentially equivalent to the distribution of a taxable dividend. Cf. Carter Tiffany, 16 T.C. 1443; Zenz v. Quinlivan, (C.A.6), 213 F.2d 914; Regs. 111, sec. 29.115–9. However, "A cancellation or redemption by a corporation of its stock pro rata among all the shareholders will generally be considered as effecting a distribution essentially equivalent to a dividend distribution to the extent of the earnings and profits accumulated after February 28, 1913." Regs. 111, sec. 29.115–9. * * * But, as pointed out by the regulations, a pro rata distribution is not always "essentially equivalent to the distribution of a taxable dividend" and each case depends upon its own particular circumstances. Commissioner v. Sullivan, (C.A.5), 210 F.2d 607, affirming John L. Sullivan, 17 T.C. 1420. The circumstances in the instant case, however, do not warrant a finding that to the extent of earnings and profits the pro rata distribution was not essentially equivalent to a taxable dividend.

Being a question of fact, the decided cases are not controlling. However, in Joseph W. Imler, 11 T.C. 836, 840, we listed some of the factors which have been considered important, viz., "the presence or absence of a real business purpose, the motives of the corporation at the time of the distribution, the size of the corporate surplus, the past dividend policy, and the presence of any special circumstances relating to the distribution." * * *

An examination of the facts reveals that the Company had a large earned surplus and an unnecessary accumulation of cash from the standpoint of business requirement, both of which could have been reduced to the extent of earnings and profits by the declaration of a true dividend. The only suggested benefit accruing to the business by the distribution in cancellation of half the stock was the elimination of a substantial amount of this excess cash. Ordinarily such cash would be disposed of by the payment of a dividend. Coupled with the fact that the stockholders' proportionate interests in the enterprise remained unchanged, these factors indicate that [§ 115(a) of the 1939 Code respecting distributions essentially equivalent to a dividend, the predecessor of §§ 302 and 346] is applicable.

Petitioners seek to avoid application of [that section] by contending that the cash distribution and redemption of stock did not represent an artifice to disguise the payment of a dividend but was occasioned by a bona fide contraction of business with a resulting decrease in the need for capital. While important, the absence of a plan to avoid taxation is not controlling. A distribution in redemption of stock may be essentially equivalent to a taxable dividend although it does not represent an attempt to camouflage such a dividend. * * * Commissioner v. Cordingley, (C.A.1), 78 F.2d 118; and Commissioner v. Quackenbos, (C.A.2), 78 F.2d 156, both of which adopted a "bad faith" test as controlling, have either been overruled or rejected by later opinions. * * * Whether a cancellation or redemption of stock is "essentially equivalent" to a taxable dividend depends primarily upon the net effect of the distribution rather than the motives and plans of the shareholders or the corporation. * * * Moreover, we cannot find from the present record that the reduction of taxes was not the motivating factor causing the stockholders to make a distribution in redemption of stock rather than to declare a dividend to the extent of earnings and profits.

Petitioners' primary contention is that the sale of the department store and the opening of the smaller ladies' ready-to-wear store resulted in a contraction of corporate business. This is a vital factor to be considered, but a contraction of business per se does not render [the section in question] inapplicable. L.M. Lockhart, 8 T.C. 436. Furthermore, even though it is clear that there was a diminution in the size of the Company's business, there was no contraction such as was present in Commissioner v. Sullivan, Joseph W. Imler, and L.M. Lockhart, all supra. In those cases there was a contraction of business with a corresponding reduction in the amount of capital used. Here, although the business was smaller, the amount of capital actually committed to the corporate business was not reduced accordingly. On December 31, 1945, before the sale of the department store to McArthur's Incorporated, the Company had $32,736.53 tied up in fixed assets and inventories. On December 31, 1946, after the ladies' ready-to-wear store was opened, it had $31,504.67 invested in those items. Undoubtedly the department store required larger reserves than the ladies' ready-to-wear store for purchasing inventories and carrying accounts receivable. But to the extent of earnings and profits the excess cash distributed was not created by a reduction in the amount of capital required for the operation of the business. Most of the excess cash had existed since prior to the sale of the department store and did not arise from fortuitous circumstances, as petitioners contend, but from an accumulation of earnings beyond the needs of the business. This excess could have been eliminated by the payment of a taxable dividend, and its distribution in redemption of stock was essentially equivalent to a taxable dividend.

It is true that the entire $67,250 distribution could not have been made in the form of an ordinary dividend and to some extent a redemption of stock was required. But [the section] applies if the distribution is only "in part" essentially equivalent to a taxable dividend, and here the distribution was essentially equivalent to a taxable dividend to the extent of earnings and profits.

Decisions will be entered for the respondent.

ILLUSTRATIVE MATERIAL

A. FIVE–YEAR SEPARATE BUSINESS SAFE HARBOR

Section 302(e)(2) deems a distribution consisting of *all* of the assets, or the proceeds from the sale, of an *active* trade or business conducted for at least five years and which was not acquired by the corporation within the five year period in a taxable transaction to be not essentially equivalent to a dividend if after the distribution the corporation continues to conduct an *active* trade or business with a similar five year history. See Rev.Rul. 79–275, 1979–2 C.B. 137 (distribution of unrelated assets rather than promissory notes received on sale of terminated business did not qualify). Whether the distribution is pro rata or not is immaterial for purposes of § 302(e)(2). I.R.C. § 302(e)(4). Thus, although technically the attribution of ownership rules apply, as a practical matter they are not a factor under § 302(e).

Satisfaction of the mechanical test of § 302(e)(2) relates only to the "not essentially equivalent to a dividend" test of § 302(e)(1). It does not *per se* qualify the transaction under § 302(e)(1); the plan and timing tests of § 302(e)(1)(B) must be met even after satisfaction of § 302(e)(2). Rev. Rul. 77–468. 1977–2 C.B. 109; Baan v. Commissioner, 51 T.C. 1032 (1969), aff'd on other grounds, *sub nom.* Gordon v. Commissioner, 424 F.2d 378 (2d Cir.1970), and Baan v. Commissioner, 450 F.2d 198 (9th Cir.1971).

The concept of an active business separately conducted for five years also is utilized with respect to corporate divisions under § 355 and is discussed more fully in relation to that section (see page 685). The regulations under § 355 provide detailed examples of what constitutes the active conduct of a trade or business, which are relevant for purposes of § 302(e). See Treas. Reg. §§ 1.346–1(c)(2); 1.355–3(c). There is, however, a significant difference between the test under § 355 and the test under § 302(e)(2). While the division of a single business may be accomplished under § 355, § 302(e)(2) requires the existence of two distinct, separate trades or businesses prior to the partial liquidation. Kenton Meadows, Inc. v. Commissioner, 766 F.2d 142 (4th Cir.1985); Krauskopf v. Commissioner, T.C. Memo. 1984–386. In Bilar Tool & Die Corp. v. Commissioner, 530 F.2d 708 (6th Cir.1976), the court held that the division of a single business because of shareholder disputes, carried out by the transfer of one-half the assets and liabilities of the business to a newly created corporation for its stock followed by the redemption of one of the shareholders' stock in the old corporation in exchange for stock of the new subsidiary, did not constitute a partial liquidation. (Such a transaction is a type (D) reorganization coupled with a split-off, discussed at page 674.) In determining whether the terminated activity constituted a separate trade or business, the inquiry focuses on (1) whether the activity produced a substantial part of the combined corporate income, and (2) whether there was separate supervision and control. Blaschka v. United States, 393 F.2d 983 (Ct.Cl. 1968); Mains v. United States, 508 F.2d 1251 (6th Cir.1975).

The distributing corporation is not required to have conducted the terminated business throughout the five year predistribution period, as long as someone conducted the business and it was not acquired in a taxable transaction. Basically, this rule disqualifies acquisitions by purchase within the five year period but permits termination of a trade or business acquired in a tax free reorganization to qualify as a partial liquidation. The provision is designed to prevent the distributing corporation from temporarily "parking" excess funds in a trade or business for a short period prior to "termination" of the newly acquired business. Since tax free reorganizations entail acquisitions in exchange for stock of the acquiring corporation rather than cash, the same considerations do not apply.

B. CONTRACTION OF THE CORPORATE BUSINESS

As noted above, contraction of the corporate enterprise as the standard for testing nondividend equivalence originated under the 1939 Code, and that test has been carried forward through successive statutory revisions. It is available with respect to transactions that fail to come within the safe harbor of § 302(e)(2).

The leading case finding sufficient corporate contraction to constitute a partial liquidation is Imler v. Commissioner, 11 T.C. 836 (1948)(A). A corporation, whose stock was held by three stockholders, owned a seven story building and several smaller buildings and was engaged in retinning and soldering metals. It also rented its excess space. A fire destroyed the upper two floors of the seven story building in 1941. Because of the shortage of building materials, the corporation did not rebuild the two floors but reduced the building to a five-story building. Finding its facilities inadequate to store materials for the retinning and soldering activities and also that a scarcity of materials made those operations unprofitable, it discontinued those operations. The corporation distributed $15,000 pro rata in redemption of part of its stock, the cash in part representing the excess of insurance proceeds over repair costs. The redemption was held not to be a dividend, the court stressing the bona fide contraction of business operations, the consequent reduction in capital needed, and the fact that except for the fire no distribution would have been made.

In Lockhart v. Commissioner, 8 T.C. 436 (1947), the sole stockholder of a corporation in the business of oil production, drilling, and operation of a recycling plant desired to operate the business as an individual. He could not completely liquidate as some of the shares were pledged to secure an obligation; in addition, he desired to retain the corporate name and to obtain limited liability respecting the drilling business. The stockholder also needed about $220,000 to pay pending income tax liabilities. Accordingly, net assets of about one million dollars, including about $250,000 in cash, were transferred to him in exchange for 16,245 out of his 17,000 shares, so that the corporation retained only the drilling assets, worth about $34,000. The court held that the reasons for and the results of the redemption did not render it essentially equivalent to a dividend.

In a case in which a corporation did not want to incur the risks of developing certain oil leases, a pro rata distribution of the leases in cancellation of some of its stock was held not to be a dividend. Commissioner v. Sullivan, 210 F.2d 607 (5th Cir.1954). A dissent stressed the pro rata aspect as being almost conclusive and that there was no business purpose for the redemption of the stock instead of a mere distribution.

The Internal Revenue Service has carried the principles of the above cases forward in Revenue Rulings issued after the 1954 Code revision. Rev.Rul. 74-296, 1974-1 C.B. 80, held that there was a genuine corporate contraction where a corporation changed from operating a large department store to a small discount clothing store. In contrast, Rev.Rul. 57–333, 1957–2 C.B. 239, involved a corporation that distributed only a small parcel of land adjacent to its place of business, which it had acquired in contemplation of expansion and leased out in the interim. There was not a contraction where the rentals represented only 2 percent of the corporation's gross receipts. Similarly, a corporation in the quarrying business distributed a portion of a condemnation award received with respect to a taking of a portion of its mineral reserves; there was no contraction because the current operations of the corporation were unaffected. Rev.Rul. 67–16, 1967–1 C.B. 77.

The contraction must be represented by the disposition of all or part of the property used by the corporation in a trade or business. Rev.Rul. 56–512, 1956–2 C.B. 173 (distribution by corporation engaged in paper business of mineral land leased for royalties did not qualify because the corporation was not engaged in a trade or business with respect to the distributed property); Rev.Rul. 76–526, 1976–2 C.B. 101 (same as to distribution of parcel of land subject to net lease); Rev.Rul. 56–513, 1956–2 C.B. 191 (distribution of one-quarter of proceeds of contraction).

In Viereck v. United States, 3 Cl.Ct. 745 (1983), a corporation distributed to its sole shareholder real estate used in its flower business. Although the real estate constituted 80 percent of the net worth of the corporation before the distribution, the court found no partial liquidation because the corporation continued to conduct its flower business on the same scale as it had done previously. See also Rev.Proc. 98–3, § 4.01(23), 1998–1 I.R.B. 100,107 (I.R.S. will not issue ruling that redemption is a partial liquidation unless corporation reduces net fair market value of assets, gross revenues, and number of employees by 20 percent).

If the contraction of corporate business test is met, the partial liquidation distribution may include the working capital attributable to the discontinued activity. Rev.Rul. 60–232, 1960–2 C.B. 115. But funds transferred from another business into the terminated business shortly before the distribution may not constitute part of the working capital of the terminated business. Rev.Rul. 76–289, 1976–2 C.B. 100. Similarly, a distribution of cash reserves for future acquisitions of equipment that are no longer needed because of a change of business operations does not qualify as a contraction. Rev.Rul. 78–55, 1978–1 C.B. 88. In determining the amount of the distribution that will be considered attributable to a contraction, the proceeds from the sale of assets and the working capital must be reduced by corporate liabilities attributable to the discontinued activity (including taxes on the sale of the assets). Rev.Rul. 77–166, 1977–1 C.B. 90.

Rev.Proc. 81–42, 1981–2 C.B. 611, provides a checklist of information required by the Internal Revenue Service to obtain an advance ruling as to the qualification of a transaction as a partial liquidation.

C. REQUIREMENTS OF "PLAN" AND "REDEMPTION"

1. "Plan"

Section 302(e)(1)(B) limits partial liquidation treatment to redemption distributions that (1) are "pursuant to a plan," and (2) occur within the taxable year in which the plan is adopted or in the succeeding taxable year. A formal plan is not required, Fowler Hosiery Co. v. Commissioner, 301 F.2d 394 (7th Cir.1962), Rev.Rul. 79–287, 1979–2 C.B. 130, but the total absence of a plan can be fatal, Blaschka v. United States, 393 F.2d 983 (Ct.Cl.1968). Adherence to the time limitations for distributions, however, is crucial. This strict enforcement of the two year window for distributions can be turned to the taxpayer's advantage if partial liquidation treatment is not desired. Section 302(e) is elective in the sense that its consequences may be avoided by failing to comply with the time requirements in § 302(e)(1)(B). See Rev.Rul. 77–468, 1977–2 C.B. 109. In some cases it may be important to determine precisely when the "plan" was adopted, a determination that may be difficult when the plan was not formally adopted. A number of cases and Revenue Rulings involving complete liquidations dealt with determining the date of adoption of an informal plan. See, e.g., Mountain Water Co. v. Commissioner, 35 T.C. 418 (1960) (A); Rev.Rul. 65–235, 1965–2 C.B. 88.

To qualify a distribution as a partial liquidation under § 302(e), the proceeds from the sale of the assets meeting either the safe harbor of § 302(e)(2) or the general "contraction" test must be distributed as soon as possible within the permissible time window. See Treas. Reg. § 1.346–1(c)(2). The distribution need not be immediate; the proceeds may be invested in portfolio securities pending distribution, but investment profits are not treated as distributions in partial liquidation. Rev.Rul. 76–279, 1976–2 C.B. 99; Rev.Rul. 71–250, 1971–1 C.B. 112. Investment of the proceeds in additional assets for use in the corporation's remaining business, however, precludes a subsequent distribution of an amount equal to the proceeds from qualifying as a partial liquidation. Rev.Rul. 67–299, 1967–2 C.B. 138. See also Rev.Rul. 58–565, 1958–2 C.B. 140 (use of proceeds to pay debts precludes treatment of subsequent distribution of equivalent amount as partial liquidation).

2. *Redemption of Shares*

An actual surrender of the shares is not required in the case of a pro rata distribution. Rev. Rul. 90–13, 1990–1 C.B. 65; *Fowler Hosiery Co.*, supra. If there is a genuine contraction of a corporate business in partial liquidation, a surrender of shares would be meaningless; thus the shareholders are deemed to have surrendered a number of shares with a total fair market value equal to the amount of the distribution. See Rev.Rul. 77–245, 1977–2 C.B. 105, for the method of valuing the shares. But if the partial liquidation distribution was not pro rata, cases decided under the predecessor of § 302(e) have disqualified transactions if there was no actual redemption of the shares. E.g., Gordon v. Commissioner, 424 F.2d 378 (2d Cir.1970); Honigman v. Commissioner, 55 T.C. 1067 (1971), aff'd on this issue, 466 F.2d 69 (6th Cir.1972).

D. EFFECT OF OPERATION THROUGH A SUBSIDIARY

If a parent corporation operating a business also owns the stock of a subsidiary operating a five-year active business, a sale of the stock and distribution of the proceeds does not satisfy § 302(e). Rev.Rul. 79–184, 1979–1 C.B. 143. Nor would a direct distribution of the stock of the subsidiary qualify under § 302(e), § 355 being the controlling section in these situations. On the other hand, the parent could liquidate the subsidiary, sell its assets, and then make a qualifying distribution of the proceeds under § 302(e). Alternatively, the subsidiary could sell the assets prior to its liquidation with the parent in turn distributing the proceeds under § 302(e). Rev.Rul. 75–223, 1975–1 C.B. 109; Rev.Rul. 77–376, 1977–2 C.B. 107.

In Rev.Rul. 77–375, 1977–2 C.B. 106, a subsidiary was indebted to its parent. The subsidiary sold all its assets for cash, liquidated, and the proceeds were distributed to the shareholders of the parent corporation in redemption of part of their stock. In the liquidation, the debt of the subsidiary to the parent was cancelled. The Ruling held that the assets the parent received in satisfaction of its debt were not received as a liquidation distribution even though no gain or loss was recognized by the subsidiary under the predecessor of § 337(b)(1). As a result, such assets, if distributed by the parent to its shareholders, would not be part of the distribution in partial liquidation of the parent corporation. Rev.Rul. 75–223 was distinguished on the ground that assets of the subsidiary used to satisfy its indebtedness reduced the amount available for distribution in partial liquidation of the parent.

If a parent corporation does not operate any active business itself but is a holding company, the holding of the stock of two operating subsidiaries presumably would not satisfy the "trade or business" requirement of § 302(e)(2). See Blaschka v. United States, 393 F.2d 983 (Ct.Cl.1968) (management of a subsidiary did not establish a separate viable business for purposes of the two-business rule); Morgenstern v. Commissioner, 56 T.C. 44 (1971) (majority control of a corporation engaged in a business does not qualify the holder as engaged in that business for purposes of the two-active-businesses rule). The parent, however, could liquidate its operating subsidiaries and retain the assets of one while distributing the assets of the other to provide qualification under § 302(e)(2).

E. DISTRIBUTIONS TO CORPORATIONS

A distribution described in § 302(e) does not qualify as a partial liquidation under § 302(b)(4) if received by a corporate shareholder. Thus, unless the redemption also is described in any of §§ 302(b)(1) through (3) with respect to the corporate shareholder, the redemption will be treated as a § 301 distribution. In determining whether the distributee is a corporation or an individual, § 302(e)(5) requires that stock owned by a trust or a partnership be treated as owned proportionately by the beneficiaries or partners.

Because a corporate distributee will be entitled to a § 243 dividends received deduction with respect to the distribution, denying partial liquidation treatment is not necessarily disadvantageous. The benefit of the dividends received deduction will be "recaptured," however, when the corporate shareholder later sells the stock with respect to which the partial liquidation distribution was received. Section 1059(e)(1) provides that a partial liquidation distribution is an "extraordinary dividend" regardless of the period for which the stock was held. See page 231. Thus under § 1059(a) the corporate shareholder must reduce the basis of the stock by an amount equal to the dividends received deduction claimed with respect to the partial liquidation distribution. As a result, the gain on a taxable disposition will increase or the loss will be reduced. If the basis would have been reduced below zero if the full amount of the dividends received deduction had been subtracted from basis, the excess deduction, which did not reduce basis, is recaptured upon disposition of the stock. Thus, the § 243 deduction operates only to defer taxes when it is claimed with respect to partial liquidation distributions.

F. EFFECT ON DISTRIBUTING CORPORATION

If the corporation distributes appreciated property in a partial liquidation, gain is recognized under § 311(b). No loss may be recognized on the distribution of depreciated property. I.R.C. § 311(a). This result is in contrast to the treatment of distributions in complete liquidation, discussed at page 333, in which losses are generally allowed by § 336.

Section 312(n)(7) governs the effect on earnings and profits of any redemption subject to § 302(a), including partial liquidations. These rules are discussed at page 236.

G. OTHER ASPECTS OF PARTIAL LIQUIDATIONS

1. *Qualification Under Section 302(b)(4) or Sections 302(b)(1)–(3)*

If a distribution fails to qualify as a redemption under § 302(b)(4), it still may qualify under one of §§ 302(b)(1) through (3) and vice versa. Whether a distribution qualifies as a redemption in partial liquidation under § 302(b)(4) or under one of the tests in §§ 302(b)(1) through (3), the basic result to an individual shareholder is the same—capital gain or loss. Under § 302(b)(4), however, in determining the basis of the stock redeemed, the number of shares deemed surrendered is considered to be the same ratio of total shares as the amount of the distribution bears to the value of all corporate assets prior to the distribution, regardless of actual shares surrendered. Rev.Rul. 56–513, 1956–2 C.B. 191; Rev.Rul. 77–245, supra. Under §§ 302(b)(1) through (3), the basis of the shares actually surrendered usually would govern. Also, a § 302(b)(1), (2), or (3) distribution apparently does not fall under § 341, relating to collapsible corporations and which results in ordinary gain treatment, while a § 302(b)(4) distribution is subject to § 341. See page 795. Thus, it may be important to determine which subsection of § 302(b) controls. Treas. Reg. § 1.302–1(a) indicates that partial liquidation treatment controls if a distribution could be treated either as a partial liquidation or as a different redemption under § 302(b). See also Rev.Rul. 82–187, 1982–2 C.B. 80 (§ 346(a)(2), statutory predecessor of §§ 302(b)(4) and (e), takes precedence over other § 302 redemptions); Treas. Reg. § 1.346–2. Also, if a distribution may be either a complete termination under § 302(b)(3) only by virtue of the waiver of family attribution or a partial liquidation, § 302(b)(5) provides that the prohibition on the acquisition of a prohibited interest within ten years under § 302(c)(2)(A) does not apply.

2. *Partial Liquidation Under Section 302(e) Versus Serial Installment in Complete Liquidation*

Distributions that are one of a series leading to complete liquidation are treated as distributions in complete liquidation under § 331, rather than as distributions in partial liquidation. See page 338. Characterization of a distribution in this regard may be important as respects the shareholder for two reasons. First, a loss may be realized and recognized on a distribution in partial liquidation. See Rev.Rul. 56–513, 1956–2 C.B. 191. But in a complete liquidation, no loss may be claimed until the series of distributions is completed. Second, corporate distributees never qualify for exchange treatment under § 302(b)(4), but always will be accorded exchange treatment if the distribution is pursuant to a plan of complete liquidation. From the perspective of the distributing corporation, the difference is significant because the corporation under § 311 recognizes only gains (with realized losses being disallowed) on the distribution of property in a partial liquidation, but recognizes both gains and losses on the distribution of property in complete liquidation under § 336.

3. *Other Recharacterizations*

If the shareholder, following the receipt of assets in a partial liquidation, transfers the assets to a new corporation, the liquidation-reincorporation issue, discussed at page 672, may be encountered; see, e.g., Rev.Rul. 76–429, 1976–2 C.B. 97 (subsidiary sold assets of one of two businesses and liquidated; parent placed assets of the other business in a newly created subsidiary; the liquidation and reincorporation were ignored and the transaction was treated as a partial liquidation). The characterization of the transaction is important with respect to whether the distributing corporation recognizes gain or loss on the distribution of the assets, and whether the shareholders currently recognize gain or loss with respect to the stock.

SECTION 6. REDEMPTIONS THROUGH THE USE OF RELATED CORPORATIONS

INTERNAL REVENUE CODE: Section 304 (omitting sections 304(b)(3)(C) and (D), (b)(4) and (b)(5)).

Regulations: SECTION 1.304–2.

Section 304 is designed to prevent a shareholder from escaping dividend treatment in a transaction involving the sale of shares in one controlled corporation to another controlled corporation. Though such a transaction formally is structured as a sale, it obviously has similarities to a redemption since it involves a distribution of cash by a corporation to the shareholder in a situation in which, because of the controlled nature of the corporations involved, there may be no real economic change in the shareholder's overall position. Section 304 requires that the sales proceeds received in such a transaction be treated as a corporate distribution which, to qualify for sale or exchange treatment, must meet the tests of § 302 or § 303.[1] Section 304 deals with two basic factual patterns, sales between brother-sister corporations and sales involving parent-subsidiary corporations.

Suppose that the shareholder owns all the stock of X Corporation and all of the stock of Y Corporation. If Y Corporation buys some of the X Corporation stock, § 304 restructures the transaction as a redemption of the Y Corporation stock. Dividend equivalence under § 302, however, is tested in terms of the shareholder's change in ownership in the corporation whose stock is sold, i.e., X Corporation. I.R.C. § 304(b)(1). The amount actually taxed as a dividend, however, is a function of the earnings and profits of *both* corporations, although § 304(b)(2) specifies that the earnings and profits of the purchasing corporation, i.e., Y Corporation are attributed to the distribution before the earnings and profits of the corporation whose stock is sold. The X Corporation stock that was actually transferred to Y Corporation is treated as a contribution to capital by the shareholder who received the distribution.

The second situation with which § 304 is concerned involves the purchase by a subsidiary of its parent's stock from the shareholders of its parent corporation (subsidiary being defined in terms of 50 percent or greater stock ownership). Under § 304(a)(2) the shareholders are treated as if the parent redeemed its stock from them. In testing for dividend equivalence under § 302, stock of the parent owned by the subsidiary after the transaction is attributed under § 318(a)(2)(C) first to the parent corporation and then, in turn, to the shareholders of the parent. Assume, for example, that A owns 80 percent (80 out of 100 shares) of the stock of P Corporation, which in turn owns 70 percent (70 out of 100 shares) of S Corporation. If A sells 40 shares of P Corporation stock to S Corporation, A now actually owns only 40 of 100 shares, or 40 percent of P Corporation. But 70 percent of the 40 shares of P Corporation owned by S (28 shares) are attributed to P Corporation under § 318(a)(3)(A) and 40 percent of the 28 X Corporation shares thus constructively owned by P are attributed to A, with the result that A constructively owns 11.2 shares of P Corporation. A's total ownership of P has therefor been reduced only from 80 percent to 51.2 percent, and dividend treatment is likely. Because § 304(b)(2) permits the earnings and profits of both the issuer and the acquiring corporation to support dividend treatment, a dividend may result even though the parent corporation has no earnings and profits.

1. For qualification for sale or exchange treatment under § 303 of a sale of stock subject to § 304, see Webb v. Commissioner, 67 T.C. 293 (1976), aff'd per curiam, 572 F.2d 135 (5th Cir.1978). Section 303 is discussed at page 286.

Fehrs Finance Co. v. Commissioner*

Tax Court of the United States, 1972.
58 T.C. 174.

■ SIMPSON, JUDGE. [Mr. and Mrs. Fehrs owned all of the stock of Fehrs Rental Corporation (Rental). In December, 1964, Mr. Fehrs made gifts of the Rental stock to members of his family and after the gifts Mr. Fehrs owned 982 shares, Mrs. Fehrs 177 shares and 221 shares were owned by his son-in-law, his daughters and his grandchildren. Approximately two months later, Fehrs Finance Company (Finance) was incorporated with two of the Fehrs daughters as its sole shareholders. Immediately thereafter Mr. and Mrs. Fehrs transferred all of the remaining Rental stock which they held to Finance in return for Finance's promise to pay them annuities totaling $70,000 per year for the rest of their lives. Finance immediately resold the Rental stock to Rental in exchange for $100,000 cash and an unsecured promissory note of $625,000. The Commissioner asserted a deficiency against Finance based on the gain it allegedly recognized on the disposition of the Rental stock.]

The issue ultimately to be decided in this case appears to be simple: Did the petitioner realize a capital gain on the sale of the Rental stock in 1965? However, to reach that ultimate issue, we must work our way through an amazing maze of preliminary issues. At no time has the respondent taken the position that Rental's acquisition of its stock constituted a redemption under section 302 and that the payments received by the petitioner should be treated as dividends; at all times, he has treated such payments as a capital gain. The controversy revolves about the petitioner's basis in the stock. The respondent contends that section 304 is applicable to the petitioner's acquisition of stock from Mr. and Mrs. Fehrs and that its basis in such stock is therefore determined under sections 304 and 362(a). He concedes that if section 304 is applicable to the petitioner's acquisition of such stock, the gain which it realized on the transfer of such stock to Rental is taxable as a long-term capital gain. Thus, the initial issue for us to consider is whether section 304 is applicable to the petitioner's acquisition of the stock.

Section 304(a)(1) provides in relevant part that, if one or more persons are in "control" of each of two corporations, and if one of those corporations acquires stock in the other corporation from the person or persons in control, then the transaction shall be treated as a redemption under section 302. The stock shall be treated by the acquiring corporation as having been received as a contribution to its capital. The term "control" is defined in section 304(c)(1) as "the ownership of stock possessing at least 50 percent of the total combined voting power of all classes of stock entitled to vote, or at least 50 percent of the total value of shares of all classes of stock." Furthermore, section 304(c)(2) states that the rules contained in section 318(a) with respect to the constructive ownership of stock shall apply for

* [Ed.: The decision of the Tax Court was affirmed in an opinion that essentially followed the reasoning of the Tax Court, 487 F.2d 184 (8th Cir.1973).].

the purpose of determining "control," except that the 50-percent limitations of sections 318(a)(2)(C) and 318(a)(3)(C) shall be disregarded for such purpose. Section 318(a) provides that an individual shall be considered as actually owning the stock which is owned by his spouse, his children, and his grandchildren.

Section 304(a)(1) applies to what is commonly referred to as a "redemption by related or brother-sister corporations." It is clear that by its terms, such section applies to the factual situation in this case. Immediately prior to the transactions here in issue, Mr. and Mrs. Fehrs actually owned 1,159 of the 1,380 outstanding shares of Rental and their daughters and grandchildren owned 196 shares; thus, a total of 1,355 shares, or 98.2 percent of the outstanding stock, was actually or constructively owned by either Mr. Fehrs or Mrs. Fehrs. Only the 25 shares owned by Mr. Vlcek were not attributed to either of the Fehrses under section 318(a). All of the outstanding shares of the petitioner were owned by the daughters of the Fehrses, and were, therefore, similarly attributable to Mr. Fehrs or Mrs. Fehrs. Thus, either Mr. Fehrs or Mrs. Fehrs, or both, were regarded as the person or persons in control of both the petitioner and Rental prior to the transactions in issue. The transaction in which the petitioner acquired stock in Rental from Mr. and Mrs. Fehrs in return for the annuities must be treated as a redemption, and the stock of Rental so acquired must be treated as having been transferred by Mr. and Mrs. Fehrs to the petitioner as a contribution to its capital, under the express mandate of section 304(a)(1). See Rose Ann Coates Trust, 55 T.C. 501 (1970), on appeal (C.A.9, June 17, 1971) * * *.

[W]e now reach the question as to what was the petitioner's basis for the Rental stock under section 304. The petitioner must treat the stock as if it received the stock from the Fehrses as a contribution to its capital; therefore, the petitioner's basis equals the basis of the transferred stock in the hands of Mr. and Mrs. Fehrs plus the amount of gain, if any, which was recognized by Mr. and Mrs. Fehrs upon the transfer. [Secs. 304(a)(1) and 362(a).] It has been stipulated that the basis of the transferred stock in the hands of the Fehrses was zero, so the only remaining question in computing the petitioner's basis in such stock is with respect to the amount of the gain, if any, which Mr. and Mrs. Fehrs recognized upon the transfer. According to the income tax regulations, there is no step-up in the petitioner's basis if the redemption is treated as essentially equivalent to a dividend under section 302 and if the payments to Mr. and Mrs. Fehrs are taxable as a dividend under sections 302(d) and 301, but if the redemption qualifies as an exchange under section 302(b), the petitioner's basis is increased by the gain recognized by Mr. and Mrs. Fehrs. Sec. 1.304–2(c), examples (1) and (3), Income Tax Regs. The validity of such rules has not been challenged. Thus, to determine whether there is any step-up in the petitioner's basis in the stock, it becomes necessary to determine first whether the redemption is essentially equivalent to a dividend under section 302 or whether it qualifies as an exchange under such section.

Section 302 sets forth in subsection (b) the conditions under which a redemption of stock shall be treated as an exchange, and provides in subsection (d) that if those conditions are not met, then the distribution is one to which section 301 applies. If the redemption meets any one of the four tests set forth in section 302(b), it is treated as an exchange, and the amount of the distribution is treated as payment for the stock. Neither party argues the applicability of section 302(b)(2) or 302(b)(4) in this case, but the petitioner argues that the redemption should be treated as an exchange because it meets the test of either section 302(b)(1) or 302(b)(3). We shall consider each such test.

Section 302(b)(1) states, in effect, that the redemption shall be treated as an exchange if it "is not essentially equivalent to a dividend." To meet this test, a redemption must result in a meaningful reduction of the shareholder's proportionate interest in the corporation, after applying the attribution rules of section 318(a) to the stock ownership interests as they existed both before and after the redemption. Secs. 1.302–1(a), 1.302–2(b), Income Tax Regs.; United States v. Davis, 397 U.S. 301, 90 S.Ct. 1041 (1970). * * *

After applying the attribution rules, Mr. and Mrs. Fehrs are considered as owning 98.2 percent of the outstanding shares of Rental—1,355 out of 1,380—both immediately before and immediately after the redemption by the petitioner. We discussed previously the method of computing the preredemption figure; the postredemption figure is reached by attributing to the Fehrses the shares owned by the petitioner as well as those owned by their descendants. The latter result obtains from attributing the petitioner's 1,159 shares to Mmes. Vlcek and May by virtue of section 318(a)(2)(C), the 50–percent requirement of which is not applicable here by reason of section 304(b)(1), and then attributing those shares in turn to the Fehrses under section 318(a)(1)(A)(ii).

The respondent contends that the correct comparison of the Fehrses' stock ownership before and after the redemption is to measure the percentage of the shares owned by them *immediately* before and *immediately* after the redemption; if such contention is accurate, it is clear that the Fehrses' stock ownership (as viewed through the prism of the attribution rules) was not changed at all by the redemption, and thus the redemption clearly fails to meet the test of section 302(b)(1) as articulated by the Supreme Court in United States v. Davis, supra, and as followed by this Court in the decisions previously cited.

* * *

The petitioner also argues that the attribution rules should be considered only for the purpose of "determining the ownership of stock," as prescribed by section 302(c)(1), but not for the purpose of determining control as part of a dividend equivalency test under section 302(b)(1); thus, the petitioner argues, we should take cognizance of the alleged fact that the redemption "eliminated the actual control of Edward J. Fehrs over the affairs of Fehrs Rental Co." However, in section 304, Congress expressly indicated that the attribution rules are to be applied in determining control. Section 304(a)(1) applies when one or more persons "control" each of two corporations; section 304(c)(1) defines control by stating that "control means the ownership" of stock possessing a specified percentage of voting rights or value; and section 304(c)(2) expressly provides, with one exception not here relevant, "Section 318(a)(relating to the constructive ownership of stock) shall apply for purposes of determining control under paragraph (1) [of section 304(c)]." The application of the attribution rules of section 318 to a redemption under section 304(a) can operate in such a way as to cause a person who actually owns no shares in a corporation to be treated as having 100–percent *control* of it. Coyle v. United States, 415 F.2d 488, 490 (C.A.4, 1968), reversing 268 F.Supp. 233 (S.D.W.Va.1967). In *Coyle*, there is no indication that the taxpayer exercised actual control over the affairs of such corporation; the Fourth Circuit regarded the attribution rules alone as sufficient to impute complete control to him. This Court, too, has applied the attribution rules to determine who controlled a corporation involved in a redemption under section 304. Ralph L. Humphrey, supra at 205.

* * * We hold that the redemption cannot be treated as an exchange under section 302(b)(1).

The next question is whether section 302(b)(3) is applicable. Such section provides that the redemption is to be treated as an exchange "if the redemption is in complete redemption of all of the stock of the corporation owned by the shareholder." However, under section 302(c)(1), the attribution rules of section 318 are applicable in determining whether a redemption has resulted in the complete termination of a shareholder's interest under section 302(b)(3), but section 302(c)(2) sets forth certain conditions under which the attribution rules are not applicable for such purposes. Obviously, Mr. and Mrs. Fehrs did actually transfer all of their stock in Rental, but whether the redemption can qualify under section 302(b)(3) depends upon whether the conditions of section 302(c)(2) have been met so that the attribution rules are not applicable.

[The court then held that section 302(b)(3) did not apply because the Fehrs had failed to file the agreements required by section 302(c)(2), discussed at page 246.]

For the foregoing reasons, the redemption in which the petitioner acquired the Rental stock from Mr. and Mrs. Fehrs does not qualify for treatment as an exchange under any of the provisions of section 302(b), and therefore, under section 302(d), the redemption shall be treated as a distribution of property governed by section 301.

Section 301(c)(1) provides in effect that, to the extent that it is made out of the corporation's earnings and profits, the distribution is treated as a dividend and is taxed as ordinary income to the recipient. Section 301(c)(2) goes on to provide that, to the extent that the distribution is not a dividend, it is first applied against the recipient's adjusted basis in the stock, and then, according to section 301(c)(3), the amount which exceeds such adjusted basis is treated as gain from the sale or exchange of property. The petitioner argues that, because it had no earnings and profits during its 1965 taxable year, the tax consequences to Mr. and Mrs. Fehrs of the annuity payments are governed by section 301(c)(2) and (3) and that the petitioner's basis in the stock acquired in the redemption should include, for purposes of computing its gain on the sale of the stock in 1965, the gains to be recognized in subsequent years by Mr. and Mrs. Fehrs as a result of the receipt of the annuity payments.

Initially, the respondent contends that there should be no increase in the petitioner's basis by reason of any gain recognized by the Fehrses under section 301. The respondent argues that section 362(a) provides for an increase in basis by reason of a gain recognized on the transfer and that such language does not apply to gains recognized under section 301(c)(3). There is nothing in the statute or the legislative history to support such contention. The words of section 362(a) are clearly broad enough to apply to a gain recognized under section 301(c)(3), and accordingly, we reject such contention of the respondent.

The petitioner's argument that the annuity payments to Mr. and Mrs. Fehrs will be taxable, after recovery of basis, as a gain under section 301(c)(3) rests on the propositions that it had no earnings and profits in its 1965 taxable year and that the tax treatment of the payments that Mr. and Mrs. Fehrs will receive in later years is determined by its earnings and profits, or lack thereof, in 1965. The petitioner showed no earnings and profits in its books and records for 1965, but the respondent contends that its computations were incorrect for the reason that it recognized a gain on the sale of the Rental stock in that year and that such gain was erroneously omitted from its computation of earnings and profits. However, we would be required to determine the amount of the petitioner's earnings and profits in 1965 only if we conclude that the amount of, or the lack of, such earnings and profits governs the tax treatment of the property distributed to Mr. and Mrs. Fehrs. Thus, we must first decide what constituted the property distributed to the Fehrses, when the distribution or distributions occurred, and for what year or years the earnings and profits of the petitioner are determinative of the tax treatment of such property.

The petitioner argues that the making of the annuity contracts in 1965 constituted distributions of property under section 301, but we do not agree. The annuity agreements were simply promises to make payments to the Fehrses at a later time, contingent, of course, upon their surviving. The agreements provided unequivocally that they, and the payments to be made under them, could not be negotiated, assigned, or anticipated by the Fehrses, and that if the Fehrses did purport to make any such negotiation, assignment, or anticipation, the petitioner would be in no way obliged to recognize or give effect to it. Moreover, the petitioner, which was the obligor under the annuity agreements, was a new corporation with no substantial assets and no history indicating its financial reliability; the Fehrses' right to receive payments was no better secured than if the obligor were a private individual. Whatever the Fehrses may have considered the agreements to be worth to them, the agreements were in no way the equivalent of cash. Unlike the recipient of an ordinary promise to make a payment at a certain time in the future, the Fehrses did not receive anything in 1965 which they could have disposed of even at a substantial discount.

Leaving aside the question of the petitioner's ability to make the payments as they come due, it is true that a so-called actuarial value could be computed for the annuity agreements, but such value could not be realized by the Fehrses in 1965. No amount was recognizable by them in that year as a result of the receipt of the annuity agreements. * * * The annuity agreements are similar in certain significant respects to the contract involved in Allan S. Vinnell, 52 T.C. 934 (1969), in which we held that the making of the contract did not constitute a distribution of property because of its contingent nature, so that the payment of each sum due under the contract constituted a separate distribution. In *Vinnell,* the shareholder's rights to the payments were subject to certain business contingencies, and his rights were expressly subordinated to the claims of a bank with which the corporation dealt. The occurrence of one of the contingencies would have resulted in the deferral or postponement or subordination of the payments, but in the present case, the occurrence of one certain contingency—the death of Mr. or Mrs. Fehrs—would terminate the obligation completely. Moreover, the corporate obligor in *Vinnell* had proven its viability as a business entity over a 14–year period, whereas the fledgling nature of the present petitioner created an additional contingency to undermine the certainty of the Fehrses' receiving the payments in the future. In Thomas Kerr, 38 T.C. 723 (1962), affd. 326 F.2d 225 (C.A.9, 1964), certiorari denied 377 U.S. 963, 84 S.Ct. 1644 (1964); and Rose Ann Coates Trust, 55 T.C. 501 (1970), on appeal (C.A.9, June 17, 1971), we held that the distribution of a corporate obligation constituted a distribution of property; but in those cases, the obligations were to pay fixed amounts over fixed periods of time, and those obligations had ascertainable fair market values. Thus, in this case, we reach the conclusion that no property distribution within the meaning of sections 301 and 317 was made in 1965. * * *

Since no annuity payments were made to Mr. and Mrs. Fehrs in 1965, and since we have concluded that the making of the annuity contracts did not constitute a distribution of property to them in that year, no amount of gain was recognized by them in 1965 as a result of the transfer of their stock to the petitioner. The petitioner argues that its basis should include the amount of gains to be recognized by Mr. and Mrs. Fehrs in subsequent years. Although there may be circumstances in which the acquiring corporation's basis in property should take into consideration the gains to be recognized by the transferors in later years—a question which we need not and do not decide—it seems clear that such a prediction of future gains could be appropriate only when there is a reasonably reliable method for ascertaining the amount of such gains. Here, it is utterly impossible to anticipate the amount of gains to be recognized in the future. By use of actuarial tables, the amounts of the annuity payments that Mr. and Mrs. Fehrs will receive, if they live out their life expectancies, can be estimated, but it is impossible to forecast whether such payments will be treated as dividends under section 301(c)(1) or as gains under section 301(c)(3). According to its books and records, the petitioner showed substantial deficits for the years 1966, 1967, and 1968, but the respondent has raised several serious objections to the petitioner's method of computing its earnings and profits for those years. Irrespective of who is right as to those years, there is no certainty that the petitioner will operate at a loss in subsequent years during the lifetimes of Mr. and Mrs. Fehrs. In any year in which it earns profits, the payments to Mr. and Mrs. Fehrs would probably be considered as dividends under section 301(c)(1). In view of this uncertainty, there is no satisfactory method of anticipating the amounts that will be recognized as gains under section 301(c)(3) by Mr. and Mrs. Fehrs. Thus, we conclude that the petitioner's basis in 1965 must be limited to any gain recognized by the transferors in that year; that is, zero. It will be necessary to postpone to 1966 and subsequent years any adjustment in the petitioner's basis in the Rental stock to reflect any gains recognized under section 301(c)(3) by Mr. and Mrs. Fehrs. Accordingly, we hold that in 1965, the petitioner's basis for the purpose of computing its gain on the sale of the Rental stock must be zero, and it must recognize as a gain the entire payment which it received in that year. * * *

Decision will be entered under Rule [155].

ILLUSTRATIVE MATERIAL

A. BROTHER–SISTER TRANSACTIONS

1. *"Control"*

Section 304(a)(1) applies to sales of stock in the brother-sister context only if "one or more persons are in control" of each corporation. "Control" for this purpose is defined in § 304(c)(1) as ownership of 50 percent or more of either combined voting power or value of all classes of stock. See Rev.Rul. 89–57, 1989–1 C.B. 90 (an individual who owned less than 50 percent of the voting stock, but more than 50 percent of the total value of the outstanding stock of a corporation, controlled the corporation).

Related sales transactions involving a number of shareholders can be subject to § 304 using a control group concept. See Treas. Reg. § 1.304–2(b). In Bhada v. Commissioner, 89 T.C. 959 (1987), aff'd, 892 F.2d 39 (6th Cir.1989) and sub nom. Caamano v. Commissioner, 879 F.2d 156 (5th Cir.1989), an exchange of shares of a publicly traded corporation was, in part, subject to § 304. In determining whether the 50 percent threshold has been met, the attribution rules of § 318 apply, with certain modifications. Thus, as was the case in *Fehrs Finance Co.,* if A owns all of the stock of X Corporation, and A sells that stock to Y corporation, all of the stock of which is owned by A's child B, § 304 applies to the transaction. However, if the selling shareholder's entire *actual* interest in the corporation has been terminated, waiver of family attribution under § 302(c) may be available to avoid dividend treatment. In Fehrs v. United States, 556 F.2d 1019 (Ct.Cl. 1977), the individual shareholders in *Fehrs Finance Co.,* who were not parties to the Tax Court litigation, and thus not collaterally estopped, argued in the Court of Claims that the § 302(c)(2) agreement was timely filed, thus qualifying the § 304(a)(1) constructive redemption for capital gain treatment under § 302(b)(3). The Court of Claims, refusing to follow the case involving the corporate taxpayer, found the filing of the agreements in "substantial compliance" with § 302(c)(2). It left open, however, the question whether a tax avoidance motive was present in the gifts of the stock by Fehrs to his family members which, if so, would prevent qualification under § 302(b)(3).

In Niedermeyer v. Commissioner, 62 T.C. 280 (1974), aff'd per curiam 535 F.2d 500 (9th Cir.1976), the taxpayers sold all of their common stock in a corporation controlled by two of their sons to another corporation, in which they actually owned no stock, controlled by three other sons. Although the selling shareholders filed a § 302(c) waiver agreement, the court held it invalid because they retained some preferred stock in the first corporation. In requiring dividend treatment, the Tax Court rejected the taxpayer's argument that due to hostility between the brothers controlling the two different corporations the attribution rules should not have been applied to determine control.

Suppose that A owned 50 percent of the stock of X Corporation and A's child B owned the other 50 percent and all of A's stock in X Corporation was redeemed in a transaction that qualified under § 302(b)(3) by virtue of a waiver of family attribution under § 302(c)(3). Subsequently, A sold all of the stock of Y Corporation to X Corporation. Rev.Rul. 88–55, 1988–2 C.B. 45, held that the prior waiver of attribution for purposes of § 302(b)(3) did not affect application of the attribution rules in determining ownership of the Y stock held by X Corporation when applying § 304 to the sale of stock by A. Thus, since A continued to own by attribution 100 percent of Y Corporation after the sale, the transaction was treated as a redemption by X Corporation that was substantially equivalent to a dividend. The Ruling also held, however, that treatment of A as receiving a distribution with respect to X Corporation stock was not a prohibited interest in X Corporation in violation of the waiver of family attribution rules.

2. *Basis Issues*

(a) Shareholder's Basis

Although § 304(b)(1) directs that the determination of whether the transaction is entitled to redemption treatment is made with respect to the stock of the issuing corporation, i.e., the corporation the stock of which was sold, the treatment of the transaction by § 304(a)(1) as a redemption by the *purchasing* corporation is important. If the combined earnings and profits of the issuing and purchasing corporations are not sufficient to support dividend treatment of the entire distribution, the excess distribution is applied against the basis of the purchasing corporation and, when that basis has been reduced to zero, the balance is taxable gain. The basis of the selling shareholder in any remaining shares of the issuer may not be applied against the distribution to avoid gain recognition.

When a sale is treated as a § 301 distribution by virtue of § 304(a)(1), the stock of the issuing corporation sold to the acquiring corporation is treated as if the issuing corporation stock were transferred to the acquiring corporation in exchange for stock of the acquiring corporation in a nonrecognition transaction under § 351. The selling shareholder and the acquiring corporation are then treated as if the acquiring corporation had redeemed its newly issued stock in a distribution that is subject to § 301. The shareholder's basis in the deemed newly issued stock of the acquiring corporation will be the same as the shareholder's basis in the stock of the issuing corporation that was sold, but was deemed to have been transferred to the acquiring corporation in the § 351 transaction. That basis is added to the basis of the shareholder's remaining stock in the acquiring corporation. See Treas. Reg. § 1.304–2(a). The basis increase apparently occurs before § 301 applies, and this may be relevant in applying § 301(c)(2) if the combined earnings and profits of the corporations are insufficient to support divided treatment for the entire amount received by the shareholder.

What happens if the selling shareholder does not actually own any stock of the purchasing corporation after the transaction, but due to attribution rules constructively controls the purchasing corporation, for example, because the selling shareholder's child controls the purchasing corporation? Rev.Rul. 71–563, 1971–2 C.B. 175, held that the basis of the sold stock should be added to the selling shareholder's basis for any remaining stock of the issuer.

What is the effect on basis if, as in *Fehrs Finance Co.,* the selling shareholder actually owns no stock of either the issuer or the purchaser after the transaction? Coyle v. United States, 415 F.2d 488 (4th Cir.1968), suggests that in such a case the basis of the selling shareholder's stock could be added to the basis of the stock in the purchasing corporation held by the related person actually owning stock of the purchasing corporation. But Rev.Rul. 70–496, 1970–2 C.B. 74, held that the basis of the stock simply disappears. In that Ruling, Y Corporation sold its wholly owned subsidiary, S Corporation, to Z Corporation. Both Y Corporation and Z Corporation were controlled by X Corporation. Due to the § 318 attribution rules, Y Corporation continued to own 100 percent of S Corporation after the sale and § 304(a)(1) recharacterized the transaction as a dividend. Because Y Corporation had no actual interest in Z Corporation, it had no basis to adjust, and X Corporation was denied a basis adjustment with respect to either Y Corporation or Z Corporation.

(b) Purchasing Corporation's Basis in Stock

Under § 304(a)(1), the treatment of a stock acquisition as a § 351 transaction means that the acquiring corporation's basis in the stock of the issuing corporation received in the transaction will be the same as the transferor's basis in the stock, increased by any gain recognized on the transfer. See I.R.C. § 362(a).

The Tax Court's holding in *Fehrs Finance Co.* that the annuity contracts transferred in the constructive redemption did not constitute a distribution of property for purposes of § 301 avoided some difficult problems with respect to the calculation of the earnings and profits of Fehrs Finance Co.,[2] which in turn would have affected both the treatment of the distributions in the hands of the selling shareholders and Fehrs Finance Co.'s basis in the stock of Fehrs Realty Corporation as well. If the annuity contracts had been considered as a distribution under § 301 (or if cash had been distributed) the question whether the distribution should be treated as a dividend or as a capital gain transaction under § 301(c)(3)(A) would have depended on the presence or absence of earnings and profits in Fehrs Finance Co. Fehrs Finance Co. had no earnings and profits except those generated by the disposition of the Rental stock. That amount, however, was determined in part by Fehrs Finance Co.'s basis in the Rental stock which, under § 362(a)(2), would be increased to the extent that the Fehrs recognized capital gain on the distribution, thus completing the circle. In effect, the amount of gain is a function of the earnings and profits and the earnings and profits are simultaneously a function of the amount of gain.

When *Fehr's Finance Co.* was decided, the last sentence of § 304(a)(1) provided as follows: "To the extent that such distribution is treated as a distribution to which section 301 applies, the stock so acquired shall be treated as having been transferred by the person from whom acquired, and as having been received by the corporation acquiring it, as a contribution to the capital of such corporation." Both *Fehr's Finance Co.* and Treas. Reg. § 1.304–2(c), Ex. (1), interpreted the interaction of this statutory rule and § 362(a) as resulting in the acquiring corporation receiving a step-up in basis as a result of any § 301(c)(3) gain recognized by the redeemed shareholder on the overall transaction. In 1997, the last sentence of § 304(a)(1) was amended to read as it now does. If the last sentence of current § 304(a)(1) is read literally, it is difficult to discern how the shareholder can recognize any gain on the "transfer" of the issuing corporation's stock to the acquiring corporation, and thus it is difficult to see how the acquiring corporation can obtain any step-up in the basis of the issuing corporation's stock. On the other hand, the same interpretative difficulties existed under the prior statutory language, which was interpreted to provide the basis step up, and that result appears to be theoretically correct.

3. *Effect of Sale of Stock for Promissory Notes*

Fehrs Finance Co. concluded that no gain was recognized under § 301(c)(3) in the year the annuity contracts were received because they could not be valued. Suppose that A controls both X Corporation and Y Corporation and sells all of the stock of X Corporation to Y Corporation for a $100,000 promissory note, bearing adequate interest, due in ten years.

2. This holding is consistent with Rev. Rul. 69–74, 1969–1 C.B. 43, which provides that gain realized on the exchange of property for a private annuity is recognized as payments are received by the annuitant.

Suppose further, that the corporations' combined earnings and profits are only $20,000 and A's basis in the Y Corporation stock is zero. May A report the $80,000 § 301(c)(3) gain using the installment method under § 453? Cox v. Commissioner, 78 T.C. 1021 (1982), held that § 453 installment reporting of gains is not available for § 301(c)(3) gain because no "sale" occurs as a result of the distribution.

4. *Interaction With Section 351*

Suppose that A owns more than 50 percent of the stock of X Corporation and transfers the stock to Y Corporation, in which A owns 80 percent of the stock, in exchange for additional stock and cash. The transaction would fall within the literal language of § 351 and, on this approach, the cash received would be boot entitled to capital gain treatment. On the other hand, if § 304, which by its terms also applies, is controlling, the cash distribution would be subject to § 301 unless it met one of the tests of § 302(b).

Section 304(b)(3) resolves this conflict by providing that § 304 controls in cases of overlap with § 351. If a shareholder transfers stock in a controlled corporation subject to a liability to a second controlled corporation and § 351 does not apply, then § 357 likewise does not apply to allow the assumption of the liability by the transferee corporation without adverse tax consequences. However, § 304(b)(3)(B) provides an exception for certain debt incurred to acquire the stock of a corporation that is assumed by a controlled corporation acquiring the stock; assumption of such debt is an alternative to a debt-financed direct acquisition by the acquiring company. In applying these rules, indebtedness includes debt to which the stock is subject as well as debt assumed by the acquiring company.

B. PARENT–SUBSIDIARY SITUATIONS

1. *Application of the Attribution Rules*

The attribution rules raise special problems under § 304(a) since two corporations, which, absent these rules, are in a brother-sister relationship, can be viewed by virtue of the attribution rules as being in a parent-subsidiary relationship. Similarly, in the converse situation, a real parent-subsidiary relationship can constructively become a brother-sister arrangement. Treas. Reg. § 1.304–2(c), without discussion, appears to take the position that "real" brother-sister corporations will not be characterized as parent-subsidiary for purposes of § 304. Broadview Lumber Co. v. United States, 561 F.2d 698 (7th Cir.1977), held in the converse situation that two corporations in a "real" parent-subsidiary relationship would not be recharacterized for purposes of § 304 as brother-sister corporations.

The application of the attribution rules in the § 304 context can create some unusual results. In Continental Bankers Life Insurance Co. v. Commissioner, 93 T.C. 52 (1989), P Corporation owned 100 percent of the stock of X Corporation and Y Corporation. P Corporation owned 56 percent of Z Corporation and Y Corporation owned 20 percent of the stock of Z Corporation. X Corporation purchased all of the stock of Z Corporation held by Y. Although Y Corporation held no X stock directly, by attribution through P Corporation, Y controlled both X and Z. Thus, the acquisition was a redemption of X stock pursuant to § 304(a)(1).

See also Rev.Rul. 74–605, 1974–2 C.B. 97, holding that the attribution rules did not cause § 304 to apply to situations involving a purchase by the parent of stock of a second tier subsidiary.

2. *Meaning of "Property" in Section 304(a)(2)*

Suppose that A controls P Corporation, which in turn owns all of the stock of S Corporation. To reverse the parent subsidiary relationship, A transfers to S Corporation more than 50 percent of the stock of P Corporation in exchange for newly issued shares constituting more than 50 percent (but less than 80 percent) of the stock of S Corporation. Does § 304(a)(2) apply to the transaction? Section 317(b) defines property so as to include all corporate stock other than "stock in the corporation making the distribution." Section 304(a)(2) recharacterizes transfers of stock to a subsidiary as a redemption by the issuer, i.e., the issuer is the distributing corporation. In the example, since P Corporation is the issuing corporation, which is deemed to make the distribution, and S Corporation stock was distributed, it is arguable that the S Corporation stock would be "property" as defined in § 317(b). However, Bhada v. Commissioner, 89 T.C. 959 (1987), aff'd 892 F.2d 39 (6th Cir.1989) and sub nom. Caamano v. Commissioner, 879 F.2d 156 (5th Cir.1989), held that the "distribution" in § 304(a) is not the deemed redemption, *but the actual transaction.* Thus, in the example, the distribution by S Corporation to A is a distribution of its own stock, which under § 317(a) is not property. The court reenforced its conclusion that the exchange was not subject to § 304 by noting that in receiving stock of the subsidiary, the shareholders of the parent did not withdraw assets from either the parent or the subsidiary. Rather, "[t]he transaction resulted in a change in the ownership structure of the two corporations. Congress did not intend to prevent such a change in corporate ownership by enacting section 304." (970)

C. RELATIONSHIP OF SECTION 304 TO PARTIAL LIQUIDATION RULES

Assume that A owns all of the stock of X Corporation, which in turn owns all of the stock of Y Corporation, and A transfers a portion of his shares in X Corporation to Y Corporation in exchange for the proceeds from the sale of all of the assets of one of its two operating divisions. This transaction is described by both § 304 and § 302(b)(4), discussed at page 260. Can the distribution be treated as a partial liquidation of Y Corporation and avoid § 301 treatment under § 304? Based upon a technical analysis of the language of a prior version of § 304 and the statutory predecessor of § 302(e), Blaschka v. United States, 393 F.2d 983 (Ct.Cl. 1968), concluded as follows:

"The function of § 304, then is to complement § 302. To that end, § 304(b)(1) provides that such a sale is defined as a redemption of the stock of the acquiring corporation, and that for purposes of § 302(b), whether such stock acquisition is to be treated as a distribution in exchange for the stock is determined by reference to the stock of the issuing corporation. * * * The essential question is whether the distribution has affected the stockholder's proportionate interest and control in the issuing corporation, and for that reason the special rule of § 304(b)(1) points to the issuing corporation to apply § 304(a) to § 302. * * * [N]o mention is made of * * * any provision in § 304 or elsewhere in the 1954 Code, as to which corporation is to be tested to determine whether there has been a partial liquidation in a stock redemption through use of related corporations. * * * [H]owever, * * * the considerations underlying the tax treatment of partial liquidations requires that a § 304 stock redemption, involving the question of a partial liquidation under [§ 302(b)(4) and § 302(e)], be tested on the level of the acquiring corporation. * * * The very nature of a partial liquidation, at least as purportedly involved in this case, is a curtailment or contraction of the activities of the acquiring corporation, and the distribution to a stockholder of unneeded funds in exchange for stock in a related corporation. It is concluded that the purported partial liquidation is not to be measured by § 302[(b)(1)–(3)], but that a general rule of § 304(a)—that the stock sale is to be treated as a redemption by the acquiring corporation—applies subject, however, to the statutory definition as to what constitutes a partial liquidation under [§ 302(b)(4)] and [§ 302(e)] * * *, applied to the acquiring corporation." (986–87)

D. EXTRAORDINARY DIVIDENDS

Under § 1059(e)(1)(A)(iii)(II), distributions to a corporate shareholder that are treated as § 301 distributions by virtue of § 304(a)(1), and thus are eligible for the dividends received deduction under § 243, are classified as extraordinary dividends. As a consequence, the corporate shareholder is required to reduce its basis in the stock of the acquiring corporation by the amount of the dividend that is not included in income. I.R.C. § 1059(a). Amounts in excess of basis are treated as exchange gain. See page 231.

SECTION 7. STOCK REDEMPTION DISTRIBUTIONS TO PAY DEATH TAX

INTERNAL REVENUE CODE: Section 303(a)–(c).

Revenue Ruling 87–132

1987–2 C.B. 82.

ISSUE

Whether the application of section 303 of the Internal Revenue Code to a stock redemption is precluded when the stock redeemed was newly distributed as part of the same transaction.

FACTS

X corporation had outstanding 300 shares of voting common stock that were owned equally by an estate and by *A*, an individual, who had no interest in the estate under section 318 of the Code. The value of the *X* stock held by the estate exceeded the amount specified in section 303(b)(2)(A). The estate wanted to effect a redemption pursuant to section 303 to pay death taxes.

In order to maintain relative voting power and to preserve continuity of management, *X* undertook the following two steps. First, *X* issued 10 shares of a new class of nonvoting common stock on each share of common stock outstanding. Thus, the estate and *A* each received 1,500 shares of this stock. Immediately thereafter, 1,000 shares of the non-voting common stock were redeemed by *X* from the estate in exchange for cash. The overall result of these two steps was that the estate obtained the cash it needed while giving up only nonvoting stock.

The redemption of the *X* nonvoting common stock occurred within the time limits prescribed by section 303(b)(1)(A) of the Code and did not exceed the amount permitted by section 303(a).

LAW AND ANALYSIS

Section 303(a) of the Code provides that a distribution of property to a shareholder by a corporation in redemption of stock of the corporation, which (for federal estate tax purposes) is included in determining the gross estate of a decedent, is treated as a distribution in full payment in exchange for the stock redeemed to the extent of the sum of certain taxes and expenses. These taxes and expenses are the estate, inheritance, legacy and succession taxes plus the amount of funeral and administrative expenses allowable as deductions for federal estate tax purposes.

Section 303(c) of the Code provides that if a shareholder owns stock of a corporation (new stock) the basis of which is determined by reference to the basis of stock of a corporation (old stock) that was included in determining the gross estate of a decedent, and section 303(a) would apply to a distribution in redemption of the old stock, then section 303(a) applies to a distribution in redemption of the new stock. Section 1.303–2(d) of the Income Tax Regulations specifically provides that section 303 applies to a distribution in redemption of stock received by an estate in a distribution to which section 305(a) applies.

Section 305(a) of the Code provides that, generally, gross income does not include the amount of any distribution of the stock of a corporation made by the corporation to its shareholders with respect to its stock. Section 305(b)(1), however, provides that if the distribution is, at the election of any of the shareholders (whether exercised before or after the declaration of the distribution), payable either in its stock or in property, then the distribution of stock is treated as a distribution to which section 301 applies. Section 305(b)(2) provides that if the distribution has the result of the receipt of property by some shareholders and an increase in the proportionate interest of other shareholders in the assets or earnings and profits of the corporation, then the distribution of stock is treated as a distribution to which section 301 applies.

Section 307(a) of the Code provides that if a shareholder already owning stock in a corporation ("old stock") receives additional stock ("new stock") in a distribution to which section 305(a) applies, then the basis of the old stock prior to the distribution is allocated between the old stock and new stock subsequent to the distribution.

Here, 3,000 shares of nonvoting common stock were distributed and 1,000 shares were subsequently redeemed by *X* as part of a plan designed to allow the estate to avail itself of the benefits of section 303 of the Code. The intent of Congress in enacting the statutory predecessor of section 303 was to provide an effective means whereby the estate of a decedent owning an interest in a family enterprise could finance the estate tax without being required to dispose of its entire interest in the family business in order to avoid the imposition of an ordinary dividend tax. H.R.Rep. No. 2319, 81st Cong., 2d Sess. 63–64 (1950). Given this intent, it follows that the estate should be able to obtain the benefits of section 303 without a substantially adverse effect on the estate's ownership of the family business.

Moreover, section 303(c) of the Code is a remedial provision that was added to expand the application of section 303 to the redemption of stock which, despite a technical change in the form of ownership, represents the same stock as that owned at death. S.Rep. No. 1622, 83rd Cong., 2nd Sess. 239 (1954). The sole requirement for application of section 303 to the redemption, under section 303(c), is that the basis of the stock redeemed ("new stock") be determined by reference to the basis of the "old stock" included in the estate. Section 1.303–2(d) of the regulations provides that stock received by an estate in a section 305(a) distribution is entitled to section 303 treatment. Rev.Rul. 83–68, 1983–1 C.B. 75, holds that a distribution of stock that is immediately redeemable at the option of a shareholder gives the shareholder an election to receive either stock or property within the meaning of section 305(b)(1) and, therefore, is a distribution to which section 301 applies. See also Rev.Rul. 76–258, 1976–2 C.B. 95.

The nature of section 303 of the Code and the limited time period for redemption provided in section 303(b)(1) are generally indicative of a Congressional intent that section 303 be applicable to stock issued as part of the same plan as the redemption. Consequently, for purposes of section 303 only, section 305 should be applied prior to, and without reference to, the subsequent redemption.

HOLDING

The exclusion from gross income provision of section 305(a) of the Code, and the carryover of basis provisions of section 307(a), apply to *X*'s distribution of its new nonvoting common stock to *A* and the estate. Section 303(a) applies to *X*'s distribution of cash to the estate in redemption of the 1,000 shares of its new nonvoting common stock. For the tax consequences to *A* (the nonredeeming shareholder) as a result of this transaction, see section 305.

* * *

ILLUSTRATIVE MATERIAL

A. GENERAL

Section 303, whose provisions were first adopted in 1951, has a significant effect upon estate planning, since it permits certain redemptions for the purpose of paying estate taxes to qualify for sale or exchange treatment, even though the redemption does not meet any of the tests of § 302. In order to qualify under § 303 the stock must (1) have been included in the decedent's gross estate for Federal estate tax purposes; (2) have comprised the specified percentage of the gross estate (less certain expenses); (3) be redeemed from a person who bears the burden of the estate tax; and (4) be redeemed within a specified period of time after the decedent's death. A redemption that qualifies under § 303 generally produces limited tax consequences to the distributee as regards gain recognition because § 1014 provides the deceased shareholder's successor in interest with a basis in the stock equal to its value on the decedent's date of death. On the other hand, if § 303 is not satisfied, dividend treatment, which would generally be the case, would not allow tax-free basis recovery so the section in this regard gives the taxpayer a substantial advantage.

B. POLICY BASIS FOR SECTION 303

By making the treasury of a closely-held corporation available as a source of funds at the death of a principal shareholder, the problem of meeting estate taxes may be substantially eased. The enactment of this provision was justified as follows:

"It has been brought to the attention of your committee that the problem of financing the estate tax is acute in the case of estates consisting largely of shares in a family corporation. The market for such shares is usually very limited, and it is frequently difficult, if not impossible, to dispose of a minority interest. If, therefore, the estate tax cannot be financed through the sale of the other assets in the estate, the executors will be forced to dispose of the family business. In many cases the result will be the absorption of a family enterprise by larger competitors, thus tending to accentuate the degree of concentration of industry in this country." S.Rep. No. 81–2375, 81st Cong., 2d Sess. 54 (1951).

Since the enactment of § 303, the Code has been amended by the addition of §§ 6166 and 6166A, which provide an extension of time for payment of the estate tax if the estate consists largely of an interest in a closely held business. It would seem that the availability of relief under these provisions should be sufficient to mitigate any hardship in paying estate taxes attributable to stock in closely held corporations and § 303 is, in fact, largely unnecessary.

C. TECHNICAL ASPECTS OF SECTION 303

Suppose the stock redeemed to pay death taxes is "§ 306" preferred stock. Since the § 306 stock was included in the decedent's estate and its basis was determined under § 1014, it would lose its § 306 "taint" and can be redeemed under § 303 so as to receive exchange treatment at the shareholder level. See I.R.C. § 306(a)(1)(C).

Section 2035(d)(3)(A) includes in a decedent's gross estate for purposes of computing the § 303(b)(2) percentages (but not for purposes of computing Federal estate taxes) the value of any stock transferred by the decedent for less than adequate consideration within three years prior to death. Such transferred shares, however, may not be redeemed under § 303. Rev.Rul. 84–76, 1984–1 C.B. 91.

CHAPTER 7

STOCK DIVIDENDS

SECTION 1. TAXABLE VERSUS NONTAXABLE STOCK DIVIDEND

A. JUDICIAL AND STATUTORY BACKGROUND

Eisner v. Macomber

Supreme Court of the United States, 1920.
252 U.S. 189.

[The taxpayer was the owner of 2,200 shares of common stock in the Standard Oil Company of California. The corporation declared a 50 percent stock dividend and the taxpayer received 1,100 additional shares of which 198.77 shares represented surplus of the corporation earned between March 1, 1913 and January 1, 1916, the latter date being the date of the stock dividend. The shares representing the post–March 1, 1913 surplus had a par value of $19,877 and the Commissioner treated the stock dividend as taxable income to the extent of the par value of such shares. Cash dividends in such an amount would have constituted taxable income. The applicable statute expressly included stock dividends in income. The taxpayer asserted that the stock dividend was not income within the meaning of the Sixteenth Amendment. The District Court rendered judgment against the Government.]

■ MR. JUSTICE PITNEY delivered the opinion of the Court. * * *

In Towne v. Eisner, [245 U.S. 418, 38 S.Ct. 158], the question was whether a stock dividend made in 1914 against surplus earned prior to January 1, 1913, was taxable against the stockholder under the Act of October 3, 1913, which provided that net income should include "dividends," and also "gains or profits and income derived from any source whatever." * * * When the case came here, after overruling a motion to dismiss made by the government upon the ground that the only question involved was the construction of the statute and not its constitutionality, we dealt upon the merits with the question of construction only, but disposed of it upon consideration of the essential nature of a stock dividend disregarding the fact that the one in question was based upon surplus earnings that accrued before the Sixteenth Amendment took effect. Not only so, but we rejected the reasoning of the District Court, saying (245 U.S. 366, 38 S.Ct. 159):

"Notwithstanding the thoughtful discussion that the case received below we cannot doubt that the dividend was capital as well for the purposes of the Income Tax Law as for distribution between tenant for life and remainderman. What was said by this court upon the latter question is equally true for the former. 'A stock dividend really takes nothing from the property of the corporation, and adds nothing to the interests of the shareholders. Its property is not diminished, and their interests are not increased. * * * The proportional interest of each shareholder remains the same. The only change is in the evidence which represents that interest, the new shares and the original shares together representing the same proportional interest that the original shares represented before the issue of the new ones.' Gibbons v. Mahon, 136 U.S. 549, 559, 560 [10 S.Ct. 1057]. In short, the corporation is no poorer and the stockholder is no richer than they were before. Logan County v. United States, 169 U.S. 255, 261 [18 S.Ct. 361]. If the plaintiff gained any small advantage by the change, it certainly was not an advantage of $417,450, the sum upon which he was taxed. * * * What has happened is that the plaintiff's old certificates have been split up in effect and have diminished in value to the extent of the value of the new.''

This language aptly answered not only the reasoning of the District Court but the argument of the Solicitor General in this court, which discussed the essential nature of a stock dividend. And if, for the reasons thus expressed, such a dividend is not to be regarded as "income" or "dividends" within the meaning of the act of 1913, we are unable to see how it can be brought within the meaning of "incomes" in the Sixteenth Amendment; it being very clear that Congress intended in that act to exert its power to the extent permitted by the amendment. In Towne v. Eisner it was not contended that any construction of the statute could make it narrower than the constitutional grant; rather the contrary. * * * We adhere to the view then expressed, and might rest the present case there, not because that case in terms decided the constitutional question, for it did not, but because the conclusion there reached as to the essential nature of a stock dividend necessarily prevents its being regarded as income in any true sense.

Nevertheless, in view of the importance of the matter, and the fact that Congress in the Revenue Act of 1916 declared that a "stock dividend shall be considered income, to the amount of its cash value," we will deal at length with the constitutional question, incidentally testing the soundness of our previous conclusion.

* * *

[I]t becomes essential to distinguish between what is and what is not "income," as the term is there used, and to apply the distinction, as cases arise, according to truth and substance, without regard to form. Congress cannot by any definition it may adopt conclude the matter, since it cannot by legislation alter the Constitution, from which alone it derives its power to legislate, and within whose limitations alone that power can be lawfully exercised.

The fundamental relation of "capital" to "income" has been much discussed by economists, the former being likened to the tree or the land, the latter to the fruit or the crop; the former depicted as a reservoir supplied from springs, the latter as the outlet stream, to be measured by its flow during a period of time. For the present purpose we require only a clear definition of the term "income," as used in common speech, in order to determine its meaning in the amendment, and having formed also a correct judgment as to the nature of a stock dividend, we shall find it easy to decide the matter at issue.

After examining dictionaries in common use (Bouv.L.D.; Standard Dict.; Webster's Internat. Dict.; Century Dict.), we find little to add to the succinct definition adopted in two cases arising under the Corporation Tax Act of 1909 (Stratton's Independence v. Howbert, 231 U.S. 399, 415, 34 S.Ct. 136, 140; Doyle v. Mitchell Bros. Co., 247 U.S. 179, 185, 38 S.Ct. 467, 469)—"Income may be defined as the gain derived from capital, from labor, or from both combined," provided it be understood to include profit gained through a sale or conversion of capital assets, to which it was applied in the Doyle Case, 247 U.S. 179, 185, 38 S.Ct. 467, 469.

Brief as it is, it indicates the characteristic and distinguishing attribute of income essential for a correct solution of the present controversy. The government, although basing its argument upon the definition as quoted, placed chief emphasis upon the word "gain," which was extended to include a variety of meanings; while the significance of the next three words was either overlooked or misconceived. "*Derived—from—capital*"; "the *gain—derived—from—capital,*" etc. Here we have the essential matter: *not* a gain *accruing to* capital; not a *growth* or *increment* of value *in* the investment; but a gain, a profit, something of exchangeable value, *proceeding from* the property, *severed from* the capital, however invested or employed, and *coming in,* being "*derived*"—that is, *received* or *drawn by* the recipient (the taxpayer) for his *separate* use, benefit and disposal—*that* is income derived from property. Nothing else answers the description.

The same fundamental conception is clearly set forth in the Sixteenth Amendment—"incomes, *from* whatever *source derived*"—the essential thought being expressed with a conciseness and lucidity entirely in harmony with the form and style of the Constitution.

Can a stock dividend, considering its essential character, be brought within the definition? To answer this, regard must be had to the nature of a corporation and the stockholder's relation to it. * * *

In the present case, the corporation had surplus and undivided profits invested in plant, property, and business, and required for the purposes of the corporation, amounting to about $45,000,000, in addition to outstanding capital stock of $50,000,000. In this the case is not extraordinary. The profits of a corporation, as they appear upon the balance sheet at the end of the year, need not be in the form of money on hand in excess of what is required to meet current liabilities and finance current operations of the company. Often, especially in a growing business, only a part, sometimes a small part, of the year's profits is in property capable of division; the remainder having been absorbed in the acquisition of increased plant, equipment, stock in trade, or accounts receivable, or in decrease of outstanding liabilities. When only a part is available for dividends, the balance of the year's profits is carried to the credit of undivided profits, or surplus, or some other account having like significance. If thereafter the company finds itself in funds beyond current needs it may declare dividends out of such surplus or undivided profits; otherwise it may go on for years conducting a successful business, but requiring more and more working capital because of the extension of its operations, and therefore unable to declare dividends approximating the amount of its profits. Thus the surplus may increase until it equals or even exceeds the par value of the outstanding capital stock. This may be adjusted upon the books in the mode adopted in the case at bar—by declaring a "stock dividend." This, however, is no more than a book adjustment, in essence not a dividend but rather the opposite; no part of the assets of the company is separated from the common fund, nothing distributed except paper certificates that evidence an antecedent increase in the value of the stockholder's capital interest resulting from an accumulation of profits by the company, but profits so far absorbed in the business as to render it impracticable to separate them for withdrawal and distribution. In order to make the adjustment, a charge is made against surplus account with corresponding credit to capital stock account, equal to the proposed "dividend"; the new stock is issued against this and the certificates delivered to the existing stockholders in proportion to their previous holdings. This, however, is merely bookkeeping that does not affect the aggregate assets of the corporation or its outstanding liabilities; it affects only the form, not the essence, of the "liability" acknowledged by the corporation to its own shareholders, and this through a readjustment of accounts on one side of the balance sheet only, increasing "capital stock" at the expense of "surplus"; it does not alter the preexisting proportionate interest of any stockholder or increase the intrinsic value of his holding or of the aggregate holdings of the other stockholders as they stood before. The new certificates simply increase the number of the shares, with consequent dilution of the value of each share.

A "stock dividend" shows that the company's accumulated profits have been capitalized, instead of distributed to the stockholders or retained as surplus available for distribution in money or in kind should opportunity offer. Far from being a realization of profits of the stockholder, it tends rather to postpone such realization, in that the fund represented by the new stock has been transferred from surplus to capital, and no longer is available for actual distribution.

The essential and controlling fact is that the stockholder has received nothing out of the company's assets for his separate use and benefit; on the contrary, every dollar of his original investment, together with whatever accretions and accumulations have resulted from employment of his money and that of the other stockholders in the business of the company, still remains the property of the company, and subject to business risks which may result in wiping out the entire investment. Having regard to the very truth of the matter, to substance and not to form, he has received nothing that answers the definition of income within the meaning of the Sixteenth Amendment. * * *

We are clear that not only does a stock dividend really take nothing from the property of the corporation and add nothing to that of the shareholder, but that the antecedent accumulation of profits evidenced thereby, while indicating that the shareholder is the richer because of an increase of his capital, at the same time shows he has not realized or received any income in the transaction.

It is said that a stockholder may sell the new shares acquired in the stock dividend; and so he may, if he can find a buyer. It is equally true that if he does sell, and in doing so realizes a profit, such profit, like any other, is income, and so far as it may have arisen since the Sixteenth Amendment is taxable by Congress without apportionment. The same would be true were he to sell some of his original shares at a profit. But if a shareholder sells dividend stock he necessarily disposes of a part of his capital interest, just as if he should sell a part of his old stock, either before or after the dividend. What he retains no longer entitles him to the same proportion of future dividends as before the sale. His part in the control of the company likewise is diminished. Thus, if one holding $60,000 out of a total $100,000 of the capital stock of a corporation should receive in common with other stockholders a 50 per cent. stock dividend, and should sell his part, he thereby would be reduced from a majority to a minority stockholder, having six-fifteenths instead of six-tenths of the total stock outstanding. A corresponding and proportionate decrease in capital interest and in voting power would befall a minority holder should he sell dividend stock; it being in the nature of things impossible for one to dispose of any part of such an issue without a proportionate disturbance of the distribution of the entire capital stock, and a like diminution of the seller's comparative voting power—that "right preservative of rights" in the control of a corporation. Yet, without selling, the shareholder, unless possessed of other resources, has not the wherewithal to pay an income tax upon the dividend stock. Nothing could more clearly show that to tax a stock dividend is to tax a capital increase, and not income, than this demonstration that in the nature of things it requires conversion of capital in order to pay the tax.

* * *

Conceding that the mere issue of a stock dividend makes the recipient no richer than before, the government nevertheless contends that the new certificates measure the extent to which the gains accumulated by the corporation have made him the richer. There are two insuperable difficulties with this: In the first place, it would depend upon how long he had held the stock whether the stock dividend indicated the extent to which he had been enriched by the operations of the company; unless he had held it throughout such operations the measure would not hold true. Secondly, and more important for present purposes, enrichment through increase in value of capital investment is not income in any proper meaning of the term. * * *

It is said there is no difference in principle between a simple stock dividend and a case where stockholders use money received as cash dividends to purchase additional stock contemporaneously issued by the corporation. But an actual cash dividend, with a real option to the stockholder either to keep the money for his own or to reinvest it in new shares, would be as far removed as possible from a true stock dividend, such as the one we have under consideration, where nothing of value is taken from the company's assets and transferred to the individual ownership of the several stockholders and thereby subjected to their disposal.

* * *

Thus, from every point of view we are brought irresistibly to the conclusion that neither under the Sixteenth Amendment nor otherwise has Congress power to tax without apportionment a true stock dividend made lawfully and in good faith, or the accumulated profits behind it, as income of the stockholder. The Revenue Act of 1916, in so far as it imposes a tax upon the stockholder because of such dividend, contravenes the provisions of article 1, § 2, cl. 3, and article 1, § 9, cl. 4, of the Constitution, and to this extent is invalid, notwithstanding the Sixteenth Amendment.

Judgment affirmed.

* * *

■ MR. JUSTICE BRANDEIS, dissenting, delivered the following opinion, in which MR. JUSTICE CLARKE concurred.

Financiers, with the aid of lawyers, devised long ago two different methods by which a corporation can, without increasing its indebtedness, keep for corporate purposes accumulated profits, and yet, in effect, distribute these profits among its stockholders. One method is a simple one. The capital stock is increased; the new stock is paid up with the accumulated profits; and the new shares of paid-up stock are then distributed among the stockholders pro rata as a dividend. If the stockholder prefers ready money to increasing his holding of the stock in the company, he sells the new stock received as a dividend. The other method is slightly more complicated. Arrangements are made for an increase of stock to be offered to stockholders pro rata at par, and, at the same time, for the payment of a cash dividend equal to the amount which the stockholder will be required to pay to the company, if he avails himself of the right to subscribe for his pro rata of the new stock. If the stockholder takes the new stock, as is expected, he may endorse the dividend check received to the corporation and thus pay for the new stock. In order to ensure that all the new stock so offered will be taken, the price at which it is offered is fixed far below what it is believed will be its market value. If the stockholder prefers ready money to an increase of his holdings of stock, he may sell his right to take new stock pro rata, which is evidenced by an assignable instrument. In that event the purchaser of the rights repays to the corporation, as the subscription price of the new stock, an amount equal to that which it had paid as a cash dividend to the stockholder.

Both of these methods of retaining accumulated profits while in effect distributing them as a dividend had been in common use in the United States for many years prior to the adoption of the Sixteenth Amendment.

They were recognized equivalents. Whether a particular corporation employed one or the other method was determined sometimes by requirements of the law under which the corporation was organized; sometimes it was determined by preferences of the individual officials of the corporation; and sometimes by stock market conditions. Whichever method was employed the resultant distribution of the new stock was commonly referred to as a stock dividend. * * *

It is conceded that if the stock dividend paid to Mrs. Macomber had been made by the more complicated method * * *; that is, issuing rights to take new stock pro rata and paying to each stockholder simultaneously a dividend in cash sufficient in amount to enable him to pay for this pro rata of new stock to be purchased—the dividend so paid to him would have been taxable as income, whether he retained the cash or whether he returned it to the corporation in payment for his pro rata of new stock. But it is contended that, because the simple method was adopted of having the new stock issued direct to the stockholders as paid-up stock, the new stock is not to be deemed income, whether she retained it or converted it into cash by sale. If such a different result can flow merely from the difference in the method pursued, it must be because Congress is without power to tax as income of the stockholder either the stock received under the latter method or the proceeds of its sale; for Congress has, by the provisions in the Revenue Act of 1916, expressly declared its purpose to make stock dividends, by whichever method paid, taxable as income. * * *

First. The term "income," when applied to the investment of the stockholder in a corporation, had, before the adoption of the Sixteenth Amendment, been commonly understood to mean the returns from time to time received by the stockholder from gains or earnings of the corporation. * * *

[W]hether a dividend declared payable from profits shall be paid in cash or in some other medium is wholly a matter of financial management. If some other medium is decided upon, it is also wholly a question of financial management whether the distribution shall be, for instance, in bonds, scrip or stock of another corporation or in issues of its own. And if the dividend is paid in its own issues, why should there be a difference in result dependent upon whether the distribution was made from such securities then in the treasury or from others to be created and issued by the company expressly for that purpose? So far as the distribution may be made from its own issues of bonds, or preferred stock created expressly for the purpose, it clearly would make no difference in the decision of the question whether the dividend was a distribution of profits, that the securities had to be created expressly for the purpose of distribution. If a dividend paid in securities of that nature represents a distribution of profits Congress may, of course, tax it as income of the stockholder. Is the result different where the security distributed is common stock? * * *

Second. It has been said that a dividend payable in bonds or preferred stock created for the purpose of distributing profits may be income and taxable as such, but that the case is different where the distribution is in common stock created for that purpose. Various reasons are assigned for making this distinction. One is that the proportion of the stockholder's ownership to the aggregate number of the shares of the company is not changed by the distribution. But that is equally true where the dividend is paid in its bonds or in its preferred stock. Furthermore, neither maintenance nor change in the proportionate ownership of a stockholder in a corporation has any bearing upon the question here involved. Another reason assigned is that the value of the old stock held is reduced approximately by the value of the new stock received, so that the stockholder after receipt of the stock dividend has no more than he had before it was paid. That is equally true whether the dividend be paid in cash or in other property, for instance, bonds, scrip or preferred stock of the company. The payment from profits of a large cash dividend, and even a small one, customarily lowers the then market value of stock because the undivided property represented by each share has been correspondingly reduced. The argument which appears to be most strongly urged for the stockholders is, that when a stock dividend is made, no portion of the assets of the company is thereby segregated for the stockholder. But does the issue of new bonds or of preferred stock created for use as a dividend result in any segregation of assets for the stockholder? In each case he receives a piece of paper which entitles him to certain rights in the undivided property. Clearly segregation of assets in a physical sense is not an essential of income. The year's gains of a partner is taxable as income, although there, likewise, no segregation of his share in the gains from that of his partners is had.

The objection that there has been no segregation is presented also in another form. It is argued that until there is a segregation, the stockholder cannot know whether he has really received gains; since the gains may be invested in plant or merchandise or other property and perhaps be later lost. But is not this equally true of the share of a partner in the year's profits of the firm or, indeed, of the profits of the individual who is engaged in business alone? And is it not true, also, when dividends are paid in cash? The gains of a business, whether conducted by an individual, by a firm or by a corporation, are ordinarily reinvested in large part. Many a cash dividend honestly declared as a distribution of profits, proves later to have been paid out of capital, because errors in forecast prevent correct ascertainment of values. Until a business adventure has been completely liquidated, it can never be determined with certainty whether there have been profits unless the returns at least exceeded the capital originally invested. Business men, dealing with the problem practically, fix necessarily periods and rules for determining whether there have been net profits—that is, income or gains. They protect themselves from being seriously misled by adopting a system of depreciation charges and reserves. Then, they act upon their own determination, whether profits have been made. Congress in legislating has wisely adopted their practices as its own rules of action.

Third. The Government urges that it would have been within the power of Congress to have taxed as income of the stockholder his pro rata share of undistributed profits earned, even if no stock dividend representing it had been paid. Strong reasons may be assigned for such a view. See

The Collector v. Hubbard, 12 Wall. 1. The undivided share of a partner in the year's undistributed profits of his firm is taxable as income of the partner, although the share in the gain is not evidenced by any action taken by the firm. Why may not the stockholder's interest in the gains of the company? The law finds no difficulty in disregarding the corporate fiction whenever that is deemed necessary to attain a just result. * * * But we have no occasion to decide the question whether Congress might have taxed to the stockholder his undivided share of the corporation's earnings. For Congress has in this act limited the income tax to that share of the stockholder in the earnings which is, in effect, distributed by means of the stock dividend paid. In other words to render the stockholder taxable there must be both earnings made and a dividend paid. Neither earnings without dividend—nor a dividend without earnings—subjects the stockholder to taxation under the Revenue Act of 1916. * * *

ILLUSTRATIVE MATERIAL

A. SUBSEQUENT DEVELOPMENTS

1. *Statutory Exemption, 1921–1936*

Starting with the Revenue Act of 1921, Congress for many years provided that "a stock dividend shall not be subject to tax." In Koshland v. Helvering, 298 U.S. 441 (1936), the Supreme Court was faced with a taxpayer who had owned cumulative non-voting preferred stock, had received a dividend in common voting stock, and who then had her preferred stock redeemed. The Commissioner, following the regulations, divided the cost of the preferred stock between that stock and the dividend stock, and then used the reduced cost allocated to the preferred to compute the gain on the redemption of the preferred. The taxpayer argued that she was entitled to her full cost as respects the preferred, and the Court agreed. It held that since the stock dividend could have been taxed because the shareholder received an interest different from her original stockholdings, its receipt represented "income" even though it was not taxed and there was therefore no statutory authority for the allocation formula of the regulations.

Helvering v. Gowran, 302 U.S. 238 (1937), involved a preferred stock dividend to holders of common stock, there being like preferred stock also outstanding, but not held pro rata by the holders of the common. The preferred had a $100 par value, with a 7 percent cumulative dividend rate. A stockholder then sold his dividend stock. The Court held that the dividend constitutionally could have been taxed, under the authority of *Koshland,* but that it was exempt by statute. Being so exempt, it had a zero cost and hence a zero basis on sale.

2. *Statutory Inclusion and Judicial Exclusion, 1936–1954*

Commencing in 1936, and continuing in the 1939 Code, Congress changed the statutory rule to provide "a distribution made by a corporation to its shareholders in its stock or in rights to acquire its stock shall not be treated as a dividend to the extent that it does not constitute income to the shareholder within the meaning of the Sixteenth Amendment to the Constitution." In 1939, the statute was amended to provide that in the case of exempt stock dividends, whenever issued, the basis of the old stock would be allocated between the old stock and the new stock, thus providing statutory authority for the allocation formula in the regulations that was held unauthorized in Koshland v. Helvering.

The first case decided by the Supreme Court under the amended statute was Helvering v. Griffiths, 318 U.S. 371 (1943), involving a common stock dividend on common stock in 1939. The Commissioner included in income the value of the dividend, $109.01, asserting a deficiency of $9.06. Mrs. Griffiths objected and the Supreme Court agreed. It pointed out that in 1939 the existing Treasury Regulations were in terms of a test of proportionate change in rights or interest and expressly stated that a distribution of common on common was not taxable.

Shortly thereafter the Court decided Helvering v. Sprouse and Strassburger v. Commissioner, 318 U.S. 604 (1943), arising under the same statutory provision. In *Sprouse* the corporation had distributed a nonvoting common stock dividend to holders of voting and nonvoting common. The Commissioner included the value of the dividend in the income of the taxpayer, who held some voting common stock. In *Strassburger*, the taxpayer owned all of the common stock and received a dividend of preferred stock, which the Commissioner included in income. The Court held against inclusion in both cases, relying on Helvering v. Griffiths.

3. *Statutory Exemption 1954–1969*

Excerpt from SENATE FINANCE COMMITTEE REPORT, INTERNAL REVENUE CODE OF 1954, S.Rep. No. 83–1622, 83rd Cong., 2d Sess. (1954):

"Your committee has followed the policy of the House bill allowing the distribution of equity interests in a corporation as a dividend to the greatest extent possible. As long as a shareholder's interest remains in corporate solution, there is no appropriate occasion for the imposition of a tax. Accordingly, the general rule is that no tax is imposed upon the distribution of stock rights and stock dividends whether or not a particular shareholder's proportionate interest in the corporation is varied, but rather is postponed through the application of the pertinent basis provisions. [The bill] provides certain exceptions to this basic rule in cases where a distribution of stock [is] in lieu of arrearages on preferred stock. * * * Your committee continues the rule of the House bill and of existing law that where a shareholder has an election to take a dividend in stock or in cash, the election to take a stock dividend will not prevent the stock being subject to tax.

"[T]he problems involved in the line of court decisions such as Koshland v. Helvering (298 U.S. 441); Helvering v. Gowran (302 U.S. 238); Wiegand v. Commissioner (194 F.2d 479), etc., wherein the taxability of a stock distribution is dependent upon whether the proportionate interest of the shareholder in the corporation has been altered, are eliminated." (44, 241).

The 1954 Code revision also provided that the receipt of preferred stock dividends paid on common stock continued to be nontaxable but special rules applied to the disposition of the preferred stock. This problem is discussed in Section 2 of this Chapter.

B. The Current Statutory Structure

INTERNAL REVENUE CODE: Sections 305; 307(a).

REGULATIONS: Sections 1.305–1(a), (b); 1.305–2; 1.305–3(a)–(c), (e) Ex. (1)–(6); 1.305–5(b); 1.305–6; 1.305–7; 1.307–1,–2.

The rules governing the treatment of stock dividends were substantially revised in 1969, and the 1969 amendments to § 305 have been carried forward in the 1986 Code.

Senate Finance Committee Report, Tax Reform Act of 1969

S.Rep. No. 91–552, 91st Cong., 1st Sess. 150–53 (1969).

[Pre-1969] law.—In its simplest form, a stock dividend is commonly thought of as a mere readjustment of the stockholder's interest, and not as income. For example, if a corporation with only common stock outstanding issues more common stock as a dividend, no basic change is made in the position of the corporation and its stockholders. No corporate assets are paid out, and the distribution merely gives each stockholder more pieces of paper to represent the same interest in the corporation.

On the other hand, stock dividends may also be used in a way that alters the interests of the stockholders. For example, if a corporation, with only common stock outstanding declares a dividend payable at the election of each stockholder, either in additional common stock or in cash, the stockholder, who receives a stock dividend is in the same position as if he received a taxable cash dividend and purchased additional stock with the proceeds. His interest in the corporation is increased relative to the interests of stockholders who took dividends in cash.

[Pre-1969] law (sec. 305(a)) provides that if a corporation pays a dividend to its shareholders in its own stock (or in rights to acquire its stock), the shareholders are not required to include the value of the dividend in income. There are two exceptions to this general rule. First, stock dividends paid in discharge of preference dividends for the current or immediately preceding taxable year are taxable. Second, a stock dividend is taxable if any shareholder may elect to receive his dividend in cash or other property instead of stock.

These provisions were enacted as part of the Internal Revenue Code of 1954. Before 1954 the taxability of stock dividends was determined under the "proportionate interest test," which developed out of a series of

Supreme Court cases, beginning with Eisner v. Macomber, 252 U.S. 189 (1920). In these cases the Court held, in general, that a stock dividend was taxable if it increased any shareholder's proportionate interest in the corporation. The lower courts often had difficulty in applying the test as formulated in these cases, particularly where unusual corporate capital structures were involved.

Soon after the proportionate interest test was eliminated in the 1954 Code, corporations began to develop methods by which shareholders could, in effect, be given a choice between receiving cash dividends or increasing their proportionate interests in the corporation in much the same way as if they had received cash dividends and reinvested them in the corporation. The earliest of these methods involves dividing the common stock of the corporation into two classes, A and B. The two classes share equally in earnings and profits and in assets on liquidation. The only difference is that the class A stock pays only stock dividends and class B stock pays only cash dividends. The market value of the stock dividends paid on the class A stock is equated annually to the cash dividends paid on the class B stock. Class A stock may be converted into class B stock at any time. The stockholders can choose, either when the classes are established, when they purchase new stock, or through the convertibility option whether to own class A stock or class B stock.

In 1956, the Treasury Department issued proposed regulations which treated such arrangements as taxable (under sec. 305(b)(2)) as distributions subject to an election by the stockholder to receive cash instead of stock. In recent years, however, increasingly complex and sophisticated variations of this basic arrangement have been created. In some of these arrangements, the proportionate interest of one class of shareholders is increased even though no actual distribution of stock is made. This effect may be achieved, for example, by paying cash dividends on common stock and increasing by a corresponding amount the ratio at which convertible preferred stock or convertible debentures may be converted into common stock. Another method of achieving this result is a systematic periodic redemption plan, under which a small percentage, such as 5 percent, of each shareholder's stock may be redeemed annually at his election. Shareholders who do not choose to have their stock redeemed automatically increase their proportionate interest in the corporation.

On January 10, 1969, the Internal Revenue Service issued final regulations (T.D.6990) under which a number of methods of achieving the effect of a cash dividend to some shareholders and a corresponding increase in the proportionate interest of other shareholders are brought under the exceptions in section 305(b), with the result that shareholders who receive increases in proportionate interest are treated as receiving taxable distributions.

General reasons for change.—The final regulations issued on January 10, 1969, do not cover all of the arrangements by which cash dividends can be paid to some shareholders and other shareholders can be given corresponding increases in proportionate interest. For example, the periodic redemption plan described above is not covered by the regulations, and the committee believes it is not covered by the present statutory language (of sec. 305(b)(2)).

Methods have also been devised to give preferred stockholders the equivalent of dividends on preferred stock which are not taxable as such under present law. For example, a corporation may issue preferred stock for $100 per share which pays no dividends, but which may be redeemed in 20 years for $200. The effect is the same as if the corporation distributed preferred stock equal to 5 percent of the original stock each year during the 20–year period in lieu of cash dividends. The committee believes that dividends paid on preferred stock should be taxed whether they are received in cash or in another form, such as stock, rights to receive stock, or rights to receive an increased amount on redemption. Moreover, the committee believes that dividends on preferred stock should be taxed to the recipients whether they are attributable to the current or immediately preceding taxable year or to earlier taxable years.

Explanation of [section 305].—The bill continues (in sec. 305(b)(1)) the provision of present law that a stock dividend is taxable if it is payable at the election of any shareholder in property instead of stock.

The bill provides (in sec. 305(b)(2)) that if there is a distribution or series of distributions of stock which has the result of the receipt of cash or other property by some shareholders and an increase in the proportionate interests of other shareholders in the assets or earnings and profits of the corporation, the shareholders receiving stock are to be taxable (under sec. 301).

For example, if a corporation has two classes of common stock, one paying regular cash dividends and the other paying corresponding stock dividends (whether in common or preferred stock), the stock dividends are to be taxable.

On the other hand, if a corporation has a single class of common stock and a class of preferred stock which pays cash dividends and is not convertible, and it distributes a pro rata common stock dividend with respect to its common stock, the stock distribution is not taxable because the distribution does not have the result of increasing the proportionate interests of any of the stockholders.

In determining whether there is a disproportionate distribution, any security convertible into stock or any right to acquire stock is to be treated as outstanding stock. For example, if a corporation has common stock and convertible debentures outstanding, and it pays interest on the convertible debentures and stock dividends on the common stock, there is a disproportionate distribution, and the stock dividends are to be taxable (under section 301). In addition, in determining whether there is a disproportionate distribution with respect to a shareholder, each class of stock is to be considered separately.

The committee has added two provisions to the House bill (secs. 305(b)(3) and (4)) which carry out more explicitly the intention of the

House with regard to distributions of common and preferred stock on common stock, and stock distributions on preferred stock. The first of these provides that if a distribution or series of distributions has the result of the receipt of preferred stock by some common shareholders and the receipt of common stock by other common shareholders, all of the shareholders are taxable (under sec. 301) on the receipt of the stock.

The second of the provisions added by the committee (sec. 305(b)(4)) provides that distributions of stock with respect to preferred stock are taxable (under sec. 301). This provision applies to all distributions on preferred stock except increases in the conversion ratio of convertible preferred stock made solely to take account of stock dividends or stock splits with respect to the stock into which the convertible stock is convertible. * * *

The bill provides (in sec. 305(c)) that under regulations prescribed by the Secretary or his delegate, a change in conversion ratio, a change in redemption price, a difference between redemption price and issue price, a redemption treated as a section 301 distribution, or any transaction (including a recapitalization) having a similar effect on the interest of any shareholder is to be treated as a distribution with respect to each shareholder whose proportionate interest is thereby increased. The purpose of this provision is to give the Secretary authority to deal with transactions that have the effect of distributions, but in which stock is not actually distributed.

The proportionate interest of a shareholder can be increased not only by the payment of a stock dividend not paid to other shareholders, but by such methods as increasing the ratio at which his stock, convertible securities, or rights to stock may be converted into other stock, by decreasing the ratio at which other stock, convertible securities, or rights to stock can be converted into stock of the class he owns, or by the periodic redemption of stock owned by other shareholders. It is not clear under present law to what extent increases of this kind would be considered distributions of stock or rights to stock. In order to eliminate uncertainty, the committee has authorized the Secretary or his delegate to prescribe regulations governing the extent to which such transactions shall be treated as taxable distributions. * * *

ILLUSTRATIVE MATERIAL

A. SCOPE OF SECTION 305

1. *General*

The blanket exclusion afforded stock dividends by § 305 prior to 1969 led to some difficulties as taxpayers probed for favorable tax techniques based on that exclusion. A variety of sophisticated schemes arose that in effect allowed shareholders to choose, sometimes on a year-to-year basis, whether to receive cash dividends or instead to obtain an increase in their equity participation in the corporation. These plans had the effect of allowing shareholders who chose the second course to substitute potential capital gain income for current ordinary income cash dividends. The Internal Revenue Service attempted to reach some of these arrangements under regulations, but as the Senate Finance Committee Report indicates, the existing statutory structure was not sufficiently broad to cover all of the situations. As a result, the 1969 legislation made some fundamental changes in the theory on which the taxation of stock dividends is based. Several related policies seem to lie behind the 1969 changes. The most dominant themes were to limit the possibility of converting ordinary income into capital gain and to limit the ability of taxpayers to defer income inclusion despite having received the economic equivalent of a dividend.

2. *Stock in Lieu of Cash*

From the beginning, Congress wished to prevent a shareholder from having an obvious choice on a year-by-year basis whether to receive cash dividends or an increase in his proportionate interest in the corporation. Thus, § 305(b)(1) provides that where the shareholder has an explicit election to receive stock or cash the stock distribution will be taxable. This is in effect a specific application of the general principle of constructive receipt, i.e., the shareholder cannot avoid taxation by simply turning his back on the possible cash dividend and taking a stock dividend instead.

3. *Disproportionate Distributions*

Even if the shareholders do not have an obvious choice to receive stock or cash, a stock distribution will be taxable under § 305(b)(2) if it has the result of (1) an increase in the proportionate interest of some shareholders coupled with (2) a receipt of property (including cash) by other shareholders in a distribution subject to § 301 or 356(a)(2), discussed at page 564. See Treas. Reg. § 1.305–3(b)(3). For example, suppose a corporation has two classes of common stock, one class paying quarterly cash dividends and the other class paying quarterly stock dividends, with the amount of the stock dividend adjusted to correspond to the amount of the cash dividend distribution. Under § 305(b)(2), the stock dividend would be treated as a taxable dividend, since some shareholders receive cash distributions (which are subject to § 301) while others receive an increase in their proportionate interest in the corporation's earnings and assets by virtue of the stock dividends. See Treas. Reg. § 1.305–3(b)(2).

Section 305(b)(3), which taxes stock distributions when some shareholders receive common stock while others receive preferred, is in effect a variation on the disproportionate distributions treated by § 305(b)(2). Under § 305(b)(3), the shareholders receiving common stock are increasing their equity interests while other shareholders receive preferred stock, which is analogous to the receipt of cash or other property in the § 305(b)(2) situation. Paragraph (b)(3) is necessary to cover the situation described because § 317 excludes the distributed stock described in paragraph (b)(3) from "property" and hence it is not "other property" under paragraph (b)(2).

Section 305(b)(5), dealing with distributions of convertible preferred stock, is likewise related to the problem of disproportionate distributions and amplifies § 305(b)(2). Suppose a corporation makes a pro rata distribution on its common stock of preferred stock convertible into common stock. If all of the convertible preferred stock is converted into common the effect of the distribution will be the same as a distribution of common on common, which would not affect the shareholder's proportionate interest in the corporation. On the other hand, if some of the recipients of the convertible preferred exercise the conversion privilege while others do not exercise but sell the preferred, the net effect will be an increase in the proportionate interest in the corporation by the converting shareholders and a corresponding receipt of cash by the selling shareholders, thus having the result that § 305(b)(2) was intended to prevent. Accordingly, § 305(b)(5) makes the distribution of convertible preferred taxable unless the distribution is not likely to result in an increase in the proportionate interest for some shareholders. See Treas. Reg. § 1.305–6(a); compare Treas. Reg. § 1.305–4(b), Ex. (2), and § 1.305–6(b), Ex. (2).

Section 305(b)(2), as reinforced by § 305(b)(3) and § 305(b)(5), thus appears to express a Congressional judgment that the same corporation should not be allowed to arrange its dividend policies to attract simultaneously both the investor who desires current cash distributions and the investor who seeks an increase in the value of her stock investment through corporate growth (and thus future capital gain rather than currently taxable cash distributions). This policy thus goes beyond the problems with which § 305(b)(1) is concerned, i.e., the year-to-year option to receive stock dividends rather than cash, and seems to express a general view that the investor must choose at the time of making a particular investment whether she wished to stress capital appreciation or current cash dividends; the same corporation cannot simultaneously offer both alternatives to the investing community. To reach this result, the statute in some way returns to the judicially developed proportionate interest test of the pre–1954 law by making increases in proportionate interests an element in the tax pattern imposed on stock dividends. However, in keeping with the policy discussed above, the increases in the proportionate interests of some of the shareholders must be accompanied by a property distribution to other shareholders. Hence, § 305 does not fully mirror the pre–1954 case law, and its basic policy stands on a somewhat different footing.

4. *Distributions on Preferred Stock*

Section 305(b)(4) responds to a different problem than those considered above. While the 1954 version of § 305 dealt to a limited extent with stock dividends on preferred stock issued in lieu of cash distributions, it was generally possible under the 1954 provision to give preferred stockholders "the equivalent, of dividends" through devices that allowed them to obtain capital gain treatment. For example, convertible preferred stock might pay no cash dividends but the ratio at which it was converted into common might increase annually by a specified percentage. On conversion, the shareholder would sell the shares that in effect were issued in lieu of cash dividend distributions at capital gain rates. Or the preferred might have a redemption price substantially in excess of the issue price, with the redemption generating capital gain that substituted for current dividend distributions. Section 305(b)(4) prevents this result by currently taxing all stock dividends, either actual or constructive, received by holders of preferred stock.

5. *Constructive Distributions*

Under § 305(c), the Treasury is given broad discretionary authority to issue regulations dealing with situations that result in an increase in a shareholder's proportionate interest in the corporation. This authority was intended to forestall taxpayer attempts to probe the limits of nontaxability under the § 305 stock distribution rules and to prevent disputes as to the authority of the Treasury to deal with the ingenious arrangements that would and do inevitably develop. Under § 305(c), a number of devices such as a change in conversion ratio or redemption price, a recapitalization, etc., that have the effect of an increase in a shareholder's proportionate interest are treated as falling under § 305(b), thus making the constructive stock distribution potentially taxable. For example, the increase in proportionate interest of some shareholders caused by the redemption of the shares of other shareholders can, in the appropriate circumstances, be treated as a constructive distribution under § 305(c).

B. TECHNICAL AND INTERPRETIVE PROBLEMS UNDER SECTION 305

1. *General*

In the years since the enactment of § 305, only a few stock dividend cases governed by its provisions have been decided, and two of those cases involved the same very narrow issue. The Internal Revenue Service, however, has issued a number of significant Revenue Rulings clarifying the application of § 305. This dearth of litigation may indicate that § 305 has had a significant prophylactic effect with respect to the stock dividend transactions that it is designed to tax.

2. *Manner of Taxation*

When a stock distribution is taxable under § 305(b), it is treated as a distribution of property to which § 301 applies, and a dividend results under § 301(c)(1) in the amount of the fair market value of the stock dividend (either actual or constructive) if the distributing corporation has sufficient earnings and profits. See Treas. Reg. § 1.305–2(b), Ex. (1).

In situations to which § 305(b)(1) applies, the amount that is taxable is the fair market value of the stock dividend itself and not the cash dividend that was foregone in lieu of the stock dividend should these two amounts for any reason not be equivalent. See Treas. Reg. § 1.301–1(d)(ii). For example, Rev.Rul. 76–53, 1976–1 C.B. 87, involved a dividend reinvestment plan pursuant to which the shareholder could elect to have the cash dividend reinvested in shares of the distributing company at a price 5 percent below the market price. The Ruling held that the amount taxable under § 305(b)(1) was the full fair market value of the stock received and not the cash dividend. On the other hand, if the corporation merely acts as the shareholder's agent to reinvest the cash dividend in shares of the distributing corporation purchased in the market then the cash dividend is taxable as a distribution under § 301 and § 305 does not apply. Rev.Rul. 77–149, 1977–1 C.B. 82.

3. *Impact on Earnings and Profits*

If the stock distribution is nontaxable under § 305(a), no reduction is made in earnings and profits. I.R.C. § 312(d)(1). On the other hand, if the distribution is taxable under § 305(b), the earnings and profits are reduced by the fair market value of the stock dividend, both in the case of individual and corporate distributees. Treas. Reg. § 1.312–1(d).

4. *Basis of Stock Dividend Shares*

If the stock distribution is taxable under § 305(b), its basis in the hand of the distributee is its fair market value at the time of the distribution. Treas. Reg. § 1.301–1(h). If the stock distribution is not taxable by virtue of § 305(a), then the basis of the stock with respect to which the stock distribution is issued is allocated between the old stock and the new stock in accordance with the fair market value of each on the date of the distribution. Treas. Reg. § 1.307–1(a). The rules with respect to the effect on earnings and profits and basis of a taxable stock dividend under § 305 apply equally when the taxable amount involved is a deemed distribution on convertible debentures under § 305(b)(2). Rev.Rul. 76–186, 1976–1 C.B. 86.

5. *The "Option" in Section 305(b)(1)*

One of the most common examples of the application of § 305(b)(1) is a dividend reinvestment plan under which shareholders may elect either to take cash dividends or to apply the dividends that they would have received to the purchase (frequently at a discount from market price) of new stock from the corporation. See Rev.Rul. 78–375, 1978–2 C.B. 130. Section 305(b)(1) also applies if the same effect is achieved by issuing a stock dividend to all shareholders and giving the shareholders an option to have the stock immediately redeemed by the corporation. Rev.Rul. 76–258, 1976–2 C.B. 295. This same result occurs even though not all of the shareholders have the option. Treas. Reg. § 1.305–2(a)(5). See Rev.Rul. 83–68, 1983–1 C.B. 75. Conversely, a purported cash dividend that the shareholder *must* apply to the purchase of additional stock from the corporation is a tax free stock dividend under § 305(a). Rev.Rul. 80–154, 1980–1 C.B. 68.

Whether a pro rata stock dividend to all shareholders coupled with an option to have stock redeemed by the corporation has the effect of a distribution described in § 305(b)(1) might depend on the effect of other laws governing the corporate capital structure. In Frontier Savings and Loan Association v. Commissioner, 87 T.C. 665 (1986), aff'd sub nom.

Colonial Savings Ass'n v. Commissioner, 854 F.2d 1001 (7th Cir.1988), the Federal Home Loan Bank of Chicago (FHLB), all of whose shareholders were banks, declared a stock dividend in December of each of several successive years. At the same time that it notified shareholders of the dividend, it also notified them that they could request the FHLB to redeem those shares held by any shareholder that exceeded the minimum shareholdings required under federal banking laws. Although the FHLB was not required to honor the requests for redemption, in both years before the court it granted all shareholder requests for redemption. The Commissioner asserted that the taxpayer, which had not requested redemption of any of its shares, received a taxable stock dividend under § 305(b)(1). Emphasizing that the FHLB did not surrender its discretionary authority to redeem or not to redeem the shares as it saw fit, the Tax Court held that the stock dividend was not taxable. The court rejected the Commissioner's argument that, because the authority was exercised so consistently in favor of redemption, the shareholders had the option to redeem their shares. An additional factor was that while the dividend was distributed in December, the shareholders generally would be unable to calculate their minimum required shareholdings in the FHLB, and thus would not be able to submit their redemption requests, until the following year. While acknowledging that the form of the transaction was admittedly motivated in part by tax considerations—to permit those shareholders of FHLB that were required to increase their shareholdings to do so through the receipt of a nontaxable stock dividend—the court concluded that the stock dividends were not a "mere subterfuge for cash distributions." A concurring opinion, joined in by four judges, noted that if discretionary redemptions of stock dividends were to become a "routine matter," the transaction should be treated differently. Nevertheless, the concurring opinion considered the redemptions in this case to be "isolated" rather than "periodic." The Court of Appeals affirmed based on the reasoning of the Tax Court. Accord Western Federal Savings and Loan Ass'n v. Commissioner, 880 F.2d 1005 (8th Cir.1989). In Rev.Rul. 90–98, 1990–2 C.B. 56, the Internal Revenue Service indicated that it will follow the Courts of Appeals decisions in *Colonial Savings Ass'n* and *Western Federal Savings and Loan Ass'n* in the case of Federal Home Bank stock dividends and redemptions. However, the Service will continue to apply Rev.Rul. 83–68 in other cases to treat a pattern of stock dividends and shareholder option redemptions as an optional stock dividend subject to § 301(b)(1).

Suppose that a corporation with ten equal shareholders issued a 1-for-1 stock dividend and simultaneously notified the shareholders that they could request redemption of any number of their shares received in the stock dividend distribution. Is the distribution nontaxable under *Frontier Savings and Loan* as long as the corporation does not "offer" to redeem the shares, but invites shareholders to "offer" their shares for redemption which offer the corporation formally would accept or reject, or is it taxable under Rev. Rul. 83–68? Should an "option" be found in the "circumstances of the distribution" pursuant to Treas. Reg. § 1.305–2(a)(4)? Although the Commissioner's "circumstances of the distribution" argument was rejected by the court in *Frontier Savings and Loan,* the bank regulatory aspects of the case may have played a role in the decision and, in the case of a closely held corporation, particularly if the shareholders are related, it would appear that the "circumstances of the distribution" argument should carry more weight.

6. *The Proscribed "Result" in Section 305(b)(2)*

Under § 305(b)(2), the stock distribution is taxable if it "has the result" of an increase in the proportionate interest of some shareholders in the corporation and the receipt of property by other shareholders in a § 301 distribution. See Treas. Reg. § 1.305–3(b)(3). Under the regulations, if the stock distribution and the property distribution are more than 36 months apart, they will be presumed not to have the proscribed statutory result unless made pursuant to a "plan." Treas. Reg. § 1.305–3(b)(4). The negative implication of the regulation is that if the property distribution and the stock distribution do take place within a 36 month period, then the stock dividend will be taxable even though there is no other connection between the two distributions. See also Treas. Reg. § 1.305–3(b).

Section 305(b)(2) does not describe as a taxable stock dividend a stock dividend (either preferred or common) on one class of common stock if no property is distributed to another class of common stock within three years of the stock dividend, even though the proportionate interest of one class of common has been increased at the expense of the other. Presumably the drafters of § 305 considered such a provision unnecessary because such a transaction is unlikely to occur due to its economic inequality. But in Hagen v. Commissioner, T.C. Memo. 1989–473, aff'd in part and rev'd in part on other issues by order, 951 F.2d 1259 (10th Cir.1991), a shareholder of a closely held corporation increased his proportionate interest in a closely held corporation through stock dividends from which other shareholders were fraudulently excluded. Because the stock dividend was not accompanied by a distribution of property to the other shareholders, the Tax Court held that it was not taxable under § 305. The court specifically rejected the Commissioner's argument that an increase in the taxpayer's equity interest, standing alone, was taxable.

7. *Increase in Proportionate Interest*

The regulations take the position that the determination of an increase in proportionate interest is to be made in terms of the class of stock taken as a whole. If the class of stock has an increase in proportionate interest, the individual shareholders of the class of stock will be deemed to have increased their respective ownership interests in the distributing corporation. Treas. Reg. § 1.305–3(b)(6). Suppose an individual owns two classes of stock pro rata and there is a distribution of additional shares on one class of stock without a distribution on the other class of stock. Or suppose the taxpayer is the sole shareholder of both classes of stock. Under the class-by-class approach, the individual might be taxed in both these situations when the stock distribution was coupled with a subsequent property distribution, as, for example, a cash dividend on the other class of stock within the 36 month period, even though viewed individually, there was no change in his proportionate interest. Compare the *Strassburger* case, discussed at page 300.

The above analysis is limited, however, by the requirement that the increased interest in the assets or earnings and profits must be at the expense of another class of stock. See Treas. Reg. § 1.305–3(e), Ex. (3). Thus, if a corporation has only one class of common stock outstanding and issues a stock dividend in shares of preferred stock, the distribution is tax free under § 305(a) (although the preferred stock would be § 306 stock, see Section 2 of this Chapter). However, if at a time when preferred stock was outstanding, a stock dividend in preferred shares was issued to the holders of the common stock, § 305(b)(2) could be applicable since the class of common shareholders would increase its proportionate interest in the distributing corporation's earnings and assets by virtue of their receipt of additional preferred stock while the preferred shareholders, on the subsequent payment of dividends, would receive the necessary cash distribution. But, a distribution of new junior preferred stock on common stock, coupled with payment of cash dividends on the senior preferred, does not invoke § 305(b)(2) since the subordination of the junior preferred prevents the required increase in proportionate interest. On the other hand, a distribution of new preferred stock on one class of common, coupled with a cash dividend on a different class of common stock, is subject to § 305(b)(2). If a corporation has outstanding both common stock and preferred stock convertible into common stock, a distribution of a common stock dividend on the common stock with no change in the conversion ratio of the convertible preferred, would, if coupled with a cash payment on the convertible preferred, make the common stock dividend taxable. See Treas. Reg. § 1.305–3(e), Ex. (4).

8. *Distributions on Preferred Stock*

Preferred stock does not normally pay stock dividends except in the event of default in the payment of cash dividends or to prevent dilution. Rev.Rul. 84–141, 1984–2 C.B. 80, involved cumulative preferred stock that gave the holders the option to elect to receive an amount of common stock equal in value to accrued past due dividends, increased by an interest factor, whenever dividends were past due for two or more successive quarters. The Ruling held that the preferred shareholders constructively received a stock dividend taxable under § 305(b)(4) upon the passage of two successive quarters without the payment of cash dividends. The common stock attributable to the interest factor was treated as a distribution, not as interest.

Treas. Reg. § 1.305–3(d) elaborates on the statutory exception for distributions in the form of an increase in the conversion ratio of convertible preferred stock to take into account a stock dividend on or a split in the common stock into which the preferred is convertible. Rev.Rul. 83–42, 1983–1 C.B. 76, held that an actual distribution of common stock to holders of convertible preferred stock to compensate for dilution as a result of a split of the common stock was taxable. The exception is limited to changes in the conversion ratio.

For the definition of preferred stock for purposes of § 305(b)(4), see Treas. Reg. § 1.305–5(a).

9. *Constructive Distributions Under Section 305(c)*

(a) Redemptions in General

A stock redemption can bring § 305 into play. I.R.C. § 305(c). The redemption involves an increase in the proportionate interest in the corporation for those shareholders whose stock is not redeemed, and because the redeemed shareholders are receiving cash in the redemption, the "receipt of property" required by § 305(b)(2) is present. Treas. Reg. § 1.305–3(b) states that the redemption transaction will not generate a taxable deemed distribution to the remaining shareholders under § 305(c) if the redemption itself is entitled to capital gains treatment by the redeemed shareholders. However, if the redemption distribution is treated as a dividend under § 302(d) and § 301, see Chapter 6, the increase in proportionate interest on the part of the other shareholders can be taxable under § 305(b)(2) and § 305(c). See Treas. Reg. § 1.305–7.

Rev.Rul. 78–60, 1978–1 C.B. 81, involved a corporation that adopted a plan whereby each shareholder was entitled to have the corporation redeem two-thirds of one percent of the shareholder's stock annually. Pursuant to the plan, in a particular year the corporation redeemed shares from 8 of the 24 shareholders. All of the redemption distributions were treated as distributions subject to § 301. The Ruling held that the shareholders whose shares were not redeemed received a taxable stock dividend, the amount of which was to be computed under Treas. Reg. § 1.305–3(e). On the other hand, Treas. Reg. § 1.305–3(b)(3) provides that redemptions that are "isolated" are not covered by § 305(c). The exact scope of this exception is unclear. See Rev.Rul. 77–19, 1977–1 C.B. 83 (§ 305(c) did not apply where over a three year period a publicly held corporation redeemed shares from 20 different retiring and deceased shareholders; the redemptions fell under the "isolated" redemption exception in Treas. Reg. § 1.305–3(b)(3)).

Suppose a publicly held corporation purchases its own shares in the market. Viewed as redemptions, such purchases technically could result in constructive stock dividends to the other shareholders of the corporation. However, Treas. Reg. § 1.305–3(e), Ex. (13), exempts such transactions from the application of § 305(b)(2) if the shares are purchased for use in connection with employee stock investment plans, for future acquisitions, etc., and there is no plan to increase the proportionate interests of some shareholders and distribute property to other shareholders.

(b) Redemptions of Callable Preferred Stock

Section 305(c) also provides that a difference between the redemption price of stock and its issue price can be treated as a constructive stock distribution to the shareholder. The provision is aimed at a technique by which the corporation issues preferred stock with an excessive redemption price on which it pays no dividends and which it subsequently redeems in a transaction qualifying for capital gain treatment under § 302(b). The transaction in effect converts what otherwise would have been current dividend income into deferred capital gain. Section 305(c) prevents this result by treating the excess redemption premium as a constructive distribution on the preferred stock, taxable under § 305(b)(4).

As amended in 1990, § 305(c) directs the Treasury to promulgate regulations treating an unreasonable call premium on preferred stock that the issuer is required to redeem at a certain time, or the holder has an option to put to the corporation, as a distribution to be taken into account by the holder under the economic accrual rules of § 1272 (see page 168). In addition, the Treasury is granted authority in § 305(c) to extend these principles to callable preferred stock bearing a redemption premium. Under this provision, "unreasonable" call premium must be recognized as income by the stockholder as if it were original issue discount. Unreasonable call premium is any call premium in excess of one-quarter of one percent of the stated redemption price of the stock multiplied by the number of years until the stock is redeemable. More technically, § 305(c)(1) limits the application of § 305(c) to a call premium that exceeds the amount ignored for OID purposes under § 1273(a)(3); this amount is 1/4 of one percent of the redemption price at maturity, multiplied by the number of years until maturity.

Treas. Reg. § 1.305–5(b) implements the 1990 amendments to § 305(c). The regulations apply the OID principles to preferred stock that the issuer has a right (but not an obligation) to redeem at a premium if "based on all the facts and circumstances as of the issue date, redemption pursuant to that right is more likely than not to occur." See Treas. Reg. § 1.305–5(b)(3)(i). Either the fact that the preferred stock will obtain voting control if not redeemed by a particular date or that the yield to the preferred stock can be minimized (thereby reducing the issuer's cost of capital) by calling it at a certain time indicates that it more likely than not will be redeemed. See Treas. Reg. § 1.305–5(d), Exs. (5) and (7). The constructive distribution rules do not apply, however, if the redemption premium "is solely in the nature of a penalty for premature redemption." This exception can apply only if the premium is paid as a result of changes in market conditions over which neither the issuer nor the holder has control. The regulations do not provide an example of such a situation. Finally, a safe harbor treats a redemption as not being "more likely than not to occur," thereby excepting callable preferred stock from the constructive distribution rule, if (1) the issuer and the holder are not related, (2) there are no arrangements effectively requiring a redemption, and (3) exercise of the issuer's redemption right would not reduce the yield of the stock. Treas. Reg. § 1.305–5(b)(3)(iii). Treas. Reg. § 1.305–5(d), Ex. (4) applies this safe harbor rule to callable convertible preferred stock that is redeemable at a very substantial premium.

Section 305(c) can also be relevant in situations in which the redemption provisions are being used to effect a sale of the corporate business, see page 492, or in the case of a corporate recapitalization, see page 643.

10. *De Minimis Aspects*

The Senate version of the 1969 bill contained a de minimis provision but it was eliminated by the Conference Committee. As a consequence, it was feared for a time that the distribution of cash in lieu of fractional shares in a stock dividend distribution might trigger the application of § 305(b)(2) since the literal terms of the statute would apply; some shareholders would receive a dividend solely in stock, increasing their proportionate interest in the corporation, while other shareholders would receive cash in lieu of their fractional shares, thus providing the necessary property distribution for purposes of § 305(b)(2). But Treas. Reg. § 1.305–3(c) takes the position that § 305(b)(2) will not apply in such situations if "[t]he purpose in distributing the cash is to save the distributing corporation the trouble, expense, and inconvenience of issuing and transferring fraction shares * * * and not to give any particular group of shareholders an increased interest in the assets or earnings and profits of the corporation."

11. *Situations To Which Section 305 Does Not Apply*

Though § 305 has a wide scope, the regulations explicitly exempt some transactions that otherwise might fall within the terms of the section. Thus, a change in conversion ratio or redemption price of stock that is in effect an adjustment in the purchase price of assets acquired in exchange for the stock will not fall within § 305. Treas. Reg. § 1.305–1(c). Similarly, if stock is issued in what is in effect a security arrangement and it is anticipated that the bulk of the corporation's earnings will be used to redeem the stock the redemptions will not be treated as subject to § 305(b)(2). Treas. Reg. § 1.305–3, Ex. (14); Rev.Rul. 78–115, 1978–1 C.B. 85.

C. STOCK OPTIONS

The general rules respecting stock options or stock rights issued on outstanding stock follow those for stock dividends. There is no income inclusion on issuance of the options, except for the cases in § 305(b). See Rev.Rul. 90–11, 1990–1 C.B. 10 (adoption by the corporation of a "poison pill" plan, which provides for the issuance of a separately tradable right to purchase a fractional share of preferred stock for every share of common stock in the event of an unfriendly takeover attempt, is not a distribution of "property" to shareholders). On a sale of the options, the proceeds would be capital gain, with the holding period of the rights being that of the stock, § 1223(5), unless the stock rights were classified as § 306 stock in which event ordinary income could result. If the value is 15 percent or more of the value of the old stock *and* the rights are either sold or exercised, the basis of the rights is an allocable portion of the basis of the old stock. I.R.C. § 307(a); Treas. Reg. § 1.307–1. If the value of the rights is less than 15 percent of the value of the old stock, the basis of the rights is zero unless an election is made under § 307(b) to allocate the stock basis between the rights and the stock. If the rights are allowed to lapse, no loss arises (regardless of the value of the rights) since for this purpose no part of the basis of the old stock is allocated to them, and the basis of the old stock is not reduced.

If the stock rights involve the option to purchase stock of another corporation, the distribution cannot be subject to § 305(a). The shareholders receive a distribution subject to § 301, and the distributing corporation may be required to recognize gain under § 311. See page 202.

SECTION 2. THE PREFERRED STOCK BAILOUT

A. THE SOURCE OF THE PROBLEM

Suppose that Z Corporation has outstanding only common stock, which is held equally by individuals A and B. At a time when Z Corporation has accumulated earnings and profits in excess of $100,000, the corporation declares a dividend payable in 100 shares of $1,000 par value 9 percent cumulative preferred stock that is subject to mandatory redemption in 5 years. A and B each receive 50 shares of preferred stock, having an aggregate par value of $50,000 and a fair market value that would in all likelihood be close to par value. This stock dividend would be tax free under § 305(a). Suppose further that before the distribution A and B each had a basis in their common stock of $60,000 and that after the distribution the fair market value of the common stock held by each shareholder was $25,000. Under § 307, A and B would each allocate a basis of $40,000 to their preferred stock. Suppose now that A and B each sell their preferred stock to X Corporation for $50,000. If the transaction is treated as an ordinary sale of stock, A and B each would recognize a capital gain of $10,000. X Corporation will have a basis in the preferred stock of $100,000 and when the stock is redeemed in 5 years, it will recognize neither gain nor loss. Even though Z Corporation effectively has distributed $100,000 of its earnings and profits to A and B, without diminishing their voting rights or percentage ownership in the assets or residual profits of the corporation (except as necessary to pay dividends on and redeem the preferred stock), they would not be required to recognize that amount as ordinary income.

Chamberlin v. Commissioner, 207 F.2d 462 (6th Cir.1953), involved just such a transaction. The taxpayers in that case asserted that the stock dividend, that was distributed in 1946, was a nontaxable distribution under the principles of *Strassburger,* discussed at page 300, which governed stock dividends under the 1939 Code. The Commissioner argued that under the circumstances there was not a true stock dividend, that in effect the taxpayers had received a cash distribution even though the corporation had not distributed the cash in 1946. The court held that the distribution was a stock dividend in substance as well as form, even though the taxpayer conceded that the form of the transaction was motivated by tax avoidance. Because the insurance company that purchased the stock acquired a bona fide investment in the corporation and the redemption features of the stock were not unreasonable, the court refused to treat the otherwise nontaxable stock dividend as taxable solely because the stock was sold soon after its receipt. Thus, the shareholders in *Chamberlin* were able not only to treat a portion of the sales proceeds as a recovery of basis, but also were able to report the gain as taxable at the preferential rate that then applied to long-term capital gains. If the principle of the *Chamberlin* case prevailed, closely held corporations in effect could have avoided ever paying taxable cash dividends.

Expressly responding to the *Chamberlin* decision, Congress foreclosed this tax avoidance route with the enactment of § 306 in the 1954 Code. Rather than adopting the Commissioner's position in *Chamberlin* that the stock distribution itself was taxable, however, Congress chose to "taint" with ordinary income treatment any future disposition of the stock as explained in the following excerpt from SENATE FINANCE COMMITTEE REPORT, INTERNAL REVENUE CODE OF 1954, S.Rep. No. 83–1622, 83d Cong., 2d Sess. 46 (1954):

"Your committee has * * * acted to close a possible loophole of existing law known as the 'preferred stock bail-out'. * * * Your committee's approach to this problem imposes a tax on the recipient of the dividend stock at the time of its sale. This dividend stock would be called 'section 306 stock' and any stock received as a dividend would be section 306 stock to the extent of its allocable share of corporate earnings at the time of issuance, except common stock issued with respect to common stock.

"The tax imposed at the time of the sale of the stock is at ordinary income rates to the extent of its allocable share of earnings and profits of the corporation at the time the stock dividend was declared. Any amount received for the section 306 stock which exceeds the earnings and profits attributable to it will be taxed as capital gain. If, instead of selling the section 306 stock, the shareholder redeems it, the proceeds received will be taxed as a dividend to the extent of corporate earnings at the time of redemption. * * * [C]ertain exceptions to this basic rule of ordinary income treatment with respect to dispositions of section 306 stock are provided."

B. OPERATION OF SECTION 306

INTERNAL REVENUE CODE: Section 306.

REGULATIONS: Section 1.306–1; –2; –3(a)–(c), (e).

Pescosolido v. Commissioner*

Tax Court of the United States, 1988.
91 T.C. 52.

■ COHEN, JUDGE:

* * *

* The Tax Court decision was affirmed, 883 F.2d 187 (1st Cir.1989).

The sole issue for decision is whether petitioners' deductions for charitable contributions of section 306 stock are allowable at fair market value or limited to cost basis in the stock.

* * *

Petitioner graduated from Deerfield Academy and, in 1934, from Harvard College. He went to work for an oil company because other jobs were not available. In 1949, petitioner invested his savings in the formation of Valley Oil Co. Through this closely held corporation, petitioner distributed fuel oil and gasoline. As petitioner's business grew, petitioner bought out several other small oil companies. Petitioner also established corporations in Maine and other parts of Massachusetts to carry out various aspects of his business.

The growth of petitioner's business was haphazard and unplanned. In 1976, petitioner decided to consolidate his enterprise into one efficient and cost-effective organization. He also planned to effect a "freeze" of the value of his stock for estate tax purposes. In a tax-free reorganization, petitioner merged his six controlled corporations into the Lido Corp. of New England, Inc. (Lido). Through counsel, petitioner obtained a ruling letter from the Internal Revenue Service with respect to the reorganization. The application for a ruling represented, among other things, that nonvoting preferred stock to be issued by Lido would not be redeemed for 5 years. Among other things, the ruling stated: "The Corp. A Preferred to be received by [petitioner] and [William Pescosolido] will constitute 'section 306 stock' within the meaning of section 306(c)."

Immediately after the reorganization, petitioner held all of the 2,500 shares of Lido class A voting stock and 11,708 shares of nonvoting preferred stock. Petitioner's sons, daughter, and brother received nonvoting common stock. The cost basis of petitioner's preferred stock was $16.32 per share.

By receiving all of the Lido voting stock, petitioner retained control over Lido's growth and development. Petitioner's children, who were employed by the company, were given an interest in Lido's welfare through their nonvoting shares. Petitioner's preferred stock also advanced the interests of petitioner's family by serving petitioner's estate planning needs. Petitioner did not plan at that time to sell or otherwise dispose of the preferred stock.

Petitioner had long been an ardent supporter of Deerfield Academy and Harvard College. As petitioner built his business, he contributed small amounts of cash and donated his time to the Harvard College Schools Committee.

* * *

As the energy crises of the early 1970's came to an end, petitioner's fortunes markedly improved. Petitioner felt that he was now in a position to make more substantial donations to Deerfield and Harvard. In 1978 and 1979, petitioner made the following donations of Lido preferred stock:

Years	*Number of preferred shares*	*Fair market value dollar amount*	*Recipient*
1978	500	$50,000	Harvard University
1979	500	50,000	Harvard University
1979	500	50,000	Deerfield Academy

Deerfield and Harvard were at all material times educational institutions described in section 501(c)(3). In each of the years in issue, the donees of the shares received 7-percent dividends.

At the time of the gifts, petitioner did not seek professional advice concerning the tax consequences of his gifts of preferred stock.

* * *

On their tax returns, petitioners deducted the contributions to Harvard and Deerfield calculated at $100 per share as follows:

Tax year	*Contributions deduction dollar amount*
1978	$50,000
1979	78,601
1980	21,399

* * *

In a notice of deficiency, respondent disallowed petitioners' charitable contribution deductions in their entirety. Respondent now concedes that petitioners are entitled to deduct their cost basis of $16.32 per share.

OPINION

Section 170(a) allows a deduction for any charitable contribution. Section 1.170–1(c), Income Tax Regs., provides that if the charitable contribution is made in property other than money, the amount of the deduction allowed under section 170(b) is the fair market value of the property on the date of the contribution. In such a case, section 170(e) imposes a significant limitation on the amount of an otherwise allowable deduction. That section provides, in pertinent part, as follows:

> SEC. 170(e). CERTAIN CONTRIBUTIONS OF ORDINARY INCOME AND CAPITAL GAIN PROPERTY.—
>
> (1) GENERAL RULE.—The amount of any charitable contribution of property otherwise taken into account under this section shall be reduced by the sum of—
>
> (A) the amount of gain which would not have been long-term capital gain if the property contributed had been sold by the taxpayer at its fair market value (determined at the time of such contribution) * * *

The property to which section 170(e)(1)(A) applies includes stock described in section 306(a). Sec. 1.170A–4(b)(1), Income Tax Regs.

Section 306 is designed to prevent "preferred stock bailouts," in which shareholders extract corporate earnings and profits as capital gain, rather than ordinary income, while retaining ownership of a corporation. Fireoved v. United States, 462 F.2d 1281, 1284–1286 (3d Cir.1972); Bialo v. Commissioner, 88 T.C. 1132, 1138–1139 (1987). Section 306(a) generally provides that if a shareholder sells or otherwise disposes of "section 306 stock," the amount realized on the disposition of the stock will be treated as ordinary income. The parties agree that the stock given by petitioner to Deerfield and Harvard was "section 306 stock." Petitioner argues, however, that his "tainted" stock was "purged" by section 306(b)(4), which provides, in pertinent part, as follows:

SEC. 306(b). EXCEPTIONS.—subsection (a) Shall Not Apply—

* * *

(4) TRANSACTIONS NOT IN AVOIDANCE.—If it is established to the satisfaction of the Secretary—

(A) that the distribution, and the disposition or redemption * * *

* * *

was not in pursuance of a plan having as one of its principal purposes the avoidance of Federal income tax.

Petitioner has the burden of proving that neither the distribution nor the disposition of section 306 stock was part of a plan of tax avoidance; that burden is a heavy one. Bialo v. Commissioner, 88 T.C. at 1138; Roebling v. Commissioner, 77 T.C. 30, 59 (1981).[2]

Petitioner testified, without contradiction, that he received Lido preferred stock in an attempt to "freeze" the value of his equity in the company for estate planning purposes. See Northern Trust Co., Transferee v. Commissioner, 87 T.C. 349 (1986), affd. sub nom. Citizens Bank & Trust Co. v. Commissioner, 839 F.2d 1249 (7th Cir.1988). There is no evidence that petitioner planned at the time of the distribution to sell or otherwise dispose of the preferred stock. Petitioner further testified that he was an ardent supporter of Deerfield Academy and Harvard College, institutions that he believes changed his life. Petitioner struggled for many years to build a prosperous family business. After years of effort he found himself in a position to repay his alma maters. Petitioner argues that he has thus

2. Respondent does not argue that the language in sec. 306(b)(4), "If it is established to the satisfaction of the Secretary," creates a special standard of review. See Fireoved v. United States, 318 F.Supp. 133 (E.D.Pa.1970), affd. in part and revd. in part 462 F.2d 1281, 1287 n. 10 (3d Cir.1972); 3B J. Mertens, Law of Federal Income Taxation, sec. 22:90 (1980): "it is questionable whether this [language] confers any greater prerogative or discretion on the Commissioner than normally resides in him with respect to the usual kind of determination which first is made on the administrative level and which receives a presumption of correctness." See also sec. 3B J. Mertens, supra at 38D.35 n. 20.

negated a tax avoidance purpose for disposition of the stock and brought himself within the exception of section 306(b)(4)(A).

According to respondent, section 306(b)(4)(A) will generally apply *only* to minority shareholders who are not in control of the distributing corporation. Thus, he argues, petitioner cannot bring himself within this exception.

Respondent's argument is based on the following language in section 1.306–2(b)(3), Income Tax Regs.:

> (b) Section 306(a) does not apply to—
>
> * * *
>
> (3) A disposition or redemption, if it is established to the satisfaction of the Commissioner that the distribution, and the disposition or redemption, was not in pursuance of a plan having as one of its principal purposes the avoidance of Federal income tax. * * * For example, in the absence of such a plan and of any other facts the first sentence of this subparagraph would be applicable to the case of dividends and isolated dispositions of section 306 stock by minority shareholders. * * *

The regulatory language pertaining to minority shareholders is prefaced by the words "For example." Thus, an isolated disposition of section 306 stock by a minority shareholder is but one instance in which disposition of "tainted" stock is not part of a tax-avoidance plan. The regulation does not purport to set forth an exhaustive list of all situations that fall within section 306(b)(4). Certainly the statute contains no reference to the taxpayer's percentage of ownership or degree of control of the corporation. Respondent's argument, therefore, is overstated.

Respondent also cites the report of the Senate Finance Committee, S.Rept. 1622, 83d Cong., 2d Sess. 243–244 (1954), which states:

> Paragraph (4) of subsection (b) excepts from the general rule of subsection (a) those transactions not in avoidance of this section where it is established to the satisfaction of the Secretary that the transaction was not in pursuance of a plan having as one of its principal purposes the avoidance of Federal income tax. Subparagraph (A) of this paragraph applies to cases where the distribution itself, coupled with the disposition or redemption was not in pursuance of such a plan. This subparagraph is intended to apply to the case of dividends and isolated dispositions of section 306 stock by minority shareholders who do not in the aggregate have control of the distributing corporation. In such a case it would seem to your committee to be inappropriate to impute to such shareholders an intention to remove corporate earnings at the tax rates applicable only to capital gains.

This legislative history was given persuasive effect in Fireoved v. United States, supra, and Bialo v. Commissioner, supra, the cases relied on by respondent. In Fireoved, the taxpayer contended that distribution and disposition of certain stock received by him as a stock dividend and later redeemed by the corporation fell within the exception of section 306(b)(4)(A). The taxpayer argued that the purpose of the stock dividend was business related, to wit, to obtain additional capital for the corporation from third parties. The Court of Appeals stated that the existence of a business purpose was not inconsistent with a conclusion in the statutory language that "one of [the] principal purposes" of the stock dividend was "the avoidance of Federal income tax." The Court of Appeals stated:

> In a situation such as the one presented in this case, where the facts necessary to determine the motives for the issuance of a stock dividend are peculiarly within the control of the taxpayer, it is reasonable to require the taxpayer to come forward with the facts that would relieve him of his liability. Here the stipulation was equivocal in determining the purpose of the dividend and is quite compatible with the thought that "one of the principal purposes" was motivated by "tax avoidance." We hold then that the district court did not err in refusing to apply the exception created by section 306(b)(4)(A). [462 F.2d at 1287; fn. ref. omitted.]

With respect to the redemption of the corporate stock by the corporation, the taxpayer argued that he had sold 24 percent of his underlying common stock in the corporation in order to give greater control to another investor and that the subsequent redemption of a part of his section 306 stock related to that business purpose. The Court of Appeals concluded:

> More important, however, is that an examination of the relevant legislative history indicates that Congress did not intend to give capital gains treatment to a portion of the preferred stock redeemed on the facts presented here. [462 F.2d at 1288.]

After quoting S.Rept. 1622, supra, the Court of Appeals continued:

> Thus, it is reasonable to assume that Congress realized the general lack of a tax avoidance purpose when a person sells *all* of his control in a corporation and then either simultaneously or subsequently disposes of his section 306 stock. However, when *only a portion* of the underlying common stock is sold, and the taxpayer retains essentially all the control he had previously, it would be unrealistic to conclude that Congress meant to give that taxpayer the advantage of section 306(b)(4)(B) when he ultimately sells his section 306 stock. Cf. United States v. Davis, 397 U.S. 301, 90 S.Ct. 1041, 25 L.Ed.2d 323 (1970).
>
> * * * although Mr. Fireoved did sell a portion of his voting stock prior to his disposition of the section 306 stock, he retained as much control in the corporation following the sale of his common stock as he had prior to the sale. Under these circumstances it is not consonant with the history of the legislation to conclude that Congress intended such a sale of underlying common stock to exempt the proceeds of the disposition of section 306 stock from treatment as ordinary income. Accordingly, the district court

> erred when it held that any of the preferred shares Mr. Fireoved redeemed were not subject to section 306(a) by virtue of section 306(b)(4)(B). [462 F.2d at 1289–1290; fn. refs. omitted; emphasis in original.]

Bialo v. Commissioner, supra, presented an easier case than Fireoved v. United States, supra, or the instant case. In Bialo, the taxpayers' closely held corporation issued a pro rata dividend of preferred stock on common stock. The preferred stock was contributed to a charitable trust and then redeemed by the corporation. The evidence did not establish the business purpose of the donation argued by the taxpayers on brief, and:

> The only document admitted into evidence, however, which was prepared prior to the distribution of stock and subsequent contribution to the Trust discusses only the tax advantages of the transaction. * * * The memorandum also notes that a contribution of stock in a privately held corporation is likely to result in quick redemption by the charitable organization. The majority shareholder who contributed such stock would thereby be restored to the status of a 100–percent shareholder. [88 T.C. at 1141.]

Thus we held that the amount of the charitable contribution deduction must be reduced under section 170(e)(1)(A).

In this case, there is evidence of the taxpayer's bona fide charitable intent in the disposition of the stock. Evidence of tax motivation is not as clear as it was in *Bialo.* The reasoning of *Fireoved,* however, is persuasive and applies to the facts of this case. Here, as in other areas of the law, the ultimate purpose of a transaction must be inferred from the objective facts rather than from the taxpayer's mere denial of tax motivation. Petitioner was a sophisticated businessman, making deliberate decisions and advised of the nature of section 306 stock at the time that he received it. We must assume that the potential tax consequences of future disposition of the section 306 stock were explained to petitioner by counsel who requested and received the ruling from the Internal Revenue Service in relation to the reorganization. That ruling specifically stated that the stock would be section 306 stock. See Roebling v. Commissioner, 77 T.C. at 60.

On his 1978 tax return, petitioner claimed a deduction for the fair market value of the stock as if he had made a $50,000 cash contribution. We are not persuaded that he was unaware that the consequence of such a deduction would be the avoidance of ordinary income tax on the bailout of corporate earnings. His testimony that he did not have tax advice at the time of the gifts does not mean that he was ignorant of the tax benefits that he was claiming.

Petitioners have presented a credible purpose other than income tax avoidance for both the distribution and the disposition of Lido stock. The statutory language and purpose and petitioner's control of the corporation, however, require that the evidence clearly negate an income-tax-avoidance plan to satisfy petitioner's burden. His control of the corporation permits an inference of unity of purpose and plan between the corporate issuer and the shareholder, and the substantial tax savings that would result from the bailout and contribution of appreciated stock permit an inference of income-tax-avoidance purpose. Unlike those of a minority shareholder, petitioner's circumstances do not require an exception to section 306 to avoid the trap for the unwary in section 306 or invoke the relief anticipated by Congress in limited circumstances. * * *

Petitioners' deduction for contributions of section 306 stock to Harvard and Deerfield are therefore limited to his cost basis in the stock, pursuant to section 170(e)(1)(A).

ILLUSTRATIVE MATERIAL

A. DEFINITION OF SECTION 306 STOCK

1. *Stock Other Than Common Stock Received As a Tax Free Stock Dividend*

Section 306(c) defines § 306 stock with reference to the potential for "bailing out" earnings and profits inherent in stock received in a tax free distribution. The basic rule, in § 306(c)(1)(A), defines § 306 stock to include any stock *other than common stock* received as a tax free stock dividend under § 305(a) by the shareholder disposing of the stock. This basic rule is limited by § 306(c)(2), which provides that stock which would otherwise have been § 306 stock will not be treated as such if the corporation had no current or accumulated earnings and profits at the time the stock dividend was issued.

2. *Definition of "Common Stock"*

Neither the Code nor the regulations provide much assistance in defining the term "common stock" beyond the rule of § 306(e)(2) that common stock that is convertible into other than common stock is not "common stock." See Treas. Reg. § 1.306–3. The scope of the term "common stock" has been clarified by a series of Revenue Rulings that illustrate that not all preferred stock is § 306 stock and that stock that is not traditional preferred stock may be § 306 stock.

In Rev. Rul. 76–387, 1976–2 C.B. 96, the Service held that if the stock in question was nonvoting and limited in either the right to dividends or the right to assets upon liquidation, it was considered to be "other than common stock" and was § 306 stock. Subsequently, Rev. Rul. 79–163, 1979–1 C.B. 131, expanded the definition of other than common stock to include any stock with restricted right to dividends or rights to assets upon liquidation, even if the stock in question is the only stock outstanding entitled to vote.

Rev.Rul. 81–91, 1981–1 C.B. 123, involved "Class B" voting stock entitled to a preferential liquidation distribution equal to par value and an annual dividend equal to 6 percent of par value prior to dividends being paid on the Class A stock. After satisfaction of the Class B preference, the Class A and Class B stock shared equally in liquidation and dividend rights. In holding that the Class B stock was "common stock" and therefore not

§ 306 stock, the Ruling stated: "[S]tock is other than 'common stock' for purposes of section 306 not because of its preferred position as such, but because the preferred position is limited and the stock does not participate in corporate growth to any significant extent." Rev.Rul. 82–191, 1982–2 C.B. 78, expanded on this explanation as follows: "[T]he factors used to determine whether the stock in question was other than common stock were whether it could be disposed of without a loss in voting control and without a loss in an interest in the unrestricted equitable growth of the corporation. In other words, if a stock in question is nonvoting and is limited in either the right to dividends or the right to assets upon liquidation then it is considered to be other than common stock * * *." Rev.Rul. 82–191 held that *voting* preferred stock was section 306 stock because it was limited as to dividends and had a fixed liquidation preference. On the other hand, non-voting common stock presumably is still "common stock."

See also Rev.Rul. 76–386, 1976–2 C.B. 95 (the fact that voting common stock is subject to a right of first refusal by the corporation in the case of sale does not prevent it from being classified as "common stock"); Rev.Rul. 57–132, 1957–1 C.B. 115 (common stock redeemable at the option of the corporation at a price in excess of its book value is not "common stock").

3. *Stock Received in Section 351 Transactions and Corporate Reorganizations*

Prior to 1982, the rule that preferred stock issued when the corporation has no earnings and profits does not constitute § 306 stock left open the possibility of bailout-motivated transactions. For example, a taxpayer could create a holding company and, in a § 351 transaction, transfer to it stock of a controlled operating corporation that had earnings and profits in exchange for holding company common and preferred stock. The preferred stock would not constitute § 306 stock, due to the absence of earnings and profits in the newly formed holding company, and gain on the sale of the preferred stock would thus be capital gain. Section 306(c)(3) was added in 1982 to block this technique by providing, in effect, that any stock other than common stock issued in a § 351 transaction will be § 306 stock if it is issued in exchange for stock of another controlled corporation that has earnings and profits. The technical rules for determining the available earnings and profits are discussed in connection with § 304 (see page 272).

Section 306(c)(2) extends the § 306 taint to stock other than common stock received in a corporate reorganization (as defined in § 368) or a corporate division (as defined in § 355) if either (a) the effect of the transaction was substantially the same as the receipt of a stock dividend, or (b) the stock was received in exchange for § 306 stock. This provision is discussed in detail at pages 579, and 650.

4. *Miscellaneous Definitional Issues*

(a) Stock Having Transferred or Substituted Basis

Section 306(c)(1)(C) brings within the meaning of § 306 stock any stock having a transferred or substituted basis determined with reference to the basis of § 306 stock. One of the principal effects of this rule is that the taint of § 306 stock carries over from a donor to a donee of such stock. However, if § 306 stock receives a fair market value basis under § 1014 when it is transferred at death, the § 306 "taint" is purged and the stock can be disposed of without ordinary income consequences. See Treas. Reg. § 1.306–3(e).

(b) Stock Rights and Convertible Stock

Section 306(d) applies the § 306 taint to stock rights to purchase stock that would have been § 306 stock if the stock had been issued directly as a stock dividend. Stock purchased pursuant to such rights also is tainted. See Treas. Reg. § 1.306–2(b).

Section 306(e) provides that if § 306 stock is converted into common stock, either through a conversion privilege or otherwise, the § 306 taint is purged. This rule will apply even though the common stock has an exchanged basis. Section 306(e) also provides that common stock convertible into other than common stock is not treated as common stock. Thus, such stock may be § 306 stock. Does such stock present the bailout potential at which § 306 is directed?

B. TAXATION OF DISPOSITIONS OF SECTION 306 STOCK

1. *Sales*

Section 306(a)(1) treats the entire amount realized on the sale of § 306 stock as ordinary income to the extent of the stock's ratable share of earnings and profits of the issuing corporation at the time of the distribution of the stock, i.e., the amount that would have been a taxable dividend if the original stock distribution had been a taxable distribution of money rather than a tax free stock dividend under § 305. The excess of any amount realized over the dividend amount is treated first as a return of capital that reduces the basis of the stock, and after the basis of the stock has been reduced to zero, any further excess is treated as capital gain on the sale of the stock. These rules are illustrated in the following example.

Suppose that X Corporation has outstanding 100 shares of common stock having a basis of $6 per share and a fair market value of $30 per share. Assume further that the X Corporation common stock is held in equal shares by A and B. At a time when X Corporation has no accumulated earnings and profits and $500 of current earnings and profits, it distributes a stock dividend of 50 shares of $10 par value preferred stock (which is § 306 stock) to each shareholder. The dividend is tax free under § 305. Assuming that after the distribution the fair market value of the common stock is $20 per share and the fair market value of the preferred stock is $10 per share, under § 307 the basis of the preferred stock is $2 per share. After five years A sells for $500 the 50 shares of preferred stock received in the distribution. Absent § 306, A would recognize a $400 capital gain. Under § 306(a)(1), however, A realizes ordinary income of $250 (50 percent of the $500 earnings and profits at the time the stock was issued), receives a return of capital of $100, and recognizes a capital gain of $150.

While the *sale* of § 306 stock may result in ordinary income, the income is not dividend income. Thus, the amount of the corporation's current and accumulated earnings and profits in the year of the sale is irrelevant; and the earnings and profits of the issuing corporation are not reduced by the amount taxed to the shareholder as ordinary income. Treas. Reg. § 1.306–1(b)(1). In the same vein, a corporate shareholder may not claim the § 243 deduction with respect to ordinary income realized on the sale of § 306 stock.

The amount that "would have been a dividend at the time of distribution" of the stock is a ceiling on the amount of ordinary income realized on the sale. Thus, in the above example, if the earnings and profits of X Corporation at the time of the distribution were $2,000 and A sold the preferred stock for $600, A would realize $500 of ordinary income and have a return of capital of $100. See Treas. Reg. § 1.306–1(b)(2), Ex. (1).

No loss is allowed on the sale of § 306 stock. I.R.C. § 306(a)(1)(C). Thus, in the above example, if A sold the 50 shares of preferred stock for only $310, A would realize $250 of ordinary income and recover $60 of basis. The remaining $40 of the basis of the preferred stock is reallocated to common stock on which the § 306 stock originally was issued. See Treas. Reg. § 1.306–1(b)(2), Ex. (2).

2. *Redemptions*

When § 306 stock is redeemed by the issuing corporation, the amount realized is treated by § 306(a)(2) as a distribution subject to § 301. The corporation's current and accumulated earnings and profits for the year of the redemption determine the portion of the distribution that will be taxed as ordinary income. Thus, even though the corporation may have had sufficient earnings and profits at the time of the distribution of the stock to support dividend treatment of a cash distribution of equal value, if the corporation has no earnings and profits at the time of the redemption, no part of the distribution is ordinary income. If the corporation has earnings and profits at the time of the redemption, however, the "ratable share" of earnings and profits rule of § 306(a)(1)(A)(ii), which applies to limit ordinary income treatment in the case of sales, does not apply to redemptions of § 306 stock (although the proration of current earnings and profits rules of Treas. Reg. § 1.316–2(b) may apply). But, if at the time of the stock distribution the corporation had no earnings and profits, no part of the amount distributed in redemption of the stock will be subject to § 306. See I.R.C. § 306(c)(2).

Application of these rules is illustrated in the following example. Suppose that Y Corporation has outstanding 100 shares of common stock that have a fair market value of $45 per share. Assume further that the Y Corporation common stock is held in equal shares by C and D who each have a basis of $9 per share. At a time when Y Corporation has no accumulated earnings and profits and $600 of current earnings and profits, it distributes a stock dividend of 50 shares of $15 par value preferred stock (which is § 306 stock) to each shareholder. Assuming that after the distribution the fair market value of the common stock is $30 per share and the fair market value of the preferred stock is $15 per share, the basis of the preferred stock is $3 per share. After five years, Y Corporation has $700 of accumulated earnings and profits and no current earnings and profits. Y Corporation then distributes $750 to C in redemption of all 50 of C's shares of preferred stock; none of D's shares are redeemed. C is treated as receiving a $700 dividend and a $50 return of capital. The remaining $100 of C's basis for the preferred stock is reallocated to C's common stock. Y Corporation reduces its accumulated earnings and profits by $700. If D's 50 shares were redeemed the following year, if Y Corporation had no current earnings and profits, no portion of the distribution would be ordinary income.

Section 306 operates independently and overrides the rules of § 302(a) and (b), discussed in Chapter 6, under which redemption distributions may be accorded capital gain treatment.

3. *Other Dispositions*

Note that § 306(a) applies if a shareholder "sells or otherwise *disposes*" of § 306 stock. Treas. Reg. § 1.306–1(a) indicates that other dispositions may include a pledge of the stock if the lender can look only to the stock to satisfy the loan (i.e., a nonrecourse loan secured by § 306 stock). Such a transaction, however, usually is not viewed as a recognition event. As is implicit in the *Pescosolido* case, a transfer by gift to a noncharitable donee of § 306 stock is not a realization event and thus is not a disposition that results in recognition of ordinary income to the donor. In such a case, however, pursuant to § 306(c)(1)(C), the stock retains its § 306 "taint" in the hands of the donee. See Treas. Reg. § 1.306–3(e). Hence § 306 income can be shifted from one member of the family group to another by means of a donative transfer.

At one time, the tax disadvantages inherent in § 306 preferred stock could be avoided by a contribution of the stock to a charitable organization. The shareholder would escape tax with respect to the § 306 stock, there being no sale, and could also treat its fair market value as a charitable contribution. See Rev.Rul. 57–328, 1957–2 C.B. 229. The Tax Reform Act of 1969 eliminated this tax advantage by adding § 170(e)(1)(A), which was applied in *Pescosolido,* requiring the charitable deduction to be reduced by the amount of potential ordinary income gain in the property. See also Bialo v. Commissioner, 88 T.C. 1132 (1987). For an example of the computations involved when § 306 stock is donated to a charity, see Rev.Rul. 76–396, 1976–2 C.B. 55.

C. EXCEPTIONS TO ORDINARY INCOME TREATMENT

Section 306(b) provides a number of exceptions to the ordinary income treatment generally accorded to § 306 stock. Two of the exceptions are straightforward in their application. Section 306(b)(2) exempts redemptions in complete liquidation of the corporation; § 306(b)(3) provides that the various nonrecognition provisions of the Code take precedence over the recognition rules of § 306. In the latter case, however, §§ 306(c)(1)(B) and (c)(1)(C) assure that the § 306 taint will attach to any stock of a corporation acquired in such a transaction, even though that stock would not otherwise be § 306 stock. See Treas. Reg. § 1.306–3(e).

Section 306(b)(1) provides an exception when the shareholder disposes (other than by redemption) of his entire interest in the corporation (taking into account the § 318 attribution rules) to a person not related to the shareholder within the § 318 attribution rules. (Section 318 is discussed at page 241.) A redemption in complete termination of the shareholder's interest in the corporation under § 302(b)(3) or in partial liquidation under § 302(b)(4) is excepted by § 306(b)(2).

Section 306(b)(4) provides two additional exceptions. Applicability of the exception in § 306(b)(4)(A) was at issue in the *Pescosolido* case. The exception in § 306(b)(4)(B) is explained in the following excerpt from the 1954 Senate Finance Committee Report:

"Subparagraph (B) of subsection (b)(4) applies to a case where the shareholder has made a prior or simultaneous disposition (or redemption) of the underlying stock with respect to which the section 306 stock was issued. Thus if a shareholder received a distribution of 100 shares of section 306 stock on his holdings of 100 shares of voting common stock in a corporation and sells his voting common stock before he disposes of his section 306 stock, the subsequent disposition of his section 306 stock ordinarily would not be considered a tax avoidance disposition since the shareholder has previously parted with the stock that allows him to participate in the ownership of the business. However, variations of the above example may give rise to tax avoidance possibilities that are not within the exception of subparagraph (B). Thus if a corporation has only one class of common stock outstanding and it issues stock under circumstances that characterize it as section 306 stock, a subsequent issue of a different class of common having greater voting rights than the original common will not permit a simultaneous disposition of the section 306 stock together with the original common to escape the rules of subsection (a) of section 306." S.Rep. No. 83–1622, 83d Cong., 2d Sess. 244 (1954).

Rev.Rul. 75–247, 1975–1 C.B. 104, held that a disposition of both a portion of the shareholder's common stock and a corresponding portion of § 306 stock that had been issued with respect to the common stock did not of itself establish the non-tax avoidance purpose required by § 306(b)(4). See also Fireoved v. United States, 462 F.2d 1281 (3d Cir.1972), in which the taxpayer failed to qualify for § 306(b)(4) relief, even though he sold a portion of his common stock prior to a redemption of § 306 stock, because he retained sufficient common stock to avoid any effective diminution in voting power and failed to prove that one of the principal purposes of the stock dividend was not tax avoidance.

Treas. Reg. § 1.306–2(b)(3) gives illustrations of non-tax avoidance transactions falling outside § 306 by reason of § 306(b)(4). In Rev.Rul. 81–81, 1981–1 C.B. 122, the Internal Revenue Service held that the exception in § 306(b)(4)(A) applied to cash received by minority shareholders in lieu of fractional shares in connection with a distribution of a dividend payable in preferred stock. Rev.Rul. 89–63, 1989–1 C.B. 90, held that the fact that § 306 stock was issued by a corporation whose stock is widely held is not sufficient grounds, standing alone, to apply the § 306(b)(4)(A) exception to a sale of the stock. See also Roebling v. Commissioner, 77 T.C. 30 (1981) (§ 306(b)(4)(A) did not apply to a redemption of § 306 stock that represented capitalized dividend arrearages); Rev.Rul. 77–455, 1977–2 C.B. 93 (§ 306(b)(4)(B) exception available because the shareholder's entire *actual* interest was terminated; attributed ownership under § 318 was not fatal); Rev.Rul. 80–33, 1980–1 C.B. 69 (reaching same result as in *Pescosolido*).

Previously the Service would issue letter rulings to the taxpayer on the § 306(b)(4) issue. Somewhat surprisingly, given the inherently factual nature of the issue, rulings were issued with some frequency. Currently, however, the Service will not ordinarily rule in advance on § 306(b)(4) issues. Rev. Proc. 98–1, § 4.01(24), 1998–1 I.R.B. 100.

D. POLICY ASPECTS OF THE TREATMENT OF PREFERRED STOCK DIVIDENDS

Why did Congress choose to address the preferred stock bailout problem by "tainting" preferred stock issued as a tax-free stock dividend rather than taxing the shareholders upon receipt of the stock dividend? First, unlike the situations that prompted Congress immediately to tax disproportionate and optional stock dividends under § 305(b), see Section 1 of this Chapter, a dividend of preferred stock on common stock does not effect any tax avoidance until the shareholder disposes of the preferred stock. As long as all of the shareholders retain the preferred stock, the effect of the preferred stock dividend is not substantially different than a common on common stock dividend; none of the shareholders have changed their proportionate interest in the corporation. Thus, it may be inappropriate to tax the dividend upon receipt.

The argument that it is inappropriate to tax preferred stock dividends upon receipt is stronger if nontax business planning objectives of closely held corporations, which are not dependent on the sale of the stock, are served by the use of preferred stock dividends. One such situation occurs, for example, when a parent owns all the common stock of a family corporation and desires on retirement or death to transfer the ownership to his children, and in addition wants to have a child who has worked in the business with him run the business while other children receive a more certain income interest that does not participate in management. After a preferred stock dividend, the parent would be in a position to leave the common stock to the participating child and the preferred stock to the other children. This rearrangement of family ownership does not appear to give rise to any tax avoidance. But if preferred stock dividends were taxable upon receipt, in all likelihood, the tax cost would deter the corporation from distributing a preferred stock dividend and the estate planning objectives of the shareholder could not be so easily achieved. By taxing preferred stock dividends only upon disposition, § 306 eliminates their income tax avoidance potential while permitting their use for estate planning purposes.

The preceding situation is not totally devoid of tax avoidance potential. For many years preferred stock dividends were useful in planning what was known as an "estate tax freeze." These transactions were designed to limit the appreciation to be realized in stock retained by members of the older generation holding stock in a family corporation, thus reducing the federal estate taxes that would be due upon their deaths, by transferring the growth potential to stock held by, or to be transferred to, the younger generation. For example, assume that the A, who is the parent of B and C, owns all 100 shares of common stock of X Corporation and the stock has an aggregate value of $1,000,000. The corporation declares a dividend of 1,000 shares of $1,000 par cumulative preferred stock, paying a dividend sufficient to justify valuing the stock at par (typically, as a matter of practice, it appeared that this condition was seldom if ever met; tax advisors instead relied on the fact that the preferred could be redeemed for no more than its par value to "freeze" the value of the preferred stock). As a result, the common stock has a very low value (applying a liquidation value theory) immediately after the distribution. A then transfers the common stock to B and C with little or no gift tax consequences. As the corporation grows in value, all of the increased value arguably inures to the common stock. Thus, even if the aggregate value of the corporation is $10,000,000 at the time of A's death, only the $1,000,000 value of the preferred stock would be included in A's taxable estate. Sections 2701–2704 now foreclose this planning device.

CHAPTER 8

CORPORATE LIQUIDATIONS

SECTION 1. INTRODUCTION

The termination of an activity conducted in the corporate form through liquidation of the corporation raises a number of important structural issues for the income tax. One issue is similar to that encountered in the redemption area: Is the corporate liquidating distribution analogous to an ongoing dividend distribution and thus to the extent of earnings and profits taxable as ordinary income in the hands of the shareholder; or is the controlling analogy a sale of the shares of stock, in which case the shareholder would receive capital gain treatment. However, since the corporation is disappearing, even if ordinary income treatment is considered to be more appropriate to the extent of earnings and profits, the shareholder logically should be allowed a tax free recovery of basis either through a cash distribution or a loss deduction; this consideration is not present in the case of redemption distributions taxed as ordinary income (except in the case of termination of interests). Alternatively, liquidation of the corporation might be likened to the tax-free incorporation transaction under § 351. If this analogy were followed, nonrecognition would be appropriate; and a mechanism for providing the shareholders with an exchanged or transferred basis in the distributed property would be necessary. In addition, if this model were applied, rules for dealing with cash distributions, which cannot be accorded nonrecognition if the distribution exceeds the shareholder's basis for his stock, would be necessary. From the corporation's perspective, the primary issue is whether gains and losses should be recognized with respect to the distribution to the shareholders of appreciated and depreciated assets.

Unlike Subchapter K, which accords nonrecognition to the liquidation of a partnership, Subchapter C long has treated a corporate liquidation as a recognition event from the shareholder's perspective.[1] As for characterization of the income, the sale of stock model generally has been accepted, and shareholders are taxed on capital gains to the extent that the distribution exceeds the basis for their stock;[2] if the amount of the distribution is less than the basis of a shareholder's stock, a capital loss is realized. See I.R.C. § 331. This characterization is of great importance because, unlike in the

1. Former § 333, which was repealed in 1986, permitted limited nonrecognition at the shareholder level for liquidating distributions if certain conditions were met. The conditions were such that § 333 was not widely used, and when it was used, it presented numerous pitfalls.

2. Section 341, discussed in Chapter 17, Section 3, treats gain on a corporate liquidation as ordinary income in certain instances.

redemption situation, the corporate accumulated earnings and profits disappear at the termination of the corporation's existence. Thus, as a result of the liquidation the accumulated earnings and profits permanently escape treatment as ordinary income to the shareholders.

As to the corporation, the Tax Reform Act of 1986 included provisions to ensure two levels of taxation of the corporation's economic profits by requiring the corporation to recognize built-in gain and loss upon the distribution of property in liquidation. Prior to 1986, the general rule was that neither gain nor loss was recognized as a result of liquidating distributions of appreciated or depreciated property. This treatment was a facet of the *General Utilities* rule, discussed at page 202, which accorded nonrecognition to the corporation on all distributions of property. This gap in the two level taxation system was filled by the repeal of the *General Utilities* doctrine in 1986, and under § 336 the liquidating corporation now must recognize gains and losses on distributed assets.

The distribution of appreciated property may result in a tax to both the corporation and the shareholder. However, because there is generally no relationship between the corporation's basis for its assets and the basis of a shareholder's stock, one may recognize gain while the other recognizes a loss. For example, assume that a corporation with a single asset having a basis of $100 and a fair market value of $400 distributes the asset in a liquidating distribution to its shareholder, who has a $500 basis for the stock. The corporation recognizes a gain of $300 while the shareholder recognizes a loss of $100. Given the potential for two taxes on liquidating distributions, including a corporate tax on gain that accrued prior to the formation of the corporation, taxpayers must be very sure that the corporate form is, and for the foreseeable future will be, the form in which they wish to carry on business. Undoing a decision to operate in corporate form can be very expensive.

Liquidation of the corporation may occur in a number of contexts. In some cases, the shareholders may use the distributed assets to continue the corporation's trade or business or another trade or business, either separately or as partners. Even though in this case some plausible arguments may be made for nonrecognition based on continuity of the business enterprise, gain and loss nevertheless always have been recognized to the shareholder. In other cases, the sale of the business may be the objective. Under one selling method, the corporation sells its assets and distributes the cash proceeds to the shareholders as a liquidating distribution. As a policy matter, in a system that adopts two level taxation of corporate profits, recognition of gain and loss at both the corporate and shareholder level is appropriate in this case. On the other hand, a sale of stock results in only a single level tax to the selling shareholder.[3]

3. From a tax perspective, however, the buyer of a going business may prefer to purchase the assets rather than the stock. The tension between the seller's desire to sell the stock and avoid the double tax and the buyer's preference to purchase assets is discussed in Chapter 11.

The nature of the shareholder also may affect issues involved in corporate liquidation. Thus, suppose the shareholder is another corporation rather than an individual. Should there be any analogy drawn to the exclusion of intercorporate dividends allowed under § 243, discussed at page 227? If so, it could be argued that a corporation which receives a liquidating distribution should be able to exclude a portion of the distribution attributable to the liquidating corporation's earnings and profits (with an appropriate basis adjustment). Nevertheless, except in the case of liquidations of controlled (80 percent or more) subsidiary corporations, the rules governing corporate liquidations generally are applied in the same manner to both individual and corporate shareholders. In the case of liquidations of controlled subsidiaries, §§ 332 and 337 generally provide for nonrecognition of gains and losses to both the liquidating corporation and the distributing corporation. As is usual in nonrecognition transactions, the transferee must take an exchanged or transferred basis. In this case § 334(b) requires that the parent corporation take the subsidiary's basis as its basis for the assets received in the liquidating distribution.

The materials in this chapter are concerned both with the rules that govern corporate liquidations in general and with the special rules governing subsidiary liquidations. Chapter 11 contrasts the problems encountered when a liquidation occurs in the context of a sale of the assets of the corporation with those encountered when the shareholders choose to dispose of the corporate business by selling the stock of the corporation. In these cases the tax treatment accorded to the purchaser may influence the form of the transaction. Chapter 13 examines the treatment of those "tax free" reorganizations that involve the disposition of either corporate stock or all of the corporation's assets in exchange for stock of another corporation.

SECTION 2. TREATMENT OF THE CORPORATION

INTERNAL REVENUE CODE: Sections 336(a)-(c), (d)(1)-(2).

Section 336(a) requires recognition to the corporation of gain or loss as if the property distributed in liquidation had been sold to the distributee for its fair market value. Gain and loss are computed separately on each asset. Generally the gain will be characterized with reference to the purpose for which the corporation held the property. Thus ordinary income will be recognized if inventory is distributed, capital gain will be recognized with respect to capital assets, § 1231 gain will be recognized with respect to depreciable property and land used in the corporation's business, and recapture income will be recognized where appropriate. As a result, in some cases the liquidating corporation may find itself with ordinary income and capital losses which may not be deducted against that income. See I.R.C. § 1211(a).

The treatment of liquidating distributions differs from current distributions in kind, which under § 311 result in recognition of gain but not of loss (see page 204). The legislative history of §§ 311 and 336 does not explain the reason for this differing treatment. Perhaps the answer is that Congress was concerned that allowing losses to be recognized on current distributions would have presented too much opportunity for manipulation, for example, by distributing an asset, such as portfolio securities, which had temporarily fallen in value but which was expected to regain its value. On the other hand, a liquidation terminates the corporate existence, and even though depreciated assets may regain value after the liquidation, the distribution is not a selective distribution subject to manipulation. Thus, it is appropriate to permit the corporation to recognize losses on liquidating distributions. To this end, § 267(a), which generally disallows deductions for losses incurred on sales and exchanges between certain related taxpayers, by its terms does not apply to losses recognized under § 336. However, Congress has provided for disallowance of losses that it considered to be artificial or duplicative of shareholder losses; § 336(d) imposes a complex web of limitations on losses that may be recognized with respect to certain distributions to majority shareholders and distributions of property that has been recently contributed to the corporation.

ILLUSTRATIVE MATERIAL

A. ISSUES WITH RESPECT TO GAIN RECOGNITION UNDER SECTION 336

1. *Distributions of Encumbered Property*

Generally, distributions of encumbered property present no special problems under § 336(a). If a liquidating corporation distributes property having a basis of $200 and a fair market value of $1,000, subject to a $600 mortgage, the amount of the mortgage is irrelevant to the computation—the corporation recognizes a gain of $800. But if the mortgage encumbering the distributed property exceeds the fair market value of the property, § 336(b) deems the value of the property to be not less than the amount of the liability. Thus, if the mortgage on the property in the immediately preceding example were $1,150, the corporation would recognize a $950 gain. This provision extends the principle of Commissioner v. Tufts, 461 U.S. 300 (1983), which applies only to nonrecourse liabilities, to recourse liabilities. Compare Treas. Reg.§ 1.1001–2(a)(1), which generally treats as discharge of indebtedness income the amount by which a recourse debt exceeds the fair market value of the encumbered property when the property is transferred subject to the debt. Because the nonrecognition rules of § 108 generally will not apply to debt discharged in the liquidation of a solvent corporation, the primary effect of the application of § 336(b) to recourse debt is to convert ordinary income into § 1231 or capital gain.

Section 336(b) should apply on an asset-by-asset basis. Where a liability does not specifically encumber a particular property but a shareholder assumes the liability in connection with the distribution, the liability should be allocated among the distributed properties relative to their respective fair market values. See Rev.Rul. 80–283, 1980–2 C.B. 108 (applying now repealed version of former § 311(c), which was analogous to present § 336(b)).

2. *Distributions of Depreciable Property to Majority Shareholders*

Section 336(a) provides that gain is recognized "as if such property were sold to the distributee." Thus, in most cases the purpose for which the corporation held the property determines the character of the gain. Section 1239, however, treats as ordinary income any gain recognized with respect to any property distributed to a shareholder who owns more than fifty percent of the value of the stock (taking into account attribution under § 267(c), excluding § 267(c)(3)) if the shareholder holds the property as depreciable property. Thus, for example, if a corporation distributes to its sole shareholder a building, having an adjusted basis of $100,000 and a fair market value of $1,000,000, the entire $900,000 gain is ordinary income to the corporation, without regard to any applicable depreciation recapture, if the shareholder holds the building for use in a trade or business. The purpose for which the corporation held the building is not relevant under § 1239.

B. LIMITATIONS ON LOSS RECOGNITION UNDER SECTION 336

1. *Distributions to Related Persons.*

(a) *Non-pro Rata Distributions to Related Shareholders*

If a specific item of loss property is distributed among the shareholders other than in undivided interests proportionate to their shareholdings, any loss attributable to the portion of the property distributed to a related person is disallowed. I.R.C. § 336(d)(1)(A)(i). This loss disallowance rule applies only with respect to property distributed to a shareholder who is "related" within the meaning of § 267, generally, a more than 50 percent shareholder. Assume, for example, that 60 percent of the stock of Y Corporation is held by B and 40 percent is held by C, who is unrelated to B. The corporation makes a liquidating distribution as follows: B receives Blackacre, having a fair market value of $60 and a basis of $70; C receives Whiteacre, having a fair market value of $40 and a basis of $50. Y Corporation may recognize the loss on the distribution of Whiteacre to C because C is not a related person. But because B is a related person and B received 100 percent of the asset, none of the loss on Blackacre may be recognized. However, if Y Corporation had distributed an undivided 6/10th's of each asset to B and an undivided 4/10th's of each asset to C, it would have been allowed to recognize the loss with respect to both assets. Like the rule disallowing losses on distributions to related persons of property contributed within five years of the distribution, this rule applies without regard to whether there was a valid business purpose for distributing the property non-pro rata. Furthermore, the disallowance rule applies regardless of how the corporation acquired the property.

The purpose of § 336(d)(1)(A)(i) is puzzling. If Y Corporation distributed Asset #1 and Asset #2 to B and C pro rata, under § 334(a) B and C each would have a basis in their respective interests in the property equal to fair market value. Thus, immediately after the distribution they could exchange the undivided interests received in the liquidating distribution without realization of gain or loss. (An undivided 4/10th's of Asset #1 is equal in value to an undivided 6/10th's of Asset #2, and each asset has a basis equal to its fair market value.) It would appear that B could end up with all of Asset #1 and C could receive all of Asset #2, and the corporation could recognize its losses. Could the Commissioner successfully apply the "sham transaction" doctrine to treat the distribution as being made by the corporation non-pro rata? What if it made good business sense for B to own all of Asset #1 and C to own all of Asset #2?

(b) *Distributions to a Related Shareholder of Recently Contributed Property*

Section 336(d)(1)(A)(ii) disallows any loss deduction to the corporation with respect to a distribution to a related shareholder if the property was acquired in a § 351 transaction or as a contribution to capital within the five year period ending on the date of the distribution. The purpose of this rule is to prevent "stuffing" property with built-in losses into the corporation in anticipation of the liquidation. In the absence of this rule the corporation could recognize losses to offset gains on property held by the corporation; the shareholder also would recognize an additional loss on the liquidation because the basis of the stock would be increased under § 358 by the basis of the appreciated asset. At the same time, only the fair market value of the asset would be taken into account as an amount realized in computing gain or loss on the liquidation. This "double loss" situation is a corollary of the double taxation of gains and is normally the appropriate result. Congress has limited the availability of double losses in this situation because of the tax avoidance potential. See H.Rep. No. 99–841, 99th Cong., 2d Sess. II–200 (1986).

In operation, however, § 336(d)(1)(A)(ii) is mechanical and applies without regard to whether the property was appreciated or depreciated at the time it was contributed to the corporation. Suppose, for example, that for a valid business purpose A contributes two items of property to X Corporation in exchange for all of its stock. The first asset has a basis of $500 and a fair market value of $1,000; the second has a basis of $1,000 and a fair market value of $1,600. Four years later X Corporation is liquidated and both properties are distributed to A. At the time of the liquidation, the first property has appreciated in value to $2,000 and its basis remains $500; the second property has depreciated in value to $600 and its basis remains $1,000. X Corporation must recognize the $1,500 gain on the first property, but may not recognize the $400 loss on the second property.

2. *Distributions to Unrelated Shareholders of Recently Contributed Property*

In cases where § 336(d)(1) is not applicable § 336(d)(2), which applies without regard to the amount of stock of the corporation owned by the distributee shareholder, might disallow losses at the corporate level with respect to distributed property. Section 336(d)(2) applies to property acquired by the corporation in a § 351 transaction or as a contribution to capital if "the acquisition of such property by the liquidating corporation was part of a plan a principal purpose of which was to recognize loss by the liquidating corporation with respect to such property in connection with the liquidation." I.R.C. § 336(d)(2)(B)(i)(II). Section 336(d)(2), which also is intended to disallow built-in double losses, is more accurately targeted than § 336(d)(1)(A)(ii). Section 336(d)(2) disallows only that portion of the loss that is attributable to the excess of the adjusted basis of the property immediately before the acquisition over the fair market value of the property at that time. In other words, only the built-in loss is disallowed; any loss accruing while the property was owned by the corporation is allowed. Mechanically, this result is accomplished by reducing the basis of the contributed property in an amount equal to the built-in loss.

The basis reduction under § 336(d)(2) applies only for purposes of computing losses. For example, if an asset was contributed to the corporation at a time when its basis was $500 and its fair market value was $400 and the asset was distributed when its adjusted basis, without regard to § 336(d)(2), was $450 and its fair market value was $150, the adjusted basis would be reduced to $350, reflecting the $100 built-in loss, and only a $200 loss would be allowed, assuming that § 336(d)(1) does not also apply. However, because the basis reduction rule does not apply when computing gain, if the property had a fair market value of at least $350 but not more than $450 at the time it was distributed, the corporation would recognize neither a gain nor a loss.

Although the general applicability of the loss disallowance rule of § 336(d)(2) is based on intent, a timing element is introduced by § 336(d)(2)(B)(ii), which conclusively deems property contributed to the corporation within two years prior to adoption of the plan of liquidation to have been contributed as part of the proscribed plan, except as otherwise provided in regulations. However, the Conference Committee Report indicates that the regulations should provide that the presumption "will be disregarded *unless* there is no clear and substantial relationship between the contributed property and the conduct of the corporation's current or future business enterprises." H.Rep. No. 99–841, 99th Cong., 2d Sess. II–201 (1986). Stated affirmatively, the presumption does not apply to assets used in the corporation's trade or business and the question reverts to one of intent. Thus, contributions of portfolio securities will be presumed to have been made for the prohibited purpose. Furthermore, the Conference Report indicates that the loss disallowance rule should not apply at all if a plan of liquidation is adopted within two years of formation of the corporation. Id.

Technically, the loss disallowance rule of § 336(d)(2) applies to property transferred to the corporation more than two years prior to adoption of the plan of liquidation if the acquisition by the corporation was pursuant to a plan having the prohibited purpose. However, the Conference Committee Report indicates that § 336(d)(2) should be applied to property contributed more than two years prior to adoption of the plan of liquidation "only in the most rare and unusual cases." Id. at II–200.

The flush material of § 336(d)(2)(B)(i) includes within property subject to the basis adjustment any property the basis of which is determined with reference to property contributed pursuant to the proscribed plan. Thus, if contributed property is subject to a basis adjustment under § 336(d)(2), the taint cannot be purged by exchanging the property for other property which takes an exchanged basis (such as in a § 351 transaction or a § 1031 like-kind exchange).

C. EXCEPTIONS TO SECTION 336

Section 336 does not apply to distributions which are part of a corporate reorganization. I.R.C. § 336(c). However, § 361(c) may require recognition of gain, but not loss, with respect to property other than stock or securities of the acquiring corporation distributed in liquidations pursuant to a corporate reorganization. Corporate reorganizations are discussed in Chapter 13.

Section 337 displaces § 336 and provides nonrecognition in the case of liquidating distributions by an 80 percent controlled corporate subsidiary.

SECTION 3. TREATMENT OF SHAREHOLDERS

INTERNAL REVENUE CODE: Sections 331; 334(a); 346(a); 453(h)(1)(A)–(C), (2).

REGULATIONS: Section 1.331–1.

Section 331 treats a distribution in complete liquidation as being received in exchange for the stock of the liquidating corporation, resulting in recognition of capital gain or loss to the shareholder. The shareholder takes a basis in any property received in the liquidation equal to its fair market value. I.R.C. § 334(a). While these basic rules generally are not difficult to apply, certain situations may cause problems. Only distributions in *complete* liquidation are accorded sale or exchange treatment under § 331. Where a liquidation is accomplished through a series of distributions, § 346(a) provides that all distributions in the series pursuant to a plan to liquidate the corporation will be treated as liquidating distributions. Generally a distribution other than one in liquidation will be subject to § 301 and will be taxed as ordinary income to its full extent if the corporation has sufficient earnings and profits. Section 346(a) eliminates the necessity to distinguish between dividend distributions and liquidating distributions once the liquidation process begins, but determining when the liquidation process begins sometimes presents difficult factual questions. The status of liquidation is important to the tax treatment of the shareholder, since capital gain and recovery of basis with respect to the liquidating distribution result only if a "liquidation" exists; otherwise, the shareholder will generally be treated as having received an ordinary dividend.

Where property is distributed in liquidation and the shareholder assumes liabilities of the corporation in connection therewith, the shareholder's gain is computed by subtracting the basis of his stock from the fair market value of the property received less any liabilities assumed.[4] See Rev.Rul. 59–228, 1959–2 C.B. 59. For purposes of computing gain on a subsequent sale, the shareholder's basis for the property under § 334(a) is the fair market value of the property at the time of distribution without any adjustment to reflect the assumed liabilities. Ford v. United States, 311 F.2d 951 (Ct.Cl.1963). This failure to take liabilities directly into account in computing basis is appropriate because the liabilities were subtracted from the fair market value of the distributed property in computing the shareholder's amount realized on the liquidation. Since the shareholder must pay the liabilities, they are a cost of acquiring the property and properly should be reflected in basis. Since only the net fair market value of the property was taken into account in computing the shareholder's gain realized in the liquidation, providing the property with a basis equal to its fair market value undiminished by liabilities indirectly includes the liabilities in its basis. For this reason, it likewise is proper not to increase basis by the amount of the assumed liabilities; to do so would take them into account twice.

Section 331 provides that a liquidating distribution is received in *exchange* for the stock, thereby providing the vital link to § 1222 that produces capital gain or loss treatment. Suppose the stock of the corporation has become worthless prior to the liquidation and the shareholder receives nothing in the liquidation. Since there is no sale or exchange of the stock because there has been no liquidating distribution, see Aldrich v. Commissioner, 1 T.C. 602 (1943), it would appear that the loss would be an ordinary rather than capital loss. This result is foreclosed by § 165(g), which provides capital loss treatment upon the worthlessness of corporate stock and securities. However, § 1244, discussed at page 166, provides for ordinary loss treatment on the sale or exchange or worthlessness of certain common stock.

Section 267(a)(1) generally disallows loss deductions on the sale or exchange of property between a shareholder and a corporation of which the shareholder directly or through attribution owns more than 50 percent of the stock. Losses incurred on the complete liquidation of a corporation, however, are exempted from disallowance under § 267 by the express terms of that provision.

ILLUSTRATIVE MATERIAL

A. EXISTENCE OF A "LIQUIDATION"

Neither the Code nor the regulations under § 331 define a "liquidation," and thus the existence of a distribution in "liquidation" may be an

4. If the amount of a liability is contingent at the time of the distribution and the shareholder later repays an amount in excess of the liability taken into account in computing his gain or loss on the distribution, the repayment will give rise to a capital loss, not an ordinary deduction. See Arrowsmith v. Commissioner, 344 U.S. 6 (1952).

issue. However, Treas. Reg. § 1.332–2(c), which defines the term "liquidation" in the context of liquidation of a corporate subsidiary, provides some guidance: "A status of liquidation exists when the corporation ceases to be a going concern and its activities are merely for the purpose of winding up its affairs, paying its debts, and distributing any remaining balance to its shareholders."

In Estate of Maguire v. Commissioner, 50 T.C. 130 (1968), the court formulated the test for determining whether a liquidation has in fact occurred as follows: "[T]here are three basic tests: (1) There must be a manifest intention to liquidate; (2) there must be a continuing purpose to terminate corporate affairs; and (3) the corporation's activities must be directed to such termination." (142). Under these tests, distributions received in 1960 were held to be dividends and not liquidating distributions; although a plan of liquidation had been adopted in 1944, the corporation after the 1960 distributions still had assets of over $48 million and annual income of over $1.5 million, and liquidation had not been completed by 1964.

The factual nature of this inquiry is illustrated by contrasting *Estate of Maguire* with Olmsted v. Commissioner, T.C.Memo. 1984–381. During 1969 and 1970, the shareholders entered into contractual agreements to wind up the corporation's affairs and liquidate it. The board of directors began selling properties in 1970, but shareholders did not approve a plan of liquidation until December, 1973. Due to difficulties in selling mineral and timber properties, the corporation leased the properties to others and received almost $1,200,000 of income from mineral royalties, timber sales, and rents during the period 1973 through 1981. It distributed over $1,900,000 to shareholders over the same period. The Tax Court held that a status of liquidation existed during 1974 and 1975. Because the corporation would have had difficulty selling its properties, the leasing and royalty arrangements were substitutes for sales and were not inconsistent with the status of liquidation; the fact that the corporation ceased exploration and development of new mineral properties evidenced an intent to wind up business.

Formal action by the directors or shareholders is not necessarily required to effect a complete liquidation for tax purposes. Distributions may be treated as having been received in a *de facto* liquidation if the facts and circumstances indicate that notwithstanding a failure to comply with the formalities of corporate law, the corporation actually has ceased to be a going business. For example, in Rendina v. Commissioner, T.C. Memo. 1996–392, a corporation distributed all of its business assets to its sole shareholder, who in connection with the distribution assumed all of the corporation's liabilities. The corporation, however, did not formally dissolve. Relying on the tests for liquidation status in Treas. Reg. § 1.332–2(c), *Estate of Maquire,* and *Olmsted*, the court found that a *de facto* liquidation had occurred and declined to uphold the Commissioner's deficiency based on treatment of the distribution as a dividend. See also Shore v. Commissioner, 286 F.2d 742 (5th Cir.1961)("loans" to shareholders of a Cuban corporation which were intended to be liquidating distributions were so treated, even though no formal plan of liquidation was ever adopted in order to avoid a Cuban law requiring completion of liquidation within 30 days after adoption of a formal plan).

B. TIMING OF RECOGNITION ON SERIAL LIQUIDATING DISTRIBUTIONS

Where the shareholder of a liquidating corporation owns a single block of stock acquired at the same time and at the same cost, and receives a single liquidating distribution, the distribution is applied first to the basis of the stock. Gain is recognized to the extent the fair market value of the assets received exceeds the basis of the stock. However, where a series of liquidating distributions are received or where the shareholder owns different blocks of stock acquired at different times and at different costs, each distribution must be allocated to each block of stock and gain or loss is computed separately for each block of stock. Treas. Reg. § 1.331–1(e). Rev.Rul. 68–348, 1968–2 C.B. 141, amplified in Rev.Rul. 85–48, 1985–1 C.B. 126, provides examples of how to make the required allocations.

Computation of gain and loss on a block-by-block basis when the shareholder receives a single liquidating distribution generally is relevant either if long term capital gains are taxed differently than short-term capital gains or if liquidating distributions are made over the course of two or more years. Thus, block-by-block computations often are unnecessary. A block-by-block computation may have an impact, however, where the taxpayer holds a block of stock as a capital asset which has depreciated in value and holds an appreciated block as an ordinary income asset, as may be the case with a dealer in securities.

Where the shareholder receives a series of distributions with respect to two or more blocks of stock, significant timing differences may occur as a result of the block-by-block computation. After each distribution has been allocated among the blocks of stock, gain is recognized with respect to a block of stock after its basis has been recovered. This treatment, ratified by Rev.Rul. 85–48, supra, reflects the "open transaction" doctrine of Burnet v. Logan, 283 U.S. 404 (1931), even though such treatment generally is not available for installment sales. See Treas. Reg. § 15a.453–1(c). However, no loss is recognized in a § 331 liquidation until after the corporation has made its final distribution. Rev.Rul. 68–348, 1968–2 C.B. 141; Schmidt v. Commissioner, 55 T.C. 335 (1970). Thus, gain may be recognized on a particular block before basis has been completely recovered on another block. Furthermore, where the series of distributions spans two or more years, it is possible for a shareholder with no overall gain to realize capital gain in one year and a capital loss in a subsequent year, without being able to offset the two.

Assume that B holds 300 shares of common stock of X Corporation. B's basis for 100 shares (Block 1) is $500; B's basis for the other 200 shares (Block 2) is $2,000. In 1996, X Corporation adopts a plan of liquidation pursuant to which it distributes $1,800 to B in 1999 and $900 in 2000. One-third of the $1,800 received in 1999, $600, is allocated to Block 1, and B recognizes a $100 gain with respect to Block 1. The remaining $1,200 received in 1999 is allocated to Block 2 and is applied against basis to reduce the basis of Block 2 from $2,000 to $800. When the $900 is received in 2000, $300 is allocated to Block 1, and B recognizes a $300 gain with respect to Block 1; $600 is allocated to Block 2, and B recognizes a $200 loss with respect to Block 2. Overall, B recognizes total net gain of $200, of which $100 is recognized in each of 1999 and 2000. Had B been permitted to aggregate the basis of both blocks and apply distributions against the aggregate basis before recognizing any gain, no gain would have been recognized in 1999, the entire $200 would have been recognized in 2000.

C. DISTRIBUTION OF INSTALLMENT NOTES

Where the corporation distributes in liquidation a § 453 installment note previously received from another person on the sale of property by the corporation, § 453B requires the corporation to include any remaining deferred gain in income. The shareholders generally are not entitled to use the installment method under § 453 with respect to the note. Instead, the shareholders must treat the fair market value of the note as an amount received from the corporation in a liquidating distribution. Any gain recognized is capital gain; and the note takes a basis in the hands of the shareholders equal to its fair market value at the time of the distribution. Rev.Rul. 66–280, 1966–2 C.B. 304. If the principal amount of the note exceeds its fair market value on the date of the distribution, the excess, when collected, is ordinary income, either pursuant to the market discount rules of § 1276 or judicial interpretation of the sale or exchange requirement of § 1222. See Weiss v. Commissioner, T.C. Memo. 1965–20 (requiring ordinary income treatment for a year prior to the enactment of § 1276).

Section 453(h) provides a very limited exception to the shareholder recognition rule (but not to the rules requiring recognition by the corporation upon distribution of the note) when the shareholders receive installment obligations arising from a sale or exchange of corporate assets occurring after the adoption of a plan of complete liquidation that is completed within twelve months after the plan was adopted. This provision is discussed in Chapter 11, Section 1.

D. DISTRIBUTIONS OF GOODWILL AND ASSETS WITH UNASCERTAINABLE VALUE

Where goodwill is distributed in a liquidation, the value of the goodwill is includible for purposes of determining shareholder gain. Cf. Carty v. Commissioner, 38 T.C. 46 (1962) (A). The valuation of goodwill and other intangible assets distributed in liquidation historically has presented difficult problems. See Jack Daniel Distillery v. United States, 379 F.2d 569 (Ct.Cl.1967) (approving "residual" method of valuing goodwill, whereby the excess of the purchase price over the fair market value of tangible assets determines the value of goodwill); Rev.Rul. 68–609, 1968–2 C.B. 327 (capitalization of earnings method of valuing goodwill). The Tax Reform Act of 1986 added § 1060, which requires that in any "applicable asset acquisition," the value of acquired goodwill be determined by the "residual" method. See Temp. Reg. § 1.1060–1T. The definition of "applicable asset acquisition" in § 1060(c), if read literally, might include corporate liquidations in which the shareholders acquire the assets of a trade or business of the corporation. In the context of liquidations of closely held corporations, application of the "residual" method to distributed goodwill is problematical because that valuation method contemplates that the consideration for the transferred assets is susceptible to valuation without reference to the assets themselves. In the case of a closely held corporation, the stock usually is valued with reference to the value of the assets, including the value of goodwill determined under a capitalization of earnings method. But see Temp. Reg. § 1.1060–1T, requiring the application of § 1060 when assets are acquired from the corporation in a stock redemption transaction.

Nevertheless, in some cases a closely held corporation might not own goodwill apart from that of its shareholder employees. In Norwalk v. Commissioner, T.C. Memo 1998–279, an accounting services professional corporation dissolved and distributed its assets to its two CPA shareholders, who in turn contributed the assets a partnership that they joined in the same year. The IRS asserted that in addition to its tangible assets, the corporation distributed to its shareholders customer based intangible assets, including the corporation's client base, client records, goodwill and going concern value, which resulted in an additional gain to the corporation under § 336 and also increased the amount realized and thus the capital gain realized by the shareholders on the liquidation. The court, however, upheld the taxpayer's argument that because any clients would have followed the individual CPAs the corporation's earning were entirely attributable to the CPA-shareholders. Thus it owned no goodwill or customer based intangibles that could be separately sold. Because clients sought the personal ability, personality, and reputation of the individual CPAs, these assets did not belong to the corporation. The corporation's name had no goodwill value.

Suppose that a corporation liquidates and distributes to the shareholders a contractual right to receive royalties with respect to sales by a licensee of a product to which the corporation holds the patent. At the time of liquidation, there is no reasonable basis for estimating future sales. May the shareholders treat the liquidation as an open transaction, applying distributions and royalty payments against the basis of the stock and reporting gain only when the basis of the stock has been recovered fully? A number of cases allowed open transaction treatment for liquidating distributions of rights with a speculative or unascertainable value which occurred in years prior to the enactment of § 453(j)(2), which limited the use of the open transaction approach generally. See, e.g., Likins–Foster Honolulu Corp. v. Commissioner, 840 F.2d 642 (9th Cir.1988) (open transaction doctrine applied at Commissioner's behest to claims for condemnation of liquidated subsidiary's property); Cloward Instrument Corp. v. Commissioner, T.C. Memo. 1986–345, aff'd by order, 842 F.2d 1294 (9th Cir. 1988) (royalty contract). In other cases, income-producing intangibles were valued and the liquidation was taxed as a closed transaction. See, e.g., Waring v. Commissioner, 412 F.2d 800 (3d Cir.1969) (patent royalty contract). Whether § 453(j)(2) applies to liquidating distributions is unclear; literally a liquidation may fall within the definition of "installment" sale in § 453(b)(1). If § 453(j)(2) is applicable, open transaction reporting of a liquidating distribution generally will be foreclosed, and the shareholder will recover the basis of the stock ratably over fifteen years, unless a different basis recovery period can be established. See Temp. Reg. § 15a.453–1(c)(4).

E. DISTRIBUTIONS IN PAYMENT OF SHAREHOLDER HELD DEBT

Payments of debts owed by the corporation to its shareholders are not treated as liquidating distributions. See, e.g., Braddock Land Co., Inc. v. Commissioner, 75 T.C. 324 (1980). Thus, a cash method shareholder generally will recognize ordinary income when in the course of liquidation, the corporation pays an account payable due to the shareholder. Suppose that a cash method shareholder forgives a corporate indebtedness on a book account prior to adoption of a plan of liquidation, but shortly thereafter the corporation liquidates. What will be the consequences of the two transactions? In *Braddock Land Co., Inc.*, the shareholder's forgiveness of indebtedness after the corporation had adopted a plan of liquidation was ignored because the court determined that there was no "business purpose" for the forgiveness. See also Dwyer v. United States, 622 F.2d 460 (9th Cir.1980) (shareholder who purportedly forgave accrued interest on debt owed to him by corporation realized ordinary income equal to "forgiven" interest upon liquidation). Furthermore, if a shareholder contributes to the corporation a corporate debt owed to the shareholder, § 108(e)(6) might require the corporation to recognize income.

F. "RECEIPT" OF DISTRIBUTION

A distribution need not actually be received for a shareholder to be taxed on the gain realized on the liquidation. Rev.Rul. 80–177, 1980–2 C.B. 109, held that a cash method shareholder had constructively received a liquidating distribution on the date announced by the corporation as the date on which it would make a liquidating distribution to any shareholder presenting a stock certificate for surrender. If a shareholder makes a gift of stock in a liquidating corporation after a plan of liquidation has been adopted but prior to receiving the liquidating distribution, the gain generally will be taxed to the donor, even though the distribution is received by the donee. See Kinsey v. Commissioner, 477 F.2d 1058 (2d Cir.1973) (charitable contribution of stock following adoption of plan of liquidation); Dayton Hydraulic Co. v. United States, 592 F.2d 937 (6th Cir.1979) (corporation taxed on gain of stock of another corporation distributed to shareholder).

Typically, distributions in complete liquidation of a corporation are pro rata to the shareholders. If, however, a non-pro rata distribution occurs in a § 331 liquidation, a shareholder who receives less than a pro rata share of the liquidating distribution is treated as having received a pro rata share and then, in a separate transaction, having conveyed a portion of the liquidating distribution (equal to the difference between a pro rata share and the share actually received) to the other shareholders as compensation, gifts, in satisfaction of obligations, or the like, as the facts indicate. Rev.Rul. 79–10, 1979–1 C.B. 140.

In some cases a liquidating distribution may be made to a trust for the benefit of the shareholders rather than directly to the shareholders. A liquidation often is structured in this manner to facilitate a post-liquidation sale of assets that are not readily divisible where there are numerous shareholders. Generally, the shareholders will be treated as receiving a liquidating distribution when the assets are transferred to the trust. See Rev.Rul. 72–137, 1972–1 C.B. 101. The trust is then treated as a grantor trust for income tax purposes. However, if a liquidation involving a liquidating trust is unreasonably prolonged or the business activities of the trust are significant enough to obscure its stated purpose of facilitating an orderly liquidation, the trust may be reclassified as an association taxable as a corporation or as a partnership. Treas. Reg.§ 301.7701–4(d). See also Rev.Proc. 82–58, 1982–2 C.B. 847, amplified, Rev.Proc. 91–15, 1991–1 C.B. 484, modified and amplified, Rev.Proc. 94–45, 1994–2 C.B. 685 (requirements for advance ruling on classification of liquidating trust).

SECTION 4. LIQUIDATION OF SUBSIDIARY CORPORATIONS—SECTION 332

INTERNAL REVENUE CODE: Sections 332; 334(b); 337(a), (b)(1), (c), (d); 381(a); 453B(d).

REGULATIONS: Sections 1.332–2, –5, –7.

Where a parent corporation completely liquidates a subsidiary corporation which it controls, under § 332 no gain or loss is recognized to the parent.[5] This provision also applies if a controlled subsidiary merges into its parent corporation. Treas. Reg. § 1.332–2(d). Under § 334(b) the basis of the assets in the parent corporation's hands remains the same as the basis of the assets to the subsidiary corporation. "Control" is defined in § 332(b)(1), through a cross reference to § 1504(a)(2), as holding both (1) 80 percent or more of the voting stock, and (2) 80 percent or more of the total value of all stock of the corporation, except that pursuant to § 1504(a)(4), nonparticipating, nonconvertible, nonvoting preferred stock is not counted in determining control. When the nonrecognition rule of § 332 applies, the parent's investment in the stock of the subsidiary is irrelevant, and any potential gain or loss inherent in the stock disappears.[6] This treatment differs from the exchanged basis rule which is more commonly encountered in tax free transactions and is the same as the transferred basis rule generally applied to the transferee corporation in a § 351 exchange or a corporate reorganization. Elimination of the potential gain

5. For a checklist of information to be submitted to the Internal Revenue Service in connection with a request for a ruling on the liquidation of a controlled subsidiary, see Rev.Proc. 90–52, 1990–2 C.B. 626.

6. Additional considerations come to bear when the parent and subsidiary have been filing a consolidated return.

inherent in the subsidiary's stock prevents two level taxation of corporate profits which have not been distributed out of corporate solution. In this regard, § 332 serves a purpose analogous to the dividends received deduction under § 243 (see page 227). The theory behind § 332 is also reflected in the consolidated return provisions of §§ 1501 through 1504, discussed in Chapter 10, which permit affiliated corporations (defined with reference to the 80 percent control test) to file a single income tax return reflecting their combined incomes. Although § 332 governs the liquidation in both cases, the results of liquidating a subsidiary with which the parent did not file a consolidated return, however, are not always the same as the results of a liquidation of a subsidiary in a group filing a consolidated return.

Under § 332, the term "property" includes money. Rev.Rul. 69–379, 1969–2 C.B. 48. Thus the parent corporation recognizes neither gain nor loss even though only cash is received on the liquidation. International Investment Corp. v. Commissioner, 11 T.C. 678 (1948), aff'd per curiam, 175 F.2d 772 (3d Cir.1949). Taxable gain or loss would have been recognized previously by the subsidiary on the conversion of its assets to cash.

When § 332 applies to the parent of a liquidating corporation, § 337 provides a general exception to the basic rule of § 336 that a liquidating corporation recognizes gain or loss on liquidating distributions.[7] Under § 337(a), no gain or loss is recognized on a distribution to an "80 percent distributee", defined in § 337(c) as a corporation that meets the stock ownership requirements of § 332(b). The final sentence of § 337(c), referring to the consolidated return regulations, requires that a single corporation meet the 80 percent requirement: it is not sufficient for two or more affiliated corporations to have aggregate holdings meeting the 80 percent test. In concert, §§ 332 and 337 provide for complete nonrecognition of gain or loss at the corporate level on the liquidation of a wholly owned subsidiary.

As a corollary to the nonrecognition treatment accorded to both the liquidating subsidiary and the distributee parent corporation, § 381(a), discussed in Chapter 16, provides that the tax attributes of the subsidiary carry over to the parent. The most notable of these attributes are net operating loss carryovers, capital loss carryovers, and the earnings and profits accumulations or deficits. If either the parent or the subsidiary has a deficit in its earnings and profits accounts, after a § 332 liquidation the parent must maintain separate earnings and profits accounts; the deficit of one corporation cannot be used to offset the surplus in the earnings and profits account of the other. I.R.C. § 381(c)(2); Luckman v. Commissioner, 56 T.C. 1216 (1971). Earnings and profits accumulated by the parent after the liquidation are used to exhaust the deficit account before the accumu-

7. To prevent the complete avoidance of tax on appreciation in the subsidiary's assets, subject to certain exceptions, § 337 does not apply to a liquidation of a subsidiary of a tax-exempt organization. I.R.C. § 337(b)(2). This provision is necessary because notwithstanding a carryover basis under § 334(b), a subsequent sale of the former subsidiary's assets generally would not be taxable.

lated earnings and profits account of the parent is increased. Treas. Reg. § 1.312–11(b)(2), (c).

H.K. Porter Company, Inc. v. Commissioner

Tax Court of the United States, 1986.
87 T.C. 689.

OPINION

■ CLAPP, JUDGE: Respondent determined deficiencies in petitioner's 1978 and 1979 Federal income tax in the amounts of $105,281 and $745,161, respectively. After concessions, the issue for decision is whether section 332 applies to bar the recognition of gain or loss on the liquidation of H.K. Porter Australia, Pty., Ltd., petitioner's subsidiary.

* * *

In 1962, petitioner paid $219,336 for all of the outstanding stock of an Australian business corporation which manufactured saws, brake linings, and clutch facings. Petitioner changed the name of the corporation to H.K. Porter Australia, Pty., Ltd. (Porter Australia), and loaned Porter Australia the funds it needed to operate. At all relevant times, petitioner owned all of Porter Australia's outstanding stock.

In 1966, Porter Australia authorized 400,000 shares of $1 par common stock and 1 million shares of $1 par preferred stock. In 1968, it authorized 2 million additional shares of preferred stock.

The preferred stock only had voting rights at meetings convened to wind up the business, reduce its capital, sanction the sale of a business, or consider any question affecting the rights and privileges of the preferred stock. It had a 5–percent, noncumulative dividend, was redeemable, and had a $2,452,000 liquidation preference over the common stock.

In September 1966, and again in December 1968, Porter Australia capitalized loans from petitioner of $1 million and issued to petitioner 896,861 shares of preferred stock on each occasion. In November 1969, it capitalized loans from petitioner totalling $452,000 and issued petitioner 405,380 shares of preferred stock. Porter Australia capitalized the loans because it was unable to "satisfy" the loans in the short term and it wanted to avoid any further claim by respondent that income should be allocated to petitioner by reason of those loans.

* * *

In October 1978, petitioner's board of directors voted to terminate Porter Australia's operations because they were unprofitable, and dispose of all its assets. In May 1979, pursuant to Australian law, a certified liquidator was appointed to liquidate Porter Australia. In December 1979, petitioner surrendered all of its common and preferred stock in Porter Australia in exchange for a $477,876 liquidating distribution which included $10,288 to satisfy an intercompany receivable. Said distribution was not enough to cover the $2,452,000 liquidation preference of the preferred stock.

As of December 31, 1978, petitioner's adjusted basis in its 182,664 shares of Porter Australia's common stock was $249,981. As of January 1, 1979, petitioner's adjusted basis in its 2,199,102 shares of Porter Australia's preferred stock was $2,425,358.

On its 1978 and 1979 Federal income tax returns, petitioner claimed losses with respect to its Porter Australia stock. In his notice of deficiency, respondent disallowed said losses because "under I.R.C. Sec. 332, no gain or loss is recognized on the receipt of property distributed in complete liquidation of a subsidiary corporation."

* * *

Respondent contends that section 332 bars the recognition of petitioner's losses. Petitioner contends that section 332 is inapplicable and cites Spaulding Bakeries, Inc. v. Commissioner, 27 T.C. 684 (1957), affd. 252 F.2d 693 (2d Cir.1958).

In *Spaulding Bakeries,* the taxpayer purchased all the outstanding common and preferred stock of Hazleton Bakeries, Inc. between 1930 and 1946. In 1950, Hazleton Bakeries was liquidated and the taxpayer received the assets distributed in the liquidation. The distributed assets failed to cover the preferred stock's liquidation preference. No assets were distributed with respect to the common stock. On its 1950 Federal income tax return, the taxpayer claimed a worthless stock deduction with respect to the common stock. Respondent disallowed the deduction because of section 112(b)(6),[4] the predecessor of section 332. The sole issue for decision was whether section 112(b)(6) barred the recognition of the taxpayer's claimed losses. Specifically, the issue focused on whether Hazleton Bakeries distributed its assets in complete cancellation or redemption of "all its stock."

In a Court-reviewed opinion, we held that the phrase "all its stock" did not include "nonvoting stock which is limited and preferred as to dividends." 27 T.C. at 688. Thus, Hazleton Bakeries' distribution, which was in respect of only the nonvoting preferred stock, was not a distribution in complete cancellation or redemption of all its stock.

The Second Circuit, in affirming this Court, stated:

> The [taxpayer], it seems to us, argues with convincing force that the two classes of stock of Hazleton cannot be treated as though they were but one class, nor can the distribution in respect

4. Sec. 112(b)(6) of the Internal Revenue Code of 1939 provided that no gain or loss shall be recognized upon the receipt by a corporation of property distributed in complete liquidation of another corporation if—

(A) the corporation receiving such property was * * * the owner of at least 80 per centum of the total number of shares of all other classes of stock (except nonvoting stock which is limited and preferred as to dividends) * * * ; and

* * *

(C) the distribution is by such other corporation in complete cancellation or redemption of *all its stock,* * * * [Emphasis added.]

> to the preferred stock be treated as though it were a distribution by Hazleton in respect to *all* its stock, all classes. It is convincingly argued as a matter of law, that there could be no distribution in respect to the common stock until the prior claim of the preferred stock had been satisfied. [252 F.2d at 697; emphasis in original.]

Respondent, in essence, advances two arguments: (1) *Spaulding Bakeries* was erroneously decided and the decision should be reconsidered; and (2) even under the rationale of *Spaulding Bakeries,* section 332 applies.

Spaulding Bakeries Reconsidered

Respondent contends that *Spaulding Bakeries* was erroneously decided because: (1) The phrase "all its stock" was misread as referring to only voting or common stock and not to nonvoting preferred stock; (2) an inappropriate analogy was constructed between preferred stock and indebtedness; and (3) the legislative history suggests that section 332 applies when a liquidating distribution is made on preferred stock only.

"all its stock"

In *Spaulding Bakeries* we stated:

> The statute is specific in that there must be a "distribution" in liquidation and the distribution must be "in complete cancellation or redemption of *all its [parent's] stock.*" What does the phrase "all its stock" mean? Clearly it means at least 80 per cent of the common or voting stock. Does it also mean to include nonvoting stock which is limited and preferred as to dividends? We think not. The statute specifically excepts such preferred stock from the classes of stock which the parent should own—it could be owned by the parent or outsiders. * * * This means the payment in liquidation, in satisfaction of the preferred stock claim, whether to the parent or outsiders, will be immaterial. * * * Here there was no payment or distribution to the parent after the payment of the preferred stock claim in liquidation. The preferred stock claim captured all of the assets. There was nothing left to distribute to the parent as a common stockholder in the subsidiary. We hold the parent received no distribution in liquidation on its common stock within the intendment of the statute. Petitioner merely received in liquidation, payment of a part of its preferred stock claim—a fact which the statute, in effect, states will be immaterial. [27 T.C. at 688; emphasis added.]

In summary, we held that "its" referred to the parent's stock, i.e., the distribution had to be in complete cancellation or redemption of all the stock the parent owned in the subsidiary. Furthermore, because the parent had to own only 80 percent of each class of stock except nonvoting stock which was limited and preferred as to dividends, any distribution with respect to only the nonvoting preferred stock was "immaterial," i.e., not with respect to all the stock.

We agree with respondent that the phrase "all its stock" might be better interpreted as all *the subsidiary's* stock. Our decision, however, was not based on this analysis alone, and, as discussed below, we are not required to reach a different result.

Analogy Between Preferred Stock and Indebtedness

In *Spaulding Bakeries,* we cited cases which set forth the proposition that where the parent was the sole stockholder and also a creditor of the subsidiary, and the liquidating distribution to the parent was insufficient to satisfy the debt, the parent has both a deductible bad debt and a deductible stock loss. We analogized those cases to the facts in *Spaulding Bakeries.* We concluded that those cases were "authority for the conclusion that nothing was or could be 'distributed' on dissolution to the common stockholders until the full liquidation preference of the preferred stockholders was satisfied." 27 T.C. at 689.

Respondent contends that it was illogical to analogize preferred stock to indebtedness rather than to common stock. We disagree. We previously thought the analogy appropriate; the Second Circuit cited our analogy with approval; and we again find said analogy logical.

We further find that the Second Circuit aptly focused on the importance of priorities on dissolution. It stated, and we hold, that "the respective priorities of indebtedness over preferred and common stock and of preferred stock over common stock must be given full force and effect." 252 F.2d at 697. Here the assets were distributed with respect to the preferred stock. No assets were distributed with respect to the common. Consequently, the distribution was not a distribution with respect to all the subsidiary's stock.

Legislative History

Respondent contends that Congress originally passed section 112(b)(6) because (1) the nonrecognition of gain or loss on the liquidation of a controlled subsidiary would encourage simplification of corporate structures, thereby destroying unnecessary holding companies, and (2) in actuality, the parent and subsidiary represent one unitary business venture and unification of such closely connected businesses should not be subject to tax consequences. Respondent further contends that the second reason, the unitary theory, supports him in the present case and cites the dissenting opinion in *Spaulding Bakeries.*

The majority opinion did not adopt the unitary theory in *Spaulding Bakeries.* The dissenting opinion adopted the theory. The Second Circuit concluded that "no help was afforded by a reading of the legislative reports." Commissioner v. Spaulding Bakeries, 252 F.2d 693, 697 (2d Cir.1958).

Respondent gives us no new reason as to why the unitary theory, a theory implicitly rejected or accorded little weight by the Second Circuit and our majority opinion, should control the disposition of this case. He simply points to the dissenting opinion in *Spaulding Bakeries.* Suffice it to say that we are not persuaded. See *Commissioner v. Spaulding Bakeries,* supra.

Respondent also contends that the Senate Finance Committee report accompanying the enactment of the Internal Revenue Code of 1954 reflects congressional intent to minimize the elective features, and hence taxpayer manipulation, of section 332. Specifically, respondent cites a Finance Committee report which stated "Your committee has removed this provision with the view to limiting the elective features of the section." S.Rept. 1622, 83d Cong., 2d Sess. 255 (1954).

The provision referred to above prohibited the parent from selling any part of the subsidiary's stock between the time of adoption of the plan of liquidation and the time of distribution. See sec. 112(b)(6)(A), I.R.C. 1939. If a sale was effected, section 112(b)(6) would not apply. This provision, however, was deleted in 1954 upon the enactment of the Internal Revenue Code of 1954.

We cannot infer from the quoted excerpt, or respondent's purported fear of taxpayer manipulation, that Congress intended the result respondent seeks. See Granite Trust Co. v. United States, 238 F.2d 670, 679 (1st Cir.1956), revg. 150 F.Supp. 276 (D.Mass.1955). First, we decided Spaulding Bakeries in 1957. The Second Circuit affirmed in 1958. Congress has had ample opportunity to address any perceived taxpayer abuse spawned by Spaulding Bakeries.

Secondly, a manipulating taxpayer need not rely on Spaulding Bakeries. Section 332 has several requirements which can easily be avoided. See, e.g., Commissioner v. Day & Zimmermann, Inc., 151 F.2d 517 (3d Cir. 1945), affg. a Memorandum Opinion of this Court (taxpayer sold stock to avoid 80–percent requirement); Granite Trust Co. v. United States, supra (taxpayer made gift and sale of stock to avoid 80–percent requirement).

Notwithstanding Spaulding Bakeries, Does Section 332 Apply?

Respondent alternatively argues that section 332 applies, even under the rationale of *Spaulding Bakeries,* because: (1) Porter Australia's preferred stock had voting rights and, therefore, the distribution in the present case cannot be considered "immaterial;" and (2) substance prevails over form and, here, petitioner in substance held only one class of stock.

Porter Australia's Preferred Stock

Respondent focuses on the voting rights of Porter Australia's preferred stock.[5] We need not. We agree that the Second Circuit's analysis was correct in that priorities on dissolution cannot be disregarded. In the instant case, Porter Australia's preferred stock had a liquidation preference. In satisfying that preference, no assets remained to distribute with respect to the common stock. Thus, the distribution was not in cancellation or redemption of *all* its stock.

5. The preferred stock in *Spaulding Bakeries* was treated as nonvoting even though, as in this case, it had certain limited voting rights on matters which affected it.

Substance Over Form

Respondent contends that the substance of the transaction indicates that petitioner held only one class of stock which, when so viewed, would render Porter Australia's liquidating distribution subject to section 332 even under the rationale of *Spaulding Bakeries.* In support of his position, he states that Porter Australia's preferred stock did not grant petitioner any benefits or privileges that it did not already possess as the only stockholder in Porter Australia.

In Weiss v. Stearn, 265 U.S. 242, 254, 44 S.Ct. 490, 492 (1924), the Supreme Court stated:

> Questions of taxation must be determined by viewing what was actually done, rather than the declared purpose of the participants; and when applying the provisions of the Sixteenth Amendment and income laws enacted thereunder we must regard matters of substance and not mere form.

In the instant case, petitioner loaned Porter Australia money which Porter Australia needed to operate. Porter Australia capitalized the loans and issued preferred stock in 1966, 1968, and 1969 because it was unable to satisfy the loans in the short term and it wanted to avoid any further claim by respondent that income should be allocated to petitioner by reason of those loans. In 1979, petitioner received the liquidating distribution with respect to its preferred stock.

The preferred stock issued in 1966, 1968, and 1969, approximately 10 years before Porter Australia liquidated, was not "illusory" or part of a financial facade constructed of shuffled papers. Cf. Gregory v. Helvering, 293 U.S. 465, 55 S.Ct. 266 (1935)(transaction in form of corporate reorganization was just an elaborate conveyance). Significant consequences attached to petitioner's decision to capitalize the loans. Petitioner capitalized the loans with preferred stock, not common. We need not know why petitioner issued preferred stock instead of common. See Granite Trust Co. v. United States, supra. What is important here is that Porter Australia authorized and issued preferred stock with specific rights and privileges. Respondent has not argued that those rights and privileges have been ignored and the record does not suggest such a finding. We find that the preferred stock was exactly what it purported to be—preferred stock.

* * *

Finally, because we have held that section 332 does not bar the recognition of petitioner's losses, we hold that, based on the record, petitioner is entitled to an ordinary loss of $249,981 in 1978 with respect to the worthlessness of its common stock and a long-term capital loss of $1,957,770 in 1979 with respect to its preferred stock. See sec. 165(a) and (g).

* * *

ILLUSTRATIVE MATERIAL

A. INSOLVENT SUBSIDIARIES

As illustrated in *H.K. Porter Co.*, for § 332 to apply there must be some distribution applicable to the common stock, so as to supply the "cancellation or redemption of *all* [the] stock" required by § 332(b)(2). Thus, if the assets of the subsidiary are insufficient to pay its debts or satisfy its preferred shares, including those held by the parent, the common stock simply becomes worthless rather than being cancelled or redeemed, and § 332 is therefore inapplicable. In such a case, a § 165(g)(3) ordinary loss deduction may be recognized by the parent on the common stock, assuming the requirements of that section are met. See Northern Coal & Dock Co. v. Commissioner, 12 T.C. 42 (1949)(A); Commissioner v. Spaulding Bakeries, Inc., 252 F.2d 693 (2d Cir.1958); Textron, Inc. v. United States, 561 F.2d 1023 (1st Cir.1977) (loss allowed even though subsidiary was subsequently reactivated). Capital gain or loss may be recognized with respect to preferred stock when there are no distributions on the common stock. Any assets received by the parent corporation in exchange for the preferred stock in this situation take a fair market value basis under § 334(a). In such cases, there is no carryover of the tax attributes of the subsidiary under § 381. Rev.Rul. 68–359, 1968–2 C.B. 161; Rev.Rul. 59–296, 1959–2 C.B. 87; Rev.Rul. 70–489, 1970–2 C.B. 53 (where the parent continued to operate the subsidiary's business as a division).

Since nonrecognition of gain or loss to the subsidiary is conditioned on the liquidation qualifying under § 332, gain or loss will be recognized by the subsidiary with respect to transfers of property to satisfy indebtedness. Gain recognition is appropriate where the parent receives no distribution on any class of stock because the corporation is insolvent and all assets are used to retire debts. But the appropriateness of recognition of gain or loss is not as clear in cases such as *H.K. Porter Co.* where the parent receives a distribution with respect to preferred stock, but none with respect to common stock, particularly when the parent owns all (or at least 80 percent) of the preferred stock. Even though the Commissioner's argument to this effect was rejected by the court in *H.K. Porter Co.*, the preferred stock represents all of the equity interest in the corporation at the time of the liquidation and is therefore tantamount to common stock. Furthermore, for all other purposes, unless the preferred stock is reclassified as debt under the general debt-equity principles, discussed at page 130, the preferred stock will be treated as stock rather than as debt. This analysis cannot be applied, however, if the parent owns less than 80 percent of any class of preferred stock which actually receives a liquidating distribution.

Where a subsidiary's insolvency is due to indebtedness to the parent, cancellation of the debt by the parent to make the subsidiary solvent followed by liquidation of the subsidiary might enable the liquidation to qualify under § 332, and hence, for example, make available to the parent a net operating loss carryover of the subsidiary; but such a cancellation of indebtedness will be ignored if it was an integral part of the liquidation. Rev.Rul. 68–602, 1968–2 C.B. 135. See also Braddock Land Co., Inc. v.

Commissioner, 75 T.C. 324 (1980). Often, however, this will not be a desirable planning technique because under § 108(e)(6), the subsidiary will recognize income as a result of the cancellation of indebtedness, even if the cancellation is classified as a contribution to capital.

For purposes of § 332, insolvency exists when the fair market value of the subsidiary's assets is less than the sum of its debts plus the liquidation preference of the preferred stock. Difficult valuation problems may exist where the subsidiary is potentially insolvent, especially where intangible assets, such as patents, copyrights, and goodwill, are involved. See, e.g., Swiss Colony, Inc. v. Commissioner, 52 T.C. 25 (1969) (judicial determination of fair market value of patents), aff'd on other issues in 428 F.2d 49 (7th Cir.1970); Continental Grain Co. v. Commissioner, T.C. Memo. 1989–155 (in determining that subsidiary was insolvent court took into account imputed interest on book account debt to parent). In addition, problems arise in determining whether advances to the subsidiary by the parent in fact constituted equity. Inductotherm Industries, Inc. v. Commissioner, T.C. Memo. 1984–281, aff'd by order, 770 F.2d 1071 (3d Cir. 1985), reclassified as equity a subsidiary's purported indebtedness to the parent, thereby eliminating an insolvency situation and bringing the liquidation within the nonrecognition rule of § 332. See Development Corp. of America v. Commissioner, T.C. Memo. 1988–127 (same).

B. RELEVANCE OF ULTIMATE DISPOSITION OF SUBSIDIARY'S ASSETS

The liquidation of a subsidiary clearly qualifies under § 332 where the parent uses the assets to continue to conduct the same business as a division following the liquidation, Rev.Rul. 70–105, 1970–1 C.B. 70, or if the parent uses the assets of the subsidiary in the parent's business even though the business of the subsidiary is discontinued, Rev.Rul. 70–357, 1970–2 C.B. 79. What if the parent does not continue in any business, but itself liquidates following the liquidation of the subsidiary? Dictum in Fairfield S.S. Corp. v. Commissioner, 157 F.2d 321 (2d Cir.1946), stated that the predecessor of § 332 did not apply where, following the liquidation of the subsidiary into the parent, the parent is then itself liquidated. The Internal Revenue Service has not followed this dictum, however. See Private Letter Rulings 8331017, 8336056, and 8413045. Kamis Engineering Co. v. Commissioner, 60 T.C. 763 (1973), and Rev.Rul. 69–172, 1969–1 C.B. 99, obsoleted by Rev. Rul. 95–71, 1995–2 C.B. 323, although not expressly dealing with the issue, reach holdings that assume that § 332 applies in situations where the parent liquidates following the liquidation of the subsidiary. Thus, it is generally understood that § 332 applies if a subsidiary liquidates and the parent thereafter also liquidates. If, however, the order of the liquidations is reversed, i.e., the parent liquidates and distributes the subsidiary stock to it shareholders, and the subsidiary then liquidates by distributing its assets to the former parent's shareholders, §§ 331 and 336 control both liquidations. See *Kamis Engineering Co.*, supra. In most cases, however, the total gain recognized at the shareholder and corporate levels, respectively, is the same as if the subsidiary were liquidated first pursuant to § 332.

C. TRANSFERS INVOLVING INTERCORPORATE INDEBTEDNESS

1. *Subsidiary Indebted to Parent*

If the subsidiary is indebted to the parent corporation and pursuant to a plan of liquidation to which § 332 applies the subsidiary distributes property in satisfaction of the debt, § 332 does not apply to provide nonrecognition if the parent's basis for the debt differs from the amount received in payment. See Treas. Reg. § 1.332–7. As long as the subsidiary is solvent, however, the parent will not realize any gain or loss upon payment of the subsidiary's obligations unless the parent purchased them from a third party to whom they were issued.[10] Under § 337(b)(1), the distributing subsidiary corporation recognizes no gain or loss, and the parenthetical clause in § 334(b)(1) provides the parent corporation with a transferred basis in the assets used to satisfy the debt. Thus, insofar as concerns liquidation of a solvent subsidiary, in most cases no distinction is made between distributions to satisfy an indebtedness to the parent and distributions in exchange for surrender of the parent's stock in the subsidiary. This treatment prevents any attempt selectively to recognize losses by satisfying indebtedness with depreciated property while distributing appreciated property in a nonrecognition distribution.

2. *Parent Indebted to Subsidiary*

In Rev.Rul. 74–54, 1974–1 C.B. 76, a note of the parent corporation held by the subsidiary was cancelled in a § 332 liquidation; the note was held to constitute property received by the parent corporation in the liquidation and it therefore did not realize cancellation of indebtedness income under either § 61(a)(12) or Treas. Reg. § 1.301–1(m). Subsequent amendments to § 108 and the original issue discount rules cast doubt on the continuing vitality of this ruling, and the preamble to Proposed Regulations under § 108(e)(4) dealing with the acquisition of debt by persons related to the issuer indicates that the Treasury intends to promulgate regulations under which the parent will recognize cancellation of indebtedness income to the extent that redemption price of the parent's note exceeds its basis in the subsidiary's hands at the time of the liquidation. See Notice of Proposed Rulemaking, Income From Discharge of

10. Note that if the parent purchased the subsidiary's indebtedness at a discount from a third party holder to whom it was originally issued, under § 108(e)(4) the subsidiary would have been required to recognize cancellation of indebtedness income equal to the discount at that time. The debt is treated as a new debt issued for the parent's purchase price, and the excess of the amount due at maturity over the purchase price is treated as original issue discount. See Treas. Reg. § 1.108–2(a), (g)(4), Ex.(1). Although the Regulations do not address the point, the preamble to the proposed regulations indicated that the Treasury intends to amend Treas. Reg. § 1.332–7 to characterize the parent's income in such a situation as cancellation of indebtedness income rather than gain. CO–90–90, Notice of Proposed Rulemaking, Income From Discharge of Indebtedness—Acquisition of Indebtedness by Person Related to the Debtor, 1991–1 C.B. 774, 777.

Indebtedness—Acquisition of Indebtedness by Person Related to the Debtor, CO–90–90, 1991–1 C.B. 774, 777.

D. EIGHTY PERCENT CONTROL REQUIREMENT AND TAX PLANNING

Section 332 is not by its terms elective. But if the taxpayer desires to avoid §§ 332 and 337 to obtain loss deductions on the parent's stock investment and the subsidiary's liquidating distributions, it may do so by a sale of stock that reduces the parent's stock ownership below the 80 percent control line prior to the adoption of the plan of liquidation. In Granite Trust Co. v. United States, 238 F.2d 670 (1st Cir.1956), after the plan of liquidation was adopted, the parent corporation made some sales and charitable gifts of stock to cause the parent's ownership of the subsidiary to drop below 80 percent. It thus sought to avoid § 332 and recognize a loss. The Commissioner argued that the transfers should have been ignored and § 332 applied. The court, however, found the stock transfers to be real in substance, not just form, and gave effect to them. The court stated:

"As for the Commissioner's 'end-result' argument, the very terms of [§ 332(b)] make it evident that it is not an 'end-result' provision, but rather one which prescribes specific conditions for the nonrecognition of realized gains or losses, conditions which if not strictly met, make the section inapplicable. * * *

"In the present case the question is whether or not there actually were sales. Why the parties may wish to enter into a sale is one thing, but that is irrelevant under the *Gregory* case so long as the consummated agreement was no different from what it purported to be.

"Even the Commissioner concedes that '[l]egal title' passed to the several transferees on December 13, 1943, but he asserts that 'beneficial ownership' never passed. We find no basis on which to vitiate the purported sales, for the record is absolutely devoid of any evidence indicating an understanding by the parties to the transfers that any interest in the stock transferred was to be retained by the taxpayer. * * *

"In addition to what we have said, there are persuasive reasons of a general nature which lend weight to the taxpayer's position. To strike down these sales on the alleged defect that they took place between friends and for tax motives would only tend to promote duplicity and result in extensive litigation as taxpayers led courts into hair-splitting investigations to decide when a sale was not a sale. It is no answer to argue that, under Gregory v. Helvering, there is an inescapable judicial duty to examine into the actuality of purported corporate reorganizations, for that was a special sort of transaction whose bona fides could readily be ascertained by inquiring whether the ephemeral new corporation was in fact transacting business, or whether there was in fact a continuance of the proprietary interests under an altered corporate form. * * *

"In short, though the facts in this case show a tax avoidance, they also show legal transactions not fictitious or so lacking in substance as to be anything different from what they purported to be, and we believe they must be given effect in the administration of [§ 332(b)]as well as for all other purposes." (675–78)

See also Commissioner v. Day & Zimmermann Inc., 151 F.2d 517 (3d Cir.1945) (sale at public auction to corporation's treasurer who purchased stock with his own funds and assumed an actual economic risk with respect to the value he ultimately might realize); Associated Wholesale Grocers, Inc. v. United States, 927 F.2d 1517 (10th Cir.1991) (step transaction doctrine applied to disallow loss claimed on a taxable merger, the transaction treated instead as a § 332 liquidation followed by an asset sale).

In the opposite situation, in Estate of Glass v. Commissioner, 55 T.C. 543 (1970) (A), aff'd per curiam, 453 F.2d 1375 (5th Cir.1972), a parent corporation was unable to utilize the step transaction doctrine to come within § 332, where it owned only 75 percent of the stock of the subsidiary at the time of adoption of the plan of liquidation and thereafter acquired the balance of the stock. The difference in result between *Granite Trust Co.* and *Day & Zimmermann, Inc.*, on the one hand, and *Estate of Glass*, on the other hand, can be explained by the statutory requirement of § 332(b)(1) that the parent meet the 80 percent control test at the time of adoption of the plan and at all times until receipt of the distribution. Thus, although control may be broken after adoption of the plan, control acquired after adoption of the plan does not meet the statutory prerequisite.

Because control acquired after adoption of a plan of liquidation does not bring the liquidation under § 332, it is important to determine when the plan was adopted. In Rev.Rul. 70–106, 1970–1 C.B. 70, the parent corporation owned 75 percent of the stock of its subsidiary and desired to liquidate the subsidiary under § 332. Pursuant to an agreement with the minority shareholders, their stock was redeemed and the subsidiary corporation was then liquidated. The Ruling held that the plan of liquidation was adopted at the time the agreement was reached with the minority shareholders and the transaction therefore did not qualify under § 332, since at that time the parent corporation owned only 75 percent of the stock of the subsidiary. All shareholders thus were taxed under § 331. On the other hand, Rev.Rul. 75–521, 1975–2 C.B. 120, applied § 332 where the parent corporation first purchased the stock of the minority shareholders and then liquidated the subsidiary. Rev.Rul. 75–521 distinguished Rev.Rul. 70–106 on the grounds that in the earlier Ruling the entire distribution was a distribution in liquidation; in Rev.Rul. 75–521, however, the purchase by the parent corporation was not a part of a distribution in liquidation and the mere sale between shareholders did not constitute the adoption of a plan of liquidation.

In George L. Riggs, Inc. v. Commissioner, 64 T.C. 474 (1975)(A), a corporation, during the time that it owned less than 80 percent of the stock of its subsidiary, voted in favor of selling substantially all of the assets of the subsidiary and took various other steps evidencing an intention to liquidate the subsidiary. Subsequently, by virtue of a redemption by the subsidiary, the parent corporation obtained 80 percent control of the subsidiary. Thereafter the subsidiary formally adopted a plan of liquidation. The Commissioner asserted that a plan of liquidation had been adopted prior to obtaining 80 percent control and thus § 332 was inapplicable. The court held, however, that although the actions taken prior to formal adoption of the plan of liquidation may have evidenced an intention to liquidate the subsidiary, the intent to liquidate is not tantamount to adoption of a plan of liquidation. The date of adoption of the plan of liquidation controlled and § 332 therefore provided nonrecognition treatment to the liquidation. The court stated that "section 332 is elective in the sense that with advance planning and properly structured transactions, a corporation should be able to render section 332 applicable or inapplicable". Rev.Rul. 70–106 was distinguished on the basis that the plan of liquidation there was adopted when the agreement regarding the redemption was reached with the minority shareholders.

Thus, if liquidation of a subsidiary is contemplated, the tax advisor has a choice of recommending a taxable or tax-free liquidation of the subsidiary. In choosing between the alternatives, the effect of §§ 336 and 337 often will be more important than the effect of § 332. Because the parent's basis in the stock of the subsidiary is unaffected by the subsidiary's earnings and profits history (unless a consolidated return has been filed), the parent may realize little or no gain on the liquidation while the subsidiary realizes a substantial gain or loss on the liquidating distribution. In general, a taxable liquidation will be advisable where the subsidiary has depreciated assets and both the subsidiary and the parent will realize a loss or the subsidiary's loss exceeds the parent's gain, or where the parent's loss exceeds the subsidiary's gain. On the other hand, the tax-free route of § 332 ordinarily will be advisable where the subsidiary's gain exceeds the parent's loss or both corporations realize a gain. Where the subsidiary has a net operating loss carryover that would be available to the parent, the determination is more complex. If the net operating loss carryover is large enough, the tax benefit to the parent of acquiring the carryover may compensate for denial of otherwise available losses, but in other cases, current loss recognition may yield a greater benefit.

E. STATUTORILY REQUIRED TIME LIMITS ON COMPLETING THE LIQUIDATION

A liquidation qualifies under § 332 either (1) if it is completed within a single taxable year or (2) if the plan requires completion of the liquidation within three years from the close of the year in which the first distribution is made *and* the liquidation is in fact completed within that period. Neither timetable requires that distributions commence within any particular period after the plan is adopted. Where a subsidiary for valid business reasons did not make a liquidating distribution until February, 1966, pursuant to a plan of liquidation adopted on July 1, 1963, § 332 treatment was upheld; the phrase "within the taxable year" in § 332(c)(2) refers to the year in which liquidating distributions are made and not to the year of the adoption of the plan of liquidation. Rev.Rul. 71–326, 1971–2 C.B. 177. See also Rev.Rul. 76–317, 1976–2 C.B. 98, which held that the "taxable year" referred to in § 332(b)(2) and (3) is the taxable year of the subsidiary corporation. No formal plan is required if a liquidation actually is completed within a single year. Burnside Veneer Co. v. Commissioner, 167 F.2d 214 (6th Cir.1948).

If the liquidation takes more than a year to complete, the Commissioner may require the corporation to post a bond. See Treas. Reg. § 1.332–4. The statute provides that if the liquidation is not completed within the required period, none of the distributions are treated as liquidating distributions within the meaning of § 332(a). However, the distributions presumably remain liquidating distributions within the meaning of §§ 331 and 336. Thus, if the conditions of § 332 are not met, both the liquidating subsidiary corporation and the parent corporation will recognize gain or loss on the liquidation. The property received by the parent would take a fair market value basis under § 334(a) rather than a transferred basis.

In general, retention of any property by a subsidiary, regardless of amount, for the purpose of continuing the operation of a business or of engaging in a new business will prevent the application of § 332. Rev.Rul. 76–525, 1976–2 C.B. 98. But Rev.Rul. 84–2, 1984–1 C.B. 92, held that the transfer to a new subsidiary by the parent of a nominal amount of the liquidated subsidiary's assets for the purpose of protecting the corporate name of the subsidiary did not disqualify the liquidation.

Suppose that both the parent and the subsidiary will recognize losses if the liquidation is taxable. Can §§ 332 and 337 be avoided by intentionally spreading liquidating distributions out over a four year period? There is no direct authority on this issue. In Cherry–Burrell Corp. v. United States, 367 F.2d 669 (8th Cir.1966), a U.S. parent received the first liquidating distribution from its British subsidiary in 1952. However, because claims were pending against the subsidiary and British law prohibited further distributions until the claims were finally settled in 1968, the court held that § 332 applied because the corporation had de facto liquidated within the required time period and the delay in distributing the remaining assets was involuntary; all the assets were converted to cash in 1952, only an amount necessary for a reasonable reserve for the claims asserted was retained as required by British law, no commercial activity was engaged in during the interim period, and the final liquidating distribution was made immediately after the settlement of claims.

F. DISTRIBUTIONS TO MINORITY SHAREHOLDERS

Section 332 applies only to the controlling corporate parent. Minority shareholders cannot take advantage of its provisions. Therefore, the liquidating distribution received by a minority shareholder will be taxable under § 331; and a minority shareholder will hold the distributed property with a basis determined under § 334(a).

Furthermore, even though § 337 shields the subsidiary from recognition of gain or loss on liquidating distributions to the parent in a § 332 liquidation, § 337(a) limits nonrecognition to gain or loss inherent in property distributed to the parent. If property is distributed to minority shareholders, § 336 applies as to gains, but § 336(d)(3) requires nonrecognition of losses with respect to property distributed to minority shareholders. This asymmetrical treatment presumably is grounded on concerns that a liquidating subsidiary with minority shareholders would selectively distribute depreciated assets to the minority shareholders in order to recognize the loss while distributing appreciated assets to the parent subject to § 332 nonrecognition. Nonrecognition of losses, however, extends to pro rata liquidating distributions to minority shareholders as well as to non-pro rata liquidations. Thus the nonrecognition rule with respect to losses appears to be overbroad.

PART II

ELECTIVE PASSTHROUGH TAX TREATMENT

CHAPTER 9

S CORPORATIONS

Internal Revenue Code: SECTIONS 1361–1378.

SECTION 1. INTRODUCTION

Overview. Subchapter S was enacted in 1958 to make it possible for "businesses to select the form of business organization desired, without the necessity of taking into account major differences in tax consequence." S.Rep. No. 85–1983, 85th Cong., 2d Sess. 87 (1958). As originally enacted, Subchapter S status was available only for corporations that had no more than ten individual stockholders. Although shareholders were taxed on undistributed corporate profits in addition to actual dividend distributions, except for capital gains, the character of items did not pass through to the shareholders as in the case of partnerships. If the corporation had a net operating loss, it also passed through to stockholders. A stockholder's stock basis was increased by undistributed taxable income and decreased by pass-through net operating losses. An electing corporation was not subject to tax unless it realized extraordinary capital gains.[1]

In 1969 the Treasury Department, in conjunction with the Tax Section of the American Bar Association, proposed revising Subchapter S to conform more closely to the complete pass-through model of the partnership rules.[2] To alleviate problems caused by the hybrid nature of the S corporation under then current law, "not quite a corporation and not quite a partnership," the Treasury study recommended adoption of complete pass-through taxation of the entity's tax-significant items under the partnership rules plus a number of other changes to simplify Subchapter S. The 1969 proposal was adopted, generally intact, in 1982. Thus, while the detailed rules of Subchapter S have metamorphosed over the years, the fundamental purpose of Subchapter S—to eliminate the corporation as a taxable entity and provide a system under which the operating profits of qualifying corporations are taxed directly to the shareholders—remains unchanged.[3]

Prior to the mid–1980's, only a relatively small number of corporations elected Subchapter S status. One reason was that prior to 1982, Subchapter S status could not be maintained if more than 20 percent of the corporation's gross receipts were derived from passive investments such as interest, dividends, rents and royalties. In many other cases, closely held corporations simply did not show a profit after paying shareholder-employees salaries. The election was mostly valuable during the early years of a venture when the corporation produced losses that could be passed through to the stockholders.

After 1986, however, Subchapter S elections by eligible corporations became vastly more popular than previously. This result occurred because, taking into account the double taxation of distributed earnings of a C corporation, the maximum effective rate of taxation of distributed C corporation income in 1987 was significantly higher than on S corporation income, 52.4 percent for C corporation shareholders compared to 28 percent for S corporation shareholders. This fact, coupled with the reduction of preferential treatment accorded long-term capital gains in the 1986 Act, resulted in the pass-through entity being the preferred form of business organization from a tax perspective.[4] But subsequent changes in the tax

1. The corporate level tax was designed to discourage a "one-shot" election by a corporation anticipating gain on the disposition of capital (or § 1231) assets.

2. U.S. Treasury Dept. Tax Reform Studies and Proposals, House Ways and Means Committee and Senate Finance Committee, 91st Cong., 1st Sess. (1969).

3. Technical aspects of Subchapter S in all likelihood will continue to evolve.

4. For 1986 24.1 percent of all corporations, 826,214 out of 3,428,515 corporations, filed S corporation returns. By 1993, the percentage of corporations electing S status had climbed to 48.39 percent, 1,909,786 out of 3,946,614 corporations. Staff of the Joint Committee on Taxation, Present Laws and Proposals Relating to Subchapter S Corporations and Home Office Deductions, p.16 (JCS–16–95, May 24, 1995). More recently, however, the trend appears to have abated. For 1994, 46.6 percent—2,023,754 of 4,342,368 corporate returns—were for S corporations. In any event, S corporations, are primarily small enterprises. The 48 percent of all corporations electing S status held less than five percent of all corporate assets in 1993. Staff of the Joint Committee on Taxation, supra, at 20.

rate schedules, the reemergence of a significant capital gains preference, and the widespread enactment by states of limited liability company statutes may reduce the attractiveness of S corporations. In the 1990s, virtually every state enacted a limited liability company (LLC) statute. Generally, LLCs are formed so as to be taxed as partnerships, even though they confer limited liability on every member. From both the tax and nontax points of view, the LLC is a more flexible form of business organization than a corporation that makes a Subchapter S election. Nevertheless, whether a partnership, an S corporation, or a limited liability company that is taxed as a partnership is the more desirable form depends on a broad range of factors.

The Basic Framework of Subchapter S. To be eligible to make a Subchapter S election, a corporation must meet a number of requirements, including limitations on the number and identity of its shareholders. First, an electing corporation, referred to as an "S corporation," may have no more than 75 stockholders. I.R.C. § 1361(b)(1)(A). Qualifying stockholders include only individuals, grantor trusts, voting trusts, "qualified Subchapter S trusts" (QSSTs), "electing small business trusts," tax exempt charitable organizations, and certain retirement pension trusts. It cannot have a stockholder who is a nonresident alien individual, a corporation (other than a tax exempt charitable organization), partnership, or LLC, and it may issue only one class of stock (although there is an exception for stock that varies in voting rights). I.R.C. § 1361(b) and (c). An S corporation may hold stock in a controlled subsidiary corporation, but may not be a subsidiary of another corporation unless it is 100 percent owned by a parent S corporation that has elected to treat the subsidiary, in effect, as an operating division rather than a separate corporation. I.R.C. § 1361(b)(3).

S corporation status may be elected only with the consent of all stockholders at the time the election is filed. An election is effective on the first day of the taxable year following the filing of the election, except that an election filed within the first two and one-half months of the taxable year may be retroactive to the first day of the taxable year. In the latter case, the corporation must have satisfied all of the requirements for S corporation status since the first day of the taxable year. I.R.C. § 1362(b). Once made, an election continues in effect until it is revoked by a majority of the stockholders, the corporation ceases to meet the qualifications as an S corporation, or the corporation has accumulated earnings and profits[5] and earns passive investment income in excess of 25 percent of gross receipts for three consecutive taxable years. I.R.C. § 1362(d).

Generally an S corporation is not subject to corporate tax. I.R.C. § 1363(a). There are two exceptions. Under § 1374, S corporations are taxable on certain gain recognized on disposition of appreciated assets or income items generated while the corporation was a C corporation, or acquired from a C corporation in a nonrecognition transaction. In addition,

5. A corporation will accumulate earnings and profits only in years it is a C corporation. Thus, this restriction does not apply to a corporation that has no tax history as a C corporation.

under § 1375, an S corporation with accumulated earnings and profits is taxable at regular corporate rates to the extent that passive investment income exceeds 25 percent of its gross receipts.

S corporation items of income, loss or deduction are passed through the entity to the stockholders, and retain their character in the stockholder's hands, in the same manner that partnership items are passed through to partners under Subchapter K. I.R.C. § 1366. Thus each item of income or deduction that may affect stockholders differently must be separately stated and reported to the stockholders. For example, tax exempt interest income retains its exemption under § 103, and interest expense must be categorized under the complex interest allocation rules to determine its deductibility by the individual stockholders. Each stockholder reports the item on his return as if the item were derived by the stockholder directly. The character of items, such as capital gain, is based on the character of income at the corporate level. The stockholder's basis in S corporation stock is increased for income items and decreased for deduction or loss items passed through to the stockholder from the corporation. I.R.C. § 1367. As under the partnership model, the stockholder's deductible loss is limited to the stockholder's basis in stock, but S corporation shareholders who lend money to the corporation may deduct losses up to their basis in the debt of the S corporation as well. I.R.C. § 1366(d)(1).

Since S corporation income is taxed to the stockholders when realized by the corporation, subsequent distributions of the previously taxed income are received by stockholders without additional tax. I.R.C. § 1368. Distributions reduce the stockholder's basis in stock of the corporation. Distributions in excess of basis result in recognition of capital gain.

A second tier of distribution rules applies to an S corporation that has accumulated earnings and profits from taxable years in which it was a C corporation. The corporation must maintain an "accumulated adjustments account" that reflects net corporate income items that have been passed through to stockholders. Distributions to the extent of this accumulated adjustments account are received by the stockholders without tax. I.R.C. § 1368(b). To the extent that distributions exceed the accumulated adjustments account, the distributions are treated as distributions of earnings and profits, to the extent thereof, and are taxed to the stockholders as dividends. Thus a "double" tax pattern is preserved for earnings originally generated in a C corporation. Any further distributions are received by the stockholders as a reduction of basis, then as capital gain to the extent that a distribution exceeds the recipient stockholder's basis.

Comparison of S Corporations and Partnerships (Including LLCs). Although Subchapter S in general adopts the partnership model for taxing S corporations, there are significant differences between the taxation of S corporations and partnerships that affect a taxpayer's choice between the two entities. (Since an LLC almost always will elect to be taxed as a partnership, the following considerations are applicable to LLCs as well.) As discussed previously, beneficial ownership of an S corporation is limited to 75 stockholders, while there is no limit on the number of persons who may be partners in a partnership. Nor is there any restriction upon the types of entities that may be partners. The partnership form provides a significant advantage in the case of leveraged investments if losses are anticipated. Partners are allowed to include their shares of partnership debt in the bases of their partnership interests, which in turn allows partners to deduct partnership losses attributable to partnership level debt. In contrast, the stockholder's basis in Subchapter S stock or debt is limited to the stockholder's actual investment in the corporation. This limitation also means that while untaxed entity level cash, e.g., from a refinancing, can be distributed by a partnership free of tax, the same distribution by an S corporation may trigger gain recognition. For these reasons, S corporations have not been used for leveraged investments such as real estate.

Subchapter S also differs from Subchapter K in its treatment of distributions of appreciated property. An S corporation is required by §§ 311(b) and 336 to recognize gain on a distribution of appreciated property to stockholders. The recognized gain is passed through to the stockholders, who increase the basis of their stock accordingly. The distributee stockholder obtains a fair market value basis in the distributed property, and decreases the basis of the S corporation stock by the same amount. Subject to some exceptions, distributions of appreciated property by a partnership generally do not trigger recognition of gain. Instead, the distributee partner takes the partnership's basis in the property and recognition of gain is deferred until the distributee disposes of the property. The Code is thus not completely neutral as to the choice between a Subchapter S corporation and a partnership.

As the following material indicates, the tax treatment of S corporations that have always been S corporations is relatively straight-forward. Technical complexities, of course, are encountered. But for such corporations, the governing provisions are not particularly difficult either in concept or in practice. Section 3 discusses Subchapter S in the context of a corporation that was formed as an S corporation and never changed that status.

While a corporation that has a C corporation history can elect S corporation status, the rules governing such corporations are much more complex than those applicable to S corporations with no C corporation history. These rules are discussed in Section 4.

Subchapter S represents one way of integrating the corporate and personal income taxes. At the end of Section 3, consider whether the S corporation regime can be applied to corporations such as General Motors or Exxon. At the end of Section 4, consider whether the rules adopted for corporations with a C corporation history can or should be used as transition rules to a fully integrated corporate and individual tax system.

SECTION 2. ELIGIBILITY, ELECTION AND TERMINATION

A. STOCKHOLDER RULES

INTERNAL REVENUE CODE: Section 1361(b)(1), (c)(1)–(3), (d).

REGULATIONS: Section 1.1361–1(e), (f).

Section 1361(b)(1) requires that the electing corporation have no more than 75 stockholders and that it have no stockholder who is not an individual, an estate, a grantor trust, a "qualified Subchapter S trust" (QSST), an "electing small business trust," a tax exempt charitable organization, or a qualified retirement pension trust. When stock is held by a nominee, guardian, or custodian, the beneficial owner is treated as the shareholder. Treas. Reg. § 1.1361–1(e). A corporation, partnership, or LLC may not be a shareholder in an S corporation other than as a nominee for the beneficial owner. See Treas. Reg. § 1.1361–1(e)(1).

Section 1361(c)(2) permits five types of domestic trusts as stockholders of an S corporation: trusts treated as owned by a United States citizen or resident (grantor trusts), grantor trusts that survive the death of the grantor (but only for a limited period), testamentary trusts (again only for a limited period), voting trusts, and "electing small business trusts" (as defined in § 1361(e)). Section 1361(d) further provides that a QSST, a trust with a single income beneficiary who has elected to be treated as the owner of S corporation stock held by the trust, is a qualified shareholder; S corporation items of income and loss pass through the trust to the beneficiary. With the exception of these permitted trusts, trusts are ineligible shareholders.

Is any significant policy goal served by limiting to seventy-five the number of shareholders permitted in an S corporation? Consider the following Revenue Ruling, which was promulgated when the ceiling was thirty-five shareholders.

Revenue Ruling 94–43

1994–2 C.B. 198.

In Rev. Rul. 77–220, 1977–1 C.B. 263, thirty unrelated individuals entered into the joint operation of a single business. The individuals divided into three equal groups of ten individuals and each group formed a separate corporation. The three corporations then organized a partnership for the joint operation of the business. The principal purpose for forming three separate corporations instead of one corporation was to avoid the 10 shareholder limitation of § 1371 of the Internal Revenue Code of 1954 (the predecessor of § 1361) and thereby allow the corporations to elect to be treated as S corporations under Subchapter S.

Rev. Rul. 77–220 concluded that the three corporations should be considered to be a single corporation, solely for purposes of making the election, because the principal purpose for organizing the separate corporations was to make the election. Under this approach, there would be 30 shareholders in one corporation and the election made by this corporation would not be valid because the 10 shareholder limitation would be violated.

The Service has reconsidered Rev. Rul. 77–220 and concluded that the election of the separate corporations should be respected. The purpose of the number of shareholders requirement is to restrict S corporation status to corporations with a limited number of shareholders so as to obtain administrative simplicity in the administration of the corporation's tax affairs. In this context, administrative simplicity is not affected by the corporation's participation in a partnership with other S corporation partners; nor should a shareholder of one S corporation be considered a shareholder of another S corporation because the S corporations are partners in a partnership. Thus, the fact that several S corporations are partners in a single partnership does not increase the administrative complexity at the S corporation level. As a result, the purpose of the number of shareholders requirement is not avoided by the structure in Rev. Rul. 77–220 and, therefore, the election of the corporations should be respected.

ILLUSTRATIVE MATERIAL

A. HUSBAND AND WIFE SHAREHOLDERS

In counting the number of stockholders, a husband and wife (and their respective estates) are treated as a single stockholder regardless of the form of ownership in which the stock is held. I.R.C. § 1361(c)(1). Aside from this one case, each family member owning shares is counted separately.

Under § 1361(b)(1)(C) an S corporation may not have a nonresident alien stockholder. In Ward v. United States, 661 F.2d 226 (Ct.Cl.1981), a corporation's Subchapter S election was held invalid because the taxpayer's nonresident alien wife was the beneficial owner of the corporation's stock under community property laws.

B. ESTATES AND TRUSTS AS ELIGIBLE STOCKHOLDERS

1. *General*

Section 1361 permits the estate of a deceased stockholder, the estate of an individual in bankruptcy, and certain trusts, including "grantor trusts" if the grantor is a United States citizen or resident, voting trusts, and, for a limited period of time, testamentary trusts to be S corporation stockholders. In the case of a grantor trust, the grantor is treated as the stockholder and in the case of voting trusts, each beneficiary of the trust is treated as a stockholder. See generally Treas. Reg. § 1.1361–1(h)(i), (v). Rev. Rul. 92–73, 1992–2 C.B. 224, held that a trust qualified as an individual retirement account is not a permitted Subchapter S corporation shareholder because its income is not currently taxed to the beneficiary.

A testamentary trust to which stock of an S corporation has been transferred is an eligible S corporation stockholder for only two years following the day on which the stock is transferred. I.R.C. § 1361(c)(2)(A)(iii). Similarly, under § 1361(c)(2)(A), a grantor trust may continue as an S corporation stockholder for two years following the death of the grantor. If grantor trust status terminates for some reason other than the death of the grantor—for example if the grantor relinquishes the powers that make the trust a grantor trust—the trust becomes an ineligible stockholder and the corporation's S corporation status is terminated immediately.

There is no statutory limit on the length of time that an estate may remain a qualified stockholder. However, Old Virginia Brick Co. v. Commissioner, 367 F.2d 276 (4th Cir.1966), held that an estate that was one of the stockholders of an S corporation and which was kept open substantially beyond the period necessary for the performance of administrative duties became in effect an ineligible testamentary trust; accordingly the corporation was disqualified from S corporation status.[6] But Rev. Rul. 76–23, 1976–1 C.B. 264, allowed retention of S corporation stock by an estate for purposes of the ten year installment payment of estate taxes in § 6166.

2. *Qualified Subchapter S Trusts*

Section 1361(d) permits a QSST to be an S corporation stockholder. A QSST is a trust that, by its terms, has only one current income beneficiary who will be the sole income beneficiary during the beneficiary's life or for the term of the trust.[7] I.R.C. § 1361(d)(3). See Rev. Rul. 93–31, 1993–1 C.B. 186 (separate and independent share of a trust within the meaning of § 663(c) cannot be a QSST if there is any possibility, however remote, that during the income beneficiary's lifetime the corpus will be distributed to someone other than the income beneficiary). To avoid any possibility of splitting S corporation income and deductions between the trust and the beneficiary, a QSST is an eligible stockholder only if the beneficiary elects in effect to treat the trust as a grantor trust with respect to the S corporation stock. Thus the income beneficiary is treated as the owner of the portion of the trust that consists of S corporation stock. The beneficiary is taxed on the income and receives the deductions allocable to the S corporation stock without regard to the normal rules of trust taxation. I.R.C. § 1361(d)(1)(B). See generally Treas. Reg. § 1.1361–1(j). However, gain from the sale of stock by a QSST trust is not taxable to the beneficiary of the trust; instead, the trust itself is taxed on any such gain. Treas. Reg. § 1.1361–1(j)(8).

The strict requirements of § 1361(d) apparently were designed to prevent the use of trusts to avoid the 35 stockholder limitation that was in

6. See also Treas. Reg. § 1.641(b)–3(a) (an estate is deemed terminated for federal tax purposes after the expiration of a reasonable period for the performance by the executor of the duties of administration).

7. In Rev. Rul. 92–64, 1992–2 C.B. 214, the QSST provided for distributions of trust income in December and June of each year. The income beneficiary died on May 1. The Ruling allowed distributions of trust income accumulated between the last distribution and the date of the beneficiary's death to be made to either the deceased beneficiary's estate under state law or the successor beneficiary under a provision of the trust. The Ruling concluded that after the date of death, the successor income beneficiary is the only income beneficiary of the trust, even though the estate may become entitled to a distribution.

In Rev. Rul. 92–48, 1992–1 C.B. 301, the Service ruled that a charitable remainder trust, qualified under § 664, cannot be qualified as a QSST. The Ruling concluded that the scheme for the taxation of charitable remainder trusts is incompatible with the requirements of the QSST rules.

force prior to 1996, while facilitating pass-through taxation of the trust beneficiary as the ultimate recipient of the S corporation income. In light of the increase in the number of permitted shareholders from 35 to 75 in 1996 and the holding of Rev. Rul. 94–43, page 366, permitting the use of a partnership to sidestep the limitation on the number of shareholders in § 1361(b)(1)(A), any valid policy based purpose for the limitations in § 1361(d) is difficult to discern.

A trust is a QSST only if a timely election is filed with the Internal Revenue Service by the beneficiary (or the beneficiary's legal representative or parent if there is no legal representative appointed). A separate election is required with respect to the stock of each S corporation owned by a QSST. Failure to file the election for a trust that becomes an S corporation stockholder will result in revocation of the corporation's status as an S corporation. See Rev. Rul. 93–79, 1993–2 C.B. 269 (retroactive judicial reformation of trust to conform to requirements for a QSST was not effective to validate S corporation election prior to reformation at a time when the trust did not qualify).

Section 1361(d)(2)(D) provides that an election to be a QSST is retroactively effective for the two month and fifteen day period preceding the filing of the election. See Treas. Reg. § 1.1361–1(j)(6) for the detailed procedural rules respecting the election.

3. *Electing Small Business Trusts*

Under § 1361(e), a trust may elect to be a "small business trust" if the only current beneficiaries of the trust are individuals, estates eligible to own S corporation stock, and tax exempt charitable organizations, and none of the beneficiaries has purchased the interest in the trust.

The election is made by the trustee of the trust. See Notice 97–12, 1997–1 C.B. 385 (procedures for election; because the trust is taxed rather than beneficiaries, even though all beneficiaries are counted against the 75 shareholder limit, only the trustee must consent to the corporation's S election). If an election is made, the portion of the trust consisting of the S corporation stock is treated as a separate trust and trust income attributable to the S corporation stock, including gain on the sale of the stock, is taxed to the trust at the highest individual rate, whether or not the income is distributed. The beneficiaries, in turn, are not taxed on any trust distributions attributable to the stock. See I.R.C. § 641(d). This provision is designed to permit discretionary, or "spray" trusts to be S corporation shareholders, which may be desired by shareholders for estate planning purposes. Since each potential current beneficiary of the trust is counted against the 75 shareholder limit, I.R.C. § 1361(c)(2)(B)(v), however, the use of this provision may result in termination of S corporation status if several trusts with a large number of beneficiaries make an election.

Notice 97–49, 1997–36 I.R.B. 8, contains specific rules regarding the identification of the beneficiaries of an electing small business trust. The beneficiaries of an electing small business trust do not include a trust that is a potential future distributee of the electing small business trust, e.g., a trust with a potential future remainder interest. Instead, the beneficiaries of the electing small business trust include the beneficiaries of the distributee trust, who are also treated as shareholders of the S corporation. A person in whose favor a power of appointment may be exercised becomes a beneficiary only on the exercise of the power of appointment. A person with a remote contingent interest that is negligible also is not considered to be a beneficiary for purposes of § 1361(e)(1)(A)(i). If a distributee trust becomes entitled to a distribution of income or principal from an electing small business trust, or may be so entitled at the discretion of any person, the S corporation's election will terminate unless the distributee trust is itself a qualified electing small business trust. A person whose entitlement to a distribution is contingent on a specified event or a specified time is not treated as a current beneficiary until occurrence of the event or passage of the time.

The literal language of § 1361(e)(1)(A)(i) appears to permit individuals as beneficiaries of an electing small business trust without qualification. Thus, the statute on its face may permit nonresident aliens as beneficiaries to hold an indirect interest in an S corporation where they could not do so directly. However, § 1361(c)(2)(B)(v) states that each potential current beneficiary of an electing small business trust shall be treated as a shareholder of the S corporation. The legislative history states that in order to qualify, "all beneficiaries of the trust must be individuals or estates eligible to be S corporation shareholders * * * ." H.R. Rep. No. 104–586, 104th Cong., 2d Sess. 82 (1996). The Internal Revenue Service stated in Notice 97–49, supra, that the potential current beneficiaries of an electing small business trust must be qualifying shareholders of the S corporation for purposes of § 1361(b)(1).

C. POLICY ASPECTS OF THE SEVENTY–FIVE SHAREHOLDER LIMITATION

The legislative history of the Subchapter S Revision Act of 1982, which increased the number of permitted shareholders from 10 to 35, indicated that the 35 stockholder limit was intended to correspond to the private placement exemption of federal securities law.[8] When the ceiling on the number of shareholders was increased from 35 to 75 in 1996, the reason given was to "facilitate corporate ownership by additional family members, employees and capital investors." H.R. Rep. No. 104–586, 104th Cong., 2d Sess. 82 (1996). There is, however, no inherent tax policy rationale for limiting pass through tax treatment to 75 stockholders, as long as the corporation is not publicly traded.[9] If there are too many stockholders,

8. S.Rep. No. 97–640, 97th Cong. 2d Sess. 7 (1982).

9. Section 7704, which treats any partnership that is publicly traded as an association, subject to the corporate income tax, evidences a Congressional intent that passthrough taxation is not appropriate for publicly traded businesses regardless of the form of organization.

however, administrative problems may arise because audits are conducted and tax deficiencies are assessed and collected at the shareholder level. Although limiting the number of stockholders allowed to an S corporation reduces the complexity of accounting for allocations of corporate items to the stockholders, experience with Subchapter K demonstrates that pass-through accounting on a large scale is possible. Nevertheless, was it appropriate for the IRS to "wink" at the form over substance avoidance of the shareholder ceiling in Rev. Rul. 94–43?

B. CORPORATE ELIGIBILITY

INTERNAL REVENUE CODE: Section 1361(a),(b)(1)(D), (b)(2)–(3), (c)(4).

REGULATIONS: Sections 1.1361–1(b), (*l*).

Only a domestic corporation may elect to be an S corporation. A controlled subsidiary of an S corporation cannot itself make an S election because its parent corporation is an ineligible shareholder. Thus, the subsidiary is a C corporation. If, however, the subsidiary is wholly owned by the parent S corporation and the subsidiary would be eligible to be an S corporation if the stock of the corporation were held directly by the shareholders of its parent S corporation, § 1361(b)(3) allows the parent S corporation to elect to ignore the separate existence of its subsidiary for tax purposes and to treat its subsidiary's assets, liabilities, income, and deduction items as its own.

Certain corporations are ineligible for S corporation status. These include small (but not large) banks, insurance companies, and other corporations subject to a special tax regime. I.R.C. § 1362(b)(2).

Under § 1361(b)(1)(D), an S corporation is allowed to have only one class of stock. The purpose of this requirement is to avoid accounting difficulties that would arise if the corporation were permitted to create different interests in income and loss in different classes of stock. Thus, unlike partnerships, S corporations are not allowed to make special allocations of income and loss among S corporation stockholders.

Section 1361(c)(4) allows differences in voting rights without violating the one-class-of-stock rule so long as the outstanding shares are identical with respect to the rights of the holders in the profits and in the assets of the corporation. The existence of debt of an S corporation that might be classified as equity creates a risk that the re-classified equity interests will be treated as a prohibited second class of stock. To reduce this risk, § 1361(c)(5) provides a safe-harbor in which certain "straight debt" will not be considered a second class of stock.

Revenue Ruling 85–161*

1985–2 C.B. 191

ISSUE

Will the stock purchase agreement described below cause a corporation to be treated as having more than one class of stock within the meaning of Section 1361(b)(1)(D) of the Internal Revenue Code?

FACTS

Corporation X has two classes of stock issued and outstanding: voting common stock and nonvoting common stock. The nonvoting stock is held by A, B, and C, siblings, and by D, an unrelated individual who is an officer of the corporation. A and B own all the voting stock. The voting and nonvoting shares are identical other than with respect to voting rights and other than as provided in a shareholder's agreement described below.

X and all the shareholders of X have entered into an agreement with respect to the transfer of D's stock. Under the agreement, D may transfer D's stock only after obtaining the consent of the holders of voting stock in X. If such consent cannot be obtained, D may sell the stock only to the corporation or the other shareholders at book value. Other provisions of the agreement give X or the other shareholders the right to purchase D's stock in the event of D's termination of employment or disability and upon D's death.

X filed an election to be an S corporation under section 1362 of the Code with respect to its taxable year beginning January 1, 1984.

LAW AND ANALYSIS

Section 1361(b)(1)(D) of the Code provides that the term "small business corporation" means a corporation that does not have more than one class of stock.

Section 1361(c)(4) of the Code provides that for purposes of section 1361(b)(1)(D), a corporation will not be treated as having more than one class of stock solely because there are differences in voting rights among the shares of common stock.

Although there may be differences in the voting rights among the shares of common stock, the outstanding shares of a corporation must be identical as to the rights of the holders in the profits and in the assets of the corporation. S. Rep. No. 97–640, 97th Cong., 2d Sess. 8 (1982), 1982–2 C.B. 718, 721.

In this case, all shares of X's stock are equal with respect to rights to profits and rights in the assets of the corporation. The agreement restricting the transfer of D's stock does not affect D's interest in corporate profits or corporate assets while D is a shareholder. Therefore, X does not have

* Obsoleted by Rev. Rul. 95–71, 1995–2 C.B. 323. The issue addressed in Rev. Rul. 85–161 is now addressed in Treas. Reg. § 1.1361–1(*l*)(2)(iii).

more than one class of stock within the meaning of section 1361(b)(1)(D) of the Code.

HOLDING

The stock purchase agreement with respect to stock held by D will not cause the corporation to be treated as having more than one class of stock for purposes of section 1361(b)(1)(D) of the Code.

ILLUSTRATIVE MATERIAL

A. ONE CLASS OF STOCK

1. *General*

Treas. Reg. § 1.1361–1(*l*)(1) provides that a corporation has one class of stock if all of the outstanding shares of stock of the corporation confer identical rights to current distributions and liquidation proceeds. Differences in voting rights are disregarded. The determination of whether stock possesses identical distribution and liquidation rights is made under the formal governing provisions applicable to the corporation, including state law, the corporate charter, articles of incorporation, bylaws, and binding agreements relating to distributions and liquidation proceeds. Treas. Reg. § 1.1361–1(*l*)(2)(i). Contractual arrangements, such as a lease or a loan, will not be treated as a binding agreement regarding distributions or liquidation proceeds, and thus not a governing instrument, unless the principal purpose of the agreement is to circumvent the one class of stock requirement. Treas. Reg. § 1.1361–1(*l*)(2)(i) provides that "distributions * * * that differ with respect to either timing or amount are to be given appropriate tax effect in accordance with the facts and circumstances." Treas. Reg. § 1.1361–1(*l*)(2)(v), Ex. (3)–(5), indicates that an agreement (that is not included in the corporate governing provisions) that results in payments to shareholder-employees of excessive compensation that are not allowed as a deduction, makes fringe benefits available to employee-shareholders, or provides below market-rate loans to shareholders, will not be treated as creating a second class of stock if the arrangement is not entered into to circumvent the one class of stock requirement.

The single class of stock limitation has been interpreted strictly. In Paige v. United States, 580 F.2d 960 (9th Cir.1978), a second class of stock was created as a result of conditions imposed by the California Department of Corporations on stock held by stockholders transferring property to the corporation. Similar conditions were not imposed on stockholders who had transferred cash to the corporation. Among the conditions were restrictions preventing dividend or liquidation distributions to the property stockholders until the cash stockholders received cumulative dividends equal to 5 percent of the purchase price. The result in *Paige* has been incorporated in Treas. Reg. § 1.1361–1(*l*)(2)(v), Ex. (1).

Treas. Reg. § 1.1361–1(*l*)(2)(i) refers to "outstanding shares of stock" for purposes of the one-class of stock rules, and Treas. Reg. § 1.1371–1(g) provides that stock is counted only if it is issued and outstanding. Thus, unissued or treasury stock of a different class than the outstanding stock should not create a second class of stock. In addition, Treas. Reg. § 1.1361–1(b)(3) provides that stock which has not been included in income by the holder under § 83 because it is substantially nonvested will not be treated as outstanding stock. However, restricted stock for which an election has been made under § 83(b) is taken into account in determining whether there is a second class of stock, but the stock will not be treated as a second class if rights to distributions and liquidation proceeds are identical to unrestricted stock. Treas. Reg. § 1.1361–1(*l*)(3). Instruments held as part of a deferred compensation plan that are not required to be taken into income by beneficiaries of the plan (e.g., stock appreciation rights) are not treated as a second class of stock. Treas. Reg. § 1.1361–1(b)(4).

2. *Voting Rights*

Section 1361(c)(4) allows variations in voting rights among the shares of common stock, including the issuance of nonvoting common stock, without creating a second class of stock. This provision settled an issue that also gave rise to litigation under the pre–1983 Subchapter S provisions. See e.g. Parker Oil Co. v. Commissioner, 58 T.C. 985 (1972) (A) (stockholders' agreement providing that the right to vote certain shares was irrevocably granted by proxy to an unrelated third party did not create a second class of stock); Rev.Rul. 73–611, 1973–2 C.B. 312 (agreed with *Parker Oil,* but stated that if differences in voting rights, etc., arise from the articles of incorporation as such, rather than from agreements between stockholders and third parties, a second class of stock would result), obsoleted by Rev. Rul. 95–71, 1995–2 C.B. 323.

3. *Options*

Call options, warrants and similar instruments will be treated as a second class of stock if, under the facts and circumstances, (1) the option is substantially certain to be exercised and (2) has an exercise price substantially below the fair market value of the underlying stock on the date the option is (a) issued (unless fair market value at exercise is used), (b) transferred by a person who is an eligible shareholder to a person who is not an eligible shareholder, or (c) materially modified. Treas. Reg. § 1.1361–1(*l*)(4)(iii)(A). A safe harbor exception applies if the exercise price is at least 90 percent of the fair market value of the underlying stock on the date the option is issued, transferred to an ineligible shareholder, or modified. Treas. Reg. § 1.1361–1(*l*)(4)(iii)(C). Additional exceptions are provided for call options issued in connection with a loan to the corporation by a person regularly engaged in the business of lending, or issued to an employee or independent contractor in connection with the performance of services if the call option is nontransferable and does not have a readily ascertainable fair market value at the time the option is issued. Treas. Reg. § 1.1361–1(*l*)(4)(iii)(B).

4. *Debt Reclassified as Equity*

The one class of stock requirement was the subject of considerable litigation for years prior to 1983, but the straight debt safe harbor of

§ 1361(c)(5), enacted in 1982, has reduced the tension in this area. The Senate Finance Committee Report explained the provision as follows:

"In order to insure that the corporation's election will not terminate in certain situations where the existence of a purported debt instrument (that otherwise would be classified as stock) may not lead to tax avoidance and does not cause undue complexity, the bill provides that an instrument which is straight debt will not be treated as a second class of stock (within the meaning of sec. 1361(b)(1)(D)), and therefore cannot disqualify a Subchapter S election. For this purpose, a straight debt instrument means a written unconditional promise to pay on demand or on a specified date a sum certain in money so long as the interest rate, and payment date are fixed. For this purpose these factors are fixed if they are not contingent on the profits of the corporation, the discretion of the corporation, or other similar factors. However, the fact that the interest rate is dependent upon the prime rate or a similar factor not related to the debtor corporation will not disqualify the instrument from being treated under the safe harbor. In order for the 'safe harbor' to apply, the instrument must not be convertible into stock, and must be held by a person eligible to hold Subchapter S stock."[10]

Section 1361(c)(5) was amended in 1996 to add to the list of eligible holders of straight debt "a person which is actively and regularly engaged in the business of lending money." This amendment was intended to extend the straight debt safe harbor to loans from financial institutions, even though most financial institutions are not eligible to be shareholders. The rationale for this provision is that it generally is unlikely that a loan from a financial institution in the business of lending money is a disguised equity interest.

Treas. Reg. § 1.1361–1(*l*)(5)(i) provides that for debt to qualify for the straight debt safe harbor it must be: (1) an unconditional written obligation to pay a sum certain on demand or on a specified date, that is not convertible into an equity interest; (2) held by a person or trust eligible to be an S corporation shareholder (a limitation that must be qualified by the subsequent amendment to § 1361(c)(5) permitting financial institutions to hold straight debt); and (3) neither the timing nor amount of payments of interest and principal can be contingent on the corporation's profits. Subordination of the debt to other corporate debt does not prevent its treatment as straight debt. Treas. Reg. § 1.1361–1(*l*)(5)(ii). Although instruments qualifying as straight debt are treated as debt for tax purposes, Treas. Reg. § 1.1361–1(*l*)(5)(iv) provides that the payment of an unreasonably high rate of interest may be classified as a payment that is not interest. The regulations add, however, that the payment will not be treated as creating a second class of stock.

Treas. Reg. § 1.1361–1(*l*)(4)(ii)(B)(*2*) provides that proportionately held debt reclassified as equity will not constitute a second class of stock. In a somewhat similar vein, Treas. Reg. § 1.1361–1(*l*)(4)(ii)(A) provides that

10. S.Rep. No. 97–640, 97th Cong., 2d Sess. 8 (1982).

debt reclassified as equity will not be treated as a second class of stock unless a principal purpose of issuing the instrument was to circumvent the rights to distribution or liquidation proceeds conferred by the outstanding shares of stock or to circumvent the limitations on eligible shareholders. Furthermore, unwritten advances from a shareholder that are reclassified as equity and that do not exceed $10,000 in the aggregate, are treated by the parties as debt, and are expected to be repaid within a reasonable period of time, will not be treated as a second class of stock. Treas. Reg. § 1.1361–1(*l*)(4)(ii)(B)(1). Failure of an unwritten advance to comply with the safe harbor will not create a second class unless the advance is reclassified as equity *and* a principal purpose of making the advance was to circumvent the rights to distribution or liquidation proceeds conferred by the outstanding shares of stock or to circumvent the limitations on eligible shareholders.

The potential classification of purported debt instruments as a second class of stock remains a problem if debt is convertible, held by a corporation related to a shareholder, or otherwise falls outside of the safe harbors. Treas. Reg. § 1.1361–1(*l*)(4)(iv) provides that debt convertible into equity will be treated as a second class of stock if the debt is reclassified as equity and a principal purpose of issuing the instrument was to circumvent the rights to distributions or liquidation proceeds conferred by the outstanding shares of stock or to circumvent the limitations on eligible shareholders. Convertible debt will also be classified as a second class of stock if it embodies rights equivalent to a call option that is substantially certain to be exercised and which has a conversion price that is substantially below the fair market value of the underlying stock on the date of issuance, on the date of transfer to a person who is not an eligible shareholder, or on the date of a material modification.

5. *Policy Analysis*

There is no strong policy or administrative reason for prohibiting S corporations from issuing nonparticipating preferred stock. In 1995, legislation that would have permitted S corporations to issue nonparticipating preferred stock was considered, but not enacted. Dividends paid with respect to such stock would be treated as interest, deductible to the corporation, i.e., the deduction would pass through to the common shareholders and the dividends would be includable by the preferred shareholders without regard to corporate earnings. S. 758, 104th Cong., 1st Sess. § 201. See Staff of the Joint Committee on Taxation, Present Laws and Proposals Relating to Subchapter S Corporations and Home Office Deductions, p.29 (JCS–16–95, May 24, 1995).

B. AFFILIATED GROUPS

1. *Eighty Percent Controlled Subchapter C Subsidiaries*

Prior to 1997, an S corporation could not be part of an affiliated group of corporations as defined in § 1504. This meant that an S corporation could not own stock of an 80 percent or more controlled subsidiary. The limitation was repealed by the 1996 Act, thereby permitting an S corporation to own 80 percent or more of the stock of a subsidiary that is a C corporation. Such a C corporation subsidiary may elect to join in the filing of a consolidated return, discussed in Chapter 10, Section 2, with its affiliated C corporations (chains of controlled corporations of which the subsidiary is the common parent), but the S corporation parent is not allowed to join in the consolidated return. See I.R.C. § 1504(b)(8). On the other hand, because a corporation that has another corporation as a shareholder is not eligible to make an S election, a subsidiary of another corporation may not be an S corporation. However, § 1361(b)(3) provides a special rule for "qualified Subchapter S subsidiaries."

2. *Qualified Subchapter S Subsidiaries*

A qualified Subchapter S subsidiary (QSSS) is any domestic corporation that (1) is not an ineligible corporation, (2) is wholly owned by an S corporation, and (3) the parent S corporation elects to treat as a QSSS. I.R.C. § 1361(b)(3)(B). Election procedures are described in Notice 97–4, 1997–1 C.B. 351 and Prop. Reg. § 1.1361–3(a) (1998). A corporation for which a QSSS election is made is not treated as a separate corporation. Transactions between the S corporation parent and the qualified S corporation subsidiary are not taken into account for tax purposes. All assets, liabilities, and items of income, deduction, and credit of the QSSS are treated as assets, liabilities, and items of income, deduction, and credit of the parent S corporation. See Prop. Reg. § 1.1361–4(a)(1) (1998). The existence of the stock of a QSSS thus is ignored for tax purposes. See Prop. Reg. § 1.1361–4(a)(4) (1998). If a QSSS election is made for a newly formed subsidiary, the subsidiary is treated as a QSSS from its inception—the parent and subsidiary both are treated as if the subsidiary never had been formed. In the case of a preexisting subsidiary, as a result of a QSSS election the subsidiary is deemed to have liquidated under §§ 332 and 337 immediately before the election is effective. See Prop. Reg. § 1.1361–4(a)(2), (b) (1998); see also S. Rep. No. 281, 104th Cong., 2d Sess. 53 (1996); H.R. Rep. No. 586, 104th Cong., 2d Sess. 89 (1996).[11]

Prop. Reg. § 1.1361–3(a)(3) (1998) would allow the effective date of a QSSS election to be any specified date within 2 months and 15 days prior to, or not more than 12 months after, the date the election is made. Unlike an S election, a QSSS election does not have to be made within 2 months and 15 days of the beginning of a taxable year.

A QSSS election may be revoked as of any specified date within 2 months and 15 days prior to, or not more than 12 months after, the date of the revocation. Prop. Reg. § 1.1361–3(b)(2) (1998). A QSSS that ceases to qualify under § 1361(b)(3)(B) or whose election has been revoked is treated as a new corporation that has acquired all of its assets and assumed all of its liabilities from its S corporation parent in exchange for the subsidiary's

11. The legislative history of a technical correction made by the 1997 Act indicates that regulations may provide exceptions to this general rule. See S. Rep. No. 33, 105th Cong., 1st Sess. 320 (1997).

stock immediately before the cessation of QSSS status. I.R.C. § 1361(b)(3)(C); Prop. Reg. § 1.1361–5(b)(1) (1998). This hypothetical transaction would be governed by § 351 and its associated sections. A QSSS whose election has terminated may not have a QSSS election made with respect to it (or, if its stock is acquired by eligible shareholders, make an S election itself) before its fifth taxable year that begins after the first taxable year for which the termination is effective without the Service's consent. I.R.C. § 1361(b)(3)(D); Prop. Reg. § 1.1361–5(d) (1998). Relief for inadvertent terminations, using the same standards as apply under § 1361(f), would be provided by Prop. Reg. § 1.1361–5(c) (1998). In addition, if a QSSS election is terminated by reason of the disposition of the stock of the subsidiary by the parent, the new owners may make an immediate S election, without the consent of the IRS, provided that there has been no intervening period in which the corporation was a C corporation. Prop. Reg. § 1.1361–5(d)(2) (1998).

C. S Corporation Election Procedures

Internal Revenue Code: Section 1362(a), (b), (c), and (f).

Regulations: Sections 1.1362–1,–6.

A Subchapter S election is made by the corporation, but the election is valid only if all of the stockholders file consents to this election. I.R.C. § 1362(a). After an election has been made, new stockholders are not required to consent. A stockholder individually cannot directly revoke or terminate an election, but undertaking a transaction that causes the corporation no longer to qualify for S corporation status may have that effect. See page 382.

An election made any time during the taxable year will be effective for the corporation's next succeeding taxable year. I.R.C. § 1362(b)(1)(A). Section 1362(b)(1)(B) provides for an election retroactive to the first day of the taxable year if the election is made on or before the fifteenth day of the third month of the taxable year. However, a retroactive election is effective for the taxable year in which made only if the corporation meets all of the requirements for S corporation status during the portion of the taxable year preceding the filing of the election and all of the stockholders consent to the election, including stockholders who were stockholders before the election was filed but who are no longer stockholders at the time of the election. I.R.C. § 1362(b)(2); Treas. Reg. § 1.1362–6(a)(2)(ii)(B). This requirement is intended to avoid an allocation of income and loss to pre-election stockholders who were either ineligible to hold S corporation stock or who did not consent to the election.[12] If the corporation and its stockholders were not qualified to elect S corporation status during each day of the portion of the taxable year preceding a retroactive election, the election will be effective on the first day of the next taxable year. I.R.C. § 1362(b)(3).

12. S.Rep. No. 97–640, 97th Cong., 2d Sess. 11 (1982).

ILLUSTRATIVE MATERIAL

A. STOCKHOLDER CONSENTS

Section 1362(a)(2) requires the consent of all stockholders of the corporation as of the day of the election. See Kean v. Commissioner, 469 F.2d 1183 (9th Cir.1972) (consent was required from the beneficial owner of stock of an electing corporation even though the person was not included on the corporate books as a stockholder of record); Cabintaxi Corp. v. Commissioner, T.C. Memo. 1994–316, aff'd, 63 F.3d 614 (7th Cir.1995) (election must be joined in by all persons who have contributed equity capital, not merely those to whom stock certificates have been issued; whether a person is a shareholder for this purpose depends on whether the person would have been required to report income from the S corporation if it were profitable and a valid election had been made). See Treas. Reg. § 1.1362–6 for procedural aspects of shareholder consents and extensions of time for filing consents.

Although husband and wife are treated as a single stockholder, Treas. Reg. § 1.1362–6(b)(2)(i) requires that both consent to the election if they own the stock as community property, tenants in common, joint tenants, or as tenants by the entirety. In Wilson v. Commissioner, 560 F.2d 687 (5th Cir.1977), the record owner of a single share of stock who lived in a community property state, held the stock as an accommodation to other stockholders. He filed a consent to the corporation's S election but his wife did not. The court held that the husband had no beneficial interest in the stock and was therefore not required to consent to the corporation's S election. Thus his wife's consent was also unnecessary.

Section 1362(f) authorizes the Commissioner to waive a defect rendering an election ineffective because all of the required shareholder consents (including QSST elections) were not obtained in a timely manner if (1) the defect was inadvertent, (2) within a reasonable period of time the corporation obtains the shareholder consents, and (3) the corporation and the shareholders all agree to report as if the S corporation had been effective originally. See also Treas. Reg. § 1.1362–6(b)(3)(iii), providing for a waiver of the timely shareholder consent requirement in certain circumstances for years prior to the amendment of § 1362(f) to deal with this problem.

B. CORPORATE ELECTION

With respect to a newly formed corporation, it is necessary to identify the date on which the taxable year begins in order to determine whether an election has been filed on or before the fifteenth day of the third month of the taxable year. Treas. Reg. § 1.1362–6(a)(2)(ii)(C) provides that the taxable year of a new corporation begins on the date the corporation has stockholders, acquires assets, or begins doing business, whichever is the first to occur. See Bone v. Commissioner, 52 T.C. 913 (1969) (first taxable year had begun when the corporation acquired assets and engaged in business even though no stock had been issued to stockholders; under state law the issuance of stock was not a prerequisite to corporate existence).

Treas. Reg. § 1.1362–6(a)(2)(ii)(C) provides that a month is measured from the first day of the corporation's taxable year to the day preceding the same numerical date of the following month, or the last day of the month if there is no corresponding date in the succeeding month. Treas. Reg. § 1.1362–6(a)(2)(iii), Ex. (1), promulgated before the 1996 amendments to § 1362(f), indicates that an election filed before the corporation begins its first taxable year will not be valid. Presumably, the 1996 amendments to § 1362(f) now permit the Service to treat such a premature election as an effective election.

Section 1362(b)(5) permits the Commissioner to waive a late election for "reasonable cause." Rev.Proc. 98–55, 1998–46 I.R.B. 27, provides detailed procedures for seeking relief from a late election under § 1362(b)(5). If the only defect was a late filed Form 2553 (the corporate election itself) and the due date for the first corporate tax return (excluding extensions) has not passed, relief is virtually automatic if the election is filed within twelve months of the original due date and there was reasonable cause for the failure to file a timely S Corporation election. Otherwise, a private letter ruling seeking relief under § 1362(b)(5) must be requested.

Under Rev.Proc. 97–48, 1997–43 I.R.B. 19, later is better. Rev.Proc. 97–48 provides automatic relief for late filed elections that are made at least six months after the date on which the corporation filed its tax return for the first year the corporation intended to be treated as an S corporation. Automatic relief is provided under Rev.Proc. 97–48 if the corporation fails to qualify as an S corporation because its election was not timely, the corporation and all of its shareholders reported their income consistent with S corporation status for the year in which the election should have been made and for all subsequent years. Automatic relief is available to the corporation and its shareholders even where the Internal Revenue Service has notified the corporation of an invalid election and has indicated that the corporation must file as a C corporation, as long as the statute of limitations has not lapsed with respect to either the corporation or any of its shareholders for years that the corporation intended to be treated as an S corporation. In order to seek automatic relief from a late filed election, the election must be signed by a corporate officer and all persons who were shareholders during the period the corporation is to be treated as an S corporation. The corporation and the shareholders must certify that returns were filed consistent with S corporation status, or in the case of a corporation notified by the service that its S status in invalid, the corporation and shareholders must agree to amend their returns to reflect S corporation status.

Rev.Proc. 98–55, supra, also provides procedures for automatic relief for late QSST elections under § 1361(d)(2), late ESBT elections under § 1361 (e)(3), and late QSSS elections under § 1361(b)(3)(B), if certain qualifying conditions have been met. Rev.Proc. 97–98, however, does not apply to elections that are invalid because of late shareholder elections, such as a failure to file a ESBT or QSST election. If relief under Rev.Proc.

98–55 is not available in one of these cases, relief must be sought through application for a private letter ruling.

D. Revocation or Termination of S Corporation Status

Internal Revenue Code: Section 1362(d), (e), (f) and (g).

Regulations: Section 1.1362–2(a) and (b),–3,–4,–5.

An S corporation election is effective for the taxable year to which it first applies and all succeeding taxable years until revoked or terminated. S corporation status may be ended in three ways: voluntary revocation by stockholders holding a majority of the S corporation stock, failure to comply with the requirements for S corporation status, or receipt of passive investment income in excess of 25 percent of gross income for three consecutive years if the corporation has Subchapter C previously accumulated and undistributed earnings and profits in those years.[13] Section 1362(d)(1) provides that a voluntary revocation of S corporation status by stockholders can be effective on the date specified by the revocation. Termination of S corporation status because the corporation or its stockholders subsequently fail to meet the initial requirements for eligibility is effective on the date the corporation ceases to qualify as an S corporation. I.R.C. § 1362(d)(2). The S corporation's taxable year ends on the day preceding the effective date of a revocation or termination and a new taxable year begins for the corporation as a C corporation on the following day. I.R.C. § 1362(e). Items of income and deduction must be allocated between the corporation's short Subchapter S and Subchapter C taxable years.

ILLUSTRATIVE MATERIAL

A. TERMINATION BY VOLUNTARY REVOCATION

Section 1362(d)(1) allows revocation of an S election by stockholders owning a majority of outstanding stock. A revocation made on or before the fifteenth day of the third month of the taxable year will be retroactively effective as of the first day of the taxable year. Otherwise, a revocation is effective on the first day of the next taxable year. Alternatively, the revocation may specify an effective date as long as the date specified is subsequent to the date of the revocation. Treas. Reg. § 1.1362–2(a)(2)(ii) requires that the date be specified in terms of a day, month, and year, rather than in terms of a particular event. Treas. Reg. § 1.1362–2(a)(4) also allows rescission of a voluntary prospective revocation at any time before the revocation becomes effective. Rescission requires the consent of any person who consented to the revocation and any person who became a stockholder of the corporation after the revocation was filed.

13. The rules governing an S corporation with a prior history as a C corporation are discussed in Section 4 of this Chapter.

Section 1362(e) requires that in any taxable year in which the S corporation election terminates effective on a date other than the first day of the taxable year, income and deduction items must be allocated between the portion of the year the corporation is qualified as an S corporation and the portion of the year the corporation is treated as a C corporation. This rule is discussed at page 396.

B. INADVERTENT TERMINATION

A corporation's S election terminates immediately upon an event that disqualifies the corporation or one of its stockholders under the initial requirements for S corporation status. I.R.C. § 1361(d)(2). However, the savings clause of § 1362(f) allows the Commissioner to overlook an inadvertent termination if (1) the Commissioner determines that disqualification was inadvertent, (2) the corporation and/or its stockholders take steps to remedy the disqualifying event within a reasonable period after discovery, and (3) the corporation and each stockholder agree to such adjustments as the Commissioner may prescribe. The Senate Finance Committee indicated that it "intends that the Internal Revenue Service be reasonable in granting waivers, so that corporations whose Subchapter S eligibility requirements have been inadvertently violated do not suffer the tax consequences of a termination if no tax avoidance would result from the continued Subchapter S treatment."[14]

Treas. Reg. § 1.1362–4(b) provides that the burden of establishing that termination is inadvertent under the facts and circumstances is on the corporation. The regulations add: "The fact that the terminating event was not reasonably within the control of the corporation and was not part of a plan to terminate the election, or the fact that the event took place without the knowledge of the corporation notwithstanding its due diligence in the course of its business to safeguard itself against such an event, tends to establish that the termination was inadvertent." See Rev. Proc. 94–23, 1994–1 C.B. 609 (granting automatic inadvertent termination relief to S corporations when stock is transferred to a QSST, whose beneficiary inadvertently fails to file an election, if the beneficiary files the election and the corporation and all shareholders report income as if a timely election had been filed). Rev.Rul. 86–110, 1986–2 C.B. 150, granted inadvertent termination relief to an S corporation that lost its eligibility because the majority stockholders transferred stock to trusts for the stockholder's children. The stockholder acted on the advice of counsel that the transfer would not disqualify the corporation's S election and would not have made the transfer but for the advice of counsel. Private letter rulings issued by the Internal Revenue Service indicate that it is quite lenient in applying the authority granted under § 1362(f).

C. TRANSFER TO INELIGIBLE OWNER BY MINORITY STOCKHOLDER

May a minority stockholder intentionally and unilaterally, to the detriment of other shareholders, terminate an S election by transferring

14. S.Rep. No. 97–640, 97th Cong., 2d Sess. 12 (1982).

stock to a disqualified person or by otherwise taking action to fail the initial requirements for S corporation status? In T.J. Henry Associates, Inc. v. Commissioner, 80 T.C. 886 (1983)(A), the controlling stockholder of a Subchapter S corporation transferred a single share of stock to himself as custodian for his children under a Uniform Gifts to Minors statute. The transfer was intended to terminate the corporation's S election.[15] The Tax Court rejected the Commissioner's assertion that the transfer was not a bona fide transfer of beneficial ownership of the stock and that the stockholder acted as a custodian for his children merely as an accommodation. The Tax Court further held that, so long as there is a bona fide transfer of beneficial ownership, a transfer deliberately made to disqualify an S election should be recognized. The Internal Revenue Service has acquiesced in this result. 1984–1 C.B. 1.

The result in *T.J. Henry Associates, Inc.* permits a single shareholder to terminate an S election without the consent of majority stockholders, which otherwise is required for voluntary revocation under § 1361(d)(1). Provisions in corporate documents and shareholder agreements often seek to limit the shareholder's ability to make a stock transfer that would terminate the corporation's S election. While not always effective to prevent termination, such provisions might give rise to civil liability for shareholders undertaking disqualifying events.

D. ELECTION FOLLOWING REVOCATION OR TERMINATION OF S CORPORATION STATUS

Under § 1362(g), if an S corporation election is revoked or terminated the corporation or its successor is not eligible to make a new election for five years unless the Commissioner consents to an earlier election. Treas. Reg. § 1.1362–5(a) provides that consent ordinarily will be denied unless it can be shown that the event causing termination was not reasonably within the control of the corporation or stockholders having a substantial interest in the corporation and was not part of a plan to terminate the election. The regulations also provide that consent should be granted if more than 50 percent of the corporation's stock is owned by persons who were not stockholders at the time the election was terminated. Private letter rulings reflect a rather relaxed approach on the part of the Commissioner in granting the requisite consent.

E. COORDINATION WITH SUBCHAPTER C

INTERNAL REVENUE CODE: Section 1371.

Section 1371 contains rules coordinating the treatment of items that affect both Subchapter S and Subchapter C years when a former C corporation elects S corporation status or an S corporation revokes or terminates its Subchapter S election.

15. With respect to the taxable year involved, § 1372(e)(1) required an affirmative consent to the election by a new stockholder in order to maintain S corporation status. The stockholder in *T.J. Henry Assoc., Inc.* did not file the requisite consent.

There are no carrybacks or carryovers of loss or other items from Subchapter C years to Subchapter S years and vice versa. I.R.C. § 1371(b). Thus, a carryover of net operating losses incurred in a Subchapter C year will not be available to reduce S corporation income taxable to the stockholders. See Rosenberg v. Commissioner, 96 T.C. 451 (1991) (shareholders of former C corporation that elected S corporation status when it had unused net operating loss carryovers attributable to the development of condominiums could not exclude gain from the subsequent sale of the condominium units under the tax benefit rule). See also Frederick v. Commissioner, 101 T.C. 35 (1993) (shareholders of an S corporation were required to include under the tax benefit rule of § 111 a "recovery" of accrued but unpaid interest expense by an S corporation deducted in a prior year when the corporation was a C corporation).

The period during which the S election is in effect will be counted in determining the number of years during which a carryforward or carryback is available. I.R.C. § 1371(b)(3). In the case of a former S corporation, however, losses will have passed through to stockholders who may carry-over losses on their individual returns to a year following revocation of the S election.

St. Charles Investment Co. v. Commissioner, 110 T.C. 46 (1998), involved an S corporation that prior to making its S election had been subject to § 469 as a closely held C corporation. The corporation had unused passive activity loss carryovers from the period that it had been a C corporation. The court held that under § 1371(b)(1), the passive activity loss carryovers from C corporation years could not be claimed against passive activity income recognized in S corporation years. Furthermore, to the extent depreciation deductions contributed to the disallowed passive activity loss, the basis of the depreciable property was reduced by the otherwise allowable depreciation deductions. On a subsequent sale of the property (that was not part of the complete disposition of the activity in which the property was used) the basis of the depreciable asset was not recomputed by adding back disallowed losses attributable to the suspended depreciation deductions to reduce gain recognized on the sale of the depreciable asset. That the depreciation deductions had not yet produced a tax benefit, and might never produce a benefit unless the conditions for releasing them from suspension were met, was said to be irrelevant.

SECTION 3. EFFECT OF THE SUBCHAPTER S ELECTION BY A CORPORATION WITH NO C CORPORATION HISTORY

A. PASSTHROUGH OF INCOME AND LOSS

(1) GENERAL PRINCIPLES

INTERNAL REVENUE CODE: Sections 1363; 1366(a)-(e); 1367; 1378; 444.

REGULATIONS: Sections 1.1367–1; 1.1367–2; 1.1368–1(g).

PROPOSED REGULATIONS: Sections 1.1366–1,–2; 1.1367–1(f), (h), Ex. 2; 1.1368–1(e)(2).

Senate Finance Committee Report, Subchapter S Revision Act of 1982

S.Rep. No. 97–640, 97th Cong., 2d Sess. 15–18 (1982).

In general

The bill sets forth new rules for the taxation of income earned by, and the allowance of losses incurred by, subchapter S corporations. These rules generally follow the * * * rules governing the taxation of partners with respect to items of partnership income and loss.

Computation of corporate items

A subchapter S corporation's taxable income will be computed under the same rules presently applicable to partnerships under section 703, except that the amortization of organization expenditures under section 248 will be an allowable deduction. As in the case of partnerships, deductions generally allowable to individuals will be allowed to subchapter S corporations, but provisions of the Code governing the computation of taxable income which are applicable only to corporations, such as the dividends received deduction (sec. 243) or the special rules relating to corporate tax preferences (sec. 291), will not apply. Items, the separate treatment which could affect the liability of any shareholder (such as investment interest) will be treated separately. Elections will generally be made at the corporate level, except for those elections which the partners of a partnership may make separately (such as the election to claim the foreign tax credit).

Generally subchapter C will apply, except that a subchapter S corporation will be treated in the same manner as an individual in transactions, such as the treatment of dividends received under section 301, where the corporation is a shareholder in a regular corporation. Provisions relating to transactions by a subchapter S corporation with respect to its own stock will be treated as if the S corporation were a regular corporation. However, the subchapter C rules are not to apply where the result would be inconsistent with the purpose of the subchapter S rules which treat the corporation as a passthrough entity.

Passthrough of items

The following examples illustrate the operation of the bill's passthrough rules:

a. *Capital gains and losses.*—Gains or losses from sales or exchanges of capital assets will pass through to the shareholders as capital gains or losses. Net capital gains will no longer be offset by ordinary losses at the corporate level.

b. *Section 1231 gains and losses.*—The gains and losses on certain property used in a trade or business will be passed through separately and will be aggregated with the shareholder's other section 1231 gains and losses. Thus, section 1231 gains will no longer be aggregated with capital gains at the corporate level and passed through as capital gains.

c. *Charitable contributions.*—The corporate 10–percent limitation will no longer apply to contributions by the corporation. As in the case of partnerships, the contributions will pass through to the shareholders, at which level they will be subject to the individual limitations on deductibility.

d. *Tax-exempt interest.*—Tax-exempt interest will pass through to the shareholders as such and will increase the shareholders' basis in their subchapter S stock. Subsequent distributions by a corporation will not result in taxation of the tax-exempt income. (See discussion below for rules relating to corporate distributions.)

* * *

f. *Credits.*—As with partnerships, items involved in the determination of credits, * * * will pass through to the subchapter S corporation's shareholders.

* * *

i. *Other items.*—Limitations on the * * * expensing of certain depreciable business assets (sec. 179), and the amortization of reforestation expenditures (sec. 194) will apply at both the corporate level and shareholder level, as in the case of partnerships. Exclusions of income from discharge of indebtedness will be determined at the shareholder level (sec. 108). * * *

Carryovers from years in which the corporation was not a subchapter S corporation will not be allowed to the corporation while in subchapter S status.

Shareholders treatment of items

In general.—As with the partners of a partnership, each shareholder of a subchapter S corporation will take into account separately his or her pro rata share of items of income, deduction, credit, etc., of the corporation. These rules parallel the partnership rules under section 702.

Each shareholder's share of the items will be taken into account in the shareholder's taxable year in which the corporation's year ends. In the case of the death of a shareholder, the shareholder's portion of subchapter S items will be taken into account on the shareholder's final income tax return. Items from the portion of the corporation's taxable year after the shareholder's death will be taken into account by the estate or other person acquiring the stock.

* * * In cases of transfers of subchapter S stock during the taxable year, income, losses, and credits will be allocated in essentially the same manner as when the election terminates during the year. Thus, the allocation generally will be made on a per-share, per-day basis unless the corporation, with the consent of its shareholders, elected to allocate according to its permanent records (including work papers).

A "conduit" rule for determining the character of items realized by the corporation and included in the shareholder's pro rata share will be the same as the partnership rule (sec. 702(b)). Under the partnership rules, this has generally resulted in an entity level characterization. Also, the "gross income" determinations made by a shareholder will parallel the partnership rule (sec. 702(c)).

Worthless stock.—If the corporation's stock becomes worthless in any taxable year of the corporation or shareholder, the corporate items for that year will be taken into account by the shareholders and the adjustments to the stock's basis will be made before the stock's worthlessness is taken into account under section 165(g).

Family members.—Under [section 1366(e)], items taken into account by members of the family (whether or not themselves shareholders) wherever it is necessary to reflect reasonable compensation to the shareholder for services rendered or capital furnished to the corporation may be properly adjusted. Both the amount of compensation and the timing of the compensation can be so adjusted.

Loss limitations.—As under [pre–1983] law, a shareholder's allowable pro rata share of the corporation's loss will be limited to the sum of the shareholder's adjusted basis in the stock of the corporation plus the shareholder's adjusted basis of any indebtedness of the corporation to the shareholder. However, unlike [pre–1983] law, disallowed losses can be carried forward or allowed in any subsequent year in which the shareholder has adequate basis in such stock or debt.

* * *

Terminated election.—Subsequent to a termination of a subchapter S election, these disallowed losses will be allowed if the shareholder's basis in his stock in the corporation is restored by the later of the following dates:

(1) One year after the effective date of the termination, or the due date for the last subchapter S return, whichever is later; or

(2) 120 days after a determination that the corporation's subchapter S election had terminated for a previous year. (A determination will be defined as a court decision which becomes final, a closing agreement, or an agreement between the corporation and the Internal Revenue Service that the corporation failed to qualify.)

3. Basis adjustment (sec. 1367)

Under [section 1367(a)], both taxable and nontaxable income and deductible and nondeductible expenses will serve, respectively, to increase and decrease a subchapter S shareholder's basis in the stock of the corporation. These rules generally will be analogous to those provided for partnerships under section 705. [Section 1368(d) requires that adjustments to basis as a result of distributions be taken into account under section 1367(a) prior to applying the rule of section 1366(d) limiting shareholder loss deductions to basis.]* Unlike the partnership rules, however, to the extent property distributions are treated as a return of basis, basis will be reduced by the fair market value of these properties * * *. Any passthrough of income for a particular year (allocated according to the proportion of stock held in the corporation) will first increase the shareholder's basis in loans to the corporation to the extent the basis was previously reduced by the passthrough of losses.

ILLUSTRATIVE MATERIAL

A. PASS THROUGH OF CHARACTER OF INCOME AND LOSS

Although the individual shareholders report the items of gain or loss on their own returns, the character of items is determined at the corporate level and passed through to the shareholders pursuant to § 1366(b), a provision analogous to § 704(b), which requires that partnership items be characterized at the partnership level. In Rath v. Commissioner, 101 T.C. 196 (1993), the Tax Court held that § 1244, discussed at page 166, cannot apply to allow an ordinary loss to be recognized on the sale of stock in another corporation held by an S corporation. Even though the loss ultimately will be reported by individuals, under § 1366(b) the character of the loss is determined at the corporate level. An S corporation shareholder does not "step into the shoes of the corporation for purposes of determining the character of a loss." Since Treas. Reg. § 1.1244(a)–1(b) provides that a corporation cannot claim an ordinary loss for § 1244 stock, the loss passes through to the shareholders as a capital loss.

After the character of an item is determined at the corporate level, whether it must be separately stated depends on whether the characterization may affect the computation of tax at the shareholder level. Thus, Rev.Rul. 93–36, 1993–1 C.B. 187, held that a nonbusiness bad debt must be separately stated as a short term capital loss under § 166(d) and passed through to its shareholders as such. Because § 166 is not an enumerated exception to § 1363(b), § 166 applies in the same manner as it does for an individual in computing the taxable income of an S corporation.

B. PERMITTED TAXABLE YEAR

Before the enactment of § 1378 in 1982, calendar year stockholders of a profitable S corporation generally preferred a taxable year for the corporation ending on January 31. Under § 1366(a), stockholders account for their share of an S corporation's items in the taxable year of the stockholder in which the taxable year of the S corporation ends. A January

* [Ed.: The material in brackets reflects amendments to §§ 1366 and 1368 made in the Small Business Job Protection Act of 1996.]

31 year-end permitted calendar year stockholders to defer income for up to eleven months. If, on the other hand, the S corporation was passing through losses to the stockholders, the stockholders preferred a calendar year so as to avoid any deferral of deductions.

The last sentence of 1378(b) prohibits stockholder deferral from being treated as a business purpose for adopting a fiscal year. Section 444, however, allows limited deferral but at the price of a corporate level payment to the government. The rules governing the use of a taxable year other than a calendar year are the same as those for partnerships.

C. STOCKHOLDER'S BASIS

1. *General*

The stockholder's basis in S corporation stock initially is determined in the same manner as the basis of any other stock. Thereafter, in general, the stockholder's basis is increased by items included in the stockholder's income (and the stockholder's share of the corporation's tax exempt income) and reduced by deductions allocated and distributions made to the stockholder. I.R.C. § 1367. Treas. Regs. §§ 1.1367–1(b)(2) and (c)(3) provide that increases and decreases to the basis of Subchapter S stock are determined on a per share per day basis. Basis adjustments generally are made at the close of the taxable year, Treas. Reg. § 1.1367–1(d)(1), but if a shareholder sells stock during the year, the adjustment to the basis of the stock sold is effective immediately prior to the disposition. Treas. Reg. § 1.1367–1(d)(1). Adjustments to the basis of the stock are made in the following order: (1) increases for income items; (2) decreases for distributions; (3) decreases for noncapital nondeductible expenses; and (4) decreases for losses. See Prop. Reg. § 1.1367–1(f) (1998).

Section 1367(a)(2)(D) requires a reduction in basis for expenses that are neither deductible nor chargeable to capital account. Treas. Reg. § 1.1367–1(c)(2) clarifies this language as applying only to expenses for which no loss or deduction is allowable, and as not applying to expenses that are deferred to a later taxable year. The regulations describe expenses to which § 1367(a)(2)(D) apply as including such things as fines, penalties, illegal bribes and kickbacks and other items disallowed under § 162(c) and (f); expenses incurred to earn tax exempt income disallowed under § 265; losses disallowed under § 267 relating to related party transactions; and the nondeductible portion of meal and entertainment expenses under § 274. This adjustment is necessary to prevent the shareholder from in effect recognizing the disallowed deduction by realizing less gain or greater loss on the subsequent sale of the stock.

2. *Effect of Corporate Level Cancellation of Indebtedness Income*

Because § 1367 provides for a stockholder basis increase with respect to the stockholder's separately stated income items in § 1366(a)(1)(A), as well as with respect to the stockholder's share of the corporation's nonseparately stated income, and § 1366(a)(1)(A) refers to "tax-exempt income," a stockholders's basis in stock of an S corporation is increased by the stockholder's share of tax exempt income. The committee reports accompanying the enactment of these rules give as an example of tax exempt income interest excluded under § 103. See S. Rep. No.97–640, page 385. Neither the Code nor the regulations, however, clearly define "tax exempt" income for this purpose, and the question arises regarding what is "tax-exempt income," which results in a current basis adjustment, versus what is "tax deferred income," which does not result in a current basis increase.

In Nelson v. Commissioner, 110 T.C. 114 (1998), the taxpayer was the sole shareholder of an S corporation that realized cancellation of indebtedness (COD) income while it was insolvent. Under § 108(a), the corporation properly excluded the COD income. Upon the subsequent disposition of the stock (in the same year), the taxpayer-shareholder nevertheless claimed an increase in the basis of his stock in the corporation pursuant to §§ 1367(a)(1)(A) and 1366(a)(1)(A), on the theory that the COD income was passed-through "exempt" income, and reported a long-term capital loss. The Commissioner disallowed the portion of the loss attributable to the untaxed COD income. The Tax Court upheld the Commissioner's position and denied the basis increase. Section § 108(d)(7)(A) provides that for purposes of Subchapter S the COD income exclusion is applied at the corporate level. Section 108, through the attribute reduction rules in § 108(b), which likewise apply at the corporate level, is generally intended to defer the recognition of income, not to totally exempt it from taxation, and pursuant to § 108(d)(7)(A), that deferral occurs at the corporate level. Thus "excludable" COD income does not pass through to the shareholders or increase their basis in the stock of the corporation. In this respect the pass-through regime for S corporations differs from the pass-through rules for partnerships.

In Winn v. Commissioner, 1998–71 T.C. Memo, which was decided on the same day as *Nelson*, the Tax Court held that cancellation of indebtedness income flowing through to an insolvent S corporation from a partnership did not pass through to the shareholders to increase their basis.

D. LIMITATION OF LOSS DEDUCTIONS TO BASIS

1. *General*

When net losses have reduced a stockholder's basis to zero, additional allocations of deduction and loss items reduce the basis of any indebtedness of the S corporation held by the stockholder. I.R.C. § 1367(b)(2)(A). See also Prop. Reg. § 1.1366–2 (1998). (If an S corporation has a qualified S corporation subsidiary, any indebtedness of the subsidiary to a shareholder of the parent is treated as indebtedness of the parent S corporation to the shareholder for this purpose. I.R.C. § 1361(b)(3)(A)(ii); H.R. Rep. No. 104–586, 104th Cong., 2d Sess. 89 (1996).) When the basis of both the stockholder's stock and corporate indebtedness have been reduced to zero, passed through losses no longer can be deducted by the stockholder. The losses are suspended and may be deducted in a later year in which the stockholder acquires basis. I.R.C. § 1366(d). Treas. Reg. § 1.1367–2(b)(3) provides that if the shareholder holds multiple indebtedness of the S Corporation, the reduction in basis is applied to each indebtedness in proportion to the relative bases of the indebtedness. The legislative history of the Small Business Job Protection Act directs the Service to promulgate regulations governing the order in which the basis of indebtedness is reduced if a shareholder holds indebtedness of both an S corporation and the corporation's qualified Subchapter S subsidiary. H.R. Rep. No. 104–586, 104th Cong., 2d Sess. 89 (1996).

The reduction in basis occurs notwithstanding the taxpayer's inability to use the losses on his own tax return. In Hudspeth v. Commissioner, 914 F.2d 1207 (9th Cir.1990), the stockholders were required to reduce the basis of bonds because of the corporation's net operating losses. However, because the stockholders' shares of losses exceeded their incomes in the taxable year of the losses and in subsequent years, they received no tax benefit with respect to the losses. The court rejected the stockholders' assertion that under the tax benefit rule the basis of the bonds should not be reduced to the extent that the corporation's losses did not produce a tax benefit. The court indicated that to so hold would nullify the limited carryback and carryforward provisions of § 172.

2. *Restoration of Basis*

If a stockholder has reduced the basis in her stock to zero and also has reduced the basis of corporate indebtedness by any amount, any "net increase in basis" attributable to passed-through income in a subsequent year (i.e., basis increase minus distributions for the year) will be applied to restore the basis of indebtedness before there is any increase in the basis of stock. I.R.C. § 1367(b)(2)(B); Treas. Reg. § 1.1367–2(c). Assume for example, that A is the sole shareholder of X Corp., which has an S election in effect. The basis of A's stock in X Corp. is $10,000 and A holds a $5,000 promissory note from X Corp. In 1999, X Corp. passes through to A a $14,000 loss, and A reduces the basis of the X Corp. stock to zero and the basis of the promissory note to $1,000. In 2000, X Corp. has $6,500 of income and distributes $3,000 to A. To the extent of the $3,000 distribution, the passed through income is allocated to increase the basis of A's stock, and because the positive and negative adjustments to the stock basis offset, its basis remains zero. The remaining $3,500 of passed-through income increases the basis of the debt to $4,500. See Treas. Reg. § 1.1367–2(e), Ex. (2).

Nevertheless, § 1367(b)(2)(B) can produce an unexpected consequence to the stockholder. To the extent that corporate earnings passed through to the stockholder under § 1366 are allocated to increase the basis of stockholder debt, the stockholder's stock basis will not be adjusted to reflect income previously taxed to the stockholder. Distributions of these earnings in a subsequent year might be taxed to the stockholder to the extent distributions exceed the stockholder's stock basis even though the stockholder has basis in the debt. Thus, if in the immediately preceding example, in 2001 X Corp. realized neither income nor loss and distributed $2,000 to

A, A would recognize a $2,000 gain under § 1368. (But if X Corp. had distributed $5,000 to A in 1999, A would have recognized no gain under § 1368 and the basis of the debt would have been increased to only $2,500.) As a consequence, the stockholder appears to be taxed twice on the same income; once as the stockholder is allocated a proportionate share of the income under § 1366, and a second time to the extent the distribution of that income exceeds the stockholder's stock basis. The "second" tax, however, can be viewed as a consequence of the pass through of losses in excess of stock basis, which has reduced the basis in the debt; the statute in effect requires those losses to be "recaptured" when distributions are made on the stock before the full basis of the debt has been accounted for.

Suppose that in 1999 a shareholder-creditor is allocated a loss that exceeds the basis of her stock by $600, and as a result reduces the basis of a $1,000 corporate debt obligation to $400. In July 2000, the corporation repays the debt and for 2000, the shareholder's share of the S corporation's income is $700. If the debt had not been repaid until January 1, 2001, its basis would have been increased from $400 to $1,000 as a result of the 2000 income, and no gain would have been recognized upon repayment. Must the shareholder recognize a $600 gain when the debt is repaid in July 2000 because the corporation's year had not closed at that time or may the basis of the debt be retroactively increased? Treas. Reg. § 1.1367–2(d) addresses this problem. Although basis adjustments to debt obligations held by shareholders generally are determined at the close of the taxable year, if the debt is repaid during the year, its basis is adjusted immediately before the repayment. As a result, the shareholder in the above example realizes no gain in 2000.

3. *Carryover of Disallowed Losses*

The loss limitation of § 1366(d)(1) prevents a stockholder from claiming losses in excess of the stockholder's investment in the S corporation. Losses disallowed by § 1366(d)(1) may be carried over indefinitely to future years and deducted whenever the stockholder has sufficient basis to support the deduction. I.R.C. § 1366(d)(2). A stockholder may have losses carried into the last taxable year of the S corporation. In such a case, the loss is treated as a loss incurred by the stockholder on the last day of a "post-termination transition period." The post-termination transition period is defined in § 1377(b) as the period beginning on the last day of the corporation's taxable year as an S corporation and ending on the later of (1) one year after the last day of the S corporation taxable year, (2) the due date for the tax return for the last taxable year as an S corporation (including extensions), (3) 120 days after any determination pursuant to a post-termination audit of a shareholder that adjusts any item of S corporation income, loss, or deduction for the period the corporation was an S corporation, or (4) if there is a judicial determination or administrative agreement that the corporation's S election terminated in an earlier taxable year, 120 days after the date of the determination. See also Treas. Reg. § 1.1377–2. The loss carryover is personal to each individual stockholder and is not a loss carryover to the corporation. I.R.C. § 1366(d)(2). Disposition of S corporation stock by the stockholder thus terminates the loss carryforward attributable to that stock.

4. *Additional Shareholder Contributions to Capital*

Cash or property contributions to capital will increase the shareholder's stock basis, thereby allowing the shareholder to deduct losses otherwise in excess of basis. In Rev.Rul. 81–187, 1981–2 C.B. 167, the stockholder of an S corporation attempted to increase basis for purposes of deducting a net operating loss by transferring the stockholder's own promissory note to the corporation. The Internal Revenue Service ruled that the note did not increase the stockholder's basis because the stockholder incurred no cost in executing the note; the stockholder's basis in the note was zero. But see Peracchi v. Commissioner, 143 F.3d 487 (9th Cir.1998), page 90; Lessinger v. Commissioner, 872 F.2d 519 (2d Cir.1989), page 101.

A contribution of additional assets will not necessarily increase basis, however, if the assets are encumbered or the corporation assumes liabilities of the shareholder in connection with the transfer. In Wiebusch v. Commissioner, 59 T.C. 777 (1973), aff'd per curiam, 487 F.2d 515 (8th Cir.1973), the taxpayer transferred the assets of a sole proprietorship to an existing S corporation that also assumed certain of the transferor's liabilities. The liabilities exceeded the taxpayer's basis for the assets, which resulted in gain to the taxpayer under § 357(c) and, as a result of § 358(d)(1), the taxpayer's basis in the stock was reduced to zero. Accordingly, the corporation's current losses could not be deducted by the taxpayer. As a result of the contribution, the taxpayer recognized gain and lost the benefit of a current loss deduction, neither of which would have occurred had the business continued to be operated in a sole proprietorship form.

E. ALLOCATIONS IF STOCK OWNERSHIP CHANGES DURING THE YEAR

Section 1377(a) provides that each shareholder's pro rata share of an S corporation's items passed through under § 1366 is determined on a day-by-day, share-by-share method if the ownership of shares changes during the year. See Treas. Reg. § 1.1377–1(a), (c), Ex.1. This rule is similar to the proration method available to partnerships under § 706(d), except that in the case of an S corporation, the pro ration method is the normal rule. Pursuant to authority granted in § 1377(a)(2), Treas. Reg. § 1.1377–1(b) allows an S corporation to close its year for purposes of allocating income among shareholders if a shareholder completely terminates his interest and the corporation and all of the shareholders who are affected consent. If stock is sold, the affected shareholders are the seller and the purchaser(s); if stock is redeemed by the corporation, however, all shareholders are affected and must consent. I.R.C. § 1377(a)(2)(B); Treas. Reg. § 1.1377–1(b)(2). Treas. Reg. § 1.1368–1(g) provides a similar election if any shareholder disposes of more than 20 percent of the outstanding stock of the corporation during the taxable year but has not disposed of all of her stock. Treas. Reg. § 1.1368–1(g) requires consent of all shareholders, not just the "affected shareholders." The Treasury has not amended Treas. Reg.

§ 1.1368–1(g) to conform to the consent requirements in § 1377(a)(2), apparently because it was not promulgated under authority of that Code section, although the policy considerations are identical. The pro ration method is not applicable, however, and allocations based on the closing corporate books method are required if there is a sale or exchange of more than 50 percent of the corporation's stock during a year in which the corporation's S election terminates. I.R.C. § 1362(e)(6)(D).

If items are allocated by closing the corporation's books, the corporation pro rates its income within each segment of the year among the shareholders in proportion to their ownership during that segment of the year and then cumulates the share of items for each shareholder for all of the segments of the year.[16] If two or more qualifying dispositions occur during the year, it apparently would be possible for the corporation to terminate its year with respect to one but to pro rate income with respect to the other.

These principles are illustrated by the following example. Assume that A, B, C, D, and E each owned 100 shares of stock of X Corp., which had made an S election. X Corp.'s income for the year was $182,500, but by quarters it was as follows: 1st quarter, ($90,000); 2nd quarter, $90,000; 3rd quarter, $229,000; 4th quarter, ($46,500). On March 31st, A sold his stock to F, and on September 30, B sold her stock to G.[17]

Under the normal method in § 1377(a), $500 of the corporation's $182,500 of income would be allocated to each day, and then $1 would be allocated to each share. The shareholders' income would be as follows:

Shareholder	Days	Shares	Income/Share/Day	Total
A	90	100	$1	$ 9,000
B	273	100	$1	$27,300
C	365	100	$1	$36,500
D	365	100	$1	$36,500
E	365	100	$1	$36,500
F	275	100	$1	$27,500
G	92	100	$1	$ 9,200

If, however, all affected shareholders consented to closing the books as of March 31st, the corporation's $90,000 loss for the first quarter would be allocated among only A, B, C, D and E, and the corporation's $272,500 income for the last three quarters ($1.98 per share-per day) would be allocated among B, C, D, E, and F, as follows:[18]

Shareholder	Days	Shares	Income/Share/Day	Total
A	90	100	($2)	($18,000)
B	90	100	($2)	($18,000)

16. See Treas. Reg. § 1.1377–1(b), (c)(2) (method of making the election to allocate items under this method; illustrating method of making computations).

17. On the day of the sale the selling shareholder rather than the purchaser is counted as the shareholder. Treas. Reg. § 1.1377–1(a)(2)(ii).

18. The income totals slightly less than $182,500 due to rounding the earnings per share per day in the last three quarters to the nearest cent.

Shareholder	Days	Shares	Income/Share/Day	Total
	183	100	$1.98	$36,234
				$18,234
C	90	100	($2)	($18,000)
	275	100	$1.98	$54,450
				$36,450
D	90	100	($2)	($18,000)
	275	100	$1.98	$54,450
				$36,450
E	90	100	($2)	($18,000)
	275	100	$1.98	$54,450
				$36,450
F	275	100	$1.98	$54,450
G	92	100	$1.98	$18,216

A and F are the only affected shareholders with respect to the March 31st sale. Thus, only A and F need consent to closing the books on March 31st. Since closing the books at the end of the first quarter results in F realizing significantly greater income than under the pro ration method, it is unlikely that F would consent unless F were compensated in some manner. In fact, however, the tax liability of each of A, B, F, and G is affected by closing of the books on March 31. Nevertheless, § 1377(a)(2)(B) and Treas. Reg. § 1.1377–1(b)(2) define affected shareholders as including only the seller and purchaser.

F. ALLOCATIONS AMONG FAMILY GROUPS

The Commissioner is given authority to allocate items described in § 1366 among those stockholders who are members of the stockholder's family (spouse, ancestors, and lineal descendants) if he determines that reallocation is necessary to reflect the value of services rendered by any of those persons. I.R.C. § 1366(e). See also Prop. Reg. § 1.1366–3 (1998). Thus, if a parent works for a low salary in an effort to shift income to the parent's stockholder-children, the Commissioner may allocate additional income to the parent or reduce the deduction for salary allocable to the parent. Unlike § 704(e)(3), which reallocates partnership income in the case of an interest purchased from a related person, § 1366(e) permits reallocation of S corporation income among family members who purchased their stock from the corporation or from an outsider in an arm's length transaction. On the other hand, § 1366(e) is more restrictive than § 704(e)(1) and (2) (which provide for reallocation of partnership income in the case of transfers by gift) in the sense that it permits reallocation only among family members.

In Davis v. Commissioner, 64 T.C. 1034 (1975), the Tax Court held that the Commissioner abused this discretion under the predecessor to § 1366(e) by allocating 100 percent of the income of two S corporations to the taxpayer. The taxpayer was an orthopedic surgeon who organized two corporations to perform X-ray and physical therapy services related to his medical practice. Ninety percent of the stock of each corporation was owned by the taxpayer's three minor children. The Tax Court indicated that the value of the taxpayer's services depended upon factors such as the nature of the services, the responsibilities involved, the time spent, the size and complexity of the business, economic conditions, compensation paid by others for comparable services, and salary paid to company officers in prior years. The court held that the 20 or so hours per year that the taxpayer spent directly performing services for the corporations was minimal and rejected the Commissioner's argument that the taxpayer's referral of patients to the corporations was personal service rendered by him to the corporations. Thus, the fees earned by the corporations were the result of the use of equipment owned by the corporations and the services of corporate employees, and not the result of services rendered by the taxpayer. The Tax Court also rejected the Commissioner's claim that income was allocable to the taxpayer under § 482 and assignment of income principles.

G. APPLICABILITY OF AT RISK AND PASSIVE ACTIVITY LOSS LIMITATION RULES

The at risk rules of § 465 apply to the stockholder of an S corporation. As a result, a loss that is passed through to a stockholder may be deducted only to the extent that the stockholder is at risk with respect to the activities that generated the loss. Under the aggregation rules of § 465(c)(3)(B), an S corporation may be treated as engaged in a single activity if its activities constitute a trade or business and 65 percent or more of the losses are allocable to persons who actively participate in the management of the trade or business. If passed through losses have been suspended by the at-risk rules and they have not been used by the shareholder prior to the termination of the corporation's S election, the suspended losses may be carried forward to the post-termination transition period (as defined in § 1377(b)) and can be deducted in the year or years within the post-termination transition period to the extent the taxpayer's at-risk amount is increased.

The passive activity loss limitation of § 469 applies to losses passed through to S corporation stockholders in the same manner as to partners. Thus net losses of an activity operated by an S corporation in which the stockholder does not materially participate are deductible by the stockholder only to the extent of the stockholder's passive activity income. Disallowed losses are carried forward and treated as passive activity deductions in the next succeeding year until offset by the taxpayer's passive activity income. Complete disposition of the activity of the S corporation allows the taxpayer to deduct the unused loss attributable to the specific activity.

H. SHORT SUBCHAPTER S AND SUBCHAPTER C TAXABLE YEARS ON TERMINATION

Section 1362(e) requires that in any taxable year in which the S corporation election terminates effective on a date other than the first day of the taxable year, income and deduction items must be allocated between the portion of the year the corporation is qualified as an S corporation and the portion of the year the corporation is treated as a C corporation.[19] The Senate Finance Committee Report explained the allocation rule as follows:

"The day before the day on which the terminating event occurs will be treated as the last day of a short Subchapter S taxable year, and the day on which the terminating event occurs will be treated as the first day of a short regular (i.e., Subchapter C) taxable year. There will be no requirement that the books of a corporation be closed as of the termination date. Instead the corporation will allocate the income or loss for the entire year (i.e., both short years) on a proration basis."[20]

Each separately stated item of the corporation's income and loss during the short Subchapter S year must be allocated to each day of the short taxable year and taken into account by the stockholders. I.R.C. § 1362(e)(2). The remaining taxable income for the taxable year is allocated to the short C corporation year. Taxable income for the short Subchapter C year is then annualized for purposes of computing the tax under § 11. First, the corporation's tax for the short Subchapter C year is determined as if it had earned a proportionate amount of taxable income for a full taxable year; then the corporation pays only the proportionate amount of the tax that corresponds to the portion of a full taxable year that it is deemed a C corporation. See Treas. Reg. § 1.1362–3(a) and (c)(2). For example, suppose S Corporation has taxable income of $100,000 in 1999. Its Subchapter S election terminates effective April 1, 1999. There have been 90 days in S Corporation's short taxable year ending on March 31, 1999, and there are 275 days in S Corporation's short Subchapter C year beginning on April 1, 1999. As a result, $24,658 of S Corporation's $100,000 taxable income is allocated to the short S corporation year ($100,000 × 90/365) and the remaining $75,342 of taxable income is allocated to S Corporation's Subchapter C year. The $75,342 of taxable income is annualized so that S Corp. is deemed to have $100,000 of taxable income for purposes of determining its corporate tax for the short Subchapter C year ($75,342 × 365/275). The tax under § 11 on $100,000 of taxable income is $22,250. S Corporation's actual tax liability for the short Subchapter C year then is calculated to be $16,764 ($22,250 × 275/365).

In lieu of a pro rata allocation of income between the short Subchapter S and C years, the corporation may elect, with the consent of *all* stockholders at any time during the S year and all shareholders on the first day of the C year, to report income and deductions on the basis of actual amounts shown on the corporate books. I.R.C. § 1362(e)(3). Allocation of amounts based on the corporate books is required if the corporation's stock is acquired by a corporation, thereby terminating the S election, if the acquiring corporation elects to treat the acquisition as an asset purchase under § 338, see page 475. I.R.C. § 1362(e)(6)(C). The "closing of the

19. Section 1362(e)(6)(A) provides that the short taxable years required by § 1362(e) shall be treated as only one year for purposes of the carryback and carryforward of corporate items such as net operating losses.

20. S.Rep. No. 97–640, 97th Cong., 2d Sess. 11 (1982).

books" method may be desirable in situations in which the parties do not want events occurring after termination to affect income determination for the S corporation portion of the year. Note, however, that a single shareholder, who may be adversely affected, can prevent the use of the closing of the books method.

(2) EFFECT OF INDIRECT CONTRIBUTIONS ON LIMITATION OF LOSS DEDUCTIONS TO SHAREHOLDER BASIS

Estate of Leavitt v. Commissioner

Court of Appeals, United States, Fourth Circuit, 1989.
875 F.2d 420.

■ MURNAGHAN, CIRCUIT JUDGE:

The appellants, Anthony D. and Marjorie F. Cuzzocrea and the Estate of Daniel Leavitt, Deceased, et al., appeal the Tax Court's decision holding them liable for tax deficiencies for the tax years 1979, 1980 and 1981. Finding the appellants' arguments unpersuasive, we affirm the Tax Court.

I.

As shareholders of VAFLA Corporation,[1] a subchapter S corporation during the years at issue, the appellants claimed deductions under § 1374 of the Internal Revenue Code of 1954 to reflect the corporation's operating losses during the three years in question. The Commissioner disallowed deductions above the $10,000 bases each appellant had from their original investments.

The appellants contend, however, that the adjusted bases in their stock should be increased to reflect a $300,000 loan which VAFLA obtained from the Bank of Virginia ("Bank") on September 12, 1979, after the appellants, along with five other shareholders ("Shareholders–Guarantors"), had signed guarantee agreements whereby each agreed to be jointly and severally liable for all indebtedness of the corporation to the Bank.[5] At the time of the loan, VAFLA's liability exceeded its assets, it could not meet its cash flow requirements and it had virtually no assets to use as collateral. The appellants assert that the Bank would not have lent the $300,000 without their personal guarantees.

VAFLA's financial statements and tax returns indicated that the bank loan was a loan from the Shareholders–Guarantors. Despite the representation to that effect, VAFLA made all of the loan payments, principal and

1. VAFLA is a Virginia corporation incorporated in February 1979 to acquire and operate the Six-Gun Territory Amusement Park near Tampa, Florida. At that time, both Cuzzocrea and Leavitt each paid $10,000 for their respective shares of VAFLA. Therefore, the adjusted bases of their stock amounted to $10,000 each, the cost of the stock.

5. All the guarantees to the Bank were unlimited except the guarantee of Cuzzocrea which was limited to $300,000. The Shareholders–Guarantors had an aggregate net worth of $3,407,286 and immediate liquidity of $382,542.

interest, to the Bank. The appellants made no such payments. In addition, neither VAFLA nor the Shareholders–Guarantors treated the corporate payments on the loan as constructive income taxable to the Shareholders–Guarantors.

The appellants present the question whether the $300,000 bank loan is really, despite its form as a borrowing from the Bank, a capital contribution from the appellants to VAFLA. They contend that if the bank loan is characterized as equity, they are entitled to add a *pro rata* share of the $300,000 bank loan to their adjusted bases, thereby increasing the size of their operating loss deductions.[7] Implicit in the appellants' characterization of the bank loan as equity in VAFLA is a determination that the Bank lent the $300,000 to the Shareholders–Guarantors who then contributed the funds to the corporation. The appellants' approach fails to realize that the $300,000 transaction, regardless of whether it is equity or debt, would permit them to adjust the bases in their stock if, indeed, the appellants, and not the Bank, had advanced VAFLA the money. The more precise question, which the appellants fail initially to ask, is whether the guaranteed loan from the Bank to VAFLA is an economic outlay of any kind by the Shareholders–Guarantors. To decide this question, we must determine whether the transaction involving the $300,000 was a loan from the Bank to VAFLA or was it instead a loan to the Shareholders–Guarantors who then gave it to VAFLA, as either a loan or a capital contribution.

Finding no economic outlay, we need not address the question, which is extensively addressed in the briefs, of whether the characterization of the $300,000 was debt or equity.

II.

To increase the basis in the stock of a subchapter S corporation, there must be an economic outlay on the part of the shareholder. See Brown v. Commissioner, 706 F.2d 755, 756 (6th Cir.1983), affg. T.C. Memo. 1981–608("In similar cases, the courts have consistently required some economic outlay by the guarantor in order to convert a mere loan guarantee into an investment."); Blum v. Commissioner, 59 T.C. 436, 440 (1972)(bank expected repayment of its loan from the corporation and not the taxpayers, i.e., no economic outlay from taxpayers).[8] A guarantee, in and of itself, cannot fulfill that requirement. The guarantee is merely a promise to pay in the future if certain unfortunate events should occur. At the present time, the

7. Former § 1374 of the 1954 tax code which was in effect during the years in issue provides that a shareholder of an electing small business corporation may deduct from gross income an amount equal to his or her portion of the corporation's net operating loss to the extent provided for in § 1374(c)(2). Such deduction is limited, however, to the sum of (a) the adjusted basis of the shareholder's stock in the corporation, and (b) the adjusted basis of any indebtedness of the corporation to the shareholder, as determined as of the close of the corporation's taxable year.

8. Even the Eleventh Circuit case on which the appellants heavily rely applies this first step. See Selfe v. United States, 778 F.2d 769, 772 (11th Cir.1985)("We agree with *Brown* inasmuch as that court reaffirms that economic outlay is required before a stockholder in a Subchapter S corporation may increase her basis.").

appellants have experienced no such call as guarantors, have engaged in no economic outlay, and have suffered no cost.

The situation would be different if VAFLA had defaulted on the loan payments and the Shareholders–Guarantors had made actual disbursements on the corporate indebtedness. Those payments would represent corporate indebtedness to the shareholders which would increase their bases for the purpose of deducting net operating losses under § 1374(c)(2)(B). Brown, 706 F.2d at 757. See also Raynor v. Commissioner, 50 T.C. 762, 770–71 (1968)("No form of indirect borrowing, be it guaranty, surety, accommodation, co-making or otherwise, gives rise to indebtedness from the corporation to the shareholders until and unless the shareholders pay part or all of the obligation.").

The appellants accuse the Tax Court of not recognizing the critical distinction between § [1366(d)(1)(A)] (adjusted basis in stock) and § [1366(d)(1)(B)] (adjusted basis in indebtedness of corporation to shareholder). They argue that the "loan" is not really a loan, but is a capital contribution (equity). Therefore, they conclude, § [1366(d)(1)(A)]applies and § [1366(d)(1)(B)] is irrelevant. However, the appellants once again fail to distinguish between the initial question of economic outlay and the secondary issue of debt or equity. Only if the first question had an affirmative answer, would the second arise.

The majority opinion of the Tax Court, focusing on the first issue of economic outlay, determined that a guarantee, in and of itself, is not an event for which basis can be adjusted. It distinguished the situation presented to it from one where the guarantee is triggered *and actual payments are made.* In the latter scenario, the first question of economic outlay is answered affirmatively (and the second issue is apparent on its face, i.e., the payments represent indebtedness from the corporation to the shareholder as opposed to capital contribution from the shareholder to the corporation). To the contrary is the situation presented here. The Tax Court, far from confusing the issue by discussing irrelevant matters, was comprehensively explaining why the transaction before it could not represent any kind of economic outlay by the appellants.

The Tax Court correctly determined that the appellants' guarantees, unaccompanied by further acts, in and of themselves, have not constituted contributions of cash or other property which might increase the bases of the appellants' stock in the corporation.

The appellants, while they do not disagree with the Tax Court that the guarantees, standing alone, cannot adjust their bases in the stock, nevertheless argue that the "loan" to VAFLA was in its "true sense" a loan to the Shareholders–Guarantors who then theoretically advanced the $300,000 to the corporation as a capital contribution. The Tax Court declined the invitation to treat a loan and its uncalled-on security, the guarantee, as identical and to adopt the appellants' view of the "substance" of the transaction over the "form" of the transaction they took. The Tax Court did not err in doing so.

Generally, taxpayers are liable for the tax consequences of the transaction they actually execute and may not reap the benefit of recasting the transaction into another one substantially different in economic effect that they might have made. They are bound by the "form" of their transaction and may not argue that the "substance" of their transaction triggers different tax consequences. Don E. Williams Co. v. Commissioner, 429 U.S. 569, 579–80, 97 S.Ct. 850, 856–57, 51 L.Ed.2d 48 (1977) * * * .[10] In the situation of guaranteed corporate debt, where the form of the transaction may not be so clear, courts have permitted the taxpayer to argue that the substance of the transaction was in actuality a loan to the shareholder. See Blum, 59 T.C. at 440. However, the burden is on the taxpayer and it has been a difficult one to meet. That is especially so where, as here, the transaction is cast in sufficiently ambiguous terms to permit an argument either way depending on which is subsequently advantageous from a tax point of view.

In the case before us, the Tax Court found that the "form" and "substance" of the transaction was a loan from the Bank to VAFLA and not to the appellants:

> The Bank of Virginia loaned the money to the corporation and not to petitioners. The proceeds of the loan were to be used in the operation of the corporation's business. Petitioners submitted no evidence that they were free to dispose of the proceeds of the loan as they wished. Nor were the payments on the loan reported as constructive dividends on the corporation's Federal income tax returns or on the petitioners' Federal income tax returns during the years in issue. Accordingly, we find that the transaction was in fact a loan by the bank to the corporation guaranteed by the shareholders.

Whether the $300,000 was lent to the corporation or to the Shareholders/Guarantors is a factual issue which should not be disturbed unless clearly erroneous. Finding no error, we affirm.

It must be borne in mind that we do not merely encounter naive taxpayers caught in a complex trap for the unwary. They sought to claim

10. On the other hand, the Commissioner is not so bound and may recharacterize the nature of the transaction according to its substance while overlooking the form selected by the taxpayer. Higgins v. Smith, 308 U.S. 473, 477, 60 S.Ct. 355, 357, 84 L.Ed. 406 (1940). In doing so, the Commissioner usually applies debt-equity principles to determine the true *nature* of the transaction. As the *Selfe* court noted:

> This principle is particularly evident where characterization of capital as debt or equity will have different tax consequences. Thus in Plantation Patterns [462 F.2d 712 (5th Cir.1972)] the court held that interest payments by a corporation on debentures were constructive stockholder dividends and could not be deducted by the corporation as interest payments. There, the former Fifth Circuit recharacterized debt as equity at the insistence of the Commissioner.

Selfe, 778 F.2d at 773.

It is important to note that those cases did not involve the question posed here of whether an economic outlay existed because it clearly did. Actual payments were made. The only question was what was the nature of the payments, debt or equity.

deductions because the corporation lost money. If, however, VAFLA had been profitable, they would be arguing that the loan was in reality from the Bank to the corporation, and not to them, for that would then lessen their taxes. Under that description of the transaction, the loan repayments made by VAFLA would not be on the appellants' behalf, and, consequently, would not be taxed as constructive income to them. See Old Colony Trust Co. v. Commissioner, 279 U.S. 716, 49 S.Ct. 499, 73 L.Ed. 918 (1929) (payment by a corporation of a personal expense or debt of a shareholder is considered as the receipt of a taxable benefit). It came down in effect to an ambiguity as to which way the appellants would jump, an effort to play both ends against the middle, until it should be determined whether VAFLA was a profitable or money-losing proposition. At that point, the appellants attempted to treat the transaction as cloaked in the guise having the more beneficial tax consequences for them.

Finally, the appellants complain that the Tax Court erred by failing to apply debt-equity principles to determine the "form" of the loan. We believe that the Tax Court correctly refused to apply debt-equity principles here, a methodology which is only relevant, if at all,[12] to resolution of the second inquiry—what is the nature of the economic outlay. Of course, the second inquiry cannot be reached unless the first question concerning whether an economic outlay exists is answered affirmatively. Here it is not.

The appellants, in effect, attempt to collapse a two-step analysis into a one-step inquiry which would eliminate the initial determination of economic outlay by first concluding that the proceeds were a capital contribution (equity). Obviously, a capital contribution is an economic outlay so the basis in the stock would be adjusted accordingly. But such an approach simply ignores the factual determination by the Tax Court that the Bank lent the $300,000 to the corporation and not to the Shareholders–Guarantors.

The appellants rely on Blum v. Commissioner, 59 T.C. 436 (1972), and Selfe v. United States, 778 F.2d 769 (11th Cir.1985), to support their position. However, the appellants have misread those cases. In *Blum,* the Tax Court declined to apply debt-equity principles to determine whether the taxpayer's guarantee of a loan from a bank to a corporation was an indirect capital contribution.[13] The Tax Court held that the taxpayer had

12. In a § [1366(d)]subchapter S corporation case, the inquiry whether or not the economic outlay, assuming there is one, is debt or equity appears not to matter since the economic outlay, regardless of its characterization as debt or equity, will increase the adjusted basis. * * * There are no different tax consequences from the point of view of the taxpayer on the narrow issue of what amount of net operating losses may be deducted. Therefore, application of debt-equity principles in a case such as this one appears to be a red herring. However, we do not reach that issue because the Tax Court's factual finding that the appellants have shown no economic outlay on their part is not clearly erroneous.

13. The *Blum* court stated:

> The respondent [Commissioner] has argued that the entire equity-contribution argument espoused by petitioner is inimical to the subch. S area. Because of our holding that the facts do not warrant the applicability of this doctrine to the present case we will not consider this rather fascinating question.

failed to carry his burden of proving that the transaction was in "substance" a loan from the bank to the shareholder rather than a loan to the corporation. The *Blum* court found dispositive the fact that "the bank expected repayment of its loan from the corporation and not the petitioner." Blum, 59 T.C. at 440.[14]

With regard to *Selfe,* the Tax Court stated:

> the Eleventh Circuit applied a debt-equity analysis and held that a shareholder's guarantee of a loan made to a subchapter S corporation may be treated for tax purposes as an equity investment in the corporation where the lender looks to the shareholder as the primary obligor. We respectfully disagree with the Eleventh Circuit and hold that a shareholder's guarantee of a loan to a subchapter S corporation may not be treated as an equity investment in the corporation absent an economic outlay by the shareholder.[15]

The Tax Court then distinguished Plantation Patterns, 462 F.2d 712 (5th Cir.1972), relied on by *Selfe,* because that case involved a C corporation, reasoning that the application of debt-equity principles to subchapter S corporations would defeat Congress' intent to limit a shareholder's pass-through deduction to the amount he or she has actually invested in the corporation.[16]

Blum, 59 T.C. at 439 n. 4. In other words, the *Blum* court never reached the second step of the analysis, if there is a second step, because it found that there was no economic outlay. The Tax Court focused on the first inquiry: "we must find that the bank in substance loaned the sums to petitioner, not the corporation, and that petitioner then proceeded to advance such funds to the corporation." Id. at 440. The court found that "there is no evidence to refute the fact that the bank expected repayment of its loan from the corporation and not the petitioner." Id.

* * *

14. The appellants and Judge Fay, in his dissent, content that the Tax Court has misread its earlier opinion. Indeed, Judge Fay was the author of *Blum.* However, the Tax Court, sitting *en banc,* has now had the opportunity to interpret more precisely the language of *Blum* in light of subsequent cases and arguments. Leavitt v. Commissioner, 90 T.C. 206 (1988)(court reviewed). We agree with the amplification the Tax Court has given *Blum.*

The confusion may be explained to some degree because the test applied in *Blum* to determine whether the bank lent the money to the corporation or to the shareholders sounds similar to one of the debt-equity factors, i.e., the source of the payments. When focusing on the proper question, however, it becomes clear that the debt-equity principles are simply irrelevant to the determination of whether the $300,000, unquestionably a loan when it left the Bank, went to VAFLA or to the appellants. In *Blum,* the fact that the bank expected repayment from the corporation indicated that it actually lent the funds to the corporation and not the shareholder. Similarly, in the case before us, the fact that VAFLA paid the principal and interest on the $300,000 loan and did not treat the payments as constructive income taxable to the Shareholders–Guarantors, indicated that the Bank actually lent the money to VAFLA and not the appellants.

15. Our reading of the *Selfe* opinion, as explained below, does not require us to reject the case completely. In this respect we disagree with the Tax Court's interpretation of Selfe in the present case and in Erwin v. Commissioner, 56 T.C.M. (CCH) 1343 (1989).

16. The Committee on Finance of the Senate stated in its report:

> The amount of the net operating loss apportioned to any shareholder pursuant

The Tax Court also distinguished In re Lane, 742 F.2d 1311 (11th Cir.1984), relied on by the *Selfe* court, on the basis that the shareholder had actually paid the amounts he had guaranteed, i.e., there was an economic outlay. In Lane, which involved a subchapter S corporation, the issue was "whether advances made by a shareholder to a corporation constitute debt or equity * * *." Id. at 1313. If the advances were debt, then Lane could deduct them as bad debts. On the other hand, if the advances were capital, no bad debt deduction would be permitted. Thus, the issue of adjusted basis for purposes of flow-through deductions from net operating losses of the corporation was not at issue. There was no question of whether there had been an economic outlay.

Although *Selfe* does refer to debt-equity principles, the specific issue before it was whether any material facts existed making summary judgment inappropriate. The Eleventh Circuit said:

> At issue here, however, is not whether the taxpayer's contribution was either a loan to or an equity investment in Jane Simon, Inc. The issue is whether the taxpayer's guarantee of the corporate loan was in itself a contribution to the corporation [as opposed to a loan from the bank] sufficient to increase the taxpayer's basis in the corporation.

The *Selfe* court found that there was evidence that the bank primarily looked to the taxpayer and not the corporation for repayment of the loan.[17] Therefore, it remanded for "a determination of whether or not the bank primarily looked to Jane Selfe [taxpayer] for repayment [the first inquiry] and for the court to apply the factors set out in In re Lane and I.R.C. section 385 to determine if the taxpayer's guarantee amounted to either an equity investment in or shareholder loan to Jane Simon, Inc. [the second inquiry]." Id. at 775. The implications are that there is still a two-step

> to the above rule is limited under § [1366(d)(1)] to the adjusted basis of the shareholder's investment in the corporation; that is, to the adjusted basis of the stock in the corporation owned by the shareholder and the adjusted basis of any indebtedness of the corporation to the shareholder.

S.Rep. No. 1983, 85th Cong., 2d Sess. at 220, (1958–3 Cum.Bull. at 1141). The word "investment" was construed to mean the actual economic outlay of the shareholder in question. Perry v. Commissioner, 54 T.C. 1293, 1296 (1970).

In other words, the economic outlay must be found to exist first.

17. The loan officer so stated during deposition testimony. Furthermore, the bank originally extended a credit line to the taxpayer in consideration of her pledge of 4500 shares of stock in another corporation. When her business was later incorporated, the bank converted the loans made on the existing credit line to corporate loans, accompanied by taxpayer's agreement guaranteeing the corporation's indebtedness to the bank. The Eleventh Circuit noted that "a guarantor who has pledged stock to secure a loan has experienced an economic outlay to the extent that the pledged stock is not available as collateral for other investments." Id. at 772 n. 7. Thus, upon remand, the district court could determine that there was an economic outlay on that basis alone, before deciding whether the form of the loan was to the taxpayer or to the corporation.

This particular situation is not before us and we decline to address the question of whether a guarantee can be an economic outlay when accompanied by pledged collateral.

analysis and that the debt-equity principles apply only to the determination of the characterization of the economic outlay, once one is found.

Granted, that conclusion is clouded by the next and final statement of the *Selfe* court: "In short, we remand for the district court to apply Plantation Patterns and determine if the bank loan to Jane Simon, Inc. was in reality a loan to the taxpayer." Id.[18] To the degree that the *Selfe* court agreed with Brown that an economic outlay is required before a shareholder may increase her basis in a subchapter S corporation, *Selfe* does not contradict current law or our resolution of the case before us. Furthermore, to the extent that the *Selfe* court remanded because material facts existed by which the taxpayer could show that the bank actually lent the money to her rather than the corporation, we are still able to agree.[19] It is because of the *Selfe* court's suggestion that debt-equity principles must be applied to resolve the question of whether the bank actually lent the money to the taxpayer/shareholder or the corporation, that we must part company with the Eleventh Circuit for the reasons stated above.

In conclusion, the Tax Court correctly focused on the initial inquiry of whether an economic outlay existed. Finding none, the issue of whether debt-equity principles ought to apply to determine the nature of the economic outlay was not before the Tax Court. * * *

ILLUSTRATIVE MATERIAL

A. DETERMINING A SHAREHOLDER'S "ACTUAL" INVESTMENT IN THE CORPORATION

1. *General*

As *Leavitt* indicates, the form in which an investment in a Subchapter S corporation is made can be crucially important. The taxpayers in *Leavitt* could have increased their stock bases by borrowing directly from the bank and contributing or lending the proceeds to the corporation, transactions which are economically essentially the same as the one which was actually carried out. The *Selfe* case, discussed in the *Leavitt* opinion, represented a rare taxpayer victory in the guaranty context. *Estate of Leavitt* was followed in Harris v. United States, 902 F.2d 439 (5th Cir.1990); Goatcher v. United States, 944 F.2d 747 (10th Cir.1991); Uri v. Commissioner, 949 F.2d 371

18. It is unclear whether the reference to *Plantation Patterns* means that debt-equity principles should be applied or refers back to an earlier statement in the *Selfe* court's opinion which related to the initial inquiry:

> In Plantation Patterns, the Fifth Circuit held that a loan is deemed to be made to a stockholder who has guaranteed a corporate note when the facts indicate that the lender is looking primarily to the stockholder for repayment.

Selfe, 778 F.2d at 771.

19. We note, however, that under the circumstances presented here, the Tax Court resolved that factual determination against the appellants because they could not overcome the uncontradicted fact that they did not treat the loan repayments made by VAFLA as constructive income to them. Such a position was inconsistent with their claim that the transaction was in actuality a loan from the Bank to them followed by their contribution of the $300,000 to the corporation.

(10th Cir.1991). See also Harrington v. United States, 605 F.Supp. 53 (D.Del.1985)(stockholders and S corporation were co-makers of a note originally executed by the stockholders only; the corporation was added at the request of the lender to perfect a pledge of corporate assets as security; the corporation was treated as a principal debtor on the note to the lender under state law and, therefore, did not receive the proceeds as a loan from the stockholders; the stockholders were not allowed to include the note in basis).

In Bolding v. Commissioner, 117 F.3d 270 (5th Cir.1997), the shareholder of an S corporation successfully argued that a bank loan was made to the shareholder who then relent the proceeds to his S corporation. The taxpayer conducted a cattle ranching business through an S corporation, "Three Forks Land & Cattle Co." The taxpayer arranged a line of credit from a bank, signing the note and security agreement "Dennis E. Bolding d/b/a Three Forks Land & Cattle Co." The taxpayer signed a UCC–1 using his name only. The bank disbursed the loan proceeds directly to the corporation's bank account and the corporation made loan payments directly to the bank. When the corporation incurred losses in excess of the taxpayer's basis in his stock, the taxpayer claimed losses against the amount of the loan. The corporation's return showed the loan as a loan from stockholders. The court upheld the taxpayer's contention because the transaction followed the form of a loan from the bank to the taxpayer individually, and rejected the Commissioner's argument that the loan was in substance made to the corporation. The taxpayer's failure to report interest income from the corporation and to claim interest deductions for payments to the bank was not contrary to the taxpayer's characterization because at the same interest rate these items were a wash.

2. *Shareholder Satisfaction of Guarantee*

If a stockholder is required to satisfy a corporate liability pursuant to a guarantee of the corporation's note, an obligation from the corporation to the stockholder is created as a result of the subrogation doctrine[21] with a basis equal to the amount paid on the guaranty. Rev.Rul. 70–50, 1970–1 C.B. 178 (holding that basis arises only in the year of payment under the guaranty); Rev.Rul. 75–144, 1975–1 C.B. 277 (same result in case in which the stockholder executed a personal note that the creditor accepted in satisfaction of the corporate obligation); but see Underwood v. Commissioner, 535 F.2d 309 (5th Cir.1976) (substitution of stockholder note for note of S corporation to another corporation controlled by the stockholder merely amounted to a guaranty since, unlike Rev.Rul. 75–144, the creditor was not an independent third party and there was no likelihood the payment would ever be required under the note; as a result no basis was acquired in the indebtedness of the S corporation until payments were actually made on

21. See Putnam v. Commissioner, 352 U.S. 82 (1956), holding that the debt of a C corporation paid by a stockholder is deductible as a bad debt upon failure of the corporation to pay the shareholder's subrogation claim because the stockholder steps into the shoes of the original creditor and becomes a creditor of the corporation.

the note to the creditor corporation); Brown v. Commissioner, 706 F.2d 755 (6th Cir.1983) (guaranteeing stockholders must make actual disbursements on the corporate indebtedness before they can increase basis).

3. *Indirect Corporate Obligations*

In Hitchins v. Commissioner, 103 T.C. 711 (1994), the taxpayer lent money to CCC Corp., a C corporation formed to develop a database for a corporation subsequently to be formed. CMB Corp. subsequently was formed with the taxpayer as a shareholder, and CMB Corp. validly elected to be an S corporation. CMB Corp. gave a note to CCC Corp. for the amount the latter had expended in developing the database. Subsequently, in partial payment of the note, CMB Corp assumed CCC Corp.'s indebtedness to the taxpayer, but CCC Corp.'s promissory note to the taxpayer was not canceled and CMB Corp. did not issue its own promissory note to the taxpayer. The court held that the amount lent by the taxpayer to CCC Corp. could not be included in his basis in the stock and indebtedness of CMB Corp. when determining the amount of CMB Corp. losses the taxpayer could deduct under § 1366(d)(1):

"There is no question that there was an economic outlay by [the taxpayer]. Nor is there any question that, by virtue of the assumption, CMB became obligated to pay to petitioner the amount owed him on the note from CCC representing his loan to it. * * *

"[The taxpayer] argue[s] that, because section 1366(d)(1)(B) refers to '*any indebtedness*' (emphasis added), without qualifying language, the debt assumed by CMB should be considered an indebtedness to petitioners.

"[The Commissioner] counters that, because of the words '*of*' and '*to*' in section 1366(d)(1)(B)(emphasis added), the indebtedness must represent an outlay from the taxpayer directly to the S corporation incurring the loss and that CMB's assumption of CCC's liability does not constitute such an outlay. * * *

"In the absence of any evidence of a direct obligation from CMB to him, [taxpayer] was simply a creditor beneficiary of CMB whose rights against it were derivative through CCC, albeit that he could probably sue CMB without joining CCC. * * * We think it significant that, as between CCC and CMB, CCC remained liable as a surety of the obligation of CMB to [taxpayer]; there was no novation relieving CCC of its liability to [taxpayer] as a primary obligor. * * * Thus, if CMB failed to pay its obligation, petitioner would have had recourse against CCC. * * * The continued obligation of CCC to [taxpayer] would, if CMB defaulted, provide a remedy to [taxpayer] which would in effect produce a reimbursement of his initial outlay by way of his loan to CCC. * * * Thus, [taxpayer's] position ultimately depended upon his status as a creditor and shareholder of CCC, and not as an investor in CMB. * * * We are satisfied that, under these circumstances, there was no 'investment' by [taxpayer] in CMB * * *."

In Frankel v. Commissioner, 61 T.C. 343 (1973), aff'd by order, 506 F.2d 1051 (3d Cir. 1974), taxpayers were stockholders of an S corporation that operated a restaurant located in a building owned by a partnership in which the taxpayers were partners. The taxpayers' interests in the corporation and the partnership were identical. The partnership loaned funds to the corporation and the taxpayers asserted that their bases for purposes of passing through a net operating loss should include the partnership loans on the theory that loans from the partnership constituted loans made by the individual partners. The court held, however, that the debt ran to the partnership and the stockholders were not entitled to reflect the loans in their bases.

B. COMPARISON OF SUBCHAPTER S AND PARTNERSHIP TREATMENT OF ENTITY–LEVEL DEBT

The requirement that only actual investment in the corporation, however determined, is included in the S corporation stockholder's stock and debt basis precludes the kind of pass through treatment provided to debt incurred by a partnership. In the case of a partnership, each partner is deemed to contribute money to the partnership to the extent of the partner's share of partnership liabilities. This deemed contribution increases the partner's basis in the partner's partnership interest. I.R.C. §§ 752(a) and 722. In this sense, a partnership is treated as an aggregate of the partners' interests with each partner sharing in the partnership's liabilities. The S corporation is treated as an entity separate from the stockholders, who do not share corporate debt as a pass through attribute. Why should the S corporation be treated differently? One possible answer is that, unlike general partners, S corporation stockholders are not responsible for corporate debt by virtue of their corporate limited liability. However, this protection is often eliminated by stockholder guarantees, as in *Leavitt.* In addition, nonrecourse partnership debt for which no partner is subject to an economic risk of loss is allocated to the partners and increases their basis in their partnership interests. However, the partnership rules also require a matching allocation of partnership income to partners who receive credit for nonrecourse partnership debt so that, as the debt is repaid, the partner whose basis was increased by the debt is charged with partnership income equivalent to the debt principal. The same matching of income allocations with payments of debt may occur in a partnership with respect to partner guarantees of partnership debt and partnership debt for which a partner is personally liable. In addition, a partner who personally assumes a non-pro rata share of partnership debt may be specially allocated the partnership income used to satisfy debt principal (as long as the allocation satisfies the substantial economic effect requirement of § 704(b)) so that the partner's basis increase and deductions claimed by the partner based on the debt are matched with an offsetting income allocation. There is no equivalent vehicle for such an allocation of S corporation income, which is shared pro rata among stockholders in proportion to stock ownership. An allocation of corporate debt to stockholders of an S corporation could be unsatisfactory because the allocation would not be adjusted to account for a particular stockholder's secondary liability through guarantees or other devices. Although these problems can be resolved with provisions similar to the partnership rules providing for adjustable allocations to S corporation stockholders, the change would add substantial complexity to Subchapter S.

B. DISTRIBUTIONS

INTERNAL REVENUE CODE: Sections 1368, 1371(c) and (e); 453B(h).

REGULATIONS: Sections 1.1367–1(d)(1), (e); 1.1368–1(a)–(c),–3, Ex. (1).

PROPOSED REGULATIONS: Sections 1.1368–1(e)(2).

Senate Finance Committee Report, Subchapter S Revision Act of 1982

S.Rep. No. 97–640, 97th Cong., 2d Sess. 20 (1982).

Explanation of Provisions

1. Taxation of shareholders (secs. 1368 and 1371(c))

Under [section 1368(a)], the amount of any distribution to a shareholder will equal the amount of cash distributed plus the fair market value of any property distributed * * *.

The amount of a distribution by a corporation without accumulated earnings and profits will be tax-free to the extent of the shareholder's basis in the stock. The distribution will be applied to reduce the shareholder's basis in his stock. To the extent the amount of the distribution exceeds basis, capital gains generally will result.

No post–1982 earnings of a subchapter S corporation will be considered earnings and profits for this purpose. Thus, under [section 1371(c)(1)], a corporation will not have earnings and profits attributable to any taxable year beginning after 1982 if a subchapter S election was in effect for that year.

* * *

2. Treatment of corporation [sec. 311]

Gain will be recognized by a subchapter S corporation on a distribution of appreciated property, other than distributions [of property permitted to be received without recognition of gain under sections 354, 355 or 356], in the same manner as if the property had been sold to the shareholder as its fair market value. Like other corporate gain, it will pass-thru to the shareholders.

Without this rule, assets could be distributed tax-free (except for recapture in certain instances) and subsequently sold without income recognition to the selling shareholder because of the stepped-up fair market value basis.

ILLUSTRATIVE MATERIAL

A. DISTRIBUTIONS OF APPRECIATED PROPERTY

1. *Generally*

In a significant departure from the partnership provisions on which treatment of S corporation distributions is generally based, § 311(b) requires recognition of gain at the corporate level on the distribution of appreciated property to stockholders. In the corresponding partnership situation, gain recognition is postponed through the rules on basis adjustments.[22] Presumably, Congress believed that the partnership approach would have been too complex to apply in a corporate context. Technically, this result is reached under § 1371(a), which provides that, except when specifically displaced, the normal Subchapter C rules, including the rules governing corporate distributions, are applicable to Subchapter S corporations. Thus, § 311(b) requires recognition of corporate level gain on the distribution of appreciated property as if the property were sold for its fair market value.[23] The recognized gain is passed through to stockholders who report the gain as income under § 1366. Under § 1368, the distribution of the property itself is tax free to the stockholder to the extent of the stockholder's basis in his stock. The stockholder's basis in the property received is its fair market value, I.R.C. § 301(d), and the shareholder reduces by a like amount the basis of the stock with respect to which the distribution was made. Thus, in comparison to the treatment accorded distributions by a partnership, the distribution of appreciated property by an S corporation accelerates the payment of tax, although there is still only one level of tax.

2. *Liquidating Distributions*

Liquidating distributions by an S corporation also are subject to the liquidation rules of Subchapter C. Section 336 requires recognition of gain or loss at the corporate level as if the property were sold for its fair market value. The gain or loss is passed through to stockholders under § 1366 and their bases in their stock are adjusted accordingly pursuant to § 1367. Under § 331 liquidating distributions are treated as received by the stockholders in exchange for their stock; gain is recognized to the extent the distribution exceeds basis, or loss is recognized if the distribution is less than the stockholder's basis. Stock gain or loss is recognized in situations where the stockholder's stock basis is not the same as the stockholder's ratable share of the corporation's asset bases, e.g., where the stockholder acquired the stock by purchase or bequest.

Distribution of a § 453 installment obligation generally results in immediate recognition, under either or both of §§ 311 and 453B, of gain to

22. Except to the extent required by § 751, no gain is recognized by a partnership on a distribution of appreciated property. The partnership basis carries over to the distributee partner to the extent of the partner's basis in the partner's partnership interest.

23. H.Rep.No. 100–795, 100th Cong., 2d Sess. 64 (1988).

the corporation, which will be passed through to the shareholders. Section 453B(h), however, provides a very narrow exception for the distribution of an installment obligation acquired by an S corporation on the sale of its assets within twelve months preceding complete liquidation of the corporation. Corporate level gain is not triggered by the distribution in liquidation of the installment obligation,[24] and the shareholder does not treat receipt of the installment obligation itself as a payment in exchange for the stockholder's stock in the liquidation. I.R.C. § 453(h). Instead, the receipt of each installment payment by the stockholder is a taxable event. Thus, S corporation stockholders are permitted to defer recognition of liquidation gain in the same manner that § 453(h) permits deferral of recognition by C corporation stockholders. See page 473. But § 453B(h) requires that the character of the stockholder's gain be determined as if the corporation had recognized the gain and the gain had passed through to the stockholders under § 1366.

B. TIMING OF BASIS ADJUSTMENTS FOR GAIN AND LOSS AND DISTRIBUTIONS

Section 1368(d) requires that positive adjustments to a stockholder's stock basis under § 1367(a)(1), reflecting the stockholder's share of corporate income, be taken into account before applying the distribution rules of § 1368(b), but that distributions be taken into account before negative adjustments to a stockholder's stock basis are made under § 1367(a)(2), reflecting the stockholder's share of corporate loss. See also Treas. Reg. § 1.1367–1(e)(4) (promulgated before the 1996 amendments). This asymmetrical rule works to the shareholder's advantage by preventing interim distributions of profits during the year from being treated as distributions in excess of basis, thereby triggering gain under § 1368(b)(2). Conversely, if the corporation loses money, distributions will not be taxed to the extent they did not exceed the shareholder's basis at the beginning of the year (subject to adjustment for items other than passed-through corporate losses).

Prior to 1997, adjustments to stock basis to reflect passed-through losses were taken into account before the distribution rules were applied. Thus, if the corporation lost money, distributions that did not exceed basis on the date of the distribution could result in recognition of capital gain when taken into account after the stockholder's basis had been reduced by the loss for the year. While this result may appear to have been detrimental to the shareholder, it was in some cases quite beneficial because it could create capital gains and ordinary losses that offset in amounts but not in character.

24. Section 453B(h) does not apply for purposes of determining the corporation's tax liability under Subchapter S. Thus the corporation is not relieved from recognition of gain on the distribution of an installment obligation that triggers the built-in gain tax of § 1374, discussed at page 420, or the tax on passive investment income of § 1375, discussed at page 417.

Suppose that A is a fifty percent shareholder of X Corp., an S Corporation. A's adjusted basis in the X Corp. stock on January 1, 1996, was $1,000. During 1996, A's share of X Corp.'s items of income and loss were a capital gain of $200 and an operating loss of $900, and during the year X Corp. distributed $700 to A. Under the pre–1997 rules, A would have recognized both the $200 capital gain and the $900 ordinary loss under § 1366; as a result A's stock basis would be reduced to $300 under § 1367. A also would have recognized a $400 gain on the distribution. The net result would have been that A recognized $600 of capital gain and $900 of ordinary loss.

Under the post–1996 rules, the loss is taken into account last. A's basis in the X Corp. stock first is increased to $1,200 ($1,000 plus $200 capital gain). The distribution then reduces A's stock basis to $500, with no gain being recognized. Finally, A is able to deduct currently $500 of the $900 loss that passed through, reducing A's basis to zero. The remaining $400 loss is carried forward pursuant to § 1366(d)(2). The net result is that A recognizes currently $200 of capital gain and $500 of ordinary loss. See Staff of the Joint Committee on Taxation, General Explanation of Tax Legislation Enacted in the 104th Congress 122–124 (Comm. Prt. 1996).

C. DISTRIBUTIONS FOLLOWING TERMINATION OF S CORPORATION STATUS

Following termination of an S election, distributions of money may be received by stockholders as a tax-free reduction of basis to the extent of the undistributed taxable income of the S corporation that has been passed through to the stockholders. I.R.C. § 1371(e)(1). The distribution must be made within the "post termination transition period" as defined in § 1377(b), generally at least a one year period after termination of S corporation status, although the period may differ in certain specified circumstances. See Treas. Reg. § 1.1377–2. If the stockholders fail to withdraw previously taxed income from the corporation within the applicable period, the privilege of tax-free distribution under § 1368 is lost and subsequent corporate distributions are taxable under § 301, i.e., subsequent distributions are taxable dividends if supported by sufficient earnings and profits. (If the corporation has always been an S corporation, earnings and profits will arise only in the period following termination of the election.)

Section 1371(e)(1) prescribes that only distributions of "money" may be tax-free during the post-termination transition period. Under a requirement of the pre–1983 Subchapter S rules, distributions of money during the first two and one-half months of the taxable year were received tax-free by the stockholders as distributions of previously taxed income of the prior taxable year.[25] Taxpayers attempted various devices to circumvent this

25. Otherwise, distributions during the taxable year were taxed as dividends to the extent of the current year's earnings and profits. After current earnings were distributed, distributions of prior years' undistributed taxable income were also received tax-free by stockholders.

"money" distribution requirement, but with a marked lack of success. This case law remains relevant under § 1371(e)(1). See, e.g., Roesel v. Commissioner, 56 T.C. 14 (1971) (NA) (cash distribution and subsequent loan to corporation by stockholders were disregarded and the transaction was treated as a taxable distribution of the debt obligations); DeTreville v. United States, 445 F.2d 1306 (4th Cir.1971) (two transactions treated as one because the stockholders purported to receive cash distributions and immediately purchased property from the corporation; the transactions were in substance a distribution of property); Stein v. Commissioner, 65 T.C. 336 (1975) (fact that stockholders were in constructive receipt of amounts credited to their accounts on the books of the corporation did not satisfy the money requirement).

D. SHAREHOLDER–EMPLOYEE FRINGE BENEFITS

For purposes of employee fringe benefit provisions, § 1372 treats an S corporation as a partnership and each more than 2 percent stockholder as a partner. As a result, S corporation stockholders holding more than 2 percent of the stock are not eligible for employee fringe benefits. Revenue Ruling 91–26, 1991–1 C.B. 184, holds that payments of health and accident insurance premiums with respect to a more than two percent shareholder/employee of an S corporation must be included in income by the shareholder/employee and are not subject to exclusion from gross income under § 106. The corporation may deduct the premiums under § 162 and is required to report the premiums as compensation to the employee/shareholder on a Form W–2.

Section 1372 does not affect the treatment of a qualified pension plan maintained by an S corporation. If an S corporation has a qualified pension plan, a shareholder of the corporation who is also an employee may participate in the corporation's qualified pension plan regardless of the amount of stock that the shareholder-employee owns. But if the shareholder is not also an employee, the shareholder may not participate in the qualified pension plan. Passed through S corporation income is not self-employment income for purposes of maintaining an H.R. 10 Plan.

SECTION 4. S CORPORATIONS THAT HAVE A C CORPORATION HISTORY

A. DISTRIBUTIONS FROM AN S CORPORATION WITH EARNINGS AND PROFITS ACCUMULATED FROM SUBCHAPTER C YEARS

INTERNAL REVENUE CODE: Section 1368(a), (c)–(e).

REGULATIONS: Sections 1.1368–1(d)–(f), –2, –3.

PROPOSED REGULATIONS: Sections 1.1368–1(d),–2(a)(1), (3)(ii), (5).

Conversion of an existing C corporation to S corporation status raises several problems that are related to the double tax regime of Subchapter C. The Subchapter S rules are structured to maintain the possibility of a second layer of tax on income earned or appreciation in assets occurring while the Subchapter S corporation was subject to Subchapter C. Thus, under § 1368(c)(1), distributions by an S corporation that has accumulated earnings and profits from its C corporation years are tax-free to stockholders only to the extent of an "accumulated adjustments account." The accumulated adjustments account, as defined in § 1368(e)(1), reflects the S corporation's taxable income that has been passed through and taxed to shareholders under § 1368 while the corporation has been subject to Subchapter S. Distributions in excess of the accumulated adjustments account are treated as taxable dividends to the stockholders to the extent of the corporation's accumulated earnings and profits. I.R.C. § 1368(c)(2). Distributions in excess of both the accumulated adjustments account and accumulated earnings and profits are treated the same as distributions from a corporation with no earnings and profits; distributions are not included in the stockholder's gross income to the extent of the stockholder's basis in the S corporation's stock, and any excess is capital gain.

ILLUSTRATIVE MATERIAL

A. SOURCES OF S CORPORATION EARNINGS AND PROFITS

Generally, corporate activities during the period when a Subchapter S election is in effect have no impact on the corporation's earnings and profits. I.R.C. § 1371(c)(1). An S corporation will have earnings and profits only (1) if it has accumulated earnings from a period before its S election during which it was a C corporation, or (2) if it inherited the earnings and profits account of a C corporation that was acquired in a merger or other transaction to which § 381 applies. (For § 381, see Chapter 16.)

B. ACCUMULATED ADJUSTMENTS ACCOUNT

1. *General*

Distributions to stockholders from an S corporation with earnings and profits are excluded from the stockholders' gross incomes only to the extent of the corporation's accumulated adjustments account. I.R.C. § 1368(c)(1). The accumulated adjustments account is basically a running total of the corporation's net taxable income while operating as an S corporation. The account is based on adjustments to the stockholders' basis under § 1367 except that the accumulated adjustments account does not include tax-exempt income, nor is it reduced by deductions not allowed in computing the corporation's taxable income. I.R.C. § 1368(e)(1); Treas. Reg. § 1.1368–2(a)(2) and (3). The exclusion of tax-exempt items from the accumulated adjustments account means that tax-exempt income of the S corporation may not be distributed tax-free to stockholders until after the taxable distributions of accumulated earnings and profits from the Subchapter C period have been made.

Operation of the stacking principle used in § 1368(c) is illustrated as follows: As of January 1, 1999, the effective date of its Subchapter S election, Y Corporation had $50,000 of Subchapter C accumulated earnings and profits. Y Corporation's sole shareholder, A, had a basis in her stock of $6,000. For 1999, Y Corporation had taxable income of $30,000 and made a cash distribution to A of $100,000. Before taking into account the effect of the distribution, the $30,000 of current taxable income generates an increase in the basis of A's stock in Y Corporation from $6,000 to $36,000 and the balance in the accumulated adjustments account is increased from zero to $30,000. The distribution is treated as follows: Pursuant to § 1368(c)(1), the first $30,000, attributable to the accumulated adjustments account, is applied against the basis of the stock, reducing A's basis in the stock to $6,000; and the balance in the accumulated adjustments account is reduced to zero. Under § 1368(c)(2), the next $50,000, attributable to the accumulated earnings and profits, is taxed as a dividend. Once accumulated earnings and profits are exhausted, § 1368(c)(3) brings § 1368(b) into play and the next $6,000 is applied against basis, reducing A's basis in the stock to zero. The final $14,000 is treated as gain from the sale or exchange of the stock.

The accumulated adjustments account is a corporate account that is not apportioned among the shareholders. Treas. Reg. § 1.1368–2(a)(1). If an S corporation makes two or more distributions during the taxable year that in the aggregate exceed the accumulated adjustments account, the accumulated adjustments account determined as of the end of the year without regard to distributions during the year, is allocated among the distributions pro rata. Treas. Reg. § 1.1368–2(b). Application of this rule is illustrated by the following example, derived from Treas. Reg. § 1.1368–3, Ex.(5). Assume that the stock of X Corporation, which as of December 31, 1999 has earnings and profits of $1,000 and an accumulated adjustments account of $400, is owned 40 percent by A and 60 percent by B. For 2000, X Corp. has taxable income of $120, which increases its accumulated adjustments account to $520. On January 31, 2000, X Corp. distributes $240 to A and $360 to B. On October 31, 2000, X Corp. distributes $80 to A and $120 to B. During the year, X Corp. distributed $800, which exceeded its $520 accumulated adjustments account by $280. A's January distribution was 30 percent of the total distributions (240/800), so thirty percent of the accumulated adjustments account as of December 31, 2000, or $156 is allocated to A's January distribution. B's January distribution was 45 percent of the total distributions for the year, so $234 of the accumulated adjustments account is allocated to that distribution. A's October distribution was 10 percent of the total distributions, so $52 of the accumulated adjustments account is allocated to that distribution; likewise 15 percent of the accumulated adjustments account, or $78 is allocated to B's October distribution. A has received a total of $208 ($156 + $52) tax-free under § 1368(c)(1) and $112 taxed as a dividend; B has received $312 ($234 + 78) tax-free and a dividend of $168. Earnings and profits are reduced to $720 to reflect the $280 of dividends.

2. *Distributions in Loss Years*

Although positive adjustments to a shareholder's stock basis under § 1367(a)(1) to reflect the stockholder's share of corporate income are taken into account before applying the distribution rules of § 1368(c), if the corporation incurs a loss, § 1368(d) directs that distributions be taken into account first. Consonantly, § 1368(e)(1)(C) directs that negative adjustments to the accumulated adjustments account to reflect losses incurred by the corporation be taken into account after distributions, thus increasing the portion of the distribution that may be treated as ordinary income under § 1368(c). The operation of this rule is illustrated by the following example derived from H.R. Rep. No. 104–586, 104th Cong., 2d Sess. 90–91 (1996):

B is the sole shareholder of X Corp., an S corporation with $500 of accumulated earnings and profits and an accumulated adjustments account of $200. B's adjusted basis in the X Corp. stock on January 1, 2000, is $1,000. During 2000, X Corp. recognizes a capital gain of $200, incurs an operating loss of $900, and distributes $600 to B. Because there is a net negative adjustment for the year, no adjustment is made to the accumulated adjustments account before determining the effect of the distribution under § 1368(c). First, B's adjusted basis in the X Corp. stock is increased from $1,000 to $1,200 to reflect the capital gain. Second, $200 of the $600 distribution to B is a distribution from X Corp.'s accumulated adjustments account, reducing the accumulated adjustments account to zero. This $200 is applied against B's adjusted basis of $1,200, reducing B's basis in the stock to $1,000. The remaining $400 of the distribution is a distribution of accumulated earnings and profits. It is taxable as a dividend to B and does not reduce B's basis in the X Corp. stock. X Corp.'s earnings and profits account is reduced by $400, to $100. X Corp.'s accumulated adjustments account is then increased by $200 to reflect the recognized capital gain and reduced by $900 to reflect the operating loss, leaving a negative balance in the accumulated adjustments account on January 1, 2001, of $700. Because B's adjusted basis is $1,000, the § 1366(d) loss limitation does not apply, and B may deduct the entire $900 operating loss. As a result, B's basis in the X Corp. stock is decreased by $900, and B's basis in the stock on January 1, 2001, is $100 ($1,000 plus $200 less $200 less $900). See Staff of the Joint Committee on Taxation, General Explanation of Tax Legislation Enacted in the 104th Congress 122–124 (Comm. Prt. 1996).

C. REDEMPTIONS

Section 1371(c) applies to redemptions by an S corporation with earnings and profits that are treated as a § 301 distribution because none of the tests for redemption treatment in § 302 or § 304 have been met. If a distribution is received by a stockholder as a redemption in exchange for stock under § 302(a) or § 303, a pro rata portion of the distribution is deemed to reduce the accumulated adjustments account. I.R.C. § 1368(e)(1)(B).[26] Rev. Rul. 95–14, 1995–1 C.B. 159, involved a redemption

26. Section 1371(c)(2) requires adjustments to the earnings and profits account in the case of redemptions, liquidations, reorganizations and other transactions to which Subchapter C is applicable. Section 1371(c)(3) provides for an adjustment to earnings and profits in the case of distributions treated as subject to § 1368(c) rather than § 302(a) where both the shareholder's basis in her stock and the corporation's accumulated adjustments account exceeded the amount of the distribution. Under § 1368(c), none of the distribution was included in income, and under § 1368(e)(1)(A), the accumulated adjustments account was reduced by an amount equal to the distribution. Section 1368(e)(1)(B) was not applicable because the redemption did not qualify under either § 302(a) or § 303.

D. ELECTIONS

Section 1368(e)(3) provides an election, with the consent of all stockholders, to treat distributions as dividends from accumulated earnings and profits before reducing the accumulated adjustments account. The election may be used to prevent termination for excess passive investment income under § 1362(d)(3), or to avoid the § 1375 tax on passive investment income of an S corporation with accumulated earnings and profits, discussed below. Treas. Reg. § 1.1368–1(f)(3) also provides for an election to reduce Subchapter C earnings and profits by a deemed dividend. The amount deemed to be received as a dividend by shareholders is treated as a cash contribution back to the corporation.

B. PASSIVE INVESTMENT INCOME OF AN S CORPORATION WITH ACCUMULATED EARNINGS AND PROFITS

INTERNAL REVENUE CODE: Sections 1362(d)(3); 1375.

REGULATIONS: Section 1.1362–2,–3(b).

There are no limitations on the type of income, e.g., passive versus active, that can be earned by an S corporation with no C corporation history.[27] On the other hand, § 1375 imposes a tax on an S corporation with accumulated Subchapter C earnings and profits in any year in which the corporation has passive investment income in excess of 25 percent of gross receipts. The tax is imposed at the highest rate under § 11(b) on "excess net passive income," which is defined in § 1375(b) as an amount that bears the same ratio to net passive income as the passive investment income in excess of 25 percent of gross receipts bears to the passive investment income for the taxable year. In other words, the taxable amount is determined from the formula—

$$\text{Net Passive Investment Income} \times \frac{\text{Passive Investment Income minus 25 percent of Gross Receipts}}{\text{Passive Investment Income}}$$

dividends under § 1368(c)(2). See Treas. Reg. § 1.1368–2(d).

27. Before 1982, former § 1375(e)(5) provided for termination of an S election for any corporation if more than 20 percent of its gross receipts constituted passive investment income, without regard to whether the corporation also had Subchapter C earnings and profits. The definition of passive investment income under this now repealed provision raised interpretive issues that continue to be important under current law.

"Net passive investment income" is defined as passive income (defined below) less deductible expenses incurred to produce the passive investment income. By virtue of this definition, the apportionment formula allocates expenses between the passive investment income in excess of 25 percent of gross receipts, which is subject to the tax, and the passive investment income that is less than 25 percent of gross receipts, which is not taxed. Finally, the amount subject to tax as net passive investment income is limited to the corporation's regular taxable income for the year. I.R.C. § 1375(b)(1)(B).

Suppose, for example, that an S corporation with earnings and profits from its C corporation history had gross receipts from an active business of $600,000, dividend income of $360,000, and expenses to earn the dividend income of $60,000. The formula in § 1375(b) is as follows:

$$(\$360{,}000 - \$60{,}000) \times \frac{(\$360{,}000 - [0.25 \times \{\$600{,}000 + \$360{,}000\}])}{\$360{,}000} = \$100{,}000$$

Thus, the § 1375(a) tax is levied on the amount of $100,000, which under the formula is the corporation's "excess net passive investment income." Applying the highest rate under § 11, 35 percent, the tax is $35,000. Pursuant to § 1366(f)(3), the amount of dividend income passed through to the shareholders will be reduced by the tax imposed on the corporation with respect to that income.

The Commissioner may waive imposition of the passive investment income tax if the corporation establishes that it determined in good faith that it had no Subchapter C earnings and profits and within a reasonable period of time the corporation distributed its earnings and profits to stockholders. I.R.C. § 1375(d).

In addition, pursuant to § 1362(d)(3), an S election is terminated if the corporation has Subchapter C earnings and profits at the close of each of three consecutive taxable years following the election and during each of the three years more than 25 percent of the corporation's gross receipts are passive investment income.[28] This provision is intended to prevent an S corporation from utilizing accumulated C corporation earnings for passive investment purposes.

A termination because of excess passive investment income is effective on the first day of the taxable year following the third consecutive year in which the corporation has disqualifying earnings and profits and investment income. Termination may be avoided if the Internal Revenue Service determines that the termination is inadvertent under the standards of § 1362(f), see page 382.

28. The termination rule does not apply with respect to earnings and profits accumulated before the effective date of the 1982 Act. Prior to 1983 it was possible for an S corporation to accumulate earnings and profits because earnings and profits could exceed pass-through taxable income.

The tax on passive investment income and termination of S status both can be avoided either by distributing accumulated earnings and profits to stockholders as a taxable dividend prior to making the S election or by making a deemed dividend and recontribution election under Treas. Regs. § 1.1368–1(f)(3).

ILLUSTRATIVE MATERIAL

A. PASSIVE INVESTMENT INCOME

For purposes of §§ 1362(d)(3) and 1375, passive investment income is defined as income from royalties, rents, dividends, interest, annuities and sales or exchanges of stock or securities (but only to the extent of gains). Passive investment income, however, does not include interest on notes acquired in the ordinary course of business on the sale of inventory, or gross receipts from the regular conduct of a lending or finance business. I.R.C. § 1362(d)(3)(C). In addition, § 1362(d)(3)(E) excludes from passive investment income dividends that are attributable to the active conduct of a trade or business of a C corporation in which the S corporation has an 80 percent or greater ownership interest (as defined in § 1504(a)(2). Prop. Reg. § 1.1362–8 (1998) provides rules for determining whether the earnings and profits of the subsidiary are "active" or "passive."

Treas. Reg. § 1.1362–2(c)(5)(ii)(B)(*2*) provides that the term "rents" does not include rents derived in an active trade or business of renting property if the corporation provides significant services or incurs substantial costs in the rental business. Thus, for example the income from hotel and motel operations is not rent. However, Feingold v. Commissioner, 49 T.C. 461 (1968), held under predecessor Regulations that rental income from summer bungalows did not fall within the "significant services" exception and constituted disqualifying income.

The list of passive interest income items in the predecessor to § 1362(d)(3)(C)(i) was held to be exclusive, so that gains from the sale of unimproved real estate did not constitute passive investment income for purposes of the limitation. Howell v. Commissioner, 57 T.C. 546 (1972)(A); Rev.Rul. 75–188, 1975–1 C.B. 276.

If an S corporation receives passive investment income specified in § 1362(d)(3)(C), the fact that it is an active operating company with respect to such income does not prevent application of the disqualification rule. See Zychinski v. Commissioner, 506 F.2d 637 (8th Cir.1974), in which a corporation's Subchapter S status was terminated because too high a percentage of its income was gains on sales of stocks and securities; that the corporation was a dealer did not change the result. This result is mitigated for lending and financing businesses, however, by § 1362(d)(3)(C)(iii), which excludes the interest received in the ordinary course by S corporations engaged in such a business from investment income for purposes of the termination rule. In a similar vein, § 1362(d)(3)(D) provides that gains or losses on certain futures contracts and options derived by commodities and options dealers will not be taken into account in determining passive investment income. There is no corresponding relief for rental income derived in the ordinary course of a business. Thus a corporation with Subchapter C earnings and profits still cannot conduct rental operations yielding rents in excess of 25 percent of its gross receipts for more than three years and retain S corporation status.

B. GROSS RECEIPTS

Treas. Reg. § 1.1362–2(c)(4)(i) provides that gross receipts are not the same as gross income. A corporation operating at a loss because its cost of goods sold exceeds its receipts will still have gross receipts. In contrast, proceeds from the sale or exchange of capital assets (except for stocks or securities) are taken into account in computing gross receipts only to the extent that gains from the sale or exchange of capital assets exceed losses from the sale or exchange of capital assets. I.R.C. § 1362(d)(3)(B). Gross receipts from the sale of stock or securities are taken into account only to the extent of gains. Losses from the sale of stock or securities do not offset the gains for this purpose. See Treas. Reg. § 1.1362–2(c)(4)(ii)(B). This rule prevents the corporation from acquiring and selling stocks to enhance artificially the amount of its gross receipts. Receipts that are not included in gross income because the corporation is a mere conduit are not included in gross receipts. See Kaiser's Estate v. Commissioner, T.C. Memo. 1997–88 (an insurance agency's gross receipts from its insurance business included only commissions received with respect to policies written by it; gross receipts did not include premiums collected from customers on behalf of the insurance company and remitted to the company).

C. BUILT-IN GAIN TAX

INTERNAL REVENUE CODE: Section 1374. See also section 1363(d).

REGULATIONS: Section 1.1374–1,–2,–3,–4(a), (b), (h)(1) and (2),–7, and–9.

Technical and Miscellaneous Revenue Act of 1988, Report of the Committee on Ways and Means, House of Representatives

H.Rep. No. 100–795, 100Th Cong., 2D Sess. 62–64 (1988).

A corporate level tax is imposed [by section 1374] on gain that arose prior to the conversion of a C corporation to an S corporation ("built-in gain") that is recognized by the S corporation through sale, distribution, or other disposition within 10 years after the date on which the S election took effect. The total amount of gain that must be recognized by the corporation, however, is limited to the aggregate net built-in gain of the corporation at the time of conversion to S status.

The 1986 Act [section 1374(c)(2)] provided that the amount of recognized built-in gains taken into account for any taxable year shall not exceed the excess (if any) of 1) the net unrealized built-in gain, over 2) the recognized built-in gains for prior years beginning in the 10–year recognition period. Also, recognized built-in gain is not taxed in a year to the extent that it exceeds the taxable income of the corporation for the year computed as if the corporation were a C corporation.

Under [section 1374(b)(2) and (3)], the corporation may take into account certain subchapter C tax attributes in computing the amount of tax on recognized built-in gains. Thus, for example, it may use unexpired net operating losses to offset the gain and may use business credit carryforwards to offset the tax.

The [1988 Act] modifies the operation of the built-in gains tax. [Section 1374(d)(2)(A)(ii)] retains the net income limitation of the [1986] Act by providing that a net recognized built-in gain for a year will not be taxed to the extent the corporation would not otherwise have taxable income for the year if it were a C corporation (determined in accordance with section 1375(b)(1)(B)). Under [section 1374(d)(2)(A)(ii)], therefore, recognized built-in gain in any post-conversion year is reduced for purposes of the built-in gains tax by any recognized built-in loss for that year, and also by any other post-conversion losses for that year.

Although the committee believes it is appropriate not to impose the built-in gains tax in a year in which the taxpayer experiences losses, the committee also believes it is appropriate to reduce the potential for taxpayers to manipulate the timing of post-conversion losses in a manner that might entirely avoid the built-in gains tax on the net unrealized built-in gain of the former C corporation. Accordingly, [section 1374(d)(2)(B)] provides that any net recognized built-in gain that is not subject to the built-in gains tax due to the net income limitation will be carried forward.

Thus, an amount equal to any net recognized built-in gain that is not subject to the built-in gains tax because of the net income limitation will be carried forward and will be subject to the built-in gains tax to the extent the corporation subsequently has other taxable income (that is not already otherwise subject to the built-in gains tax) for any taxable year within the 10 year recognition period. * * *

The provision is illustrated by the following example: Corporation A elects S status on March 31, 1988. The corporation has two assets, one with a value of $200 and an adjusted basis of $0 and the other with a value of $0 and an adjusted basis of $100. It has no other items of built-in gain or loss. The corporation thus has a net unrealized built-in gain of $100. In its first taxable year for which it is an S corporation, the corporation sells both assets for their fair market value and has a net recognized built-in gain of $100. It also has an additional $100 loss from other post-conversion activities. The corporation is not subject to any built-in gains tax in that year because its net recognized built-in gain ($100) exceeds its net income determined in accordance with section 1375(b)(1)(B)($0). In its next taxable year, the corporation has $200 of taxable income. $100 is subject to the built-in gains tax in that year, because of the carryforward of the $100 of net unrecognized built-in gain that had been untaxed due to the net income limitation.

[Section 1374(d)(8)] clarifies that the built-in gain provision applies not only when a C corporation converts to S status but also in any case in which an S corporation acquires an asset and the basis of such asset in the hands of the S corporation is determined (in whole or in part) by reference to the basis of such asset (or any other property) in the hands of the C corporation. In such cases, each acquisition of assets from a C corporation is subject to a separate determination of the amount of net built-in gain, and is subject to the provision for a separate 10–year recognition period. * * *

[Section 1374(d)(5)(A)] clarifies that, for purposes of this built-in gains tax under section 1374, any item of income which is properly taken into account for any taxable year in the recognition period but which is attributable to periods before the first taxable year for which the corporation was an S corporation is treated as a recognized built-in gain for the taxable year in which it is properly taken into account. Thus, the term "disposition of any asset" includes not only sales or exchanges but other income recognition events that effectively dispose of or relinquish a taxpayer's right to claim or receive income. For example, the term "disposition of any asset" for purposes of this provision also includes the collection of accounts receivable by a cash method taxpayer and the completion of a long-term contract performed by a taxpayer using the completed contract method of accounting.

Similarly, [section 1374(d)(5)(B)] clarifies that amounts that are allowable as a deduction during the recognition period but that are attributable to periods before the first S corporation taxable year are thus treated as recognized built-in losses in the year of the deduction.

As an example of these built-in gain and loss provisions, in the case of a cash basis personal service corporation that converts to S status and that has receivables at the time of the conversion, the receivables, when received, are built-in gain items. At the same time, built-in losses would include otherwise deductible compensation paid after the conversion to the persons who performed the services that produced the receivables, to the extent such compensation is attributable to such pre-conversion services. To the extent such built-in loss items offset the built-in gains from the receivables, there would be no amount subject to the built-in gains tax.

[Section 1374(b)(2)] clarifies that capital loss carryforwards may also be used to offset recognized built-in gains.

ILLUSTRATIVE MATERIAL

A. SCOPE OF SECTION 1374: DOUBLE TAXATION OF GAIN ECONOMICALLY ACCRUING DURING S CORPORATION'S PRIOR C CORPORATION HISTORY

Section 1374 is intended to impose double taxation of appreciation that occurred while assets were held by a C corporation that subsequently made an S election if the corporation does not continue to hold the assets for a substantial period of time after making the S election. Double taxation is achieved by imposing a corporate level tax on recognized built-in gain with respect to assets held by the corporation at the time of conversion from C to S corporation status in addition to taxing the shareholders on the gain under § 1366. The tax also applies to built-in gain recognized on the disposition of an asset acquired from a C corporation in a nonrecognition transaction with a transferred basis to the acquiring S corporation. Section 1374 is not applicable to a corporation that never was a C corporation or that has no assets acquired from a C corporation in a nonrecognition transaction. I.R.C. § 1374(c)(1). Nor is § 1374 applicable to assets purchased by the corporation or contributed to it during the period an S election is in effect.

Built-in gain recognized by an S corporation during the ten year recognition period[29] is subject to tax at the highest corporate tax rate under § 11(b), currently 35 percent. Recognized built-in gain is then subject to a second tax at the stockholder level as the recognized gain is passed through to stockholders under § 1366. Each stockholder's proportionate share of recognized built-in gain is reduced by the stockholder's proportionate share of the § 1374 tax. I.R.C. § 1366(f)(2). For example, if S Corporation sells a built-in gain asset with a basis of $10 for $110, the corporation's recognized gain of $100 is subject to tax of 35 percent. Stockholders are allocated their proportionate share of the $100 of gain, less the tax of $35, or a net taxable gain of $65. Then the stockholders pay a tax equal to 39.6 percent of $65. The total taxes of $60.74 are the same as would be imposed on a C corporation selling the assets and distributing the after-tax proceeds as a dividend, thus preserving the effects of the double tax regime.

Section 1374(e) grants to the Treasury Department broad authority to promulgate regulations to ensure that the double tax on assets that were appreciated at the time the corporation converted from C to S corporation status is not circumvented. Treas. Regs. §§ 1.1374–1 through 1.1374–10 provide detailed rules governing the application of § 1374.

B. AMOUNT OF GAIN SUBJECT TO THE BUILT–IN GAIN TAX

The technical operation of § 1374 is somewhat convoluted. Section 1374(a) imposes the tax on the corporation's "net recognized built-in gain." The term net recognized built-in gain is, in turn, defined in § 1374(d)(2)(A) as the amount that would be the corporation's taxable income for the year if only "recognized built-in gains" and "recognized built-in losses" were taken into account (but not more than the corporation's actual taxable income for the year). Recognized built-in gain is defined in § 1374(d)(3) as the amount of the gain recognized with respect to any asset disposed of during the year that was held by the corporation on the first day of its first

29. Treas. Reg. § 1.1374–1(d) provides that the "recognition period" during which the § 1374 tax applies is the 120 month period beginning on the first day that the corporation is an S corporation (or acquires an asset from a C corporation in a transferred basis transaction), and provides rules for determining taxable recognized built-in gain when the recognition period ends within the corporation's taxable year.

taxable year as an S corporation to the extent the property's fair market value exceeded its basis on that day. Similarly, recognized built-in loss is defined in § 1374(d)(4) as the loss recognized with respect to any asset disposed of during the year that was held by the corporation on the first day of its first taxable year as an S corporation to the extent the fair market value of the property was less than its basis on that day. Section 1374(c)(2) then limits the net recognized built-in gain taxable under § 1374(a) for the year to the excess of the corporation's "net unrealized built-in gain" over the net recognized built-in gain for previous years. "Net unrealized built-in gain" is defined in § 1374(d)(1) as the excess of the fair market value of the corporation's assets on the first day of its first taxable year as an S corporation over the aggregate basis of those assets on that day.

The purpose of this maze of statutory rules is to assure that the aggregate amount taxed under § 1374 if assets held on the day the S election was made are sold over a number of years does not exceed the gain that would have been recognized if the corporation had sold all of its assets immediately before making the S election. Furthermore, since the precise wording of § 1374(d)(3) creates rebuttable presumptions that all recognized gain on any asset sold during the ten year recognition period is built-in gain and that no loss recognized during the period is built-in loss, it is incumbent on the corporation to appraise all of its assets as of the effective date of an S election.

The limitation in § 1374(c) is illustrated in the following example. Assume that X Corporation made an S election on July 1, 1998. At that time X Corporation had the following assets:

Asset	Basis	Fair Market Value	Built-in Gain/Loss
Blackacre	$150	$225	$ 75
Whiteacre	$300	$550	$250
Greenacre	$450	$350	($100)
			$225

In 2000, when it has operating profits of $500, X Corporation sells Whiteacre for $650 and Greenacre for $300. The corporation recognizes a gain of $350 on Blackacre and a loss of $150 on Greenacre. Assuming that X Corporation satisfies its burden of proof as to the properties' fair market values on July 1, 1998, the recognized built-in gain on Whiteacre is $250 and the recognized built-in loss on Greenacre is $100. The net recognized built-in gain for the year is $150. Since the corporation's net unrealized built-in gain with respect to all of its assets is $225, the entire net recognized built-in gain is taxed under § 1374(a) in 2000. If Blackacre is sold the following year for $225, the entire gain is net recognized built-in gain, and since the ceiling in § 1374(c)(2) is $75 ($225 net unrealized built-in gain minus $175 net recognized built-in gain from 2000), the entire $75 gain is taxed at the corporate level under § 1374(a).

Now assume alternatively that in 2000, X Corporation sells Blackacre for $225 and Greenacre for $300. X Corporation recognizes a gain of $75 on

Blackacre and a loss of $150 on Greenacre. Assuming that X Corporation satisfies its burden of proof as to the properties' fair market values on July 1, 1998, the recognized built-in gain on Blackacre is $75 and the recognized built-in loss on Greenacre is $100. Its net recognized built-in loss for the year is $25, and no tax is due under § 1374(a). If Whiteacre is sold the following year for $650, the corporation recognizes a gain of $350, of which $250 is net recognized built-in gain. But since the corporation's net unrealized built-in gain is only $225, only $225 of that gain is subject to corporate level tax under § 1374(a).

Although § 1371(b) generally proscribes the use by an S corporation of net operating loss carryovers from years when it was a C corporation, there is an exception if built-in gains are required to be recognized and taxed to the S corporation under § 1374. Section 1374(b) permits Subchapter C NOL carryovers to offset net recognized built-in gain for a Subchapter S year solely for the purpose of computing the § 1374 tax.

Treas. Regs. §§ 1.1374–9 and 1.1374–10(b)(3) provide anti-abuse rules directed to the acquisition of property for the purpose of avoiding the § 1374 tax.

C. EFFECT OF ACCOUNTING METHOD ON APPLICATION OF SECTION 1374 TO GAINS FROM PROPERTY

Treas. Reg. § 1.1374–7 provides that the inventory method maintained by a corporation will be used to determine whether goods required to be included in inventory were on hand with built-in gain at the time of conversion to S corporation status. Reliable Steel Fabricators, Inc. v. Commissioner, T.C. Memo. 1995–293, held that the valuation of inventory work in progress on the effective date of an S election must include some profit margin for completed work, but not for raw materials.

Treas. Reg. § 1.1374–4(h) imposes the tax under § 1374 on all gains from an installment sale under § 453 recognized during or after the 120 month recognition period if the sale occurred prior to or during the 120 month recognition period. Tax is imposed under this provision, however, only to the extent that the gain would have been included in net recognized built-in gain if the entire gain had been recognized in the year of sale, taking into account the taxable income limitation. In determining the limitation, if the sale occurred before commencement of the recognition period (generally speaking, while the corporation was still a C Corporation), the sale is deemed to have occurred in the first year of the recognition period.

D. INCOME ITEMS OTHER THAN GAIN FROM THE SALE OF PROPERTY SUBJECT TO SECTION 1374

Under Treas. Reg. § 1.1374–4(b)(1) and (2), items of income and deduction attributable to prior periods that are taken into account as built-in gain items under § 1374(d)(5) include items that would have been taken into account before the beginning of the recognition period if the corporation had used the accrual method of accounting. Thus, for example, accounts receivable accrued before conversion to S Corporation status, but collected by a cash method S corporation after conversion, are treated as built-in gain items. See Treas. Reg. § 1.1374–4(b)(3), Ex.(1); Leou, M.D., P.A. v. Commissioner, T.C. Memo. 1994–393 (§ 1374 built-in gains tax applied to collection of cash method accounts receivable of a corporation that elected S status in 1988 and previously had been a C corporation).

Argo Sales Company, Inc. v. Commissioner, 105 T.C. 86 (1995), involved a year prior to the effective date of Treas. Reg. § 1.1374–4(d), which now dictates the same result. The corporation changed from the cash method of accounting to the accrual method in a year in which it was a C corporation. Pursuant to § 481, a positive adjustment to income to reflect accrual of its accounts receivable and payable was spread over ten years. Three years later, the corporation elected S corporation status. Application of § 1374(d)(5) to impose the corporate level tax on the § 481 adjustments was upheld.

Treas. Reg. § 1.1374–4(f) provides that discharge of indebtedness income or bad debt deductions attributable to indebtedness that exists prior to the beginning of the recognition period will be treated as built-in gain or loss. In addition, built-in gain or loss includes adjustments to income required under § 481 as a result of a change in accounting method effective before the beginning of the second year of the recognition period. Treas. Reg. § 1.1374–4(d).

Under Treas. Reg. § 1.1374–4(i)(1), an S corporation's distributive share of income or loss from a partnership interest owned by the S corporation will be treated as built-in gain or loss to the extent that the item would have been so treated if it had been taken into account directly by the corporation. Among other limitations, the amount of built-in gain or loss recognized by an S corporation as its distributive share of partnership items will be limited to the corporation's built-in gain or loss in the partnership interest itself. Treas. Reg. § 1.1374–4(i)(4). Subject to an anti-abuse rule, these partnership rules do not apply if the fair market value of an S corporation's partnership interest is less than $100,000 and represents less than 10 percent of the partnership capital and profits. Treas. Reg. § 1.1374–4(i)(5).

E. APPLICATION OF BUILT-IN GAINS TAX TO QUALIFIED SUBCHAPTER S SUBSIDIARY

If an election is made under § 1361(b)(3) to treat an existing wholly owned subsidiary corporation as a qualified Subchapter S subsidiary, the subsidiary is treated as having been liquidated immediately before the election is effective. Section 332 provides nonrecognition to the parent S corporation, and § 337 provides nonrecognition to the subsidiary. The basis of the subsidiary's assets remains the same under § 334(b). Pursuant to § 381, the S corporation parent also inherits any earnings and profits of its subsidiary. If the subsidiary previously was a C corporation, the § 1374 built-in gains tax will apply to the subsidiary's assets as if the subsidiary had made an S election. (The LIFO recapture tax under § 1363(d), if applicable, will apply immediately.) H.R. Rep. No. 104–586, 104th Cong., 2d Sess. 89 (1996).

D. POLICY ASPECTS OF THE TREATMENT OF SUBCHAPTER S CORPORATIONS WITH A SUBCHAPTER C HISTORY

The policy basis of the various rules dealing with Subchapter S corporations that have previously operated as C corporations is not clearly articulated in the legislative history of the provisions. With respect to the built-in gain rules, the provisions can perhaps best be understood as a variation on the *General Utilities* problem. The conversion from C status to S status and the consequent move to a single tax regime is in many ways like a liquidation of the corporation and a transfer of the assets out of corporate solution. If this change in taxing pattern had been achieved through a liquidation, § 336 would have required recognition of gain at the corporate level, followed by a shareholder level gain. In the Subchapter S situation, rather than impose an immediate tax at the time of conversion, the statute defers the tax until a sale of the assets and in effect turns that deferral into an exemption if the assets are held for ten years.

As to the passive income limitations, if the liquidation model is continued, on a liquidation the accumulated but undistributed corporate level earnings would not be subject to dividend taxation when distributed in liquidation, but would incur a shareholder level capital gains tax, the size of which would depend on the stock basis. Since the conversion to S status does not result in any shareholder level tax, Congress apparently felt that it was inappropriate to allow those earnings, unreduced by any second level tax, to be reinvested in assets generating passive income unrelated to the basic business operations of the corporation. Initially the sanction is an additional level of tax, with the corporation ultimately losing its S status if the situation goes on for too long.

If conversion from C to S status were treated as a liquidation of the old corporation and formation of a new corporation, these rules designed to safeguard the double tax regime with respect to gains accrued during the time the corporation was a C corporation could be eliminated and Subchapter S simplified. The Treasury Department advanced such a proposal in 1995 as part of a broader debate on the extent to which passthrough treatment should be available to small businesses, however organized, in light of the phenomenal growth in the popularity of limited liability companies, which provide limited liability for all members under state law but, if properly organized, partnership taxation under federal tax laws. The Treasury Department recommended to Congress that S corporations generally should be permitted to elect to be taxed as a partnership notwithstanding that the corporation was organized as such under state law. Furthermore, the election would not be treated as a liquidation and accrued gains would not be taxed at that time. To offset the revenue loss from this proposal, the Treasury Department further recommended that Congress should consider treating an S election by an existing C corporation as a constructive liquidation. This proposal mirrored a recommendation of the

Joint Committee on Taxation in 1990. See Statement of Leslie B. Samuels, Assistant Secretary (Tax Policy), Department of the Treasury, Before the House Committee on Ways and Means (July 28, 1995).

SECTION 5. POLICY ASPECTS OF SUBCHAPTER S

Subchapter S raises significant questions both in theory and in practice. Given the fundamental decision to have a separate corporate income tax, the question is whether there are situations that justify departure from that model. The argument in favor of Subchapter S is that taxes should be as neutral as possible as respects the form of doing business for a closely held enterprise. That argument may justify the special passthrough treatment of S corporations. On the other hand, Subchapter S contains significant differences from the other major form of passthrough enterprise, the partnership, which create significant advantages and disadvantages depending upon particular circumstances. Compared to partnerships, Subchapter S provides a less complex device for passthrough taxation of a joint enterprise. The differences between Subchapters K and S are substantial, however, and require tax motivated choices between the forms of doing business. Does the reduced complexity of Subchapter S justify its variations from the partnership model?

While the partnership rules of Subchapter K adopt an aggregate approach to many issues, with attendant complexity attributable to the aggregate treatment of liabilities and the partners' aggregate shares of the partnership's inside basis if they so elect, the S corporation can be characterized as an entity with a specific passthrough of designated income and loss items. The aggregate versus entity distinction is apparent in the divergent treatment of distributions of appreciated property; distributions by partnerships do not trigger recognition by the partnership and the partners take a carryover basis; and distributions of appreciated property by an S corporation require recognition of gain by all the stockholders and the recipient stockholder receives a step-up in basis to fair market value. Entity level recognition by the S corporation avoids the partnership problems addressed in § 751(b) and the need for adjustments to aggregate basis provided for in § 734, both highly complex provisions. On the other hand, the entity level recognition operates as a disincentive to non-pro rata distributions since the nonrecipient shareholders recognize current gain and the tax effect of that recognition may not be reversible until liquidation (by means of a capital loss deduction).

These disparate distribution rules also affect liquidations. Subject to the exceptions of § 751(b), a partnership can be liquidated and assets distributed to the partners without current taxation. The partners substitute their outside basis in their partnership interests for the partnership's basis in the assets distributed to them. The liquidation of an S corporation is subject to the normal rules of Subchapter C (§§ 331 and 336) that require recognition of gain at the corporate level. In tandem these provisions require recognition of at least corporate level gain on distributed appreciated assets, and perhaps additional gain at the stockholder level depending upon the relationship between the stockholders' stock bases and the value of distributed property. As a result of the taxable nature of the transaction, the stockholders take a fair market value basis in the distributed assets.

Similar disparities exist in comparing the redemption (under § 302) of an S corporation stockholder with the retirement of a partner. A distribution of appreciated property to an S corporation stockholder in a stock redemption will result in recognition of gain by the corporation. The gain is passedthrough to all shareholders in proportion to stockholdings, while only the redeemed stockholder receives the distributed property. The redeemed stockholder may or may not recognize gain depending on the basis of redeemed stock. A distribution of appreciated property in retirement of a partner's partnership interest will not trigger partnership level recognition of gain or loss, unless § 751 assets are involved. The distributee partner will recognize gain, loss, or in some cases (if § 736(a) is involved) both ordinary gain and a capital loss.

The entity approach to Subchapter S also affects the potential for shifting income from one stockholder to another as a result of a contribution of appreciated property to the corporation. Section 704(c) operates in Subchapter K to prevent a shift of pre-contribution appreciation or losses to the non-contributing partners by requiring that the difference between basis and fair market value at the time of contribution be reflected in allocations to the partners. There is no provision for equivalent adjustments under Subchapter S where each stockholder is required to report the stockholder's proportionate share of corporate income and loss items.

The restrictions of Subchapter S on the number and types of S corporation stockholders may also be analyzed as a response to perceived problems of complexity. Although Subchapter K demonstrates that passthrough accounting on a large scale is a possible alternative for income tax purposes, the limited number of permissible stockholders of an S corporation and the restrictions on the types of permissible stockholders, excluding other passthrough entities and corporations, substantially reduces the burden of accounting for the passthrough of S corporation income.

However, the goal of simplicity in Subchapter S creates its own complexity. Differences in the passthrough treatment under Subchapters K and S require careful planning choices regarding the choice of entity. The flexibility permitted by Subchapter K with respect to allocations of income and loss items can be contrasted with the rather rigid requirements of a single class of stock under Subchapter S. Stockholder attempts to create preferential interests in an S corporation through the use of purported debt instruments have been a source of considerable litigation. Additional difficulty is created by the detailed requirements for electing S corporation status. Failure to comply with the statutory requirements regarding timing and form can defeat the attempts of well-intentioned taxpayers to elect S corporation status. No such requirements are imposed on operation as a partnership, an entity also requiring participants to report their share of entity level income and loss, though the question of entity classification represents a somewhat similar problem. Nevertheless, provisions for notifying the Internal Revenue Service of an intent to operate a corporation as a pass-through entity and requiring stockholders to consent to the pass-through of tax significant items are warranted.

Beyond the question of the relationship between Subchapter S and partnership taxation, the Subchapter S provisions raise the more fundamental issue of the extent to which operation in corporate form should be coupled with a double level of tax on distributions. Absent a decision to adopt some general form of integration of corporate and individual taxes, why should closely held corporations with only common stock be subject to a single level of tax while all other corporate entities operate in a two tax world? Do these characteristics have any bearing on whether double tax or single tax is appropriate?

PART III

AFFILIATED CORPORATION

CHAPTER 10

AFFILIATED CORPORATIONS

Business activities linked by common ownership may be conducted as separate divisions in a single corporation or divided into separate corporate entities. Related corporate entities may share common ownership through identity of stockholders, i.e., each corporation is owned pro rata by the same group of stockholders, (brother-sister corporations), or may be linked through a chain of parent subsidiary corporations in which the ultimate stockholders own the stock of the common parent corporation.

The corporate tax system must identify whether and under what circumstances separate incorporation of activities under common control will be recognized for tax purposes. If separate business activities are conducted within a single corporation, the income and operating losses of each activity are netted to produce a single taxable income or loss for the combined operation within the corporation. Earnings and profits, net operating losses, and many corporate elections, such as the taxable year, are combined and shared by each of the separate activities. On the other hand, separation of business activities related by common ownership and control into different corporations may result in very different tax consequences. The taxable income of each activity might be separately computed and subject to different marginal rates under § 11. The operating losses of one activity will be separated from the taxable income of another. Thus one activity may be subject to tax on its income while the other has unused operating losses that will be carried back or forward to other taxable years of that corporation. Elections, taxable years, accounting methods, all may vary among the entities. The conduct of business activities through different entities also makes it possible to attempt to affect the profitability of each activity by manipulating the price of goods and services in transactions between jointly owned corporations. Thus X Corporation could reduce its taxable income by selling goods to related Y Corporation at a price less than its cost of manufacturing the goods, and thus increase the taxable income of Y Corporation, which could sell the goods outside of the related group at a higher price.

The Code contains two different regimes for dealing with some of these issues. Sections 1561 and 1563 are intended to prevent the multiple use of the lower tax brackets of § 11 by a group of affiliated corporations. Other rules prevent creation of losses between related entities, I.R.C. § 267, and the use of intercompany pricing among controlled corporations to avoid tax, I.R.C. § 482, which is significant mostly with respect to foreign operations. The second regime, the consolidated return provisions of §§ 1501 through 1504, accommodate affiliated groups of parent-subsidiary corporations that want to combine the incomes and losses of separately incorporated activities into a single consolidated income for the entire group.

SECTION 1. TAX REDUCTION WITH MULTIPLE CORPORATE TAXPAYERS

INTERNAL REVENUE CODE: Sections 1561; 1563.

A. BACKGROUND

For tax years ending before 1978, the corporate tax consisted of a normal tax plus a surtax on taxable income in excess of the "surtax exemption." As an example, for taxable years ending in 1977, the tax on corporate income under § 11 included the normal tax of 20 percent on the first $25,000 of taxable income and 22 percent of income in excess of $25,000, plus a surtax of 26 percent on income in excess of the $50,000 surtax exemption. Prior to enactment of the limitations of §§ 1561–1563 by the Tax Reform Act of 1969, taxpayers utilized multiple corporations to obtain multiple surtax exemptions and, to a lesser extent, multiple accumulated earnings tax credits, discussed at page 780. Each of several controlled corporations would be structured to earn only enough taxable income to remain taxable at the lower tax rates of the normal tax.

The Commissioner has had a number of weapons, both statutory and judicial, to combat tax avoidance through controlled corporations, but with mixed success. Section 269 permits the Commissioner to disallow multiple surtax exemptions and other allowances in the case of the acquisition of control of a corporation when the "principal purpose for which such acquisition is made is evasion or avoidance of Federal income tax by securing the benefit of a deduction, credit or other allowance * * *."

Section 482 permits the Commissioner to reallocate income, deductions or other items among controlled corporations if necessary to prevent evasion of taxes or in order to clearly reflect income. Section 1551 denies the multiple use of the lower corporate tax brackets in the event of a transfer of property to a controlled corporation by a group of five or fewer controlling stockholders, or by a controlling corporation, if the taxpayers are unable to establish by a preponderance of the evidence that securing the benefits of lower brackets was not a major purpose of the transfer. Additionally, the Commissioner could invoke judicially developed doctrines to disregard the separate entity status of a corporation, discussed at page 47, or use assignment of income principles to tax the true earner of income.

B. SECTIONS 1561–1563

The objective tests of §§ 1561 through 1563, allowing only a single surtax exemption to the "component members of a controlled group of corporations," were enacted in 1964 to overcome inadequacies of the former potentially operative sections and the continuing judicial doctrines which required a subjective finding of tax avoidance. The Revenue Act of 1978 replaced the normal tax and surtax structure with a five-step graduated rate structure with rates ranging from 17 to 46 percent. Currently § 11 contains four rate brackets and a five percent surtax on taxable income between $100,000 and $334,000 to phase out the benefits of first two brackets, and a three percent surtax on taxable income of between $15,000,000 and $18,333,333 to eliminate the benefit of the third bracket, as discussed at page 3. The restrictions on multiple surtax exemptions were modified correspondingly to provide that a controlled group of corporations collectively is limited to one amount in each of the taxable income brackets of the corporate rate table of § 11(b). For example, if there are five members of a controlled group, and if no plan of unequal apportionment is adopted, each member is subject to tax at a rate of 15 percent on its first $10,000 of taxable income (1/5 of $50,000), 25 percent on the next $5,000 of taxable income, 34 percent on the next $5,000 of taxable income, and 35 percent on taxable income in excess of $2,000,000. In addition, the five percent surtax of § 11(b) applies to the income of each corporation in excess of $20,000 (1/5 of $100,000) until each corporation pays $2,350 of additional tax. The additional three percent surtax applies to the income of each corporation in excess of $3,000,000 (1/5 of $15,000,000) until each corporation pays $20,000 of additional tax. Section 1561(a) permits the members of a controlled group to consent to an unequal allocation of the amounts limited by the provision.

The limitations of § 1561 apply to any group that meets the objective control test of § 1563. A business reason for operating through multiple corporations will not defeat application of the multiple bracket limitation of § 1561. Tribune Publishing Company v. Commissioner, 731 F.2d 1401, 1404 (9th Cir.1984).

Section 1561 applies to both parent-subsidiary and brother-sister controlled groups, or a combined group of both. A parent-subsidiary controlled group is one or more chains of corporations connected through stock ownership with a common parent if 80 percent of the voting power and value of each corporation (except the common parent) is owned by another member of the group, and the common parent owns at least 80 percent of the voting power and value of all classes of stock of at least one of the other corporations (determined by excluding stock of any member of the group held directly by another member of the group). I.R.C. § 1563(a)(1). A brother-sister controlled group is defined under a two part test that requires both common ownership of two or more corporations and a degree of common control through an identity of cross-ownership of the corporations. A brother-sister controlled group exists if five or fewer stockholders who are individuals, estates, or trusts (1) own 80 percent of the voting power and value of all classes of stock of each corporation, and (2) own more than 50 percent of the voting power and value of each corporation after taking into account the stock ownership of each stockholder only to the extent that the stock ownership is identical with respect to each corporation. I.R.C. § 1563(a)(2). For example, A, B and C own the stock of corporations X and Y in the following proportions:

	A	B	C	Total
X Corporation	35	50	15	100
Y Corporation	5	20	75	100
Total Identity	5	20	15	40

X Corporation and Y Corporation are not a brother-sister controlled group. A, B and C own 100 percent of the stock of each corporation. However, taking their identical stock ownership into account, A, B and C own only 40 percent for purposes of § 1561(a)(2)(B). Thus, while there is common ownership of X and Y Corporations, there is not common control. If, however, A owned only 24 percent of the X Corporation stock, and C owned 26 percent of the X Corporation stock, X and Y Corporations would qualify as a brother-sister controlled group.

X Corporation	24	50	26	100
Y Corporation	5	20	75	100
Total Identity	5	20	26	51

Finally, a group of three or more corporations will be combined into a single controlled group if one of the corporations is the common parent of a parent-subsidiary controlled group and also part of a brother-sister group. I.R.C. § 1563(a)(3).

In addition to limiting a controlled group to a single amount of taxable income in each tax rate bracket, § 1561 limits the group to one exemption credit under the accumulated earnings tax, page 780, and one $40,000 exemption for purposes of the alternative minimum tax, page 6. Other provisions of the Code specifically treat a controlled group as a single corporation. See, for example, § 179(d)(6) (members of a controlled group are treated as one taxpayer for purposes of the limit on the first year depreciation allowance of § 179) and § 414(b) (anti-discrimination rules and other provisions regarding qualified pension and employee benefit plans all applied to a controlled group as if it were a single employer).

ILLUSTRATIVE MATERIAL

A. STOCK OWNERSHIP AND CONTROL

Section 1563(c) excludes certain stock from consideration in determining whether corporations are members of a controlled group. These provisions result in a concentration of stock ownership that makes it easier to establish the existence of control. Stock that is limited and preferred as to dividends and treasury stock are not counted. I.R.C. § 1563(c)(1)(A) and (B). In the case of a parent-subsidiary group in which the parent owns 50 percent or more of the voting power or value, control is determined without regard to (a) stock held by an employee deferred compensation trust, (b) stock of the subsidiary that is owned by an individual stockholder who is also a 50 percent or greater stockholder in the parent corporation or an officer of the parent, (c) stock owned by an employee of a subsidiary that is restricted by limitations on the right of the employee to dispose of the stock which run in favor of the parent or subsidiary corporation, and (d) stock in a subsidiary corporation held by an organization exempt from tax under § 501 which is controlled by the parent corporation, a principal stockholder of the parent, or by an officer of the parent corporation. I.R.C. § 1563(c)(2)(A).

Section 1563(e) provides its own set of constructive ownership rules for determining control. For purposes of applying the ownership tests to determine the existence of either a parent-subsidiary or brother-sister controlled group, (a) an option holder is treated as the owner of optioned stock, (b) stock owned by a partnership is attributed to five percent or greater partners, (c) stock owned by a trust is attributed to a person who is treated as the owner of trust property under the grantor trust rules, and (d) stock owned by an estate or a non-grantor trust is attributed to beneficiaries who have a five percent or greater interest in the trust. I.R.C. § 1563(d)(1) and (e)(1) through (3). In addition, only with respect to determining the ownership of stock of a brother-sister group, (a) stock owned by a corporation is attributed to five percent or greater stockholders in proportion to the value of stock held by the five percent stockholder, (b) stock is attributed to a spouse (with an exception for a spouse who holds no direct interest and is not a director, employee or manager of the corporation, as long as not more than 50 percent of the corporation's income is derived from passive sources), (c) an individual is attributed stock owned by minor children, (d) a minor child is attributed stock owned by her parents, and (e) a more than 50 percent individual stockholder is treated as owning stock held by parents, grandparents, and children and grandchildren who have reached the age of twenty-one. I.R.C. § 1563(d)(2) and (e)(4) through

(6). In Complete Finance Corp. v. Commissioner, 766 F.2d 436 (10th Cir.1985), the court held that under § 1563(e)(5), attribution of stock to a spouse does not dilute the interest of the direct stockholder and each spouse is counted as owning both all of the stock owned by the individual directly plus the stock attributed from his or her spouse.

B. COMPONENT MEMBERS OF A CONTROLLED GROUP

The limitations of § 1561 apply to the component members of a controlled group. Under § 1563(b), a corporation is a component member of a group if the corporation is a member of the controlled group on December 31 of the taxable year. However, a corporation is treated as a component member of a group only if it is a member of the group for more than one-half of the year. Under § 1563(b)(3) a corporation that was not a member of the controlled group on December 31 will be included as a component member if it was a member of the group for one-half or more of the number of days in the taxable year preceding December 31. Conversely, under § 1563(b)(2), a corporation that is a member of the controlled group on December 31 of the taxable year but was not a member of the group for one-half of the number of days preceding December 31 will be excluded from the controlled group. Component members of a controlled group do not include certain corporations subject to special tax provisions such as corporations exempt from tax under § 501, foreign corporations, insurance companies, and a franchise corporation which the parent corporation is obligated to sell (as defined in § 1563(f)(4)).

C. BROTHER–SISTER CONTROLLED GROUP

As described above, a brother-sister controlled group exists under § 1563(a)(2) if five or fewer stockholders who are individuals, estates, or trusts own 80 percent of the voting power and value of all classes of stock of each corporation, and own more than 50 percent of the voting power and value of each corporation after taking into account the stock ownership of each stockholder only to the extent that the stock ownership is identical with respect to each corporation. In United States v. Vogel Fertilizer Co., 455 U.S. 16 (1982), the Court held that a person's stock ownership may not be taken into account for purposes of the 80 percent requirement of § 1563(a)(2)(A) unless that person also owns stock in another member of the corporate group. Arthur Vogel owned 77.49 percent of the Vogel Fertilizer Company. The remaining 22.51 percent was owned by Richard Crain, who was unrelated to Vogel. Vogel also owned 87.5 percent of the voting stock and 93 percent of the value of Vogel Popcorn. Applying Treas.Reg. § 1.1563–1(a)(3), the Commissioner took the position that Crain and Vogel's ownership of more than 80 percent of Vogel Fertilizer, and Vogel's ownership of more than 80 percent of Vogel Popcorn, satisfied the 80 percent test of § 1563(a)(2)(A), and that Vogel's ownership of more than 50 percent of each corporation satisfied the 50 percent test of § 1563(a)(2)(B). The Court concluded that the limitations of §§ 1561–1563 only are intended to apply to related corporations and held that the 50 percent limitation of § 1563(a)(2)(B) is a "safeguard" to "insure that the

* * * definition is limited to cases where the brother-sister corporations are, in fact, controlled by the group of stockholders as one economic enterprise." (30) The Court also observed that 80 percent ownership by five or fewer persons indicates only that the two corporations are closely held. The Court thus declared the regulations invalid to the extent that they permitted a stockholder who owned stock in only one corporation to be taken into account for purposes of the 80 percent requirement. Treas.Reg. § 1.1563–1(a)(3) was amended in 1988 to follow the result in *Vogel Fertilizer*.

In Complete Finance Corp. v. Commissioner, 766 F.2d 436 (10th Cir.1985), the court rejected the taxpayer's argument that under *Vogel Fertilizer* persons must directly own stock in each brother-sister corporation to be counted as part of the five or fewer persons in control under § 1563(a)(2)(A). Thus, the stock attribution rules of § 1563(d)(2) are applied to determine whether the 80 percent and 50 percent tests of § 1563(a)(2) are satisfied.

D. POLICY ISSUES UNDER SECTION 1561

It is still possible for a corporate enterprise to avoid the § 1561 limitations if its constituent corporations are not members of a "controlled group" as defined in § 1563(a). Thus 79 percent ownership of a subsidiary will allow use of multiple lower rate brackets under § 11. Proper arrangement of stock ownership in a brother-sister group to avoid the more than 50 percent limitation of § 1563(a)(2)(B) also will permit avoidance of the multiple bracket limitations of § 1561. Presumably the Commissioner still could utilize the approaches available to him prior to enactment of §§ 1561–1563.

An interesting policy aspect of the multiple corporation legislation is the success with which multi-corporate groups were able to resist effective legislation for so long by invoking the argument that they had a "business purpose" for conducting their business operations in multiple rather than single corporate form. There may be valid "business reasons" to operate in multiple corporation form, but this factor hardly justifies a difference in tax liability from a single corporation conducting the same number of businesses through branches. But in this, as in other areas, Congress was willing to be persuaded for a considerable period of time that if there was a "business reason" for engaging in a certain kind of conduct, favorable tax consequences should also flow from that business decision. It appears difficult for Congress consistently to apply the principle that all businesses should be taxed on the same basis regardless of what genuine business decisions may be controlling as to their forms of operation.

C. REALLOCATION OF INCOME UNDER SECTION 482

The cases arising under § 482 discussed at page 65, involved attempts by taxpayers to channel income between the corporation and its stockholder so as to take advantage of the differences between individual and corporate tax rates. The issues under § 482 as it applies to related corporations involve the same strategic goal of reduced taxation, though the situations are somewhat different. However, after enactment of § 1561 there is no longer much in the way of tax savings to be obtained by strategic arrangements of transactions among domestic corporations. Nonetheless, special situations still exist which prompt such arrangements and in turn prompt the Commissioner to apply § 482. For example, a tax advantage can be obtained by the artificial shifting of income from a profitable corporation to a related corporation with a net operating loss that it would not otherwise be able to use. See, e.g., Ballentine Motor Co. v. Commissioner, 321 F.2d 796 (4th Cir.1963) (appreciated inventory was transferred by a parent to a subsidiary with a loss carryover, the subsidiary subsequently realizing the income; held, Commissioner properly allocated the income on the sale to the parent under § 482); Likins–Foster Honolulu Corp. v. Commissioner, 417 F.2d 285 (10th Cir.1969) (§ 482 allocation prevented use of losses in a consolidated return). For other cases applying § 482 in a domestic context, see Engineering Sales, Inc. v. United States, 510 F.2d 565 (5th Cir.1975); Liberty Loan Corp. v. United States, 498 F.2d 225 (8th Cir.1974).

Section 482 is of greatest importance in the international area. Here the significance of transactions between related corporations arises because of the deferral of U.S. tax on the profits of foreign subsidiaries controlled by U.S. parent corporations that operate in countries with tax rates lower than the United States. If, for example, a U.S. parent corporation sells its products to its controlled foreign subsidiary at an artificially low price and the subsidiary then sells the products in the foreign market, there would be an understatement of the parent's portion of the profits on the transactions, and an overstatement of the subsidiary's portion. In addition, even if the foreign related corporation is taxed at rates comparable to U.S. rates, so that no overall tax saving is involved, § 482 is necessary to insure that the U.S. obtains its appropriate share of revenues from international transactions. For representative cases see Eli Lilly & Co. v. Commissioner, 856 F.2d 855 (7th Cir.1988), and G.D. Searle & Co. v. Commissioner, 88 T.C. 252 (1987) (§ 482 applied to reallocate income from the manufacture of pharmaceuticals in Puerto Rico based on patents and research developed by the United States parent corporation); Bausch & Lomb v. Commissioner, 933 F.2d 1084 (2d Cir.1991) (Commissioner's increase of sales price of soft contact lenses from Irish manufacturing subsidiary to domestic parent corporation was an abuse of discretion, but 5% royalty for use of intangibles paid to parent was too low; the court rejected the Commissioner's assertion that a royalty in the range of 27% to 33% was proper and adopted a royalty of 20%); Seagate Technology, Inc. v. Commissioner, 102 T.C. 149 (1994) (Commissioner's reallocation of income from a Singapore manufacturing subsidiary to its U.S. parent for sales of component parts and completed disk drives was arbitrary and capricious, the subsidiary's 1% royalty rate to its parent on direct sales was increased to 3%, compensation for procurement services rendered to the subsidiary was adequate, and research and development expenses were reallocated between the parent and subsidiary).

Congress steadily has tightened the application of § 482 in the international context, particularly as applied to intangibles. See § 367 and § 482 (last clause). Treas.Reg. § 1.482–4 reflects these changes.

The Commissioner has promulgated a complex set of regulations under § 482 to ensure that taxpayers clearly reflect income attributable to controlled transactions by placing commonly controlled taxpayers on "a tax parity with an uncontrolled taxpayer by determining the true taxable income of the controlled taxpayer." Treas.Reg. § 1.482–1(a)(1). True taxable income results from a transaction under an "arms length" standard, which attempts to equate a controlled transaction with the result that would have occurred if the uncontrolled taxpayers had engaged in the same transaction under similar circumstances. Treas.Reg. § 1.482–1(b)(1). The regulations contain detailed methodologies for determining arm's length pricing in a variety of transactions. See Treas.Regs. §§ 1.482–2 through–6. Treas.Reg. § 1.482–1(a)(2) authorizes the Commissioner to reallocate items affecting taxable income among members of a controlled group. Although § 482 does not authorize taxpayers to invoke its terms to reallocate income or deductions, Treas.Reg. § 1.482–1(a)(3) permits a taxpayer to report income on a return using prices that vary from the prices actually charged in a controlled transaction in order to reflect an arm's length result.

The treatment of intercompany transactions under § 482 should be compared with the approach in the consolidated return context where a deferred accounting technique is used to postpone the recognition of gain or loss on intercompany sales until the property is sold outside the group.

SECTION 2. CONSOLIDATED RETURNS

INTERNAL REVENUE CODE: Sections 1501; 1503(b); 1504(a)-(b).

REGULATIONS: Sections 1.1502–1(f), (g),–2,–11(a),–12,–13(a) to (d), (f), –15A, –19, –20(a) to (c), –21A,, –22, –31, –32(a) and (b).

TEMPORARY REGULATIONS: Sections 1.1502 –15T, –21T and –22T.

Section 1501 provides that all members of an affiliated group of corporations may elect to file a consolidated return. A consolidated return permits the includible members of an affiliated group of corporations to combine their incomes into a single return. Section 1502 authorizes the Secretary to promulgate regulations as necessary in order "that the tax liability of any affiliated group of corporations making a consolidated return and of each corporation in the group * * * may be returned, determined, computed, assessed, collected, and adjusted, in such manner as clearly to reflect the income-tax liability and the various factors necessary for the determination of such liability, and in order to prevent avoidance of such tax liability." The detailed rules for filing consolidated returns are found in regulations promulgated pursuant to this broad delegation of authority. These regulations have been in a state of transition in recent years. In general, the recently adopted regulations reflect a "single entity" approach, which attempts to treat the several members of a consolidated group in the same manner as divisions of a single corporation.

The members of an affiliated group includible in a consolidated return are identified under § 1504(a) as the common parent corporation and one or more corporations affiliated through a chain or chains of corporations connected by ownership of stock representing 80 percent of the voting control and value of each affiliated member. Any corporation that is connected to the common parent or another member of an affiliated group by meeting this ownership requirement is treated as an "includible corporation" and must be included on the consolidated return. I.R.C. § 1501.

The principal advantage of filing consolidated returns is the ability to combine the income and loss of each member of an affiliated group into a single taxable income. Treas.Reg. § 1.1502–11(a). Thus, net operating losses of one member of the group can be used to reduce the taxable income of another member. In addition, net operating losses of a member of the group incurred during consolidated return years of the group can be carried back or forward against income of other members. There are, however, limitations on carryovers of losses incurred by a corporation in separate return years before the corporation became a member of the affiliated group. Temp.Reg. § 1.1502–21T(c). Filing a consolidated return also permits the members of the affiliated group to ignore intercompany dividends in computing taxable income and to defer recognition of gain or loss on intercompany transactions. Similar to the passthrough model of partnerships and Subchapter S, the basis of stock of one member of a consolidated group held by another member is adjusted to reflect taxable income, loss and the other items of the lower-tier member. Intercompany distributions and contributions also affect the basis of stock of a member of an affiliated group that is held by the common parent or other members, thereby increasing or decreasing gain or loss on disposition of the stock. In addition, deferred intercompany gains and losses may be recognized in the event that a member leaves the consolidated group, even if the transaction otherwise would be accorded nonrecognition treatment as a tax-free reorganization. Filing consolidated returns requires that all members of the consolidated group use the taxable year of the common parent, but the individual members may use different accounting methods. Treas.Regs. §§ 1.1502–76(a), –17(a).

Even through the federal tax liability of an affiliated group filing a consolidated return is based on the combined taxable incomes of the members of the affiliated group, the separate tax identity of each member of the group is respected through maintenance of individual earnings and profits accounts and basis adjustments with respect to the stock of each member. Treas.Regs. §§ 1.1502–19, –31, –32, and –33. As a result, while certain intercompany transactions are disregarded in computing taxable income of the group under the consolidated return rules, those transactions will affect the earnings and profits and stock basis of the component members. Accounting for the separate tax identity of each member is required to determine tax consequences in the event that an includible corporation enters or leaves the affiliated group.

Treas.Reg. § 1.1502–32 contains a series of "investment adjustments" to the basis of stock of subsidiaries held by other members of an affiliated group. These adjustments are intended to eliminate potential double tax consequences as the separate taxable income or loss of each member of the consolidated group is reflected on the consolidated return. Treas.Reg. § 1.1502–32(a)(1). Investment adjustments begin with the stock of the lowest tier subsidiary in a chain and work their way up to stock of includible corporations held by the common parent. Treas.Reg. § 1.1502–32(a)(3)(iii). Positive adjustments increase the basis of the stock of a subsidiary member of the group held by another member, negative adjustments decrease basis. Treas.Reg. § 1.1502–32(b)(2). Following the partnership model, adjustments are made for the net amount of the subsidiary's taxable income or loss, tax-exempt income, non-deductible non-capital expenses (e.g. fines and disallowed losses), and distributions with respect to the stock of the subsidiary. Losses of a subsidiary and/or distributions may exceed the upper-tier corporation's basis in the stock of the subsidiary. In that case, Treas.Reg. § 1.1502–32(a)(3)(ii) provides for the creation of an "excess loss account", which is the equivalent of a negative basis in the subsidiary's stock.[1] The amount of an excess loss account attributable to the stock of an includible subsidiary is recognized (1) on a sale of the stock, (2) whenever either the subsidiary or the includible corporation holding the stock ceases to be a member of the consolidated group, or (3) if the subsidiary's stock becomes worthless. Treas.Reg. § 1.1502–19(a)(1), (b). The gain is generally treated as gain from the disposition of stock, and is thus capital gain. However, to the extent that the subsidiary is insolvent, gain is ordinary except to the extent that the excess loss account is attributable to distributions. Treas.Reg. § 1.1502–19(a)(2).

In general, under Treas.Reg. § 1.1502–13(a)(2), the tax consequences of intercompany transactions between members of the same consolidated group generally are accounted for in consolidated taxable income as transactions between divisions of a single corporation. In the case of payment for services or a sale or exchange of property, gain or loss that is recognized by the selling member under its method of accounting is deferred until the item can be matched with the buying member's accounting of its corresponding item in the form of a deduction or a recovery of basis when the expenditure is capitalized. Treas.Reg. § 1.1502–13(c)(2). Thus, in the case of an intercompany sale of property, the selling member defers accounting for its recognized gain or loss until the date on which the buying member sells the property outside of the consolidated group. In this manner the gain or loss is deferred until the property is disposed of outside of the consolidated group, as would be the case with respect to an exchange of property between divisions of a single corporation. The character of the

1. Treas.Reg. 1.1502–19(a)(2)(B)(ii) refers to the amount of an excess loss account as "negative basis."

selling member's deferred gain and the buying member's recognized gain on sale outside of the group also will be determined by single entity principles. The activities of each, therefore, may affect the character of the other's gain. Treas.Reg. § 1.1502–13(c)(1)(i). For example, assume that S Corporation and B Corporation are members of an affiliated group filing a consolidated return. S Corporation sells appreciated investment real estate to B Corporation. Subsequently, B Corporation develops the land as residential real estate for sale to customers in the ordinary course of B Corporation's trade or business. When B Corporation disposes of the land, S Corporation must recognize its deferred gain. Even though S Corporation held the land for investment at the time of its sale to B Corporation, both S Corporation and B Corporation's gain will be treated as ordinary income. Treas.Reg. § 1.1502–13(c)(7)(ii), Ex. (2).

In the case of a sale of depreciable property, the selling member will defer its gain or loss to the time when the buying member claims increased capital cost recovery deductions. Treas.Reg. § 1.1502–13(c)(7)(ii), Ex.(4). Under the single entity approach of the regulations, increased capital recovery deductions that result from the buying member's cost basis will be offset by the corresponding gain taken into account by the selling member. In this fashion, these transactions have no net effect on the consolidated return of the group, the same result that would occur if the selling and buying members were divisions of a single corporation. Any increased deduction or basis recovery by the buying member will be offset on the consolidated return by an equivalent recognition of deferred gain by the selling member.

Deferred gain or loss from intercompany transactions is accelerated into a year in which it becomes no longer possible to match the buying member's corresponding item with the selling member's deferred gain or loss. Treas.Reg. § 1.1502–13(d). Thus, gain or loss deferred by the selling member will be accounted for if either the buying member or the selling member ceases to be a member of the consolidated group before the buying member accounts for its matching item corresponding to the selling member's deferred gain or loss.

Distributions from one member of an affiliated group to another are also treated under the single entity principle. Distributions are not included in the income of the recipient, but only so long as there is a matching reduction in the basis of the stock of distributing member held by the recipient member under the investment adjustment rules of Treas.Reg. § 1.1502–32. Treas.Reg. § 1.1502–13(f)(2)(ii). Gain recognized by the distributing member under § 311(b) is deferred under the matching principle until the stock of the distributing member is sold outside of the consolidated group. Treas.Reg. § 1.1502–13(f)(2)(iii).

An election to file a consolidated return may not be revoked without the consent by the Commissioner. Permission to discontinue filing a consolidated return will be granted only on a showing of good cause. Treas.Reg. § 1.1502–75(c). Treas.Reg. § 1.1502–75(c)(1)(ii) describes good cause as including a change in the Code, regulations, or other law which has a substantial adverse effect on the tax liability of an affiliated group relative to the aggregate tax liability of the members of the group filing separate returns. Treas.Reg. § 1.1502–75(c)(2) gives the Commissioner additional authority to grant blanket permission to discontinue filing consolidated returns to all groups, or to a class of groups, in the event of a change in the law of the type that will have a substantial adverse effect on the filing of consolidated returns. The election to file a consolidated return will, therefore, affect the tax liability of an affiliated group for the current and future tax years. Thus, a proposal to file a consolidated return must be carefully analyzed.

ILLUSTRATIVE MATERIAL

A. ELIGIBILITY AND INCLUDIBLE CORPORATIONS

1. *Stock Ownership*

An affiliated group consists of the common parent and one or more chains of corporations connected through stock ownership with the common parent. I.R.C. § 1504(a)(1). The common parent must own stock of at least one other corporation that represents at least 80 percent of the total voting power of the stock of the corporation and has value equal to at least 80 percent of the total value of the stock of the corporation. I.R.C. § 1504(a)(1) and (2). In addition, each includible corporation must be connected to the common parent or to one or more corporations owned by the common parent with the requisite 80 percent of voting power and value. Thus, a single chain of connected corporations or parallel brother-sister corporations connected to a common parent corporation can qualify as an affiliated group. All shares of stock within a class are treated as having the same value. Control premiums, minority discounts and blockage discounts are not taken into account. Treas.Reg. § 1.1504–4(b)(2)(iv).

In Alumax, Inc. v. Commissioner, 109 T.C. 133 (1997), aff'd, 165 F.3d 822 (11th Cir. 1999), the court was required to interpret the 80 percent voting control requirement of § 1502(a)(2) in the face of a complicated voting arrangement. Alumax had two classes of stock outstanding. The class C stock, which was owned by an affiliated group claiming control, was entitled to elect four of six voting members of the Alumax Board. The class B stock was entitled to elect two of six voting members. The class B and class C directors, in the aggregate and not voting by class, elected one of two special nonvoting directors. By agreement between the two class stockholders, the class B directors were permitted to name this special director. The other special nonvoting director was the CEO of Alumax. Each of the two class B directors had one vote. Each of the four class C directors had two votes. However, a majority of the directors of each of the two classes was required to approve certain corporate actions. Likewise, with respect to shareholder votes, each share of class C stock had four votes while each share of class B stock had one vote. A majority vote of each class of stock was required with respect to a number of restricted stockholder matters. The court rejected the taxpayer's assertion that a mechanical application of these voting formulae represented 80 percent voting control. The court held that the impact of various restrictions on the actions of elected directors must be taken into account in assessing the existence of voting control under § 1502(a)(2). Accordingly the control test was not met and Alumax was not part of the affiliated group.

Certain stock that possesses more "debt-like" features than equity features is not included for purposes of determining whether the voting power and value tests of § 1504(a)(2) are satisfied. Section 1504(a)(4) provides that "stock" does not include non-voting stock that is limited and preferred as to dividends and does not participate in corporate growth to any significant extent, if its liquidation and redemption rights do not exceed its issue price (except for a reasonable liquidation or redemption premium), and it is not convertible into another class of stock. In addition, § 1504(a)(5) authorizes regulations that treat certain convertible instruments as not constituting stock.

The regulations provide in general that options will not be treated as stock, or as deemed exercised, unless it can be reasonably anticipated that the issue or transfer of the underlying stock will result in a substantial federal income tax saving, and it is reasonably certain that the option will be exercised. Treas.Reg. § 1.1504–4(b)(1) and (2)(i). The regulations broadly define options as including any instrument that provides for the transfer of stock. Treas.Reg. § 1.1504–4(d)(1). This definition, therefore, includes convertible stock. The inquiry is undertaken at the time of issue or transfer of an option, the "measurement date", with some exceptions.[2] Treas.Reg. § 1.1504–4(c)(4). If an option is treated as exercised, it will be taken into account in determining the percentage of the value of stock held by the option holder and other parties, but not for purposes of determining ownership of voting power. Treas.Reg. § 1.1504–4(b)(2)(iii).

2. *Includible Corporations*

Each corporation includible on a consolidated return must consent to the application of the consolidated return regulations, although filing a consolidated return will be deemed to be consent. I.R.C. § 1501. An includible corporation is any domestic corporation that is a member of the affiliated group at any time during the taxable year under the stock ownership tests of § 1504(b). Includible corporations do not include, among others, tax-exempt corporations, insurance companies[3], possessions corporations under § 936 (certain U.S. owned corporations doing business in Puerto Rico), regulated investment companies (mutual funds) and real

2. A "measurement date" does not include a transfer between spouses that is covered by § 1041, or a transfer between persons none of whom is a member (or related to a member) of an affiliated group that includes the issuing corporation. Treas.Reg. § 1.1504–4(c)(4)(ii).

3. Section 1504(c) permits insurance companies to form a consolidated group that includes only affiliated insurance companies. In addition, the common parent of an affiliated group can elect to include an insurance company on the consolidated return of the group after the insurance company has been a member of the affiliated group for five consecutive years.

estate investment trusts. An includible corporation must be included in the consolidated return of an affiliated group for the part of any year during which the includible corporation meets the stock ownership tests. I.R.C. § 1501. If a corporation ceases to be a member of an affiliated group, absent the consent of the Commissioner, the corporation may not again be included within the consolidated return of the affiliated group for five years after the close of the taxable year in which the corporation ceased to be a member of the group. I.R.C. § 1504(a)(3).

In Elko Realty Co. v. Commissioner, 29 T.C. 1012 (1958), aff'd per curiam, 260 F.2d 949 (3d Cir.1958), the court held that two subsidiaries acquired for the purpose of using losses to offset income of the profitable acquiring corporation were not includible on a consolidated return. The court indicated that if ownership of a subsidiary's stock serves no business purpose other than a tax reduction purpose, the subsidiary is not an affiliate for purposes of the consolidated return provisions. The court also disallowed loss deductions under the predecessor to § 269.

B. CONSOLIDATED TAXABLE INCOME

The consolidated group computes its federal income tax liability on the basis of its combined consolidated taxable income. The computation of consolidated taxable income begins with the determination of the separate taxable incomes of each member of the consolidated group. Treas.Reg. § 1.1502–11(a)(1). In general, each member of the consolidated group computes its separate taxable income as a separate corporation. Treas.Reg. § 1.1502–12(a). However, separate taxable income excludes distributions with respect to the stock of other members of the group, deferred gains and losses from intercompany transactions, capital gains and losses and § 1231 gains and losses, and charitable contributions. Items excluded from the taxable income of members are separately consolidated and accounted for in consolidated taxable income as provided in specific regulations. Treas. Reg. § 1.1502–11(a)(2) through (8). Tax liability for the consolidated group is determined by applying the rates of § 11, and other relevant provisions of the Code, to the consolidated taxable income of the group. Tax liability is reduced by consolidated credits attributable to members of the group. Each member of a consolidated group is severally liable for the tax on consolidated taxable income. Treas.Reg. § 1.1502–6(a).

C. NET OPERATING LOSSES

1. *General*

The consolidated net operating loss of a consolidated group generally includes the consolidated net operating loss carrybacks and carryovers of the consolidated group. Temp.Reg. § 1.1502–21T(a). In addition, Temp. Reg. § 1.1502–21T(b) allows the net operating losses of a member of an affiliated group to be carried over from a pre-consolidation return period against the consolidated income of the group. This general rule, is, however, subject to two limitations: (1) if the loss year was a "separate return limitation year" (SRLY), then the loss may be carried over only against the income of the member of the group that generated the loss, Temp.Reg. § 1.1502–21T(c) and–22T(c) applicable to capital loss carryovers; and (2) if § 382 is applicable then the carryovers are limited accordingly, see Temp. Reg. § 1.1502–91T. Section 382 is discussed in Chapter 16.

2. *Separate Return Limitation Year*

Treas.Reg. § 1.1502–1(f) provides the definition for "separate return limitation year." In general it is a year in which any member of the consolidated group filed a separate return. But there are exceptions. One important exception is that a SRLY does not include a separate return year for a subsidiary which was a member of the group at the time the loss was incurred, although a consolidated return was not filed in that year. See Treas.Reg. § 1.1502–1(f)(2)(ii). In addition, the exception in Treas.Reg. § 1.1502–1(f)(2)(i) permits a loss corporation to acquire a profitable subsidiary and apply its own loss carryovers against the profits of the newly acquired subsidiary. Acquisition of a corporation with built-in gain, however, is subject to the limitations of § 384, discussed at page 774, which restricts the use of preacquisition losses against recognized built-in gain of either the acquired or acquiring corporation.

Wolter Construction Co., Inc. v. Commissioner, 634 F.2d 1029 (6th Cir.1980), upheld the validity of the SRLY Regulations. In that case losses incurred by a subsidiary in separate return years could not be used by the consolidated group even though the corporations in their separate return years were commonly controlled by individual stockholders as brother-sister corporations. Since the stockholders were individuals and not corporations, the group did not fall within the "common parent" exception in Treas.Reg. § 1.1502–1(f)(2)(i). The court in *Wolter Construction Co.* described the operation of the SRLY rule as follows:

"Reg. 1.1502–21(b)(1) is concerned with the use of net operating losses on a consolidated return. That regulation permits an affiliated group to use net operating losses sustained by any members of the group in 'separate return years' if the losses could be carried over pursuant to the general principles of § 172 of the Code. A 'separate return year' is defined as any year in which a company filed a separate return or in which it joined in the filing of a consolidated return by another group. Reg. 1.1502–1(e).

"As a general rule, then, net operating losses reported on a separate return can be carried over to and used on a consolidated return. An important exception to this rule is found in Reg. 1.1502–21(c). That section provides that the net operating loss of a member of an affiliated group arising in a 'separate return limitation year' which may be included in the consolidated net operating loss deduction of the group shall not exceed the amount of consolidated taxable income contributed by the loss-sustaining member for the taxable year at issue. The term 'separate return limitation year' is defined in Reg. 1.1502–1(f), in essence, as a separate return year in which the member of the group (except, with qualifications, the common parent) was either: 1) not a member of the group for its entire taxable year; or 2) a member of the group for its entire taxable year, that enjoyed the benefit of multiple surtax exemptions. In summary, losses incurred by a brother-sister corporation or by a corporation which is unrelated at the time of its losses to its subsequent affiliates, before it becomes a member of an affiliated group filing a consolidated return, can only be carried forward and used on the consolidated return to the extent that the corporation that incurred the losses has current income reflected on the consolidated return." (1032–1033)

In *Wolter Construction Co.*, the fact that the regulations provided a greater limitation on net operating loss carryovers in the context of the consolidated return than is contained in §§ 381 and 382 did not invalidate the Regulations.

Under Temp.Reg. § 1.1502–21T(c)(1), deduction of a SRLY loss by the consolidated group in any taxable year is limited to the taxable income contributed to the group by the member with the SRLY loss. The member's contribution to consolidated taxable income is measured on a cumulative basis over the entire period during which the SRLY corporation is a member of the group. Thus, a member's SRLY losses may be absorbed in any consolidated return year to the extent of the member's cumulative net contribution to consolidated taxable income in prior consolidated return years of the group, even though the member may not have consolidated taxable income in the year the loss is absorbed.

Temp.Reg. § 1.1502–21T(c)(2) applies similar rules on the basis of a SRLY subgroup, rather than fragmenting the limitation on a corporation-by-corporation basis. A SRLY subgroup consists of corporations affiliated with the loss corporation continuously from the year in which the loss was incurred to the year into which the loss is carried.

3. *Reverse Acquisition*

Since the SRLY limitation does not apply in the case of a change of ownership of the common parent, there remains a possibility that the assets of a profitable corporation may be merged into the common parent in exchange for more than 50 percent of the stock of the common parent of the loss group. For example, assume that a profitable P Corporation merges into L Corporation, which is the common parent of a consolidated group of corporations, and as a result of the merger the persons who were shareholders of former P Corporation immediately before the merger end up owning more than 50 percent of the stock of L Corporation. SRLY does not limit the losses of the L Corporation consolidated group none of which were incurred in a separate return limitation year.[4] Treas.Reg. § 1.1502–1(f)(3), however, treats this transaction as a "reverse acquisition" to deny the net operating loss carryover against the profits of the "acquired corporation."

In *Wolter Construction Co.* the taxpayer argued that the common parent exception to the SRLY limitation and the reverse acquisition excep-

4. The § 382 limitation applies where there is a more than 50% change in ownership of the loss corporation.

tion to the exception were intended to insure that loss carryovers were available only to the stockholders who owned the corporation when the losses were incurred, and that this policy should be applied to allow use of losses by the common parent affiliated with its former sister corporation. The court rejected the argument and described the reverse acquisition rule as follows:

"In a typical reverse acquisition in the loss carryover context, substantially all the assets or stock of a profit corporation are nominally acquired by a loss corporation in exchange for more than 50 percent of the latter's stock, so that control of the loss corporation has shifted to the stockholders of the profit corporation as they existed prior to the acquisition. The Regulations essentially treat the loss corporation as having been acquired, and under Section 1.1502–1(f)(3) of the Treasury Regulations, all taxable years of the loss corporation prior to the reverse acquisition are treated as separate return limitation years, notwithstanding its status as the common parent corporation of the new affiliated group consisting of it and the profit corporation. Conversely, the separate return years of the profit corporation prior to the acquisition are not treated, in general, as the separate return limitation years. Accordingly, the net operating losses sustained by the loss corporation, but not the profit corporation, in its separate return years are subject to the carryover limitation contained in Section 1.1502–21(c). The purpose and effect of the reverse acquisition rules is to prevent trafficking in loss corporations. This is accomplished by redirecting the SRLY limitation to the ostensibly acquiring corporation. This 'simple technical rule thwarts the attempts of those who would seek to present that the ailing David is trying to improve its financial strength by drawing on the earning power of Goliath.' Gans [A Practical Guide to Consolidated Returns (1976)], at 828.2." (1035–1036.)

4. *Built-In Deductions*

Under Temp.Reg. § 1.1502–15T, if losses are economically incurred in a prior separate return year but recognized for tax purposes in a consolidated year, the losses are treated as arising in a separate return limitation year (SRLY) and thus may not be applied against consolidated income but may be used only to offset the income of the corporation which realized the loss. Net unrealized built-in losses are thus subject to the SRLY limitations of Temp.Regs. §§ 1.1502–21T(c) and–22T(c). The temporary regulations adopt the definitions of built-in loss contained in § 382(h)(3), discussed at page 769, which refers to the excess of adjusted basis of assets over their fair market value.[5] Under Temp.Reg. § 1.1502–15T, the SRLY limitation applies to the recognition of "net unrealized built-in losses" of a new member of a consolidated group (as determined under § 382(h)(3)) but only during a five year recognition period after the new member joins the group.

5. Built-in loss under § 382(h) includes deduction items that are attributable to a SRLY but which are accounted for in a consolidated return year. See I.R.C. § 382(h)(6)(B).

5. *Post Acquisition Losses of an Acquired Member*

Treas.Reg. § 1.1502–21T(b)(1) provides for the carryback and carry-over of the consolidated net operating loss of the group under the principles of § 172(b)(two year carryback and twenty year carryforward). However, the consolidated net operating loss does not include losses apportioned under Treas.Reg. § 1.1502–79(a) to a separate return year of a member of the consolidated group. In Amorient, Inc. v. Commissioner, 103 T.C. 161 (1994), the taxpayer incurred a consolidated net operating loss that was allocable in part to separate return years of a corporation that had been a Subchapter S corporation prior to acquisition by the consolidated group. The Tax Court held that the portion of the taxpayer's consolidated net operating loss allocable to separate return years of the former S corporation was to be carried back to the S corporation's separate return year even though deduction of net operating losses by an S corporation is barred by § 1373(d). The Tax Court justified its result in part on its conclusion that losses that are not deductible in carryback separate return years of the S corporation are to be carried forward to a year when either the former S corporation or the consolidated group can utilize the loss. Treas.Reg. § 1.1502–21T(b)(2)(i) partially addresses the issues raised in *Amorient* by providing that the portion of a consolidated net operating loss that is apportioned to a member and carried back to a separate return year of the member may not be carried back to an equivalent or earlier year of the consolidated group. Likewise, if a consolidated net operating loss is carried forward to a separate return year of a member of the group, that carryforward loss may not be used in an equivalent or later consolidated return year of the group.

D. INVESTMENT ADJUSTMENTS

1. *Stock Basis*

Treas.Reg. § 1.1502–32 requires that each member of the group owning stock in another member of the group adjust its basis for that stock annually to account for income, losses and other items attributable to the subsidiary that are reflected in consolidated taxable income. The purpose of the investment adjustment rule is to prevent gain or loss which has been recognized by the subsidiary from being recognized a second time as investment gain or loss by the parent upon disposition of the subsidiary's stock. These rules treat the consolidated group as a single entity by accounting for gains and losses within the consolidated group only once.

Under Treas.Reg. § 1.1502–32(a) and (b), a parent corporation's basis in the stock of its consolidated subsidiary is increased or decreased annually by the net amount of the subsidiary's taxable income or loss, tax exempt income, nondeductible noncapital expenses, and distributions to the parent corporation. A positive adjustment increases basis, a negative adjustment decreases basis. These items cause an adjustment to the parent's basis in subsidiary stock in the taxable year in which the item is taken into account in determining consolidated taxable income. Thus, just as a partnership's income, losses, and distributions affect the partners' bases under § 705, items of income and loss, and distributions, will result in adjustments to the parent's basis in the stock of a consolidated subsidiary.

For purposes of the investment adjustment rules, a member's taxable income or loss includes items of income or loss attributable to the member that are included in the consolidated taxable income of the group. Treas. Reg. § 1.1502–32(b)(3)(i). Operating losses are included in the investment adjustment in the year the loss is absorbed into consolidated taxable income. Thus, a net operating loss carryforward is reflected in a basis adjustment for the year to which the loss is carried. A carryback loss is reflected as an adjustment in the year in which it arose. Treas.Reg. § 1.1502–32(b)(3)(i)(A) and (B). Tax-exempt income that increases the basis of a subsidiary's stock is defined as income or gain that is permanently excluded from income. Tax-exempt income includes intercompany dividends received by the subsidiary and tax-exempt interest that is permanently excluded from income under § 103. Gain that is not recognized in a § 1031 exchange, but which is deferred into the basis of property received, is not treated as tax-exempt income. Treas.Reg. § 1.1502–32(b)(3)(ii)(A). Similarly, expenses or losses that are taken into account but which are permanently disallowed or eliminated from determining taxable income, such as federal taxes and losses not allowed by § 311(a), give rise to a negative adjustment. Treas.Reg. § 1.1502–32(b)(3)(iii). Failure to adjust basis upwards for tax-exempt income, or downwards for expenditures not allowed as deductions or recoverable as capital items, would result in taxation of the gain or allowance of the expenditure on disposition of the stock.

2. *Excess Loss Accounts*

Under Treas.Reg. § 1.1502–11, the utilization by the consolidated group of the operating losses of a subsidiary is not limited by the group's current investment in the subsidiary. When the losses are utilized, however, the parent's investment adjustments under Treas.Reg. § 1.1502–32 may reduce the basis in the subsidiary stock below zero. This negative basis creates an "excess loss account" with respect to the subsidiary's stock. Treas.Reg. § 1.1502–32(a)(3)(ii). The purpose of the excess loss account is to allow losses in excess of basis and to ensure the subsequent recapture in consolidated taxable income of negative adjustments to the stock of a subsidiary upon the occurrence of specified events. Treas.Reg. § 1.1502–19(a)(1). The excess loss account is treated as a "negative basis" reflecting the fact that the group has been able to utilize current deductions in excess of the investment in the subsidiary. The negative basis reflected in an excess loss account is used as adjusted basis to determine the tax consequence of transactions involving the stock. Treas.Reg. § 1.1502–19(a)(2)(ii).

The existence of an excess loss account has an important impact on a number of corporate transactions involving the stock of the subsidiary. For example, if the stock of the subsidiary is sold to a third party outside the group, under Treas.Reg. § 1.1502–19, the amount of gain realized by the parent on the transaction includes not only the sales proceeds received but also the amount of the parent's excess loss account for the subsidiary. Treas.Reg. § 1.1502–19(b)(1).

The amount of gain on the sale resulting from the excess loss account is treated as capital gain. Arguably the gain attributable to the excess loss account should be treated as ordinary income when it represents deductions previously taken against ordinary income. However, the regulations allow capital gain treatment, apparently on the theory that, had the subsidiary realized the appreciation in its assets prior to the disposition, the earnings and profits so generated would have eliminated the excess loss account and this is in effect what is happening when the parent sells the stock at a gain. If the subsidiary is insolvent at the time of the disposition, however, then ordinary income results from the transaction to the extent of the insolvency. Treas.Reg. § 1.1502–19(b)(4)(i).[6] The amount treated as ordinary income is limited to the amount of the excess loss account redetermined to exclude distributions to the parent. Treas.Reg. § 1.1502–19(b)(4)(ii).

The existence of an excess loss account also can affect transactions that otherwise would be tax-free. For example, the disposition of stock in a reorganization involving an unrelated corporation will trigger a recognition of gain if the subsidiary involved had generated an excess loss account. Treas.Reg. § 1.1502–19(b)(2)(ii), (c)(1)(ii). On the other hand, tax-free reorganizations within the group generally do not require the inclusion of the excess loss account in income; instead the excess loss account is applied to the stock received without recognition of gain or loss under § 354, either reducing basis or adding to the excess loss account of that stock. Treas.Reg. § 1.1502–19(b)(2)(i). A liquidation to which §§ 332 and 334(b) apply eliminates the excess loss account; here apparently the theory is that since the "normal" basis is eliminated in such a transaction, similar treatment should apply to the "negative" basis represented by the excess loss account. The transaction is in effect treated as if the parent had owned the subsidiary's assets directly from the beginning.

Other events, such as the discontinuation of filing consolidated returns or the worthlessness of the stock of the subsidiary, also can require the inclusion in income of the amount of the excess loss account. Treas.Reg. § 1.1502–19(c)(1)(iii), (2). Treas.Reg. § 1.1502–19(c)(1)(iii) defers recognition of gain attributable to an excess loss account of a worthless subsidiary from the date the stock becomes worthless under the normal facts and circumstances test of § 165(g) to the date on which substantially all of the subsidiary's assets are disposed of or abandoned or the date on which the subsidiary recognizes discharge of indebtedness income under § 108(a).

6. Covil Insulation Co. v. Commissioner, 65 T.C. 364 (1975), upheld the validity of Treas.Reg. § 1.1502–19, and required the parent corporation to include as ordinary income the excess loss account with respect to a subsidiary whose stock had become worthless. Both the treatment of the stock's worthlessness as an income generating event with respect to the excess loss account and characterization of the gain as ordinary were "permissible exercise[s] of the rule-making power granted by § 1502."

In Garvey, Inc. v. United States, 726 F.2d 1569 (Fed.Cir.1984), the parent corporation acquired stock of a subsidiary in a tax-free type (B) reorganization (an exchange of stock for stock without recognition of gain or loss, § 368(a)(1)(B)) that resulted in a $250,000 basis to the common parent under § 358. Subsequent to acquisition the subsidiary distributed $4.9 million in dividends out of pre-affiliation earnings and profits. Under Treas.Reg. § 1.1502–32(b)(2)(iii)(B), the dividend distribution created an excess loss account of $4.65 million which was required to be recognized as income when the group disaffiliated. The court rejected the taxpayer's argument that application of the regulations unfairly created phantom income that would not have existed had the group filed separate tax returns. The court pointed out that in electing consolidated treatment the taxpayer "must take the bitter with the sweet."[7]

3. *Loss Disallowance Rules*

In some cases, application of the investment adjustment rules conflicts with the principles of §§ 311 and 336, discussed at pages 202 and 333, because it permits assets which are sold out of the consolidated group to obtain a step up in basis without the payment of a current corporate level tax. Suppose, for example, that S Corporation holds a single asset with a basis of $100 and a fair market value of $300. P Corporation purchases all of the stock of S Corporation for $300, P and S do not make a § 338 election, and P and S Corporations elect to file a consolidated return. S Corporation then sells the asset for $300. S Corporation recognizes a $200 gain, and P Corporation increases its basis in the S Corporation stock from $300 to $500. P Corporation then sells the stock of S Corporation for $300, realizing a $200 loss, which offsets the $200 gain. Absent a limitation on the recognition of this loss, tax on the sale of the asset effectively would be eliminated by P Corporation's loss on the sale of the stock of S. P Corporation's tax loss is artificial; it does not reflect an economic loss. The same problem arises if the asset is a depreciable asset which is consumed in the course of S Corporation's business.

Treas.Reg. § 1.1502–20(a)(1) responds to this problem by disallowing any loss realized by a member of a consolidated group upon the disposition of the stock of a subsidiary. The loss disallowance rule does not apply to the extent that gain also is recognized on a related sale of the same class of stock (such as where one block of stock is sold at a gain and another block is sold at a loss) or to the extent that the sale results in the recognition of deferred intercompany gain. Even though the loss on the sale of the subsidiary stock is disallowed as a deduction, the selling corporation nevertheless reduces its earnings and profits by the amount of the loss.

7. Proposed regulations, pending at the time of the *Garvey* transaction would have provided a basis adjustment in the case of a (B) reorganization. The court rejected the taxpayer's argument that the Commissioner was estopped from applying the existing Treas.Reg. § 1.1502–32(b)(2)(iii)(B), because of the proposed regulation. When the proposed regulations were finalized in 1972, the relief for (B) reorganizations was not included. See Treas.Reg. § 1.1502–19(b)(2)(ii).

The broad loss disallowance rule of Treas.Reg. § 1.1502–20(a), which applies to real economic losses as well as the artificial losses, is tempered by the provisions of Treas.Reg. § 1.1502–20(c)(1). Under this provision, the amount of loss that is disallowed is limited to the sum of (i) income or gain resulting from "extraordinary gains dispositions," which are defined as dispositions of capital assets, depreciable property used in the trade or business, certain bulk asset dispositions, and discharge of indebtedness income, (ii) positive investment adjustments (other than those attributable to extraordinary gain dispositions), and (iii) "duplicated loss," which is the aggregate of the subsidiary's asset bases and loss carryovers over the value of the subsidiary's assets. Recognition of losses in excess of these amounts is not barred by Treas.Reg. § 1.1502–20(a). Thus, in the example above, P Corporation's $200 loss on the sale of its S Corporation stock is disallowed. P Corporation's loss is equal to the income from the disposition of S Corporation's asset, which meets the definition of an extraordinary gain disposition. However, if some of the loss is attributable to an economic decline in value, that portion of the loss would be deductible. For example, if the fair market value of S Corporation's asset declined and S Corporation sold the asset for $150, S Corporation would recognize a $50 gain and, under the investment adjustment rules, P Corporation's basis in its S Corporation stock would be increased to $350. If P Corporation then sold its S Corporation stock for $150, it would realize a loss of $200. Since there are no other items involved, the amount of P Corporation's disallowed loss is limited to the gain recognized by S Corporation on the "extraordinary gain disposition" of its asset. Only $50 of P Corporation's loss is offset by S Corporation's extraordinary disposition gain. P Corporation is allowed to deduct $150 of its loss. See Treas.Reg. § 1.1502–20(c)(4), Ex.(1).

A positive investment adjustment attributable to operating income also can create an artificial loss on disposition of the stock of a subsidiary. Assume, for example, that P Corporation purchases the stock of T Corporation for $100. T Corporation's assets are worth $100 and have a zero basis. T Corporation earns $100 of operating income which increases P Corporation's basis in the T Corporation stock to $200. At the same time, the fair market value of T Corporation's assets declines to zero, as a result of which the value of the T Corporation stock remains $100. A sale of the T Corporation stock for $100 at a time when P Corporation's basis in the stock is $200 would result in a loss of $100. Because the loss is attributable to a positive adjustment to the basis of T Corporation stock, the loss is disallowed. Treas.Reg. § 1.1502–20(c)(1)(ii), (c)(4), Ex.(3). This loss disallowance superficially appears to thwart the function of the investment adjustment rules, but actually reaches a result identical to the result that would occur if T Corporation sold the asset for fair market value and then liquidated. Section 332, discussed at page 345, prevents the recognition of loss on liquidation of a controlled subsidiary.

A duplicated loss arises where P Corporation forms S Corporation as a subsidiary and S Corporation thereafter incurs net operating losses that cannot be used currently on the consolidated return, or S Corporation's assets decline in value producing a built-in loss. In this case, the economic loss at the subsidiary level has not resulted in any current tax deduction and the parent's basis for the subsidiary stock is not reduced. (Basis is not reduced until the NOL is absorbed in consolidated taxable income. Treas. Reg. § 1.1502–32(b)(3).) Accordingly, P Corporation would realize a loss upon the sale of the stock of S Corporation. This loss is duplicated when, after leaving the group, S Corporation uses its NOL or recognizes its unrealized losses.[8] P Corporation's loss on sale of the S Corporation stock is disallowed to the extent of the duplicated loss. Treas.Reg. § 1.1502–20(c)(1)(iii). Treas.Reg. § 1.1502–20(g) permits the parent of the group to elect to retain as a consolidated loss carryover of the group any loss incurred by a subsidiary that was not usable in the year incurred. However, the loss is treated as absorbed and for purposes of the investment adjustment rules the parent's basis in the stock of the subsidiary must be reduced by the amount of the loss. A double deduction is thus prevented.

Treas.Reg. § 1.1502–20(b)(1) provides a related basis reduction when a subsidiary corporation ceases to be a member of the consolidated group—is "deconsolidated"—but one or more members of the group continue to hold stock of the subsidiary. This basis reduction rule applies, for example, if a parent corporation sells more than twenty percent of the stock of a wholly owned subsidiary or a previously controlled subsidiary issues to a person other than a member of the consolidated group an amount of stock sufficient to break affiliation under § 1504. As a result of the deconsolidation, if the basis of the stock of the subsidiary is greater than its fair market value, the basis must be reduced to its fair market value immediately before the deconsolidation. Treas.Reg. § 1.1502–20(b)(1). The amount of the basis reduction is also limited by Treas.Reg. § 1.1502–20(c)(1) to extraordinary gains, increases attributable to positive investment adjustments, and duplicated losses.

E. INTERCOMPANY TRANSACTIONS

1. *Transactions Between Members of a Consolidated Group*

(a) General

Treas.Reg. § 1.1502–13 provides rules for transactions between members of the same consolidated group involving the sale or exchange of property, the provision of services by one member of the group to another, the licensing or rental of tangible and intangible property, and the lending of money. The regulation also controls the treatment of intercompany distributions with respect to the stock of a member. Treas.Reg. § 1.1502–13(f). The intercompany transaction rules are treated as a method of accounting that is applied in addition to the member's other methods of accounting. Treas.Reg. § 1.1502–13(a)(3). The timing rules of the intercompany transaction regulations control over other accounting methods, however.

8. S Corporation retains its unused NOL upon leaving the group. Treas.Reg. § 1.1502–79(a).

In general, the intent of the regulations is to treat the tax consequences of intercompany transactions on the consolidated taxable income of the group as if the transactions occurred between divisions of a single entity. Thus, consolidated taxable income generally is not increased or decreased by an intercompany transaction until the property subject to the transaction is no longer within the consolidated group. However, intercompany transactions are also accounted for by each party to the transaction on a separate entity basis to determine the amount and location of an item related to the transaction. The regulations accomplish this result with two sets of rules, the matching rule and the acceleration rule.

(b) Matching Intercompany Items Related to Deferred Gains and Losses

Under Treas.Reg. § 1.1502–13(c)(2), gain or loss recognized by the selling member in an intercompany transaction is accounted for by the selling member under its method of accounting, but is not accounted for in consolidated taxable income until the "corresponding item" resulting from the transaction (see Treas.Reg. § 1.1502–13(b)(3)) is taken into account by the buying member under its method of accounting. For example, on a sale of property, the selling member's gain or loss is not accounted for in consolidated taxable income until the buying member disposes the property outside of the consolidated group, or otherwise recovers its corresponding basis in the acquired property. In this fashion, items resulting from an intercompany transaction are taken into account in a manner that produces the same net result in terms of consolidated taxable income as if the transaction occurred between divisions of a single entity. Any reduction of gain or increased loss realized by the buying member on its sale of property outside the consolidated group that is attributable to the purchase price paid to the selling member is offset in consolidated taxable income by the selling member's deferred gain. Under this single entity principle, the character, source, and other attributes of intercompany transactions are determined with reference to the activities of both the selling and buying members of the consolidated group. Treas.Reg. § 1.1502–13(c)(1). However, for purposes of identifying the amount and location of specific items, each party to an intercompany transaction is treated as a separate entity. Treas.Reg. § 1.1502–13(c)(3).

Treas.Reg. § 1.1502–13(c)(7)(ii), Ex.(1)(f), illustrates the single entity approach with the following example. In year one, S Corporation sells property for $100 that it has held for investment with a basis of $70 to B Corporation, which is a member of the consolidated group that includes S Corporation. The accounting in consolidated taxable income for S Corporation's recognized gain on the sale is deferred. As a separate entity, B Corporation holds the property with an adjusted basis of $100 and S Corporation will be required to recognize its deferred gain when B Corporation takes advantage of the $30 basis increase. See Treas.Reg. § 1.1502–13(a)(2). In year three B Corporation resells the property for $90 to a customer in the ordinary course of B Corporation's business. If S Corporation and B Corporation were divisions of a single entity, B Corporation would succeed to S Corporation's $70 basis in the land and realize $20 of gain. Under the matching principles of Treas.Reg. § 1.1502–13(c), in the year of B Corporation's sale, S Corporation must take into income an amount that reflects the difference for the year between the "corresponding item," which is the amount actually taken into account by B Corporation as a separate entity ($10 loss), Treas.Reg. § 1.1502–13(b)(3), and the "recomputed corresponding item," which is the amount that B Corporation would take into account if S Corporation and B Corporation were divisions of a single entity ($20 gain), Treas.Reg. § 1.1502–13(b)(4). See Treas.Reg. § 1.1502–13(c)(7)(ii), Ex.(1)(d). Thus, in year three, S Corporation is required by Treas.Reg. § 1.1502–13(c)(2)(ii) to recognize $30 [$20–($10) = $30]. B Corporation recognizes its $10 loss in year three. Treas.Reg. § 1.1502–13(c)(2)(i). The net effect on consolidated taxable income is $20 gain.[9] The character of S Corporation's and B Corporation's gain (or loss) is also determined as if S Corporation and B Corporation were divisions of a single entity. Thus, if B Corporation's activities with respect to the property convert the property from investment property into property described in section 1221(1), both S Corporation's and B Corporation's gain or loss will be ordinary. Treas.Reg. § 1.1502–13(c)(1) and (7)(ii), Ex.(2). The gain and loss recognized by S Corporation and B Corporation will be preserved on a separate entity basis for purposes of stock basis and earnings and profits adjustments as required by Treas.Reg. § 1.1502–32 and–33. See Treas.Reg. § 1.1502–13(a)(2).

The matching principle of the regulations also requires an accounting for the selling member's deferred gain as the buying member claims capital recovery deductions on its purchase price basis of depreciable property in an intercompany transaction. Assume for example, that S Corporation and B Corporation are members of the same consolidated group. In 1997 S Corporation acquires depreciable five year property for $150 and claims capital recovery deductions in 1997 and 1998. On the first day of its 1999 taxable year, S Corporation sells the property to B Corporation for $110. At the time of sale, S Corporation's basis in the property is $72 ($150–[$30+48]). S Corporation recognizes $38 of gain, which is deferred. Under § 168(i)(7), B Corporation must use the same depreciation rate as S Corporation with respect to so much of the adjusted basis of the property in B Corporation's hands as does not exceed S Corporation's adjusted basis at the time of the transfer. Thus, in taxable year 1999, B Corporation deducts

9. The original technique of the pre-1966 consolidated return regulations for the elimination of intercorporate gain on sales between affiliated corporations involved a carryover basis for the transferred asset in the hands of the corporation purchasing the asset. That technique also would produce $20 of gain in the example. This technique in effect deferred the recognition of gain until the asset was disposed of outside of the consolidated group. At that point, the deferred gain would be taken into account by the corporation making the outside sale. This approach, however, proved inadequate as it was possible to avoid recognition of the deferred gain in certain circumstances by a disposition of the stock of the corporation that had purchased an appreciated asset in a prior intercompany transaction. See for example Henry C. Beck Builders, Inc. v. Commissioner, 41 T.C. 616 (1964). In addition, in the event that the buying member left the consolidated group, its basis in the property would not appropriately reflect its cost on a separate entity basis.

$28.80, which is the depreciation deduction that would have been available to S Corporation under § 168. In addition, B Corporation is permitted to recover its remaining basis as if the property were new five year property. Thus, in 1999 B Corporation claims an additional $7.60 depreciation deduction (20% of adjusted basis of $38, applying the 1/2 year convention as if the property were new five year property). The additional depreciation deduction claimed by B Corporation requires that S Corporation take into account $7.60 of its deferred intercompany gain. In 2000, B Corporation deducts $17.28 of depreciation with respect to the basis transferred from P, plus $12.16 of depreciation based on its $28 basis increase from the intercompany transaction. S Corporation is required to take into account $12.16 of its deferred intercompany gain in 2000. See Treas.Reg. § 1.1502–13(c)(7)(ii), Ex.(4). Under the single entity principle, which treats S and B as divisions of a single corporation, the character of S Corporation's recognized gain will reflect the tax consequence of B Corporation's depreciation. Treas.Reg. § 1.1502–13(c)(1)(i) and (c)(4)(i). Thus, because S Corporation's deferred gain offsets B Corporation's increased depreciation, S Corporation's gain is treated as ordinary income. See also Treas.Reg. § 1.1502–13(c)(7)(ii), Ex.(4)(d). In this fashion, the regulations recognize separate entity aspects of the transaction as reflected in B Corporation's increased basis and depreciation, but treat the overall consequence to consolidated taxable income as though the property were transferred between divisions of a single entity through the matching of B Corporation's increased depreciation deductions with restoration of S Corporation's deferred intercompany gain.

If, on the first day of its 2001 taxable year, B Corporation sells the property to X Corporation, which is not a member of the S–B consolidated group, for $120 payable in two annual installments with adequate interest, both B Corporation and S Corporation must account for recognized gain. B Corporation recognizes gain of $75.84 ($120–$44.16).[10] As a consequence of B Corporation's sale, S Corporation must also recognize recapture gain. If S and B Corporations were divisions of a single entity, on its 2001 sale of the property the Corporation would have realized $94.08 of gain, determined by subtracting from the $120 amount realized an adjusted basis of $25.92 computed without regard to B Corporation's purchase from S Corporation ($150 original cost less 4 year's capital recovery deductions totaling $94.08). The difference between the gain recognized on a single entity basis and the gain recognized by B Corporation as a separate entity, $18.24 ($94.08–$75.84), is B Corporation's "recomputed corresponding item," which must be accounted for by S Corporation at the time of B Corporation's disposition.[11] As a consequence, the consolidated taxable income of the group reflects the tax consequence of the sale of the property on a single entity basis; S Corporation's gain of $18.24 plus B Corporation's gain of $75.84 is

10. B Corporation's adjusted basis is its $110 purchase price minus $65.84 of depreciation for 1999 and 2000.

11. The recomputed corresponding item is equivalent to S's deferred gain of $38 less gain recognized by S in 1999 and 2000 as B claimed increased capital recovery deductions.

the equivalent of the gain that would have been recognized on the sale of the property outside of the group without the intervention of the intercompany sale from S Corporation to B Corporation. Continuing with the single entity model, because all of the gain recognized on disposition of the property would have been recaptured as ordinary income under § 1245, the gain recognized by both S Corporation and B Corporation is treated as ordinary gain. Treas.Reg. § 1.1502–13(c)(1)(i). Under § 453(i) none of the gain is eligible for installment reporting. If B Corporation had sold the property to X for $160, an amount that would have produced $10 of § 1231 gain in addition to depreciation recapture, B Corporation would have been eligible to report $5 of its gain on the installment method in each of the two years payments are received from X. S Corporation's deferred gain accounted for in the year of sale would not have been eligible for installment reporting, however, because all of S Corporation's deferred gain on its intercompany sale to B Corporation is § 1245 gain. See Treas.Reg. § 1.1502–13(c)(7)(ii), Ex.(5)(f).[12]

(c) Acceleration of Deferred Gains and Losses

Under the acceleration rule, the presence of deferred intercompany gain or loss within the consolidated group also will affect transactions involving the stock of subsidiaries. The regulations address stock transactions by requiring "acceleration" of deferred intercompany items in the case of an event that prevents accounting for an item under the matching rules. Treas.Reg. § 1.1502–13(d)(1). For example, if either the selling or buying member leaves the consolidated group, it is no longer possible to match the selling member's deferred gain or loss with the buying member's subsequent accounting for its corresponding item. Thus, if either member ceases to be a member of the consolidated group, the selling member is required to account for its deferred gain or loss. In the first example above at page 456, where S Corporation sold investment property with a $70 basis to B Corporation for $100, if B Corporation should cease being a member of the consolidated group in year two before selling the property, S Corporation would be required to account for its deferred $30 gain in that year. See Treas.Reg. § 1.1502–13(d)(3), Ex.(1). As a separate entity, or as a member of a different consolidated group, B Corporation would continue to hold the property with a $100 basis. The character of S Corporation's gain would be determined under the matching principles of Treas.Reg. § 1.1502–13(c) as if S Corporation and B Corporation were divisions of the same entity. Treas.Reg. § 1.1502–13(d)(1)(ii). Thus B Corporation's activities with respect to the property could convert S's deferred investment gain into ordinary gain.

Treas.Reg. § 1.1502–13(e)(3) permits the common parent of a consolidated group to request the Commissioner's consent to account for inter-

12. In the case of an installment sale, the regulation also provides that B and S must account for the interest charge of § 453A on gains deferred under the installment method if the aggregate tax installment obligations of the group outstanding at the end of the taxable year exceed $5 million. Treas.Reg. § 1.1502–13(c)(7)(ii), Ex. (5)(b).

company transactions on a separate entity basis. This consent may be granted for all items or a class of items of the consolidated group.

2. *Distributions with respect to the Stock of a Member*

(a) Section 301 Distributions

Treas.Reg. § 1.1502–13(f) also applies the single entity approach to intercompany transactions involving the stock of the members of a consolidated group. Intercompany distributions with respect to the stock of a member of the consolidated group that are subject to § 301 are excluded from the gross income of the distributee member, but only to the extent that the distributee reflects a corresponding negative adjustment to the basis of the stock of the distributing member. Treas.Reg. § 1.1502–13(f)(2)(ii). Thus an intercompany distribution will increase recognized gain, or decrease loss, on a disposition of the stock of the distributing member. Under the investment adjustment rules of Treas.Reg. § 1.1502–32, if the distribution exceeds the recipient member's basis in the stock of the distributing member, the recipient's negative basis creates an excess loss account. The existence of an excess loss account will trigger recognition of gain if either the distributing or recipient member ceases to be a member of the consolidated group. Treas.Reg. § 1.1502–19.

(b) Intercompany Distributions of Appreciated and Depreciated Property

Both gain and loss on intercompany distributions of appreciated or depreciated property with respect to the stock of the distributing member are recognized under the principles of § 311(b) but are accounted for as deferred intercompany gain or loss under the matching rule if the property is sold to a non-member. Treas.Reg. § 1.1502–13(f)(2)(iii). If either member leaves the consolidated group, it will no longer be possible to match accounting for the distributing corporation's deferred item with the recipient's corresponding item, and the acceleration rule of Treas.Reg. § 1.1502–13(d)(1) will require the distributing corporation to account for deferred gain or loss recognized on the distribution. However, while deferred § 311(b) gain is included in consolidated taxable income, loss is treated as a permanently disallowed item. Treas.Reg. § 1.1502–13(c)(6) and (f)(7), Ex.(4)(d). The application of these rules in the context of a transaction that creates an excess loss account is illustrated by Treas.Reg. § 1.1502–13(f)(7), Ex.(2), as follows:

"(a) Facts. S owns all of T's only class of stock with a $10 basis and $100 value. S has substantial earnings and profits, and T has $10 of earnings and profits. On January 1 of Year 1, S declares and distributes a dividend of all of the T stock to P. Under section 311(b), S has a $90 gain. Under section 301(d), P's basis in the T stock is $100. During Year 3, T borrows $90 and declares and makes a $90 distribution to P to which section 301 applies, and P's basis in the T stock is reduced under § 1.1502–32 from $100 to $10. During Year 6, T has $5 of earnings that increase P's basis in the T stock under § 1.1502–32 from $10 to $15. On December 1 of

Year 9, T issues additional stock to X and, as a result, T becomes a nonmember.

"(b) Dividend exclusion. Under paragraph (f)(2)(ii) of this section, P's $100 of dividend income from S's distribution of the T stock, and its $10 of dividend income from T's $90 distribution, are not included in gross income.

"(c) Matching and acceleration rules. Under § 1.1502–19(b)(1), when T becomes a nonmember P must include in income the amount of its excess loss account (if any) in T stock. P has no excess loss account in the T stock. Therefore P's corresponding item from the deconsolidation of T is $0. Treating S and P as divisions of a single corporation, the T stock would continue to have a $10 basis after the distribution, and the adjustments under § 1.1502–32 for T's $90 distribution [which decrease basis] and $5 of earnings [which increase basis] would result in a $75 excess loss account [$10–$90 + $5]. Thus, the recomputed corresponding item from the deconsolidation is $75. Under the matching rule, S takes $75 of its $90 gain into account in Year 9 as a result of T becoming a nonmember, to reflect the difference between P's $0 gain taken into account and the $75 recomputed gain. S's remaining $15 of gain is taken into account under the matching and acceleration rules based on subsequent events (for example, under the matching rule if P subsequently sells its T stock, or under the acceleration rule if S becomes a nonmember)."

In the example, if the basis of the T stock had not been adjusted as a result of S's distribution of the T stock to P, the $90 distribution to P would have resulted in an excess loss account with respect to the T stock. On a single entity basis, the excess loss account would have been $75, the original $10 of basis, increased by $5 of earnings and profits and decreased by the $90 distribution. Accordingly, S is required to take into account $75 of deferred gain when T ceases to be a member of the consolidated group. The remaining $15 of S's deferred gain remains a deferred item for S, which can be matched with P's disposition of its remaining T stock, or accelerated if either S or P cease to be members of the same consolidated group. Treas.Reg. § 1.1502–19.

(c) Transactions in which a Member Acquires its own Stock

As a consequence of the nonrecognition rules of § 1032, when a corporation acquires its own stock, there will be no subsequent transaction in which the basis of the acquired stock is accounted for. To deal with this situation, Treas.Reg. § 1.1502–13(f)(4) provides in effect that if a member of a consolidated group acquires its own stock in an intercompany transaction, gain or loss recognized by the selling member must be accounted for at the time of the transaction under the acceleration rule. The gain or loss is accelerated to the date of the intercompany transaction under the acceleration rule because there is no corresponding item with which to match deferred gain. See Treas.Reg. § 1.1502–13(f)(7), Ex.(4). If a corporation acquires its own stock in a redemption subject to § 302(a), the selling member must account for its gain. If a corporation acquires its own stock in a § 301 distribution from another member, the distributing member must account for gain recognized under § 311(b). Treas.Reg. § 1.1502–13(f)(7), Ex.(4)(c). If the selling or distributing corporation realizes a loss on the transaction, the loss is accounted for as a noncapital, nondeductible amount. Treas.Reg. § 1.1502–13(c)(6) and (f)(7), Ex.(4)(d).

(d) Liquidation of a Subsidiary

An intercompany sale of the stock of a member of the consolidated group, followed by a liquidation of the subsidiary creates an interesting problem under the single entity approach. The problem is illustrated by the following example, which is based on Treas.Reg. § 1.1502–13(f)(7), Ex.(5). B Corporation, S Corporation and T Corporation are members of the same consolidated group. S Corporation owns all of the T Corporation stock, which has a fair market value of $100. S Corporation's basis in the T Corporation stock is $70. The fair market value of T Corporation's assets is $100 and the assets have a basis of $10. On July 1 of year 1, B Corporation purchases the T Corporation stock from S Corporation for $100. S Corporation's $30 gain on the intercompany sale to B Corporation in year 1 is not accounted for in consolidated taxable income. On July 1 of year 3, when T Corporation's assets are still worth $100, T Corporation distributes all of its assets to B Corporation in a complete liquidation governed by § 332. B Corporation's basis in the T Corporation stock is $100. On liquidation of T Corporation, B Corporation receives a $100 distribution and thus has zero realized gain. In addition, B Corporation recognizes no gain or loss on the liquidation under § 332. If the transfer of T Corporation stock from S Corporation to B Corporation had been between divisions of a single entity, B Corporation's realized gain on liquidation of T Corporation would have been $30, but the gain would not have been recognized under § 332. Thus, B Corporation's recomputed corresponding item is $30 of unrecognized gain, which must be taken into account by S Corporation in year 3. Although Treas.Reg. § 1.1502–13(c)(1)(i) provides that the attributes of S Corporation and B Corporation's gain, including its status as a nonrecognition item, are determined as if S Corporation and B Corporation were divisions of a single entity, Treas.Reg. § 1.1502–13(c)(6)(ii) provides that gain subject to a nonrecognition provision that is not permanently and explicitly disallowed is not treated as having the attribute of an item excluded from income. Thus, S Corporation's $30 of deferred gain is taken into account as capital gain in year 3. This result seems to be necessary because B Corporation inherits T Corporation's asset basis and the T Corporation stock is no longer available as a corresponding item to match S Corporation's deferred gain from the sale of the T Corporation stock to B Corporation.

Treas.Reg. § 1.1502–13(c)(6)(ii) only applies to gains. As a consequence, deferred intercompany loss on an intercompany sale of stock of a subsidiary followed by a § 332 liquidation of the subsidiary is not taken into account by the selling member. See Treas.Reg. § 1.1502–13(f)(7), Ex.(5)(c). The examples suggest that relief from S Corporation's accounting for its deferred gain may be available under Treas.Reg. § 1.1502–13(f)(5)(ii) if the liquidation of T Corporation is followed by a transfer of the T Corporation assets to New T Corporation. In this case, the stock of New T Corporation would be a successor asset to B Corporation's stock in old T Corporation.

(e) Anti–Abuse Rules

In language designed to force tax practitioners to bang their heads against a brick wall for pleasure, Treas.Reg. § 1.1502–13(h)(1) provides that, "If a transaction is structured with a principal purpose to avoid the purposes of this section, (including, for example, by avoiding treatment as an intercompany transaction), adjustments must be made to carry out the purposes of this section." Specific examples of abusive transactions described in the regulation include the transfer of property to a partnership to avoid the SRLY limitation, the use of corporations formed under § 351 or partnerships to mix assets for the purpose of avoiding gain on disposition of appreciated property, and the use of a sale-leaseback transaction to create gain for the purpose of absorbing losses subject to the SRLY limitation. Treas.Reg. § 1.1502–13(h)(2). Similar anti-abuse language is attached to other consolidated return regulations. See e.g., Treas.Regs. §§ 1.1502–19(e),–32(e), and–33(g).

F. EARNINGS AND PROFITS

Special adjustments are required in the earnings and profits accounts of the parent corporation in a consolidated group to reflect the consolidated situation. If the parent of the group were not required to include in its earnings and profits the earnings and profits of subsidiaries in the group, under § 301 a parent corporation with profitable subsidiaries and no earnings and profits of its own could make tax-free distributions to its stockholders despite the group as a whole having current or accumulated earnings. Under Treas.Reg. § 1.1502–33(a) and (b), the earnings and profits of a consolidated subsidiary are determined under the applicable provisions of the Code (see § 312, page 196), and passed up through higher-tier entities to be consolidated in the earnings and profits of the common parent.

Treas.Reg. § 1.1502–33(c) requires a separate determination of the parent's basis in the stock of a consolidated subsidiary for purposes of determining the increase or decrease in earnings and profits resulting from the sale of the subsidiary's stock. Gain or loss on the disposition of the stock of a member of the consolidated group is determined from the basis of the stock as adjusted by the investment adjustment rules of Treas.Reg. § 1.1502–32, which are based on the subsidiary's contribution to taxable income. There are differences in the computation of earnings and profits and taxable income, however, primarily because § 312(k) and (n) require adjustments to earnings and profits for a number of items including depreciation, inventory amounts, and installment sales, which differ from the amounts taken into account in computing taxable income or loss. To account for these differences in determining the effect on the parent's earnings and profits of the sale of stock in a subsidiary, the basis of a subsidiary's stock must be determined using earnings and profits as the basis for investment adjustments. Thus, the basis of stock of a subsidiary for earnings and profits purposes is increased by the earnings and profits of the subsidiary and decreased by a deficit in earnings and profits. Treas.Reg. § 1.1502–33(c)(1).

Under § 1552, tax liability of the consolidated group is apportioned against the earnings and profits of each of the members in proportion to the member's contribution to consolidated taxable income, as a percentage of the total tax attributable to the member if the tax of each member were computed on a separate return basis, on the basis of each member's actual contribution to consolidated taxable income including reductions in income, or by any other method selected by the group and approved by the Commissioner. Section 1552 does not provide a device to account for the effect of the absorption of one member's tax attributes by another member, e.g., one member's income may be absorbed by another member's losses. Treas.Reg. § 1.1502–33(d) contains rules to account for the impact of the absorption of tax attributes which are intended to reflect in earnings and profits the reduction of one member's tax liability by attributes of another that would have reduced the latter member's earnings and profits in a different year if not used by the first member.

*

PART IV

CORPORATE ACQUISITION TECHNIQUES

CHAPTER 11

TAXABLE ACQUISITIONS: THE PURCHASE AND SALE OF A CORPORATE BUSINESS

The material considered up to this point has focused on the provisions of Subchapter C from the perspective of their function in the statutory structure provided for the taxation of corporations and shareholders. The material in this Part changes from this structural focus to concentrate on the application of the corporate rules to a specific transaction, the purchase and sale of a corporate business. This Chapter and Chapter 12 deal with the tax aspects of a taxable purchase and sale of the corporate business;[1] the various techniques for tax free acquisitions are considered in Chapter 13.

A taxable purchase and sale of a business often involves a fairly straightforward application of the general principles that have previously

1. Chapter 12 examines the problems that arise when corporate distributions are made in connection with the sale of a corporate business.

been considered. Suppose that A owns all of the stock of X Corporation, which operates a business consisting of two assets, Asset #1, having a basis of $50 and a fair market value of $500, and Asset #2, having a basis of $250 and a fair market value of $200. Also assume that the basis of A's stock is $200. If Y Corporation desires to acquire the business of X Corporation it might purchase the assets of X Corporation for $700. X Corporation would realize a net gain of $400 on the sale of its assets. If this gain were taxed at the maximum corporate rate of 35 percent, X Corporation would pay taxes of $140 and make a $560 liquidating distribution to A, who would recognize a capital gain of $360. A would pay a tax, at 20 percent, of $72 and would receive net proceeds of $488. Y Corporation would take a basis of $500 for Asset #1 and $200 for Asset #2. On a subsequent sale of the assets, assuming that their fair market values were unchanged, Y Corporation would realize neither gain nor loss. In some situations, however, issues peculiar to the sale of a corporate business have arisen and rules have been fashioned, either by the Congress or by the courts, to deal with these problems. The materials in Section 1 deal with the sale of a business that takes the form of a sale of corporate assets and explore the problems that this form of transaction historically has generated and the currently applicable rules.

Rather than purchasing the X Corporation's assets, Y Corporation might purchase the stock of X Corporation from A. If Y Corporation paid $700 for the stock, A would recognize a gain of $500. The basis of the assets in X Corporation's hands would be unaffected by the sale of the stock, and on a subsequent sale of the assets, X Corporation would recognize an aggregate gain of $400. Since the economic burden of the tax on this gain would be borne by Y Corporation, presumably it would offer A less than $700 for the stock of X Corporation to reflect this inherent tax burden. If the gain were to be realized and taxed contemporaneously with the purchase, it could be expected that Y Corporation would offer A only $560 for the stock, the same amount that he would receive in a liquidating distribution following a taxable sale of its assets by X Corporation. But if the gain were not expected to be realized until sometime in the future, Y Corporation could be expected to be willing to pay somewhat more for the stock.

Section 2 of this Chapter focuses on this second basic alternative form for the sale of a corporate business, the sale of the shares of stock of the corporation and again focuses on the corporate tax rules designed for this form of transaction.

In examining these materials keep in mind that the manner in which the parties have structured transactions involving the sale of a corporate business historically has been influenced by three major tax factors: the seller's desire to maximize the portion of the gain that would be taxed as capital gain rather than as ordinary income; the buyer's desire to obtain as high a basis as possible for the corporation's assets, particularly inventory and depreciable property; and, finally, the ability to avoid recognition of gain at the corporate level under either the *General Utilities* doctrine or the pre–1987 version of § 337.[2] The elimination of this last factor by the 1986 Tax Reform Act has significantly altered the stakes in many transactions, but important issues remain.[3]

Tax results are not the only factors that influence the form of a sale and purchase of a corporate business. Indeed, tax results in many cases are of lesser importance than nontax factors. In many cases, a single purchaser for all of the corporation's business activities cannot be located, and one line of business is sold to one purchaser while another line of business is sold to a second purchaser. In other cases, a purchaser might be unwilling to acquire the stock of a corporation because of concerns regarding contingent or unascertained liabilities. On the other hand, an asset purchase might be ruled out if the acquired business owns contract rights that are not assignable; in such a case the acquisition must be structured as a sale and purchase of stock. Other important factors to be considered include state law rights of dissenting shareholders, federal and state securities laws, and the authority of state and federal regulatory agencies to approve or disapprove a transaction.

SECTION 1. ASSETS ACQUISITIONS

INTERNAL REVENUE CODE: Sections 197(a)–(e)(f)(1), (3), (7); 453(h); 1060.

REGULATIONS: Section 1.1060–1T(a)(1), (b)(1), (c), (d), (e)(1), (h)(1)–(2).

If a corporation sells its business by selling its assets to the purchaser, it recognizes gain or loss with respect to each separate asset, as would a partnership or sole proprietorship selling its business. On liquidation the shareholders recognize capital gain or loss under the rules governing complete liquidations, discussed in Chapter 8, subject to the exception under § 332 for liquidations of controlled subsidiaries. Thus, gain or loss generally results to both the corporation and the shareholders. The same tax results follow if the corporation liquidates first, recognizing gain or loss under § 336, with the shareholders again taxable under § 331. In this case the shareholders take a fair market value basis in the corporation's assets pursuant to § 334, and they realize no gain or loss upon the immediate sale of the assets.

In an asset sale, both buyer and seller must allocate the purchase price to the various assets transferred, the seller in order to determine the amount of gain or loss on each asset and the buyer to establish the tax

2. The general rule of former § 337, as in effect from 1954–1987, was that a corporation recognized neither gain nor loss on the sale or exchange of assets after the adoption of a plan of liquidation, if all of the assets (including proceeds from the sale of assets) were distributed in liquidation within twelve months of adoption of the plan. Elimination of the corporate tax through nonrecognition of gain depended, however, on following mechanical formulae involving time intervals, bulk inventory sales of a certain nature, and the like.

3. The history summarized above is detailed in an earlier edition of this work, see McDaniel, Ault, McMahon and Simmons, Federal Income Taxation of Business Organizations 689–693 (Foundation Press 1991).

basis for each of the newly acquired assets. These allocations generally present no problem if the parties have bargained on an asset-by-asset basis, but that is rarely the case. More commonly the parties bargain for the sale and purchase based on a lump sum price. After the total purchase price has been determined the parties often then bargain as to the allocation among all of the assets. The parties' objectives in this *ex post* allocation are to a large extent determined by tax considerations. Generally, allocations of the purchase price by the parties have been respected by the Internal Revenue Service and the courts on the theory that the parties had adverse tax interests and that a bargained-for allocation is therefore presumptively correct.

There was, however, the danger that the Treasury could be "whip-sawed" by inconsistent allocations in which each party allocated the purchase price in the manner most advantageous to that party and differently from the other party. This was a particularly serious problem prior to the enactment in 1993 of § 197, allowing 15-year amortization of almost all purchased intangible assets. Prior to the enactment of § 197, goodwill and going concern value were not depreciable. Thus, purchasers preferred to minimize the amount allocated to those assets and maximize the amount allocated to depreciable assets and inventory. From the seller's perspective, however, it was more desirable to allocate purchase price to goodwill and going concern value, because the gain on those assets was capital gain, rather than to inventory and depreciable equipment, which resulted in ordinary income. In addition, purchasers attempted to allocate all or part of a "premium" payment in excess of the value of the assets among all of the assets, rather than allocating the premium solely to goodwill or going concern value.[4] Congress responded to these problems with the enactment in 1986 of § 1060, requiring the use by both the buyer and the seller of the "residual method" of valuing goodwill.[5] This provision was intended not only to prevent the allocation of any purchase price premium to depreciable assets, but to help insure that the seller and purchaser allocate the price consistently.

With the enactment of § 197, providing for uniform amortization of purchased intangible assets over 15 years, however, the former function of § 1060 has diminished in importance and the latter function has become more significant. Pursuant to its statutory authority, the Treasury Department has promulgated regulations requiring both parties to file information returns with respect to the purchase price allocation thus allowing the

4. Purchasers had sometimes applied a so-called "proportional allocation method" in determining purchase price premiums. Under this approach, an independent value was established for goodwill, often by a capitalization of earnings method, and then the premium was allocated proportionately to all assets, including goodwill. See United States v. Cornish, 348 F.2d 175 (9th Cir.1965) (allowing premium paid for partnership interest to be allocated among partnership assets in making basis adjustment under § 743).

5. For earlier judicial application of the residual method of valuing goodwill, see Carty v. Commissioner, 38 T.C. 46 (1962); compare Rev.Rul. 68–609, 1968–2 C.B. 327 (capitalization of earnings method).

Internal Revenue Service to identify situations in which allocations have been made on an inconsistent basis. See Temp. Reg. § 1.1060–1T(h).

ILLUSTRATIVE MATERIAL

A. ALLOCATION OF PURCHASE PRICE

1. *General*

Section 1060 refers to preexisting regulations under § 338(b)(5), discussed at page 485, which contain a detailed set of rules for the allocation of the purchase price among acquired assets. Temp. Reg. § 1.1060–1T(d) sets forth the allocation rules, which divide all assets into five classes. Class I assets include cash, bank deposits, and similar assets; Class II includes certificates of deposit, United States Government securities, and readily marketable stock or securities; Class III includes all other assets except § 197 intangibles; Class IV includes all § 197 intangibles other than goodwill and going concern value, and Class V, which is the residual basis category, includes only goodwill and going concern value. The term "§ 197 intangibles" is intended to be broader than the term "amortizable § 197 intangibles" and includes, for example, § 197 intangibles that are amortizable by the buyer but not by the seller. See T.D. 8711, 1997–1 C.B. 85, 86. Class III thus typically contains most tangible assets and some depreciable intangible assets, such as computer software, while Class IV typically contains intangible assets, such as patents, copyrights, trademarks, tradenames, franchises, customer lists, and covenants not to compete.

The purchase price is allocated first to Class I assets based on their aggregate fair market value, then to Class II assets, and so on through Class IV. Within each class, the price is allocated among assets relative to their respective fair market values. Since each asset in Classes I–IV should be allocated a portion of the purchase price equal to its fair market value, any amount designated as paid for goodwill or going concern value, as well as the entire premium, if any, is allocated to Class V. Conversely, if a going business is purchased for less than its liquidation value, the Class IV assets, and the Class III assets, if the Class IV assets are insufficient enough or the discount is deep enough, are allocated an amount less than their individual fair market values.

Nevertheless, even after the enactment of § 197, under Temp. Reg. § 1.1060–1T, some conflict of interest between buyer and seller remains. Since all § 197 intangibles are amortized over 15 years, the division of § 197 amortizable intangibles between two classes for purposes of determining basis is significant only if some, but not all, of the amortizable intangibles acquired in a single transaction are subsequently sold at a gain, necessitating calculation of individual bases of the intangibles that were sold. From the seller's side, however, it is more likely that § 1245 recapture will apply with respect to Class IV assets than with respect to Class V assets, since Class IV may contain amortizable self-created intangibles, but Class V intangibles are amortizable, and thus subject to § 1245 on sale, only if purchased. Furthermore, the allocation of price between Classes IV and V on the one hand and between assets within Class III itself can be important and the parties can have differing interests. Class III contains both depreciable and nondepreciable assets, such as land. Purchasers will want to establish as high a fair market value as is possible for depreciable assets and inventory, but for the seller such an allocation may give rise to ordinary income (including § 1245 recapture income) instead of capital gain. Generalizations as to which of the seller or purchaser is benefited by an allocation to Class III versus Class IV are impossible because the analysis is fact specific. Class III contains many assets for which cost recovery under § 168 is more rapid than is cost recovery under § 197 for Class IV and Class V assets, but it also contains important assets, e.g., real property, for which cost recovery under § 168 is not as rapid as cost recovery for intangibles under § 197.

In addition, the purchase and sale of a corporate business often is accompanied by the shareholders' agreement not to compete with the buyer in the field of business involved. Section 1060 did not completely address the problem of artificial allocations between goodwill and covenants not to compete. A covenant not to compete, even though created in the sale transaction, is a Class IV asset, Temp.Reg. § 1.1060–1T(d)(2)(ii), (g), Ex.4. Goodwill, however, is a Class V asset. Because a covenant not to compete is as difficult to value as goodwill itself, the tension continued. The enactment of § 197 did not eliminate this tension. Both a covenant not to compete and purchased goodwill must be amortized over 15 years under § 197, regardless of the term of the covenant or the payment schedule, and no loss deduction is allowed for the basis allocated to one as long as the other is retained, I.R.C. § 197(f)(1). The buyer is thus indifferent as to the allocation between the two. As to the seller, however, payments received for a covenant not to compete are ordinary income, Hamlin's Trust v. Commissioner, 209 F.2d 761 (10th Cir.1954), Rev.Rul. 69–643, 1969–2 C.B. 10, while amounts received for self-created goodwill produce capital gain and amounts received for purchased goodwill produce § 1231 gain, see I.R.C. § 197(f)(7), which will result in capital gain treatment. Thus, if the seller enjoys a preferential rate for capital gains, the seller will want as much as possible of the purchase price that exceeds the fair market value of other assets allocated to goodwill rather than a covenant not to compete. If, however, the covenant not to compete involves the shareholders of the corporation whose assets are acquired, they might prefer an allocation to a covenant not to compete because, although the payments are taxed as ordinary income rather than capital gain, they will not be subject to the double tax regime as they would be if they were allocated to goodwill of the corporate business. Furthermore, in many cases the buyer's business need for an enforceable covenant not to compete will prevent the parties from omitting a covenant not to compete from the transaction entirely. See Beaver Bolt, Inc. v. CIR, T.C. Memo. 1995–549 (buyer's allocation of $380,000 of price to seller's covenant not to compete was reduced to $324,000; a substantial allocation was proper, even though the parties had no adverse tax interests, because seller had the ability to compete and realistically might have competed in the absence of the covenant). Artificial allocations nevertheless might continue to be a problem.

Section 1060(a) binds both the transferor and transferee to any written agreement between them with respect to the allocation of the purchase price or the fair market value of the assets, unless the Commissioner determines that the allocation is not appropriate. The legislative history states that the agreement will be binding on both parties unless a party is able to refute the allocation under the standards of Commissioner v. Danielson, 378 F.2d 771 (3d Cir.1967). H.Rep. 101–964, 101st Cong., 2d Sess. 95 (1990). *Danielson* allows a party to refute an agreement only on proof admissible in an action to show unenforceability because of mistake, undue influence, fraud, or duress. The Internal Revenue Service, however, is not restricted from challenging the taxpayers' allocations. S.Rep. No. 99–313, 99th Cong., 2d Sess. 255 (1986). In general, there is no requirement in § 1060 or in the regulations that the parties agree on an allocation or that they file consistent information returns. As a practical matter, however, the purchaser usually requires a contractual provision that consistent information returns be filed.

2. *Applicable Asset Acquisition*

The legislative history indicates that § 1060 applies to any sale and purchase of assets that constitute an active trade or business under § 355, discussed at page 685, or to which "goodwill or going concern value could under any circumstances attach." S.Rep. No. 99–313, 99th Cong., 2d Sess. 255 (1986). Temp.Reg. § 1.1060–1T(b)(2) and (3), Ex. (1)–(4) indicates that the term "applicable asset acquisition" is to be broadly construed. Thus, if a liquidating corporation sells a portion of its assets to each of several purchasers, several applicable asset acquisitions may have occurred. Conversely, if a purchasing corporation acquires assets of a seller that constituted a trade or business of the seller, an applicable asset acquisition has occurred even though the purchaser discontinues the seller's trade or business and uses the assets in a different trade or business conducted by it. Section 1060 does not apply to a stock purchase treated as an asset purchase under § 338, discussed in Section 2 of this Chapter. See H.Rep. 101–882, 101st Cong., 2d Sess. 102 (1990).

B. LIABILITIES

Assumption by the buyer of the seller's liabilities generally is treated as a payment received by the seller. Treas. Reg. § 1.1001–2. The proper treatment in cases in which those liabilities would have given rise to a deduction when paid, however, is not so clear. In Commercial Security Bank v. Commissioner, 77 T.C. 145 (1981), the purchaser of all of the business assets of a cash method corporation assumed the seller's accounts payable as part of the consideration paid. The court held that the selling corporation properly should include the payables in the amount realized on the sale but is entitled to an offsetting deduction because it in effect paid the liabilities at the time of the sale. The court stated that the purchaser was required to capitalize the assumed liabilities and could not deduct them when paid. This treatment, however, is inconsistent with Crane v. Commissioner, 331 U.S. 1, 13 n. 34 (1947), which held that otherwise deductible liabilities assumed by the buyer are not included in the amount realized on the sale of assets. This aspect of *Crane* was applied in the context of § 357 in Focht v. Commissioner, 68 T.C. 223 (1977)(A), and appears to reflect the current policy of the Internal Revenue Service. See Rev. Rul. 95–74, page 99 . Under this view, the buyer does not capitalize the amount of such assumed liabilities but instead deducts them when paid. James M. Pierce Corp. v. Commissioner, 326 F.2d 67 (8th Cir.1964), reached a similar result. Nevertheless, *Commercial Security Bank* reached the theoretically correct result.

Corporate acquisitions may involve the assumption of contingent liabilities, such as environmental damage, products liability, pension plan, and other employment related claims. Such contingent liabilities also present tax problems. For example, in Albany Car Wheel Co. v. Commissioner, 40 T.C. 831 (1963), aff'd per curiam, 333 F.2d 653 (2d Cir.1964), the purchaser of a business assumed the seller's contingent liability for severance pay under a union contract if the purchased factory was closed. Because the obligation was "speculative," the court held that it could not be taken into account until paid. There is, however, little authority on whether the purchaser must capitalize the payment when made, even if it would have been deductible by the seller. Pacific Transport Co. v. Commissioner, 483 F.2d 209 (9th Cir.1973), rev'g T.C. Memo. 1970–41, required capitalization of such payments, but United States v. Minneapolis & St. Louis Ry., 260 F.2d 663 (8th Cir.1958), allowed a deduction, and Rev. Rul. 95–74, supra, implies that the payment should be either capitalized or deducted depending upon its character. If a contingent liability would have been deductible if paid by the seller, the seller should be permitted to exclude the liability from the amount realized under the principle of *Crane* and *Focht*, supra. Furthermore, Rev. Rul. 95–74, supra, also implies that a contingent liability that would have been capitalized if paid by the seller also should be ignored in computing the seller's gain. This is logical because if the liability were included in the amount realized, the seller's basis should be increased by a like amount, leaving the amount of gain unchanged.

When a contingent obligation related to the acquisition of property is satisfied, the amount of the satisfied debt is added to basis. If the property is depreciable, the taxpayer may deprecate the increased basis over the property's remaining cost recovery period; a new cost recovery period is not commenced. See Meredith Corp. v. Commissioner, 102 T.C. 406, 462–463 (1994). If the property's cost recovery period has expired prior to the contingent obligation having been satisfied, however, an ordinary loss deduction is allowable. See Meredith Corp. v. Commissioner, 108 T.C. 89 (1997).

C. INSTALLMENT REPORTING BY ACQUIRED CORPORATION'S SHAREHOLDERS

1. *General*

If the consideration in an asset sale consists in whole or in part of the acquiring corporation's bonds or other debt instruments, the possibility of installment reporting under § 453 must be considered. In situations in which the selling corporation liquidates, the possibilities for installment reporting are quite limited. Installment reporting of gains from inventory and depreciation recapture is not permitted in any event. See I.R.C. § 453(b)(2), (i)(2). In addition, as a result of distribution of installment obligations in liquidation, under § 453B the corporation must recognize all of its gain on any installment notes for which § 453 installment sale accounting otherwise would have been available. Then the question is whether the shareholders may report their gain on the installment method when they receive the purchaser's debt obligations in the liquidating distribution. If the seller receives purchaser's bonds that are readily tradable, § 453(f)(4) precludes installment sale reporting. Furthermore, if the stock of the selling liquidating corporation was publicly traded, § 453(k)(2) might deny installment sale treatment. If neither of these disqualifying facts is involved, then, if the conditions of § 453(h) are satisfied, the shareholders of the selling corporation may be eligible to report gain using the installment method in either an asset sale followed by a liquidation or a taxable merger.

Suppose that under the terms of the merger agreement, the shareholders of T Corporation may elect to receive either cash or installment obligations of A Corporation. Will those shareholders electing to receive the installment obligations nonetheless be found to be in constructive receipt of cash and thus currently taxable? Rev.Rul. 73–396, 1973–2 C.B. 160, held that the constructive receipt doctrine did not apply in a situation in which the purchaser was willing to pay cash but a buyer insisted on deferred payments.

2. *Section 453(h)*

Section 453(h) provides a very limited exception to the shareholder recognition rule (but not to the rules requiring recognition by the corporation upon distribution of the note) when the shareholders receive installment obligations arising from a sale or exchange of corporate assets occurring after the adoption of a plan of complete liquidation that is completed within twelve months after it was adopted,[6] and it applies whether the installment sale is pursuant to a complete acquisition of the seller's business or a dispersal sale. This provision applies only if the liquidation is completed within twelve months following adoption of the plan.[7] If this requirement is met, shareholders recognize gain on the

6. Section 453(k)(2), denying installment sale treatment for sales of marketable stock and securities, might render § 453(h) unavailable in the liquidation of a publicly traded corporation, but it is highly unlikely that a publicly traded corporation ever would liquidate in a manner to which § 453(h) could apply.

7. Section 453(h) is a vestige of the pre–1987 rules under which a corporation did not recognize gain or loss on the sale or exchange of certain assets if the assets were sold after the adoption of a plan of liquidation and the liquidation was completed within twelve months. Although those rules were repealed by the Tax Reform Act of 1986, installment reporting of shareholder gain was continued.

liquidation with respect to the notes under the installment method of § 453 as they receive payments on the obligations. If an installment obligation arises from the sale of inventory, however, deferred recognition is available only if substantially all of the inventory attributable to a particular trade or business of the corporation was sold in bulk to a single purchaser.

Assume, for example, that C is the sole shareholder of Y Corporation. C's basis for her stock is $1,000. Y Corporation owns a factory and inventory. If Y Corporation sells the factory and inventory for a $10,000 promissory note, payable in five equal principal installments (with interest), and then distributes the note to C in complete liquidation, C recognizes no gain at the time of the liquidation, but instead recognizes $1,800 of gain under § 331 as each $2,000 installment is received (C also recognizes interest income). If the factory were sold for $6,000 cash and the inventory were sold in bulk for a $4,000 note, due in four equal principal installments (with interest), and Y Corporation liquidated, C would allocate a pro rata portion of the $1,000 basis in the stock, $600 ($1,000 x $6,000/($6,000 + $4,000)) to the cash distribution and C would recognize a $5,400 gain upon receipt of the cash distribution; C would allocate $100 of basis to each $1,000 payment received on the note and recognize $900 of gain as each payment is received.

Section 453(h) has some limitations. If the property sold for an installment obligation is depreciable property and the purchaser is related to the shareholder (i.e., the shareholder's spouse, a trust of which the shareholder or the shareholder's spouse is a beneficiary, or a corporation or partnership more than 50 percent controlled by the shareholder of the selling corporation), installment reporting is not available to the shareholder. Where a corporation distributes cash or property (other than qualifying installment obligations) in one tax year and then in a subsequent tax year (but within 12 months) distributes installment obligations qualifying under § 453(h), the gain included in the first year must be recomputed—usually on an amended return—to reflect treatment of the earlier cash distribution as an installment payment. In turn, a portion of the basis for the stock originally used to offset the cash distribution must be allocated to the installment obligation, thereby increasing the gain recognized in the first year. Treas. Reg. § 1.453–11 provides detailed rules regarding the application of § 453(h).

D. TAXABLE "CASH" MERGERS

The use of a statutory merger under state law allows an acquisition to take place on a tax-free basis if the various requirements of § 368, discussed in Chapter 13, are met. The statutory merger technique frequently has been used instead of a direct asset sale to carry out a taxable acquisition in which the acquiring corporation pays the shareholders of the target corporation cash, corporate bonds (installment obligations), or a combination of cash and installment obligations in connection with the merger. One of the reasons for using a "cash" merger is to effect a transfer of the properties of the acquired corporation directly to the acquiring corporation as a matter of state law, avoiding the need to document separately each transfer. In addition, a merger forces out any minority shareholders in the acquired corporation who dissented from the merger. Furthermore, if the acquisition takes the form of a "reverse" merger in which the acquired corporation is the surviving corporation, problems can be avoided with regard to assets which cannot be assigned or transferred, for example, assets subject to a restriction on transferability in connection with a loan agreement.

To take the simplest case, suppose T Corporation is merged into A Corporation in a transaction in which the T Corporation shareholders all receive cash or debt instruments of A Corporation. For tax purposes, the transaction is treated as a sale of assets followed by the liquidation of T Corporation. See West Shore Fuel, Inc. v. United States, 598 F.2d 1236 (2d Cir.1979) (all debt merger treated as corporate assets sale); Rev.Rul. 69–6, 1969–1 C.B. 104 (merger of mutual savings banks). Thus, both the acquired corporation and its shareholders recognize gain or loss on the transaction. This double tax treatment of cash mergers may be avoided through the use of a "reverse" triangular merger, the merger of a subsidiary of the acquiring corporation into the target corporation, with the shareholders of the target receiving cash from the parent. Rev. Rul. 90–95, 1990–2 C.B. 67, and Rev.Rul. 79–273, 1979–2 C.B. 125, indicate that this transaction will be treated as a sale and purchase of shares of the target corporation.

SECTION 2. STOCK ACQUISITIONS

INTERNAL REVENUE CODE: Section 338.

In the transactions considered in Section 1, the purchaser of the corporate business desired to acquire assets and the seller agreed to this form of the transaction. Often, however, the seller desires to structure the transaction as a sale of corporate stock. One of the prime motivations for a stock sale is that the preferential tax rate accorded to capital gains applies to the entire recognized gain. In addition, depending on the extent to which the purchaser reduces the offering price to reflect the lower asset basis attendant to a stock purchase and sale, by avoiding double taxation the seller may expect to net a larger after-tax profit even without taking the capital gains preference into account.

Often, however, for a variety of reasons the purchaser does not want to purchase the stock but prefers to purchase the assets directly. First, the corporation may have liabilities which the purchaser does not wish to assume indirectly. Second, if the assets have a basis lower than their market value, and hence lower than the price to be paid for the business, the assets will retain that low basis when the ownership of the corporation changes hands. This basis result may be unsatisfactory to the purchaser, especially with respect to inventory or depreciable property. Third, a stock purchase involves taking over other tax attributes such as accumulated earnings and profits. However, a stock purchase will permit the use of the acquired corporation's net operating loss carryovers, subject to the limitations of § 382, discussed in Chapter 16.

Suppose the purchaser, desiring to buy the assets but unable to persuade the seller to agree, buys the stock and then proceeds to liquidate the corporation to obtain the assets, thereby making it clear that the purchase of the stock was but a step in the direction of an asset purchase. This was the problem presented in Kimbell–Diamond Milling Company v. Commissioner, 14 T.C. 74 (1950), aff'd per curiam, 187 F.2d 718 (5th Cir.1951), in which the Commissioner successfully contended that the stock purchase should be disregarded. In that case, and cases following it, the courts took the view that if the liquidation was part of an overall plan for the acquisition of assets, the stock purchase and liquidation would in effect be disregarded, no gain or loss would result to the purchaser, and the purchaser's basis for the assets would be the price paid for the stock. Prior to the repeal of the *General Utilities* doctrine, if the purchaser was an individual, the result would have been the same whether the liquidation was held to have substance or not, since the price paid for the stock would generally reflect the value of the assets and thus there would be no additional gain in the liquidation transaction. But if a corporation was the purchaser and § 332(a) governed the liquidation, the basis of the assets would remain the same under § 334(b) and would be unaffected by the amount paid for the stock; hence the need for the step-transaction approach of *Kimbell–Diamond.*

The *Kimbell–Diamond* approach proved to be unsatisfactory because it relied on the intent of a corporate purchaser to acquire assets. This subjective approach was difficult to administer, and it was replaced in 1954 by an objective standard codified in former § 334(b)(2). That section replaced the subjective intent test of *Kimbell–Diamond* with a set of objective standards to determine whether a stock purchase would be treated as a purchase of assets for tax purposes. In general terms, under § 334(b)(2), if a corporation "purchased" 80 percent or more of the stock of another corporation and then liquidated it within two years, the basis of the assets acquired in the liquidation would be determined by the purchase price of the stock, i.e., in the same manner as if the assets had been purchased directly.

Although nominally not elective, § 334(b)(2) in fact provided significant flexibility to the purchasing corporation to obtain a purchase price basis for only selected assets, particularly where the acquired corporation was the parent of an affiliated group. In addition, the computations of asset basis if the liquidation was delayed raised problems of their own. For these reasons, in 1982 § 334(b)(2) was repealed and replaced by § 338.

General Explanation, Tax Equity and Fiscal Responsibility Act of 1982

Staff of the Joint Committee on Taxation, 131–139 (1982).

[Pre–TEFRA] Law

Upon the complete liquidation of a subsidiary corporation, 80 percent of the voting power and [80 percent of the total value] (other than nonvoting preferred stock) of which is owned by the parent corporation, gain or loss is generally not recognized and the basis of the subsidiary's assets and its other tax attributes are carried over (secs. 332, 334(b)(1), and 381(a)).

Under [pre-TEFRA] law, however, if the controlling stock interest was acquired by purchase within a 12–month period and the subsidiary was liquidated pursuant to a plan of liquidation adopted within 2 years after the qualifying stock purchase was completed, the transaction was treated as in substance a purchase of the subsidiary's assets (sec. 334(b)(2)). The acquiring corporation's basis in the "purchased" assets was the cost of the stock purchased as adjusted for items such as liabilities assumed, certain cash or dividend distributions to the acquiring corporation, and postacquisition earnings and profits of the subsidiary. The liquidating distributions could be made over a 3–year period beginning with the close of the taxable year during which the first of a series of distributions occurs (sec. 332(b)(3)). Thus, this treatment applied even though the liquidation could extend over a 5–year period after control had been acquired.

In these cases, when the assets were treated as purchased by the acquiring corporation, recapture income was taxed to the liquidating corporation, * * * and tax attributes, including carryovers, of the liquidated corporation were terminated.

Cases interpreting the law applicable before the rules in section 334(b)(2) were adopted, treated the purchase of stock and prompt liquidation in some cases as a purchase of assets (Kimbell–Diamond Milling Co. v. Commissioner, 14 T.C. 74, aff'd per curiam, 187 F.2d 718 (5th Cir.), cert. denied, 342 U.S. 827 (1951)). It is not clear whether such treatment still applied after the enactment of section 334(b)(2) in cases where the requirements of that provision were not met.

A stock purchase and liquidation was treated as a purchase of all the assets of the acquired corporation under [pre-TEFRA] law if section 334(b)(2) applied. Revision of the special treatment of partial liquidations under [TEFRA] restricts the options of a corporate purchaser seeking to treat a purchase of a corporation as a purchase of assets in part combined with a continuation of the tax attributes of the acquired entity. Neither [pre-TEFRA] law nor [TEFRA's] revision of the treatment of partial liquidations restrict a corporate purchaser from achieving such selectivity by purchasing assets directly from a corporation while concurrently purchasing the corporation's stock. Selectivity could also be achieved if an acquired corporation, prior to the acquisition, dispersed its assets in tax-free transactions among several corporations which could be separately purchased. The corporate purchaser then through selective qualifying liquidations could obtain asset purchase treatment for one or more acquired corporations while preserving the tax attributes of one or more other corporations.

Reasons for Change

While section 334(b)(2) did not permit selectivity within the context of a single corporation in that the transaction was treated as wholly an asset purchase or wholly a stock purchase, inconsistency was inherent in permitting a continuation of the acquired corporation's tax attributes for up to 5 years after a stock purchase while also treating the transaction as though assets had been purchased.

* * *

[T]he extended period that could elapse between stock purchase and liquidation required complex adjustments for earnings or deficits of the acquired corporation during the intervening period as well as for sales of assets and other items during such period in order to properly allocate the cost of the stock to the assets upon their ultimate distribution. Existing case law permitted a stepped-up basis for assets distributed in liquidation that in some cases exceeded the cost basis that would be applicable if the assets were purchased directly by the controlling corporation. See, R.M. Smith, Inc., 69 T.C. 317 (1977).

[Pre–TEFRA] law also provided unwarranted tax motivations for structuring a corporate acquisition as in part a purchase of assets and in part a purchase of stock or as a purchase of several corporations historically operated as a unit in order to preserve selectivity of tax treatment. These motivations included the ability to achieve a stepped-up basis for some assets while avoiding recapture tax and other unfavorable tax attributes with respect to other assets.

Explanation of Provisions

General treatment of stock purchase as asset purchase

[TEFRA] repeals the provision of prior law (sec. 334(b)(2)) that treated a purchase and liquidation of a subsidiary as an asset purchase. The amendments made by the Act were also intended to replace any nonstatutory treatment of a stock purchase as an asset purchase under the *Kimbell–Diamond* doctrine. Instead, an acquiring corporation, within [8 1/2 months] after a qualified stock purchase, except as regulations may provide for a later election, may elect to treat an acquired subsidiary (target corporation) as if it sold all its assets pursuant to a plan of complete liquidation at the close of the stock acquisition date. The target corporation will be treated as a new corporation that purchased the assets on the day following such date. Gain or loss will not be recognized to the target corporation, except for gain or loss attributable to stock held by minority shareholders as described below, to the same extent gain or loss is not recognized (sec. 337) when a corporation sells all its assets in the course of a complete liquidation.**

** [Ed.: When § 338 was enacted in 1982, former § 337 provided generally for nonrecognition on the sale of assets by a corporation pursuant to a plan requiring the liquidation of the corporation within a twelve month period. This provision had been intended to provide nonrecognition of gain or loss to the same extent that gain or loss would not be recognized under § 336 if there were an actual liquidation of the target corporation on the acquisition date to which prior law § 334(b)(2) applied.]

ILLUSTRATIVE MATERIAL

A. GENERAL

In many important respects § 338 eliminated or resolved the problems and discontinuities that arose under former § 334(b)(2). An acquiring corporation may obtain a step-up in basis without liquidating a newly acquired subsidiary which for independent business reasons the acquiring corporation wishes to continue to operate as a subsidiary. Conversely, a newly acquired subsidiary may be liquidated for independent business reasons either with or without a step-up (or step-down) in the basis of its assets. Inevitably, § 338 has given rise to its own complexity: new interpretive issues have been raised and different avenues for manipulation of the rules governing taxable acquisitions have been created.

One by-product of § 338 has been to create a form of corporate acquisition which was not previously possible—the purchase of the stock in the target corporation followed by immediate liquidation of the target in which all tax attributes of the target corporation are preserved. Under the mechanical rules of former § 334(b)(2), the transaction resulted in a step-up in basis of the acquired assets, but elimination of all the tax attributes of the target corporation. If no § 338 election is made with respect to the acquisition, the liquidation of the target will be governed by § 332, the acquired corporation's basis in the assets will be carried over under § 334(b), and all corporate attributes such as earnings and profits, net operating loss carryovers, etc., will be preserved under § 381(a). Such a procedure might be preferable to the § 338 route where, for example, the target corporation's basis in its assets is high relative to the stock purchase price and the target has net operating loss carryovers that could be utilized by the acquiring corporation. (See Chapter 16 for limitations that are applicable to the use of such carryover items following a corporate acquisition.)

B. IMPACT OF *GENERAL UTILITIES* REPEAL

1. *General*

When § 338 originally was enacted, the pre–1987 version of § 337 provided nonrecognition to the target corporation on the deemed sale of its assets under § 338(a) when a § 338 election was made. Thus, except to the extent that one of the exceptions to former § 337 required that gain be recognized on the sale of a liquidating corporation's assets, the effect of a § 338 election was to secure a step-up in basis without an attendant gain. Because of this highly advantageous treatment, § 338 elections frequently were made when the qualifying conditions were satisfied. Section 338 was amended by the 1986 Act to conform it with the repeal of the *General Utilities* doctrine.

Section 338(a)(1) provides that if an election is made under § 338(g), the target corporation will be treated as having sold all of its assets in a transaction in which gain or loss is fully recognized. This corresponds to the treatment that the target corporation would have received if it had distributed all of its assets in liquidation or had made a direct sale of the assets. Thus, in all circumstances in which the purchaser obtains, directly or indirectly, a step-up in basis for the target corporation's assets, the target corporation will be required to recognize gain currently. This change substantially reduces the advantage of a § 338 election. The tax benefit of increased future depreciation or amortization deductions generated by the step-up in basis must be "purchased" at the price of a present tax liability with respect to any appreciation in the acquired corporation's assets. And since there is no preferential treatment for corporate capital gains, the tax price is at full rates. Thus, only in very unusual circumstances, for example, where the target corporation has a net operating loss which would shield the gain required to be recognized under § 338, would an election make economic sense from the point of view of the purchaser. See I.R.C. § 382(h), permitting the net operating loss of an acquired corporation to be used to offset recognized built-in gain without regard to the limitations otherwise imposed by § 382, discussed in Chapter 16.

2. *Example*

Generally, as long as the parties take into account tax burdens in negotiating the price and the seller does not have otherwise unusable capital loss deductions, from a tax perspective it makes no difference to either the seller or the buyer whether a purchase and sale is structured as an asset sale or as a stock sale followed by a § 338 election and a § 332 liquidation.

Suppose that individual C owns all of the stock of T Corporation. C's basis for the stock is $2,000. T Corporation's sole asset has a basis of $1,000 and a fair market value of $4,000. If T Corporation sold the asset to A Corporation (assuming that T Corporation was subject to a flat corporate tax of 35 percent), it would owe taxes of $1,050 on its $3,000 gain and would distribute $2,950 to C in a liquidating distribution. C would pay taxes of $190 (assuming a 20 percent rate) on the $950 gain, leaving C with $2,760 of net proceeds.

Alternatively, A Corporation could pay C $2,950 in cash for the stock, again leaving C with $2,760 after taxes. A Corporation could make a § 338 election, which would give rise to a $1,050 tax liability on the deemed sale of T Corporation's asset. The asset would acquire a $4,000 basis, which under § 334 would carryover to A corporation if it liquidated T Corporation. Again, A Corporation has paid a total of $4,000 to acquire T Corporation's asset with a basis of $4,000.

In actual practice, however, things will work somewhat differently. Although the two levels of tax theoretically cannot be avoided, the corporate level tax can be deferred through a sale and purchase of stock without a § 338 election. Alternatively, one level of tax can be deferred through an installment purchase of assets coupled either with continuation of the selling corporation or the use of § 453(h). If the acquiring corporation is willing to buy stock, it will not likely be willing to make the § 338 election; hence it will not pay the shareholders of the target corporation the full net asset value (including goodwill and going concern value) of the target corporation, but will discount the offset for the corporate level tax to reflect the deferral of that tax. Thus, in the preceding example, A Corporation likely would pay C more than $2,950 but less than $4,000 for the stock of T Corporation. Thus § 338 is something of an anachronism after 1986, providing a complex solution to a situation that seldom arises.

3. *Policy Issues*

Recall that the broad purpose of § 338 and its statutory predecessor, former § 334(b)(2), is to equalize the treatment of stock and asset acquisitions by providing a stepped-up basis in either case, albeit at the price of an immediate corporate level tax on asset appreciation. The treatment of the two transactions is not always equalized, however, because of the elective aspects of the transaction. This situation raises the question whether the tax treatment of stock and asset acquisitions should be fully equalized by amending the Code to apply § 338 to every "qualified stock purchase" on a mandatory basis.

C. QUALIFYING CONDITIONS

1. *General*

An election under § 338 is available only to a corporation that makes a "qualified stock purchase" of stock of another corporation. A "qualified stock purchase" is defined in § 338(d)(3), through a cross reference to § 1504(a)(2), as the acquisition by purchase within a twelve month period of 80 percent or more of the voting stock and 80 percent or more of the total value of all stock of the corporation, excluding nonvoting stock that is limited and preferred as to dividends and does not participate in corporate growth to any significant extent. Stock of the target corporation already owned by the acquiring corporation is not counted toward the 80 percent requirement. Thus, for example, if P Corporation has owned 21 percent of the stock of T Corporation for one year or more, P Corporation cannot thereafter complete a "qualified stock purchase." Note that § 338(h)(8) provides that all acquisitions by corporations that are part of an affiliated group are treated as made by one corporation. Thus, if P Corporation purchases 40 percent of the stock of T Corporation and P Corporation's controlled subsidiary, S Corporation, purchases an additional 40 percent of the T Corporation stock, a qualified stock purchase has been made, presumably by P Corporation.

2. *The "Purchase" Requirement*

A "purchase" under § 338(h)(3) includes any "acquisition" that is not specifically excluded. Section 338(h)(3) provides three specific exclusions: (1) stock the basis of which is determined in whole or in part with reference to the transferor's basis, i.e., transferred basis stock, and stock acquired from a decedent; (2) stock acquired in certain nonrecognition transactions, including § 351 transactions and corporate reorganizations: and (3) stock acquired from a person from whom it would be attributed to the purchaser under § 318. Thus, for example, stock of a subsidiary acquired by another corporate subsidiary from its parent is not "purchased" at the time of the transfer. See Matter of Chrome Plate, Inc., 614 F.2d 990 (5th Cir.1980). Stock acquired in a § 301 distribution is "purchased" (unless received from a corporation of which the shareholder owns 50 percent or more of the stock), since it was "acquired" in a transaction that is not excluded. See Rev.Rul. 74–211, 1974–1 C.B. 76. The purchase requirement in § 338 is derived from former § 334(b)(2), and cases decided under that provision remain relevant.

In Madison Square Garden Corp. v. Commissioner, 500 F.2d 611 (2d Cir.1974), the taxpayer purchased 52 percent of the stock of another corporation. The acquired corporation then redeemed some of its stock. Following the redemption, the taxpayer owned approximately 79 percent of the stock of the acquired corporation, and it then acquired by purchase additional stock sufficient to give it 80.22 percent ownership. The acquired corporation was then merged into the taxpayer. Under Treas. Reg. § 1.332–2(d) and (e), the merger was treated as a liquidation for tax purposes, and the taxpayer argued that § 334(b)(2) was applicable. The Commissioner asserted that the 80 percent requirement applied to the shares of stock outstanding at the time the purchase of the stock began, and thus former § 334(b)(2) was not satisfied. The Court of Appeals, affirming the Tax Court, held that the taxpayer had acquired the requisite 80 percent by "purchase". See also Yoc Heating Corp. v. Commissioner, 61 T.C. 168 (1973). The issue posed by *Madison Square Garden* is relevant in determining whether a redemption affects a "qualified stock purchase" under § 338. Treas. Reg. § 1.338–2(b)(5) follows the result in *Madison Square Garden Corp.* and provides that redemptions from unrelated shareholders are taken into account in determining whether the target stock purchased within the twelve month acquisition period satisfies the 80 percent ownership requirement.

In Rev.Rul. 90–95, 1990–2 C.B. 67, P Corporation formed a subsidiary, S Corporation, for the purpose of merging S Corporation into T Corporation. The T Corporation shareholders received cash in exchange for their T Corporation stock and T Corporation became a subsidiary of P Corporation in a reverse cash merger. The Ruling held that the existence of S Corporation should be disregarded and P Corporation was treated as acquiring the T Corporation stock in a qualified stock purchase under § 338. If as part of a plan, T Corporation were liquidated, the transaction would be treated as a qualified stock purchase under § 338 followed by a liquidation of T Corporation into S Corporation under § 332.

3. *The Timetable*

The statutory twelve month period within which a "qualified stock purchase" must be made begins to run on the date of the first "purchase" of stock by the acquiring corporation, I.R.C. § 338(h)(1), but each purchase starts a new twelve month period running. For example, if P Corporation purchases 10 percent of the stock of T Corporation on January 1, 1997, and another 10 percent on February 1, 1997, the purchase of an additional 70 percent of the stock of T Corporation anytime before February 2, 1998 will constitute a "qualified stock purchase." Section 338(g) gives the acquiring corporation 8 1/2 months after the end of the month in which a qualified stock purchase is completed to make the election. For example, if P Corporation acquires 70 percent of the stock of T Corporation on March 1, 1996, 10 percent on April 1, 1996, and 20 percent on June 1, 1996, the period for making the election begins to run on May 1, 1996 and the election must be made by January 15, 1997. The deadline will not be extended by P Corporation's purchase of additional T Corporation stock on June 1, 1996.

D. CONSISTENCY REQUIREMENTS

Section 338 imposes two statutory consistency requirements. Section 338(f) requires that the acquiring corporation make consistent elections with respect to all "qualified stock purchases" of target corporations which are members of the same affiliated group that are made within the consistency period defined in § 338(h)(4). Generally, the consistency period begins one year before the first stock purchase of a series that culminates in a qualified stock acquisition and extends until one year after the stock acquisition transaction by which control has been obtained, i.e., a "qualified stock acquisition" has been completed. Section § 338(h)(4)(B) extends the consistency period in limited circumstances. The second consistency rule is in § 338(e), which statutorily provides for a deemed § 338 election if the acquiring corporation or any of its affiliates purchases any assets (other than in the ordinary course of business) from the target corporation or any of its affiliates during the period beginning one year before the first stock acquisition which is part of a qualified stock purchase and ending one year after the date of the transaction by which the acquiring corporation acquired 80 percent control of the target corporation.

Both of these consistency rules are vestigial provisions of the era when due to the *General Utilities* rule a § 338 election resulted in a tax free step-up in basis. The consistency rules were designed to minimize the possibilities for an acquiring corporation to structure an acquisition to obtain a tax free step-up in basis for appreciated assets while avoiding a step-down in the basis of depreciated assets, for which no loss deduction was allowed. Generally, after 1986 this problem no longer exists because the step-up in basis under § 338 is coupled with recognition of gain and loss. Thus, Treas. Reg. § 1.338–4(a) provides that neither the asset consistency rules of § 338(e) nor the stock consistency rules of § 338(f) will be applied except in narrow circumstances.

Under the regulations, the asset consistency rules will be applied to situations in which an asset is acquired from a target corporation and the target corporation is a member of an affiliated group filing a consolidated return (see Chapter 10). This rule is necessary because the asset purchase would result in an investment adjustment (see page 449) increasing the parent's basis in its stock in the target corporation, thereby reducing the gain realized on the sale of the target corporation stock. The asset consistency rules also apply in situations in which a nonconsolidated target corporation pays a dividend to its selling parent prior to the sale of the target stock and the dividend is subject to the 100 percent dividends paid deduction under § 243. This rule is required because the transaction might have a result similar to that in the investment adjustment accounts in consolidated returns; the tax free dividend reduces the gain realized on the sale even though the overall before-tax proceeds realized by the selling corporation, including the dividend, equal the amount that would have been realized on a sale of the subsidiary's stock without the prior payment of the dividend. Finally, the asset consistency rules apply in the case of assets acquired from affiliates of the target if an arrangement to avoid the consistency requirement exists. See Treas. Reg. § 1.338–4(a)(3), (f), (j).

When these limited asset consistency rules apply, rather than imposing a deemed § 338 election when none has been made (as provided in § 338(e)), Treas. Reg. § 1.338–4(d) requires that the purchasing corporation take a carryover basis for all assets acquired from the target corporation during the consistency period. Thus, for example, if S Corporation and its controlled subsidiary T Corporation are members of an affiliated group filing a consolidated return, the consistency rules apply if P Corporation on July 1, 1996, purchases an asset from T and then anytime before July 2, 1997, makes a qualified stock purchase of the stock of T Corporation from S Corporation. The asset purchased from T corporation on July 1, 1996, will have a carryover basis in P Corporation's hands unless a § 338 election is made with respect to the qualified stock purchase. Treas. Reg. § 1.338–4(e)(2), Ex.(1). If P Corporation makes a § 338 election, the asset consistency rules are not applicable. As a result, the purchasing corporation is given the choice of having all of the assets of the target corporation acquired during the consistency period take either a transferred basis or a stepped-up basis by making or not making a § 338 election.

Treas. Reg. § 1.338–4(a)(6) provides that the stock consistency rules of § 338(f) normally will not be applied. Thus, for example, if P Corporation purchases all of the stock of T Corporation, which owns controlled subsidiary S Corporation, P Corporation normally may make a § 338 election with respect to T Corporation without making an election with respect to S Corporation. See Treas. Reg. § 1.338–4(e)(2), Ex.(6). Similarly, if P Corporation purchases at least 80 percent of the stock of S Corporation from T Corporation on July 1, 1996 and then also purchases at least 80 percent of the stock of R Corporation from T Corporation within the consistency period, the stock consistency rules normally should not apply. The stock consistency rules will be applied only if necessary to prevent avoidance of the asset consistency rules.

E. DEEMED SALES PRICE

1. *General*

Section 338(a)(1) provides that as a result of a § 338 election the target corporation is treated as having sold all of its assets at "fair market value."

In general, this definition should obviate the need separately to account for the target corporation's liabilities in computing its gain. However, since § 338 applies to stock sales and purchases, not asset transactions, there is no market valuation of the corporation's assets to which to look for the relevant valuation. Thus, Treas. Reg. § 1.338–3 provides mechanical rules for determining the "aggregate deemed sale price" (ADSP) of the target's assets. Under this formula the ADSP is the sum of the "grossed-up basis" of the purchasing company's "recently purchased stock" of the target, liabilities of the target, including tax liabilities arising from the § 338 election, and "other relevant items." Recently purchased stock is stock acquired in the "qualified stock purchase," and the grossed-up basis of the recently purchased stock for purposes of computing the ADSP is the basis of that stock divided by percentage of target corporation that is recently purchased stock. Treas. Reg. § 1.338–3(d). The purpose of the "grossed-up basis" concept is to approximate the fair market value of 100 percent of the stock of the target in cases where the acquiring corporation purchases less than 100 percent of the target stock within the twelve month acquisition period.

2. *Acquisition of Target With Subsidiaries*

If the target corporation owns stock in a subsidiary corporation and the acquiring corporation makes a § 338 election, the acquisition by the "new" target corporation of the subsidiary corporation's stock in the § 338 deemed sale will itself qualify as a "purchase" for purposes of § 338. I.R.C. § 338(h)(3)(B). The acquiring corporation may make a § 338 election with respect to only T Corporation or both of T and S Corporations. See Treas. Reg. § 1.338–4(e)(2), Ex.(6).

Application of the statutory rules of § 338 present a special problem where a target corporation has subsidiary corporations and the acquiring corporation makes a § 338 election with respect to both the target and its subsidiaries. Assume that P Corporation purchases 100 percent of the stock of T Corporation, which owns 100 percent of the stock of S Corporation and P Corporation makes a § 338 election with respect to both. (Under § 338(h)(3)(B) the deemed sale and repurchase of the stock of S Corporation by T Corporation constitutes a "purchase" of that stock for purposes of § 338, thus enabling T Corporation to make the election with respect to S Corporation.) There could be a double tax at the corporate level if T Corporation is taxed on the deemed sale of the S Corporation stock and S Corporation is taxed on the deemed sale of its assets. The Internal Revenue Service has concluded that Congress did not intend for the repeal of the *General Utilities* rule to lead to such double taxation. Accordingly, Treas. Reg. § 1.338–3(c) provides that T Corporation does not recognize any gain on the deemed sale of the S Corporation stock; the deemed gain on the sale by S Corporation of its assets is recognized.

F. DETERMINATION OF ASSET BASIS

1. *General*

In general, § 338 is intended to produce the same tax consequences as a direct asset acquisition. However, § 338 does not directly assign to each asset of the target corporation a fair market value basis. Instead, under § 338(b) the aggregate basis of the assets, termed "adjusted grossed-up basis" (AGUB) by Treas. Reg. § 1.338(b)–1, is first determined according to a formula based on the acquiring corporation's basis for all of the stock of the target corporation which it owns, adjusted for liabilities assumed, and the aggregate basis then is allocated among the assets as provided in Temp. Reg. § 1.338(b)–2T. The basis allocation rules are substantially the same as the allocation rules under § 1060, discussed at page 469, and many of the same valuation issues arise.

2. *Adjusted Grossed–Up Basis*

Section 338(b)(1) provides that the starting point for determining the AGUB, the deemed purchase price of the target corporation's assets, is the sum of (1) the "grossed-up basis" of the "recently purchased stock" of the target, plus (2) the basis of the "nonrecently purchased stock." Treas. Reg. § 1.338(b)–1 provides detailed rules for computing the AGUB. Recently purchased stock generally is defined as stock acquired in the "qualified stock purchase." Nonrecently purchased stock is stock owned by the acquiring corporation prior to commencement of the acquisition period, which is not counted toward the "qualified stock purchase." I.R.C. § 338(b)(6). The grossed-up basis of the recently purchased stock is the basis of that stock multiplied by a fraction, the numerator of which is 100 minus the percentage of target corporation stock owned by the acquiring corporation which is not recently purchased stock and the denominator of which is the percentage of stock of the target which is recently purchased stock. I.R.C. § 338(b)(4); Treas. Reg. § 1.338(b)–1(d). (Note that the definition of "grossed-up basis" for purposes of determining AGUB under Treas. Reg. § 1.338(b)–1 differs from the definition for computing ADSP under Treas. Reg. § 1.338–3. See Treas. Reg. § 1.338(b)–1(e)(4).) Section 338(b)(3) permits the acquiring corporation to elect to recognize gain attributable to any nonrecently purchased stock and add that amount to its deemed purchase price. In such a case, the gross-up formula is adjusted accordingly.

The purpose of the "grossed-up basis" concept is to assign to the target's assets a basis equal to the aggregate fair market value of the target corporation's stock where the acquiring corporation purchases more than 80 percent but less than all of the target corporation's stock. For example, assume that A Corporation, which previously owned none of the stock of T Corporation, purchases 85 percent of the T Corporation stock for $850. The grossed-up basis of the stock is $1,000, computed as follows: $850 × (100 – 0) / 85.

Section 338(b)(2) provides for an adjustment to the deemed purchase price in computing AGUB to reflect the acquired corporation's liabilities that would have been included in the purchaser's basis if the transaction had been an asset sale. Treas. Reg. § 1.338(b)–1(f). These liabilities include the target corporation's tax liability arising from the deemed sale of its assets under § 338(a)(1). Treas. Reg. § 1.338(b)–1(h)(2), Ex.(1).

G. COMPUTATION AND ALLOCATION OF TAX LIABILITY

A § 338 election results in closing the taxable year of the target. As long as the target corporation was not purchased from a parent that was a member of an affiliated group filing a consolidated return, the old target's final return includes the deemed sale. Treas. Reg. § 1.338–1(b)(6), (e)(1). Section 338(h)(9) provides that except as provided in § 338(h)(10) a target corporation is not treated as a member of any affiliated group with respect to the deemed sale of its assets. As a general rule, if the target corporation otherwise would have been included in a consolidated return, it is required to file a special "deemed sale return" reporting the items from the § 338 sale. Temp. Reg. § 1.338–1T(e)(2). Section 338(h)(9) requires that the target not be treated as a member of an affiliated group for purposes of reporting the sale, thereby precluding the use of net operating losses or capital losses of the purchaser (or its consolidated group) to offset the gain recognized on the deemed sale. However, if the acquiring corporation on the same acquisition date made qualified stock purchases with respect to two or more corporations that were members of the same consolidated group prior to the purchases, a consolidated deemed sale return covering all of such corporations may be filed. I.R.C. § 338(h)(15); Treas. Reg. § 1.338–1(e)(4).

While the target corporation nominally bears the liability for any taxes generated by the § 338 deemed sale, economically the burden is borne by the purchasing corporation, except to the extent that the purchase price is reduced to reflect the tax burden.

H. ACQUISITION OF SUBSIDIARY FROM AFFILIATED GROUP: SECTION 338(h)(10)

A special rule applies when a corporation makes a qualified stock purchase of the stock of a controlled subsidiary of another corporation and the target corporation and the selling parent corporation filed a consolidated return or were members of an affiliated group filing separate returns. Section 338(h)(10) allows a joint election by the acquiring corporation and the former consolidated (or affiliated) group of the target corporation pursuant to which the gain or loss on the sale of the stock will not be recognized by the selling parent, but the selling group or parent will include on its tax return the gain and loss recognized under § 338(a)(1) by virtue of the § 338 election. In essence, this election permits the selling corporation to treat the sale as if its subsidiary first had made a taxable sale of its assets that was followed by a § 332 liquidation. See Treas. Reg. § 1.338(h)(10)–1(e)(2). As a result, the selling shareholder corporation bears the tax liability for any gain recognized with respect to the § 338 election. The existence of § 338(h)(10) allows the parties to keep the form of the transaction as a sale of stock but have the tax results of an asset sale. Since this situation does not involve a double tax on the sale of the stock and the deemed liquidating sale of assets, a § 338 election remains a viable tax planning technique when § 338(h)(10) is available, despite the repeal of the *General Utilities* doctrine. It is a particularly attractive planning device when the selling group has losses from other activities which will offset the gains on the consolidated return, since § 338(h)(9) does not apply where a § 338(h)(10) election has been made.

If the § 338(h)(10) route is followed, the tax attributes of the target corporation are inherited by the selling parent corporation. See Treas. Reg. § 1.338(h)(10)–1(g), Ex.(1).

I. EXTENSION OF SECTION 338(h)(10) PRINCIPLES

Section 336(e) authorizes regulations under which a sale of all of the stock of a controlled subsidiary may be treated as a sale of assets coupled with nonrecognition of the gain or loss on the sale of the stock. This is analogous to § 338(h)(10), but the statute does not limit the application of the regulations, which have not yet been promulgated, to corporate purchasers from consolidated groups.

Thus, for example, § 336(e) may apply where individual A owns all of the stock of P Corporation, which in turn owns all of the stock of T Corporation, and B, who may be either an individual or a corporation, purchases all of the T Corporation stock from P Corporation. In some cases treatment of this transaction as an asset sale with nonrecognition of the gain or loss on the stock is necessary to prevent "triple" taxation as a result of the repeal of *General Utilities.* If this transaction were taxed under the normal rules, P Corporation would recognize a taxable gain on the sale of the stock of T Corporation; if A were to liquidate P Corporation to acquire the proceeds from the sale of T Corporation, A would recognize a taxable gain on the liquidation (assuming that P Corporation's sole asset was the cash proceeds from the sale of T Corporation, P Corporation would recognize no gain on the liquidation). In addition, if B were an individual, T Corporation would recognize gain under § 336 if B liquidated T Corporation to acquire its assets (assuming that the purchase price equaled the value of the assets, B would not realize any gain on the liquidation). Thus, a triple tax would have resulted from the removal of both the assets and the sale proceeds from corporate solution.

By treating the transaction as an asset sale, however, the bases of T Corporation's assets presumably are increased to the stock purchase price when B acquires T Corporation, and thus the corporation does not realize any gain on its liquidation. The legislative history does not indicate whether P Corporation or T Corporation reports the taxable gain on the deemed asset sale. See H.R.Rep. No. 99–841, 99th Cong., 2d Sess. II–204 (1986). By analogy to § 338(h)(10), the gain and tax liability ought to be on P Corporation's tax return. Otherwise, the purchaser would bear the direct corporate tax burden with respect to appreciation of assets occurring prior to the purchase, and the burden could be shifted to the seller only through a price adjustment. This conclusion is further supported by analogy to § 336(e), i.e., it replicates the results if P Corporation had liquidated T Corporation in a § 332 liquidation and then sold the assets directly to B.

J. ACQUISITIONS INVOLVING S CORPORATIONS

1. *Acquisitions by S Corporations*

If an S corporation acquires all of the stock of another corporation, it may make a QSSS election with respect to the newly acquired subsidiary regardless of whether the subsidiary previously was a QSSS of another S corporation, a Subchapter S corporation itself, or a C corporation. See H.R. Rep. No. 104–586, 104th Cong., 2d Sess. 88–89 (1996). As a result of the election, the subsidiary is deemed to have liquidated under §§ 332 and 337 immediately before the election is effective. If the subsidiary previously was a C corporation, the § 1374 built-in gains tax and § 1363(d) LIFO recapture might apply.

If the stock of the subsidiary was acquired by the S corporation in a qualified stock purchase, a § 338 election may be made with respect to the subsidiary. See H.R. Rep. No. 104–586, 104th Cong., 2d Sess. 88–89 (1996). If both a § 338 election and a QSSS election are made, then the QSSS election is not effective until after the consequences of the § 338 election are taken into account. The subsidiary must file a final return for the § 338 election as a C corporation. Prop. Reg. § 1.1361–4(b)(3) (1998).

2. *Acquisitions of Qualified Subchapter S Subsidiaries*

If a QSSS subsidiary is acquired, the original QSSS election is terminated. If the new owners of the stock are all eligible to be shareholders of an S corporation, an immediately effective S election can be made notwithstanding the provisions of § 1361(b)(3)(D), as long as there is no intervening day on which the corporation was a C corporation. If the purchaser of the QSSS stock is another S corporation, the new 100 percent parent likewise may make an immediately effective QSSS election with respect to the newly acquired subsidiary. See Prop. Reg. § 1.1361–5(d)(2) and (3) (1998).

SECTION 3. MEDIUM OF PAYMENT: SPECIAL PROBLEMS OF SUBORDINATED CONVERTIBLE DEBENTURES

INTERNAL REVENUE CODE: Section 279.

Suppose the purchaser does not have sufficient cash or borrowing power to finance the purchase of either the stock or assets of the target corporation's assets or stock. In this case, the purchasing corporation may try to bootstrap the transaction by utilizing the future earnings of the acquired corporation and, optimally, to pay out those earnings in a deductible manner, i.e., as interest on debt incurred to finance the acquisition. In the late 1960's Congress became concerned over acquisition activities that involved as the payment vehicle the use of various kinds of debt instruments, frequently convertible into the common stock of the acquiring corporation. This use of convertible debt had several advantages in the acquisition. Because interest on the debentures was deductible the corporation was willing to pay a much higher price for the acquired corporation; if the selling shareholders could report the gain under the installment method of § 453, taxation of the gain realized on the transaction could be deferred for many years; and the convertibility feature gave to the shareholders of the acquired corporation the opportunity to secure an equity interest in the acquiring corporation at a future date.

In the Tax Reform Act of 1969, Congress took several steps to restrict the use of convertible debentures by corporations engaged in aggressive acquisition programs. Installment payment treatment under § 453 was denied to selling shareholders who received readily marketable debentures.[8] See I.R.C. § 453(f)(4). The original issue discount rules, discussed at page 168, required the debenture holders to include the discount in income over the life of the debentures. Finally, Congress added § 279, which disallows the interest deduction to the acquiring corporation on certain "corporate acquisition indebtedness".

In brief, § 279 disallows a deduction for interest on debt obligations issued by a corporation to acquire the stock or assets of another corporation (in the case of asset acquisitions only if such assets constitute at least two-thirds of the value of all of the assets used in the trades or businesses carried on by the acquired corporation) if all of the following conditions are met:

(1) The obligation is subordinated to the claims of trade creditors generally or expressly subordinated to any substantial amount of unsecured indebtedness, whether presently outstanding or subsequently issued, of the issuing corporation;

(2) The obligation is convertible into the stock of the issuing corporation or is part of an investment unit that includes an option to acquire stock in the issuing corporation (through warrants, rights, etc.); and

(3) Either the ratio of debt to equity of the issuing corporation after the issuance of the obligation exceeds 2:1, or the "projected earnings" of the issuing corporation (or of the combined corporations, if "control" has been acquired), do not exceed three times the annual interest to be paid or incurred with respect to the obligation.

In order to avoid the disallowance of the interest deduction under § 279, a corporation need only avoid any one of the conditions. Thus, for example, a corporation's obligations will not be affected by § 279 if not subordinated to trade creditors generally, even though the obligations may be subordinated to a very substantial amount of secured debt. In addition, as another hurdle to the application of § 279, interest on "acquisition indebtedness" must exceed $5 million annually in order for the provision to apply. And then, only the acquisition indebtedness interest in excess of the $5 million safe harbor threshold is disallowed. For a corporation which pays 8 percent interest, this means that it can have outstanding $62.5 million dollars of debt without running afoul of § 279. There is also a de minimis

8. Section 453 has since been amended also to preclude installment reporting of gains from the sale of publicly trade stock.

rule which provides that § 279 will not apply where the issuing corporation after the transaction owns less than 5 percent of the voting stock of the corporation whose stock has been acquired with the debt. Finally, the provisions in § 279(d)(3) and (4) offer means for removing the § 279 "taint" once acquired.

The debt-equity principles discussed at page 130, take precedence over § 279, so that it would be possible for an obligation to fall outside the conditions of § 279 but for a deduction for the interest on the obligation still to be disallowed on the grounds that the instrument constituted an equity instrument. See Treas. Reg. § 1.279–1,–7. In addition, the earnings stripping rules, discussed at page 180, may apply to deny an interest deduction even if § 279 does not apply.

CHAPTER 12

DISTRIBUTIONS MADE IN CONNECTION WITH THE SALE OF A CORPORATE BUSINESS: "BOOTSTRAP" ACQUISITIONS

If the sale of a corporate business is accomplished by the sale of stock, the parties may at the same time desire to reduce the size of the corporation prior to the sale. There can be a variety of motivations for structuring the transaction in this manner. The corporation may have assets which the purchaser does not wish to acquire. Alternatively, the purchaser may not be able to afford the "full" corporation and may wish to have it reduced in size prior to the acquisition, thus acquiring a smaller corporation for a correspondingly smaller purchase price. Finally, tax planning to maximize the after-tax proceeds to the seller sometimes may be a principal purpose for the structure of the sale and purchase.

The reduction in size of the corporation can take place either through a redemption of some of the shares of an existing shareholder or through a dividend distribution to the shareholder. Which technique is preferable may depend in part on the status of the shareholder. A redemption distribution taxed as a capital gain under § 302 is more advantageous to an individual shareholder than the ordinary income treatment that a normal dividend distribution would receive. On the other hand, if the shareholder is a corporation, dividend treatment, with a corresponding intercorporate dividend deduction under § 243, may be preferable to recognizing capital gain on the sale of the stock, depending on the basis of the stock. In addition, the timing of the distribution is important because the redemption or dividend distribution may be deemed to have taken place after the actual ownership of the stock has been transferred to the purchaser by the seller. In some cases whether the distribution is characterized as a redemption or as a dividend turns on when the distribution is considered to have been made. The materials that follow are concerned with various aspects of the issues created by distributions to individual shareholders and corporate shareholders, respectively, in connection with the sale of corporate stock.

SECTION 1. BOOTSTRAP TRANSACTIONS INVOLVING INDIVIDUALS: CAPITAL GAIN VERSUS ORDINARY INCOME

Holsey v. Commissioner

United States Court of Appeals, Third Circuit, 1958.
258 F.2d 865.

■ MARIS, CIRCUIT JUDGE. This is a petition to review a decision of the Tax Court. * * * The facts as found by the Tax Court, some of which were stipulated, may be summarized as follows:

J.R. Holsey Sales Company, a New Jersey corporation, was organized on April 28, 1936, as an Oldsmobile dealership. Taxpayer has been president and a director of the company since its organization. Only 20 shares were issued out of the 2,500 shares of no par value stock authorized; these 20 shares were issued to Greenville Auto Sales Company, a chevrolet dealership, in exchange for all of the latter's right, title, and interest to the Oldsmobile franchise and other assets with respect to the franchise which had been owned and operated by the Greenville Company. the 20 shares issued were assigned a value of $11,000. Taxpayer's father, Charles V. Holsey, in 1936, owned more than two-thirds of the outstanding stock of the Greenville Company, and taxpayer was vice-president and a director of that corporation.

On April 30, 1936, taxpayer acquired from the Greenville Company an option to purchase 50% of the outstanding shares of the Holsey Company for $11,000, and a further option to purchase, within ten years after the exercise of the first option, all the remaining shares for a sum to be agreed upon. The Greenville Company owned all of the outstanding stock of the Holsey Company from its organization in 1936 until November, 1939, when taxpayer exercised his first option and purchased 50% of the outstanding stock of the Holsey Company for $11,000.

On June 28, 1946, the further option in favor of taxpayer was revised. Under the terms of the revised option, taxpayer was granted the right to purchase the remaining outstanding shares of the Holsey Company at any time up to and including June 28, 1951, for $80,000. The revised option was in favor of taxpayer individually and was not assignable by him to anyone other than a corporation in which he owned not less than 50% of the voting stock. On the date of the revision of this option, taxpayer's father owned 76% of the stock of the Greenville Company and taxpayer was a vice-president and director of that corporation. On April 28, 1948, the Holsey Company declared a 3-for-1 stock dividend and the common stock was allocated a value of $750 per share. This stock dividend increased the outstanding stock to 80 shares which was held in equal amounts by taxpayer and the Greenville Company.

On January 19, 1951, taxpayer assigned his revised option to the Holsey Company; on the same date the Holsey Company exercised the option and paid the Greenville Company $80,000 for the stock held by it. This transaction resulted in taxpayer becoming the owner of 100% of the outstanding stock of the Holsey Company. In his income tax return for the year 1951, taxpayer gave no effect to this transaction.

The principal officers and only directors of the Holsey Company from April 28, 1936, to December 31, 1951, were taxpayer, his brother, Charles D. Holsey, and their father, Charles V. Holsey. On January 19, 1951, when the revised option was exercised, the earned surplus of the Holsey Company was in excess of $300,000.

The Oldsmobile franchise, under which the Holsey Company operated, was a yearly contract entered into by the Corporation and the manufacturer in reliance upon the personal qualifications and representations of taxpayer as an individual. It was the manufacturer's policy to have its dealers own all of the stock in dealership organizations.

The Commissioner determined that the effect of the transaction of January 19, 1951, wherein the Holsey Company paid $80,000 to the Greenville Company for 50% of the outstanding stock of the Holsey Company, constituted a dividend to taxpayer, the remaining stockholder. The Commissioner therefore asserted a deficiency against taxpayer in the sum of $41,385.34. The Tax Court sustained the Commissioner. 28 T.C. 962.

The question presented for decision in this case is whether the Tax Court erred in holding that the payment by the Holsey Company of $80,000 to the Greenville Company for the purchase from that company of its stock in the Holsey Company was essentially equivalent to the distribution of a taxable dividend to the taxpayer, the remaining stockholder of the Holsey Company. To determine that question we must begin with the applicable statute [reference is made to the predecessors of §§ 316(a) and 302].

It will be observed that [§ 316(a)] defines a dividend as a distribution made by a corporation "to its shareholders". Accordingly unless a distribution which is sought to be taxed to a stockholder as a dividend is made to him or for his benefit it may not be regarded as either a dividend or the legal equivalent of a dividend. Here the distribution was made to the Greenville Company, not to the taxpayer. This the Government, of course, concedes but urges that it was made for the benefit of the taxpayer. It is true that it has been held that a distribution by a corporation in redemption of stock which the taxpayer stockholder has a contractual obligation to purchase is essentially the equivalent of a dividend to him since it operates to discharge his obligation. Wall v. United States, 4 Cir., 1947, 164 F.2d 462; Ferro v. Commissioner of Internal Revenue, 3 Cir., 1957, 242 F.2d 838; Zipp v. Commissioner of Internal Revenue, 6 Cir., 1958, 259 F.2d 119. But where, as here, the taxpayer was never under any legal obligation to purchase the stock held by the other stockholder, the Greenville Company, having merely an option to purchase which he did not exercise but instead assigned to the Holsey Company, the distribution did not discharge any obligation of his and did not benefit him in any direct sense.

It is, of course, true that the taxpayer was benefited indirectly by the distribution. The value of his own stock was increased, since the redemption was for less than book value, and he became sole stockholder. But these benefits operated only to increase the value of the taxpayer's stock holdings; they could not give rise to taxable income within the meaning of the Sixteenth Amendment until the corporation makes a distribution to the taxpayer or his stock is sold. Eisner v. Macomber, 1920, 252 U.S. 189, 40 S.Ct. 189, 64 L.Ed. 521; Schmitt v. Commissioner of Internal Revenue, 3 Cir., 1954, 208 F.2d 819. * * * We think that the principle thus stated is equally applicable here. Indeed the Tax Court itself has so held in essentially similar cases. S.K. Ames, Inc. v. Commissioner, 1942, 46 B.T.A. 1020; Fred F. Fischer v. Commissioner, 1947, 6 T.C.M. 520.

The question whether payments made by a corporation in the acquisition and redemption of its stock are essentially equivalent to the distribution of a taxable dividend has been often before the courts and certain criteria have been enunciated. The most significant of these is said to be whether the distribution leaves the proportionate interests of the stockholders unchanged as occurs when a true dividend is paid. Ferro v. Commissioner of Internal Revenue, 3 Cir., 1957, 242 F.2d 838, 841. The application of that criterion to the facts of this case compels the conclusion that in the absence of a direct pecuniary benefit to the taxpayer the Tax Court erred in holding the distribution in question taxable to him. For in his case prior to the distribution the taxpayer and the Greenville Company each had a 50% interest in the Holsey Company whereas after it was over the taxpayer had 100% of the outstanding stock and the Greenville Company none.

The Government urges the lack of a corporate purpose for the distribution and the taxpayer seeks to establish one. But we do not consider this point for, as we have recently held, "It is the effect of the redemption, rather than the purpose which actuated it, which controls the determination of dividend equivalence." Kessner v. Commissioner of Internal Revenue, 3 Cir., 1957, 248 F.2d 943, 944. Nor need we discuss the present position of the Government that the transaction must be treated as a sham and the purchase of the stock as having been made by the taxpayer through his alter ego, the Holsey Company. For the Tax Court made no such finding, doubtless in view of the fact that at the time the taxpayer owned only 50% of the stock and was in a minority on the board of directors. On the contrary that court based its decision on the benefit which the distribution by the corporation to the Greenville Company conferred upon the taxpayer, which it thought gave rise to taxable income in his hands.

For the reasons stated we think that the Tax Court erred in its decision. The decision will accordingly be reversed and the cause remanded for further proceedings not inconsistent with this opinion.

■ MCLAUGHLIN, CIRCUIT JUDGE (dissenting). I think that the net effect of the facile operation disclosed in this case amounts to the distribution of a taxable dividend to the taxpayer. I do not think that the Schmitt decision controls here. Quite the contrary to the Schmitt facts, this taxpayer himself acquired a valuable option to buy the shares and solely on the theory of a gift of the option rights would make the corporation the true purchaser. I agree with the Tax Court that "The assignment of the option contract to J.R. Holsey Sales Co. was clearly for the purpose of having that company pay the $80,000 in exercise of the option that was executed for petitioner's personal benefit. The payment was intended to secure and did secure for petitioner exactly what it was always intended he should get if he made the payment personally, namely, all of the stock in J.R. Holsey Sales Co."

I would affirm the Tax Court decision.

Zenz v. Quinlivan

United States Court of Appeals, Sixth Circuit, 1954.
213 F.2d 914.

■ GOURLEY, DISTRICT JUDGE.

The appeal relates to the interpretation of [§ 302]of the Internal Revenue Code and poses the question—

Is a distribution of substantially all of the accumulated earnings and surplus of a corporation, which are not necessary to the conduct of the business of the corporation, in redemption of all outstanding shares of stock of said corporation owned by one person *essentially equivalent to the distribution of a taxable dividend under the Internal Revenue Code*?

* * *

Appellant is the widow of the person who was the motivating spirit behind the closed corporation which engaged in the business of excavating and laying of sewers. Through death of her husband she became the owner of all shares of stock issued by the corporation. She operated the business until remarriage, when her second husband assumed the management. As a result of a marital rift, separation, and final divorce, taxpayer sought to dispose of her company to a competitor who was anxious to eliminate competition.

Prospective buyer did not want to assume the tax liabilities which it was believed were inherent in the accumulated earnings and profits of the corporation. To avoid said profits and earnings as a source of future taxable dividends, buyer purchased part of taxpayer's stock for cash. Three weeks later, after corporate reorganization and corporate action, the corporation redeemed the balance of taxpayer's stock, purchasing the same as treasury stock which absorbed substantially all of the accumulated earnings and surplus of the corporation.

Taxpayer, in her tax return, invoked [the predecessor of § 302(b)] as constituting a cancellation or redemption by a corporation of all the stock of a particular shareholder, and therefore was not subject to being treated as a distribution of a taxable dividend.

The District Court sustained the deficiency assessment of the Commissioner that the amount received from accumulated earnings and profits was ordinary income since the stock redeemed by the corporation was "at such time and in such manner as to make the redemption thereof essentially equivalent to the distribution of a taxable dividend" * * * .

The District Court's findings were premised upon the view that taxpayer employed a circuitous approach in an attempt to avoid the tax consequences which would have attended the outright distribution of the surplus to the taxpayer by the declaration of a taxable dividend.

The rationale of the District Court is dedicated to piercing the external manifestations of the taxpayer's transactions in order to establish a subterfuge or sham.

Nevertheless, the general principle is well settled that a taxpayer has the legal right to decrease the amount of what otherwise would be his taxes or altogether avoid them, by means which the law permits. Gregory v. Helvering, 293 U.S. 465, 469, 55 S.Ct. 266 * * * . The taxpayer's motive to avoid taxation will not establish liability if the transaction does not do so without it. Chamberlain v. Commissioner of Internal Revenue, 6 Cir., 207 F.2d 462 * * *.

The question accordingly presented is not whether the overall transaction, admittedly carried out for the purpose of avoiding taxes, actually avoided taxes which would have been incurred if the transaction had taken a different form, but whether the sale constituted a taxable dividend or the sale of a capital asset. * * *

It is a salutary fact that [§ 302(b)] is an exception to [§§ 301 and 316] that all distributions of earning and profits are taxable as a dividend.

The basic precept underlying the capital gains theory of taxation as distinguished from ordinary income tax is the concept that a person who has developed an enterprise in which earnings have been accumulated over a period of years should not be required to expend the ordinary income tax rate in the one year when he withdraws from his enterprise and realizes his gain.

Common logic dictates that a fair basis of measuring income is not determined upon the profits on hand in the year of liquidation but is properly attributable to each year in which the profits were gained.

We cannot concur with the legal proposition enunciated by the District Court that a corporate distribution can be essentially equivalent to a taxable dividend even though that distribution extinguishes the shareholder's interest in the corporation. To the contrary, we are satisfied that where the taxpayer effects a redemption which completely extinguishes the taxpayer's interest in the corporation, and does not retain any beneficial interest whatever, that such transaction is not the equivalent of the distribution of a taxable dividend as to him. Tiffany v. Commissioner of Internal Revenue, 16 T.C. 1443.

The statutory concept of dividend is a distribution out of earnings and profits, and normally it is proportionate to shares and leaves the shareholder holding his shares as his capital investment. Flinn v. Commissioner of Internal Revenue, 37 B.T.A. 1085.

Complete and partial liquidations are treated for the purpose of the statute, as sales with a consequent measure of gain or loss, even though the proceeds may to some extent be derived from earnings. Hellmich v. Hellman, 276 U.S. 233, 48 S.Ct. 244, 72 LEd. 544.

The use of corporate earnings or profits to purchase and make payment for all the shares of a taxpayer's holdings in a corporation is not controlling, and the question as to whether the distribution in connection with the cancellation or the redemption of said stock is essentially equivalent to the distribution of a taxable dividend under the Internal Revenue Code and Treasury Regulation must depend upon the circumstances of each case.

Since the intent of the taxpayer was to bring about a complete liquidation of her holdings and to become separated from all interest in the corporation, the conclusion is inevitable that the distribution of the earnings and profits by the corporation in payment for said stock was not made at such time and in such manner as to make the distribution and cancellation or redemption thereof essentially equivalent to the distribution of a taxable dividend.

* * *

We do not feel that a taxpayer should be penalized for exercising legal means to secure a tax advantage. The conduct of this taxpayer does not appear to contravene the purport or congressional intent of the provisions of the Internal Revenue Act which taxpayer invoked.

We conclude that under the facts and circumstances of the present case the District Court was in error, and the taxpayer is not liable as a distributee of a taxable dividend * * *.

ILLUSTRATIVE MATERIAL

A. HOLSEY SITUATION IN GENERAL

Suppose A and B each own 50 percent of the stock of a corporation. A desires to end his participation and B buys A's stock for its fair market value, $150,000. In effect, B has decided to invest $150,000 more in the corporation, and now owns 100 percent of a $300,000 corporation. Alternatively, suppose that B did not have sufficient funds or never contemplated buying A's stock. Instead of the above arrangement, therefore, the corporation redeems A's stock for $150,000. B now owns 100 percent of a corporation worth $150,000. Was the Tax Court, which was reversed by the Court of Appeals in the *Holsey* opinion, supra, saying that in this latter case B has a dividend of $150,000? How has B benefitted? While he is now the sole owner, he is the sole owner of a corporation half as large. Another possible view of the Tax Court decision, which does not rest on a dividend distribution, is that the redemption and consequent change in the interests of the shareholders may be treated as an appropriate occasion to tax any increase in the value of the shares of the remaining shareholders over the tax basis for their shares. But to treat this event as a realization of that gain would be a departure from existing rules. These questions are related to the problem of the proper treatment of the increase in the shareholder's proportionate interest in the corporation caused by a stock dividend, either actual or constructive, see Chapter 17, Section 1.

Going back to the first situation, suppose that B first had agreed to buy A's stock and then, after B had received the stock and undertaken this obligation, the obligation was assumed by the corporation and it paid A. Here in form and legal effect an obligation of B has been discharged by the corporation and he should have dividend income. The relief from a $150,-000 debt is the receipt of income. This was the situation in Zipp v. Commissioner, referred to in the *Holsey* opinion. Suppose then, as the next case, A and B are about to conclude a contract for the purchase by B, and B's lawyer, thinking of taxes, suddenly says the corporation should buy A's stock. The contract is hastily redrawn and the corporation acquires A's stock. Is the case to fall on the dividend side or on the nondividend side? The question here is whether the parties proceeded so far along the "purchase" by B that the taking over of B's obligation by the corporation came too late.

Where does the *Holsey* case itself fall? Certainly the parties were moving along the "purchase by B" route and then changed. Also, the option was a favorable one, since $80,000 was less than the value of 50 percent of the stock. Let us assume that value was $200,000. To gain this $120,000 benefit, the taxpayer B had to have $80,000. By taking over this option and providing the $80,000, the corporation produced a benefit for the taxpayer B. Is this what the Tax Court had in mind? If so, is the dividend $80,000 or $120,000?

Rev.Rul. 58–614, 1958–2 C.B. 920, states that the Service will follow the *Holsey* case where the stock was not in reality purchased by the continuing shareholder.

B. TREATMENT OF THE CONTINUING SHAREHOLDER

1. *Was the Corporation or the Continuing Shareholder the Purchaser of the Stock?*

(a) Conditional Versus Unconditional Obligation to Purchase Shares

The cases dealing with this issue turn on the factual question whether the continuing shareholder is regarded as the purchaser, so that the corporation in either paying funds to the selling shareholder as in the *Zipp* and *Wall* cases referred to in the *Holsey* opinion, or in taking the stock from the continuing shareholder and paying him for it, as in Lowenthal v. Commissioner, 169 F.2d 694 (7th Cir.1948), is in effect paying a dividend to the continuing shareholder. Here the primary issue is whether the continuing shareholder has a "personal, unconditional, primary obligation" to purchase the stock which is discharged by the corporation. In Sullivan v. United States, 363 F.2d 724 (8th Cir.1966), the majority shareholder in a corporation was obligated personally to purchase stock from a minority shareholder on the latter's leaving the employ of the corporation. When the minority shareholder left the employ of the corporation, however, instead of purchasing it himself, the majority shareholder caused the corporation to redeem the minority shareholder's stock. The redemption of the employee's shares in lieu of purchase by the majority shareholder under the agreement resulted in a dividend.

In general, however, both the cases and the Rulings in this area have been quite favorable to taxpayers. Thus, for example, in Priester v. Commissioner, 38 T.C. 316 (1962), a minority shareholder agreed to purchase the majority interest in a corporation but was financially unable to meet his commitment under the agreement. He then assigned the contract of sale to a third party with an understanding that the shares to be purchased by the third party would be redeemed by the corporation within a short period of time. Seven months following the purchase the shares were redeemed. The court found no dividend to the continuing shareholder since his obligation to the original owner of the stock was extinguished by the third party's purchase of the shares and not by the corporate distribution; the court refused to view the third party as a "straw man" through whom the taxpayer indirectly received the benefit of the corporate distribution. In addition, the Tax Court indicated that it would follow the Court of Appeals holding in *Holsey* that the benefit derived by the shareholder in becoming the sole shareholder of the corporation as a result of the redemption was not a taxable event.

Rev.Rul. 69–608, 1969–2 C.B. 42, discussed a number of commonly recurring situations in which the redemption of stock from retiring shareholders will not result in a constructive dividend to the continuing shareholder. In general, the Ruling allows the continuing shareholder to avoid dividend consequences as long as at the time of the redemption there is no existing primary and unconditional obligation on his part to purchase the redeemed shares. Thus, in one situation, A and B owned all of the outstanding stock of a corporation and had an agreement that, on the death of either, the survivor would purchase the decedent's shares from his estate. The cancellation of the agreement prior to the death of either shareholder, in favor of a new contract under which the corporation would redeem the shares of the decedent, was held not to result in a constructive dividend since at the time of the revision of the agreement there was no unconditional obligation to purchase the shares. In another situation dealt with by the Ruling, an individual entered into a contract for the purchase of the stock of a corporation. The contract provided that it could be assigned to another corporation, thereby releasing the purchaser from his obligations under the contract. The individual organized a corporation and assigned the stock purchase contract to it, the corporation borrowing funds to consummate the transaction. The purchasing corporation was subsequently merged into the acquired corporation, which then satisfied the loan liabilities. The Ruling, following Kobacker v. Commissioner, 37 T.C. 882 (1962), found no dividend on the repayment of the loan since the shareholder was not unconditionally obligated to purchase the stock. See also Smith v. Commissioner, 70 T.C. 651 (1978) (taxpayer was found to be unconditionally obligated to purchase stock under a stock purchase agreement with one shareholder but not so obligated with respect to another shareholder who only had an option to sell the stock to the taxpayer; consequently only redemptions in connection with the binding stock purchase agreement constituted dividends to the taxpayer).

On the other hand, Rev.Rul. 69–608 makes clear that where the continuing shareholder has become unconditionally bound to purchase the retiring or deceased shareholder's stock, a redemption by the corporation will give rise to a constructive dividend to the continuing shareholder. Thus, a constructive dividend was found where A and B agreed that upon the death of either the survivor would purchase the decedent's stock, and after the death of B, A caused the corporation to redeem the stock from B's estate. But, if the obligation is not unconditional, constructive dividend treatment may be avoided. Thus, the Ruling holds that no constructive dividend occurred where A and B and the corporation agreed that upon the death of either A or B, the corporation would redeem the decedent's shares and, to the extent that the corporation did not so redeem the shares, the survivor would purchase them. The same result follows where A agrees that if B desires to sell his shares, A will purchase the shares or cause another person to purchase the shares, and A causes the corporation to purchase the shares.

The results in individual cases turn on whether under state contract law the continuing shareholder has a contractual obligation. For example, in Apschnikat v. United States, 421 F.2d 910 (6th Cir.1970), the court found that the negotiations and correspondence between the purchaser and the sellers resulted in a binding obligation on the purchaser to purchase the stock and were not simply pre-contract dealings. Accordingly, payments for the stock by a corporation to which the purchaser had transferred the sales contract resulted in dividends to him.

In Hayes v. Commissioner, 101 T.C. 593 (1993), a husband and wife owned all the stock of a corporation operating a McDonald's franchise. When divorce proceedings were commenced, McDonald's insisted that Mrs. Hayes dispose of her stock if Mr. Hayes were to retain the franchise. A separation agreement executed on April 2, 1986 included a provision requiring Mr. Hayes to purchase Mrs. Hayes' stock for $128,000. Two days later, Mr. Hayes' attorney proposed to Mrs. Hayes' attorney that the corporation instead redeem Mrs. Hayes' stock in order to avoid the federal tax liability that would result from a dividend to Mr. Hayes to fund the purchase price. This proposal was accepted and payments in redemption of Mrs. Hayes' stock were made by the corporation to her on December 31, 1986, and March 31, 1987. On March 4, 1987, the divorce court entered a *nunc pro tunc* order, to "correct" its original divorce decree, requiring the corporation to purchase Mrs. Hayes' stock. Neither Mr. or Mrs. Hayes included the corporate distribution in income. Finding that the *nunc pro tunc* order was invalid under applicable state law, the Tax Court upheld the Commissioner's determination that the redemption transaction constituted a constructive dividend to Mr. Hayes. The Commissioner treated the constructive payment to Mrs. Hayes as nontaxable under § 1041. On the other hand, Blatt v. Commissioner, 102 T.C. 77 (1994), held that the spouse receiving the redemption payment was taxable in a situation where the divorce decree created no obligation in the other spouse to purchase the stock. The Tax Court in *Blatt* distinguished and indicated its disagreement with Arnes v. United States, 981 F.2d 456 (9th Cir.1992), which held that a redemption of the wife's stock pursuant to a divorce was for the husband's benefit and the wife was therefor entitled to nonrecognition under § 1041. Under the reasoning of the Court of Appeals in *Arnes,* Mr. Arnes, who was not joined in Mrs. Arnes' action, would be treated as receiving a distribution from the corporation. Mr. Arnes, however, litigated his tax liability in the Tax Court, which held that the redemption of Mrs. Arnes stock was not for Mr. Arnes benefit and he was not taxable. Arnes v. Commissioner, 102 T.C. 522 (1994). As a result of separate litigation of the cases, neither Mr. nor Mrs. Arnes was taxed on the redemption of the stock by the corporation.

If a shareholder of X Corporation is obligated to purchase stock of Y Corporation and, rather than purchasing the Y Corporation stock directly, the shareholder assigns the contractual obligation to X Corporation, which purchases the stock, there is no dividend to the shareholder. In this case X Corporation has not redeemed its own stock. Rather it has received fair value for the amount paid and thus it is not a distribution. See Citizens Bank & Trust Co. v. United States, 580 F.2d 442 (Ct.Cl.1978).

(b) Continuing Shareholder as Agent of Corporation

In situations in which the shares first pass through the continuing shareholder, the court sometimes may regard him as an agent acquiring the stock on behalf of the corporation, which was the real purchaser, so that no dividend results. In Bennett v. Commissioner, 58 T.C. 381 (1972), the majority shareholder in the corporation wished to terminate his interest. The taxpayer, a minority shareholder, suggested that the corporation redeem the shares but the retiring shareholder (in order not to incur a possible liability to creditors of the corporation because of a depletion of corporate assets) insisted that the taxpayer appear as the purchaser of the shares. It was agreed that the corporation would borrow money to advance to the taxpayer, the latter would then purchase the shares from the retiring shareholder and the corporation would immediately redeem. The transaction was consummated in this manner and the Tax Court found no dividend, distinguishing the *Wall* case, relied on by the Commissioner, as follows:

"In *Wall,* the taxpayer in one transaction acquired stock, paid an amount of cash, and obligated himself personally to pay additional amounts; in a subsequent, separate transaction the corporation paid the notes. In contrast, [the taxpayer here] never intended to acquire personal ownership of the Jones stock and never incurred any personal obligation to do so; at all times, he was serving as a conduit or agent for the Corporation in a single, integrated transaction in which it acquired the stock." (388)

A similar result was reached in Ciaio v. Commissioner, 47 T.C. 447 (1967), where, as a result of disagreements, two shareholders agreed to sell their stock to the corporation, leaving the taxpayer as the sole shareholder. To finance the transaction, the corporation obtained a bank loan. The bank, as a condition of the loan (imposed under banking law), required that the stock be deposited with it as security and that the documents reflect the continuing shareholder and not the corporation as the buyer of the stock. The continuing shareholder was also required to guarantee the bank loan. The loan proceeds were used to redeem the shares of the two retiring shareholders. The court found no dividend to the continuing shareholder on account of the redemption since he was at all times acting as an agent for the corporation. Compare Deutsch v. Commissioner, 38 T.C. 118 (1962), rejecting the agency argument where the contract for the purchase of the stock was at all times between the individual taxpayer and the seller, and Glacier State Electric Supply Co. v. Commissioner, 80 T.C. 1047 (1983), holding that a parent corporation was the true owner of redeemed stock of its wholly owned subsidiary, rather than an agent of the parent corporation's shareholders who were asserted to be the beneficial owners of the stock of the subsidiary.

In Schroeder v. Commissioner, 831 F.2d 856 (9th Cir.1987), the selling shareholder, after initially agreeing to cause the corporation to redeem 90 percent of her stock and to sell 10 percent of her stock to the purchaser, on the advice of counsel changed her mind and insisted on selling all of the stock to the purchaser. The bank which was financing the acquisition, however, required that the permanent loan be made to the corporation as primary obligor and be guaranteed by the purchaser. In order to effect the acquisition of all of the stock directly by the purchaser a "bridge" loan was made directly to the purchaser, subject to an agreement between the purchaser and the bank that immediately after the acquisition, the corporation would assume primary responsibility for the loan in consideration of a redemption of a proportionate amount of its stock. In fact, the corporation assumed approximately two-thirds of the loan two months after the acquisition, and it redeemed a proportionate amount of stock. The taxpayer argued that the purchase and the redemption were part of a single transaction which should have been treated as a redemption from the seller. The court rejected this argument as follows:

"The Tax Court found that 'there was no common or mutually agreed plan of action between the estate of Fred Collins [the seller], Schroeder [the buyer], and Skyline [the corporation] whose object was the ultimate redemption by Skyline of a part of its stock. * * *' We agree with the Tax Court. The record confirms Schroeder's stated intentions, but also shows that this intention was particular to him. Donna Collins, as the personal representative of her husband's estate and as the seller of Skyline's stock, made it clear to Schroeder by April 13, 1976, that she would not agree to Skyline redeeming its stock as part of a bootstrap acquisition of Skyline proposed by Schroeder. Instead, she insisted that Schroeder buy the stock personally, which Schroeder undertook to do. In addition, Skyline cannot have had any intention different from Donna's, since she controlled 100 percent of Skyline's stock.

"Schroeder, because of Donna's insistence, could not undertake a bootstrap acquisition and had to buy the Skyline stock himself. He had business reasons for choosing the form of the transaction that he did. He cannot now argue that he is immunized from tax because the transaction was really something that never occurred. * * *

"Schroeder's contention that he acted as an agent or conduit of the corporation pursuant to a prearranged plan is without merit. First, as noted above, there was no mutually agreed plan between Collins and Schroeder or between Schroeder and Skyline. The intention to have the corporation redeem its own stock was Schroeder's intention alone. Second, when he acquired the stock on April 30, 1976, 'Schroeder was neither an officer, director nor a shareholder of Skyline, and he had no apparent authority to bind or commit Skyline to acquire its own stock or to borrow $600,000 from the bank in Skyline's name.' * * * It was not until he acquired sole ownership of the Skyline stock, on July 1, 1976, when the debt to State Bank was restructured, and on August 1, 1976, when Skyline redeemed his stock, that Schroeder caused his intention to become Skyline's as well. Schroeder was not Skyline's agent or conduit on April 30, 1976." (859)

Can *Schroeder* be distinguished from *Bennett* and *Ciaio?*

(c) Post–Acquisition Redemption From Purchaser

While a well-tailored plan for the purchase of a corporate business can use part of the corporation's assets to finance the transaction, the formalities generally must be observed. If an agency argument fails, a distribution to the purchaser following the acquisition of all of the stock, for the purpose of reducing the net out-of-pocket purchase price paid for the corporate business, will be a dividend to the purchaser. In Television Industries, Inc. v. Commissioner, 284 F.2d 322 (2d Cir.1960), the purchasing shareholder borrowed money to complete the purchase of all the shares then had some of the shares redeemed to obtain funds to repay the loan; a dividend resulted. Accord, Adams v. Commissioner, 594 F.2d 657 (8th Cir.1979) (pro-rata redemption of shares following purchase taxed as dividend even though pursuant to prearranged plan of which sellers had knowledge). Even though in economic effect and intent this transaction may not differ from a pre-acquisition redemption from the seller, the form of the transaction will control for tax purposes. See Jacobs v. Commissioner, T.C. Memo. 1981–81, aff'd, 698 F.2d 850 (6th Cir.1983), in which upon finding that the corporation acted as the continuing shareholders' agent in acquiring the seller's shares, the Tax Court observed as follows: "Petitioners could very easily have avoided dividend treatment of this transaction had they obtained tax advice from the start. * * * Unfortunately, this is another area of the law in which 'the formalities of handling a particular transaction assume a disproportionate importance and * * * a premium is placed upon consulting one's lawyer early enough in the game.' * * * Petitioners have chosen the wrong form and consequently must suffer the consequences." (953). Is the agency theory employed in *Bennett* and *Ciaio* inconsistent with the "form controls" theory of *Jacobs?*

2. *Section 305 Aspects*

While the case law after *Holsey* was unanimous in rejecting the Government's argument that the continuing shareholder's increase in his proportionate interest in the corporation as a result of the redemption of other shareholders constituted a taxable dividend to him, increase in proportionate interest again became relevant with the amendments to § 305 in 1969, see page 301. Under § 305(b)(2) the increase in the proportionate interests of some shareholders in the earnings or assets of the corporation caused by a stock dividend, when coupled with the receipt of property by other shareholders, can result in a taxable distribution to the former group. Under § 305(c), the increase in proportionate interest caused by a redemption can be treated as a constructive stock dividend for purposes of § 305(b)(2). The regulations, however, provide that in a situation like *Holsey,* where the redemption distribution is entitled to capital gains treatment under § 302(b), no constructive dividend will result to the continuing shareholders. Treas. Reg. § 1.305–3(b)(2). In addition, an isolated redemption will not trigger a constructive stock dividend under § 305(c). Treas. Reg.§ 1.305–7(a). See Treas. Reg.§ 1.305–3(b)(3), (e) Ex. (10) (no constructive dividend as a result of isolated redemption even though redemption was treated as a § 301 distribution). For an example of a redemption situation in which § 305(b)(2) was applicable by virtue of § 305(c), see Rev.Rul. 78–60, 1978–1 C.B. 81.

C. TREATMENT OF THE REDEEMED SHAREHOLDER

Where a prospective purchaser of the stock is unwilling to pay for all the stock at its present value and the parties arrange for the corporation to redeem some of the shares of the existing shareholders contemporaneously with the sale of the balance of their stock to the purchaser, who thus is required to pay a lesser figure (but who also receives a corporation with fewer assets), the courts generally have followed the approach of Zenz v. Quinlivan. See Auto Finance Co. v. Commissioner, 24 T.C. 416 (1955), aff'd per curiam, 229 F.2d 318 (4th Cir.1956); In re Lukens' Estate, 246 F.2d 403 (3d Cir.1957) (father had part of his stock redeemed at book value and gave the balance to his adult children, who also were shareholders and who managed the corporation). The Internal Revenue Service has ruled that it will follow *Zenz,* Rev.Rul. 55–745, 1955–2 C.B. 223, and that the actual sequence of the redemption and the sale will be ignored in a *Zenz*-type corporate sale as long as the two steps are both part of an integrated plan to reduce the outgoing shareholders' interest. Thus, the fact that the redemption precedes the sale of the shares will not cause the outgoing shareholders to receive dividend treatment; the formal order of the steps in the transaction is not crucial. Rev.Rul. 75–447, 1975–2 C.B. 113; accord Monson v. Commissioner, 79 T.C. 827 (1982). See also Rev.Rul. 77–226, 1977–2 C.B. 90 (corporate shareholder tendered part of its shares for redemption and sold the remaining shares of stock on the market; it treated the redemption as a § 301 distribution under § 302(d) qualifying for the intercorporate dividends deduction and claimed a capital loss on the disposition of the remaining shares which were attributed the basis of the shares which were redeemed; held, the entire transaction resulted in a termination of the corporate shareholder's interest and hence a taxable capital gain).

It is not necessary for the selling shareholder's interest to be completely terminated in order for the *Zenz* principle to apply. Rev.Rul. 75–447, 1975–2 C.B. 113, held that the reduction in interest effected through a combined sale and redemption should be aggregated to determine whether the redemption qualified for sale or exchange treatment under § 302(b)(2), discussed at page 238. Furthermore, in private letter rulings the Internal Revenue Service has applied *Zenz* to qualify a redemption under § 302(b)(1). See Ltr.Rul. 8540074.

A variation on Zenz v. Quinlivan was involved in McDonald v. Commissioner, 52 T.C. 82 (1969). There the shareholder, who owned all of the preferred stock and most of the common stock in a corporation, had the preferred stock redeemed and, as part of a prior arrangement, exchanged his common stock for the common stock of a public corporation in a tax-free exchange. The Commissioner argued that the preferred stock redemption constituted a dividend, distinguishing *Zenz,* since in this situation the shareholder retained a continuing interest in the assets of old corporation by virtue of his stock ownership in the acquiring corporation. The court found the redemption and subsequent reorganization effected a "substantial change" in the shareholder's interest and refused to treat the redemption as a dividend. For the reorganization aspects of *McDonald* see page 599.

An interesting twist on the *Zenz* principle is found in Estate of Durkin v. Commissioner, 99 T.C. 561 (1992). The taxpayer purchased a corporate asset for a price substantially below fair market value. At the same time, the taxpayer's stock was redeemed by the corporation for a price equal to its basis, the taxpayer reporting no gain or loss on the redemption. The Commissioner asserted that the bargain sale of corporate assets was a constructive dividend to the taxpayer. The taxpayer argued that the substance of the transaction was a redemption qualified under § 302(b)(3) under *Zenz.* The Tax Court sustained the Commissioner's assertion of dividend treatment with respect to the bargain purchase holding that the taxpayer is to be held to the form of the transaction that he chose, which was selected in an attempt to avoid recognition of gain on the redemption.

D. DIVIDENDS DISTRIBUTED IN CONNECTION WITH THE SALE OF A CORPORATE BUSINESS

While the treatment of redemptions made as part of the sale of a corporate business is fairly well established since the initial decisions in

Holsey and *Zenz,* the appropriate treatment of dividend distributions in similar situations raises different questions.

In Casner v. Commissioner, 450 F.2d 379 (5th Cir.1971), substantial shareholders in the corporation wished to withdraw by selling their stock to the remaining shareholders. The buyers did not have enough cash to finance the transaction. It was agreed that a distribution of some of the cash of the corporation would be made pro rata to all the shareholders, thus reducing the value of the corporation and giving the remaining shareholders some cash to pay a portion of the purchase price. Accordingly, the corporation made a cash distribution and contemporaneously the retiring shareholders sold their shares. The selling shareholders treated all the payments as sales proceeds; the buying shareholders regarded themselves as conduits. The Tax Court treated the corporate distributions to both the selling and buying shareholders as dividends. T.C. Memo. 1969–98. The Court of Appeals reversed, finding that the distributions to the *selling* shareholders were in fact part of the payment of the purchase price and as such resulted in dividends to the *buying* shareholders (in addition to the latter's own direct dividends). The court found alternatively that the buying stockholders were the beneficial owners of the stock at the time of the dividend distribution.

The *Casner* treatment of the distributions to the selling shareholders as dividends to the buying shareholders followed by a payment of the purchase price to the sellers is clearly inconsistent with the redemption line of cases dealing with a similar factual pattern. The Internal Revenue Service will not apply *Casner* to tax the buyer where the payment of the dividend to the selling shareholder does not reduce the buyer's obligation to pay an agreed upon purchase price, Rev.Rul. 75–493, 1975–2 C.B. 108. This position is consistent with the redemption cases which likewise focus on the question of whether the distribution by the corporation discharges the buying shareholder's personal obligation. It similarly places a premium on the careful timing of the transactions since very different tax consequences result depending on whether the distribution is made before or after entering into a binding purchase agreement.

Even where the dividend does not reduce the buying shareholder's obligation under the purchase agreement, a dividend to the buyer may still be found on the theory that the buyer had become the beneficial owner of the stock at the time the dividend was declared. See Steel Improvement and Forge Co. v. Commissioner, 314 F.2d 96 (6th Cir.1963); Walker v. Commissioner, 544 F.2d 419 (9th Cir.1976).

SECTION 2. BOOTSTRAP TRANSACTIONS INVOLVING CORPORATIONS

Different problems arise where a dividend in connection with a sale is paid to a selling shareholder which is itself a corporation and thus able to take advantage of the reduction or elimination of tax on intercorporate dividends under § 243. Suppose that X Corporation owns 100 percent of the stock of Y Corporation, which has a basis of $200 and a fair market value of $500. (Also assume that X Corporation and Y Corporation do not file a consolidated return.) If X Corporation sold the stock of Y Corporation to Z Corporation for $500, after paying taxes (at 35 percent) on its $300 gain, X Corporation would have net after-tax proceeds of $395. Now suppose that prior to the sale Y Corporation declared a dividend of $200, which was eligible for 100 percent exclusion under § 243(a)(3), following which X Corporation sold the stock of Y Corporation for $300. In this case, X Corporation would pay taxes on only a $100 gain, and after taxes it would receive $465.

The Commissioner generally argues that such a dividend payment was in fact additional purchase price, and therefore constituted capital gain which was not eligible for the § 243 deduction. See Rev.Rul. 75–493, 1975–2 C.B. 108, characterizing such a transaction as a "sham designed to disguise the true substance of the transaction." The Commissioner has had mixed success with this argument in the courts.

Litton Industries, Inc. v. Commissioner

Tax Court of the United States, 1987.
89 T.C. 1086.

[The taxpayer's board of directors began to consider a sale of its subsidiary, Stouffer, in July of 1972. In late August, Stouffer declared a $30 million dividend, which was paid in the form of a negotiable promissory note for $30 million; and on September 7, Litton announced that it was interested in selling Stouffer. After considering a public offering of the Stouffer stock in late 1972, on March 1, 1973, Litton sold its Stouffer stock to Nestle for $75 million; simultaneously, it sold the promissory note to Nestle for $30 million. The Commissioner contended that the $30 million "dividend" was in fact part of the purchase price and disallowed Litton's dividends received deduction.]

OPINION

* * *

The instant case is substantially governed by Waterman Steamship Corp. v. Commissioner, 50 T.C. 650 (1968), revd. 430 F.2d 1185 (5th Cir.1970), cert. denied 401 U.S. 939 (1971). [The Commissioner] urges us to follow the opinion of the Fifth Circuit * * *. [Taxpayer] contends that the reasoning of the Fifth Circuit in *Waterman Steamship* should not apply since the facts here are more favorable to petitioner. Additionally, petitioner points out that several business purposes were served by the distribution here which provide additional support for recognition of the distribution as a dividend. For the reasons set forth below, we conclude that the $30 million distribution constituted a dividend which should be recognized as such for tax purposes. * * *

In many respects, the facts of this case and those of *Waterman Steamship* are parallel. The principal difference, and the one which we find to be most significant, is the timing of the dividend action. In *Waterman Steamship,* the taxpayer corporation received an offer to purchase the stock of two of its wholly owned subsidiary corporations, Pan–Atlantic and Gulf Florida, for $3,500,000. The board of directors of Waterman Steamship rejected that offer but countered with an offer to sell the two subsidiaries for $700,000 after the subsidiaries declared and arranged for payments of dividends to Waterman Steamship amounting in the aggregate to $2,800,000. Negotiations between the parties ensued, and the agreements which resulted therefrom included, in specific detail, provisions for the declaration of a dividend by Pan–Atlantic to Waterman Steamship prior to the signing of the sales agreement and the closing of that transaction. Furthermore, the agreements called for the purchaser to loan or otherwise advance funds to Pan–Atlantic promptly in order to pay off the promissory note by which the dividend had been paid. Once the agreement was reached, the entire transaction was carried out by a series of meetings commencing at 12 noon on January 21, 1955, and ending at 1:30 p.m. the same day. * * *

As the Fifth Circuit pointed out, "By the end of the day and within a ninety minute period, the financial cycle had been completed. Waterman had $3,500,000, hopefully tax-free, all of which came from Securities and McLean, the buyers of the stock." 430 F.2d at 1190. This Court concluded that the distribution from Pan–Atlantic to Waterman was a dividend. The Fifth Circuit reversed, concluding that the dividend and sale were one transaction. 430 F.2d at 1192.

The timing in the instant case was markedly different. The dividend was declared by Stouffer on August 23, 1972, at which time the promissory note in payment of the dividend was issued to Litton. There had been some general preliminary discussions about the sale of Stouffer, and it was expected that Stouffer would be a very marketable company which would sell quickly. However, at the time the dividend was declared, no formal action had been taken to initiate the sale of Stouffer. It was not until 2 weeks later that Litton publicly announced that Stouffer was for sale. There ensued over the next 6 months many discussions with various corporations, investment banking houses, business brokers, and underwriters regarding Litton's disposition of Stouffer through sale of all or part of the business to a particular buyer, or through full or partial public offerings of the Stouffer stock. All of this culminated on March 1, 1973, over 6 months after the dividend was declared, with the purchase by Nestle of all of Stouffer's stock. * * *

In the instant case, the declaration of the dividend and the sale of the stock were substantially separated in time in contrast to *Waterman Steamship* where the different transactions occurred essentially simultaneously. In *Waterman Steamship,* it seems quite clear that no dividend would have been declared if all of the remaining steps in the transaction had not been lined up in order on the closing table and did not in fact take place. Here, however, Stouffer declared the dividend, issued the promissory note, and definitely committed itself to the dividend before even making a public announcement that Stouffer was for sale. Respondent argues that the only way petitioner could ever receive the dividend was by raising revenue through a sale of Stouffer. Therefore, respondent asserts the two events (the declaration of the dividend and then the sale of the company) were inextricably tied together and should be treated as one transaction for tax purposes. In our view, respondent ignores the fact that Stouffer could have raised sufficient revenue for the dividend from other avenues, such as a partial public offering or borrowing. Admittedly, there had been discussions at Litton about the sale of Stouffer which was considered to be a very salable company. However, there are many slips between the cup and the lip, and it does not take much of a stretch of the imagination to picture a variety of circumstances under which Stouffer might have been taken off the market and no sale consummated. Under these circumstances, it is unlikely that respondent would have considered the dividend to be a nullity. On the contrary, it would seem quite clear that petitioner would be charged with a dividend on which it would have to pay a substantial tax. Petitioner committed itself to the dividend and, thereby, accepted the consequences regardless of the outcome of the proposed sale of Stouffer stock. See Crellin v. Commissioner, 17 T.C. 781, 785 (1951), affd. 203 F.2d 812 (9th Cir.1953), cert. denied 346 U.S. 873, 74 S.Ct. 123 (1953).

Since the facts here are distinguishable in important respects and are so much stronger in petitioner's favor, we do not consider it necessary to consider further the opinion of the Fifth Circuit in *Waterman Steamship.*

* * * [T]he $30 million distribution by Stouffer would clearly constitute a dividend if the sale of Stouffer had not occurred. We are not persuaded that the subsequent sale of Stouffer to Nestle changes that result merely because it was more advantageous to Litton from a tax perspective.

It is well established that a taxpayer is entitled to structure his affairs and transactions in order to minimize his taxes. This proposition does not give a taxpayer carte blanche to set up a transaction in any form which will avoid tax consequences, regardless of whether the transaction has substance. Gregory v. Helvering, 293 U.S. 465, 55 S.Ct. 266 (1935). A variety of factors present here preclude a finding of sham or subterfuge. Although the record in this case clearly shows that Litton intended at the time the dividend was declared to sell Stouffer, no formal action had been taken and no announcement had been made. There was no definite purchaser waiting in the wings with the terms and conditions of sale already agreed upon. At that time, Litton had not even decided upon the form of sale of Stouffer. Nothing in the record here suggests that there was any prearranged sale agreement, formal or informal, at the time the dividend was declared.

Petitioner further supports its argument that the transaction was not a sham by pointing out Litton's legitimate business purposes in declaring the dividend. Although the Code and case law do not require a dividend to have a business purpose, it is a factor to be considered in determining whether the overall transaction was a sham. T.S.N. Liquidating Corp. v.

United States, 624 F.2d 1328 (5th Cir.1980). Petitioner argues that * * * since Litton was considering disposing of all or part of Stouffer through a public or private offering, the payment of a dividend by a promissory note prior to any sale had two advantages. First, Litton hoped to avoid materially diminishing the market value of the Stouffer stock. At that time, one of the factors considered in valuing a stock, and in determining the market value of a stock was the "multiple of earnings" criterion. Payment of the dividend by issuance of a promissory note would not substantially alter Stouffer's earnings. Since many investors were relatively unsophisticated, Litton may have been quite right that it could increase its investment in Stouffer by at least some portion of the $30 million dividend. Second, by declaring a dividend and paying it by a promissory note prior to an anticipated public offering, Litton could avoid sharing the earnings with future additional shareholders while not diminishing to the full extent of the pro rata dividend, the amount received for the stock. Whether Litton could have come out ahead after Stouffer paid the promissory note is at this point merely speculation about a public offering which never occurred. The point, however, is that Litton hoped to achieve some business purpose, and not just tax benefits, in structuring the transaction as it did.

Under these facts, where the dividend was declared 6 months prior to the sale of Stouffer, where the sale was not pre-arranged, and since Stouffer had earnings and profits exceeding $30 million at the time the dividend was declared, we cannot conclude that the distribution was merely a device designed to give the appearance of a dividend to a part of the sales proceeds. In this case, the form and substance of the transaction coincide; it was not a transaction entered into solely for tax reasons, and it should be recognized as structured by petitioner.

ILLUSTRATIVE MATERIAL

A. OTHER JUDICIAL DECISIONS

As in *Waterman Steamship,* discussed in the excerpt from *Litton Industries,* supra, the Commissioner met with success in the District Court in TSN Liquidating Corp. v. United States, 77–2 U.S.T.C. ¶ 9741 (N.D.Tex. 1977), but on appeal the decision was reversed, 624 F.2d 1328 (5th Cir.1980). In that case, Union Mutual agreed to purchase from TSN the stock of TSN's subsidiary, CLIC, but Union Mutual insisted that prior to the acquisition CLIC distribute to TSN certain securities, primarily stock of closely held corporations, constituting some 78 percent of CLIC's total assets. Although Union Mutual did not desire CLIC to hold the particular securities distributed pursuant to the agreement, neither did it desire to own a "smaller" corporation. To the contrary, for reasons having to do with state law it desired to maintain the net assets of CLIC, and shortly after the closing, Union Mutual contributed to CLIC cash and marketable securities slightly in excess of the amount distributed to TSN.

Emphasizing that the distribution of investment assets immediately prior to the sale of the stock was matched by a post acquisition infusion of investment assets, the Commissioner argued that the conduit rationale of *Waterman Steamship* applied. Although it agreed with the District Court that "the substance of the transaction controls over the form," the Court of Appeals found *Waterman Steamship,* upon which the District Court had relied, to be distinguishable. The earlier case involved a "sham transaction," which even the Commissioner did not argue was the case in *TSN Liquidating.* Instead, the Commissioner argued, successfully in the District Court, that from CLIC's perspective there was no business purpose for the distribution which could not have occurred other than in the context of the sale. The Court of Appeals, however, concluded as follows:

"We agree that the transaction must be viewed as a whole and we accept the district court's finding of fact that the dividend of the unwanted assets was 'part and parcel of the purchase arrangement with Union Mutual,' motivated specifically by Union Mutual's unwillingness to take and pay for such assets. That being the case, we decline to focus on the business purpose of one participant in the transaction—a corporation controlled by the taxpayer—and instead find that the business purpose for the transaction as a whole, viewed from the standpoint of the taxpayer, controls. The facts found by the district court clearly demonstrate a business purpose for the presale dividend of the unwanted assets which fully explains that dividend. We note that there is no suggestion in the district court's opinion of any tax avoidance motivation on the part of the taxpayer TSN. The fact that the dividend may have had incidental tax benefit to the taxpayer, without more, does not necessitate the disallowance of dividend treatment." (1336)

In Basic, Inc. v. United States, 549 F.2d 740 (Ct.Cl.1977), the court refused to respect the taxpayers' structure of the transaction even though payment of an intercorporate dividend was not in effect a conduit device to transfer funds from the purchaser to the seller. Basic owned all the shares of Falls which in turn owned all the shares of Carbon. A corporate purchaser was interested in buying the shares of Falls and Carbon but, in order to take advantage of a now repealed provision governing a subsequent liquidation of the subsidiaries, it desired to purchase the stock of both Falls and Carbon directly rather than simply purchasing the Falls stock and obtaining the Carbon stock on a liquidation of Falls. After an irrevocable offer by the purchaser to purchase the Falls and Carbon stock, Falls distributed the Carbon stock to Basic as a dividend. The dividend of the stock was entitled to the dividends received deduction under § 243(a)(1) but because under § 301(d) the basis of the Carbon stock was not reduced to reflect the dividends received deduction, Basic acquired an essentially "cost free" basis in the Carbon stock against which to offset the sales price to be paid for the stock of the two corporations. The Court of Claims held that the transfer of the Carbon stock to Basic did not qualify as a dividend. The court rested its decision on general notions of tax avoidance, citing Gregory v. Helvering, 293 U.S. 465 (1935), and took the position that for a corporate distribution to qualify as a dividend it must have an independent "business purpose":

"These facts leave no room for a conclusion that a business interest was served by the claimed dividend. From all that appears, the case is plain that Falls, through its controlling parent, was caused to transfer the property whose sale the parent had decided upon for its own separate purposes. Nothing therefore remains save the obvious: the transaction reduced the tax that Basic would otherwise have incurred in the sale of its own property, i.e., the shares of Falls. * * *

"Under the facts and circumstances presented here, plaintiff has not shown that there was a reason for the transfer of the Carbon stock from Falls to Basic aside from the tax consequences attributable to that move. Accordingly, for purposes of taxation, the transfer was not a dividend within the meaning of § 316(a)(1). Instead, it should be regarded as a transfer that avoided part of the gain to be expected from the sale of the business to Carborundum, and should, therefore, be now taxed accordingly. Such a treatment is in keeping with the results reached in like situations. Waterman Steamship Corp. v. Commissioner, supra; Steel Improvement & Forge Co. v. Commissioner, 314 F.2d 96, 98 (6th Cir.1963); Commissioner v. Transport Trading & Terminal Corp., supra." (746, 749).

The *Basic, Inc.* opinion cannot be reconciled with *Litton Industries* and *TSN Liquidating. Basic, Inc.* appears to require that the payor have a business purpose for paying the dividend totally apart from the business purpose of the parent. It will be difficult, if not impossible, ever to establish an independent business purpose for the payment of an extraordinary dividend by a controlled subsidiary.

The cases involving intercorporate dividends associated with a bootstrap acquisition requiring that a dividend distribution must have a "business purpose" are in marked contrast to the cases in the redemption area in which the form which the taxpayer has selected for the extraction of corporate assets prior to a sale of the corporation is in general respected without regard to any inquiry into purposes. Does the fact that intercorporate dividends are in general either tax free or subject to reduced taxation mean that special safeguards are required with respect to such distributions in the context of corporate acquisitions? If so is the introduction of a "business purpose" doctrine an appropriate response? Compare the treatment given intercorporate dividends in the consolidated return situation discussed at page 459, where the parent corporation upon receipt of an excluded intercorporate dividend must reduce its basis in the stock of the subsidiary by an amount equal to the dividend. Thus, in a consolidated return context, the intercorporate dividend prior to the sale does not produce a tax advantage to the seller.

B. SECTION 1059

Section 1059 requires that a corporate shareholder which receives an "extraordinary dividend" under certain circumstances must, in computing the gain or loss realized upon the sale of the stock, reduce the basis of the stock by the amount of the untaxed portion of the dividend. See page 231. As long as the stock has been held for more than two years prior to the dividend announcement date, however, only a distribution in partial liquidation of the corporation (as defined in § 302(e), discussed at page ___) or a non-pro rata redemption distribution generally will be treated as an extraordinary distribution. Furthermore, § 1059 never applies to "qualifying dividends" paid by an 80 percent owned subsidiary to its parent corporation. I.R.C. § 1059(e)(2). Thus § 1059 is of limited application in this context, and it would not apply, for example, to a transaction identical to that in *Litton*.

Section 1059 was not enacted for the purpose of dealing with *Litton* type transactions, but the mechanical approach of § 1059 could be extended to apply to such transactions if Congress considered bootstrap acquisitions involving intercorporate dividends to involve inappropriate tax avoidance.

CHAPTER 13

TAX FREE ACQUISITIVE REORGANIZATIONS

SECTION 1. EARLY JUDICIAL BACKGROUND

Marr v. United States

Supreme Court of the United States, 1925.
268 U.S. 536.

■ MR. JUSTICE BRANDEIS delivered the opinion of the Court.

Prior to March 1, 1913, Marr and wife purchased 339 shares of the preferred and 425 shares of the common stock of the General Motors Company of New Jersey for $76,400. In 1916, they received in exchange for this stock 451 shares of the preferred and 2,125 shares of the common stock of the General Motors Corporation of Delaware which (including a small cash payment) had the aggregate market value of $400,866.57. The difference between the cost of their stock in the New Jersey corporation and the value of the stock in the Delaware corporation was $324,466.57. The Treasury Department ruled that this difference was gain or income * * *.

The exchange of securities was effected in this way. The New Jersey corporation had outstanding $15,000,000 of 7 per cent. preferred stock and $15,000,000 of the common stock; all shares being of the par value of $100. It had accumulated from profits a large surplus. The actual value of the common stock was then $842.50 a share. Its officers caused to be organized the Delaware corporation with an authorized capital of $20,000,000 in 6 percent nonvoting preferred stock and $82,600,000 in common stock; all shares being of the par value of $100. The Delaware corporation made to stockholders in the New Jersey corporation the following offer for exchange of securities: For every share of common stock of the New Jersey corporation, five shares of common stock of the Delaware corporation. For every share of the preferred stock of the New Jersey corporation, one and one-third shares of preferred stock of the Delaware corporation. In lieu of a certificate for fractional shares of stock in the Delaware corporation, payment was to be made in cash at the rate of $100 a share for its preferred and at the rate of $150 a share for its common stock. On this basis all the common stock of the New Jersey corporation was exchanged and all the preferred stock except a few shares. These few were redeemed in cash. For acquiring the stock of the New Jersey corporation only $75,000,000 of the common stock of the Delaware corporation was needed.

The remaining $7,600,000 of the authorized common stock was either sold or held for sale as additional capital should be desired. The Delaware corporation, having thus become the owner of all the outstanding stock of the New Jersey corporation, took a transfer of its assets and assumed its liabilities. The latter was then dissolved.

It is clear that all new securities issued in excess of an amount equal to the capitalization of the New Jersey corporation represented income earned by it; that the new securities received by the Marrs in excess of the cost of the securities of the New Jersey corporation theretofore held were financially the equivalent of $324,466.51 in cash; and that Congress intended to tax as income of stockholders such gains when so distributed. The serious question for decision is whether it had power to do so. Marr contends that, since the new corporation was organized to take over the assets and continue the business of the old, and his capital remained invested in the same business enterprise, the additional securities distributed were in legal effect a stock dividend; and that under the rule of Eisner v. Macomber, 252 U.S. 189, 40 S.Ct. 189, applied in Weiss v. Stearn, 265 U.S. 242, 44 S.Ct. 490, he was not taxable thereon as income, because he still held the whole investment. The government insists that identity of the business enterprise is not conclusive; that gain in value resulting from profits is taxable as income, not only when it is represented by an interest in a different business enterprise or property, but also when it is represented by an essentially different interest in the same business enterprise or property; that, in the case at bar, the gain actually made is represented by securities with essentially different characteristics in an essentially different corporation; and that, consequently, the additional value of the new securities, although they are still held by the Marrs, is income under the rule applied in United States v. Phellis, 257 U.S. 156, 42 S.Ct. 63; Rockefeller v. United States, 257 U.S. 176, 42 S.Ct. 68; and Cullinan v. Walker, 262 U.S. 134, 43 S.Ct. 495. In our opinion the government is right.

In each of the five cases named, as in the case at bar, the business enterprise actually conducted remained exactly the same. In United States v. Phellis, in Rockefeller v. United States, and in Cullinan v. Walker, where the additional value in new securities distributed was held to be taxable as income, there had been changes of corporate identity. That is, the corporate property, or a part thereof, was no longer held and operated by the same corporation; and, after the distribution, the stockholders no longer owned merely the same proportional interest of the same character in the same corporation. In Eisner v. Macomber and in Weiss v. Stearn, where the additional value in new securities was held not to be taxable, the identity was deemed to have been preserved. In Eisner v. Macomber the identity was literally maintained. There was no new corporate entity. The same interest in the same corporation was represented after the distribution by more shares of precisely the same character. It was as if the par value of the stock had been reduced, and three shares of reduced par value stock had been issued in place of every two old shares. That is, there was an exchange of certificates but not of interests. In Weiss v. Stearn a new corporation had, in fact, been organized to take over the assets and business of the old. Technically there was a new entity; but the corporate identity was deemed to have been substantially maintained because the new corporation was organized under the laws of the same state, with presumably the same powers as the old. There was also no change in the character of securities issued. By reason of these facts, the proportional interest of the stockholder after the distribution of the new securities was deemed to be exactly the same as if the par value of the stock in the old corporation had been reduced, and five shares of reduced par value stock had been issued in place of every two shares of the old stock. Thus, in Weiss v. Stearn, as in Eisner v. Macomber, the transaction was considered, in essence, an exchange of certificates representing the same interest, not an exchange of interests.

In the case at bar, the new corporation is essentially different from the old. A corporation organized under the laws of Delaware does not have the same rights and powers as one organized under the laws of New Jersey. Because of these inherent differences in rights and powers, both the preferred and the common stock of the old corporation is an essentially different thing from stock of the same general kind in the new. But there are also adventitious differences, substantial in character. A 6 per cent. nonvoting preferred stock is an essentially different thing from a 7 per cent. voting preferred stock. A common stock subject to the priority of $20,000,000 preferred and a $1,200,000 annual dividend charge is an essentially different thing from a common stock subject only to $15,000,000 preferred and a $1,050,000 annual dividend charge. The case at bar is not one in which after the distribution the stockholders have the same proportional interest of the same kind in essentially the same corporation.

Affirmed.

■ The separate opinion of MR. JUSTICE VAN DEVANTER, MR. JUSTICE MCREYNOLDS, MR. JUSTICE SUTHERLAND, and MR. JUSTICE BUTLER.

We think this cause falls within the doctrine of Weiss v. Stearn, 265 U.S. 242, 44 S.Ct. 490, and that the judgment below should be reversed. The practical result of the things done was but the reorganization of a going concern. The business and assets were not materially changed, and the stockholder received nothing actually severed from his original capital interest—nothing differing in substance from what he already had.

Weiss v. Stearn did not turn upon the relatively unimportant circumstance that the new and old corporations were organized under the laws of the same state, but upon the approved definition of income from capital as something severed therefrom and received by the taxpayer for his separate use and benefit. Here stockholders got nothing from the old business or assets except new statements of their undivided interests, and this, as we carefully pointed out, is not enough to create taxable income.

ILLUSTRATIVE MATERIAL

A. STATUTORY NONRECOGNITION

By the time *Marr* was decided the Internal Revenue Code already contained rudimentary provisions for nonrecognition in certain corporate reorganizations. The first such provisions were enacted in 1918 (and thus did not apply to the transaction in *Marr,* which occurred in 1916), and these early statutes were exceedingly simplistic. For example, both the 1924 and 1928 Acts defined a tax-free reorganization as follows:

"[A] merger or consolidation (including the acquisition by one corporation of at least a majority of the voting stock and at least a majority of the total number of shares of all other classes of stock of another corporation, or substantially all the properties of another corporation)." The statutory definition of reorganization was expanded and refined through the 1930's. Most of the basic principles regarding nonrecognition, however, were in place by 1928. Further changes were made when the 1954 Code was adopted, and a number of refinements have been enacted since that time.

SECTION 2. THE FUNDAMENTAL RULES GOVERNING REORGANIZATIONS

A. THE BASIC STATUTORY SCHEME

INTERNAL REVENUE CODE: Sections 1001; 354(a), (b); 356; 357; 358; 361; 362; 368 (omitting (a)(2)(F) and (a)(3)).

REGULATIONS: Section 1.368–1(a)–(c);–2(a), (f), (g).

The corporate reorganization sections cover a great variety of corporate transformations. In general these sections are designed to permit business transactions involving certain corporate acquisitions and readjustments to be carried out without a tax being incurred by the participating corporations or their shareholders at the time of the transaction. The policy rationale for according nonrecognition to these transactions is that while such acquisitions and readjustments may produce changes in the form of a business enterprise, these changes do not involve a change in the nature or character of the relation of the owners of the enterprise to that enterprise sufficient to warrant taxation of gain (generally it would have been as capital gain) or allowance of loss. Since the sections, like the other nonrecognition provisions, permit nonrecognition and hence postponement of gain, and as a corollary require nonrecognition and postponement of loss, special provisions are needed to reflect such nonrecognition in the basis of the corporate assets and stock involved.

In this Chapter the sale and purchase of a corporate business are viewed from the standpoint of the provisions permitting deferral of gain recognition in such transactions (usually referred to as "tax free" reorganizations). The transactions covered are the same in form as those considered in Chapter 11, i.e., the sale may be effected by the transfer of stock or assets of the target corporation. But the purchasing medium is different. In general, the acquiring corporation utilizes its own stock (or in some cases the stock of its parent corporation), rather than cash or notes, to make the acquisition. As a policy matter, consider whether this difference justifies such a radical difference in tax treatment, particularly where publicly traded corporations are involved. Further, within the tax free reorganization provisions themselves, small differences in form can produce significantly different tax results. Consider whether these differences are either justified or necessary. Perhaps in no other area of corporate taxation is Professor Eustice's dictum more apt: "In subchapter C, form *is* the substance."

In addition to "acquisitive" reorganizations, there are a number of other corporate readjustments that are governed by the reorganization provisions. Although the acquisition of one corporation by another may be furthered by one of these types of reorganization, more frequently they involve a realignment of ownership of a single corporation. Such nonacquisitive reorganizations are considered in subsequent chapters.

1. *Definition Of Reorganization*

The essential nonrecognition sections are § 354(a) and § 361(a). But they operate only after it has been determined that a "reorganization," a term that is narrowly defined in the Code, has occurred. Thus, reference must first be made to the definition of that term in § 368(a). Seven basic situations are covered; and these are the only situations included within the term "reorganization." Section 368(a)(1) states that the term "reorganization" "*means*"rather than "*includes*."

The reorganizations considered in this Chapter are defined as follows:

Type (A) Mergers. Section 368(a)(1)(A) describes a merger or consolidation in compliance with the state statutes permitting such transactions—as where the target corporation merges into the acquiring corporation or two corporations and consolidate into a new corporation.[1] The target and acquiring corporations may be existing parent and subsidiary corporations, or may be corporations that have not previously been related. Where the acquiring corporation acquires the assets of the target corporation in a statutory merger, the acquiring corporation may then transfer part or all of the assets to its controlled subsidiary without disqualifying the (A) reorganization. See I.R.C. § 368(a)(2)(C).

In addition, § 368(a)(2)(D) permits a subsidiary corporation, which may either be an existing or a newly-created subsidiary, to acquire the assets of the target corporation in a statutory merger between the subsidiary corporation and target corporation in which the shareholders of the target corporation receive the stock of the acquiring subsidiary's parent corporation, for "substantially all" of the properties of the target corporation if (1) the transaction would have qualified as an (A) reorganization if the merger had been directly into the parent corporation,[2] and (2) no stock

1. See Treas. Reg. § 1.368–2(b); Russell v. Commissioner, 40 T.C. 810, 822 (1963), aff'd per curiam, 345 F.2d 534 (5th Cir.1965)(failure to follow state merger laws prevented (A) reorganization).

2. The restriction that the transaction "would have qualified" as an (A) reorganization if it had involved the acquiring corporation directly does not require that the hypothetical merger would have been permissible under state merger statutes; it has reference

of the acquiring subsidiary corporation is used in the transaction. If these conditions are met, the transaction will be treated as an (A) reorganization. The § 368(a)(2)(D) transaction frequently is referred to as a "forward" triangular reorganization.

Section 368(a)(2)(E) permits a "reverse" triangular merger to qualify under certain specified conditions. Here, rather than a merger of the target corporation into the acquiring subsidiary corporation (using the stock of the parent corporation), the acquiring subsidiary corporation is merged into the target corporation, with the shareholders of the target corporation receiving stock of acquiring subsidiary's parent corporation. This transaction qualifies if (1) after the transaction the surviving target corporation holds substantially all of its properties and the properties of the acquiring subsidiary corporation (other than stock of parent corporation which may have been issued to the subsidiary corporation to be distributed in the transaction to the shareholders of the target corporation), and (2) in the transaction, the former shareholders of the target corporation exchange for voting stock of the acquiring subsidiary's parent corporation an amount of stock in the target corporation that constitutes *control* of the target corporation. If these conditions are met, the transaction will qualify as an (A) reorganization.

Under § 368(a)(2)(E), the target corporation ends up as a subsidiary of acquiring parent corporation, replacing the original subsidiary corporation. In contrast, in a § 368(a)(2)(D) transaction, the target corporation ends up as a part of the acquiring subsidiary corporation. In both cases, however, the shareholders of the target corporation become shareholders of acquiring parent corporation. The "triangular merger" leaves the shareholders of the target corporation in the same position as in the "two corporation" direct merger of the target corporation and acquiring parent corporation, but with the assets of the target corporation transferred to a subsidiary of acquiring corporation. The same result occurs under § 368(a)(2)(C), which permits the acquiring corporation to transfer the target corporation's assets to a subsidiary after the merger. In effect, all of the subparagraphs are designed to qualify as tax-free the differing merger mechanics utilized to obtain the same end result. However, the statutory development has not been an orderly one and as outlined above, there are different technical requirements to be satisfied depending on the route chosen to reach the end result. These technical differences are of such a magnitude—for example the requirement in § 368(a)(2)(E) that the acquiring corporation use its voting stock as consideration as opposed to the allowance of the use of nonvoting stock in a § 368(a)(2)(D) transaction—that it is often more useful to think of § 368(a)(2)(D) and (E) transactions as representing two separate and independent forms of corporate reorganization.

Type (B) Stock-for-Stock Exchanges. Section 368(a)(2)(B) defines as a tax-free reorganization the acquisition of stock of the target corporation in

to qualification under judicially developed restrictions on tax-free reorganizations such as "business purpose," "continuity of interest," etc. See Treas. Reg. § 1.368–2(b)(2).

exchange for the stock of the acquiring corporation if, following the exchange, the acquiring corporation is in control of the target corporation. The shareholders of the target corporation become shareholders in the acquiring corporation. They may be minority or majority shareholders, depending on the amount of stock issued by the acquiring corporation, which depends on the relative size of the target and acquiring corporations. If the target corporation is liquidated (which may be accomplished under § 332 without recognition of gain or loss), the end result is the same as either a statutory merger under (A) above or a stock-for-assets acquisition under (C), below.

In order to qualify as a (B) reorganization, after the stock-for-stock exchange, the acquiring corporation must have *control* of the target corporation, as defined by the 80 percent standard in § 368(c).[3] In addition, the acquisition of stock of the target corporation, if it is to constitute a reorganization, must be *solely* in return for *voting stock* of the acquiring corporation. No other consideration is permissible.

There is no requirement that 80 percent or more of the stock of the target corporation be acquired in one transaction. Thus, any particular acquisition is a reorganization if after that acquisition the acquiring corporation has "control" of the target corporation. Hence, while a previous acquisition of some shares of the target corporation for cash or non-voting stock, or for voting stock but without "control", would not constitute a reorganization, the earlier acquisition would not prevent a later separate acquisition for voting stock from being a reorganization if after the latter acquisition the requisite 80 percent of the shares of the target corporation are held by the acquiring corporation as a result of the several acquisitions. This acquisition of control over a period of time is called "creeping control." Even though this rule has been in the statute for nearly fifty years, its application is uncertain, in that an acquisition for cash related in time or by plan to an acquisition for stock may be treated as one transaction and prevent a reorganization, since the "acquisition" would not be solely for voting stock. Treas. Reg. § 1.368–2(c).

A transaction is not disqualified as a (B) reorganization if, after the transaction, the acquiring corporation in turn transfers the stock of the target corporation to its subsidiary. I.R.C. § 368(a)(2)(C). In addition, a controlled subsidiary corporation may acquire the stock of the target corporation solely in return for the *voting* stock of its parent corporation.

Type (C) Stock-for-Assets Exchanges. The acquisition by one corporation of substantially all the assets of another corporation—as where the acquiring corporation acquires the assets of the target corporation rather than its stock (as in (B) above)—may qualify as a reorganization under § 368(a)(1)(C). Subject to a limited exception, the acquisition must be *solely* by means of the *voting* stock of the acquiring corporation. This asset

3. "Control" is defined in § 368(c) as ownership of 80 percent of the total combined voting power of all classes of stock entitled to vote and 80 percent of the total number of shares of all other classes of stock. Rev.Rul. 59–259, 1959–2 C.B. 115, interpreted the statute to require ownership of 80 percent of each class of nonvoting stock.

acquisition is sometimes referred to as a "practical merger". Because of this analogy, the acquiring corporation must obtain all or substantially all of the target corporation's assets. The Internal Revenue Service considers a transfer of 90 percent of the net assets and 70 percent of the gross assets as clearly qualified under the "substantially all the assets" requirement.[4] Depending on the circumstances, however, lower percentages may qualify, particularly if the retained assets are used to pay creditors. Also analogous to a statutory merger, as part of the overall transaction the target corporation must be liquidated, distributing the acquiring corporation stock it receives, as well as any other assets it has retained, to the target corporation's shareholders. See I.R.C. § 368(a)(2)(G).

While the acquisition in general must be solely for the voting stock of the acquiring corporation, several exceptions allow the use of other consideration. First, the assumption by the acquiring corporation of the liabilities of the target corporation or the acquisition subject to its liabilities does not prevent the acquisition from being regarded as solely for voting stock. Second, cash or other property may be used if at least 80 percent of *all* of the assets of the target corporation are acquired for voting stock. See I.R.C. § 368(a)(2)(B). Any additional assets may be acquired for cash, other property, or other stock. However, in applying the 20 percent limitation, liabilities of the target corporation that are assumed are treated as cash.

Finally, the assets of the target corporation may be acquired by a controlled subsidiary corporation for the voting stock of its parent, the acquiring corporation. Similarly, if the acquisition was made directly by the acquiring corporation, it may then transfer the assets to a controlled subsidiary corporation without destroying the reorganization. Or if the acquisition was by a controlled subsidiary corporation, but for the voting stock of its controlling parent corporation, the acquiring subsidiary corporation may then transfer the assets to its own controlled subsidiary. See I.R.C. § 368(a)(2)(C).

Type (G) Bankruptcy Reorganization. A transfer of the assets of a corporation involved in a bankruptcy reorganization, or a receivership, foreclosure, or similar judicial proceeding in a federal or state court is a tax-free reorganization under § 368(a)(1)(G) if the stock or securities received from the insolvent corporation are distributed pursuant to a plan of reorganization in a transaction that qualifies under §§ 354, 355 or 356. Section 368(a)(1)(G) applies only to judicially supervised insolvency proceedings. Thus a nonjudicial reorganization of an insolvent corporation must qualify under one of the other provisions of § 368 in order to achieve reorganization status. But, where a transaction qualifies both as a type (G) and, as a result of its form, as another type of reorganization, for example a type (C), it will be qualified as a type (G). I.R.C. § 368(a)(3)(C).

Subparagraphs (A), (B), (C) and (G) of § 368(a)(1), together with subparagraphs (D) and (E) of § 368(a)(2), thus cover various methods by which several corporations may be combined into one ownership, e.g., a

4. See Rev.Proc. 77–37, 1977–2 C.B. 568.

chain store swallowing a corner grocery store (obtaining its assets directly under (C), or obtaining its stock under (B) and then liquidating it or keeping it alive as a subsidiary, or pursuing a statutory merger under (A)), so that the owners of the grocery are really "selling" their business for stock. While the various statutorily deferred reorganizations overlap to a considerable extent, there are differences among them that can influence the choice of the particular reorganization route to be utilized.

2. *Corporate Transferors And Transferees: Nonrecognition And Basis*

Section 368 does not govern the tax consequences of a reorganization; it merely defines a reorganization. The operative provisions that provide for nonrecognition and the attendant basis consequences appear in other sections of the Code. Section 361(a) provides for nonrecognition of gain or loss to the corporation transferring its assets, the target corporation, in the situations constituting reorganizations under § 368(a). Thus, the target corporation does not recognize gain or loss with respect to the assets transferred by it in type (A) and (C) reorganizations.[5] Section 361(a) is applicable only if the exchange is solely for stock or securities. Qualification as an (A) reorganization does not guarantee complete nonrecognition under § 361(a) since property other than stock or securities may form part of the consideration under the merger or consolidation (as long as some stock is present). If the reorganization qualifies as a type (C) reorganization, however, this condition usually is satisfied because in most cases only voting stock will be involved. An assumption of liabilities does not violate either the "solely for voting stock" or "solely for stock or securities" requirements under the express provisions of §§ 368(a)(1)(C) and 357(a). However, because in a type (C) reorganization a limited amount of property other than voting stock may pass from the acquiring corporation to the target corporation under § 368(a)(2)(B), qualification as a type (C) reorganization does not automatically guarantee compliance with § 361(a).

If *boot* (money, property or obligations not qualifying as stock or securities) is received by the target corporation, § 361(a) does not apply and § 361(b) and (c) determines the consequences to the target corporation.[6] Under § 361(b), no gain is recognized to the target corporation as a result of the receipt of the boot if the boot is transferred to its shareholders or creditors pursuant to the plan of reorganization. In a type (A) reorganization such transfer takes place automatically under the state law merger statute. In a type (C) reorganization, the requirement in § 368(a)(2)(G) that the target corporation be liquidated generally will insure the required distribution. If the boot is distributed, the target corporation recognizes no gain on receipt of the boot, but under § 361(c), it recognizes gain (but not

5. A merger under § 368(a)(1)(A) is regarded as involving such a transfer of property. See Rev.Rul. 69-6, 1969-1 C.B. 104.

6. Technically speaking, § 361(c)(2) permits the distribution of stock, rights to acquire stock, or "obligations" of "another corporation which is a party to the reorganization." The scope of the term "obligations" presumably is broader than the term "securities."

loss) upon the distribution of the boot if at the time of the distribution the boot property has a fair market value in excess of basis.

Section 358 prescribes the basis that the target corporation in type (A), (C) and (G) reorganizations takes in the stock, securities, and boot received in the exchange. Under § 358 the basis of property allowed to be received without recognition of gain or loss is the same as the basis of the property transferred, increased by gain recognized and decreased by the amount of any cash and the fair market value of other property. Because the target corporation disappears in a type (A) reorganization, and must be liquidated in a type (C) reorganization, this basis is seldom of any consequence.

Section 362(b) prescribes the basis for property received by the acquiring corporation in type (A) and (C) reorganizations. Both the acquiring and target corporations end up with the original basis of the target corporation (aside from adjustments where boot is involved), so that possibilities of two gains or two losses exist. While § 362(b), transferring the target corporation's basis in its property to the acquiring corporation, adds to that basis any gain recognized to the target corporation on the transfer, as indicated above, the reorganization provisions allow little room for gain to be recognized to the target corporation. By virtue of the second clause of its second sentence, § 362(b) also applies to carry over to the acquiring corporation the basis of the target shareholders in stock acquired in a type (B) reorganization. If a reorganization does not exist, then the general rule of "cost" applies to fix the basis for the acquiring corporation. Treas. Reg. § 1.1032–1(d).

3. *Shareholders And Security Holders: Extent Of Nonrecognition And Basis*

Sections 354 and 356 control taxation of the shareholders in acquisitive reorganization transactions. Section 358(a) prescribes exchanged basis rules for the shareholders in § 354 and § 356 exchanges.

In type (A), (B), and (C) reorganizations, the shareholders of the target corporation are exchanging their target corporation stock for stock of the acquiring corporation. In type (A) and (B) reorganizations, the exchange is made between the target corporation's shareholders and the acquiring corporation; in a type (C) reorganization, the exchange is made upon the liquidation of the target corporation. The acquiring and target corporations are both parties to the reorganization under § 368(b). In type (A) and (C) reorganizations, the target corporation's shareholders also may receive securities of the acquiring corporation (although the receipt of securities in a type (C) reorganization is limited by § 368(a)(2)(B)). These exchanges are covered by § 354 and generally any gain or loss realized by the shareholders will not be recognized.

Section 354(a) applies only to an exchange *solely* for stock or securities, so that the presence of boot prevents its application. Suppose, however, that the target corporation transfers its assets to the acquiring corporation for stock of the acquiring corporation and cash in a transaction that qualifies as a (C) reorganization by virtue of § 368(a)(2)(B). Pursuant to

§ 361(b), the target corporation avoids recognition of gain by distributing the cash. This distribution, however, constitutes boot to the distributee shareholders. When the target corporation liquidates, as is required to qualify the transaction as a (C) reorganization, the accompanying exchange by the shareholders of their target corporation stock for the acquiring corporation stock is not accorded complete nonrecognition under § 354(a). Section 356(a)(1) operates to provide partial nonrecognition; any realized gain is recognized but only to the extent of the boot. Loss may be not recognized.

Determination of the gain that must be recognized under the rule of § 356(a)(1) is illustrated as follows. Suppose that in a type (A) reorganization (statutory merger) individual A, a shareholder of the target corporation, surrendered shares of stock of the target corporation having a basis to A of $100 in exchange for $40 of cash and shares of the acquiring corporation having a fair market value of $110. A realizes a gain of $50, but only $40, an amount equal to the cash boot, must be recognized. Under § 358(a), A's basis in the acquiring corporation stock would be only $100, thus accounting for the $10 of realized but unrecognized gain. If A's basis for the target corporation stock were $120, then A would realize a gain of only $30, all of which would be recognized. The receipt of the other $10 of cash "tax-free" would be taken into account by reducing the basis of the acquiring corporation stock received in the exchange from $120 to $110 pursuant to § 358(a)(1)(A).

In all of these situations, the transfer of boot to shareholders of the target corporation constitutes a distribution by a corporation to its shareholders. A safeguard is necessary to insure that distributions which in substance are dividends rather than additional consideration for the exchange of stock will be appropriately taxed. Section 356(a)(2) provides generally that if the distribution of boot pursuant to the plan of reorganization has the *effect of the distribution of a dividend*, the amount of the gain shall be taxed as a dividend and not as part of the exchange transaction. The resemblance to § 302 is apparent, but there are some differences. This provision is considered at page 567.

An exchange of securities other than stock gives rise to boot under § 354(a)(2) if the corporation distributes securities with a principal amount in excess of the securities received in return. In such a case the amount of the boot as determined under § 356(d) is the fair market value of the excess principal amount, which, due to the operation of the OID rules, in most cases equals the excess principal amount.[7]

Section 357 does not apply to § 356(a), so that if any liabilities of the shareholders of the target corporation are assumed by the acquiring corporation, the liabilities are boot. If the initial corporate transaction involves a situation that will qualify as a reorganization only if the exchange is solely for voting stock, such as a type (B) reorganization, then the presence of

7. Note that application of the original issue discount rules can produce a principal amount that differs from the face amount of the bond.

boot will prevent a reorganization and §§ 354(a) and 356 will not be applicable at all.

If §§ 354 and 356 do not apply, then the distributions are considered under §§ 301, 302 and 331. Sections 354 and 356 thus operate as exceptions to these other provisions respecting corporate distributions and exchanges, though the other sections do not contain any explicit references to the reorganization exceptions.

B. THE CONTINUITY OF INTEREST REQUIREMENT

REGULATIONS: Sections 1.368–1(a), (b), (e), –2(a). See also 1.338–2(c)(3).

TEMPORARY REGULATIONS: Section 1.368–1T(e)(a)(ii)(A) and (B).

Le Tulle v. Scofield

Supreme Court of the United States, 1940.
308 U.S. 415.

■ MR. JUSTICE ROBERTS delivered the opinion of the court.

* * *

The Gulf Coast Irrigation Company was the owner of irrigation properties. Petitioner was its sole stockholder. He personally owned certain lands and other irrigation properties. November 4, 1931, the Irrigation Company, the Gulf Coast Water Company, and the petitioner, entered into an agreement which recited that the petitioner owned all of the stock of the Irrigation Company; described the company's properties, and stated that, prior to conveyance to be made pursuant to the contract, the Irrigation Company would be the owner of certain other lands and irrigation properties. These other lands and properties were those which the petitioner individually owned. The contract called for a conveyance of all the properties owned, and to be owned, by the Irrigation Company for $50,000 in cash and $750,000 in bonds of the Water Company, payable serially over the period January 1, 1933, to January 1, 1944. The petitioner joined in this agreement as a guarantor of the title of the Irrigation Company and for the purpose of covenanting that he would not personally enter into the irrigation business within a fixed area during a specified period after the execution of the contract. Three days later, at a special meeting of stockholders of the Irrigation Company, the proposed reorganization was approved, the minutes stating that the taxpayer, "desiring also to reorganize his interest in the properties," had consented to be a party to the reorganization. The capital stock of the Irrigation Company was increased and thereupon the taxpayer subscribed for the new stock and paid for it by conveyance of his individual properties.

The contract between the two corporations was carried out November 18, with the result that the Water Company became owner of all the properties then owned by the Irrigation Company including the property theretofore owned by the petitioner individually. Subsequently all of its assets, including the bonds received from the Water Company, were distributed to the petitioner. The company was then dissolved. The petitioner and his wife filed a tax return * * * in which they reported no gain as a result of the receipt of the liquidating dividend from the Irrigation Company. The latter reported no gain for the taxable year in virtue of its receipt of bonds and cash from the Water Company. The Commissioner of Internal Revenue assessed additional taxes against the * * * taxpayers, by reason of the receipt of the liquidating dividend, and against the petitioner as transferee of the Irrigation Company's assets in virtue of the gain realized by the company on the sale of its property. The tax was paid and claims for refund were filed. * * * [The taxpayer] alleged that the transaction constituted a tax-exempt reorganization as defined by the Revenue Act. The * * * causes were * * * tried by the District Court without a jury. The respondent's contention that the transaction amounted merely to a sale of assets by the petitioner and the Irrigation Company and did not fall within the statutory definition of a tax-free reorganization was overruled by the District Court and judgment was entered for the petitioner.

* * *

The Circuit Court of Appeals concluded that, as the Water Company acquired substantially all the properties of the Irrigation Company, there was a merger of the latter within the literal language of the statute, but held that, in the light of the construction this Court has put upon the statute, the transaction would not be a reorganization unless the transferor retained a definite and substantial interest in the affairs of the transferee. It thought this requirement was satisfied by the taking of the bonds of the Water Company, and, therefore, agreed with the District Court that a reorganization had been consummated. * * *

[Ed.: The Circuit Court then reversed the District Court as to part of the petitioner's tax liability on grounds that had not been raised by the parties. The Circuit Court concluded that the petitioner was taxable on the gain attributable to the transfer of his individually owned assets to the Irrigation Company for transfer to the Water Company. The petitioner sought to overturn the Circuit Court decision on this ground. The Commissioner, having won in the Circuit Court, did not seek certiorari.]

We find it unnecessary to consider petitioner's contention that the Circuit Court of Appeals erred in deciding the case on a ground not raised by the pleadings, not before the trial court, not suggested or argued in the Circuit Court of Appeals, and one as to which the petitioner had never had the opportunity to present his evidence, since we are of opinion that the transaction did not amount to a reorganization and that, therefore, the petitioner cannot complain, as the judgment must be affirmed on the ground that no tax-free reorganization was effected within the meaning of the statute.

Section 112 (I) provides, so far as material:

"(1) The term 'reorganization' means (A) a merger or consolidation (including the acquisition by one corporation of at least a majority of the voting stock and at least a majority of the total number of shares of all other classes of stock of another corporation, or substantially all the properties of another corporation) * * * "

As the court below properly stated, the section is not to be read literally, as denominating the transfer of all the assets of one company for what amounts to a cash consideration given by the other a reorganization. We have held that where the consideration consists of cash and short term notes the transfer does not amount to a reorganization within the true meaning of the statute, but is a sale upon which gain or loss must be reckoned.[3] We have said that the statute was not satisfied unless the transferor retained a substantial stake in the enterprise and such a stake was thought to be retained where a large proportion of the consideration was in common stock of the transferee,[4] or where the transferor took cash and the entire issue of preferred stock of the transferee corporation.[5] And, where the consideration is represented by a substantial proportion of stock, and the balance in bonds, the total consideration received is exempt from tax under § 112 (b)(4) and 112 (g).[6]

In applying our decision in the Pinellas case the courts have generally held that receipt of long term bonds as distinguished from short term notes constitutes the retention of an interest in the purchasing corporation. There has naturally been some difficulty in classifying the securities involved in various cases.[7]

We are of opinion that the term of the obligations is not material. Where the consideration is wholly in the transferee's bonds, or part cash and part such bonds, we think it cannot be said that the transferor retains any proprietary interest in the enterprise. On the contrary, he becomes a creditor of the transferee; and we do not think that the fact referred to by the Circuit Court of Appeals, that the bonds were secured solely by the assets transferred and that, upon default, the bondholder would retake only the property sold, changes his status from that of a creditor to one having a proprietary stake, within the purview of the statute.

We conclude that the Circuit Court of Appeals was in error in holding that, as respects any of the property transferred to the Water Company, the transaction was other than a sale or exchange upon which gain or loss must be reckoned in accordance with the provisions of the revenue act dealing with the recognition of gain or loss upon a sale or exchange.

Had the respondent sought and been granted certiorari the petitioner's tax liability would, in the view we have expressed, be substantially in-

3. Pinellas Ice & Cold Storage Co. v. Commissioner, 287 U.S. 462.

4. Helvering v. Minnesota Tea Co., 296 U.S. 378.

5. Nelson Co. v. Helvering, 296 U.S. 374.

6. 45 Stat. 816, 818. See Helvering v. Watts, 296 U.S. 387.

7. Worcester Salt Co. v. Commissioner, 75 F.2d 251; Lilienthal v. Commissioner, 80 F.2d 411, 413; Burnham v. Commissioner, 86 F.2d 776; Commissioner v. Kitselman, 89 F.2d 458; Commissioner v. Freund, 98 F.2d 201; * * * L. & E. Stirn, Inc. v. Commissioner, 107 F.2d 390.

creased over the amount found due by the Circuit Court of Appeals. Since the respondent has not drawn into question so much of the judgment as exempts from taxation gain to the irrigation Company arising from transfer of its assets owned by it on and prior to November 4, 1931, and the part of the liquidating dividend attributable thereto, we cannot afford him relief from that portion of the judgment which was adverse to him.

* * *

The judgment of the Circuit Court of Appeals is affirmed * * *.

ILLUSTRATIVE MATERIAL

A. HISTORICAL BACKGROUND

Le Tulle v. Scofield is one of a long line of Supreme Court decisions developing the "continuity of interest" doctrine. The first pronouncement by the Supreme Court regarding the requisite consideration in a reorganization was in Pinellas Ice & Cold Storage Co. v. Commissioner, 287 U.S. 462 (1933). In that case, on December 15, 1926, the taxpayer corporation transferred all of its assets to the acquiring corporation in consideration of $400,000 cash (which was used to pay off debts) and promissory notes for $500,000, due on January 31, 1927, $250,000, due on March 1, 1927, and $250,000, due on April 1, 1927. As the notes were paid, the taxpayer distributed the proceeds to its shareholders in liquidation.

The Commissioner asserted that the taxpayer was required to recognize a gain on the sale of its assets, but the taxpayer contended that the transaction was a "reorganization" as defined in the Revenue Act of 1926, and that, accordingly, the predecessor of § 361 provided for nonrecognition of the gain. Notwithstanding that the statutory provision imposed no requirements or limits on the nature of the consideration required to qualify the transaction as a reorganization, the Court rejected the taxpayer's argument: "[T]he mere purchase for money of the assets of one company by another is beyond the evident purpose of the provision, and has no real semblance to a merger or consolidation. Certainly, we think that to be within the exemption the seller must acquire an interest in the affairs of the purchasing company more definite than that incident to ownership of its short-term purchase-money notes." (470).

In Helvering v. Minnesota Tea Co., 296 U.S. 378 (1935), a transfer of assets for common stock (value, $712,195.90, amounting to 7 ½ percent of the transferee's outstanding stock) and cash ($426,842.52) was considered a reorganization. After referring to the *Pinellas* statement that an "interest" must be acquired in the transferee, the Court said:

"And we now add that this interest must be definite and material; it must represent a substantial part of the value of the thing transferred. This much is necessary in order that the result accomplished may genuinely partake of the nature of merger or consolidation. * * *

"The transaction here was no sale, but partook of the nature of a reorganization, in that the seller acquired a definite and substantial interest in the purchaser.

"True it is that the relationship of the taxpayer to the assets conveyed was substantially changed, but this is not inhibited by the statute. Also, a large part of the consideration was cash. This, we think, is permissible so long as the taxpayer received an interest in the affairs of the transferee which represented a material part of the value of the transferred assets." (385–6)

John A. Nelson Co. v. Helvering, 296 U.S. 374 (1935), found the requisite continuity of interest where assets were transferred for $2,000,000 in cash and preferred stock worth approximately $1,250,000. The preferred stock was non-voting in the absence of a default in dividends and presumably non-participating. The Court stated:

"The owner of preferred stock is not without substantial interest in the affairs of the issuing corporation, although denied voting rights. The statute does not require participation in the management of the purchaser; nor does it demand that the conveying corporation be dissolved."

In its most recent pronouncement in this area, Paulsen v. Commissioner, 469 U.S. 131 (1985), the Supreme Court held that an exchange of stock in a savings and loan association for certificates of deposit in a mutual savings and loan (where the certificates of deposit represented ownership interests in the mutual savings and loan association) lacked the requisite continuity of interest. The court concluded that the debt aspects of the certificates of deposit, which permitted withdrawal of cash after one year, outweighed their equity characteristics and that the certificates of deposit were cash equivalents.[8] The Court acknowledged that when two mutual associations merge an exchange of interests in deposits in one mutual savings for an equivalent interest in the other, notwithstanding the slight equity interest reflected in the shares, will be treated as a reorganization because the shares received are essentially equivalent to the shares given up as long as the cash value of the shares on each side of the exchange is the same. Rev. Rul. 78–286, 1978–2 C.B. 145, reaches this result.

As a result of these opinions, an ownership interest cannot be turned into a creditor interest, though long-term in nature, and still have the exchange qualify as a reorganization. *A fortiori*, the ownership interest cannot be turned into cash or its equivalent in the form of notes or other evidences of a short-lived creditor status. See *Le Tulle v. Scofield*, supra. An equity interest in the transferee thus has to be obtained by the transferor

8. In Estate of Silverman v. Commissioner, 98 T.C. 54 (1992), the taxpayers exchanged stock in a state chartered savings and loan association for certificates of deposit in the acquiring federally chartered mutual savings and loan association. The certificates of deposit could not be withdrawn for six years and were subject to limitations on transfer. After *Paulsen* was decided, the taxpayers filed an amended return reporting their gain on the sale of the stock using the installment sales method under § 453. The Tax Court rejected the Commissioner's argument that the certificates of deposit were equivalent to cash and allowed the taxpayers to report gain on the installment method.

of the property. The equity interest obtained, moreover, has to be substantial, so that a non-equity interest that is too extensive might disqualify the exchange. But the nature of the equity interest can be either that of a common stockholder or that of a preferred stockholder, whether voting or non-voting. Obviously, the line drawn between preferred stock and bonds may in some instances come very close to one of form since the participation in earnings and assets and effective control can be drafted nearly alike for both types of instruments. For example, in Roebling v. Commissioner, 143 F.2d 810 (3d Cir.1944), the target corporation had leased all its properties to the acquiring corporation for 900 years. As a result of a merger, the former shareholders of the target corporation received 100 year bonds of the acquiring corporation that paid annual interest equal to the amount previously paid as rent. The court rejected the taxpayer's argument that the former shareholders' interests after the merger were substantially equivalent to their interests before the merger and applied *Le Tulle v. Scofield* to find that there was not a reorganization.

B. QUANTITATIVE ASPECTS

The statutory provisions for type (B) and type (C) reorganizations provide for continuity of interest with requirements that the stock or assets of the target corporation be acquired *solely* for voting stock. There are no specific statutory requirements concerning continuity of interest in an (A) reorganization. The subjective standards developed by the Supreme Court require an exploration of the sufficiency of equity consideration in specific cases.

In Southwest Natural Gas Company v. Commissioner, 189 F.2d 332 (5th Cir.1951), continuity of interest was held to be lacking in a statutory merger in a situation in which those shareholders of the transferor (target) corporation who chose to receive some stock in the merger had received about 16 percent of the common stock of the acquiring corporation, but such interest was worth only about $5,500 out of a total consideration of about $660,000 in bonds, cash, assumptions of liabilities, and stock. However, prior to the merger a group that owned 35 percent of the common stock of the target corporation also held 85 percent of the acquiring corporation's common stock and after the merger this group owned 88 percent of the acquiring corporation's stock. Thus, an underlying equity interest in the acquiring corporation actually existed, as a dissent pointed out, though "control" did not exist because 80 percent of the preferred stock was not held by the group.

The opinion in *Southwest Natural Gas* phrased the continuity of interest test as follows:

"Where no precise formula has been expressed for determining whether there has been retention of the requisite interest, it seems clear that the requirement of continuity of interest consistent with the statutory intent is not fulfilled in the absence of a showing: (1) that the transferor corporation or its shareholders retained a substantial proprietary stake in the enterprise represented by a material interest in the affairs of the transferee corporation, and, (2) that such retained interest represents a substantial part of the value of the property transferred."

Taken literally, the first requirement would in general depend on the relative size of the two corporations that are merged. This measure of the *quantitative* aspect is not stressed in the cases and does not appear to be a significant factor in Internal Revenue Service policy.

The focus instead is primarily on the second factor, the relation between the value of the stock received and the value of the equity interest in the target corporation. Although the case law has not established a specific minimum percentage of the total consideration which must be received in the form of stock of the acquiring corporation, the Service will grant advance rulings in type (A) reorganizations under the following conditions:

"The 'continuity of interest' requirement of section 1.368–1(b) of the Income Tax Regulations is satisfied if there is a continuing interest through stock ownership in the acquiring or transferee corporation (or a corporation in 'control' thereof within the meaning of § 368(c) of the Code) on the part of the former shareholders of the acquired or transferor corporation which is equal in value, as of the effective date of the reorganization, to at least 50 percent of the value of all of the formerly outstanding stock of the acquired or transferor corporation as of the same date. It is not necessary that each shareholder of the acquired or transferor corporation receive in the exchange stock of the acquiring or transferee corporation in 'control' thereof, which is equal in value to at least 50 percent of the value of his former stock interest in the acquired or transferor corporation, so long as one or more of the shareholders of the acquired or transferor corporation have a continuing interest through stock ownership in the acquiring or transferee corporation (or a corporation in 'control' thereof) which is, in the aggregate, equal in value to at least 50 percent of the value of all of the formerly outstanding stock of the acquired or transferor corporation." Rev.Proc. 77–37, § 3.2, 1977–2 C.B. 568.

Note, however, that in John A. Nelson Co. v. Helvering, 296 U.S. 374 (1935), page 530, the Supreme Court found the continuity of interest requirement to have been satisfied where only 38.46 percent of the consideration was stock of the acquiring corporation. See also Kass v. Commissioner, 60 T.C. 218 (1973), aff'd by order, 491 F.2d 749 (3d Cir.1974) (16 percent insufficient); Yoc Heating Corp. v. Commissioner, 61 T.C. 168 (1973) (15 percent insufficient); Civic Center Finance Co. v. Kuhl, 83 F.Supp. 251 (E.D.Wis.1948), aff'd per curiam, 177 F.2d 706 (7th Cir.1949) (participation by 40 percent of the former stockholders was held insufficient to provide continuity of interest); Western Mass. Theatres, Inc. v. Commissioner, 236 F.2d 186 (1st Cir.1956) (67 percent participation was held sufficient in a bankruptcy reorganization).

Rev.Rul. 66–224, 1966–2 C.B. 114, held that the continuity of interest requirement is to be applied with reference to the aggregate consideration received by the entire group of the shareholders of the acquired corporation. Thus, for example, if A, B, C, and D each owns 25 percent of the stock of the target corporation, and the target corporation is merged into the acquiring corporation in consideration of $100,000 cash and $100,000 worth of the acquiring corporation stock, the transaction will qualify as a type (A) reorganization regardless of how the consideration is distributed among A, B, C, and D; thus A and B could receive only cash while C and D received only stock. The gain attributable to the cash boot that must be recognized by each shareholder, however, will be determined individually.

Suppose that the target corporation is insolvent so that the shareholders receive little or no equity interest in the acquiring corporation, while the creditors of the insolvent target corporation receive an equity interest in the acquiring corporation. Has the continuity of interest requirement been satisfied? In Helvering v. Alabama Asphaltic Limestone Co., 315 U.S. 179 (1942), the Supreme Court held that a transfer of assets pursuant to which creditors of a bankrupt concern became the controlling stockholders of a new corporation provided the requisite continuity of interest. Although the old continuity of proprietary interest was broken when the creditors took steps to enforce their demands against the insolvent concern, by such action they stepped into the shoes of the stockholders and hence continuity was present on the subsequent exchange. See also Norman Scott, Inc. v. Commissioner, 48 T.C. 598 (1967) (statutory merger between the surviving corporation and its insolvent sister corporation qualified as an (A) reorganization; the continuity of interest test was satisfied since the principal shareholder-creditors of the insolvent corporation received stock in the surviving corporation). The special aspects of reorganizations involving insolvent corporations are considered at page 626.

C. "CONTINUITY OF INTEREST" AND "PARTY TO A REORGANIZATION"

In Groman v. Commissioner, 302 U.S. 82 (1937), P Corporation desired to acquire T Corporation. Accordingly, P Corporation organized S Corporation, and held all of its common stock. The shareholders of T Corporation transferred their T stock to S Corporation in return for preferred stock of S Corporation, preferred stock of P Corporation, and cash. S Corporation then liquidated T Corporation. In effect, the assets of T Corporation went to a newly-formed subsidiary of P Corporation. The Court held that the preferred stock of P Corporation was not stock in a "party to a reorganization" and hence was boot received by the T Corporation shareholders. The Court relied on the continuity of interest doctrine and stated that since P Corporation had not received the T Corporation assets, the possession of the P stock by the T shareholders did not represent a continuing interest in those assets. This case was followed in Helvering v. Bashford, 302 U.S. 454 (1938), where there was a transitory ownership of the T Corporation stock by P Corporation but it was then immediately transferred by P Corporation to its subsidiary S Corporation. The T Corporation shareholders received some common stock of S Corporation and some preferred and common stock of P Corporation. Since the ownership of the T stock by P Corporation was only transitory and the transfer to S Corporation was part of a plan, the transitory ownership did not serve to distinguish the *Groman* case.

In the *Groman* and *Bashford* cases the former stockholders had divided their ownership—they now owned some stock (preferred stock in the *Groman* case, minority common stock in the *Bashford* case) in the corporation to which the assets had been transferred and also some stock (preferred in the *Groman* case, preferred and minority common in the *Bashford* case) in the parent corporation of the corporation to which the assets had been transferred. They were thus free to dispose of one interest without the other. Suppose, however, that the assets had gone to a wholly-owned subsidiary of the parent and the former owners had received only stock in the parent? The courts held that the results were the same: stock of the parent does not provide continuity of interest and make the parent a party to the reorganization where the assets go to another corporation even though it is a wholly owned subsidiary of the parent and even though a reorganization would obviously be present if the assets had gone to the parent. This was also the result under some decisions where the assets were first transferred to the parent and then by it transferred to the subsidiary if the latter step was contemplated as part of the plan of reorganization. Anheuser–Busch, Inc. v. Helvering, 115 F.2d 662 (8th Cir.1940); Hedden v. Commissioner, 105 F.2d 311 (3d Cir.1939); Mellon v. Commissioner, 12 T.C. 90 (1949)(NA), other issues aff'd 184 F.2d 157 (3d Cir.1950); Campbell v. Commissioner, 15 T.C. 312 (1950)(A).

Subsequent statutory developments have changed these results to some extent. Section 368(a)(2)(C) permits the acquiring corporation to drop assets of the target corporation down to a controlled subsidiary following the merger. As long as there is no splitting of interests, as was present in the *Groman* and *Bashford* cases themselves, § 368(a)(2)(D) defines as a reorganization a "triangular merger," a merger in which the shareholders of the acquired corporation receive stock of the acquiring corporation's parent; and § 368(a)(2)(E) permits "reverse triangular mergers" subject to several restrictive conditions. Triangular acquisitions are considered in detail at page 617.

Rules and Regulations, Department of the Treasury, Internal Revenue Service, Continuity of Interest and Continuity of Business Enterprise

T.D. 8760, 1998–14 I.R.B. 4.

Explanation of Provisions

The Internal Revenue Code of 1986 provides general nonrecognition treatment for reorganizations specifically described in section 368. In addition to complying with the statutory requirements and certain other requirements, a transaction generally must satisfy the continuity of interest requirement and the continuity of business enterprise requirement.

A. Continuity of Interest

The purpose of the continuity of interest requirement is to prevent transactions that resemble sales from qualifying for nonrecognition of gain or loss available to corporate reorganizations. The final regulations provide that the COI requirement is satisfied if in substance a substantial part of the value of the proprietary interest in the target corporation (T) is preserved in the reorganization. A proprietary interest in T is preserved if, in a potential reorganization, it is exchanged for a proprietary interest in the issuing corporation (P), it is exchanged by the acquiring corporation for a direct interest in the T enterprise, or it otherwise continues as a proprietary interest in T. The issuing corporation means the acquiring corporation (as the term is used in section 368(a)), except that, in determining whether a reorganization qualifies as a triangular reorganization (as defined in § 1.358–6(b)(2)), the issuing corporation means the corporation in control of the acquiring corporation. However, a proprietary interest in T is not preserved if, in connection with the potential reorganization, it is acquired by P for consideration other than P stock, or P stock furnished in exchange for a proprietary interest in T if the potential reorganization is redeemed. All facts and circumstances must be considered in determining whether, in substance, a proprietary interest in T is preserved.

Rationale for the COI Regulations

The * * * regulations permit former T shareholders to sell P stock received in a potential reorganization to third parties without causing the reorganization to fail to satisfy the COI requirement. Some commentators have questioned whether the regulations are consistent with existing authorities.

The COI requirement was applied first to reorganization provisions that did not specify that P exchange a proprietary interest in P for a proprietary interest in T. Supreme Court cases imposed the COI requirement to further Congressional intent that tax-free status be accorded only to transactions where P exchanges a substantial proprietary interest in P for a proprietary interest in T held by the T shareholders rather than to transactions resembling sales. See LeTulle v. Scofield, 308 U.S. 415 (1940); Helvering v. Minnesota Tea Co., 296 U.S. 378 (1935); Pinellas Ice & Cold Storage Co. v. Commissioner, 287 U.S. 462 (1933). See also Cortland Specialty Co. v. Commissioner, 60 F.2d 937 (2d Cir.1932), cert. denied 288 U.S. 599 (1933).

None of the Supreme Court cases establishing the COI requirement addressed the issue of whether sales by former T shareholders of P stock received in exchange for T stock in the potential reorganization cause the COI requirement to fail to be satisfied. Since then, however, some courts have premised decisions on the assumption that sales of P stock received in exchange for T stock in the potential reorganization may cause the COI requirement to fail to be satisfied. McDonald's Restaurants of Illinois, Inc. v. Commissioner, 688 F.2d 520 (7th Cir.1982); Penrod v. Commissioner, 88 T.C. 1415 (1987); Heintz v. Commissioner, 25 T.C. 132 (1955), nonacq.,

1958–2 C.B. 9 * * * . The apparent focus of these cases is on whether the T shareholders intended on the date of the potential reorganization to sell their P stock and the degree, if any, to which P facilitates the sale. Based on an intensive inquiry into nearly identical facts, some of these cases held that as a result of the subsequent sale the potential reorganization did not satisfy the COI requirement; others held that satisfaction of the COI requirement was not adversely affected by the subsequent sale. The IRS and Treasury Department have concluded that the law as reflected in these cases does not further the principles of reorganization treatment and is difficult for both taxpayers and the IRS to apply consistently.

Therefore, consistent with Congressional intent and the Supreme Court precedent which distinguishes between sales and reorganizations, the final regulations focus the COI requirement generally on exchanges between the T shareholders and P. Under this approach, sales of P stock by former T shareholders generally are disregarded.

The final regulations will greatly enhance administrability in this area by both taxpayers and the government. The regulations will prevent "whipsaw" of the government, such as where the former T shareholders treat the transaction as a tax-free reorganization, and P later disavows reorganization treatment to step up its basis in the T assets based on the position that sales of P stock by the former T shareholders did not satisfy the COI requirement. See, e.g., *McDonald's Restaurants*, supra. In addition, this approach will prevent unilateral sales of P stock by former majority T shareholders from adversely affecting the section 354 nonrecognition treatment expected by former minority T shareholders.

Dispositions of T Stock

* * * The IRS and Treasury Department believe that issues concerning the COI requirement raised by dispositions of T stock before a potential reorganization correspond to those raised by subsequent dispositions of P stock furnished in exchange for T stock in the potential reorganization. * * * [T]he final regulations apply the rationale of the proposed COI regulations to transactions occurring both prior to and after a potential reorganization. Cf. J.E. Seagram Corp. v. Commissioner, 104 T.C. 75 (1995) (sales of T stock prior to a potential reorganization do not affect COI if not part of the plan of reorganization). The final regulations provide that, for COI purposes, a mere disposition of T stock prior to a potential reorganization to persons not related to P is disregarded and a mere disposition of P stock received in a potential reorganization to persons not related to P is disregarded. But see § 1.368–1T(e)(1)(ii)(A) and (B).

In soliciting comments on the effect upon COI of dispositions of T stock prior to a potential reorganization, the preamble to the proposed COI regulations specifically requests comments on King Enterprises, Inc. v. United States, 418 F.2d 511 (Ct.Cl.1969) (COI requirement satisfied where, pursuant to a plan, P acquires the T stock for 51 percent P stock and 49 percent debt and cash, and T merges upstream into P), and Yoc Heating Corp. v. Commissioner, 61 T.C. 168 (1973) (COI requirement not satisfied where, pursuant to a plan, P acquires 85 percent of the T stock for cash and notes, and T merges into P's newly formed subsidiary with minority shareholders receiving cash). Consistent with these cases, where the step transaction doctrine applies to link T stock purchases with later acquisitions of T, the final regulations provide that a proprietary interest in T is not preserved if, in connection with the potential reorganization, it is acquired by P for consideration other than P stock. Whether a stock acquisition is made in connection with a potential reorganization will be determined based on the facts and circumstances of each case. See generally § 1.368–1(a). This regulation does not address the effect, if any, of section 338 on corporate transactions (except for conforming changes to § 1.338–2(c)(3)). See generally § 1.338–2(c)(3) (certain tax effects of a qualified stock purchase without a section 338 election on the post-acquisition elimination of T).

Related Person Rule

* * * The final regulations provide * * * that a proprietary interest in T is not preserved if, in connection with a potential reorganization, a person related (as defined below) to P acquires, with consideration other than a proprietary interest in P, T stock or P stock furnished in exchange for a proprietary interest in T in the potential reorganization. The IRS and Treasury Department believe, however, that certain related party acquisitions preserve a proprietary interest in T and therefore, the rule includes an exception to the related party rule. Under this exception, a proprietary interest in T is preserved to the extent those persons who were the direct or indirect owners of T prior to the potential reorganization maintain a direct or indirect proprietary interest in P. See, e.g., Rev. Rul. 84–30 (1984–1 C.B. 114).

* * * [The] regulations adopt a * * * related person definition which has two components in order to address two separate concerns.

First, the IRS and Treasury Department were concerned that acquisitions of T or P stock by a member of P's affiliated group were no different in substance from an acquisition or redemption by P, because of the existence of various provisions in the Code that permit members to transfer funds to other members without significant tax consequences. Accordingly, § 1.368–1(e)(3)(i)(A) includes as related persons corporations that are members of the same affiliated group under section 1504, without regard to the exceptions in section 1504(b).

Second, because the final regulations take into account whether, in substance, P has redeemed the stock it exchanged for T stock in the potential reorganization, the final regulations treat two corporations as related persons if a purchase of the stock of one corporation by another corporation would be treated as a distribution in redemption of the stock of the first corporation under section 304(a)(2) (determined without regard to § 1.1502–80(b)).

Because the final regulations focus generally on the consideration P exchanges, related persons do not include individual or other noncorporate shareholders. * * *

T Stock Not Acquired in Connection With a Potential Reorganization

* * * The final regulations provide that a proprietary interest in T is preserved if it is exchanged by the acquiring corporation (which may or may not also be P) for a direct interest in the T enterprise, or otherwise continues as a proprietary interest in T.

Redemptions of T Stock or Extraordinary Distributions With Respect to T Stock

In addition to the final regulations, the IRS and Treasury Department are contemporaneously issuing temporary regulations and proposed regulations cross-referencing the temporary regulations published elsewhere in this issue of the Federal Register with the same effective date as these final regulations. The temporary and proposed regulations provide that a proprietary interest in T is not preserved if, in connection with a potential reorganization, it is redeemed or acquired by a person related to T, or to the extent that, prior to and in connection with a potential reorganization, an extraordinary distribution is made with respect to it.

Transactions Following a Qualified Stock Purchase

As stated above, these final regulations focus the COI requirement generally on exchanges between the T shareholders and P. Accordingly, the language of § 1.338–2(c)(3) is conformed to these final COI regulations to treat the stock of T acquired by the purchasing corporation in the qualified stock purchase as though it was not acquired in connection with the transfer of the T assets.

* * *

ILLUSTRATIVE MATERIAL

A. CONTINUITY OF INTEREST AND HISTORIC SHAREHOLDERS

As discussed in T.D. 8760, prior to 1998, usually at the Commissioner's behest, a number of decisions imposed the requirement that continuity of interest be tested with respect to the "historic" shareholders of the acquired corporation, not those persons who owned the stock of the acquired corporation immediately before the merger. In Superior Coach of Florida, Inc. v. Commissioner, 80 T.C. 895 (1983), individuals A and B, the majority shareholders of P Corporation, purchased all of the stock of T Corporation from its shareholders, who were unrelated to A or B. Immediately thereafter, T Corporation was merged into P Corporation. To prevent P Corporation from utilizing T Corporation's net operating loss carryovers under § 381 and a prior version of § 382, the Commissioner argued that the merger was not a reorganization under § 368(a)(1)(A) because there was no continuity of interest. The court held for the Commissioner, stating that in order for shareholders to be considered historic shareholders the acquired corporation's shares must be "old and cold" in their hands. A contrary result was reached in J.E. Seagram Corp. v. Commissioner, 104 T.C. 75 (1995). In that case, as a result of competing tender offers by several different corporate suitors seeking to acquire Conoco, 78 percent of the stock of Conoco changed hands in purchase and sale transactions prior to Conoco's merger into DuPont. Nevertheless, 54 percent of the consideration provided by DuPont was in the form of stock. The Tax Court held that the pre-reorganization sales and purchases of Conoco stock did not vitiate the continuity of interest requirement, the court thereby largely abandoning any "historic shareholder" continuity of interest requirement.

In adopting current Treas. Reg. § 1.368–1(e), the Treasury rejected the *Superior Coach* approach in favor of the *J.E. Seagram* approach. But if the acquiring corporation (or a related corporation) itself purchases stock of the target corporation prior to the reorganization, as noted in T.D. 8760, vestiges of the historic shareholder continuity of interest requirement come into play.

In Kass v. Commissioner, 60 T.C. 218 (1973), aff'd by order, 491 F.2d 749 (3d Cir.1974), individuals A and B, minority shareholders in the target corporation, desired to obtain control of the target corporation. To accomplish this goal, A and B organized the acquiring corporation and contributed their target corporation stock to the acquiring corporation. As a result, the acquiring corporation held 10.23 percent of the stock of the target corporation. Shortly thereafter, the acquiring corporation purchased for cash an additional 83.95 percent of the stock of the target corporation. Finally, the target corporation was merged into the acquiring corporation, with the remaining shareholders of the target corporation stock, who held 5.82 percent of the target corporation stock, receiving the acquiring corporation stock. The taxpayer, who was one of the minority shareholders who received the acquiring corporation stock in the merger, claimed that the transaction was a type (A) reorganization. The court agreed with the Commissioner's argument that as far as the shareholders were concerned the transaction was a taxable sale because shareholders of the acquiring corporation had held only 16 percent of the stock of the target corporation prior to the commencement of the series of transactions culminating in the merger. Thus the continuity of interest requirement was not satisfied. A similar result was reached on similar facts in Yoc Heating Corp. v. Commissioner, 61 T.C. 168 (1973), which involved the tax treatment of the target corporation.

As noted in T.D. 8760, under Treas. Reg. § 1.368–1(e), the shareholders in cases such as *Kass* and *Yoc Heating* generally will not be considered to have participated in a reorganization if the cash purchases by the acquiring corporation are of such a magnitude relative to the stock consideration that the continuity of interest requirement has not been met. See Treas. Reg. § 1.368–1(e)(2)(i) and (e)(6), Ex(2). Pre-reorganization redemptions of stock by the target corporation also can have the same effect. See Temp. Reg. § 1.368–1T(e)(1)(ii)(A) and (B), (e)(3), Ex(10).

As far as the corporations themselves are concerned, however, Treas. Reg. § 1.338–2(c)(3) might produce a different result. Suppose P Corporation makes a qualified stock purchase of T Corporation, i.e., it purchases at least 80 percent (by vote and value) of the stock of T, but does not make a § 338 election, see page 475. P then causes the assets of T to be transferred to P (or another member of P's affiliated group, such as another subsidiary) in a reorganization defined in § 368. The regulation states that P will be treated as the relevant owner, i.e., "historic owner" of the T stock for purposes of testing continuity of interest under Treas. Reg. § 1.368–1(b) and (e). Any minority shareholders of T, however, will continue to be tested under generally applicable principles. As a result of the treatment under the regulations, the reorganization may qualify under § 368 for the P affiliation group; it will not be a "taxable merger" (see page 474). T will not recognize gain or loss on the transfer of its assets, and P (or a related corporation that acquires T's assets in the reorganization) will not obtain a step up in basis for the T assets. Thus, the result in *Yoc Heating* has been changed by the regulations, but the result in *Kass* has not been affected. The position of the regulations that a reorganization can exist with respect to some shareholders but not with respect to other shareholders is difficult to justify.

C. THE CONTINUITY OF BUSINESS ENTERPRISE REQUIREMENT

REGULATIONS: Sections 1.368–1(d), –2(k).

Revenue Ruling 81–92

1981–1 C.B. 133.

ISSUE

Does the acquisition by one corporation of all of the stock of another corporation solely in exchange for voting stock of the acquiring corporation qualify as a tax-free reorganization under section 368(a)(1)(B) if the acquired corporation's assets consist solely of cash that it realized from the sale of assets it previously used in its manufacturing business?

FACTS

T, a corporation engaged in manufacturing, sold all of its assets for cash to *Z,* an unrelated corporation. The sale was made as part of a plan of reorganization in which *P,* a corporation engaged in the manufacture of products different than those previously manufactured by *T,* acquired all of the outstanding stock in *T* from *T*'s shareholders, in exchange solely for *P* voting stock. *T,* as a wholly owned subsidiary of *P,* then used the cash realized on the sale of its manufacturing assets to engage in a business entirely unrelated to its previous manufacturing business.

LAW AND ANALYSIS

Section 368(a)(1)(B) of the Code provides, in pertinent part, that the term "reorganization" means the acquisition by one corporation, in exchange solely for shares of its voting stock, of the outstanding stock of another corporation if, immediately after the transaction, the acquiring corporation has control of such other corporation.

Section 1.368–1(b) of the Income Tax Regulations states that in order for a reorganization to qualify under section 368(a)(1) of the Code there must be a continuity of the business enterprise under the modified corporate form.

Section 1.368–1(d) of the regulations provides, in general, that the continuity of business enterprise requirement of section 1.368–1(b) is satisfied if the transferee in a corporate reorganization either (I) continues the transferor's historic business or (ii) uses a significant portion of the transferor's historic business assets in a business. Because the continuity of business enterprise requirement must be met for a transaction to qualify as a reorganization, section 1.368–1(d) is applicable to a transaction intended to qualify as a tax free reorganization under section 368(a)(1)(B) of the Code. See section 1.368–1(d)(1)(iii). Therefore, the transferee corporation must continue the transferor's historic business, or continue to use a significant portion of the transferor's historic business assets, in modified corporate form as a subsidiary of the transferee corporation for the transaction to qualify under section 368(a)(1)(B).

HOLDING

In the instant transaction, the acquisition by *P* of the *T* stock solely for *P*'s voting stock does not qualify as a tax-free reorganization under section 368(a)(1)(B) since *P* did not continue *T*'s historic (the manufacturing) business or use a significant portion of *T*'s historic business assets (those used in the manufacturing business) in a business conducted as a subsidiary of *P* after the transaction.

Accordingly, gain or loss is realized and recognized to the former shareholders of *T* upon the receipt by them from *P* of the *P* voting stock in exchange for their *T* stock under section 1001 of the Code.

ILLUSTRATIVE MATERIAL

A. BACKGROUND

Treas. Reg. § 1.368–1(b) states that one prerequisite to a "reorganization" is "a continuity of the business enterprise under the modified corporate form." Prior to 1981, establishing the scope of this requirement was left to case law and Revenue Rulings. In general, the requirement was not particularly difficult to satisfy; as long as the acquiring corporation used the assets of the acquired corporation in some business, even though different than the historic business of the acquired corporation, the continuity of business enterprise test was met. See, e.g., Bentsen v. Phinney, 199 F.Supp. 363 (S.D.Tex.1961) (merger of land development business into insurance company, which thereafter conducted only an insurance business); Atlas Tool Co. v. Commissioner, 614 F.2d 860 (3d Cir.1980) (continuity of business enterprise existed where acquired corporation's business was discontinued and its assets were held in reserve for future use in acquiring corporation's business; assets were restored to use within three months following acquisition). The requirement also was satisfied where the acquiring corporation discontinued its own historic business and continued the business of the acquired corporation. Rev.Rul. 63–29, 1963–1 C.B. 77 (corporation that had discontinued its toy business acquired the property of a steel distributor in a (C) reorganization and continued the steel business; held, continuity of business enterprise established). However, Wortham Machinery Co. v. United States, 521 F.2d 160 (10th Cir.1975), found no continuity of business enterprise where the transferor corporation in a purported (C) reorganization was engaged in no business activity at the time of the transfer and the acquiring corporation merely tried to dispose of the acquired assets; there was more than a "temporary suspension" of business activities. Consequently there was no reorganization: "Liquidation of assets is not continuation of a business enterprise." (163)

B. REGULATIONS

Treas. Reg. § 1.368–1(d), issued in 1981, expanded substantially the continuity of business enterprise requirement applicable to post–1981 acquisitions. The regulation requires that the acquiring corporation either (1) continue at least one of the acquired corporation's historic businesses, or (2) use a significant portion of the acquired corporation's historic assets in a business. Thus, as under prior law, the historic business of either corporation may be discontinued as long as some business is conducted after the acquisition. Examples in the regulations indicate that continuity of business enterprise does not exist where the historic assets of the acquired corporation are sold either before the acquisition (thereby rendering it an investment company) or shortly after the acquisition. See also Rev.Rul. 81–25, 1981–1 C.B. 132 (Rev.Rul. 63–29, supra, applies to post–1981 acquisitions).

Appeal of Laure, 653 F.2d 253 (6th Cir.1981), involved a tax year prior to the 1981 regulations, but the court noted that the regulations supported its conclusion that the retention of 27 percent of the acquired corporation's operating assets for use in the acquiring corporation's business satisfied the continuity of business requirement. Prior to the merger the acquired corporation had operated an air charter service, using leased aircraft. After the merger all of the air charter business assets, other than land and an airport hangar on the land, were sold. The hangar was leased to the purchaser of the bulk of the assets, who in turn provided air charter services to the taxpayer. The Court of Appeals held the Tax Court's finding of a lack of continuity of business enterprise was clearly erroneous because the retained assets were "substantial both in relation to the other assets transferred and in importance to the acquiring corporation."

Where the target corporation is a holding company, the continuity of business requirement is satisfied as long as a significant business of one of the target holding company's subsidiary corporations is conducted directly or indirectly by the acquiring corporation, for example by a second tier subsidiary of the acquiring corporation. Rev.Rul. 85–198, 1985–2 C.B. 120. Where a holding company is merged into its operating subsidiary, the continuity of business interest requirement is satisfied by looking through the holding company to treat the operating subsidiary's business as the business of the holding company. Rev.Rul. 85–197, 1985–2 C.B. 120.

Suppose that, following the acquisition, the acquiring corporation drops all or part of the assets of the acquired corporation into one or more of its subsidiaries, as is permitted under § 368(a)(2)(C). Rev.Rul. 81–247, 1981–2 C.B. 87, held that as long as the assets of the acquired corporation held by the acquiring corporation and any of its controlled subsidiaries, taken in the aggregate, constituted a significant portion of the acquired corporation's historic business assets, the continuity of business enterprise requirement was satisfied even if no one corporation held a significant portion of the assets.

C. REMOTE CONTINUITY OF BUSINESS ENTERPRISE

1. *Background*

In January, 1998 the Treasury issued amended Treas. Reg. § 1.368–1(d) and promulgated Treas. Reg. § 1.368–2(k) to provide that certain post-reorganization transfers by the acquiring corporation of the target corporation's assets or stock to controlled corporations or the target corporation's assets to partnerships would not cause the transaction to fail to satisfy either the continuity of interest or continuity of business enterprise requirements. The purpose of these amendments to the regulations is to reflect that "a valid reorganization may qualify as tax-free even if the acquiring corporation does not directly carry on the historic T business or use the historic T assets in a business." T.D. 8760, Rules and Regulations, Department of the Treasury, Internal Revenue Service, Continuity of Interest and Continuity of Business Enterprise, 1998–14 I.R.B. 4, 6. Thus, for example, a merger followed by a drop of the acquired corporation's assets to a third tier subsidiary would qualify under § 368. See Treas. Reg. §§ 1.368–1(d)(6), Ex.6; see also Treas. Reg. §§ 1.368–2(k). However, the regulations do not expand the scope of triangular reorganizations to permit an acquisition using stock of a grandparent or higher tier corporation to qualify. Rev. Rul. 74–565, 1974–2 C.B. 125, disqualifies such transactions.

2. *Transfers To Related Corporations*

Under the regulations, the assets of the acquired corporation (or the stock of the acquired corporation if the reorganization is in the form of a stock acquisition) can be transferred among the members of the acquiring corporation's "qualified group" without violating either the continuity of interest or continuity of business enterprise requirements. The qualified group consists of one or more chains of controlled corporations, within the meaning of § 368(c) or, in the case of any triangular reorganization, the parent of the acquiring corporation. Treas. Reg. § 1.368–1(d)(4)(I),(ii). The regulations do not address the issue of whether the "solely for voting stock" requirement of a § 368(a)(1)(C) reorganization is satisfied when a member of the "qualified group" other than the acquiring corporation assumes the acquired corporation's liabilities in connection with the transfer, but Rev. Rul. 70–224, 1970–1 C.B. 79, page 610, should permit such an indirect assumption of liabilities.

3. *Transfer of Acquired Corporation's Assets to a Partnership*

If after the potential reorganization the acquiring corporation transfers assets of the target corporation to a partnership of which it (or one or more members of its qualified group) is a member, Treas. Reg. § 1.368–1(d)(4)(iii) imposes a facts and circumstances test for determining whether the continuity of business enterprise requirement has been satisfied. See also Treas. Reg. § 1.368–1(d)(5), Exs. (5), (7), (8).

D. JUDICIAL LIMITATIONS

REGULATIONS: Section 1.368–1(a)–(c).

In an earlier edition of this book, Professor Stanley S. Surrey wrote:

"The reorganization sections are written against a background of many varied business transactions. They are stated in terms of specific rules which chart a tax-free corridor through which may flow the corporate transactions intended to be so favored. But the very breadth of the transactions to which the rules could extend and the mechanical terms in which they are written combine to make that corridor a tempting avenue of tax avoidance to persons who were not intended to be the recipients of such a safe-conduct pass. This is especially true in the case of closely-held family corporations where the corporation may be readily maneuvered by the shareholders. From the very beginning the courts, prompted by the Commissioner, have undertaken the task of policing this tax-free corridor. Their guarding has been vigorous and diligent, and many a corporation or shareholder who presented a pass carefully prepared to match the literal language of the sections has nevertheless been denied entrance. As a consequence, the literal language of the sections cannot be relied upon,[12] and safe passage depends upon knowledge of the rules of the judicial gendarmerie. An attorney who reads section 368(a)(1)(A) and believes that a statutory merger always constitutes a reorganization may be sadly mistaken—his particular statutory merger may be on the judicial proscribed list if it fails to possess the necessary continuity of interest. Some of these judicial rules have been incorporated in the statute; part of their flavor is in the Regulations.[13] But most of them still remain as they originated—judicial safeguards devised to protect the underlying statutory policy. Nor is the role of the judiciary confined to enforcing rules previously announced. Anyone applying for passage through the corridor runs the risk

12. E.g., Helvering v. Alabama Asphaltic Limestone Co., 315 U.S. 179 (1942): "It has been recognized that a transaction may not qualify as a 'reorganization' under the various revenue acts though the literal language of the section is satisfied." (182).

13. See, e.g., Regulations, sections 1.368–1(b); 1.368–1(c), referring to "plan of reorganization"; 1.368–2(a); 1.368–2(g); 1.1002–1(b), (c).

of the judicial policeman inventing a new rule on the spot if he thinks such action is demanded. And the Internal Revenue Service, in administering the statutory provisions, is alert to bring these situations before the courts. It must be remembered that most of the taxpayers who thus prompt administrative and judicial ingenuity have no real business in the corridor. But when such trespassers are in the throng, the barriers designed to separate them may catch an innocent, or may force the innocent to take added precautions to identify himself. The rules may also produce some uncertainty and confusion where the innocent too closely resembles a trespasser. Some have criticized the judicial vigilance on this score. Others believe that any effort to prescribe statutory rules covering all of the everyday transactions of the business world is bound to fail unless courts and administrators are able to cope with transactions that would otherwise involve a distorted application of those rules."

Professor Surrey's words apply with equal force today. The various judicial doctrines of which he spoke will be examined throughout this chapter in the context of specific acquisition transactions. But since they apply to all forms of reorganizations, a general discussion of the most important principles follows at this point.

(1) BUSINESS PURPOSE

Gregory v. Helvering

Supreme Court of the United States, 1935.
293 U.S. 465.

[*The Facts*. Mrs. Gregory in 1928 owned all of the stock of United Mortgage Corporation. That corporation held among its assets 1,000 shares of Monitor Securities Corporation. The value of the Monitor shares exceeded their basis. Mrs. Gregory's problem was to have the Monitor shares sold and to obtain in her hands the cash received on such sale. One method would be to have the Monitor shares distributed as a dividend and then sold by her. But this would result in a tax on the value of the shares as ordinary income, which she wished to avoid. She was willing to pay some capital gains tax. The key to Mrs. Gregory's maneuvers to achieve her goals was § 112(g) of the 1928 Act. That section provided for no gain to the shareholder on the distribution by a corporation, a party to a reorganization, of stock or securities of another corporation, also a party to the reorganization, even though the shareholder did not surrender any shares, so that it in effect exempted a dividend distribution of such stock or securities. It was thus similar to present § 355 but without the latter's conditions.

Mrs. Gregory proceeded to follow the statute in literal fashion. To that end, she caused the Averill Corporation to be organized under the laws of Delaware on September 18, 1928. Three days later, the United Mortgage Corporation transferred to the Averill Corporation the 1,000 shares of Monitor stock, for which all the shares of the Averill Corporation were issued to Mrs. Gregory. This was a short-cutting step, whose effect was the same as the issuance of the Averill shares to United and their distribution by United to Mrs. Gregory. On September 24, the Averill Corporation was dissolved, and liquidated by distributing all its assets, namely the Monitor shares, to its sole shareholder, Mrs. Gregory. No other business was ever transacted, or intended to be transacted, by Averill. She immediately sold the Monitor shares for $133,333.33. She then contended that the transfer to Averill was a reorganization as United controlled Averill; the distribution to her of Averill shares was tax free under old § 112(g); the Averill shares took part ($57,325.45) of the basis of her United shares (originally $350,000) on an allocation of her United basis based on the market values of the United and Averill shares; the liquidation of Averill and her acquisition thereby of the Monitor shares worth $133,333.33 produced a capital gain (of $76,007.88) taxable at capital gain rates; the sale of the Monitor shares resulted in no gain since the taxable liquidation resulted in a basis in her hands equal to their market value.

The Commissioner argued that the creation of the Averill Corporation was without substance and must be disregarded; consequently, the entire transaction must be considered as a distribution of the Monitor shares as a dividend, producing ordinary income of $133,333.33, the value of such shares. The sale of the Monitor shares had no tax effect under his theory, since, once taxed as a dividend, they had a basis equal to their value.

The Decision of the Board of Tax Appeals, 27 B.T.A. 223 (1932). The Board held for Mrs. Gregory:

"A statute so meticulously drafted must be interpreted as a literal expression of the taxing policy, and leaves only the small interstices for judicial consideration. The general legislative plan apparently was to recognize the corporate entity and, in view of such recognition, to specify when the gains or losses would be recognized and upon what basis they should be measured. We may not destroy the effectiveness of this statutory plan by denying recognition to the corporation and thus preventing consideration of its transactions." (225–6)

The Decision of the Circuit Court of Appeals, Second Circuit, 69 F.2d 809 (1934). The Circuit Court held for the Commissioner, in an opinion by Judge Learned Hand:

"We agree with the Board and the taxpayer that a transaction, otherwise within an exception of the tax law, does not lose its immunity, because it is actuated by a desire to avoid, or, if one choose, to evade, taxation. Any one may so arrange his affairs that his taxes shall be as low as possible; he is not bound to choose that pattern which will best pay the Treasury; there is not even a patriotic duty to increase one's taxes. U.S. v. Isham, 17 Wall. 496, 506; Bullen v. Wisconsin, 240 U.S. 625, 630, 36 S.Ct. 473. Therefore, if what was done here, was what was intended by [the section corresponding to present § 368(a)(1)(D), but without the present requirement of a distribution of the stock], it is of no consequence that it was all an elaborate scheme to get rid of income taxes, as it certainly was. Nevertheless, it does not follow that Congress meant to cover such a transaction, not even though the facts answer the dictionary definitions of each term used in the statutory definition. It is quite true, as the Board has very well said, that as the articulation of a statute increases, the room for interpretation must contract; but the meaning of a sentence may be more than that of the separate words, as a melody is more than the notes, and no degree of particularity can ever obviate recourse to the setting in which all appear, and which all collectively create. The purpose of the section is plain enough; men engaged in enterprises—industrial, commercial, financial, or any other—might wish to consolidate, or divide, to add to, or subtract from, their holdings. Such transactions were not to be considered as 'realizing' any profit, because the collective interests still remained in solution. But the underlying presupposition is plain that the readjustment shall be undertaken for reasons germane to the conduct of the venture in hand, not as an ephemeral incident, egregious to its prosecution. To dodge the shareholders' taxes is not one of the transactions contemplated as corporate 'reorganizations.'

"We do not indeed agree fully with the way in which the Commissioner treated the transaction; we cannot treat as inoperative the transfer of the Monitor shares by the United Mortgage Corporation, the issue by the Averill Corporation of its own shares to the taxpayer, and her acquisition of the Monitor shares by winding up that company. The Averill Corporation had a juristic personality, whatever the purpose of its organization; the transfer passed title to the Monitor shares and the taxpayer became a shareholder in the transferee. All these steps were real, and their only defect was that they were not what the statute means by a 'reorganization,' because the transactions were no part of the conduct of the business of either or both companies; so viewed they were a sham, though all the proceedings had their usual effect. But the result is the same whether the tax be calculated as the Commissioner calculated it, or upon the value of the Averill shares as a dividend." (810–811)

On this theory the value of the Averill shares, and hence the amount taxed as a dividend, would be $133,333.33, the value of the underlying Monitor shares. The later liquidation of Averill and sale of the Monitor shares would have no tax effect since the Averill shares, taxed as a dividend, thereby obtained a basis equal to the value of the Monitor shares.]

■ MR. JUSTICE SUTHERLAND delivered the opinion of the Court. * * *

It is earnestly contended on behalf of the taxpayer that since every element required by [the section of the 1928 Act corresponding to present § 368(a)(1)(D), but without the present requirement of a distribution of the stock] is to be found in what was done, a statutory reorganization was effected; and that the motive of the taxpayer thereby to escape payment of a tax will not alter the result or make unlawful what the statute allows. It is quite true that if a reorganization in reality was effected within the meaning of [that provision], the ulterior purpose mentioned will be disregarded. The legal right of a taxpayer to decrease the amount of what otherwise would be his taxes, or altogether avoid them, by means which the law permits, cannot be doubted. United States v. Isham, 17 Wall. 496, 506; Superior Oil Co. v. Mississippi, 280 U.S. 390, 395, 396, 50 S.Ct. 169; Jones v. Helvering, * * * 71 F.2d 214, 217. But the question for determination is whether what was done, apart from the tax motive, was the thing which the statute intended. The reasoning of the court below in justification of a negative answer leaves little to be said.

When [the statutory provision] speaks of a transfer of assets by one corporation to another, it means a transfer made "in pursuance of a plan of reorganization" * * * of corporate business; and not a transfer of assets by one corporation to another in pursuance of a plan having no relation to the business of either, as plainly is the case here. Putting aside, then, the question of motive in respect of taxation altogether, and fixing the character of the proceeding by what actually occurred, what do we find? Simply an operation having no business or corporate purpose—a mere device which put on the form of a corporate reorganization as a disguise for concealing its real character, and the sole object and accomplishment of which was the consummation of a preconceived plan, not to reorganize a business or any part of a business, but to transfer a parcel of corporate shares to the petitioner. No doubt, a new and valid corporation was created. But that corporation was nothing more than a contrivance to the end last described. It was brought into existence for no other purpose; it performed, as it was intended from the beginning it should perform, no other function. When that limited function had been exercised, it immediately was put to death.

In these circumstances, the facts speak for themselves and are susceptible of but one interpretation. The whole undertaking, though conducted according to the terms of [the statutory provision], was in fact an elaborate and devious form of conveyance masquerading as a corporate reorganization, and nothing else. The rule which excludes from consideration the motive of tax avoidance is not pertinent to the situation, because the transaction upon its face lies outside the plain intent of the statute. To hold otherwise would be to exalt artifice above reality and to deprive the statutory provision in question of all serious purpose.

Judgment affirmed.

ILLUSTRATIVE MATERIAL

A. REPEAL AND RESTORATION OF FORMER SECTION 112(g).

The tax avoidance potential of former § 112(g) had led to its elimination in 1934, prior to the Supreme Court's decision in *Gregory*. But in 1951 the provision was revived in altered form as the predecessor of current § 355, discussed in Chapter 15.

B. JUDGE HAND ON THE GREGORY DECISION

A year after *Gregory* was decided, in Chisholm v. Commissioner, 79 F.2d 14 (2d Cir.1935), Judge Learned Hand described the *Gregory* case as follows:

"It is important to observe just what the Supreme Court held in that case. It was solicitous to reaffirm the doctrine that a man's motive to avoid taxation will not establish his liability if the transaction does not do so without it. The question always is whether the transaction under scrutiny is in fact what it appears to be in form; a marriage may be a joke; a contract may be intended only to deceive others; an agreement may have a collateral defeasance. In such cases the transaction as a whole is different from its appearance. True, it is always the intent that controls; and we need not for this occasion press the difference between intent and purpose. We may assume that purpose may be the touchstone, but the purpose which counts is one which defeats or contradicts the apparent transaction, not the purpose to escape taxation which the apparent, but not the whole, transaction would realize. In Gregory v. Helvering, supra, 293 U.S. 465, 55 S.Ct. 266, the incorporators adopted the usual form for creating business corporations; but their intent, or purpose, was merely to draught the papers, in fact not to create corporations as the court understood that word. That was the purpose which defeated their exemption, not the accompanying purpose to escape taxation; that purpose was legally neutral. Had they really meant to conduct a business by means of the two reorganized companies, they would have escaped whatever other aim they might have had, whether to avoid taxes, or to regenerate the world." (15)

And in 1948, Judge Hand said in Commissioner v. National Carbide Corporation, 167 F.2d 304 (2d Cir.1948), aff'd, 336 U.S. 422 (1949):

"In Gregory v. Helvering the taxpayer had organized a corporation only to serve as a means of transfer; it was used once and only for that purpose, and was dissolved as soon as it had done so. The Court held that it was not a 'corporation' within the meaning of that term, as Congress must be understood to have used it, because in common speech, it means a jural person created to conduct industry, commerce, charity or some other commonly practiced activity, and not to serve merely as an escape from taxation. Such a corporation might be in some contexts a 'corporation'; but words are chameleons, which reflect the color of their environment, and in a tax statute 'corporation' could not have been so intended.

"This decision has at times been thought to trench upon the doctrine—which courts are never tired of repeating—that the rights resulting from a legal transaction otherwise valid, are not different, vis-a-vis taxation, because it has been undertaken to escape taxation. That is a doctrine essential to industry and commerce in a society like our own, in which, so far as possible, business is always shaped to the form best suited to keep down taxes. Gregory v. Helvering, supra, was no exception, in spite of the fact that it was the purpose for which the taxpayer created the corporation that determined the event; for it is not the presence of an accompanying motive to escape taxation that is ever decisive, but the absence of any motive which brings the corporation within the group of those enterprises which the word ordinarily includes. Indeed, a corporation may be a 'sham' and 'unreal,' when the only reason for its creation was 'to deter the creditors of one of the partners,' who organized it, for that is not an activity commonly understood to be corporate." (306–7)

C. OTHER ASPECTS OF GREGORY

As Randolph Paul stated: "Few cases have been the subject of such violent disagreement and confusion as the *Gregory* case. The case is all things to all men."[9] The disagreement is between those who follow the philosophy of the Board of Tax Appeals in that case and those who follow the view of Judge Hand and the Supreme Court. But while the dispute may be heated, every wise tax advisor realizes that the attitude of the *Gregory* decision is still alive today in the tax world. Tax avoidance schemes must reckon with that attitude and with judicial and administrative ingenuity in applying it. The principle of the decision is not limited to the reorganization provisions, but pervades the entire Code. The *Gregory* decision is expressed in many ways and words, all of which come to the pointed warning, "Beware—Proceed with Caution," that faces tax reduction plans having any element of artificiality or non-conformance with normal business or family conduct.

There are, as the quotations above from Judge Hand's opinions indicate, many facets to the *Gregory* "business purpose" doctrine. While the facets often overlap, there are some recognizable patterns. For example:

1. *Sham Situations.* The business purpose test is applied to disregard the existence of a particular entity or the effect of a particular status where its existence serves no function apart from its tax-saving function. This is the *Gregory* case itself.

2. *Transactions Lacking Economic Reality.* Suppose that a transaction is entered into which involves binding legal obligations not of a transitory character, so it is not a "sham," and that in its arrangements and end result complies with the statutory requirements, so that it is not defeated by the end-result or step transaction argument. The transaction, however, lacks economic or business reality in the sense that it would not be entered into except for the benefit that results solely from the expected tax consequences. Here courts sometimes will apply the "business purpose" doctrine to defeat such plans on the ground that they represent a distortion of the function of the particular statutory provisions in question or will require that the transaction involve some "purposive" activity apart from the tax benefits to be derived. For example, Wortham Machinery Co. v. United States, 521 F.2d 160 (10th Cir.1975), denied a net operating loss carryover (otherwise available under § 381 and § 382, discussed in Chapter 16) to the acquiring corporation in a transaction that literally complied with the statutory requirements for a type (C) reorganization. In the transaction a corporation transferred its assets, which consisted primarily of a net operating loss carryover, to its sister corporation in exchange for that corporation's stock. The stock was distributed to the controlling shareholders of both corporations in a liquidating distribution. The court

9. Paul, Studies in Federal Taxation, Third Series (1940) 125 and references cited.

held that while the "questioned transaction was within the 'inert language' of section 368(a)(1)(C) the only attraction shown by the record for the acquisition of [the assets of the transferor] was the net operating loss carryover which [the acquiring corporation] used in its tax return to reduce its tax liability." (163) Hence, there was no business purpose for the transaction.

One or more of the above doctrines often are loosely applied by a court invoking the principles of "substance over form". As far as corporate reorganizations are concerned, the business purpose doctrine has been incorporated into Treas. Reg. § 1.368–1(c) and–2(g), but the *Gregory* decision and the ramifications of the business purpose doctrine stand primarily as judicial warnings that *some* provisions are off limits in *some* situations. This combination of the existence of a rule permitting transactions to be disregarded but uncertainty as to when the rule will be applied has an *in terrorem* effect that dampens the enthusiasm of some would-be tax manipulators but prompts others to take a chance where little is at risk if the scheme fails. But it is difficult to see how the Internal Revenue Code could be applied successfully without the safeguards afforded by the *Gregory* doctrine and its various facets. It is a technique of statutory interpretation difficult to apply but essential to our tax system as it now operates.

3. *Step Transactions.* The business purpose test may be applied to disregard the separate existence of several steps and instead to judge the transaction by its end result with the intervening steps omitted.

(2) STEP TRANSACTION DOCTRINE

The step transaction doctrine, like the business purpose doctrine, is especially important in the area of corporate reorganizations. When this judicial doctrine is applied, the tax treatment of several transactions is determined by examining their overall effect rather than giving effect to each of the several transactions in sequence. In some cases, however, the form of a transaction will be allowed to control. Predicting when the step transaction doctrine will be applied is difficult.

King Enterprises, Inc. v. United States

United States Court of Claims, 1969.
418 F.2d 511.

■ PER CURIAM:

* * *

This is an action to recover Federal income taxes paid by petitioner for the fiscal year ended June 30, 1960. The issues involve the proper characterization for tax purposes of the transaction in question, and the tax treatment of the resulting gain. * * *

Petitioner, King Enterprises, Inc., * * * was one of 11 shareholders in Tenco, Inc. * * * Tenco was financially successful over the years, and by

1959 had become the second largest producer of soluble coffee in the United States. Despite its financial success there was stockholder discontent.

Minute Maid Corporation had become by 1958 one of the nation's principal producers of frozen concentrated citrus juices. * * * Between January and July 29, 1959, Minute Maid submitted and the Tenco directors rejected three separate proposals for acquisition of Tenco stock. A fourth proposal was approved by the respective boards on August 25, 1959, and on September 3, 1959, petitioner and other Tenco shareholders signed an agreement with Minute Maid entitled "Purchase and Sale Agreement".

Pursuant to the Agreement providing for the sale of their Tenco stock to Minute Maid, the Tenco shareholders received a total consideration consisting of $3,000,000 in cash, $2,550,000 in promissory notes, and 311,996 shares of Minute Maid stock valued at $5,771,926. Petitioner's share of the total consideration consisted of $281,564.25 in cash, $239,-329.40 in promissory notes, and 29,282 shares of Minute Maid stock valued at $541,717. The Minute Maid stock received by Tenco stockholders represented 15.62 percent of the total outstanding Minute Maid shares, and constituted in excess of 50 percent of the total consideration received.

On December 10, 1959, the Minute Maid directors approved the November 24th recommendation of its general counsel to merge the company's four subsidiaries, including Tenco, into the parent company, and authorized that the merger be submitted to its stockholders for approval at a meeting scheduled for February 1960. Minute Maid's annual report to stockholders announced the merger plan about December 3, 1959. On January 5, 1960, Minute Maid requested a ruling from the Commissioner of Internal Revenue whether in the event of the proposed Tenco merger the basis of Tenco assets in Minute Maid's hands would be determined under [former] section 334(b)(2) of the Internal Revenue Code of 1954. This was approved by the Commissioner by ruling of February 25, 1960 that "Under the provisions of section 334(b)(2) that basis of the property received by Minute Maid upon the complete liquidation of Tenco will be determined by reference to the adjusted basis of the Tenco stock in the hands of Minute Maid." On April 30 and May 2, 1960, in accordance with the applicable state laws, Tenco and certain other subsidiaries were merged into Minute Maid.

On its income tax return for the fiscal year ended June 30, 1960, * * * [t]he value of the Minute Maid stock received by petitioner was not reported, it being petitioner's position that such stock was received in connection with a nontaxable corporate reorganization. The District Director of Internal Revenue assessed a deficiency on the ground that the gain portion of the total consideration received (cash, notes, and Minute Maid stock) constituted taxable capital gain from the sale of a capital asset.

* * *

Petitioner contends that the transfer by the Tenco stockholders of their Tenco stock to Minute Maid in exchange for Minute Maid stock, cash and notes, followed by the merger of Tenco into Minute Maid, were steps in a unified transaction qualifying as a reorganization under section 368(a)(1)(A) of the 1954 Code. * * * The Government asserts that the transfer of Tenco stock to Minute Maid was an independent sales transaction; therefore, the entire gain realized by petitioner on the payment to it of cash, notes and Minute Maid stock is taxable as gain from the sale of a capital asset.

I

The Reorganization Issue

The threshold issue is whether the transfer of Tenco stock to Minute Maid is to be treated for tax purposes as an independent transaction of sale, or as a transitory step in a transaction qualifying as a corporate reorganization. Significant tax consequences turn on which characterization is determined to be proper.

The general rule is that when property is sold or otherwise disposed of, any gain realized must also be recognized, absent an appropriate nonrecognition provision in the Internal Revenue Code. One such nonrecognition provision, section 354(a)(1), provides in pertinent part:

> No gain or loss shall be recognized if stock or securities in a corporation a party to a reorganization are, in pursuance of the plan of reorganization, exchanged solely for stock or securities in such corporation or in another corporation a party to the reorganization.

By its terms, this exception to the general rule of taxation depends for its operation on the existence of a corporate reorganization. The term "reorganization", moreover, is a word of art in tax law and is specifically defined in section 368(a)(1) as comprising six types of transactions, exclusively.

* * *

It is not disputed that there was a Type A reorganization in April 1960 when Tenco and Minute Maid were merged in accordance with state law. Nor does the Government dispute that Minute Maid continued the business of Tenco following the merger, or that the former Tenco shareholders had a continuity of interest in the enterprise by virtue of their ownership of stock in Minute Maid received in the exchange. The disagreement centers on whether the initial exchange of stock was a step in a unified transaction pursuant to a "plan of reorganization".

The underlying theory of the petitioner's claim is that the tax consequences of business transactions are properly determined by their substance and not by the form in which they are cast. Thus petitioner views the substance of the transaction under review to be an acquisition by Minute Maid of Tenco's assets in exchange for transferring Minute Maid stock, cash and notes to Tenco's stockholders. * * * The value of the Minute Maid stock received, which exceeded 50 percent of the total consideration, constituted a sufficient continuity of interest to support a Type A reorganization.[5] Petitioner concludes, therefore, that the net result of the entire transaction is a reorganization, not to be altered by splitting the entire transaction into its component transitory steps. * * * Petitioner's conclusion is justified in fact and in law.

The problem of deciding whether to accord the separate steps of a complex transaction independent significance, or to treat them as related steps in a unified transaction, is a recurring problem in the field of tax law.[6] The principle that even extended business transactions have determinate limits for tax purposes is based on a strong preference for "closed transactions" upon which to impose tax consequences. This preference is tempered, however, with respect for the integrity of an entire transaction. Accordingly, the essence of the step transaction doctrine is that an "integrated transaction must not be broken into independent steps or, conversely, that the separate steps must be taken together in attaching tax consequences". Bittker and Eustice, Federal Income Taxation of Corporations and Shareholders, p. 18 (1966) * * * . The mere recitation of the doctrine, however, does not clarify the necessary relationship between the steps requisite to characterization as an integrated transaction.

Analysis of the reported cases and the diverse business transactions they encompass reveals that there is no universal test applicable to step transaction situations. See * * * American Bantam Car Co. v. Commissioner of Internal Revenue, 11 T.C. 397 (1948), aff'd, 177 F.2d 513 (3d Cir.1949); * * * Commissioner of Internal Revenue v. Gordon, 391 U.S. 83, 88 S.Ct. 1517, 20 L.Ed.2d 448 (1968). It has been persuasively suggested that "the aphorisms about 'closely related steps' and 'integrated transactions' may have different meanings in different contexts, and that there may be not one rule, but several, depending on the substantive provision of the Code to which they are being applied". Mintz and Plumb, Step Transactions, pp. 247, 252–253 (1954).

In their attempt to define the criteria upon which application of step transaction principles depend, the courts have enunciated two basic tests. The "interdependence test" requires an inquiry as to 'whether on a reasonable interpretation of objective facts the steps were so interdependent that the legal relations created by one transaction would have been fruitless without a completion of the series'. Paul and Zimet, Step Transactions, Selected Studies in Federal Taxation (2d Series, 1938), pp. 200, 254. * * * The "end result" test, on the other hand, establishes a standard whereby:

5. In Rev.Rul. 66–224, 1966–2 C.B. 114, the Internal Revenue Service ruled that the continuity of interest requirement of section 1.368–1(b) is satisfied when, pursuant to a statutory merger, 50 percent of the consideration received by stockholders of the dissolved corporation is comprised of stock of the surviving corporation.

6. In coping with this and related problems, courts have enunciated a variety of doctrines, such as step transaction, business purpose, and substance over form. Although the various doctrines overlap and it is not always clear in a particular case which one is most appropriate, their common premise is that the substantive realities of a transaction determine its tax consequences.

> * * * purportedly separate transactions will be amalgamated into a single transaction when it appears that they were really component parts of a single transaction intended from the outset to be taken for the purpose of reaching the ultimate result.[7]

Despite the real differences between the tests, each is faithful to the central purpose of the step transaction doctrine; that is, to assure that tax consequences turn on the substance of a transaction rather than on its form.

In support of its position that the step transaction doctrine is inapplicable to the facts of this case the Government correctly points out that there was no binding commitment for the merger of Tenco to follow the acquisition of its stock. Defendant erroneously concludes, however, that the absence of such a commitment here renders the step transaction doctrine inapplicable. The binding commitment requirement relied upon by the Government, was enunciated by the Supreme Court in Commissioner of Internal Revenue v. Gordon, supra, * * * wherein the Court said "if one transaction is to be characterized as a 'first step' there must be a binding commitment to take the later steps". Analysis of the statement in its proper context, however, dispels its application to the case before us. In Gordon, Pacific transferred certain of its assets to a new company, Northwest, in exchange for all of the latter's common stock, and debt paper. In 1961 Pacific distributed to its shareholders rights to purchase about 57 percent of Northwest's common stock at $16 per share, a price below its market value. Pacific notified its stockholders that "[i]t is expected that within about three years * * * the Company by one or more offerings will offer for sale the balance of such stock * * *." 391 U.S., at 97, 88 S.Ct., at 1525. In 1963 the remaining Northwest stock was offered to Pacific stockholders through distributed rights. Taxpayers were minority stockholders of Pacific who received rights in the 1961 distribution. Taxpayers sold four rights and exercised the balance, but they reported no income for the year 1961 from these transactions.

The primary issue in Gordon was whether the 1961 distribution was part of a Type D reorganization. To qualify as a D reorganization, Pacific must have distributed all or an amount constituting control (80 percent) of the Northwest stock. Sec. 355(a)(1)(D). In disposing of taxpayers' contention that the 1963 distribution (43 percent), taken in conjunction with the 1961 distribution (57 percent), satisfied the statutory requirement, the Supreme Court said at pp. 96–97, 88 S.Ct. at pp. 1524–1525:

> * * * The Code requires that 'the distribution' divest the controlling corporation of all of, or 80% control of, the controlled corporation. Clearly, if an initial transfer of less than a controlling interest in the controlled corporation is to be treated for tax purposes as a mere first step in the divestiture of control, it must

7. Herwitz, Business Planning, p. 804 (1966). See also, Helvering v. Alabama Asphaltic Limestone, supra; Anheuser–Busch v. Helvering, supra; South Bay Corp. v. Commissioner of Internal Revenue, supra.

at least be identifiable as such at the time it is made. Absent other specific directions from Congress, Code provisions must be interpreted so as to conform to the basic premise of annual tax accounting. It would be wholly inconsistent with this premise to hold that the essential character of a transaction, and its tax impact, should remain not only undeterminable but unfixed for an indefinite and unlimited period in the future, awaiting events that might or might not happen. This requirement that the character of a transaction be determinable does not mean that the entire divestiture must necessarily occur within a single tax year. It does, however, mean that if one transaction is to be characterized as a 'first step' there must be a binding commitment to take the later steps.

Here, it was little more than a fortuity that, by the time suit was brought alleging a deficiency in taxpayers' 1961 returns, Pacific had distributed the remainder of the stock. * * *.

The opinion in Gordon contains not the slightest indication that the Supreme Court intended the binding commitment requirement as the touchstone of the step transaction doctrine in tax law. Nor is there any indication that the Court intended to overrule any prior decisions applying the step transaction doctrine to other types of transactions where there were no binding commitments. On the contrary, the opinion addressed a narrow situation (a D reorganization) involving a specific statutory requirement (divestiture of control), and limited the potential for dilution and circumvention of that requirement by prohibiting the indefinite extension of divestiture distributions. Its interpretation should be so limited.[8] Clearly, the step transaction doctrine would be a dead letter if restricted to situations where the parties were bound to take certain steps.

The doctrine derives vitality, rather, from its application where the form of a transaction does not require a particular further step be taken; but, once taken, the substance of the transaction reveals that the ultimate result was intended from the outset. * * * In the majority of cases, it is the Government that relies on the step transaction doctrine for tax characterization. General application of the binding commitment requirement would effectively insure taxpayers of virtual exemption from the doctrine merely by refraining from such commitments. Such an untoward result cannot be intended by the Gordon opinion; indeed, defendant acknowledges as much in its brief by stating "the Supreme Court seems to have restricted the step transaction doctrine at least in one type of transaction, a corporate distri-

8. See Mintz v. Plumb, supra, at 285, where in regard to the similarly restrictive interdependence test it is concluded:

> [The interdependence test] applies * * * in cases * * * where the concept of a "plan or reorganization" is not pertinent. In reorganization cases, except possibly in applying the "control" requirement * * * the determinative test seems to be whether the step was intended, or even contemplated as an alternative possibility, under the plan or reorganization, and the test of "interdependence" has not been applied.

bution of stock in a controlled corporation". The present case involves no such transaction.

In the alternative, the Government asserts that the step transaction doctrine has no application to this case because the merger of Tenco into Minute Maid was not the intended end result from the outset. Although the appropriate standard is invoked, defendant's assertion is inconsistent with the inferences to be drawn from the record.

The operative facts emerging from the record in this case suggest that Minute Maid, desirous of diversifying its operations in order to stabilize its income, was presented with the opportunity to acquire the entire stock of Tenco for a bargain "price". Tenco's record of financial success and its asking price for Tenco stock of seven or eight times its earnings (while other companies were asking 20 times their earnings), without more, constituted an attractive investment. After the stock acquisition, moreover, Minute Maid was at liberty to operate Tenco as a wholly owned subsidiary, if it so desired. There is no persuasive evidence, however, that Minute Maid's appetite was limited to these goals, though worthy, when there was more in sight. On the contrary, the record reveals that, prior to the acquisition of Tenco stock, the officers of Minute Maid considered merging its existing subsidiaries into the parent in order to eliminate some of the general ledgers and extra taxes, and to bring about other savings. In fact, the merger of subsidiaries as a money-saving device was Mr. Speeler's (Minute Maid's vice president and general counsel) pet idea, which he discussed with Minute Maid's President Fox before the initial agreement with Tenco.

Shortly after the stock acquisition, Minute Maid instituted steps to consummate the merger of Tenco into Minute Maid. The proposed merger was motivated by a desire to avoid additional income tax on intercorporate dividends, to eliminate duplicate costs in the approximate amount of $50,000, and to obtain a stepped-up basis for stock in foreign corporations and other assets owned by Tenco. The potential step-up in basis for the foreign stock was estimated at $750,000 and the step-up for Tenco's other assets, although unable to be precisely ascertained, was considerable and probably sufficient as a justification for the merger independent of the other assigned reasons.[10]

Minute Maid applied for on January 5, 1960, and received on February 25, 1960, a ruling by the Internal Revenue Service that Minute Maid's basis in property received upon the complete liquidation of Tenco would be determined under section 334(b)(2) by reference to the adjusted basis of Tenco stock in Minute Maid's hands. Subsequently, on April 30 and May 2, 1960, in accordance with applicable state laws, Tenco and certain other subsidiaries were merged into Minute Maid.

10. Petitioner asserts that the potential step-up in basis of Tenco assets is approximately $5,525,000. There is also evidence that Minute Maid believed such step-up to be approximately $5,950,000. The actual step-up, though undisclosed by the available facts, is probably at least several million dollars.

No express intention on the part of Minute Maid to effect a merger of Tenco surfaces in the record until after the initial agreement to exchange stock. It strains credulity, however, to believe other than that the plan to merge was something more than inchoate, if something less than announced, at the time of such exchange. One gains the impression that the record of intentions is edited, so in reconstruction we must lean heavily on the logic of tell-tale facts and lightly on chameleon words. It is difficult to believe that sophisticated businessmen arranging a multimillion dollar transaction fraught with tax potentials were so innocent of knowledge of the tax consequences as the testimony purports. Perhaps testimony from private tax authorities serving the parties would have yielded more explicit knowledge of the questions asked and the advice given, but a trial record is rarely perfect in retrospect and a decision must be reached on an objective appraisal of the facts, including the inferences to be squeezed from them.

The operative facts in this case clearly justify the inference that the merger of Tenco into Minute Maid was the intended result of the transaction in question from the outset, the initial exchange of stock constituting a mere transitory step. Accordingly, it is concluded that the initial exchange and subsequent merger were steps in a unified transaction qualifying as a Type A reorganization, and that petitioner received its Minute Maid stock pursuant to the plan of reorganization shown by the facts and circumstances above to have existed.[11]

* * *

ILLUSTRATIVE MATERIAL

A. VARIATIONS OF THE STEP TRANSACTION DOCTRINE

As should be evident from the opinion in *King Enterprises, Inc.*, the difficulty in predicting when the step transaction doctrine will be applied is compounded by the fact that there are several different variations of the step transaction doctrine. It is likewise difficult to predict which variation of the doctrine will be applied. These variations on a theme were synopsized by the Tax Court in Penrod v. Commissioner, 88 T.C. 1415 (1987):

"* * * There is no universally accepted test as to when and how the step transaction doctrine should be applied to a given set of facts. Courts have applied three alternative tests in deciding whether to invoke the step transaction doctrine in a particular situation.

"The narrowest alternative is the 'binding commitment' test, under which a series of transactions are collapsed if, at the time the first step is entered into, there was a binding commitment to undertake the later step. See Commissioner v. Gordon, 391 U.S. 83, 96 (1968) * * *. The binding commitment test has the advantage of promoting certainty in the tax planning of shareholders. Under such test, a court must make an objective

11. A formal plan or reorganization is not necessary if the facts of the case show a plan to have existed. See William H. Redfield, 34 B.T.A. 967 (1936).

determination as to whether the acquired shareholders were bound by an obligation to sell the shares received in an acquisition. Other factors, such as intent by such shareholders to sell their shares, are not considered. However, there have been objections to that test on the ground that the result is easily manipulable by taxpayers. * * *

"At the other extreme, the most far-reaching alternative is the 'end result' test. Under this test, the step transaction doctrine will be invoked if it appears that a series of formally separate steps are really prearranged parts of a single transaction intended from the outset to reach the ultimate result. See King Enterprises, Inc. v. United States, 418 F.2d at 516 * * *. The end result test is based upon the actual intent of the parties as of the time of the merger. It can be argued that any test which requires a court to make a factual determination as to a party's intent promotes uncertainty and therefore impedes effective tax planning. However, in contrast to the binding commitment test, the end result test is flexible and bases tax consequences on the real substance of the transactions, not on the formalisms chosen by the participants.

"The third test is the 'interdependence' test, which focuses on whether 'the steps are so interdependent that the legal relations created by one transaction would have been fruitless without a completion of the series.' Redding v. Commissioner, 630 F.2d at 1177 * * * American Bantam Car Co. v. Commissioner, 11 T.C. 397 (1948), affd. 177 F.2d 513 (3d Cir.1949). This test concentrates on the relationship between the steps, rather than on their 'end result.' * * * However, since the interdependence test requires a court to find whether the individual steps had independent significance or whether they had meaning only as part of the larger transaction, the court may be called upon to determine the result the participants hoped to achieve. Thus, the interdependence test is a variation of the end result test.

"Courts have applied each of these three alternatives to a variety of transactions to determine whether the transactions should be 'stepped.' * * * " (1429–1430)

The impact of variation of the step transaction doctrine that the court chooses to apply can be significant. For example, if the court in *King Enterprises, Inc.* had determined that the mutual interdependence test or the binding commitment test ought to have been applied, rather than the end result test, *King Enterprises, Inc.*, and its shareholders would not have been involved in a reorganization.

B. OTHER EXAMPLES OF APPLICATION OF THE STEP TRANSACTION DOCTRINE

As in *King Enterprises, Inc.*, in some cases the step transaction doctrine is applied to find a reorganization where none would have existed if each step of the overall transaction were viewed independently. Unlike in the *King Enterprises* case, however, in most of these cases, the step transaction doctrine is applied at the Commissioner's behest to produce a tax-free reorganization, thereby denying a loss deduction, where following the form of the several steps would have produced a taxable transaction. For example, in Heller v. Commissioner, 2 T.C. 371 (1943), aff'd, 147 F.2d 376 (9th Cir.1945), the shareholders of a Delaware corporation organized a California corporation, contributing borrowed cash for the stock of the California corporation. The California corporation then borrowed additional cash and purchased the assets of the Delaware corporation, which paid its existing indebtedness and distributed the balance of the cash to its shareholders in liquidation. The taxpayer claimed a deductible loss on the liquidation of the Delaware corporation because his basis for his stock in that corporation exceeded the amount of the liquidating distribution. The Commissioner disallowed the loss, asserting that the series of steps was in fact a single transaction which was a reorganization under the predecessors of § 368(a)(1)(D) or § 368(a)(1)(F) and that, accordingly, pursuant to the predecessor of § 354(a)(1), no loss was recognizable. In response, the taxpayer argued that even if the transaction had the same result as a reorganization, no exchange of stock for stock as required by the predecessor of § 354(a)(1), had occurred.

The Tax Court held for the Commissioner, reasoning as follows:

"In determining the substance of a transaction it is proper to consider the situation as it existed at the beginning and end of the series of steps as well as the object sought to be accomplished, the means employed, and the relation between the various steps. * * *

"Petitioner and two others, the stockholders and directors of the Delaware corporation, decided to have the business, assets, and liabilities of that company taken over by a new California corporation. The desired end was accomplished by a series of steps, all of which were planned in advance. * * * The net result was that petitioner and the other two stockholders had substituted their interest in the Delaware corporation for substantially the same interest in the California corporation. The nonrecognition of gain or loss provisions of the statute are 'intended to apply to cases where a corporation in form transfers its property, but in substance it or its stockholders retain the same or practically the same interest after the transfer.' * * *

"The result achieved under the plan could have been accomplished by having the California corporation acquire the assets of the Delaware corporation for its stock, and by having the latter distribute the stock to its stockholders in complete liquidation. Petitioner and his associates apparently chose the longer route, hoping that they might thereby become entitled to a loss deduction. However, as the Supreme Court pointed out in Minnesota Tea Co. v. Helvering, 302 U.S. 609, 613, 'a given result at the end of a straight path is not made a different result because reached by following a devious path.' The effect of all the steps taken was that petitioner made an exchange of stock of one corporation for stock of another pursuant to a plan of reorganization." (383–84)

In Rev.Rul. 67–448, 1967–2 C.B. 144, P Corporation formed a subsidiary, S Corporation, and contributed P's stock to the subsidiary. S Corporation was then merged into unrelated corporation Y with shareholders of Y receiving P Corporation stock in the merger. The Ruling treated the series of transactions as the direct acquisition by P of the Y stock in exchange of its own shares, thereby qualifying the transaction as a type (B) reorganization. "It is evident that the shortest route to the end result described above would have been achieved by a transfer of P voting stock directly to the shareholders of Y in exchange for their stock. This result is not negated because the transaction was cast in the form of a series of interrelated steps. The transitory existence of the new subsidiary, S, will be disregarded. The effect of all the steps taken in the series is that Y became a wholly owned subsidiary of P, and P transferred solely its voting stock to the former shareholders of Y." (145) The Ruling dealt with a situation arising before the enactment of § 368(a)(2)(E).

In yet other cases, the step transaction doctrine may be applied to find that no reorganization meeting the statutory definition existed in substance, even though one existed in form. In McDonald's Restaurants of Illinois, Inc. v. Commissioner, 688 F.2d 520 (7th Cir.1982), McDonald's acquired a number of corporations that owned franchised McDonald's restaurants in a merger in which it gave the shareholders of the acquired corporations only McDonald's common stock. Pursuant to the merger agreement, McDonald's facilitated the subsequent sale on the New York Stock Exchange by the shareholders of the McDonald's stock acquired in the merger. The Court of Appeals reversed the Tax Court's decision that the step transaction doctrine did not apply. It held that because the shareholders intended all along to sell the stock they received in the merger, McDonald's knew of their intent, and McDonald's was obligated by the merger agreement to facilitate their sale, the "spirit" of the binding commitment test had been met. Accordingly, as argued by the taxpayer—McDonald's Corporation—the transaction was treated as a cash merger, taxed as a sale and purchase, not as a tax free reorganization. McDonald's thus received a stepped-up purchase price basis in the assets of the acquired corporations. On nearly identical facts, in Penrod v. Commissioner, 88 T.C. 1415 (1987), the Tax Court held that regardless of the appropriate variation of the step transaction doctrine that applied, the merger and subsequent sale of the stock should not be stepped together because there was no evidence that at the time they received it the shareholders intended to sell their McDonald's stock. Accordingly, the transaction in *Penrod* was treated as a tax-free reorganization, and the acquiring corporation took a transferred basis in the acquired corporation's assets. Under Treas. Reg. § 1.368–1(e), page 534, the specific continuity of interest issue with which these two case dealt no longer arises, but the analytical methodology employed in them continues to be relevant to application of the step transaction doctrine.

In yet other cases, a reorganization undoubtedly has occurred, but the question is the scope the reorganization and the identification of the transactions that will be accorded nonrecognition as occurring "pursuant to the plan of reorganization." This type of issue was the question addressed in *King Enterprises, Inc.* Another case raising a similar issue was J.E. Seagram Corp. v. Commissioner, 104 T.C. 75 (1995). This case involved a battle of corporate giants for control of Conoco. J.E. Seagram, approached Conoco to negotiate for a friendly takeover. After negotiations broke down, Seagram made a public tender offer to acquire for cash at least 33 percent of the Conoco shares. In the meantime, Conoco entered into an agreement with DuPont pursuant to which DuPont agreed to acquire at least 51 percent of Conoco's shares for either stock or cash, provided a minimum number of shares had been acquired for stock. Pursuant to the agreement, after the requisite number of shares had been acquired, Conoco would then be merged into a subsidiary of DuPont and Conoco shareholders would receive DuPont stock. Mobil Oil then entered the fray and an escalating round of purchase price increases ensued. Seagram acquired 32 percent of the Conoco stock for cash. Mobil dropped out. DuPont's tender offer was successful, and it acquired 51 percent of the Conoco shares for either stock or cash, including approximately 16 million newly issued Conoco shares acquired pursuant to an option granted to Conoco by DuPont. At this point, Seagram decided to accept DuPont stock, which constituted a little over 20 percent of the outstanding stock of DuPont, in exchange for its Conoco stock, and this exchange was completed pursuant to the tender offer. DuPont then completed its agreement with Conoco by merging Conoco into a DuPont subsidiary. Seagram claimed a loss on the exchange on the theory that because approximately 78 percent of the original Conoco shareholders had sold their stock for cash, the transaction lacked the requisite continuity of interest to qualify as a reorganization, even though approximately 54 percent of the Conoco shares were acquired by DuPont in exchange for its own shares. The Commissioner denied the loss, claiming that there was an integrated plan of reorganization and § 354 was thus applicable.

The first issue in *J.E. Seagram Corp.* was whether the exchange of Conoco stock held by J.E. Seagram for DuPont stock was "in pursuance of the plan of reorganization," as required by § 354 as a condition for nonrecognition. J.E. Seagram argued that the exchange of its Conoco common stock for DuPont common stock was not done in pursuance of a plan of reorganization, as required by § 354, and that therefore it could recognize a loss on the exchange. It claimed that DuPont's tender offer and the subsequent merger were separate independent transactions.

The Tax Court rejected J.E. Seagram's argument:

"The concept of "plan of reorganization" * * *is one of substantial elasticity. * * * One commentator has stated that

> The courts, and the Service where it has served its purposes, have adopted a functional approach to the problem that is undoubtedly consistent with congressional intent. They have held that a plan of reorganization is a series of transactions intended to accomplish a transaction described as a reorganization in section 368, regardless of how and in what form the plan is expressed and whether the parties intended tax free treatment. * * * [Faber, "The Use and Misuse of the Plan of Reorganization Concept," 38 Tax L. Rev. 515, 523 (1982–1983).]

"The DuPont/Conoco Agreement was the definitive vehicle spelling out the interrelated steps by which DuPont would acquire 100 percent of Conoco's stock. To explain the mechanics of the type of procedure utilized by DuPont and Conoco, respondent submitted an 'Expert Affidavit' of Bernard S. Black. Black is a Professor of Law at the Columbia University School of Law, where he teaches courses in Corporate Finance, Securities and Capital Markets Regulations, and Corporate Acquisitions. * * *

"In the affidavit, Professor Black states that

> In substance, DuPont's bid for Conoco was a minor variant on a standard two-step acquisition, in which the parties sign a merger agreement that contemplates a first-step cash tender offer, to be followed by a second-step merger. The parties to an acquisition often use this transaction form, rather than a single-step merger (without a tender offer), because a tender offer can close faster than a merger, which increases the likelihood that the acquisition will be completed. * * *

Professor Black goes on to observe that 'DuPont added a third step to this transaction form—an exchange offer of DuPont stock for Conoco stock.'

"The DuPont/Conoco Agreement, which definitively states the terms for 'the acquisition of [Conoco] by [DuPont] * * *', sets out the steps referred to by Professor Black in his affidavit—the series of transactions which in their totality were intended to accomplish a section 368 reorganization. * * *

"It has been said that 'reorganizations, like other commercial events, must have a discrete start and a finish.' See Bittker & Eustice, Federal Income Taxation of Corporations and Shareholders, par. 12.21.[10]. Uncertainty in this regard can present questions as to whether various steps can be considered together as a unified transaction constituting a reorganization. * * *

"The Agreement provides a discrete start and finish, and the record discloses no steps agreed to outside the Agreement, or pre-Agreement activity by DuPont or its shareholders, that would invalidate the contemplated reorganization. * * *

"In Commissioner v. Gordon, supra * * *, the Supreme Court held that the requirement that the character of a transaction be determinable means that 'if one transaction is to be characterized as a "first step" there must be a binding commitment to take the later steps.' This requirement has been met. While DuPont's acquisition of control of Conoco by means of the tender offer unquestionably had economic significance, 'independent' or not, and unquestionably was not a 'meaningless step,' DuPont * * * [was] under a binding and irrevocable commitment to complete the culminating merger—the second step—upon the successful completion of the DuPont tender offer—the first step.

"Petitioner argues that DuPont had a 'plan' to engage in a series of transactions that might 'ultimately may include a reorganization,' but not a 'plan of reorganization'. For reasons already discussed, we disagree. We hold that, because DuPont was contractually committed to undertake and complete the second step merger once it had undertaken and completed the first step tender offer, these carefully integrated transactions together constituted a plan of reorganization within the contemplation of section 354(a)." (93–99)

Despite the existence of the step transaction doctrine, in some situations, the tax result may in the end become one turning purely on form alone, with one route leading to one tax consequence and another route leading to a different tax consequence, though the non-tax end result is the same. See Granite Trust Co. v. United States, 238 F.2d 670 (1st Cir.1956), page 356. In the end, determining when the form of a particular transaction will be respected and when a step transaction approach will be applied is a complex process that resists a simple verbal formulation. Nonetheless, it is central to understanding the reorganization provisions and corporate taxation generally.

C. THE STEP TRANSACTION DOCTRINE AND THE CONTINUITY OF INTEREST REGULATIONS

Although Treas. Reg. § 1.368–1(e), promulgated in 1998, eliminated the application of the step transaction doctrine in determining whether pre-reorganization sales of target corporation stock and post-reorganization sales of acquired corporation stock by former shareholders of the target affect whether the continuity of interest requirement is satisfied, Treas. Reg. § 1.368–1(a) was amended at the same time specifically to require that "[i]n determining whether a transaction qualifies as a reorganization under section 368(a), the transaction must be evaluated under the relevant provisions of law, including the step transaction doctrine." An example of the application of the step transaction that results in failure to meet the continuity of interest requirement even though the acquiring corporation putatively acquires 100 percent of the stock of the target in exchange for stock is provided in Treas. Reg. § 1.368–1(e)(6), Ex. 5:

"Redemption in substance by issuing corporation. A owns 100 percent of the stock of T and none of the stock of P. T merges into P. In the merger, A receives P stock. In connection with the merger, B buys all of the P stock received by A in the merger for cash. Shortly thereafter, in connection with the merger, P redeems the stock held by B for cash. Based on all the facts and circumstances, P in substance has exchanged solely cash for T stock in the merger. The continuity of interest requirement is not satisfied, because in substance P redeemed the stock exchanged for a proprietary interest in T, and a substantial part of the value of the proprietary interest in T is not preserved."

E. TAX RESULTS TO THE PARTIES TO A REORGANIZATION

The consequences to the parties to a reorganization generally do not vary significantly as result of which of the several different subsections of § 368 defines the reorganization. The type (A) reorganization represents the simplest type of acquisitive reorganization. Section 368(a)(1)(A) defines an (A) reorganization as a "statutory merger or consolidation." See Treas. Reg. § 1.368–2(b)(1). Thus, generally speaking, any type of amalgamation or consolidation of corporate entities under state merger statutes meets the statutory definition. The assets and liabilities of the target corporation are transferred to the acquiring corporation by operation of state law; the shareholders of the target corporation receive the consideration agreed upon in the merger agreement in exchange for their stock. The consideration may include property other than stock or securities. There are no statutory requirements regarding the proportion of the consideration that must include stock. Thus, the judicially developed continuity of interest requirement, now incorporated in the regulations, is determinative in qualification as a type (A) reorganization.

The type (C) reorganization is treated very similarly to a statutory merger, and the forward triangular merger (§ 368(a)(2)(D)) and reverse triangular merger (§ 368(a)(2)(E)) reorganizations are merely variations of the type (A) reorganization as far as treatment of parties to the reorganization is concerned. The type (B) reorganization, however, is the only form of tax free reorganization that involves a direct transaction between the acquiring corporation and the shareholders of the target corporation. In addition, it is the only reorganization that does not involve at least one corporation that disappears in the transaction. As a result, it can produce somewhat different tax results to the parties to the reorganization.

This section examines the overarching principles involving taxation of the parties to a reorganization and deals comprehensively with the tax treatment of parties to a type (A) reorganization. Special aspects of the treatment of parties to other forms of reorganizations are discussed in succeeding sections, along with the detailed rules for qualifying as a tax-free reorganization under those subsections of § 368.

(1) SHAREHOLDERS AND SECURITY HOLDERS

INTERNAL REVENUE CODE: Sections 354(a); 356(a), (c), (d), (e); 358(a), (b); 368(b).

REGULATIONS: Sections 1.354–1(a), (b), (d),Ex.4, (e); 1.356–1,–3,–4; 1.358–1,–2; 1.368–2(f), (g).

Commissioner v. Clark

Supreme Court of the United States, 1989.
489 U.S. 726.

■ JUSTICE STEVENS delivered the opinion of the Court.

This is the third case in which the Government has asked us to decide that a shareholder's receipt of a cash payment in exchange for a portion of his stock was taxable as a dividend. In the two earlier cases, Commissioner v. Estate of Bedford, 325 U.S. 283, 65 S.Ct. 1157 * * * (1945), and United States v. Davis, 397 U.S. 301, 90 S.Ct. 1041 * * * (1970), we agreed with the Government largely because the transactions involved redemptions of stock by single corporations that did not "result in a meaningful reduction of the shareholder's proportionate interest in the corporation." Id., at 313, 90 S.Ct. at 1048. In the case we decide today, however, the taxpayer in an arm's length transaction exchanged his interest in the acquired corporation for less than one percent of the stock of the acquiring corporation and a substantial cash payment. The taxpayer held no interest in the acquiring corporation prior to the reorganization. Viewing the exchange as a whole, we conclude that the cash payment is not appropriately characterized as a dividend. We accordingly agree with the Tax Court and with the Court of Appeals that the taxpayer is entitled to capital gains treatment of the cash payment.

I

In determining tax liability under the Internal Revenue Code, gain resulting from the sale or exchange of property is generally treated as capital gain, whereas the receipt of cash dividends is treated as ordinary income. The Code, however, imposes no current tax on certain stock-for-stock exchanges. In particular, § 354(a)(1) provides, subject to various limitations, for nonrecognition of gain resulting from the exchange of stock or securities solely for other stock or securities, provided that the exchange is pursuant to a plan of corporate reorganization and that the stock or securities are those of a party to the reorganization. 26 U.S.C. § 354(a)(1).

Under § 356(a)(1) of the Code, if such a stock-for-stock exchange is accompanied by additional consideration in the form of a cash payment or other property—something that tax practitioners refer to as "boot"—"then the gain, if any, to the recipient shall be recognized, but in an amount not in excess of the sum of such money and the fair market value of such other property." 26 U.S.C. § 356(a)(1). That is, if the shareholder receives boot, he or she must recognize the gain on the exchange up to the value of the boot. Boot is accordingly generally treated as a gain from the sale or exchange of property and is recognized in the current tax-year.

Section 356(a)(2), which controls the decision in this case, creates an exception to that general rule. * * * [If] the "exchange * * * has the effect of the distribution of a dividend," the boot must be treated as a dividend and is therefore appropriately taxed as ordinary income to the extent that gain is realized. In contrast, if the exchange does not have "the effect of the distribution of a dividend," the boot must be treated as a payment in exchange for property and, insofar as gain is realized, accorded capital gains treatment. The question in this case is thus whether the exchange between the taxpayer and the acquiring corporation had "the effect of the distribution of a dividend" within the meaning of § 356(a)(2).

The relevant facts are easily summarized. For approximately 15 years prior to April 1979, the taxpayer was the sole shareholder and president of Basin Surveys, Inc. (Basin), a company in which he had invested approximately $85,000. The corporation operated a successful business providing various technical services to the petroleum industry. In 1978, N.L. Industries, Inc. (NL), a publicly owned corporation engaged in the manufacture and supply of petroleum equipment and services, initiated negotiations with the taxpayer regarding the possible acquisition of Basin. On April 3, 1979, after months of negotiations, the taxpayer and NL entered into a contract.

The agreement provided for a "triangular merger," whereby Basin was merged into a wholly owned subsidiary of NL. In exchange for transferring all of the outstanding shares in Basin to NL's subsidiary, the taxpayer elected to receive 300,000 shares of NL common stock and cash boot of $3,250,000, passing up an alternative offer of 425,000 shares of NL common stock. The 300,000 shares of NL issued to the taxpayer amounted to approximately 0.92% of the outstanding common shares of NL. If the taxpayer had instead accepted the pure stock-for-stock offer, he would have held approximately 1.3% of the outstanding common shares. The Commissioner and the taxpayer agree that the merger at issue qualifies as a reorganization under § 368(a)(1)(A) and (a)(2)(D).

Respondents * * * reported the cash boot as taxable gain. In calculating the tax owed, respondents characterized the payment as long-term capital gain. The Commissioner on audit disagreed with this characterization. In his view, the payment had "the effect of the distribution of a dividend" and was thus taxable as ordinary income up to $2,319,611, the amount of Basin's accumulated earnings and profits at the time of the merger. * * *

Respondents petitioned for review in the Tax Court, which, in a reviewed decision, held in their favor. 86 T.C. 138 (1986). The court started from the premise that the question whether the boot payment had "the effect of the distribution of a dividend" turns on the choice between "two judicially articulated tests." Id., at 140. Under the test advocated by the Commissioner and given voice in Shimberg v. United States, 577 F.2d 283 (C.A.5 1978), cert. denied, 439 U.S. 1115, 99 S.Ct. 1019 * * * (1979), the boot payment is treated as though it were made in a hypothetical redemption by the acquired corporation (Basin) immediately *prior* to the reorganization. Under this test, the cash payment received by the taxpayer indisputably would have been treated as a dividend.[6] The second test, urged by

6. The parties do not agree as to whether dividend equivalence for the purposes of § 356(a)(2) should be determined with reference to § 302 of the Code, which concerns dividend treatment of redemptions of stock by a single corporation outside the context of a reorganization. Compare Brief for the United States 28–30 with Brief for Respondent 18–24. They are in essential agreement, however, about the characteristics of a dividend. Thus, the Government correctly argues that the "basic attribute of a dividend, derived from Sections 301 and 316 of the Code, is a pro rata distribution to shareholders out of corporate earnings and profits. When a distribution is made that is not a formal dividend, 'the fundamental test of dividend equivalency' is whether the distribution is proportionate to the shareholders' stock interests (United States v. Davis, 397 U.S. 301, 306 [90 S.Ct. 1041, 1044, 25 L.Ed.2d 323] (1970))." Brief for Petitioner 7. Citing the same authority, but with different emphasis, the taxpayer argues that "the hallmark of a non-dividend distribution is a 'meaningful reduction of the shareholder's proportionate interest in the corporation.' United States v. Davis, 397 U.S. 301, 313 [90 S.Ct. 1041, 1048, 25 L.Ed.2d 323] (1970)." Brief for Respondents 5.

the taxpayer and finding support in Wright v. United States, 482 F.2d 600 (C.A.8 1973), proposes an alternative hypothetical redemption. Rather than concentrating on the taxpayer's pre-reorganization interest in the acquired corporation, this test requires that one imagine a pure stock-for-stock exchange, followed immediately by a post-reorganization redemption of a portion of the taxpayer's shares in the acquiring corporation (NL) in return for a payment in an amount equal to the boot. Under § 302 of the Code, which defines when a redemption of stock should be treated as a distribution of dividend, NL's redemption of 125,000 shares of its stock from the taxpayer in exchange for the $3,250,000 boot payment would have been treated as capital gain.[7]

The Tax Court rejected the pre-reorganization test favored by the Commissioner because it considered it improper "to view the cash payment as an isolated event totally separate from the reorganization." 86 T.C., at 151. Indeed, it suggested that this test requires that courts make the "determination of dividend equivalency fantasizing that the reorganization does not exist." Id., at 150 (footnote omitted). The court then acknowledged that a similar criticism could be made of the taxpayer's contention that the cash payment should be viewed as a post-reorganization redemption. It concluded, however, that since it was perfectly clear that the cash payment would not have taken place without the reorganization, it was better to treat the boot "as the equivalent of a redemption *in the course of implementing the reorganization,*" than "as having occurred *prior to and separate from the reorganization.*" Id., at 152 (emphasis in original).[8]

Under either test, a pre-reorganization distribution by Basin to the taxpayer would have qualified as a dividend. Because the taxpayer was Basin's sole shareholder, any distribution necessarily would have been pro rata and would not have resulted in a "meaningful reduction of the [taxpayer's] proportionate interest in [Basin]."

7. * * * As the Tax Court explained, receipt of the cash boot reduced the taxpayer's potential holdings in NL from 1.3% to 0.92%. 86 T.C., at 153. The taxpayer's holdings were thus approximately 71% of what they would have been absent the payment. Ibid. This fact, combined with the fact that the taxpayer held less than 50% of the voting stock of NL after the hypothetical redemption, would have qualified the "distribution" as "substantially disproportionate" under § 302(b)(2).

8. The Tax Court stressed that to adopt the pre-reorganization view "would in effect resurrect the now discredited 'automatic dividend rule' * * *, at least with respect to pro rata distributions made to an acquired corporation's shareholders pursuant to a plan of reorganization." 86 T.C., at 152. On appeal, the Court of Appeals agreed. 828 F.2d 221, 226–227 (C.A.4 1987).

The "automatic dividend rule" developed as a result of some imprecise language in our decision in Commissioner v. Estate of Bedford, 325 U.S. 283, 65 S.Ct. 1157, 89 L.Ed. 1611 (1945). Although *Estate of Bedford* involved the recapitalization of a single corporation, the opinion employed broad language, asserting that "a distribution, pursuant to a reorganization, of earnings and profits 'has the effect of a distribution of a taxable dividend' within [§ 356(a)(2)]." Id., at 292, 65 S.Ct., at 1161. * * * The courts have long since retreated from the "automatic dividend rule," see, e.g., Idaho Power Co. v. United States, 161 F.Supp. 807, 142 Ct.Cl. 534, cert. denied, 358 U.S. 832, 79 S.Ct. 53, * * * (1958), and the Commissioner has followed suit, see Rev.Rul. 74–515, 1974–2 C.B. 118. As our decision in this case makes plain, we agree that *Estate of Bedford* should not be read to require that all payments of boot be treated as dividends.

The Court of Appeals for the Fourth Circuit affirmed. 828 F.2d 221 (1987). Like the Tax Court, it concluded that although "[s]ection 302 does not explicitly apply in the reorganization context," id., at 223, and although § 302 differs from § 356 in important respects, id., at 224, it nonetheless provides "the appropriate test for determining whether boot is ordinary income or a capital gain," id., at 223. Thus, as explicated in § 302(b)(2), if the taxpayer relinquished more than 20% of his corporate control and retained less than 50% of the voting shares after the distribution, the boot would be treated as capital gain. However, as the Court of Appeals recognized, "[b]ecause § 302 was designed to deal with a stock redemption by a single corporation, rather than a reorganization involving two companies, the section does not indicate which corporation [the taxpayer] lost interest in." Id., at 224. Thus, like the Tax Court, the Court of Appeals was left to consider whether the hypothetical redemption should be treated as a pre-reorganization distribution coming from the acquired corporation or as a post-reorganization distribution coming from the acquiring corporation. It concluded:

> "Based on the language and legislative history of § 356, the change-in-ownership principle of § 302, and the need to review the reorganization as an integrated transaction, we conclude that the boot should be characterized as a post-reorganization stock redemption by N.L. that affected [the taxpayer's] interest in the new corporation. Because this redemption reduced [the taxpayer's] N.L. holdings by more than 20%, the boot should be taxed as a capital gain." Id., at 224–225.

This decision by the Court of Appeals for the Fourth Circuit is in conflict with the decision of the Fifth Circuit in *Shimberg,* 577 F.2d 283 (1978), in two important respects. In *Shimberg,* the court concluded that it was inappropriate to apply stock redemption principles in reorganization cases "on a wholesale basis." Id., at 287 * * *. In addition, the court adopted the pre-reorganization test, holding that "§ 356(a)(2) requires a determination of whether the distribution would have been taxed as a dividend if made prior to the reorganization or if no reorganization had occurred." Id., at 288.

* * *

II

We agree with the Tax Court and the Court of Appeals for the Fourth Circuit that the question under § 356(a)(2) of whether an "exchange * * * has the effect of the distribution of a dividend" should be answered by examining the effect of the exchange as a whole. We think the language and history of the statute, as well as a common-sense understanding of the economic substance of the transaction at issue, support this approach.

The language of § 356(a) strongly supports our understanding that the transaction should be treated as an integrated whole. Section 356(a)(2) asks whether "*an exchange* is described in paragraph (1)" that "has the effect of the distribution of a dividend." (Emphasis supplied.) The statute does not provide that boot shall be treated as a dividend if its payment has the effect of the distribution of a dividend. Rather, the inquiry turns on whether the "exchange" has that effect. Moreover, paragraph (1), in turn, looks to whether "the property received in *the exchange* consists not only of property permitted by section 354 or 355 to be received without the recognition of gain but also of other property or money." (Emphasis supplied.) Again, the statute plainly refers to one integrated transaction and, again, makes clear that we are to look to the character of the exchange as a whole and not simply its component parts. Finally, it is significant that § 356 expressly limits the extent to which boot may be taxed to the amount of gain realized in the reorganization. This limitation suggests that Congress intended that boot not be treated in isolation from the overall reorganization.

* * *

Our reading of the statute as requiring that the transaction be treated as a unified whole is reinforced by the well-established "step-transaction" doctrine, * * *.

Viewing the exchange in this case as an integrated whole, we are unable to accept the Commissioner's pre-reorganization analogy. The analogy severs the payment of boot from the context of the reorganization. Indeed, only by straining to abstract the payment of boot from the context of the overall exchange, and thus imagining that Basin made a distribution to the taxpayer independently of NL's planned acquisition, can we reach the rather counterintuitive conclusion urged by the Commissioner—that the taxpayer suffered no meaningful reduction in his ownership interest as a result of the cash payment. We conclude that such a limited view of the transaction is plainly inconsistent with the statute's direction that we look to the effect of the entire exchange.

The pre-reorganization analogy is further flawed in that it adopts an overly expansive reading of § 356(a)(2). As the Court of Appeals recognized, adoption of the pre-reorganization approach would "result in ordinary income treatment in most reorganizations because corporate boot is usually distributed pro rata to the shareholders of the target corporation." 828 F.2d, at 227. * * * Such a reading of the statute would not simply constitute a return to the widely criticized "automatic dividend rule" (at least as to cases involving a pro rata payment to the shareholders of the acquired corporation), see n. 8, supra, but also would be contrary to our standard approach to construing such provisions. The requirement of § 356(a)(2) that boot be treated as dividend in some circumstances is an exception from the general rule authorizing capital gains treatment for boot. In construing provisions such as § 356, in which a general statement of policy is qualified by an exception, we usually read the exception narrowly in order to preserve the primary operation of the provision. * * * Given that Congress has enacted a general rule that treats boot as capital gain, we should not eviscerate that legislative judgment through an expansive reading of a somewhat ambiguous exception.

The post-reorganization approach adopted by the Tax Court and the Court of Appeals is, in our view, preferable to the Commissioner's approach. Most significantly, this approach does a far better job of treating the payment of boot as a component of the overall exchange. Unlike the pre-reorganization view, this approach acknowledges that there would have been no cash payment absent the exchange and also that, by accepting the cash payment, the taxpayer experienced a meaningful reduction in his potential ownership interest.

Once the post-reorganization approach is adopted, the result in this case is pellucidly clear. Section 302(a) of the Code provides that if a redemption fits within any one of the four categories set out in § 302(b), the redemption "shall be treated as a distribution in part or full payment in exchange for the stock," and thus not regarded as a dividend. As the Tax Court and the Court of Appeals correctly determined, the hypothetical post-reorganization redemption by NL of a portion of the taxpayer's shares satisfies at least one of the subsections of § 302(b). In particular, the safe harbor provisions of subsection (b)(2) provide that redemptions in which the taxpayer relinquishes more than 20% of his or her share of the corporation's voting stock and retains less than 50% of the voting of stock after the redemption, shall not be treated as distributions of a dividend. * * * Here, we treat the transaction as though NL redeemed 125,000 shares of its common stock (i.e., the number of shares of NL common stock foregone in favor of the boot) in return for a cash payment to the taxpayer of $3,250,000 (i.e., the amount of the boot). As a result of this redemption, the taxpayer's interest in NL was reduced from 1.3% of the outstanding common stock to 0.9%. See 86 T.C., at 153. Thus, the taxpayer relinquished approximately 29% of his interest in NL and retained less than a 1% voting interest in the corporation after the transaction, easily satisfying the "substantially disproportionate" standards of § 302(b)(2). We accordingly conclude that the boot payment did not have the effect of a dividend and that the payment was properly treated as capital gain.

III

The Commissioner objects to this "recasting [of] the merger transaction into a form different from that entered into by the parties," Brief for the United States 11, and argues that the Court of Appeals' formal adherence to the principles embodied in § 302 forced the court to stretch to "find a redemption to which to apply them, since the merger transaction entered into by the parties did not involve a redemption," id., at 28. There are a number of sufficient responses to this argument. We think it first worth emphasizing that the Commissioner overstates the extent to which the redemption is imagined. As the Court of Appeals for the Fifth Circuit noted in *Shimberg,* "[t]he theory behind tax-free corporate reorganizations is that the transaction is merely 'a continuance of the proprietary interests in the continuing enterprise under modified corporate form.' " * * * As a result, the boot-for-stock transaction can be viewed as a partial repurchase of stock by the continuing corporate enterprise—i.e., as a redemption. It is of course true that both the pre-and post-reorganization analogies are somewhat artificial in that they imagine that the redemption occurred outside the confines of the actual reorganization. However, if forced to choose between the two analogies, the post-reorganization view is the less artificial. Although both analogies "recast the merger transaction," the post-reorganization view recognizes that a reorganization has taken place, while the pre-reorganization approach recasts the transaction to the exclusion of the overall exchange.

Moreover, we doubt that abandoning the pre-and post-reorganization analogies and the principles of § 302 in favor of a less artificial understanding of the transaction would lead to a result different from that reached by the Court of Appeals. Although the statute is admittedly ambiguous and the legislative history sparse, we are persuaded—even without relying on § 302—that Congress did not intend to except reorganizations such as that at issue here from the general rule allowing capital gains treatment for cash boot. 26 U.S.C. § 356(a)(1). The legislative history of § 356(a)(2), although perhaps generally "not illuminating," Estate of Bedford, 325 U.S., at 290, 65 S.Ct., at 1160, suggests that Congress was primarily concerned with preventing corporations from "siphon[ing] off" accumulated earnings and profits at a capital gains rate through the ruse of a reorganization. * * * This purpose is not served by denying capital gains treatment in a case such as this in which the taxpayer entered into an arm's length transaction with a corporation in which he had no prior interest, exchanging his stock in the acquired corporation for less than a one percent interest in the acquiring corporation and a substantial cash boot.

* * *

Moreover, the legislative history of § 302 supports this reading of § 356(a)(2) as well. In explaining the "essentially equivalent to a dividend" language of § 302(b)(1)—language that is certainly similar to the "has the effect * * * of a dividend" language of § 356(a)(2)—the Senate Finance Committee made clear that the relevant inquiry is "whether or not the transaction by its nature may properly be characterized as a sale of stock. * * * " S.Rep. No. 1622, 83d Cong., 2d Sess., 234 (1954); cf. United States v. Davis, 397 U.S., at 311, 90 S.Ct., at 1047.

Examining the instant transaction in light of the purpose of § 356(a)(2), the boot-for-stock exchange in this case "may properly be characterized as a sale of stock." Significantly, unlike traditional single corporation redemptions and unlike reorganizations involving commonly owned corporations, there is little risk that the reorganization at issue was used as a ruse to distribute dividend. Rather, the transaction appears in all respects relevant to the narrow issue before us to have been comparable to an arm's length sale by the taxpayer to NL. This conclusion, moreover, is supported by the findings of the Tax Court. The court found that "[t]here is not the slightest evidence that the cash payment was a concealed distribution from BASIN." 86 T.C., at 155. As the Tax Court further noted, Basin lacked the funds to make such a distribution:

"Indeed, it is hard to conceive that such a possibility could even have been considered, for a distribution of that amount was not only far in excess of the accumulated earnings and profits ($2,319,611), but also of the total assets of BASIN ($2,758,069). In fact, only if one takes into account unrealized appreciation in the value of BASIN's assets, including good will and/or going-concern value, can one possibly arrive at $3,250,000. Such a distribution could only be considered as the equivalent of a complete liquidation of BASIN. * * * " Ibid.

In this context, even without relying on § 302 and the post-reorganization analogy, we conclude that the boot is better characterized as a part of the proceeds of a sale of stock than as a proxy for a dividend. As such, the payment qualifies for capital gains treatment.

The judgment of the Court of Appeals is accordingly

AFFIRMED.

■ JUSTICE WHITE, dissenting.

* * *

[T]he question today is whether the cash payment to Clark had the *effect* of a distribution of a dividend. We supplied the straightforward answer in United States v. Davis, 397 U.S. 301, 306, 312, 90 S.Ct. 1041, 1044, 1047, * * * (1970), when we explained that a pro rata redemption of stock by a corporation is "essentially equivalent" to a dividend. A pro rata distribution of stock, with no alteration of basic shareholder relationships, is the hallmark of a dividend. This was precisely Clark's gain. As sole shareholder of Basin, Clark necessarily received a pro rata distribution of monies that exceeded Basin's undistributed earnings and profits of $2,319,611. Because the merger and cash obligation occurred simultaneously on April 18, 1979, and because the statutory merger approved here assumes that Clark's proprietary interests continue in the restructured NLAC, the exact source of the pro rata boot payment is immaterial, which truth Congress acknowledged by requiring only that an exchange have the *effect* of a dividend distribution.

To avoid this conclusion, the Court of Appeals—approved by the majority today—recast the transaction as though the relevant distribution involved a single corporation's (NL's) stock redemption, which dividend equivalency is determined according to § 302 of the Code. Section 302 shields distributions from dividend taxation if the cash redemption is accompanied by sufficient loss of a shareholder's percentage interest in the corporation. The Court of Appeals hypothesized that Clark completed a pure stock-for-stock reorganization, receiving 425,000 NL shares, and thereafter redeemed 125,000 of these shares for his cash earnings of $3,250,000. The sum escapes dividend taxation because Clark's interest in NL theoretically declined from 1.3% to 0.92%, adequate to trigger § 302(b)(2) protection. Transporting § 302 from its purpose to frustrate shareholder sales of equity back to their own corporation, to § 356(a)(2)'s reorganization context, however, is problematic. Neither the majority nor the Court of Appeals explains why § 302 should obscure the core attribute of a dividend as a pro rata distribution to a corporation's shareholders,[1] nor offers insight into the mechanics of valuing hypothetical stock transfers and equity reductions; nor answers the Commissioner's observations that the sole shareholder of an acquired corporation will always have a smaller interest in the continuing enterprise when cash payments combine with a stock exchange. Last, the majority and the Court of Appeals' recharacterization of market happenings describes the exact stock-for-stock exchange, without a cash supplement, that Clark refused when he agreed to the merger.

Because the parties chose to structure the exchange as a tax-free reorganization under § 354(a)(1), and because the pro rata distribution to Clark of $3,250,000, during this reorganization had the *effect* of a dividend under § 356(a)(2), I dissent.

ILLUSTRATIVE MATERIAL

A. NONRECOGNITION OF GAIN

Section 354 protects the shareholders from gain recognition to the extent they receive stock of the acquiring corporation. Where cash or other non-qualifying property, including debt securities, is received in addition to stock, the shareholders will recognize gain under § 356, but only to the extent of the amount of cash or the fair market value of the other property received. If a shareholder exchanges more than one block of stock in exchange for stock and boot, the gain must be computed separately on each block; gain may be recognized on one block of stock while an unrecognized loss is realized on the other. Rev.Rul. 68–23, 1968–1 C.B. 144. If a loss has been realized, it may not be recognized even though boot has been received. I.R.C. § 356(c). Section 356(a)(2) provides that gain recognized under § 356(a) sometimes may be treated as a dividend depending upon the characterization of boot under the test of *Clark*. Problems also can arise if shareholders of the acquired corporation receive the right to obtain additional stock conditioned, for example, on the earnings level of the corporation. See page 601.

For the nonrecognition protection of § 354 to apply the stock must be received as part of the reorganization exchange. Thus, in Rev.Rul. 73–233, 1973–1 C.B. 179, where minority shareholders in a merger refused to vote in favor of the merger unless they received a disproportionate amount of stock in the acquiring corporation, the amount of stock received in excess of

1. The Court of Appeals' zeal to excoriate the "automatic dividend rule" leads to an opposite rigidity—an automatic nondividend rule, even for pro rata boot payments. Any significant cash payment in a stock-for-stock exchange distributed to a sole shareholder of an acquired corporation will automatically receive capital gains treatment. Section 356(a)(2)'s exception for such payments that have attributes of a dividend disappears. Congress did not intend to handicap the Commissioner and courts with either absolute; instead, § 356(a)(1) instructs courts to make fact-specific inquiries into whether boot distributions accompanying corporate reorganizations occur on a pro rata basis to shareholders of the acquired corporation, and thus threaten a bailout of the transferor corporation's earnings and profits escaping a proper dividend tax treatment.

their proportionate interest was taxable under § 61. A contribution to capital by the majority shareholder was disregarded and the transaction was treated as if all of the parties had received their proportionate shares of stock in the acquiring corporation with the majority shareholder then transferring to the minority shareholders additional shares of stock as consideration for their voting in favor of the merger.

B. CHARACTERIZATION OF GAIN

1. *Dividend versus Capital Gain*

The decision in *Clark* settled a long standing dispute regarding the manner in which dividend equivalency under § 356(b) is to be tested. The rule announced in *Clark* rejected the position taken by the Internal Revenue Service that the transaction was to be treated as if there had been a pre-reorganization redemption of shares of the acquired corporation. The pre-reorganization redemption analysis urged by the Internal Revenue Service in *Clark* leads to a dividend in all cases in which the boot is paid pro rata to the shareholders of the acquired corporation.

Contrary to the protestations of the dissent, however, the post-reorganization constructive redemption analysis adopted in *Clark* does not eliminate dividend treatment in all cases. Under the analysis adopted in *Clark*, proportionately larger cash distributions to the shareholders of the target corporation are more likely to receive capital gains treatment than relatively smaller amounts of boot, which remain susceptible to dividend characterization. Suppose that A and B each own 200 shares of common stock of T Corporation, which has outstanding 400 shares. Each of their blocks of stock has a basis of $50,000 and a fair market value of $200,000. In a valid type (A) reorganization, T Corporation is merged into P Corporation. Prior to the merger, P Corporation had outstanding 800 shares of common stock, which had an aggregate fair market value of $400,000. Each corporation has retained earnings and profits in excess of $200,000. Pursuant to the merger, A and B each receive in exchange for their T stock 240 newly issued shares of P Corporation common stock having a fair market value of $120,000 plus $80,000 of cash. Under the analysis of *Clark*, if A and B had received stock instead of cash, they each would have received 400 shares of P stock. Each would have held 25 percent of the outstanding P stock (400/1600 shares). After the $80,000 cash redemption, A and B each would have had 18.75 percent of the outstanding P stock (240/1280 shares). The boot thus qualifies for capital gain treatment as a redemption under § 302(b)(2) (18.75% is less than 80% of 25%). If A and B each were to receive $25,000 of cash and 350 shares of P stock, the boot is more likely to be treated as a dividend. A and B each would own 23.33 percent of the outstanding P stock (350 of 1500 outstanding shares). Under the analysis of *Clark*, the reduction in their interest from the 25 percent interest they would have held if they had received all stock to 23.33 percent is not enough to qualify the distribution as a redemption under § 302(b)(2). However, the boot might qualify for capital gain treatment under § 302(b)(1), although that result is anything but clear. See Rev.Rul. 76–

364, 1976–2 C.B. 91 and Rev.Rul. 75–512, 1975–2 C.B. 112, page 257, both of which involved additional circumstances.

2. *Earnings and Profits*

The opinion in *Clark* does not identify which corporation's earnings and profits are to be used to determine whether a distribution of boot is a dividend under § 316. Under § 381(a) and (c)(2), discussed at page 729, the acquiring corporation in a type (A) or type (C) reorganization inherits the earnings and profits of the target corporation. Following the post-acquisition redemption analysis of *Clark*, which views the exchange as an integrated whole, the distribution that is treated as a post-acquisition distribution by the acquiring corporation may be deemed to come from the earnings and profits of the acquiring corporation as enhanced by the earnings and profits of the target corporation. However, in cases involving type (D) reorganizations, the Tax Court has held that dividend status is measured by the earnings and profits of the target (transferor) corporation, rejecting the Commissioner's argument that dividend status should be determined from the combined earnings and profits of the acquiring and target corporations. Atlas Tool Co. v. Commissioner, 70 T.C. 86 (1978); American Manufacturing Co. v. Commissioner, 55 T.C. 204 (1970); but see Davant v. Commissioner, 366 F.2d 874 (5th Cir.1966) (looking to the earnings and profits of both corporations where there is identity of ownership). These authorities may be distinguished as predating *Clark* and by differences between type (A) and type (D) reorganizations, particularly in the context of the liquidation/reincorporation transactions at issue. See page 672.

What if neither the target corporation nor the acquiring corporation has accumulated earnings and profits as of the date of a reorganization, but the acquiring corporation has current earnings and profits for the taxable year in which it distributes boot that is taxable as a dividend under § 356(a)(2)? The reference of § 356(a)(2) to the distributee's "ratable share of earnings and profits accumulated after February 28, 1913," suggests that dividend status is dependent upon earnings and profits accumulated to the date of the distribution. See also Treas. Reg. § 1.356–1(b)(1).

C. BASIS CONSIDERATIONS

The basis for the stock of the acquiring corporation received by the shareholders of the target corporation without recognition of gain under § 354 is determined under § 358(a). That section provides that the basis of the stock is the same as the stock in the target corporation that was surrendered in the reorganization transaction. If, in addition to stock or securities of the acquiring corporation, nonqualifying "boot" is received, the aggregate basis of all property received in the exchange, including both qualified stock and securities and boot, first is increased by the sum of the gain recognized and the amount treated as a dividend under § 356(b). I.R.C. § 358(a)(1)(B). Then the amount of cash received is subtracted, and the boot is assigned a basis equal to its fair market value. The remaining basis is allocated among the qualified stock and securities, as provided in Treas. Reg. § 1.358–2.

Generally speaking, Treas. Reg. § 1.358–2 requires that the basis be allocated among the stock or securities received in proportion to their fair market values. Where a single class of stock or securities has been surrendered, the regulations permit the aggregate basis of the stock or securities to be used as the starting point in a single computation. Treas. Reg. § 1.358–2(a)(2) and (3), (c), Ex. (2). But where multiple blocks of stock or both stock and securities have been exchanged, the basis for each class of stock or securities surrendered must be assigned to the particular stock and securities received in exchange therefor. Treas. Reg. § 1.358–2(a)(4), (c), Ex. (3) and (4).

D. RECEIPT OF SECURITIES

1. *Amount of Boot*

Section 354(a) extends nonrecognition treatment to an exchange of "stock or securities * * * for stock or securities."[10] Thus, where the target corporation's securities become securities of the acquiring corporation under state law in a statutory merger, no gain or loss is recognized. However, § 354(a)(2) and § 356(d) treat the receipt of securities as boot if the principal amount of securities received is greater than the principal amount of any securities surrendered. The fair market value of the excess principal amount of securities received is treated as "other property." Where securities are received in exchange for only stock, the entire fair market value of the securities is treated as boot. Treas. Reg. § 1.356–3(b), Ex. (1). Where securities are received in exchange for other securities, only the fair market value of the excess principal amount constitutes boot. The value of the excess principal amount is determined by the following formula:

$$\text{Fair Market Value of Securities Received} \times \frac{\text{Principal Amount of Securities Received} \text{ minus } \text{Principal Amount of Securities Surrendered}}{\text{Principal Amount of Securities Received}}$$

In determining the "principal amount" of securities exchanged in the reorganization, the original issue discount rules of §§ 1272 and 1274, discussed at page 168, must be taken into account. If the OID rules do not apply, generally speaking, the amount of any excess face value of a security received over the face value of securities surrendered also will be the value of the excess. However, if the OID rules apply the principal amount of the securities exchanged must be reduced as required by those rules to an amount less than their face value when computing gain under § 356. Thus,

10. Generally under state law in a statutory merger outstanding securities of the target corporation become liabilities of the acquiring corporation. Without intervention of a nonrecognition provision the exchange of securities may be a taxable transaction. See Treas. Reg. § 1.1001–3. However, Treas. Reg. § 1.1001–3(e)(4)(i)(B) provides that a change in the obligor of a debt instrument in a transaction to which § 381 applies, which includes reorganizations qualified under § 368(a)(1)(A), is not a significant modification of the debt resulting in a taxable exchange.

receipt of a security having a *face* value in excess of the principal amount of the security surrendered will not give rise to boot under § 356 if under the OID rules the imputed principal amount of the security received does not exceed the principal amount of the security surrendered. Section 1273(b) applies to the determination of the amount of OID if either the securities surrendered or the securities received are publicly traded. In such a case, the "issue price" and thus the "principal amount" of the securities received will be equal to the fair market value of the publicly traded securities. If the securities received are not publicly traded, but the securities surrendered are so traded, then the issue price is the value of the securities surrendered. Section 1274 controls if the securities involved in the exchange are not publicly traded. See also Treas. Reg. § 1.356–3(d), Ex. (2)–(6). The application of these rules is discussed in greater detail at page 653.

2. *Installment Reporting*

Gain recognized on the receipt of securities in a reorganization may be reported using the installment method under § 453 unless either the stock or securities surrendered were readily tradable on an established securities market (§ 453(h)(1)) or the securities received are readily tradable (§ 453(f)(4)). See Prop. Reg. § 1.453–1(f)(2) (1984). In the case of gain reported under the installment method, the basis of the stock received in the reorganization is computed under Prop. Reg. § 1.453–1(f)(2) (1984) in the same manner as the basis of stock received in a § 351 transaction is computed if an installment note is received as boot. See page 84.

E. STOCK RIGHTS AND WARRANTS

For many years, exchanges involving stock warrants that were issued pursuant to a plan of reorganization appeared to be taxable notwithstanding that the transaction otherwise qualified for nonrecognition. Bateman v. Commissioner, 40 T.C. 408 (1963), held that warrants were not "stock" but did not resolve the issue whether they were securities or "other property," since in the situation involved the tax result would have been the same by virtue of § 354(a)(2)(A)(ii). Baan v. Commissioner, 51 T.C. 1032 (1969), aff'd on other grounds sub nom. Gordon v. Commissioner, 424 F.2d 378 (2d Cir.1970), held that stock rights were neither stock nor securities.

As amended in 1998, Treas. Regs. §§ 1.354–1(e) and 1.356–3(b) treat rights to acquire stock of a corporation (options and warrants) that is a party to a reorganization as securities of the corporation having no principal amount. The term "rights to acquire stock" of an issuing corporation has the same meaning as for purposes of §§ 305(d)(1) and 317(a). Thus, an exchange of options to purchase stock of the target corporation for options to purchase stock of the acquiring corporation is accorded nonrecognition, as is an exchange of target corporation bonds for acquiring corporation options. Likewise, an exchange of stock for stock and an option or an exchange of an option for stock and an option is not taxable. See Treas. Reg. § 1.356–3(c), Exs.(7) and (8). If, however, warrants are exchanged for debt securities, gain must be recognized. Treas. Reg. § 1.356–3(c), Ex.(9).

Arguably, however, because the receipt solely of warrants in exchange for stock is not covered by § 354, see Treas. Reg. § 1.354–1(d), Ex. 4, and § 356 technically applies only if some permissible consideration under § 354 is received in the exchange—an exchange of target stock solely for options to purchase stock of the acquiring corporation is not entitled to nonrecognition. The regulations do not address this point and it is not clear whether or not the ambiguity was intended. (In any event, a purported reorganization involving the exchange of target stock for only options to purchase stock of the acquiring corporation would fail the continuity of interest requirement.)

Rights exercisable against persons other than the issuer of the stock are not covered by Treas. Reg. § 1.354–1(e). Rev. Rul. 69–265, 1969–1 C.B. 109, held that a conversion privilege contained in a stock or debt instrument generally is not considered to be a separate property right received in the reorganization, and the regulations do not change that result. Treas. Regs. §§ 1.354–1(e) and 1.356–3(b) apply only in determining the amount of gain recognized in an otherwise qualifying reorganization. Thus, the regulations do not affect pre-existing law under which stock rights are not taken into account in determining whether the continuity of shareholder interest test has been satisfied. See Notice of Proposed Rulemaking and Notice of Public Hearings, Reorganizations, Receipt of Securities, REG–249819–96, 1997–1 C.B. 793, 794.

F. PREFERRED STOCK

1. *Section 306 Aspects*

If pursuant to the reorganization the shareholders of the acquired corporation surrender common stock and receive both common stock and preferred stock, the preferred stock will be characterized as § 306 stock pursuant to § 306(c)(1)(B) if "the effect of the transaction was substantially the same as the receipt of a stock dividend." See Treas. Reg. § 1.306–3(d). (Section 306 is discussed in Chapter 7.) The regulations and Rev.Rul. 56–586, 1956–2 C.B. 214, indicate that unless a cash distribution in lieu of the preferred stock would have been a dividend under § 356(a)(2), the stock will not be § 306 stock. As a result of the decision in *Clark,* classification of preferred stock received in an acquisitive reorganization as § 306 stock depends on the ratio of common stock to preferred stock received by the shareholder in the reorganization. Generally speaking, the higher the ratio of common to preferred, the more likely the preferred stock will be characterized as § 306 stock and the lower the ratio the more likely the preferred stock will not be so characterized.

Rev.Rul. 89–63, 1989–1 C.B. 90, held that where both common and preferred stock of a publicly held acquiring corporation were issued to the former holders of the common stock of a publicly held target corporation in a type (A) statutory merger, the preferred stock was § 306 stock. The Ruling did not provide any rationale for its conclusion that the stock was § 306 stock, and if cash had been distributed in lieu of the preferred stock, under *Clark* the cash would not have been substantially equivalent to a dividend. The fact that the corporations were publicly held, standing alone, was not sufficient to bring the preferred stock within the § 306(b)(4) exception for transactions not involving tax avoidance.

Preferred stock received for preferred stock in acquisitive reorganizations will not be § 306 stock if it is of equal value to the preferred stock surrendered, the terms of the new preferred stock are not substantially different from the terms of the old preferred stock, and the preferred stock surrendered in the exchange was not itself § 306 stock. Rev.Rul. 88–100, 1988–2 C.B. 46 (holding that Treas. Reg. § 1.306–3(d), Ex. (2), applies to acquisitive reorganizations); Rev.Rul. 82–118, 1982–1 C.B. 56. The Rulings emphasize that in such cases the new preferred stock is merely a substitute for the old preferred stock, and the distribution therefore does not have the effect of a distribution of earnings and profits. However, if the surrendered preferred stock was § 306 stock, then any preferred stock (or common stock) received in exchange for the tainted preferred stock will be § 306 stock. I.R.C. § 306(c)(1)(C).

2. *Nonqualified Preferred Stock*

Sections 354(a)(2)(C) and 356(e) require that "nonqualified preferred stock" be treated as boot for purposes of §§ 354 and 356. Nonqualified preferred stock is defined in § 351(g)(2), page 86. Preferred stock is stock that is limited and preferred as to dividends and which does not participate in corporate growth. I.R.C. § 351(g)(3)(A). Preferred stock is "nonqualified" only if within 20 years after issue, the issuer or a related person (1) may be required by the holder to redeem the stock, (2) is required to redeem the stock, or (3) has a right to redeem the stock, and, in any of those three instances it is more likely than not that the right to redeem will be exercised. I.R.C. § 351(g)(2). Preferred stock also is nonqualified preferred stock if the dividend rate is determined in whole or in part by reference to interest rates, commodity prices, or similar indices. See Temp. Reg. § 1.356–6T.

(2) TREATMENT OF THE CORPORATIONS PARTICIPATING IN AN (A) REORGANIZATION

INTERNAL REVENUE CODE: Sections 357(a), (b); 358(a), (b)(1), (e), (f); 361; 362(b); 368(b).

ILLUSTRATIVE MATERIAL

A. TARGET CORPORATION

Section 361 protects the target corporation from gain recognition in a type (A) reorganization transaction regardless of the nature of the consideration received from the acquiring corporation. If only stock or securities of the acquiring corporation are received in the reorganization, § 361(a) provides nonrecognition upon receipt of the stock or securities. (Section 361(b)(2) bars the recognition of any loss.) No gain or loss is recognized by the target corporation on the distribution of the acquiring corporation's stock or securities. I.R.C. § 361(c)(1), (2)(B). If boot is received, § 361(b)(1) requires that the target corporation recognize gain upon receipt only if that boot is not distributed to either its shareholders or creditors pursuant to the plan of reorganization. See also § 361(c). Since in an (A) reorganization the target corporation disappears by operation of law, all of the boot must be distributed and no gain can be recognized under § 361(b).

Section 361(c)(2) provides for recognition of gain to the target corporation upon the distribution of appreciated boot. However, because § 358(a)(2) provides the target corporation with a fair market value basis in any boot received in the reorganization transaction, no gain will be realized.

B. ACQUIRING CORPORATION

1. *Nonrecognition of Gain*

The acquiring corporation in an (A) reorganization is protected from gain recognition on the issue of its stock by § 1032. However, if the acquiring corporation also transfers non-qualifying "boot" (other than its own securities) that has appreciated in value, none of the reorganization nonrecognition provisions apply and gain must be recognized on the transfer. Rev.Rul. 72–327, 1972–2 C.B. 197. Loss is similarly recognized if the basis of the boot property is less than its fair market value.

2. *Basis of Assets*

Under § 362(b), the acquiring corporation takes as its basis in the acquired assets the basis that the assets had in the hands of the transferor corporation. The statute provides that the basis of the assets in the hands of the acquiring corporation is increased by any gain recognized by the target-transferor corporation in the reorganization transaction, but since gain is only recognized if the property received is not distributed in a type (A) reorganization, the acquiring corporation always takes a transferred basis in the assets without any increase for gain recognized to the transferor.

3. *Carryover of Corporate Attributes*

Under § 381, the tax attributes of the target corporation, e.g., net operating loss carryovers, earnings and profits accounts, etc., carryover to the acquiring corporation. The limitations of § 382(b) are, however, applicable. See Chapter 16.

C. CAPITAL EXPENDITURE ASPECTS

Costs involved in acquisition transactions must generally be capitalized rather than deducted currently under § 162 or § 212. United States v. Hilton Hotels Corp., 397 U.S. 580 (1970), so held with respect to the expenses of an appraisal proceeding involving payments to dissenting shareholders in a merger transaction. INDOPCO, Inc. v. Commissioner, 503 U.S. 79 (1992), held that legal, investment banking, and other expenses incurred in a friendly merger by the target corporation to evaluate the offer and make recommendations to its shareholders must be capitalized, rather than deducted under § 162(a). In A.E. Staley Mfg. Co. v. Commissioner, 105 T.C. 166 (1995), rev'd in part and aff'd in part, 119 F.3d 482 (7th Cir.1997), the Tax Court reached the same result in a situation in which the acquisition originated as a hostile take over, but the Court of Appeals for the Seventh Circuit reversed, holding that expenses incurred to fight a hostile takeover are currently deductible. See also Victory Markets, Inc. v. Commissioner, 99 T.C. 648 (1992) (professional fees incurred in assessing a hostile takeover offer required to be capitalized). Stokely–Van Camp, Inc. v. United States, 974 F.2d 1319 (Fed.Cir.1992), required capitalization of premiums paid to acquire stock from shareholders to avoid an unfriendly take-over bid. The court applied the origin of the claim test of Woodward v. Commissioner, 397 U.S. 572 (1970), to conclude that the premium had its origin in a capital transaction, a voluntary stock redemption. Rev.Rul. 73–580, 1973–2 C.B. 86, requires that the salary of corporate employees who spend a "substantial" amount of time on acquisition work, e.g., legal accounting and other such activities in connection with mergers and acquisitions, must similarly be capitalized. If a proposed reorganization is abandoned a capital loss under § 165 is permitted. Obviously difficult allocation questions arise in the application of the Ruling.

D. MERGER OF CONTROLLED SUBSIDIARY INTO PARENT

If an 80 percent controlled subsidiary is merged into its parent, Treas. Reg. § 1.332–2(d) and (e) provide that the transaction will be taxed as if the subsidiary had been liquidated. In certain cases, Kass v. Commissioner, page 539, will require that minority shareholders of the subsidiary who receive parent corporation stock in the merger recognize gain or loss on the exchange of their shares. See also Treas. Reg. § 1.338–2(c).

In *Kass* the Government conceded that "theoretically" it would be possible for the same transaction to be treated as a liquidation under § 332 and § 334(b) at the corporate level and as a reorganization from the point of view of minority shareholders. While no case has expressly so held, such treatment was implicit in King Enterprises, Inc. v. United States, 418 F.2d 511 (Ct.Cl.1969), page 549. See also Kansas Sand & Concrete, Inc. v. Commissioner, 462 F.2d 805 (10th Cir.1972). Treas. Reg. § 1.332–2(d) also seems to imply that the same transaction can be both a liquidation under § 332 and a reorganization as far as minority shareholders are concerned.

In Rev.Rul. 69–617, 1969–2 C.B. 57, a parent corporation owned more than 80 percent of the stock of its subsidiary. In order to operate its subsidiary as a wholly-owned subsidiary, it merged the subsidiary into itself and the minority shareholders of the subsidiary received the parent's stock. The parent then transferred all of the assets acquired from the subsidiary to a newly created wholly-owned subsidiary. The Ruling held that the transaction constituted an (A) reorganization; § 332 was not applicable because the immediate transfer of the subsidiary's assets to the newly created subsidiary meant that there was not a complete liquidation of the former subsidiary. Thus the minority shareholders of the former subsidiary received tax-free reorganization treatment, whereas under liquidation treatment, gain would have resulted to them.

See also FEC Liquidating Corp. v. United States, 548 F.2d 924 (Ct.Cl. 1977), holding that the reorganization provisions preempted the pre–1986 Act liquidation provisions. Compare General Housewares v. United States, 615 F.2d 1056 (5th Cir.1980)(rejecting the approach of *FEC Liquidating Corp.*)

SECTION 3. STOCK FOR STOCK ACQUISITIONS: TYPE (B) REORGANIZATIONS

INTERNAL REVENUE CODE: Sections 354; 362(b); 368(a)(1)(B), (a)(2)(C), (c).

REGULATIONS: Section 1.368–2(c).

Chapman v. Commissioner

United States Court of Appeals, First Circuit, 1980.
618 F.2d 856.

■ LEVIN H. CAMPBELL, CIRCUIT JUDGE.

* * * We must decide whether the requirement of Section 368(a)(1)(B) that the acquisition of stock in one corporation by another be solely in exchange for voting stock of the acquiring corporation is met where, in related transactions, the acquiring corporation first acquires 8 percent of the acquiree's stock for cash and then acquires more than 80 percent of the acquiree in an exchange for voting stock. The Tax Court agreed with the taxpayers that the latter exchange constituted a valid tax-free reorganization. Reeves v. Commissioner, 71 T.C. 727 (1979).

THE FACTS

Appellees were among the more than 17,000 shareholders of the Hartford Fire Insurance Company who exchanged their Hartford stock for shares of the voting stock of International Telephone and Telegraph Corporation pursuant to a formal exchange offer from ITT dated May 26, 1970. On their 1970 tax returns, appellees did not report any gain or loss from these exchanges. * * *

* * * In October 1968, ITT executives approached Hartford about the possibility of merging the two corporations. This proposal was spurned by Hartford, which at the time was considering acquisitions of its own. In November 1968, ITT learned that approximately 1.3 million shares of Hartford, representing some 6 percent of Hartford's voting stock, were available for purchase from a mutual fund. After assuring Hartford's directors that ITT would not attempt to acquire Hartford against its will, ITT consummated the $63.7 million purchase from the mutual fund with Hartford's blessing. From November 13, 1968 to January 10, 1969, ITT also made a series of purchases on the open market totaling 458,000 shares which it acquired for approximately $24.4 million. A further purchase of

400 shares from an ITT subsidiary in March 1969 brought ITT's holdings to about 8 percent of Hartford's outstanding stock, all of which had been bought for cash.

In the midst of this flurry of stock-buying, ITT submitted a written proposal to the Hartford Board of Directors for the merger of Hartford into an ITT subsidiary, based on an exchange of Hartford stock for ITT's $2 cumulative convertible voting preferred stock. Received by Hartford in December of 1968, the proposal was rejected in February of 1969. A counterproposal by Hartford's directors led to further negotiations, and on April 9, 1969 a provisional plan and agreement of merger was executed by the two corporations. * * *

* * * By private letter ruling, the Service notified the parties on October 13, 1969 that the proposed merger would constitute a nontaxable reorganization, provided ITT unconditionally sold its 8 percent interest in Hartford to a third party before Hartford's shareholders voted to approve or disapprove the proposal. On October 21, the Service ruled that a proposed sale of the stock to Mediobanca, an Italian bank, would satisfy this condition, and such a sale was made on November 9.

On November 10, 1969, the shareholders of Hartford approved the merger, which had already won the support of ITT's shareholders in June. On December 13, 1969, however, the merger plan ground to a halt, as the Connecticut Insurance Commissioner refused to endorse the arrangement. ITT then proposed to proceed with a voluntary exchange offer to the shareholders of Hartford on essentially the same terms they would have obtained under the merger plan. After public hearings and the imposition of certain requirements on the post-acquisition operation of Hartford, the insurance commissioner approved the exchange offer on May 23, 1970, and three days later ITT submitted the exchange offer to all Hartford shareholders. More than 95 percent of Hartford's outstanding stock was exchanged for shares of ITT's $2.25 cumulative convertible voting preferred stock. The Italian bank to which ITT had conveyed its original 8 percent interest was among those tendering shares, as were the taxpayers in this case.

In March 1974, the Internal Revenue Service retroactively revoked its ruling approving the sale of Hartford stock to Mediobanca, on the ground that the request on which the ruling was based had misrepresented the nature of the proposed sale. Concluding that the entire transaction no longer constituted a nontaxable reorganization, the Service assessed tax deficiencies against a number of former Hartford shareholders who had accepted the exchange offer. Appellees, along with other taxpayers, contested this action in the Tax Court, where the case was decided on appellees' motion for summary judgment. For purposes of this motion, the taxpayers conceded that questions of the merits of the revocation of the IRS rulings were not to be considered; the facts were to be viewed as though ITT had not sold the shares previously acquired for cash to Mediobanca. The taxpayers also conceded, solely for purposes of their motion for summary judgment, that the initial cash purchases of Hartford stock had been made for the purpose of furthering ITT's efforts to acquire Hartford.

THE ISSUE

Taxpayers advanced two arguments in support of their motion for summary judgment. Their first argument related to the severability of the cash purchases from the 1970 exchange offer. Because 14 months had elapsed between the last of the cash purchases and the effective date of the exchange offer, and because the cash purchases were not part of the formal plan of reorganization entered into by ITT and Hartford, the taxpayers argued that the 1970 exchange offer should be examined in isolation to determine whether it satisfied the terms of Section 368(a)(1)(B) of the 1954 Code. The Service countered that the two sets of transactions—the cash purchases and the exchange offer—were linked by a common acquisitive purpose, and that they should be considered together for the purpose of determining whether the arrangement met the statutory requirement that the stock of the acquired corporation be exchanged "solely for * * * voting stock" of the acquiring corporation. The Tax Court did not reach this argument; in granting summary judgment it relied entirely on the taxpayers' second argument.

For purposes of the second argument, the taxpayers conceded arguendo that the 1968 and 1969 cash purchases should be considered "parts of the 1970 exchange offer reorganization." Even so, they insisted upon a right to judgment on the basis that the 1970 exchange of stock for stock satisfied the statutory requirements for a reorganization without regard to the presence of related cash purchases. The Tax Court agreed with the taxpayers, holding that the 1970 exchange in which ITT acquired more than 80 percent of Hartford's single class of stock for ITT voting stock satisfied the requirements of Section 368(a)(1)(B), so that no gain or loss need be recognized on the exchange under section 354(a)(1). The sole issue on appeal is whether the Tax Court was correct in so holding.

I.

* * *

The single issue raised on this appeal is whether "the acquisition" in this case complied with the requirement that it be "solely for * * * voting stock." It is well settled that the "solely" requirement is mandatory; if any part of "the acquisition" includes a form of consideration other than voting stock, the transaction will not qualify as a (B) reorganization. See Helvering v. Southwest Consolidated Corp., 315 U.S. 194, 198, 62 S.Ct. 546, 550 (1942)(" 'Solely' leaves no leeway. Voting stock plus some other consideration does not meet the statutory requirement"). The precise issue before us is thus how broadly to read the term "acquisition." The Internal Revenue Service argues that "the acquisition * * * of stock of another corporation" must be understood to encompass the 1968–69 cash purchases as well as the 1970 exchange offer. If the IRS is correct, "the acquisition" here fails as a (B) reorganization. The taxpayers, on the other hand, would limit "the acquisition" to the part of a sequential transaction of this nature which meets the requirements of subsection (B). They argue that the 1970 exchange of stock for stock was itself an "acquisition" by ITT of stock in Hartford solely in exchange for ITT's voting stock, such that after the exchange took place ITT controlled Hartford. Taxpayers contend that the earlier cash purchases of 8 percent, even if conceded to be part of the same acquisitive plan, are essentially irrelevant to the tax-free reorganization otherwise effected.

The Tax Court accepted the taxpayers' reading of the statute, effectively overruling its own prior decision in Howard v. Commissioner, 24 T.C. 792 (1955), rev'd on other grounds, 238 F.2d 943 (7th Cir.1956). The plurality opinion stated its "narrow" holding as follows:

> "We hold that where, as is the case herein, 80 percent or more of the stock of a corporation is acquired in one transaction,[18] in exchange for which only voting stock is furnished as consideration, the 'solely for voting stock' requirement of section 368(a)(1)(B) is satisfied.
>
> 18. In determining what constitutes 'one transaction,' we include all the acquisitions from shareholders which were clearly part of the same transaction."

71 T.C. at 741. The plurality treated as "irrelevant" the 8 percent of Hartford's stock purchased for cash, although the opinion left somewhat ambiguous the question whether the 8 percent was irrelevant because of the 14–month time interval separating the transactions or because the statute was not concerned with transactions over and above those mathematically necessary to the acquiring corporation's attainment of control.[15]

II.

For reasons set forth extensively in section III of this opinion, we do not accept the position adopted by the Tax Court. Instead we side with the Commissioner on the narrow issue presented in this appeal, that is, the correctness of taxpayers' so-called "second" argument premised on an assumed relationship between the cash and stock transactions. As explained below, we find a strong implication in the language of the statute, in the legislative history, in the regulations, and in the decisions of other courts that cash purchases which are concededly "parts of" a stock-for-stock exchange must be considered constituent elements of the "acquisi-

15. If the holding rested on the former basis, it would be difficult to credit the Tax Court's repeated assertions that it was not reaching or deciding the severability issue. As the taxpayers conceded their cash purchases were "parts of the 1970 exchange offer reorganization," the Tax Court had no reason to consider the actual lapse of time which occurred as a factor in treating the cash purchases as legally irrelevant. We assume, therefore, that any indications in the Tax Court's opinion that the separation in time was necessary to its holding were inadvertent, and that the holding actually rests on the Tax Court's reading of the statute. If the Tax Court wishes explicitly to articulate a rule regarding the time period which will suffice to separate two transactions for purposes of Section 368(a)(1)(B), we think it will have an adequate opportunity to do so in considering on remand the issue of severability raised by taxpayers' first argument.

tion" for purposes of applying the "solely for * * * voting stock" requirement of Section 368(a)(1)(B). We believe the presence of non-stock consideration in such an acquisition, regardless of whether such consideration is necessary to the gaining of control, is inconsistent with treatment of the acquisition as a nontaxable reorganization. It follows for purposes of taxpayers' second argument—which was premised on the assumption that the cash transactions were part of the 1970 exchange offer reorganization—that the stock transfers in question would not qualify for nonrecognition of gain or loss.

Our decision will not, unfortunately, end this case. The Tax Court has yet to rule on taxpayers' "first" argument. * * * The question of what factors should determine, for purposes of Section 368(a)(1)(B), whether a given cash purchase is truly "related" to a later exchange of stock requires further consideration by the Tax Court, as does the question of the application of those factors in the present case. We therefore will remand this case to the Tax Court for further proceedings on the question raised by the taxpayers' first argument in support of their motion for summary judgment.

We view the Tax Court's options on remand as threefold. It can hold that the cash and stock transactions here in question are related as a matter of law—the position urged by the Commissioner—in which case, under our present holding, there would not be a valid (B) reorganization. On the other hand, the Tax Court may find that the transactions are as a matter of law unrelated, so that the 1970 exchange offer was simply the final, nontaxable step in a permissible creeping acquisition. Finally, the court may decide that, under the legal standard it adopts, material factual issues remain to be decided, so that a grant of summary judgment would be inappropriate at this time.[17]

17. We do not intend to dictate to the Tax Court what legal standard it should apply in determining whether these transactions are related. We would suggest, however, that the possibilities should include at least the following; perhaps others may be developed by counsel or by the Tax Court itself.

One possibility—advanced by the taxpayers—is that the only transactions which should be considered related, and so parts of "the acquisition," are those which are included in the formal plan of reorganization adopted by the two corporations. The virtues of this approach—simplicity and clarity—may be outweighed by the considerable scope it would grant the parties to a reorganization to control the tax treatment of their formal plan of reorganization by arbitrarily including or excluding certain transactions. A second possibility—urged by the Commissioner—is that all transactions sharing a single acquisitive purpose should be considered related for purposes of Section 368(a)(1)(B). Relying on an example given in the legislative history, see S.Rep. No. 1622, 83d Cong., 2d Sess. 273, reprinted in [1954] U.S.Code Cong. & Admin.News, pp. 4621, 4911 [hereinafter cited as 1954 Senate Report], the Commissioner would require a complete and thoroughgoing separation, both in time and purpose, between cash and stock acquisitions before the latter would qualify for reorganization treatment under subsection (B).

A third possible approach, lying somewhere between the other two, would be to focus on the mutual knowledge and intent of the corporate parties, so that one party could not suffer adverse tax consequences from unilateral activities of the other of which the former had no notice. Cf. Manning, "In Pursuance of the Plan of Reorganization": The Scope of the Reorganization Provisions of the Internal Revenue Code, 72 Harv.L.Rev. 881,

III.

A.

* * * We begin with the words of the statute itself. The reorganization definitions contained in Section 368(a)(1) are precise, technical, and comprehensive. They were intended to define the exclusive means by which nontaxable corporate reorganizations could be effected. See Treas. Reg. § 1.368–1 (1960) * * *. In examining the language of the (B) provision, we discern two possible meanings. On the one hand, the statute could be read to say that a successful reorganization occurs whenever Corporation X exchanges its own voting stock for stock in Corporation Y, and, immediately after the transaction, Corporation X controls more than 80 percent of Y's stock. On this reading, purchases of shares for which any part of the consideration takes the form of "boot" should be ignored, since the definition is only concerned with transactions which meet the statutory requirements as to consideration and control. To take an example, if Corporation X bought 50 percent of the shares of Y, and then almost immediately exchanged part of its voting stock for the remaining 50 percent of Y's stock, the question would arise whether the second transaction was a (B) reorganization. Arguably, the statute can be read to support such a finding. In the second transaction, X exchanged only stock for stock (meeting the "solely" requirement), and after the transaction was completed X owned Y (meeting the "control" requirement).

The alternative reading of the statute—the one which we are persuaded to adopt—treat the (B) definition as prescriptive, rather than merely descriptive. We read the statute to mean that the entire transaction which constitutes "the acquisition" must not contain any nonstock consideration if the transaction is to qualify as a (B) reorganization. In the example given above, where X acquired 100 percent of Y's stock, half for cash and half for voting stock, we would interpret "the acquisition" as referring to the entire transaction, so that the "solely for * * * voting stock" requirement would not be met. We believe if Congress had intended the statute to be read as merely descriptive, this intent would have been more clearly spelled out in the statutory language.[18]

* * *

912–13 (1959). Such a rule would prevent, for example, the situation where the acquiree's shareholders expect to receive favorable tax treatment on an exchange offer, only to learn later that an apparently valid (B) reorganization has been nullified by anonymous cash purchases on the part of the acquiring corporation. See Bruce v. Helvering, 64 App.D.C. 192, 76 F.2d 442 (D.C.Cir.1935), rev'g, 30 B.T.A. 80 (1934).

Difficulties suggest themselves with each of these rules, and without benefit of thorough briefing and argument, as well as an informed decision by the lower court, we are reluctant to proceed further in exploring this issue. We leave to the Tax Court the task of breaking ground here.

18. For example, Congress could have used the word "any" rather than the word "the" before "acquisition" in the first line of the (B) definition. This would have tended to negate the implication that this definition prescribes the conditions a transaction *must* meet to qualify, rather than simply describing that part of a transaction which is entitled to the statutory tax deferral.

The Tax Court's interpretation of the statute suffers from a * * * fundamental defect * * *. In order to justify the limitation of its holding to transactions involving 80 percent or more of the acquiree's stock, the Tax Court focused on the *passage* of control as the primary requirement of the (B) provision. This focus is misplaced. Under the present version of the statute, the *passage* of control is entirely irrelevant; the only material requirement is that the acquiring corporation *have* control immediately after the acquisition. As the statute explicitly states, it does not matter if the acquiring corporation already has control before the transaction begins, so long as such control exists at the completion of the reorganization. * * * In our view, the statute should be read to mean that the related transactions that constitute "the acquisition," whatever percentage of stock they may represent, must meet both the "solely for voting stock" and the "control immediately after" requirements of Section 368(a)(1)(B). Neither the reading given the statute by the Tax Court, nor that proposed as the first alternative above, adequately corresponds to the careful language Congress employed in this section of the Code.

B.

The 1924 Code defined reorganization, in part, as "a merger or consolidation (including the acquisition by one corporation of at least a majority of the voting stock and at least a majority of the total number of shares of all other classes of stock of another corporation, or substantially all the properties of another corporation)." Pub.L. No. 68–176, c. 234, section 203(h)(1), 43 Stat. 257. Although the statute did not specifically limit the consideration that could be given in exchange for stock or assets, courts eventually developed the so-called "continuity of interest" doctrine, which held that exchanges that did not include some quantum of stock as consideration were ineligible for reorganization treatment for lack of a continuing property interest on the part of the acquiree's shareholders. See, e.g., Cortland Specialty Co. v. Commissioner, 60 F.2d 937, 939–40 (2d Cir.1932), cert. denied, 288 U.S. 599, 53 S.Ct. 316 (1933); Pinellas Ice Co. v. Commissioner, 287 U.S. 462, 470, 53 S.Ct. 257, 260 (1933).

* * * In 1934, the House Ways and Means Committee proposed abolition of the stock-acquisition and asset-acquisition reorganizations which had appeared in the parenthetical section of the 1924 Act quoted above. See H.R.Rep. No. 704, 73d Cong., 2d Sess. 12–14 (1939–1 C.B. (Part 2) 554, 563–65). The Senate Finance Committee countered with a proposal to retain these provisions, but with "restrictions designed to prevent tax avoidance." S.Rep. No. 558, 73d Cong., 2d Sess. 15 (1939–1 C.B. (Part 2) 586, 598).[20] One of these restrictions was the requirement that the acquiring corporation obtain at least 80 percent, rather than a bare majority, of the stock of the acquiree. The second requirement was stated in the Senate

20. The Senate's purpose in retaining these provisions was apparently to make available an alternative to statutory merger or consolidation in those states where merger statutes were overly restrictive or nonexistent. See Howard v. Commissioner, 238 F.2d 943, 946 (7th Cir.1956).

Report as follows: "the acquisition, whether of stock or of substantially all the properties, must be in exchange solely for the voting stock of the acquiring corporation." Id. at 17. The Senate amendments were enacted as Section 112(g)(1) of the Revenue Act of 1934, 48 Stat. 680, which provided in pertinent part:

"(1) The term 'reorganization' means (A) a statutory merger or consolidation, or (B) the acquisition by one corporation in exchange solely for all or a part of its voting stock: of at least 80 per centum of the voting stock and at least 80 per centum of the total number of shares of all other classes of stock of another corporation; or of substantially all the properties of another corporation * * *."

* * *

The next major change in this provision occurred in 1954. In that year, the House Bill, H.R. 8300, would have drastically altered the corporate reorganization sections of the Tax Code, permitting, for example, both stock and "boot" as consideration in a corporate acquisition, with gain recognized only to the extent of the "boot." See H.R.Rep. No. 1337, 83d Cong., 2d Sess. A118–A119, A132–A134 * * * The Senate Finance Committee, in order to preserve the familiar terminology and structure of the 1939 Code, proposed a new version of Section 112(g)(1), which would retain the "solely for * * * voting stock" requirement, but alter the existing control requirement to permit so-called "creeping acquisitions." Under the Senate Bill, it would no longer be necessary for the acquiring corporation to obtain 80 percent or more of the acquiree's stock in one "reorganization." The Senate's proposal permitted an acquisition to occur in stages; a bloc of shares representing less than 80 percent could be added to earlier acquisitions, regardless of the consideration given earlier, to meet the control requirement. The Report of the Senate Finance Committee gave this example of the operation of the creeping acquisition amendment:

> "[C]orporation A purchased 30 percent of the common stock of corporation W (the only class of stock outstanding) for cash in 1939. On March 1, 1955, corporation A offers to exchange its own voting stock, for all the stock of corporation W tendered within 6 months from the date of the offer. Within the 6 months period corporation A acquires an additional 60 percent of the stock of W for its own voting stock. As a result of the 1955 transactions, corporation A will own 90 percent of all of corporation W's stock. No gain or loss is recognized with respect to the exchanges of the A stock for the W stock."

1954 Senate Report, supra note 17, at 273, U.S.Code Cong. & Admin.News 1954, p. 4911. See also Treas. Reg. § 1.368–2(c)(1960).

At the same time the Senate was revising the (B) provision, (while leaving intact the "solely for * * * voting stock" requirement), it was also rewriting the (C) provision to explicitly permit up to 20 percent of the consideration in an asset acquisition to take the form of money or other nonstock property. See 26 U.S.C. § 368(a)(2)(B). The Senate revisions of subsections (B) and (C) were ultimately passed, and have remained largely unchanged since 1954. * * * Proposals for altering the (B) provision to allow "boot" as consideration have been made, but none has been enacted.[22]

As this history shows, Congress has had conflicting aims in this complex and difficult area. On the one hand, * * * [Congress] evidences a strong intention to limit the reorganization provisions to permit forms of tax avoidance that had proliferated under the earlier revenue acts. This intention arguably has been carried forward in the current versions through retention of the "solely for * * * voting stock" requirement in (B), even while the (C) provision was being loosened. On the other hand, both the 1939 and 1954 revisions represented attempts to make the reorganization procedures more accessible and practical in both the (B) and (C) areas. In light of the conflicting purposes, we can discern no clear Congressional mandate in the present structure of the (B) provision, either in terms of the abuses sought to be remedied or the beneficial transactions sought to be facilitated. At best, we think Congress has drawn somewhat arbitrary lines separating those transactions that resemble mere changes in form of ownership and those that contain elements of a sale or purchase arrangement. In such circumstances we believe it is more appropriate to examine the specific rules and requirements Congress enacted, rather than some questionably delineated "purpose" or "policy," to determine whether a particular transaction qualifies for favorable tax treatment.

To the extent there is any indication in the legislative history of Congress' intent with respect to the meaning of "acquisition" in the (B) provision, we believe the intent plainly was to apply the "solely" requirement to all related transactions. In those statutes where Congress intended to permit cash or other property to be used as consideration, it made explicit provision therefor. See, e.g., 26 U.S.C. § 368(a)(2)(B). It is argued that in a (B) reorganization the statute can be satisfied where only 80 percent of the acquiree's stock is obtained solely for voting stock, so that additional acquisitions are irrelevant and need not be considered. In light of Congress' repeated, and increasingly sophisticated, enactments in this area, we are unpersuaded that such an important question would have been left unaddressed had Congress intended to leave open such a possibility. We are not prepared to believe that Congress intended—either when it enacted the 1934, the 1939, or the 1954 statutes—to permit a corporation to exchange stock tax-free for 80 percent of the stock of another and in a related transaction to purchase the remaining 20 percent for cash. The only question we see clearly left open by the legislative history is the degree of

22. See, e.g., H.R.Rep. No. 4459, 86th Cong., 1st Sess. § 26 (1959). * * *

Furthermore, the legislative report accompanying a later revision of Section 368(a)(1) explicitly stated that cash is not permitted in a (B) reorganization:

"[I]n order to qualify as a tax-free stock-for-stock [B] reorganization it is necessary that the acquisition be *solely* for voting stock and that no stock be acquired for cash or other consideration." (Emphasis in original.)

S.Rep. No. 1533, 91st Cong., 2d Sess. 2–3, * * *.

separation required between the two transactions before they can qualify as a creeping acquisition under the 1954 amendments. This is precisely the issue the Tax Court chose not to address, and it is the issue we now remand to the Tax Court for consideration.

C.

Besides finding support for the IRS position both in the design of the statute and in the legislative history, we find support in the regulations adopted by the Treasury Department construing these statutory provisions.

* * *

When we turn to the regulations under the 1954 Act, the implication that the entire transaction must be judged under the "solely" test is strong* * *.

> "In order to qualify as a 'reorganization' under section 368(a)(1)(B), the *acquisition* by the acquiring corporation of stock of another corporation must be in exchange solely for all or a part of the voting stock of the acquiring corporation * * * and the acquiring corporation must be in control of the other corporation immediately after *the transaction*. If, for example, Corporation X in one transaction exchanges nonvoting preferred stock or bonds *in addition to* all or a part of its voting stock in the acquisition of stock of Corporation Y, the transaction is not a reorganization under section 368(a)(1)(B)." (Emphasis supplied.)

Treas. Reg. § 1.368–2(c)(1960). The equation of "transaction" and "acquisition" in the above-quoted passage is particularly significant, since it seems to imply a functional test of what constitutes "the acquisition" as opposed to a view of "the acquisition" as simply that part of a transaction which otherwise satisfies the statutory requisites.[23] The regulation also goes on to say, in explaining the treatment of creeping acquisitions:

> "The acquisition of stock of another corporation by the acquiring corporation solely for its voting stock * * * is permitted tax-free even though the acquiring corporation already owns some of the stock of the other corporation. Such an acquisition is permitted tax-free in a single transaction or in a series of transactions taking place over a relatively short period of time such as 12 months."

23. Furthermore, the regulation explicitly states that the presence of "boot" in addition to stock as consideration would prevent treatment of the transaction as a (B) reorganization. This language is not wholly dispositive, however; it could be read as reaching only cases where "boot" was present in the consideration given for each share exchanged. It is clear that the "solely for * * * voting stock" requirement prevents stock acquired for such "mixed" consideration from qualifying for reorganization treatment. The "in addition to" language in the regulation could be construed as reaching only this situation, and not the contrasting case where Corporation X acquires 80 percent of Y's stock solely for voting stock and another separate 20 percent for some other consideration. The *Reeves* case is, of course, of the latter type; with respect to every single share transferred, the consideration was either wholly in stock or wholly in cash.

Treas. Reg. § 1.368–2(c). This regulation spells out the treatment afforded related acquisitions, some of which occur before and some after the acquiring corporation obtains the necessary 80 percent of stock in the acquiree. It would be incongruous, to say the least, if a series of stock-for-stock transactions could be combined so that the tax-free treatment of later acquisitions applied to earlier ones as well, yet a related cash purchase would be ignored as irrelevant. This section reinforces our view that all related transactions must be considered part of "the acquisition" for purposes of applying the statute.

D.

Finally, we turn to the body of case law that has developed concerning (B) reorganizations to determine how previous courts have dealt with this question. Of the seven prior cases in this area, all to a greater or lesser degree support the result we have reached, and none supports the result reached by the Tax Court. We recognize that the Tax Court purported to distinguish these precedents from the case before it, and that reasonable persons may differ on the extent to which some of these cases directly control the question raised here. Nevertheless, after carefully reviewing the precedents, we are satisfied that the decision of the Tax Court represents a sharp break with the previous judicial constructions of this statute, and a departure from the usual rule of stare decisis, which applies with special force in the tax field where uncertainty and variety are ordinarily to be avoided.

Of the seven precedents, the most significant would seem to be Howard v. Commissioner, 238 F.2d 943 (7th Cir.1956), rev'g, 24 T.C. 792 (1955), which stands out as the one case prior to *Reeves* that specifically addressed the issue raised herein. In *Howard,* the Truax–Traer Coal Company acquired 80.19 percent of the outstanding stock of Binkley Coal Company solely in exchange for Truax–Traer voting stock. At the same time and as part of the same plan of acquisition, Truax–Traer purchased the other 19.81 percent of Binkley's stock for cash. The taxpayers, former shareholders of Binkley who had exchanged their shares solely for voting stock, sold some of the Truax–Traer stock they had received in August 1950, the same year as the exchange. The Commissioner, treating the exchange as a taxable event and not a reorganization, employed a new holding period, beginning with the effective date of the exchange, and treated the taxpayers' gain on their sale of the Truax–Traer stock as a short-term capital gain. The Tax Court sustained the Commissioner, concluding the exchange had not been made "solely for * * * voting stock," as required by the 1939 Act, even though the cash purchases were not essential to Truax–Traer's acquisition of control. 24 T.C. at 804.

The Seventh Circuit, after reviewing the legislative history of Section 112(g)(1)(B) of the 1939 Code, agreed with the Tax Court's conclusion that the presence of cash purchases prevented the transaction from meeting the "solely" requirement of the statute. * * * The principal linchpin of the Seventh Circuit's decision was Helvering v. Southwest Consolidated Corp.,

315 U.S. 194, 62 S.Ct. 546 (1942), in which the Supreme Court denied tax-free treatment to an asset acquisition under the 1934 Act because a substantial amount of the consideration was given in the form of stock warrants and cash. The Court first noted that under the law existing before 1934, this transaction would have been a perfectly valid tax-free reorganization. The revised statute, see text at notes 20–21 supra, had made the continuity of interest test much stricter, however:

> "Congress has provided that the assets of the transferor corporation must be acquired in exchange 'solely' for 'voting stock' of the transferee. 'Solely' leaves no leeway. Voting stock plus some other consideration does not meet the statutory requirement."

315 U.S. at 198, 62 S.Ct. at 550. The Seventh Circuit noted that in the 1934 Act the asset and stock acquisition reorganizations were dealt with in the same clause both in the statutory language and in the legislative history. It therefore seemed reasonable to the Seventh Circuit to conclude that the Supreme Court's "no leeway" rule for asset acquisitions applied with equal force to stock acquisitions.

* * *

Our reading of the statute is reinforced by another more recent circuit decision as well. In Mills v. Commissioner, 331 F.2d 321 (5th Cir.1964), *rev'g*, 39 T.C. 393 (1962), the issue was whether cash payments for fractional shares in an exchange prevented a nontaxable reorganization. General Gas Corporation, the acquiror, offered the three taxpayers, sole stockholders in three small gas corporations, shares of General common stock in exchange for all of their stock. The number of General shares to be exchanged—at a value of $14 per share—was to be determined by measuring the net book value of the three small corporations. In the event the purchase price was not evenly divisible by 14, cash was to be paid in lieu of fractional shares. As a result, each taxpayer received 1,595 shares of General Stock and $27.36 in cash. The Tax Court held this transaction invalid as a tax-free reorganization, declining to adopt a *de minimis* rule. 39 T.C. at 400.[36] The Fifth Circuit agreed that cash could not form any part of the consideration in a (B) reorganization, but concluded in reversing the Tax Court that the fractional-share arrangement was merely a bookkeeping convenience and not an independent part of the consideration. 331 F.2d at 324–25.

* * *

36. The Tax Court in *Mills* stated:

"We construe the word 'solely' as meaning precisely what it purports to mean, namely that the receipt by the stockholders of an acquired corporation of any consideration whatsoever other than voting stock forbids a transaction from being a reorganization as defined under § 368(a)(1)(B) * * *. We cannot assume that Congress was incapable of expressing a grant of leeway when that was its purpose."

39 T.C. at 400.

IV.

We have stated our ruling, and the reasons that support it. In conclusion, we would like to respond briefly to the arguments raised by the Tax Court, the District Court of Delaware, and the taxpayers in this case against the rule we have reaffirmed today. The principal argument, repeated again and again, concerns the supposed lack of policy behind the rule forbidding cash in a (B) reorganization where the control requirement is met solely for voting stock. It is true that the Service has not pointed to tax loopholes that would be opened were the rule to be relaxed as appellees request. We also recognize, as the Tax Court and others have highlighted, that the rule may produce results which some would view as anomalous. For example, if Corporation X acquires 80 percent of Corporation Y's stock solely for voting stock, and is content to leave the remaining 20 percent outstanding, no one would question that a valid (B) reorganization has taken place. If Corporation X then decides to purchase stock from the remaining shareholders, the *Howard* rule might result in loss of nontaxable treatment for the stock acquisition if the two transactions were found to be related. See 71 T.C. at 740–41. The Tax Court asserted that there is no conceivable Congressional policy that would justify such a result. Further, it argued, Congress could not have felt that prior cash purchases would forever ban a later successful (B) reorganization since the 1954 amendments, as the legislative history makes clear, specifically provided that prior cash purchases would not prevent a creeping acquisition.

While not without force, this line of argument does not in the end persuade us. First of all, as already discussed, the language of the statute, and the longstanding interpretation given it by the courts, are persuasive reasons for our holding even in the absence of any clear policy behind Congress' expression of its will. Furthermore, we perceive statutory anomalies of another sort which the Tax Court's rule would only magnify. It is clear from the regulations, for example, that a corporation which already owned as much as 80 percent of another's stock, acquired solely for cash, could in some circumstances acquire all or a part of the remainder solely for voting stock as a valid (B) reorganization.[38] Why, then, could not as little as 10 percent of an acquisition constitute a (B) reorganization, if made solely for voting stock, even though the remaining transactions—totaling more than 80 percent—were made for nonstock consideration? If it is true that Congress did not view related cash transactions as tainting a stock-acquisition reorganization, why would it enact a "solely for * * * voting stock" requirement at all, except to the extent necessary to prevent mixed consideration of the sort employed in the "disguised sales" of the twenties?

Possibly, Congress' insertion of the "solely for * * * voting stock" requirement into the 1934 Act was, as one commentator has suggested, an overreaction to a problem which could have been dealt with through more precise and discriminating measures.[39] But we do not think it appropriate

38. See Treas.Reg. § 1.368–2(c).

39. See Dailey, *The Voting Stock Requirement of B and C Reorganizations,* 26 Tax L.Rev. 725, 731 (1971) * * *.

for a court to tell Congress how to do its job in an area such as this. If a more refined statutory scheme would be appropriate, such changes should be sought from the body empowered to make them. While we adhere to the general practice of construing statutes so as to further their demonstrated policies, we have no license to rework whole statutory schemes in pursuit of policy goals which Congress has nowhere articulated. Appellees have not shown us any reason to believe that reaffirmation of the settled rule in this area will frustrate the Congressional purpose of making the (B) reorganization provision generally available to those who comply with the statutory requirements.[40]

* * *

Finally, we see no merit at all in the suggestion that we should permit "boot" in a (B) reorganization simply because "boot" is permitted in some instances in (A) and (C) reorganizations. Congress has never indicated that these three distinct categories of transactions are to be interpreted *in pari materia*. In fact, striking differences in the treatment of the three subsections have been evident in the history of the reorganization statutes. We see no reason to believe a difference in the treatment of "boot" in these transactions is impermissible or irrational.

Accordingly, we vacate the judgment of the Tax Court insofar as it rests on a holding that taxpayers were entitled to summary judgment irrespective of whether the cash purchases in this case were related by purpose or timing to the stock exchange offer of 1970. The case will be remanded to the Tax Court for further proceedings consistent with this opinion.

Vacated and remanded.

ILLUSTRATIVE MATERIAL

A. PERSPECTIVES ON *CHAPMAN*

Heverly v. Commissioner, 621 F.2d 1227 (3d Cir.1980), reached the same result as *Chapman* in a case involving other taxpayers involved in the Hartford–ITT acquisition.

The taxpayers in *Chapman* and *Heverly* petitioned for a writ of certiorari but the petitions were dismissed pursuant to agreement of the parties. 451 U.S. 1012 (1981). Under the agreement, ITT paid $18.5 million in taxes and the IRS agreed not to contest the tax-free treatment of the former Hartford shareholders on the exchange for ITT stock so long as the shareholders did not attempt to claim a stepped-up basis in the ITT shares. IR 81–53 (1981). If the case had not been settled, on remand the Tax Court

40. We do not see how the argument that cash purchases are necessary to buy out the interests of "dissenting shareholders" who decline to take part in the exchange advances taxpayers' cause. One of the purposes of stock-acquisition arrangements, as opposed to statutory mergers, is to provide the option to minority shareholders not to take part. In this case, had such protection not been afforded, the Connecticut Insurance Commissioner evidently would not have approved the acquisition.

would have had to decide whether the two acquisition transactions constituted a single transaction and, if so, whether the "sale" of the stock acquired for cash to the Italian bank in fact transferred the burdens and benefits of ownership so that the subsequent stock exchange could qualify as a (B) reorganization.[11]

Prior to the decision of the Tax Court in Reeves v. Commissioner, 71 T.C. 727 (1979), the decision that was reversed in *Chapman,* it was generally accepted that the presence of nonqualifying consideration would defeat a (B) reorganization even though the requisite 80 percent control had been acquired solely for voting stock. See, e.g., Rev.Rul. 75–123, 1975–1 C.B. 115. Most of the prior case law and rulings in situations similar to *Chapman* were concerned with the taxpayer's alternative argument in *Chapman* that the nonqualifying consideration was not part of the "plan of reorganization" and therefore should not be taken into account in determining if the solely for voting stock requirement was met. After *Chapman,* the focus of attention in the (B) reorganization area will continue to be on whether any nonqualifying consideration was received pursuant to the plan of reorganization.

B. THE SOLELY FOR VOTING STOCK REQUIREMENT.

1. *"Voting" Stock*

In Rev.Rul. 72–72, 1972–1 C.B. 104, a corporation acquired all the outstanding shares of a second corporation in exchange for its voting stock. The shareholders of the target corporation agreed that the former sole shareholder of the acquiring corporation would have the irrevocable right to vote the new shares received by the target shareholders for five years, after which time the target shareholders would receive their right to vote the stock of the acquiring corporation without restriction. The Ruling held that the transaction did not qualify as a (B) reorganization; it was in effect an acquisition for non-voting common stock that would be converted to voting common stock in five years, and thus did not meet the voting stock test. Compare Federal Grain Corp. v. Commissioner, 18 B.T.A. 242 (1929), in which the fact that voting shares received by the transferors of property were immediately placed in a voting trust was ignored in determining whether the transferors had "control" for purposes of the predecessor of § 351.

Rev.Rul. 63–234, 1963–2 C.B. 148, held that preferred stock entitled to elect two of the members of the Board of Directors of the issuing corporation qualified as "voting stock" in a (B) reorganization. The Ruling indicates that to qualify as "voting stock" the shares must confer "upon the holders * * * the right to significant participation in the management of the affairs of the corporation." (149) See also Rev.Rul. 70–108, 1970–1 C.B. 78 (exchange involving voting convertible preferred stock under the terms of which the shareholder had an option upon conversion to purchase

11. See McMahon, Defining the "Acquisition" in B Reorganizations Through the Step Transaction Doctrine, 67 Iowa L. Rev. 31 (1981).

an additional share of stock at a stipulated price did not satisfy the "solely for voting stock" requirement; the right to purchase the additional stock constituted property other than voting stock).

2. *The Presence of Cash Payments*

Rev.Rul. 85–139, 1985–2 C.B. 123, held that the "solely for voting stock" requirement had been violated where the acquiring corporation acquired 90 percent of the stock of the target corporation for the acquiring corporation's voting stock and pursuant to the overall plan the acquiring corporation caused its wholly owned subsidiary to purchase the remaining 10 percent of the target corporation stock for cash.

If the cash transaction is separate from the stock transaction, however, the solely for voting stock requirement is not violated. See, e.g., Rev.Rul. 69–91, 1969–1, C.B. 106 (separate purchase for cash of convertible debentures); Rev.Rul. 68–562, 1968–2 C.B. 157 (unrelated purchase of shares by majority shareholder of acquiring corporation); Rev.Rul. 72–522, 1972–2 C.B. 215 (cash paid by the acquiring corporation to the target corporation in a (B) reorganization to provide it with working capital did not affect the solely for voting stock exchange at the shareholder level); Rev.Rul. 75–33, 1975–1 C.B. 115 (provision for payment of additional dividend on convertible preferred stock of acquiring corporation to insure that the shareholders of the target corporation would receive as large a dividend as they would have received had they accepted a competing offer from another corporation did not constitute "other property;" the right to the additional dividend inhered in the stock itself, since the right was lost if the conversion privilege was exercised and purchasers of the preferred stock also obtained the right to the extra dividend).

As *Chapman* indicates, the Internal Revenue Service originally took the position that cash issued in lieu of fractional shares violated the solely for voting stock requirement, but this position was rejected in Mills v. Commissioner, 331 F.2d 321 (5th Cir.1964). The Service subsequently indicated that it would follow *Mills* unless the cash received for the fractional shares was "separately bargained-for consideration," Rev.Rul. 66–365, 1966–2 C.B. 116. The cash received is not treated as "boot" but as a payment in redemption of the taxpayer's stock, the transaction thus being viewed as in effect the transfer of voting stock to the shareholder followed by a redemption.

Does payment by the acquiring corporation of expenses of transferor shareholders incurred in connection with the (B) reorganization constitute disqualifying consideration? Rev.Rul. 73–54, 1973–1 C.B. 187, held that the solely for voting stock requirement is not violated in such a case if the expenses were "solely and directly related to the reorganization." But the Ruling cautions that payment of shareholders' expenses "for legal, accounting or investment advice or counsel pertaining to participation in, or action with respect to, the reorganization" will result in disqualification. Payment of shareholders' transfer taxes similarly results in disqualification. However, the Service has ruled that the acquiring corporation may pay the costs necessary to register the voting shares used in the acquisition with the Securities and Exchange Commission without violating the "solely for voting stock" requirement, on the theory that such costs are properly costs of the acquiring corporation and not of the transferor shareholders. Rev. Rul. 67–275, 1967–2 C.B. 142.

If the payment of cash or other property is made by the target corporation rather than the acquiring corporation, the solely for voting stock requirement is not violated. See e.g., Rev.Rul. 68–435, 1968–2 C.B. 155 (dividend paid by the target corporation based on the dividend its shareholders would have received from the acquiring corporation had the final transaction been consummated as originally planned held not to violate the solely for voting stock requirement); Rev.Rul. 75–421, 1975–2 C.B. 108 ((B) reorganization upheld where the target corporation paid the fees of a financial consultant and accountant employed by its sole shareholder to determine the value of the acquiring company's stock; the fees were paid before the reorganization was consummated and constituted a dividend to the shareholder). Similarly, the target corporation can make cash payments to shareholders who dissent without endangering the reorganization as long as the funds for the payment do not come from the acquiring corporation. See Rev.Rul. 68–285, 1968–1 C.B. 147. Compare Rev.Rul. 75–360, 1975–2 C.B. 110 (in McDonald v. Commissioner, 52 T.C. 82 (1969), discussed at page 506, stock of the target corporation was redeemed prior to the (B) reorganization exchange for funds provided indirectly by the acquiring corporation; the Ruling stated that the case had been wrongly argued solely as a redemption case (with a separate valid (B) reorganization conceded); the redemption and stock exchange were steps in a single transaction and the receipt of cash thus prevented (B) reorganization treatment). However, under Temp. Reg. § 1.368–1T(e)(1)(ii), extraordinary pre-reorganization redemptions of stock by the target corporation can result in the transaction failing the continuity of interest requirement. See also Temp. Reg. § 1.368–1T(e)(3), Ex(10).

3. *The Presence of Non-Cash Consideration*

An exchange will fail to qualify as a (B) reorganization if shareholders of the target corporation who are also debenture holders exchange their shares and debentures for voting stock and new debentures of the acquiring corporation and some of the new debentures are determined to be part of the consideration attributable to the shares transferred. In Rev.Rul. 69–142, 1969–1 C.B. 107, the stockholders of the target corporation exchanged one share of the target corporation stock for one share of the stock of the acquiring corporation. In addition, outstanding debentures of the target corporation were exchanged for an equivalent amount of debentures of the acquiring corporation. Not all of the debentures of the target corporation were held by stockholders. The Internal Revenue Service held that the transaction qualified as a (B) reorganization specifically noting that all of the stock of the target corporation was exchanged for stock of the acquiring corporation. Although the exchange of debentures was part of the overall reorganization transaction, the Service ruled that the exchange of debentures of the acquiring corporation did not constitute additional consideration for the stock of the target corporation. The ruling adds that because the exchange of debentures was not part of the reorganization exchange, the exchange of debentures was a taxable transaction under § 1001. But see Rev.Rul. 98–10, page 606.

Rev.Rul. 70–269, 1970–1 C.B. 82, and Rev.Rul. 78–408, 1978–2 C.B. 203, held that the acquiring corporation could substitute its stock options for options of the target corporation without affecting qualification as a (B) reorganization; the acquiring corporation's options were not given in consideration of stock of the target corporation. Treas. Regs. §§ 1.354–1(e) and 1.356–3(b) treat stock options of a corporation that is a party to a reorganization as securities of the corporation having no principal amount. Accordingly, a holder of options of the target corporation who, pursuant to the plan of reorganization, exchanges them for options of the acquiring corporation is entitled to nonrecognition under § 354(a) and § 356(d)(2). See Rev. Rul. 98–10, 1998–10 I.R.B. 11.

An assumption of indebtedness of the shareholders of the target corporation in connection with the acquisition of their stock can prevent the qualification of the transaction as a (B) reorganization. In Rev.Rul. 70–65, 1970–1 C.B. 77, sixty percent of the stock of the target corporation was owned by Z Corporation and the balance by unrelated parties. The acquiring corporation obtained Z's target stock from Z along with the remaining Z assets in exchange for the acquiring corporation's voting stock and the assumption of Z's liabilities. The acquiring corporation then exchanged its voting stock for the remaining forty percent of the shares of the target corporation. The acquisition of the target corporation's stock from Z (along with the remaining Z assets) qualified as a (C) reorganization, but neither of the acquisitions of the target corporation stock qualified as a (B) reorganization because of the assumption of Z's liabilities, the two transactions being treated as one for purposes of testing the transaction as a (B) reorganization. However, in most stock for stock acquisitions, the liabilities of the target corporation simply stay with the corporation. But see Rev.Rul. 79–4, 1979–1 C.B. 150, where the target corporation was thinly capitalized and a shareholder-guaranteed loan was treated as a direct loan by the shareholder. The acquiring corporation's assumption of the obligation as a condition of the reorganization exchange was treated as disqualifying consideration. See also, Fisher v. Commissioner, 62 T.C. 73 (1974) (additional shares of stock paid by the acquiring corporation in lieu of cash dividend held to constitute a separate transaction from otherwise valid (B) reorganization; the additional stock constituted a taxable stock dividend under the former version of § 305(b)(2)).

Dealings between the acquiring corporation and the target corporation's creditors that are separate from the "plan of reorganization" do not disqualify an otherwise valid (B) reorganization. See Rev.Rul. 79–89, 1979–1 C.B. 152 (contribution of cash to the target corporation used to pay debt of the corporation guaranteed by a shareholder was not disqualifying additional consideration where the payment of the debt was not a condition of the exchange of stock).

4. *Compensation Arrangements*

The shareholders of the target corporation may enter into employment contracts in connection with the reorganization. In Rev.Rul. 77–271, 1977–2 C.B. 116, the president of the target corporation as part of the plan of reorganization entered into an employment contract with the target corporation and received additional stock of the acquiring corporation as consideration for entering into the contract. The Service treated the employment arrangement as a transaction separate from the otherwise valid (B) reorganization; the additional stock received by the president constituted ordinary income to him. If part of the alleged compensation for services is in fact paid for stock of the target corporation, however, the solely for voting stock requirement would not be met.

5. *Contingent Stock Payouts*

The shareholders of the target corporation also may receive the right to obtain additional voting shares in the future if specified conditions are met, e.g., the earnings of the target corporation reaching a certain level. Generally, such contingent stock payout agreements are utilized in situations in which the parties to the reorganization are unable to agree on the fair market value of the target corporation's stock. The right to receive voting shares in the future is not the same as the present receipt of voting shares as such and hence arguably could violate the solely for voting stock restriction.

Carlberg v. United States, 281 F.2d 507 (8th Cir.1960), held that certificates representing a contingent interest in shares in the acquiring corporation should be treated as "stock" for purposes of nonrecognition under § 354 (a result disputed by the Service because the certificates in question were negotiable). In Hamrick v. Commissioner, 43 T.C. 21 (1964), the court treated a nonnegotiable contingent right to receive additional shares of stock as the equivalent of stock for purposes of § 351. Neither case had to decide whether the contingent interest represented "voting stock," a somewhat more difficult question. That question was resolved, however, in Rev.Rul. 66–112, 1966–1 C.B. 68, which held that the receipt of a contingent contractual right to additional voting shares that was not assignable and could only ripen into additional voting shares did not violate the solely for voting stock requirement in a (B) reorganization.

After the issuance of Rev.Rul. 66–112, the following transactions were held not to violate the solely for voting stock requirement: Rev.Rul. 73–205, 1973–1 C.B. 188 (the conversion ratio of convertible preferred stock received in a (B) reorganization was subject to upward adjustment after five years based on the target corporation's earnings performance; the right to additional shares, if any, was forfeited by those shareholders who converted within the 5–year period); Rev.Rul. 75–456, 1975–2 C.B. 128 (subsequent to a (B) reorganization in which a contingent stock payout provision was employed, the acquiring corporation changed its place of incorporation by means of an (F) reorganization in which a new corporation was formed in another state and the acquiring corporation merged into it; the fact that the new corporation assumed the acquiring corporation's contingent stock payout obligation and agreed to issue its own additional shares of stock in lieu of the acquiring corporation's stock did not affect the status of the prior (B) reorganization); Rev.Rul. 75–237, 1975–1 C.B. 116 (acceleration of contingent stock payout agreement by acquiring corporation in a (B) reorganization prior to the transfer of all of its assets to a third corporation in a (C) reorganization did not affect the validity of the earlier (B) reorganization; same result if the earlier reorganization had itself been a (C) reorganization).

Rev.Proc. 77–37, § 3.03, 1977–2 C.B. 568, amplified by Rev.Proc. 84–42, 1984–1 C.B. 521, sets forth nine conditions under which a favorable ruling will be issued on the solely for voting stock question in a contingent stock payout situation. The principal requirements are that all the additional stock must be issued within five years from the date of the original reorganization transaction, there must be a valid business reason for not issuing all the stock immediately, such as the difficulty of valuing the stock of one or both of the corporations, the maximum number of shares that may be issued is stated, and at least one-half of the total number of shares to be issued must be issued in the initial distribution.

Regulations under § 483 in force prior to the adoption of the comprehensive rules in §§ 1272 through 1275 (governing the imputation of interest, see page 168) provided that a portion of the additional stock received in a contingent stock transaction constituted interest, taxable as ordinary income and not entitled to nonrecognition. Taxpayers challenged the validity of the § 483 regulations, arguing that treatment of the receipt of additional stock as a "payment" under § 483 is inconsistent with the conclusion that the receipt of the right to additional stock does not violate the solely for voting stock requirements in the reorganization provisions. The position taken in the regulations, however, was upheld by the courts. See Kingsley v. Commissioner, 72 T.C. 1095 (1979); Catterall v. Commissioner, 68 T.C. 413 (1977), aff'd sub nom., Vorbleski v. Commissioner, 589 F.2d 123 (3d Cir.1978); Jeffers v. United States, 556 F.2d 986 (Ct.Cl.1977) ((A) reorganization); Solomon v. Commissioner, 570 F.2d 28 (2d Cir.1977); Katkin v. Commissioner, 570 F.2d 139 (6th Cir.1978) ((A) reorganization). The OID regulations do not deal with contingent stock payout situations because the OID rules apply only to "debt instruments," and a contingent stock right is not a debt instrument. Section 483, however, applies to impute interest on "contingent payments," and Treas.Reg. § 1.483–4(b), Ex. (2) applies § 483 to a contingent stock payout. As a result, upon receipt of the contingent stock, a portion of the stock will be characterized as interest taxable as ordinary income and not entitled to nonrecognition under § 354.

Rev.Rul. 75–94, 1975–1 C.B. 111, dealt with a variation on a contingent stock payout situation. In 1973, a type (B) reorganization took place. In the following year it was discovered that the acquiring corporation had misrepresented its earnings because of an improper accounting practice. Upon correction of the improper practice, the earnings were reduced and the target corporation's stockholders asserted that they were entitled to additional stock of the acquiring corporation to satisfy the negotiated acquisition price. After discussions between the parties, the acquiring corporation did issue additional stock. The Ruling concluded that the additional shares received were part of the original "plan of reorganization" and hence qualified as part of the (B) reorganization.

Another technique that is employed where the parties cannot agree upon the value of the corporations is the "escrowed stock" arrangement. Under such an arrangement, the acquiring corporation issues its stock to the shareholders of the target corporation, but part of the stock is placed in escrow to be returned to the acquiring corporation upon the occurrence of a specified event, for example, the failure of the target corporation to reach a specified earnings level. If the earnings level is reached, the stock is transferred out of escrow to the former shareholders of the target corporation. Since the stock is actually issued, subject to subsequent forfeiture, some problems of contingent stock payouts are avoided. For example, interest will not be imputed under § 483 if the transaction is properly structured. Rev.Rul. 70–120, 1970–1 C.B. 124 (shareholders entitled to unrestricted voting rights and received dividends on stock); Feifer v. United States, 500 F.Supp. 102 (N.D.Ga.1980) (same even though voting rights were restricted).

Rev.Rul. 76–42, 1976–1 C.B. 102, held that no gain or loss is recognized by the shareholders of the target corporation if the escrowed stock is returned to the acquiring corporation where the number of shares to be returned was based on their initially negotiated value. The adjusted basis of the returned shares is added to the basis of those received by the shareholders of the target corporation. Compare Rev.Rul. 78–376, 1978–2 C.B. 149 (because the number of shares to be returned from the escrow to discharge an indemnity obligation was based on the value of the shares on the date of the return from escrow and not on the initially negotiated price, the taxpayer was required to realize gain since he received a benefit from the appreciation in value that was used to discharge his obligations).

Rev.Proc. 77–37, § 3.06, 1977–2 C.B. 568, amplified by Rev.Proc. 84–42, 1984–1 C.B. 521, sets forth nine conditions under which a favorable ruling will be issued in escrowed stock transactions. The principal requirements are that there must be a valid reason for establishing the arrangement, the stock subject to the escrow agreement must be treated as issued and outstanding stock of the acquiring corporation for all purposes, voting rights must be exercisable by the shareholders or their agent, all shares must be released from the escrow within five years, and not more than 50 percent of the total number of shares to be issued may be subject to the escrow.

Contingent stock and escrowed stock arrangements are not unique to type (B) reorganizations. They may be used in connection with any type acquisition, but different problems may arise with respect to qualifying the transaction under different provisions of § 368. For example, Rev.Rul. 76–334, 1976–2 C.B. 108, involved the use of an escrow arrangement in a type (C) reorganization in which the transferor corporation liquidated and distributed all rights in the escrowed stock to its shareholders. The purpose of the escrow was to protect the acquiring corporation from a breach of representations and warranties made by the target corporation as a part of the reorganization transaction. The acquiring corporation asserted a breach and the escrow agent returned part of the escrowed stock to the acquiring corporation, with the balance being distributed to the target corporation's shareholders. However, those shareholders disputed the validity of the acquiring corporation's claim to a return of part of the escrowed stock. Negotiations between the parties resulted in a settlement pursuant to which the acquiring corporation paid cash equal to one-half the value of the escrowed shares distributed to the shareholders and the shareholders returned the balance of the escrowed shares to the acquiring corporation. The Ruling held that the cash payment was separate from, and did not violate the solely for voting stock requirement of, the (C) reorganization. There was a redemption of one-half the escrowed stock under § 302 and the other one-half was simply returned pursuant to the escrow arrangement with no gain or loss being recognized by the target corporation's shareholders under the principles of Rev.Rul. 76–42.

C. MULTI–STEP ACQUISITIONS

The taxpayer's alternative argument in *Chapman* was that the cash purchases of the stock and the exchange of stock for voting stock were separate transactions. If the cash acquisitions were separated from the stock exchange, the exchange by itself would have qualified as a (B) reorganization. The Tax Court did not face the factual issue of whether the stock purchases were "old and cold" and thus did not taint the share exchange because of its holding that in any event a (B) reorganization was present. The Court of Appeals remanded for consideration of the factual question whether the cash purchase and the exchange were connected. However, the case was settled prior to consideration of this issue by the Tax Court. There is only sparse authority regarding the extent to which prior or subsequent acquisitions for nonqualifying consideration will defeat the (B) reorganization. Treas. Reg. § 1.368–2(c) gives as an example of a qualifying reorganization a situation where the corporation purchased 30 percent of the stock for cash and then 16 years later acquired an additional 60 percent in exchange for its voting stock. Whether the various steps in the acquisition will be considered together or separately depends in part on the time interval between the steps and in part on other circumstances that indicate that the various steps in the acquisition are part of the "same transaction". See Rev.Rul. 75–123, 1975–1 C.B. 115 (cash acquisition and stock exchange pursuant to the "same plan" resulted in a taxable exchange and not a (B) reorganization). The step transaction doctrine, discussed at page 551, is relevant in this determination.

A similar question is involved when the acquisition is made solely in exchange for voting stock but the stock of the acquired company is obtained in a series of transactions. Treas. Reg. § 1.368–2(c) seems to require that the requisite 80 percent control be acquired within a 12–month period. If this time limitation is satisfied, the series of acquisitions is in effect treated as a single transaction and all shares acquired in the 12–month period will qualify for tax free treatment. If the 12–month time limitation in the regulations is not met, then possibly only those shares acquired for stock that provide or exceed the 80 percent control requirement qualify for (B) reorganization treatment and the other exchanges would be treated as taxable transactions. However, in American Potash & Chemical Corp. v. United States, 402 F.2d 1000 (Ct.Cl.1968), the Government took the position that a transaction qualified as a (B) reorganization even though the series of acquisitions to obtain control of the target corporation occurred over a 14–month period, asserting that the 12–month rule in Treas. Reg. § 1.368–2(c) "is merely a guideline to determine which exchanges of a series of exchanges of stock for stock qualify as tax-free under the B reorganization provisions." (1001) In *American Potash,* the Government unsuccessfully sought reorganization treatment to prevent a step-up in basis on the subsequent liquidation of the acquired corporation; it seems doubtful that the Commissioner would accept a similar argument by a taxpayer seeking to qualify for reorganization treatment.

See also Rev.Rul. 69–585, 1969–2 C.B. 56 (subsidiary distributed its previously acquired 25% of the stock of the target corporation to its parent as a dividend and the parent then acquired the remaining 75% of the stock of the target corporation from the latter's shareholders; parent's acquisitions held to constitute a valid (B) reorganization); Rev.Rul. 69–294, 1969–1 C.B. 110 (parent liquidated subsidiary to obtain 80% stock interest in target corporation that was held by the liquidated subsidiary, and then acquired the balance of the target stock in a stock-for-stock exchange; parent's acquisition held not to constitute a valid (B) reorganization since part of the acquired corporation's stock was obtained in the liquidation in exchange for the subsidiary's stock).

D. THE "CONTROL" REQUIREMENT

Rev.Rul. 59–259, 1959–2 C.B. 115, holds that "control" as defined by section 368(c) requires ownership of stock possessing at least 80 percent of the total combined voting power of all classes of voting stock and the ownership of at least 80 percent of the total number of shares of *each* class of outstanding non-voting stock. In Rev.Rul. 76–223, 1976–1 C.B. 103, the target corporation had outstanding 81 shares of voting common stock and 19 shares of non-voting preferred stock. The acquiring corporation wished to obtain all of the common, but none of the preferred stock in exchange for its voting stock. This transaction, however, would not have qualified as a (B) reorganization, since the "control" test requires ownership of 80 percent of each class of non-voting stock in addition to 80 percent of the voting stock. Accordingly, prior to the reorganization, the target corporation amended its charter to grant voting rights to the preferred stock.

Voting stock of the acquiring corporation was then exchanged for the common stock of the target corporation. The Ruling held that the control requirement was met since the acquiring corporation received over 80 percent of all the classes of stock entitled to vote at the time of the acquisition, there being at that time no non-voting classes of stock outstanding in the target corporation.

E. PARTIES TO THE REORGANIZATION

Section 368(a)(2)(C) provides that the acquiring corporation in a (B) reorganization may transfer the stock of the target corporation to a subsidiary without disqualifying the reorganization. The target corporation, as a result, becomes a second tier subsidiary of the acquiring corporation. Moreover, by virtue of the first parenthetical provision in § 368(a)(1)(B) itself, a valid (B) reorganization can occur if an 80 percent controlled subsidiary is the acquiring corporation, using the stock of its parent in the reorganization. Again, as a result, the target corporation becomes a second tier subsidiary in the corporate group.

Treas. Reg. § 1.368–2(k), discussed at page 533, allows post-reorganizations transfers by the acquiring corporation of the target corporation's stock to related corporations without violating the continuity of interest requirement, even though the continuity is more remote than specifically permitted in §§ 368(a)(1)(B) and (a)(2)(C). For example, a stock-for-stock acquisition followed by a drop of the acquired corporation's stock to a third tier controlled subsidiary is permitted.

F. RELATIONSHIP OF (B) AND (C) REORGANIZATIONS

A valid (B) reorganization followed by the immediate liquidation of the acquired corporation may be treated by the Internal Revenue Service as a (C) reorganization. See Rev.Rul. 67–274, 1967–2 C.B. 141. See also page 614.

G. TREATMENT OF PARTIES TO A TYPE (B) REORGANIZATION

1. *Shareholders of Target Corporation*

In a (B) reorganization the shareholders of the target corporation do not recognize any gain or loss. I.R.C. § 354(a). Section 356 does not come into play since receipt of "other property" disqualifies the transaction as a "reorganization" under § 368(a)(1)(B). The shareholders of the target corporation take as their basis in the acquiring corporation's shares received the basis of their stock in the target corporation. I.R.C. § 358(a).

2. *Bondholders of the Target Corporation*

In Rev. Rul. 98–10, 1998–10 I.R.B. 11, X Corporation acquired all of the outstanding stock of Y Corporation in exchange for its voting stock. Also pursuant to the plan of reorganization, X Corporation acquired the outstanding debentures of Y Corporation in exchange for its own debentures of an equal principal amount. Some debenture holders held Y Corporation stock but a substantial portion of the debentures were held by persons who owned no Y Corporation stock. The ruling held that the stock-for-stock exchange qualified as a B reorganization. The separate debenture for debenture exchange was pursuant to the plan of reorganization, and thus, under § 354, no gain or loss was recognized by the debenture holders.

3. *Acquiring Corporation*

No gain or loss is recognized by the acquiring corporation in a valid (B) reorganization. I.R.C. § 1032. If the acquiring corporation uses stock of its parent as is permitted by the parenthetical in § 368(a)(1)(B), § 1032 does not apply on its face, but Treas. Reg. § 1.1032–2, provides nonrecognition.

The acquiring corporation's basis in the stock of the target corporation is the aggregate of the bases of the transferring shareholders. I.R.C. § 362(b). If the target corporation is widely held, this information may be difficult to obtain. Rev.Proc. 81–70, 1981–2 C.B. 729, provides guidelines for estimating the transferor shareholders' bases, including, where appropriate, the use of standard statistical methods using a probability sample.

The target corporation itself is unaffected by the reorganization exchange. The bases of the target corporation's assets are therefore unchanged and it retains its tax attributes.

SECTION 4. STOCK FOR ASSETS ACQUISITIONS: TYPE (C) REORGANIZATIONS

INTERNAL REVENUE CODE: Sections 354; 356(a), (c); 357(a), (b); 358(a); 361; 362(b); 368(a)(1)(C), (a)(2)(B), (C), and (G).

REGULATIONS: Section 1.368–2(d).

The type (C) reorganization resembles an (A) reorganization in that the assets of the target corporation are transferred to the acquiring corporation in exchange for stock of the acquiring corporation. Indeed, the (C) reorganization is often referred to as a "practical merger." But requirements are imposed that are not present in an (A) reorganization. "Substantially all" the assets of the target corporation must be exchanged in the transaction and, since the target corporation in a (C) reorganization does not automatically disappear as in an (A) reorganization, § 368(a)(2)(G) requires the target corporation to liquidate. Moreover, the (C) reorganization has elements in common with a (B) reorganization that are not present in an (A) reorganization, notably the requirement that the consideration for the target assets be "solely" voting stock of the acquiring corporation. But, in turn, the solely for voting stock requirement is less stringently applied in the (C) reorganization, which allows up to 20 percent of the consideration (including debt assumption) to be other than voting stock. Thus, a number of the issues considered in connection with (A) and (B) reorganizations are also present in (C) reorganizations.

ILLUSTRATIVE MATERIAL

A. SOLELY FOR VOTING STOCK REQUIREMENT

1. *General*

As in the case of a (B) reorganization, § 368(a)(1)(C) imposes the requirement that the acquisition be "solely for voting stock." This phrase has the same meaning as in the context of a (B) reorganization and the materials discussed beginning at page 583 are equally applicable in interpreting the requirement in a (C) reorganization. The rigors of the solely for voting stock requirement are, however, relaxed to some extent where a (C) reorganization is involved. The (C) reorganization definition allows up to 20 percent of the consideration used in the acquisition to be other than voting stock. I.R.C. § 368(a)(2)(B). The 20 percent leeway for (C) reorganizations is of limited scope, however. If any consideration other than voting stock is used in the acquisition, liabilities of the target that are assumed or to which its property are subject are also applied against the permissible 20 percent consideration that may be in a form other than voting stock. Moreover, the 80 percent voting stock consideration is tested by reference to "all" and not "substantially all" of the target's assets and thus presents significant valuation problems if some of the target's assets are not transferred but are instead distributed to the target's shareholders in the liquidation of the target.

2. *Assumption of Liabilities*

If assets are acquired for voting stock in a (C) reorganization, assumption of indebtedness by the acquiring corporation does not prevent qualification as a reorganization (except as to the effect on the operation of § 368(a)(2)(B)). Consequently in a (C) reorganization, the acquiring corporation may, in addition to issuing voting stock, issue debt securities to the creditors of the target. Southland Ice Co. v. Commissioner, 5 T.C. 842, 850 (1945)(A). If all of the consideration consists of voting stock and assumption of liabilities, there is no specific limitation on the portion of the consideration that may be in the form of assumption of liabilities, although if too high a percentage of the total consideration is debt assumption there is some possibility that the "substantially all the assets" requirement may be violated. But if any portion of the consideration is boot as permitted by § 368(a)(2)(B), then the total amount of boot plus the liabilities assumed may not exceed 20 percent of the value of *all* of the target corporation's assets. This requirement effectively eliminates the possibility of using any boot in a (C) reorganization whenever the target corporation's net assets are not more than 80 percent of its gross assets. See Rev.Rul. 85–138, 1985–2 C.B. 122.

Even where boot is not present, not all debt assumptions are permitted. In Helvering v. Southwest Consolidated Corp., 315 U.S. 194 (1942), the acquiring corporation had assumed a bank loan entered into by the bondholders' committee to obtain cash to pay nonparticipating security holders. The Court held that the bank loan did not fall within the assumption of liabilities clause, since the requirement to pay cash arose out of the reorganization plan itself and could not therefore be regarded as an obligation of the "other corporation." Subsequent cases, however, limited the scope of *Southwest Consolidated.* See Claridge Apartments Co. v. Commissioner, 1 T.C. 163 (1942) (assumption of expenses of bankruptcy reorganization did not disqualify transaction); Alcazar Hotel, Inc. v. Commissioner, 1 T.C. 872 (1943) (same); Roosevelt Hotel Co. v. Commissioner, 13 T.C. 399 (1949) (loans used to pay preexisting liabilities did not disqualify transaction). In Rev.Rul. 73–54, 1973–1 C.B. 187, the Service declined to apply the holding of *Southwest Consolidated* to the fullest extent possible by ruling that the payment by the acquiring corporation of valid reorganization expenses of the target corporation is not a violation of the solely for voting stock requirement: "Although the acquired corporation and its shareholders are relieved of the reorganization expenses otherwise attributable to them, nevertheless they will be receiving solely voting stock of the acquiring corporation." On the other hand, in Rev.Rul. 73–102, 1973–1 C.B. 186, where the acquiring corporation assumed the obligation of the target corporation to pay the claims of dissenting shareholders, the assumption was treated as in substance a payment of cash (and thus not within the exception of § 368(a)(1)(C) for liability assumptions) and also did not fall within the exception for reorganization expenses set out in Rev.Rul. 73–54. Reorganization treatment was still possible, however, as the cash payment fell within the leeway allowed under § 368(a)(2)(B).

In Rev.Rul. 76–365, 1976–2 C.B. 110, prior to a (C) reorganization, the target corporation had employed an accountant and a financial consultant to value the stock of each of six prospective acquiring corporations, including the stock of the corporation with which the transaction was ultimately consummated. As part of the reorganization, the acquiring corporation paid the fees of the consultants. The Ruling held that the expenses of valuing the stock of the acquiring corporation itself were covered by Rev.Rul. 73–54 and did not violate the solely for voting stock requirement. The expenses of evaluating the other five potential acquiring corporations were treated as liabilities of the target corporation assumed by the acquiring corporation. Hence, such assumption of liabilities fell within the exception in § 368(a)(1)(C) and the solely for voting stock requirement was satisfied.

Care must be taken that only existing liabilities are assumed and that new liabilities of the acquiring corporation are not created. In Stoddard v. Commissioner, 141 F.2d 76 (2d Cir.1944), the issuance of mortgage bonds to replace unsecured indebtedness of the target corporation was held to go beyond assumption of the target corporation's debts and to constitute additional impermissible consideration. But where new bonds issued by the acquiring corporation to replace outstanding bonds of the target vary only somewhat from the terms of the old bonds the courts have tended to treat the replacement as an assumption. See, e.g. Southland Ice Co. v. Commissioner, page 608, and the Service likewise allows some leeway here. See Rev.Rul. 79–155, 1979–1 C.B. 153 (replacement of 8% nonconvertible bonds due in 1995 with 9% convertible bonds due in 1990 was treated as "assumption").

The relaxation of the solely for voting stock requirement in § 368(a)(1)(C) applies only to the assumption of liabilities by "the acquiring corporation." Thus the Service has ruled that where a subsidiary acquires by means of its parent's stock the assets of a third corporation, as is permitted under § 368(a)(1)(C), the assumption by the parent of liabilities of the target corporation violated the solely for voting stock requirement since the subsidiary is technically the acquiring corporation. Rev.Rul. 70–107, 1970–1 C.B. 78. Treas. Reg. § 1.368–1(d)(4), discussed at page 542, which was promulgated in 1998, allows certain post-reorganization transfers by the acquiring corporation of the target corporation's assets to related corporations without running afoul of the continuity of business enterprise requirement, but Treas. Reg. § 1.368–1(d)(4) does not affect the result in Rev. Rul. 70–107. However, if the parent retains the right to direct the transfer of the assets to the subsidiary, the parent is then considered the acquiring corporation and its assumption of liabilities falls within the exception. Rev.Rul. 70–224, 1970–1 C.B. 79.

Section 357(b), discussed at page 107, treats all of the target corporation's debts assumed by the acquiring corporation as boot if a tax avoidance motive is present with respect to any of the assumed indebtedness. See Rev.Rul. 79–258, 1979–2 C.B. 143 (on facts, declining to apply § 357(b) to assumption of liabilities in a type (D) reorganization).

B. THE "SUBSTANTIALLY ALL OF THE PROPERTIES" REQUIREMENT

The "substantially all of the properties" requirement in § 368(a)(1)(C) appears to reflect the view that reorganization treatment should be allowed only if there is a continuation of the business enterprise. Perhaps too, the requirement may reflect elements of the continuity of interest requirement, i.e., that the shareholders of the target corporation retain a continuing interest in the assets which had comprised their pre-transfer investment.

In Smith v. Commissioner, 34 B.T.A. 702 (1936)(A), the Board of Tax Appeals permitted 71 percent of the gross assets to qualify where the balance was retained for the sole purpose of liquidating liabilities. The Board, in distinguishing other cases, stressed the purpose of the retention and emphasized it was not to engage in business or to distribute assets to shareholders. Referring to this decision, the Tax Court in Southland Ice Company v. Commissioner, 5 T.C. 842 (1945), said "Even this [the 'substantially all'] provision has been subjected to a construction which in effect applies a continuity test rather than mere blind percentages." Rev.Rul. 57–118, 1957–2 C.B. 253, following a statement in the *Smith* case, stressed that a transaction will not qualify as a (C) reorganization if the net assets transferred are too low a percentage of gross assets. Thus, the Ruling stated that where net assets equal only 10 percent of gross assets, the requirement clearly could not be satisfied. The Ruling held, however, that a transfer of 70 percent of the target corporation's assets satisfied the "substantially all the assets" requirements where the assets retained were not in excess of those sufficient to discharge liabilities. In National Bank of

Commerce of Norfolk v. United States, 158 F.Supp. 887 (E.D.Va.1958), a transfer of 81 percent of the assets was held not "substantially all" where the remaining assets were not retained to meet liabilities but were to be distributed to shareholders.

In Rev.Proc. 77–37, § 3.01, 1977–2 C.B. 568, the Service stated that it would issue advance rulings on the "substantially all" issue where the transferred assets represent at least 90 percent of the fair market value of the net assets and at least 70 percent of the fair market value of the gross assets of the corporation immediately prior to the transfer; this test, as with the continuity of interest test, page 526, is only an "operating rule" and does not "define, as a matter of law, the lower limits of 'continuity of interest' or 'substantially all of the properties'." Rev.Proc. 77–37 also stated that payments to dissenters and pre-acquisition redemptions and extraordinary dividends that are part of the plan of reorganization are considered assets held immediately prior to the transfer for purposes of determining whether substantially all the assets are transferred to the acquiring corporation. See also Rev.Rul. 74–457, 1974–2 C.B. 122 (cash used in payment of regular cash dividend prior to the reorganization by the target corporation is not taken into account in applying the "substantially all" test; however, if the payment occurred after the reorganization, the cash required to pay the dividend and the liability for payment of the dividend are taken into account).

Rev.Rul. 88–48, 1988–1 C.B. 117, found the "substantially all" requirement to have been met where the target corporation sold for cash one of its two historic businesses, which represented 50 percent of its historic business assets, and then transferred the cash and all its remaining assets to the acquiring corporation for the acquiring corporation's voting stock and assumption of the target corporation's liabilities. The sale of the assets was pursuant to the overall plan because the acquiring corporation did not wish to acquire the business that was sold. The Ruling stressed that the Service views the purpose of the "substantially all" requirement as preventing the use of § 368(a)(1)(C) to effect a divisive reorganization. Since the sale was to unrelated persons and no part of the proceeds was directly or indirectly retained by the shareholders of the target corporation, the test was met.

In Helvering v. Elkhorn Coal Co., 95 F.2d 732 (4th Cir.1937), the Elkhorn Coal and Coke Co. desired to transfer a part of its mining property to Mill Creek Company for stock. To qualify as a reorganization since Mill Creek would not obtain control of Elkhorn Coal Co., Elkhorn would have had to transfer substantially all its assets. To accomplish this, Elkhorn first formed a new company, transferred the other Elkhorn properties to it for its stock, and distributed such stock to its shareholders, this distribution being nontaxable under the predecessors of §§ 368(a)(1)(D) and 355. It then transferred the mining properties, now "all its properties," to Mill Creek for stock, technically a reorganization. The new company then acquired the Elkhorn stock for its stock and dissolved Elkhorn so that the old Elkhorn stockholder ended up as the shareholders of a corporation that owned the remaining Elkhorn properties and stock of Mill Creek. The transaction predated the enactment of the liquidation requirement in § 368(a)(2)(G). Applying *Gregory* principles, the court disregarded the distribution of the stock of the new company and held that Elkhorn had not transferred substantially all of its assets to Mill Creek. Hence no reorganization had occurred and the transaction was taxable. Compare Rev.Rul. 70–434, 1970–2 C.B. 83 (preacquisition spin-off of assets does not preclude (B) reorganization treatment).

C. LIQUIDATION REQUIREMENT

Section 368(a)(2)(G) requires that the target corporation liquidate and distribute the stock and securities it receives in the reorganization as well as its other properties to its shareholders in pursuance of the plan of reorganization. This requirement was added in 1984 to forestall tax avoidance effected by keeping the target corporation in existence as an investment company following the acquisition. This tax avoidance potential arose because under § 381 all of the target corporation's tax attributes are transferred to the acquiring corporation as a result of the reorganization. See Chapter 16. Thus if not required to liquidate, the target corporation would have substantial assets, against which it might borrow to make distributions, but would have no earnings and profits to support dividend treatment. See H.Rep. No. 98–861, 98th Cong., 2d Sess. 205 (1984).

The distribution requirement may be waived by the Internal Revenue Service in circumstances in which an actual distribution would result in substantial hardship. However, the waiver will be granted only on the condition that the target corporation and its shareholders be treated as if the retained assets were distributed and then recontributed to a new corporation. See H.Rep. No. 98–861, 98th Cong., 2d Sess. 845–46 (1984). This constructive liquidation and contribution will trigger recognition of gain and loss to the target corporation under § 361(c)(2)(A) as well as recognition of gain to the shareholders of the target corporation under § 356(a).

As a further safeguard, the 1984 Act also amended § 312(h)(2) to authorize the Treasury to promulgate regulations requiring that the earnings and profits of the target corporation be allocated between the acquiring and the target corporations.

In Rev.Rul. 84–30, 1984–1 C.B. 114, X Corporation owned all the stock of Y Corporation and Z Corporation; Z Corporation, in turn, owned all of the stock of N Corporation. Y acquired substantially all the assets of N for its voting stock. N was liquidated and Z received the Y stock, which it immediately distributed to X. The Ruling held that the continuity of interest requirement of Treas. Reg. § 1.368–1(b) is satisfied where the stock of Y Corporation exchanged for the assets of X Corporation is distributed through Y Corporation's 100 percent parent to that corporation's 100 percent parent. It does not appear to have been crucial to the result in the Ruling that X Corporation was the common parent of both Y and Z. Furthermore, there is no obvious reason why the holding should apply only if the ultimate distributee is a 100 percent parent corporation, rather than individual shareholders. Note, however, that the distribution from Y Corporation's parent to its own shareholders should be treated as a dividend, which may result in recognition to both the distributing corporation and the shareholders.

D. MULTI–STEP ACQUISITIONS

1. *Treated as Separate Transactions*

The problems of "creeping acquisitions," as in the case of a (B) reorganization, discussed at page 604, also are encountered in the (C) reorganization context.

Bausch & Lomb Optical Co. v. Commissioner, 267 F.2d 75 (2d Cir. 1959), and Rev.Rul. 54–396, 1954–2 C.B. 147, denied (C) reorganization status under the 1939 Code where the acquiring corporation, which earlier had acquired 79 percent of the stock of the target corporation for cash, issued its stock for the assets of the target corporation and then liquidated it. The Ruling stated that only 21 percent of the assets had been acquired solely for voting stock, since the balance had been in effect acquired because of the stock purchased for cash. Grede Foundries, Inc. v. United States, 202 F.Supp. 263 (E.D.Wis.1962), followed *Bausch & Lomb* on similar facts. However, Rev.Rul. 57–278, 1957–1 C.B. 124, would permit the above transaction to be accomplished by the acquiring corporation forming a subsidiary corporation by exchanging the acquiring corporation's stock for the subsidiary's stock, the subsidiary corporation then acquiring the assets of the target corporation with the new acquiring corporation stock, and the target corporation then liquidating. The minority shareholders of the target corporation have become minority shareholders of the acquiring corporation, which was intended, although the subsidiary corporation remains as a subsidiary. The Ruling stresses the fact that the acquiring corporation could have acquired the minority shares of the target corporation in a (B) reorganization and the above route ends the same way. See also Rev.Rul. 58–93, 1958–1 C.B. 188 (upholding the foregoing transaction as an (A) or (C) reorganization, even though, in order to satisfy a requirement of state law, the transfer to the subsidiary corporation occurred prior to the merger). Rev.Rul. 57–278 was held not to apply in a transaction in which the acquiring corporation acquired part of the stock of the target corporation for cash, followed by the acquisition by the subsidiary corporation of the assets of the target corporation, where the cash purchase was an integral step in a pre-conceived plan to acquire substantially all of the properties of the target corporation; the acquisition of the assets of the target corporation was for cash plus voting stock, and the solely for voting stock requirement of a (C) reorganization was not met. Rev.Rul. 69–48, 1969–1 C.B. 106.

Other means are available to avoid the adverse tax consequences of *Bausch & Lomb* where a corporation finds itself in the predicament of owning part, but not all, of the stock of a subsidiary in which it desires 100 percent ownership. The acquiring and target corporations could each transfer their assets to new corporation in return for its stock in (C) reorganizations and then liquidate. Rev.Rul. 68–526, 1968–2 C.B. 156; George v. Commissioner, 26 T.C. 396 (1956). In Rev.Rul. 69–413, 1969–2 C.B. 55, (C) reorganization treatment was upheld where the acquiring corporation, owning 99 percent of the stock of the target corporation, created a new subsidiary that then exchanged the acquiring corporation stock for the target corporation assets and the target corporation then liquidated.

2. *Treated as a Single Transaction*

The Internal Revenue Service may regard a stock for stock type (B) acquisition followed by liquidation of the target corporation as a (C) reorganization. Rev.Rul. 67–274, 1967–2 C.B. 141; Resorts International, Inc. v. Commissioner, 60 T.C. 778 (1973), aff'd on this issue, 511 F.2d 107 (5th Cir.1975) (no intention to operate target corporations as subsidiaries; the liquidations were part of a series of continuing transactions that constituted a (C) reorganization); American Potash & Chemical Corp. v. United States, 399 F.2d 194 (Ct.Cl.1968). One result of this treatment, is that, if the acquiring corporation had previously owned stock of the target corporation, the *Bausch & Lomb* doctrine, discussed above, may be applicable.

The Service's recharacterization of a (B) reorganization-liquidation as a (C) reorganization is grounded on the theory that under Kimbell–Diamond Milling Co. v. Commissioner, 14 T.C. 74 (1950), aff'd per curiam 187 F.2d 718 (5th Cir.1951), the transaction is actually an asset acquisition (see page 476). See Rev.Rul. 74–35, 1974–1 C.B. 85 (holding that *Kimbell–Diamond* reasoning and Rev.Rul. 67–254 do not apply to recast a (B) reorganization where the target corporation does not transfer substantially all its assets to the acquiring corporation); Rev.Rul. 72–405, 1972–2 C.B. 217 ((C) reorganization upheld where a newly-created subsidiary acquired the assets of another corporation in a merger utilizing the parent corporation's stock, followed by a liquidation of the subsidiary).

Where one of the steps in a multi-step acquisition is a cash purchase of stock of the target corporation, which is followed by an asset acquisition using voting stock, the transaction may fail to qualify as a (C) reorganization because the "solely for voting stock" requirement has been violated. In Rev.Rul. 85–138, 1985–2 C.B. 122, P Corporation owned all of the stock of S1 and S2. Pursuant to a plan by which S1 would acquire substantially all the properties of the target corporation in consideration of P voting stock and the assumption by S1 of the target corporation's liabilities, S2 purchased some of the outstanding stock of the target corporation for cash in order to eliminate any possible adverse minority interest in the target corporation. The liabilities of the target corporation assumed by S1 exceeded 20 percent of the value of the target corporation's assets. Because the cash purchases of stock by S2 were part of a prearranged plan, the cash was treated as additional consideration provided by S1 and, since the cash and liabilities together exceeded the 20 percent limit in § 368(a)(2)(B), the acquisition did not qualify as a (C) reorganization.

E. PARTIES TO THE REORGANIZATION

Section 368(a)(2)(C) allows the acquiring corporation in a (C) reorganization to transfer the target's assets to a controlled subsidiary. See Rev. Rul. 68–261, 1968–1 C.B. 147 (where the target corporation operated through six divisions and merged into the acquiring corporation, which then transferred each division to six wholly-owned subsidiaries, § 368(a)(2)(C) applied). See also Rev.Rul. 81–247, 1981–2 C.B. 87 (drop down of assets acquired in merger does not violate continuity of business enterprise requirement of Treas. Reg. § 1.368–1(d)). The transfer down can also be made to a "second tier" subsidiary controlled indirectly by the parent. Rev.Rul. 64–73, 1964–1 C.B. 142. See Treas.Reg. § 1.368–2(k).

In addition, by virtue of the parenthetical clause in § 368(a)(1)(C), a subsidiary can be utilized as the acquiring corporation, exchanging voting stock of its parent for substantially all the assets of the target corporation.

F. RELATIONSHIP OF (TYPE (C) REORGANIZATIONS TO OTHER PROVISIONS

Section 368(a)(2)(A) provides that if a (C) reorganization also constitutes a (D) reorganization it will be treated only as a (D) reorganization, thus insuring that the (C) reorganization provisions cannot be used to accomplish a disguised tax-free division of a corporation that does not comply with the requirements of § 355. See Chapter 15.

Rev.Rul. 76–188, 1976–1 C.B. 99, involved a transaction in which a parent corporation transferred all its assets to its wholly-owned subsidiary and the subsidiary assumed all of the parent corporation's liabilities. The liabilities assumed exceeded the basis of the assets transferred to the subsidiary. Section 357(c) was held to be applicable, since the transaction was one "described in" § 351 (a provision to which § 357(c) applies); the fact that it also constituted a (C) reorganization did not prevent the application of § 357(c), and the parent corporation accordingly recognized a gain on the transaction. If brother-sister corporations are involved, it is possible for a (C) reorganization to overlap with § 304, page 272. It is not clear which provision will control.

G. TREATMENT OF PARTIES TO A TYPE (C) REORGANIZATION

1. *Target Corporation and Shareholders*

No gain or loss is recognized by the target corporation on the exchange with the acquiring corporation regardless of the nature of the property received from the acquiring corporation. If only stock or securities of the acquiring corporation is received in the reorganization, § 361(a) provides nonrecognition. If nonqualifying boot is received, § 361(b) requires that the target corporation recognize gain upon receipt only if the boot is not distributed to either its shareholders or creditors pursuant to the plan of reorganization. Because § 368(a)(2)(G) requires the target corporation to liquidate, all of the boot must be distributed and, in general, no gain can be recognized under § 361(b). However, if boot is received and expended, for example to pay ongoing expenses, so that it is not distributed, then gain will be recognized.

As for the liquidating distributions, no gain or loss is recognized by the target corporation on the distribution of qualified stock or securities. I.R.C. § 361(c)(1), (2)(B). Distribution of appreciated boot in the liquidation results in recognition of gain (but not loss) under § 361(c)(2), but because § 358(a)(2) provides the target corporation with a fair market value basis in any boot received in the reorganization transaction, no gain will be realized unless there is a change in value between the receipt and the liquidating distribution. If any property was retained by the target corporation, gain may be recognized by the corporation as a result of distributing such property in the liquidation.

The operative rules of § 361 leave little room for the target corporation to recognize gain in a (C) reorganization. However, although § 361(c)(3) accords tax free treatment to the receipt and distribution of stock in satisfaction of creditors' claims, if stock of the acquiring corporation received in the reorganization is *sold* by the target corporation and the proceeds used to pay creditors' claims, the target corporation must recognize gain on the sale; the receipt of the stock remains nontaxable.

For the shareholders of the target corporation, the tax results are similar to those in an (A) reorganization. No gain or loss is recognized if they receive solely the stock of the acquiring corporation in exchange for their stock in the target corporation. I.R.C. § 354(a). If the permissible amount of "boot" is involved and it is distributed to the shareholders, they may recognize gain under § 356, either as capital gain or as a dividend, depending on the circumstances, as discussed at page 565. Section 358 then provides an exchanged basis for the acquiring corporation's stock. If any boot is received, however, the basis is determined by first increasing the basis by the amount of any gain recognized by the shareholders as the result of the receipt of boot, and then decreasing it by the amount of cash or the fair market value of any other property received.

2. *Acquiring Corporation*

Pursuant to § 1032, the acquiring corporation recognizes no gain or loss on the transfer of its shares in a (C) reorganization. If, however, the acquiring corporation transfers any boot other than cash or its own stock or securities, it must recognize gain or loss with respect to the boot transferred.

Under § 362(b) the acquiring corporation's basis in the acquired assets is equal to the target corporation's basis in those assets. Although § 362(b) provides that the acquiring corporation's basis in the assets is to be increased by any gain recognized under § 361(b) by the target corporation on the transfer of its assets to the acquiring corporation, it is not likely that the target corporation will recognize gain as a result of the transfer of its assets to the acquiring corporation because the target liquidates and distributes all of its property to shareholders.

Under § 381, the tax attributes of the target corporation, e.g., net operating loss carryovers, earnings and profits accounts, etc., carry over to the acquiring corporation. The limitations of § 382(b) are, however, applicable. See Chapter 16.

SECTION 5. TRIANGULAR REORGANIZATIONS

INTERNAL REVENUE CODE: Sections 368(a)(2)(D), (E); 368(c).

REGULATIONS: Sections 1.358–6; 1.368–2(b)(2), (j), (k); 1.1032–2.

PROPOSED REGULATIONS: Section 1.1032–3 (1998).

There is no policy objection to allowing acquisitions involving the use of a subsidiary corporation to be tax-free. As discussed in the preceding materials, a series of amendments to the reorganization definitions made it possible to transfer assets or stock acquired in a reorganization transaction to a controlled subsidiary (§ 368(a)(2)(C)) or to employ the subsidiary itself as the acquiring vehicle in a type (B) or type (C) reorganization, using stock of the parent company as consideration for the acquisition. However, these amendments did not cover two situations that were important in practice. In the first place, a direct acquisition by the subsidiary of the target company's assets in an (A) reorganization in exchange for the parent stock was not possible since the parent was not considered to be a party to the reorganization under § 368(b). In addition, though the subsidiary could acquire assets in a (C) reorganization for the parent stock, the parent could not assume liabilities of the target corporation directly since § 368(a)(1)(C) applies only to liabilities assumed by the "acquiring" corporation, in this case the subsidiary. The desired results could have been obtained through other somewhat complicated means, such as the acquisition by the parent of the assets in a (C) reorganization and the subsequent transfer of the target assets to a newly formed subsidiary under § 368(a)(2)(C), with the parent assuming the liabilities of the target corporation.

In successive amendments to § 368 in 1968 and 1971, described in the following Senate Finance Committee Report, Congress made such arrangements unnecessary. In 1968 Congress added § 368(a)(2)(D), which, together with a corresponding amendment to the § 368(b) definition of "party to a reorganization," permits the direct use of the parent's stock by the subsidiary as consideration for assets acquired in an (A) reorganization. See Treas. Reg. § 1.368–2(b)(2).

Section § 368(a)(2)(E), added in 1971, covers the so-called "reverse triangular merger" situation by allowing the subsidiary to be merged into the target corporation using stock of the parent in an (A) reorganization. Thus, the target corporation becomes a subsidiary of the acquiring parent corporation. The stockholders of the target corporation exchange their target corporation stock for the stock of the acquiring parent corporation.

Senate Finance Committee Report, Public Law 91–693

S.Rep. No. 91–1533, 91st Cong., 2d Sess. 622–23 (1971).

[H.R. 19562] amends the tax law to permit a tax-free statutory merger when stock of a parent corporation is used in a merger between a controlled subsidiary of the parent and another corporation, and the other corporation survives—here called a "reverse merger."

In 1968 Congress added a provision to the tax laws permitting statutory mergers where the stock of the parent of the corporation making the acquisition was used in the acquisition (sec. 368(a)(2)(D)). At the time that statute was enacted, the use of stock of a parent corporation was permitted in the type of reorganization involving the acquisition of stock (subparagraph (B)) and in the type of reorganization involving the acquisition of assets (subparagraph (C)) but was not permitted in the case of a statutory merger of a subsidiary. After noting this fact, the House committee report went on to explain the reasons for the amendment as follows:

> Apparently the use of a parent's stock in statutory mergers was not initially provided for because there was no special concern with the problem at the time of the adoption of the 1954 code. However, this is no longer true. A case has been called to the attention of your committee in which it is desired to have an operating company merged into an operating subsidiary in exchange for the stock of the parent holding company. Your committee sees no reason why tax-free treatment should be denied in cases of this type where for any reason the parent cannot or, for business or legal reasons, does not want to acquire the assets (even temporarily) through a merger.
>
> For the reasons set forth above your committee concluded that it was desirable to permit the use of the stock of the parent corporation in a statutory merger in acquiring a corporation in essentially the same manner as presently is available in the case of other tax-free acquisitions. (House report on H.R. 18942 (90th Cong.))

Thus, under existing law, corporation X (an unrelated corporation) may be merged into corporation S (a subsidiary) in exchange for the stock in corporation P (the parent of S) in a tax-free statutory merger. However, if for business and legal reasons (wholly unrelated to Federal income taxation) it is considered more desirable to merge S into X (rather than merging X into S), so that X is the surviving corporation—a "reverse merger"—the transaction is not a tax-free statutory merger.

Although the reverse merger does not qualify as a tax-free statutory merger, it may, in appropriate circumstances, be treated as tax-free as a stock-for-stock reorganization (subparagraph (B)). However, in order to qualify as a tax-free stock-for-stock reorganization it is necessary that the acquisition be *solely* for voting stock and that no stock be target for cash or other consideration. Thus, if a small amount of the stock of X (the unrelated corporation) is target for cash before the merger of S into X, there often may be doubt as to whether or not the transaction will meet the statutory requirements of a stock-for-stock reorganization.

The committee agrees with the House, that there is no reason why a merger in one direction (S into X in the above example) should be taxable, when the merger in the other direction (X into S), under identical circumstances, is tax-free. Moreover, it sees no reason why in cases of this type the acquisition needs to be made solely for stock. For these reasons the amendment makes statutory mergers tax-free in the circumstances described above.

In discussions on this bill, the Treasury Department has expressed concern that the corporate reorganization provisions need review and modification. The committee in agreeing to this amendment does not intend to foreclose consideration of any substantive changes which the Treasury may propose in the corporate reorganization provisions in any future presentations.

ILLUSTRATIVE MATERIAL

A. GENERAL

The Senate Fiancee Committee report suggests that a merger in one direction, the target corporation into the acquiring subsidiary, should not be treated differently than the reverse, the acquiring subsidiary into the target corporation. Note however, that in the case of a reverse triangular merger, § 368(a)(2)(E)(ii) requires that the original shareholders of the surviving corporation exchange stock representing control of the surviving corporation for voting stock of the acquiring parent corporation. There is no such limitation applicable to a forward triangular merger under § 368(a)(2)(D). The reason for this requirement in § 368(a)(2)(E) is not grounded in a policy distinction between the two forms but rather on the difference in structures used by the taxpayers who sought the remedial legislation to effect these transactions before the remedial legislation was enacted. As noted in the Senate Finance Committee Report, a reverse triangular merger is functionally equivalent to a stock for stock exchange under § 368(a)(1)(B), but the reverse triangular merger allows somewhat more latitude with respect to non-stock consideration. The relationship of § 368(a)(2)(E) to § 368(a)(1)(B) is highlighted by Rev.Rul. 67–448, 1967–2 C.B. 144, which, prior to the enactment of § 368(a)(2)(E), held that a reverse triangular merger into corporate shell subsidiary in consideration solely for parent's voting stock was a type (B) reorganization. Is there a continuing justification for the stricter statutory continuity of interest requirements of § 368(a)(2)(E)?

On the other hand, the prohibition against a splitting of interests, reflected in the *Groman* and *Bashford* decisions, is present in the requirement in § 368(a)(2)(D) that no stock of the subsidiary corporation be used in the transaction. In contrast, § 368(a)(2)(E) contains no such express prohibition, although the stricter continuity of interest requirement leaves little room for shareholders of the target corporation to continue to hold a minority interest in it after the acquisition.

B. FORWARD TRIANGULAR MERGERS

1. *Permissible Consideration*

Since § 368(a)(2)(D) is grafted onto the basic type (A) reorganization definition, there is no restriction on the consideration that may be used by the subsidiary in the acquisition other than the general continuity of interest limitation in an (A) reorganization (see discussion at page 526 and the express statutory restriction that no stock of the subsidiary be used. Thus, the stock of dissenting shareholders may be acquired for cash. In addition, the requirements of an (A) reorganization can be met where the subsidiary uses as consideration non-voting stock of the parent and other securities of either the subsidiary or the parent corporation. Treas. Reg. § 1.368–2(b)(2). The assumption of liabilities of the target corporation by the parent will not prevent the transaction from qualifying as a reorganization, nor will the assumption be treated as "boot" under § 361(b). See Rev.Rul. 73–257, 1973–1 C.B. 189 (both parent and subsidiary may assume target corporation's debts). In Rev.Rul. 79–155, 1979–1 C.B. 153, the holders of convertible securities of the target corporation in a forward triangular merger received securities on which the parent and the subsidiary were jointly and severally liable and which were convertible into stock of the parent, unless the parent sold the subsidiary, in which case the securities were convertible into stock of the subsidiary. The Ruling held that the exchange of securities, which had identical principal amounts, was tax-free under § 354; in addition, conversion of the securities into stock of the parent was not a realization event. Would the result have differed if the securities were convertible into stock of the subsidiary from the outset?

2. *Substantially all of the Properties*

In a § 368(a)(2)(D) acquisition, the acquiring subsidiary must *acquire* substantially all of the properties of the target corporation. Treas. Reg. § 1.368–2(b)(2) indicates that the "substantially all" criteria developed in the context of (C) reorganizations (page 610) are to be applied.

3. *Hypothetical Merger Requirement*

The requirement in § 368(a)(2)(D) that the merger "would have qualified" as an (A) reorganization if the transaction had taken place between the target corporation and the parent is not interpreted literally. It need not be established that the merger actually could have taken place under state or federal law; it is sufficient that the "general requirements of a reorganization (such as a business purpose, continuity of business enterprise and continuity of interest)" are met. Treas. Reg. § 1.368–2(b)(2). Section 368(a)(2)(D) applies only to a merger; a consolidation of the target corporation with the acquiring subsidiary in a new corporation is not covered. See e.g. Rev.Rul. 84–104, 1984–2 C.B. 94 (§ 368(a)(2)(E) applies only to state law mergers, not to "consolidations" involving a subsidiary, but consolidation under federal banking law where the target corporation survived was treated as a merger).

C. REVERSE TRIANGULAR MERGERS

1. *Permissible Consideration*

The requirement of § 368(a)(2)(E)(ii) that former shareholders of the surviving corporation exchange a controlling interest in the target corporation for voting stock of the acquiring parent corporation assures that the continuity of interest test will be satisfied. While this requirement is reminiscent of the (B) reorganization, which is the antecedent to the reverse triangular merger, it also has aspects of a (C) reorganization in that a 20 percent leeway for other consideration is permissible. Within this exception there are no limits on the character of the boot that may be exchanged; theoretically stock of the surviving subsidiary, i.e. new stock of the target, is permissible. See also Treas. Reg. § 1.368–2(j)(4), permitting the acquiring parent to assume the target corporation's liabilities.

State law requirements that shareholders exercising statutory dissenters rights be redeemed for cash can present problems with respect to the 80 percent requirement of § 368(a)(2)(E)(ii). Treas. Reg. § 1.368–2(j)(3)(i) provides that stock of the target corporation that is redeemed for cash or property of the target corporation (in contrast to cash or property provided by the acquiring parent or its subsidiary) is not counted as outstanding immediately prior to the reorganization. Thus, for example, if the holders of 100 out of 1000 shares of the target corporation dissent from the merger, the target corporation may redeem those shares, and to qualify under § 368(a)(2)(E) the acquiring parent's stock need be exchanged only for 80 percent of the remaining 900 shares, or 720 shares; the remaining 120 shares may be acquired for cash. But if the funds to redeem the stock are provided by the acquiring parent or subsidiary, then all 1000 shares are taken into account and 800 shares must be acquired for parent's voting stock. Furthermore, although a redemption of stock by the target corporation does not necessarily prevent compliance with the continuity of interest requirement (Treas. Reg. § 1.368–2(j)(6), Ex. (3)), extraordinary pre-reorganization redemptions can violate the continuity of interest requirement. See Temp. Reg. § 1.368–1T(e)(1)(ii)(A) and (B), (e)(6), Ex(10). Furthermore, cash and property of the target corporation used to redeem the stock of its own dissenting shareholders are taken into account in determining whether the "substantially all the properties" test has been met. Treas. Reg. § 1.368–2(j)(7), Ex. (3). If the cash or property distributed in redemption of the dissenting stockholders' shares constitutes too high a percentage of the target corporation's assets, the transaction may fail to meet the "substantially all the properties" test.

2. *Substantially all of the Properties*

In the case of a § 368(a)(2)(E) acquisition, the surviving corporation must *hold* substantially all of its properties and the properties of the merged subsidiary corporation (other than the stock of the parent distributed in the acquisition). Treas. Reg. § 1.368–2(j)(3)(iii) indicates that the "substantially all" criteria developed in the context of (C) reorganizations are to be applied, but assets transferred from the controlling corporation to the merged corporation pursuant to the plan of reorganization are not taken into account. Thus, for example, cash transferred from the controlling corporation to the merged corporation to pay dissenting shareholders of the surviving corporation pursuant to state law or to pay reorganization expenses would not be considered in determining whether the resulting corporation held "substantially all" the assets of the two corporations involved in the acquisition transaction. See also Rev.Rul. 77–307, 1977–2 C.B. 117 (same result prior to issuance of regulations).

3. *"Creeping" Acquisitions*

As in the (B) and (C) reorganization situations, discussed at pages 582 and 607, prior ownership by the parent corporation of stock in the target corporation can present problems in the (a)(2)(E) context. There is no such thing as a "creeping" reverse triangular merger under § 368(a)(2)(E). If the parent corporation already owns over 20 percent of the stock of the target corporation, an (a)(2)(E) reorganization is not possible because of the statutory requirement that an amount of stock constituting "control" in the target corporation be exchanged in the reorganization transaction for voting stock of the acquiring parent corporation. Rev.Rul. 74–564, 1974–2 C.B. 124. However, a failed § 368(a)(2)(E) reverse triangular merger may be recharacterized as a (B) reorganization under the principles of Rev.Rul. 67–448, page 560, if the requirements for a (B) reorganization have been met. See Treas. Reg. § 1.368–2(j)(6), Ex. (4) and (5). This recharacterization will save the reorganization only if the sole consideration used is voting stock of the parent. The 20 percent leeway granted by § 368(a)(2)(E) is not available. Compare the *Bausch & Lomb* situation discussed, at page 613.

These problems are not presented in a § 368(a)(1)(D) forward triangular merger situation. Indeed, a forward triangular merger often is used as the second step in a "two-step acquisition" in which the acquiring corporation first purchases a majority of the stock of the target corporation and then causes the target to be merged into another subsidiary with the minority shareholders of the target receiving stock of the acquiring parent corporation. See, e.g., J.E. Seagram Corp. v. Commissioner, 104 T.C. 75 (1995), page 561.

D. "REMOTE" "CONTINUITY"

While various subsections of § 368 permit the use by a first tier subsidiary of its parent's stock in a reorganization acquisition, the problem of "remote" continuity of interest still exists where stock of a corporation further removed in the chain of ownership is used in the acquisition transaction. Thus, Rev.Rul. 74–565, 1974–1 C.B. 125, held that an acquisition made by a second tier subsidiary using the stock of its "grandparent" did not qualify under § 368(a)(2)(E). However, since the second tier subsidiary that formally made the acquisition was formed solely for the purpose of the acquisition and disappeared as a result of the "reverse" merger, its existence was ignored; because the sole consideration was now parent's voting stock the transaction was viewed as an acquisition by the now first tier subsidiary of the stock of the target company in exchange for its parent's stock that qualified as a (B) reorganization under the principles of Rev.Rul. 67–448, page 560. Treas. Reg. §§ 1.368–1(d)(4) and 1.368-2(k) permit certain post-reorganization transfers by the acquiring corporation of the target corporation's assets or stock to controlled corporations or to partnerships without violating the continuity of interest or continuity of business enterprise requirements. One of the purposes of these regulations is to reflect the relaxation by Congress, in § 368(a)(2)(D) and (E), among other provisions, of the judicially developed doctrine, discussed at page 533, that remote continuity of interest did not suffice to support reorganization treatment. See Notice of Proposed Rulemaking and Notice of Public Hearing, Continuity of Interest and Continuity of Business Enterprise, REG–252233–96, 1997–1 C.B. 802. Thus, for example, a forward triangular merger followed by a transfer of the acquired corporation's assets to a sister corporation can qualify under § 368. However, the regulations do not permit an acquisition using stock of a grandparent or higher tier corporation to qualify. Rev. Rul. 74–565 continues to disqualify such transactions.

On a different, but related point, Rev.Rul. 79–250, 1979–2 C.B. 156, held that an (F) reorganization entered into for the purpose of changing the state of incorporation of a subsidiary immediately following the merger of an target corporation into the subsidiary in a forward triangular merger under § 368(a)(2)(D) did not cause the acquisition transaction to fail to be tax-free, even though the two reorganizations were part of a single overall plan. In Rev.Rul. 96–29, 1996–1 C.B. 50, the Service modified Rev.Rul. 79–250 by limiting its principle that two successive reorganizations do not affect the validity of either to cases in which one of the reorganizations is a type (F) reorganization, discussed at page 656, which the Service described as "unique."

E. TREATMENT OF PARTIES TO A TRIANGULAR REORGANIZATION

1. *Section 368(a)(2)(D) Forward Triangular Merger*

(a) Target Corporation and Shareholders

No gain or loss is recognized by the target corporation on the exchange with the acquiring corporation regardless of the nature of the property received from the acquiring corporation. Because the target corporation disappears by operation of state law, any nonqualifying boot not directly distributed to its shareholders or creditors is deemed to have been distributed to its shareholders or creditors, and thus no gain can be recognized under § 361(b).

As to the shareholders of the target corporation, no gain or loss will be recognized if they receive solely the stock of the acquiring parent corporation in exchange for their stock in the target corporation. I.R.C. § 354(a). If "boot" is involved, the shareholders may recognize gain under § 356, either as capital gain or as a dividend, depending on the circumstances. See page 565. Section 358 provides an exchanged basis for the acquiring parent corporation's stock. If any boot is received, however, the basis is determined by first increasing the basis by the amount of any gain recognized by the shareholders as the result of the receipt of boot, and then decreasing it by the amount of cash and the fair market value of any other property received.

(b) Acquiring Corporation

Neither the acquiring subsidiary nor its parent generally recognizes any gain or loss on the transfer of the parent's shares in a forward triangular merger. Treas. Reg. § 1.1032–2 prevents gain recognition to the acquiring subsidiary corporation so long as the parent corporation stock was received by the subsidiary pursuant to the plan or reorganization. The acquiring subsidiary would be required to recognize gain, however, if it acquired some of its parent corporation's stock in a prior unrelated transaction and used that stock in the reorganization. If the acquiring subsidiary or its parent transfers any boot other than cash or its own securities, gain or loss must be recognized with respect to the boot transferred. Under § 362(b) the acquiring corporation's basis in the assets is equal to the target corporation's basis in those assets. The acquiring parent corporation's basis in its subsidiary's stock is increased by the basis of the target corporation's assets. See Treas.Reg. § 1.358–6.

Under § 381, the tax attributes of the target corporation e.g., net operating loss carryovers, earnings and profits accounts, etc., carryover to the acquiring subsidiary corporation. The limitations of § 382(b) are applicable, however. See Chapter 16.

2. *Section 368(a)(2)(E) Reverse Triangular Merger*

(a) Target Corporation and Shareholders

Generally, no gain or loss is recognized by the target corporation on the exchange with the acquiring corporation because boot, if any is involved, will be distributed to the shareholders. Section 361(b).

The shareholders of the target corporation recognize no gain or loss if they receive solely the stock of the parent of the acquiring corporation in exchange for their stock in the target corporation. I.R.C. § 354(a). If "boot" is involved, the shareholders may recognize gain under § 356, as in the case of a forward triangular merger. Section 358 provides an exchanged basis of the stock received in the reorganization, subject to the same adjustments as are made in a forward triangular merger if boot is involved.

(b) Acquiring Corporation

Neither the acquiring subsidiary corporation nor its parent generally recognizes any gain or loss on the transfer of the parent's shares in a § 368(a)(2)(E) reorganization. I.R.C. § 1032; Treas.Reg. § 1.1032–2; Prop. Reg. § 1.1032–3 (1998) (subsidiary recognizes no gain on transfer of parent corporation's shares). If the acquiring corporation or its parent transfers any boot other than cash or its own securities, gain or loss must be recognized with respect to the boot transferred. Because the target corporation remains in existence, its basis for its assets is unchanged. The acquiring parent corporation's basis in the stock of the surviving subsidiary is generally determined in the same manner as in a forward triangular merger.

Under § 381, the target corporation retains its tax attributes, but the § 382(b) limitations are applicable. See infra, Chapter 16.

F. THE PARENT CORPORATION'S BASIS FOR THE STOCK OF THE SUBSIDIARY

There is no statutory provision to adjust the basis of the acquiring parent corporation in the stock of its subsidiary to reflect the subsidiary's basis in property acquired in a reorganization described in § 368(a)(2)(D) or (E). Presumably the parent corporation's basis in its own shares is zero. As a consequence, the parent's basis in the stock of the acquiring subsidiary formed by transfer of the parent's stock will also be zero. Similarly, the subsidiary will have a zero basis in shares of the parent's stock transferred to the shareholders of the target corporation. See Rev.Rul. 74–503, 1974–2 C.B. 117, so holding, although the Ruling explicitly stated that the transfer of the parent shares to the subsidiary "was not for the purpose of enabling [the subsidiary] to acquire property by the use of such stock." In a § 368(a)(2)(E) transaction this could mean that the parent corporation has a zero basis in the shares it holds in the surviving corporation. Furthermore § 1032, which generally provides nonrecognition treatment to the acquiring corporation in a reorganization transaction on the issue of its shares for property, does not apply to the subsidiary corporation's transfer of its parent's shares in a reorganization.

The statutory lacuna in the triangular reorganization area arose because of the grafting of §§ 368(a)(2)(D) and (E) onto the preexisting reorganization structure without adequate analysis of the implications of the change in structure. The issues are addressed in Treas. Reg. §§ 1.358–6 and 1.1032–2, which apply a common set of rules to forward and reverse triangular mergers, triangular (B) reorganizations (page 606) and triangular (C) reorganizations (page 615). In general, the regulations adopt an "over-the-top" model, i.e., the basis and gain results parallel those that occur if the parent corporation were to acquire the stock or assets of the target corporation and transfer them to its controlled subsidiary.See also Prop.Reg. § 1.1032–3 (1998), which extends nonrecognition to a subsidiary upon the transfer of its parent corporation's stock in an acquisition (and certain other circumstance) if the parent corporation transferred the stock to the subsidiary immediately before the acquisition for the purpose of making the acquisition.

In a forward triangular merger and a triangular (C) reorganization, the acquiring parent corporation's basis in its subsidiary's stock after the transaction is adjusted as if the parent corporation had acquired the target corporation's assets in a transaction in which the parent corporation's basis in the assets was determined under § 362(b) and the parent corporation then transferred those assets to its subsidiary in a transaction in which the parent corporation's basis in the subsidiary corporation's stock was determined under § 358. As a result, the parent corporation's basis in the subsidiary's stock and the subsidiary's basis in the target's assets will be the same (assuming that the parent has a zero basis in the subsidiary's stock before the transaction). The rules are employed solely to determine the parent corporation's basis in its subsidiary's stock; thus no adjustment for liabilities under § 358(d) or gain recognition under § 357(c) results. Treas. Reg. § 1.358–6(c)(1). Similar rules apply to a triangular (B) reorganization, i.e., the parent corporation is treated as having acquired the target corporation's stock directly and as having dropped the stock down to its subsidiary.

The acquiring parent corporation's basis in the surviving subsidiary in a reverse triangular merger is also determined as if the target corporation's assets were acquired directly by the parent corporation and transferred to a subsidiary in a forward triangular merger. Treas. Reg. § 1.358–6(c)(2)(i)(A). If the acquiring parent corporation acquires less than all of the target corporation's stock in a reverse triangular merger, the parent corporation's basis in the surviving subsidiary is adjusted to reflect an allocable portion of the target corporation's basis in its assets. Treas. Reg. § 1.358–6(c)(2)(i)(B). A special rule applies if a reverse triangular merger is effected using a shell subsidiary corporation, organized for purposes of the merger, and the parent's voting stock is the only consideration. Because under Rev.Rul. 67–448, 1967–2 C.B. 144, such a transaction qualifies as a type (B) reorganization, the parent corporation may elect to take a basis in the target corporation's stock computed with reference to the aggregate basis of the former target corporation shareholders. Treas. Reg. 1.358–6(c)(2)(ii).

The regulations for triangular reorganizations also apply in the consolidated return context. Treas. Reg. 1.1502–30. However, in the consolidated return context, liabilities are taken into account in determining the parent corporation's basis in the stock of the acquiring subsidiary. As a result, the parent corporation will have an excess loss account (see page 450) to the extent liabilities exceed basis. This adjustment is possible in the consolidated return context because the excess loss account rules in effect permit the use of negative basis. Outside of consolidated returns, negative basis is not permitted.

SECTION 6. BANKRUPTCY REORGANIZATIONS: TYPE G REORGANIZATIONS

INTERNAL REVENUE CODE: Section 368(a)(1)(G), (a)(3).

Senate Finance Committee Report, Bankruptcy Tax Act of 1980

S.Rep. No. 96–1035, 96th Cong., 2d Sess. 8 (1980).

* * *

C. Corporate Reorganization Provisions

[Pre–1981] Law

Definition of reorganization.—A transfer of all or part of a corporation's assets, pursuant to a court order in a proceeding under chapter X of the Bankruptcy Act (or in a receivership, foreclosure, or similar proceeding), to another corporation organized or utilized to effectuate a court-approved plan may qualify for tax-free reorganization treatment under special rules relating to "insolvency reorganizations" (secs. 371–374 of the Internal Revenue Code).

These special rules for insolvency reorganizations generally allow less flexibility in structuring tax-free transactions than the rules applicable to corporate reorganizations as defined in section 368 of the Code. Also, the special rules for insolvency reorganizations do not permit carryover of tax attributes to the transferee corporation, and otherwise differ in important respects from the general reorganization rules.[1] While some reorganizations under chapter X of the Bankruptcy Act may be able to qualify for nonrecognition treatment under Code section 368, other chapter X reorganizations may be able to qualify only under the special rules of sections 371–374 and not under the general reorganization rules of section 368.

Triangular reorganizations.—In the case of an insolvency reorganization which can qualify for nonrecognition treatment only under the special rules of Code sections 371–374, the stock or securities used to acquire the assets of the corporation in bankruptcy must be the acquiring corporation's own stock or securities. This limitation generally precludes corporations in bankruptcy from engaging in so-called triangular reorganizations, where the acquired corporation is acquired for stock of the parent of the acquiring corporation. By contrast, tax-free triangular reorganizations generally are permitted under the general rules of Code section 368.

Transfer to controlled subsidiary.—In the case of an insolvency reorganization which can qualify for nonrecognition treatment only under the special rules of Code sections 371–374, it is not clear under [pre–1981] law whether and to what extent the acquiring corporation may transfer assets received into a controlled subsidiary. In the case of other corporate reorganizations, the statute expressly defines the situations where transfers to subsidiaries are permitted (Code sec. 368(a)(2)(C)).

* * *

1. Under [pre–1981] law, it is not clear to what extent creditors of an insolvent corporation who receive stock in exchange for their claims may be considered to have "stepped into the shoes" of former shareholders for purposes of satisfying the nonstatutory "continuity of interest" rule, under which the owners of the acquired corporation must continue to have a proprietary interest in the acquiring corporation. Generally, the courts have found the "continuity of interest" test satisfied if the creditors' interests were transformed into proprietary interests prior to the reorganization (e.g., Helvering v. Alabama Asphaltic Limestone Co., 315 U.S. 179 (1942); Treas.Reg. § 1.371–1(a)(4)). It is unclear whether affirmative steps by the creditors are required or whether mere receipt of stock is sufficient.

Reasons for Change.—The committee believes that the provisions of existing Federal income tax law which are generally applicable to tax-free corporate reorganizations should also apply to reorganizations of corporations in bankruptcy or similar proceedings, in order to facilitate the rehabilitation of financially troubled businesses.

Also, the committee believes that a creditor who exchanges securities in a corporate reorganization (including an insolvency reorganization) should be treated as receiving interest income on the exchange to the extent the creditor receives new securities, stock, or any other property for accrued but unpaid interest on the securities surrendered.

Explanation of Provisions.—[The Act] generally conforms the tax rules governing insolvency reorganizations with the existing rules applicable to other corporate reorganizations. * * *

Definition of reorganization.—*In general.*—The bill adds a new category—"G" reorganizations—to the general Code definition of tax-free reorganizations (sec. 368(a)(1)). The new category includes certain transfers of assets pursuant to a court-approved reorganization plan in a bankruptcy case under new title 11 of the U.S. Code, or in a receivership, foreclosure, or similar proceeding in a Federal or State court.

* * *

In order to facilitate the rehabilitation of corporate debtors in bankruptcy, etc., these provisions are designed to eliminate many requirements which have effectively precluded financially troubled companies from utilizing the generally applicable tax-free reorganization provisions of present law. To achieve this purpose, the new "G" reorganization provision does not require compliance with State merger laws (as in category "A" reorganizations), does not require that the financially distressed corporation receive solely stock of the acquiring corporation in exchange for its assets (category "C"), and does not require that the former shareholders of the financially distressed corporation control the corporation which receives the assets (category "D").

The "G" reorganization provision added by the bill requires the transfer of assets by a corporation in a bankruptcy or similar case, and the distribution (in pursuance of the court-approved reorganization plan) of stock or securities of the acquiring corporation in a transaction which qualifies under sections 354, 355, or 356 of the Code. This distribution requirement is designed to assure that either substantially all of the assets of the financially troubled corporation, or assets which consist of an active business under the tests of section 355, are transferred to the acquiring corporation.

"Substantially all" test.—The "substantially all" test in the "G" reorganization provision is to be interpreted in light of the underlying intent in adding the new "G" category, namely, to facilitate the reorganization of companies in bankruptcy or similar cases for rehabilitative purposes. Accordingly, it is intended that facts and circumstances relevant to this intent, such as the insolvent corporation's need to pay off creditors or

to sell assets or divisions to raise cash, are to be taken into account in determining whether a transaction qualifies as a "G" reorganization. For example, a transaction is not precluded from satisfying the "substantially all" test for purposes of the new "G" category merely because, prior to a transfer to the acquiring corporation, payments to creditors and asset sales were made in order to leave the debtor with more manageable operating assets to continue in business.[5]

Relation to other provisions.—A transaction which qualifies as a "G" reorganization is not to be treated as also qualifying as a liquidation under section 332, an incorporation under section 351, or a reorganization under another category of section 368(a)(1) of the Code.[6]

A transaction in a bankruptcy or similar case which does not satisfy the requirements of new category "G" is not thereby precluded from qualifying as a tax-free reorganization under one of the other categories of section 368(a)(1). For example, an acquisition of the stock of a company in bankruptcy, or a recapitalization of such a company, which transactions are not covered by the new "G" category, can qualify for nonrecognition treatment under sections 368(a)(1)(B) or (E), respectively.

Continuity of interest rules.—The "continuity of interest" requirement which the courts and the Treasury have long imposed as a prerequisite for nonrecognition treatment for a corporate reorganization must be met in order to satisfy the requirements of new category "G". Only reorganizations—as distinguished from liquidations in bankruptcy and sales of property to either new or old interests supplying new capital and discharging the obligations of the debtor corporation—can qualify for tax-free treatment.

It is expected that * * * shareholders or junior creditors, who might previously have been excluded, may now retain an interest in the reorganized corporation.

For example, if an insolvent corporation's assets are transferred to a second corporation in a bankruptcy case, the most senior class of creditor to receive stock, together with all equal and junior classes (including shareholders who receive any consideration for their stock), should generally be considered the proprietors of the insolvent corporation for "continuity" purposes. However, if the shareholders receive consideration other than

5. Because the stated intent for adding the new "G" category is not relevant to interpreting the "substantially all" test in the case of other reorganization categories, the comments in the text as to the appropriate interpretation of the "substantially all" test in the context of a "G" reorganization are not intended to apply to, or in any way to affect interpretations under present law of, the "substantially all" test for other reorganization categories.

6. However, if a transfer qualifying as a "G" reorganization also meets the requirements of section 351 or qualifies as a reorganization under section 368(a)(1)(D) of the Code, the "excess liability" rule of section 357(c) applies if any former shareholder of the transferor corporation receives consideration for his stock, but does not apply if no former shareholder of the transferor corporation receives any consideration for his stock (i.e., if the corporation is insolvent). * * *

stock of the acquiring corporation, the transaction should be examined to determine if it represents a purchase rather than a reorganization.

Thus, short-term creditors who receive stock for their claims may be counted toward satisfying the continuity of interest rule, although any gain or loss realized by such creditors will be recognized for income tax purposes.

Triangular reorganizations.—[Section 368(a)(1)(G)] permits a corporation to acquire a debtor corporation in a "G" reorganization in exchange for stock of the parent of the acquiring corporation rather than for its own stock.

In addition, [section 368(a)(1)(G) and (a)(3)(E)] permits an acquisition in the form of a "reverse merger" of an insolvent corporation (i.e., where no former shareholder of the surviving corporation receives any consideration for his stock) in a bankruptcy or similar case if the former creditors of the surviving corporation exchange their claims for voting stock of the controlling corporation which has a value equal to at least 80 percent of the value of the debt of the surviving corporation.

Transfer to controlled subsidiary.—[Section 368(a)(1)(G)] permits a corporation which acquires substantially all the assets of a debtor corporation in a "G" reorganization to transfer the acquired assets to a controlled subsidiary without endangering the tax-free status of the reorganization. This provision places "G" reorganizations on a similar footing with other categories of reorganizations.

* * *

"Principal amount" rule; "boot" test.—* * * "G" reorganizations are subject to the rules governing the tax treatment of exchanging shareholders and security holders which apply to other corporate reorganizations.

Accordingly, an exchanging shareholder or security holder of the debtor company who receives securities with a principal amount exceeding the principal amount of securities surrendered is taxable on the excess, and an exchanging shareholder or security holder who surrenders no securities is taxed on the principal amount of any securities received. Also, any "boot" received is subject to the general dividend-equivalence test of Code section 356.

Treatment of accrued interest.—[Section 354(b)(2)(B) provides that] a creditor exchanging securities in any corporate reorganization described in section 368 of the Code (including a "G" reorganization) is treated as receiving interest income on the exchange to the extent the security holder receives new securities, stock, or any other property attributable to accrued but unpaid interest (including accrued original issue discount) on the securities surrendered. This provision, which reverses the so-called *Carman* rule, applies whether or not the exchanging security holder realizes gain on the exchange overall. Under this provision, a security holder which had previously accrued the interest (including original issue discount) as income recognizes a loss to the extent the interest is not paid in the exchange.

Example.—The reorganization provisions of the bill are illustrated in part by the following example.

Assume that Corporation A is in a bankruptcy case commenced after December 31, 1980. Immediately prior to a transfer under a plan of reorganization, A's assets have an adjusted basis of $75,000 and a fair market value of $100,000. A has a net operating loss carryover of $200,000. A has outstanding bonds of $100,000 (on which there is no accrued but unpaid interest) and trade debts of $100,000.

Under the plan of reorganization, A is to transfer all its assets to Corporation B in exchange for $100,000 of B stock. Corporation A will distribute the stock, in exchange for their claims against A, one-half to the security holders and one-half to the trade creditors. A's shareholders will receive nothing.

The transaction qualifies as a reorganization under new section 368(a)(1)(G) of the Code, since all the creditors are here treated as proprietors for continuity of interest purposes. Thus, A recognizes no gain or loss on the transfer of its assets to B (Code sec. 361). B's basis in the assets is: $75,000 (sec. 362), and B succeeds to A's net operating loss carryover (sec. 381).

* * * [T]he pro-rata distribution of B stock to A's creditors does not result in income from discharge of indebtedness or require attribute reduction.

Assume the same facts as above except that B also transfers $10,000 in cash, which is distributed by A to its creditors. Although A would otherwise recognize gain on the receipt of boot in an exchange involving appreciated property, the distribution by A of the $10,000 cash to those creditors having a proprietary interest in the corporation's assets for continuity of interest purposes prevents A from recognizing any gain (Code sec. 361(b))

ILLUSTRATIVE MATERIAL

A. GENERAL

Inside or outside of a formal bankruptcy proceeding, a financially troubled corporation generally has three options available to it. It can try to work with its creditors to reduce or restructure existing debt. It can issue stock for debt, thus replacing debt with equity on its balance sheet. Or it can seek to be acquired by another corporation. The first two transactions, each of which envisions a recapitalization of the corporation within the confines of a single entity, are discussed in greater detail in Chapter 14. The transfer of assets by an insolvent corporation in exchange for the stock of the acquiring corporation may be accomplished as a nonrecognition transaction under § 368(a)(1)(A), (C) or (G).

In any of these transactions, the insolvent corporation may realize discharge of indebtedness income. In general, however, a corporation involved in a bankruptcy proceeding or an insolvent corporation will avoid recognition of discharge of indebtedness income under § 108(a)(1)(A) or (B). This issue is discussed in the context of debt for debt exchanges and stock for debt exchanges beginning at page 648.

B. ACQUISITION REORGANIZATIONS IN BANKRUPTCY

A transfer by the target corporation of all or part of its assets to the acquiring corporation in a bankruptcy reorganization or a receivership, foreclosure, or similar judicial proceeding in a federal or state court is a tax-free reorganization under § 368(a)(1)(G) if the stock or securities received from the acquiring corporation are distributed pursuant to the plan of reorganization in a transaction that qualifies under §§ 354, 355, or 356. The target corporation recognizes no gain or loss if any boot that it receives is distributed. I.R.C. § 361(b).

Section 368(a)(1)(G) applies only to judicially supervised insolvency proceedings. Thus a nonjudicial reorganization of an insolvent corporation must qualify under one of the other provisions of § 368 in order to achieve reorganization status, assuming the continuity of interest test can be met. But, if a transaction qualifies both as a type (G) and, as a result of its form, as another type of reorganization, for example a type (C), it will be classified solely as a type (G). I.R.C. § 368(a)(3)(C).

When an insolvency reorganization qualifies as a type (G) reorganization, §§ 354 and 356 continue to control taxation of the shareholders and creditors. Thus, for example, short-term creditors who do not hold "securities" will have a taxable exchange; shareholders and other securities holders will be subject to the usual pattern of reorganization taxation.

C. CONTINUITY OF INTEREST IN A BANKRUPTCY REORGANIZATION

In Helvering v. Alabama Asphaltic Limestone Co., 315 U.S. 179 (1942), a creditor's committee formed a new corporation to acquire the assets of an insolvent corporation. An involuntary bankruptcy proceeding was instituted in which the creditors' claims were satisfied by the transfer of assets to the new corporation pursuant to a judicial sale. Ninety-five percent of the stock of the new corporation was issued to note holders and the balance was issued to unsecured creditors of the insolvent corporation. The new corporation claimed depreciation based on a transferred basis from the old corporation, arguing that a reorganization had taken place. The Commissioner contended that the assets were acquired by purchase because the continuity of shareholder interest requirement had not been satisfied. Citing LeTulle v. Scofield, 308 U.S. 415 (1940), page 526, the Commissioner argued that for a transaction to qualify as a reorganization, a substantial ownership interest in the transferee company must be retained by the holders of the ownership interest in the transferor. In holding that the assets had been acquired in a tax-free reorganization, the Supreme Court explained the application of the continuity of interest rules to insolvent acquired corporations as follows:

"We conclude, however, that it is immaterial that the transfer shifted the ownership of the equity in the property from the stockholders to the creditors of the old corporation. Plainly, the old continuity of interest was broken. Technically, that did not occur in this proceeding until the judicial sale took place. For practical purposes, however, it took place not later than the time when the creditors took steps to enforce their demands against the insolvent debtor. In this case, that was the date of the institution of the bankruptcy proceedings. From that time on, they had effective command over the disposition of the property. The full priority rule * * * in bankruptcy * * * gives creditors, whether secured or unsecured, the right to exclude the stockholders entirely from the reorganization plan when the debtor is insolvent. When the equity owners are excluded and the old creditors become the stockholders of the new corporation, it conforms to realities to date their equity ownership from the time when they invoked the process of the law to enforce their rights to full priority. At the time they stepped into the shoes of the old stockholders. * * *

"That conclusion involves no conflict with the principals of the *Le Tulle* case. A bondholder interest in a solvent corporation plainly is not the equivalent of a proprietary interest * * *." (183–84)

This approach continues under the (G) reorganization provisions. In testing for continuity, all classes of creditors who receive stock in the reorganized corporation are considered to be the historic shareholders of the corporation. In addition if the shareholders receive anything for their shares, they too will be taken into account in the continuity test. Thus, for example, if all the stock in the reorganized company is received by junior creditors, with the secured creditors receiving cash and the shareholders receiving nothing, continuity of interest would be present. On the other hand, if the secured creditors also receive stock, they too would be counted in testing for continuity, which might be lacking if the amount of the cash payment is too large in relation to the stock. If shareholders receive cash, the Committee Report indicates that the transaction may be considered a purchase rather than a reorganization.

D. SECURITIES

In Neville Coke & Chemical Co. v. Commissioner, 148 F.2d 599 (3d Cir.1945), the taxpayer held stock, bonds, three-, four-, and five-year notes, and accounts receivable of an insolvent corporation. Pursuant to a bankruptcy proceeding the debtor corporation was recapitalized and the taxpayer received new common stock for its stock, new debentures for its bonds, and new debentures and common stock for its notes and accounts receivable. The Commissioner asserted that the taxpayer recognized a gain on the exchange of the notes and accounts receivable for debentures and common stock. The taxpayer asserted that the notes and accounts receivable were "securities" within the meaning of the predecessor of § 354(a)(1) and that it had exchanged "securities" for "stock and securities," thereby entitling it to nonrecognition on the exchange. In holding for the Commissioner, the court held that "securities" has the same meaning in the context of the interest surrendered as it does in the context of the interest received, that a "security" entails having a "proprietary" interest in the corporation, and that the rights of the taxpayer as a note holder were merely those of a creditor.

Under § 368(a)(1)(G), while short-term creditors who receive stock in the reorganization will be counted for continuity purposes, the exchange of their debt claims for stock presumably will be a taxable transaction, since the "securities" test has not been met.

E. TREATMENT OF PARTIES TO A TYPE (G) REORGANIZATION

1. *Target Corporation and Shareholders*

No gain or loss is recognized by the target corporation on the exchange with the acquiring corporation regardless of the nature of the property received from the acquiring corporation. If only stock or securities of the acquiring corporation is received in the reorganization, § 361(a) provides nonrecognition. If nonqualifying boot is received, § 361(b) requires that the target corporation recognize gain upon receipt only if the boot is not distributed to either its shareholders or creditors pursuant to the plan of reorganization.

The target corporation may realize discharge of indebtedness income, but because a type (G) reorganization is limited to a corporation involved in a bankruptcy proceeding, discharge of indebtedness income is excluded under § 108(a)(1)(A).

As for the liquidating distributions, no gain or loss is recognized by the target corporation on the distribution of qualified stock or securities. I.R.C. § 361(c)(1), (2)(B). Distribution of appreciated boot in the liquidation results in recognition of gain (but not loss) under § 361(c)(2), but because § 358(a)(2) provides the target corporation with a fair market value basis in any boot received in the reorganization, no gain will be realized unless there is a change in value between the receipt and the liquidating distribution. If any property was retained by the target corporation, gain may be recognized by the corporation as a result of distributing such property in the liquidation.

For the shareholders of the target corporation, the tax results are similar to those in an (A) reorganization. No gain or loss will be recognized if they receive solely the stock of the acquiring corporation in exchange for their stock in the target corporation. I.R.C. § 354(a). If the permissible amount of "boot" is involved and it is distributed to the shareholders, they may recognize gain under § 356, either as capital gain or as a dividend, depending on the circumstances, as discussed at page 565. Section 358 then provides an exchanged basis for the acquiring corporation's stock. If any boot is received, however, the basis is determined by first increasing the basis by the amount of any gain recognized by the shareholders as the result of the receipt of boot, and then decreasing it by the amount of cash or the fair market value of any other property received. If, as may be the case, the shareholders of the target corporation receive nothing in the reorganization, they may recognize losses under § 165(g).

2. *Acquiring Corporation*

Pursuant to § 1032, the acquiring corporation recognizes no gain or loss on the transfer of its shares in a (G) reorganization. If, however, the acquiring corporation transfers any boot other than cash or its own stock or securities, it must recognize gain or loss with respect to the boot transferred.

Under § 362(b) the acquiring corporation's basis in the assets is equal to the target corporation's basis in those assets. Although § 362(b) provides that the acquiring corporation's basis in the assets is to be increased by any gain recognized under § 361(b) by the target corporation on the transfer of its assets to the acquiring corporation, the target corporation will not recognize gain as a result of the transfer of its assets if the target corporation distributes all of its property to shareholders.

Under § 381, the tax attributes of the target corporation, most significantly net operating loss carryovers, which may be an important asset of the target corporation, carry over to the acquiring corporation. The limitations of § 382(b) are, however, applicable. Under § 382, a corporation's net operating loss carryover is limited if there has been a greater than 50 percent change in ownership over a three year testing period (an "ownership change"). See Chapter 16. However, as discussed in greater detail beginning at page 772, in the case of a bankruptcy or insolvency proceeding, the § 382 limitation is not applied if, following an ownership change, the creditors and former stockholders of the loss corporation own at least 50 percent of the loss corporation stock. I.R.C. § 382(*l*)(5)(A).

SECTION 7. TAX POLICY: ACQUISITION TRANSACTIONS

As the last paragraph of the Senate Finance Committee report reproduced in the preceding section (page 618) indicates, the addition of layers of statutory complexity to the already complicated reorganization provisions with enactment of § 368(a)(2)(D) and (E) has been a source of concern. Many analysts believe that a thorough-going review of the technical issues in the reorganization is required. The following is the recommendations of one such analysis.

Report by the Staff of the Senate Finance Committee, the Subchapter C Revision Act of 1985*

S.Prt. 99–47, 99th Cong., 1st Sess. 50–53 (1985).

IV. Summary of Proposals

* [Ed.: The Subchapter C Revision Act of 1985 was not enacted into law.]

The principal proposals contained in the bill are described below. A more detailed description of the proposals is set forth in the Technical Explanation accompanying the bill.

A. Definition of Qualified Acquisition (New Section 364 of the Code)

In general, the bill consolidates, simplifies, and makes uniform the rules classifying corporate mergers and acquisitions, whether treated under current law as a "reorganization", a liquidating sale * * *, or a section 338 stock acquisition.

New section 364 defines "qualified acquisition" as meaning any "qualified stock acquisition" or any "qualified asset acquisition." A qualified stock acquisition is defined as any transaction or series of transactions during the 12–month acquisition period in which one corporation acquires stock representing control of another corporation. A qualified asset acquisition means (1) any statutory merger or consolidation, or (2) any other transaction in which one corporation acquires at least 70 percent of the gross fair market value and at least 90 percent of the net fair market value of the assets of another corporation held immediately before the acquisition, and the target corporation distributes, within 12 months of the acquisition date, all of its assets (other than assets retained to meet claims) to its shareholders or creditors.

For these purposes, the definition of "control" is conformed to that contained in section 1504(a)(2) of the Code.

Where an acquiring corporation makes a qualified stock acquisition of a target corporation and the target corporation owns stock in a subsidiary, a special rule would treat the acquiring corporation as having also acquired the stock of the subsidiary, for purposes of determining whether the acquiring corporation has made a qualified stock acquisition of the subsidiary.

A special rule is also provided where an acquisition might qualify as both a qualified asset acquisition and a qualified stock acquisition. For example, where an acquiring corporation acquires all of the assets of a target corporation, and certain of those assets consist of all of the stock of a subsidiary, the transaction is treated as a qualified stock acquisition of the subsidiary and a qualified asset acquisition of all of the other assets of the target corporation.

The common-law doctrines of continuity of interest, continuity of business enterprise, and business purpose would have no applicability in determining whether a transaction qualifies as a qualified acquisition.

The bill repeals section 368. Acquisitive reorganizations ("A" "B" and "C" reorganizations and subsidiary mergers) under current law would be replaced by the rules for qualified acquisitions. The "D" reorganization rules would be replaced by special rules (described below) relating to qualified acquisitions between related parties. Transactions qualifying under current law as an "E" reorganization (a recapitalization) and an "F" reorganization (a mere change in identity, form, or place of organization of one corporation) are conformed to the definition of qualified acquisitions. Finally, the "G" reorganization rules (bankruptcy reorganizations), developed largely in response to continuity of interest problems in those types of transactions, are no longer needed and therefore are repealed.

B. Elective Tax Treatment of Qualified Acquisitions (New Section 365 of the Code)

The corporate level tax consequences of a qualified acquisition are explicitly made elective. Under new section 365, all qualified acquisitions are treated as "carryover basis acquisitions" unless an election to be treated as a "cost basis acquisition" is made.

In general, elections may be made on a corporation-by-corporation basis. Thus, for example, if an acquiring corporation makes a qualified stock acquisition of both a target corporation and a target subsidiary, a cost basis election may be made for the target corporation but, if desired, no such election need be made for the target subsidiary.

Within a single corporation, the same election must generally apply for all of the assets of the corporation. A consistency rule would provide that assets that are acquired which were held by a single corporation during the consistency period must be treated consistently, either as all cost basis or all carryover basis.

* * *

In general, no cost basis election may be made with respect to any qualified acquisition between related parties. These generally refer to transactions where, after application of the attribution rules, there is 50 percent or greater common ownership between the target and acquiring corporations. In addition, no cost basis election may be made with respect to a transaction qualifying as an "E" or "F" reorganization under current law. Finally, a mandatory cost basis election generally applies to a qualified asset acquisition where the acquiring corporation is a non-taxable entity (such as a tax-exempt entity, a regulated investment company, or a foreign corporation).

An election must be made before the later of (1) the 15th day of the 9th month following the month in which the acquisition date occurs, or (2) the date prescribed in regulations. Once made, an election is irrevocable.

C. Corporate Level Tax Consequences of Qualified Acquisitions (Sections 361, 362 and 381 of the Code)

The corporate level tax consequences of a qualified acquisition result directly from the election made at the corporate level. For example, in the case of a carryover basis acquisition, no gain or loss is recognized by the target corporation and the acquiring corporation obtains a carryover basis in any assets target. Attributes carry over under section 381.

In the case of a cost basis acquisition, the target corporation recognizes gain or loss and the acquiring corporation obtains a basis in any assets target determined under section 1012. Attributes do not carry over. Where the cost basis acquisition is a qualified stock acquisition, the target corporation is deemed to have sold all of its assets for fair market value at the close of the acquisition date in a transaction in which gain or loss is recognized, and then is treated as a new corporation which purchased all of such assets as of the beginning of the day after the acquisition date.

A special rule is provided in the case where a target corporation is a member of an affiliated group and a cost basis election is made. In general, unless the parties elect otherwise, a target corporation in that situation shall not be treated as a member of such group with respect to the gain or loss recognized in the transaction.

The basis of any property received by a target corporation in a qualified asset acquisition is the fair market value of such property on the acquisition date. The basis of stock target by an acquiring corporation in a qualified stock acquisition is determined under new section 1020 of the Code (see description below for rules concerning basis of stock of controlled subsidiaries).

Under the bill, section * * * 338 of current law [is] repealed.

D. Shareholder Level Tax Consequences of Qualified Acquisitions (Sections 354, 356, and 358 of the Code)

In general, shareholder level tax consequences of a qualified acquisition are determined independent of the corporate level tax consequences and independent of the election made at the corporate level. Thus, even if a transaction is treated as a cost basis acquisition at the corporate level, it may be wholly or partly tax free at the shareholder level. In addition, shareholder level consequences are generally determined shareholder-by-shareholder, and the consequences to one shareholder do not affect the tax treatment of other shareholders or investors of the target corporation.

As a general rule, nonrecognition treatment is provided to shareholders or security holders of the target corporation upon receipt of "qualifying consideration," i.e., stock or securities of the acquiring corporation and, where the acquiring corporation is a member of an affiliated group, of the common parent of such group and any other member of such group specified in regulations. The nonrecognition rule applies to the receipt of securities only to the extent the issue price of any securities received does not exceed the adjusted basis of any securities surrendered.

A special rule is provided in the case of investment company stock. In general, stock or securities of an investment company does not qualify as qualifying consideration. An exception applies, however, and such stock or securities will qualify as qualifying consideration, if the target corporation is a diversified investment company. The term "investment company" and "diversified investment company" generally have the same meaning as under current law. In short, the existence of an investment company as the acquiring corporation may affect the tax treatment of the transaction at the shareholder level, but does not affect the corporate level tax consequences.

Receipt of "nonqualifying consideration" (i.e., any consideration other than qualifying consideration) generally results in recognition of gain to the shareholder or security holder. Such gain is treated as gain from the sale or exchange of property unless the receipt of nonqualifying consideration has the effect of a distribution of a dividend. The determination of dividend effect is made by treating the shareholder as having received only qualifying consideration in the exchange, and then as being redeemed of all or a portion of such qualifying consideration (to the extent of the nonqualifying consideration received). For these purposes, earnings and profits of both the target and acquiring corporations are generally taken into account.

Special rules are provided where there is a controlling corporate shareholder of the target corporation. In general, these rules are designed to avoid a second corporate level tax where the target corporation is target in a cost basis acquisition. In addition, where the target corporation is acquired in a carryover basis acquisition and all or part of the consideration is nonqualifying consideration, these rules are designed to insure that the controlling corporate shareholder or a distributee of such shareholder will recognize gain on the receipt of the nonqualifying consideration.

In general, shareholders or security holders obtain a substitute basis in any [qualifying] consideration received, and a fair market value basis in any nonqualifying consideration received. Controlling corporate shareholders of the target corporation generally obtain a basis in any qualifying consideration received equal to the lesser of substitute basis or fair market value basis.

ILLUSTRATIVE MATERIAL

The 1985 proposals of the Staff of the Senate Finance Committee were based in part on proposals in the American Law Institute Federal Income Tax Project—Subchapter C (1980). The following excerpt explains the reasons for the ALI proposals:

"[The] search for substantive differences among acquisitions by which to determine their tax classification has been essentially fruitless. * * * So are many of the criteria for reorganization treatment. In the context of a complete acquisition of all shareholders' interests in all corporate assets, even the distinction between a stock and an asset acquisition is one of corporate procedure rather than financial import. Indeed, for financial reporting purposes, no distinction is drawn between a stock purchase and an asset purchase, or between a pooling of interests effected by an acquisition of stock and one effected by an acquisition of assets.

"A better approach would begin by acknowledging that the choice between carryover and cost-basis treatment is essentially elective.

* * *

"E. *Recommended Revisions*

"1) *Making electivity explicit and independent of corporate procedural choices.* The trouble with present law, in this view, is not that tax classification of acquisitions is effectively elective, but that the election is tied unnecessarily to matters of corporate procedure. The solution to the trouble is to make tax classification explicitly elective and as independent as possible of corporate procedural considerations. * * *

"2) *Classification in the absence of election.* In the absence of effective election, acquisitions should be classified as simply and as consistently as possible with the likely expectations of those who are most apt to neglect to make a specific election. These criteria suggest that any stock acquisition should be a carryover-basis acquisition and any asset purchase should be a cost-basis acquisition, unless there is a specific election to the contrary. * * *"

PART V

NONACQUISITIVE REORGANIZATIONS

CHAPTER 14

SINGLE CORPORATION REORGANIZATIONS

SECTION 1. STATUTORY STRUCTURE

While the reorganization provisions historically have been most important in the context of acquisition transactions, several forms of reorganizations involve only changes or adjustments in the form or capital structure of a single corporation. In this context, the reorganization provisions allow exchanges of stock or securities to modify some aspects of the corporate capital structure without requiring the current recognition of gain (or allowing the recognition of loss). The controversies involving nonacquisitive reorganizations have primarily involved attempts by taxpayers to avoid dividend treatment on cash or other property extracted from the corporation. In some situations, the issue has been whether the reorganization rules themselves, as properly applied, should result in the receipt of a dividend when, in the context of an admitted reorganization, a shareholder receives property. In other cases, the question is whether the transaction is in fact a reorganization at all or is more appropriately characterized as some form of sale or liquidation transaction, which qualifies for capital gain treatment. In these latter cases, it often has been the Internal Revenue Service that was arguing for characterization as a reorganization in order to apply the reorganization rules requiring dividend treatment.

The requirements of § 311 and § 336 that the corporation recognize gain on the distribution of appreciated property have curtailed taxpayer attempts to convert potential dividend income into capital gain by extracting property from the corporation. There remains, however, the fundamental question of whether an otherwise taxable transaction should be given nonrecognition treatment when it takes place in the context of a corporate adjustment or restructuring. Here the present statutory structure provides for reorganization treatment in three situations. Section 368(a)(1)(E) deals with corporate "recapitalizations", i.e., adjustments to the corporation's capital structure, as when a bondholder exchanges his bonds for stock in the corporation. Section 368(a)(1)(F) deals with a change in corporate structure involving a change in the place of incorporation or form of organization, as when a California corporation reincorporates in Delaware. Finally, § 368(a)(1)(D) describes reorganizations involving a transfer of assets by a corporation to a subsidiary corporation and the distribution of the stock of the subsidiary corporation to the corporation's shareholders.

Section 368 provides the following definitions of the reorganizations considered in this Chapter:

Type (E) Recapitalizations. Section 368(a)(1)(E) covers the recapitalization of an existing corporation, such as the exchange of one type of common stock for another, or of one type of preferred stock for another, or of new preferred stock for old bonds, of new preferred stock for old stock or of new common stock for old preferred stock, or of new bonds for old bonds. Here only one corporation and its shareholders (or bondholders) are involved. These same transactions, however, can be implemented under sections 368(a)(1)(A), (B) or (C), for example, by a corporation which creates a new subsidiary corporation and has the new corporation issue to the parent, in return for the parent's assets, stock and securities of the nature desired that the parent will then distribute to its shareholders on its liquidation. Type (E) reorganizations are considered in Section 2.

Type (F) Change of Identity, Form, or Place of Organization. A mere change in identity, form, or place of organization of one corporation, however effected, is governed by § 368(a)(1)(F). For example, X Corporation may change its state of incorporation from New Jersey to Delaware by forming Y Corporation, a Delaware subsidiary into which X Corporation merges with the shareholders (and bondholders) of X Corporation receiving identical securities of Y Corporation in exchange for their interests in X Corporation. But if X Corporation simultaneously effects a recapitalization, for example, by exchanging both common and preferred shares of Y Corporation for X Corporation common stock (as was the case in Marr v. United States, 268 U.S. 536 (1925), page 515), then the transaction is not an (F) reorganization. Furthermore, it probably is not an (E) reorganization either. In this case, the transaction will be a reorganization only if it fits within the definition of one of the other subparagraphs, such as type (A). Type (F) reorganizations are considered in Section 3.

Type (D) Transfer of Assets to New Corporation. The transfer of some or all of the parent's assets to a newly created or existing subsidiary—as where X Corporation transfers some of its assets to new or existing Y Corporation—is governed by § 368(a)(1)(D) if following the transfer to the subsidiary the parent, X Corporation, distributes a controlling amount of the stock of the subsidiary, Y Corporation, to its shareholders. The nature of the securities received, if any (a contribution to capital without additional stock may be involved), is immaterial as long as immediately after the transfer either X Corporation, its shareholders, or a combination of the two, control Y Corporation. Thus, unless Y Corporation is a newly formed corporation, the use of voting stock is not an essential factor in the reorganization. The quantity of assets transferred, however, can be material. Although a type (D) reorganization generally involves the division of an enterprise, in contrast to the amalgamation or acquisition transactions of the first three subparagraphs of § 368(a)(1), subsection (D) also can describe a single corporation reorganization where all of the assets of X Corporation are transferred to Y Corporation. The inclusion of these two substantially different transactions under one definitional paragraph of the reorganization provisions complicates matters.

Where X Corporation desires to create controlled subsidiary Y Corporation or to transfer assets to existing Y Corporation without recognition of gain but wishes to retain Y Corporation as a subsidiary, a (D) reorganization would not be the statutory vehicle. This type of transfer falls under § 351. Where there is no distribution of Y Corporation stock to the shareholders of X Corporation, there is no division in the sense considered in a type (D) reorganization. Instead, the shareholders, through their ownership of X Corporation, have become the owners of a corporate chain of parent and subsidiary corporations. If X Corporation does distribute some or all of the Y Corporation stock, which it may do under § 351(c) without disturbing the tax-free character of the initial transfer of the assets, the situation begins to resemble a divisive (D) situation. Nondivisive type (D) reorganizations are considered in Section 4. Divisive type (D) reorganizations are considered in Chapter 15.

SECTION 2. RECAPITALIZATIONS

INTERNAL REVENUE CODE: Sections 108(e)(8), (10); 368(a)(1)(E); 354(a); 356(a), (c)–(e); 306(c)(1)(B), (C).

REGULATIONS: Sections 1.354–1(d), (e); 1.356–1,–3,–4,–5; 1.368–2(e); 1.306–3(d), (e); 1.301–1(1).

Bazley v. Commissioner*

Supreme Court of the United States, 1947.
331 U.S. 737.

■ MR. JUSTICE FRANKFURTER delivered the opinion of the Court.

The proper construction of provisions of the Internal Revenue Code relating to corporate reorganizations is involved in both these cases. Their importance to the Treasury as well as to corporate enterprise led us to grant certiorari, 329 U.S. 695, 67 S.Ct. 62; 329 U.S. 701, 67 S.Ct. 77. While there are differences in detail to which we shall refer, the two cases may be disposed of in one opinion.

In the Bazley case, No. 287, the Commissioner of Internal Revenue assessed an income tax deficiency against the taxpayer for the year 1939. Its validity depends on the legal significance of the recapitalization in that year of a family corporation in which the taxpayer and his wife owned all but one of the Company's one thousand shares. These had a par value of $100. Under the plan of reorganization the taxpayer, his wife, and the holder of the additional share were to turn in their old shares and receive in exchange for each old share five new shares of no par value, but of a stated value of $60, and new debenture bonds, having a total face value of $400,000, payable in ten years but callable at any time. Accordingly, the taxpayer received 3,990 shares of the new stock for the 798 shares of his old holding and debentures in the amount of $319,200. At the time of these transactions the earned surplus of the corporation was $855,783.82.

The Commissioner charged to the taxpayer as income the full value of the debentures. The Tax Court affirmed the Commissioner's determination, against the taxpayer's contention that as a "recapitalization" the transaction was a tax-free "reorganization" and that the debentures were "securities in a corporation a party to a reorganization," "exchanged solely for stock or securities in such corporation" "in pursuance of a plan of reorganization," and as such no gain is recognized for income tax purposes. [The Court cites the predecessors of §§ 368(a)(1)(E) and 354(a)(1)].** The Tax Court found that the recapitalization had "no legitimate corporate business purpose" and was therefore not a "reorganization" within the statute. The distribution of debentures, it concluded, was a disguised dividend, taxable as earned income under [the predecessors of §§ 61(a), 301, 302 and 318(a)]. 4 T.C. 897. The Circuit Court of Appeals for the Third Circuit, sitting en banc, affirmed, two judges dissenting. 155 F.2d 237.

Unless a transaction is a reorganization contemplated by [the predecessor of § 368(a)(1)], any exchange of "stock or securities" in connection with such transaction, cannot be "in pursuance of the plan of reorganization" under [the predecessor of § 354(a)(1)]. While [§ 368(a)(1)]informs us that "reorganization" means, among other things, "a recapitalization," it

* Together with No. 209, Adams v. Commissioner of Internal Revenue.

** [Ed.: The case arose under the 1939 Code which did not contain provisions corresponding to §§ 354(a)(2) and 356(d).]

does not inform us what "recapitalization" means. "Recapitalization" in connection with the income tax has been part of the revenue laws since 1921. Congress has never defined it and the Treasury Regulations shed only limited light. [Citing the predecessor of Treas. Reg. § 1.368–2(e).] One thing is certain. Congress did not incorporate some technical concept, whether that of accountants or of other specialists, into [§ 368(a)(1)], assuming that there is agreement among specialists as to the meaning of recapitalization. And so, recapitalization as used in [§ 368(a)(1)] must draw its meaning from its function in that section. It is one of the forms of reorganization which obtains the privileges afforded by [§ 368(a)(1)]. Therefore, "recapitalization" must be construed with reference to the presuppositions and purpose of [§ 368(a)(1)]. It was not the purpose of the reorganization provision to exempt from payment of a tax what as a practical matter is realized gain. Normally, a distribution by a corporation, whatever form it takes, is a definite and rather unambiguous event. It furnishes the proper occasion for the determination and taxation of gain. But there are circumstances where a formal distribution, directly or through exchange of securities, represents merely a new form of the previous participation in an enterprise, involving no change of substance in the rights and relations of the interested parties one to another or to the corporate assets. As to these, Congress has said that they are not to be deemed significant occasions for determining taxable gain.

These considerations underlie [§ 368(a)(1)] and they should dominate the scope to be given to the various sections, all of which converge toward a common purpose. Application of the language of such a revenue provision is not an exercise in framing abstract definitions. In a series of cases this Court has withheld the benefits of the reorganization provision in situations which might have satisfied provisions of the section treated as inert language, because they were not reorganizations of the kind with which [§ 368] in its purpose and particulars, concerns itself. See Pinellas Ice & Cold Storage Co. v. Commissioner, 287 U.S. 462, 53 S.Ct. 257; Gregory v. Helvering, 293 U.S. 465, 55 S.Ct. 266; Le Tulle v. Scofield, 308 U.S. 415, 60 S.Ct. 313.

Congress has not attempted a definition of what is recapitalization and we shall follow its example. The search for relevant meaning is often satisfied not by a futile attempt at abstract definition but by pricking a line through concrete applications. Meaning frequently is built up by assured recognition of what does not come within a concept the content of which is in controversy. Since a recapitalization within the scope of [§ 368(a)(1)] is an aspect of reorganization nothing can be a recapitalization for this purpose unless it partakes of those characteristics of a reorganization which underlie the purpose of Congress in postponing the tax liability.

No doubt there was a recapitalization of the Bazley corporation in the sense that the symbols that represented its capital were changed, so that the fiscal basis of its operations would appear very differently on its books. But the form of a transaction as reflected by correct corporate accounting opens questions as to the proper application of a taxing statute; it does not close them. Corporate accounting may represent that correspondence between change in the form of capital structure and essential identity in fact which is of the essence of a transaction relieved from taxation as a reorganization. What is controlling is that a new arrangement intrinsically partake of the elements of reorganization which underlie the Congressional exemption and not merely give the appearance of it to accomplish a distribution of earnings. In the case of a corporation which has undistributed earnings, the creation of new corporate obligations which are transferred to stockholders in relation to their former holdings, so as to produce, for all practical purposes, the same result as a distribution of cash earnings of equivalent value, cannot obtain tax immunity because cast in the form of a recapitalization-reorganization. The governing legal rule can hardly be stated more narrowly. To attempt to do so would only challenge astuteness in evading it. And so it is hard to escape the conclusion that whether in a particular case a paper recapitalization is no more than an admissible attempt to avoid the consequences of an outright distribution of earnings turns on details of corporate affairs, judgment on which must be left to the Tax Court. See Dobson v. Commissioner, 320 U.S. 489, 64 S.Ct. 239.

What have we here? No doubt, if the Bazley corporation had issued the debentures to Bazley and his wife without any recapitalization, it would have made a taxable distribution. Instead, these debentures were issued as part of a family arrangement, the only additional ingredient being an unrelated modification of the capital account. The debentures were found to be worth at least their principal amount, and they were virtually cash because they were callable at the will of the corporation which in this case was the will of the taxpayer. One does not have to pursue the motives behind actions, even in the more ascertainable forms of purpose, to find, as did the Tax Court, that the whole arrangement took this form instead of an outright distribution of cash or debentures, because the latter would undoubtedly have been taxable income whereas what was done could, with a show of reason, claim the shelter of the immunity of a recapitalization-reorganization.

The Commissioner, the Tax Court and the Circuit Court of Appeals agree that nothing was accomplished that would not have been accomplished by an outright debenture dividend. And since we find no misconception of law on the part of the Tax Court and the Circuit Court of Appeals, whatever may have been their choice of phrasing, their application of the law to the facts of this case must stand. A "reorganization" which is merely a vehicle, however elaborate or elegant, for conveying earnings from accumulations to the stockholders is not a reorganization under [§ 368(a)(1)]. This disposes of the case as a matter of law, since the facts as found by the Tax Court bring them within it. And even if this transaction were deemed a reorganization, the facts would equally sustain the imposition of the tax on the debentures under [the predecessors of § 356(a)(1) and (2)]. Commissioner v. Estate of Bedford, 325 U.S. 283, 65 S.Ct. 1157.

In the Adams case, No. 209, the taxpayer owned all but a few of the 5914 shares of stock outstanding out of an authorized 6000, par value $100.

By a plan of reorganization, the authorized capital was reduced by half, to $295,700, divided into 5914 shares of no par value but having a stated value of $50 per share. The 5914 old shares were cancelled and the corporation issued in exchange therefor 5914 shares of the new no-par common stock and 6 per cent 20 year debenture bonds in the principal amount of $295,700. The exchange was made on the basis of one new share of stock and one $50 bond for each old share. The old capital account was debited in the sum of $591,400, a new no-par capital account was credited with $295,700, and the balance of $295,700 was credited to a "Debenture Payable" account. The corporation at this time had accumulated earnings available for distribution in a sum not less than $164,514.82, and this account was left unchanged. At the time of the exchange, the debentures had a value not less than $164,208.82.

The Commissioner determined an income tax deficiency by treating the debenture bonds as a distribution of the corporation's accumulated earnings. The Tax Court sustained the Commissioner's determination, 5 T.C. 351, and the Circuit Court of Appeals affirmed. 155 F.2d 246. The case is governed by our treatment of the Bazley case. The finding by the Tax Court that the reorganization had no purpose other than to achieve the distribution of the earnings, is unaffected by the bookkeeping detail of leaving the surplus account unaffected. See [the predecessor to § 316(a), second sentence], and Commissioner v. Wheeler, 324 U.S. 542, 546, 65 S.Ct. 799.

* * *

Judgments affirmed.

ILLUSTRATIVE MATERIAL

A. DEFINITION OF "RECAPITALIZATION" IN GENERAL

Section 368(a)(1)(E) includes within the definition of a reorganization a "recapitalization." The term "recapitalization" is not defined in either the Code or regulations, however, and its scope and contours have been left to judicial development. Speaking generally, a recapitalization involves a "reshuffling of a capital structure within the framework of an existing corporation," Helvering v. Southwest Consolidated Corporation, 315 U.S. 194, 202 (1942), and encompasses transactions involving exchanges of one class of stock or securities in a corporation for another class issued by the same corporation. Treas. Reg. § 1.368–2(e) provides examples of five different recapitalization exchanges, but those examples are not exhaustive.[1]

The Courts of Appeals and the Tax Court held in the *Bazley* and *Adams* cases that no corporate business purpose existed and that the business purpose test must be viewed in terms of the corporation qua

1. Rev.Proc. 98–3, § 3.01(27), 1998–1 I.R.B. 10, provides that the Service will not rule on whether a transaction constitutes a recapitalization if either (1) the corporation is closely held, or (2) the issues involved are substantially similar to those in published revenue rulings, unless the recapitalization is part of a larger overall reorganization.

corporation and apart from the shareholders. Dissenting opinions in both courts contended that the shareholders had persuasive business reasons for the transaction (obtaining a more marketable security and one that could be sold without reducing stock control of the corporation, an equal footing with creditors to the extent of the debentures, and a more permanent dedication of the accumulated profits to the business). They rejected the view that shareholder business purposes do not supply the necessary corporate business purpose, stating that such a distinction between "corporate" and "shareholder" purposes lacked substance since a corporation did not have purposes apart from its shareholders. The Government's brief stressed the argument that the transaction was not actuated by a purpose germane to the corporation's business, relied strongly on the *Gregory* case, and stated in effect that the stockholders' purposes were not relevant. In the light of this background, note the Supreme Court's avoidance of direct "business purpose" terminology. For a similar issue in the context of divisive reorganizations, see page 685.

Rev.Rul. 77–238, 1977–2 C.B. 115, found an (E) reorganization existed where the certificate of incorporation required retiring employees owning common stock to exchange that stock for preferred. The purpose of the provision was to eliminate common stockholdings by employees no longer with the corporation, thus supplying the business purpose necessary to support the reorganization.

Rev.Rul. 82–34, 1982–1 C.B. 59, held that the continuity of business enterprise doctrine embodied in Treas. Reg. § 1.368–1(d) does not apply to a recapitalization. Thus, incident to a recapitalization a corporation may sell all of its assets and purchase new assets to engage in a different line of business. Presumably, the corporation also could sell its assets and acquire investment assets, thereby becoming a holding company.

B. EXCHANGE OF OUTSTANDING STOCK FOR NEW STOCK OR NEW BONDS

1. *General*

The exchange of outstanding preferred stock for new preferred stock or of outstanding common stock for new common stock constitutes a recapitalization.[2] The exchange of outstanding preferred stock for common stock is likewise a recapitalization as is an exchange of common stock for common and preferred stock. Treas. Reg. § 1.368–2(e). In the latter situation, however, special rules apply to limit the "bailout" potential of the transaction.

It is not necessary that all shareholders in a recapitalization exchange their stock. Thus, a valid (E) reorganization results where only one of three

2. Where the exchange is of stock for stock, there is an overlap of § 368(a)(1)(E) and § 1036. That section applies both to an exchange between shareholders and one between the shareholder and the issuing corporation. See Treas. Reg. § 1.1036–1(a). However, both sections produce the same result, at least where no boot is involved. Rev.Rul. 72–57, 1972–1 C.B. 103, held that where boot is involved, only the reorganization provisions apply.

shareholders exchanges common stock for preferred stock and the fair market value of the preferred equals the fair market value of the common stock exchanged. If there is a difference in value between the common and the preferred stock, the difference may constitute a gift, compensation, etc. Rev.Rul. 74–269, 1974–1 C.B. 87. See also Rev.Rul. 89–3, 1989–1 C.B. 278 (recapitalization whereby shareholder who had acquired shares by gift from controlling shareholder exchanged common stock for new voting common and donor shareholder exchanged common stock for new common stock with restricted voting rights resulted in a taxable gift).

2. *Stock Surrendered in Exchange for Securities*

(a). General—Continuity of Interest

In Hickok v. Commissioner, 32 T.C. 80 (1959)(A), the Tax Court held that the continuity of interest doctrine, discussed at page 526, does not apply to recapitalizations. The Service has followed this principle in Revenue Rulings. See Rev.Rul. 77–415, 1977–2 C.B. 311. Thus, for example, if A, B, C, and D each held 25 percent of the stock of X Corporation, a transaction whereby A exchanged common stock for new common stock and new preferred stock, while B, C, and D exchanged their stock for debentures, could qualify as a recapitalization. B, C, and D would recognize gain, but A would be entitled to nonrecognition. Likewise, a pre-arranged sale of newly issued stock received in an (E) reorganization does not impair the validity of the reorganization. Rev.Rul. 77–479, 1977–2 C.B. 119.

(b). Security Bailouts

Sections 354(a)(2) and 356(d) extend the rationale of the *Bazley* case to all recapitalization and other reorganization exchanges since the value of the excess in principal amount of securities received by the shareholder over the principal amount of securities given up is considered "other property" or "boot." Hence if a shareholder exchanges stock, whether common or preferred, for new stock, whether common or preferred, and debt securities, the securities will be boot and governed by § 356(a). If stock is exchanged for securities alone, § 354(a)(2) renders § 354(a)(1) inapplicable entirely, § 356(a)(1)(B) does not come into play, and the treatment of the exchange is determined under §§ 301, 302, and 331. Treas. Reg. § 1.354–1(d), Ex. (3); Rev.Rul. 77–415, 1977–2 C.B. 311.

Thus, although lack of continuity of equity interest does not destroy the validity of a type (E) reorganization, § 354(a)(2) in effect applies a continuity of interest concept on a shareholder by shareholder basis. Where the recapitalization exchange "has the effect" of a dividend distribution, dividend income is recognized to the extent of the gain realized on the exchange. I.R.C. § 356(a)(2).[3] See Commissioner v. Estate of Bedford, 325

3. The effect of § 1036 must also be considered. On the face of the statute, there is an overlap of § 368(a)(1)(E) and § 1036 in these various situations. Where boot is involved in a § 1036 exchange, § 1031(b), which applies to § 1036 transactions, controls taxation of the boot. But in cases of an overlap between § 1036 and § 368(a)(1)(E),

U.S. 283 (1945). Dividend equivalency of boot distributions made in connection with a recapitalization is determined by applying the principles of § 302, which governs redemptions (discussed in Chapter 6). See Johnson v. Commissioner, 78 T.C. 564 (1982) ($850 per share boot in recapitalization which converted nonvoting common stock into voting common stock was a dividend because it was pro rata and compensated nonvoting shareholders for dividends previously withheld). The reasoning in *Clark,* page 565, which significantly limits the application of § 356(a)(2) in the case of acquisitive reorganizations, should not affect the application of that section to recapitalizations because only a single corporation is involved. The Service has so ruled in the context of a divisive reorganization of a single corporation under § 355. See Rev.Rul. 93–62, 1993–2 C.B. 118, page 681. In addition, in the appropriate circumstances, the Internal Revenue Service might argue that under the approach of *Bazley,* the full amount of the boot was a dividend. Treas. Reg. § 1.301–1(*l*) preserves this contention.

3. *Preferred Stock Bailouts—Exchange of Outstanding Common Stock for New Preferred Stock*

Suppose holders of common stock exchange some common stock for new preferred, or exchange all of their common stock for new common stock and new preferred, so that after the exchange they own both common stock and preferred stock. This is of course a recapitalization variant of the preferred stock dividend bailout, dealt with by § 306. Section 306(c)(1)(B) extends the § 306 solution to the recapitalization exchange if "the effect of the transaction was substantially the same as the receipt of a stock dividend." Treas. Reg. § 1.306–3(d) refers to § 356(a)(2) and states that if any cash received in lieu of the stock would have been a dividend under § 356(a)(2), then the stock is § 306 stock. If a cash distribution would not have been taxable under § 356(a)(2) because of the "dividend within the gain" limitation, then the stock apparently is not § 306 stock.

Do the § 318 attribution of ownership rules apply in determining whether preferred stock received in a recapitalization is § 306 stock? For example, if a husband retains his common stock but his wife receives preferred stock in a recapitalization, is the preferred stock § 306 stock? Rev.Rul. 81–186, 1981–2 C.B. 85, suggests that the attribution rules do not apply and that the stock is not § 306 stock. That Ruling held that where a sole shareholder exchanged some of his common stock for preferred stock in a recapitalization and gave his remaining common stock to his children, the preferred stock was not § 306 stock because if the shareholder had received cash it would not have been a dividend since he would have

Treas. Reg. § 1.1031(b)–1(a)(3) defers to the reorganization provisions, See Rev.Rul. 72–57, 1972–1 C.B. 103 (exchange of outstanding stock for stock and cash as part of a transaction to eliminate minority shareholders was a recapitalization and therefore, under Treas. Reg. § 1.1031(b)–1(a)(3), was not a § 1036 exchange coupled with the receipt of nonqualifying property by the majority shareholder under § 1031(b)); Rev.Rul. 78–351, 1978–2 C.B. 148, modifying Rev.Rul. 72–57, held the cash was a § 356(a)(2) dividend to the majority shareholder.

terminated his entire interest in the corporation. See Zenz v. Quinlivan, 213 F.2d 914 (6th Cir.1954), page 496.

Where, in a reorganization, boot is distributed in exchange for § 306 stock, § 356(e) applies to treat the boot under § 301. In Rev.Rul. 76–14, 1976–1 C.B. 97, the majority shareholder desired to transfer control of the business to an employee-minority shareholder. Under a recapitalization plan, the majority shareholder turned in his common stock for cash and his preferred stock (which was § 306 stock) for a new class of nonvoting common stock. The Ruling held § 356(e) applied; thus the cash received was applied first to the § 306 stock, with a resulting dividend. But if cash is distributed to minority shareholders in lieu of fractional shares, the exception in § 306(b)(4)(A) applies, and the cash will be treated as received in a redemption subject to § 302. Rev.Rul. 81–81, 1981–1 C.B. 122. If in the reorganization, stock which is other than common stock is issued for § 306 stock under § 306(c)(1)(B), the new stock is § 306 stock.

A recapitalization exchange can occur without a direct exchange of stock. Thus, in Rev.Rul. 56–654, 1956–2 C.B. 216, a corporation with outstanding common and preferred stock amended its charter to increase the liquidation value of the preferred stock. The Ruling states that this represented an exchange of all preferred stock and a portion of the common stock for new preferred stock; presumably the increase in value of the preferred stock is § 306 stock. See also Rev.Rul. 66–332, 1966–2 C.B. 108, holding that a "reclassification" of outstanding common stock together with the issuance of additional classes of stock could result in the reclassified stock being treated as § 306 stock.

4. *Relation of Security Bailout to Preferred Stock Bailout*

The Service's view of *Bazley* type recapitalizations prior to the 1954 Code was that the vice lay in splitting a common stockholder's interest into common stock which could be retained and another interest, preferred stock or debt, which could be sold, thereby obtaining capital gain treatment for a part of the accumulated earnings without reducing the shareholder's common stock interest. The current Code embodies the view that an exchange of outstanding stock for debt must meet the tests of the dividend sections. It is akin to the policy of § 306 respecting preferred stock bailouts, in that it seeks to block the efforts to convert situations having potential dividend taxation into situations involving capital gain potential only. The solution for the "security bailout," however, is that of an immediate tax, while under § 306 the solution for the "preferred stock bailout" is that of "tainting" by giving the preferred stock an ordinary income status on future disposition.

C. EXCHANGE OF DEBT SECURITIES FOR DEBT SECURITIES

1. *Qualification as a Recapitalization*

The regulations under § 368(a)(1)(E) and its predecessors never have expressly provided that an exchange of only debt securities qualifies as a recapitalization. See Treas. Reg. § 1.368–2(e). Treatment of the exchange of outstanding debentures for new corporate debentures as a recapitalization was first established judicially.

Commissioner v. Neustadt's Trust, 131 F.2d 528 (2d Cir.1942), involved the exchange of outstanding 20 year, 6 percent debentures for a like face amount of 10 year, 3¼ percent convertible debentures of the corporation. The Commissioner contended that a taxable gain resulted, but the court disagreed and applied the reorganization provisions:

"The first question is whether the debentures are 'securities' within the meaning of [the predecessor of § 354(a)(1)]. The word is used in contrast to 'stock'; it necessarily refers to bonds of some sort, since bonds are the most usual, if not the only, form of corporate securities to contrast with stock. * * * [It] is usual financial practice to speak of debentures as 'securities' and the term should be given its ordinary meaning. In Helvering v. Watts, 296 U.S. 387, 56 S.Ct. 275, bonds with a maximum maturity of seven years were held to be 'securities' within the corresponding provision of the Revenue Act of 1924. We do not understand that the authority of this case has been destroyed by the subsequent decision in LeTulle v. Scofield, 308 U.S. 415, 60 S.Ct. 313. There it was held that continuity of proprietary interest must be found if the transaction is to be deemed within the definition of reorganization, and that a transfer of all the assets of one corporation to another in exchange for cash and bonds of the latter did not fall within such a definition. It was not held that an exchange of bonds for bonds pursuant to a plan of reorganization is not an exchange of 'securities' within the meaning of [the predecessor of § 354(a)(1)]. * * * We think the debentures involved in the case at bar are 'securities' within that section.

"It remains to determine whether they were exchanged pursuant to a plan of reorganization and this turns on whether the exchange amounts to a 'recapitalization,' as that word is used in [the predecessor of § 368(a)(1)(E)]. * * * The Commissioner contends that only a change in authorized or outstanding capital stock of a corporation can properly be denominated a recapitalization or a reshuffling of the capital structure. He describes an exchange of old debentures for new debentures in the same corporation as a mere refinancing operation. * * * But in common financial parlance the long term funded debt of a corporation is usually regarded as forming part of its capital structure. * * * The Security and Exchange Commission has required the funded debt of a corporation to be listed under the caption of 'capital securities.' The Interstate Commerce Commission treats funded debt as part of the corporate capital structure. St. Louis, San Francisco Ry. Co., Reorganization, 240 I.C.C. 383, 406 * * *. [T]he purpose of the statutory nonrecognition of gain or loss from reorganization transactions, favors ascribing to the word 'recapitalization' a broad rather than a restricted meaning. Such purpose, as indicated by the Congressional reports * * * was apparently twofold: To encourage legitimate reorganizations required to strengthen the financial condition of a corporation, and to prevent losses being established by bondholders, as well as stockholders, who have received the new securities without substantially changing their original investment. The transaction in the case at bar meets both of these tests. By changing the interest rate and date of maturity of its old bonds and adding a conversion option to the holders of the new, the corporation could strengthen its financial condition, while the bondholders would not substantially change their original investments by making the exchange. 'Recapitalization' seems a most appropriate word to describe that type of reorganization and it is the very kind of transaction were Congress meant the recognition of gain or loss to be held in suspense until a more substantial change in the taxpayer's original investment should occur. We hold that the exchange of securities was made pursuant to a plan of 'recapitalization.' "(529–530)

The Committee Reports under the 1954 Act approve the *Neustadt* rule. Senate Finance Committee Report, S.Rep. No. 83–1622, 83rd Cong., 2d Sess. 51 (1954). Rev.Rul. 77–415, 1977–2 C.B. 311, accepted the principle that an exchange of new debentures for outstanding debentures is a recapitalization under § 368(a)(1)(E). Thus, the exchange of new ten-year, 10 percent debentures for outstanding 20–year, 8 percent debentures did not result in gain or loss to the exchanging debenture holders since the principal amounts of the two issues were the same.

2. *Treatment of Bondholders*

Although an exchange of bonds for bonds qualifies as a recapitalization, § 354(a)(2) excludes from the complete nonrecognition rule the receipt of securities in a principal amount greater than the principal amount of any securities surrendered. In such a case, § 356(d) treats the fair market value of the excess principal amount as boot. See Treas. Reg. § 1.356–3(d), Exs. (2)–(6). The value of the "excess principal amount" is determined by the following formula:

$$\text{Fair Market Value of Securities Received} \times \frac{\text{Principal Amount of Securities Received} \quad \text{minus} \quad \text{Principal Amount of Securities Surrendered}}{\text{Principal Amount of Securities Received}}$$

In determining the "principal amount" of securities received in the reorganization, the original issue discount rules of §§ 1272 through 1274, discussed in Chapter 4, must be taken into account. If either the securities surrendered or the securities received are publicly traded, pursuant to § 1273(b) the "issue price," and thus the "principal amount" of the securities received, equals their fair market value. Where neither security is publicly traded, whether a security issued in a recapitalization is an OID instrument is determined by treating the instrument as issued for property. I.R.C. § 1275(a)(4). Thus, the issue price (and principal amount) are determined by discounting to net present value the payments due on the instrument (including both principal and interest), using the proper "applicable federal rate." See I.R.C. § 1274, discussed at page 168. In either case, if the stated principal amount exceeds the issue price, the principal amount of the securities received will be an amount less than their face value when computing gain under § 356. Thus, receipt of a security having a *face* value in excess of the principal amount of the security surrendered will not give rise to boot under § 356 if under the OID rules the imputed principal amount of the security received does not exceed the principal amount of the security surrendered.

Boot can result under § 354(a)(2) and give rise to taxable gain under § 356(d) even where the value of the securities given up is the same as the value of those received. For example, if a 9½ percent, $100 face amount bond with basis of $100 is exchanged for a new 6 percent, $120 face amount publicly traded bond, and the value of each is $120, the value of the excess $20 in principal amount, i.e., $120 × 20/120, is boot. See Treas. Reg. § 1.356–3. The new bond has a basis under § 358 of $120 ($100 basis of old bond + $20 gain).

Under Rev.Rul. 60–37, 1960–1 C.B. 309, if the old bonds had an original issue discount element, the new bonds were to be similarly treated. This rule is now embodied in the "issue price" rules in § 1273(b)(3) where either security is publicly traded.

A single transaction can involve recognition of gain attributable to boot, the creation of OID, and the preservation of market discount. Suppose a publicly traded 9½ percent, $100 face amount bond with a basis of $90 (because it was purchased at a discount in the secondary market) is exchanged for a new 6 percent, $130 face amount publicly traded bond and the values of both are $120. The issue price, and thus the principal amount, of the new bond is $120. The value of the excess $20 of principal amount, i.e., $20 ($120 × ($20/$120)), is boot, and that amount of gain must be recognized currently. Because the face amount of the security received ($130) exceeds the fair market value of the security surrendered ($120) the excess amount ($10) is OID. The new bond has a basis under § 358 of $110 ($90 basis of the old bond plus $20 gain), and upon redemption at maturity the holder will recognize gain of $10. This gain will be ordinary income under § 1276 because it is market discount. See I.R.C. § 1278(a)(1)(D)(iii).

If the excess principal amount is in satisfaction of accrued interest, § 354(a)(2)(B) requires that the entire amount of the excess so attributable be recognized as ordinary income. To the extent the excess is not attributable to accrued interest, the value of the excess principal amount is treated as boot taxable under § 356(a), and the boot gain should be treated as capital gain under § 356(a)(1).

3. *Treatment of the Corporation*

If a corporation issues new bonds in exchange for outstanding bonds having a higher principal amount, an (E) reorganization exists but the corporation may have to recognize cancellation of indebtedness income under § 61(a)(12), subject to the exceptions and technical rules of § 108. Neither § 361(a) nor § 1032 applies to relieve the corporation from tax. Rev.Rul. 77–437, 1977–2 C.B. 28. If the corporation is solvent and not in bankruptcy at the time of the recapitalization it must recognize cancellation of indebtedness income equal to the amount by which the principal amount of the obligations surrendered, plus accrued but unpaid interest, exceeds the issue price/principal amount of the newly issued securities. See I.R.C. § 108(e)(10). Note that the amount of discharge of indebtedness income realized by the corporation is determined by comparing the amount owed on the surrendered obligations to the issue price/principal amount of the newly issued bonds, while the creation of OID is determined by comparing the fair market value of the surrendered obligations with the stated principal amount of the newly issued obligations. Thus, both cancellation of indebtedness income and OID may be created simultaneously in a debt-for-debt recapitalization. This result would occur, for example, if outstanding publicly traded bonds with a stated principal amount of $100 and a fair market value of $80 were exchanged for new bonds with a stated principal amount of $90.

If the corporation is *insolvent* (as defined in § 108(d)(3)) both before and after the recapitalization, no cancellation of indebtedness income is recognized. If an insolvent corporation is rendered solvent, cancellation of indebtedness income results only to the extent the recapitalization results in a positive net worth. See I.R.C. § 108(a)(1)(B) and (3). In either case, the insolvent corporation is required to reduce its tax attributes, such as net operating loss carryovers, by the amount of income excluded by the insolvency exception, and in the order specified in § 108(b)(2). The corporation may elect to reduce the basis of depreciable assets under § 1017 in lieu of the tax attribute reduction. I.R.C. § 108(b)(5). If the recapitalization was pursuant to a bankruptcy proceeding, the corporation is not required to recognize any cancellation of indebtedness income that might result from debt restructuring, even if the reorganization renders the corporation solvent. I.R.C. § 108(a)(1)(A). As in the case of an insolvent corporation, however, the reorganized corporation's tax attributes must be reduced under § 108(b).

Regardless of the reorganized corporation's financial status, if the new bonds have a *higher principal amount* than the old bonds (determined under OID principles), the corporation may deduct the retirement premium as an additional cost of borrowing, unless a portion of the premium is attributable to extinguishment of a conversion feature in the old bonds. See I.R.C. § 249, discussed at page 181.

D. EXCHANGE OF OUTSTANDING BONDS FOR NEW STOCK

Treas. Reg. § 1.368–2(e)(1) provides that the issuance by a corporation of new preferred stock in exchange for existing bonds is a recapitalization. See also Commissioner v. Capento Securities Corporation, 140 F.2d 382 (1st Cir.1944). An exchange of outstanding bonds for new common stock would likewise be a recapitalization. In either case, the former security owners are accorded nonrecognition under § 354 (subject to recognition under § 354(a)(2)(B) to the extent that the stock is attributable to interest arrearages). From the corporation's perspective, however, if the corporation is solvent the transaction gives rise to taxable discharge of indebtedness income to the extent that the sum of the principal amount of the securities plus accrued but unpaid interest exceeds the fair market value of the stock issued in the transaction. I.R.C. § 108(e)(8). To the extent of the fair market value of the stock, § 1032 provides nonrecognition to the corporation.

If the holder of a security that is an OID instrument receives stock in exchange for the instrument in a recapitalization, the balance of the original issue discount will not be included in the income of the exchanging bondholder. See Rev.Rul. 75–39, 1975–1 C.B. 272. The stock will take a basis under § 358 equal to the basis of the debt instrument, which includes all previously accrued OID.

On a related point, the exercise of a conversion privilege of a bond convertible into stock of the same corporation is not an "exchange" and hence the recapitalization provision and § 354 are not involved, Rev.Rul. 72–265, 1972–1 C.B. 222. See also Rev.Rul. 79–155, 1979–1 C.B. 153 (parent of subsidiary which issued debt obligations convertible into stock of parent was treated as a joint obligor on debt, thereby resulting in conversion not being a taxable event).

E. SECTION 305 ASPECTS

A recapitalization, which would be tax-free under the reorganization provisions, is one of the transactions that can result in a constructive stock dividend under § 305(c). See page 312. For example, in a recapitalization in which a shareholder exchanges preferred stock with dividend arrearages for new common and preferred stock, the exchange would be a tax-free recapitalization under § 368. See e.g., Kaufman v. Commissioner, 55 T.C. 1046 (1971) (A). When viewed from the perspective of § 305, however, the recapitalization has the effect of a distribution of additional shares of stock to the preferred stockholder which would result in a taxable dividend under sections 305(c) and 305(b)(4). Treas. Reg. § 1.305–5(d), Ex. (1) (taxable stock dividend if arrearages are eliminated). However, see Treas. Reg. § 1.305–3(e), Ex. (12), illustrating that § 305 is inapplicable to a "single and isolated" recapitalization transaction.

In Rev.Rul. 83–119, 1983–2 C.B. 57, pursuant to a recapitalization a corporation issued preferred stock with an issue price of $600, which was according to its terms required to be redeemed for $1,000 upon the holder's death. The Ruling held that under sections 305(c) and 305(b)(4), $340 of the redemption premium was a taxable stock dividend that was includable ratably over the holder's life expectancy. Upon the holder's death, any portion of the $340 not yet included in income would be includable. For valuation of preferred stock issued in a recapitalization, see Rev.Rul. 83–120, 1983–2 C.B. 170.

SECTION 3. CHANGES IN IDENTITY, FORM, OR PLACE OF ORGANIZATION: TYPE (F) REORGANIZATIONS

INTERNAL REVENUE CODE: Section 368(a)(1)(F).

Section 368(a)(1)(F) treats as a reorganization a change in "identity, form or place of organization of one corporation." The definition of an (F) reorganization focuses on purpose and effect, not the form of the transaction. Thus, the (F) reorganization definition overlaps with other forms of reorganizations. For example, in order to change its state of incorporation, X Corporation might form a new Y Corporation in another jurisdiction and then merge into it. The transaction is both an (A) and an (F) reorganization, but the Internal Revenue Service has indicated that in these circumstances the transaction will be characterized as an (F) reorganization. Rev.Rul. 57–276, 1957–C.B. 126.[4] The phrase "of one corporation" in § 368(a)(1)(F) precludes ever treating a merger of two or more pre-existing operating companies as a type (F) reorganization.[5]

Classifying a transaction as a type (F) reorganization has two principal effects: (1) the old corporation's taxable year does not end; and, (2) the new corporation is entitled under § 172 to carry back to taxable years of the old corporation post-reorganization net operating losses.[6] See I.R.C. § 381(b). These results reflect the fact that the reorganized corporation is "really" unchanged by the reorganizing transaction. In other respects, the new (or acquiring) corporation succeeds to the old (or acquired) corporation's tax attributes under § 381, discussed in Chapter 16, in the same manner as in any other reorganization.

Revenue Ruling 96–29

1996–1 C.B. 50

ISSUE

Do the transactions described below qualify as reorganizations under § 368(a)(1)(F) of the Internal Revenue Code?

4. See also Rev.Rul. 88–25, 1988–1 C.B. 116 (conversion of foreign corporation to domestic corporation by filing domestication certificate under state law); Rev.Rul. 87–27, 1987–1 C.B. 134 (reincorporation of domestic corporation in foreign country is a type (F) reorganization); Rev.Rul. 87–66, 1987–2 C.B. 168 (reincorporation of foreign corporation in U.S. is a type (F) reorganization); Rev.Rul. 80–105, 1980–1 C.B. 78 (conversion of federal mutual savings and loan association to state stock savings and loan association was a type (F) reorganization).

5. The statute was amended in 1982 to add the phrase "of one corporation" to make it clear that the provision does not apply to the merger of pre-existing operating companies. See H.Rep. No. 97–760, 97th Cong., 2d Sess. 540–541 (1982). Prior to the amendment, some courts had permitted (F) reorganization treatment in such circumstances. See, e.g., Home Construction Corp. v. United States, 439 F.2d 1165 (5th Cir.1971).

6. In cases where the type (F) and type (D) reorganization overlap, classification as a type (F) has an additional effect. Type (F) reorganizations differ from Type (D) reorganizations in that § 357(c) applies to type (D) reorganizations but not to type (F) reorganizations. Rev.Rul. 79–289, 1979–2 C.B. 145 (§ 357(c) does not apply to reorganization meeting requirements for both (D) and (F)). For example, if X Corporation, whose sole asset is land and a building which has a basis of $50,000 and is subject to a $70,000 mortgage, reincorporates in a different state by merging into Y Corporation, a wholly owned subsidiary formed solely for the reincorporation transaction, no gain is recognized to X Corporation and Y Corporation takes a $50,000 basis in the land and building.

FACTS

Situation 1. Q is a manufacturing corporation all of the common stock of which is owned by twelve individuals. One class of nonvoting preferred stock, representing 40 percent of the aggregate value of Q, is held by a variety of corporate and noncorporate shareholders. Q is incorporated in state M. Pursuant to a plan to raise immediate additional capital and to enhance its ability to raise capital in the future by issuing additional stock, Q proposes to make a public offering of newly issued stock and to cause its stock to become publicly traded. Q entered into an underwriting agreement providing for the public offering and a change in its state of incorporation. The change in the state of incorporation was undertaken, in part, to enable the corporation to avail itself of the advantages that the corporate laws of state N afford to public companies and their officers and directors. In the absence of the public offering, Q would not have changed its state of incorporation. Pursuant to the underwriting agreement, Q changed its place of incorporation by merging with and into R, a newly organized corporation incorporated in state N. The shares of Q stock were converted into the right to receive an identical number of shares of R stock. Immediately thereafter, R sold additional shares of its stock to the public and redeemed all of the outstanding shares of nonvoting preferred stock. The number of new shares sold was equal to 60 percent of all the outstanding R stock following the sale and redemption.

Situation 2. W, a state M corporation, is a manufacturing corporation all of the stock of which is owned by two individuals. W conducted its business through several wholly owned subsidiaries. The management of W determined that it would be in the best interest of W to acquire the business of Z, an unrelated corporation, and combine it with the business of Y, one of its subsidiaries, and to change the state of incorporation of W. In order to accomplish these objectives, and pursuant to an overall plan, W entered into a plan and agreement of merger with Y and Z. In accordance with the agreement, Z merged with and into Y pursuant to the law of state M, with the former Z shareholders receiving shares of newly issued W preferred stock in exchange for their shares of Z stock. Immediately following the acquisition of Z, W changed its place of organization by merging with and into N, a newly organized corporation incorporated in state R. Upon W's change of place of organization, the holders of W common and preferred stock surrendered their W stock in exchange for identical N common and preferred stock, respectively.

LAW AND ANALYSIS

Section 368(a)(1)(F) provides that a reorganization includes a mere change in identity, form, or place of organization of one corporation, however effected. This provision was amended by the Tax Equity and Fiscal Responsibility Act of 1982, Pub.L. No. 97–248, in order to limit its application to one corporation. Certain limitations contained in § 381(b), including those precluding the corporation acquiring property in a reorganization from carrying back a net operating loss or a net capital loss for a taxable year ending after the date of transfer to a taxable year of the transferor, do not apply to reorganizations described in § 368(a)(1)(F) "in recognition of the intended scope of such reorganizations as embracing only formal changes in a single operating corporation." H.R.Rep. No. 760, 97th Cong., 2d Sess. 540, 541 (1982). Although a change in the place of organization usually must be effected through the merger of one corporation into another, such a transaction qualifies as a reorganization under § 368(a)(1)(F) because it involves only one operating corporation. The 1982 amendment of § 368(a)(1)(F) thus overruled several cases in which a merger of two or more operating corporations could be treated as a reorganization under § 368(a)(1)(F). See, e.g., Estate of Stauffer v. Commissioner, 403 F.2d 611 (9th Cir.1968); Associated Machine, Inc. v. Commissioner, 403 F.2d 622 (9th Cir.1968); and Davant v. Commissioner, 366 F.2d 874 (5th Cir.1966).

A transaction does not qualify as a reorganization under § 368(a)(1)(F) unless there is no change in existing shareholders or in the assets of the corporation. However, a transaction will not fail to qualify as a reorganization under § 368(a)(1)(F) if dissenters owning fewer than 1 percent of the outstanding shares of the corporation fail to participate in the transaction. Rev.Rul. 66–284, 1966–2 C.B. 115.

The rules applicable to corporate reorganizations as well as other provisions recognize the unique characteristics of reorganizations qualifying under § 368(a)(1)(F). In contrast to other types of reorganizations, which can involve two or more operating corporations, a reorganization of a corporation under § 368(a)(1)(F) is treated for most purposes of the Code as if there had been no change in the corporation and, thus, as if the reorganized corporation is the same entity as the corporation that was in existence prior to the reorganization. See § 381(b); § 1.381(b)–1(a)(2); see also 87–110, 1987–2 C.B. 159; 80–168, 1980–1 C.B. 178; 73–526, 1973–2 C.B. 404; 64–250, 1964–2 C.B. 333.

In 69–516, 1969–2 C.B. 56, the Internal Revenue Service treated as two separate transactions a reorganization under § 368(a)(1)(F) and a reorganization under § 368(a)(1)(C) undertaken as part of the same plan. Specifically, a corporation changed its place of organization by merging into a corporation formed under the laws of another state and, immediately thereafter, it transferred substantially all of its assets in exchange for stock of an unrelated corporation. The ruling holds that the change in place of organization qualified as a reorganization under § 368(a)(1)(F).

Accordingly, in *Situation 1*, the reincorporation by Q in state N qualifies as a reorganization under § 368(a)(1)(F) even though it was a step in the transaction in which Q was issuing common stock in a public offering and redeeming stock having a value of 40 percent of the aggregate value of its outstanding stock prior to the offering.

In *Situation 2*, the reincorporation by W in state N qualifies as a reorganization under § 368(a)(1)(F) even though it was a step in the transaction in which W acquired the business of Z.

HOLDING

On the facts set forth in this ruling, in each of *Situations 1* and *2*, the reincorporation transaction qualifies as a reorganization under § 368(a)(1)(F), notwithstanding the other transactions effected pursuant to the same plan.

EFFECT ON OTHER REVENUE RULINGS

79–250, 1979–2 C.B. 156, addressed a similar issue on facts that are substantially similar, in all material respects, to those of *Situation 2*. The ruling holds that a merger of Z with and into Y in exchange for the stock of W qualifies as a reorganization under § 368(a)(1)(A) by reason of § 368(a)(2)(D), even though W is reincorporated in another state immediately after the merger. The ruling also holds that the reincorporation qualifies as a reorganization under § 368(a)(1)(F). Rev.Rul. 79–250 did not apply the step transaction doctrine in order to combine the two transactions, stating that the merger and the subsequent reincorporation were separate transactions because "the economic motivation supporting each transaction is sufficiently meaningful on its own account, and is not dependent upon the other transaction for its substantiation."

Although the holding of 79–250 is correct on the facts presented therein, in order to emphasize that central to the holding in 79–250 is the unique status of reorganizations under § 368(a)(1)(F), and that 79–250 is not intended to reflect the application of the step-transaction doctrine in other contexts, 79–250 is modified.

ILLUSTRATIVE MATERIAL

A. (F) REORGANIZATION FOLLOWING OR PRECEDING AN ACQUISITION

Suppose that X Corporation purchases all of the stock of Y Corporation and immediately thereafter merges Y Corporation into Z Corporation, a subsidiary of X Corporation with no assets which was formed solely for the purpose of changing the state of incorporation of Y Corporation. Does the merger qualify as an (F) reorganization?

In Security Industrial Insurance Co. v. United States, 702 F.2d 1234 (5th Cir.1983), OIC, a holding company, purchased all of the stock of Southern, following which OIC liquidated Southern and then contributed OIC's operating assets to Security, another subsidiary of OIC. The taxpayer argued that the transaction was an (F) reorganization. Applying the step transaction doctrine, the court held that no (F) reorganization had occurred because the intended result of the transaction was an acquisition of the assets of OIC. The court tested shareholder continuity of interest by comparing ownership of Southern before the acquisition with ownership of OIC after the entire transaction had been completed. Since the historic shareholders of Y corporation had been eliminated, the transaction failed to meet the continuity of interest requirement. A key element in the reasoning of *Security Industrial Insurance Co.*, however, was the application of the step transaction doctrine. See also Cannonsburg Skiing Corporation v. Commissioner, T.C. Memo. 1986–150, aff'd sub nom. Russell v. Commissioner, 832 F.2d 349 (6th Cir.1987) (step transaction doctrine applied to treat the overall transaction as an asset acquisition, and concluded that no (F) reorganization had occurred because there was a 98 percent shift in ownership "which clearly violates the identity of shareholders and their proprietary interests as required for an F reorganization").

Treas. Reg. § 1.338–3(c)(3) ameliorates these problems to a large extent by providing that for purposes of applying the continuity of interest requirement, an acquiring corporation will be treated as the historic shareholder of a target corporation if it made a "qualified stock purchase," as defined in § 338(d)(3). Under Treas. Reg. § 1.338–3(c)(3) the merger of Y Corporation into Z Corporation in the above example could qualify as a type (F) reorganization. Although the regulation does not apply to purchases by individual shareholders, it would be incongruous not to apply the same principle if individual A (or a group of individuals) purchased 100 percent of the stock of X Corporation and then merged X Corporation into Y Corporation, a shell corporation wholly owned by A (or the group who purchased X), for the purpose of changing the state of incorporation.

In Dunlap & Associates, Inc. v. Commissioner, 47 T.C. 542 (1967), the merger of a New York corporation into its Delaware subsidiary as part of an overall plan subsequently to acquire stock of two other corporations in type (B) reorganizations prior to making a public offering of stock in the Delaware corporation, was held to be an (F) reorganization.

B. "FUNCTIONALLY UNRELATED" TRANSACTIONS

Suppose that X Corporation, which is incorporated in California, wishes to reincorporate in Delaware and simultaneously to redeem the stock of A, a 20 percent shareholder. To this end, X Corporation forms Y Corporation (a Delaware corporation) and then merges into Y Corporation with A receiving cash and all of the other X shareholders receiving Y Corporation stock. Does the transaction qualify as an (F) reorganization or does it qualify only as an (A) reorganization? This will be an important issue if, for example, Y Corporation incurs a net operating loss, which can be carried back to an X Corporation year only if the transaction qualifies as an (F) reorganization.

If the payment of cash to A can be viewed as functionally unrelated to the merger effected to change the place of organization, then the transaction might be divided into a redemption and an (F) reorganization. This analysis is suggested by Rev.Rul. 61–156, 1961–2 C.B. 62. In that ruling X Corporation liquidated and distributed its assets to its shareholders, who in turn contributed the operating assets received in the liquidation to newly formed Y Corporation, but who retained liquid assets received in the liquidation. Other individuals who had not been shareholders of X Corporation also contributed property to Y Corporation. To treat the shareholders of X Corporation as receiving a dividend with respect to the liquid assets, the Service held that the issuance of stock to the new shareholders was "functionally unrelated" to the "liquidation-reincorporation" and did not prevent the finding of an (F) reorganization. There is also some support in the case law for application of the "functionally unrelated" analysis. In Reef Corp. v. Commissioner, 368 F.2d 125 (5th Cir.1966), two groups of shareholders controlled a corporation. One group desired to buy out the other and a plan was developed whereby a new corporation was formed and then it issued stock in exchange for a portion of the stock in the old corporation held by the shareholders desiring to continue in the business. Both groups then sold the remaining stock in the old corporation to a third party with the outgoing shareholders receiving cash and notes. The old corporation then sold its assets to the new corporation in exchange for notes of the new corporation. Those notes were then distributed to the old shareholders in discharge of the third party's obligation for the purchase price. The outgoing group was thus left with notes of the new corporation and cash while the continuing group now controlled the new corporation and held its notes as well. The court found that an (F) reorganization had occurred:

"Distilled to their pure substance, two distinct and unrelated events transpired. First, the holders of 48 percent of the stock in Reef Fields had their stockholdings completely redeemed. Second, new Reef was formed and the assets of Reef Fields were transferred to new Reef. The business enterprise continued without interruption during both the redemption and the change in corporate vehicles.

"Much confusion flows from the fact that the corporate reorganization took place simultaneously with the stock redemption. But taking the Code as a standard, these two elements were functionally unrelated. Reef Fields could have completely redeemed the stock of 48 percent of its shareholders without changing the state of its incorporation. A complete redemption is not a characteristic of a reorganization. Congress clearly indicated this when it defined reorganization in section 368. Section 368(a)(1)(A) speaks of a 'merger or consolidation' which looks to the joining of two or more corporations. Section 368(a)(1)(B) and (C) look to one corporation acquiring the assets of another or control of another corporation solely for its voting stock. Section 368(a)(1)(D) looks to the consolidation of two or more corporations or the division of two or more going businesses into separate corporations. Only sections 368(a)(1)(E) and (F) look to adjustments within a corporation. But none of these provisions focuses on a complete redemption as a characteristic of a reorganization. Congress did not have redemption of stock as a primary purpose of any of the forms of a reorganization. That subject came under consideration when it undertook to enact specific legislation on complete and partial redemptions, section 302.

"The boot provision, section 356, is adequate to cover a complete redemption when it occurs incident to a reorganization * * *. When the primary characteristics of the reorganization conform to those described by 368(a)(1)(F), we should parse the occurrences into their functional elements. * * * To effectuate the intention of Congress manifested in the Code, we must separate this transaction into its two distinctly separate functional parts. The test of whether events should be viewed separately or together as part of a single plan is not temporal but is functional.

"Applying this test to the instant case, it is clear that the redemption and the change of corporate vehicles must be viewed as separate and distinct occurrences. Cf. Bazley v. Commissioner, 1947, 331 U.S. 737, 67 S.Ct. 1489." (134)

In The Aetna Casualty and Surety Co. v. United States, 568 F.2d 811 (2d Cir.1976), Aetna Life, which held 61 percent of the stock of Old Aetna, formed a new corporation, New Aetna, to which it transferred its stock of Old Aetna. Old Aetna was then merged into New Aetna with the minority shareholders in Old Aetna receiving shares of Aetna Life. The minority shareholders of Old Aetna thus became shareholders of Aetna Life and New Aetna became a wholly owned subsidiary of Aetna Life. Subsequent to the reorganization, New Aetna operated at a loss and attempted to carry that loss back against part of Old Aetna's taxable income, arguing that the transaction constituted an (F) reorganization and that the carryback was thus permitted under § 381(b)(3). The court held that the transaction constituted an (F) reorganization despite the fact that the minority shareholders in Old Aetna emerged from the transaction with a substantially changed interest in the reorganized corporate structure. The court treated the transaction as if the minority shareholders' interests in Old Aetna had been redeemed (i.e., by exchanging their Old Aetna shares for shares in Aetna Life) in the course of an (F) reorganization: "Clearly a corporation which merely redeems its minority shareholders' stock has not undergone a reorganization at all under § 368(a)(1) and is entitled to carryback its losses under § 172. We see no reason why the result should be different simply because the redemption occurs in the course of merging one corporation into a different shell. * * * If the redemption, reorganization and carryback provisions were not intended to preclude carrybacks where there has been a simple redemption, we do not believe those provisions should be construed to preclude the carryback here involved."

In Casco Products Corp. v. Commissioner, 49 T.C. 32 (1967), "New Casco" corporation acquired 91 percent of the stock of "Old Casco" by means of a public tender. Solely to acquire 100 percent ownership of Old Casco, New Casco formed a subsidiary and Old Casco was merged into it, with the dissenting shareholders receiving cash. The Tax Court treated the overall transaction, including the merger, as a "reorganization in form" only, and regarded the subsidiary as "merely a meaningless detour" to accomplish the effect of a redemption of the remaining 9 percent of the shares. Thus a net operating loss of the now wholly owned subsidiary was allowed to be carried back to the taxable years of Old Casco.

C. "LIQUIDATION–REINCORPORATION" TRANSACTIONS AND THE TYPE (F) REORGANIZATION

Prior to 1986, when the *General Utilities* doctrine permitted corporations to distribute appreciated property without recognizing gain, shareholders often attempted to extract property from corporate solution at capital gains rates while continuing to operate the business in corporate form. In a typical transaction, the corporation would be liquidated and simultaneously or within a short period the operating assets of the corporation would be reincorporated in a new corporation with the shareholders retaining the liquid assets. If the form of the transaction was respected, the liquidation would generate capital gains to the shareholders under § 331 and the incorporation would be tax free under § 351.

In attacking such transactions, the Commissioner often argued that the overall effect of the transaction was an (F) reorganization with the retained assets representing "boot" in the reorganization taxable as a dividend. This argument was generally successful where the shareholders in the "old" and "new" corporations were substantially identical. See, e.g., Pridemark v. Commissioner, 42 T.C. 510 (1964) (A), aff'd in part and rev'd in part, 345 F.2d 35 (4th Cir.1965). However, where some shareholders were eliminated in the transaction, it was harder to characterize the transaction as a "mere" change of form. Here the Commissioner argued that the aspect of the transaction which resulted in the change in share ownership was "unrelated" to the (F) reorganization transaction. See, e.g., Rev.Rul. 61–156, page 661. The Commissioner's approach had only mixed success in the courts with the Tax Court insisting on complete identity of share ownership as a precondition for finding an (F) reorganization. See, e.g., Gallagher v. Commissioner, 39 T.C. 144 (1962); Reef Corp. v. Commissioner, T.C. Memo. 1965–72, rev'd, 368 F.2d 125 (5th Cir.1966). Type (D) reorganization aspects of the liquidation-reincorporation transaction are discussed at page 672.

Because § 336 now requires that gain be recognized by a corporation distributing appreciated assets in liquidation, intentionally structured transactions of this sort no longer occur. However, the case law developed in connection with liquidation-reincorporation transactions has had some effect on the case law involving "normal" (F) reorganizations. Compare Romy Hammes, Inc. v. Commissioner, 68 T.C. 900, 906 note 8 (1977) ("The (F) reorganization received relatively little judicial or administrative attention until [the government] began to use the (F) reorganization as a weapon in the liquidation-reincorporation area. * * * Although the litigating positions of the Service and the taxpayer are reversed when the scope of the (F) reorganization is to be determined for purposes of § 381(b)(3) loss carryback, the judicial interpretation of § 368(a)(1)(F) must obviously be consistent."); The Aetna Casualty and Surety Co. v. United States, 568 F.2d 811, 823 (2d Cir.1976) ("We specifically declin[e] to decide whether classifying a reorganization as an (F) reorganization for purposes of § 381(b)(3) will necessarily mean it is an (F) reorganization for purposes of other provisions of the Code.").

SECTION 4. NONDIVISIVE TYPE (D) REORGANIZATIONS

INTERNAL REVENUE CODE: Sections 354(b); 368(a)(1)(D), (a)(2)(A), (a)(2)(H), (c); 312(h)(2).

The transfer of some or all of a corporation's assets to a newly created or existing subsidiary—as where X Corporation transfers some of its assets to new or existing Y Corporation—is a type (D) reorganization if, following the transfer, X Corporation distributes a controlling amount of the stock of Y Corporation to its shareholders in a distribution that meets the requirements of § 354, § 355, or § 356. A type (D) reorganization usually is the first step in dividing a corporate enterprise into two separate corporations by a distribution of stock of the subsidiary to the parent's shareholders in a transaction subject to § 355. See Chapter 15. However, § 368(a)(1)(D) also can describe a single corporation reorganization. In this case, the stock distribution must qualify under § 354, which requires that (1) X Corporation transfer *substantially all* of its assets to Y Corporation and (2) all of the properties of X Corporation, including the stock of Y Corporation, be distributed to the X Corporation shareholders. The purpose of the "substantially all the assets" requirement in § 354(b) is to insure that the provisions of § 355 be met in any transaction that potentially could involve the division of a corporation. Rev. Rul. 74–545, 1974–2 C.B. 122, held that the distribution requirement means that the transferor corporation must liquidate. As a result of these two overlapping rules, a nondivisive (D) reorganization generally occurs when X Corporation transmutes itself into Y Corporation through an asset transfer and a liquidation. A nondivisive (D) reorganization also may occur, however, when X Corporation transfers all of its assets to Y Corporation, which is owned by the same shareholders as owned X Corporation.

The first step of a nondivisive (D) reorganization—the asset transfer—usually overlaps with a § 351 incorporation transfer, which, like a reorganization, is a nonrecognition event. The second step overlaps with the liquidation provisions, which require corporate and shareholder gain or loss recognition. However, when the liquidation is pursuant to a plan of reorganization, § 354 provides nonrecognition to the shareholders, except to the extent of boot, which is governed by § 356. Section 361 displaces § 336 to provide nonrecognition to the liquidating corporation, X Corporation in the preceding example, with respect to the distribution of the Y Corporation stock. However, § 361(c) requires that the liquidating corporation recognize gain (but not loss) with respect to all other property distributed in the liquidation.

Warsaw Photographic Associates, Inc. v. Commissioner

Tax Court of the United States, 1985.
84 T.C. 21.

■ CHABOT, JUDGE:

[Warsaw Studios, Inc. (Studios) conducted a photography business in leased premises on Madison Avenue and East 34th Street in New York City. Warsaw & Co., Inc., which was wholly owned by J.J. Warsaw, owned all the preferred stock and 7,549 shares of common stock of Studios. Approximately 2,000 shares of Studio's common stock were owned by ten employees of Studios. For a number of years Studios incurred significant net operating losses, due in part to unfavorable terms of the 34th Street lease. Shawn, one of the employee-shareholders, thought the corporation could be made profitable if the corporation could rid itself of the burden of the lease. Shawn and the nine other employee-shareholders of Studios formed Warsaw Photographic Studios, Inc. (Photographic) which issued 100 shares of common stock to each of the ten shareholders. At the same time, Studios transferred its operating assets (but not the adverse lease) to Photographic for $21,000. The employee-shareholders surrendered their stock in Studios. No Photographic stock was transferred to Studios or to Warsaw & Co. Photographic took the position that the transaction constituted a (D) reorganization, claiming depreciation deductions on the operating assets based on a transferred basis from Studios and utilizing Studios' net operating loss carryover deductions.]

OPINION

I. D Reorganization

Ordinarily, a corporation is a separate entity for Federal income tax purposes; its tax attributes are not combined with those of its shareholders or other corporations. One of the major exceptions to this normal rule is part of the complex of provisions relating to corporate reorganizations, in particular that part of the complex that allows a corporation to use for income tax purposes certain parts of the income tax history of another corporation.

Corporate reorganizations, as defined in one or another of the subparagraphs of section 368(a)(1), qualify for special treatment for Federal income tax purposes under certain rules. The dispute in the instant case is as to whether petitioner is entitled to the special treatment provided under two of these rules. One of these rules gives a transferee corporation a carryover basis (subject to certain adjustments) in the assets acquired from the transferor corporation. Sec. 362(b). The other of these rules allows the transferee corporation to "succeed to and take into account" certain tax attributes of the transferor, including net operating loss carryovers (the tax attribute in issue in the instant case). Secs. 381(a), 381(c).

Of the various definitions of corporate reorganization, the parties have apparently limited the controversy to whether the transaction qualifies as nondivisive D reorganization (sec. 368(a)(1)(D)); we have chosen in the instant case to adhere to the parties' view of the parameters of the controversy. * * *

In order to qualify as a nondivisive D reorganization (and thus, permit petitioner to (1) use Studios' bases for calculating depreciation, and (2) under sections 368(a)(1)(D) and 354, deduct Studios' net operating losses), the transaction in the instant case must satisfy a series of statutory requirements and also a series of judicial requirements.

Respondent contends that the transfer from Studios to petitioner does not qualify as a nondivisive D reorganization because it does not satisfy certain of the statutory and judicial requirements. Instead, respondent contends, the transfer of assets from Studios to petitioner is a sale. Respondent maintains that the transaction does not satisfy the statutory requirement that stock of the transferee corporation (i.e., petitioner) be issued and distributed in the purported reorganization. * * *

Petitioner contends that the transaction between Studios and petitioner qualifies as a nondivisive D reorganization because it satisfies all the statutory and judicial requirements. In particular, petitioner contends that the 100 shares were given as consideration for Studios' assets and that the 100 shares were worth at least $42,727, far more than the $21,000 of cash and other property transferred by petitioner to Studios. Petitioner further contends that the fact that the 100 shares were issued directly to the 10 shareholders, rather than first to Studios and then distributed from Studios to the 10 shareholders, does not mean that petitioner's stock was not distributed within the meaning of section 354(b)(1)(B). * * *

We agree with respondent that the transaction is not a D reorganization because of the failure to satisfy the statutory requirement that petitioner's stock be transferred to Studios and distributed in a transaction which qualifies under sec. 354.

In order for a transaction to be a D reorganization, the transaction must be one "which qualifies under section 354." (Sec. 368(a)(1)(D); Baan v. Commissioner, 51 T.C. 1032, 1040 (1969), affd. sub nom. Gordon v. Commissioner, 424 F.2d 378 (2d Cir.1970), affd. 450 F.2d 198 (9th Cir. 1971).) In order for petitioner to succeed to Studios' net operating losses under a D reorganization, Studios must have received stock of petitioner, and Studios must have distributed the stock it thus received (secs. 354(a)(1) and 354(b)(1)(B)). The July 2, 1973, agreement between petitioner and Studios provides * * * that, as part of the consideration flowing from petitioner to Studios, "The Buyer is hereby issuing 10 shares of Common Stock, $.05 par value, of the Buyer to each of the shareholders of the Seller other than Warsaw & Co., Inc. who are the only shareholders of the Buyer." There was not literally a transfer of petitioner's stock from petitioner to Studios and a distribution of this stock by Studios to Studios' shareholders. Accordingly, we conclude that the statute's formal requirements have not been met in this regard.

It is true that "we have repeatedly held that, when the stock ownership of transferor and transferee is identical, the actual distribution would be a mere formality and the statute [sec. 368(a)(1)(D)] may be satisfied without it. See American Manufacturing Co. v. Commissioner, 55 T.C. 204, 221 (1970); James Armour, Inc. v. Commissioner, 43 T.C. 295, 307 (1964)." Atlas Tool Co. v. Commissioner, 70 T.C. 86, 97 (1978), affd. 614 F.2d 860, 865 (3d Cir.1980). * * * However, in the instant case, the stock ownerships of petitioner and Studios were not identical. Warsaw & Co., Inc., which owned about 80 percent of Studios' common stock and all of Studios' preferred stock, was not a shareholder in petitioner. The 10 shareholders, each holding 10 percent of petitioner's shares, had differing holdings in Studios. These holdings ranged from Zad's 375 shares down to Sinn's 92 shares. Indeed, apart from Shawn and Neil (each holding 250 shares), none of the 10 shareholders held the same number of Studios' shares as any of the others among the 10 shareholders * * * even though all were equal shareholders in petitioner.

Thus, the instant case does not qualify for the one exception that the courts have created regarding the stock transfer and distribution rule. Compliance with this rule is essential for the net operating loss carryover benefit sought by petitioner (secs. 381(a)(2) and 354(b)(1)(B)) and the carryover basis benefit sought by petitioner (secs. 362(b), 368(a)(1)(D), 354(b)(1)(B)). Accordingly, we conclude that petitioner is entitled to use neither of the tax benefits it seeks to carry over from Studios.

On brief, petitioner makes the following contention regarding the stock transfer and distribution requirement:

> Code section 354(b)(1)(B) requires that all properties of the transferor corporation must be distributed in pursuance of the plan of reorganization. This provision is satisfied whenever, pursuant to the plan of reorganization, the shareholders of the transferor receive shares of the transferee sufficient to satisfy the control requirements of Code section 368(a)(1)(D). A direct issuance of shares of the transferee corporation to shareholders of the transferor corporation will suffice. An actual exchange of the transferor corporation's assets for shares of the transferee corporation, followed by a distribution of those shares to the transferor corporation's shareholders is not required. See Commissioner v. Morgan, 288 F.2d 676 (3d Cir.[1961]), cert. denied, 368 U.S. 836 (1961). Accord, South Texas Rice Warehouse Co., 43 T.C. 540 (1965), aff'd sub nom., Davant v. Commissioner, 366 F.2d 874 (5th Cir.1966). * * *.
>
> * * *. Where as in the case at bar the acquiring corporation issues stock directly to the shareholders of the transferor corporation in consideration of the assets received from the transferor corporation, the transfer is treated as if the shares were first issued to the transferor corporation and then distributed in redemption of the outstanding shares of the transferor corporation.

We believe petitioner's reliance on the cases it cites is misplaced.

In Commissioner v. Morgan, 288 F.2d 676 (3d Cir.1961), the Court of Appeals for the Third Circuit reversed this Court (Morgan v. Commissioner, 33 T.C. 30 (1959)), holding that an actual transfer and distribution of the transferee corporation's stock "would have been a meaningless gesture" in that case, since one individual held all the stock in both the transferor corporation and the transferee corporation (288 F.2d at 680, see 33 T.C. at 32). In South Texas Rice Warehouse Co. v. Commissioner, 43 T.C. 540 (1965), we rejected the taxpayers' contention that a transaction did not qualify as a D reorganization because no stock was transferred and distributed. In that case, each of the 14 individuals who were the shareholders held the same percentage of the transferor corporation's stock as he or she held in the transferee corporation. (43 T.C. at 544.) The Court of Appeals for the Fifth Circuit noted the identity of ownership, followed the rationale of *Morgan,* and affirmed on this point. (Davant v. Commissioner, 366 F.2d 874, 886–887.) * * *

All of these authorities on which petitioner relies are distinguishable from the instant case in that the transferors and transferees in those instances had identical ownership, while in the instant case, the ownership interests in petitioner and Studios differed widely. Further, in each of these cases in which a court has held that the requirement of an actual stock transfer and distribution may be ignored, it was respondent who urged on the court that the realities of the situation belied the form chosen by the taxpayer. In those situations where the courts have departed from the literal language of the statute, it was to counter a perceived abuse by the taxpayer, these courts having concluded that the taxpayer should not be permitted to shape the form of the transaction so as to secure an unwarranted benefit. * * * We have not found, and petitioner has not cited us to, any case in this area in which the court has acceded to a taxpayer's urging that the taxpayer be permitted to obtain a D reorganization tax benefit even though the form of the transaction which the taxpayer shaped did not meet the literal requirements of the statute.

Petitioner contends that the "transaction in form and in substance qualified as a reorganization described in Code section 368(a)(1)(D)". * * *

When we examine the substance of what was done, we conclude that it points toward "sale" at least as much as toward "reorganization". Ten people put up an aggregate of $100,000 to acquire and bankroll a going business. The business had suffered substantial losses. The 10 shareholders trimmed the work force and avoided the burdens of an unfavorable lease, and apparently succeeded in reviving the business. The 10 shareholders had owned about 20 percent of the old corporation's common stock and none of its preferred. If they had purchased the remaining common stock or a controlling interest, then (as petitioner notes on brief) the corporation's tax characteristics would not be affected by the substance of the change in ownership and control. Apparently, for a legitimate business reason (escaping from the burdens of the 34th Street lease), the 10 shareholders specifically turned down an opportunity to buy the old corporation, thus turning down the simple route toward retention of the old corporation's tax attributes.

If the 10 shareholders (or petitioner, their new corporation) had merely purchased Studios' assets, then the transaction would be a sale, the normal tax rules would apply (i.e., petitioner would not be entitled to use Studios' tax attributes) even though petitioner carried on the business that Studios had carried on and did so with essentially the same work force at the "same old stand."

What, in these circumstances, is the matter of substance that distinguishes the transaction from a sale? Petitioner contends that the issuance of the 100 shares is an element of substance that (1) enables the transaction to satisfy the statutory requirement of stock distribution, (2) enables the transaction to satisfy the judicial requirement that its stock be a substantial part of the consideration given by it * * *. In connection with the latter [point], petitioner contends that the 100 shares were worth $349,000.

After examining the transaction with care in light of petitioner's contentions, we note the following:

Firstly, the 100 shares effected no change, not even a subtle one, in the positions of the 10 shareholders. Each of the 10 shareholders merely had one extra piece of paper. See Eisner v. Macomber, 252 U.S. 189 (1920). None involved in the transaction—not petitioner, Studios, the 10 shareholders, Warsaw & Co., Inc., or J.J. Warsaw—were any richer or any poorer on account of the issuance of the 100 shares, than they would have been if no shares were issued or if 1 million shares were issued.

Secondly, care was taken to be sure that the 100 shares were not held by Studios at any time. This element is of some significance because Studios made a general assignment for the benefit of creditors only 3 weeks after the transaction in dispute, and the assignee was not able to find assets to make any payments to the creditors.

Thirdly, although the 100 shares were supposed to be issued to the 10 shareholders in their capacities as Studios' shareholders, they were issued * * * in proportion to the 10 shareholders' ownership of petitioner and not in proportion to the 10 shareholders' ownership of Studios.

Fourthly, petitioner contends that the 100 shares were worth a total of $349,000, while at the same time the initial 1,000 shares were worth a total of $100,000. The contentions, as to identical shares issued virtually simultaneously, are manifestly inconsistent. We are not given any hint as to why the 100 shares would be worth $3,490, each, while the 1,000 shares were worth $100, each.

On answering brief, petitioner tells us that "Taxation is a practical art; labels will not replace or substitute for judgment as to the roles played by the parties and whether or not those roles were acted out in such a way as to effect a reorganization described by the Internal Revenue Code". We agree. We conclude that, as a practical matter, the appearance of the 100 shares in the transaction provides only a smell of reorganization. We will not speculate as to why the July 2, 1973, agreement provided for the issuance of the 100 shares in such a manner that their issuance satisfies neither the form nor the substance of section 368(a)(1)(D). We conclude that the 100 shares did not constitute any part of petitioner's consideration for the assets, tangible or intangible, that petitioner received from Studios. * * *

To sum up: petitioner is not entitled to use Studios' bases for depreciation of assets and is not entitled to deduct Studios' net operating losses unless petitioner shows that it has complied with the requirements of a D reorganization. Baan v. Commissioner, supra. See also Corn Products Co. v. Commissioner, 350 U.S. 46, 52 (1955), where, in another context, the Supreme Court stated that "an exception from the normal tax requirements of the Internal Revenue Code, * * * must be narrowly applied and its exclusions interpreted broadly." Petitioner acknowledges that the transaction failed to comply with one of the requirements of the statute, but seeks to excuse this failure by citing certain authorities. Those authorities rest on circumstances (identical ownership of the corporations that are parties to the reorganization) which are materially different from the facts of the instant case. Atlas Tool Co. v. Commissioner, supra; Baan v. Commissioner, 51 T.C. at 1038–1039. There was no substance to the issuance of the 100 shares. Petitioner cannot escape from the failure of the transaction to comply with the statute. Petitioner is not entitled to the tax benefits of another corporation's bases and net operating losses.

We hold for respondent on this issue.

ILLUSTRATIVE MATERIAL

A. DEFINITIONAL PROBLEMS

A transaction meeting the definition of a type (D) reorganization also may meet the definition of a type (C) reorganization, discussed at page 607. Suppose that X Corporation owns all of the stock of both Y Corporation and Z Corporation. If Z Corporation transfers all of its assets to Y Corporation for Y stock and then liquidates, the transaction meets the definitions of both a (C) and a (D) reorganization. In such a case, § 368(a)(2)(A) requires that the transaction be treated as a type (D) reorganization. As discussed in *Warsaw Photographic,* the asset transfer from Z to Y would be classified as a (D) reorganization even if no additional Y Corporation stock were issued since X would own 100 percent of Y in any event. As a consequence, Y succeeds to Z's tax attributes under § 381. An overlap between a type (D) and type (F) reorganization results in classification as a type (F). Rev.Rul. 57–276, 1957–1 C.B. 126; Rev.Rul. 87–27, 1987–1 C.B. 134 (reincorporation of domestic corporation in foreign country which is both a type (F) and type (D) reorganization is treated as type (F)); Rev.Rul. 87–66, 1987–2 C.B. 168 (reincorporation of foreign corporation in U.S. which is both a type (D) and a type (F) reorganization treated as a type (F)).

Suppose that X Corporation owns 50 percent of the stock of Y Corporation and 100 percent of the stock of Z Corporation, and that Z Corporation owns the other 50 percent of the stock of Y Corporation. If Y Corporation transfers all of its assets to Z Corporation in exchange for Z stock, which is distributed equally to X Corporation and Z Corporation in liquidation of Y, is the transaction a (D) reorganization or does the *Bausch & Lomb* doctrine, which applies in type (C) reorganizations, see page 613, apply to treat Z Corporation as having received 50 percent of Y's assets in liquidation rather than in exchange for its stock, thereby violating the "substantially all" requirement. Rev.Rul. 85–107, 1985–2 C.B. 121, held that the *Bausch & Lomb* doctrine will not be applied to a reorganization which otherwise qualifies as a type (D) reorganization because there is no "solely for voting stock" requirement applicable to type (D) reorganizations.

B. LIQUIDATION–REINCORPORATION TRANSACTIONS AND THE (D) REORGANIZATION PROVISIONS

1. *Background*

Historically, the nondivisive (D) reorganization provision was used principally by the Commissioner as a weapon to attack the liquidation-reincorporation transactions, described at page 663, in connection with (F) reorganizations. Indeed, the definition of "control" for purposes of (D) reorganizations subject to § 354 is reduced from the 80 percent benchmark in § 368(c) to 50 percent (§ 368(a)(2)(H)) to make it easier to fit liquidation-reincorporation transactions under the (D) reorganization definition when there is a change in the shareholder ownership between the "new" and "old" corporations. See S.Rep. No. 98–169, 98th Cong., 2d Sess. 207–209 (1984)

In general, the courts were quite liberal in interpreting the (D) reorganization requirements in order to find a reorganization with an accompanying dividend to block the tax avoidance possibilities in the liquidation-reincorporation situations. In testing whether "substantially all" the assets have been transferred, as is required by § 354(b)(1)(A), the focus has been on the operating assets of the corporation. See, e.g., Smothers v. United States, 642 F.2d 894 (5th Cir.1981):

"To maintain the integrity of the dividend provisions of the Code, 'substantially all assets' in this context must be interpreted as an inartistic way of expressing the concept of 'transfer of a continuing business.' * * * Properly interpreted, therefore, the assets looked to when making the 'substantially all assets' determination should be all the assets, and only the assets, necessary to operate the corporate business—whether or not those assets would appear on a corporate balance sheet. * * * Inclusion of assets unnecessary to the operation of the business in the 'substantially all assets' assessment would open the way for the shareholders of any enterprise to turn dividends into capital gains at will. * * * [E]xclusion of assets not shown on a balance sheet * * * would offer an unjustified windfall to owners of service businesses conducted in the corporate form. The most important assets of such a business may be its reputation and the availability of skilled management and trained employees * * *. [F]or example a sole legal practitioner who owns nothing but a desk and chair could incorporate himself, accumulate earnings, and then set up a new corporation and liquidate the old at capital gain rates—as long as he is careful to buy a new desk and chair for the new corporation, rather than transferring the old." (901)

2. *Control and Continuity of Interest*

The requirement that the transferor corporation or its shareholders be in control of the transferee corporation after the transfer has been strictly construed. For example, in Breech v. United States, 439 F.2d 409 (9th Cir.1971), a corporation sold all of its assets to a second corporation the stock of which was owned 20 percent by one of its shareholders and 80 percent by a third corporation in which its shareholders had a 75 percent interest. The court refused to ignore the separate existence of the third corporation or to apply the attribution rules in § 318 (which by their terms did not then apply) to find control of the transferee in the shareholders of the transferor. Hence a (D) reorganization was not present. A similar result was reached in Commissioner v. Berghash 361 F.2d 257 (2d Cir.1966). Section 368(a)(2)(H) now incorporates the attribution rules of § 318 for purposes of determining controlling stock ownership.

Can the "functionally unrelated" concept be applied to "disaggregate" a transaction in order to create a reorganization in which the continuity of interest requirement has been met? Suppose for example that X Corporation transfers its operating assets to Y Corporation in exchange for Y Corporation stock. Y Corporation is controlled by a group of X Corporation shareholders who own less than 50 percent of the X stock. X Corporation then liquidates, distributing the Y Corporation stock to its shareholders who control Y and liquid assets to its shareholders who do not own Y stock. Could this be treated as a (D) reorganization and a separate redemption of the stock owned by the shareholders who received the liquid assets? A type (D) (or an (F)) reorganization could be present since, under this analysis, there would be no change in the continuing shareholders of the corporation.

As in the (F) reorganization area, the Commissioner attempted to fit liquidation-reorganization transactions into the (D) reorganization definition by considering pieces of the transaction which might defeat reorganization treatment as "functionally unrelated" to the reorganization. Reef Corporation v. Commissioner, 368 F.2d 125 (5th Cir.1966), discussed at page 662, upheld the Commissioner in finding a (D) reorganization (as well as an (F) reorganization) coupled with a redemption in a series of transactions having substantially the same result as described above, where the continuing shareholders held 52 percent of the old corporation's stock at a time when the control test for type (D) reorganizations was 80 percent, not 50 percent as it now is. Other cases hesitated to separate related transactions in order to find a reorganization. Thus, in Commissioner v. Berghash, 361 F.2d 257 (2d Cir.1966), the sole shareholder of a corporation agreed to transfer to a corporate employee a 50 percent ownership in the business which the employee demanded as a condition of his continued employment. The employee was willing to invest $25,000 in the business but, because of the size of the business, this would not have entitled him to a 50 percent interest. Accordingly, the corporation was liquidated and its operating assets transferred to a new corporation in exchange for notes and 50 percent of the stock. The additional 50 percent of the stock was issued to the employee for cash. The old shareholder treated the transaction as a liquidation entitled to capital gain treatment under § 331. The Government argued that the sale of stock to the employee should be disregarded as an "unrelated step" and thus the transaction would fit the pattern of a (D) or an (F) reorganization and an accompanying boot distribution under § 356. The Tax Court, however, finding the sale a "critical fact" in evaluating the transaction, refused to find a reorganization and a boot distribution, and the Court of Appeals affirmed.

CHAPTER 15

CORPORATE DIVISIONS: SPIN-OFFS, SPLIT-OFFS, AND SPLIT-UPS

SECTION 1. CORPORATE DIVISIONS: GENERAL RULES

INTERNAL REVENUE CODE: Sections 355; 368(a)(1)(D), (2)(A), (2)(H)(ii); 354(b); 356(b); 358; 312(h).

REGULATIONS: Sections 1.355–1 to–4; 1.356–3(b).

In contrast to provisions for acquisitive reorganizations, which allow the merger or consolidation of separate corporate entities, § 355 provides nonrecognition treatment for the division of a corporation's existing trades or business into separate corporate entities owned by the shareholders. A divisive transaction under § 355 may take one of three forms—

1. *Spin-Off.* A spin-off occurs when a corporation transfers assets to a subsidiary and distributes the stock of the subsidiary pro rata to its stockholders (a type (D) reorganization), or distributes the stock of an existing subsidiary to its stockholders pro rata. Thus, X Corporation, conducting businesses A and B, may divide by transferring business B to a newly formed subsidiary, Y Corporation, and then distributing the stock of Y Corporation pro rata to the stockholders of X Corporation. The same division may be undertaken by a corporation operating a single business that is capable of division into two separate independently functioning trades or businesses. X Corporation divides its single business into two parts by transferring some of its assets to Y Corporation which, following the transaction, is also actively engaged in the conduct of a trade or business. X Corporation then distributes all of the stock of Y Corporation to the X Corporation stockholders. Alternatively, X Corporation, which conducts business A, may already own all of the stock of Y Corporation, which conducts business B. For valid business reasons X Corporation may spin-off Y Corporation by distributing the Y corporation stock to its stockholders.

2. *Split-off.* In a split-off, the distributing corporation distributes the stock of a subsidiary to its stockholders in exchange for a portion of the outstanding stock of the distributing corporation. For example, X Corporation, conducting business A, owns the stock of Y Corporation, which conducts business B. X Corporation distributes the stock of Y Corporation to the stockholders of X Corporation in exchange for X Corporation stock. While this transaction does not involve a reorganization of either X Corporation or Y Corporation, the ownership of each corporation is changed as a result of the exchange. Alternatively, X Corporation, which conducts both business A and business B, might transfer business B to newly formed Y Corporation and then distribute the Y Corporation stock to

its stockholders in exchange for a portion of its own outstanding stock (a type D reorganization). A split-off distribution that results in a pro rata exchange of stock among the stockholders of the distributing corporation is functionally equivalent to a "spin-off". A non-pro rata split-off, however, results in a change in proportionate ownership of both businesses.

3. *Split-Up.* In a split-up the original corporation transfers a separate trade or business to each of two or more subsidiaries. The distributing corporation then transfers the stock of the subsidiaries to its stockholders and liquidates. Each separate trade or business, still in corporate solution, may be distributed to different stockholders. Thus, X Corporation, which owns businesses A and B, transfers business A to a new Y Corporation and business B to a new Z Corporation. X Corporation then liquidates distributing the stock of Y to one group of X stockholders, and the stock of Z to the other group of X stockholders.

As noted above, each of these divisive transactions may involve as the initial step a transfer of a trade or business to a new subsidiary followed by a distribution of the subsidiary's stock to stockholders. A divisive transaction that involves the reorganization of the corporate structure is a type (D) reorganization. To qualify as a reorganization under § 368(a)(1)(D), the distribution to stockholders must comply with § 355, the pivotal section in the treatment of transactions seeking to accomplish a corporate division. In addition to providing nonrecognition to both the distributing corporation and its shareholders for corporate divisions following a type (D) reorganization, § 355(a)(1) also provides nonrecognition treatment to both the distributing corporation and the recipient stockholders in a division of an existing parent-subsidiary group that does not involve a corporate reorganization.

The essence of a § 355 division is the separate ownership at the stockholder level of the corporate businesses. In many cases the businesses already are divided or separated prior to the distribution to the stockholders. In the first example of a spin-off, businesses A and B could have been conducted as separate branches or divisions of X Corporation; in the third example they were conducted separately through parent-subsidiary operation. X Corporation in the first example could separate the businesses simply by placing business B in new Y Corporation under § 351 and operating it as a subsidiary. If the desired separation is a degree of insulation of one business from the other, it will be accomplished through parent-subsidiary operation. Section 355 entails to a different type of separation, that of separate ownership at the stockholder level.

The separate ownership at the stockholder level may be pro rata or non-pro rata. Thus, § 355 applies to very different divisions of corporate ownership. Suppose X Corporation is owned by individuals C and D. If X Corporation distributes the stock of its subsidiary Y Corporation pro rata in a spin-off, each individual stockholder now owns what the stockholder owned before—a one-half interest in each business—but the stockholders have separated the form of ownership. X and Y Corporations have been transmuted from a parent-subsidiary group to brother-sister corporations. If the distribution of the Y Corporation stock is completely non-pro rata, as where stockholder D surrenders his stock in X Corporation for all the stock of Y Corporation in a split-off, then a complete division of ownership has been accomplished at the stockholder level in addition to the division at the corporate level. The corporations are no longer related in any way, assuming there is no family or other special relationship between C and D.

A pro rata corporate division into brother-sister corporations presents the potential for a bail-out of corporate profits taxable to the stockholders at capital gains rates. Thus, in the examples above, if the stockholders of X and Y Corporations sell the stock of Y Corporation, they end up with stock of X Corporation and cash taxed at capital gain rates. This situation, it will be recalled, is also the end result of a "preferred stock bail-out" or a "security bail-out." The limitations on divisive transactions contained in § 355 are intended to insure that the tax-free corporate division privilege is not abused as a bail-out of corporate earnings.

The tax stakes for the distributee shareholders in a corporate division are whether they receive a current taxable dividend equal to the fair market value of the stock received or a distribution of stock on which tax is deferred until recognition as capital gain on a subsequent sale. Qualification under § 355 thus provides the dual advantage of the deferral of tax until the distributed stock is disposed of in a taxable transaction and recognition of gain at preferential capital gain rates at the time of sale. In addition, gain realized on the sale will be reduced by some portion of original basis in the stock of the distributing corporation. With respect to the distributing corporation, the tax issue is whether the spun-off stock can be distributed without recognition of gain by the corporation under § 311.

Most of the statutory pattern for qualifying a division as a tax-free transaction can be understood in terms of its attempt to prevent the bail-out of corporate earnings as capital gains. These safeguards are found in both § 355 itself and in other sections governing corporate reorganizations.

With respect to § 355:

1. The transaction must not be used principally as a *device* for the distribution of the earnings and profits of either of the corporations. I.R.C. § 355(a)(1)(B).

2. To prevent the isolation of cash or passive investments into a separate corporation with its potential for ready sale, each corporation after the division must be operating an active trade or business. In addition, to prevent either the distributing corporation or the controlled corporation from utilizing accumulated earnings to acquire the active business, the active businesses must have been operated for five years preceding the distribution and must not have been acquired in a taxable transaction within the five year period. I.R.C. § 355(a)(1)(C), (b).

3. All of the stock and securities which the parent owns in the controlled corporation being separated must be distributed to the stockholders (or at least 80 percent of the stock of the controlled corporation if retention of the balance of stock and securities can be justified). I.R.C. § 355(a)(1)(D). This requirement was originally designed to differentiate

between genuine separations and incidental distributions of a controlled corporation's stock which took the place of current cash dividends. If, in addition, boot is distributed, § 356 applies and the distribution may be taxed as a dividend to the extent of the boot under the principles discussed at page 565. The distributing corporation also must recognize gain with respect to appreciated property distributed as boot. § 355(c). Further, the distributing corporation is required to recognize gain on the distribution of stock of the controlled corporation to a person who, by virtue of an acquisition by purchase of the stock of either the distributing or the controlled corporation within the five year period ending on the date of the distribution, holds a 50 percent or greater interest in either the distributing corporation or the controlled corporation. § 355(d). This requirement is aimed at preventing a transfer of ownership of the distributed corporation that avoids corporate level recognition of gain on the disposition.

4. A "security bail-out" is not permitted as part of a corporate division, and rules similar to § 354(a)(2), page 649, are utilized to treat the excess principal amount of securities received over the principal amount of securities surrendered as boot. I.R.C. §§ 355(a)(3), (a)(4)(A); 356(b), (d)(2)(C).

With respect to the reorganization provisions generally:

A reorganization transaction which has the potential of a corporate division, must, if reorganization status is desired, either:

1. comply with the requirement of § 354(b)(1)(A) that substantially all of the assets of the distributing corporation be transferred to the controlled corporation so as to eliminate the effect of a division (see page 664), or

2. be channeled into § 355 so that the resulting division is tested by the rules of that section.

Thus, the attempt is to provide unified treatment of corporate divisions regardless of the form of the transaction.

This plan explains the addition of the last clause in § 368(a)(1)(D), which requires that a corporation forming a controlled subsidiary must, to qualify as a reorganization, distribute the stock of the subsidiary to its stockholders in a transaction qualifying under §§ 354 or 355 (and 356). The reference to § 355 thus brings into play the tests for qualifying corporate divisions. The reference to § 354 brings into play § 354(b), which makes § 354 inapplicable unless substantially all the assets are transferred and the transferor liquidates. As a result, a transfer that divides the distributing corporation cannot qualify under § 354. If the requirements of § 354(b) are not met, as where only some of the assets are transferred or where the transferor does not liquidate, then a corporate division is present since the stockholders will now own stock in the old and the new corporations. Section 354(a) is not applicable, and the exchange with the stockholders is thrown into § 355 to see if it meets the corporate division tests.[1]

1. Section 368(a)(2)(A) is intended to prevent a transaction which otherwise would fit the definition of both a type (C) and a type (D) reorganization, as in the case of the

The "device" restriction of § 355 is intended to prevent the bail-out of corporate earnings at capital gains rates rather than as a dividend.[2] The limitations of § 355 may also have a role in ensuring that a corporate division is not used to avoid corporate level tax on appreciated assets that would be otherwise recognized under § 311 or § 336. A corporate division permits the transfer of stock to the distributee stockholders without recognition of gain by either the distributing corporation or the stockholders. The business purpose test and continuity of interest requirements inherent in the "device" clause may serve to identify corporate reorganizations that are appropriate transactions for this nonrecognition treatment. In this connection, compare the direct distribution of a corporate trade or business in partial liquidation under § 302(b)(4) and (e), discussed at page 260. These sections require recognition of gain by the corporation on distribution of appreciated assets under § 311 and a second level recognition by the distributee stockholders of capital gain on the distribution. However, an economically similar transaction that meets the requirements of § 355 can be completed on a tax-free basis. As is the case with acquisitive reorganizations, nonrecognition and carryover basis are justified, if at all, by the stockholders' continued ownership of assets in corporate solution.

ILLUSTRATIVE MATERIAL

A. SCOPE OF SECTION 355

Under Treas.Reg. § 1.355–4, § 355 does not apply to transactions that are in effect exchanges of interests between stockholders of brother-sister corporations. Thus, assume that A and B each own 50 percent of the stock of X and Y Corporations. A and B transfer their stock to a newly created Z

transfer of substantially all the assets to a controlled subsidiary, from escaping the requirements regarding corporate divisions by being treated as a type (C) reorganization. Although the subsequent enactment of § 368(a)(2)(G) requiring complete liquidation of the target corporation in a type (C) reorganization precludes the use of a type (C) reorganization as a divisive transaction, any overlap possibility is intended to be eliminated by exclusively regarding the transaction as a type (D) reorganization, so that the mechanisms described above to channel the reorganization into § 355 are operative. If a corporation desires to transfer some of its assets in a tax-free transaction to a controlled subsidiary and retain the stock of the latter, it therefore cannot proceed under the reorganization provisions, but it can proceed under § 351, which does not require distribution of the transferee's stock to the stockholders of the transferor. Also, see Rev. Rul. 74–545, 1974–2 C.B. 122 (a transaction may be one that is described in § 368(a)(1)(D) and thus subject to the requirements of that section even though it does not satisfy all of the requirements for nonrecognition as a type (D) reorganization).

2. The term "bail-out" is something of a misnomer because the combined earnings and profits of the distributing and distributed corporations are the same as they were before the transaction. It would be more appropriate to refer to the problem as a "conversion" issue, i.e., converting cash received by the recipient shareholders on a subsequent sale of the distributed stock into capital gain from ordinary income if cash had been paid as a dividend by the distributing corporation. Nonetheless, the term "bail-out" is so deeply entrenched in the tax jargon that the term is used here.

Corporation in a transaction to which § 351 applies. In a split-up, Z Corporation then distributes the stock of X Corporation to A and the stock of Y Corporation to B. As a result, A owns all the stock of X Corporation and B owns all the stock of Y Corporation. In effect, A and B have made a taxable exchange of their 50 percent interests in X and Y Corporations and the transaction will not qualify under § 355.

In Portland Mfg. Co. v. Commissioner, 56 T.C. 58 (1971) (A), aff'd by order, 75–1 U.S.T.C. ¶ 9449 (9th Cir.1975), two corporations each owned 50 percent of a third corporation and 50 percent of a joint venture. Because of disagreements between the two corporations, the mechanics of a tax-free split-off under § 355 were implemented at the conclusion of which one corporation owned all the stock of the third corporation. The court upheld the Commissioner's treatment of the transaction as a taxable exchange. A similar result was reached in Atlee v. Commissioner, 67 T.C. 395 (1976) (A), where the taxpayers sought to avoid having the transaction characterized as a taxable exchange by making pre-spin-off contributions to capital.

B. THE "CONTROL" REQUIREMENT OF § 355(a)(1)(A)

Two different "control" tests are relevant in determining the status of divisive transactions. First, immediately prior to the distribution, the distributing corporation must have "control," as defined in § 368(c), of the corporation whose stock is being distributed. I.R.C. § 355(a)(1)(A). Pre-distribution transfers to the distributing corporation solely for the purpose of giving it the requisite 80 percent stock ownership under § 368(c) may be disregarded. In Rev.Rul. 63–260, 1963–2 C.B. 147, the sole stockholder of a corporation, which owned 70 percent of the stock of a subsidiary, transferred an additional 10 percent of the subsidiary stock to the parent corporation which then spun off the subsidiary shares to the sole stockholder. The Ruling held that § 355 was inapplicable because the distributing corporation did not have "control" except in a "transitory and illusory sense."

But if there is greater economic reality to the transaction in which the distributing corporation obtains control, then § 355 treatment is allowed. Rev.Rul. 69–407, 1969–2 C.B. 50, involved a situation in which X Corporation owned 70 percent of the stock of Y Corporation and A and B, two individuals, owned the remaining 30 percent. In an (E) recapitalization, two classes of voting stock were created, A and B receiving shares of one class and X Corporation receiving the other class. The relative values of the interests of X Corporation, A, and B did not change, but after the recapitalization, X Corporation held over 80 percent of the total voting power. X Corporation then distributed the Y Corporation stock to its stockholders. The Ruling held that the transaction constituted a valid (E) recapitalization followed by a § 355 distribution; the recapitalization resulted in a permanent realignment of voting control and hence Rev.Rul. 63–260 was distinguishable. See also Rev.Rul. 71–593, 1971–2 C.B. 181, in which a transfer of additional assets to a 75 percent owned subsidiary in exchange for sufficient stock to give the parent 90 percent control, followed by a spin-off of the subsidiary's stock, was held to constitute a "meaningful exchange" and § 355 was applicable. In Rev.Rul. 70–18, 1970–1 C.B. 74, A, an individual, owned 100 percent of the stock of X and Y Corporations. In turn Y Corporation owned 60 percent of Z Corporation and X Corporation owned 40 percent of Z Corporation. X Corporation was required by a regulatory agency to divest itself of its Z stock. Y Corporation merged into X Corporation and X Corporation then distributed all of the Z stock to A. The Ruling held that there were substantial business reasons for the merger other than giving X Corporation control of Z Corporation for the purposes of a spin-off and the transaction qualified under § 355.

In Rev.Rul. 77–11, 1977–1 C.B. 93, A and B each owned 50 percent of the stock of X and Y Corporations, each of which was engaged in the construction business. The parties desired B to be the sole owner of a corporation engaged in the construction business. X and Y Corporations each contributed one-half of their assets to Z Corporation in exchange for Z stock, with X receiving 84 percent of the Z stock and Y 16 percent. X then distributed all the Z stock to B for B's X stock and Y distributed all its Z stock to B for B's Y stock. As a result, A owned all the stock of X and Y, and B owned all the stock of Z. The Ruling held: (1) The transfers by X and Y to Z followed by the distribution of the Z stock constituted a valid § 351 transaction and a good (D) reorganization; (2) the distribution of Z stock by X to B qualified under § 355 because before the distribution X had the requisite control over Z (the predecessor to Treas.Reg. § 1.355–4, did not require treatment of the transaction as a taxable exchange because Z received operating assets and A remained as a stockholder in X and Y); and (3) the distribution of Z stock by Y to B did not qualify under § 355 because Y owned less than 80 percent of the Z stock before the distribution; this aspect of the transaction was treated as a redemption under § 302 which qualified for capital gain treatment under § 302(b)(3).

The second control test is imposed by § 355(a)(1)(D), which requires that the distributing corporation distribute to its shareholders no less than a controlling interest, as defined in § 368(c), in the subsidiary. This requirement is discussed in Section 3.

C. BOOT IN A SECTION 355 TRANSACTION

1. *Distributions of Cash or Other Property*

The shareholder nonrecognition rule of § 355(a) is limited to the distribution of stock or securities of the controlled corporation, or the exchange of stock or securities solely for stock or securities of the controlled corporation. However, § 356 allows for the receipt of cash or other property (including the receipt of securities in excess of the securities transferred) with the recognition of gain to the extent of the boot. Section 356(a)(2) provides for ordinary income treatment of recognized gain to the extent of the distributee's pro rata share of earnings and profits if the distribution is essentially equivalent to a dividend. In Rev.Rul. 74–516, 1974–2 C.B. 121, the Internal Revenue Service ruled that a distribution of boot in a § 355 transaction is tested for dividend equivalency under § 302 as if the boot were distributed prior to the divisive transaction in redemption of an amount of stock of the distributing corporation equal to the value of the boot. As a consequence, a pro rata distribution of boot to the stockholders of the distributing corporation will result in dividend treatment whenever the distributing corporation has sufficient earnings and profits. In Rev.Rul. 93–62, 1993–2 C.B. 118, which supersedes Rev.Rul. 74–515, the Service indicated that the result of Rev.Rul. 74–516 is not changed by the holding of *Commissioner v. Clark*, 489 U.S. 726 (1989), page 565. *Clark* held that in an acquisitive reorganization dividend status is tested under § 356(a)(2) by hypothesizing a *post-reorganization* redemption of an amount of stock of the distributing corporation equal to the fair market value of the boot.

2. *Stock of the Controlled Corporation as Boot*

Section 355(a)(3)(B) provides that stock of the controlled corporation which has been acquired by the distributing corporation in a taxable transaction within the five year period preceding distribution to stockholders will be treated as other property taxable to the stockholders as boot.

Trust of E.L. Dunn v. Commissioner, 86 T.C. 745 (1986) (A in result), narrowly interpreted the meaning of "acquired" in a taxable transaction. In a taxable reverse triangular merger consummated on May 12, 1982, AT&T acquired all of the stock of Pacific Telephone and Telegraph with the exception of nonvoting preferred stock held by institutional investors. Following this transaction, AT&T owned the only share of Pacific common stock outstanding. The reverse triangular merger was a taxable transaction because, by virtue of the outstanding nonvoting preferred stock, AT&T did not meet the control requirement of § 368(c). On August 24, 1982, a long standing antitrust action between AT&T and the United States government was settled with a judicially approved agreement that AT&T would divest itself of each of its regional telephone operating companies, including Pacific. At that time, AT&T was the common parent of a group of corporations known as the Bell System. The divestiture plan required AT&T to group its 22 operating companies into seven regional holding companies. The stock of the regional holding companies was distributed to AT&T stockholders pro rata. As part of this plan, Pacific was reorganized under § 368(a)(1)(E) to convert the single share of Pacific stock held by AT&T into 224,504,982 shares of voting common stock (the number of shares outstanding before AT&T's taxable reorganization of Pacific) and to convert the nonvoting preferred stock into voting preferred stock. By virtue of this transaction the holding company to which Pacific was transferred, the PacTel Group, would acquire control of Pacific within the meaning of § 368(c). AT&T transferred its Pacific stock along with other assets to the PacTel Group in exchange for all of the stock of the PacTel Group which was then distributed to AT&T stockholders in the divestiture.

The Commissioner asserted that the receipt of PacTel Group stock was taxable in part to the AT&T stockholders as a dividend under § 355(a)(3)(B) because a portion of the value of the PacTel Group stock represented the stock of Pacific that was acquired by AT&T in a taxable merger within five years of the distribution. The Tax Court rejected the Commissioner's argument and held that the distribution was completely tax free to the AT&T stockholders. The court read § 355(a)(3)(B) literally, concluding that the provision applied only to the stock of the controlled corporation that is distributed to the stockholders of the distributing corporation. The controlled corporation is the corporation that the distributing corporation controls immediately before the distribution. The Tax Court refused to look through the controlled corporation, in this case the PacTel Group, to examine the stock of its subsidiaries for purposes of applying the boot rule of § 355(a)(3)(B). The court reasoned in part that since Congress carefully provided a look-through rule for purposes of identifying under § 355(b)(2)(D) whether a trade or business had been acquired "directly (or through 1 or more corporations)" in a taxable transaction by the controlled corporation, Congress would have specifically provided a similar look-through rule in subdivision (a)(3)(B) if it had intended such a rule to be applied.

D. EXCHANGES OF OPTIONS TO PURCHASE STOCK OF DISTRIBUTING AND CONTROLLED CORPORATION

Treas. Regs. §§ 1.355–1(c) and 1.356–3(b) treat rights to acquire stock of a corporation (options and warrants) issued by either the distributing corporation or the controlled corporation as securities of the respective corporations having no principal amount. The term "rights to acquire stock" of an issuing corporation has the same meaning for purposes of §§ 355 and 356 as for purposes of §§ 305(d)(1) and 317(a). Accordingly, as long as the other requirements of § 355, particularly the "distribution" of stock constituting "control" of the distributed corporation, have been met, the recipient of stock rights in either corporation is not required to recognize gain under § 356(d)(2)(B). Thus, for example, a shareholder of the distributing corporation who surrenders stock in the distributing corporation for stock of the controlled corporation in a split-off and also exchanges options to purchase stock of the distributing corporation in exchange for options to purchase stock of the controlled corporation does not recognize any gain or loss on the exchange of options. Likewise, nonrecognition is available in the case of a split-up of a corporation having outstanding options, which must be replaced by options to purchase stock of the distributed corporations. Rights exercisable against persons other than the issuer of the stock are not covered by Treas. Reg. § 1.355–1(c).

E. RECOGNITION OF GAIN BY THE DISTRIBUTING CORPORATION

1. *Distributions of Appreciated Property as Boot*

Under § 355(c) the distributing corporation must recognize gain on the distribution of appreciated property as boot. The statute requires recognition of gain with respect to the distribution of any property with a fair market value in excess of basis that is not "qualified property." Qualified property is limited to stock or securities of the controlled corporation. I.R.C. § 355(c)(2)(B). Gain is recognized as if the nonqualified property were sold to the distributee for its fair market value. If the distributed property is subject to liabilities (or liabilities are assumed by the distributee), the fair market value of distributed property is deemed to be at least the amount of the liabilities. I.R.C. § 355(c)(2)(C).

2. *Stockholder's Disqualified Stock*

Section 355(d) requires recognition of gain by the distributing corporation (but not the stockholder) on a distribution of *stock of the controlled corporation* to a stockholder who holds "disqualified stock," even though the transaction otherwise qualifies under § 355. A stockholder holds disqualified stock if immediately after the distribution the stockholder holds stock that constitutes either (1) a 50 percent or greater interest in the distributing corporation acquired by purchase within the five year period ending on the date of the distribution, or (2) a 50 percent or greater interest in the controlled corporation which was received as a distribution on stock of the distributing corporation that was purchased within the five year period. I.R.C. § 355(d)(3). An acquisition by purchase is generally defined as any acquisition in which the basis of the property in the hands of the acquiring stockholder is not determined by reference to its basis in the hands of the transferor. I.R.C. § 355(d)(5)(A). However, acquisition by purchase includes the acquisition of property in a § 351 exchange to the extent that the property is acquired in exchange for cash, marketable securities, or debt of the transferor. In the case of a transferred basis acquisition from a person who acquired the stock by purchase, the five year period will begin with the date of purchase by the person transferring the stock to the stockholder. The five year period is suspended during any period in which the holder's risk of loss is substantially diminished by an arrangement such as an option, short sale, a special class of stock or any other such device or transaction. I.R.C. § 355(c)(6).

The legislative history explains that the purpose of these provisions is to prevent avoidance of corporate level tax in a manner that is inconsistent with repeal of the *General Utilities* doctrine by precluding acquisition of a corporate subsidiary by an individual purchaser, or a corporate purchaser who acquires less than 80 percent of the stock of the parent corporation, without recognition of gain by the selling parent corporation. H.R.Rep. No. 101–882, 101st Cong., 2d Sess. 90–92 (1990).

3. *Post-Distribution Dispositions of Distributee Corporation*

Sections 355(e) and (f) require corporate level recognition of gain with respect to the stock of the controlled distributee corporation if pursuant to a plan or arrangement in connection with a corporate division there is a change of ownership of a majority interest of either the distributing corporation or the controlled corporation. In such cases, the distributing corporation generally must recognize gain as if the stock of the controlled corporation had been sold for fair market value on the date of distribution. (If the distributee corporation was formed in a § 368(a)(1)(D) reorganization in contemplation of the distribution, § 368(a)(2)(H)(ii) preserves the tax-free status of that transaction even if the controlling corporation's shareholders dispose of the stock of the distributed corporation in a transaction subject to § 355(e).) Acquisitions occurring within two years before or after the date of the distribution are presumed to have occurred pursuant to a plan or arrangement. If, however, a divisive distribution of stock is from one member of an affiliated group of corporations (as defined in § 1504(a)) to another member of the group, e.g., S_1 distributes the stock of its subsidiary, S_2 to S_1's parent, P, § 355(f) provides that § 355 does not apply at all if the distribution is part of a plan or series of related transactions pursuant to which a 50 percent or greater interest in the distributing corporation or controlled corporation will be transferred to new owners. The effects of § 355(e) and (f) are discussed at page 718.

F. TREATMENT OF CORPORATE ATTRIBUTES

Section 381, which provides for the carryover of corporate attributes (including earnings and profits) in certain reorganizations and liquidations, discussed in Chapter 16, is not applicable to a corporate division under § 355. However, § 312(h) provides that the earnings and profits of the two corporations must be allocated as provided in regulations. In the case of a newly created controlled corporation, earnings and profits are allocated between the distributing corporation and the controlled corporation in proportion to the fair market value of assets transferred to the controlled corporation. In other cases, earnings and profits are allocated with respect to the relative net bases of assets transferred to the controlled corporation and assets retained by the distributing corporation, or by some other appropriate method. Treas.Reg. § 1.312–10.

The treatment of net operating loss carryovers in a § 355 transaction is discussed in Rev.Rul. 77–133, 1977–1 C.B. 96. In a split-off under § 355, M Corporation transferred assets constituting a business to S, a newly formed corporation, and distributed all of the S stock to one of M's two stockholders in exchange for all of stockholder's M stock. The Internal Revenue Service held that no part of M's net operating loss carryforward was transferred to S in the split-off but that M could continue to use its loss carryover. However, where the transaction is a split-up under § 355 in which the loss corporation transfers separate businesses to each of two new corporations and distributes the stock of each corporation to different stockholders in complete liquidation, Rev.Rul. 56–373, 1956–2 C.B. 217, held that neither of the successor corporations can take advantage of the distributing corporation's unused net operating loss carryover. The Ruling concluded that because all of the assets of the distributing corporation were transferred to two corporations, the type (D) reorganization is not a transaction described by § 354(b)(1) and therefore was not subject to attribute carryover under § 381(a)(2). Thus the survival of net operating loss carryovers in a divisive type (D) reorganization depends upon whether the transaction is structured as a split-off or a split-up, even though the economic results of the two transactions may be identical.

The limitations on net operating loss carryforwards of § 382, discussed in Chapter 16, will apply to unused net operating loss carryforwards that survive a split-off as described in Rev.Rul. 77–133 if the continuing stockholders of the loss corporation increase their ownership interest by more than 50 percentage points.

SECTION 2. "ACTIVE CONDUCT OF A TRADE OR BUSINESS," "DEVICE," AND OTHER LIMITATIONS

INTERNAL REVENUE CODE: Section 355(a)(1)(B) and (C), (b).

Rafferty v. Commissioner

United States Court of Appeals, First Circuit, 1971.
452 F.2d 767.

■ MCENTEE, CIRCUIT JUDGE. Taxpayers, Joseph V. Rafferty and wife, appeal from a decision of the Tax Court, 55 T.C. 490, which held that a distribution to them of all the outstanding stock of a real estate holding corporation did not meet the requirements of § 355 of the Internal Revenue Code of 1954 and therefore was taxable as a dividend. Our opinion requires a construction of § 355 and the regulations thereunder.

The facts, some of which have been stipulated, are relatively simple. The taxpayers own all the outstanding shares of Rafferty Brown Steel Co., Inc. (hereinafter RBS), a Massachusetts corporation engaged in the processing and distribution of cold rolled sheet and strip steel in Longmeadow, Massachusetts. In May 1960, at the suggestion of his accountant, Rafferty organized Teragram Realty Co., Inc., also a Massachusetts corporation. In June of that year RBS transferred its Longmeadow real estate to Teragram in exchange for all of the latter's outstanding stock. Thereupon Teragram leased back this real estate to RBS for ten years at an annual rent of $42,000. In 1962 the taxpayers also organized Rafferty Brown Steel Co., Inc., of Connecticut (RBS Conn.), which corporation acquired the assets of Hawkridge Brothers, a general steel products warehouse in Waterbury, Connecticut. Since its inception the taxpayers have owned all of the outstanding stock in RBS Conn. From 1962 to 1965 Hawkridge leased its real estate in Waterbury to RBS Conn. In 1965 Teragram purchased some unimproved real estate in Waterbury and built a plant there.[2] In the same year it leased this plant to RBS Conn. for a term of fourteen years. Teragram has continued to own and lease the Waterbury real estate to RBS Conn. and the Longmeadow realty to RBS, which companies have continued up to the present time to operate their businesses at these locations.[4]

During the period from 1960 through 1965 Teragram derived all of its income from rent paid by RBS and RBS Conn. Its earned surplus increased from $4,119.05 as of March 31, 1961, to $46,743.35 as of March 31, 1965.

2. Teragram contracted for the construction of the plant, arranged mortgage financing by using the Longmeadow and Waterbury properties as security, and became solely obligated on the mortgage.

4. Both properties are also suitable for use by other companies in other types of business.

The earned surplus of RBS increased from $331,117.97 as of June 30, 1959, to $535,395.77 as of June 30, 1965. In August 1965, RBS distributed its Teragram stock to the taxpayers. Other than this distribution, neither RBS nor Teragram has paid any dividends.

Joseph V. Rafferty has been the guiding force behind all three corporations, RBS, RBS Conn., and Teragram. He is the president and treasurer of Teragram which, while it has no office or employees, keeps separate books and records and filed separate tax returns for the years in question.

On various occasions Rafferty consulted his accountant about estate planning, particularly about the orderly disposition of RBS.[5] While he anticipated that his sons would join him at RBS, he wanted to exclude his daughters (and/or his future sons-in-law) from the active management of the steel business. He wished, however, to provide them with property which would produce a steady income. The accountant recommended the formation of Teragram, the distribution of its stock, and the eventual use of this stock as future gifts to the Rafferty daughters. The taxpayers acted on this advice and also on the accountant's opinion that the distribution of Teragram stock would meet the requirements of § 355.

In their 1965 return the taxpayers treated the distribution of Teragram stock as a nontaxable transaction under § 355. The Commissioner viewed it, however, as a taxable dividend and assessed a deficiency. He claimed (a) that the distribution was used primarily as a device for the distribution of the earnings and profits of RBS or Teragram or both, and (b) that Teragram did not meet the active business requirements of § 355.

We turn first, to the Tax Court's finding that there was no device because there was an adequate business purpose for the separation and distribution of Teragram stock. In examining this finding we are guided by the rule that the taxpayer has the burden of proving that the transaction was not used principally as a device. Wilson v. Commissioner of Internal Revenue, 42 T.C. 914, 922 (1964), rev'd on other grounds, 353 F.2d 184 (9th Cir.1965). Initially, we are disturbed by the somewhat uncritical nature of the Tax Court's finding of a business purpose. Viewing the transaction from the standpoint of RBS, RBS Conn., or Teragram, no immediate business reason existed for the distribution of Teragram's stock to the taxpayers. Over the years the businesses had been profitable, as witnessed by the substantial increase of the earned surplus of every component, yet none had paid dividends. The primary purpose for the distribution found by the Tax Court was to facilitate Rafferty's desire to make bequests to his children in accordance with an estate plan.[6] This was a personal motive. Taxpayers seek to put it in terms relevant to the corporation by speaking of avoidance of possible interference with the operation of the steel business by future sons-in-law, pointing to Coady v.

5. Rafferty's concern is understandable in view of the fact that he had nine children.

6. This plan incorporated two objectives: (1) the exclusion of daughters and sons-in-law from active management of the steel business and (2) providing his daughters with investment assets, safe and independent from the fluctuations of the steel business.

Commissioner of Internal Revenue, 33 T.C. 771 (1960), aff'd per curiam 289 F.2d 490 (6th Cir.1961).

In *Coady,* however, the separation was in response to a seemingly irreconcilable falling-out between the owners of a business. This falling-out had already occurred and, manifestly, the separation was designed to save the business from a substantial, present problem. See also Olson v. Commissioner of Internal Revenue, 48 T.C. 855, 867 modified, 49 T.C. 84 (1967). In the case at bar there was, at best, only an envisaged possibility of future debilitating nepotism. If avoidance of this danger could be thought a viable business purpose at all, it was so remote and so completely under the taxpayers' control that if, in other respects the transaction was a "device," that purpose could not satisfy the taxpayers' burden of proving that it was not being used "principally as a device" within the meaning of the statute.

Our question, therefore, must be whether taxpayers' desire to put their stockholdings into such form as would facilitate their estate planning, viewed in the circumstances of the case, was a sufficient personal business purpose to prevent the transaction at bar from being a device for the distribution of earnings and profits. While we remain of the view, which we first expressed in Lewis v. Commissioner of Internal Revenue, 176 F.2d 646 (1st Cir.1949), that a purpose of a stockholder, qua stockholder, may in some cases save a transaction from condemnation as a device, we do not agree with the putative suggestion in Estate of Parshelsky v. Commissioner of Internal Revenue, 303 F.2d 14, 19 (2d Cir.1962), that any investment purpose of the stockholders is sufficient. Indeed, in *Lewis,* although we deprecated the distinction between stockholder and corporate purpose, we were careful to limit that observation to the facts of that case, and to caution that the business purpose formula "must not become a substitute for independent analysis." 176 F.2d at 650. For that reason we based our decision on the Tax Court's finding that the transaction was "undertaken for reasons germane to the continuance of the corporate business." Id. at 647.

This is not to say that a taxpayer's personal motives cannot be considered, but only that a distribution which has considerable potential for use as a device for distributing earnings and profits should not qualify for tax-free treatment on the basis of personal motives unless those motives are germane to the continuance of the corporate business. Cf. Commissioner of Internal Revenue v. Wilson, 353 F.2d 184 (9th Cir.1965); Treas.Reg. § 1.355–2(c). We prefer this approach over reliance upon formulations such as "business purpose," and "active business." * * * The facts of the instant case illustrate the reason for considering substance. Dividends are normally taxable to stockholders upon receipt. Had the taxpayers received cash dividends and made investments to provide for their female descendants, an income tax would, of course, have resulted. Accordingly, once the stock was distributed, if it could potentially be converted into cash without thereby impairing taxpayers' equity interest in RBS, the transaction could easily be used to avoid taxes. The business purpose here alleged, which could be fully satisfied by a bail-out of dividends, is not sufficient to prove that the transaction was not being principally so used.

Given such a purpose, the only question remaining is whether the substance of the transaction is such as to leave the taxpayer in a position to distribute the earnings and profits of the corporation away from, or out of the business. The first factor to be considered is how easily the taxpayer would be able, were he so to choose, to liquidate or sell the spun-off corporation. Even if both corporations are actively engaged in their respective trades, if one of them is a business based principally on highly liquid investment-type, passive assets, the potential for a bail-out is real. The question here is whether the property transferred to the newly organized corporation had a readily realizable value, so that the distributee-shareholders could, if they ever wished, "obtain such cash or property or the cash equivalent thereof, either by selling the distributed stock or liquidating the corporation, thereby converting what would otherwise be dividends taxable as ordinary income into capital gain. * * * "Wilson v. Commissioner, supra, 42 T.C. at 923. In this connection we note that the Tax Court found that a sale of Teragram's real estate properties could be "easily arranged." 55 T.C. at 353. Indeed, taxpayers themselves stressed the fact that the buildings were capable of multiple use.

There must, however, be a further question. If the taxpayers could not effect a bail-out without thereby impairing their control over the on-going business, the fact that a bail-out is theoretically possible should not be enough to demonstrate a device because the likelihood of it ever being so used is slight. "[A] bail-out ordinarily means that earnings and profits have been drawn off without impairing the shareholder's residual equity interest in the corporation's earning power, growth potential, or voting control." B. Bittker & J. Eustice, Federal Income Taxation of Corporations and Shareholders (3d ed. 1971) § 13.06. If sale would adversely affect the shareholders of the on-going company, the assets cannot be said to be sufficiently separated from the corporate solution and the gain sufficiently crystallized as to be taxable. See Lewis v. Commissioner of Internal Revenue, supra, 176 F.2d at 650. In this case, there was no evidence that the land and buildings at which RBS carried on its steel operations were so distinctive that the sale of Teragram stock would impair the continued operation of RBS, or that the sale of those buildings would in any other way impair Rafferty's control and other equity interests in RBS.[7]

In the absence of any direct benefit to the business of the original company, and on a showing that the spin-off put saleable assets in the hands of the taxpayers, the continued retention of which was not needed to continue the business enterprise, or to accomplish taxpayers' purposes, we find no sufficient factor to overcome the Commissioner's determination that the distribution was principally a device to distribute earnings and profits.

7. Our conclusion is reinforced by the fact that RBS and RBS Conn. were guaranteed occupancy of Teragram property under long term leases at fixed rents.

The taxpayers fail for a further reason. The Tax Court found that Teragram was not an active business within the meaning of § 355(b). The Commissioner contends that this result is mandated by Treas.Reg. § 1.355–1(c) and the examples in Treas.Reg. § 1.355–1(d). The correctness of these regulations is questionable in view of the rejection of the separate business requirement of § 1.355–1(a) in United States v. Marett, 325 F.2d 28 (5th Cir.1963) and Coady v. Commissioner of Internal Revenue, supra. In fact, Revenue Ruling 64–147, 1964–1 C.B. pt. I, at 136, indicates that the Commissioner recognized a need to modify the § 355 regulations. Moreover, we find that the regulations in this area are so broadly drawn that they may in some instances defeat the congressional purpose behind the enactment of § 355,[12] and we decline to rest our decision on so tenuous a foundation.

It is our view that in order to be an active trade or business under § 355 a corporation must engage in entrepreneurial endeavors of such a nature and to such an extent as to qualitatively distinguish its operations from mere investments. Moreover, there should be objective indicia of such corporate operations. Prior to 1965 Teragram's sole venture was the leasing back to its parent of its only asset for a fixed return, an activity, in economic terms, almost indistinguishable from an investment in securities. Standing by itself this activity is the type of "passive investment" which Congress intended to exclude from § 355 treatment. Furthermore, there are hardly any indicia of corporate operations. Prior to 1965 Teragram paid neither salaries nor rent. It did not employ independent contractors, and its only activity appears to have been collecting rent, paying taxes, and keeping separate books. Prior to 1965 it failed to meet either set of criteria for an active trade or business. We need not reach the more difficult question of whether its activities in 1965 constituted an active trade or business.

Affirmed.

ILLUSTRATIVE MATERIAL

A. POST-*RAFFERTY* REGULATIONS

As the discussion in *Rafferty* indicates, the scope and interpretation of the tests specified in § 355 have been the object of considerable dispute and continued development. Much of the uncertainty is created by the statutory structure itself, which raises a number of questions. What is the role of the "active trade or business" requirement? What is the nature and degree of activity required before an "active" trade or business is present? What is the relationship of the active business requirement to the "device" prohibi-

12. For example, the regulations could be construed to deny § 355 treatment to a large hotel chain which spun-off its land purchasing, hotel construction, and leasing activities from its hotel management operations if the spun-off corporation leased the completed hotels exclusively to the management corporation. We are reluctant to approve such regulations which appear to fly in the face of congressional intent.

tion? How do the business purpose and continuity of interest requirements of the regulations relate to those issues?

Prior to 1973, the Internal Revenue Service relied primarily on the "active trade or business" requirement to police divisive reorganizations. The Service seemed to exclude absolutely from the active trade or business category investment activities and transactions involving owner-occupied real estate. Moreover, it was the Service's position that two separate pre-division businesses were required before § 355 could be employed by a taxpayer. The *Coady* case discussed in *Rafferty,* rejected the second position and the *Rafferty* court articulated an entirely different standard to test for "active" business operations.

Beginning in 1973, the Internal Revenue Service appeared to shift its position to conform more closely to the approach adopted in *Rafferty.* Thus, in its published rulings, the Service seemed to rely to a greater extent upon the "device" limitation and adopted a view of the active trade or business requirement patterned on the *Rafferty* test. Regulations proposed in 1977 and finally adopted in 1989, confirmed these developments. The regulations place greater emphasis on the "device" limitation as the principal technique for insuring that spin-off transactions do not involve bail-outs of earnings and profits. The regulations also elevate the business purpose requirement discussed in *Rafferty* to the level of an independent test and add a specific continuity of interest requirement which theretofore had played only a subsidiary role. These latter two requirements are important with respect to a divisive transaction designed to avoid double tax on appreciated corporate assets but which may not involve any attempt to bail out accumulated earnings. The active trade or business requirement is substantially modified by the regulations and its close interaction with the device requirement is more clearly spelled out. In addition, the regulations relax the prior requirements concerning the types of business activities which may be split up.[3]

A. THE "DEVICE" LIMITATION

INTERNAL REVENUE CODE: Section 355(a)(1)(B).

REGULATIONS: Section 1.355–2(d).

The "device" language of § 355(a)(1)(B) is aimed at preventing a division from being merely a step in a bail-out of earnings and profits through the sale of the stock of one of the corporations or its liquidation. The division of a part of one corporation into distributed stock of another corporation provides an opportunity to dispose of the distributed assets in a stock sale that produces capital gains and basis recovery deferred to the date of sale, in contrast to immediate recognition of ordinary income in the amount of the full fair market value of the distributed property in the form of a dividend.

3. See Rev.Proc. 96–30, 1996–1 C.B. 696, for a check list of information that must be submitted to obtain an advance ruling under § 355.

Although analysis of a transaction under § 355 may not always start with an exploration of the device requirement, each of the substantive requirements of § 355 traces its origin in part to the same purpose—identifying a distribution that is a step in a bail-out of earnings and profits. The requirement of § 355(b) that following a distribution each of the resulting corporations be engaged in the active conduct of a trade or business prevents the distribution of stock of a subsidiary that can easily be sold because it possesses only passive assets unnecessary to the conduct of the business of the distributing corporation. The five year history required by § 355(b)(2) prevents the distributing corporation from converting cash or passive assets into a going trade or business to be distributed under section 355. The presence of a business purpose obviates the use of the transaction as a "device." The continuity of interest requirement provides nonrecognition treatment only if the recipient stockholders retain their interest in the distributed stock rather than disposing of the stock with the attendant capital gains treatment.

What constitutes a "device" is far from clear. Is it akin to a distribution essentially equivalent to a dividend? Or does it refer to tax avoidance of the Gregory v. Helvering type? Treas.Reg. § 1.355–2(d)(1) states: "Section 355 recognizes that a tax-free distribution of the stock of a controlled corporation presents a potential for tax avoidance by facilitating the avoidance of the dividend provisions of the Code through the subsequent sale or exchange of stock of one corporation and the retention of the stock of another corporation." The presence of the "device" test in § 355 focuses the inquiry on the circumstances under which the corporate division has taken place. Since every corporate division carries with it the potential for extracting earnings from the corporation with no dividend consequences, the problem is how to identify those situations in which dividend treatment is nonetheless proper. Compare, however, the treatment of partial liquidations under § 302(b)(4) and (e)(2), page 260, in which a corporate "division" is involved, but no "device" limitation is imposed.

ILLUSTRATIVE MATERIAL

A. NON-PRO RATA DISTRIBUTIONS

Pro rata divisions represent a clear situation in which there is a bail-out potential in a divisive distribution. Thus, Treas.Reg. § 1.355–2(d)(2)(ii) treats the fact that a distribution is pro rata, or substantially pro rata, as evidence that the transaction is used as a device to effect a distribution of earnings and profits. At the other extreme, however, Treas.Reg. § 1.355–2(d)(5) provides that a non-pro rata distribution which qualifies as a redemption under § 302(a), page 235, ordinarily will not be considered to be a device. There is no "bail-out" potential in a transaction that would produce capital gains in any event. See also Rev.Rul. 64–102, 1964–1 C.B. 136 (transfer to a previously existing subsidiary of assets representing more than 50 percent of the value of the subsidiary to equalize the value of the subsidiary stock with the value of the parent company stock owned by a minority stockholder, followed by a distribution of the subsidiary stock in exchange for the minority stockholder's parent stock, did not amount to a "device" since the transaction as to the minority stockholder would have entitled him to capital gain treatment under § 302(b)(3)); Rev.Rul. 71–383, 1971–2 C.B. 180 (a distribution which was substantially disproportionate under § 302(b)(2) did not constitute a "device" since under that section the taxpayer was entitled to capital gain treatment). For the same reason, Treas.Reg. § 1.355–2(d)(5)(ii) provides that there is ordinarily no device present if neither the distributing nor controlled corporations have earnings and profits (including built-in gain property that would create earnings if distributed) which would cause taxable dividend treatment on a distribution to stockholders. Rev.Rul. 71–384, 1971–2 C.B. 181, is to the same effect. In these situations, however, the "business purpose" and "continuity of interest" requirements of the regulations still must be met.

B. POST–DISTRIBUTION SALE OR EXCHANGE

Treas.Reg. § 1.355–2(d)(2)(iii) provides that a sale or exchange of the stock of either the distributing or the spun-off corporation following a division is evidence that the transaction was used principally as a device for distribution of the earnings and profits of either or both of the corporations. The percentage of stock sold and the period of time before the stock sale affect the strength of this evidence of a "device." If the stock sale is negotiated or agreed upon before the § 355 division occurs, the evidence of "device" is elevated by the regulations to the level of "substantial evidence", while a sale or exchange arranged only after the division is merely "evidence" of a "device." Treas.Reg. § 1.355–2(d)(2)(iii)(B) and (C).

Treas.Reg. § 1.355–2(d)(2)(iii)(E) also provides that a post-distribution exchange of stock of either the distributing or the controlled corporation in a reorganization in which no more than an insubstantial amount of gain is recognized will not be treated as a subsequent sale or exchange constituting evidence of a "device." This portion of the regulations adopts the holding of Commissioner v. Morris Trust, 367 F.2d 794 (4th Cir.1966). In *Morris Trust,* a state bank desired to merge into a national bank. However, the state bank operated an insurance department, an operation which could not be continued by the national bank. To avoid a violation of the national banking laws, the state bank organized a new corporation to which it transferred the insurance business assets and then distributed the stock in the insurance corporation to its stockholders. Following the distribution, the state bank was merged into the national bank. The Commissioner argued in part that there was "an inherent incompatibility in substantially simultaneous divisive and amalgamating reorganizations." The court rejected the Commissioner's argument, holding that there was no "discontinuance of the [distributing corporation's] banking business" even though conducted in a different corporate form, and that the stockholders of the distributing corporation retained the requisite continuity of interest through their majority stock interest in the resulting national bank.[4] See

4. Curtis v. United States, 336 F.2d 714 (6th Cir.1964), was to the contrary, holding that § 355 did not apply where following the distribution of the stock of the corporation

also Rev.Rul. 70–434, 1970–2 C.B. 83, in which the stockholders of the distributing corporation, after receiving the stock of the spun-off corporation, then exchanged their stock in the distributing corporation in a (B) reorganization. Helvering v. Elkhorn Coal Company, 95 F.2d 732 (4th Cir.1937), indicates, however, that a (C) reorganization is not available following a spin-off because of the requirement that the acquired corporation transfer "substantially all" its assets in the (C) reorganization.

In Rev.Rul. 77–377, 1977–2 C.B. 111, an estate owned 80 percent of the stock of X Corporation. In a split-up transaction, X transferred its assets to new Y and Z Corporations, and then liquidated. Prior to the split-up, the estate had contemplated a § 303 redemption of a part of its X stock to pay estate taxes. The § 303 redemption could not be completed before the split-up. Therefore, after the split-up, new Y and Z Corporations redeemed part of the estate's stock in each under § 303. The Ruling held that no "device" was involved since the dividend provisions of the Code had not been avoided. See Treas.Reg. § 1.355–2(d)(5)(iii) (a transaction is generally not considered to be a device if the distribution would have been treated as a redemption under § 303).

Finally, the 1997 Act added §§ 355(e) and (f), which are colloquially referred to as "the anti-*Morris Trust* rules," even though they would not actually apply to the specific transaction in that case if it were to occur today. If pursuant to a plan or arrangement in connection with a corporate division there is a change of ownership of a majority interest of either the distributing corporation or the controlled corporation, under § 355(e) the distributing corporation generally must recognize gain as if the stock of the controlled corporation had been sold for fair market value on the date of distribution. The distributee shareholders, however, continue to receive nonrecognition treatment if § 355 otherwise applies. Acquisitions occurring within two years before or after the date of the distribution are presumed to have occurred pursuant to a plan or arrangement. Special rules under § 355(f) apply to divisive distributions of stock from one member of an affiliated group of corporations (as defined in § 1504(a)) to another member of the group followed by a sale outside the group. These issues are discussed in greater detail at page 718.

holding the unwanted assets, the distributing corporation merged into another corporation. It construed § 355 to require the distributing corporation to stay in existence.

The Commissioner also argued in *Morris Trust* that the active business requirements of § 355(b)(1)(A) were not met since the state bank's business was not continued in unaltered corporate form. The court found no specific limitation in § 355 preventing continuation of the active conduct of the business of the distributing corporation in altered corporate form and concluded that permitting nonrecognition under § 355 did not violate the principles underlying the provision.

In Rev.Rul. 68–603, 1968–2 C.B. 148, the Service announced that it would follow the *Morris Trust* decision to the extent that it held (1) the active trade or business requirement is met even though the distributing corporation merges following the distribution; (2) the control requirement of a (D) reorganization implies no limits on the reorganization of the distributing corporation after the spin-off; and (3) there is a business purpose for the spin-off and the merger.

C. NATURE AND USE OF ASSETS

Treas.Reg. § 1.355–2(d)(2)(iv)(A) provides that in determining whether a transaction is principally a device for the distribution of earnings and profits, consideration will be given to the "nature, kind, amount, and use" of the assets of both corporations immediately after the transaction. There are two aspects to this consideration.

1. *Nonbusiness Assets*

The presence of assets not related to the trade or business of one of the corporations, such as cash and other liquid assets, is evidence of a device. Treas.Reg. § 1.355–2(d)(2)(iv)(B). The presence of unrelated assets is particularly damaging if the amount of unrelated assets transferred to or retained by one corporation is disproportionate to the relative value of the business assets in that corporation. See Treas.Reg. § 1.355–2(d)(4), Ex. (3). In Rev.Rul. 86–4, 1986–1 C.B. 174, the Internal Revenue Service held that the transfer of investment assets to the controlled corporation in a spin-off is a factor to be considered in determining whether the transaction is a device regardless of the percentage of the investment assets relative to the total amount of assets transferred to the controlled corporation.

In Rev.Rul. 73–44, 1973–1 C.B. 182, clarified by Rev.Rul. 76–54, 1976–1 C.B. 96, the distributing corporation conducted three businesses: (1) a manufacturing and distribution business which it had conducted for more than five years and which constituted over one-half the value of the corporation's total business assets; (2) a newspaper business, acquired in a taxable transaction within the preceding five years, which had been transferred to a newly created subsidiary in a nontaxable transaction; and (3) a separate manufacturing business conducted for more than five years. The distributing corporation transferred business (3) to the existing subsidiary and then distributed all the stock of the subsidiary to its shareholders. Business (3) represented a "substantial portion" of the value of the spun-off corporation, but less than one-half. The Ruling held that a "device" was not present since the newspaper business acquired in the taxable transaction represented "operating businesses and not assets that would be used" as a device.

A contribution to the capital of the controlled corporation preceding a spin-off of the subsidiary's stock also may provide an opportunity for the distribution of earnings to stockholders. In Rev.Rul. 83–114, 1983–2 C.B. 66, the Service held that a predistribution capital contribution to the controlled corporation was not per se a device. P was required by an antitrust decree to divest itself of its subsidiary S. In order to improve S's capital and expand S's business opportunities, P discharged S's indebtedness to it. The debt discharge increased S's net worth by more than 100 percent. P distributed S stock to P stockholders. The Ruling concluded that there was no device since both the distribution of S stock and the discharge of S's indebtedness were undertaken for valid business reasons.

2. *Related Business Activities*

The second part of the inquiry into the nature of transferred assets concerns the relationship of the businesses of the two corporations. Although the regulations recognize that § 355 can be employed to divide a single business or to effect a functional division of the business, there is evidence of a device if the businesses of the distributing and controlled corporations are functionally related in the sense that one of the businesses is a secondary business of the other, and the secondary business can be sold without adversely affecting the other. Treas.Reg. § 1.355–2(d)(2)(iv)(C). Example (10) of Treas.Reg. § 1.355–3(c), illustrates this concept. A corporation engaged in the manufacture of steel products spins off a subsidiary which owns a coal mine supplying the steel plant. Evidence of a device exists if the principal function of the coal mine is to satisfy the requirements of the steel business for coal and the stock of the coal mine could be sold without adversely affecting the steel business by depriving it of the supply of coal from the mine.

The related function test of Treas.Reg. § 1.355–2(d)(2)(iv)(C) is closely related to the situation involved in *Rafferty*, and is not wholly inconsistent with the result in that case. In King v. Commissioner, 458 F.2d 245 (6th Cir.1972), a transportation company distributed stock of subsidiaries which owned and leased terminals and other real estate necessary to the operation of the distributing corporation's business. Distinguishing *Rafferty*, the court in *King* rejected the Commissioner's argument that the distribution failed the device requirement pointing out that a sale or liquidation of the spun-off corporation would have hindered the business operation of the distributing corporation.

The *Rafferty* court's reliance on the factor of "readily realizable value" to determine the bail-out potential refers to the division of liquid from illiquid assets; even if the spun-off corporation is in an active trade or business, the bail-out potential may be high because of the nature of the assets (as would be the case with real estate). But further, if the sale or liquidation of the spun-off corporation would seriously impair the ability of the distributing corporation to operate, then a "device" is not likely to be present. Thus, the court in *King* upheld § 355 treatment for the spin-off of real estate leased solely to the distributing corporation on the ground that, while the real estate operations were highly liquid (net leases were involved), the properties were uniquely suited to the distributing company's needs and a sale would have impaired the company's ability to obtain financing. Under the *Rafferty* approach, transactions involving real estate must be closely scrutinized. For example, long-term leases on the real estate may make possible a sale of the stock of the distributed corporation without impairing in any way the operating functions of the distributing corporation. In such a case, the transaction should constitute a "device" under the *Rafferty* test.

B. ACTIVE CONDUCT OF A TRADE OR BUSINESS

INTERNAL REVENUE CODE: Section 355(a)(1)(C) and (b).

REGULATIONS: Section 1.355–3.

The "active business" requirements of § 355(a)(1)(C) and (b) are directed at several different, though related, aspects of divisive transactions and raise a number of interpretive problems. The technical rules of § 355(a)(1)(C) and (b) require each of the surviving corporations following a division to be actively engaged in the conduct of a trade or business. In addition, the business in each corporation must have been actively conducted for the five year period preceding the distribution to stockholders. These rules require not only the classification of assets in each of the corporations surviving a divisive reorganization as an active trade or business, but also identification of the scope of the trade or business conducted during the five year qualifying period.

At the first level, the provisions are designed to prevent the tax-free separation of liquid assets from operating assets because of the substantial bail-out potential involved in such transactions. Here the principal interpretive problems concern the classification of owner-occupied real estate (and real estate leased by a subsidiary to its parent) as an active trade or business or as property that constitutes an investment asset. In such situations, the question is whether the nature and extent of the taxpayer's activities are sufficient to qualify as an "active business."

A second set of issues arises when the plan is to divide a single business, to divide a business along geographical lines, to separate different lines of business (e.g., wholesaling from retailing), or to separate a particular function (e.g., research). Here the issues are whether there are separate businesses following division, each of which consists of an individual profit-making enterprise, and whether each of the separated businesses may inherit the five-year operating history of the original business.

The purpose of the five-year rule is to prevent the use of corporate earnings generated by one business—and otherwise available for dividend distributions to its stockholders—to establish or acquire another business that could be spun-off and sold creating capital gains. The difficult questions in this area involve a determination of the point at which simple expansion of an existing business becomes the acquisition of a new business which must then establish its own five-year history. As a backstop to the basic five-year rule, sections 355(b)(2)(C) and (D) preclude tax-free distribution of a business acquired in a taxable transaction during the five years preceding the spin-off.

ILLUSTRATIVE MATERIAL

A. ACTIVE TRADE OR BUSINESS

1. *What is "Active" Trade or Business?*

The operation and maintenance of rental real estate, as well as other rental property, readily may be classified as the operation of a trade or business. The principal question that arises in the case of dividing off the rental business is whether the relationship of the distributing corporation to the rental activity is the *active* conduct of that business. The problem is further complicated when the distributing corporation occupies the rental property.

Another question is whether the form in which property is held should matter in the analysis of the active trade or business requirement. Suppose in *Rafferty* the property had been owned directly by the parent and managed and operated as a real estate division, with the real estate division "charging" rent to the operating division for internal accounting purposes. The Internal Revenue Service appears to regard the parent-subsidiary rental situation as a variation on the owner-occupied real estate situation and uses the same tests in each to determine whether the requisite level of business activity is present.

The pre-1989 regulations refused to find an active trade or business if owner-occupied real estate was involved unless the rental activities with respect to, and the rental income from, third parties were substantial. Some cases used a similar approach; see, e.g. Appleby v. Commissioner, 35 T.C. 755 (1961), aff'd per curiam, 296 F.2d 925 (3d Cir.1962) (rental of less than 50 percent of space in building occupied by insurance agency where rentals were small part of total income did not constitute an active trade or business); Bonsall v. Commissioner, 317 F.2d 61 (2d Cir.1963) (lease of small part of owner-occupied building as an accommodation to a supplier and rental of another building was not a trade or business where rental income small).

Furthermore, the Service held the view that if "investment" property was involved, no amount of activity with respect to the investment would constitute an active trade or business. See Rev.Rul. 66-204, 1966-2 C.B. 113 (substantial activity in managing an investment portfolio of a broker-dealer not an active trade or business).

But *Rafferty* signaled a new approach to the treatment of investment property and property used in the trade or business of the owner under the active trade or business test of § 355. Under *Rafferty,* the satisfaction of the active trade or business test turns on the question whether the corporation engaged "in entrepreneurial endeavors of such a nature and to such an extent as to qualitatively distinguish its operations from mere investments." Thus under the *Rafferty* approach, it is possible for the operation of owner-occupied real estate to constitute an active trade or business under § 355, even though no renting of the property to third parties is present.

King v. Commissioner, 458 F.2d 245 (6th Cir.1972), applied the *Rafferty* approach in a transaction in which a transportation company owned three subsidiaries formed earlier to acquire real estate, erect terminals, and lease the terminals on a net lease basis to the parent company. To facilitate a merger with another operating company, the transportation company decided to put all of the transportation operations in one corporate group and the nonoperating corporations in a separate corporate group. The stock of the real estate subsidiaries was distributed to the stockholders of the transportation company who then transferred the stock to a sister corporation and the business activities were operated as before. In reversing the Tax Court, the court concluded, that the financing and construction activities of the real estate group constituted an active trade or business, even though performed by the identical persons who were employees of the operational group and no third party leasing was involved.

Rev.Rul. 73–234, 1973–1 C.B. 180, reflected a shift in the Internal Revenue Service interpretation of the active conduct of a trade or business requirement. The Ruling stated that an actively conducted business denoted "substantial management and operational activities directly carried on by the corporation itself." There a corporation which engaged in farming through tenant farmers, who were independent contractors, was held to be engaged in an active trade or business because it did perform substantial management activities with respect to the farm business.

Rev.Rul. 89–27, 1989–1 C.B. 106, discussed the role of services performed by outside contractors:

> "[I]n order for a trade or business to be actively conducted, substantial management and operational activities generally must be directly carried on by the corporation itself and such activities generally do not include the activities of others outside the corporation, including independent contractors. However, the fact that a portion of a corporation's business activities is performed by others will not preclude the corporation from being engaged in the active conduct of a trade or business if the corporation itself directly performs active and substantial management and operational functions."

The Ruling held that the owner of a working interest in an oil lease was actively engaged in the conduct of a business despite outside work by independent contractors. See also Rev.Rul. 73–237, 1973–1 C.B. 184 (construction corporation acting as a general contractor was in an active trade or business even though it utilized independent subcontractors for actual construction work, the general contractor's activities were substantial); Rev.Rul. 79–394, 1979–2 C.B. 141 (corporation engaged in an active business even though it had no paid employees of its own; all of the corporation's operational and management activity was performed by employees of its parent corporation which was reimbursed by the controlled corporation); Rev.Rul. 80–181, 1980–2 C.B. 121 (clarifying Rev.Rul. 79–394 and indicating that the controlled corporation would be actively engaged in the conduct of a business if the parent had not been reimbursed for the services provided by its employees). However, in Rev.Rul. 86–125, 1986–2 C.B. 57, the Service held that a subsidiary's ownership of an office building that was operated and managed by an independent real estate management company was not the active conduct of a business. The subsidiary's limited managerial and operational activities were compared to those of a prudent investor.

Treas.Reg. § 1.355–3(b)(2)(iii) incorporates a requirement that to satisfy the "active conduct" test the corporation must "perform active and substantial management and operational functions." The current regulations modify the strict rule of the prior regulations by stating that the holding of real or personal property used in a trade or business can satisfy the active conduct test if the owner performs significant services with respect to the operation and management of the property. Treas.Reg. § 1.355–3(b)(2)(iv)(B). See also Rev.Rul. 92–17, 1992–1 C.B. 142 (a corporation that was a general partner of a real estate limited partnership, and whose officers performed active and substantial management functions for the partnership, was engaged in an active trade or business).

Despite the modification in principle of the Internal Revenue Service's prior strict rule regarding investment property (other than stocks, securities and similar portfolio type investments)and owner-occupied real estate, however, Examples (1)–(3), (12), and (13) in Treas.Reg. § 1.355–3(c) indicate that the Service will continue to scrutinize closely divisive transactions involving investment assets and owner-occupied real estate. Indeed, only one of the examples, Example (12), concludes that an active trade or business is involved. In that example, the owner of a building occupied only one of eleven floors and the spun-off corporation continued the prior practice of renting the other ten floors to unrelated tenants. Example (13) indicates that if the controlled corporation leases the property it owns back to the distributing corporation, it will be difficult to establish that an active trade or business is present.

For advance ruling purposes the Service also imposes a quantitative test. Rev. Proc. 98–3, § 4.01(33), 1998–1 I.R.B. 100, provides that the Service will not ordinarily issue advance rulings with respect to the active business test under § 355 if the gross assets of the businesses relied upon to satisfy the test with respect to any corporation would be less than five percent of the gross assets of the corporation.

2. *Vertical Division of a Single Business Activity*

As noted by the court in *Rafferty,* the Internal Revenue Service position for many years was that § 355 could not be applied to divide a single business, which did have the requisite five-year active trade or business history, into two separate corporations. The Service position was rejected in Coady v. Commissioner, 33 T.C. 771 (1960) (A), aff'd per curiam, 289 F.2d 490 (6th Cir.1961), the court holding invalid regulations which provided that § 355 did not apply to the separation of a single business. Accord, United States v. Marett, 325 F.2d 28 (5th Cir.1963); Lester v. Commissioner, 40 T.C. 947 (1963)(A). In Rev.Rul. 64–147, 1964–1 C.B. 136, the Service announced that it would follow *Coady* and *Marett.*

Treas.Reg. § 1.355–3(c), Ex. (4) and (5), specifically sanctions the use of § 355 to divide a single business with the requisite five-year predistribution history. See also Treas.Reg. § 1.355–1(b) and–3(c), Ex. (6) and (7).

3. *Single Business Versus Two Separate Businesses*

As a result of the *Coady* and *Marett* cases, the Commissioner and taxpayers tended to shift sides in the single business versus separate businesses controversy. The Commissioner contended that an activity involved two separate businesses, and one of the two did not satisfy the five-year rule; the taxpayer argued that the activities constituted a single business, which could be divided under *Coady*. The question of whether an activity constitutes a single business, or two separate businesses may arise in several different contexts.

(a) Geographical Division

Suppose that a multi-state business operates through branches in each of its market states. Is each branch a separate business, or is there but a single business? In Burke v. Commissioner, 42 T.C. 1021 (1964), the Commissioner asserted that establishing a second retail store in another town constituted the creation of a separate trade or business as to which the five-year rule was not satisfied. The court upheld the taxpayer's assertion that under the *Coady* rule the second store constituted a branch of a single retail business which satisfied the five-year rule. In Estate of Lockwood v. Commissioner, 350 F.2d 712 (8th Cir.1965), a corporation operated in the Midwest through branches that were ultimately separately incorporated and spun-off. In 1949 it began to make sales in New England and in 1954 established a branch office in Maine. In 1956, the branch was incorporated separately and the stock distributed. No sales activity was present in Maine from 1951 to 1953 and the Commissioner asserted that the business had not been actively conducted in the Maine location for the five years preceding the division in 1956. The court rejected the Commissioner's reliance on its "geographical area" test:

"Nothing in the language of § 355 suggests that prior business activity is only to be measured by looking at the business performed in a geographical area where the controlled corporation is eventually formed. In this case, when the entire Lockwood market is viewed, it can be seen that Lockwood was engaged in active business as required by § 355 for the five years prior to the incorporation of Maine, Inc. Since its incorporation Maine, Inc. has carried on the same kind of manufacturing and selling business previously and concurrently performed by Lockwood. Thus all § 355 prerequisites are met. * * *

"Since there is no Congressional intent evidenced to the contrary, the test, restated, is not whether active business had been carried out in the geographic area later served by the controlled corporation. But, simply, whether the distributing corporation, for five years prior to distribution, had been actively conducting the type of business now performed by the controlled corporation without reference to the geographic area." (715, 717).

Treas.Reg. § 1.355–3(c), Ex. (7), follows the *Burke* and *Estate of Lockwood* cases. Example (6) likewise approves the separation of the downtown and suburban branches of a retail clothing store.

(b) Separate Lines of Business

In Lester v. Commissioner, 40 T.C. 947 (1963)(A), a corporation was both a warehouse distributor (in which capacity it sold to "jobbers") and a "jobber" (in which capacity it sold to retailers). Jobber customers objected to purchasing from a corporation which was also a competitor, and the warehouse activity was spun-off. The court reaffirmed *Coady,* but in any event found that the activities constituted two separate businesses, each with its own five-year history. See also Wilson v. Commissioner, 42 T.C. 914 (1964), rev'd on other grounds, 353 F.2d 184 (9th Cir.1965) (furniture business and its financing activities were two separate businesses). In Rev.Rul. 56–451, 1956–2 C.B. 208, the Service ruled that the publication of a trade magazine for one industry was a business separate from the publication of three magazines for another industry, and the former could be spun-off since the requirements of § 355 were met.

The problems in this area are closely related to the "functional division" situations discussed above, and the position in the regulations that there can be a valid functional division of a single business under § 355 will presumably have an impact in the single business-two separate businesses context as well. As discussed below, Treas.Reg. § 1.355–2(d)(2)(iv)(C), focuses on the device test in this context.

4. *Functional Division of a Single Business*

For purposes of § 355, Treas.Reg. § 1.355–1(b)(2)(ii) defines a "business" as a specific group of activities consisting of the operations necessary to the process of earning income or profit. Activities which merely contributed to the process of earning income before the distribution may themselves constitute a business. Treas.Reg. § 1.355–3(c), Ex. (9), provides that a research department of a manufacturing activity may be spun-off as a separate business. The Example states that the status of the research department as a separate business is independent of whether it furnishes services solely to the distributing corporation or undertakes to contract with others. The Example cautions, however, that if the research department continues to function as a secondary business providing service solely to the distributing corporation, that fact is evidence of a "device" under Treas.Reg. § 1.355–2(d)(2)(iv), discussed at page 695. See also Examples (10) (sales function separated from manufacturing function), and (11) (captive coal mine separated from steel products manufacturing). Treas. Reg. § 1.355–2(d)(2)(iv)(C) indicates that the functional relationship between the active trade or businesses of the distributing and controlled corporations may be evidence of a "device."

B. FIVE YEAR HISTORY

1. *Taxable Acquisitions of a Going Business Within the Five Year Period*

The active trades or businesses of the distributing corporation must be the historic trades or businesses of the distributing corporation or its subsidiary. Section 355(b)(2)(C) and (D) stand as barriers to bailing out corporate earnings and profits through the acquisition of a new business shortly before it is distributed. Section 355(b)(2)(C) disqualifies an active trade or business that was acquired in a taxable transaction within the five year period ending on the date of the distribution. Section 355(b)(2)(D) disqualifies a trade or business in a controlled corporation that was acquired by the distributing corporation or any distributee corporation in a taxable transaction within the five year period.

In Boettger v. Commissioner, 51 T.C. 324 (1968), a corporation had operated a hospital since 1956. In 1961 it acquired another hospital in a separate location by means of a taxable purchase. Because of disagreement between the two groups of stockholders, a split-up was effected in 1964. The taxpayers who received the 1956 hospital argued that the acquisition in 1961 simply represented an expansion of a single business and *Coady* applied. The Tax Court did not reach the question of whether there was one or two businesses. It held that the word "such" in § 355(b)(2)(C) referred to the business engaged in by the distributed corporation after the distribution and since this business, viewed alone, was acquired in a taxable transaction within five years preceding the distribution, § 355 was inapplicable. Subsequently, in Nielsen v. Commissioner, 61 T.C. 311 (1973), a case involving the stockholders who received the 1961 hospital, the Tax Court concluded that two separate businesses were involved, only one of which had the requisite five-year history. Each hospital had been run separately, there was not shared staff or patients, and each was a separate income-producing activity. On this factual basis, the Court distinguished the *Burke* and *Estate of Lockwood* cases, page 700. See also Russell v. Commissioner, 40 T.C. 810 (1963), aff'd per curiam, 345 F.2d 534 (5th Cir.1965) (taxable acquisition within five-year period preceding distribution disqualified transaction under § 355); Rev.Rul. 78–442, 1978–2 C.B. 143 (corporation transferred assets and liabilities of one business to a newly formed corporation and then distributed the stock; gain was recognized in the transaction under § 357(c) because liabilities exceeded the bases of the assets transferred; despite the fact that gain was recognized on the transfer § 355(b)(2)(C) was held not applicable because it was not intended to apply to an acquisition of a trade or business by a controlled corporation from the distributing corporation).

2. *Diversification and Expansion of an Existing Business With a Five-Year History*

The active trades or businesses in the distributing and controlled corporations must be the same as those conducted earlier. Thus, if the distributing corporation or the distributed controlled corporation contains only a new business started within the preceding five years, the active trade or business test is not satisfied. What about changes in product, location, or methods? What about growth itself? Is a small rental business started in 1990 the same business as a large rental activity with many more properties in 1999; is the operation of a single retail store in 1990 the same business as the operation in 1999 of a chain of 50 stores? See Treas.Reg. § 1.355–3(b)(3)(D)(ii).

The Internal Revenue Service addressed the expansion issue in Rev. Rul. 59–400, 1959–2 C.B. 114:

"M corporation was engaged in two businesses, operating a hotel and renting improved real estate (both commercial and residential). The hotel business was started upon organization in 1920 and has been actively conducted up to the present time. In 1934, M corporation also entered into the rental real estate business when it purchased property, constructed a garage and automobile agency facilities thereon and rented it to a dealer. In the intervening years, it acquired other rental properties which it has continued to operate. In 1954 the hotel had a fair market value of 550x dollars and a net book value of 167x dollars.

"During the five-year period commencing with 1954, the operation of the hotel business resulted in earnings, after taxes, of 240x dollars, and the operation of the real estate business resulted in earnings of approximately 75x dollars. In 1958, a new rental office building was built for 400x dollars, some 175x dollars thereof being provided by loans from banks. At the beginning of 1959, the hotel business was placed in a new corporation N, and the stock thereof distributed to the stockholders of M on a pro rata basis. N corporation received the hotel, plus certain receivables and other hotel business assets. M corporation retained the real estate liabilities and assets, which at that time had a net book value of 372x dollars and a fair market value of 705x dollars.

* * *

"The purpose behind the five-year limitation of § 355 is to prevent the corporate earnings of one business from being drawn off for such a period and put into a new business and thereby, through the creation of a marketable enterprise, convert what would normally have been dividends into capital assets that are readily saleable by the stockholders.

"It is the position of the Internal Revenue Service that where a corporation which is devoted to one type of business also engages in the rental business, and substantial acquisitions of new rental property are made within the five-year period preceding the separation of these businesses, a spin-off transaction will not qualify under § 355 unless it can be shown that the property acquisitions were substantially financed out of the earnings of the rental business and not out of the earnings of the other business.

"From the facts presented herein, it is readily apparent that there has been a very substantial increase in the rental properties subsequent to 1954, primarily as a result of the addition of the large office building in 1958. Further, it is also apparent that, viewing the transaction most favorably to the taxpayer, earnings properly attributable to the hotel business, in the amount of approximately 150x dollars, have been employed in increasing the real estate business. In view of this substantial financing out of the earnings of the hotel business, it is held that the distribution of the stock of N corporation to the stockholders of M corporation will not qualify as a nontaxable distribution under § 355 of the Code."

What is the basis for the Ruling? Is it that the infusion of funds into the real estate business so changed its character that it became a "new" business which required a five-year aging period? Or was the transaction struck down by the "device" language of § 355(a)(1)(B)? The Ruling is unclear on these questions, but stands as a warning that substantial infusions of funds into a going business may create problems if a spin-off is contemplated.

In a related fashion, the parent corporation in a parent subsidiary group already conducting separate businesses may use its earnings to make a capital contribution to the subsidiary prior to distribution of the subsidiary's stock. The expansion of the subsidiary's business with the parent's earnings does not affect the presence of the group's historic business, but may be evidence of a "device."

3. *Conduct of the Business for the Five Year Period*

Occasionally a question arises as to whether the business has been conducted for the requisite five-year period. An unusual case is W.E. Gabriel Fabrication Co. v. Commissioner, 42 T.C. 545 (1964) (A). There two brothers, who owned a corporation which was actively engaged in three businesses, decided to divide up the corporation because of disputes between them. The taxpayer-brother was to receive two of the businesses. Pursuant to an agreement entered into in 1955, the corporation loaned the assets of the two businesses to the taxpayer who operated the businesses as a sole proprietor for about 14 months. In 1956 a new corporation was formed to which the assets of the businesses were formally transferred and this corporation was spun-off to the taxpayer. The taxpayer then transferred his sole proprietorship interest (in which the "loaned" assets had been used) to the new corporation. Under the facts, the distributing corporation had ceased to engage in the spun-off businesses for the 14–month period prior to the distribution and the new corporation itself had not engaged in the business until after the distribution. The court upheld the taxpayer's argument that § 355 nonetheless applied since it concluded that there was no requirement that the business in the five-year period preceding the distribution be conducted by either the distributing corporation or the distributee corporation. It was sufficient that the business itself was conducted during the five-year period, and the taxpayer was permitted to add on the 14–month operation as a sole proprietorship to the time when the businesses had been conducted by the distributing corporation for the purpose of satisfying the five-year requirement.

In Rev.Rul. 82–219, 1982–2 C.B. 82, a subsidiary corporation that manufactured pollution control equipment for a single unrelated automobile manufacturer was required to cease its production activities for a year when the automobile manufacturer unexpectedly filed for bankruptcy. During the year in which it was shut down, the subsidiary pursued new customers for its products. The subsidiary was spun-off by its parent corporation for valid business reasons. The fact that the subsidiary had income in only four of the five years preceding the distribution of its stock to its parent's stockholders did not defeat the five-year active conduct of business requirement.

C. SALE OF ASSETS FOLLOWING DISTRIBUTION

Suppose that shortly after the distribution, the distributed corporation sells all of its operating assets and winds up its business. Martin Ice Cream Co. v. Commissioner, 110 T.C. 189 (1998), held that a post-distribution sale of all of the assets of the distributed controlled corporation six weeks after a split-off, but pursuant to a pre-arranged plan, resulted in the distribution failing to qualify under § 355 because the active business requirement of § 355(a)(1)(A) had not been met after the distribution. The same result should occur if the distributing corporation sells all of its assets and liquidates immediately after the distribution.

D. HOLDING COMPANIES

§ 355(b)(2)(A) provides that a holding company will be engaged in the active conduct of a trade or business if "substantially all" of its assets consists of stock or securities of controlled corporations that are each actively engaged in the conduct of a business. For advance ruling purposes, the "substantially all" requirement is met if at least 90 percent of the fair market value of the *gross* corporate assets consist of stock and securities in controlled corporations that have actively been engaged in a trade or business for the requisite five-year period. Rev.Proc. 96–30, § 4.03(5), 1996–1 C.B. 696; Rev.Proc. 77–37, § 3.04, 1977–2 C.B. 568, 570. See also Rev.Rul. 74–382, 1974–2 C.B. 120 (same result where first tier subsidiary is a holding company but all the second tier subsidiaries are actively engaged in a trade or business); Rev.Rul. 74–79, 1974–1 C.B. 81 (operating subsidiaries acquired in taxable transactions within five-year period are treated as stock in corporations not actively engaged in a trade or business).

E. ACQUISITION OF CONTROL OF THE DISTRIBUTING CORPORATION BY A DISTRIBUTEE CORPORATION

Following repeal of the *General Utilities* doctrine by the 1986 Act, there was concern that a § 355 division could be used to thwart recognition of corporate level gain in a corporate acquisition followed by a disposition of unwanted assets. For example, T Corporation operates two separate businesses. X Corporation wishes to acquire business number 1, but not business number 2. T is not willing to dispose of the businesses separately. To accomplish the transaction, T transfers each business into separate subsidiaries, S1 and S2, in a nontaxable transaction under § 351. X acquires the T stock from the T stockholders. X causes T to distribute the stock of S1, the wanted subsidiary, to it in a § 355 distribution. Subsequently, X sells the T stock thereby disposing of the unwanted assets of business number 2 (held in S2) without corporate level recognition of unrealized gain in the assets of business number 2.[5] The final phrase of

5. This transaction was thought to have been approved by Rev.Rul. 74–5, 1974–1 C.B. 82, obsoleted by Re. Rul. 89–37, 1989–1 C.B. 107, in which P Corporation in 1969 acquired all of the stock of X Corporation for cash. X Corporation in turn owned all of the stock of Y Corporation which it had acquired in 1965. In 1971, X distributed the Y stock to P and in 1972 P distributed the Y stock to its stockholders. The Ruling held that the 1971 distri-

§ 355(b)(2)(D) was amended in 1987 to apply the five-year rule to the acquisition of control by the distributee corporation of a corporation conducting a trade or business. Thus, in the example, because X, the distributee of the S1 stock, indirectly acquired control of S1 and S2 within the five-year period preceding the distribution, § 355 would not apply to the distribution of S1 stock to X. T will be required to recognize gain on the distribution of S1 stock to X under § 311.

Note that the transaction as described above would have difficulty satisfying both the business purpose and continuity of interest requirements, discussed in the next sections. Section 355(b)(2)(D) was amended to avoid the need to rely on these general subjective tests.

C. THE "BUSINESS PURPOSE" REQUIREMENT

REGULATIONS: Sections 1.355–2(b) and (d)(3)(ii).

The role of "business purpose" in the § 355 framework is important and has several aspects. Under Treas.Reg. § 1.355–2(d)(3)(ii) the presence of a corporate business purpose for the transaction is evidence that a "device" is not present. The stronger the device factors, the stronger the evidence of business purpose necessary to overcome the presence of a device. In addition, Treas.Reg. § 1.355–2(b) independently requires a corporate business purpose for nonrecognition treatment in order to limit nonrecognition to "distributions that are incident to readjustments of corporate structures required by business exigencies and that effect only readjustments of continuing interests in property under modified corporate forms." This business purpose test is independent of the "device" language, so that even upon a finding of no "device," the transaction nonetheless may fail to qualify for want of a "business purpose." The regulations are consistent with the decision in Commissioner v. Wilson, 353 F.2d 184 (9th Cir.1965), holding that § 355 was inapplicable where, although the transaction was not a "device" because there was no tax avoidance motive, no affirmative business purpose was demonstrated for the transaction, and that under the *Gregory* doctrine "business purpose" is an essential ingredient of the law. *Rafferty,* on the other hand, appears to deal with "business purpose" only as a factor under the "device" prohibition.

ILLUSTRATIVE MATERIAL

A. BUSINESS PURPOSE FOR THE DISTRIBUTION OF STOCK

Treas.Reg. § 1.355–2(b)(3) indicates that the "business purpose" must relate not only to the need for separate operations in corporate form of the

bution satisfied § 355(b)(2)(D), since P was neither the distributing nor the controlled corporation but simply the stockholder of the distributing corporation. On the other hand, the 1972 distribution did not satisfy § 355(b)(2)(D), since the business of controlled Corporation Y was acquired indirectly by P through another Corporation (X) in a transaction within five years in which gain or loss had been recognized. See also Rev.Rul. 69–461, 1969–2 C.B. 52.

two businesses, but that the corporate business purpose must extend also to the distribution of the stock to the stockholders. There may be business reasons for separate corporate operations, but these frequently can be satisfied by a parent-subsidiary operation. Thus, a distribution will not qualify for nonrecognition treatment under § 355 if the corporate business purpose can be achieved through a nontaxable separation of the businesses into two corporations without a distribution to stockholders. To illustrate, in Treas.Reg. § 1.355–2(b)(5), Ex. (3), X Corporation is engaged in the manufacture and sale of toys and candy. The stockholders of X wish to protect the candy business from the risks of the toy business. To achieve this business purpose X transfers the assets of the toy business to a new corporation Y, and distributes the Y stock to X stockholders. The regulations conclude that since the purpose of protecting the candy business from the risks of the toy business is accomplished at the moment the separate businesses are divided into separate corporations, the distribution of Y stock to X's stockholders is not carried out for a corporate business purpose.

The requisite business purpose must be a nontax business purpose of one or both of the corporations involved in a division. Treas.Reg. § 1.355–2(b)(2). The regulations expressly provide that a shareholder purpose such as personal planning is not a corporate business purpose. The regulations recognize, however, that a stockholder purpose may be "so nearly coextensive" with the corporation's business purpose as to preclude any distinction between them. Compare the decision in *Rafferty,* which employed the business purpose test as one factor relevant to a determination of the "device" issue, with the taxpayer having the burden of proving that no device was involved. The court stated that if the only purpose for the distribution is a "stockholder" purpose, the bail-out potential of the transaction is to be closely scrutinized.

Rev.Rul. 75–337, 1975–2 C.B., 124, concluded that a stockholder's purpose could supply the requisite "business purpose" if the estate planning problem faced by the stockholder was immediate and was directly related to the ability of the corporation to carry on its business without interruption or loss. X Corporation held an automobile sales franchise and its subsidiary Y was in the automobile rental business. Fifty-three percent of the X Corporation stock was held by A and the remainder was held by A's five daughters. Three of the daughters were active in X's automobile sales business. To facilitate A's estate planning, Y Corporation stock was distributed pro-rata to the X Corporation stockholders. The spin-off was justified by the fact that the franchise policy of the automobile manufacturer required that the stockholders of a corporation owning a franchise be actively involved in the business. On A's death, the inactive stockholders would receive their inheritance in Y stock and assets and no interest in X. The Ruling distinguished *Rafferty* on the basis that the stockholder problem involved there had only a "remote and conjectural" impact on the business.

B. NONTAX BUSINESS PURPOSE

Treas.Reg. § 1.355–2(b)(2) stresses that the requisite business purpose must be a purpose unrelated to federal taxes and germane to the business of the corporations involved. A corporate separation to save state taxes satisfies the business purpose requirement only if there is no corresponding federal income tax savings that is greater than or substantially co-extensive with the state tax savings. Under this provision, a parent corporation cannot justify distribution of the stock of a subsidiary with a claim that the distribution is necessary to qualify for elective status under a state pass-through taxation provision similar to Subchapter S of the Code, which bars the election by affiliated groups, if the distribution also would allow qualification for federal Subchapter S status. See Treas.Reg. § 1.355–2(b)(5), Ex. (7). See also Rev.Rul. 76–187, 1976–1 C.B. 97 (valid business purpose to distribute stock of subsidiary to reduce state and local taxes on the capital value of the subsidiary); Rev.Rul. 89–101, 1989–2 C.B. 67 (distribution to domestic parent corporation by foreign first tier subsidiary of all of the stock of second tier foreign subsidiary for purposes of reducing foreign taxes satisfied business purpose requirement).

C. EXAMPLES

The adequacy of business purpose for nonrecognition under § 355 is generally a question which depends upon the facts and circumstances of particular cases. Treas.Reg. § 1.355–2(b)(1) provides that the potential for tax avoidance is relevant in determining the extent to which the distribution is motivated by a bona fide corporate business purpose. There are numerous authorities identifying valid business purposes for a distribution under § 355. For example, Pulliam v. Commissioner, T.C. Memo. 1997–274, found a valid business purpose for a spin-off of a corporation holding one of two funeral homes originally operated directly by the distributing corporation where 49 percent of the stock of the spun-off corporation was sold to a valued employee, who operated the spun-off funeral home, after the spin-off. The purpose for the distribution was that state law required funeral home corporations to be PSCs in which a majority interest was owned directly by licensed funeral directors, so the original corporation could not hold a majority interest in a subsidiary in which the employee licensed funeral director owned the other 49 percent. See Lester v. Commissioner, 40 T.C. 947 (1963)(A) (corporation was both warehouse distributor and jobber of auto parts; valid business purpose to separate the two businesses where warehouse business sold to other jobbers who objected to doing business with a company that was a competitor insofar as its jobber business was concerned); Olson v. Commissioner, 48 T.C. 855 (1967) A) (desire to confine union difficulties to one corporation was valid business purpose for spin-off distribution); Rev.Rul. 69–460, 1969–2 C.B. 51 (valid business purpose for distribution of a subsidiary corporation was upheld where necessary to permit key employees to buy into the parent corporation at a price which they could afford; but if the key employees desired to buy into the subsidiary corporation, there was no business purpose for distribution of the subsidiary); Rev.Rul. 72–530, 1972–2 C.B. 212 (valid business purpose to distribute stock of subsidiary to facilitate a merger involving the parent corporation, because state law restrictions imposed serious disadvantages on handling transaction through creation of a new corporation); Rev.Rul. 76–527, 1976–2 C.B. 103 (valid business purpose to distribute stock of subsidiary to enable subsidiary to acquire an unrelated corporation, because the acquired corporation would not accept the subsidiary stock if it were controlled by the distributing corporation); Rev.Rul. 77–22, 1977–1 C.B. 91 (valid business purpose to distribute stock of subsidiary to enable each corporation to obtain separate borrowing limits from a bank, the aggregate borrowing limits of the two separate corporations being greater than that of the parent-subsidiary); Rev.Rul. 82–130, 1982–2 C.B. 83 (valid business purpose to distribute stock of real estate subsidiary with long-term indebtedness to facilitate financing by parent in high-technology business; underwriters stated that subsidiary's long-term debt would make it difficult for the parent to raise equity in a public offering and that significant commitment to subsidiary's real estate activities made the parent corporation less attractive to investors; also notes that a holding company with parent and subsidiary as subsidiaries would raise the same problems); Rev.Rul. 82–131, 1982–2 C.B. 83 (valid business purpose to distribute stock of unregulated subsidiary by regulated parent to justify parent's rate increase for its regulated business; regulatory agency included subsidiary's earnings in rate base to deny rate increase to parent); Rev.Rul. 83–23, 1983–1 C.B. 82 (valid business purpose for spin-off to satisfy foreign decree requiring 60 percent direct ownership of local business by nationals); Rev.Rul. 85–122, 1985–2 C.B. 118 (valid business purpose for the separation of an unprofitable ski resort from profitable golf and tennis resort in order to meet the recommendation of securities underwriter on marketing of debentures); Rev.Rul. 88–33, 1988–1 C.B. 115 (valid business purpose to distribute stock of subsidiary to allow parent to escape burdensome administrative compliance costs imposed on it because of subsidiary's business; subsidiary was subject to state regulatory scheme which also required burdensome registration and compliance by the parent; stock of the subsidiary spun-off pro rata to the parent's stockholders in order to free the parent of the registration requirement).

Rev.Proc. 96–30 (Appendix A), 1996–1 C.B. 696, 706–712, describes numerous business purposes acceptable to seek an advance ruling.

SECTION 3. DISTRIBUTION OF "CONTROL" AND CONTINUITY OF INTEREST REQUIREMENTS

INTERNAL REVENUE CODE: Section 355(a)(1)(A), and (D); 368(a)(2)(H)(ii).

REGULATIONS: Section 1.355–2(a),–2(c).

The nonrecognition principles of § 355 apply to the distribution of stock of a corporation that is "controlled" by the distributing corporation immediately before the distribution. Control is defined in § 368(c) as ownership of 80 percent of voting power and 80 percent of all other classes of stock of a corporation. In addition, § 355(a)(1)(D) requires the distributing corporation to distribute all of the stock or securities of the controlled corporation held by it immediately before the distribution, or, with the permission of the Commissioner, at least 80 percent of the stock of the controlled corporation. This distribution requirement results, at least initially, in continued ownership of the business of the controlled corporation by the shareholders of the distributing corporation.

The Supreme Court addressed these requirements in Commissioner v. Gordon, 391 U.S. 83 (1968). The taxpayers were minority shareholders in the Pacific Telephone and Telegraph Company (Pacific). Ninety percent of the Pacific stock was owned by A.T. & T. In 1961 A.T. & T. decided to split Pacific into two separate corporations, Pacific and Pacific Northwest Bell. Pacific transferred all of the assets and liabilities related to its business in Oregon, Washington and Idaho to Northwest Bell in exchange for all of the Northwest Bell stock and some debt instruments. Pacific retained assets related to its business in California. Also in 1961, Pacific distributed warrants entitling Pacific stockholders to purchase Pacific Northwest Bell stock representing 57 percent of the outstanding stock at a price substantially below the market price at which the stock traded on a public exchange. In 1963, Pacific distributed additional warrants to its stockholders entitling the Pacific stockholders to purchase the remaining 43 percent of Pacific Northwest Bell. The Commissioner argued that the transaction failed the requirements of § 355 because Pacific did not distribute enough stock of Pacific Northwestern Bell in 1961 to constitute control. The Commissioner thus asserted that the taxpayers realized ordinary income in an amount equal to the difference between the value of the Pacific Northwest Bell stock and the purchase price paid on exercise of the warrants. The Supreme Court agreed with the Commissioner, rejecting the taxpayers' argument that in combination the 1961 and 1963 distributions satisfied the requirements of § 355(a)(1)(D).[6]

"* * * The Code requires that 'the distribution' divest the controlling corporation of all of, or 80% control of, the controlled corporation. Clearly, if an initial transfer of less than a controlling interest in the controlled corporation is to be treated for tax purposes as a mere first step in the divestiture of control, it must at least be identifiable as such at the time it is made. Absent other specific directions from Congress, Code provisions must be interpreted so as to conform to the basic premise of annual tax accounting. It would be wholly inconsistent with this premise to hold that the essential character of a transaction, and its tax impact, should remain not only undeterminable but unfixed for an indefinite and unlimited period in the future, awaiting events that might or might not happen. This requirement that the character of a transaction be determinable does not

6. The Commissioner also argued that the transaction failed under § 355 because the Pacific Northwestern Bell stock received by the taxpayers was not distributed to them by Pacific, but was instead sold to the taxpayers for cash under the terms of the warrants. The Court declined to address this argument.

One of the taxpayers sold some warrants for cash. The taxpayer was required to treat the sales proceeds as ordinary income.

mean that the entire divestiture must necessarily occur within a single tax year. It does, however, mean that if one transaction is to be characterized as a 'first step' there must be a binding commitment to take the later steps." (96)

Along with the statutory requirement that "control" of the subsidiary be distributed to the shareholders, Treas.Reg. § 1.355–2(c) imposes a "continuity of interest" requirement in § 355 transactions. This requirement is closely related to the "device" provision in terms of preventing post-distribution sales. See Rev.Rul. 59–197, 1959–1 C.B. 77, treating a pre-distribution sale of stock in the distributing corporation as in effect a binding contract to sell stock in the newly-created corporation after the distribution; but the transaction did not constitute a "device" in view of the valid business purpose for the spin-off, i.e., to permit a key employee to obtain a proprietary interest in the spun-off business. Nonetheless, continuity of interest is an independent requirement aimed at limiting nonrecognition in corporate separations to transactions in which shareholders of the original corporation maintain a continuing interest in each of the corporations surviving a division.

The continuity of interest doctrine in the divisive distribution context does not require that every stockholder in the distributing corporation maintain a continuing interest in each corporation surviving the division. A non-pro rata division may result in some of the stockholders of the divided corporation owning no interest at all in a business in which they were stockholders prior to the divisive reorganization.

The continuity of interest requirement of Treas.Reg. § 1.325–2(c) is satisfied in a divisive reorganization as long as one or more of the stockholders of the original corporation retain sufficient continuing interest in each of the divided corporations, but not necessarily in both. Thus, the regulations indicate that the continuity of interest requirement is satisfied in the following example: A and B own all of the stock of X Corporation. X in turn owns the stock of S Corporation. C acquires 49 percent of A's stock in X. Immediately thereafter, and as part of a prearranged plan, X distributes its S stock to B in exchange for B's stock in X. There is sufficient continuity of interest for nonrecognition treatment under § 355 since the former stockholders of X have a continuing interest in one of the businesses formerly undertaken by X. A has a 51 percent continuing interest in X, B has 100 percent continuing interest in S. Treas.Reg. § 1.355–2(c)(2), Ex. (2).[7]

Treas.Reg. § 1.355–2(c)(2), Ex's. (3) and (4), further indicate that if C purchased all of A's X stock, or purchased 80 percent of A's X stock, before the division, continuity would not exist because the original stockholders of X would have an insufficient continuing interest in one of the two corporations following division. However, this result also is indirectly precluded by

7. The example in the regulations provides that B acquires 50% of A's stock. In that case, however, § 355(d)(3) would require recognition of gain by the distributing corporation, X, on distribution of stock to B.

§ 355(d), discussed at page 683, which was enacted after the examples in Treas. Reg. § 1.355–2(c)(2) were promulgated. Section 355(d) would require recognition of gain by the distributing corporation, X, on the distribution of S stock to B, because C acquired by purchase within the five year period ending on the date of distribution stock representing a 50 percent interest in the distributing corporation immediately after the distribution. Section 355(d) thus indirectly creates a continuity of interest requirement in certain circumstances.

Recent amendments to § 368(a)(2)(H)(ii), however, may have eliminated the continuity of interest requirement. See page 715.

ILLUSTRATIVE MATERIAL

A. THE DISTRIBUTION REQUIREMENT

1. *General*

In Redding v. Commissioner, 630 F.2d 1169 (7th Cir.1980), rev'g. 71 T.C. 597 (1979), the court was presented with a transaction similar to that before the Supreme Court in *Gordon.* In *Redding,* the parent corporation distributed transferable rights to its stockholders which enabled the stockholders to subscribe to shares of stock of the parent corporation's wholly owned subsidiary. The rights could be exercised only for a two-week period. A stockholder could receive one share of the subsidiary's stock for two rights plus $5. During the two-week period the fair market value of the subsidiary's stock ranged from $5.70 per share to $7 per share. An over-the-counter market for the warrants developed during this subscription period. After the two-week period, the warrants became worthless. The Commissioner and the taxpayers stipulated that, as the result of the exercise of the stock rights, more than 80 percent of the subsidiary's stock was distributed in the offering. The parties stipulated further that there was a good business purpose for the distribution of the subsidiary stock, the distribution was not a device for the distribution of earnings and profits, and the 20 percent of the subsidiary's stock retained by the parent corporation was not held for tax avoidance purposes under § 355(a)(1)(D)(ii).

The Commissioner asserted that the rights distribution constituted a taxable dividend under § 301, relying on Rev.Rul. 70–521, 1970–2 C.B. 72, to that effect. The taxpayers, on the other hand, asserted that the transaction was an integrated transaction and qualified under § 355. The Tax Court held that the requirements of § 355(a)(1)(A) and (D) were met. The issuance of the rights by the distributing corporation "was merely a procedural device to give [the distributing corporation] stockholders the opportunity to be included or excluded from the [subsidiary] stock distribution." Having found that the distribution of the stock rights was "merely a brief transitory phase of the corporate separation," the Tax Court concluded that the requirements of § 355(a)(1)(A) and (D) were met. The requisite 80 percent of the subsidiary stock was in fact distributed and after the transaction the stockholders held only stock of the subsidiary.

The Court of Appeals disagreed with the Tax Court's finding that the issuance of the warrants was only a procedural step and concluded that the warrants had independent economic significance in light of their readily ascertainable market value and transferability on an open market. The issuance of the warrants could not, therefore, be disregarded as a mere transitory step in the distribution of the stock of the subsidiary to stockholders of the distributing corporation. The Court of Appeals concluded further that the distribution of the stock of the subsidiary failed the requirement of § 355(a)(1)(A) that the stock of the controlled corporation be distributed with respect to the stock of the distributing corporation. Since the warrants had independent significance, the distribution of the subsidiary's stock was made with respect to the warrants rather than the stock of the distributing corporation. The court held that the distribution of warrants was a dividend to the stockholders.[8]

Although it felt bound by the parties' stipulation that 80 percent control of the subsidiary was distributed to the stockholders of the distributing corporation, the Court of Appeals in *Redding* questioned whether the control requirement of § 355(a)(1)(D) was in fact satisfied. For valid business reasons the distributing corporation retained 1 share less than 20 percent of the subsidiary's stock. Fifty thousand shares of the subsidiary's stock were distributed to underwriters. The remaining shares distributed with respect to exercised warrants represented approximately 76 percent of the subsidiary's stock. The Court of Appeals read § 355(a)(1)(D) in conjunction with § 355(a)(1)(A) to require the distribution of control to persons who were the stockholders of the distributing corporation before the division. That requirement was not satisfied in *Redding* because of the distribution of stock to the underwriters.

The Internal Revenue Service has indicated that it will use the step transaction doctrine to find a qualifying distribution in a § 355 transaction in appropriate cases. In Rev.Rul. 83–142, 1983–2 C.B. 68, a foreign subsidiary of a United States parent corporation distributed assets to a new subsidiary, the controlled corporation, in exchange for stock. To satisfy a requirement of the foreign country in which it was incorporated, the subsidiary sold the stock of the controlled corporation to its parent for cash. The subsidiary thereupon redistributed the cash to its parent as a dividend. The Service held that the transfer of stock of the controlled corporation to the parent was a § 355 distribution by the subsidiary. The subsidiary's sale of stock and subsequent return of cash as a dividend were disregarded for Federal tax purposes as transitory steps taken for the purpose of complying with local law.

2. *Retention of Stock or Securities*

Section 355(a)(1)(D) permits the distributing corporation to retain up to 20 percent of the stock of the spun-off corporation if it is established that

8. Receipt of the warrants was not sheltered from dividend treatment under § 305 because the warrants did not represent rights to acquire the stock of the distributing corporation. 630 F.2d at 1181.

the retention of the stock was not motivated by tax avoidance purposes. Treas.Reg. § 1.355–2(e)(2) warns, however, that ordinarily the corporate business purpose for a divisive reorganization will require the distribution of all the stock and securities of the controlled corporation. The Internal Revenue Service, in addition to examining whether there is a good business purpose for retention of any stock or securities, also looks to whether the retained stock gives the distributing corporation "practical control" over the spun-off corporation. See Rev.Rul. 75–321, 1975–2 C.B. 123 (pursuant to federal banking laws, distributing corporation was required to divest itself of at least 95 percent of the stock of a bank subsidiary; retention of a percent of the bank stock to use as collateral for short-term financing for the distributing corporation's remaining business enterprises was for a valid business purpose and the retained interest did not give the distributing corporation practical control); Rev.Rul. 75–469, 1975–2 C.B. 126 (stock of controlled corporation was pledged as collateral for bank loan; to eliminate dissident stockholders, the distributing corporation desired to spin-off the subsidiary's stock, but the bank required substitute collateral for the loan; debenture issued by the subsidiary to the parent, which was pledged to the bank to secure the loan, could be retained since it gave the distributing corporation no practical control over the spun-off corporation).

B. CONTINUITY OF INTEREST

1. *General*

Some Rulings, mostly issued before the current regulations were proposed in 1977, illustrate the application of the continuity of interest requirement under § 355. In Rev.Rul. 62–138, 1962–2 C.B. 95, regulatory authorities required a bank subsidiary to divest itself of two apartment buildings which it owned. The subsidiary transferred the two apartment buildings to a new corporation and distributed the stock of that corporation to the bank, which in turn distributed the stock to its stockholders. The required continuity of interest was found to exist. See also Rev.Rul. 70–18, 1970–1 C.B. 74 (A, an individual, owned 100 percent of the stock of X and Y Corporations; Y Corporation owned 60 percent and X Corporation owned 40 percent of Z Corporation; Y Corporation was required to divest itself of its interest in Z Corporation; Y Corporation merged into X Corporation, which then distributed all of the Z stock to A; continuity of interest was satisfied under these circumstances); Rev.Rul. 76–528, 1976–2 C.B. 103 (continuity of interest requirement satisfied despite pre-split-up dissolution of partnership that owned 60 percent of the stock of the distributing corporation).

On the other hand, Rev.Rul. 69–293, 1969–1 C.B. 102, disqualified a § 355 transaction for want of continuity of interest where two stockholders who owned all of the stock of a private university spun off a subsidiary trade school and then converted the distributing corporation into a § 501(c)(3) organization in order to qualify for federal financial aid; the stockholder proprietary interests were converted into non-proprietary interests and the requisite continuity of interests was therefore lacking.

2. *Post-Distribution Sales and Reorganizations*

Commissioner v. Morris Trust, 367 F.2d 794 (4th Cir.1966), discussed at page 692, held that a post-distribution tax-free reorganization of the distributing corporation in which its shareholders received a majority of the stock of the surviving corporation did not invalidate a § 355 transaction. On the other hand, in Rev.Rul. 79–273, 1979–2 C.B. 125, continuity of interest was found lacking where P Corporation distributed the stock of its subsidiary to P stockholders as part of a reverse cash merger in which P was acquired by an unrelated corporation. Since the former P stockholders had no continuing interest in P, the distribution of S stock to the P stockholders did not qualify for nonrecognition treatment under § 355.

A result similar to that in Rev. Rul. 79–273 was reached on different reasoning in Rev.Rul. 70–225, 1970–1 C.B. 80, obsoleted by Rev. Rul. 98–44, 1998–37 I.R.B. 4. In Rev. Rul. 79–273, the Service held that an attempted post-distribution (B) reorganization involving the stock of the controlled subsidiary defeated nonrecognition treatment because of the control requirement of § 368(a)(1)(D). T Corporation desired to acquire one of two businesses of R Corporation. Pursuant to a prearranged plan, R Corporation transferred the assets of the desired business to a newly created subsidiary and then distributed the stock of the subsidiary to its sole stockholder. The stockholder then immediately exchanged the stock of the subsidiary for stock of T Corporation in an attempted (B) reorganization. The spin-off failed because the stockholder did not acquire control of the distributed corporation. The transaction was treated in effect as a transfer by R Corporation of part of its assets in exchange for stock of T Corporation, followed by a distribution of the T Corporation stock as a dividend to the sole stockholder of R Corporation. The result in Rev.Rul. 70–225 appears to have been reversed by a 1998 amendment to § 368(a)(2)(H)(ii).

On the other hand, Rev. Rul. 75–406, 1975–2 C.B. 125, modified by Rev. Rul. 96–30, 1996–1 C.B. 36, obsoleted by Rev. Rul. 98–27, 1998–22 I.R.B. 4, held that a spin-off prior to the merger of the distributing corporation into another corporation was a valid § 355 transaction as long as the shareholders were free to vote either for or against the merger after the spin-off.

A wrinkle on the applicability of the continuity of interest requirement in Treas. Reg. § 1.355–2(c) was added by the enactment of § 355(e), discussed at page 718, in 1997. It was the enactment of this provision that led the IRS to declare Rev.Rul. 70–225 and Rev. Rul. 96–30 to be obsolete. The legislative history accompanying § 355(e) states as follows:

"The House bill does not change the present law requirement under section 355 that the distributing corporation must distribute 80 percent of the voting power and 80 percent of each other class of stock of the controlled corporation. It is expected that this requirement will be applied by the Internal Revenue Service taking account of the provisions of the proposal regarding plans that permit certain types of planned restructuring of the distributing corporation following the distribution, and to treat similar restructurings of the controlled corporation in a similar manner.

Thus, the 80–percent control requirement is expected to be administered in a manner that would prevent the tax-free spin-off of a less-than–80–percent controlled subsidiary, but would not generally impose additional restrictions on post-distribution restructurings of the controlled corporation if such restrictions would not apply to the distributing corporation." H.R.Rep. No. 105–220, at 529–30 (1997).

In Rev. Rul. 98–27, 1998–22 I.R.B. 4, the Service interpreted this language as follows:

"[T] the Service will not apply *Court Holding* [324 U.S. 331 (1945)] (or any formulation of the step transaction doctrine) to determine whether the distributed corporation was a controlled corporation immediately before the distribution under § 355(a) solely because of any postdistribution acquisition or restructuring of the distributed corporation, whether prearranged or not. In otherwise applying the step transaction doctrine, the Service will continue to consider all facts and circumstances. See, e.g., Rev. Rul. 63–260, 1963–2 C.B. 147. An independent shareholder vote is only one relevant factor to be considered."

It is unclear whether this statement means that the Service believes that there no longer is any post-distribution continuity of interest requirement, apart from the "device" and business purpose tests, that must be satisfied in order to qualify for § 355 treatment. But it is difficult to understand how the enactment of § 355(e), which in effect overrides only § 355(c), dealing with tax treatment of the corporations, could be interpreted to eliminate a requirement for qualifying the shareholders for nonrecognition under § 355(a).

However, the legislative history of the 1998 amendments to §§ 351(c)(2) and 368(a)(2)(H)(ii) infer that there no longer should be any shareholder continuity of interest requirement imposed with respect to § 355 transactions. S.Rep. No. 105–174, 105th Cong., 2d Sess. (1998) describes the 1998 amendments as follows:

"* * * [I]n the case of certain divisive transactions in which a corporation contributes assets to a controlled corporation and then distributes the stock of the controlled corporation in a transaction that meets the requirements of section 355 (or so much of section 356 as relates to section 355), solely for purposes of determining the tax treatment of the transfers of property to the controlled corporation by the distributing corporation, the fact that the shareholders of the distributing corporation dispose of part or all of the distributed stock shall not be taken into account for purposes of the control immediately after requirement of section 351(a) or 368(a)(1)(D). For purposes of determining the tax treatment of transfers of property to the controlled corporation by parties other than the distributing corporation, the disposition of part or all of the distributed stock continues to be taken into account, as under prior law, in determining whether the control immediately after requirement is satisfied.

"*Example 1*: Distributing corporation D transfers appreciated business X to subsidiary C in exchange for 100 percent of C stock. D distributes its stock of C to D shareholders. As part of a plan or series of related transactions, C merges into unrelated acquiring corporation A, and the C shareholders receive 25 percent of the vote or value of A stock. If the requirements of section 355 are met with respect to the distribution, then the control immediately after requirement will be satisfied solely for purposes of determining the tax treatment of the transfers of property by D to C. Accordingly, the business X assets transferred to C and held by A after the merger will have a carryover basis from D. Section 355(e) will require D to recognize gain as if the C stock had been sold at fair market value.

"*Example 2*: Distributing corporation D transfers appreciated business X to subsidiary C in exchange for 85 percent of C stock. Unrelated persons transfer appreciated assets to C in exchange for the remaining 15 percent of C stock. D distributes all its stock of C to D shareholders. As part of a plan or series of related transactions, C merges into acquiring corporation A; and the interests attributable to the D shareholders' receipt of C stock with respect to their D stock in the distribution represent 25 percent of the vote and value of A stock. If the requirements of section 355 are met with respect to the distribution, then the control immediately after requirement will be satisfied solely for purposes of determining the tax treatment of the transfers of property by D to C. Section 355(e) will require recognition of gain as if the C stock had been sold for fair market value. The business X assets transferred to C and held by A after the merger will have a carryover basis from D. The persons other than D who transferred assets to C for 15 percent of C stock will recognize gain on the appreciation in their assets transferred to C if the control immediately after requirement is not satisfied after taking into account any post-spin-off dispositions that would have been taken into account under prior law.

"*Example 3*: The facts are the same as in example 2, except that the interests attributable to the shareholders' receipt of C stock with respect to their D stock in the distribution represent 55 percent of the vote and value of A stock in the merger. If the requirements of section 355 are met with respect to the distribution, then the control immediately after requirement will be satisfied solely for purposes of determining the tax treatment of the transfers by D to C. The business X assets in C (and in A after the merger) will therefore have a carryover basis from D. Because the D shareholders retain more than 50 percent of the stock of A, section 355(e) will not apply. The persons other than D who transferred property for the 15 percent of C stock will recognize gain on the appreciation in their assets transferred to C if the control immediately after requirement is not satisfied after taking into account any post-spin-off dispositions that would have been taken into account under prior law."

Although the introductory paragraph of the legislative history quoted above refers only to the impact of the amendments with respect to the treatment of the transfer of assets to the controlled subsidiary, it is important to note that the examples presume that a post-distribution disposition of the stock received in the spin-off does not necessarily destroy the § 355 treatment of the distribution by the shareholders even though the shareholders who received the distribution do not even indirectly retain a majority interest in the distributed corporation. If this is so, the continuity of interest requirement in Treas.Reg. § 1.355–.2(c) has been *sub silentio* repealed.

C. COMPARISON WITH PARTIAL LIQUIDATIONS

Apart from the principal focus of § 355 as preventing a corporate bail-out of earnings and profits, § 355 is significant with respect to the question of recognition of corporate level gain on appreciated assets when there is a change of ownership. A comparison of the tax treatment of the spin-off or split-off of a trade or business under § 355 with the tax consequence of the distribution of a trade or business to stockholders in a partial liquidation under § 302(b)(4), page 260, is illustrative. Both transactions involve the distribution of a trade or business with a five year history. If appreciated property is distributed to stockholders in a partial liquidation, gain is recognized at both the corporate and stockholder levels. However, under § 355, if the distributed trade or business is housed in a corporation, no gain or loss is recognized at either level. This different treatment is justified in a § 355 transaction by the stockholders' continued interest in business assets that remain in corporate solution. The double tax regime is protected because gain or loss will ultimately be recognized at the stockholder and corporate levels on disposition of the stock and assets, respectively. A distribution in partial liquidation removes the business assets from corporate solution thus eliminating the opportunity for future taxation of corporate level appreciation. See Simon and Simmons, The Future of Section 355, 40 Tax Notes 291, 296–7 (1988).

SECTION 4. DIVISIVE DISTRIBUTIONS IN CONNECTION WITH ACQUISITIONS

INTERNAL REVENUE CODE: Sections 351(c)(2), 355(e), (f); 368(a)(2)(H)(ii).

As is evident from the preceding material, a source of continuing tension has been whether, and the extent to which, tax-free treatment under § 355 is warranted in the case of a divisive transaction prior to and in contemplation of a subsequent acquisition (whether by taxable purchase or tax-free reorganization) of either the distributing or distributed corporation. Generally speaking, a prearranged spin-off of the corporation to be acquired was denied § 355 nonrecognition. On the other hand, as illustrated by Morris Trust v. Commissioner, page 692, a spin-off followed by a merger in which the distributing corporation's shareholders retained more than 50 percent of the merged entity clearly could be tax-free under § 355. The controversial issue was whether a corporation that was the target of an acquisition could be "customized" by spinning-off to its pre-acquisition shareholders the stock of a subsidiary that the acquiring corporation did not want to acquire. Nevertheless, a number of highly publicized transactions of this nature in the mid-1990s led to congressional concerns that "customizing" tax-free spin-offs were inappropriate, and Congress responded to this issue in 1997 by enacting §§ 355(e) and (f).

General Explanation of Tax Legislation Enacted in 1997

Staff of the Joint Committee on Taxation, 197–203, 205 (1997).

2. Require Gain Recognition on Certain Distributions of Controlled Corporation Stock (Sec. 1012 of the Act and Secs. 355, 358, 351(c), and 368(a)(2)(H) of the Code)

Prior Law

A corporation generally is required to recognize gain on the distribution of property (including stock of a subsidiary) as if such property had been sold for its fair market value. The shareholders generally treat the receipt of property as a taxable event as well. Section 355 of the Internal Revenue Code provides an exception to this rule for certain "spin-off" type distributions of stock of a controlled corporation, provided that various requirements are met, including certain restrictions relating to acquisitions and dispositions of stock of the distributing corporation ("distributing") or the controlled corporation ("controlled") prior and subsequent to a distribution.

In cases where the form of the transaction involves a contribution of assets to the particular controlled corporation that is distributed in connection with the distribution, there are specific Code requirements that distributing corporation's shareholders own "control" of the corporation immediately after the distribution. Control is defined for this purpose as 80 percent of the voting power of all classes of stock entitled to vote and 80 percent of each other class of stock (secs. 368(a)(1)(D), 368(c), and 351(a) and (c)). In addition, it is a requirement for qualification of any section 355 distribution that the distributing corporation distribute control of the controlled corporation (defined by reference to the same 80–percent test). [Pre–1997] law has the effect of imposing more restrictive requirements on certain types of acquisitions or other transfers following a distribution if the company acquired is the controlled corporation rather than the distributing corporation.

* * *

Reasons for Change

The Congress believed that section 355 was intended to permit the tax-free division of existing business arrangements among existing shareholders. In cases in which it is intended that new shareholders will acquire ownership of a business in connection with a spin-off, the transaction more closely resembles a corporate level disposition of the portion of the business that is acquired.

The Congress also believed that the difference in treatment of certain transactions following a spin-off, depending upon whether the distributing or controlled corporation engages in the transaction, should be minimized.

* * *

Explanation of Provision

The Act adopts additional restrictions under section 355 on acquisitions and dispositions of the stock of the distributing or controlled corporation.

Under [section 355(e)], if either the controlled or distributing corporation is acquired pursuant to a plan or arrangement in existence on the date of distribution, gain is recognized as of the date of the distribution.

In the case of an acquisition of either the distributing corporation or the controlled corporation, the amount of gain recognized is the amount that the distributing corporation would have recognized had the stock of the controlled corporation been sold for fair market value on the date of the distribution. Such gain is recognized immediately before the distribution and is treated as long-term capital gain. No adjustment to the basis of the stock or assets of either corporation is allowed by reason of the recognition of the gain.

Whether a corporation is acquired is determined under rules similar to those of * * * section 355(d), except that acquisitions would not be restricted to "purchase" transactions. Thus, an acquisition occurs if one or more persons acquire 50 percent or more of the vote or value of the stock of the controlled or distributing corporation pursuant to a plan or arrangement. For example, assume a corporation ("P") distributes the stock of its wholly owned subsidiary ("S") to its shareholders in a transaction that otherwise qualifies as a section 355 spin-off. If, pursuant to a plan or arrangement, 50 percent or more of the vote or value of either P or S is acquired by one or more persons, the Act requires gain recognition by the distributing corporation. Except as provided in Treasury regulations, if the assets of the distributing or controlled corporation are acquired by a successor in a merger or other transaction under section 368(a)(1)(A), (C) or (D) of the Code, the shareholders (immediately before the acquisition) of the corporation acquiring such assets are treated as acquiring stock in the corporation from which the assets were acquired. Under Treasury regulations, other asset transfers also could be subject to this rule.

Under [section 355(e)(4)(C)], certain aggregation and attribution rules apply for determining whether one or more persons has acquired a 50–percent or greater interest in distributing or controlled. * * *

A public offering of sufficient size can result in an acquisition that causes gain recognition under the provision.

Acquisitions occurring within the four-year period beginning two years before the date of distribution are presumed to have occurred pursuant to a plan or arrangement. Taxpayers can avoid gain recognition by showing that an acquisition occurring during this four-year period was unrelated to the distribution.

* * *

Certain transactions not considered acquisitions

Under the Act, certain specific types of transactions do not cause gain recognition or are not counted as acquisitions for purposes of determining whether there has been an acquisition of a 50-percent or greater interest in the distributing or the controlled corporation.

Single affiliated group

Under [section 355(e)(2)(C)], a plan (or series of related transactions) is not one that will cause gain recognition if, immediately after the completion of such plan or transactions, the distributing corporation and all controlled corporations are members of a single affiliated group of corporations (as defined in section 1504 without regard to subsection (b) thereof).

* * *

Continuing direct or indirect ownership

Under [section 355(e)(3)(A)], except as provided in Treasury regulations, certain acquisitions are not taken into account in determining whether a 50-percent or greater interest in distributing or controlled has been acquired. Generally, in any transaction, stock received directly or indirectly by former shareholders of distributing or controlled, in a successor or new controlling corporation of either, is not treated as acquired stock if it is attributable to such shareholders' stock in distributing or controlled that was not acquired as part of a plan or arrangement to acquire 50 percent or more of such successor or other corporation.

* * *

Example 2: Individual A owns all the stock of P corporation. P owns all the stock of a subsidiary corporation, S. Subsidiary S is distributed to individual A in a transaction that otherwise qualifies under section 355. As part of a plan, P then merges with corporation X, also owned entirely by individual A. There is not an acquisition that requires gain recognition under the provision, because individual A owns directly or indirectly 100 percent of all the stock of both X, the successor to P, and S before and after the transaction.[225] * * *

Example 3: Assume the facts are the same as in Example 2 except that corporations P and X are each owned by the same 20 individual 5-percent shareholders (rather than wholly by individual A). The transaction described in Example 2, in which S is spun off by P to P's shareholders and P

225. The example assumes that A did not acquire his or her stock in P as part of a plan or series of related transactions that results in the direct or indirect ownership of 50 percent or more of S or P separately by A. If A's stock in P was acquired as part of such a plan, the transaction would be one requiring gain recognition on the spin-off of S.

is acquired by X, would not cause gain recognition, because each shareholder that owned stock of distributing and controlled before the transaction continues to own the same percentage of stock of each corporation after the transaction.

* * *

Except as provided in Treasury regulations, certain other acquisitions also are not taken into account. For example, under section 355(e)(3)(A), the following other types of acquisitions of stock are not subject to the provision, provided that the stock owned before the acquisition was not acquired pursuant to a plan or series of related transactions to acquire a 50-percent or greater ownership interest in either distributing or controlled:

* * *

[Section 355(e)] does not apply to distributions that would otherwise be subject to section 355(d) * * *, which imposes corporate level tax on certain disqualified distributions.

[Section 355(e)] does not apply to a distribution pursuant to a title 11 or similar case.

Section 355(f)

[Section 355(f)] provides that, except as provided in Treasury regulations, section 355 (or so much of section 356 as relates to section 355) shall not apply to the distribution of stock from one member of an affiliated group of corporations (as defined in section 1504(a)) to another member of such group (an "intragroup spin-off") if such distribution is part of a plan (or series of related transactions) described in subsection (e)(2)(A)(ii), pursuant to which one or more persons acquire directly or indirectly stock representing a 50-percent or greater interest in the distributing corporation or any controlled corporation.

Example 5: P corporation owns all the stock of subsidiary corporation S. S owns all the stock of subsidiary corporation T. S distributes the stock of T corporation to P as part of a plan or series of related transactions in which P then distributes S to its shareholders and then P is merged into unrelated X corporation. After the merger, former shareholders of X corporation own 50 percent or more of the voting power or value of the stock of the merged corporation. Because the distribution of T by S is part of a plan or series of related transactions in which S is distributed by P outside the P affiliated group and P is then acquired under section 355(e), section 355 in its entirety does not apply to the intragroup spin-off of T to P, under section 355(f). Also, the distribution of S by P is subject to section 355(e).

In determining whether an acquisition described in subsection (e)(2)(A)(ii) occurs, all the provisions of new subsection 355(e) are applied. For example, an intragroup spin-off in connection with an overall transaction that does not cause gain recognition under section 355(e) because it is described in section 355(e)(2)(C), or because of section 355(e)(3), * * * is not subject to the rule of section 355(f).

* * *

ILLUSTRATIVE MATERIAL

A. ASPECTS OF SECTION 355(e)

1. *Corporate Level Issues*

Even though § 355(e) requires corporate level recognition of gain with respect to stock in transactions that otherwise qualify for nonrecognition under § 355, nonrecognition at the shareholder level is still the order of the day. What is the precise tax policy justification for § 355(e)? Section 355(e) can, and often will, apply even though neither the distributing corporation nor the distributed corporation has itself received any consideration, let alone any cash consideration, and the only consideration that the shareholders have received is stock in one or more corporations. Furthermore, none of the assets held in corporate solution has received a step-up in basis. Given these parameters, why should the distributing corporation recognize gain with respect to the stock of the distributed corporation?

Nevertheless, customizing spin-offs do have the potential for abuse. Assume, for example, that T manufactures toys and airplanes. P wants to acquire the airplane business, but not the toy business, and is willing to pay in stock and deferred cash. To effectuate the transaction, T borrows an amount equal to one-half of the negotiated purchase price. T then contributes the cash and the toy business to S, which is spun-off to the T shareholders. Thereafter, T, which retained the liability for the borrowed money that has been transferred to S, is merged into P and the T shareholders (who also are the S shareholders) receive P stock. Since S holds cash equal to one half of the total consideration effectively provided by P, the transaction has significant overtones of a sale of the airplane division at the corporate level. If this perceived abuse is the real problem with which Congress was concerned, could it have drafted a more narrowly targeted remedy?

Another strange aspect of § 355(e) is the measure of gain. Regardless of whether the controlling corporation or the distributed corporation is the corporation that is subsequently acquired, the recognized gain is measured with reference to the stock of the distributed subsidiary.[9] This might be a reasonable measure of the gain to be recognized in cases where the subsidiary is the subsequently acquired corporation, but if the original controlling corporation is the corporation that is acquired, as in the above example, it is difficult to understand why Congress considered the proper measure of gain to be the appreciation in the stock of the distributed

9. If the distributee corporation was formed in a § 368(a)(1)(D) reorganization in contemplation of the distribution, § 368(a)(2)(H)(ii) preserves the tax-free status of that transaction even if the controlling corporation's shareholders dispose of the stock of the distributed corporation in a transaction subject to § 355(e).

corporation, which is retained by the shareholders of the acquired target corporation.

2. *Shareholder Level Issues*

In Rev. Rul. 96–30, 1996–1 C.B. 36, obsoleted by Rev. Rul. 98–27, 1998–22 I.R.B. 4, D Corporation distributed the stock of a controlled subsidiary, C Corporation, to its shareholders. Soon after the distribution, Y Corporation proposed to acquire C Corporation and subsequently C Corporation was merged into Y Corporation in a tax-free merger in which the former C Corporation shareholders received 25 percent of the stock of Y Corporation. No negotiations had occurred between D Corporation and Y Corporation, and the C Corporation shareholders were free to vote their stock as they saw fit. The Service ruled that the step transaction doctrine must be applied to determine whether the substance on the transaction was the same as its form or whether in substance C Corporation had been merged into Y Corporation prior to the distribution by D Corporation, followed by a constructive distribution by D Corporation to its shareholders of the Y Corporation stock received in the merger. In the latter case the transaction would not have qualified under § 355. Based on the facts and circumstances, particularly the fact that there had been no pre-distribution negotiations regarding the acquisition of C Corporation by Y Corporation, the Service ruled that the form of the transaction would be respected and § 355 thus applied.

Following the enactment of § 355(e), in Rev. Rul. 98–27, 1998–22 I.R.B. 4 the Service obsoleted Rev. Rul. 96–30. Rev. Rul. 98–27 states that the Service no longer will apply *Court Holding Company* principles (or any other variant of the step transaction doctrine) to determine whether for purposes of § 355(a) the distributed corporation qualifies as a controlled corporation solely because of any post-distribution acquisition or restructuring of the distributed corporation, whether prearranged or not. According to the ruling, any implication that § 355(a) restricts post-distribution acquisitions or restructurings of a controlled corporation is inconsistent with § 355(e) and its legislative history (citing H.R.Rep. No. 105–220, at 529–30). In applying the step transaction doctrine to divisive transactions for other purposes, however, the Service will continue to consider all facts and circumstances.

B. ASPECTS OF SECTION 355(f)

1. *Background*

The effect of § 355(e), which triggers gain to the distributing corporation if it applies, is rather straightforward. The effect of § 335(f), which removes the transaction from the ambit of § 355 entirely, however, is not so clear. Since § 355(f) applies only when the distributee shareholders are one or more corporations that are members of the same affiliated group of corporations as the distributing and controlled corporations, special rules control the taxation of the distribution even though § 355 does not apply. The precise treatment of the transaction depends on whether or not the corporations involved in the transaction file consolidated returns, which are discussed in Chapter 10.

2. *Effect of Section 355(f)*

(a) Corporations That Do Not File Consolidated Returns

If the corporations involved in the transaction do not file consolidated returns, under § 311 (discussed at page 202) the distributing corporation generally must recognize gain (but not loss) with respect to the distributed stock of the controlled corporation.[10] The distributee corporation recognizes dividend income equal to the fair market value of the stock, but the income item is entirely offset by a 100 percent dividends received deduction under § 243 (discussed at page 227). Nevertheless, pursuant to § 301(d), the distributee corporation takes a fair market value basis in the stock of the controlled corporation. The distributee corporation's basis in the distributing corporation stock that it continues to hold is not affected. See I.R.C. § 1059(e)(2). Thus, whether the distributing corporation or the controlled corporation is acquired after the spin-off, the tax consequence of the spin-off is limited to recognition of gain by the distributing corporation with respect to the controlled corporation's stock.

(b) Corporations That File Consolidated Returns

The effect of § 355(f) is different if the distributing and distributee shareholder corporation file consolidated returns. First, although the distributing corporation recognizes gain on the distribution of the controlled corporation under § 311(a), the dividend distribution is a deferred intercompany transaction, and pursuant to Treas. Reg. § 1.1502–13(f)(2)(iii), discussed at page 459, the gain is not immediately recognized. The distributee corporation excludes the dividend from gross income, Treas. Reg. §§ 1.1502–13(f)(2)(iii), but must reduce its basis in the stock of the distributing corporation by the amount of the excluded dividend, i.e., the fair market value of the stock of the controlled corporation received in the distribution. Treas. Reg. §§ 1.1502–32 (discussed at page 449). If the distributee corporation subsequently disposes of the controlled corporation received in the spin-off, the distributing corporation must recognize its deferred gain without regard to whether the disposition is a sale or a tax-free reorganization. Treas. Reg. §§ 1.1502–13. The same result occurs if the distributee corporation disposes of the stock of the distributing corporation.

3. *Pyramiding Sections 355(e) and 355(f)*

It is possible for both § 355(e) and § 355(f) to apply to a series of transactions involving an intragroup spin-off followed by a spin-off out of the group as part of a plan by which a majority interest in either of the distributing corporations or the distributed controlled corporation subsequently is acquired by new owners. Assume that X Corporation is publicly

10. If, however, the distributing corporation liquidates as part of the transaction, § 337 (discussed at page 345) may provide nonrecognition of gain or loss with respect to the stock of the controlled corporation.

held and owns all of the stock of Y Corporation, which in turn owns all of the stock of Z Corporation. The corporations file a consolidated return. To facilitate the acquisition of X Corporation by P Corporation, Y Corporation distributes all of the stock of Z Corporation to X Corporation, which in turn distributes the Z Corporation stock to its public shareholders. Thereafter, X Corporation is merged into P Corporation. After the merger the former shareholders of X Corporation hold less than 50 percent of the P Corporation stock. Pursuant to § 355(f), § 355 does not apply to the distribution of Z Corporation stock to X Corporation by Y Corporation. The distribution is a taxable distribution, but Y Corporation can defer its intercompany gain and X Corporation can eliminate the dividend from gross income. X Corporation takes a fair market value basis in the Z Corporation stock, but must reduce its basis in its Y Corporation stock by a like amount. Section 355(e) applies to the distribution by X Corporation to its shareholders of the Z Corporation stock, but because X Corporation's basis in the Z Corporation stock equals its fair market value on the day it was received, if the distribution follows promptly, it is likely that little, if any, gain will be realized. As a result of the spin-off of Z Corporation by X Corporation, Y Corporation recognizes its deferred intercompany gain, and X Corporation increases its basis in Y Corporation by the amount of gain recognized. The same consequences would follow if P acquired Z Corporation.

C. SPECIAL BASIS PROBLEMS IN INTRAGROUP SPIN–OFFS

In the case of an intragroup spin-off, i.e, a divisive distribution of stock from one member of an affiliated group of corporations (as defined in § 1504(a)) to another member of the group, the issues involving the appropriate effects on basis are essentially the same whether or not the spin-off is part of an acquisition. Spin-offs in the consolidated return context present special problems even if an acquisition is not in the wind. In this case, the basis of the distributed corporation is generally determined with reference to the basis of the distributing corporation. The basis allocation rules generally eliminate any excess loss account in the stock of a controlled corporation that is distributed within the group. See I.R.C. §§ 355(c), 358; Treas. Reg. § 1.1502–19(b)(2)(i). Congress also was concerned that a § 355 distribution within an affiliated group that does not file a consolidated return also could result in similar basis results, which it considered inappropriate. Congress addressed these issues by giving the Treasury Department broad regulatory authority in § 358(g), which is discussed in the following excerpt from Staff of the Joint Committee on Taxation, General Explanation of Tax Legislation Enacted in 1997, 203–204 (1997).

"[Section 358(g)] provides that in the case of any distribution of stock of one member of an affiliated group of corporations to another member under section 355 ('intragroup spin-off'), the Secretary of the Treasury is authorized under section 358(g) to provide adjustments to the basis of any stock in a corporation which is a member of such group, to reflect appropriately the proper treatment of such distribution. It is understood that the approach of any such regulations applied to intragroup spinoffs that do not involve an acquisition may also be applied under the Treasury regulatory authority to modify the rule of section 355(f) as may be appropriate.

"Congress believed that the concerns relating to basis adjustments in the case of intragroup spin-offs are essentially similar, whether or not an acquisition is currently intended as part of a plan or series of related transactions. The concerns include the following. First, under present law consolidated return regulations, it is possible that an excess loss account of a lower tier subsidiary may be eliminated. This creates the potential for the subsidiary to leave the group without recapture of the excess loss account, even though the group has benefitted from the losses or distributions in excess of basis that led to the existence of the excess loss account.

"Second, under present law, a shareholder's stock basis in its stock of the distributing corporation is allocated after a spin-off between the stock of the distributing and controlled corporations, in proportion to the relative fair market values of the stock of those companies. If a disproportionate amount of asset basis (as compared to value) is in one of the companies (including but not limited to a shift of value and basis through a borrowing by one company and contribution of the borrowed cash to the other), present law rules under section 358(c) can produce an increase in stock basis relative to asset basis in one corporation, and a corresponding decrease in stock basis relative to asset basis in the other company. Because the spin-off has occurred within the corporate group, the group can continue to benefit from high inside asset basis either for purposes of sale or depreciation, while also choosing to benefit from the disproportionately high stock basis in the other corporation. If, for example, both corporations were sold at a later date, a prior distribution can result in a significant decrease in the amount of gain recognized than would have occurred if the two corporations had been sold together without a prior spin off (or separately, without a prior spin-off).

"*Example 6:* P owns all the stock of S1 and S1 owns all the stock of S2. P's basis in the stock of S1 is 50; the inside asset basis of S1's assets is 50; and the total value of S1's stock and assets (including the value of S2) is 150. S1's basis in the stock of S2 is 0; the inside basis of S2's assets is 0; and the value of S2's stock and assets is 100. If S1 were sold, holding S2, the total gain would be 100. S1 distributes S2 to P in a section 355 transaction. After this spin-off, under present law, P's basis in the stock of 51 is approximately 17 (50/150 times the total 50 stock basis in 51 prior to the spin-off) and the inside asset basis of S1 is 50. P's basis in the stock of S2 is 33 (100/150 times the total 50 stock basis in 51 prior to the spin-off) and the inside asset basis of S2 is 0. After a period of time, S2 can be sold for its value of 100, with a gain of 67 rather than 100. Also, since S1 remains in the corporate group, the full 50 inside asset basis can continue to be used. S1's assets could be sold for 50 with no gain or loss. Thus, S1 and S2 can be sold later at a total gain of 67, rather than the total gain of 100 that would have occurred had they been sold without the spin-off.

"As one variation on the foregoing concern, taxpayers have attempted to utilize spin-offs to extract significant amounts of asset value and basis, (including but not limited to transactions in which one corporation decreases its value by incurring debt, and increases the asset basis and value of the other corporation by contributing the proceeds of the debt to the other corporation) without creation of an excess loss account or triggering of gain, even when the extraction is in excess of the basis in the distributing corporation's stock.

"The Treasury Department may promulgate any regulations necessary to address these concerns and other collateral issues. As one example, the Treasury Department may consider providing rules that require a carryover basis within the group (or stock basis conforming to asset basis as appropriate) for the distributed corporation (including a carryover of an excess loss account, if any, in a consolidated return). Similarly, the Treasury Department may provide a reduction in the basis of the stock of the distributing corporation to reflect the change in the value and basis of the distributing corporation's assets. The Treasury Department may determine that the aggregate stock basis of distributing and controlled after the distribution may be adjusted to an amount that is less than the aggregate basis of the stock of the distributing corporation before the distribution, to prevent inappropriate potential for artificial losses or diminishment of gain on disposition of any of the corporations involved in the spin-off. The Treasury Department may provide separate regulations for corporations in affiliated groups filing a consolidated return and for affiliated groups not filing a consolidated return, as appropriate to each situation."

PART VI

CORPORATE ATTRIBUTES IN REORGANIZATIONS AND OTHER TRANSACTIONS

CHAPTER 16

CARRY OVER AND LIMITATION OF CORPORATE TAX ATTRIBUTES

SECTION 1. CARRY OVER OF TAX ATTRIBUTES

INTERNAL REVENUE CODE: Section 381.

REGULATIONS: Section 1.381(a)–1(b)(1) and (2).

Commissioner v. Sansome

United States Court of Appeals, Second Circuit, 1932.
60 F.2d 931.

[In 1921 Corporation X transferred all its assets to newly-formed Corporation Y in return for all of the latter's stock, which went to the Corporation X shareholders. Corporation X had a large amount of earnings and profits. Corporation Y did not earn profits after its formation but instead suffered some losses. Corporation Y then made cash distributions in 1923 which under the applicable statute, § 201 of the 1921 Act, were taxable if those distributions were out of "its earnings and profits." If the earnings and profits of Corporation X were taken into account, then the distributions would be taxable. The 1921 transaction was a reorganization under the applicable statute, § 202(c)(2) of the 1921 Act.]

■ L. Hand, Circuit Judge. * * * It seems to us that [§ 202(c)(2) of the 1921 Act] should be read as a gloss upon [§ 201 of the 1921 Act]. That section provides for cases of corporate "reorganization" which shall not result in any "gain or loss" to the shareholder participating in them, and it defines them with some particularity. He must wait until he has disposed of the new shares, and use his original cost as the "base" to subtract from what he gets upon the sale. Such a change in the form of the shares is "an exchange of property," not a "sale or other disposition" of them * * *. It appears to us extremely unlikely that what was not "recognized" as a sale or disposition for the purpose of fixing gain or loss, should be "recognized" as changing accumulated profits into capital in a section which so far overlapped the latter. That in substance declared that some corporate transactions should not break the continuity of the corporate life, a troublesome question that the courts had beclouded by recourse to such vague alternatives as "form" and "substance," anodynes for the pains of reasoning. The effort was at least to narrow the limits of judicial inspiration, and we cannot think that the same issue was left at large in the earlier section. Hence we hold that a corporate reorganization which results in no "gain or loss" under [§ 202(c)(2) of the 1921 Act], does not toll the company's life as a continued venture under [§ 201 of the 1921 Act], and that what were "earnings or profits" of the original * * * company remain, for purposes of distribution, "earnings and profits" of the successor * * *.

Order reversed; cause remanded for further proceedings in accord with the foregoing.

ILLUSTRATIVE MATERIAL

A. GENERAL

The *Sansome* doctrine respecting earnings and profits is but one facet of a larger problem-to what extent is the acquiring corporation to be regarded as succeeding to the tax characteristics, benefits and obligations possessed by the transferor corporation, where both are parties to a tax-free reorganization. Prior to 1954, the rules regarding carry over of corporate attributes were found mainly in court decisions.

Section 381, enacted in 1954, contains detailed but non-exclusive statutory rules regarding the carry over of items in corporate liquidations and reorganizations in which the acquiring corporation steps into the shoes of the transferor or distributing corporation. Under § 381(a), corporate attributes carry over on the liquidation of a controlled subsidiary in which the parent takes the basis of the subsidiary's assets pursuant to §§ 332 and 334(b), discussed at page 345, and in type (A), (C), and (F) reorganizations and nondivisive type (D) and (G) reorganizations. In general, § 381 applies to transactions in which the transferor corporation is absorbed by the acquiring corporation in a tax free transaction, such as a reorganization. Section 381 does not apply to taxable acquisitions, for example, a "cash merger".

Under Treas.Reg. § 1.381(a)–1(b)(2), the acquiring corporation that succeeds to tax attributes of the transferor is the corporation that acquires directly or indirectly all of the assets transferred by the transferor. Under the regulations, there may be only one acquiring corporation. Thus, if X Corporation acquires all of the assets of T in a type (C) reorganization and thereafter transfers one-half of the assets to its wholly owned subsidiary, S1 and the remaining one-half of the T assets to a wholly owned subsidiary S2, X, as the corporation which first acquired all of T's assets, is treated as the acquiring corporation so that neither S1 nor S2 succeeds to T's corporate attributes. See Treas.Reg. § 1.381(a)–1(b)(2)(ii), Ex. (4).

B. CARRY OVER OF EARNINGS AND PROFITS

Sections 381(a) and 381(c)(2) provide in general that in the transactions covered under § 381(a) the earnings and profits, or deficit in earnings and profits, of the transferor or distributing corporation carry over to the acquiring corporation, but that any deficit in earnings and profits of the corporations involved shall be used only to offset earnings and profits accumulated after the date of transfer or distribution. Treas.Reg. § 1.381(c)(2)–1(a)(5). Thus, a deficit earnings account of one corporation cannot be used to offset pre-transfer accumulated earnings of the other. Treas.Reg. § 1.381(c)(2)–1(a)(2). If both corporations either have accumulated earnings, or a deficit in accumulated earnings, the earnings and profits accounts are consolidated into a single account in the surviving corporation. Treas.Reg. § 1.381(c)(2)–1(a)(4). Treas.Reg. § 1.381(c)(2)–1(a)(2) also provides that earnings and profits inherited by the acquiring corporation become part of its accumulated earnings and profits, but not part of current earnings and profits for purposes of § 316(a)(2).

The rule that a deficit in accumulated earnings can offset only profits accumulated after the date of transfer requires identification of the transfer date. Treas.Reg. § 1.381(b)–1(b)(1) provides that the relevant date is the date on which the transfer is finally completed. Treas.Reg. § 1.381(b)–1(b)(2) and (3) also allow the taxpayer to specify a transfer date by filing a statement indicating the date on which substantially all of the assets of the transferor are transferred and the transferor has ceased business operations.

Treas.Reg. § 1.381(c)(2)–1(c) requires an adjustment to the earnings and profits of the transferor corporation to reflect distributions. In the case of a reorganization in which the transferor distributes other property along with stock or securities allowed to be received under § 354 without recognition of gain, the earnings and profits of the transferor corporation as of the transfer date are reduced by the amount attributable to the distribution. In the case of a liquidation of the transferor corporation under § 332, the earnings and profits of the transferor must be adjusted to account for distributions of property to minority stockholders. In both cases, the adjustments are required whether the distributions are made before or after the transfer date.

C. CARRY OVER OF NET OPERATING LOSSES

1. *General*

Net operating losses are probably the most significant corporate tax attribute affected by § 381. Normally a corporation with a net operating loss for the taxable year is entitled to carryback its loss to the two taxable years preceding the loss year, and then forward for the next twenty taxable years. I.R.C. § 172(b)(1)(A), (B). Section 381(c)(1) allows the transfer of an acquired corporation's net operating loss carryover to the acquiring corporation in a transaction covered by § 381(a), but limits the carryover to taxable income of the acquiring corporation attributable to the period following the transfer date. If the transfer date is any day other than the last day of the acquiring corporation's taxable year, the taxable year of the acquiring corporation is divided into two periods and taxable income is allocated to each period on a daily basis. An inherited loss carryover may be deducted by the acquiring corporation in the year of the transfer only against income allocated to the period subsequent to the transfer date. This rule results in the creation of two separate years for carry over purposes; one carryover year for the transferor corporation ending on the transfer date, and a second period ending on the last day of the acquiring corporation's taxable year. If the acquiring corporation acquires several loss corporations during a taxable year, the taxable year of the acquiring corporation will be divided into several short periods, one for the transfer date of each acquisition. Treas.Reg. § 1.381(c)(1)–2(b)(2). If the transfer occurs on the last day of the acquiring corporation's taxable year, the inherited loss carryover may be used only in subsequent taxable years.

Even though § 381 provides for the carry over of net operating losses to the acquiring corporation, § 382, discussed in Section 2, restricts the rate at which those losses may be claimed against post-acquisition income, including income that is derived from the business of the acquired corporation.

The taxable year of the transferor corporation ends on the transfer date. I.R.C. § 381(b)(1). Under § 381(b)(3), net operating losses of the acquiring corporation may not be carried back to taxable years of the transferor corporation preceding the transfer date, except in an (F) reorganization. Thus, for example, if X Corporation acquires the assets of Y Corporation in a statutory merger, and following the transfer date the combined enterprise incurs a net operating loss, the loss cannot be carried back to pre-acquisition profitable years of Y, even if the loss is attributable entirely to a trade or business acquired from Y. The loss may be carried back, however, and deducted from pre-acquisition taxable income of X, the acquiring corporation.

In Bercy Industries v. Commissioner, 640 F.2d 1058 (9th Cir.1981), the Court of Appeals declined to strictly interpret § 381(b)(3). The taxpayer was acquired by another corporation in a reverse triangular merger in which the newly formed subsidiary acquired all of the assets of the taxpayer in exchange for its parent corporation's stock. Immediately after the acquisition the acquiring subsidiary corporation changed its name to that of the taxpayer (the transaction occurred prior to enactment of § 368(a)(2)(E)). The Court held that the purpose of § 381(b)(3) was to avoid accounting difficulties in allocating post acquisition losses of the surviving corporation between pre-acquisition carryback years of the acquired corporation and the surviving corporation. The court concluded that when the acquiring corporation in a triangular reorganization is merely a shell corporation formed for the purpose of the acquisition, the policy of § 381(b)(3) is not violated. (640 F.2d at 1061–1062.) Thus post-reorganization losses of the surviving corporation were allowed to be carried back to pre-reorganization years of the acquired corporation. The court also noted that the surviving corporation was essentially the same entity as the acquired corporation. See also Aetna Casualty & Sur. Co. v. United States, 568 F.2d 811 (2d Cir.1976).

2. *Liquidation of a Worthless Subsidiary*

In the case of a parent-subsidiary relationship, there is an interplay between § 381 and § 165(g)(3). If § 332 applies to the liquidation of a controlled subsidiary, see page 345, § 381 provides for the carry over to the parent of the subsidiary's tax attributes. But § 332 does not apply to the liquidation of an 80 percent controlled subsidiary unless some assets of the liquidating subsidiary are allocable to the common stock after payment of all creditors and preferred stockholders including the parent. If the common stock of the subsidiary is worthless, then § 332 is not applicable and § 381(a) does not permit a carry over of net operating losses. See Rev.Rul. 68–359, 1968–2 C.B. 161; Rev.Rul. 68–602, 1968–2 C.B. 135. However, if the parent owns 80 percent of the subsidiary stock (and the subsidiary was operating a business), then § 165(g)(3) applies to give the parent an ordinary loss on its stock and security investment in the subsidiary. "Securities" here means any debt obligation that is in registered form or with interest coupons. If the debt obligation is not a security, an ordinary loss still results under § 166. These ordinary losses in turn can create both loss carrybacks and carryovers for the parent, the duration of which starts with the year of worthlessness. If § 165(g)(3) does not apply, the parent's worthless stock and security losses are capital losses, with other worthless debt losses being ordinary.

In Marwais Steel Co. v. Commissioner, 354 F.2d 997 (9th Cir.1965), a subsidiary corporation borrowed operating capital from its parent and incurred net operating losses. The parent claimed bad debt deductions with respect to loans made to the subsidiary. The subsidiary was subsequently liquidated and the parent attempted to use the subsidiary's net operating losses under § 381. Despite the literal satisfaction of § 381, the court denied the carryover since the net operating losses had formed the rationale for the previous bad debt deductions, and a double deduction was not permitted. But in Textron Inc. v. United States, 561 F.2d 1023 (1st Cir.1977), a parent corporation was allowed to claim a deduction for the worthless stock of its subsidiary despite the fact that the subsidiary was subsequently able to acquire a new profitable business and use its net operating loss carryovers to offset the income from the new business. Section 382(g)(4)(D) now limits the use of net operating losses in a Textron type situation. See page 770.

D. CAPITAL LOSS CARRYOVERS

Under § 381(c)(3), the transferor's excess capital losses carryover to the acquiring corporation on much the same terms as net operating losses. The inherited capital loss carryover becomes a capital loss carryover of the acquiring corporation for purposes of § 1212, the capital loss carryover provision. The transferor's capital losses are available to the acquiring corporation in the acquiring corporation's first taxable year ending after the transfer date. I.R.C. § 381(c)(3)(A). The amount of the transferor's capital loss that can be utilized by the acquiring corporation in the year of the transfer is limited to the proportion of the acquiring corporation's capital gain net income that is allocable on a daily basis to the portion of the acquiring corporation's taxable year remaining after the transfer date. I.R.C. § 381(c)(3)(B). In addition, under § 381(b)(3), any net capital loss of the acquiring corporation incurred after the transfer date cannot be carried back to offset capital gain net income of the transferor derived in a taxable year ending on or prior to the transfer date.

E. CARRY OVER OF OTHER ATTRIBUTES

In addition to earnings and profits and loss carryovers, § 381(c) lists a number of separate corporate attributes that carry over in a transaction described by § 381(a). Several of these provisions deal with accounting issues. In general, § 381(c)(4) provides for continuation of the transferor's method of accounting, but authorizes regulations to prescribe the method to be used if the parties to the transfer use different methods. Under Treas.Reg. § 1.381(c)(4)–1(b)(2), if the acquiring corporation maintains the assets of the transferor as a separate and distinct trade or business, the acquiring corporation must continue to use the accounting method of the transferor with respect to that trade or business. If the transferor's assets are integrated into a trade or business of the acquiring corporation, the acquiring corporation must adopt whichever accounting method is determined to be the "principal method of accounting" based on a comparison of the relative asset bases and gross receipts of the component businesses immediately preceding the transfer date. Treas.Reg. § 1.381(c)(4)–1(b)(2), (c). In any event, the method adopted must clearly reflect income of the acquiring corporation and the acquiring corporation may apply for permission from the Commissioner to adopt a different method of accounting. Any change in a method of accounting under these provisions may require adjustments under § 481, which is intended to avoid double counting of income and deduction items. A method of accounting for purposes of § 381(c)(4) includes, under § 446, the accounting treatment of any material item of income or deduction in addition to the taxpayer's overall method of accounting. Treas.Reg. § 1.382(c)(4)–1(a)(2). Thus, § 381(c)(4) applies broadly to numerous items not specifically enumerated in § 381(c).

Several accounting matters are specifically described in § 381(c): inventory accounting carries over under rules similar to accounting methods, § 381(c)(5); the acquiring corporation inherits the transferor's depreciation and capital recovery elections and methods, § 381(c)(6); the transferor's installment sales reporting continues without change, § 381(c)(8); amortization of premium and discount on the transferor's bonds for which the acquiring corporation becomes liable are reported by the acquiring corporation as they would have been by the transferor, § 381(c)(9); and the acquiring corporation is entitled to the benefits of § 111 with respect to the recovery of items previously deducted by the transferor, § 381(c)(12).

The acquiring corporation steps directly into the shoes of the transferor with respect to some deduction and credit items: the acquiring corporation may deduct contributions to employee benefit plans under § 404, § 381(c)(11); the acquiring corporation inherits an obligation to replace property involuntarily converted if nonrecognition treatment was claimed by the transferor under § 1033, § 381(c)(13); the acquiring corporation becomes entitled to general business credit carryovers and is potentially liable for credit recapture, § 381(c)(24); and the acquiring corporation becomes entitled to the transferor's § 53 credit for prior year alternative minimum tax liability, § 381(c)(25).

Section 381(c)(16) allows the acquiring corporation to deduct payments of liabilities that result from obligations of the transferor assumed by the acquiring corporation if the liability would have been deductible by the transferor if paid by it. This provision permits the acquiring corporation to avoid capitalization of such liabilities as part of the cost of the acquired assets. Section 381(c)(16) provides, however, that deductibility is available only if the assumed obligation is not reflected in the amount of stock or securities transferred by the acquiring corporation for the assets of the transferor. Treas.Reg. § 1.381(c)(16)–1(a)(5) provides that if the liability is known at the time of transfer, and the amount of consideration transferred by the acquiring corporation is reduced to account for the liability, the liability will be treated as reflected in the stock transfer. Otherwise, it is presumed that a liability is not reflected in the consideration transferred. Treas.Reg. § 1.381(c)(16)–1(a)(1) provides that a liability not subject to § 381(c)(16) is subject to the general accounting provision of § 381(c)(4). Although this reference may be read to require that a liability assumed as part of the consideration for the acquisition must be capitalized, that is not necessarily the case. In Rev.Rul. 83–73, 1983–1 C.B. 84, the taxpayer acquired the assets of Y Corporation in a type (A) reorganization. The assets were subject to an outstanding contingent claim against Y which the taxpayer settled for $700x. Pursuant to an agreement entered into at the time of the reorganization, the former stockholders of Y reimbursed the taxpayer for $500x. The $500x reimbursement was based on the taxpayer's cost of settling the claim, taking into account the taxpayer's § 162 deduction for the payment. The Internal Revenue Service held that, because of the former stockholders' indemnity agreement, the contingent liability was reflected in the consideration given for the transfer of the assets. Thus, payment of the liability was not covered by § 381(c)(16). The Ruling further held, however, that the $500x reimbursement from Y's former stockholders was to be deemed a nontaxable contribution by them to Y's capital, and that the taxpayer's satisfaction of the claim was deductible under Y's accounting method which carried over to the taxpayer under § 381(c)(4) and Treas.Reg. § 1.381(c)(4)–1(a)(1).

SECTION 2. LIMITATIONS ON NET OPERATING LOSS CARRYOVERS FOLLOWING A CHANGE IN CORPORATE OWNERSHIP

INTERNAL REVENUE CODE: Sections 382; 383; 384; 269.

REGULATIONS: Sections 1.382–2T(a)(1) and (2)(i).

General Explanation of the Tax Reform Act of 1986

Staff of the Joint Committee on Taxation 288–299 (1987).

Overview

In general, a corporate taxpayer is allowed to carry a net operating loss ("NOL(s)") forward for deduction in a future taxable year, as long as the corporation's legal identity is maintained. After certain nontaxable asset acquisitions in which the acquired corporation goes out of existence, the acquired corporation's NOL carryforwards are inherited by the acquiring corporation. Similar rules apply to tax attributes other than NOLs, such as net capital losses and unused tax credits. Historically, the use of NOL and other carryforwards has been subject to special limitations after specified transactions involving the corporation in which the carryforwards arose (referred to as the "loss corporation"). [Pre–1986] law also provided other rules that were intended to limit tax-motivated acquisitions of loss corporations.

The operation of the special limitations on the use of carryforwards turned on whether the transaction that caused the limitations to apply took the form of a taxable sale or exchange of stock in the loss corporation or one of certain specified tax-free reorganizations in which the loss corporation's tax attributes carried over to a corporate successor. After a purchase (or other taxable acquisition) of a controlling stock interest in a loss corporation, NOL and other carryforwards were disallowed unless the loss corporation continued to conduct its historical trade or business. In the case of a tax-free reorganization, NOL and other carryforwards were generally allowed in full if the loss corporation's shareholders received stock representing at least 20 percent of the value of the acquiring corporation.

NOL and other carryforwards

Although the Federal income tax system generally requires an annual accounting, a corporate taxpayer was allowed to carry NOLs back to the three taxable years preceding the loss and then forward to each of the 15 taxable years following the loss year (sec. 172). The rationale for allowing the deduction of NOL carryforwards (and carrybacks) was that a taxpayer should be able to average income and losses over a period of years to reduce the disparity between the taxation of businesses that have stable income and businesses that experience fluctuations in income.

In addition to NOLs, other tax attributes eligible to be carried back or forward include unused investment tax credits (secs. 30 and 39), excess foreign tax credits (sec. 904(c)), and net capital losses (sec. 1212). Like NOLs, unused investment tax credits were allowed a three-year carryback and a 15-year carryforward. Subject to an overall limitation based on a taxpayer's U.S. tax attributable to foreign-source income, excess foreign tax credits were allowed a two-year carryback and a five-year carryforward. For net capital losses, generally, corporations had a three-year carryback (but only to the extent the carrybacks did not increase or create a NOL) and a five-year carryforward.

NOL and other carryforwards that were not used before the end of a carryforward period expired.

Carryovers to corporate successors

In general, a corporation's tax history (e.g., carryforwards and asset basis) was preserved as long as the corporation's legal identity was continued. Thus, under the general rules of [pre–1986] law, changes in the stock ownership of a corporation did not affect the corporation's tax attributes. Following are examples of transactions that effected ownership changes without altering the legal identity of a corporation:

(1) A taxable purchase of a corporation's stock from its shareholders (a "purchase"),

(2) A type "B" reorganization, in which stock representing control of the acquired corporation is acquired solely in exchange for voting stock of the acquiring corporation (or a corporation in control of the acquiring corporation)(sec. 368(a)(1)(B)),

(3) A transfer of property to a corporation after which the transferors own 80 percent or more of the corporation's stock (a "section 351 exchange"),

(4) A contribution to the capital of a corporation, in exchange for the issuance of stock, and

(5) A type "E" reorganization, in which interests of investors (shareholders and bondholders) are restructured (sec. 368(a)(1)(E)).

Statutory rules also provided for the carry over of tax attributes (including NOL and other carryforwards) from one corporation to another in certain tax-free acquisitions in which the acquired corporation went out of existence (sec. 381). These rules applied if a corporation's assets were acquired by another corporation in one of the following transactions:

(1) The liquidation of an 80–percent owned subsidiary (sec. 332),

(2) A statutory merger or consolidation, or type "A" reorganization (sec. 368(a)(1)(A)),

(3) A type "C" reorganization, in which substantially all of the assets of one corporation is transferred to another corporation in exchange for voting stock, and the transferor completely liquidates (sec. 368(a)(1)(C)),

(4) A "nondivisive D reorganization," in which substantially all of a corporation's assets are transferred to a controlled corporation, and the transferor completely liquidates (secs. 368(a)(1)(D) and 354(b)(1)),

(5) A mere change in identity, form, or place of organization of a single corporation, or type "F" reorganization (sec. 368(a)(1)(F)), and

(6) A type "G" reorganization, in which substantially all of a corporation's assets are transferred to another corporation pursuant to a court approved insolvency or bankruptcy reorganization plan, and stock or securities of the transferee are distributed pursuant to the plan (sec. 368(a)(1)(G)).

In general, to qualify an acquisitive transaction (including a B reorganization) as a tax-free reorganization, the shareholders of the acquired corporation had to retain "continuity of interest." Thus, a principal part of the consideration used by the acquiring corporation had to consist of stock, and the holdings of all shareholders had to be traced. Further, a tax-free reorganization was required to satisfy a "continuity of business enterprise" test. Generally, continuity of business enterprise requires that a significant portion of an acquired corporation's assets be used in a business activity (see Treas.Reg. sec. 1.368–1(d)).

Acquisitions to evade or avoid income tax

The Secretary of the Treasury was authorized to disallow deductions, credits, or other allowances following an acquisition of control of a corporation or a tax-free acquisition of a corporation's assets if the principal purpose of the acquisition was tax avoidance (sec. 269). This provision applied in the following cases:

(1) where any person or persons acquired (by purchase or in a tax-free transaction) at least 50 percent of a corporation's voting stock, or stock representing 50 percent of the value of the corporation's outstanding stock;

(2) where a corporation acquired property from a previously unrelated corporation and the acquiring corporation's basis for the property was determined by reference to the transferor's basis; and

(3) where a corporation purchased the stock of another corporation in a transaction that qualified for elective treatment as a direct asset purchase (sec. 338), a section 338 election was not made, and the acquired corporation was liquidated into the acquiring corporation (under sec. 332).

Treasury regulations under section 269 provided that the acquisition of assets with an aggregate basis that is materially greater than their value (i.e., assets with built-in losses), coupled with the utilization of the basis to create tax-reducing losses, is indicative of a tax-avoidance motive (Treas. Reg. sec. 1.269–3(c)(1)).

* * *

1954 Code special limitations

The application of the special limitations on NOL carryforwards was triggered under the 1954 Code by specified changes in stock ownership of the loss corporation (sec. 382). In measuring changes in stock ownership, section 382(c) specifically excluded "nonvoting stock which is limited and preferred as to dividends." Different rules were provided for the application of special limitations on the use of carryovers after a purchase and after a tax-free reorganization. Section 382 did not address the treatment of built-in losses.

If the principal purpose of the acquisition of a loss corporation was tax avoidance, section 269 would apply to disallow NOL carryforwards even if section 382 was inapplicable.

* * *

Special limitations on other tax attributes

Section 383 incorporated by reference the same limitations contained in section 382 for carryforwards of investment credits, foreign tax credits, and capital losses.

* * *

Reasons for Change

* * *

Preservation of the averaging function of carryovers

The primary purpose of the special limitations is the preservation of the integrity of the carryover provisions. The carryover provisions perform a needed averaging function by reducing the distortions caused by the annual accounting system. If, on the other hand, carryovers can be transferred in a way that permits a loss to offset unrelated income, no legitimate averaging function is performed. With completely free transferability of tax losses, the carryover provisions become a mechanism for partial recoupment of losses through the tax system. Under such a system, the Federal Government would effectively be required to reimburse a portion of all corporate tax losses. Regardless of the merits of such a reimbursement program, the carryover rules appear to be an inappropriate and inefficient mechanism for delivery of the reimbursement.

Appropriate matching of loss to income

[Amendments to § 382 enacted in 1976 which never became effective] reflect the view that the relationship of one year's loss to another year's income should be largely a function of whether and how much the stock ownership changed in the interim, while the *Libson Shops* business continuation rule* measures the relationship according to whether the loss and the income were generated by the same business. The Act acknowledges the merit in both approaches, while seeking to avoid the economic distortions and administrative problems that a strict application of either approach would entail.

A limitation based strictly on ownership would create a tax bias against sales of corporate businesses, and could prevent sales that would increase economic efficiency. For example, if a prospective buyer could increase the income from a corporate business to a moderate extent, but not enough to overcome the loss of all carryovers, no sale would take place because the business would be worth more to the less-efficient current owner than the prospective buyer would reasonably pay. A strict ownership limitation also would distort the measurement of taxable income generated by capital assets purchased before the corporation was acquired, if the tax deductions for capital costs economically allocable to post-acquisition years were accelerated into pre-acquisition years, creating carryovers that would be lost as a result of the acquisition.

Strict application of a business continuation rule would also be undesirable, because it would discourage efforts to rehabilitate troubled businesses. Such a rule would create an incentive to maintain obsolete and inefficient business practices if the needed changes would create the risk of

* [Ed.: In Libson Shops, Inc. v. Koehler, 353 U.S. 382 (1957), the Court held that following a merger of seventeen separate entities (all of which were engaged in the same line of business and owned by the same stockholders) into a single corporation, the loss carryovers of three of the merged entities could not be deducted from the income of the combined enterprise. The Court held that the prior year's loss could be offset against the current year's income only to the extent that income was derived from the operation of substantially the same business that produced the loss. The Court stated that it could find no indication in the legislative history to the predecessor of § 172 that it was intended "to permit the averaging of the pre-merger losses of one business with the post-merger income of some other business which had been operated and taxed separately before the merger." Maxwell Hardware Company v. Commissioner, 343 F.2d 713 (9th Cir.1965), held that enactment of the predecessor to § 382 in the 1954 Code destroyed the precedential value of *Libson Shops*. *Maxwell Hardware* was followed in Frederick Steel Co. v. Commissioner, 375 F.2d 351 (6th Cir.1967); Euclid–Tennessee, Inc. v. Commissioner, 352 F.2d 991 (6th Cir.1965); United States v. Adkins–Phelps, Inc., 400 F.2d 737 (8th Cir.1968). However, the Internal Revenue Service announced that it would continue to apply the *Libson Shops* doctrine to any loss carryover case under the 1954 Code where there has been both a 50% or more shift in beneficial interests in a loss carryover and a change of business. T.I.R. No. 773, 657 CCH 6751 (1965).]

discontinuing the old business for tax purposes, thus losing the benefit of the carryovers.

Permitting the carry over of all losses following an acquisition, as is permitted under the 1954 Code if the loss business is continued following a purchase, provides an improper matching of income and loss. Income generated under different corporate owners, from capital over and above the capital used in the loss business, is related to a pre-acquisition loss only in the formal sense that it is housed in the same corporate entity. Furthermore, the ability to use acquired losses against such unrelated income creates a tax bias in favor of acquisitions. For example, a prospective buyer of a loss corporation might be a less efficient operator of the business than the current owner, but the ability to use acquired losses could make the loss corporation more valuable to the less efficient user and thereby encourage a sale.

Reflecting the policies described above, the Act addresses three general concerns: (1) the approach of prior law (viz., the disallowance or reduction of NOL and other carryforwards), which is criticized as being too harsh where there are continuing loss-corporation shareholders, and ineffective to the extent that NOL carryforwards may be available for use without limitation after substantial ownership changes, (2) the discontinuities in the prior law treatment of taxable purchases and tax-free reorganizations, and (3) defects in the prior law rules that presented opportunities for tax avoidance.

General approach

After reviewing various options for identifying events that present the opportunity for a tax benefit transfer (e.g., changes in a loss corporation's business), it was concluded that changes in a loss corporation's stock ownership continue to be the best indicator of a potentially abusive transaction. Under the Act, the special limitations generally apply when shareholders who bore the economic burden of a corporation's NOLs no longer hold a controlling interest in the corporation. In such a case, the possibility arises that new shareholders will contribute income-producing assets (or divert income opportunities) to the loss corporation, and the corporation will obtain greater utilization of carryforwards than it could have had there been no change in ownership.

To address the concerns described above, the Act adopts the following approach: After a substantial ownership change, rather than reducing the NOL carryforward itself, the earnings against which an NOL carryforward can be deducted are limited. This general approach has received wide acceptance among tax scholars and practitioners. This "limitation on earnings" approach is intended to permit the survival of NOL carryforwards after an acquisition, while limiting the ability to utilize the carryforwards against unrelated income.

The limitation on earnings approach is intended to approximate the results that would occur if a loss corporation's assets were combined with those of a profitable corporation in a partnership. This treatment can be justified on the ground that the option of contributing assets to a partnership is available to a loss corporation. In such a case, only the loss corporation's share of the partnership's income could be offset by the corporation's NOL carryforward. Presumably, except in the case of tax-motivated partnership agreements, the loss corporation's share of the partnership's income would be limited to earnings generated by the assets contributed by the loss corporation.

For purposes of determining the income attributable to a loss corporation's assets, the Act prescribes an objective rate of return on the value of the corporation's equity. Consideration was given to the arguments made in favor of computing the prescribed rate of return by reference to the gross value of a loss corporation's assets, without regard to outstanding debt. It was concluded that it would be inappropriate to permit the use of NOL carryforwards to shelter earnings that are used (or would be used in the absence of an acquisition) to service a loss corporation's debt. The effect of taking a loss corporation's gross value into account would be to accelerate the rate at which NOL carryforwards would be used had there been no change in ownership, because interest paid on indebtedness is deductible in its own right (thereby deferring the use of a corresponding amount of NOLs). There is a fundamental difference between debt capitalization and equity capitalization: true debt represents a claim against a loss corporation's assets.

Annual limitation

The annual limitation on the use of pre-acquisition NOL carryforwards is the product of the prescribed rate and the value of the loss corporation's equity immediately before a proscribed ownership change. The average yield for long-term marketable obligations of the U.S. government was selected as the measure of a loss corporation's expected return on its assets.

The rate prescribed by the Act is higher than the average rate at which loss corporations actually absorb NOL carryforwards. Indeed, many loss corporations continue to experience NOLs, thereby increasing-rather than absorbing-NOL carryforwards. On the other hand, the adoption of the average absorption rate may be too restrictive for loss corporations that out-perform the average. Therefore, it would be inappropriate to set a rate at the lowest rate that is theoretically justified. The use of the long-term rate for Federal obligations was justified as a reasonable risk-free rate of return a loss corporation could obtain in the absence of a change in ownership.

Anti-abuse rules

The mechanical rules described above could present unintended tax-planning opportunities and might foster certain transactions that many would perceive to be violative of the legislative intent. Therefore, the Act includes several rules that are designed to prevent taxpayers from circumventing the special limitations or otherwise appearing to traffic in loss corporations by (1) reducing a loss corporation's assets to cash or other passive assets and then selling off a corporate shell consisting primarily of NOLs and cash or other passive assets, or (2) making pre-acquisition infusions of assets to inflate artificially a loss corporation's value (and thereby accelerate the use of NOL carryforwards). In addition, the Act retains the prior law principles that are intended to limit tax-motivated acquisitions of loss corporations (e.g., section 269), relating to acquisitions to evade or avoid taxes * * *.

* * *

Continuity-of-business enterprise

The requirement under the 1954 Code rules that a loss corporation continue substantially the same business after a purchase presented potentially difficult definitional issues. Specifically, taxpayers and the courts were required to determine at what point a change in merchandise, location, size, or the use of assets should be treated as a change in the loss corporation's business. It was also difficult to identify a particular business where assets and activities were constantly combined, separated, or rearranged. Further, there was a concern that the prior law requirement induced taxpayers to continue uneconomic businesses.

The Act eliminates the business-continuation rule. The continuity-of-business-enterprise rule generally applicable to tax-free reorganizations also applies to taxable transactions.

* * *

Built-in gains and losses

Built-in losses should be subject to special limitations because they are economically equivalent to pre-acquisition NOL carryforwards. If built-in losses were not subject to limitations, taxpayers could reduce or eliminate the impact of the general rules by causing a loss corporation (following an ownership change) to recognize its built-in losses free of the special limitations (and then invest the proceeds in assets similar to the assets sold).

The Act also provides relief for loss corporations with built-in gain assets. Built-in gains are often the product of special tax provisions that accelerate deductions or defer income (e.g., accelerated depreciation or installment sales reporting). Absent a special rule, the use of NOL carryforwards to offset built-in gains recognized after an acquisition would be limited, even though the carryforwards would have been fully available to offset such gains had the gains been recognized before the change in ownership occurred. (Similarly, a partnership is required to allocate built-in gain or loss to the contributing partner.)

Although the special treatment of built-in gains and losses may require valuations of a loss corporation's assets, the Act limits the circumstances in which valuations will be required by providing a generous de minimis rule.

* * *

Explanation of Provisions

Overview

The Act alters the character of the special limitations on the use of NOL carryforwards. After an ownership change, as described below, the taxable income of a loss corporation available for offset by pre-acquisition NOL carryforwards is limited annually to a prescribed rate times the value of the loss corporation's stock immediately before the ownership change. In addition, NOL carryforwards are disallowed entirely unless the loss corporation satisfies continuity-of-business enterprise requirements for the two-year period following any ownership change. The Act also expands the scope of the special limitations to include built-in losses and allows loss corporations to take into account built-in gains. The Act includes numerous technical changes and several anti-avoidance rules. Finally, the Act applies similar rules to carryforwards other than NOLs, such as net capital losses and excess foreign tax credits.

Ownership change

The special limitations apply after any ownership change. An ownership change occurs, in general, if the percentage of stock of the new loss corporation owned by any one or more 5-percent shareholders (described below) has increased by more than 50 percentage points relative to the lowest percentage of stock of the old loss corporation owned by those 5-percent shareholders at any time during the testing period (generally a three-year period)(new sec. 382(g)(1)).[27] The determination of whether an ownership change has occurred is made by aggregating the increases in percentage ownership for each 5-percent shareholder whose percentage ownership has increased during the testing period. For this purpose, all stock owned by persons who own less than five percent of a corporation's stock generally is treated as stock owned by a single 5-percent shareholder (new sec. 382(g)(4)(A)). The determination of whether an ownership change has occurred is made after any owner shift involving a 5-percent shareholder or any equity structure shift.

Determinations of the percentage of stock in a loss corporation owned by any person are made on the basis of value. Except as provided in regulations to be prescribed by the Secretary, changes in proportionate ownership attributable solely to fluctuations in the relative fair market values of different classes of stock are not taken into account (new sec. 382(1)(3)(D)).

In determining whether an ownership change has occurred, changes in the holdings of certain preferred stock are disregarded. Except as provided in regulations, all "stock" (not including stock described in section 1504(a)(4)) is taken into account (new sec. 382(k)(6)(A)). Under this standard, the term stock does not include stock that (1) is not entitled to vote, (2) is limited and preferred as to dividends and does not participate in

27. Unless specifically identified as a taxable year, all references to any period constituting a year (or multiple thereof) means a 365-day period (or multiple thereof).

corporate growth to any significant extent, (3) has redemption and liquidation rights that do not exceed the stock's issue price upon issuance (except for a reasonable redemption premium), and (4) is not convertible to any other class of stock. If preferred stock carries a dividend rate materially in excess of a market rate, this may indicate that it would not be disregarded.

Under grants of regulatory authority, the Treasury Department is expected to publish regulations disregarding, in appropriate cases, certain stock that would otherwise be counted in determining whether an ownership change has occurred, when necessary to prevent avoidance of the special limitations (new sec. 382(k)(6)(B)). For example, it may be appropriate to disregard preferred stock (even though voting) or common stock where the likely percentage participation of such stock in future corporate growth is disproportionately small compared to the percentage value of the stock as a proportion of total stock value, at the time of the issuance or transfer. Similarly, there is a concern that the inclusion of voting preferred stock (which is not described in section 1504(a)(4) solely because it carries the right to vote) in the definition of stock presents the potential for avoidance of section 382. * * *

In addition, the Treasury Department will promulgate regulations regarding the extent to which stock that is not described in section 1504(a)(4) should nevertheless not be considered stock. For example, the Treasury Department may issue regulations providing that preferred stock otherwise described in section 1504(a)(4) will not be considered stock simply because the dividends are in arrears and the preferred shareholders thus become entitled to vote.

Owner shift involving a 5-percent shareholder

An owner shift involving a 5-percent shareholder is defined as any change in the respective ownership of stock of a corporation that affects the percentage of stock held by any person who holds five percent or more of the stock of the corporation (a "5-percent shareholder") before or after the change (new sec. 382(g)(2)). For purposes of this rule, all less-than-5-percent shareholders are aggregated and treated as one 5-percent shareholder. Thus, an owner shift involving a 5-percent shareholder includes (but is not limited to) the following transactions:

(1) A taxable purchase of loss corporation stock by a person who holds at least five percent of the stock before the purchase;

(2) A disposition of stock by a person who holds at least five percent of stock of the loss corporation either before or after the disposition;

(3) A taxable purchase of loss corporation stock by a person who becomes a 5-percent shareholder as a result of the purchase;

(4) A section 351 exchange that affects the percentage of stock ownership of a loss corporation by one or more 5-percent shareholders;

(5) A decrease in the outstanding stock of a loss corporation (e.g., by virtue of a redemption) that affects the percentage of stock ownership of the loss corporation by one or more 5–percent shareholders;

(6) A conversion of debt (or pure preferred stock that is excluded from the definition of stock) to stock where the percentage of stock ownership of the loss corporation by one or more 5–percent shareholders is affected; and

(7) An issuance of stock by a loss corporation that affects the percentage of stock ownership by one or more 5–percent shareholders.

* * *

Equity structure shift

An equity structure shift is defined as any tax-free reorganization within the meaning of section 368, other than a divisive "D" or "G" reorganization or an "F" reorganization (new sec. 382(g)(3)(A)). In addition, to the extent provided in regulations, the term equity structure shift may include other transactions, such as public offerings not involving a 5–percent shareholder or taxable reorganization-type transactions (e.g., mergers or other reorganization-type transactions that do not qualify for tax-free treatment due to the nature of the consideration or the failure to satisfy any of the other requirements for a tax-free transaction)(new secs. 382(g)(3)(B), (g)(4), and [(m)(4))]. A purpose of the provision that considers only owner shifts involving a 5–percent shareholder is to relieve widely held companies from the burden of keeping track of trades among less-than–5–percent shareholders. For example, a publicly traded company that is 60 percent owned by less-than–5–percent shareholders would not experience an ownership change merely because, within a three-year period, every one of such shareholders sold his stock to a person who was not a 5–percent shareholder. There are situations involving transfers of stock involving less-than–5–percent shareholders, other than tax-free reorganizations (for example, public offerings), in which it will be feasible to identify changes in ownership involving such shareholders, because, unlike public trading, the changes occur as part of a single, integrated transaction. Where identification is reasonably feasible or a reasonable presumption can be applied, the Treasury Department is expected to treat such transactions under the rules applicable to equity structure shifts.

For purposes of determining whether an ownership change has occurred following an equity structure shift, the less-than–5–percent shareholders of each corporation that was a party to the reorganization will be segregated and treated as a single, separate 5–percent shareholder (new sec. 382(g)(4)(B)(i)). The Act contemplates that this segregation rule will similarly apply to acquisitions by groups of less-than–5–percent shareholders through corporations as well as other entities (e.g., partnerships) and in transactions that do not constitute equity structure shifts (new sec. 382(g)(4)(C)). Moreover, the Act provides regulatory authority to apply similar segregation rules to segregate groups of less than 5–percent shareholders in cases that involve only a single corporation, (for example, a public offering or a recapitalization). (new sec. [382(m)(4)]).

* * *

To the extent provided in regulations that will apply prospectively from the date the regulations are issued, a public offering can be treated, in effect, as an equity structure shift with the result that the offering is a measuring event, even if there is otherwise no change in ownership of a person who owns 5–percent of the stock before or after the transaction. Rules also would be provided to segregate the group of less-than–5–percent shareholders prior to the offering and the new group of less than–5–percent shareholders that acquire stock pursuant to the offering. Under such regulations, therefore, the less-than–5–percent shareholders who receive stock in the public offering could be segregated and treated as a separate 5–percent shareholder. * * * The Act contemplates that the regulations may provide rules to allow the corporation to establish the extent, if any, to which existing shareholders acquire stock in the public offering.

Attribution and aggregation of stock ownership

Attribution from entities.—In determining whether an ownership change has occurred, the constructive ownership rules of section 318, with several modifications, are applied (new sec. 382(1)(3)). Except to the extent provided in regulations, the rules for attributing ownership of stock (within the meaning of new section 382(k)(6)) from corporations to their shareholders are applied without regard to the extent of the shareholders' ownership in the corporation. Thus, any stock owned by a corporation is treated as being owned proportionately by its shareholders. Moreover, except as provided in regulations, any stock attributed to a corporation's shareholders is not treated as being held by such corporation. Stock attributed from a partnership, estate or trust similarly shall not be treated as being held by such entity. The effect of the attribution rules is to prevent application of the special limitations after an acquisition that does not result in a more than 50 percent change in the ultimate beneficial ownership of a loss corporation. Conversely, the attribution rules result in an ownership change where more than 50 percent of a loss corporation's stock is acquired indirectly through an acquisition of stock in the corporation's parent corporation.

* * *

3–year testing period

In general, the relevant testing period for determining whether an ownership change has occurred is the three-year period preceding any owner shift involving a 5–percent shareholder or any equity structure shift (new sec. 382(i)(1)). Thus, a series of unrelated transactions occurring during a three-year period may constitute an ownership change. A shorter period, however, may be applicable following any ownership change. In such a case, the testing period for determining whether a second ownership change has occurred does not begin before the day following the first ownership change (new sec. 382(i)(2)).

In addition, the testing period does not begin before the first day of the first taxable year from which there is a loss carryforward (including a current NOL that is defined as a pre-change loss) or excess credit (new sec. 382(i)(3)). Thus, transactions that occur prior to the creation of any attribute subject to limitation under section 382 or section 383 are disregarded. Except as provided in regulations, the special rule described above does not apply to any corporation with a net unrealized built-in loss. The Act contemplates, however, that the regulations will permit such corporations to disregard transactions that occur before the year for which such a corporation establishes that a net unrealized built-in loss first arose.

Effect of ownership change

Section 382 limitation

For any taxable year ending after the change date (i.e., the date on which an owner shift resulting in an ownership change occurs or the date of the reorganization in the case of an equity structure shift resulting in an ownership change), the amount of a loss corporation's (or a successor corporation's) taxable income that can be offset by a pre-change loss (described below) cannot exceed the section 382 limitation for such year (new sec. 382(a)). The section 382 limitation for any taxable year is generally the amount equal to the value of the loss corporation immediately before the ownership change multiplied by the long-term tax-exempt rate (described below)(new sec. 382(b)(1)).

The Treasury Department is required to prescribe regulations regarding the application of the section 382 limitation in the case of a short taxable year. These regulations will generally provide that the section 382 limitation applicable in a short taxable year will be determined by multiplying the full section 382 limitation by the ratio of the number of days in the year to 365. Thus, taxable income realized by a new loss corporation during a short taxable year may be offset by pre-change losses not exceeding a ratable portion of the full section 382 limitation.

If there is a net unrealized built-in gain, the section 382 limitation for any taxable year is increased by the amount of any recognized built-in gains (determined under rules described below). Also, the section 382 limitation is increased by built-in gain recognized by virtue of a section 338 election (to the extent such gain is not otherwise taken into account as a built-in gain). Finally, if the section 382 limitation for a taxable year exceeds the taxable income for the year, the section 382 limitation for the next taxable year is increased by such excess.

If two or more loss corporations are merged or otherwise reorganized into a single entity, separate section 382 limitations are determined and applied to each loss corporation that experiences an ownership change.

* * *

Special rule for post-change year that includes the change date.—In general, the section 382 limitation with respect to an ownership change that occurs during a taxable year does not apply to the utilization of losses against the portion of the loss corporation's taxable income, if any, allocable to the period before the change. For this purpose, except as provided in regulations, taxable income (not including built-in gains or losses, if there is a net unrealized built-in gain or loss) realized during the change year is allocated ratably to each day in the year. The regulations may provide that income realized before the change date from discrete sales of assets would be excluded from the ratable allocation and could be offset without limit by pre-change losses. Moreover, these regulations may provide a loss corporation with an option to determine the taxable income allocable to the period before the change by closing its books on the change date and thus forgoing the ratable allocation.

Value of loss corporation

The value of a loss corporation is generally the fair market value of the corporation's stock (including preferred stock described in section 1504(a)(4)) immediately before the ownership change (new sec. 382(e)(1)). If a redemption occurs in connection with an ownership change-either before or after the change-the value of the loss corporation is determined after taking the redemption into account (new sec. 382(e)(2)). The Treasury Department is given regulatory authority to treat other corporate contractions in the same manner as redemptions for purposes of determining the loss corporation's value. The Treasury Department also is required to prescribe such regulations as are necessary to treat warrants, options, contracts to acquire stock, convertible debt, and similar interests as stock for purposes of determining the value of the loss corporation (new sec. 382(k)(6)(B)(i)).

In determining value, the price at which loss corporation stock changes hands in an arms-length transaction would be evidence, but not conclusive evidence, of the value of the stock. Assume, for example, that an acquiring corporation purchased 40 percent of loss corporation stock over a 12–month period. Six months following this 40 percent acquisition, the acquiring corporation purchased an additional 20 percent of loss corporation stock at a price that reflected a premium over the stock's proportionate amount of the value of all the loss corporation stock; the premium is paid because the 20–percent block carries with it effective control of the loss corporation. Based on these facts, it would be inappropriate to simply gross-up the amount paid for the 20–percent interest to determine the value of the corporation's stock. Under regulations, it is anticipated that the Treasury Department will permit the loss corporation to be valued based upon a formula that grosses up the purchase price of all of the acquired loss corporation stock if a control block of such stock is acquired within a 12–month period.

* * *

Long-term tax-exempt rate

The long-term tax-exempt rate is defined as the highest of the Federal long-term rates determined under section 1274(d), as adjusted to reflect differences between rates on long-term taxable and tax-exempt obligations, in effect for the month in which the change date occurs or the two prior months (new sec. 382(f)). The Treasury Department will publish the long-term tax-exempt rate by revenue ruling within 30 days after the date of enactment and monthly thereafter. The long-term tax-exempt rate will be computed as the yield on a diversified pool of prime, general obligation tax-exempt bonds with remaining periods to maturity of more than nine years.

The use of a rate lower than the long-term Federal rate is necessary to ensure that the value of NOL carryforwards to the buying corporation is not more than their value to the loss corporation. Otherwise there would be a tax incentive to acquire loss corporations. If the loss corporation were to sell its assets and invest in long-term Treasury obligations, it could absorb its NOL carryforwards at a rate equal to the yield on long-term government obligations. Since the price paid by the buyer is larger than the value of the loss company's assets (because the value of NOL carryforwards are taken into account), applying the long-term Treasury rate to the purchase price would result in faster utilization of NOL carryforwards by the buying corporation. The long-term tax-exempt rate normally will fall between 66 (1 minus the maximum corporate tax rate of 34 percent) and 100 percent of the long-term Federal rate.

* * *

Continuity of business enterprise requirements

Following an ownership change, a loss corporation's NOL carryforwards (including any recognized built-in losses, described below) are subject to complete disallowance (except to the extent of any recognized built-in gains or section 338 gain, described below), unless the loss corporation's business enterprise is continued at all times during the two-year period following the ownership change. If a loss corporation fails to satisfy the continuity of business enterprise requirements, no NOL carryforwards would be allowed to the new loss corporation for any post-change year. This continuity of business enterprise requirement is the same requirement that must be satisfied to qualify a transaction as a tax-free reorganization under section 368. (See Treasury regulation section 1.368–1(d)). Under these continuity of business enterprise requirements, a loss corporation (or a successor corporation) must either continue the old loss corporation's historic business or use a significant portion of the old loss corporation's assets in a business. Thus, the requirements may be satisfied even though the old loss corporation discontinues more than a minor portion of its historic business. Changes in the location of a loss corporation's business or the loss corporation's key employees, in contrast to the results under the business-continuation rule in the 1954 Code version of section 382(a), will not constitute a failure to satisfy the continuity of business enterprise requirements under the conference agreement.

Reduction in loss corporation's value for certain capital contributions

Any capital contribution (including a section 351 transfer) that is made to a loss corporation as part of a plan a principal purpose of which is to avoid any of the special limitations under section 382 shall not be taken into account for any purpose under section 382. For purposes of this rule, except as provided in regulations, a capital contribution made during the two-year period ending on the change date is irrebuttably presumed to be part of a plan to avoid the limitations. The application of this rule will result in a reduction of a loss corporation's value for purposes of determining the section 382 limitation. The term "capital contribution" is to be interpreted broadly to encompass any direct or indirect infusion of capital into a loss corporation (e.g., the merger of one corporation into a commonly owned loss corporation). Regulations generally will except (i) capital contributions received on the formation of a loss corporation (not accompanied by the incorporation of assets with a net unrealized built-in loss) where an ownership change occurs within two years of incorporation, (ii) capital contributions received before the first year from which there is an NOL or excess credit carryforward (or in which a net unrealized built-in loss arose), and (iii) capital contributions made to continue basic operations of the corporation's business (e.g., to meet the monthly payroll or fund other operating expenses of the loss corporation). The regulations also may take into account, under appropriate circumstances, the existence of substantial nonbusiness assets on the change date (as described below) and distributions made to shareholders subsequent to capital contributions, as offsets to such contributions.

* * *

Losses subject to limitation

The term "pre-change loss" includes (i) for the taxable year in which an ownership change occurs, the portion of the loss corporation's NOL that is allocable (determined on a daily pro rata basis, without regard to recognized built-in gains or losses, as described below) to the period in such year before the change date, (ii) NOL carryforwards that arose in a taxable year preceding the taxable year of the ownership change and (iii) certain recognized built-in losses and deductions (described below).

For any taxable year in which a corporation has income that, under section 172, may be offset by both a pre-change loss (i.e., an NOL subject to limitation) and an NOL that is not subject to limitation, taxable income is treated as having been first offset by the pre-change loss (new sec. 382(*l*)(2)(B)). This rule minimizes the NOLs that are subject to the special limitations. For purposes of determining the amount of a pre-change loss that may be carried to a taxable year (under section 172(b)), taxable income for a taxable year is treated as not greater than the section 382 limitation for such year reduced by the unused pre-change losses for prior taxable years. (New sec. 382(*l*)(2)(A)).

Built-in losses

If a loss corporation has a net unrealized built-in loss, the recognized built-in loss for any taxable year ending within the five-year period ending at the close of the fifth post-change year (the "recognition period") is treated as a pre-change loss (new sec. 382(h)(1)(B)).

Net unrealized built-in losses.—The term "net unrealized built-in loss" is defined as the amount by which the fair market value of the loss corporation's assets immediately before the ownership change is less than the aggregate adjusted bases of a corporation's assets at that time. Under a de minimis exception, the special rule for built-in losses is not applied if the amount of a net unrealized built-in loss does not exceed [15] percent of the value of the corporation's assets immediately before the ownership change. For purposes of the de minimis exception, the value of a corporation's assets is determined by excluding any (1) cash, (2) cash items (as determined for purposes of section 368(a)(2)(F)(iv)), or (3) marketable securities that have a value that does not substantially differ from adjusted basis.

* * *

Recognized built-in losses.—The term "recognized built-in loss" is defined as any loss that is recognized on the disposition of an asset during the recognition period, except to the extent that the new loss corporation establishes that (1) the asset was not held by the loss corporation immediately before the change date, or (2) the loss (or a portion of such loss) is greater than the excess of the adjusted basis of the asset on the change date over the asset's fair market value on that date. The recognized built-in loss for a taxable year cannot exceed the net unrealized built-in loss reduced by recognized built-in losses for prior taxable years ending in the recognition period.

The amount of any recognized built-in loss that exceeds the section 382 limitation for any post-change year must be carried forward (not carried back) under rules similar to the rules applicable to net operating loss carryforwards and will be subject to the special limitations in the same manner as a pre-change loss.

* * *

Built-in gains

If a loss corporation has a net unrealized built-in gain, the section 382 limitation for any taxable year ending within the five-year recognition period is increased by the recognized built-in gain for the taxable year (new sec. 382(h)(1)(A)).

Net unrealized built-in gains.—The term "net unrealized built-in gain" is defined as the amount by which the value of a corporation's assets exceeds the aggregate bases of such assets immediately before the ownership change. Under the de minimis exception described above, the special rule for built-in gains is not applied if the amount of a net unrealized built-in gain does not exceed [15] percent of the value of a loss corporation's assets.

Recognized built-in gains.—The term "recognized built-in gain" is defined as any gain recognized on the disposition of an asset during the recognition period, if the taxpayer establishes that the asset was held by the loss corporation immediately before the change date, to the extent the gain does not exceed the excess of the fair market value of such asset on the change date over the adjusted basis of the asset on that date. The recognized built-in gain for a taxable year cannot exceed the net unrealized built-in gain reduced by the recognized built-in gains for prior years in the recognition period.

* * *

Carryforwards other than NOLs

The Act also amends section 383, relating to special limitations on unused business credits and research credits, excess foreign tax credits, and capital loss carryforwards. Under regulations to be prescribed by the Secretary, capital loss carryforwards will be limited to an amount determined on the basis of the tax liability that is attributable to so much of the taxable income as does not exceed the section 382 limitation for the taxable year, with the same ordering rules that apply under present law. Thus, any capital loss carryforward used in a post-change year will reduce the section 382 limitation that is applied to pre-change losses. In addition, the amount of any excess credit that may be used following an ownership change will be limited, under regulations, on the basis of the tax liability attributable to an amount of taxable income that does not exceed the applicable section 382 limitation, after any NOL carryforwards, capital loss carryforwards, or foreign tax credits are taken into account. The Act also expands the scope of section 383 to include passive activity losses and credits and minimum tax credits.

* * *

ILLUSTRATIVE MATERIAL

A. GENERAL

The *General Explanation* indicates that net operating loss carryovers are provided to average the loss years of a business with a fluctuating income against its profitable years. The averaging rationale is not applicable to the new owners of a loss business who have not borne the burden of pre-acquisition losses. The existence of a net operating loss carryover which is transferable to new owners, however, allows the previous owners to recoup a portion of their loss from the new owners who are willing to pay for the future tax savings available from an acquired net operating carryover.[1] The *General Explanation* indicates that eliminating net operating

1. In re Prudential Lines Inc., 928 F.2d 565 (2d Cir.1991), recognized a corporate net operating loss carryforward as a property interest of the loss corporation's bankruptcy

loss carryovers completely following a substantial ownership change would discourage the sale of a loss corporation and hence the partial recoupment of the losses by the historic shareholders who have borne the losses. Thus, Congress adopted the "limitation of earnings" approach which focuses on the market value of the loss to the loss corporation.

In general terms, the market value of a net operating loss carryover to a loss corporation (and indirectly to its existing shareholders) is the present value of its anticipated tax savings on future earnings. The present value of a loss carryover is dependent on the net return the loss corporation can expect to derive from its invested capital. Likewise the value of a loss carryover to a purchaser is the present value of anticipated tax savings on the future earnings which will be offset by acquired losses. Since a profitable enterprise may be expected to achieve a higher rate of return on its investment than a loss corporation (whose rate of return may be negative), an unlimited loss carryover will be more valuable to a profitable purchaser than to the loss corporation. The difference in value may result in a sale of loss carryovers for a price substantially less than the value of the carryover to the purchaser or, in any event, at a price somewhere between the value to the purchaser and the value to the loss corporation. Thus, an unlimited loss carryover not only provides a form of recoupment of prior losses for the seller of a loss corporation, but also provides a windfall profit for the purchaser financed by the Treasury. Section 382 is intended to eliminate this windfall potential by limiting the value of a loss carryover following a substantial ownership change to an approximation of the value of the carryover to the loss corporation. So limited, the carryover has the same value to both seller and purchaser. The cost of this limitation falls, in part, on the loss corporation which is limited in the amount it can receive for the transfer of loss carryovers.

Theoretically, because the loss carryover has the same value to each, the seller and the purchaser should be neutral with respect to the presence of a loss carryover as part of an asset transfer. This "neutrality" principle works only if the limitation on the use of acquired loss carryovers does not reduce the value of loss carryovers to an amount less than the present value of the losses to the loss corporation. An overly restrictive limitation will inhibit the transfer of assets to more efficient operators. A limitation that is too generous, however, will provide a windfall profit to one of the parties. Section 382 attempts to strike a balance by limiting the annual recovery of a net operating loss carryover following an ownership change to the fair market value of the equity interests in the loss corporation multiplied by a federal tax exempt rate. This formula is based on the theory that a loss corporation could dispose of its assets and invest the proceeds in risk-free taxable government bonds thereby earning an annual rate of return at least equal to the rate on long-term federal instruments. Senate

estate and enjoined the loss corporation's parent corporation from taking an action (claiming a worthless stock deduction) that would jeopardize the subsidiary's loss carryforward.

Finance Committee, Final Report on Subchapter C, The Subchapter C Revision Act of 1985 (Staff Report), S. Prt. 99–47, 99th Cong., 1st Sess. 71 (1985). The Conference Report on the 1986 Act indicates that the rate is reduced to a tax-exempt rate, in part, because Congress believed that the fair market value of the loss corporation includes the value of the loss carryover itself. The loss carryover is an asset which could not be individually sold and the proceeds reinvested. See H. Rep. No. 99–841, 99th Cong., 2d Sess. II–188 (1986). In addition, Congressional studies have indicated that loss corporations typically have absorbed net operating losses at the rate of 4.4 percent of book net worth.[2] Senate Finance Committee, Final Report on Subchapter C, The Subchapter C Revision Act of 1985 (Staff Report), S. Prt. 99–47, 99th Cong., 1st Sess. 71 (1985). The federal tax-exempt rate, which has varied between approximately 4.6 percent and 8 percent since § 382 was enacted,[3] is generous when compared with actual experience. Some commentators have argued, however, that the limitation based on the federal exempt rate is too low thereby undervaluing the loss corporation's loss carryovers. See, e.g., N.Y. State Bar Ass'n Tax Section, Comm. on Net Operating Losses, The Net Operating Loss and Excess Credit Carryforwards Under H.R. 3838, 31 Tax Notes 725, 729 (1986).

B. OWNERSHIP CHANGE

1. *In General*

The limitation on loss carryovers in § 382 is triggered by an "ownership change," in general, a greater than 50 percentage point increase in the ownership of the stock of a loss corporation by one or more five percent stockholders over a three year testing period. I.R.C. § 382(g)(1). Disposition of a corporate business by a majority of the investors who suffered the burden of losses terminates the averaging function of loss carryovers as to those investors and thus eliminates this particular justification for further loss carryovers. The only remaining justification for allowing loss carryovers to the new owners of a loss corporation is to provide the former investors with some recovery of a portion of their loss in the form of consideration paid for the carryover. Thus, a more than 50 percentage point change of ownership of the loss corporation is deemed an appropriate trigger for imposing limitations on loss carryovers.

Under the statutory language, an ownership change may result from an "owner shift," defined as any change in ownership of a loss corporation's stock involving a five percent stockholder, or an "equity structure shift," which is a reorganization of a loss corporation (with the exception of divisive (D) and (G) reorganizations, and (F) reorganizations). Under the statutory definitions, an equity structure shift that results in an ownership change also will qualify as an owner shift. This is true even for a publicly held corporation with no single five percent stockholder because of rules

2. This rate will itself overstate the true rate of recovery on the fair market value of assets if book values are less than fair market value.

3. The federal tax-exempt rate is determined monthly by the Internal Revenue Service and announced in Revenue Rulings.

that aggregate the stock ownership of non-five percent stockholders. I.R.C. § 382(g)(4)(B) and (C). The preamble to the § 382 temporary regulations states that there are no substantive differences (except for some transitional rule purposes) between classifying a transaction as an owner shift or an equity structure shift. T.D. 8149, 52 Fed. Reg. 29,668, 29,670 (1987); See also Temp.Reg. § 1.382–2T(e)(2)(iii) (an equity structure shift which affects the stock ownership of a five percent stockholder is also an owner shift). There is no apparent reason for the distinction, which appears to be attributable to an early version of the statute that was changed during the drafting process.

The recipient of stock by reason of death, as a gift, or in a transfer from a spouse by reason of divorce or separation, is treated as the owner of the stock for the period the stock was held by the transferor. I.R.C. § 382(*l*)(3)(B). These transfers, therefore, are not counted in testing for an ownership change.

Technically, the § 382 limitation applies to losses carried over to any "post change year" of a "new loss corporation." I.R.C. § 382(a). A new loss corporation is defined as a corporation entitled to a net operating loss carryover following an ownership change. I.R.C. § 382(k)(1) and (3). A "post change year" is any taxable year ending after the date of an ownership change. I.R.C. § 382(d)(2). A loss corporation to which the limitation applies following an ownership change is any corporation entitled to a net operating loss carryover or which incurred a net operating loss in the year of an ownership change. I.R.C. § 382(k)(1). The term "loss corporation" also includes a corporation with built-in losses, page 769, which are also subject to the § 382 limitation. A corporation which is a loss corporation before the date of an ownership change is referred to as an "old loss corporation." I.R.C. § 382(k)(2).

2. *Counting Owner Shifts During the Testing Period*

An ownership change occurs if the percentage stock ownership of five percent stockholders on the date of any owner shift or equity structure shift (the "testing date") has increased by more than 50 percentage points over the lowest percentage of stock ownership of five percent stockholders at any time within the three-year period preceding the testing date. I.R.C. § 382(g)(1). An ownership change may result from the sum of unrelated stock transfers by five percent stockholders and transfers from less than five percent stockholders to persons who become five percent stockholders. A loss corporation is thus required during a rolling three-year period to keep track of all stock transfers from or to persons who are or become five percent stockholders.

A full three year look-back is not necessary in all cases. The testing period does not begin until the first day of a taxable year in which a loss corporation incurs a net operating loss which is carried over into a taxable year ending after the testing date. I.R.C. § 382(i)(3). Thus, stock transfers occurring in a year in which a corporation has neither a net operating loss nor loss carryover do not count towards an ownership change. In addition, a new testing period begins following an ownership change. I.R.C. § 382(i)(2). Stock transfers predating an ownership change will not be counted again towards a subsequent ownership change.

The basic operation of these rules is illustrated by the following example. As of January 1, 1996, A, B, C, D, and E each owned 20 of the 100 outstanding shares of L Corporation. L Corporation had no net operating loss carryovers as of that date and did not incur a net operating loss in 1996. On July 1, 1996, A sold her 20 shares of L Corporation stock to P Corporation, which previously owned no L Corporation stock. In 1997, L Corporation incurred a net operating loss which is carried forward. On January 1, 1997, B sold his 20 shares to P Corporation, and on June 30, 1999, C sold her 20 shares to P Corporation. Although P has increased its stock ownership of L from zero percent to 60 percent during the three-year period ending on June 30, 1999, because L Corporation did not have any net operating loss carryovers from 1996 or earlier years, the owner shift effected by the July 1, 1996 purchase from A is not counted in determining whether there has been an ownership change. On December 31, 1999, D sold his 20 shares to P Corporation. Looking backwards from December 31, 1999, P has increased its stock ownership by 60 percentage points, from 20 percent to 80 percent. Because L had a net operating loss in 1997 which was carried forward to subsequent years, all the purchases from B, C, and D are taken into account and an ownership change has occurred. Because the ownership change starts a new testing period, if E were to sell her stock to F on June 1, 2002, there would be no ownership change, even though in the three-year period ending June 1, 2002, P Corporation would have increased its stock ownership by 40 percentage points (from 40 percent to 80 percent) and F would have increased his stock ownership by 20 percentage points, for a total shift of 60 percentage points.

In some circumstances, the requirement of § 382(g)(1)(B) that an ownership change be tested with respect to the lowest percentage of stock owned by a five percent stockholder during the testing period can have a surprising result. For example, L Corporation has 200 shares of stock outstanding of which A owns 100 shares and B and C each own 50 shares. On January 2, 1998, A sells 60 shares of L stock to B. B's ownership interest increases by 30 percentage points, from 25 percent of L stock to 55 percent. A's interest drops to 20 percent. On January 1, 1999, A acquires all of C's L stock. A and B have in the aggregate increased their percentage ownership of L by only 25 percentage points during the testing period; B's interest has increased by 30 percentage points and A's percentage interest has declined by five percentage points. Nonetheless, Temp.Reg. § 1.382–2T(c)(4)(i) treats A's acquisition of C's stock as an ownership change. The temporary regulation concludes that, as a result of A's purchase of C's stock, A's percentage interest increased from a low of 20 percent, the lowest percentage of A's ownership interest during the testing period, to 45 percent. A's 25 percentage points increase plus B's 30 percentage points increase within the testing period are sufficient to trigger an ownership change despite the fact that their aggregate overall increase in stock ownership during the testing period is only 25 percentage points. The temporary regulation reaches this result even if A's sale to B and purchase from C are part of an integrated plan. Temp.Reg. § 1.382–2T(c)(3).

Arguably, the temporary regulation misreads § 382(g)(1) and reaches an unduly harsh result. Section 382(g)(1) can be interpreted as requiring that the increased interests of A and B be aggregated for purposes of both subsections (A) and (B). To paraphrase the statutory language, A and B's stock ownership of L has increased by only 25 percentage points over the lowest percentage of stock owned by A and B together ("such shareholders") at any time during the testing period (from a low of 75% [20% plus 55%] to 100%). Given the Treasury's broad regulatory authority under § 382(m) to interpret § 382, however, it is not likely that its interpretation of § 382(g)(1) could be challenged successfully.

3. *Stock Ownership and Five Percent Stockholders*

(a) Identifying Five Percent Stockholders

The § 382 trigger focuses on stock transfers to or by persons who own five percent or more of the loss corporation stock. Proportionate stock ownership is determined by the value of stock held by the stockholder. I.R.C. § 382(k)(6)(C). A person is treated as a five percent stockholder if the person was a five percent stockholder at any time during the testing period, even though the person may not own five percent of the loss corporation stock on the testing date. Temp.Reg. § 1.382–2T(g)(1)(iv). The five percent figure was chosen to relieve companies from the burden of keeping track of trades among stockholders with a minor interest. H.Rep. No. 99–841, 99th Cong., 2d Sess. II–176 (1986).[4] Thus stock transfers between less than five percent stockholders are not counted in testing for an ownership change. Temp.Reg. § 1.382–2T(e)(1)(ii). The less than five percent stockholders as a group, however, are treated as a single five percent stockholder regardless of the percentage interest held by such persons. I.R.C. § 382(g)(4)(A). Temp.Reg. § 1.382–2T(f)(13) refers to the group of less than five percent stockholders as a "public group." As a single five percent stockholder, transfers to or by a public group can trigger an ownership change. Thus, for example, a public issue of more than 50 percent of the stock of a closely held loss corporation to less than five percent stockholders will trigger an ownership change because the public group of new stockholders increases its ownership interest from zero preceding the public offering to more than 50 percent following the public offering. See Temp.Reg. § 1.382–2T(e)(1)(iii), Ex. (5). Various groups of less than five percent stockholders separately may represent five percent stockholders and transfers between those groups can be an ownership change. See page 763.

(b) Attribution Rules

With certain modifications, the attribution rules of § 318 apply to identify proportionate stock ownership. I.R.C. § 382(*l*)(3). In general, the

4. In general, any person who acquires five percent or more of the stock of a publicly traded corporation is required to register the acquisition with the Securities and Exchange Commission.

modifications to § 318 have two effects. First, members of a family who are subject to stock attribution under § 318(a)(1) are treated as a single individual. Thus, stock transfers among family members will not trigger an ownership change. If an individual is a member of more than one family group under the attribution rules, that individual will be treated as a member of the family which results in the smallest increase in stock held by five percent stockholders on a testing date. Temp.Reg. § 1.382–2T(h)(6)(iv). The regulations also provide that an individual who is not otherwise a five percent stockholder will not be treated as a five percent stockholder as a result of family attribution. Second, stock of a loss corporation owned by any entity (corporation, partnership or trust) which has a five percent or greater interest is attributed up the ownership chain to the last person from whom no further attribution is possible. I.R.C. § 382(*l*)(3)(A)(ii)(II); Temp.Reg. § 1.382–2T(g)(2), (h)(2)(i). Intermediate entities are disregarded. Temp.Reg. § 1.382–2T(h)(2)(i)(A). Treas.Reg. § 1.382–3(a)(1)(i) includes as an entity for this purpose any group of less than five percent shareholders who act pursuant to a plan to acquire five percent of the stock of a loss corporation.

Temp.Reg. § 1.382–2T(g)(4), Ex. (1), illustrates application of these attribution rules as follows. The stock of L, a loss corporation is owned 20 percent by A, 10 percent by corporation P1, and 20 percent by E, a joint venture. The remaining 50 percent of L stock is publicly held ("Public Group L"). B owns 15 percent of the stock of P1 corporation. The remaining 85 percent of the shares of P1 are publicly held ("Public Group P1"). E, the joint venture, is owned 30 percent by corporation P2 and 70 percent by corporation P3. Both P2 and P3 are publicly held ("Public Group P2" and "Public Group P3"). L's ownership structure is illustrated as follows:

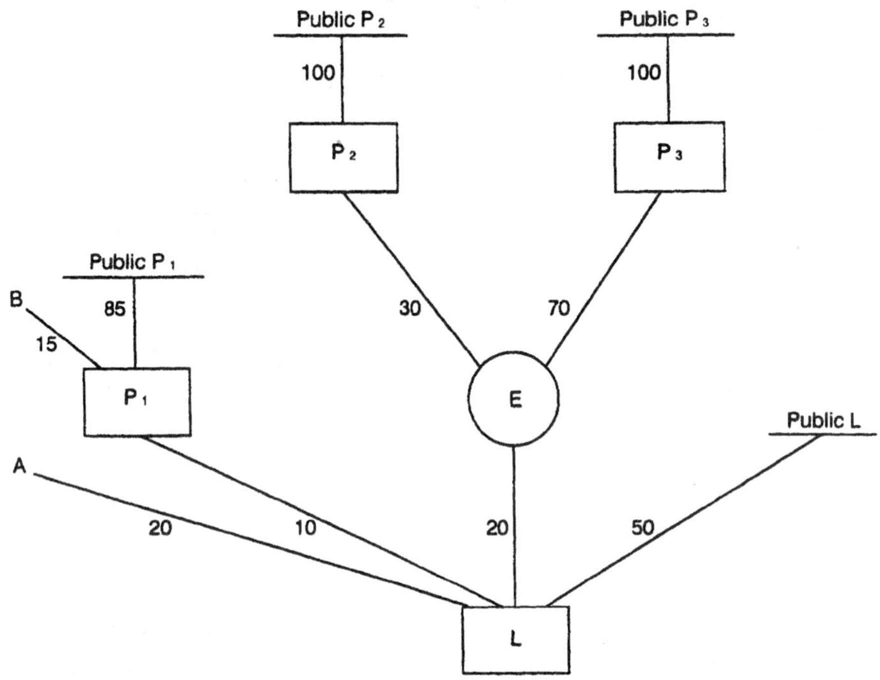

A is a five percent stockholder of L because of A's direct ownership of 20 percent of L stock. Public Group L is a single five percent stockholder by virtue of its collective 50 percent interest in L.

B is not a five percent stockholder. Although B is a five percent stockholder of P1, and thereby indirectly owns the L stock owned by P1, Temp.Reg. § 1.382–2T(g)(2), B's ownership interest in L is only 1.5 percent (15% of P1's 10%). Because B is not a five percent stockholder of L, B is treated as a member of the Public Group P1. See Temp.Reg. § 1.382–2T(j)(1)(iv). P1 is not a five percent stockholder because its interest is attributable to its stockholders. P1's public stockholders, Public P1, are treated as a single five percent stockholder of L owning 10 percent of the L stock, 8.5 percent plus B's 1.5 percent.

Public Group P2 is also a five percent stockholder. P2 has a six percent interest attributed from P2's 30 percent interest in E, which in turn owns 20 percent of L (30% x 20% = 6%). P2's six percent interest is attributed to the P2 public group which owns 100 percent of P2. Public Group P3 is also a five percent stockholder with a 14 percent interest attributed to it ([20% x 70%] x 100%).

(c) Option Attribution

Even in the absence of a direct stock transfer, outstanding options and other rights to acquire stock (including convertible debt) may create an owner shift, which must be taken into account in determining whether there is an ownership change during a testing period. Section 382(*l*)(3)(A)(iv) provides that, except to the extent provided in the regulations, an option or other right to acquire stock will be treated as exercised if the deemed exercise results in an ownership change. However, Treas.Reg. § 1.382–4(d)(2) provides that an option will be treated as exercised on the date of its issue, transfer, or on a subsequent testing date, only if the option satisfies one of three tests, an ownership test, a control test, or an income test.

Under the *ownership* test of Treas.Reg. § 1.382–4(d)(3), an option will be treated as exercised if a principal purpose of the issuance, transfer, or structure of the option is to avoid or ameliorate the impact of an ownership change by providing its holder with a substantial portion of the attributes of ownership of the underlying stock. Under Treas.Reg. § 1.382–4(d)(6)(i), factors that indicate the presence or absence of a purpose to avoid or ameliorate the impact of an ownership change (under all three of the tests) include whether there are business purposes for the issuance, transfer or structure of the option, the likelihood of exercise of the option, and the consequences of treating the option as having been exercised. Treas.Reg. § 1.382–4(d)(6)(ii) specifically identifies additional factors that indicate that an option provides its holder with the attributes of ownership. These include the relationship between the exercise price of the option at the time of its issue or transfer and the value of the underlying stock, whether the option provides a right to participate in management or other rights that ordinarily would be held by stock owners, and the existence of reciprocal options (e.g. offsetting put and call options held by the prospective seller and purchaser). The ability of the option holder to participate in future appreciation in the value of the underlying stock may be considered, but is not of itself sufficient to satisfy the ownership test. Conversely, the absence of risk of loss does not preclude treating an option as exercised.

An option will be treated as exercised under the control test of Treas.Reg. § 1.382–4(d)(4) if a principal purpose of the issuance, transfer, or structure of the option is to avoid or ameliorate the impact of an ownership change and the option holder (or a related person) directly or indirectly has a more than 50 percent interest in the loss corporation determined by including the ownership interest that would result from exercise of the option. Treas.Reg. § 1.382–4(d)(6)(iii) indicates that economic interests in the loss corporation and influence over management of the loss corporation held by the holder and related persons will be taken into account in applying the control test.

The *income* test of Treas.Reg. § 1.382–4(d)(5) treats an option as exercised if a principal purpose of the issuance, transfer, or structure of the option is to avoid or ameliorate the impact of an ownership change of the loss corporation by facilitating the creation of income or value in the loss corporation prior to the exercise of the option. Under this test, an option will be treated as exercised if in connection with the issuance or transfer of an option the loss corporation engages in transactions that accelerate income thereby utilizing loss carryovers prior to an ownership change, or the option holder or related person purchases stock or makes a capital contribution that increases the value of the loss corporation. Treas.Reg. § 1.382–4(d)(6)(iv).

Treas.Reg. § 1.382–4(d)(7) contains a list of safe harbors that exclude some options from the deemed exercise rules. Commercially reasonable contracts to acquire stock when obligations to complete the transaction are subject only to reasonable closing conditions, and which close on a change date within one year after the contract is entered into, will not be treated as exercised under the ownership test or the control test. These contracts will be subject to the income test. In addition, the safe harbors shelter options that are part of a security agreement in a lending transaction, options issued as compensation for performance of services, options exercisable only on death, disability or retirement, and a "bona fide" right of first refusal with "customary terms." The deemed exercise rules are not applicable to transfers of options if neither party to the transfer is a five percent shareholder, the transfer is between members of separate public groups, or the transfer occurs by reason of death, gift, divorce or separation. Treas. Reg. § 1.382–4(d)(11).

(d) The Definition of Stock

By reference to § 1504(a)(4), § 382(k)(6)(A) defines stock for § 382 purposes as excluding nonvoting, nonconvertible stock interests that are limited as to dividends and which do not participate in corporate growth "to any significant extent." This provision prevents a loss corporation from increasing the amount of its outstanding stock with equity interests that are insignificant in order to avoid an ownership change. In addition, § 382(k)(6)(B) directs the Treasury to promulgate regulations treating certain stock that is stock under § 1504(a)(4) (such as voting stock with no significant participation in growth) as nonstock for § 382 purposes. Temp. Reg. § 1.382–2T(f)(18)(ii) contains a three part test for the identification of such "nonstock stock:" (A) the likely participation of the interest of a five percent stockholder at the time of the stock's issue is disproportionately small compared to the fair market value of outstanding stock of the corporation, (B) treating the interest as nonstock would result in an ownership change, and (C) net operating losses and built-in losses are at least twice the annual limitation (two times the value of the loss corporation times the tax-exempt rate).

To cover the field completely, under the authority of § 382(k)(6)(B)(ii), Temp.Reg. § 1.382–2T(f)(18)(iii) treats certain interests that are not normally classified as stock (potential equity disguised as debt) as constituting stock for § 382 purposes if (A) at the time of issue, a nonstock interest issued to a five percent stockholder offers the potential for significant participation in corporate growth, (B) treating the interest as stock would result in an ownership change, and (C) the loss corporation's net operating losses and built-in losses are at least twice the annual limitation. This provision is designed to prevent avoidance of the ownership change rules by the issue of equity-flavored instruments that are not equity in form. This provision does not apply to treat an option (such as a convertible instrument), whether or not deemed to be exercised, as stock. Treas.Reg. § 1.382–4(d)(12). The rules treating nonstock interests as stock are thus independently applicable to only a narrow range of nonconvertible nonstock instruments such as a debt instrument with a contingent payout large enough to constitute a significant participation in future growth. Such an instrument likely would be classified as stock under debt-equity rules, but the drafters of the regulations were not willing to leave the question open to the vagaries of litigation. Identifying instruments that provide a significant participation in future growth may prove to be no less difficult, however.

Under Treas.Reg. § 1.382–2(a)(3)(ii), convertible stock is treated as stock. Thus, preferred stock that is classified as nonstock under the § 1504(a)(4) rules, but which is convertible into stock, is treated as stock. Convertible stock is also treated as an option if the terms of the conversion feature permit or require consideration other than the stock being converted. Treas.Reg. § 1.382–4(d)(9)(ii). As a consequence, the presence of convertible stock may trigger an ownership change if the conversion is deemed exercised under the tests of Treas.Reg. § 1.382–4(d)(2).

(e) Aggregation and Segregation of Less Than Five Percent Stockholders

All stockholders of a corporation who individually own less than five percent of the stock are aggregated into a group (a "public group") and treated as a single five percent stockholder regardless of the percentage of stock held by less than five percent stockholders either individually or as a group. I.R.C. § 382(g)(4)(A). Sections 382(g)(4)(B) and (C) provide for the segregation of identifiable groups of less than five percent stockholders for purposes of determining whether an ownership change has occurred with respect to five percent stockholders following either an equity structure shift or an owner shift. In certain transactions, particularly equity structure shifts, it is possible to trace the changes in ownership of separate identifiable public groups. For example, in the merger of a publicly held loss corporation into another publicly held corporation, there are two identifiable groups of less than five percent stockholders, the public group of the loss corporation and the public group of the acquiring corporation. The transfer of ownership of the loss corporation from its pre-merger public stockholders to the public stockholders of the acquiring corporation may be treated as a stock transfer from the loss corporation public group to the pre-merger public group of the acquiring corporation. Similar transfers by or to a public group can be identified with respect to other reorganizations (whether taxable or nonrecognition transactions), a public offering (the new stockholders are a separate five percent stockholder), or a redemption (stockholders whose interests are increased are a separate five percent stockholder).

Temp.Reg. § 1.382–2T(j)(1) first aggregates groups of less than five percent stockholders of a loss corporation into different public groups depending upon direct and indirect ownership of stock in a loss corporation. For example, all individuals who directly own less than five percent of the stock of the loss corporation are treated as a single five percent stockholder.

Temp. Reg. § 1.382–2T(j)(2) then segregates into two or more public groups any public group of less than five percent stockholders that can be separately identified as having acquired their stock in a particular transaction, such as a prior reorganization or a stock issue covered by § 1032 (e.g., a public issue of stock). Similar principles apply if some individuals in the public group increase their interest in the corporation through a redemption of shares; the public group is divided into the group whose shares were not redeemed and the group whose shares were redeemed. The same aggregation and segregation rules apply to stockholders who are less than five percent stockholders of a loss corporation by attribution from an entity which directly or indirectly owns five percent or more of the loss corporation stock. Temp.Reg. § 1.382–2T(j)(3).

Once an ownership change has occurred following a transaction that requires segregation of different groups of less than five percent stockholders, the groups are no longer treated as separate five percent stockholders. Temp.Reg. § 1.382–2T(j)(2)(iii)(B), Ex. (3)(iv).

Treas.Reg. § 1.382–3(j) exempts certain small stock issues from the segregation requirement so that the loss corporation is not required to treat recipients of a small stock issue as a separate group of less than five percent stockholders. A stock issue is subject to the exception if the value of all stock issued during the taxable year does not exceed ten percent of the total value of outstanding stock at the beginning of the year, or if, on a class-by-class basis, the total number of shares of any class of stock issued during the taxable year does not exceed ten percent of the number of shares of stock of that class outstanding at the beginning of the taxable year. Treas.Reg. § 1.382–3(j)(2).

In addition, Treas.Reg. § 1.382–3(j)(3) exempts from the segregation rules stock issued for cash if the total amount of the newly issued stock does not exceed one-half of the stock ownership of direct public groups immediately preceding the stock issue. Stock exempted from the segregation rules under these provisions is treated as acquired by existing direct public groups in proportion to the existing public groups' pre-issuance ownership interests. Treas.Reg. § 1.382–3(j)(5). However, if the loss corporation has actual knowledge that a particular direct public group acquired a greater percentage of newly issued stock than its proportionate share, the loss corporation may treat that public group as receiving the higher percentage. Treas.Reg. § 1.382–3(j)(5)(ii).

The small issue and cash issue exemptions from the segregation rules also apply to stock issues of first tier and higher tier entities. Treas.Reg. § 1.382–3(j)(11).

The operation of the aggregation and segregation rules is illustrated by the following example:

L, a loss corporation, P1, and P2 each have 1000 shares of stock outstanding. The stock of L is owned 600 shares by P1, 200 shares by P2, and 170 shares by a public group, none of whom owns more than five percent of the L stock, and A who owns 30 shares. A owns 50 shares of the

P1 stock. The remaining 950 shares of P1 stock are owned by public stockholders none of whom owns more than five percent of P1 stock. A owns 100 shares of P2 stock. The remaining 900 shares of P2 stock are held by public stockholders none of whom owns more than five percent of P2 stock. The ownership structure of L is as follows:

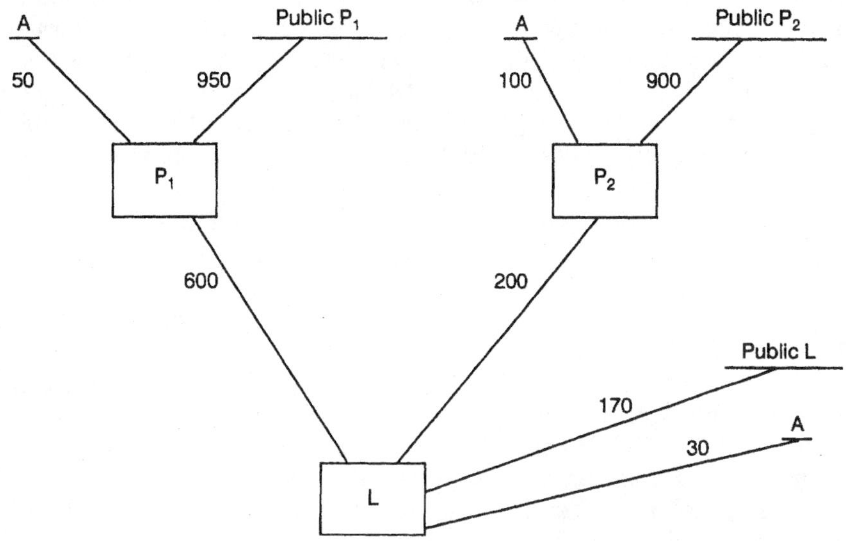

L's stock is held by three separate public groups, each of which is treated as a single five percent stockholder: the public group that directly holds L stock, the public group of P1 stockholders which by attribution holds 60 percent of L stock, and the public group of P2 stockholders which by attribution holds 20 percent of L stock.

Although A directly and indirectly owns more than five percent of L stock, A is not a five percent stockholder of L. A owns 3 percent of L directly. As a five percent owner of P1, A is attributed a proportionate share of P1's L stock, an interest of 3 percent (5% x 60%). Since A's interest is less than five percent, A is treated as a member of the P1 public group. Temp.Reg. § 1.382–2T(j)(1)(iv)(A). As a 10 percent owner of P2, A indirectly owns an additional 2 percent of L, but again A's stock interest is included as part of the interest of the P2 public group. Temp.Reg. § 1.382–2T(j)(1)(iii) contains a presumption that stockholders, including five percent owners of a higher tier entity which owns stock in a loss corporation, who are not five percent stockholders of a loss corporation are not members of more than one public group. Thus, A's three percent direct interest, A's three percent interest through P1, and A's two percent interest through P2 are not accumulated to make A a five percent stockholder of L. Because L is required to keep track of only five percent stockholders who can be traced through a chain of at least five percent ownership interests, L is presumed not to have knowledge of A's existence as a five percent stockholder. However, A will be treated as a five percent stockholder if L has actual knowledge of A's ownership interests. Temp.Reg. § 1.382–2T(j)(1)(iii), (k)(2). As the example demonstrates, this distinction can be significant.

On April 1, 1999, L issues 111 shares of new stock to the public. The stock is not purchased by any person who owns five percent of L stock. The issue of L stock to less than five percent stockholders creates a new public group which is treated as a five percent stockholder.[5] This new group ("New Public L") increased its interest in L during the testing period from 0 percent before the stock offering to 10 percent (111/1111) afterwards. Temp.Reg. § 1.382–2T(j)(1)(iii) presumes that there is no cross-ownership between the old public stockholders of L and the new public stockholders. Thus, absent actual knowledge by L, any acquisition of the newly issued L stock by existing stockholders will be ignored. The stock issue is, therefore, a 10 percent owner shift.

On April 1, 2000, all of the assets of P1, including the L stock, are acquired by P2 in a statutory merger. The P1 stockholders receive one share of P2 stock for every four shares of P1 stock. A receives 12.5 shares of P2 stock, the remaining P1 stockholders receive 237.5 shares of P2 stock. P2 now owns 72 percent (800/1111 shares) of L. The transaction is tested for an ownership change by segregating the post-merger stockholders of P2 into two public groups, the original P2 stockholders, who now own 72 percent of P2 ("Old Public P2"), and the pre-merger P1 stockholders ("New Public P2"). (As will be discussed below, A has become a five percent stockholder of L and is therefore no longer included in a P2 public group.) Before the reorganization, the original P2 public group, including A, owned 18 percent of L by attribution from P2 ([200/1111] x 100%). After the reorganization, the original P2 public group owns 51.8 percent of L ([800/1111] x [900/1250]). Thus, Old Public P2 has increased its ownership interest in L by 33.8 percent.

Following the merger, the ownership structure of L is as follows:

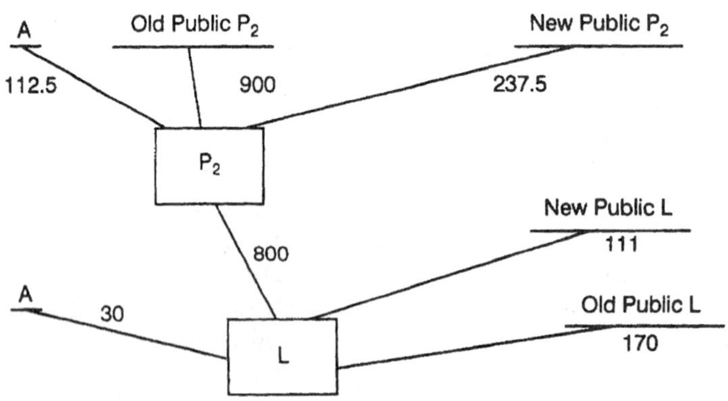

Within the testing period, the 33.8 percent owner shift in L from New

5. Treas.Reg. § 1.382–3(j) does not prevent segregation of the new public group because the stock issue exceeds ten percent of the outstanding stock and is more than one-half of the stock held by direct public groups immediately preceding the stock issue.

Public P2 to Old Public P2, plus the 10 percent owner shift from Old Public L to New Public L, are not sufficient to trigger an ownership change of L. However, A's interest in the transaction causes an ownership change to be triggered. Before the merger of P1 into P2, A's cross-ownership was disregarded under the presumption of Temp.Reg. § 1.382–2T(j)(1)(iii), and A was treated as a less than five percent stockholder whose stock interests are part of public groups. In contrast to A's pre-merger ownership interests, after the merger A has an identifiable interest greater than five percent that is traceable through a connection of five percent ownership interests. A thus becomes a distinct five percent stockholder who must be counted. After the merger A owns 112.5 shares of P2 stock, 9 percent of P2. A is, therefore, deemed to own 6.5 percent of L by attribution from P2 (9% x 72%). Even though A is now identified as a five percent stockholder, A's ownership interest is presumed to include only A's 6.5 percent interest through P2. A's 2.7 percent direct interest in L is still treated as part of the Old Public L group. Temp.Reg. § 1.382–2T(j)(1)(vi), Ex. (5). As a result, A's interest as an identified five percent stockholder increased from zero before the transaction to 6.5 percent after the merger. A's 6.5 percent owner shift, when added to the increased interests of Old Public P2 and New Public L, result in an increased interest by five percent stockholders of 50.3 percent, sufficient to trigger an ownership change.

If L has actual knowledge of A's pre-merger stock ownership interest, L may overcome the presumption of Temp.Reg. § 1.382–2T(j)(1)(iii), and avoid the ownership change. See Temp.Reg. § 1.382–2T(k)(2). After L's public offering, but before the merger of P1 and P2, A's lowest actual percentage interest during the testing period was 7.2 percent, 2.7 percent direct interest in L stock, 2.7 percent attributed through P1, and 1.8 percent attributed through P2. A's percentage interest in L after the merger is 9.2, of which 6.5 percent is attributed from P2 and 2.7 percent is direct. Based on actual knowledge, the owner shift attributable to A is only two percent. In addition, without A as a member, Public P2's ownership interest goes from 16.2 percent (200/1111 x 90%) to 51.8 percent, an ownership change of 35.6 percent. That is not sufficient to trigger an ownership change on the merger of P1 into P2 (35.6% + 10% + 2% = 47.6%).

(f) Reporting Requirements

Temp.Reg. § 1.382–2T(a)(2)(ii) and (iii) impose extensive information reporting and record keeping requirements that require the corporation to monitor its status under § 382 even if there is only a remote possibility of an ownership change. In any taxable year in which a corporation is a loss corporation (see § 382(k)(1)), the corporation must file a statement with its tax return indicating whether there has been a testing date during the year, identifying any testing dates on which an ownership change occurred, identifying testing dates that occurred closest to the end of each calendar quarter of the taxable year, indicating the percentage stock ownership of each five percent stockholder on each testing date reported and the percentage increase of each five percent stockholder during the testing period, and identifying the extent to which the corporation relied on presumptions provided in Temp.Reg. § 1.382–2T(k)(1). Temp.Reg. § 1.382–2T(k)(1) allows a publicly held loss corporation to rely on filings with the Securities and Exchange Commission to disclose the existence of five percent stockholders. A loss corporation is also allowed to rely on statements by responsible persons (such as officers, trustees, partners, etc.), signed under penalties of perjury, which disclose the ownership interests and changes in interest of the owners of an upper-tier entity that owns an interest in the loss corporation. The temporary regulations also require a loss corporation to maintain records adequate to identify five percent stockholders and ascertain whether an ownership change has occurred. In many cases, it is possible that the cost of providing information returns will outweigh the value of loss carryovers.

C. COMPUTING THE SECTION 382 LIMITATION

1. *Valuing the Loss Corporation*

The annual limitation on income of a loss corporation that can be offset by net operating loss carryovers following an ownership change is computed by multiplying the value of the loss corporation by the federal long-term tax-exempt rate. I.R.C. § 382(b)(1). Value is based on the value of the stock of the loss corporation on the date immediately preceding an ownership change. I.R.C. § 382(e)(1). As noted in the *General Explanation*, the value of a loss corporation includes the value of interests that are not treated as stock under § 1504(a)(4). The value of the loss corporation also includes nonstock that is treated as stock under Temp.Reg. § 1.382–2T(f)(18)(iii).

To prevent a loss corporation from artificially enhancing its value on the eve of an ownership change, § 382(*l*) provides that any capital contributed to the loss corporation as part of a plan to increase the limitation shall not be taken into account in determining value. Section 382(*l*)(2) provides that, except as otherwise provided in regulations, any capital contribution within 2 years of the date of an ownership change shall be treated as part of a forbidden plan.

Additional anti-abuse rules are found in § 382(*l*)(4), which reduces the value of a loss corporation that has substantial nonbusiness assets. The value of the loss corporation is reduced by the fair market value of nonbusiness assets, less liabilities attributable to such assets. A loss corporation has substantial nonbusiness assets if more than one-third of the total value of the loss corporation consists of investment assets. This limitation is intended to prevent the sale of carryovers by a loss corporation which has disposed of its operating assets. However, given the severity of the limitation imposed by § 382, a market for shell corporations with loss carryovers is not likely to exist in any event. The provision ultimately works only to reduce the sales price of a loss corporation with substantial investment assets.

Under § 382(e)(2), if an ownership change occurs in connection with a redemption or other corporate contraction, the value of the loss corporation immediately before the ownership change must be adjusted to account for assets distributed in the redemption.

2. *Valuing Members of Controlled Groups of Corporations*

Temp.Reg. § 1.382–8T contains rules for the valuation of a loss corporation that is a member of a controlled group of corporations (as defined in § 1563(a), page 432). These rules are designed to avoid duplication of the value of assets of one member of a controlled group by including in the value of the stock of an upper-tier corporation the value of stock of a subsidiary member of the controlled group held directly by the upper-tier corporation. Thus, in general, for purposes of determining the § 382 limitation with respect to a loss of a controlled group, the value of the stock of each component member of the controlled group (as defined in § 1563(b), page 432) is reduced by the value of the stock of any other member of the controlled group held directly by the component member of the controlled group. Temp.Reg. § 1.382–8T(c)(1).

3. *Built-in Gains and Losses*

Section 382 also deals with unrealized losses of a loss corporation which could be utilized to offset future income following an ownership change in the same manner as a net operating loss carryforward. Without application of the limitation, the loss corporation could realize the losses after an ownership change to offset post-change income. Net unrealized losses existing at the time of an ownership change are subject to the annual § 382 limitation in the taxable year the losses are recognized. I.R.C. § 382(h)(1)(B). Recognized built-in losses that are not deductible in the taxable year because of the § 382 limitation are carried forward into subsequent taxable years (subject to the limitation in future years) in the same manner as a net operating loss which arose in the year of recognition. I.R.C. § 382(h)(4).

With respect to built-in gains, § 382 takes into account the fact that a loss corporation could at any time absorb its loss carryovers by disposing of assets with unrealized appreciation. Section 382(h)(1)(A) thus allows a loss corporation to increase its annual limitation following an ownership change by built-in gain recognized during the taxable year.

The built-in gain or loss rules of § 382(h) apply only to unrealized gains or losses recognized by the loss corporation within five years of an ownership change, and only if the corporation has net unrealized gain or loss on the date of an ownership change. Net unrealized built-in gains and losses are based on the difference between the fair market value and adjusted bases of the assets of a loss corporation immediately before an ownership change. I.R.C. § 382(h)(3)(A). Net unrealized loss also includes any depreciation or other capital recovery deductions attributable to the excess of the adjusted basis of an asset over its fair market value on the date of an ownership change. Thus, a valuation of the corporation's assets is required as of the date of an ownership change. Net unrealized built-in gain or loss is ignored, however, if the amount of unrealized gain or loss is not greater than the lesser of $10,000,000 or 15 percent of the fair market value of the loss corporation's assets (computed without regard to cash or marketable securities the value of which approximates cost) immediately prior to the date of an ownership change. I.R.C. § 382(h)(3)(B). In the case of a corporation with respect to which a § 338 election is in effect following an ownership change, the § 382 limitation is increased by the lesser of gain recognized by reason of the § 338 election, or built-in gain determined without regard to the limitation of § 382(h)(3)(B). I.R.C. § 382(h)(1)(C).

Section 382(h)(6) provides that income earned prior to the date of an ownership change, but which has not been taken into account by the loss corporation, will be treated as built-in gain recognized in the year the item is properly taken into account. Thus earned but unreported income items increase the annual limitation in the year the item is properly accounted for by the loss corporation. Conversely, deduction items attributable to periods predating the date of an ownership change, but which have not been deducted by the loss corporation, are treated as recognized built-in losses in the year the item is deducted. These items are thus subject to the § 382 limitation in the year deducted. Whether items of income or deduction are attributable to a period prior to the change date is determined as an economic matter, not by the taxpayer's method of accounting.

Temp.Reg. § 1.382–2T(d)(3)(ii) provides a special rule for commencement of the three year testing period in the case of a corporation with built-in losses. As described at page 756, the testing period generally begins on the earlier of the first day of a taxable year from which there is a loss or excess tax credit carryforward, or the first day of a taxable year in which a testing date occurs. In the case of a corporation with a net unrealized built-in loss, the testing date extends back a full three years from the date of an owner shift or equity structure shift that requires testing for an ownership change. The testing period may be shortened, however, if the corporation can show that unrealized built-in losses accrued at an earlier date, in which case the testing period will begin on the first day of the taxable year in which the losses accrued, from which there is a loss carryover, or the year the transaction being tested occurs, whichever is earlier.

4. *Worthless Stock Deduction by a 50 Percent Stockholder*

In Textron, Inc. v. United States, 561 F.2d 1023 (1st Cir.1977), a parent corporation claimed a worthless stock deduction for the stock of its controlled subsidiary. The court held that the net operating loss carryover of the subsidiary was unaffected by the parent's worthless stock deduction and thus the subsidiary was permitted to claim its loss carryover as a deduction against future income. In effect, *Textron, Inc.* allowed the same loss to be counted twice, once at the corporation level and once at the stockholder level. Section 382(g)(4)(D) was enacted in 1987 to overrule this result.

Section 382(g)(4)(D) treats a worthless stock deduction by a greater than 50 percent stockholder, who continues to own the stock at the close of the taxable year, as an owner shift. The stockholder is treated as acquiring the stock on the first day of the taxable year following the year in which the stock is claimed to have become worthless, and as not having any stock ownership preceding that date. The consequence is an owner shift from zero percent to an ownership interest of more than 50 percent. This owner shift triggers an ownership change thereby subjecting the corporation's loss carryovers to the § 382 limitation. The value of the loss corporation subject to a worthless stock deduction will be zero. See I.R.C. §§ 165(a) and (g)(1), 382(e)(1). As a result, the annual limitation on carryovers of the loss corporation will be zero and the loss carryovers will not be available to offset the corporation's post change income. H.R.Rep. No. 100–495 (Conf. Rep.), 100th Cong., 1st Sess. A–40 (1987).

D. CONTINUITY OF BUSINESS ENTERPRISE

Prior to the 1986 revision of § 382, loss carryovers survived a change in ownership of the loss corporation in a purchase transaction if the corporation continued to conduct business substantially the same as before the ownership change. See editors' note at page 740. Section 382(c) retains a vestige of the business continuity requirements by disallowing loss carryovers following an ownership change if the corporation "does not continue the business enterprise" of the loss corporation for a period of at least 2 years. The legislative history indicates that § 382(c) is intended to adopt the continuity of business requirement applied to reorganizations by Treas.Reg., § 1.368–1(d). See page 534. Thus, the continuity requirement is satisfied if the new loss corporation either continues the trade or business which existed before an ownership change, or uses a significant portion of the business assets of the old loss corporation in a business. The Conference Report makes it clear that loss carryovers survive an ownership change even if the new loss corporation discontinues more than a minor portion of the historic business of the old loss corporation. H.Rep. No. 99–841, 99th Cong., 2d Sess. II–189 (1986).

The insistence on continuity of business is to some extent inconsistent with the basic theory behind the limitation of § 382. The § 382 limitation is based, in part, on the assumption that the loss corporation could dispose of its assets, invest the proceeds in income generating securities, and absorb its loss carryover with interest income. There is no continuity of business restriction preventing use of loss carryovers following such a transaction. Why is it necessary to encourage continued investment in a loss operation following an ownership change? Perhaps the answer is that the continuity of business requirement is necessary to prevent the acquisition of a corporation to acquire only loss carryovers. However, the § 382 limitation itself is sufficiently restrictive to eliminate transactions motivated by only tax reduction. To the extent the continuity requirement inhibits the purchaser, it restrains the sale of the loss corporation, encourages continuation of an unprofitable business, and thereby violates the neutrality principle on which § 382 is based.

E. LIMITATIONS ON CARRYOVERS UNDER SECTION 383

Section 383 applies the limitation of § 382 following an ownership change to capital loss carryovers, general business credits, minimum tax credits under the alternative minimum tax, and foreign tax credits. Section 383(b) states that regulations are to be issued to provide that capital losses carried forward from a year pre-dating an ownership change are limited under § 382 principles and shall reduce the § 382 limitation on net operating losses. Section 383(a) and (c) provide for regulations to limit the use of tax credit carryforwards to tax liability computed on income up to the § 382 limitation. Tax credits are thereby converted into their taxable income equivalents for limitation purposes. See Treas.Reg. § 1.383–1.

F. APPLICATION OF SECTION 382 IN BANKRUPTCY AND INSOLVENCY PROCEEDINGS

1. *Stock for Debt Exchange*

In the case of a loss corporation involved in a Title 11 or similar bankruptcy proceeding, the § 382 limitation is not applied if, following an ownership change, the creditors and former stockholders of the loss corporation own at least 50 percent of the loss corporation stock. I.R.C. § 382(*l*)(5)(A). In effect, the creditors of the financially distressed corporation are treated as stockholders for purposes of testing for an ownership change. Under this provision, an exchange of debt for stock by creditors does not trigger the § 382 limitation. The relief of § 382(*l*)(5)(A) is available only with respect to an exchange of stock for indebtedness that has been held by the creditor for at least eighteen months preceding the date of filing of the bankruptcy or insolvency proceeding, or with respect to indebtedness incurred in the ordinary course of business of the old loss corporation which at all times has been held by the same person. I.R.C. § 382(*l*)(5)(E).

There is a substantial cost imposed for avoiding the general § 382 limitation under the exception provided by § 382(*l*)(5)(A). Section 382(*l*)(5)(B) requires that loss carryovers be reduced by the amount of interest on indebtedness converted into stock that has been paid or accrued during the taxable year of the ownership change and the three year period preceding the taxable year of the ownership change. Theoretically, debt of the bankrupt corporation has had the characteristics of equity during this period so that the interest deduction should not be available to increase loss carryovers.

Under § 382(*l*)(5)(C), discharged indebtedness for interest that is taken into account to reduce net operating loss carryovers does not create discharge of indebtedness income under § 108(e)(8). Discharge of indebtedness income is created under § 108(e)(8) in the amount by which the fair market value of stock issued in exchange for debt is less than the amount of the debt.

If there is a second ownership change within two years with respect to a corporation that avoided the § 382 limitation under § 382(*l*)(5)(A), the § 382 limitation following the second ownership change will be zero. I.R.C. § 382(*l*)(5)(D).

2. *Qualified Debt Holders*

Relief from an ownership change under § 382(*l*)(5) is available only with respect to debt held by the creditor for eighteen months preceding the ownership change, or trade or business debt held at all times by the same person. Under Treas.Reg. § 1.382–9(d)(3), debt held by a person who is a less than five percent shareholder after the ownership change will be treated as owned by the same creditor for the 18 month period preceding the filing of a bankruptcy or insolvency petition. Thus, qualification under § 385(*l*)(5) does not require tracing of ownership during this "continuity period" of widely held debt that is converted into equity. This provision does not apply to an entity through which a five percent shareholder owns an indirect ownership interest in the loss corporation. In addition, if the loss corporation has knowledge of the acquisition of its debt by a group of persons with the principal purpose of exchanging the debt for stock, the indebtedness and stock will be treated as owned by an entity. Treas.Reg. § 1.382–9(d)(3)(ii)(A). Treas.Reg. § 1.382–9(d)(4) also provides that indebtedness held by a beneficial owner that is a five percent shareholder after the ownership change of the loss corporation and which is a corporation (or other entity) that has itself experienced an ownership change, will not be treated as indebtedness qualified for § 385(*l*)(5) treatment if the indebtedness represents more than 25 percent of the beneficial owner's gross assets on the beneficial owner's ownership change date.

For purposes of determining whether the eighteen month holding period is met, Treas.Reg. § 1.382–9(d)(5) provides that the transferee of indebtedness in certain transactions is treated as holding the indebtedness during the transferor's holding period. Transfers subject to this "tacking rule" include (1) transfers between related parties, (2) transfers pursuant to customary loan syndications, (3) transfers by an underwriter in the course of an underwriting, (4) transfers in which the transferee's basis is determined under § 1014 (death-time transfers), § 1015 (gifts), or with reference to the transferor's basis (nonrecognition transactions in general), (5) transfers in satisfaction of a pecuniary bequest, (6) transfers pursuant to a divorce or separation agreement, and (7) transfers by reason of subrogation. The tacking rule does not apply, however, if the transfer is for the principal purpose of taking advantage of the losses of the loss corporation. In addition, Treas.Reg. § 1.382–9(d)(5)(iv) provides for tacking of the holding period and character of indebtedness incurred in the course of a trade or business in the case of indebtedness received from the loss corporation in exchange for old indebtedness. This tacking rule also applies to a change in the terms of an indebtedness which constitutes an exchange under § 1001.

3. *Election Out*

A loss corporation may elect under section 382(*l*)(5)(H) not to have section 382(*l*)(5) apply to it. Treas.Reg. § 1.383–9(i) provides that the election is irrevocable and specifies the language that must be filed with the electing corporation's tax return by the due date (including extensions) for the loss corporation's return for the taxable year that includes the change date.

If an ownership change in a bankruptcy reorganization or Title 11 case does not qualify for the benefits of § 382(*l*)(5), or the loss corporation has elected out of the provision, under § 382(*l*)(6) the value of the loss corporation will reflect any increase in value that results from the surrender of debt in the transaction. Although § 382(*l*)(1) provides that capital contributions intended to increase the value of the loss corporation shall not be taken into account, Treas.Reg. § 1.382–9(j) recognizes that economically the direct conversion of debt into stock, or a stock issuance for cash which is used to satisfy creditors, have the same effect on the corporation. See CO–88–90, 1992–2 C.B. 616. Subject to a number of anti-abuse rules (see Treas.Reg. § 1.382–9(k)), Treas.Reg. § 1.382–9(j)(1) and (2) basically provide that the value of a loss corporation to which § 382(*l*)(6) applies is the lesser of the value of the stock of the loss corporation immediately after the ownership change or the value of the loss corporation's pre-change assets. Limiting the value of the loss corporation to the value of pre-change assets, if less than stock value, in effect removes from the valuation the benefit of contributions to capital that are not used to satisfy creditors and which would otherwise be reflected in stock value.

4. *Continuity of Business Requirement*

Treas.Reg. § 1.382–9(m)(1) provides that the continuity of business requirement for utilizing net operating loss carryovers imposed by § 382(c) does not apply to a loss corporation that is not subject to the § 382 limitation by virtue of § 382(*l*)(5). As a corollary, Treas.Reg. § 1.269–6, Ex. (3), indicates that a change of control in an ownership change covered by § 382(*l*)(5) will be considered under § 269 to be made for the principal purpose of tax avoidance unless the corporation carries on more than an insignificant amount of an active trade or business during and subsequent to the Title 11 or similar case.

G. ACQUISITION OF BUILT–IN GAIN PROPERTY BY A LOSS CORPORATION: SECTION 384

The § 382 limitation does not apply to restrict loss carryovers if, instead of being acquired by new owners, the loss corporation directly or indirectly acquires appreciated assets of a profitable enterprise in a carryover basis transaction and uses its loss carryover to avoid tax on gain recognized on disposition of the acquired assets. Section 384 was enacted in 1987 to deal with this situation. The legislative history explains the provision as follows:

"[Section 384] provides that loss corporations will be precluded from using their losses to shelter built-in gains of an acquired company recognized within five years of the acquisition. Built-in gains for this purpose includes any item of income which is attributable to periods before the acquisition date. For example, built-in gains for this purpose include so-called 'phantom' gains on property on which depreciation had been taken prior to the acquisition. It is likewise expected that built-in gains for this purpose will also include any income recognized after an acquisition in which the fair market value of the property acquired is less than the present value of the taxes that would be due on the income associated with the property (for example, in the case of a 'burnt-out' leasing subsidiary with built-in income transferred to a loss corporation). No inference is intended that such situations are not subject to § 269 of present law." H.Rep. No. 100–391, 100th Cong., 1st Sess. 1093–1094 (1987).

Section 384 applies to built-in gain recognized during the five-year period following the corporate acquisition of control of another corporation, or the acquisition of corporate assets in an (A), (C) or (D) reorganization, when either the acquiring corporation or the acquired corporation has a "net unrealized built-in gain" at the time of acquisition. By reference to § 382(h), net unrealized built-in gain exists if the aggregate value of transferred assets at the time of acquisition exceeds the aggregate adjusted bases of such assets. I.R.C. § 384(c)(1) and (8). Section 384 prohibits the use of pre-acquisition losses (including recognized built-in losses) of one corporation to offset recognized built-in gain of the gain corporation. It does not prevent a loss corporation from acquiring an on-going profitable enterprise for the purpose of using its loss carryovers to offset future income (other than recognized built-in gain) of the acquired business. However, such an acquisition may be subject to § 269.

H. SECTION 269 AND LOSS CARRYOVERS

Section 269 allows the Commissioner to deny the benefit of deductions made possible by an acquisition of control of another corporation or assets with a carryover basis when the principal purpose of the acquisition is tax avoidance. Before 1986, § 269 was a moderately important weapon for the Commissioner to prevent abusive acquisitions of shell corporations with loss carryovers. For example, in Scroll, Inc. v. Commissioner, 447 F.2d 612 (5th Cir.1971), the stock of the taxpayer, which had a substantial net operating loss carryforward, was acquired by another corporation, Keller. Several months after the acquisition, Keller merged the operations of a profitable subsidiary into the loss corporation. As a result of the merger, the income of the profitable business was offset by the loss corporation's operating loss carryforward. The taxpayer asserted that the transaction enabled the profitable subsidiary to reduce state income taxes and provided the loss corporation with the benefit of the marketing skills of the profitable enterprise. The Court of Appeals affirmed the Tax Court's finding that the forbidden tax avoidance motive was present:

"Regardless of whether these non-tax motives were actual or illusory, however, the practical effect of the entire transaction was to enable the corporation to set off substantial pre-acquisition losses against subsequent earnings and thereby to obtain a tax benefit not otherwise available. According to the Treasury Regulations (§ 1.269–3), such a result by itself indicates a tax-avoidance motive irrespective of whether any other evidence points to the proscribed principal purpose. And, contrary to Taxpayer's contention that the disallowance fails for want of verbal testimony linking (i) the initial acquisition of [the taxpayer] with (ii) the soon-to-follow merger of [the profitable subsidiary into the taxpayer], the Tax Court was entitled to treat both acquisition and merger as interrelated steps in a single transaction. [Citation omitted.]

"There is a good deal of practical wisdom in the regulation, whether its principle comes from the mind of Judge or the pen of a regulation redactor. A 269 problem is not one of torts in which the judicial inquiry artificially cuts off at the moment of wrong. What was intended by such a merger-acquisition can properly be ascertained both by initial actions and those taken shortly thereafter, especially when the subsequent steps are so obviously necessary that they must have been in the minds of the strategists. The record here is undisputed that Keller's top management—including a former practicing certified public accountant—was aware in detail of this $600,000 loss carryover. We think a court experienced in the affairs of Federal income taxation was entitled to believe that no businessman in his right mind would allow this plum to go unplucked. To do nothing was to forsake forever the hope of a tax savings. To try, the structural change had to be made. If it worked, all was well. If it didn't, the try was worth the risk-indeed, there was no risk at all because what is here 'lost' is what would have been paid had the game plan not been chosen. The burden of proof on the taxpayer is not an easy one, and when the disputed tax benefits are so disproportionate to the value of the other asserted advantages, that burden may be practically impossible to sustain. * * * "(617–618)

The legislative history of the 1986 Act indicates that § 382 does not alter the application of § 269 to acquisitions made to evade or avoid taxes. H.Rep. No. 99–841, 99th Cong., 2d Sess. II–194. However, after 1986, § 382 so severely discounts net operating loss carryforwards following an ownership change that there is no longer a significant tax avoidance potential in a transaction subject to the limitation. Thus, Treas.Reg. § 1.269–7 provides that § 269 may be applied following an ownership change subject to § 382, but the reduced value of net operating loss carryforwards under the § 382 limitation will be taken into account in determining whether the change of control was undertaken with the prohibited tax avoidance motive. Nonetheless, because the more than 50 percent ownership change rules of § 382 and the acquisition of control provisions of § 269 are not identical, there is a possibility that an acquisition will fall within § 269 without triggering an ownership change under § 382. For example, P, which owns 49 percent of L, a loss corporation, acquires an additional 31 percent of the loss corporation stock. P then liquidates L under § 332 thereby inheriting L's loss carryover under § 381. If there have been no other owner shifts with respect to the L stock during the three year testing period, P has acquired control of L for § 269 purposes without triggering the § 382 limitation on L's loss carryovers. If P's acquisition of L, or its assets, is undertaken with the requisite tax avoidance purpose, § 269 may be invoked to deny P the benefit of L's loss carryforward even though the transaction escapes the reach of § 382.

The § 382 limitation is applicable only to an ownership change of the loss corporation itself. Although § 384 restricts the acquisition of assets with built-in gain by a loss corporation, there is nothing in the statutory scheme to prevent a loss corporation from acquiring a profitable business in a taxable or nontaxable transaction to generate income to absorb the corporation's loss carryforward. In Rev.Rul. 63–40, 1963–1 C.B. 46, the Internal Revenue Service indicated that it would not contend that an acquisition is undertaken for tax avoidance purposes under § 269 if a loss corporation acquires the stock of a profitable corporation, liquidates the profitable business, and discontinues the loss business. The Ruling does not apply, however, if the purchase price for the profitable business is paid over a long period of time or exceeds the fair market value of the acquired business. Could the Service ever successfully overcome a loss corporation's assertion that its acquisition of a profitable enterprise was undertaken for valid business purposes? Indeed, would imposition of § 269 restrictions on this transaction achieve a desirable policy goal? If the stockholders who suffered the losses are still in the picture, there is not the windfall that is present in the case in which newcomers acquire a loss corporation, the typical "trafficking in loss corporation" case.

I. NET OPERATING LOSS CARRYOVERS OF A CONSOLIDATED GROUP

If after a change of ownership of a loss corporation, the corporation is a member of a controlled group of corporations filing a consolidated return, discussed in Chapter 10, under current law net operating loss carryovers are subject to two principal limitations: the Separate Return Limitation Year (SRLY) restriction of Temp.Reg. § 1.1502–21T(c), which allows the use of losses from a separate return year of member of the group only to the extent of income produced by that member (page 445); and § 382 (see Temp.Reg. § 1.1502–91T). Temp.Regs. §§ 1.1502–90T through 1.1502–99T adopt complex rules applying the § 382 limitation in the consolidated return context.

The temporary regulations generally treat the members of a consolidated group as a single entity for purposes of determining whether an ownership change has occurred with respect to a loss corporation and ascertaining the value of the loss corporation stock. Before an ownership change, a consolidated group of corporations is able to absorb net operating losses of some members against the income of other members as a single entity. Following an ownership change, the consolidated taxable income of a group that may be offset by pre-ownership change losses and built-in losses of the group is limited by the § 382 consolidated limitation applied to the group as a whole. Temp.Reg. § 1.1502–91T(a)(1). Under Temp.Reg. § 1.1502–92T(b)(1), a consolidated loss group has an ownership change for purposes of § 382 and Temp.Reg. § 1.382–2T if there has been an ownership change of the common parent. In determining whether an ownership change has occurred, losses of the group are treated as the losses of the common parent, and the testing period is measured by losses of members of the loss group. Temp.Reg. § 1.1502–92T(b)(1)(A) and (B).

Temp.Reg. § 1.1502–91T(d) provides for the identification of loss subgroups within a consolidated group for the purpose of applying the § 382 limitation on the basis of the loss subgroup. There is an ownership change with respect to a loss subgroup if there is an ownership change of the common parent of the loss subgroup. Temp.Reg. § 1.1502–92T(b)(1)(B)(ii).

The § 382 limitation, which under § 382(b)(1) is based on the value of the stock of the loss corporation multiplied by the applicable long-term tax-exempt rate, is determined from the value of the stock of the consolidated loss group or subgroup as a single entity. Temp.Reg. § 1.1502–93T(a). The value of the consolidated loss group immediately before an ownership change is the value of the stock of each member of the group, other than the value of stock of a member of the group which is held directly by another member of the group. Temp.Reg. § 1.1502–93T(b)(1).

In some circumstances, a subsidiary will be required to recognize an ownership change on a separate corporation basis with respect to its portion of the consolidated return net operating loss of the group. See Temp.Reg. § 1.1502–96T(b)(1).

Temp.Reg. § 1.1502–94T contains a separate set of rules applicable to carryover losses of a new member of a consolidated group which are subject to both the SRLY rule and the § 382 limitation. In general, a new loss member of a consolidated group is treated as a separate entity for purposes of applying the § 382 limitation. Thus, the amount of consolidated taxable income of the group that may be offset with losses of the new member is limited by a § 382 limitation that is computed with respect to the value of the new member corporation's stock at the time of its ownership change. Temp.Reg. § 1.1502–94T(b)(1). Under the SRLY limitation, the amount of the new member's losses that may be absorbed by the consolidated group is also limited to the new member's aggregate contribution to the consolidated taxable income of the group. Temp.Reg. § 1.1502–21T(c).

As noted, a consolidated loss group subject to the § 382 limitation is treated as a single entity subject to the limitation on the basis of the stock value of the entire group. If a loss corporation leaves a consolidated loss group or subgroup which has had an ownership change while the departing corporation was a member of the group, losses apportioned to the corporation under Temp.Reg. § 1.1502–21T(b) remain subject to the § 382 limitation. Under Temp.Reg. § 1.1502–95T, the § 382 limitation applicable to the departing loss corporation will be zero unless the common parent (not a loss subgroup parent) elects to apportion part of the § 382 limitation of the consolidated loss group to the departing loss corporation. The § 382 limitation apportioned to the departing member will reduce the § 382 limitation of the remaining consolidated loss group. Temp.Reg. § 1.1502–95T(c)(2).

PART VII

Special Rules to Prevent Avoidance of Shareholder Level Tax

CHAPTER 17

Penalty Taxes

The Code contains three sets of provisions to prevent the use of a corporation to accumulate income in avoidance of progressive individual tax rates and to convert ordinary income at the corporate level into stockholder capital gain. First, the accumulated earnings tax of §§ 531–537 imposes a penalty tax on corporate earnings that are accumulated beyond the reasonable needs of the business. Second, the personal holding company tax of §§ 541–547 imposes a penalty tax on undistributed passive investment income of closely held holding companies. Finally, the collapsible corporation rules of § 341 are designed to prevent the conversion of unrealized corporate income into stockholder capital gain.

The changes in corporate and individual income taxation resulting from various tax acts beginning with the Tax Reform Act of 1986, have reduced the significance of these penalty tax provisions. At one time, individual marginal rates were substantially higher than the top rate on corporate income thereby creating an incentive for accumulating earnings at the corporate level. As originally enacted, the 1986 Act imposed a higher rate on corporate taxable income (34%) than the highest marginal rate for individuals (28%). Currently the highest individual marginal rate is less than five percentage points above the highest marginal corporate rate. Thus, after 1986, there is little advantage to accumulating earnings at the corporate level. Further, the double tax regime creates a tax disadvantage to corporate income that eliminates any incentive to use the corporate form as a holding company for personal investments. The requirement that corporate level built-in gain be taxed on liquidation of the corporation defeats the benefit of the collapsible corporation. Nonetheless, all three provisions remain in the Code and under some factual circumstances provide traps for the unwary. Perhaps the penalty provisions, especially the accumulated earnings tax, now best can be viewed as appropriate to accelerate full imposition of the two-level tax, but many believe they are no longer necessary.

SECTION 1. THE ACCUMULATED EARNINGS TAX

INTERNAL REVENUE CODE: Sections 531–537.

REGULATIONS: Sections 1.532–1(a); 1.533–1(a); 1.537–1(a), (b),–2,–3.

Sections 531 and 532 impose a tax of 39.6 percent on the "accumulated taxable income" of a corporation which has been formed or availed of for the purpose of avoiding the imposition of income tax on its shareholders, or the shareholders of another corporation, by permitting earnings and profits to accumulate instead of being distributed.[1] In Ivan Allen Company v. United States, 422 U.S. 617 (1975), at a time when the top individual rate was significantly higher than the top corporate rate, the Court described the purpose and function of the accumulated earnings tax as follows:

"Under our system of income taxation, corporate earnings are subject to tax at two levels. First, there is the tax imposed upon the income of the corporation. Second, when the corporation, by way of a dividend, distributes its earnings to its shareholders, the distribution is subject to the tax imposed upon the income of the shareholders. Because of the disparity between the corporate tax rates and the higher gradations of the rates on individuals, a corporation may be utilized to reduce significantly its shareholders' overall tax liability by accumulating earnings beyond the reasonable needs of the business. Without some method to force the distribution of unneeded corporate earnings, a controlling shareholder would be able to postpone the full impact of income taxes on his share of the corporation's earnings in excess of its needs. * * *

"In order to foreclose this possibility of using the corporation as a means of avoiding the income tax on dividends to the shareholders, every revenue act since the adoption of the Sixteenth Amendment in 1913 has

1. The constitutionality of the predecessor of the accumulated earnings tax, was sustained by the Supreme Court in Helvering v. National Grocery Co., 304 U.S. 282 (1938). The Court said that tax was on net income and the fact that the incidence was determined by a state of mind was not unknown to the tax field.

imposed a tax upon unnecessary accumulations of corporate earnings effected for the purpose of insulating shareholders.[8]

"The Court has acknowledged the obvious purpose of the accumulation provisions of the successive acts:

> 'As the theory of the revenue acts has been to tax corporate profits to the corporation, and their receipt only when distributed to the stockholders, the purpose of the legislation is to compel the company to distribute any profits not needed for the conduct of its business so that, when so distributed, individual stockholders will become liable not only for normal but for surtax on the dividends received." Helvering v. Chicago Stock Yards Co., 318 U.S. 693, 699, * * * (1943).

This was reaffirmed in United States v. Donruss Co., 393 U.S. 297 * * * (1969).

"It is to be noted that the focus and impositions of the accumulated earnings tax is upon 'accumulated taxable income,' § 531. This is defined in § 535(a) to mean the corporation's 'taxable income,' as adjusted. The adjustments consist of the various items described in § 535(b), including federal income tax, the deduction for dividends paid defined in § 561, and the accumulated earnings credit defined in § 535(c). The adjustments prescribed by § 535(a) and (b) are designed generally to assure that a corporation's 'accumulated taxable income' reflects more accurately than 'taxable income' the amount actually available to the corporation for business purposes. This explains the deductions for dividends paid and for federal income taxes; neither of these enters into the computation of taxable income. Obviously, dividends paid and federal income taxes deplete corporate resources and must be recognized if the corporation's economic condition is to be properly perceived. Conversely, § 535(b)(3) disallows, for example, the deduction, available to a corporation for income tax purposes

8. The accumulated earnings tax originated in § II A, Subdivision 2, of the Tariff Act of October 3, 1913, 38 Stat. 166. This imposed a tax on the shareholders of a corporation "formed or fraudulently availed of for the purpose of preventing the imposition of such tax through the medium of permitting such gains and profits to accumulate instead of being divided or distributed." Accumulations "beyond the reasonable needs of the business shall be prima facie evidence of a fraudulent purpose to escape such tax." Id., at 167. The same provision appeared as § 3 of the Revenue Act of 1916, 39 Stat. 758, and again as § 220 of the Revenue Act of 1918, 40 Stat. 1072 (1919), except that in the 1918 Act the word "fraudulently" was deleted. This change was effected inasmuch as the Senate felt that the former phraseology "has proved to be of little value, because it was necessary to its application that intended fraud on the revenue be established in each case." S.Rep. No. 617, 65th Cong., 3d Sess., 5 (1918).

This pattern of tax on the shareholders was changed with the Revenue Act of 1921, § 220, 42 Stat. 247. The incidence of the tax was shifted from the shareholders to the corporation itself. Judge Learned Hand opined that the change was due to doubts "as to the validity of taxing income which the taxpayers had never received, and in 1921 it was thought safer to tax the company itself." United Business Corp. v. Commissioner, 62 F.2d 754, 756 (CA2), cert. denied, 290 U.S. 635 * * * (1933).

Although the statutory language has varied somewhat from time to time, the income tax law, since the change effected by the Revenue Act of 1921, consistently has imposed the tax on the corporation, rather than upon the shareholders. * * *

under § 243, on account of dividends received; dividends received are freely available for use in the corporation's business.

"The purport of the accumulated earnings tax structure established by §§ 531–537, therefore, is to determine the corporation's true economic condition before its liability for tax upon 'accumulated taxable income' is determined. The tax, although a penalty and therefore to be strictly construed, Commissioner v. Acker, 361 U.S. 87, 91, * * * (1959), is directed at economic reality.

* * *

"Accumulation beyond the reasonable needs of the business, by the language of § 533(a), is 'determinative of the purpose' to avoid tax with respect to shareholders unless the corporation proves the contrary by a preponderance of the evidence. The burden of proof, thus, is on the taxpayer. A rebuttable presumption is statutorily imposed. To be sure, we deal here, in a sense, with a state of mind. But it has been said that the statute, without the support of the presumption, would 'be practically unenforceable without it.' United Business Corp. v. Commissioner, 62 F.2d 754, 755 (CA2), cert. denied, 290 U.S. 635 * * *(1933). What is required, then, is a comparison of accumulated earnings and profits with 'the reasonable needs of the business.' Business needs are critical. And need, plainly, to use mathematical terminology, is a function of a corporation's liquidity, that is, the amount of idle current assets at its disposal. The question, therefore, is not how much capital of all sorts, but how much in the way of quick or liquid assets, it is reasonable to keep on hand for the business."

Generally, the Commissioner has attempted to apply the accumulated earnings tax only to closely held corporations. The requirement that the corporation be formed or availed of to avoid shareholder tax is less likely to exist in the case of publicly owned companies. In some instances, the tax has been applied to widely held companies that were controlled by a small group of stockholders;[2] and since 1984 § 532(c) has provided that the accumulated earnings tax is to be applied without regard to the number of stockholders.

2. See Trico Products Corp. v. Commissioner, 137 F.2d 424 (2d Cir.1943) and Trico Products v. McGowan, 169 F.2d 343 (2d Cir. 1948) (corporation owned by 2,000 stockholders but 74% of the stock was held by six stockholders). But in Golconda Mining Corp. v. Commissioner, 507 F.2d 594 (9th Cir. 1974), the appellate court reversed the Tax Court's holding that the accumulated earnings tax was applicable to a corporation whose management group owned from 12% to 17% of the stock. The court held that the accumulated earnings tax could apply only if a relatively small group of stockholders exercised control, a situation which could exist only if a small group of stockholders owned more than 50% of the stock of the corporation.

In Technalysis Corp. v. Commissioner, 101 T.C. 397 (1993), the court held that the accumulated earnings tax is applicable to a publicly held corporation without regard to whether control was exercised by a relatively small group of shareholders. However, the court concluded that although the corporation's accumulations were beyond the reasonable needs of the business, the corporation was not formed or availed of to avoid income tax with respect to its shareholders.

ILLUSTRATIVE MATERIAL

A. THE RELATIONSHIP BETWEEN THE PROSCRIBED ACCUMULATION "PURPOSE" AND THE REASONABLE NEEDS OF THE BUSINESS

In United States v. Donruss Co., 393 U.S. 297 (1969), the Court resolved a conflict as to whether, as urged by the Government, a taxpayer to rebut the presumption contained in § 533(a) must establish that tax avoidance with respect to the shareholders was not "one" of the purposes for the accumulation or whether, as some Courts of Appeals had held, the presumption could be rebutted by demonstrating that tax avoidance was not the "dominant, controlling, or impelling" purpose for the accumulation. The Court sustained the Government's position.

To understand the impact of the holding in *Donruss*, consider the situation of the taxpayer in that case on remand. Since the jury that decided the case below had already found that the accumulation was beyond the reasonable needs of the business, the presumption in § 533(a) that the purpose was to avoid income taxes with respect to the shareholders had been brought into play. It would thus now be up to the taxpayer to prove by a preponderance of the evidence the negative proposition that not one of the purposes of the accumulation was tax avoidance, an almost impossible task. Though the statute makes a finding of the proscribed purpose the crucial event for the imposition of the tax, the *Donruss* holding made the finding as to the reasonableness of the accumulation the determinative factor in the vast majority of cases. See e.g., Bahan Textile Machinery Co., Inc. v. United States, 453 F.2d 1100 (4th Cir.1972) (after an accumulation beyond the reasonable needs of the business was established, the taxpayer unsuccessfully tried to overcome the presumption as to purpose by showing that the controlling shareholder was "an overly cautious man, fearful of long-term debt and conservative in financial outlook"). Compare Bremerton Sun Publishing Co. v. Commissioner, 44 T.C. 566 (1965) ("Although we feel that the total accumulation was somewhat beyond the reasonable foreseeable business needs of petitioner, we are convinced that the only reason for the excessive retention of earnings was the conservative policies of the directors and not their concern for the surtax liability of [the shareholders]." (590)); Starman Investment, Inc. v. United States, 534 F.2d 834 (9th Cir.1976) (even if accumulation beyond reasonable needs, lack of tax avoidance motive precludes imposition of tax).

In Magic Mart, Inc. v. Commissioner, 51 T.C. 775 (1969), the court concluded that since accumulations beyond the reasonable needs of the business were not present, a finding as to the purpose of the accumulations was unnecessary in light of the credit in § 535(c) for reasonable accumulation, and the *Donruss* issue was not reached. In contrast to Magic Mart, some courts have apparently been of the view that, to escape tax, the accumulations, in addition to being reasonable in an objective sense, must have been motivated by business needs and not tax avoidance purposes. See Apollo Industries, Inc. v. Commissioner, 358 F.2d 867 (1st Cir.1966), remanding the case to the Tax Court for an answer to the following question: "[E]ven if accumulated earnings did not exceed reasonably anticipated business needs in one or both years, was avoidance of taxes on shareholders nevertheless a dominant purpose?" The Court of Appeals in *Donruss* apparently was of the same view (384 F.2d 292, 294 (6th Cir. 1967)), though the cases it cited for this proposition were decided prior to the enactment of § 535(c). The Tax Court uniformly has taken the view that if the accumulations do not exceed the reasonable needs of the business so that a sufficient credit would be present quite apart from any issue as to the purpose for the accumulation, the issue as to the purpose of the accumulations is irrelevant. John P. Scripps Newspapers v. Commissioner, 44 T.C. 453 (1965); Dielectric Materials Co. v. Commissioner, 57 T.C. 587 (1972).

B. FACTORS BEARING ON REASONABLE BUSINESS NEEDS

1. *General*

Determining the "reasonable business needs" involves a complex factual inquiry into all aspects of the corporation's business. Courts generally start with the statement that they are reluctant to substitute their judgment for the business judgment of the management as to the need for the accumulations (see e.g., Dielectric Materials Co. v. Commissioner, 57 T.C. 587 (1972)), and then proceed with an exhaustive analysis of the corporation's financial and business history. While the cases are not easily classified, each turning on its own facts, they typically involve the factors discussed below.

2. *Accumulations for Expansion or Diversification*

The expansion or replacement of existing business facilities often is given as a justification for accumulations. Treas.Reg. § 1.537–1(b)(1) requires that the corporation "must have specific, definite, and feasible plans for the use of such accumulations." The courts have applied this requirement with varying degrees of strictness. See, e.g., Faber Cement Block Co., Inc. v. Commissioner, 50 T.C. 317 (1968)(A) (taxpayer's operations on its property constituted a nonconforming use under the local zoning ordinances and any expansion would have required an additional variance; accumulations over a long period of time for a proposed expansion were justified).

In addition to expansion of facilities, accumulations often are justified on the ground that they are needed to diversify the existing business. Treas.Reg. § 1.537–3(a) defines the "business" of a corporation very broadly as "not merely that which it has previously carried on but includ[ing], in general, any line of business which it may undertake." On the other hand, investments that are "unrelated" to the activities of the business of the taxpayer are an indication of unreasonable accumulations, Treas.Reg. § 1.537–2(c)(4), and the line between an "unrelated investment" and the beginning of a new "business" is not a clear one. See, e.g., Electric Regulator Corp. v. Commissioner, 336 F.2d 339 (2d Cir.1964) (taxpayer produced a small patented voltage regulator that was successful commercially, resulting in large accumulated profits; taxpayer's justification for the accumulation based on the desire to develop new products was sustained); Hughes Inc. v. Commissioner, 90 T.C. 1 (1988) (purchase of an orange grove and interests in partnerships holding real estate were justified as part of efforts to diversify the business of owning and leasing improved real and tangible personal properties); J. Gordon Turnbull, Inc. v. Commissioner, 41 T.C. 358 (1963) (fact that an architectural and engineering firm invested large sums in real estate was found indicative of an accumulation beyond the reasonable needs of its business); Cataphote Corp. of Miss. v. United States, 535 F.2d 1225 (Ct.Cl.1976) (acquisition of 26 fractional working interests in oil and gas ventures by a corporation in the truck leasing business did not mean that the corporation was also in the oil and gas business for accumulated earnings tax purposes; the corporation did not have the necessary business responsibilities and the interests constituted mere investments unrelated to the active business of the corporation).

3. *Working Capital Needs*

Treas.Reg. § 1.537–2(b)(4) recognizes the need to accumulate earnings "to provide necessary working capital for the business." The courts have struggled to develop standards for the determination of a reasonable allowance for working capital. Earlier cases allowed an accumulation of working capital to cover some arbitrary period of time, such as one year, or stressed the relationship between current liabilities and current assets in assessing working capital needs. More recent cases, following the approach taken initially in Bardahl Mfg. Corp. v. Commissioner, T.C.Memo. 1965–200, attempt to relate the corporation's need for working capital to its "operating cycle." In J.H. Rutter Rex Mfg. Co. v. Commissioner, 853 F.2d 1275 (5th Cir.1988), the court described the operating cycle approach as follows:

"An operating cycle for a manufacturing business like Rutter Rex is the period of time needed to convert cash into raw materials, raw materials into inventory, inventory into accounts receivable, and accounts receivable into cash. In other words, an operating cycle is the time a corporation's working capital is tied up in producing and selling its product. * * *

"The 'operating cycle' as originally formulated in *Bardahl Manufacturing* is broken down into two sub-cycles: an inventory cycle and an accounts receivable cycle. These cycles are measured in terms of days. An inventory cycle is the time necessary to convert raw materials into finished goods and to sell those goods. An accounts receivable cycle is the time necessary to convert the accounts receivable created by the sale of finished goods into cash. These two cycles are added together to determine the total number of days in the operating cycle. The number of days in the operating cycle is then divided by 365; the resulting fraction is multiplied by the amount of the corporation's operating expenses for one year, including costs of goods sold, selling expenses, general and administrative expenses, and estimated federal and state income tax payments (but excluding depreciation). The resulting figure is the amount of liquid assets necessary to meet the ordinary operating expenses for the complete operating cycle."

The *Bardahl* formula is also applied by taking account of a credit cycle. The credit cycle is based on the amount of time between the corporation's receipt of raw materials, supplies, labor, and other inputs, and the corporation's payment for these items. The deferral of payment reduces the corporation's need for capital and thus the credit cycle is subtracted from the operating cycle determined from inventory and receivables cycles. See C.E. Hooper, Inc. v. United States, 539 F.2d 1276 (Ct.Cl.1976). In *J.H. Rutter Rex Mfg. Co.*, supra, the taxpayer convinced the appellate court that application of a credit cycle to reduce its working capital needs was inappropriate because of the lack of evidence that the corporation utilized an extension of credit from its major suppliers to any significant degree.

Despite the seeming exactness of the operating cycle formula, its limitations must be recognized. See Dielectric Materials Co. v. Commissioner, 57 T.C. 587 (1972) (*Bardahl* not strictly applied because the formula was not sufficiently "flexible" to take into account the fact that taxpayer had additional working capital needs in the light of a threatened labor dispute); Ready Paving and Construction Co. v. Commissioner, 61 T.C. 826 (1974) ("special investment warrants" received as payment for contracting work done for municipal governments constituted assets available for use as working capital under the *Bardahl* formula; correspondingly, the warrants did not constitute accounts receivable for determining the amount of accumulated earnings needed for working capital; consistent treatment of the items was required in both aspects of the *Bardahl* formula).

4. *Provision for Contingencies*

Fears, both real and imagined, of contingent liabilities also have been used to justify accumulations of earnings. In Halby Chemical Co., Inc. v. United States, 180 Ct.Cl. 584 (1967), the court allowed accumulations for self-insurance against the "enduring possibility of a disastrous fire or explosion" which could not adequately be covered by insurance because of the risk of taxpayer's operations. In Hughes Inc. v. Commissioner, 90 T.C. 1 (1988), a closely held corporation which rented warehouses to a publicly held corporation used accumulated earnings to purchase stock of the public corporation in order to prevent a hostile takeover of its lessee. The court said that investments in marketable securities which bear some relationship to a corporation's business are considered a proper business application of funds and may be accumulated with impunity. On the other hand, in Oyster Shell Products Corp. v. Commissioner, 313 F.2d 449 (2d Cir. 1963), the taxpayer unsuccessfully attempted to justify accumulations on the ground that possible flooding of the river on which its operations were located could result in large expenses; the court rejected the argument as "conjured up" after the accumulated earnings tax issue was first raised by the Government.

Section 537(b)(4) specifically provides for the accumulation of a reserve for reasonably anticipated product liability losses.

5. *Accumulations to Fund Stock Redemptions*

If a redemption is treated as a dividend under § 301, no accumulated earnings tax issue arises because the distribution is fully taxed at the shareholder level. But redemptions qualifying under § 302(b) or § 303 are not treated as dividends and thus raise an accumulated earnings tax issue. Pelton Steel Casting Co. v. Commissioner, 251 F.2d 278 (7th Cir.1958), held that the accumulated earnings tax applied in a case in which the corporation accumulated income to redeem the stock of two of its three shareholders rather than paying its earnings out as dividends to all of the shareholders and, presumably, then redeeming the stock at a lower price. The purpose of the redemption was to prevent the redeemed shareholders from selling their stock to outsiders, which was found not to be a corporate business purpose.

Mountain State Steel Foundries, Inc. v. Commissioner, 284 F.2d 737 (4th Cir.1960), held that the accumulated earnings tax did not apply to earnings in 1951 through 1954 used to pay a promissory note issued by the corporation in redemption of 50 percent of its shares in 1950. The Court emphasized that there was a business purpose for the redemption because the redeemed shareholders, who were inactive, had conflicting interests regarding corporate management with the continuing shareholders, who were active.

Is a business purpose such as was found in Mountain State Steel Foundries sufficient to justify a pre-redemption accumulation, as occurred in *Pelton Steel Casting Co.*? The lower courts have found a proper "corporate purpose" sufficient to avoid the accumulated earnings tax in a number of situations involving minority shareholders or retiring employee-shareholders. See Ted Bates & Co., Inc. v. Commissioner, T.C.Memo. 1965–251 (redemption made in order to assure "continuity of [taxpayer's] management"); Farmers & Merchants Investment Co. v. Commissioner, T.C.Memo. 1970–161 ("promotion of harmony in the conduct of the business"). In contrast, accumulations to redeem uncontentious large shareholders have been held subject to the tax. See John B. Lambert & Associates v. United States, 76–2 U.S.T.C. ¶ 9776 (Ct.Cl.1976); Lamark Shipping Agency, Inc. v. Commissioner, T.C.Memo. 1981–284.

Section 537(a)(2) specifically provides that accumulations to fund redemptions which qualify under § 303 are to meet the reasonable need of the business. However, § 537(b)(1) limits qualification under this rule to accumulations in the year the shareholder dies and subsequent years. Accumulations in years prior to the year of death cannot be justified by subsequent use for a § 303 redemption. See S.Rep. No. 91–522, 91st Cong., 1st Sess. 291 (1969).

6. *Shareholder Loans, Dividend Record and Shareholder Tax Bracket*

While the fact that the corporation has paid no dividends is, of course, not conclusive on the issue of the proscribed purpose, it is a factor. Failure to pay dividends together with loans to shareholders by the corporation indicate an availability of funds to make dividend distributions. See, e.g.,

Bahan Textile Machinery, Co. v. United States, 453 F.2d 1100 (4th Cir. 1972) (loans to shareholders and relatives "show not only that the company was dissipating funds which it claimed were needed for the business, but also indicated a purpose to distribute corporate profits indirectly rather than as dividends that would be taxable to the recipients").

In GPD, Inc. v. Commissioner, 60 T.C. 480 (1973), rev'd, 508 F.2d 1076 (6th Cir.1974), the Tax Court held that the corporation was subject to the accumulated earnings tax for a year in which there had been a decrease in the corporation's earnings and profits. The Tax Court took the position that since there was no accumulation of earnings and profits, the accumulated earnings tax could not apply, even though in that year, the corporation did have accumulated taxable income under § 535.[3] The Court of Appeals reversed the Tax Court, holding that the legislative history of the accumulated earnings tax did not show any intent to require the accumulations of earnings and profits in the current year as a condition precedent to the imposition of the tax. The Court of Appeals observed that if the Tax Court position were adopted, and a corporation distributed the exact amount of its earnings and profits for a year, no accumulated earnings tax could be imposed on accumulated taxable income of the corporation in that year; on the other hand, one cent of undistributed earnings and profits for the year would subject the entire accumulated taxable income to the tax. Moreover, the Court of Appeals observed that the Tax Court rule in effect gave a corporation a double accumulated earnings tax credit, since a corporation would be protected both in the year of accumulation and also in the year in which the actual redemption reduced earnings and profits.

Atlantic Properties, Inc. v. Commissioner, 519 F.2d 1233 (1st Cir. 1975), involved a corporation owned by four equal shareholders but whose corporate charter required an 80 percent vote of the shareholders for any corporate action. Three of the shareholders desired to have the corporation adopt a policy of dividend distributions; one shareholder did not, in part because of the adverse tax consequences of the dividend distribution to him. The court held that the accumulated earnings tax applied since the corporation was availed of for a proscribed purpose, even though a majority of the shareholders did not agree with that purpose.

7. *Accumulations by and for Subsidiaries*

Treas.Reg. § 1.537–3(b) provides that under certain circumstances the accumulated earnings of a parent corporation may be justified by the reasonably anticipated business needs of its subsidiary. In the converse situation, the Court of Appeals in Inland Terminals, Inc. v. United States, 477 F.2d 836 (4th Cir.1973), held that it was also possible to justify a controlled subsidiary's accumulated earnings with reference to the parent corporation's reasonably anticipated business needs which the parent corporation itself could not satisfy. On remand, the District Court held that

3. Accumulated taxable income was present despite a reduction in earnings and profits because stock redemptions, not being dividends, had no effect on the determination of accumulated taxable income.

the parent corporation's alternative diversification or relocation plans were such as would take all or substantially all of its own earnings and those of the subsidiary; thus the combined earnings of the two corporations did not exceed the reasonable needs of the parent's business. 73–2 U.S.T.C. ¶ 9724 (D.Md.1973).

In Chaney & Hope, Inc. v. Commissioner, 80 T.C. 263 (1983), the court held that accumulations for the business needs of a brother or sister corporation cannot generally be considered as accumulations to meet reasonable business needs because the business of the sister corporation is not the business of the brother corporation. The court also held, however, that the taxpayer could accumulate its earnings to meet the reasonably anticipated future needs of an expanded business to be conducted by its successor corporation, a sister corporation into which the taxpayer would be merged. Permissible accumulations were limited to earnings accumulated after the time plans for the merger became definite.

8. *Valuation Aspects*

In Ivan Allen v. United States, 422 U.S. 617 (1975), page 780, the issue was whether in determining the reasonable needs of the business marketable securities owned by the corporation should be counted at cost, as the taxpayer asserted, or their net liquidation value as claimed by the Commissioner. The Court pointed out that the accumulated earnings tax itself is imposed only on accumulated taxable income, which includes only realized gains. The Court held, however, that in determining whether accumulations exceed the reasonable needs of the business the full value of readily available liquid assets should be taken into account.

The decision of the Supreme Court in *Ivan Allen* was correct from the standpoint of the policy behind the accumulated earnings tax. The actual value which the corporation could realize from its investments and distribute to its shareholders is the best measure of the amount and reasonableness of its total accumulation; the cost basis of the investments is not relevant to that determination. Nevertheless, there are some difficulties in implementing the Court's decision. The majority in *Ivan Allen* assumed that the proper time for valuation of the securities was the end of the taxable year of the corporation. In some instances, other dates, for example, the date on which the Board of Directors makes its dividend decision for the year, might be more appropriate. There are also some technical problems. In other areas of the tax law, valuation of securities is made by taking a "blockage" factor into account, i.e., the size of the block of stock held by a particular shareholder can reduce the total value below a fair market value based on the quoted per share value because a single sale of the entire stock would depress the market. Valuation of closely held stock will present similar difficulties.

The majority in *Ivan Allen* went to some length to emphasize that its opinion was directed toward "readily marketable portfolio securities." But, as the dissenters pointed out, the majority's "rationale is not so easily contained." If a corporation holds securities which are not readily marketable but are still unrelated to its business, the majority's reasoning appears equally applicable; the lack of marketability or difficulties in disposition would be relevant to the valuation issue but do not lead to the conclusion that cost basis should be employed. Likewise, a finding that investments in real estate, timber land, and other such assets are unrelated to the business of the corporation should call into play the fair market value approach adopted by the majority.

In footnote 9 of the opinion, the majority stated that it was expressing no view with respect to the valuation of items such as inventory or accounts receivable. Motor Fuel Carriers, Inc. v. Commissioner, 559 F.2d 1348 (5th Cir.1977), held that accounts receivable should be treated as liquid assets for accumulated earnings tax purposes and valued at fair market value.

C. PROCEDURAL ASPECTS

In addition to the presumptions in § 533, discussed above, § 534 sets forth a complicated allocation of the burden of proof on certain issues in Tax Court proceedings. The provision is intended to ease the burden on the taxpayer in an accumulated earnings tax case. See, Senate Finance Committee Report, S.Rep. No. 83–1622, 83rd Cong., 2d Sess. 70–71 (1954). The provision, however, has not been of much help to taxpayers because the Tax Court has been quite strict regarding the required content of the taxpayer's statement under § 534(c). It must contain adequate factual material and not simply "conclusory" statements. See, J.H. Rutter Rex Mfg. Co. v. Commissioner, 853 F.2d 1275, 1283 (5th Cir.1988), in which the taxpayer's statement was found wanting because of its failure to quantify working capital needs and provide financial information supporting its claim: "Obviously the statute does not contemplate shifting the burden of proof when a taxpayer merely tells the Commissioner it is going to challenge the imposition of the accumulated earnings tax. There must be notice of the specific grounds and contentions." See also, Hughes Inc. v. Commissioner, supra, 90 T.C. 1(1988)(taxpayer provided sufficient detail which, if proven, would support the alleged business needs for the accumulation with respect to some but not all of the grounds asserted). The significance of the shift in the burden of proof provided by § 534 is reduced by § 7491, enacted in 1998, which shifts the burden of proof to the Commissioner after the taxpayer has produced credible evidence in support of the taxpayers position, but only if the taxpayer has cooperated with the Commissioner.

Sections 561–563 provide a deduction for dividends paid within two and one-half months of the close of the taxable year, which dividends reduce the taxpayer's accumulated earnings and profits for the prior year for purposes of the accumulated earnings tax.

SECTION 2. THE PERSONAL HOLDING COMPANY TAX

INTERNAL REVENUE CODE: Sections 541–547; 6501(f).

Section 541 imposes a special tax on the undistributed personal holding company income of a corporation which qualifies as a personal holding company. Historically, the personal holding company tax has been imposed on corporate income at the highest individual tax rate. A corporation is classified as a personal holding company under § 542(a) if at least 60 percent of its adjusted ordinary gross income is personal holding company income and more than 50 percent in value of its stock is directly or indirectly owned by five or fewer individuals.[4]

The tax operates as an automatic obstacle to corporate accumulations intended to avoid the individual tax on the shareholders, since it does not turn on the need, reasonableness, or purpose of an accumulation but instead is applied if its objective conditions are met. After 1986, the corporate tax structure provides little inducement to accumulate earnings because the top corporate rate is not significantly less than the highest marginal rate for individuals. Nonetheless, a closely held corporation with personal holding company income still may be subject to the penalty tax. Even an apparent operating company unexpectedly may find itself with a sufficiently high proportion of personal holding company income to trigger the tax. See Eller v. Commissioner, 77 T.C. 934 (1981). Similarly, an active corporation that is in the process of liquidating and selling its assets can become a personal holding company by virtue of the passive investment income that is generated by investments of the sales proceeds prior to distribution in liquidation. See Lachinski v. Commissioner, T.C.Memo. 1986–334 (interest on installment sale of active business received pending liquidation triggered personal holding company tax; the court rejected the taxpayer's argument that personal holding company income is limited to passive rather than active income).

ILLUSTRATIVE MATERIAL

A. PERSONAL HOLDING COMPANY INCOME

1. *Incorporated Passive Investments*

A personal holding company has been called an "incorporated pocketbook," a corporation used by the taxpayer to derive investment income at lower corporate rates. Personal holding company income includes passive rents,[5] dividends, interest,[6] non-mineral royalties, produced film rents,

4. Rev.Rul. 89–20, 1989–1 C.B. 170, holds that for purposes of determining whether five or fewer persons own 50 percent or more of the stock of a corporation, stock held directly or indirectly by a shareholder will only be counted once. Thus, stock that is attributed from one person to another under the family and partnership attribution rules of § 544(a)(2) is not taken into account a second time either as stock of the person who owns it directly or as stock of a third person to whom it is also attributable. If stock owned directly by one person is attributed to another and counted as the stock of that second person, the first person may nevertheless be counted among the five largest shareholders by virtue of attribution to that person of stock that is directly owned by others and that has not otherwise been taken into account for purposes of § 542(a)(2).

5. As to whether receipts constitute rents, see e.g., Hilldun Corp. v. Commissioner, 408 F.2d 1117 (2d Cir.1969); Rev.Rul. 67–

amounts under certain personal service contracts, and mineral royalties.[7] Personal holding company income excludes "active rental income" (rental income earned by a corporation if such income is more than 50% of adjusted ordinary gross income) but only if undistributed personal holding company income (not including rents) does not exceed ten percent of the corporation's ordinary gross income. The 10 percent rule, in effect, requires $900 of adjusted income from rents to shield $100 of dividend income from the personal holding company tax. Similar limitations apply with respect to oil, gas and mineral royalties, and copyright royalties. I.R.C. § 543(a)(3) and (4). Section 543(a)(1)(C) excludes royalties received from computer software from the definition of personal holding company income.

2. *Incorporated Personal Services*

The personal holding company provisions are also aimed at an "incorporated talent," a corporation formed to shelter the personal service income of a particular individual from individual income tax rates and to provide fringe benefits such as an employer provided health plan or retirement plan. Under § 543(a)(7) personal holding company income includes amounts received under personal service contracts if someone other than the corporation has the right to designate the person who is to perform the services and that designated person owns more than 25 percent of the outstanding stock of the corporation. For example, in Kenyatta Corp. v. Commissioner, 86 T.C. 171 (1986), former pro-basketball star Bill Russell formed a corporation to contract for his promotional services. The corporation entered into contracts with different media outlets and the Seattle SuperSonics (who separately employed Russell as a coach) for promotional appearances and a newspaper column. On examination of the taxpayer's contracts, the Tax Court found that the contracting party was contracting specifically for Russell's services.

In general, however, the Internal Revenue Service has been surprisingly liberal in its interpretation of the "right to designate" requirement of § 543(a)(7). For example, Rev.Rul. 75–67, 1975–1 C.B. 169, held that no personal services income resulted from a contract to render medical services between a patient and a professional corporation even though the principal shareholder-doctor was the only medical doctor employed by the corporation. Since the contract between the patient and the corporation did not explicitly state that the doctor would personally perform the services, no "designation" was present despite the fact that it was clear that both parties anticipated that the doctor would perform the services. See also Rev.Rul. 75–249, 1975–1 C.B. 171 (the fact that a client may solicit and expect the services of a professional entertainer is not a designation as long as there is no personal obligation to perform). Thus as long as the person

423, 1967–2 C.B. 221; Rev.Rul. 70–153, 1970–1 C.B. 139.

6. Personal holding company interest includes interest imputed to the taxpayer from interest free loans to related persons. See Likins–Foster Honolulu Corp. v. Commissioner, 840 F.2d 642 (9th Cir.1988); Krueger Co. v. Commissioner, 79 T.C. 65 (1982).

7. As to whether receipts constitute mineral royalties, see Bayou Verret Land Co., Inc. v. Commissioner, 450 F.2d 850 (5th Cir. 1971); Rev.Rul. 72–148, 1972–1 C.B. 170.

contracting for the services of a professional is willing to run the slight, but real, risk that the professional in theory has the right to substitute the performance of another, the personal holding company provisions can be avoided. In RAS of Sand River, Inc. v. Commissioner, T.C. Memo. 1990–322, aff'd by order, 935 F.2d 270 (6th Cir.1991), the taxpayer's sole shareholder incorporated the taxpayer to provide engineering services. Although the written contract between the corporation and its customer did not designate a particular person to perform the work or give the customer the right to designate the person to perform the work, the court found that an oral agreement with the customer required the work to be performed by the taxpayer's sole shareholder. The court reached this result even though the shareholder's services were not so valuable or unique as to be irreplaceable.

3. *Incorporated Personal Use Assets*

The third device targeted by the personal holding company provisions is incorporation of personal use property such as a yacht or vacation home. Individuals would put personal use property in a corporation along with passive investments producing sufficient income to maintain the personal use property. The more aggressive taxpayer would then attempt to deduct the cost of maintaining the personal use property from income produced by the passive investment, thereby maintaining the personal use property with tax-free income. In a modified form, the taxpayer might rent the personal use property from the corporation for an arm's-length rental which was less than the cost of maintenance, and fund the difference with income from passive assets. To combat these attempts, § 543(a)(6) includes as personal holding company income amounts received as compensation for the use of tangible property of the corporation if a 25 percent or greater shareholder is entitled to personal use of the property. In addition, § 545(b)(6) provides that in computing taxable income subject to the personal holding company tax, no deduction for depreciation and maintenance expense shall be allowed against rental income from property held by a personal holding company unless the corporation can establish (A) that the rent received was the highest rent attainable, (B) that the property is held in the course of a business carried on for bona fide profit, and (C) that there is either an expectation that operation of the property would produce a profit or that the property is necessary for the conduct of the business. Section 545(b)(6) is intended to insure that deductions attributable to property used by a shareholder do not reduce other personal holding company income.

B. COMPUTING THE PERSONAL HOLDING COMPANY TAX BASE

Section 541 imposes the personal holding company tax on the corporation's "undistributed personal holding company income." Section 545 defines this undistributed taxable income as the current year's taxable income less deductions for other taxes,[8] dividends[9] (including consent dividends not involving actual distributions), and other disbursements. In addition, § 547 allows a deficiency dividend deduction under which a deficiency in personal holding company tax may be avoided by a dividend distribution to shareholders after a determination of the deficiency. This device is helpful, for example, if the corporation does not realize it is a personal holding company or if, even though it realizes it is a personal holding company, believes that it has distributed all of its income only to find that undistributed income exists either because the Commissioner has found additional income items or has disallowed deductions. This device is not available, however, if fraud is present or there was a willful failure to file an income tax return.

C. ADDITIONAL ASPECTS OF THE PERSONAL HOLDING COMPANY PROVISIONS

There are several facets of the relationship between the accumulated earnings tax and the personal holding company tax. A corporation may escape the accumulated earnings tax, which is based upon the accumulation of earnings and profits, but still be subject to the personal holding company tax, because the latter tax depends upon the existence of undistributed personal holding company income, a concept entirely distinct from earnings and profits. Also the concept of "accumulation" is essentially absent from the personal holding company tax. On the other hand, if the corporation is a personal holding company, the accumulated earnings tax does not apply. § 532(b)(1). But, a corporation that avoids personal holding company status must still face the possibility that its accumulations will be reached under the accumulated earnings tax.

An active manufacturing company with some investment income may fall accidentally into personal holding company status. For manufacturing companies, "gross income" is not "gross receipts," but instead constitutes gross receipts less cost of goods sold. Thus, in a bad year in which the cost of goods sold exceeded gross receipts, the corporation might find itself with less than 40 percent of its adjusted ordinary gross income from non-personal holding income sources.

The at-risk provisions of § 465, limiting the taxpayer's ability to take deductions in connection with nonrecourse financing, apply to "closely

8. The deduction for taxes paid is limited to taxes accrued during the taxable year. Contested tax liabilities are not properly accrued and therefore not allowed as a deduction in computing income subject to the personal holding company tax. Kluger Associates, Inc. v. Commissioner, 617 F.2d 323 (2d Cir.1980); LX Cattle Company v. United States, 629 F.2d 1096 (5th Cir.1980).

9. Treas.Reg. § 1.562–1(a) provides that the reduction in income for dividends if appreciated property is distributed as a dividend in kind is limited to the adjusted basis of the property. The Supreme Court in Fulman v. United States, 434 U.S. 528(1978), resolving a conflict in the Circuits, upheld the regulation as it applies to distributions of appreciated property. The Court, after describing a rather confusing legislative history, found a "reasonable basis" for the regulation limiting the corporate deduction to the basis of the property despite the fact that the full fair market value of the property is included in the income of the shareholder as a dividend. The limitation to adjusted basis no longer may be appropriate as the distributing corporation is required to recognize gain on the distribution of appreciated property.

held" corporations that meet the stock ownership requirements of § 542(a)(2). This limitation in turn can have an impact on the calculation of adjusted ordinary gross income and thus on the status of the corporation as a personal holding company.

SECTION 3. COLLAPSIBLE CORPORATIONS

INTERNAL REVENUE CODE: Section 341.

In a tax regime with a generous capital gain preference, there is an advantage to producing an ordinary income asset in a corporation and selling the stock before the income is realized, thereby converting the gains from ordinary income into capital gains. The collapsible corporation provisions of § 341 are intended to prevent this device. Generally, § 341 provides ordinary income treatment for any gain recognized on the sale, exchange, or liquidation of the stock of a collapsible corporation (or on a distribution with respect to stock subject to § 301(c)(3)) that otherwise would be treated as capital gain. A collapsible corporation is defined in § 341(b)(1) as a corporation formed or availed of principally for the manufacture, construction, production, or purchase of certain types of property (mostly ordinary income property), with a view to the sale or exchange by the shareholders of their stock, or to the liquidation of the corporation (its collapse), before the realization by the corporation of two-thirds of the income to be derived from the property.

ILLUSTRATIVE MATERIAL

A. SECTION 341 IN GENERAL

1. *Historical Background*

O'Brien v. Commissioner, 25 T.C. 376 (1955), illustrates the problem that originally led to enactment of § 341. The taxpayers, Pat O'Brien and Phil L. Ryan, were a movie actor and director interested in acquiring rights to the story "Pile Buck" for purposes of making a motion picture. O'Brien and Ryan, along with a third person, formed a corporation with cash contributions totaling $12,500. The corporation employed O'Brien to star in the picture, employed Ryan as the producer, hired actors and a director, entered into a distribution agreement with Columbia Pictures, and obtained bank financing for production costs. After completion of the film, the corporation was liquidated. The corporation's film rights, including the right to payments from Columbia under the distribution contract, were distributed to the taxpayers as a liquidation distribution. The taxpayers reported the difference between the value of the film rights and their basis in corporate stock as a capital gain.[10] The Commissioner asserted that the

10. This transaction was viable because it occurred prior to the enactment of § 311(b), when the *General Utilities* doctrine, discussed at page 202, provided nonrecognition to the corporation with respect to any gain realized on the liquidating distribution.

corporation was taxable on income earned from the motion picture under assignment of income principles and, as an alternative, that the corporation should recognize gain on distribution of the film rights under Commissioner v. Court Holding Company, 324 U.S. 331 (1945), as if it had sold the movie rights before liquidation. The Tax Court refused to ignore the fact that the corporation had been liquidated before earning the income which the Commissioner sought to tax to it and rejected the Commissioner's position.[11] As a result, by collapsing the corporation before it earned income from production of the film, the taxpayers converted the corporation's earnings into capital gain of the stockholders.

Section 341 is a statutory attempt to cope with the tax avoidance potentials of the collapsible corporation device. The section first appeared in 1950 limited in its scope to what is now the "manufacture, construction or production" aspect of § 341(b). As such, the section was aimed at the single motion picture or real estate venture. In 1951 the section was amended to include the "purchase" aspect of § 341(b) so as to cover situations in which appreciated inventory was transferred to a corporation and the stock of the corporation then sold. In 1954 the "purchase" aspect of § 341(b) was extended to § 1231(b) assets, i.e., land and depreciable assets used in trade or business but not held for sale to customers. The provision apparently was aimed at improved real estate held for rental income but it also extends to television and motion picture films, patents, copyrights, and natural resources, all of which would not necessarily require manufacturing, construction or production activity and which could appreciate in value over a short period. The presumptions of § 341(c) also were added in 1954, making § 341 applicable if the corporation held inventory, unrealized receivables, or § 1231 assets which had appreciated 20 percent in value and which assets represented 50 percent of the total assets, unless the taxpayer could prove under § 341(b) that the corporation was not formed or availed of for the proscribed purpose. Section 341(c) provides an objective test to supplement the subjective test of § 341(b). In the case of a corporation with LIFO inventory, these rules can make the corporation collapsible though it has been in existence for many years. Treas.Reg. § 1.341–5(c)(1), and Rev.Rul. 56–244, 1956–1 C.B. 176, temper this result by finding a non-collapsible status if the volume of inventory is at an average level at the time of liquidation. The § 341(e) exception was added in 1958 to supplement the escape clauses in § 341(d). In 1964, a further exception was added in § 341(f). In 1984, § 341(b)(1)(A) was amended to replace the requirement that the corporation realize a "substantial part" of the income attributable to collapsible property, with an objective requirement that the corporation realize two-thirds of the income to be derived from collapsible property.

11. The taxpayers also asserted that payments from Columbia Pictures in excess of the fair market value of the distributed film rights were capital gains. The Tax Court treated the payments as ordinary income by pointing out that the value of the contract rights distributed in liquidation was fixed. Since the liquidation was a closed transaction, payments in excess of the fixed value of the liquidation distribution were not received as liquidation distributions.

The abuse targeted by § 341 is not significant after 1986. The requirement of § 336 that built-in gain be recognized by the distributing corporation on a liquidation eliminates the incentive to form or use a collapsible corporation in a liquidation. However, in some circumstances a taxpayer may accumulate income in a corporation with an eye towards selling the stock at lower capital gains tax rates before the income has been realized.

2. *General Scope*

The remedy of § 341 for the tax avoidance potential of the collapsible corporation is to treat the entire gain realized by the shareholder on the sale of the stock or liquidation of the corporation as ordinary income. This overshoots the mark to the extent that a portion of the gain, if realized at the corporate level, would have been capital gain or would not have been gain from collapsible activity because, in such a case, the conversion of ordinary income to capital gain is not present. Section 341(d)(2) compensates for this defect to a limited extent by providing that § 341 is inapplicable unless more than 70 percent of the stockholder gain is attributable to the collapsible property. In addition, ordinary income will not result to the stockholder if two-thirds of the collapsible gain has been realized at the corporate level. I.R.C. § 341(b)(1)(A). Hence, the price of avoidance of ordinary gain to the stockholder is ordinary gain to the corporation followed by capital gain to the stockholders.

Section 341 bristles with words and phrases whose applicability depends largely on the facts of the particular case: "formed or availed of principally for the purpose of;" "with a view to;" "gain attributable to the property so produced." As a consequence it has an *in terrorem* effect which restrains some adventures in tax avoidance, but it also may inhibit some transactions motivated by genuine business considerations.

Section 341 is not by its terms exclusive. Hence the Commissioner could resort to other arguments if a case does not fall within § 341. But as the *O'Brien* decision indicates, the Commissioner's chances of success are not high in view of both the adoption of § 341 itself and the considerable detail with which the rules of that section are formulated. Many courts, disliking the escape from tax presented by the collapsible device, however, have seized on § 341 to find ordinary gain and have appeared quite willing to give a favorable interpretation, from the Government's viewpoint, to the details of the section, although there are limits to this general statement. See e.g. Commissioner v. Kelley, 293 F.2d 904 (5th Cir.1961), interpreting the "substantial part" language of § 341(b)(1)(A) before amendment in 1984 to require realization of only one-third of the taxable income to be derived from collapsible property.

3. *Absence of Tax Avoidance Motive*

Taxpayers initially asserted that § 341 did not apply if the stockholders would have been entitled to capital gain treatment had they realized the gain in their individual capacities without employing the corporate form. This argument was accepted in United States v. Ivey, 294 F.2d 799 (5th

Cir.1961), but rejected in Braunstein v. Commissioner, 305 F.2d 949 (2d Cir.1962). The Supreme Court resolved the issue in favor of the Commissioner in Braunstein v. Commissioner, 374 U.S. 65 (1963), a case involving the construction of a single apartment building for sale, with the stockholder not in the business of selling apartment buildings:

"There is nothing in the language or structure of the section to demand or even justify reading into these provisions the *additional* requirement that the taxpayer must in fact have been using the corporate form as a device to convert ordinary income into capital gain. If a corporation owns but one asset, and the shareholders sell their stock at a profit resulting from an increase in the value of the asset, they have 'gain attributable to' that asset in the natural meaning of the phrase regardless of their desire, or lack of desire, to avoid the bite of federal income taxes." (70)

B. TECHNICAL ASPECTS OF SECTION 341

1. *The "View" Requirement*

(a) Must the Intent Be Principally to Collapse the Corporation or Principally to Manufacture, Construct, etc.

The courts have held that while there must be a "view" to "collapse" the corporation, the requisite principal intent need only be to manufacture, construct, etc., the collapsible asset rather than to possess a view to engage in tax avoidance through the collapse of the corporation. In Weil v. Commissioner, 252 F.2d 805, 806 (2d Cir.1958) the court said, "We read the word 'principally' as modifying the phrase 'manufacture, construction, or production of property * * *.' Under this reading, the corporation may be treated as collapsible if 'manufacture, construction, or production' was a principal corporate activity even if the 'view to' collapse was not the principal corporate objective when the corporation was 'formed or availed of * * *.'" Burge v. Commissioner, 253 F.2d 765 (4th Cir.1958), and Mintz v. Commissioner, 284 F.2d 554 (2d Cir.1960), are in accord; see also Treas.Reg. § 1.341–5(b)(3).

The Internal Revenue Service ordinarily will not issue an advance ruling on the issue whether a corporation is a collapsible corporation, that is whether it was formed or availed of with the requisite view, but will rule if the corporation has been in existence for at least twenty years or can demonstrate that it has realized two-thirds of the taxable income to be derived from collapsible property, and, during the twenty year period, has had substantially the same owners and has conducted substantially the same trade or business. Rev.Proc. 98–3, § 4.01, par. 27, 1998–1 I.R.B. 100.

(b) Time at Which Collapsible View Must Be Held

Treas.Reg. § 1.341–2(a)(3) states that if the requisite "view" exists at any time during the manufacture, construction, etc., the section is satisfied. Thus the view need not exist before the collapsible activity is started but it must exist before it is completed. Some courts have thought the Treasury's interpretation too restrictive from the Government's standpoint, as the following excerpt from Glickman v. Commissioner, 256 F.2d 108 (2d Cir. 1958), indicates:

"[The taxpayers] contend that * * * the requisite 'view' must exist when the corporation is formed or at least when construction is begun. We agree with Judge Parker's statement in [Burge v. Commissioner, 253 F.2d 765 (4th Cir., 1958)]: 'It is not necessary that the "view" exist when the corporation is formed. It is sufficient that it exist when the corporation is "availed of" * * *.' Since the corporation may at any time during its corporate life be 'availed of' for the proscribed purpose, subject, of course, to the limitations imposed by [§ 341(b)(1)], it seems surprising that the Regulations have adopted a narrower interpretation of the statute, and require the requisite view to exist 'during the construction * * * ' or to be 'attributable' to 'circumstances which reasonably could be anticipated at the time of such * * * construction.' We are disposed to disagree with so narrow an interpretation, but whether the Regulation is valid need not be determined now."

The Second Circuit, however, in Braunstein v. Commissioner, 305 F.2d 949 (2d Cir.1962), referred to the *Glickman* statement quoted above as "dictum." Most courts have adopted the position of the regulations that the requisite view must arise prior to the completion of manufacture, construction, or production, see, e.g. Payne v. Commissioner, 268 F.2d 617 (5th Cir.1959); Tibbals v. United States, 362 F.2d 266 (Ct.Cl.1966); F.T.S. Associates, Inc. v. Commissioner, 58 T.C. 207 (1972); Jacobson v. Commissioner, 281 F.2d 703 (3d Cir.1960). As to the facts evidencing the time at which the "view" arises, see, e.g., Manassas Airport Industrial Park, Inc. v. Commissioner, 66 T.C. 566 (1976) (view present when corporation's "policymakers considered dissolution a recognized possibility").

If the view to collapse arises only after the construction or production of the property has been completed, the corporation will not be treated as collapsible, thus making the factual determination of when construction or production is completed a crucial question. See e.g., Computer Sciences Corp. v. Commissioner, 63 T.C. 327(1974) (production of computer program was completed before the time the taxpayers considered disposing of the stock, despite the fact that subsequent improvements and changes were still being made in the program at that time).

(c) Change of Circumstances

Treas.Reg. § 1.341–2(a)(3) indicates that the requisite view will not exist if the sale, exchange, or distribution is attributable to circumstances arising after manufacture, construction, production, or purchase, "other than circumstances which reasonably could be anticipated at the time of such manufacture, construction, production, or purchase." In Commissioner v. Lowery, 335 F.2d 680 (3d Cir.1964), the taxpayer was a minority stockholder in two corporations which began the construction of apartment houses in 1950. Before construction was completed, the taxpayer was informed that more funds would be required to complete the projects. He did not have the additional funds and did not want to put more money in the projects. Therefore he sold his stock in the corporations in 1951 and 1952 to investors who were willing to put up the required funds. The corporations were never in fact liquidated. The court held for the taxpayer: "We are of the opinion that [§ 341] contemplates a freedom of choice in reaching a decision to sell stock in determining whether a shareholder had the 'view' proscribed by the section, and that where a sale is compelled by circumstances beyond control the 'view' does not exist." By basing its conclusion on the lack of the requisite view, the Court of Appeals did not have to deal with the Tax Court conclusion that § 341 does not apply to minority stockholders because a minority stockholder has no control over corporate policies and the "view" to be ascertained is that of the controlling stockholders, see (d) below.

In Commissioner v. Solow, 333 F.2d 76 (2d Cir.1964), a minority stockholder in 16 real estate corporations was forced to sell his stock because of a disagreement that arose between him and the majority stockholder, the majority stockholder insisting that the taxpayer sell his stock or he would cause the latter's financial ruin. The taxpayer "reluctantly agreed to the sale" and the court held that the requisite view was not present because of the coercive circumstances. But see Braunstein v. Commissioner, 305 F.2d 949 (2d Cir.1962) (unexpected decline in profitability did not constitute a change in circumstances).

(d) Minority Stockholders

Treas.Reg. § 1.341–2(a)(2)(second sentence) provides that the intent to form or avail of a corporation for the proscribed purpose exists when such action is contemplated by persons in a position to determine the policies of the corporation by virtue of majority control or otherwise. In Goodwin v. United States, 320 F.2d 356 (Ct.Cl.1963), a minority stockholder's stock was redeemed in circumstances that would have made § 341 applicable. Following the Tax Court position in *Solow*, the court held that the predecessor of § 341 did not apply to the minority stockholder.

2. *Realization of Two–Thirds of the Taxable Income*

The opinion in Payne v. Commissioner, 268 F.2d 617 (5th Cir.1959), implies that under the pre–1985 "substantial part" standard if the "view" exists to distribute before a realization of a substantial part of the income the Commissioner need not show that the distribution was made before the actual realization of a substantial part. Under this analysis, if an initial distribution is made prior to the realization of two-thirds of the taxable income to be derived from the property and the requisite view existed, then the corporation remains a collapsible corporation even though at the time of later distributions, the corporation has earned more than two-thirds of its income. In Heft v. Commissioner, 294 F.2d 795 (5th Cir.1961), the court stated:

"It may well be that shareholders who liquidate their corporation by a series of distributions may be caught under § [341] even though most or even all of the corporation's income is eventually realized by the corporation and taxed to it, whereas by waiting until a substantial part of the income has been realized they could have avoided § [341] and yet have acquired a major part of the corporation's property without the income attributable to it being taxed to the corporation. However, the statute is not directed at the avoidance of corporate income taxes. Section [341] is aimed at preventing taxpayers using a corporation to avoid individual stockholder gains from stock sales or corporate distributions from being accorded capital gain treatment. These are separate problems. * * * To screen out the most flagrant cases abusing the favored capital gains treatment accorded to sales or exchanges of stock, Congress selected a test based on the sequence of transactions rather than a test geared to the amount of tax paid by the corporation. Under the chosen test, the statute unmistakably applies to the taxpayers in this case." (798).

Difficulties may be encountered in determining the amount of the total gain that is to be realized from the property for purposes of deciding whether two-thirds of that gain has been realized at the time of the transaction in question. Thus, in the case of rental properties, is the gain to be realized confined to proceeds from sale of the property, or does it also include future rents? The courts in Commissioner v. Kelley, 293 F.2d 904 (5th Cir.1961), and in Payne v. Commissioner, 268 F.2d 617 (5th Cir.1959), seemed to indicate that the pre–1985 "substantial part" test required some estimate of the future operation of the property beyond an ascertainment of its value at the time of the transaction resulting in stockholder gain. See also Manassas Airport Industrial Park v. Commissioner, 66 T.C. 566 (1976), indicating the calculations appropriate to estimate the anticipated future expenses which would reduce the total gain to be realized and thus affect the amount of gain necessary to be realized to avoid collapsible status.

3. *What Constitutes the "Property"*

When more than one asset is held by the corporation, identification of the "property" with respect to which the two-thirds of income test of § 341(b)(1)(A) applies is an important aspect of the test. See Treas.Reg. § 1.341–2(a)(4). A similar problem of identification of the collapsible property is presented by the "70–30" exception of § 341(d)(2) discussed at page 803. In Rev.Rul. 68–476, 1968–2 C.B. 139, 60 percent of the gain from the sale of stock in a collapsible corporation was attributable to a building and the balance to a general increase in the value of land that had been purchased more than three years prior to the sale of the stock. The Ruling held that "property under § 341(d)(2) encompassed both the land and the building, which comprised a 'single unit of constructed real property.'" Hence, since all of the gain was attributable to such constructed property, the exception of § 341(d)(2) did not apply. See also Glickman v. Commissioner, 256 F.2d 108 (2d Cir.1958) (held in effect that as respects the 70% test both land and the building constructed on it were the collapsible property and not just the building so that appreciation attributable to the value of the land was collapsible gain).

Computer Sciences Corp. v. Commissioner, 63 T.C. 327 (1974), held that constructed property includes intangible assets produced by the taxpayer, in that case a computer program for the computerized preparation of income tax returns. It rejected the taxpayer's argument that the program was simply know-how and good will arising from its operation of a service business. *Manassas Airport Industrial Park, Inc.*, page 799, held that vacant land could be the object of "construction" and § 341 was not limited in its application to depreciable property.

4. *What Constitutes "Construction"*

Section 341(b)(2) requires a determination of what constitutes "construction." Abbott v. Commissioner, 258 F.2d 537 (3d Cir.1958), held that subdivision of land, coupled with acts such as installation of streets and utilities constituted "construction." Rev.Rul. 56–137, 1956–1 C.B. 178, stated that the obtaining of a rezoning permit was a part of "construction" activity. See also Farber v. Commissioner, 312 F.2d 729 (2d Cir.1963) (retention of architect, application for building permit, making of utility deposits and application for loan commitment constituted "construction"); Sproul Realty Co. v. Commissioner, 38 T.C. 844 (1962) (rezoning of land for commercial use, obtaining of lease commitments, hiring of architect and general contractor, and attempting to get permanent financing constituted "construction").

In Rev.Rul. 69–378, 1969–2 C.B. 49, a corporation leased land to a second corporation on which the latter was to construct a shopping center. The lessor corporation had the right to approve plans and share rents, and it agreed to subordinate its mortgage to enable the lessee to obtain a construction loan. The Ruling held that the lessor corporation's activities were "integral steps" in the construction of the shopping center; the fact that it did not engage in physical construction of the shopping center was irrelevant and its activities constituted "construction." However, where the lessor does not assist in the financing of the construction or participate in the profits of the lessee, no "construction" by the lessor will be deemed to take place. Rev.Rul. 77–306, 1977–2, C.B. 103.

It is also important under § 341(b)(3) and (d)(3) to determine when construction is completed. In Rev.Rul. 69–378, supra, construction was not completed from the standpoint of the lessor corporation until the date of actual completion of construction of the shopping center (even though its activities with respect to the property had ended with the subordination of its mortgage one year earlier). Rev.Rul. 63–114, 1963–1 C.B. 74, held that minor alterations in the three years following completion of construction of an office building, which alterations did not increase the rental space or the character of the building and did not increase the fair market value of or the net income from the property, did not constitute "construction;" Section 341(d)(3) would be satisfied three years from the date of the completion of the office building. Rev.Rul. 72–422, 1972–2 C.B. 211, indicated that neither the amount expended for alterations nor the ratio of the cost of alterations to the original cost of the property are determinative factors under Rev.Rul. 63–114. In Weil v. Commissioner, 28 T.C. 809 (1957), aff'd per curiam, 252 F.2d 805 (2d Cir.1958), a shopping center was held not completed since the construction of a retaining wall and the completion of a parking lot still remained to permit effective operation, the Tax Court saying that final completion would not be fixed earlier than the time when the project was ready to begin earning a substantial part of the net income. This last aspect hardly seems the decisive factor; thus, the construction of some houses available for rent in a housing project before the remaining houses are built does not mark the completion of the construction.

5. *Transactions to Which Section 341 Applies*

Section 341 by its terms applies to sales or exchanges of the stock of a collapsible corporation, to distributions in complete or partial liquidation, and to distributions not in redemption of stock that are treated as sales or exchanges under § 301(c)(3)(A). However, since under § 336 gain will be recognized by the distributing corporation on the liquidation distribution of appreciated property, thereby causing a realization of more than two-thirds of the taxable income to be derived from the property, only sales of stock actually are subject to § 341. In addition, § 341 does not appear to cover a § 302(a) redemption; Treas.Reg. § 1.341–1 refers to gain from an "actual" sale or exchange, which presumably excludes the "treated as" exchange gain of § 302(a).

For § 341 to apply, gain must be recognized on the exchange of the stock of the collapsible corporation so if the stock is disposed of in a nonrecognition transaction § 341 will not apply. Rev.Rul. 73–378, 1973–2 C.B. 113 (§ 341(a) was not triggered by an exchange of collapsible corporation stock for stock of the acquiring corporation in a reorganization; since the acquiring corporation was not itself a collapsible corporation, the collapsible "taint" disappeared entirely and gain on the subsequent disposition of the stock in the acquiring corporation by the former stockholder of the collapsible corporation was entitled to capital gain treatment).

6. *Section 341(d) Exceptions*

Section 341(d) provides three exceptions whereby stockholders of collapsible corporations can qualify for capital gain treatment despite the fact that the corporation is a collapsible corporation as defined in § 341(b).

The first exception, § 341(d)(1), a de minimis rule, protects from ordinary income treatment a stockholder owning (or considered as owning under the attribution rules specified in § 341(d)) five percent or less in value of the outstanding stock of a corporation.

Under the second exception, § 341(d)(2), § 341(a) will not apply to the gain recognized by a stockholder in a collapsible corporation unless more than 70 percent of such gain recognized by the stockholder during the taxable year is attributable to the manufacture, construction or production of the property, or purchase of property described in § 341(b)(3). The meanings of the terms "property" and "construction," discussed above, are thus also important with respect to this exception. Taxpayers frequently have argued that in the case of land and a building, gain should be attributable to the increase in the value of the land for purposes of bringing more of the gain into the 30 percent side of the equation. Thus, for example, in Benedek v. Commissioner, 429 F.2d 41 (2d Cir.1970), the taxpayer, relying on the 70 percent rule, asserted that distributions were attributable to an increase in land value and did not result from the construction of apartment houses. The court held that the test was "what caused the distributions, or what property—land or buildings—generated them?" The court concluded that the distributions were caused by and generated by the construction of the buildings and not by an increase in the value of the land. Loan proceeds distributed resulted from the construction and the shareholder's gain was therefore attributable entirely to construction. In King v. United States, 641 F.2d 253 (5th Cir.1981), the court held that the construction of pipelines undertaken by related corporations and contributed to a collapsible corporation contributed to the gain attributable to construction realized on sale of the collapsible corporation stock. The court also concluded that the corporation's actual construction of utility facilities enhanced the value of its other assets, including franchises, customer lists and connection lines, so that gain on these assets was attributable to the construction.

Under the third exception, § 341(d)(3), gain realized after the expiration of three years following the completion of manufacture, construction, production, or purchase of § 341(b)(3) property is protected from ordinary income treatment. The problems of time of completion of manufacture or construction, discussed at page 802, thus also are involved in this exception. Rev.Rul. 60–68, 1960–1 C.B. 151, held that if the sale of stock for cash would result in ordinary income under § 341, then the same result follows under § 453; the fact that receipt of an installment occurs more than three years after the time limit of § 341(d)(3) does not affect the ordinary income treatment. But where an executory contract of sale was entered into within the three-year period, the taxpayer was able to utilize the exception of § 341(d)(3) because the closing date occurred after the expiration of the three-year period and the burdens and benefits of ownership remained with the seller until the closing date. Rev.Rul. 79–235, 1979–2 C.B. 135, provides that the three year period with respect to property received in a like-kind exchange under § 1031 in exchange for property constructed by the taxpayer begins to run on the date that construction of the original property was completed.

Suppose that a part of a stockholder's gain is protected under the exception of § 341(d)(3) and the stockholder attempts to use the "70–30" exception for the balance of the gain. Does the amount qualifying under the § 341(d)(3) exception fall on the 70 percent or the 30 percent side of the equation? Rev.Rul. 65–184, 1965–2 C.B. 91, held that the two exceptions operate independently; the exception in § 341(d)(2) does not become applicable simply because 30 percent or more of the gain of the stockholder is attributable to property to which the exception of § 341(d)(3) applies.

7. *Section 341(e) Exception*

Section 341(b)(3)(D) extends § 341 to the purchase of § 1231(b) assets, i.e., land and depreciable property used in business but not held for sale to customers. This means that although an individual who owns such assets outright would have had capital gain, the same individual as a stockholder of a corporation owning such assets could end up with ordinary income on sale of its stock or on liquidation. To prevent this result, § 341(e) provides a general exception to § 341. If the tests of § 341(e) are met, the corporation is not a collapsible corporation. If the tests are not met, then the other provisions of § 341 still must be applied to see if collapsible status exists.

Section 341(e) is extremely complicated. Speaking very generally, as long as the unrealized appreciation of those assets of the corporation which, if sold either by the corporation or any stockholder owning more than 20 percent of its stock would result in ordinary income (other than assets which result in ordinary income because of the application of the various recapture rules specified in § 341(e)(12)), does not exceed 15 percent of the corporation's net worth, then the rules of § 341(e) may apply and the corporation will not be a collapsible corporation as respects the sale or exchange of stock by any stockholder who also meets an additional test described below. This is the "general corporate test" of Treas.Reg. § 1.341–6(a)(4). In determining the stockholder ownership percentages under § 341(e), the attribution rules specified in § 341(e)(8) are applicable.

Once the "general corporate test" is met, the "specific stockholder test" of Treas.Reg. § 1.341–6(a)(5) also must be satisfied. This test recalculates the 15 percent ceiling on ordinary income assets (so-called subsection (e) assets) of the "general corporate test" by recharacterizing certain assets, not otherwise considered to be ordinary income assets, with reference to the shareholder in question. Thus, for example, a more than 5 percent but less than 20 percent stockholder would have the ordinary or capital status of a corporate asset tested, as respects the particular stockholder, but not other stockholders, by what its character would be in that stockholder's hands if the stockholder were a more than 20 percent stockholder. (This is to prevent a dealer from obtaining capital asset status by placing the assets in a corporation along with other non-dealer stockholders.) A more than 20 percent stockholder will have the status of a corporate asset tested, as respects that individual, but no other stockholders, by considering the stockholder as owning certain assets of other corporations in which the stockholder has a substantial interest. (This to prevent an individual from using a separate corporation for each venture to avoid dealer status.) Treas.Reg. § 1.341–6(a)(5)(ii), (c)(3)(ii), and (d).

The § 341(e) exception does not apply to a sale of stock by a 20 percent shareholder to a related person as defined in § 341(e)(8). I.R.C. § 341(e)(1), last sentence.

Section 341(e) and the regulations thereunder must be studied with great care by the tax advisor since this relief provision, if operable, completely removes the collapsible corporation "taint" for the stockholder. The regulations under § 341(e) clarify many of the uncertainties in the statutory language. There remains, however, a certain aura of unreality to the section even under the regulations. For example, in applying the specific stockholder test to determine whether a more than 20 percent stockholder is a dealer, a stockholder who is not a dealer may be deemed to be a dealer by hypothesizing what the stockholder would have done with respect to corporate property if he had owned it. See Treas.Reg. § 1.341–6(b)(4).

8. *Section 341(f) Exception*

Section 341(f) provides relief from the collapsible corporation rules with respect to sales by a stockholder of a collapsible corporation if the corporation consents to recognize the gain upon a subsequent disposition of the "subsection (f) assets," as defined in § 341(f)(4). If the corporation files its consent, then shares sold by a stockholder within six months of the date of the corporation's consent will be protected from § 341(a)(2). Rev.Rul. 69–32, 1969–1 C.B. 100, specifies the rules for the filing of the requisite consent by the corporation. The general purpose of § 341(f) was to give relief to current stockholders if there is assurance that gain would ultimately be recognized by the corporation at the corporate level. Since, after 1986, § 311(b) and § 336 require a corporation to recognize gain on any distribution of corporate assets, there is no corporate level cost to making an election under § 341(f). But then again, since corporate level gain must be recognized on any distribution made after 1986, no corporation can be formed or availed of to collapse after that date without recognition of corporate level gain.

INDEX

References are to Pages

1-56662-774-5
9 781566 627740
90000